Community care and the law
fifth edition

Luke Clements is a consultant solicitor with Scott-Moncrieff and Associates LLP, London and a Professor at Cardiff Law School, Cardiff University, where he is Director of the Centre for Health and Social Care Law. He is a consulting editor to the *Journal of Community Care Law and Practice* and *Social Care Law Today* (Arden Davies Publishing) and on the editorial board of the *Community Care Law Reports* (Legal Action Group).

Pauline Thompson is currently a freelance trainer on aspects of community care. She was until recently a policy adviser on care finance for Age Concern England (now Age UK). Her background is in social work and welfare rights advice. For many years she wrote the chapters on community care in the *Disability Rights Handbook* (Disability Alliance), and was one of the original authors of the *Paying for Care Handbook* (CPAG). She is a member of the Law Society's Mental Health and Disability Committee and is on the editorial board of the *Community Care Law Reports* (Legal Action Group) and the *Elder Law Journal* (Jordans). She is about to retire from working on community care law to pursue other interests.

Luke Clements can be contacted by e-mail at **clementslj@cf.ac.uk**

Community care and the law

FIFTH EDITION

Luke Clements and Pauline Thompson

with

Carolyn Goodall
Jean Gould
Edward Mitchell
Camilla Palmer
Alison Pickup

 Legal Action Group
2011

This edition published in Great Britain 2011
by LAG Education and Service Trust Limited
242 Pentonville Road, London N1 9UN

First edition 1996
Reprinted with revisions 1997
Second edition 2000
Third edition 2004
Fourth edition 2007

While every effort has been made to ensure that the details in this text are correct, readers must be aware that the law changes and that the accuracy of the material cannot be guaranteed and the author and the publisher accept no responsibility for any losses or damage sustained.

The right of Luke Clements to be identified as the author of this work has been asserted by him in accordance with the Copyright, Designs and Patents Act 1988.

British Library Cataloguing in Publication Data
A CIP catalogue record for this book is available from the British Library

Crown copyright material is produced with the permission of the Controller of HMSO and the Queen's Printer for Scotland.

This book has been produced using Forest Stewardship Council (FSC) certified paper. The wood used to produce FSC certified products with a 'Mixed Sources' label comes from FSC certified well-managed forests, controlled sources and/or recycled material.

Print ISBN: 978 1 903307 80 9
Ebook ISBN: 978 1 903307 91 5

Typeset by RefineCatch Ltd, Bungay, Suffolk
Printed by Hobbs the Printer, Totton, Hampshire

Preface

Community care law results from a hotchpotch of statutes, many of which originated as private members' bills (and are all the better for it). Although there are a number of general rules which can be applied to the subject, the most important appears to be that for every general rule there is at least one exception.

As with the previous editions, it has been difficult to decide what to exclude. How can any text do justice to the subject and yet exclude detailed consideration of welfare benefits or special education? And so on. These subjects, however, are not covered in detail. We have tried to keep to the central community care statutes as listed in section 46 of the National Health Service and Community Care Act 1990. Welfare benefits are not covered for two reasons: the first is that they change so frequently and the second is that the Child Poverty Action Group and the Disability Alliance already publish comprehensive and indispensable annual guides. The same can also be said for the excellent *Education Law and Practice* published by Jordans.

We have tried to keep to a minimum the use of abbreviations, but have had to shorten references to the commonly used statutes. Likewise we have referred throughout to the early and important general policy guidance, *Community Care in the Next Decade and Beyond: policy guidance* (1990) as the '1990 Policy Guidance'. In several chapters or sections a particular piece of policy or practice guidance is important and in that section we have given it a shortened title, having of course explained what the shortened title refers to.

A terminological difficulty arises in England concerning references to social services departments. As a result of the Children Act 2004 local authority children's services responsibilities have been effectively merged with their education responsibilities. These organisational reconfigurations do not apply in Wales, and in England the change only affects children: on reaching 18, social care responsibility shifts to the relevant Adult Social Services Department. For the sake of simplicity we continue to refer to social services departments in this text, although depending upon the context, this may be a reference to a Children's Services Department or and Adult Services Department – or indeed to both.

In writing this book very special thanks are due to our contributors: Carolyn Goodall, Jean Gould, Edward Mitchell, Camilla Parker and Alison Pickup – who have variously taken the lead on revising key chapters or editorial themes – and without whose genius this edition would not have been possible.

Special thanks are also due to:

- The Welsh Assembly officers who have helped us try and understand the distinct community care regime in Wales and in doing so shown considerable patience.
- Those officials at the Department of Health who have shown no less patience as we have pestered them concerning the many and on-going changes particularly in letting us know which were likely to have been published by the time of this new edition.

Special apologies and thanks are due to our publisher, Esther Pilger, for all the missed deadlines and the support in getting this latest edition into print.

In writing this book we have received enormous assistance from countless kind and wise people. Many important concepts have been explained to us by social workers in particular, and our clients have taught us far more than (we hope) they will ever realise. Special thanks are due to: Karen Ashton, John Bangs, Richard Bartholomew, Caroline Bielanska, Steve Brett, Simon Bull, Julie Burton, Andy Butler, Jim Crowe, Angela Downing, Julie Duggan, Phil Fennell, Jo Fitzgerald, David Forsdick, Conor Gearty, Jenny Hambidge, Carolyn James, Byron Jones, Stephen Knafler QC, Frances Lipman, Peter Loose, Jay McCully, Michael Mandelstam, Paul Morgan, Janet Read, Frank and Sue Redmond, Lindsey Rhodes, Michael Roche, Christine Rowley, Vin West and Helen Winfield. We have almost certainly omitted from this list many who have also assisted us and to them we apologise.

What is wrong in this text is entirely our own doing and we would welcome any critical feedback.

Luke Clements
Pauline Thompson
September 2011

Contents

APPENDICES

Table of cases

Table of statutes

Entries in **bold** are reproduced in full in appendix A.

Table of statutory instruments

Abbreviations

AD	Advance decision
ADD	Attention deficit disorder
ADHD	Attention deficit hyperactivity disorder
ADASS	Association of Directors of Social Services
CA 1989	Children Act 1989
CAF	Common assessment framework
CC(DD)A 2003	Community Care (Delayed Discharges etc) Act 2003
CC(DP)A 1996	Community Care (Direct Payments) Act 1996
CCLR	Community Care Law Reports
CDCA 2000	Carers and Disabled Children Act 2000
C(EO)A 2004	Carers (Equal Opportunities) Act 2004
CHC	Community health council
CMHT	Community mental health team
CQC	Care Quality Commission
CPA	Care programme approach
CPR	Civil Procedure Rules
CRAG	Charging for Residential Accommodation Guide
CRB	Criminal Records Bureau
C(RS)A 1995	Carers (Recognition and Services) Act 1995
CSA 2000	Care Standards Act 2000
CSCI	Commission for Social Care Inspection
CSDPA 1970	Chronically Sick and Disabled Persons Act 1970
CSSIW	Care and Social Services Inspectorate Wales
CVI	Certificate of vision impairment
CYPA 2008	Children and Young Person's Act 2008
DAT	Drug and alcohol action team
DVCVA 2004	Domestic Violence, Crime and Victims Act 2004
DDA 1995/2005	Disability Discrimination Act 1995/2005
DFG	Disable facilities grant
DHSS	Department of Health and Social Security
DLA	Disability living allowance
DOLS	Deprivation of Liberty Safeguards
DP(SCR)A 1986	Disabled Persons (Services, Consultation and Representation) Act 1986

DST	Decision support tool
DWP	Department for Work and Pensions
ECHR	European Convention on Human Rights
EHB	Enhanced housing benefit
EMI	Elderly mentally ill
EPA	Enduring power of attorney
EqA 2010	Equality Act 2010
EPIOC	Electric powered indoor/outdoor wheelchair
ESA	Employment and Support Allowance
FACS	Fair access to care services
FSS	Formula spending share
GP	General practitioner
HA	Housing Act/Health Act
HASSASSAA 1983	Health and Social Services and Social Security Adjudications Act 1983
HGCRA 1996	Housing Grants, Construction and Regeneration Act 1996
HRA 1998	Human Rights Act 1998
HSCA 2001	Health and Social Care Act 2001
HSCA 2008	Health and Social Care Act 2008
HSC(CHS)A 2003	Health and Social Care (Community Health and Standards) Act 2003
HSCWB	Health, social care and well-being
HSO	Housing Service Ombudsman
HSPHA 1968	Health Services and Public Health Act 1968
HTCS	Healthcare travel costs scheme
IAA 1999	Immigration and Asylum Act 1999
ILF	Independent Living Fund
IMCA	Independent mental capacity advocate
IRP	Independent review panel
IUT	Independent user trust
JIP	Joint investment plan
JSNA	Joint strategic needs assessment
LAA	Local area agreement
LAC	Local authority circular
LASSA 1970	Local Authority Social Services Act 1970
LASSL	Local authority social services letter
LDIAG	Learning Disability Implementation Advisory Group
LGA 2000	Local Government Act 2000
LGO	Local Government Ombudsman
LHB	Local health board
LINks	Local Involvement networks
LPA	Lasting power of attorney
LRR	Local reference rent
MCA 2005	Mental Capacity Act 2005
MHA 1983	Mental Health Act 1983
NAA 1948	National Assistance Act 1948
NAM	New Asylum Model

NASS	National Asylum Support Service
NCSC	National Care Standards Commission
NHS	National Health Service
NHSA 2006	National Health Service Act 2006
NHS(W)A 2006	National Health Service (Wales) Act 2006
NHSCCA 1990	National Health Service and Community Care Act 1990
NIAA 2002	Nationality, Immigration and Asylum Act 2002
NMS	National minimum standard
NSF	National service framework
NTA	National Treatment Agency for Substance Misuse
OFT	Office of Fair Trading
OPG	Office of the Public Guardian
OT	Occupational therapist
PALS	Patient advice and liaison service
PCT	Primary care trust
PEA	Personal expenses allowance
PSED	Public sector equality duty
PSO	Public Services Ombudsman
PSSRU	Personal Social Services Research Unit
PTS	Patient transport services
RAP	Referrals, assessments and packages of care
RHA 2000	Registered Homes Act 2000
RNCC	Registered nursing care contribution
RRO 2002	Regulatory Reform (Housing Assistance) (England and Wales) Order 2002
SAP	Single assessment process
SCIE	Social Care Institute for Excellence
SHA	Strategic health authority
SVGA 2004	Safeguarding Vulnerable Groups Act 2004
UASC	Unaccompanied Asylum Seeking Child
UFSAMC	Unified and fair system for assessing and managing care
WAG	Welsh Assembly Government
WG	Welsh Government
WRS	Worker Registration Scheme

Flowcharts contained in this text

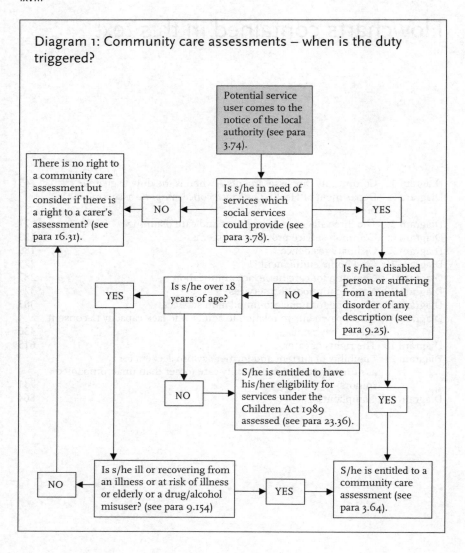

Diagram 1: Community care assessments – when is the duty triggered?

Diagram 2: Department of Health Guidance concerning the assessment process

For the Welsh Government equivalent guidance see para 3.26 footnotes 38 and 44.

General Assessment Guidance Adults with community care needs

- *Prioritising Need in the Context of Putting People First: a whole system approach to eligibility for Social Care 2010* (See para 3.31)
- *Community Care – Community Care in the Next Decade and Beyond: policy guidance,* 1990 [1990 Policy Guidance] (see para 3.28)
- *Care Management And Assessment: Practitioners' Guide,* 1991 (see para 3.92)

•

Carers

Guidance on carers' assessments is in *The Carers and Disabled Children Act 2000: a practitioners guide to carers' assessments,* 2001 (see para 16.8) and general guidance is in the practice guide to the Carers (Equal Opportunities) Act 2004 (see para 16.8)

Disabled children

FACS guidance is not of direct relevance. Specific guidance exists as *The Framework for the Assessment of Children in Need and their Families,* 2000, policy and practice guidance (see para 23.15)

Specific user group assessment guidance

Older people

- NSF for Older People (see para 3.33)
- Single assessment process, 2002 (see para 3.35)

Mental health service users

- NSF for Mental Health, 1999 (see para 3.38)
- *Effective Care Co-ordination in Mental Health Services – Modernising the Care Programme Approach,* 1999.

People with learning disabilities

- *Valuing people: White Paper,* 2001 (see para 3.36)
- *Valuing people: implementation policy guidance,* LAC (2001) 23
- *Valuing People Now: a new three year strategy* (2009) 18.8

Diagram 3: The three stages in assessment and care planning

Information Gathering

The social services department obtain sufficient information in order to make a decision about the most appropriate way of meeting the person's community care needs (see para 3.91).

Note

Note
Depending on the extent of the person's care needs, this may be a brief process, or more complex, potentially requiring input from carers (see para 16.12), and others with relevant information such as health (see para 3.127) and housing (see para 3.130). It may also require consideration of factors such as the person's emotional, cultural and psychological needs and preferences (see para 3.93).

Service provision decision

The social services department decides which of the 'needs' and 'requirements' that have been identified in the assessment 'call for the provision of services' (see para 3.136).

Note

Note
The social services department may not consider that it is 'necessary' to provide everything which is identified in the assessment as being of potential benefit to the person. In general it will only provide services which are essential or for which the assessed need meets its 'eligibility criteria' (see para 3.149).

Care plan

The social services department now prepares a 'care plan' which explains what 'care needs' must be met and details the services that are to be provided in order to do this. The care plan also explains what health or housing services are to be provided by the housing or health authority (if any). The plan will take account of the user's preferences and also identify those 'unmet needs' which do not qualify for services (see para 4.31).

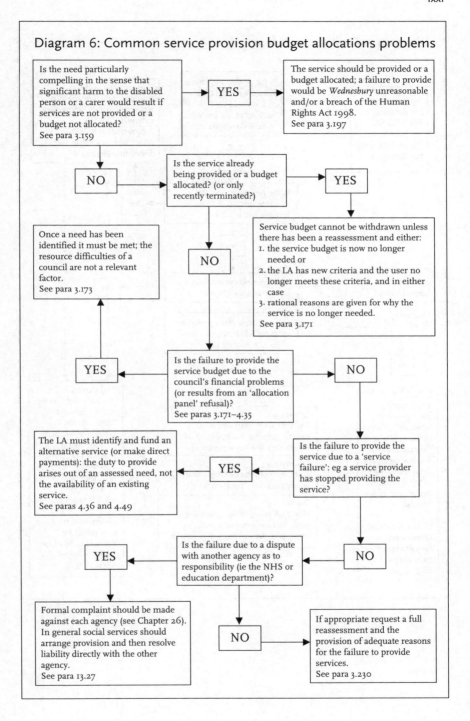

Diagram 6: Common service provision budget allocations problems

Is the need particularly compelling in the sense that significant harm to the disabled person or a carer would result if services are not provided or a budget not allocated?
See para 3.159

YES → The service should be provided or a budget allocated; a failure to provide would be *Wednesbury* unreasonable and/or a breach of the Human Rights Act 1998.
See para 3.197

NO

Is the service already being provided or a budget allocated? (or only recently terminated?)

YES

Once a need has been identified it must be met; the resource difficulties of a council are not a relevant factor.
See para 3.173

NO

Service budget cannot be withdrawn unless there has been a reassessment and either:
1. the service budget is now no longer needed or
2. the LA has new criteria and the user no longer meets these criteria, and in either case
3. rational reasons are given for why the service is no longer needed.
See para 3.171

YES ← Is the failure to provide the service budget due to the council's financial problems (or results from an 'allocation panel' refusal)?
See paras 3.171–4.35 → **NO**

The LA must identify and fund an alternative service (or make direct payments): the duty to provide arises out of an assessed need, not the availability of an existing service.
See paras 4.36 and 4.49

← **YES** ← Is the failure to provide the service due to a 'service failure': eg a service provider has stopped providing the service?

NO

YES ← Is the failure due to a dispute with another agency as to responsibility (ie the NHS or education department)? ← **NO**

Formal complaint should be made against each agency (see Chapter 26). In general social services should arrange provision and then resolve liability directly with the other agency.
See para 13.27

NO → If appropriate request a full reassessment and the provision of adequate reasons for the failure to provide services.
See para 3.230

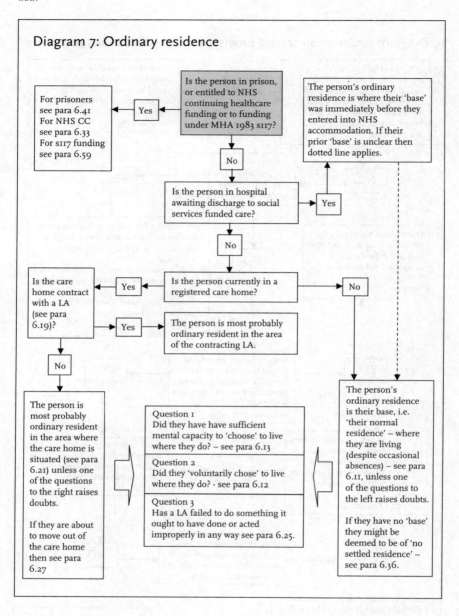

Diagram 7: Ordinary residence

Is the person in prison, or entitled to NHS continuing healthcare funding or to funding under MHA 1983 s117?

Yes → For prisoners see para 6.41 For NHS CC see para 6.33 For s117 funding see para 6.59

The person's ordinary residence is where their 'base' was immediately before they entered into NHS accommodation. If their prior 'base' is unclear then dotted line applies.

No

Is the person in hospital awaiting discharge to social services funded care?

Yes

No

Is the person currently in a registered care home?

Yes → Is the care home contract with a LA (see para 6.19)?

No

Yes → The person is most probably ordinary resident in the area of the contracting LA.

The person is most probably ordinary resident in the area where the care home is situated (see para 6.21) unless one of the questions to the right raises doubts.

If they are about to move out of the care home then see para 6.27

Question 1
Did they have have sufficient mental capacity to 'choose' to live where they do? – see para 6.13

Question 2
Did they 'voluntarily chose' to live where they do? - see para 6.12

Question 3
Has a LA failed to do something it ought to have done or acted improperly in any way see para 6.25.

The person's ordinary residence is their base, i.e. 'their normal residence' – where they are living (despite occasional absences) – see para 6.11, unless one of the questions to the left raises doubts.

If they have no 'base' they might be deemed to be of 'no settled residence' – see para 6.36.

Diagram 10: Care home entitlement

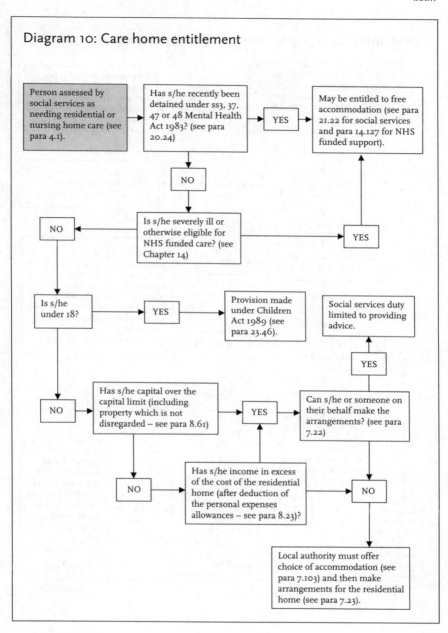

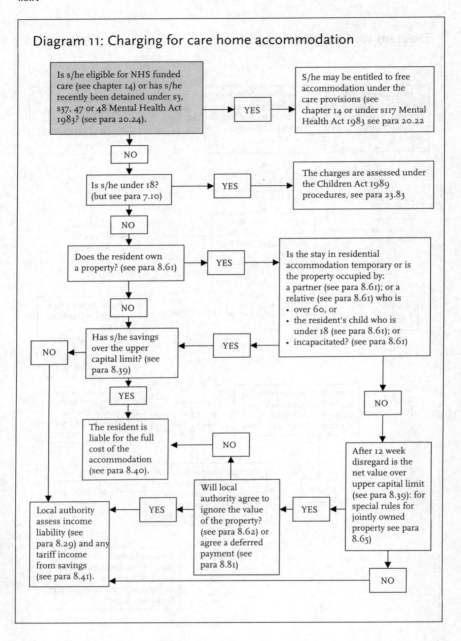

Diagram 11: Charging for care home accommodation

Is s/he eligible for NHS funded care (see chapter 14) or has s/he recently been detained under s3, s37, 47 or 48 Mental Health Act 1983? (see para 20.24).

→ YES → S/he may be entitled to free accommodation under the care provisions (see chapter 14 or under s117 Mental Health Act 1983 see para 20.22

NO

Is s/he under 18? (but see para 7.10)

→ YES → The charges are assessed under the Children Act 1989 procedures, see para 23.83

NO

Does the resident own a property? (see para 8.61)

→ YES → Is the stay in residential accommodation temporary or is the property occupied by: a partner (see para 8.61); or a relative (see para 8.61) who is
• over 60, or
• the resident's child who is under 18 (see para 8.61); or
• incapacitated? (see para 8.61)

NO

Has s/he savings over the upper capital limit? (see para 8.39)

← YES ←

NO

YES

The resident is liable for the full cost of the accommodation (see para 8.40).

← NO ←

Will local authority agree to ignore the value of the property? (see para 8.62) or agree a deferred payment (see para 8.81)

← YES ←

← YES ←

After 12 week disregard is the net value over upper capital limit (see para 8.39): for special rules for jointly owned property see para 8.65)

NO

Local authority assess income liability (see para 8.29) and any tariff income from savings (see para 8.41).

← YES ←

NO

Diagram 12: Non-accommodation services

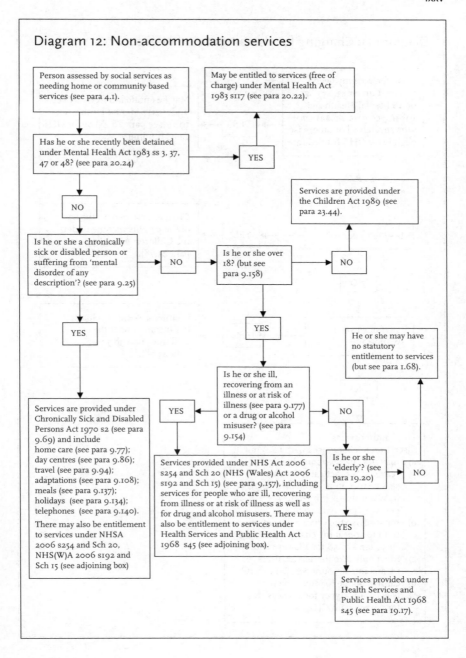

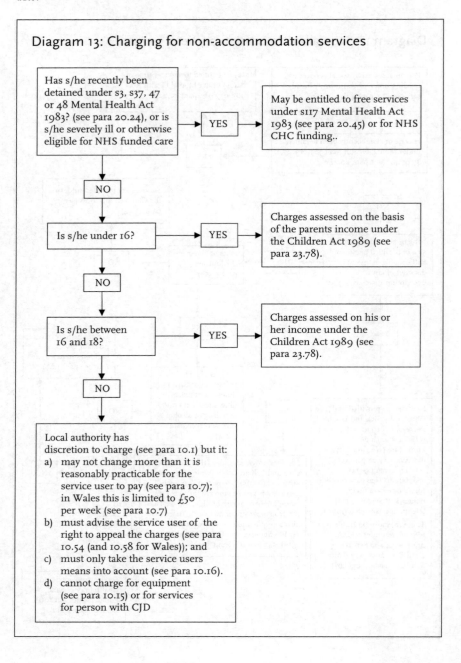

Diagram 13: Charging for non-accommodation services

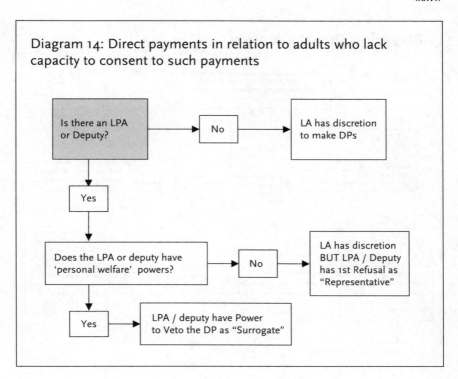

Diagram 14: Direct payments in relation to adults who lack capacity to consent to such payments

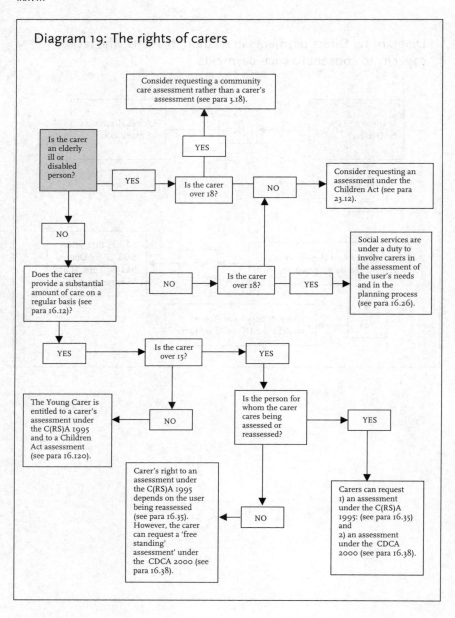

Diagram 19: The rights of carers

Is the carer an elderly ill or disabled person?

YES → Is the carer over 18? → YES → Consider requesting a community care assessment rather than a carer's assessment (see para 3.18).

Is the carer over 18? → NO → Consider requesting an assessment under the Children Act (see para 23.12).

NO → Does the carer provide a substantial amount of care on a regular basis (see para 16.12)?

NO → Is the carer over 18? → YES → Social services are under a duty to involve carers in the assessment of the user's needs and in the planning process (see para 16.26).

YES → Is the carer over 15? → YES → Is the person for whom the carer cares being assessed or reassessed?

NO → The Young Carer is entitled to a carer's assessment under the C(RS)A 1995 and to a Children Act assessment (see para 16.120).

Is the person for whom the carer cares being assessed or reassessed? → YES → Carers can request 1) an assessment under the C(RS)A 1995: (see para 16.35) and 2) an assessment under the CDCA 2000 (see para 16.38).

NO → Carer's right to an assessment under the C(RS)A 1995 depends on the user being reassessed (see para 16.35). However, the carer can request a 'free standing' assessment' under the CDCA 2000 (see para 16.38).

Diagram 21: Eligibility of current and former asylum seekers for asylum support and community care (other than unaccompanied minors)

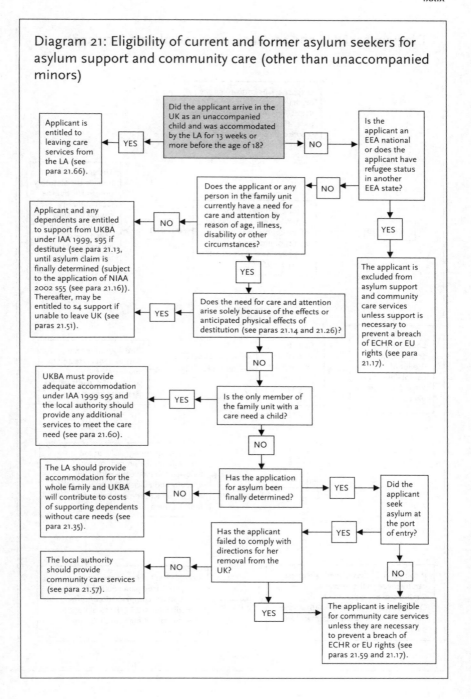

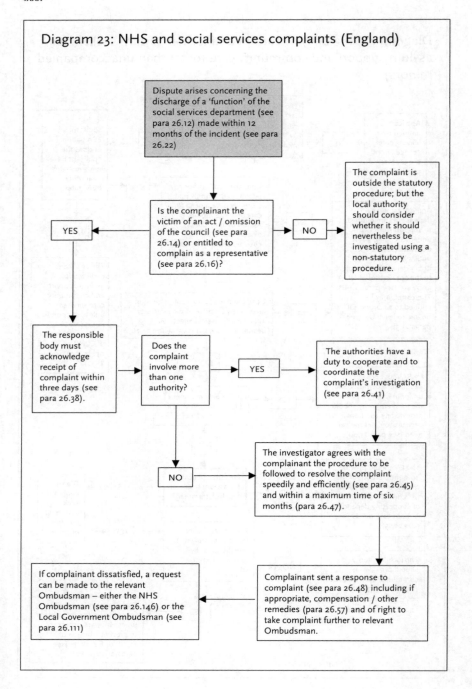

Diagram 23: NHS and social services complaints (England)

Dispute arises concerning the discharge of a 'function' of the social services department (see para 26.12) made within 12 months of the incident (see para 26.22)

Is the complainant the victim of an act / omission of the council (see para 26.14) or entitled to complain as a representative (see para 26.16)?

NO → The complaint is outside the statutory procedure; but the local authority should consider whether it should nevertheless be investigated using a non-statutory procedure.

YES

The responsible body must acknowledge receipt of complaint within three days (see para 26.38).

Does the complaint involve more than one authority?

YES → The authorities have a duty to cooperate and to coordinate the complaint's investigation (see para 26.41)

NO → The investigator agrees with the complainant the procedure to be followed to resolve the complaint speedily and efficiently (see para 26.45) and within a maximum time of six months (para 26.47).

If complainant dissatisfied, a request can be made to the relevant Ombudsman – either the NHS Ombudsman (see para 26.146) or the Local Government Ombudsman (see para 26.111)

Complainant sent a response to complaint (see para 26.48) including if appropriate, compensation / other remedies (para 26.57) and of right to take complaint further to relevant Ombudsman.

Introduction

1.1   When Sir William Beveridge declared war on the five giant evils in society he had in mind Giant Want; Giant Disease; Giant Ignorance; Giant Squalor and Giant Idleness. At the end of the Second World War legislation was brought forward with the purpose of slaying some of these monsters: the Education Act 1944, the NHS Act 1946 and the National Assistance Act (NAA) 1948. Giant Squalor was to be slain by a concerted programme of slum clearance and the building, within ten years, of three million new houses.[1]

1.2   The neglect of disabled, elderly and ill people living in the community was in many respects the forgotten sixth Giant. NAA 1948 Part III did however contain the means by which Giant Neglect was to be slain, namely the provision of 'community care services for ill, elderly and disabled people' and indeed accommodation for anyone else who was 'in need of care and attention which is not otherwise available'.[2]

1.3   It is difficult to lay down strict rules as to the nature of these 'services'. In general they are provided by social services departments, although the NHS also has community care responsibilities (see chapter 14); in general they are personal care services although social services departments may now provide the disabled person with cash by a direct payment or offer a monetary amount through a personal budget which is only loosely linked with services (see chapters 4 and 12). While the service is primarily concerned with personal care rather than health care, on occasions it will involve the provision of nursing (see para 14.20). Likewise, while community care is not primarily concerned with the provision of housing or education services, at its margins it does embrace obligations in both these areas (see paras 7.45 and 9.91). At its heart community care is about provision 'in the community' of home helps, adaptations, day centres and meals on wheels and when necessary the provision of accommodation in care homes. As an arm of the welfare state it commands £16.8 billion per annum of public resources in services.[3]

1.4   The state's assumption of responsibility for the provision of community care services predates Beveridge, by almost 400 years and

---

1   N Timmins, *The Five Giants*, Fontana, 1996.
2   NAA 1948 s21.
3   The gross current expenditure on residential care, home care and other community-based services for adults, England 2009–10; Personal Social Services expenditure and unit costs: England – 2009–10 – Final Council Data.

although NAA 1948 s1 boldly proclaimed abolition of the 'Poor Law', the present scheme bears many traits of its infamous forebear.

I.5   Sir William Holdsworth[1] considered that the poor law system commenced with a Statute of 1535–36 (27 Henry VIII c 25), the preamble to which declared that the former Acts were defective because no provision was made in them for providing work for the unemployed. Sir William listed six principles, which he considered as underlying the early poor law development, namely:

1) the duty to contribute to the support of the poor was a legal duty of the state;
2) the parish (via the justices) was the administrative unit for assessing need and payments;
3) the impotent poor were to be supported in the places in which they were settled (but not necessarily where they were born – previously they would have been directed to return to their birth place);
4) the children of people who could not work had to be taught a trade to enable them to support themselves;
5) the able bodied vagrant and beggar should be suppressed by criminal law;
6) the able bodied should have work provided for them and it be compulsory for them to do that work.

I.6   We see, particularly in 1–3, signs of this parentage today. The obligation still rests with local councils (albeit social services authorities rather than the parish). The concept of ordinary residence persists, as does the importance of the inter-relationship between community care and education, housing and employment. While categories 5 and 6 are of relevance to our present welfare benefits system, they too have echoes in the concept of work fare, claimants' availability for work and indeed under NAA 1948 s51 it still remains a criminal offence to 'neglect to maintain oneself'.

I.7   With the abolition of the 'Poor Law' in 1948, local resources (principally the workhouses) had to be redistributed. The best of these were absorbed into the fledgling NHS and the remainder were put to use in meeting the new obligations created by Part III of the 1948 Act.[2]

I.8   Part II replaced the poor law system with a national means tested benefits system known as national assistance administered by the National Assistance Board, rather than by local councils. In due course Part II was repealed and national assistance replaced by supplementary benefit, which itself has been replaced by income support. Income support (now itself largely replaced by Employment and Support Allowance ESA) and pension credit is, however, based upon essentially the same means tested national principles which characterised national assistance.

I.9   Part III of the Act tackled the needs of vulnerable people for residential accommodation and community or home-based (domiciliary) care services. Section 21 obliged authorities to provide residential accommodation

1   W Holdsworth, *A History of English Law* vol IV, 3rd impression, 1977, pp390 et seq.
2   For an excellent account of the evolution of 'community care' see R Means and R Smith, *Community Care*, Macmillan, 1994.

for elderly and disabled people as well as temporary residential accommodation for homeless people where their homelessness had arisen through unforeseen circumstances. The accommodation obligations were met by the use of workhouses: as hostels for the homeless and as 'homes' for the disabled and elderly. The residential accommodation obligations under section 21 have changed little since 1948; it is still the statutory basis for the vast majority of local authority residential accommodation placements. In 1977 the primary duty to accommodate homeless people was transferred to housing authorities via Stephen Ross MP's private member's bill which became the Housing (Homeless Persons) Act 1977: its enactment addressing many of the appalling problems highlighted in the film 'Cathy Come Home'. A further amendment occurred in 1989 when the duty to accommodate disabled became a Children Act responsibility.

I.10 The only other significant change to section 21 resulted from the National Health Service and Community Care Act (NHSCCA) 1990. The 1990 Act repealed a provision under NHS Act 1977 Sch 8 which enabled social services authorities to provide residential accommodation for people who needed it through illness, and by amendment this accommodation obligation was transferred to section 21. The 1990 Act also amended section 21 so as to enable social services authorities to purchase nursing home accommodation in addition to residential care accommodation.

I.11 In the context of the rationing and general shortages in the post war years, the NAA 1948 obligation to provide residential care together with other social welfare duties (the house building programme, the creation of the new NHS and the education reforms) represented a huge public spending commitment. Perhaps not surprisingly therefore, when it came to the provision of community or domiciliary care services, authorities were not obliged to provide these services, although they were given discretion to do so if they were able.

I.12 NAA 1948 s29 empowered[1] authorities to provide four general types of service:

- advice and guidance;
- the preparation of a register of disabled people;
- the provision of 'occupational activities' (such as workshops) for disabled people; and
- facilities which assist disabled people to overcome limitations of communication or mobility.

I.13 The power to provide such services was limited to disabled people. This represented the concern in 1948 to ensure that those people who had sacrificed their health for peace should be given priority when it came to the provision of scarce resources.[2] In 1948 there was in relative terms a

1 These discretionary powers were subsequently converted to 'target duties' (see para 1.26) by directions issued as LAC (93)10.
2 H Bolderson, *Social Security, Disability and Rehabilitation*, Jessica Kingsley Publishers, 1991, p115.

greater number of younger disabled people – in the form of wounded soldiers returning home and those injured in the bombing. This legislative prioritisation of the needs of disabled people (as opposed to those of the temporarily ill or elderly) remains anachronistically today, albeit to a lesser extent.

I.14   Given the enormous obligations placed on authorities in the post-war austerity years, the community care services provided under section 29 were in general modest. Authorities were not under a statutory duty to provide them and in any event the community care services available under section 29 were vaguely expressed, eg, 'assistance in overcoming limitations of mobility or communication'. What was required therefore was a statutory provision (similar in nature to section 21) which provided, as of right, specific community care services for all those in need.

I.15   Although the post-war austerity years gave way to the increasingly prosperous 1950s and the relatively affluent 1960s, the provision of community care services remained a Cinderella area in social welfare terms. The mid and late 1960s were also characterised by a change in social philosophical attitudes – with, for instance, the enactment of the Family Law Reform Act 1969, the Children and Young Persons Act 1969 and the creation of social services departments in 1971 consequent upon the Seebohm report. This attitude was at considerable variance with that which promoted NAA 1948 s29; the cross-heading to which section blandly states 'services for blind, deaf, dumb and crippled persons, etc'. While therefore the pressure for a change in the statutory framework of community care services was present by the mid-1960s, reform was slow in coming.

I.16   We will never again see major social welfare legislation of the type enacted during the period 1945–1951. Since that time, beneficial social welfare legislation has generally originated from one of two sources. The first is the European Court of Human Rights; into this category one might place the Mental Health Act (MHA) 1983 and the Children Act 1989. In terms of community care, questions concerning physical or learning difficulties, age and (non-mental) ill health have attracted few complaints to the Strasbourg Court. The second source is Acts of Parliament which started life as private members' bills, such as the Housing (Homeless Persons) Act 1977.

I.17   On 6 November 1969 it was announced that Alf Morris MP had won first place in the annual ballot for private members' bills. He chose to promote his own bill (which he himself drafted), the Chronically Sick and Disabled Persons Bill. The Act received Royal Assent on 29 May 1970, the day that parliament was dissolved for the 1970 general election.[1] The most important section of that Act has proved to be section 2. It is drafted so as to make the provision of services under NAA 1948 s29 obligatory (rather than discretionary) and in place of section 29's vague wording, to spell out precisely what services are to be provided. The 1970 Act remains the finest community care statute, providing disabled people with specifically

1   For an account of the passing of the Act, see RADAR, *Be it enacted . . .*, 1995.

enforceable legal rights to specific services. Despite the significance of section 2, however, history has shown it to have three defects.

I.18   The first is that its services are only available to disabled people (as with NAA 1948 s29). Other statutory provisions are therefore required to cater for people who need such services not because they are 'permanently and substantially handicapped',[1] but because they are either frail elderly or ill (but not permanently ill). The second defect concerns two particular drafting imperfections with this section, which are considered below. The third is that the section has proved to be simply too generous – from the perspective of social services authorities. On any reasonable interpretation it entitles disabled people to receive high quality services 'as of right'. In 1970, at the end of the 'Golden Phase' of the 20th century,[2] such rights were perhaps seen as a logical next step in the development of the welfare state. The subsequent turmoil in the west, precipitated by the oil crisis in the early 1970s, led to a general retreat from such specific and (in budgetary terms) open-ended welfare rights. As a consequence, subsequent community care legislation has been cloth of a duller weave; generally 'resource' rather than 'rights' oriented. Section 2 is, sadly, out of step with all the other community care legislation and this incongruity is becoming ever more obvious.

I.19   Section 2 provided disabled people with the right to good quality community care services. The need for elderly people to have such services (when they were not themselves 'permanently and substantially handicapped') was satisfied by the enactment of Health Services and Public Health Act 1968 s45 which enabled authorities to make similar arrangements for 'promoting the welfare of old people'.[3] Likewise authorities were empowered to provide such services for ill people (ie, those not 'chronically sick') by virtue of NHS Act 1977 Sch 8. Thus by 1977 social services authorities were under varying degrees of obligation to provide an array of community care services to the three main client groups: ill, elderly and disabled people.

I.20   During the late 1970s and in the 1980s the closure of long-stay mental hospitals gathered pace, such that community care became linked in the public mind with the care of people with mental health difficulties in the community rather than by incarceration in isolated hospitals. MHA 1983 s117 accordingly made particular provision for community care services to be provided for certain patients on their discharge from hospital. Section 117 services are only available to a restricted number of people.[4] Most people with a mental health difficulty receive their community care services under CSDPA 1970 s2.

I.21   When the term 'community care services' is used today in its generic legal sense, it means (as defined by NHSCCA 1990 s46):

---

1   The definition applied under the 1948 Act, see para 9.25.
2   See E Hobsbawm, *Age of Extremes*, Michael Joseph, 1994.
3   Sections 2 and 45 came into force on the same date, 29 August 1970.
4   People who are discharged after detention under section 3 or one of the criminal provisions of MHA 1983, see para 20.24.

... services which a local authority may provide or arrange to be provided under any of the following provisions –

(a) Part III of the National Assistance Act 1948;
(b) section 45 of the Health Services and Public Health Act 1968;
(c) section 254 and Sch 20 NHS Act 2006 and section 192 and Sch 15 NHS (Wales) Act 2006;
(d) section 117 of the Mental Health Act 1983;

1.22   Although section 46 does not mention services under CSDPA 1970 s2 as being 'community care services', this is because the Department of Health has always considered section 2 to be part of section 29 of the 1948 Act. This somewhat confusing statement is explained at para 9.142 below. The question of the status of CSDPA 1970 s2 constitutes the first of its two drafting problems. The second concerns the question of when the duty under the Act crystallises in favour of a disabled person. Section 2 services are only owed to an individual when the authority is 'satisfied' that the services are necessary in order to meet his or her needs. What happens if the authority simply fails to decide whether or not it is 'satisfied' as to the person's need? In essence the duty to provide services requires a collateral duty to 'assess' a person's eligibility for that service. While Tom Clarke MP endeavoured (unsuccessfully) to fill this lacuna via his private member's bill in 1986,[1] it was only as a result of NHSCCA 1990 s47 that a comprehensive duty to assess potential service users for their possible need for services under the community care statutes was created.

1.23   A significant motivation for the 1990 Act was the soaring social security expenditure on private residential care and nursing home accommodation: this had increased from about £10 million per annum in 1979 to £2.5 billion per annum in 1993. Hospitals were closing long-stay geriatric and psychiatric wards and discharging the patients into private nursing homes where the cost could be funded by the Department of Health and Social Security (DHSS), essentially, therefore, transferring the cost from one central government department's budget (the NHS) to another (Social Security). At the same time social services authorities were doing much the same, by closing their own residential care homes and transferring the residents to independent-sector homes, which again were capable of being funded via the DHSS, thus transferring the cost from local to central government.

1.24   The 1990 Act sought to cap this expenditure by transferring most of the funding responsibility to social services authorities and restricting access to residential and nursing homes if the person was to be supported by public funds. Access to such care was to be conditional on the authority being satisfied that such a placement was appropriate. Social services authorities were provided with a 'Special Transitional Grant' to compensate them for their extra costs in implementing the community care reforms and in particular for assuming responsibility for funding such accommodation. In the first full year of the reforms (1994–95) the Grant

---

1   Disabled Persons (Services, Consultation and Representation) Act 1986 s4.

amounted to £735.9 million of which 85 per cent was ring-fenced to the extent that it had to be spent on independent sector care services.[1]

1.25   The Act also endeavoured to bring together the disparate statutes which governed individual entitlement to community care services and, by various amendments, create a degree of coherence in this field of law. It was preceded by a white paper, *Caring for People*,[2] which owed much to a report prepared in 1988 by Sir Roy Griffiths for the Secretary of State for Social Services.[3] The NHSCCA 1990 does not, however, convert into law many of the themes which infused the white paper, the Griffiths report and many of the subsequent practice guides issued by the Department of Health.

1.26   The white paper set out six key objectives in relation to the community care reforms (at para 1.11), namely:

- **to promote the development of domiciliary, day and respite services to enable people to live in their own homes wherever feasible and sensible.**
  Existing funding structures have worked against the development of such services. In future, the Government will encourage the targeting of home-based services on those people whose need for them is greatest;

- **to ensure that service providers make practical support for carers a high priority.**
  Assessment of care needs should always take account of the needs of caring family, friends and neighbours;

- **to make proper assessment of need and good case management the corner stone of high quality care.**
  Packages of care should then be designed in line with individual needs and preferences;

- **to promote the development of a flourishing independent sector alongside good quality public services.**
  The Government has endorsed Sir Roy Griffiths' recommendation that social services authorities should be 'enabling' agencies. It will be their responsibility to make maximum possible use of private and voluntary providers, and so increase the available range of options and widen consumer choice;

- **to clarify the responsibilities of agencies and so make it easier to hold them to account for their performance.**
  The Government recognises that the present confusion has contributed to poor overall performance;

- **to secure better value for taxpayers' money by introducing a new funding structure for social care.**
  The Government's aim is that social security provisions should not, as

---

1   For further details see B Meredith, *The Community Care Handbook*, Age Concern England, 1995, p165.

2   Department of Health (1989) *Caring for People: Community Care in the Next Decade and Beyond*. Cm 849.

3   R Griffiths, *Community Care: Agenda for Action*, HMSO, 1988.

they do now, provide any incentive in favour of residential and nursing home care.

I.27   The NHSCCA 1990 was however largely silent on these themes. It provided no practical support for carers – this was left to Malcolm Wicks MP and his private member's bill which became the Carers (Recognition and Services) Act 1995. As to the emphasis on individual choice (or 'preferences'), this concept appears nowhere in any of the legislation, with the exception of the NAA 1948 (Choice of Accommodation) Directions 1992.

I.28   The reforms of the 1990s coincided with the emergence, at a national political level, of the disability rights movements. Many disabled people viewed the community care regime as disabling and disempowering and sought greater control, by way of direct payments and involvement at a strategic planning level. On the positive side, the Disability Discrimination Act 1995, the Community Care (Direct Payments) Act 1996 (and their successor statutes) together with the Human Rights Act 1998 have begun to address – directly or indirectly – some of these issues.

I.29   The period between 1993 and 2011 did not see any radical new thinking by the governments in England and Wales. The Royal Commission on Long Term Care's 1999 report *With Respect to Old Age* recommending a fundamental change in the funding arrangements was rejected (or more accurately, in Wales 'not implemented'). Instead the focus has been on structural/administrative reform with the Health and Social Care Act 2001 providing for the effective merger of social and health care bodies. During this period of organisational turbulence, health and social care staff have additionally been subjected to a plethora of targets, performance indicators, auditing regimes, National Service Frameworks and central government micro-guidance. As Onora O'Neill observed in the 2002 Reith lecture, 'central planning may have failed in the Soviet Union but it is alive and well in Britain today'.[1]

I.30   In the last five years, policy initiatives that have come to be called the 'personalisation agenda' have sought to create the illusion of radical new thinking and reform. However, like many of its similarly branded forebears, there must be significant doubt as to whether this programme has the ability to transform the lives of the majority of people in need of community care services.[2]

I.31   As this edition goes to print community care law remains a hotchpotch of conflicting statutes, enacted over a period of 60 years, with each statute embodying a slightly different philosophical attitude: the one prevalent at its enactment. Whilst this may be the last edition that seeks to piece together so many disparate Acts (as consolidating adult care legislation reflecting the recommendations of the Law Commission has been chalked in for 2012) this reform will not of itself do anything practical for disabled, older and ill people. What the current system requires (a system that the House of Commons Health Committee in 2010 declared 'no

1   O O'Neill, *A Question of Trust*, Cambridge University Press, 2002.
2   See in this context, L Clements 'Individual Budgets and irrational exuberance' (2008) 11 CCLR 413–430.

longer fit for purpose'[1]) is very substantial additional funding. Where these extra resources are to come from remains unclear. A succession of Commissions have suggested mechanisms for placing the funding of social care on a sustainable footing – most recently the Dilnot Commission[2] – but politically, there appears to be little enthusiasm to take action.

I.32   The law reform, that this book has been calling for since its first publication 15 years ago, now looks likely to take place. It is to be hoped that the funding reform, that is now so desperately required, will be somewhat quicker to arrive.

---

1   House of Commons Health Committee – Third Report Social Care 2010 para 78 at www.publications.parliament.uk/pa/cm200910/cmselect/cmhealth/22/2202.htm
2   Commission on Funding of Care and Support (2011) *Fairer Care Funding: The Report of the Commission on Funding of Care and Support* (the 'Dilnot' Report).

CHAPTER 1

The statutory scheme underpinning social care and the NHS services

Introduction

1.1   Primary responsibility for the delivery of community care services rests with local (social services) authorities. In a number of instances, however, obligation is shared with the NHS and in certain situations it may be the NHS's exclusive responsibility.

1.2   This chapter commences with an outline of the statutory regimes regulating these two bodies in relation to the discharge of their community care responsibilities. It then considers the nature of their public law obligations and concludes by considering Part I of the Local Government Act (LGA) 2000 which has significantly widened the powers of local authorities to promote the economic, social or environmental well-being of their area (see para 1.68 below).

Local authority social services functions

The structure of social services authorities

1.3   The community care obligations created by the National Assistance Act (NAA) 1948 were initially discharged by the welfare departments of county and county borough councils. Concern over the effectiveness of these local arrangements culminated in a critical report – the 'Seebohm report'[1] – that led to the enactment of the Local Authority Social Services Act (LASSA) 1970 which required major reform of the way councils dealt with their social care responsibilities and resulted in the creation of 'social services departments'. The 1970 Act remains the primary statute governing authorities that discharge social services functions (the material parts of the Act are in appendix 1 below). These permitted 'functions' are listed in the first schedule to LASSA 1970. The list is regularly updated and comprises a familiar (and long) list of statutory provisions, such as the NAA 1948, the Children Act (CA) 1989, the Carers (Equal Opportunities) Act 2004 and so on. The local authorities concerned are county councils, the London and metropolitan boroughs and other unitary authorities as well as the Common Council of the City of London and the Council of the Isles of Scilly (section 1).

1.4   LASSA 1970 s6 required all social services authorities to appoint a director of social services and this requirement remains in Wales. However, since the enactment of the Children Act (CA) 2004, social services in England are obliged to appoint a Director of Children's Services (section 18). CA 2004 amends LASSA 1970 s6 requiring the appointment of an officer who fulfils the functions of a Director of Adult Social Services. Accordingly social services in England are now the responsibility of two departments, namely an adult social services department (not uncommonly combining other functions – eg housing and 'well-being' in some

---

1   *Report of the Committee on Local Authority and Allied Personal Social Services* Cmnd 3703, 1968.

unitary authorities) and a children's services department (incorporating education and children's social services functions). The 2004 legislative programme anticipated the creation of non-statutory 'children's trusts' in England, but these have, it appears, proved to be of limited effectiveness.[2]

1.5   As a consequence of LGA 2000 s102, social services authorities now have considerable flexibility as to how their elected members supervise the discharge of their social services responsibilities: this may be by way of a traditional social services committee, or by way of the new executive arrangements (sometimes called the 'cabinet system').[3]

1.6   The Department of Health has issued two guidance documents concerning the role of the Director of Adult Social Services in England,[4] one being policy guidance under LASSA 1970 s7(1) (see para 1.46 below) and the other being best practice guidance.

1.7   The policy guidance requires among other things that local authorities ensure that the director is responsible/ accountable for:

- the authority's delivery of social services for adults;
- promoting social inclusion and well-being with a view to (among other things) developing sustainable services that promote independence and minimise the need for intensive home care and residential services;
- maintaining clear and effective arrangements to support the joint planning, monitoring and delivery of local authority social services with the NHS, housing authorities, Supporting People programme and other statutory agencies;
- ensuring (with the director of children's services) 'adequate arrangements' are in place 'to ensure that all young people with long-term social care needs have been assessed and, where eligible, receive a service which meets their needs throughout their transition to becoming adults' (see para 23.67 below).

1.8   By LASSA 1970 s6(6) it is the authority's duty to 'secure the provision of adequate staff[5] for assisting' in the exercise of the director's functions. Whilst authorities will be given a wide discretion by the courts in deciding

---

2   A critical Audit Commission report (2008) *Are We There Yet? Improving governance and resource management in children's trusts*, described children's trusts as 'unincorporated associations . . . [that] do not own assets, or employ staff. They are not legally accountable bodies for spending public money, or for achieving public objectives' (para 158) and concluded that was little evidence that they had 'improved outcomes for children and young people or delivered better value for money, over and above locally agreed cooperation' (summary).

3   The Localism Bill (2011) Part 3 (if enacted) will permit the secretary of state in England to implement changes to the governance arrangements of local authorities, and see also Local Government and Public Involvement in Health Act 2007 s236.

4   Department of Health (2006) *Guidance on the Statutory Chief Officer Post of Director of Adult Social Services issued under s7(1) Local Authority Social Services Act 1970*; Department of Health (2006) *Best Practice Guidance on the role of the Director of Adult Social Services*.

5   As well as the parallel duty, under the National Health Service Act (NHSA) 2006 s254 and Sch 20, to provide 'sufficient' approved social workers for the purposes of the Mental Health Act 1983, see para 9.175 below.

what is an 'adequate' staff (for the purposes of section 6(6)), the question may be raised in judicial review proceedings (or ombudsman complaints[6]) particularly where the applicant is challenging the non-provision of a service dependent upon 'human resources'.[7] Such proceedings are, however, unlikely to be appropriate where the complaint concerns the interruption of services due to unpredictable staff absences,[8] although where the complaint concerns a repeated failure of the service due to predictable interruptions, this would seem at least a matter of maladministration and amenable to remedy via the local authority complaints system.

1.9   LASSA 1970 (as amended) sets out the broad framework as to how social services departments are to be organised. As with many social welfare statutes, reserve powers were retained by the secretary of state to enable 'orders', 'directions' and 'guidance' to be issued; however, in the early years of the Act, central government exercised a 'positive philosophy of as little interference as is possible'[9] – or at least a lightness of touch over these levers of control:

> . . . there was no notion of a direct line of command from central government dictating either the organisational structure of social work at the local level or the detailed policies to be implemented within and through that structure in response to legislation. Within loose overall financial controls there was room for local authority social services departments to shape structures and policies within the framework of central government's legislation and general policy guidance.[10]

1.10   This is no longer the case. Through the provisions of LASSA 1970 s7 (see below), and array of performance indicators, performance ratings and inspection regimes the Department of Health and the Welsh Government (WG) exercise a degree of control over the actions of social services departments – which is at times best characterised as micromanagement (see para 2.17 below where performance indicators are further considered).

NHS community care functions

1.11   At the beginning of the 20th century the majority of institutional health and social care services were provided via the poor law boards. Gradually as the century progressed, local authorities assumed greater

6   Report on complaint no 05/C/18474 against Birmingham City Council, 4 March 2008 which referred to the council's 'corporate failure to ensure adequate resourcing and performance of its services to highly vulnerable people' (para 55).
7   To establish a case under this ground, useful evidence can be obtained from social services committee minutes, which not infrequently record unsuccessful requests by the director for extra staff.
8   *R v Islington LBC ex p McMillan* (1997–98) 1 CCLR 7 at 10, (1995) *Times* 21 June QBD.
9   J Griffith, *Central departments and local authorities*, Allen and Unwin, 1966, p515 cited by R Means and R Smith, *From Poor Law to Community Care*, Policy Press, 1998, at p156.
10   J Harris, *The Social Work Business*, Routledge, 2003, p18.

responsibilities for both functions. The 1929[11] poor law reforms led to the creation of local authority health committees, which took control of the better poor law hospitals (then known as public health hospitals). The remaining poor law institutions, workhouses and basic poor law hospitals were also transferred from the poor law boards, becoming the responsibility of the county and county borough councils.

1.12   The creation of the NHS in 1948 did not initially wrest responsibility for health services from local authorities. Although today it is convenient to see the National Health Service Act (NHSA) 1946 and NAA 1948 as demarcating the responsibilities of what we now call social services departments and the NHS, this separation of responsibilities has in fact developed largely as a consequence of subsequent legislation. The NHSA 1946 stipulated that many services we would today label as 'health services', such as ambulances (section 27), midwifery (section 23), health visitors (section 24), were to be the responsibility of local authority health committees (called 'local health authorities').[12] Indeed NAA 1948 s21(7)(b), as originally enacted, authorised the provision by local authorities of 'health services,[13] not being specialist services or services of a kind normally provided only on admission to hospital'.

1.13   While minor changes to the health/social care responsibilities of NHS/local authorities occurred over the next 25 years,[14] major reform did not take place until 1974, when LGA 1972 and the NHS Reorganisation Act 1973 came into force. The 1973 Act sought to transfer all nursing functions (whether in hospital, at home or elsewhere) to the NHS. It abolished local health authorities (ie local authority health committees) and in their place created free standing regional, area and district health authorities.

1.14   Since the early 1970s the NHS has been the subject of continual reform – a process that shows no evidence of abating. In 1977, the 1946 Act was repealed and replaced by a consolidating Act, NHSA 1977, and in 2006 this itself was repealed and consolidated – into three Acts, NHSA 2006, the NHS (Wales) Act (NHS(W)A) 2006 and the NHS (Consequential Provisions) Act (NHS(CP)A) 2006, of which the former is the principal Act (see para 13.8 below).

Primary care trusts, care trusts and local health boards

1.15   The reforms, which have been described elsewhere,[15] have produced the current commissioning arrangements in England where the commission-

---

11 Local Government Act 1929.
12 NHSA 1946 Part II Sch 4.
13 Including nursing services by virtue of NHSA 1946 s25.
14 Most notably the Health Services and Public Health Act 1968 which transferred to local health authorities responsibility for health visitors and nursing other than in a person's home; and LASSA 1970 which in its first schedule sought to delineate the responsibilities of local authority social services departments.
15 See eg the third edition of this text at paras 10.3–10.11.

ing of health services is the responsibility of approximately 150 PCTs[16] or care trusts whose performance is assessed and directed by ten strategic health authorities[17] (SHAs). In Wales, services are primarily commissioned by 7 local health boards[18] (LHBs) whose performance is assessed and directed by the Welsh Government. The commissioning scheme in England will be radically reformed if the Health and Social Care Bill (2011) is enacted (see para 13.6 below).

1.16   In England, PCTs are able to effectively 'merge' with the social services arm of a local authority[19] and create a 'care trust'.[20] As at May 2011 17 care trusts had been established in England. Care trusts are separate entities and legally responsible for the discharge of their health and social care functions (which should be compared with the situation in relation to partnership working arrangements – see para 13.127 below). Some concern has been expressed that care trusts have tended to prioritise health services over social care.[21]

NHS trusts and foundation trusts

1.17   PCTs, LHBs and care trusts have the primary responsibility for commissioning services to ensure, so far as is possible, that there is a 'comprehensive' health service (see para 13.13 below). They discharge this obligation by providing and commissioning primary care services, and by contracting with NHS trusts[22] and NHS foundation trusts (ie hospitals).

1.18   NHS trusts are semi-autonomous bodies which came into being as a result of the National Health Service and Community Care Act (NHSCCA) 1990 reforms and are responsible for the ownership and management of hospitals or other NHS facilities.

1.19   As a result of the Health and Social Care (Community and Health Standards) Act 2003 s1, NHS trusts in England are able to achieve semi-independence from the Department of Health and greater financial flexibilities by becoming an NHS foundation trust. There were (at May 2011) 129 such trusts, which are now governed by NHSA 2006 s30. The Coalition Government proposes in its 2010 White Paper a greatly expanded role for such trusts, and that all NHS trusts become foundation trusts by 2013.[23]

---

16 NHSA 2006 ss18–24.
17 NHSA 2006 s13.
18 NHS(W)A 2006 ss11; The Local Health Boards (Establishment and Dissolution) (Wales) Order 2009. Prior to October 2009 commissioning was in the hands of 22 Local Health Boards.
19 Care Trusts (Applications and Consultation) Regulations 2001 SI No 3788 – which requires consultation following a period of established partnership working arrangements by the two bodies (see para 13.127).
20 NHSA 2006 s77.
21 See eg Commission for Social Care Inspection, *Inspection of social care services for older people, Northumberland County Council*, 2006, para 9.12.
22 NHSA 2006 ss25–27; NHS(W)A 2006 ss18–21.
23 Secretary of State for Health (2010) *Equity and excellence: Liberating the NHS*, Cm7881, para 4.21 and 4.23.

1.20   NHS trusts and foundation trusts do not receive funding in the way that PCTs, LHBs and care trusts do, but rather through the contracts they conclude with these bodies.[24]

Statutory duties and powers

1.21   Social services and NHS functions are normally expressed as being obligatory (ie a statutory duty) or discretionary (ie a statutory power). Accordingly the use of the words 'can' and 'may' in a statute are interpreted as conferring a permissive power rather than a duty. Conversely, the appearance of the words 'shall' or 'must' are in general construed as creating a duty – an obligation to do or refrain from doing something. This is not, however, always the case. As *de Smith* points out,[25] a local authority empowered to approve building plans has been held to be obliged to approve plans that were in conformity with its bylaws,[26] whereas a local authority required by statute to provide suitable alternative accommodation for those displaced by a closing order has been held not to be obliged to place them at the top of the housing waiting list.[27]

Powers

1.22   Where an authority has a power to act, but not a duty, it must (when the possible use of that power arises) exercise its discretion in each case. Authorities are generally free to refuse to use a power, provided they reach such a decision in accordance with the principles of administrative law (and the refusal does not result in a breach of the European Convention on Human Rights[28]). They must not, for instance, ignore circular guidance,[29] operate a perverse policy which (in practice) fetters their discretion[30] or in certain situations fail to consult before reaching a decision.[31]

24 Under NHSA 2006 s9 and NHS(W)A 2006 s7, 'NHS contracts' are not legally enforceable but are subject to arbitration by the secretary of state/ Welsh Government. For details of the contracting and commissioning responsibilities of PCTs, see generally *The NHS Contractors' Companion*, Department of Health.
25 De Smith, Woolf and Jowell, *Judicial Review of Administrative Action*, 5th edn, Sweet & Maxwell, 1995, p301.
26 *R v Newcastle-upon-Tyne Corporation* (1889) 60 LT 963.
27 *R v Bristol Corporation ex p Hendy* [1974] 1 WLR 498.
28 See para 26.237 below.
29 *R v North Derbyshire Health Authority ex p Fisher* (1997–98) 1 CCLR 150, QBD (see para 1.41 below).
30 *R v North West Lancashire Health Authority ex p A* [2000] 1 WLR 977, (1999) 2 CCLR 419, CA and see para 13.19 below generally.
31 See eg *R v North West Lancashire Health Authority ex p A* [2000] 1 WLR 977, (1999) 2 CCLR 419, CA and *R (Morris) v Trafford Healthcare NHS Trust* [2006] EWHC 2334 (Admin), (2006) 9 CCLR 648.

Duties

1.23   Statutory duties owed by public bodies can be divided into two categories, general public law duties (known as 'target' duties) and specific duties owed to individuals. Specific duties are worded in precise and personal terms, so that it is clear that they are intended to confer enforceable rights upon individuals, and also make clear when these rights arise. Accordingly a failure to comply with a specific law duty may entitle an aggrieved party to a court order compelling the authority to carry out its duty (for instance an order requiring it to undertake a lawful community care assessment or to provide a specific community care service). Such duties do not, in themselves, create a 'duty of care' at common law which could found a claim for damages for injuries sustained due to their non-performance[32] – although the Ombudsman may consider non-performance to be maladministration for which a compensatory payment might be appropriate (see para 26.139 below).

1.24   Duties cannot be frustrated by fixed or 'blanket' policies – for example, by placing an absolute upper limit on the amount of support that will be provided or on the amount of a direct payment, or of never providing small items of equipment: indeed, rigid policies of this type are not permitted even where the statute provides for a discretion rather than a duty (see para 26.209 below).

1.25   In *R v Gloucestershire CC ex p Mahfood*[33] McCowan LJ held that Chronically Sick and Disabled Persons Act 1970 s2 created specific public law duties. In his opinion, once an authority had decided that it was under a duty to make arrangements under section 2, it was 'under an absolute duty to make them. It is a duty owed to a specific individual and not a target duty'.[34] The duty under section 117 of the Mental Health Act 1983 has also been held to be capable of being an individual public law duty.[35]

1.26   In contrast, general public law (or 'target') duties are worded in broad and impersonal terms, and contain a 'degree of elasticity'[36] in their interpretation – such that it is generally left to the authority in question to decide when (and to what extent) the duty comes into being. Callaghan[37] argues that target duties are essentially aspirational in nature, requiring

---

32 See for instance *Sandford v Waltham Forest LBC* [2008] EWHC 1106 (QBD) which concerned a claim for injuries allegedly suffered as a result of the failure of the local authority to provide cot sides for a bed – which it had assessed as being required under Chronically Sick and Disabled Persons Act 1970 s2. The High Court, however, did suggest that there was a common law duty on social workers to use reasonable skill when undertaking a community care assessment.

33 (1997–98) 1 CCLR 7, (1995) *Times* 21 June, QBD.

34 (1997–98) 1 CCLR 7 at 16G, (1995) *Times* 21 June, QBD.

35 *R (IH) v Secretary of State for the Home Department and others* [2003] UKHL 59, [2003] 3 WLR 1278, (2004) 7 CCLR 147.

36 Per Woolf LJ in *R v Inner London Education Authority ex p Ali* (1990) 2 Admin LR 822, p828D.

37 C Callaghan, 'What is a "target duty"?' (2000) 5(3) *Judicial Review* 184–187: In *R (G) v Barnet LBC* [2003] UKHL 57, [2003] 3 WLR 1194, (2003) 6 CCLR 500 Lord Scott (at para 115) referred to such a duty being 'expressed in broad aspirational terms that would not easily lend themselves to mandatory enforcement'.

an authority to 'do its best',[38] and that 'courts will permit public authorities to take into account practical realities, including budgetary and resource considerations, in determining how best to fulfil the target duty'.

1.27   A notable example of such a general duty is to be found in NHSA 2006 s1[39] which places a duty on the secretary of state to 'continue the promotion in England of a comprehensive health service'. The duty is not expressed as being owed to any specific individual and it is particularly difficult for a court to decide when it has been breached. To mount a successful action, an aggrieved patient would have to show, not only that he or she failed to receive a health service due to the service not being 'comprehensive' (whatever that may mean) but also that the secretary of state had effectively abandoned any intention of 'promoting' such a service. As the Court of Appeal held in *R v North and East Devon Health Authority ex p Coughlan*:[40]

> 25. When exercising his judgment [the secretary of state] has to bear in mind the comprehensive service which he is under a duty to promote as set out in section 1. However, as long as he pays due regard to that duty, the fact that the service will not be comprehensive does not mean that he is necessarily contravening either section 1 or section 3.

The section 1 duty is considered further at paras 13.9 and 13.16 below.

1.28   It is not always clear whether a particular obligation falls into the specific or target category. As Scott-Baker J observed in *R (A) v Lambeth LBC*:[41]

> Community care legislation has grown up piecemeal through numerous statutes over the past half century. There are many statutes aimed at different targets whose provisions are drawn in differing language. Each Act contains its own duties and powers. Specific duties have to be distinguished from target or general duties and duties from discretions. Sometimes a local authority has several ways in which it can meet an obligation. Some provisions overlap with others and the inter-relationship is not always easy.

1.29   A number of community care duties can be characterised as hybrid in nature; that is to say that although drafted in general terms, they can 'crystallise'[42] during the assessment process (see para 3.137) into specific public law duties owed to individual service users. Thus the general duty under NAA 1948 s21(1)(a) to provide residential accommodation for adults in need of care and attention (see paras 3.176 and 7.12) may be converted by a community care assessment into a specific public law duty.[43] In

---

38 *R v Radio Authority ex p Bull* [1998] QB 294 at 309, CA.
39 In Wales, NHS(W)A 2006 s1.
40 [2000] 2 WLR 622, (1999) 2 CCLR 285, CA.
41 [2001] EWHC 376 (Admin), [2001] 2 FLR 1201; the quotation also appears in the subsequent Court of Appeal judgment, *R (A) v Lambeth LBC* [2001] EWCA Civ 1624, (2001) 4 CCLR 486 at 499–450.
42 See the comments of Laws LJ in *R (A) v Lambeth LBC* [2001] EWCA Civ 1624, (2001) 4 CCLR 486 at 499D where he adopted Richard Gordon QC's use of this phrasing.
43 See eg *R v Sefton MBC ex p Help the Aged and Blanchard* [1997] 4 All ER 532, (1997–98) 1 CCLR 57, CA, and *R v Kensington and Chelsea RLBC ex p Kujtim* [1999] 4 All ER 161, (1999) 2 CCLR 340, CA.

R (T, D and B) v Haringey LBC[44] Ouseley J accepted that, in principle, obligations under the Human Rights Act 1998 could 'crystallise' target duties into specific law duties.

1.30   Arguments concerning the enforceability of such statutory provisions are becoming increasing rarefied and difficult to follow.[45] In *R (W) v Lambeth LBC*[46] and *R (G) v Barnet LBC*,[47] for example, the Court of Appeal and the House of Lords grappled with the differing phrasing of the obligations to provide care services for disabled children and disabled adults. They concluded that although the assessment process for adults (under NHSCCA 1990 s47) could result in specific public law duties, this was not the case in relation to children (whose assessment process was governed by CA 1989 s17). Not only is it difficult to follow the logic of the court's analysis in reaching this conclusion, it is particularly difficult to see the sense in (effectively) prioritising the rights of disabled adults to services over the rights of disabled children.

1.31   It has been argued that what we are seeing in such cases is an 'attempt to shore up the increasingly questionable public policy approach towards the state delivery of community care services'.[48] In effect, that the artificial distinction between target and specific public law duties stems from the judiciary's anxiety over the resource implications of their judgments,[49] and that this entirely artificial construct is proving to be insufficiently flexible to mediate between the complexities of state responsibilities (in a post Human Rights Act 1998 era) and individual need. Increasingly the courts appear to be using the imperative (if not the logic) of the European Convention on Human Rights in determining the enforceability of statutory obligations – and this approach is considered in greater detail at para 3.197 below.

Regulations

1.32   In common with many other Acts, NHS and local authority statutes empower the secretary of state/Welsh Government to issue various forms of delegated legislation – most commonly as regulations, rules and orders. These flesh out the bare bones of the duty or power imposed by the primary statute. In relation to residential accommodation, for

44 [2005] EWHC 2235 (Admin), (2006) 9 CCLR 58 at [142].
45 See eg the comments of Potter LJ in *R v Kensington and Chelsea RLBC ex p Kujtim* [1999] 4 All ER 161, (1999) 2 CCLR 340 at 353J, CA where he admitted to finding difficulty in following the arguments of Sedley J (concerning a parallel set of target duties) in *R v Islington LBC ex p Rixon* (1997–98) 1 CCLR 119, 15 March 1996, QBD.
46 [2002] EWCA Civ 613, [2002] 2 All ER 901, (2002) 5 CCLR 203.
47 [2003] UKHL 57, [2003] 3 WLR 1194, (2003) 6 CCLR 500 (see para 23.49 below).
48 L Clements, 'The collapsing duty: a sideways look at community care and public law' [1997] *Judicial Review Journal* 162.
49 Lord Hoffman put the position frankly when delivering the 2001 Commercial Bar Lecture ('The Separation of Powers', unpublished) commenting 'even when a case appears to involve no more than the construction of a statute or interpretation of a common law rule, the courts are very circumspect about giving an answer which would materially affect the distribution of public expenditure'.

instance, NAA 1948 s22(1) requires authorities to charge for such accommodation and section 22(5) authorises the secretary of state to issue regulations detailing how this shall be done. These were subsequently issued as the National Assistance (Assessment of Resources) Regulations 1992.[50]

1.33 Such delegated legislation has the force of law, and the procedure by which it is promulgated is set out in the Statutory Instruments Act 1946, as modified in relation to Wales by the Government of Wales Acts 1998 and 2006. These Acts detail the requirements for publication and the various types of procedures by which the legislation is laid before Parliament/Welsh Government. Delegated legislation must not, therefore, stray outside the ambit of its enabling statutory provision. Accordingly, in the example of the 1948 Act above, the regulations issued under section 22(5) could only lawfully address the question of the assessment of charges for residential accommodation. Judicial review will lie where the statutory instrument exceeds such limits.[51] In similar terms, delegated legislation must not derogate from provisions in the enabling legislation; thus where rights are conferred by a statute, any subsequent regulations must not detract from those rights[52] (see para 26.212 below where this question is further considered).

Directions and guidance

1.34 LASSA 1970 ss7(1) and 7A require social services authorities to be administered under the general supervision of the secretary of state/Welsh Government. The provisions state as follows:

> *Local authorities to exercise social services functions under guidance of Secretary of State*
> 7(1) Local authorities shall, in the exercise of their social services functions, including the exercise of any discretion conferred by any relevant enactment, act under the general guidance of the secretary of state.
> *Directions by the Secretary of State as to exercise of social services functions*
> 7A(1) Without prejudice to section 7 of this Act, every local authority shall exercise their social services functions in accordance with such directions as may be given to them under this section by the secretary of state.
> (2) Directions under this section –
> (a) shall be given in writing; and
> (b) may be given to a particular authority, or to authorities of a particular class, or to authorities generally.

1.35 The distinction between 'directions' and 'guidance' is therefore a distinction between having to act 'in accordance with' directions as opposed to having to act 'under' guidance.

---

50 SI No 2977: see para 8.9.
51 See eg *Re Ripon* [1939] 2 KB 838 and *Dunkley v Evans* [1981] 1 WLR 1522.
52 See eg *King v Henderson* [1898] AC 720.

Directions

1.36   Directions have the force of law. The power of the secretary of state/Welsh Government to issue directions, contained in LASSA 1970 s7A (above), are replicated in the NHS Acts 2006. NHSA 2006 s8 empowers the secretary of state to issue directions to NHS bodies in England and NHS(W)A 2006 ss12 and 19 give the corresponding power to the Welsh Ministers. NHSA 2006 s20 empowers SHAs in England to issue directions to PCTs.

1.37   In relation to social services functions, examples of such directions include the National Assistance Act (Choice of Accommodation) Directions 1992 (see para 7.103 below) and the Community Care Assessment Directions 2004 (see para 3.24 below). Examples of NHS directions are the NHS Continuing Healthcare (Responsibilities) Directions 2009 (see para 14.42 below) and the Directions Concerning Dowry Payments HSG (95)45 (see para 13.130 below). These have the force of law and are set out as would be any statutory instrument.

1.38   Directions are problematical constitutional instruments. Many of them are not issued as statutory instruments;[53] they are not in general subject to parliamentary scrutiny; and they can be difficult (sometimes almost impossible) to obtain. In England the Department of Health website has a list – by no means exhaustive – of some relevant directions,[54] whereas in Wales the situation is lamentable. The Welsh Government's website lists some of the directions issued after 2005 but it appears that there is no central register of those that were issued prior to this date. The Welsh Government puts this down to the difficulty 'in defining what amounts to non-statutory instrument subordinate legislation' and (in 2006) indicated that it was undertaking a 'feasibility study to consider the issue of indexing non-statutory instrument subordinate legislation made between 1999 and 2005'.[55] It is highly questionable whether such a policy complies with the Welsh Government's publication scheme under the Freedom of Information Act 2000 and indeed whether any of the inaccessible directions can be deemed to be 'law' – given that it is a 'fundamental requisite of the rule of law that the law should be made known'.[56]

1.39   To add to the confusion, directions are not always published separately: they may appear as appendices to guidance issued by the Department of Health or the Welsh Government. In this context important directions were issued as appendices to local authority circular LAC (93)10/Welsh Office Circular WOC 35/93 (concerning NAA 1948 Part III and the then

---

53 Directions are only published in the form of a statutory instrument if this requirement is stipulated in the primary Act: see eg NHSA 2006 s273(4) and NHS(W)A 2006 s204(3).

54 For instance LAC (93) 10 is not in the list of Directions on the website in spite of being pivotal in relation to establishing powers and duties across social care, although it is available if typed into the search engine.

55 Letter, First Minister for Wales to Lord Evans of Temple Guiting, 22 June 2006.

56 *R (Salih) v Secretary of State for the Home Department* [2003] EWHC 2273 (Admin) at [45], per Stanley-Burnton J where he held that this requirement extended to certain extra-statutory policy documents issued by the government.

NHSA 1977 Sch 8[57]), and DHSS Circular 19/71 (concerning Health Services and Public Health Act 1968 s45[58]).

1.40   In *Godbold v Mahmood*,[59] Mitting J noted that leading counsel had been unable to trace a direction (in this case LAC(93)10 – see para 7.25 below) and that he (Mitting J) had come across it 'by chance' whilst hearing a separate judicial review. The judge himself commented on the unusual nature and effect of such instruments since 'the duty is imposed not by primary legislation or even by secondary legislation, but by a combination of primary legislation and ministerial direction. The ministerial direction can be changed or withdrawn at any time without recourse to Parliament.'

1.41   Given the uncertain nature of directions, it will not always be clear if a departmental instruction to a local authority or the NHS is a direction or guidance. Such a question arose in *R v North Derbyshire Health Authority ex p Fisher*[60] where Dyson J had to decide whether an executive letter[61] was a 'direction' under the then NHSA 1977,[62] and if not, how much weight a health authority was required to afford it. He held that directions could be contained in such a circular, but that the wording of the circular was not sufficiently mandatory to be a 'direction'.

> If it is the intention of the secretary of state to give directions which attract a statutory duty of compliance, then he should make it clear that this is what he is doing. The difference between a policy which provides mere guidance and one which the . . . authority is obliged to implement is critical. Policy which is in the form of guidance can be expressed in strong terms and yet fall short of amounting to directions.

1.42   Accordingly it was to be construed as 'strong guidance'. This meant that the health authority, although not obliged to follow the circular, could only depart from it by giving clear reasons for so doing and that those reasons would be susceptible to a *Wednesbury* challenge (see para 26.196 – and see also para 26.231 below). In finding against the health authority the judge held that it had failed to understand the circular properly and therefore its actions were defective (as if it had had no regard to the circular at all).

1.43   Many of the directions that concern NHS responsibilities were issued in relation to the (now repealed) NHSA 1977. These continue to apply by virtue of NHS(CP)A 2006 s4 and Sch 2 para 1(2) which provide that directions issued in relation to the 1977 Act continue and apply with equal effect to the consequent provisions in the NHS Acts 2006.

---

57 See paras 7.25 and 9.45 below where these directions are considered further.
58 See paras 7.8 and 9.159 below where this direction is considered in detail.
59 [2005] EWHC 1002 (QB), [2005] Lloyd's Rep Med 379 at [24]–[26].
60 (1997–98) 1 CCLR 150, 11 July 1997, QBD.
61 EL(95)97, concerning the prescribing of Beta-Interferon drugs to people with MS.
62 At that time the relevant section was section 13.

Guidance

1.44   As noted above (see para 1.9 above), the original scheme for health and social care legislation was for a loose legislative framework within which there was room for local bodies to shape structures and policies. The enabling Acts, however, provided central government with the powers to exert control if needs be, by (for example) issuing regulations, directions and guidance. Over the last 50 years these powers have been used with increasing frequency to the point today that it could be argued that the mass of detailed guidance that now exists – particularly in relation to social services activities – is itself a major problem, inhibiting innovation and undermining local initiative. The Law Commission has expressed its concern about the 'increasing importance is being given to policy documents in areas where legal guidance is needed'[63] and recommended that if practice guidance is issued in relation to a revised legislative scheme – that it:

> should be kept to a minimum and the legal status of the guidance should be clarified and stated clearly in the guidance itself. Future policy documents should state that they are not legal documents and should be understood as indicating the direction of Government policy.[64]

Social services guidance

1.45   There are two basic types of social services guidance:

- *formal guidance* (often referred to as 'policy guidance') issued by the secretary of state specifically declaring that it is issued under LASSA 1970 s7(1) (ie 's7(1) guidance');
- *general guidance* (often called 'practice guidance' or 'best practice guidance') of the classic form, ie advice to which an authority should have regard when reaching a decision, but which it is not required to follow slavishly.

Policy guidance

1.46   Social services policy guidance (sometimes referred to as statutory guidance) is a higher-status form of guidance and is generally labelled as such: frequently it commences with the statement 'this guidance is issued under s7(1) Local Authority Social Services Act 1970'.

1.47   The wording of section 7(1) is such that local authorities (and care trusts)[65] are not merely required to bear such advice in mind when making decisions; they must 'act under' it, which is a significantly more powerful obligation.

1.48   Examples include guidance issued concerning the charging for residential accommodation rules, generally known as CRAG (see para 8.9

---

63   Law Commission (2011) *Adult Social Care*, Law Com No 326 HC941.
64   Law Commission (2011) *Adult Social Care*, Law Com No 326 HC941, Recommendation 4.
65   NHSA 2006 s77(11).

below) and guidance concerning the community care assessment process, such as the 'Prioritising need in the context of Putting People First' guidance issued in February 2010 (see para 3.30 below).[66] Such guidance covers the breadth of social services responsibilities and so far there has been no attempt to rationalise and bring it together – a point highlighted by the Law Commission (see para 1.44 above).

1.49   The question of how far policy guidance must be followed has been the subject of a number of court judgments. In *R v Islington LBC ex p Rixon*[67] Sedley J held:

> In my judgment Parliament in enacting s7(1) did not intend local authorities to whom ministerial guidance was given to be free, having considered it, to take it or leave it. Such a construction would put this kind of statutory guidance on a par with the many forms of non-statutory guidance issued by departments of state. While guidance and directions are semantically and legally different things, and while 'guidance does not compel any particular decision' (*Laker Airways Ltd v Department of Trade* [1967] QB 643, 714 per Roskill LJ), especially when prefaced by the word 'general', in my view Parliament by s7(1) has required local authorities to follow the path charted by the secretary of state's guidance, with liberty to deviate from it where the local authority judges on admissible grounds that there is good reason to do so, but without freedom to take a substantially different course.

1.50   This was also the approach adopted in *R v Gloucestershire CC ex p Barry and others*[68] where Hirst LJ contrasted the binding nature of policy guidance with other social services guidance which he considered to be merely of 'persuasive authority on the proper construction of the legislation'.[69]

1.51   Accompanying the enactment of the NHSCCA 1990, the government issued a substantial volume of general policy guidance, entitled *Community Care in the Next Decade and Beyond: policy guidance.*[70] This guidance remains of considerable importance:[71] it represents the first and still the most definitive general statement of the key policy objectives underpinning the 1990 community care reforms. In this text it is referred to as the '1990 policy guidance'.

1.52   The consequences of failing to take into account section 7(1) policy guidance were spelt out by Sedley J in *ex p Rixon* (above):

> . . . if this statutory guidance is to be departed from it must be with good reason, articulated in the course of some identifiable decision-making

---

66 This guidance illustrates the difficulty of construing the status of such documents: it describes itself as 'best practice guidance' initially, and only at para 15 states that it is in fact policy guidance issued under s7.

67 (1997–98) 1 CCLR 119 at 123, 15 March 1996, QBD.

68 [1996] 4 All ER 421, (1997–98) 1 CCLR 19 at 24, CA.

69 Hirst LJ's dissenting opinion was approved by the majority in the House of Lords: [1997] 2 WLR 459, (1997–98) 1 CCLR 40.

70 Department of Health (1990) *Community Care in the Next Decade and Beyond: policy guidance.* The guidance is no longer in available from HMSO or accessible on the internet. Extensive extracts are, however, cited in this text.

71 See eg the comments in *R (B) v Cornwall County Council* [2009] EWHC 491 (Admin), (2009) 12 CCLR 381 para 9.

process even if not in the care plan itself. In the absence of any such considered decision, the deviation from statutory guidance is in my judgment a breach of law . . .

1.53   It follows that if a local authority decides not to follow policy guidance it must give clear and adequate reasons for its decision and its departure from the guidance must be as limited as is possible in the particular circumstances.[72]

1.54   Although policy guidance has quasi-legal characteristics, it cannot amend or frustrate primary or subordinate legislation, and can of course be the subject of judicial review if, for example, it contains an error of law[73] or an misleading explanation of the law.[74] It can, in addition be struck down if its purpose is to circumvent or frustrate a statutory provision[75] or public law requirement (for instance an affected party's legitimate expectation).[76]

1.55   In *R (B and H) v Hackney LBC*[77] Keith J suggested that policy guidance might not be 'strong guidance' if it concerned a process for which the statute provided that guidance could be issued by way of directions (see para 23 below).

Codes of practice

1.56   Codes of practice are another example of 'guidance'. Many (but not all) codes of practice are 'statutory' in the sense that they are prepared as a result of a statutory requirement. For example, Mental Capacity Act 2005 s42 requires that a code of practice (see para 17.3 below) be prepared and obliges certain persons to have regard to it when discharging their functions and for courts/tribunals to take notice of any material failures in this respect. It follows that the extent to which such guidance is binding will depend upon the specific context of any decision, but in many cases it is likely to have equivalent force to policy guidance.[78] Guidance of similar effect is to be found in relation to local authorities' duties to house homeless people (see para 15.19 below) and in relation to general obligations under the Equality Act 2010. The code of practice issued under Mental Health Act 1983 s118 is guidance to which all professionals working in the mental health field must have regard. In *R (Munjaz) v Mersey Care NHS Trust*[79] the House of Lords concluded that the code was not absolutely binding, but, like policy guidance, could be departed from where justification for the departure was explained in very considerable detail.

72 In this respect see, by way of analogy, *B v X Metropolitan Council* [2010] EWHC 467 (Admin) para 29.
73 See eg *R v North and East Devon Health Authority ex p Coughlan* [2000] 2 WLR 622, (2000) 2 CCLR 285, CA and *Gillick v West Norfolk Area Health Authority* [1986] AC 112, HL.
74 See eg *R (YA) v Secretary of State for Health* [2009] EWCA Civ 225.
75 *R v Secretary of State for Health ex p Pfizer Ltd* (1999) 2 CCLR 270, QBD and *R v Worthing BC ex p Birch* (1985) 50 P & CR 53.
76 *R (Bapio Action Ltd) v Secretary of State Home Department* [2008] UKHL 27.
77 [2003] EWHC 1654 (Admin).
78 See eg *R (Brown) v Secretary of State for Work and Pensions* [2008] EWHC 3158 (Admin).
79 [2005] UKHL 58, [2005] 3 WLR 793.

Practice guidance

1.57 The majority of guidance issued by the Department of Health/Welsh Government concerning community care issues is not issued under section 7(1), but is general guidance. Such guidance is advice as to how an authority might go about implementing or interpreting a particular statutory responsibility. It is often said that policy guidance tells an authority what it must do, whereas practice guidance suggests how it might go about doing it. Such guidance is common to other areas of social welfare law – for instance in relation to children, CA 2004 s10(8) requires children's services authorities to 'have regard to any guidance given to them' by the secretary of state, and Housing Act 1996 s182(1) places a similar obligation on housing authorities when exercising their homelessness functions.[80]

1.58 Although authorities (including care trusts)[81] are not therefore required to 'act under' such guidance, they are required to have regard to it when reaching a decision in respect of which it may be material (see para 26.207). It follows that a failure to have regard to it (rather than a failure to follow it) may result in the subsequent decision being quashed by the courts or condemned by the ombudsman. In *R v Islington LBC ex p Rixon*[82] Sedley J referred to practice guidance in the following terms:

> While such guidance lacks the status accorded by s7(1) of Local Authority Social Services Act 1970, it is, as I have said, something to which regard must be had in carrying out the statutory functions. While the occasional lacuna would not furnish evidence of such a disregard, the series of lacunae which I have mentioned does . . .[83]

1.59 Practice guidance takes many forms. Previously Department of Health guidance was given a sequential reference number and a status – for instance some were labelled 'LAC' (local authority circular) which had a higher standing than those identified as 'LASSL' (local authority social services letter). This system was abandoned in 2002,[84] making it more difficult to ascertain the precise status of guidance issued since that time.[85]

Cancelled guidance

1.60 Some guidance issued by the Department of Health has a self-destruct date – ie containing a statement that 'this guidance will be cancelled on' a specified date. This does not of course mean that it ceases thereafter to be

---

80 See eg *R (Khatun, Zeb and Iqbal) v Newham LBC* [2004] EWCA Civ 55, [2004] 3 WLR 417 at [23].
81 NHSA 2006 s77(11).
82 *R v Islington LBC ex p Rixon* (1997–98) 1 CCLR 119, 15 March 1996, QBD.
83 (1997–98) 1 CCLR 119 at 131E, QBD.
84 As a consequence of Department of Health (2002) *Shifting the Balance of Power: the next steps*, which stated that the change was designed to increase local autonomy with the central government adopting a 'a less hands-on approach' – a noble ambition that demonstrably failed.
85 Or indeed to locate it – guidance lacks an easily identifiable reference, and can appear on a range of websites, as the many and varied footnotes to this book testify.

of relevance, since it will generally remain a statement of good practice (unless specifically contradicted by subsequent guidance). Some guidance expresses this proposition in explicit terms: for example, the circular LAC (2001)8 concerning social care arrangements for 'deafblind people' states 'The circular ... will be cancelled on 28 February 2006. Though the Department will not be reissuing this document, councils are reminded that the principles of good practice the Guidance contains continue to be valid'.

National Minimum Standards and National Service Frameworks

1.61   Certain guidance issued by the Department of Health and the Welsh Government is entitled a 'National Minimum Standards' or a 'National Service Framework' (NSF). NSF's are non-statutory in origin and are essentially aspirational – setting out the Department of Health's and the Welsh Government's's long term strategies for improving specific areas of care. They are NHS led but define both health and social services obligations and detail measurable goals within set time frames, generally being ten-year programmes. They cover a wide variety of subjects including services for older people (see para 19.3 below), for children (see para 23.63), for people with long term conditions (see para 13.60 below) and for mental health services (see para 20.3 below).

1.62   National minimum standards were the product of the Care Standards Act 2000 s23 which authorised the appropriate minister to publish 'national minimum standards' for the provision of care homes and elsewhere. Such standards are no longer of direct relevance in England[86] but remain so in Wales.

1.63   Such 'standards' and 'frameworks' although not legally binding must be taken into account by the relevant authorities when making decisions and are frequently cited by the Ombudsmen as benchmarks when seeking to determine whether the actions of a public body have fallen below an acceptable standard.

NHS guidance

1.64   While the NHS Acts 2006 authorise the issuing of directions (see para 1.36 above) in much the same way as authorised under LASSA 1970, there is no specific provision in the 2006 Acts concerning the issuing of guidance.[87] Under section 2(1)(b) of both the English and Welsh NHS Acts 2006, however, the secretary of state/Welsh Government have power to do 'anything whatsoever which is calculated to facilitate or is conducive or incidental to, the discharge of' the duty to promote a comprehensive

---

86   In relation to adults in England these have been replaced by Health and Social Care Act 2008 (Regulated Activities) Regulations 2010 SI No 781 – see Care Quality Commission (2010) *Guidance about compliance: Essential standards of quality and safety*: see paras 7.100 and 9.20 below.

87   Although by virtue of NHSA 2006 s77(11), care trusts (see para 1.15) are subject to such section 7 guidance, and section 75(6) of the same Act empowers the secretary of state to issue guidance concerning consultation processes.

health service. Such a power clearly authorises the issuing of guidance. In all other respects, though, the Acts are silent on the effect of such guidance.

1.65   The extent to which NHS guidance is binding on local NHS bodies is therefore a contextual question that will depend in most cases on the wording of the guidance, the nature of the process in question and the particular facts of an individual case. In some situations it would appear that guidance will have the same coercive effect as social services 'policy guidance' – as indeed Dyson J so concluded in *R v North Derbyshire Health Authority ex p Fisher*[88] (see para 1.41 above). In similar vein it would appear that where joint policy guidance is issued to social services and NHS bodies – but is primarily aimed at the latter – it is not unreasonable to assume that its legal force is no less in relation to the NHS than it is for social services.

1.66   The Autism Act 2009 incorporates an innovative device that provides for binding policy guidance to be issued to NHS bodies. Section 3(2) provides that guidance issued under section 2 of the Act 'is to be treated as if it were general guidance of the secretary of state under section 7 of the Local Authority Social Services Act 1970'. Section 3(3) then provides that for the purposes of such guidance NHS bodies are, in essence to be treated as they are local social services authorities.

Accessing guidance

1.67   Guidance is generally only accessible via the internet. The Department of Health website[89] has an archive of 'circulars and letters' and a moderately efficient search engine that is generally helpful when trying to access these documents. Accessing guidance issued by the Welsh Government (or the Welsh Assembly Government/Welsh Office) is, however, a daunting exercise, although on occasions its website's[90] search engine has been known to be of assistance.

Local Government Act 2000 Part I

1.68   As outlined above (at para 1.5), LGA 2000 s2[91] provides local authorities with considerable flexibility in that it empowers them to do anything they consider likely to promote or improve the economic, social or environmental well-being of their area (whether for the benefit of all or part of it; or for all or any persons resident in it). In exercising these powers councils are required to have regard to guidance issued by the

---

88 (1997–98) 1 CCLR 150, 11 July 1997, QBD.
89 www.dh.gov.uk.
90 http://new.wales.gov.uk/topics/health/?lang=en.
91 As amended by the Local Government and Public Involvement in Health Act 2007.

secretary of state (section 3(5)).[92] The most recent guidance was issued in 2009[93] and at para 8 explains that the purpose in introducing the well-being power was 'to move away from their necessarily cautious approach to innovation and joint action' between local authorities and their partners to improve communities'.

1.69   By virtue of LGA 2000 s3, local authorities are unable to use the power to do anything which is specifically prohibited, or limited by other statutory provisions, nor can it be used to raise money (whether by precepts, borrowing or otherwise). By way of example, in *R (Khan) v Oxfordshire CC*[94] the applicant was excluded from assistance under National Assistance Act 1948 s21 as she was a person to whom the Immigration and Asylum Act 1999 s115 applied (see para 21.86 below). On the basis of this explicit prohibition Moses J concluded that LGA 2000 s3 applied and so support under section 2 could not be provided.

1.70   The prohibition on using the power as a money raising device does not prevent a local authority charging for any services provided under section 2, nor does it prevent companies established by local authorities under the section 2 power from raising money. This power has been further widened by LGA 2003 s93 which specifically enables local authorities to charge for discretionary services (but not services the authority is 'required' to provide). Guidance on the use of the LGA 2003 charging power[95] advises that there is some flexibility in the amounts raised by charging, provided that, taking one financial year with another, the income from charges does not exceed the costs of provision. This means therefore that (for instance) when establishing a new service it would be lawful for the authority initially to accumulate a small surplus – provided that at the end of the year this is no longer the case.

1.71   A 2006 evaluation of the use by local authorities of their section 2 powers[96] suggested that this had been patchy, but that in relation to councils' health and social care responsibilities they had been used to:

- charge for topping-up packages of day care where clients would like assistance beyond that for which they have been assessed but for which they are willing to pay;
- fill perceived gaps in the legislation for housing with care schemes;

---

92   Where a local authority decides to use its powers under section 2, regulation 3(2)(b) of the Local Authorities (Executive Arrangements) (Access to Information)(England) Regulations 2000 SI No 69 requires that a written record of the reasons for using the power be prepared as soon as reasonably practicable – and a failure to comply with this requirement may result in the use of the power being declared invalid see *Brent LBC v Risk Management Partners Ltd and others* [2009] EWCA Civ 490 para 186.

93   Department for Communities and Local Government (2009) *Power to promote well-being of the area: statutory guidance for local councils* at www.communities.gov.uk/publications/communities/1149100.

94   [2004] EWCA Civ 309, (2004) 7 CCLR 215.

95   Office of the Deputy Prime Minister (2003) *General power for best value authorities to charge for discretionary services – guidance on the power in the Local Government Act 2003*, para 21.

96   Office of the Deputy Prime Minister (2005) *Formative evaluation of the take-up and implementation of the well-being power, 2003–2006*, available from the website of the Department for Communities and Local Government at www. communities.gov.uk.

- provide assistance to vulnerable young people and families in the home;
- support elderly residents leaving hospital;
- take a charge on property and pay contributions to the costs of housing to allow families to remain in their own home rather than incur extra costs of care and new accommodation;
- provide grants (in most cases, relatively small grants);
- charge for providing 'community alarm systems', ie personal alarms for older people if they fall/get attacked, which could previously be done for council tenants, but is now provided more widely.

1.72   Although general empowering provisions of this nature are not new,[97] Part I of the 2000 Act provides considerably more freedom for councils than was previously the case.[98] *R (J) v Enfield LBC and Secretary of State for Health (intervener)*,[99] for example, concerned HIV positive applicant and her child who sought accommodation from the local authority. The applicant was unlawfully within the UK having overstayed her visa and at the time of the hearing it was considered that there was no power under CA 1989 s17 to provide accommodation.[100] Elias J concluded that in the absence of any express statutory power to provide for the applicant and her daughter, such a power existed under LGA 2000 s2. He further held that if the use of this power were 'the only way in which [the local authority] could avoid a breach of the claimant's Article 8 rights, then . . . it would be obliged to exercise its discretion in that way'.[101] This analysis was accepted in *R (Grant) v Lambeth LBC*[102] which concerned a family who were unlawfully within the UK and who had no right to be accommodated. The council concluded that to avoid a breach of the family's convention rights (within the provisions of Nationality, Immigration and Asylum Act 2002 Sch 3 para 3 – see paras 21.41 and 21.46 below) it would offer to pay for their travel back to their country of origin. The Court of Appeal held that once an authority had reached this conclusion it was obliged to consider 'whether there was some other power by the exercise of which a breach of Mrs Grant's Convention rights could be avoided' and, in that context, the use of the power conferred by section 2.

97   LGA 1972 s111, for instance, empowers authorities to 'do anything (whether or not involving the expenditure, borrowing or lending of money or the acquisition or disposal of any property or rights) which is calculated to facilitate, or is conducive or incidental to, the discharge of any of their functions'; see eg *R (A and B) v East Sussex CC* [2002] EWHC 2771 (Admin), (2003) 6 CCLR 117, where the use of this power in relation to community care services was considered.

98   See eg *R (Theophilus) v Lewisham LBC* [2002] EWHC 1371 (Admin), [2002] 3 All ER 851 which concerned further education funding.

99   [2002] EWHC 432 (Admin), (2002) 5 CCLR 434.

100 The Court of Appeal having held in *R (A) v Lambeth LBC* [2001] EWCA Civ 1624, (2001) 4 CCLR 486, that no such power existed: this finding was set aside by a differently constituted Court of Appeal in *R (W) v Lambeth LBC* [2002] EWCA Civ 613, [2002] 2 All ER 901, (2002) 5 CCLR 203.

101 [2002] EWHC 432 (Admin), (2002) 5 CCLR 434 at [72]: a view affirmed by the Court of Appeal in *R (W) v Lambeth LBC* [2002] EWCA Civ 613, [2002] 2 All ER 901, (2002) 5 CCLR 203 at [74]–[75].

102 [2004] EWCA Civ 1711, [2005] 1 WLR 1781 at [50].

CHAPTER 2

Strategic planning, public sector equality duties and information to the public

2.1   This chapter considers the wider public health and social care planning functions of social services authorities and NHS bodies, including the obligation of social services departments to prepare registers of disabled people. In addition this chapter discusses the new equality duties of public bodies under the Equality Act 2010 and how these requirements affect the planning of services. It also considers the obligations to provide information about the services offered locally, and other non-confidential recorded information held by public authorities under the Freedom of Information Act 2000. Individual care planning is considered separately in chapter 4 and the data protection and confidentiality obligations of public authorities in chapter 25.

Social services strategic planning obligations

2.2   The duties upon social services authorities to plan can be subdivided into a specific obligation to compile registers about the needs of disabled people in their area, and a more general duty to prepare strategic plans as to how best to deliver services to those 'in need' within their area, and generally to promote 'well-being'.

Registers of disabled people

2.3   The obligation on local authorities to compile registers derives from the 16th century requirement that parishes maintain registers of their 'impotent poor'.[1] The National Assistance Act (NAA) 1948 s29(4)(g) and the directions made under that section[2] oblige social services authorities to maintain a register of disabled adults ordinarily resident in their area.[3] This duty is supplemented by CSDPA 1970 s1, which requires local authorities to 'inform themselves' of the number of persons in their area to whom NAA 1948 s29 applies. The purpose of such registers is to facilitate the obligation on social services authorities to inform 'persons to whom [section 29] relates of the services available for them [under section 29]'.[4]

2.4   The guidance accompanying the directions (LAC (93)10 appendix 4, para 2) explains that, for certain statutory purposes (ie to establish a right to certain social security and tax benefits[5]) unconnected with NAA 1948 s29, there is a need to keep a register of the persons who come within the

---

1   Poor Law Act 1572 s16 'and shall make a register book of the names and surnames of such . . . aged poor impotent and decayed persons'.
2   LAC (93)10 appendix 2 para 2(2). The material parts of which are to be found in appendix B, below: for a discussion concerning this Direction, see para 9.45.
3   See Chapter 6 for the definition of 'ordinary residence'.
4   LAC (93)10 appendix 2 para 2(1)(2) and s29(4)(g).
5   Various benefits for blind people remain dependent upon registration – most notably an extra income tax allowance; the Blue Badge Scheme which is granted automatically to people registered blind; and relief from non-dependent deductions for housing benefit and council tax benefit, a small reduction in the TV licence and access to free NHS eye examinations.

section's client group. The guidance points out that in addition the registers serve an important community care planning role – by helping to
ascertain the demand and potential demand for domiciliary care services.
Although the form of the registers is not prescribed, the guidance
requires that they contain sufficient information to produce the annual
statistical returns required by the Department of Health.[6] The register
aims at recording all persons who come within the NAA 1948 s29 client
group – including 'mentally disordered persons'.

2.5   Information on the numbers of people with visual and hearing
impairments who fall within the scope of section 29 and are recorded on
the registers, is collected every three years in England[7] using two separate
statistical returns – SSDA 902 (Registration of blind persons and partially
sighted persons) and SSDA 910 (Registers of people who are deaf or hard
of hearing).[8] More recently guidance asks local authorities to 'identify,
make contact with and keep a record of deafblind people in their catch-
ment area'.[9]

2.6   In many authorities the maintenance of a register of disabled people
is seen as an administrative chore of little practical value. Potentially,
however, these registers could be used for strategic planning purposes
and as important proactive tools for disseminating information about
new services and resources and as databases to facilitate, for example
consultation exercises.

2.7   For community care purposes, however, the register is purely a planning tool; where a person comes within the NAA 1948 s29 client group[10]
and is assessed as requiring domiciliary services, those services must be
provided irrespective of whether he or she is registered. Indeed, the guidance makes clear that an individual has the right not to have his or her
name included on the formal register if he or she so chooses.[11]

2.8   The Law Commission in its' 2011 report[12] found that as a general rule
registers failed to be effective as a strategic planning tool and (other than

---

6   LAC (93)10 appendix 4 para 2.
7   The Welsh Government also has forms for collecting information on people with
    learning disabilities and physical/sensory disabilities which are sent out to local
    authorities annually – see www.wales.gov.uk/topics/statistics/about/data-collection/
    social/disabled/?lang=en
8   See eg Department of Health (2010) *People Registered as Deaf or Hard of Hearing Year
    ending 31 March 2010, England;* Department of Health (2008) *Registered Blind and
    Partially Sighted People Year ending 31 March 2008, England* – this return was brought
    forward a year from 2009 due to concerns about the fall in numbers of newly
    registered people. The new reduced list of national indicators produced by the
    coalition government proposes that the register for deaf and hard of hearing people
    should be deleted – see Department for Communities and Local Government (2011)
    Single Data List 2011–12.
9   LAC (DH)(2009)6 para 14 for England and, for Wales see chapter 2 of the Welsh
    Assembly Government (2008) *Moving Forward: Services to Deafblind People.*
10 See para 9.25 for details of this client group. Joint strategic needs assessments (see
    para 2.26 below) also require information on social care profiles and levels of need
    within an area.
11 LAC (93)10 appendix 4 para 3.
12 Law Commission (2011) *Adult Social Care,* Law Com No 326 HC941, para 12.15.

for blind and partially sighted people) were of little value in proving eligibility for services.[13] Accordingly it recommended that (other than for blind and partially sighted people) the duty to establish and maintain registers should be downgraded to a 'power'.[14]

2.9   An equivalent registration duty in relation to disabled children is found in Children Act (CA) 1989 Sch 2 Part I para 2 – see para 23.10 below.

The social services duty to prepare strategic plans

2.10   The Chronically Sick and Disabled Persons Act (CSDPA) 1970 s1(1) sought to increase the planning obligation on social services authorities by making them take a more proactive role. The section requires the authority to 'inform themselves' of the number of disabled people in its area (rather than passively waiting for people to register themselves as disabled), and provides as follows:

> It shall be the duty of every local authority having functions under section 29 of the National Assistance Act 1948 to inform themselves of the number of persons to whom that section applies within their area and of the need for the making by the authority of arrangements under that section for such persons.

2.11   DHSS circular 12/70 explained the planning purpose underlying CSDPA 1970 s1(1) thus:

> . . . it requires the authorities concerned to secure that they are adequately informed of the numbers and needs of substantially and permanently handicapped persons in order that they can formulate satisfactory plans for developing their services. . . . It is not a requirement of the Section that authorities should attempt 100% identification and registration of the handicapped. This would be a difficult, expensive and time-consuming exercise, diverting excessive resources from effective work with those who are already known, involving a restrictive and artificial definition and likely to be counter-productive.[15]

2.12   The need for a more effective planning obligation was highlighted by the white paper *Caring for People*[16] which stated the government's intention that authorities would be required to draw up and publish plans for community care services, in consultation with health authorities and other interested agencies.[17] The intention was realised via National Health Service and Community Care Act (NHSCCA) 1990 s46 which gives to the secretary of state powers to direct local authorities to prepare annual plans concerning the provision in their area of community care services. In 1991, detailed directions and guidance gave effect to this legislative

---

13   Law Commission (2011) *Adult Social Care*, Law Com No 326 HC941, para 13.7.
14   Law Commission (2011) *Adult Social Care*, Law Com No 326 HC941, Recommendation 73.
15   Para 5.
16   CM 849, HMSO, November 1989.
17   At para 5.3.

intention:[18] namely that community care plans were to be the main vehicle for the strategic planning of adult care services by social services authorities.

2.13 Since 1991 the frequency with which the Department of Health in England has changed its requirements for local strategic plans is indicative of a central strategic planning failure. In the last ten years these planning obligations have included: the preparation of community care charters; community care plans; local action plans and local strategic partnerships; health improvement programmes; local health partnership and modernisation board plans; health and modernisation plans; joint investment plans (JIPs); Better Care, Higher Standards charters; local community strategy initiatives; carers strategies; and Best Value plans; local area agreements and comprehensive area assessments.[19]

2.14 NHSCCA 1990 s46 envisaged that the key strategic planning tool for adult care services would be community care plans, but the increased emphasis on joint health and social services collaboration marginalised their importance such that in 2003 the duty to prepare such plans in England was repealed.[20] Since that time, as noted above, new strategic planning requirements have arisen with considerable frequency, only to be eclipsed by the next obligation – such that it is difficult to know at any one time which plan is in vogue and which is passé.[21]

2.15 In Wales the section 46 duty to prepare and review community care plans still applies: indeed they are an essential component of the statutory Health, Social Care and Well-Being Strategies that local authorities and Local Health Boards (LHBs) are required to produce.[22] Local authorities are required to have regard to their section 46 plans when formulating and implementing their health and well-being strategies[23] and LHBs are also subject to equivalent duties when formulating their strategies. The policy objective being that, so far as is possible to harmonise the content and the timing of the health and social care strategic plans with each other and with the Children and Young People's Plans.[24]

18 The Community Care Plans Direction 1991 and its accompanying guidance LAC (91)6. This was followed by Community Care Plans (Consultation) Directions 1993 and accompanying guidance in LAC (93)4.
19 It is indicative of the speed of change that the latter two had just come into effect when the fourth edition of this book was published and in the meantime have been abolished by the Coalition Government from April 2011 along with a reduction on the number of performance indicators: Hansard Written Ministerial Statement, 10 October 2010.
20 Care Plans (England) Directions 2003.
21 The Law Commission described the legal framework for strategic planning as complex and often confusing. It considered that in order to be effective, such planning needed to involve many other agencies and accordingly that it made little sense to retain a duty on social services alone to provide strategic plans: Law Commission (2011) *Adult Social Care*, Law Com No 326 HC941, para 12.25.
22 NHS (Wales) Act 2006 s40; see also the statutory guidance to the scheme – namely Welsh Government (2011) *Health Social Care and Well-being Strategy Guidance 2011/12 – 2013/14.*
23 Health, Social Care and Well-being Strategies (Wales) Regulations 2003 as amended, regs 7(1) and (2).
24 The local authorities' lead role in strategic 'community planning' derives from The Local Government (Wales) Measure 2009 and is the subject of 2010 Welsh Government guidance *A Summary of Community Planning Arrangements in Wales.*

Performance indicators and targets

2.16   In practice, it is arguable that councils have concentrated not so much on meeting their strategic goals (or indeed their legal obligations) but on meeting non-statutory targets. Although targets have the potential to improve performance, there are concerns that they have become a distraction which has undermined good practice. Harris,[25] for instance, has described how those being audited, 'adapt their behaviour to the audit process, distorting reality so that it conforms to an auditable reality', and how councils have engaged in 'fabricating impression management' and performing to the audience of regulation.

2.17   Currently in England there appears to be a retreat from performance indicators and star ratings, with councils being required to complete a much reduced data set on social care activities.[26] Likewise the Care Quality Commission has abandoned the star rating system and adopted a new model of regulation assessing 'essential standards of quality and safety'. It has also been announced that it will no longer conduct annual performance assessments of local authority commissioning, and that in its place, councils will be required to produce 'local accounts' on the standard of services, to be reviewed by other councils or user-led groups. Inspections by the CQC will only occur when risks are identified.[27]

2.18   Wales too appears to be moving to a 'lighter touch' regulatory framework. In *Sustainable Social Services for Wales: a framework for action*[28] it proposes the development of a new National Outcomes Framework that will measure progress through a small number of high level indicators.[29]

The NHS duty to prepare strategic plans

2.19   The National Health Service Act (NHSA) 2006 s24[30] requires every PCT (in partnership with the local authorities it covers) to prepare and keep under review (in accordance with directions issued by the secretary of state) a plan which sets out a strategy for improving:

(a)   the health of the people for whom they are responsible, and
(b)   the provision of healthcare to such people.

2.20   NHSA 2006 s242,[31] further places a duty on NHS organisations to have arrangements for involving patients and the public in planning develop-

---

25   J Harris, *The Social Work Business*, Routledge, 2003, p94.
26   Department for Communities and Local Government (2011) *Single Data List 2011–12*.
27   Department of Health (2010) *A consultation on proposals – transparency in outcomes: a framework for adult social care* and see also the response to the consultation and the new framework published in February 2011.
28   Welsh Assembly Government (2011) WAG10–11086.
29   Para 3.14.
30   Under NHS (Wales) Act (NHS(W)A) 2006 s17, local health boards have equivalent obligations.
31   NHS(W)A 2006 s183.

ment and provision of services. In England this duty was augmented by the obligation under NHSA 2006 s237 to establish patients' forums which have been replaced[32] by 'Local Involvement Networks' (or LINks). Set up from April 2008 their role is (amongst other things) to scrutinise adult social services care and health services. This function is achieved by authorities entering into contracts to secure that (amongst other things) there are means by which the 'involvement of people' in 'the commissioning, provision and scrutiny of local care services' can be promoted and so that 'people' can monitor local care services (NHS and social care).

2.21   Section 226 of the Local Government and Public Involvement in Health Act 2007 provides that where a LINks refer a social care matter to a local authority's overview and scrutiny committee, it must consider the matter and decide whether to exercise any of its powers in response. The Local Involvement Networks (Duty of Service-Providers to Allow Entry) Regulations 2008 require local authorities and most NHS bodies to allow 'authorised representatives' of LINks to have access to their premises.

2.22   It appears that LINks are likely to be abolished and their functions discharged by local Health Watch Organisations (from October 2012).[33]

2.23   In Wales eight Community Health Councils (CHCs)[34] continue to be the main bodies for involving the public in planning and developing health services.[35] CHCs have the duty (amongst other things) to scrutinise the operation of the health service in their areas and to make recommendations for the improvement of services.[36] Welsh NHS bodies have a duty to involve CHCs in the planning and provision of services and the development and considerations for proposals for changing the way services are provided.[37]

Joint Strategic Needs Assessments

2.24   The need for collaboration between the NHS and local authority welfare agencies has been the subject of discussion since the formation of the modern welfare state in 1948. With the unremitting structural reconfigurations of social services and NHS bodies the importance of joint planning has assumed greater importance.

---

32 By virtue of the Local Government and Public Involvement in Health Act 2007 ss221–229.

33 The Health and Social Care Bill 2011, (currently) clause 179.

34 The regulations relating to community health councils are now contained in The Community Health Councils (Constitution, Membership and Procedures) (Wales) Regulations 2010 SI No 288.

35 Guidance has been produced for Welsh NHS bodies – *Guidance for engagement and consultation on changes to health services*, 31 March 2011, which emphasises the need for continuous engagement.

36 Community Health Councils (Constitution, Membership and Procedures) (Wales) Regulations 2010 SI No 288 reg 26.

37 Ibid, reg 27.

2.25   Chapter 2 of the 1990 Policy Guidance[38] gave general advice on what
authorities were expected to achieve through planning, and throughout it
placed considerable emphasis on the need for partnership and collaboration between authorities and the NHS.[39] The Audit Commission report
The Coming of Age: improving care services for older people (1997)[40] stressed
that 'Health authorities and social services departments must map needs
and the services available to meet them. They should share this information with each other as the basis for joint planning and commissioning'.

2.26   Currently the Local Government and Public Involvement in Health Act
2007 s116 requires local authorities along with their partner primary care
trusts to prepare and publish a Joint Strategic Needs Assessment (JSNA)
of the health and social care needs of people within their local area. Best
Practice Guidance states that the JSNA identifies the current and future
health and well-being needs in the light of existing services and informs
future service planning taking into account evidence of effectiveness, and
gives the big picture in terms of health and well-being needs and inequalities in a local population.[41]

2.27   Directors of Public Health, Directors of Adult Social Care and Directors
of Children's Services undertake the JSNA and PCTs are required to feed
into the JSNA for their area (along with a range of other stakeholders in
the statutory and voluntary sector). The guidance envisages that the JSNA
will cover needs over a period of three to five years, but will also look at the
longer term (five to ten years) to take account of demographic changes to
inform strategic planning.[42]

2.28   The Health and Social Care Bill (which at the time of writing is progressing through Parliament) proposes[43] that local authorities and Clinical
Commissioning Groups (which may replace PCTs – see para 13.6) will
be required to undertake the JSNA through the proposed Health and
Well-Being Board and then develop their commissioning plans in line
with the Health and Well-being Strategy. Although the Bill does not
specify the form the strategy should take, the explanatory note with the
original Bill states (para 1153):

> . . . the strategy could be high level and strategic, focusing on the interface
> between the NHS, social care and public health commissioning, rather
> than being a detailed study of all the commissioning across health and
> social care in the local authority area. The joint health and well-being
> strategy is not limited in its scope and could potentially include wider
> health determinants such as housing, if the health and well-being board
> wishes to consider this.

---

38   *Community Care in the Next Decade and Beyond: policy guidance*, HMSO, 1990.
39   Most notably at para 2.11 'At an early stage [*social services and health authorities /
      primary care trusts*] should draw up joint resource inventories and analyses of need
      which enable them to reach agreement on key issues of 'who does what' for whom,
      when, at what cost and who pays'.
40   (1997) Recommendation 1, p77.
41   Department of Health (2007) *Guidance on Joint Strategic Needs Assessment* p7.
42   Department of Health (2007) *Guidance on Joint Strategic Needs Assessment* p10.
43   Clauses 189 and 193 as at September 2011.

2.29 It is also proposed to impose a requirement that local authorities and clinical commissioning groups consider whether the needs in the JSNA could best be met using the flexibilities under NHSA 2006 s75 (see para 13.127 below.

2.30 As noted above (at para 2.15) Wales already has a statutory requirement to have Health, Social Care and Well-Being Strategies (HSCWBS). The guidance advises that current strategic plans should concentrate on improving health and well-being and reducing health inequalities and improving the provision, quality, integration, and sustainability of 'over-lapping services' (eg services provided by the NHS, local government and their partners)[44] and that the HSCWBS should set out clearly:

> how services will be jointly planned, developed and managed to improve integration, eliminate waste, duplication and confusion, and minimise the likelihood of harm resulting from poor co-ordination of care how they will measure outcomes of care and improve them over time.[45]

2.31 A LHB is also one of a Welsh local authority's 'community planning partners' under Local Government (Wales) Measure 2009 Part 2. As a result, a LHB must participate in community planning for the authority's area (section 37(3) of the Measure). Community planning results in the production of a community strategy, which specifies actions to be per-formed or functions to be exercised by the local authority and its com-munity planning partners, for the purpose of improving the long-term well-being of the authority's area (section 39). A local authority and LHB must, where a specified action or function relates to them, take all reason-able steps to perform the action or exercise the function in accordance with the strategy (section 43).

Public sector equality duties and planning[46]

2.32 In April 2011 the three separate public sector equality duties (relating to race, disability and gender) were consolidated into a single duty (Equality Act 2010 s149) which additionally includes as 'protected characteristics' age, gender reassignment, pregnancy and maternity, religion or belief, and sexual orientation.

2.33 Section 149 of the Equality Act 2010 provides:

> (1) A public authority must, in the exercise of its functions, have due regard to the need to—
> > (a) eliminate discrimination, harassment, victimisation and any other conduct that is prohibited by or under this Act;

---

44 Welsh Government (2011) *Health Social Care and Well-being Strategy Guidance 2011/12–2013/14*, p8.

45 Welsh Government (2011) *Health Social Care and Well-being Strategy Guidance 2011/12–2013/14*, p19. The groups for whom such plans are to be made are listed on page 20 and 21 and cover the majority of people with whom social services and health services will be jointly involved.

46 See para 4.67 below for details of how the provisions affect individual cases.

(b) advance equality of opportunity between persons who share a relevant protected characteristic and persons who do not share it;

(c) foster good relations between persons who share a relevant protected characteristic and persons who do not share it.

(2) A person who is not a public authority but who exercises public functions must, in the exercise of those functions, have due regard to the matters mentioned in subsection (1).

(3) Having due regard to the need to advance equality of opportunity between persons who share a relevant protected characteristic and persons who do not share it involves having due regard, in particular, to the need to—

(a) remove or minimise disadvantages suffered by persons who share a relevant protected characteristic that are connected to that characteristic;

(b) take steps to meet the needs of persons who share a relevant protected characteristic that are different from the needs of persons who do not share it;

(c) encourage persons who share a relevant protected characteristic to participate in public life or in any other activity in which participation by such persons is disproportionately low.

(4) The steps involved in meeting the needs of disabled persons that are different from the needs of persons who are not disabled include, in particular, steps to take account of disabled persons' disabilities.

(5) Having due regard to the need to foster good relations between persons who share a relevant protected characteristic and persons who do not share it involves having due regard, in particular, to the need to—

(a) tackle prejudice, and

(b) promote understanding.

(6) Compliance with the duties in this section may involve treating some persons more favourably than others; but that is not to be taken as permitting conduct that would otherwise be prohibited by or under this Act.

2.34   In the following paragraphs we provide an overview of the key elements of public sector equality duty (PSED). The impact of this duty is considered elsewhere in this book – particularly at para 3.212 which considers the implications of the judgment in *R (W) v Birmingham CC*.[47]

2.35   In *R (Brown) v Secretary of State for Work and Pensions*[48] the Administrative Court identified six key principles associated with the PSED. Although these related to a disability discrimination claim (under what was then the Disability Discrimination Act 1995 s49A) they read across into discrimination engaging all other 'protected characteristics' under what is now section 149 of the 2010 Act.[49] These can be summarised as follows:

47 [2011] EWHC 1147 (Admin), (2011) 14 CCLR 516.
48 [2008] EWHC 3158 (Admin) at [84]–[96].
49 For an excellent review of the duty, see J Halford and S Khan (2011) *The Equality Act 2010: a source of rights in a climate of cuts?* Discrimination Law Association Briefing 584 v42, March 2011 pp 11–16; and see also E Mitchell (2010) '*Pieretti v Enfield LBC*', *Social Care Law Today*, Issue 78, December 2010.

1) *A general obligation*

The duty to have 'due regard' to requirements of section 149 is 'broad and wide ranging' (para 35) and arises in many routine situations, essentially whenever a public body is exercising a public function, including an exercise of judgment that might affect disabled people;[50]

2) *Consideration before decision made*

The consideration of the potential impact of the decision must take place 'before and at the time that a particular policy that will or might affect disabled people is being considered by the public authority in question' and 'involves a conscious approach and state of mind'.[51] As the Court noted in *Brown* 'attempts to justify a decision as being consistent with the exercise of the duty when it was not, in fact, considered before the decision, are not enough to discharge the duty';[52]

3) *The duty is a substantial one*

The word 'due' is of importance.[53] It is not enough to 'have regard' to the duty – the public body must pay this 'due regard'. This means that it is a duty of 'substance' that must be exercised 'with rigour and with an open mind'; it is 'not a question of "ticking boxes"'.[54] Although the courts will be wary of 'micro challenges' to 'macro decisions',[55] nevertheless, where the impact of the policy is potentially 'devastating' for disabled people, then in order to satisfy the 'due regard' obligation the review process must be more than 'a 'high level and generalised' description of the likely impact of' the policy – it must make 'some attempt at assessment of the practical impact on those' who would be affected.[56] In such cases, even where the council is facing severe resource constraints the adoption of a fixed view that financially there is 'no more room for manoeuvre' might itself be irrational[57] – as Sedley LJ phrased the question in *R (Domb) v Hammersmith and Fulham*

---

50   *Pieretti v Enfield LBC* [2010] EWCA Civ 1104.

51   At para 91; and see *R (Elias) v Secretary of State for Defence* [2006] 1 WLR 3213 para 274 and *R (C) v Secretary of State for Justice* [2008] EWCA Civ 882 para 49.

52   See *R (C) v Secretary of State for Justice* [2008] EWCA Civ 882 para 49.

53   See eg *R (Meany, Glynn and Saunders) v Harlow DC* [2009] EWHC 559 (Admin) where it was held that the word 'due' must 'add something' and that 'a reduction in almost any community services is likely disproportionately to affect minority groups' – and that the equality duty is to pay 'due regard' to the 'need' (amongst other things) to eliminate unlawful discrimination and to promote equality of opportunity: and see also *R (Rahman) v Birmingham CC* [2011] EWHC 944 (Admin) where it was held that 'even where the context of decision making is financial resources in a tight budget, that does not excuse compliance with the PSEDs and indeed there is much to be said for the proposition that even in the straightened times the need for clear, well-informed decision making when assessing the impacts on less advantaged members of society is as great, if not greater'.

54   Para 92 and see *R (Kaur and Shah) v Ealing LBC* [2008] EWHC 2062 (Admin) at paras 24–25 and see also *R (Boyejo and others) v Barnet LBC and Portsmouth CC* [2009] EWHC 3261 (Admin), (2010) 13 CCLR 72.

55   *R (W) v Birmingham CC* [2011] EWHC 1147 (Admin), (2011) 14 CCLR 516 para 161.

56   *R (W) v Birmingham CC* [2011] EWHC 1147 (Admin), (2011) 14 CCLR 516 paras 157 and 183.

57   *R (W) v Birmingham CC* [2011] EWHC 1147 (Admin), (2011) 14 CCLR 516 paras 182–183.

LBC[58] 'can a local authority, by tying its own fiscal hands for electoral ends, rely on the consequent budgetary deficit to modify its perform-ance of its statutory duties?'

The duty does not, however, oblige authorities to 'take steps them-selves, or to achieve results' (para 84). It is not a duty to eliminate discrimination or to promote equality of opportunity and good rela-tions – but a duty to have 'due regard to the need to achieve these goals'.[59] Where, however, the decision may have an adverse impact on the goals advocated by s149, then the public body should consider what it can feasibly do to mitigate this negative impact. In such cases it is 'incumbent upon the borough to consider the measures to avoid that impact before fixing on a particular solution';[60]

4) *A non–delegable duty*

   In *Brown* the court considered that it would be possible for another body to undertake the 'practical steps to fulfil a policy' but in such cases the relevant public authority would have to maintain 'a proper supervision over the third party to ensure it carries out its 'due regard' duty' (para 94);

5) *It is a continuing duty.*

6) *Duty to record*

   Public authorities must keep 'an adequate record showing that they had actually considered their disability equality duties and pondered relevant questions'.[61] In *R (JL) v Islington LBC* (2009)[62] the council claimed it had considered its public sector equality duty but Black J found against it on the grounds (amongst others) that there was 'no audit trail' to establish this and 'no documentation to demonstrate a proper approach to the question'.

2.36   The regulations in England detailing the procedural obligations on public bodies concerning (amongst other things) the content, the nature of the consultation and publication of materials concerning their discharge of their PSEDs were made on 9 September 2011. The Equality and Human Rights Commission's statutory Code of Practice on the Public Sector Equality Duty under the 2010 Act is due for consultation in the Autumn.

2.37   It appears that there could be considerable difference between the Eng-lish and Welsh regulations in regard to the specific duties. The coalition government's 2011 consultation on the regulations in England announced its intention to 'strip out' unnecessary process requirements and to move away from a 'process driven approach' and focus on performance.[63]

---

58 [2009] EWCA Civ 941 para 80.
59 *R (Baker) v Secretary of State for Communities and Local Government* [2008] EWCA Civ 141.
60 *R (Kaur and Shah) v Ealing LBC* [2008] EWHC 2026 (Admin) para 43.
61 *See eg R (Bapio Action Limited) v Secretary of State for the Home Department* [2007] EWHC 199 (Admin) para 69 and *R (Eisai Limited) v National Instituted for Health and Clinical Excellence* [2007] EWHC 1941 (Admin), (2007) 10 CCLR 638 paras 92 and 94.
62 [2009] EWHC 458 (Admin) para 121.
63 Government Equalities Office (2011) *Equality Act 2010: the public sector equality duty: reducing bureaucracy.*

2.38   The 2011 Welsh Regulations[64] require listed public bodies (which includes local authorities and health bodies) to have a Strategic Equality Plan and publish their equality objectives by April 2012 and review them at least every four years. There is a requirement for authorities to assess the likely impact of their proposed policies and practices (and also existing policies when they are reviewed) on their ability to comply with the general duty. Bodies are required to publish reports of the assessments where they show a substantial impact (or likely impact) and to monitor the impact of policies and practices on their ability to meet the general duty. In contrast, the English regulations[65] merely require listed public bodies to publish information to demonstrate compliance with the Act, by January or April 2012 in relation to employees (where there are over 150 employees) or other persons affected by its policies and practices, and publish by April 2012 one or more objectives it thinks it should achieve in relation to section 149(1)(a)–(c), and subsequently at four-yearly intervals.[66]

The general duty to inform

2.39   The duty to prepare strategic plans and the duty to disseminate information about available services are complimentary obligations. Information derived from assessments,[67] complaints and user group representations should inform the strategic planning process. In turn information should be disseminated to service users, their carers and user groups as to what services are available, how they can be accessed and all other relevant factors – including for instance the charges that will accompany them and how complaints can be made concerning service deficiencies.

2.40   The following section reviews the obligations that local authorities and health bodies have to inform community care service users (and potential service users) of their rights. It is essentially a proactive obligation – to disseminate information regardless of an individual request. In para 2.49 we consider the obligations these bodies have to provide specific information when asked – the reactive obligation.

2.41   Although the duty on social services to provide general information is primarily statutory (and in particular under CSDPA 1970 s1) all public bodies have general public law obligations to provide information in certain situations. As discussed in chapter 26 there is a developing duty to provide reasons for certain decisions (see para 26.229). In addition the

---

64 Equality Act 2010 (Statutory Duties) (Wales) Regulations 2011 SI No 1064 (W155) and the Equality Act 2010 (Specification of Relevant Welsh Authorities) Order 2011 SI No 1063 (W154).
65 Equality Act (Specific Duties) Regulations 2011 SI No 2260.
66 The Equality and Human Rights Commission has issued a non-statutory *Essential Guide to the Public Sector Equality Duties* for Welsh authorities, and intends to publish the statutory code of practice for Wales in 2011.
67 See eg *R v Bristol CC ex p Penfold* (1997–98) 1 CCLR 315, QBD where Scott Baker J held that community care assessments were of importance in relation to strategic planning 'even if there is no hope' of the disabled person being deemed to be in need of services since they 'serve a useful purpose in identifying for the local authority unmet needs which will help it to plan for the future. Without assessment this could not be done'.

European Court of Human Rights has held that Article 8 of the Convention may oblige state authorities to provide information – particularly when that information will enable individuals to make crucial decisions about the extent of a physical risk they may face.[68]

2.42   NAA 1948 s29(1)(a)[69] empowers authorities to make arrangements 'for informing' disabled adults 'of the services available for them' under that section.

2.43   CSDPA 1970 s1(2) converts this discretionary power into an obligation and spells out in greater detail the nature of that duty. The duty only applies to disabled people and leaves considerable discretion as to the way in which the information is published. It remains, however, the most important statutory provision in relation to the duty to provide general information. It provides as follows:

> (2) Every such local authority –
>
> (a) shall cause to be published from time to time at such times and in such manner as they consider appropriate general information as to the services provided under arrangements made by the authority under the said section 29 which are for the time being available in the area; and
>
> (b) shall ensure that any such person as aforesaid who uses any of those services is informed of any other service provided by the authority (whether under any such arrangements or not) which in the opinion of the authority is relevant to his needs and of any service provided by any other authority or organisation which in the opinion of the authority is so relevant and of which particulars are in the authority's possession.

2.44   DHSS Circular 12/70, para 5 explains the purpose of CSDPA 1970 s1(2) as ensuring that 'those who might benefit by help, and their families, should know what help is available to them and this is to be secured both by general publicity and by personal explanations'. Whilst the duty to provide information to an individual service user is an essential part of the assessment process under NHSCCA 1990 s47, the general duty to publicise services is not specifically addressed by the 1990 Act. The 1990 policy guidance[70] only deals with this issue as an aspect of community care planning, requiring that plans include details of what arrangements authorities intend to make to inform service users and their carers about services.

2.45   The current English policy guidance on information is found in the Prioritising Needs Guidance (para 80):[71]

68 See *McGinley and Egan v UK* (1998) 27 EHRR 1; and *KH v Slovakia* (App No 32881/04) 28 April 2009.

69 As authorised by the secretary of state's directions – LAC (93)10 appendix 2 para 2(1) (see para 9.50).

70 *Community Care in the Next Decade and Beyond: policy guidance*, HMSO, 1990, para 2.25.

71 Department of Health (2010) *Prioritising need in the context of Putting People First: A whole system approach to eligibility for social care. Guidance on Eligibility Criteria for Adult Social Care, England 2010*. A principle endorsed by the Department of Health's 2010 policy paper *A vision for adult social care: capable communities and active citizens* (at para 4.9) that 'Information about care and support is available for all local people, regardless of whether or not they fund their own care'.

Councils should help individuals who may wish to approach them for support by publishing and disseminating information about access, eligibility and social care support, including personal budgets, in a range of languages and formats. The information should also describe what usually happens during assessment and care management processes, related time-scales, and how individuals can benefit from self-directed support. Councils should promote the development of services that provide interpreters, translators, advocates, and supporters to help individuals access and make best use of the assessment process.

2.46   In relation to the NHS, the NHS Constitution (see para 13.24 below) pledges to make information about healthcare services available, locally and nationally, and to offer easily accessible, reliable and relevant information to enable patients to participate fully in healthcare decisions, including information on the quality of clinical services where there is robust and accurate information available. [72]

2.47   In Wales the principal advice stems from the policy guidance *Creating a unified and fair system for assessing and managing care*,[73] which requires agencies to 'work together to publish and disseminate a coordinated set of information about services and eligibility in a range of languages and accessible formats. The information should also say what usually happens during assessment and care management processes,[74] related time-scales, and how individuals might access direct payments.' In relation to the NHS bodies, the relevant guidance requires 'timely communication and information sharing' on the 'full range and location of services they provide'.[75]

2.48   The requirement that NHS bodies and local authorities have information dissemination strategies is a public law, rather than a private law obligation. In essence this means that although a failure properly to discharge this duty could result in criticism by the ombudsman or censure in a judicial review, it cannot in general form the basis for a private law claim for damages. In *Qazi v Waltham Forest LBC*[76] the applicants sought to argue that a failure by a local authority to provide accurate information concerning the processing of disabled facilities grants could found an action based upon negligent misstatement in accordance with the

---

72   Department of Health (2010) *The NHS Constitution* p7. At the time of writing (July 2011) the outcome of a Department of Health (2010) consultation exercise '*Liberating the NHS: an information revolution*' is awaited.

73   National Assembly for Wales (2002) *Creating a unified and fair system for assessing and managing care* NAFWC 09/2002 para 2.17 onwards and annex 10.

74   Section 10 of the Social Care Charges (Wales) Measure 2010 also imposes specific information-provision obligations upon Welsh local authorities in relation to charging for non-residential care services. Authorities must make arrangements to ensure that they bring to the attention of persons who do or may use chargeable service information about their charging policies. This includes information about services for which charges are or are not imposed and standard charges for particular types of service.

75   Welsh Government (2010) *Doing Well, Doing Better: standards for health services in Wales*. Standard 18 Ministerial Letter EH/ML/014/10.

76   (2000) 32 HLR 689.

principles established in *Hedley Byrne and Co Ltd v Heller and Partners Ltd.*[77] Rejecting this approach, Richards J observed:

> It was a normal and legitimate incident of the defendant's statutory functions to provide information and advice about the system to those making inquiries about the availability of grants or applying for grants. I do not see how, by providing such information or advice, the defendant could be said to have assumed a responsibility in private law towards would-be or actual applicants.

2.49   The Law Commission in its original consultation proposed that there should be a duty on local social services authorities to provide information about services available in the local area.[78] However, in its final report it proposed that local authorities be subject to a statutory duty on to 'provide information, advice and assistance services in their area and to stimulate and shape the market for services'.[79]

Children

2.50   The obligations under the 1948 and 1970 Acts in relation to the provision of information relate only to persons aged 18 or over. The concomitant duty to inform in relation to services for disabled children and other children in need exists in CA 1989 Sch 2 Part I para 1. This duty is considered in volume 6 of the Children Act 1989 Guidance (Children with Disabilities),[80] which makes the following observations:

> 3.6 . . . SSD's should build on their existing links with community groups, voluntary organisations and ethnic minority groups to involve them in planning services and as a sounding board when formulating policies. The publicity required must include information about services provided both by the SSD and, to the extent they consider it appropriate, about such provision by others (eg voluntary organisations). Publicity should be clearly presented and accessible to all groups in the community, taking account of linguistic and cultural factors and the needs of people with communication difficulties. SSD's should take reasonable steps to ensure that all those who might benefit from such services receive the relevant information.

2.51   The guidance is endorsed by the 2007 transformation programme *Aiming High for Disabled Children,* which in addition to emphasising the importance of involving disabled children in the planning services also stress the need to have access to information.[81]

---

77 [1964] AC 465.
78 Law Commission (2010) *Adult Social Care: a consultation paper No 192.* Provisional Proposal 13–3, p164.
79 Law Commission (2011) *Adult Social Care,* Law Com No 326 Recommendation 6, p27.
80 Department of Health (1991) *The Children Act 1989 Guidance and Regulations, Volume 6: children with disabilities.*
81 HM Treasury and Department of Education and Skills (2007) *Aiming High for Disabled Children: Better Support for Families,* chapter 2: Access and Empowerment. In Wales, see Welsh Assembly Government (2008) *We are on the way: a policy agenda to transform the lives of disabled children and young people,* chapter 1.

The specific duty to inform

2.52   Access to non-confidential publicly-held information is presently regulated by a variety of statutory and non-statutory provisions, including:

Local Government Act 1972

2.53   Prior to the coming into force of the Freedom of Information Act 2000 (below) the principal statute governing access to local authority information was the Local Government Act 1972 (as amended). The relevant provisions of this Act (ss100A–100K), which remain in force, are concerned primarily with the public's right of access to meetings, and the papers considered at these meetings, including 'background papers' relating to reports considered at the meetings. Papers, agendas and minutes of meetings must generally be available three clear days prior to the date of the meeting. With the advent of the internet, many authorities (and government bodies) argue that they comply with this obligation by placing the information on their websites: given the problems in navigating such sites (the Welsh Government site is a prime example) this assertion may be open to challenge.

Freedom of Information Act 2000

2.54   The Freedom of Information Act 2000 gives any person (which includes not only individuals but also companies, other organisations and other public authorities) the general right of access to all types of 'recorded' information[82] held by public authorities[83] (and those providing services for them), sets out exemptions from that right, and places a number of obligations on public authorities. A 'public authority' is widely defined and includes parliament, government departments and local authorities, NHS bodies, GPs etc. Authorities must comply with a request within 20 working days – although if a 'conditional exemption' (see below) applies – the timescale is then such period as is reasonable in the circumstances.

2.55   The Act places two main responsibilities on public authorities, namely:

1) the adoption and maintenance of a 'publication scheme', and
2) the provision of information in response to requests from the public.

2.56   A publication scheme must specify the types of information the authority publishes, the form in which that information is published, and details of any charges for accessing that information. The scheme must be approved by the Information Commissioner[84] who is additionally responsible for enforcing and overseeing the Data Protection Act 1998.

82   This is widely defined: there is no time limit for when the material was compiled and it may include photos, plans etc.
83   The Health and Social Care Bill Schedule 5 as currently drafted (at September 2011) will if enacted amend the 2000 Act by inserting references to clinical commissioning groups and the NHS Commissioning Board as 'public authorities' for the purposes of the Act.
84   See www.ico.gov.uk.

2.57   The 2000 Act provides that anyone requesting information from a public authority is entitled to be informed in writing whether it holds information, and if so to have that information communicated to him or her. The application must, however, (1) be in writing, (2) state the applicant's name and address, and (3) describe the information requested. There is therefore no special form or precedent to use for such requests, although it is wise to describe as precisely as possible what information is sought (as otherwise the authority might refuse to provide it on costs grounds) and to state that the request is being made under 'the Freedom of Information Act 2000'.

2.58   Regulations[85] made under the Act stipulate that requests for information below a ceiling of £600 staff time for central government (eg Department of Health[86] or Welsh Government) or £450 for other authorities must be provided free of charge: it has been suggested that this equates to 2.5 days of staff time. Where the fee would exceed this limit, the public body can refuse to supply the information, or decide to supply it subject to payment of the full costs of doing so. Authorities are, however, entitled to be paid for disbursements, such as the cost of photocopying/printing and postage etc.

2.59   Authorities are exempted from providing the information in certain situations – depending upon whether an 'absolute' or 'conditional' exemption applies. Where an absolute exemption applies, the authority is not even under a duty to confirm or deny the existence of the information. All that is required is a letter, within 20 working days, explaining that the exemption is being invoked and advising the applicant of his or her right to appeal or complain about the decision. Absolute exemptions include information otherwise accessible; information concerning security matters; information in court records; parliamentary privileged material; personal information (that relates to the applicant); information provided in confidence; and information whose disclosure is restricted by law.

2.60   Conditional exemptions apply where it may be in the public interest not to have disclosure. In some cases there is a presumption that disclosure will be against the public interest, whereas in others the authority is required to provide credible evidence of the particular prejudice, before it can use the ground as a reason for withholding disclosure. Those cases where no prejudice need be established include information that is intended for future publication as well as information that concerns public inquiries, government policy formulation, and legal professional privilege. Those cases where prejudice needs to be established include such matters as: national security; law enforcement; audit functions; effective conduct of public affairs; and health and safety.

2.61   Where a request concerns personal information, the 2000 Act defers to the Data Protection Act 1998 and in general the information should be

85   Freedom of Information and Data Protection (Appropriate Limit and Fees) Regulations 2004 SI No 3244.
86   The Freedom of Information releases are accessible at www.dh.gov.uk/en/ Publicationsandstatistics/Freedomofinformationpublicationschemefeedback/FOIreleases/index.htm.

sought under the 1998 Act. Sometimes, it will not be clear which Act is relevant – for instance a request for information concerning the salary paid to a public officer. The Information Commissioner has advised that in general, where information is sought concerning someone acting in an official capacity, it should be provided under the 2000 Act.[87] The data protection regime regulating the retention and accessibility of personal information is considered further at chapter 25 below.

2.62   Anyone dissatisfied with a response to their request has a number of options, including a right to have the refusal reviewed by the authority, and a right of appeal to the Information Commissioner and to the Information Rights Tribunal.

2.63   The Ministry of Justice has published two codes of practice under the 2000 Act ss45 and 46.[88] The section 45 code sets out the practices which public authorities should follow when dealing with requests for information under the Act. It included guidance on advice and assistance to applicants, consulting third parties, the use of confidentiality clauses and the provision of internal complaints procedures. The section 46 code gives guidance on good practice in records management.[89]

Code of Practice on Openness in the NHS

2.64   A Code of Practice on Openness in the NHS in England was issued in 1995 and subsequently revised and reissued in 2003.[90] The underlying principle of the code is that information (not necessarily the documents from which the information derives) should be made available unless it can be shown to fall into one of the exempt categories, such as personal information, information about internal discussions and debate (unless this would be outweighed by public interest), and a variety of other restrictions.[91]

2.65   The code requires that (i) each health body must publish the name of an individual in their employ responsible for the operation of the code, and (ii) the method for requesting information through that individual should be publicised locally. Complaints about non-disclosure, or about delays in disclosure, or charges for information, should be made to that individual. The code provides that if complainants are dissatisfied with the response they receive they should write to the chief executive of the health body concerned. Time limits are set for each stage. Complainants

---

87 See the Information Commissioner's guidance (2005) *Freedom of Information: access to information about public authorities' employees.*

88 The section 45 code was published in 2004 and the section 46 code was revised in 2009. See also Ministry of Justice (2009) *Summary guidance to local authorities on publishing freedom of information data.*

89 The National Assembly for Wales has issued (2007) *A Code of Practice on Access to Information.*

90 Department of Health (2003) *Code of Practice on Openness in the NHS in England*: a similar but separate code was issued by the Welsh Office in 1995. It is currently still on the Department of Health website but is likely to be archived soon as it has largely been superseded by the Freedom of Information Act 2000.

91 Para 9 of the code.

still dissatisfied after receiving a reply from the chief executive are then entitled to complain to the Health Service Commissioner.

2.66   The Health Service Commissioner issued a special report on the workings of the scheme in 1996[92] in which he stated that, unlike his practice with other complaints (where individuals must show some prima facie reason for their claim and have suffered some hardship or injustice), in relation to complaints about non-disclosure he regarded the refusal as of itself a ground on which to claim injustice or hardship.

92   Health Service Commissioner, *First Report for Session 1996–97: Selected Investigations – Access to Official Information in the NHS*, HC 6, HMSO, 1996.

Community care assessments

continued

continued

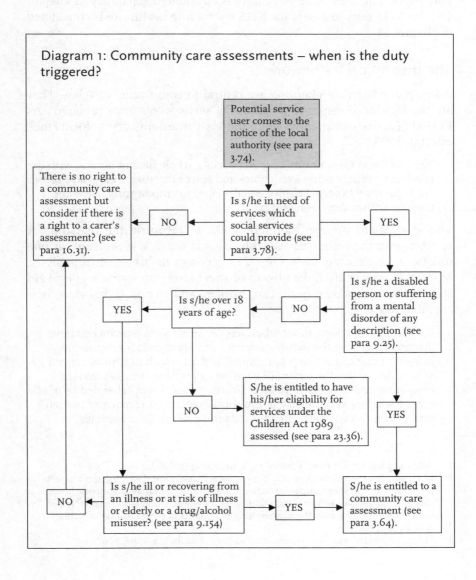

Diagram 1: Community care assessments – when is the duty triggered?

Introduction

3.1   The public provision of community care services is dependent in each case on a public authority making an administrative decision that the particular individual could not only benefit from the service, but also that the service should be provided. The decision-making procedure is known as the assessment process. The assessment process commences with the potential service user coming to the notice of the social services authority and ends with a decision as to whether or not he or she is entitled to services. If services are required, the next stage is the preparation of a care/support plan which describes and quantifies the services and speci-fies how (and by whom) they are to be delivered. This chapter is concerned with social services assessments and the following chapter with the sup-port plans. The duty to assess carers is considered separately in chapter 16. The NHS duty to assess for NHS continuing healthcare is considered in chapter 14.

The theoretical framework

3.2   Assessment and care planning are central to community care law. They are the legislative response to the social services 'resource problem'. As Phyllida Parsloe commented when the key community care reforms took effect in 1993:[1]

> The NHS and Community Care Act backs a whole field of horses, with the two front-runners being user choice and scarce resources. Local authorities are apparently expected to give equal weight to empowering users and keeping within their own budget.

3.3   The assessment process therefore seeks to reconcile the demand for services with the resources available. This is not a new problem, or one unique to community care. Over 25 years ago in his seminal analysis, Michael Lipsky[2] charted the growth of street-level bureaucracies (legal aid lawyers, social workers, healthcare workers and so on). In his view their essential role is:

> . . . to make decisions about other people. Street-level bureaucrats have discretion because the nature of service provision calls for human judgment that cannot be programmed and for which machines cannot substitute . . . It is the nature of what we call human services that the unique aspects of people and their situations will be apprehended by public service workers and translated into courses of action responsive to each case within (more or less broad) limits imposed by their agencies.[3]

---

1   'Making a bid for fair play', *Community Care*, 5 August 1993.
2   M Lipsky, *Street-Level Bureaucracy*, Russell Sage Foundation, 1989: the term 'street-level bureaucracies' encompasses 'schools, police and welfare departments, lower courts, legal services officers, and other agencies whose workers interact with and have wide discretion over the dispensation of benefits or the allocation of public sanctions' (p xi).
3   M Lipsky, *Street-Level Bureaucracy*, Russell Sage Foundation, 1989, p162.

3.4   Lipsky argued that for this function to be exercised effectively, such employees had to be accountable both to their employers' preferences and to their clients' claims and that in order to maintain client confidence (given these twin roles) it was essential that the exercise of discretion was perceived as being independent: this in turn necessitated that street-level bureaucrats be seen to act as 'professionals'.[4] The organisational response to this quasi-independence has been to make:

> ... street-level bureaucrats more accountable by reducing their discretion and constraining their alternatives. [To] write manuals to cover contingencies. [To] audit performance of workers to provide retrospective sanctions in anticipation of which it is hoped future behaviour will be modified.[5]

3.5   This trend continues, with Seddon[6] noting in 2008 that staff were not given time to reflect on and shape practice, develop good working relationships with others and explore the communities in which they work:

> Like the police service, adult social care is designed as a bureaucracy to feed the regime, not a service to meet older people's needs. The regime constrains method. It is a bureaucracy of call centres, functional specialisation, activity targets, budget management, form-filling and counting, designed according to the requirements of the regime. And the bureaucracy is cemented with information technology, all of which has been designed from the point of view of electronic data management and reporting, not solving people's problems.

3.6   Many community care practitioners would identify with this analysis. The development of 'managerialism'[7] within social services has unquestionably undermined the ability of social workers to carry out 'needs led' assessments and instead captured them within the 'bureaucratic/rationing regime' – that is adult care today.[8] The Commission for Social Care Inspection (CSCI) concluded in 2008 that 'demand was often managed by tightening procedural guidelines to reduce scope for interpretation by front-line workers'.[9] Thus increasingly assessments are budget or audit led exercises whose primary purpose is to conform to internal administrative imperatives, rather than the empowerment of service users and their carers. The cost of the increasing bureaucratisation of adult social care is high. In 2009–10 the assessment and care planning process absorbed over 12 per cent of the entire social services expenditure in England – £2.06 billion.[10]

---

4   M Lipsky, *Street-Level Bureaucracy*, Russell Sage Foundation, 1989.
5   M Lipsky, *Street-Level Bureaucracy*, Russell Sage Foundation, 1989.
6   J Seddon, *Systems thinking in the public sector: the failure of the reform regime ... and a manifesto for a better way*, Triarchy Press, 2008 as described by N Andrews, D Driffield and V Poole (2009) 'All Together Now', *Quality in Ageing and Older Adults* Vol 10 Issue 3 pp 12 – 23 at 15.
7   See in particular, J Harris, *The Social Work Business*, Routledge, 2003.
8   B Hudson, 'Captives of Bureaucracy' (2009) *Community Care* 31 (9 April 2009).
9   *The State of Social Care in England 2006–7* CSCI 2008, p23.
10   Information Centre (2011) *Personal Social Services Expenditure and Unit Costs England 2009–10*. Leeds: The Information Centre – see table 2.3.

Personalisation

3.7   Personalisation, despite being a creature of policy not law[11], represents a significant departure from the pre-existing model of assessment and service provision. It has been promoted with an evangelical fervour. At the end of 2007, six Government departments, together with local authority bodies, the NHS, regulators and representatives of independent sector providers all signed up to an 'historic protocol' *Putting People First: a shared commitment to the transformation of adult social care.*[12] The Coalition Government is maintaining the drive towards personalisation,[13] and it has been widely endorsed by the voluntary sector and providers.[14] It is also seen by some as an important and positive step towards independent living.

3.8   The aim is to increase personal choice and independence through the allocation of a personal budget (following self/supported assessments (see para 3.100 below)) to service users who are eligible for care support enabling them to determine how to spend it, generally referred to as 'self-directed support'. In theory this marks a welcome shift from service-led decisions, often reliant on poor quality care services, to a panoply of choice to find innovative ways to fulfill 'desired outcomes'. Personalisation also encourages a preventative approach to service provision with 'universal services' available to all regardless of eligibility. This dramatic re-configuration, which it is claimed will enable social workers to become advocates and brokers rather than assessors and gatekeepers,[15] is to be achieved within current resource constraints.

3.9   What this means is fleshed out more by the current English Prioritising Needs guidance (see para 3.30 below) and analysed below in the context of assessments and eligibility for service provision. To criticise a social care system which promotes independence, well-being and dignity would be heresy, but its implementation in the face of swingeing public sector cuts and a methodology of the kind characterised by Seddon (see para 3.5 above) is problematic. As CSCI observed the trend towards tightly circumscribed council help with social care needs does not sit well with the personalisation agenda and with wider concepts of health and well-being.[16]

3.10   At the heart of the dilemma is the issue of resources, and the extent to which the courts are prepared to defer to the problems of government (central and local) in ensuring that the state's finite resources are applied equitably. An analysis of the courts' approach to this question is provided at para 3.168 below.

11 Though given limited legal expression in Disabled People's Right to Control (Pilot Scheme)(England) Regulations 2010 (see chapter 4).
12 Department of Health (2007) *Putting People First: a shared vision and commitment to the transformation of Adult Social Care.*
13 See, for instance, Department of Health (2010) *A vision for adult social care: capable communities and active citizens.*
14 *Think local, act personal: a sector-wide commitment to moving forward with personalisation and community-based support* 2011 at www.thinklocalactpersonal.org.uk/_library/ Resources/Personalisation/TLAP/THINK_LOCAL_ACT_PERSONAL_5_4_11.pdf
15 LAC (2008) 1 *Transforming Social Care.*
16 *The State of Social Care in England, 2006–7, Executive Summary,* CSCI 2008 p32.

The duty to assess – the legislative and administrative framework

3.11   The community care assessment obligation, although underpinned by statute, is fleshed out by directions and considerable volumes of guidance.

The statutory framework

3.12   Arguably social services authorities have always been under a public law obligation to assess potential community care service users. Where a council has a duty to provide services for people if 'satisfied' they are 'necessary',[17] there must be a concomitant obligation on that council to have a procedure for making determinations as to when, in any given case, the duty crystallises.

Disabled Persons (Services, Consultation and Representation) Act 1986 s4

3.13   Because of doubt about the extent of this obligation, in relation to the provision of services under Chronically Sick and Disabled Persons Act (CSDPA) 1970 s2, the Disabled Persons (Services, Consultation and Representation) Act (DP(SCR)A) 1986 s4 gave to disabled people (and their carers) the right to request an assessment. The circular accompanying the 1986 Act (LAC (87)6) explained the position thus:

> 3. However, s2(1) does not make it explicit whether a local authority has a duty to determine the needs of a disabled person. It was suggested in the course of debates in Parliament on the Disabled Persons (Services, Consultation and Representation) Bill that as the duty to 'make arrangements' could be interpreted as applying only after the local authority are satisfied that such arrangements are necessary in order to meet particular needs, local authorities might refuse to come to a view as to what are those needs as a means of avoiding the obligation to make arrangements. It has never been the Government's view that subsection 2(1) should be interpreted in that way, and it is clear that this is shared by the vast majority of local authorities. However, it was agreed that the matter should be put beyond doubt.

> 4. Section 4 of the 1986 Act accordingly makes it clear that local authorities have a duty to decide whether the needs of a disabled person call for the provision of services under section 2 of the 1970 Act, if they are requested to do so by a disabled person (section 4(a)) or by anyone who provides care for him or her (section 4(c)) in the circumstances mentioned in section 8 of the 1986 Act.

3.14   Section 4 of the 1986 Act provides:

> When requested to do so by–
> (a) a disabled person,

---

17   Chronically Sick and Disabled Persons Act (CSDPA) 1970 s2(1).

(b) . . .[18]

(c) any person who provides care for him in the circumstances mentioned in section 8,[19] a local authority shall decide whether the needs of the disabled person call for the provision by the authority of any services in accordance with section 2(1) of the 1970 Act (provision of welfare services).

3.15   Although the section 4 duty remains, it is largely a historical curiosity: now effectively subsumed by the subsequent legislation. The right to request an assessment proved to be an unsatisfactory mechanism to access services under the CSDPA 1970, as it required people to know of the existence of their right to services before they could access those services. As most people did not know of their rights under that Act, they were unable to make the necessary request under DP(SCR)A 1986 s4. What was required, therefore, was a duty to assess regardless of any request from the potential service user: a duty that extended not only to services under CSDPA 1970 s2, but to all services under all the community care statutes.

3.16   The intention to create such a general duty to assess was announced in the 1989 white paper *Caring for People* (Cm 849) which at para 3.1.3 stated that social services authorities would be responsible for:

. . . carrying out an appropriate assessment of an individual's need for social care (including residential and nursing home care), in collaboration as necessary with medical, nursing and other agencies, before deciding what services should be provided.

3.17   The effect of the changes has been to make social services departments the 'gate-keepers', controlling access to state-supported community care services. Such services can only be provided at public expense after an assessment of need has occurred[20] and a decision has been made by the social services authority that, having regard to the assessment of need, services should be provided. Despite government rhetoric distancing itself from this gate-keeping role[21], the reality shows the trend moving in the opposite direction. The Care Quality Commission (CQC) in its first report in 2010 found that 72 per cent of English councils limited care support to those with critical and substantial needs.[22]

The assessment obligation under NHS and Community Care Act 1990 s47(1)

3.18   National Health Service and Community Care Act (NHSCCA) 1990 s47(1) is the general assessment duty presaged by the white paper. It provides:

18 This provision, which related to requests by 'authorised representatives', has not been brought into force.
19 That is, someone 'who provides regular and substantial care for the disabled person – see para 16.12.
20 Except in emergencies: NHSCCA 1990 s47(5), see para 4.114.
21 See, for instance, the executive summary of Department of Health (2005) *Independence, Well-being and Choice*, and LAC (2008) 1 *Transforming Social Care*.
22 Care Quality Commission (2010), *The state of health care and adult social care in England: key themes and quality of services in 2009*, HC 343.

(1) Subject to subsections (5) and (6) below, where it appears to a local authority that any person for whom they may provide or arrange for the provision of community care services may be in need of any such services, the authority–

(a) shall carry out an assessment of his needs for those services; and

(b) having regard to the results of that assessment, shall decide whether his needs call for the provision by them of any such services.

3.19　Section 47(1) obliges social services authorities to carry out an assessment of an individual's needs for community care services even where the individual has made no request for an assessment. All that is required in order to trigger the assessment obligation is that:

a)　the individual's circumstances have come to the knowledge of the authority;

b)　he or she may be in need of community care services.

3.20　The NHSCCA 1990 s47(1) duty lies at the very centre of all community care law – it is central to virtually all social services community care responsibilities and the nature of this obligation is considered in detail at para 3.87 and in the succeeding sections of this chapter.

The assessment obligation under NHS and Community Care Act 1990 s47(2)

3.21　In addition to the section 47(1) assessment obligation, section 47(2) states:

If at any time during the assessment of the needs of any person under subsection (1)(a) above it appears to a local authority that he is a disabled person, the authority –

(a) shall proceed to make such a decision as to the services he requires as is mentioned in section 4 of the Disabled Persons (Services, Consultation and Representation) Act 1986 without his requesting them to do so under that section; and

(b) shall inform him that they will be doing so and of his rights under that Act.

3.22　Detailed practice guidance issued by the Department of Health in its *Care Management and Assessment: a practitioners guide*[23] (referred to in this chapter as the 1991 practice guidance) advised that NHSCCA 1990 s47(2) entitled all disabled people to a 'comprehensive assessment' regardless of the complexity of their needs. This was, however, incorrect, as Carnwath J explained in *R v Gloucestershire CC ex p RADAR*.[24] In his opinion the Department of Health had misunderstood the effect of section 47(2). The subsection is, in effect, merely a modest provision aimed at flagging up the duty to provide services under CSDPA 1970 s2 as Lord Clyde explained in *R v Gloucestershire CC ex p Barry*:[25]

So far as the twofold provision in s47(1) and (2) is concerned the obligation on the local authority introduced by s47(1) was to carry out an assessment

23　Department of Health Social Services Inspectorate, 1991.

24　(1997–98) 1 CCLR 476 at 484, 21 December 1995, QBD.

25　[1997] 2 WLR 459, (1997–98) 1 CCLR 40, HL.

on its own initiative and the separate provision made in subs (2) cannot have been intended merely to achieve that purpose. It seems to me that there is sufficient reason for the making of a distinctive provision in sub-s (2) in the desire to recognise the distinctive procedural situation relative to the disabled. But it does not follow that any distinction exists in the considerations which may or may not be taken into account in making an assessment in the case of the disabled as compared with any other case.

Directions

3.23   NHSCCA 1990 s47(4) empowers the secretary of state to give directions as to the form community care assessments should take.[26] As noted in paras 1.55 and 3.45, in *R (B and H) v Hackney LBC*[27] the judge suggested that the terms of section 47(4) had the effect of limiting the binding nature of the policy guidance issued in respect of the section 47(1) assessment obligation. This interesting argument has not, however, been adopted by any other court and is at variance with a number of Court of Appeal decisions.

England

3.24   Directions have been issued in England by the Department of Health, as the Community Care Assessment Directions 2004:[28] Direction 2 of which requires social services authorities, when undertaking a community care assessment, to:

- consult the person to be assessed;
- consider whether the person has any carers and, if so, also consult them if the authority 'thinks it appropriate';
- take all reasonable steps to reach agreement with the person and, where they think it appropriate, any carers of that person, on the community care services which they are considering providing to meet his or her needs;
- provide information to the person and, where they think it appropriate, any carers of that person, about the amount of the payment (if any) which the person will be liable to make in respect of the community care services which they are considering providing to him or her.

3.25   The circular that accompanies the Directions (LAC (2004)24)[29] provides further information about their intended effect and is considered further in the context of carers at para 16.25 below.

---

26 See also Carers (Recognition and Services) Act 1995 s1(4), where a similar provision applies.
27 [2003] EWHC 1654 (Admin).
28 26 August 2004; at www.dh.gov.uk/en/Publicationsandstatistics/publications/ publicationslegislation DH_4088476.
29 Accessible at www.dh.gov.uk/en/Publicationsandstatistics/Lettersandcirculars/ LocalAuthorityCirculars/AllLocalAuthority/DH_4088369

Wales

3.26   It appears[30] that no equivalent directions have been issued in Wales. In the absence of directions NHSCCA 1990 s47(4) provides that assessments are to be carried out in such manner and take such form as the local authority considers appropriate. It follows that the adequacy of an assessment in any given case will depend upon its compliance with the relevant principles of public law, including:

1) that the aim of the process adopted by the social services department must be to determine the section 47(1)(b) question, ie, which of the applicant's needs 'call for' the provision of services. This therefore requires the local authority to:
    (a) gather sufficient data about the applicant in order to make an informed decision about what his or her needs are; and
    (b) have some general standard or formula by which it can make consistent decisions as to when needs do and do not 'call for' services;
2) that the process must be conducted fairly – ie, ensuring the individual understands what is occurring and has a full opportunity to contribute and respond to any third party evidence; that the process be non-discriminatory and completed within a reasonable period of time, etc;
3) that all relevant matters are taken into account – ie, central and local government guidance; the views of important persons (the service user, relevant professionals, carers and friends, etc) who have relevant information to the section 47(1)(b) judgment.

Policy and practice guidance

3.27   A plethora of guidance exists concerning the assessment process: some of it of general application and some of it specific to certain user groups.

3.28   The original policy guidance accompanying the community care reforms contained only six paragraphs concerning the assessment process.[31] Although this was buttressed by the 1991 practice guidance, the lack of firm policy guidance, combined with severe financial pressures on local authorities, led to a fragmented system which was, in the opinion of an influential 1996 Audit Commission report, unfair and extremely confusing for service users. The report commented:

> The effect of all this is to produce a maze of different criteria which are complex and difficult for people to understand. People who qualify for care in one authority may not qualify in another. The price of freedom of local decision-making is considerable variation in access to services between areas. Authorities may be able to reduce the worst effects of the inequities that result by comparing approaches and, here again, guidance may be useful.[32]

---

30 The Welsh Government has failed to keep track of what directions it has issued prior to 2005 – see para 1.38 above.
31 *Community Care in the Next Decade and Beyond: policy guidance*, HMSO, 1990, paras 3.15–3.20.
32 *Balancing the Care Equation: Progress with Community Care*, HMSO, 1996, para 32.

3.29   The government in England, in its 1998 white paper *Modernising Social Services* accepted these criticisms and committed itself to setting national standards and to defining service models for specific services or care groups.[33] The product of this commitment in England and Wales has been a series of national service frameworks (NSFs)[34] and (particularly in England) other guidance concerning the assessment of various care groups. The relationship between the various guidance documents is depicted in diagram 2 below.

Diagram 2: Department of Health Guidance concerning the assessment process

For the Welsh Government equivalent guidance see para 3.26 footnotes 38 and 44.

General Assessment Guidance Adults with community care needs	Carers	Disabled children
• *Prioritising Need in the Context of Putting People First: a whole system approach to eligibility for Social Care 2010* (See para 3.31) • *Community Care – Community Care in the Next Decade and Beyond: policy guidance,* 1990 [1990 Policy Guidance] (see para 3.28) • *Care Management And Assessment: Practitioners' Guide,* 1991 (see para 3.92) •	Guidance on carers' assessments is in *The Carers and Disabled Children Act 2000: a practitioners guide to carers' assessments,* 2001 (see para 16.8) and general guidance is in the practice guide to the Carers (Equal Opportunities) Act 2004 (see para 16.8)	FACS guidance is not of direct relevance. Specific guidance exists as *The Framework for the Assessment of Children in Need and their Families,* 2000, policy and practice guidance (see para 23.15)

Specific user group assessment guidance

Older people	Mental health service users	People with learning disabilities
• NSF for Older People (see para 3.33) • Single assessment process, 2002 (see para 3.35)	• NSF for Mental Health, 1999 (see para 3.38) • *Effective Care Co-ordination in Mental Health Services – Modernising the Care Programme Approach,* 1999.	• *Valuing people: White Paper,* 2001 (see para 3.36) • *Valuing people: implementation policy guidance,* LAC (2001) 23 • *Valuing People Now: a new three year strategy* (2009) 18.8

---

33 Cm 4169, TSO, 1998 at para 2.34.
34 The principle NSFs of direct relevance to social services are those that relate to (1) older people (see para 19.3 below), (2) mental health (see para 20.3 below) and (3) children (see para 23.63 below). See generally para 1.6 above.

3.30   Additionally the government undertook to 'introduce greater consistency in the system for deciding who qualifies' for community care services. This commitment produced in 2002 generic policy and practice guidance on 'Fair Access to Care Services' (FACS) which has now been updated (and superseded) by 2010 policy guidance entitled 'Prioritising need in the context of Putting People First'[35] (Prioritising Needs Guidance). A similar approach was taken by the Welsh Assembly Government in Wales, where the equivalent guidance to FACS is known as the 'Creating a Unified and Fair System for Assessing and Managing Care' (UFSAMC) 2002.[36]

3.31   All community care assessments should be undertaken in accordance with the Prioritising Needs Guidance in England and the UFSAMC guidance in Wales (both statutory guidance issued under s7 Local Authority Social Services Act 1970 (see para 1.46)). This guidance does not replace all the earlier guidance (for instance the 1991 practice guidance). It is supplemented in England by further practice guidance, Facts about FACS 2010: A guide to Fair Access to Care Services issued by the Social Care Institute for Excellence (SCIE)[37], and by specific user group guidance.

Specific user group assessment guidance

3.32   In addition to complying with the Prioritising Needs Guidance in England and the UFSAMC guidance in Wales, social services are also required to take into account 'user group specific' guidance – which can be broken down into the various categories listed below. The guidance relating to the assessment of older people and those with dual sensory impairment is considered briefly in this chapter, whereas the guidance specifically relating to people with mental health problems, learning disabilities, disabled children and carers is dealt with in the subsequent chapters that deal with these client groups.

Older people specific guidance

3.33   The specific guidance concerning the process by which older people should be assessed comprises:

- *NSF for Older People*, March 2001;[38]
- *Single Assessment Process (SAP) Policy Guidance*, 2002.[39]

3.34   Standard Two of the English NSF[40] outlined the SAP which had been first

---

35 Department of Health (2010) *Prioritising need in the context of Putting People First: A whole system approach to eligibility for social care. Guidance on Eligibility Criteria for Adult Social Care, England 2010.*
36 NAFWC 09/2002 http://wales.gov.uk/pubs/circulars/2002/english/NAFWC09–02Guidance-e.pdf?lang=en.
37 SCIE, *Adult Services Guide 33* at www.scie.org.uk/publications/guides/guide33/files/guide33.pdf.
38 *Strategy for Older People in Wales* (January 2003).
39 UFSAMC (Wales) 2002 incorporates the key elements of both FACS and SAP.
40 *Strategy for Older People in Wales* (January 2003) para 33 confirmed that the NSF for older people in Wales would build upon the unified assessment guidance already issued. A summary version only is available at the time of writing.

proposed in *The NHS Plan*.[41] The SAP for older people would (the NSF stated at para 2.27) ensure that:

- a more standardised assessment process is in place across all areas and agencies;
- standards of assessment practice are raised;
- older people's needs are assessed in the round.

3.35   Guidance[42] on the SAP was issued to health and social services bodies and required that they had fully integrated commissioning arrangements and integrated provision of services including community services and continence services by April 2004.[43] In Wales the UFSAMC 2002 policy guidance includes the equivalent guidance.

3.36   The raison d'être of the process is both organisational – in compelling health and social services bodies to work together in assessing and providing care services – and cultural – to provide what the guidance calls a 'person-centred approach'. The aim is to ensure that older people are not subjected to ineffective (and inefficient) multiple assessments. Such assessments cannot in fact be 'unified' in the legal sense, unless the agencies have entered into formal partnership arrangements under NHSA 2006 ss75–76 and 256–257 (see para 13.124 below).

3.37   The increasing tendency in practice for the resource allocation self-assessment questionnaire to form the core of the assessment process (see para 3.96 below), together with problems of non-integrated IT systems and anxieties about confidentiality have resulted in SAP falling into disuse. Nevertheless it is still current statutory guidance and is useful in setting out a reasonably comprehensive list of the domains applicable to older people (see para 3.100 below).

Mental health service user specific guidance

3.38   The specific guidance concerning the process by which people with mental health needs are assessed comprises:

- *NSF for Mental Health*, September 1999;[44]
- *Effective Care Co-ordination in Mental Health Services – Modernising the Care Programme Approach*, 1999;[45]
- *Refocusing the Care Programme Approach: Policy and positive practice guidance*, 2008.[46]

---

41   Department of Health White Paper, *The NHS Plan* Cm 4818-I, 2000, para 7.3.
42   In particular HSC 2002/001 and LAC (2002)1, *Guidance on the Single Assessment Process for Older People*, January 2002.
43   Updated implementation guidance and advice on 'off the shelf' assessment tools continues to be provided by the Department of Health, accessible at www.dh.gov.uk/ PolicyAndGuidance/HealthandSocialCareTopics/ SocialCare/ SingleAssessmentProcess/fs/en.
44   *Adult Mental Health Services: A National Service Framework for Wales*, April 2002.
45   *Adult Mental Health Services in Wales: Equity, Empowerment, Effectiveness, Efficiency: A Strategy Document*, 2001.
46   Adult Mental Health Services: *Stronger in Partnership* 2008.

3.39   This guidance is considered at paras 20.3 and 20.7 below.

Learning disabled people's specific guidance

3.40   The specific guidance concerning the process by which people with learning disabilities should be assessed comprises:

- *Valuing people: a new strategy for learning disability for the 21st century,
  2001;*
- *Valuing people: a new strategy for learning disability for the 21st century:
  implementation, LAC (2001)23.*[47]

3.41   This guidance is considered at para 18.5 below.

Deafblind children and adults specific guidance

3.42   Specific statutory guidance in the form of *Social Care for Deafblind
Children and Adults*[48] exists in recognition of the particular needs of this
client group. The guidance includes the following useful requirements in
relation to assessment and care planning. Councils must ensure that:

- assessments are carried out by specifically trained individuals/teams
  and include communication, one-to-one human contact, social
  interaction and emotional well-being, support with mobility, assistive
  technology and rehabilitation;
- assessments also take account of needs that will occur in the near
  future to maximize early recognition and support;
- services to deafblind people are appropriate bearing in mind that
  services designed for single rather than dual impairment may not be;
- deafblind people are able to access specifically trained one to one
  support workers if needed[49]

Disabled children's specific guidance

3.43   The right of disabled children to be assessed stems primarily from the
Children Act (CA) 1989, although they also have certain rights under the
community care regime (see para 23.61 below). However, the Prioritising
Needs and UFSAMC are not of direct application: the specific guidance
(considered further at para 23. 15 below) of relevance being:

- *Framework for the Assessment of Children in Need and their Families, 2000
  policy guidance;*[50]
- *Assessing Children in Need and their Families, 2000 practice guidance.*

47 In Wales, see *Learning Disability Strategy: Section 7 guidance on service principles and
    service responses,* 2004 and *Statement on policy and practice for adults with a learning
    disability,* 2007.
48 Department of Health LAC(2009)6: the equivalent Welsh statutory guidance: NAWC
    10/01 *Social Care for Deafblind Children and Adults.* Supplementary practice guidance:
    Moving Forward: Services for Deafblind Children and Adults WAG 2008.
49 Paras 21–25 in Welsh and English guidance.
50 In Wales, *Framework for the Assessment of Children in Need and their Families,* 2001
    policy guidance.

Disabled parents' specific guidance

3.44   Specific 2007 guidance concerning the needs of learning disabled parents exists as *Working with parents with a learning disability.*[51] Other good practice guidance (as outlined below) exists concerning the needs of all parents with a disability. The important point being that the 'presenting needs' of a disabled parent will include the need to discharge his or her parental responsibilities. Accordingly if, for instance, as a result of an impairment a parent is unable to get his or her child to school, this 'need' should, prima facie, be seen as a 'presenting need' of the parent and not a need of the child under the CA 1989. Unfortunately, in this context, two major impediments affect disabled parents. They may face doubts about their parenting ability, rather than receiving the additional support they need; and they may experience significant problems of poor coordination between adult and children services. The CSCI[52] referred to a gap between services through which disabled parents fell, and found this was exacerbated by the administrative separation of children and adult social care services as a result of the CA 2004 (see chapter 23).

3.45   There are statutory duties on both adult and children's services in this context, and no hard and fast answers as to which arm of the local authority should lead. The Welsh unified guidance simply says[53] that local authorities should ensure that they offer a holistic and equitable approach to disabled parents and their children, and they should be similarly provided with help irrespective of whether they approached the services through a child care or adult care route. Research[54] suggests that addressing the parent's needs, including the need to discharge their parenting role will go at least some way to safeguarding and promoting the welfare of the child. In the course of assessing a disabled adult, councils should recognise that adults, who may have parenting responsibilities for a child under 18 years, may require help with these responsibilities.[55] *Supporting disabled parents and parents with additional support needs*, a SCIE resource guide[56] provides useful advice on good practice in developing local protocols as recommended in the guidance. The obligations owed to children in need are considered in chapter 23.

Carers' specific guidance

3.46   Carers' assessments are not governed by NHSCCA 1990 s47 and accordingly the guidance outlined above is not of direct relevance. Practice

51 Department of Health (2007) *Good practice guidance on working with parents with a learning disability.*
52 *Supporting disabled parents: a family or fragmented approach?* CSCI 2009.
53 *UFSAMC* 2002, annex 1, para 6.
54 Olsen and Tyers, *Think parent: disabled adults as parents,* National Family and Parenting Institute 2004.
55 Prioritising Needs guidance, para 26.
56 J Morris and M Wates, *Supporting disabled parents and parents with additional support needs,* adult services resource guide 9, SCIE 2007.

guidance on carers' assessments is provided in both England and Wales as *The Carers and Disabled Children Act 2000: a practitioner's guide to carers' assessments* (2001) and additionally in England by a further guide issued by the Social Care Institute for Excellence (SCIE).[57] These are considered at para 16.8 below.

Guidance and section 47(4)

3.47   As has noted above (see paras 1.55 and 3.23), in *R (B and H) v Hackney LBC*[58] Keith J held that policy guidance issued under Local Authority Social Services Act (LASSA) 1970 s7(1) was not 'strong guidance' in relation to the assessment process under NHSCCA 1990 s47. In his view, since section 47(4) states that in the absence of directions local authorities are entitled to conduct assessments as they deem appropriate – it then logically follows that it is only a direction that can materially restrict this latitude. If this controversial view is correct, it conflicts with other High Court decisions and the Court of Appeal in the *Gloucestershire* judgment (albeit that this argument was not considered in these cases). It would also downgrade the force of the key Prioritising Needs, SAP and UFSAMC guidance (see para 3.30 above) – although only so far as this guidance relates to the actual assessment process under section 47 (ie information gathering and the service provision decision): the guidance would remain strong 'policy guidance' in so far as it relates to care planning and service provision.

3.48   The courts do not insist (save perhaps in cases involving 'severe care needs' decisions – see para 3.227 below) that practitioners stick scrupulously to their designated assessment documentation: in the words of McCombe J[59] 'whatever boxes are or are not ticked in the assessment form and in the care plan documents, local authorities will provide services to meet "eligible needs" as they perceive them to be'.

Delegation of duty to assess

3.49   The duty to assess under NHSCCA 1990 s47[60] is a social services function (for the purposes of LASSA 1970 Sch 1, see para 1.3 above). There is no general power for social services authorities to delegate this function to other bodies.[61] The only situations in which it can be legally delegated, are (1) where the social services authority has entered into a formal partnership arrangement with an NHS body (either a primary care trust (PCT) or an NHS trust under the National Health Service Act (NHSA) 2006

---

57   SCIE practice guide to the Carers (Equal Opportunities) Act 2004.
58   [2003] EWHC 1654 (Admin).
59   *R (F, J, S, R and others) v Wirral BC* [2009] EWHC 1626 (Admin) at para 74.
60   Or indeed, under the Carers Acts – see para 16.46 below.
61   *R v Kirklees MBC ex p Daykin* (1997–98) 1 CCLR 512 at 525D, 26 November 1996, QBD.

ss75–76 and 256–257; or under a pilot programme established by the secretary of state.[62] (see para 13.124).

3.50   In the absence of such partnership arrangements, there is currently no express power for the authority to delegate the function to another agency. However, the Localism Bill (if enacted) may change the landscape of local authority powers (see para 3.53 below). In practice authorities often request third parties to carry out key tasks in the assessment – for instance, an occupational therapist employed by an NHS trust in assessing the need for home adaptations. In such cases, an authority may be, to all intents and purposes, bound by that third party's view on need – especially if it has expertise which the social services authority lacks[63] (see also para 3.143 below).

3.51   A not uncommon situation where key assessment functions are in effect delegated, concerns the assessment of detained drug and alcohol misusers wishing to attend community rehabilitation facilities: frequently key aspects of such assessments are carried out by expert probation officers on behalf of social services (see para 23.16 where this is further considered).

3.52   It has been suggested that local authorities might be able to delegate their assessment functions by virtue of Local Government (Contracts) Act 1997 s1, which empowers councils to contract with third parties to discharge certain of their functions. Section 4(3) of the Act, however, places a significant limitation on such delegation, restricting its application to contracts 'for the provision or making available of services'. In the context of the 1997 Act, which in section 1 refers to 'assets or services, or both, (whether or not together with goods)' it seems unlikely that an assessment could be deemed a 'service'. It is also doubtful that an assessment could be described as the 'making available of services': it is a qualitatively different function – namely the decision as to whether or not there is any need to make any such arrangements. Such an interpretation is strongly supported by the relevant policy guidance.[64]

3.53   The general powers of local authorities, as currently set out in clause 1 of the Localism Bill, would enable councils to act as individuals except where there is an express restriction. This would significantly change the administrative law principle that public authorities as 'creatures of statute' can only act pursuant to specific powers and duties; and would enable, inter alia, the delegation of the carrying out of assessments.

62 The Contracting Out (Local Authorities Social Services Functions) (England) Order 2011 SI No 1568 permitted delegation of social services functions in England in very limited conditions – namely where the secretary of state has established an 'adult social work practice pilot scheme'; it also permits the delegation of community care assessments where a pilot 'in control' site has been established – provided the local authority is one listed in the Schedule to the Community Care Services: Disabled People's Choice and Control (Pilot Scheme) (England) Directions 2010 (see para 4.128 above).

63 This will not invariably be the case, particularly if the opinion only addresses one particular aspect of an individual's circumstances – see eg *R (Goldsmith) v Wandsworth LBC* [2004] EWCA Civ 1170, (2004) 7 CCLR 472.

64 See eg SAP 2002 policy guidance, p16; the UFSAMC 2002 policy guidance, p10 fn 2 and the combined policy guidance under the 2000 and 2004 Carers Acts, para 45.

Timescale for assessments

3.54   There is no general statutory timescale for the completion of community care assessments – although such timescales have been prescribed in policy guidance for assessments under the CA 1989 (see para 23.18) and in directions under the Community Care (Delayed Discharge etc) Act 2003 (see para 5.29).

3.55   As a matter of statutory interpretation, where a provision is silent on the time for compliance, the law implies that it be done within a reasonable time, and that what is a 'reasonable time' is a question of fact, depending on the nature of the obligation and the purpose for which the computation is to be made.[65]

3.56   The Prioritising Needs guidance requires a range of information about the assessment and care planning process, including related time-scales, to be made available in a range of languages and formats[66]. When considering complaints about delayed assessments, the local government ombudsman has had regard to the timescales set out in the relevant local authority's charter[67] – and such published information would appear to be an appropriate starting point for a review. In 2011 the ombudsman expressed the view that a reasonable time for an assessment should normally be 'between four and six weeks from the date of the initial request'[68] and in a 2006 complaint he held that a three-month delay in assessing for adaptations was 'simply unacceptable – (the Council's own targets for assessments were one month for urgent cases and two months for others)'.[69]

3.57   Authorities frequently adopt a grading scheme for assessments – with a view to prioritising the most urgent. While the idea of a scheme setting priorities for assessment is to a degree anomalous (given that in general the object of assessment is to identify the extent and urgency of need), the local government ombudsman has accepted that such a system 'does not seem unreasonable'.[70] LAC (93)2 (although primarily aimed at the particular needs of persons who misuse alcohol and/or drugs) makes a number of observations of more general application to assessments.[71] It supports the idea of some assessments being carried out faster than others, stating that authorities 'should have criteria for determining the level of assessment that is appropriate to the severity or complexity of the need' (at para 14).

---

65   See eg *Re North ex p Hasluck* [1895] 2 QB 264; *Charnock v Liverpool Corporation* [1968] 3 All ER 473.
66   Para 80.
67   See eg complaint no 01/C/15434 against South Tyneside Metropolitan BC, 20 January 2003, where the Charter stipulated 21 days for the completion of community care assessments.
68   Local Government Ombudsman (2011) Fact Sheet Complaints about councils that conduct community care assessments at www.lgo.org.uk/publications/fact-sheets/complaints-about-community-care-assessments/
69   Complaint no 05/C/07195 against Northumberland CC, 18 April 2006, paras 7, 29 and 30.
70   Para 33, Complaint no 00/B/00599 against Essex CC, 3 September 2001.
71   See eg paras 26–27 concerning the applicability of its observations to the needs of homeless people.

It further advocates the need for authorities to develop 'fast-track assessment' procedures (at paras 16–20). The circular is considered in detail in chapter 22.

3.58   The local government ombudsman has investigated a considerable number of complaints concerning delayed assessments relating to home adaptations (see paras 9.121 and 15.102 below). By way of example, a 1996 report found seven months for an assessment and a further four months' delay by the authority in processing the disabled facilities grant approval to be maladministration.[72] In this complaint the local ombudsman reiterated her view that if the authority has a shortage of occupational therapists, it should not use them for assessment purposes if this will result in unreasonable delay, stating, '[i]f such expertise is not available, councils need to find an alternative way of meeting their statutory responsibilities'. While the local government ombudsman has approved in principle the idea of prioritising certain assessments, she has criticised the way such a scheme is administered. In a 1995 complaint[73] she stated:

> The Council's system of priorities is over-simple. Within the category of 'complex' cases there is no provision for relatively simple solutions to tide people over until a full assessment can be made. Also, there will be cases which cannot be described as 'emergencies' but need to be dealt with more urgently within the 'complex' category than others. The Council's over-simple system of priorities resulted in a failure to meet [the complainants' disabled daughter's] needs promptly and I consider that to be an injustice resulting in maladministration.

3.59   Where there is unreasonable delay in assessing (or an intimation that there will be), the complaints process may be invoked (see para 26.8 below). The effect of this,[74] is that some element of a fixed timescale is introduced into the process. The complainant should emphasise (if it be the case) that the duty to assess commenced when his or her potential needs first came to the notice of the authority, rather than at the time of any later request being made for an assessment.

3.60   In cases of urgency councils have power to provide services before completing the assessment. The obligation to consider doing so will have particular force if the urgent need has been exacerbated by the authority's delay. Section 47(6) provides that if such services are provided without an assessment, 'as soon as practicable there-after, an assessment of his needs shall be made in accordance with the preceding provision of this section'. The provision of support pursuant to the section 47(5) power is further considered at para 4.114 below.

Reform – a common assessment framework

3.61   There is considerable anecdotal evidence to suggest that the proliferation of different assessment regimes for different client groups has created a

72 Complaints nos 94/C/0964 and 94/C/0965 against Middlesbrough DC and Cleveland CC.
73 Complaint no 93/C/3660 against Rochdale Metropolitan BC.
74 See para 26.22 below

complex and confusing assessment bureaucracy, dramatically increasing the time spent by care managers in 'form filling', significantly reducing their face to face contact with service users and doing little or nothing to improve the quality of services or decision making. Arguably, much of the bureaucracy that now accompanies assessments is driven by a need to satisfy statistical returns to the Department of Health or Welsh Government rather than to maximise the quality of the support provided for individual service users.

3.62   The white paper, *Our Health, Our Care, Our Say* (January 2006) proposed to develop a new assessment process, to be known as the Common Assessment Framework (CAF) for Adults. The Department of Health in its statements concerning CAF[75] accepts that having different assessment regimes for different client groups causes 'difficulties . . . particularly for individuals with multiple needs who have to negotiate the different systems'. It suggests that a CAF would overcome many of these problems, particularly if 'geared towards self-determination and planning for independence'. The statement acknowledges that 'there has been significant investment in SAP' and that 'this investment must not go to waste'. It proposes to satisfy this objective by ensuring that 'the momentum behind the implementation of SAP, including developing and implementing e-SAP solutions, continues in local communities' – presumably being harnessed by the new CAF.

3.63   Following consultation CAF is currently being developed and tested using 'demonstrator sites' (led by adult social care authorities, but involving health services, mental health trusts, housing support and IT suppliers). Sites were chosen, as SCIE puts it, 'to lead the way in creating a more efficient and transparent system of information-sharing, to avoid duplication in assessments and ensure that people receive the best quality care and support[76]' They will continue until March 2012 and be evaluated nationally.

The duty to assess: when does it arise?

Social services authority awareness of the individual

3.64   The first requirement for the triggering of the duty to assess is that the person in need comes to the knowledge of the social services authority. It is the authority that must have the requisite knowledge, rather than the individual social services department. By way of example, in the case of a unitary authority (which has responsibility for both housing and social services) the duty to assess will in general be triggered when a 'vulnerable'[77] person presents him/herself as homeless (see para 15.18 below).

---

75 See eg Department of Health (2006) *Common Assessment Framework*, Care Services Improvement Partnership.
76 SCIE (2010) *Common Assessment Framework for Adults* at www.scie.org.uk/publications/nqswtool/statements/assessment/legislation.asp
77 Under Housing Act 1996 s189.

3.65   In *R (Patrick) v Newham LBC*[78] the applicant, who had physical and mental health difficulties was living rough after the authority had determined that she was intentionally homeless. Lawyers acting on her behalf wrote to the authority, enclosing a doctor's letter confirming her significant psychiatric problems and requested urgent accommodation. In the subsequent judicial review proceedings it was argued (among other things) that this should have triggered an assessment under NHSCCA 1990 s47. Henriques J held:[79]

> I am wholly unable to accept any suggestion that the respondent has discharged its duty under section 47. The authority has not carried out any assessment of the applicant's needs for community care services. There is no record of any consideration of the applicant's individual circumstances at all . . .
>
> An assessment of needs is a formal task to be carried out in accordance with Central Government Guidance and involves collation of medical evidence, psychiatric evidence, etc, with a view thereafter to matching accommodation to needs. I am satisfied that the Council have not complied with their duty under section 47. That duty plainly accrued [on the date when] the applicant's solicitors wrote to the respondent describing the applicant's circumstances and requesting urgent accommodation.

3.66   It follows that authorities should ensure that they have the necessary internal organisational networks so that the needs of vulnerable individuals are automatically referred to the relevant community care team irrespective of the point at which first local authority contact with that individual occurs.[80] A failure to make such arrangements may amount to maladministration.

Individuals who 'may be in need' of community care services

3.67   The second requirement for the triggering of the duty to assess is that the authority have knowledge[81] that the person may be in need of services. In *R v Bristol CC ex p Penfold*[82] the court held that this was 'a very low threshold test'. ADASS guidance on the implementation of personalisation reminds local authorities, 'It is lawful to refuse assessment to only a very few people'[83]

---

78   (2000) 4 CCLR 48, QBD.
79   (2000) 4 CCLR 48, QBD at 51–52.
80   See FACS 2002 policy guidance, para 68, which states (among other things) 'if individuals need other services, officers of the council should help them to find the right person to talk to in the relevant agency or organisation, and make contact on their behalf (see Better Care, Higher Standards)'.
81   Presumably this may include constructive knowledge.
82   (1997–98) 1 CCLR 315, 23 January 1998, QBD.
83   ADASS (2009) *Personalisation and the law: Implementing Putting People First in the current legal framework* p17.

What of a 'future need' for services?

3.68   NHSCCA 1990 s47(1) speaks of a possible – rather than a present – need: it must appear that the individual '*may*' be in need'. Since everyone 'may' at some future time be in need of community care services, the courts and the guidance have adopted a pragmatic approach to the interpretation of the provision. If a person seeks an assessment on the basis of a future need, the key questions appear to be (1) how likely and (2) how imminent?

3.69   In relation to patients expected to be discharged from hospital, the guidance is phrased in mandatory terms[84] even though they will not be in need of community care services until their actual discharge. For such patients, however, the predictability and imminence of need is a given. The hospital discharge assessment duty is now reinforced by legislation – Community Care (Delayed Discharges etc) Act 2003 s2 (see para 5.5 below).

3.70   In *R (B) v Camden LBC*[85] the court was required to consider the interpretation of the provision in the context of a patient detained under the Mental Health Act 1983, who was seeking discharge. Stanley Burnton J held that the phrase 'a person . . . may be in need of such services' referred:

> . . . to a person who may be in need at the time, or who may be about to be in need. A detained patient who is the subject of a deferred conditional discharge decision of a tribunal, which envisages his conditional discharge once section 117 after-care services are in place, is a person who 'may be in need of such services', since if such services are available to him he will be discharged and immediately need them. Whether a patient who may reasonably be considered to be liable to have such an order made in an impending tribunal hearing is an issue I do not have to decide in the instant case, but I incline to the view that he is.

> However, the duty under section 47 does not arise until it 'appears' to the local authority that a person may be in need, and it cannot appear to it that he may be in need unless it knows of his possible need. It is presumably for this reason that the Community Care (Delayed Discharges etc) Act 2003 was enacted. . . .

3.71   *R v Mid-Glamorgan CC ex p Miles*[86] concerned a similar problem: a prisoner whose only hope of parole was dependent upon a prior confirmation that the local authority would fund a drug rehabilitation hostel for him. The authority was not prepared to assess him until parole was granted. The case was settled on terms that the local authority undertook the assessment.

3.72   Concern has been expressed by disabled people about the current lack of provision enabling portability of services, and the extent to which that limits freedom of movement. A proactive approach to assessments would help facilitate this. The Prioritising Needs guidance, reflecting this concern, states:

84 The first key step in the English guidance (see para 5.8) is to start planning for discharge or transfer before or on admission, (including by implication the section 47 community care assessment process).
85 [2005] EWHC 1366 (Admin), (2005) 8 CCLR 422 at [66]–[67].
86 Unreported, January 1994 *Legal Action* 21.

This pragmatic approach [taken in *R (B) v Camden LBC* above] should also be taken in relation to people with firm plans to move to another local authority's area, for example, a person with a job offer who intends to take it up, subject to suitable community care services being available. Such people could be described as "about to be in need" in the local authority's area, even though they may already be in receipt of services in the area which they are leaving. The person's move must be reasonably certain: local authorities would not be obliged to assess a person who was simply considering a move to the area.[87]

3.73   While inter-authority consultation is good practice and useful, the Court of Appeal held that there was neither a statutory duty under NHSCCA 1990 s47(3), nor did fairness require consultation when one local authority reached an assessment decision resulting in an individual moving from residential care into supported living in a second local authority's area (see paras 3.134 and 6.28 below).[88]

No need to 'request' an assessment

3.74   As has been noted above, NHSCCA 1990 s47(1) marked a major advance on the previous assessment obligation (under DP(SCR)A 1986 s4) by dispensing with the need for a 'request' in order to activate the obligation. In *R v Gloucestershire CC ex p RADAR*[89] it was held that the local authority could not discharge its obligation to potential service users (who had previously received services) simply by writing to them, asking them to reply if they wanted to be considered for assessment. Carnwath J stated:

> The obligation to make an assessment for community care services does not depend on a request, but on the 'appearance of need' . . . . Of course, the authority cannot carry out an effective reassessment without some degree of co-operation from the service user or his helpers. However, that is a very different thing from saying that they can simply rest on having sent a letter of the type to which I have referred.

3.75   In reaching this decision the court emphasised the essential frailty of many of the potential service users:

> In some areas of law that might be an adequate response, where those affected can be assumed to be capable of looking after their own interests, and where silence in response to an offer can be treated as acceptance or acquiescence. However, that approach cannot be and is not valid in the present context.[90]

3.76   Clearly it will be a question of fact and degree, whether a local authority has, in any particular situation, sufficient knowledge of a potential service user, so as to trigger the duty to assess. In *R v Bexley LBC ex p B*[91] for instance the court held that:

---

87   Para 50.
88   *Buckinghamshire CC v Royal Borough of Kingston upon Thames* [2011] EWCA Civ 457, (2011) 14 CCLR 427.
89   (1997–98) 1 CCLR 476, QBD.
90   (1997–98) 1 CCLR 476 at 482D, QBD.
91   (2002) 3 CCLR 15 at 22J.

Authorities are, however, under an obligation to make provision . . . whenever they are satisfied that the relevant conditions have been met. A request by or on behalf of a disabled person is not one of those conditions. It seems to me that the Court should look at the reality of the situation. In the present case, although no formal request was made by the applicant's mother for an assessment of the applicant's needs, that was the effect of what happened in the early months of 1994.

3.77   Not only is the duty to assess independent of any request from the potential service user, it also arises irrespective of:

a)   there being any prospect of the potential service user actually qualifying for any services;[92]

b)   the financial circumstances of the service user;[93] or

c)   the service user being ordinarily resident[94] in the local authority's area.[95]

Entitlement to services is not relevant

3.78   The duty to assess is triggered when the authority is aware of an 'appearance of need', and not the likelihood of entitlement to services. *R v Bristol CC ex p Penfold*[96] concerned a 52-year-old person who suffered from anxiety and depression. The authority refused to carry out a community care assessment on the grounds (among others) that there was no prospect of meeting any needs that might have emerged in the course of the assessment (because their eligibility criteria were so tightly drawn, that only people at considerable risk were likely to be offered services). In relation to this argument, Scott Baker J held[97]

Even if there is no hope from the resource point of view of meeting any needs identified in the assessment, the assessment may serve a useful purpose in identifying for the local authority unmet needs which will help it to plan for the future. Without assessment this could not be done.

If the Respondent's argument on construction is accepted, the consequence will be that not only can authorities set wholly disparate eligibility criteria for services they intend to provide but they may also utilise such criteria as a basis for whether they will undertake a community care assessment at all. This cannot be right. The mere fact of unavailability of resources to meet a need does not mean that there is no need to be met. Resource implications in my view play no part in the decision whether to carry out an assessment.

92   See *R v Bristol CC ex p Penfold* (1997–98) 1 CCLR 315, QBD (discussed below) although in such cases the assessment may be rudimentary.

93   LAC (98)19 [WOC 27/98 in Wales] para 8 and Prioritising Needs guidance, para 77 [UFSAMC 2002, para 2.33 in Wales].

94   See chapter 6 where 'ordinary residence' is considered further.

95   See *R v Berkshire CC ex p P* (1997–98) 1 CCLR 141, QBD (discussed below), although in general this will only be necessary for a local authority to carry out an assessment of someone who is not ordinarily resident in its area, if the person's residence is disputed or he or she has no settled residence.

96   (1997–98) 1 CCLR 315, QBD.

97   (1997–98) 1 CCLR 315 at 322, QBD.

The duty to assess arises where entitlement exists to NHS continuing care

3.79   As noted at para 14.142 below, the fact that it is the policy of the Department of Health and the Welsh Assembly that individuals eligible for NHS continuing healthcare should have all their care needs met by the NHS, does not in itself displace the statutory duties owed to them under the community care legislation – most importantly under NHSA 2006 s254 and Sch 20 (NHS (Wales) Act (NHS(W)A) 2006 s192 and Sch 15). Such people may still remain 'in need' of such services and as a consequence the duty to assess under the 1990 Act is triggered. The Department of Health has expressed its view on this question (following the abuse inquiry concerning people with learning disabilities accommodated by the Cornwall Partnership NHS Trust[98]) in the following terms:[99]

> One of the key contributing factors identified in Cornwall was a clear absence of person-centred planning together with a failure to provide comprehensive, local authority-led assessments for people living in NHS accommodation. Assessments and person-centred planning – a fundamental tenet of Valuing People – are essential in ensuring that services meet an individual's needs and are in their best interests.
>
> It is a matter of significant concern that this was allowed to happen and I am writing to remind you of your duty to ensure that such assessments are provided under section 47(1) of the NHS and Community Care Act (1990).

The duty to assess arises even when services are discretionary

3.80   The duty to assess is not dependent upon a collateral statutory duty 'to provide' or upon the person being ordinarily resident in the local authority's area. In *R v Berkshire CC ex p P*[100] the respondent local authority refused to assess the applicant, because it claimed that he was not 'ordinarily resident' within its area. Laws J held:[101]

> I reject the respondent's submission that s47(1) imports a condition requiring the physical availability of services to a person before the duty of assessment arises in relation to that person. The word 'may' in the subordinate clause in question means, in the context of the subsection as a whole, that the duty to assess arises where the local authority possesses the

98   See in particular the joint investigation by the CSCI and the Commission for Healthcare Audit and Inspection into allegations of abuse suffered by people with learning disabilities in accommodation provided by the Cornwall Partnership NHS Trust, July 2006.
99   Letter from the Director General for Social Care dated 2 November 2006 sent to all social services authorities.
100   (1997–98) 1 CCLR 141, 9 July 1996, QBD.
101   (1997–98) 1 CCLR 141 at 147F, 9 July 1996, QBD.

legal power[102] to provide or arrange for the provision of community care services to the individual in question.

3.81   Accordingly the duty to assess is not conditional upon whether the service user is resident in the authority's area or indeed whether the local authority is prepared to exercise its discretion to make any such services available. The rationale behind this decision (in relation to the ordinary residence question) must be that without such a duty, persons whose residence was disputed by two or more authorities would effectively be in limbo until their residence was resolved. However, in *R (J) v Southend BC*[103] Newman J held that where the 'ordinarily resident' authority accepts responsibility to assess, the authority in whose area the service user is actually physically present, cannot (absent unusual factors) be compelled to undertake an assessment.

Returning UK nationals

3.82   The principle established in *R v Berkshire CC ex p P* is of relevance in relation to returning UK nationals who may have been living for an extended period abroad. If on arrival they present with community care needs, it may be that they have no settled residence (see para 36 below) or at least their ordinary residence is disputed. The receiving authority will therefore have a duty to assess their community care needs – even if an ordinary residence determination is being sought (see para 6.63 below): UK nationals (unlike other EEA nationals or non-European nationals) are not disentitled to community care services (see para 21.71 below). Any such assessment may have to rely (initially at least) to a greater or lesser extent upon information provided by the overseas authorities.

Financial circumstances are not relevant

3.83   The financial circumstances of a person are irrelevant for the purposes of assessment. This point is made explicit by policy guidance in relation to residential care LAC (98)19[104] which states:

> 8. Local authorities are under a legal duty under the NHS and Community Care Act 1990 to assess the care needs of anyone who, in the authority's view, may be in need of community care services. It is the Department's view that the law does not allow authorities to refuse to undertake an assessment of care needs for anyone on the grounds of the person's financial resources, eg because they have capital in excess of the capital limit for residential accommodation. Even if someone may be able to pay the full cost of an services, or make their own arrangements independently

---

102   Social services authorities have the power under National Assistance Act (NAA) 1948 s29 to provide services for people who are not ordinarily resident in their area, see para 9.56.
103   [2005] EWHC 3547 (Admin).
104   WOC 27/98, para 8 in Wales.

... they should be advised about what type of care they require, and informed about what services are available.[105]

3.84   This view is reinforced by the Prioritising Needs guidance, which states at para 77:[106]

> From the beginning of the process, councils should make individuals aware that their individual financial circumstances will determine whether or not they have to pay towards the cost of the support provided to them. However, an individual's financial circumstances should have no bearing on the decision to carry out a community care assessment providing the qualifying requirements of section 47(1) of the NHS and Community Care Act 1990 are met. Neither should the individual's finances affect the level or detail of the assessment process.

The nature of an assessment

3.85   Despite the central importance of the assessment in community care law, there is no effective legislative description of the process. DP(SCR)A s3 described with some precision the procedure to be followed in an assessment, but this section has not been brought into force because of its 'resource and administrative implications'. However, given that such procedures have received royal assent, it may be difficult for the executive to issue directions that are radically different to the scheme prescribed by the 1986 Act.[107]

3.86   The only provisions in NHSCCA 1990 in relation to how local authorities should carry out assessments are:

- s47(3) which specifies when the NHS and the housing authority should be invited to be involved (see para 3.125 below); and
- s47(4) which requires assessments to be carried out in accordance with any directions issued by the secretary of state. As noted above (para 3.23), directions have been issued in England.[108] But other than

---

105 The circular is expressed as being issued under LASSA 1970 s7(1); see also para 7.22 below where it is further considered. See also the statement of Liam Byrne, Parliamentary Under Secretary of State for Care Services, in response to a written question from Paul Burstow MP, HC Debates col 1799W, 12 December 2005, that 'an individual's financial circumstances should have no bearing on whether a LA carries out a community care assessment or not. Once an individual's care needs have been assessed and a decision made about the care to be provided, an assessment of his/her ability to pay charges should be carried out promptly. Written information about any charges payable, and how they have been calculated, should be communicated to the individual.'

106 UFSAMC 2002, para 2.33 in Wales makes the same point, but more briefly.

107 See eg *R v Secretary of State for the Home Department ex p Fire Brigades Union* [1995] 2 All ER 244, where 'the secretary of state could not validly ... resolve to give up his statutory duty to consider from time to time whether or not to bring the statutory scheme into force' (per Lord Browne-Wilkinson at 256B) and so could not introduce a conflicting non-statutory criminal injuries compensation scheme.

108 26 August 2004; accessible at www.dh.gov.uk/en/publicationsandstatistics/ publications/publicationslegislation

requiring that the person to be assessed and 'where appropriate' carers are consulted, and that reasonable steps are taken to reach agreement about the care plan, the directions are remarkably short on the procedure to be followed in an assessment.

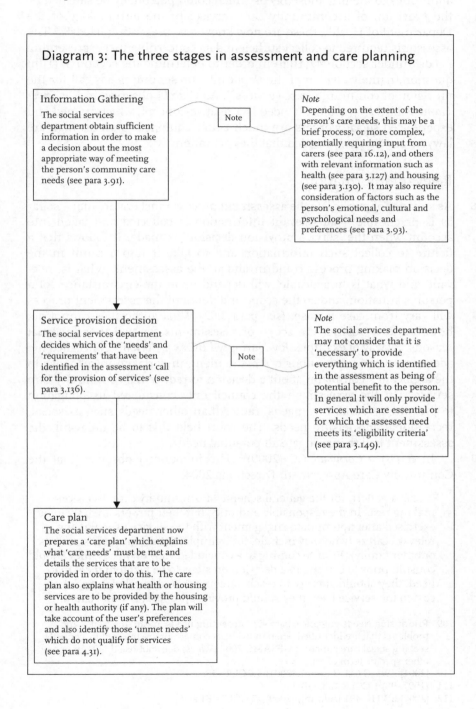

Diagram 3: The three stages in assessment and care planning

Information Gathering

The social services department obtain sufficient information in order to make a decision about the most appropriate way of meeting the person's community care needs (see para 3.91).

Note
Depending on the extent of the person's care needs, this may be a brief process, or more complex, potentially requiring input from carers (see para 16.12), and others with relevant information such as health (see para 3.127) and housing (see para 3.130). It may also require consideration of factors such as the person's emotional, cultural and psychological needs and preferences (see para 3.93).

Service provision decision

The social services department decides which of the 'needs' and 'requirements' that have been identified in the assessment 'call for the provision of services' (see para 3.136).

Note
The social services department may not consider that it is 'necessary' to provide everything which is identified in the assessment as being of potential benefit to the person. In general it will only provide services which are essential or for which the assessed need meets its 'eligibility criteria' (see para 3.149).

Care plan

The social services department now prepares a 'care plan' which explains what 'care needs' must be met and details the services that are to be provided in order to do this. The care plan also explains what health or housing services are to be provided by the housing or health authority (if any). The plan will take account of the user's preferences and also identify those 'unmet needs' which do not qualify for services (see para 4.31).

The assessment and 'presenting needs'

3.87   The first stage of the NHSCCA 1990 s47(1) assessment process obliges authorities to identify those needs which could potentially be satisfied by the provision of a community care service. In the terminology of the Department of Health, these are now known as 'presenting needs'.[109] The assessor is required to collect sufficient data concerning these 'presenting needs' (under section 47(1)(a)) in order to determine the section 47(1)(b) question, namely: 'which of the applicant's presenting needs call for the provision of community care services?'. As Hale LJ observed in *R v Tower Hamlets LBC ex p Wahid*,[110] 'need is a relative concept, which trained and experienced social workers are much better equipped to assess than are lawyers and courts, provided that they act rationally'.

Relevant information

3.88   As a matter of public law the assessment process must ensure that – so far as is practicable – all relevant information is collected and taken into account when the 'service provision decision' is made. It follows that a failure to collect such information and to take it into account in the decision-making process could invalidate the assessment. What is 'relevant' and what is 'practicable' will depend upon the circumstances of a person's situation, and so the scope and depth of the assessment process will vary from case to case. (see para 3.97) What authorities cannot do, however, is to restrict the scope of assessments for policy or financial reasons. By way of example, *R v Haringey LBC ex p Norton*[111] concerned the adequacy of the local authority's assessment, undertaken in response to the applicant's complaint about a decision to reduce his community care services. In the assessment the council only considered its obligation to provide 'personal care needs' rather than other needs such as social, recreational and leisure needs. The court held this to be unlawful; the assessment had to investigate all potential needs.

3.89   In *R (B) v Cornwall CC* (2009)[112] Hickinbottom J observed that the Community Care Assessment Directions 2004:

> . . . set a pattern for the general scheme of community care. Decision-making rests in the responsible authority, but their powers are only to be exercised after appropriate engagement with the service user and any relevant carers (who may include, for example, the service user's parents or other family). Prior to coming to a concluded view on needs, they should consult: prior to coming to a decision on steps to be taken to meet that need, they should attempt to reach agreement: and in relation to the on-cost to the service user, they should provide appropriate information.

109 Prioritising Needs guidance, para 47: 'presenting needs' mean 'the issues and problems that are identified when individuals contact, or are referred to, councils seeking social care support': UFSAMC 2002 (Wales) does not use this term or any other specific term of art.
110 [2001] EWHC 641 (Admin), (2001) 4 CCLR 455.
111 (1997–98) 1 CCLR 168, QBD.
112 [2009] EWHC 491 (Admin), (2009) 12 CCLR 381 at [9].

Assessments prepared by other social services authorities

3.90 Relevant information will also include any assessments and associated evidence prepared by other authorities, the opinions of experts and other professionals and other people with knowledge of the person being assessed. In this respect the Prioritising Needs guidance states:[113]

> When a service user permanently moves from one council area to another (or has a clear intention to move to another council – See 'Determining eligibility in respect of individuals' section of this guidance), the council whose area they move into should take account of the support that was previously received and the effect of any substantial changes on the service user when carrying out the assessment and making decisions about what level of support will be provided. If the new council decides to provide a significantly different support package, they should produce clear and written explanations for the service user.

Presenting needs

3.91 The Prioritising Needs guidance distinguishes between 'presenting needs' and eligible (or 'assessed') needs. A presenting need is a need that is identified by the person being assessed or some other on his or her behalf. It is not, however, a 'need' that the local authority is under a duty to meet: such a duty only arises when the authority decides that the need is sufficiently important that it is 'eligible' for services – ie that the result of the assessment is that the 'need' should be met.

3.92 Early (1991) practice guidance on the assessment process[114] described the concept of 'presenting needs' (without using the term) as follows:

> 11. Need is a complex concept which has been analysed in a variety of different ways. In this guidance, the term is used as a shorthand for the requirements of individuals to enable them to achieve, maintain or restore an acceptable level of social independence or quality of life, as defined by the particular care agency or authority.
>
> 16 . . . Need is a multi-faceted concept which, for the purposes of this guidance, is sub-divided into six broad categories, each of which should be covered in a comprehensive assessment of need:
> • Personal/social care
> • healthcare
> • accommodation
> • finance
> • education/employment/leisure
> • transport/access.

3.93 Some presenting needs (such as those listed above) tend to suggest specific services, for instance a need for accommodation, whereas some will condition the way a service is delivered, for instance a person might have a

---

113 Para 87; UFSAMC 2002 para 5.43 in Wales.
114 Department of Health Social Services Inspectorate (1991) *Care Management and Assessment: a practitioners' guide.*

need for 'a rigid routine'.[115] In *R v Avon CC ex p M*[116] the applicant formed an entrenched view, specified in a psychologist's report as attributable to his Down's syndrome, that he wanted to go to a particular residential home even though an alternative, cheaper home objectively catered for all his other needs. The authority refused to fund the more expensive home on the ground that it would set a precedent by accepting psychological need as being part of an individual's needs which could force it to pay more than it would usually expect to pay in such cases. Rejecting this argument, Henry J held:[117]

> The [local authority's report] . . . proceeds on the basis that the psychological need can simply be 'excluded': . . . M's needs are thus arbitrarily restricted to the remainder of his needs, which are then described as 'usual'. Meeting his psychological needs is then treated as mere 'preference', a preference involving payments greater than usual.
>
> The law is clear. The council have to provide for the applicant's needs. Those needs may properly include psychological needs.

3.94   The SAP policy guidance (2002)[118] gives a table outlining the range of the more common and specific 'presenting needs' for older people (the table is reproduced as a diagram 4 below). For younger disabled people, additional factors might need greater emphasis, for instance the need to discharge one's obligations as a parent (see para 3.44 above).

Diagram 4: Single assessment process (SAP) Annex F

The domains and sub-domains of the single assessment process

User's perspective

- Needs and issues in the users' own words
- Users' expectations, strengths, abilities and motivation

Clinical background

- History of medical conditions and diagnoses
- History of falls
- Medication use and ability to self-medicate

Disease prevention

- History of blood pressure monitoring
- Nutrition, diet and fluids
- Vaccination history
- Drinking and smoking history
- Exercise pattern
- History of cervical and breast screening

---

115   See eg complaint no 03/C/16371 against Stockton-on-Tees BC, 18 January 2005.
116   (1999) 2 CCLR 185, [1994] 2 FLR 1006, QBD.
117   (1999) 2 CCLR 185, QBD at 195–196.
118   At Annex F. A similar list for Wales appears at UFSAMC 2002 para 4.24.

Personal care and physical well-being
- Personal hygiene, including washing, bathing, toileting and grooming
- Dressing
- Pain[119]
- Oral health
- Foot-care
- Tissue viability
- Mobility
- Continence and other aspects of elimination
- Sleeping patterns

Senses
- Sight
- Hearing
- Communication

Mental health
- Cognition and dementia, including orientation and memory
- Mental health including depression, reactions to loss, and emotional difficulties

Relationships
- Social contacts, relationships, and involvement in leisure, hobbies, work, and learning
- Carer support and strength of caring arrangements, including the carer's perspective

Safety
- Abuse and neglect
- Other aspects of personal safety
- Public safety

Immediate environment and resources
- Care of the home and managing daily tasks such as food preparation, cleaning and shopping
- Housing – location, access, amenities and heating
- Level and management of finances
- Access to local facilities and services

119   see also para 3.143 below.

The assessment process

The scope of the assessment

3.95   The scope and depth of an assessment will be determined in large meas-ure by the complexity of the person's needs. The assessment may consist of little more than a single conversation with a social worker or may involve complex analysis of data, protracted interviews and multi-disciplinary meetings spanning many months. The 1991 practice guid-ance advice (at para 3.3) expressed this point thus:

> . . . the scope of an assessment should be related to its purpose. Simple needs will require less investigation than more complex ones. In the interests of both efficiency and consumer satisfaction, the assessment process should be as simple, speedy and informal as possible.[120]

3.96   The Prioritising Needs guidance reiterated this advice, stating (at para 69) that:

> Councils should not operate eligibility criteria to determine the complexity of the assessment offered; rather the depth and breadth of the assessment should be proportionate to individuals' presenting needs and circumstances, including how much support carers are able to provide, where appropriate[121].

3.97   Advice in the now superseded FACS policy guidance[122] suggested a grad-ing of types of assessment – initial, taking stock of wider needs, specialist and complex assessments. This is the approach of the Welsh guidance[123] reflecting SAP guidance which categorises assessments into four types: contact; overview; specialist, and comprehensive. This classification, although it relates specifically to older people, could be applied equally to other service groups[124]. In practice, this approach has been overtaken in England by the dominance in the assessment process of self-assessment questionnaires (see para 3.100 below)

3.98   The courts have been unenthusiastic about guidance that dictates an overly prescriptive approach to the assessment process. The 1991 practice guidance, for instance, put forward six models of assessment, from sim-ple to comprehensive and then stated that all disabled people had the right to a comprehensive assessment (regardless of how complex their needs might be). This advice was considered by Carnwath J in *R v Gloucestershire CC ex p RADAR*,[125] where (referring to the 1991 practice guidance) he held:

> I have some sympathy with those trying to write these sort of guides since the complexity of the legislative chain, combined with the length of the

---

120   FACS 2002 policy guidance, para 35 advises that they be 'as simple and timely as possible'.
121   *UFSAMC* 2002 also refers to the need for assessments to be proportionate, para 2.9
122   Para 34.
123   *UFSAMC* para 2.13
124   Department of Health (2002) *The Single Assessment Process Guidance for Local Implementation* policy guidance, para 12(IX).
125   (1997–98) 1 CCLR 476 at 484, QBD.

titles of most of the Acts, makes short and accurate exposition particularly difficult. However, if what is intended is to define the legal obligation in respect of the disabled, then it can only be intended as a reference to the decision referred to in s4 Disabled Persons (Services, Consultation and Representation) Act 1986, that is, as to the range of services required under s2 of the 1970 Act. I take that to be the intended meaning of the word 'comprehensive'. If it is intended to mean anything else, it is misleading.

3.99   In *R (McDonald) v Royal Borough of Kensington and Chelsea*, the majority of the Supreme Court rejected the appellant's claim that two 'care plan reviews' carried out by the respondent did not amount to a lawful re-assessment of her needs. Although Lord Kerr (at para 39) felt there had been no 'authentic re-evaluation' of her needs, Lord Brown, cited with approval Rix LJ in the Court of Appeal decision:[126]

> In my judgment, the 2009 and 2010 reviews are to be read as including a reassessment of Ms McDonald's needs. It is irrelevant that there has been no further separate 'Needs Assessment' document. Such a document is not, it seems, necessary in the first place, because a care plan could incorporate a needs assessment; but in any event FACS itself contemplates that a care plan review will incorporate a review of assessed needs.

Self-assessment

3.100   The use of multiple choice self-assessment questionnaires has begun to proliferate in some parts of England. The concept of self-assessment reflects the emphasis of the personalisation agenda on placing the individual at the heart of the process, respecting their expert knowledge of their own needs. However, the multiple choice nature of the question-naires currently in use is a response to the perceived need to produce a set of standardised answers to generate points for the purposes of resource allocation. This aspect, including resource allocation schemes, is analysed in more detail in chapter 4. Given the currently non-delegable nature of the assessment duty (see paras 3.49–3.53 above) pure self-assessment is not lawful. As Hickinbottom J held in *R (B) v Cornwall County Council*[127] an authority:

> . . . cannot avoid its obligation to assess needs etc by failing to make an appropriate assessment themselves, in favour of simply requiring the service user himself to provide evidence of his needs.

3.101   The Prioritising Needs guidance promotes person-centred assessment while characterising self-assessment as a stage in the overall assessment process (at paras 83 and 84):

> The assessment process should be person-centred throughout and also consider the wider family context. Councils should recognise that individuals are the experts on their own situation and encourage a partnership approach, based on a person's aspirations and the outcomes they wish to achieve, rather than what they are unable to do. Professionals should fully involve the person seeking support by listening to their views

---

126   [2011] UKSC 33, (2011) 14 CCLR 341 at [12].
127   [2009] EWHC 491 (Admin), (2009) 12 CCLR 381 at para 68.

about how they want to live their lives and the type of care and support that best suits them and by helping them to make informed choices. This includes identifying the support the person needs to make a valued contribution to their community.

Councils may wish to consider encouraging those who can and wish to do so to undertake an assessment of their own needs prior to the council doing so. Although self-assessment does not negate a council's duty to carry out its own assessment, which may differ from the person's own views of their needs, it can serve as a very useful tool for putting the person seeking support at the heart of the process.'

The term 'supported assessments' is often used in practice, and more accurately reflects the legal position.

Screening assessments

3.102   The CSCI reported in 2008 that:

Almost one in five carers and one in eight of those who said they could benefit from social care reported they had failed to have an assessment of their needs. One third of these respondents understood this was because they did not meet financial eligibility criteria for help (suggesting they were asked about their financial resources prior to any needs assessment, which contravenes current policy).[128]

3.103   The Prioritising Needs guidance, para 76,[129] cautions against individuals being screened out of the assessment process before sufficient information is known about them. This is most likely to occur in two instances; either because a pre-emptive decision is made about eligibility, a process found to be unlawful in *R v Bristol City Council ex p Penfold*[130] (see para 3.78 above), or because an individual is deemed to be a 'self-funder' before any form of community care assessment is carried out. The Prioritising Needs guidance confirms that, 'An assessment of a person's ability to pay for services should only take place after they have been assessed as having an eligible need for services'.[131]

3.104   Certain basic matters must be considered in even the most rudimentary interview for it to amount to an assessment. In *R v Bristol CC ex p Penfold* the respondent sought to argue that a mere consideration by the council of an applicant's request for an assessment, was itself an assessment. Rejecting this, Scott Baker J held that an assessment 'cannot be said to have been carried out unless the authority concerned has fully explored the need in relation to the services it has the power to supply. In some cases the exercise will be very simple; in others more complex'.[132]

3.105   Thus there is a distinction to be made between screening people out of the process altogether, as happened to Mrs Penfold, and carrying out an assessment by telephone which includes a determination as to whether or

---

128   *Cutting the Cake Fairly*, CSCI report 2008.
129   UFSAMC 2002, para 2.23 in Wales. See also para 3.20 of the 1990 policy guidance.
130   (1997–98) 1 CCLR 315, QBD.
131   Prioritising Needs Guidance 2010, para 71.
132   (1997–98) 1 CCLR 315 at 321C, QBD.

not the individual's needs call for the provision of any services. There is nothing intrinsically unlawful about a telephone assessment, provided it complies with certain minimum criteria – as detailed below. Indeed such procedures enable authorities to conserve their limited human resources and target scarce officer time on more detailed assessments of those in most need.

3.106   However, the quality (including training and supervision) of telephone assessors, needs to be such as to ensure that they are able to identify the need for a face to face assessment, for instance if there is any indication of cognitive impairment or mental illness rendering a telephone assessment unreliable. By way of further example, a disabled person phoning to enquire about a blue badge for parking may be unaware of the possibilities of additional care support, but is by definition someone demonstrating an 'appearance of need',[133] requiring further investigation in order to satisfy the NHSCCA 1990 s47(1) duty. The advice of ADASS is as follows:

> Staff dealing with first contact need enough social work skill and experience to recognise indicators of mental impairment which may affect insight and understanding of the options, and the processes involved in assessment, so that those applicants may be assured of their right to assessment.[134]

Steps in data gathering

3.107   The data gathering element of an assessment must, at the very minimum, be structured in such a way that it seeks to obtain/provide the following information:

1) The applicant's name and contact details.
2) The applicant's choice of the setting for the assessment. If the applicant is content, the assessment may take place over the telephone but it is essential that the person being assessed has a real choice over the setting of the assessment and (if it be the case) freely chooses the telephone option.
3) Whether there is a need for an interpreter or other facilitator (such as an advocate) or indeed if there is a duty on the authority to involve an Independent Mental Capacity Advocate (see para 17.67. below).
4) The applicant's care needs – this requires (in the absence of good reasons):
   a) the user's involvement and (with his or her consent) the involvement of any carer[135];
   b) the applicant's opinion as to what his or her needs are;
   c) that the full spectrum of potential needs be considered (see *R v Haringey LBC ex p Norton* at para 3.88 above);

---

133   *R v Gloucestershire CC ex p RADAR* (1997–98) 1 CCLR 476, QBD.
134   ADASS (2009) *Personalisation and the law: implementing putting people first in the current legal framework* p5.
135   Even where consent is withheld, the duty to take into account the ability of the carer to care still applies pursuant to DP(SCR)A 1986 s8 (see para 16.23).

    d) the particular risk factors that the applicant faces as well as his or her aptitudes, abilities and access to existing social support networks;

    e) what outcomes/services the applicant wants, and his or her preferences as to how those outcomes are to be achieved.

5) Whether there is any carer who may potentially be entitled to an assessment under the Carers (Recognition and Services) Act 1995 or the Carers and Disabled Children Act 2000.[136]

6) Any associated health or housing difficulties the applicant may have. If such exist then there must be a referral to the health or housing authority and it would seem therefore that the assessment cannot be finally concluded until a response has been received to that referral and the contents of that response fully considered.

7) The applicant should also be advised of his or her right to:

    a) have a written copy of the assessment; and

    b) make representations/use the complaints procedures if he or she believes that services have been unreasonably refused.

The setting of an assessment

3.108 The 1991 practice guidance (at paras 3.12–3.15) emphasises the importance of the assessment being conducted in an appropriate location, as this may have a material effect on its outcome. It points out that office interviews, whilst administratively convenient and less costly than domiciliary assessments, may give false results if the interviewee is not at ease, and that the applicant is more likely to relax in the home setting. The following important points are also made:

> 3.13 Where the assessment is concerned with the maintenance of a person at home, the assessment should take place in that setting. If users are considering admission to residential or nursing home care, involving irreversible loss of their home, they should always be given the opportunity of experiencing that setting before making their final decision.

> 3.14 There may be advantages to some part of the assessment being undertaken in settings external to the home, for example, day or residential care settings, so that staff have longer contact with the individual. In such circumstances, assessors will be working in close collaboration with service providers.

> 3.15 In considering such options, care should be taken to avoid exposing individuals to unnecessary disruption. In addition, it is necessary to avoid assuming that behaviour will be replicated in other settings. Such considerations may, occasionally, affect assessment arrangements for hospital discharges.

User involvement

3.109 The Community Care (Assessment) Directions (see para 3.23 above) requirement to consult the user, cited, for example, in *R (B) v Cornwall*

---

136 Community Care (Assessment) Directions 2004, direction 2.

CC,[137] is amplified in the Prioritising Needs guidance which advises that (at para 83):

> The assessment process should be person-centred throughout and also consider the wider family context. Councils should recognise that individuals are the experts on their own situation and encourage a partnership approach, based on a person's aspirations and the outcomes they wish to achieve, rather than what they are unable to do. Professionals should fully involve the person seeking support by listening to their views about how they want to live their lives and the type of care and support that best suits them and by helping them to make informed choices. This includes identifying the support the person needs to make a valued contribution to their community.

3.110 The 1991 policy guidance also stressed the importance of involving users in the assessment process so that the resulting services fully take into account their preferences (and so far as possible those of their carers).[138] It highlighted the need for the assessor to establish a relationship of trust and to clarify what the assessment will entail. The Prioritising Needs guidance at paragraph 79 states that assessments should be carried out in such a way, and be sufficiently transparent, for individuals to:

- Gain a better understanding of the purpose of assessment and its implications for their situation;
- Actively participate in the process;
- Identify and articulate the outcomes they wish to achieve;
- Identify the options that are available to meet those outcomes and to support their independence and well-being in whatever capacity;
- Understand the basis on which decisions are reached.

3.111 In *R v North Yorkshire CC ex p Hargreaves*[139] the social services authority came to a service provision decision without taking into account the preferences of the disabled person – largely because (in Dyson J's opinion) her carer was very protective and probably considered by the social services authority as obstructing its ability to communicate with the disabled person. Nevertheless this did not discharge the authority's obligation to discover what her preferences were, and accordingly the decision was quashed.

Disputed assessments

3.112 If an assessment is disputed the view of the social worker or care manager will prevail, subject to the overall lawfulness of the assessment process and decision-making. This follows since the local authority is charged by NHSCCA 1990 s47(1) with the duty to assess and determine, with regard to the assessment, whether the needs call for the provision of services. Where a dispute arises and agreement cannot be reached, the correct

---

137 [2009] EWHC 491 (Admin), (2009) 12 CCLR 381 at para 68.
138 At paras 3.16 and 3.25.
139 (1997–98) 1 CCLR 104, QBD.

procedure is for the council to record on the completed document the areas of disagreement: it may be maladministration for a council to delay finalising the assessment (and implementing the support plan) pending resolution of the differences.[140]

Persons unable to participate fully in the assessment process

3.113   Individual involvement in the assessment process becomes a more difficult question where the potential service user is unable to participate fully due to lack of ability to communicate or mental capacity (see also chapter 17 where questions of mental capacity are further considered). The Code of Practice for the Mental Capacity Act 2005 gives detailed guidance on good practice for assessing capacity (see para 17.3 below).

3.114   Much of the general and specific user group assessment guidance stresses the importance of endeavouring to communicate with service users, no matter how severe their impairments, and of the particular importance of advocacy services in this respect.[141]

3.115   The 1990 policy guidance states that 'where a user is unable to participate actively [in the assessment] it is even more important that he or she should be helped to understand what is involved and the intended outcome'.[142] The 1991 practice guidance elaborates on this advice, stating that where it is clear that a user or carer would benefit from independent advocacy, he or she should be given information about any schemes funded by the authority or run locally. It goes on to state that it is consistent with the aims of basing service provision on the needs and wishes of users that those who are unable to express their views – for example, those with severe learning disabilities or dementia – or those who have been previously disadvantaged – for example, those from minority ethnic groups – should, as a matter of priority, be supported in securing independent representation.[143]

3.116   In *R (A and B) v East Sussex CC (No 2)*,[144] a case concerning the appropriate way to lift and move two young women (X and Y) with profound physical and learning difficulties, Munby J stressed the importance of ascertaining their views on the process:

> 132. I have said that the assessment must take account of the disabled person's wishes, feelings and preferences. How are these to be ascertained?
>
> 133. In a case where the disabled person is, by reason of their disability, prevented, whether completely or in part, from communicating their wishes and feelings it will be necessary for the assessors to facilitate the ascertainment of the person's wishes and feelings, so far as they may be

---

140   Complaint no 07/A/11108 against Surrey County Council, 11 November 2008, para 42.
141   See para 18.29 for further considerations of the role of advocacy services.
142   At para 3.16 of the policy guidance.
143   At paras 3.25–3.27, of the policy guidance.
144   [2003] EWHC 167 (Admin), (2003) 6 CCLR 194.

deduced, by whatever means, including seeking and receiving advice – advice, not instructions – from appropriate interested persons such as X and Y involved in the care of the disabled person.

134. Good practice, Miss Foster suggests, would indicate, and I am inclined to agree that:

i) A rough 'dictionary' should be drawn up, stating what the closest carers (in a case such as this, parents and family, here X and Y) understand by the various non verbal communications, based on their intimate long term experience of the person. Thus with familiarisation and 'interpretation' the carers can accustom themselves to the variety of feelings and modes of expression and learn to recognise what is being communicated.

ii) Where the relatives are present with the carers and an occasion of 'interpretation' arises, great weight must be accorded to the relatives' 'translation'.

iii) As I commented in *Re S* (2003)[145]
'the devoted parent who . . . has spent years caring for a disabled child is likely to be much better able than any social worker, however skilled, or any judge, however compassionate, to "read" his child, to understand his personality and to interpret the wishes and feeling's which he lacks the ability to express.'

iv) That said, in the final analysis the task of deciding whether, in truth, there is a refusal or fear or other negative reaction to being lifted must . . . fall on the carer, for the duty to act within the framework given by the employer falls upon the employee. Were the patient not incapacitated, there could be no suggestion that the relative's views are other than a factor to be considered. Because of the lack of capacity and the extraordinary circumstances in a case such as this, the views of the relatives are of very great importance, but they are not determinative.

3.117 The practice of requiring assessments to be signed by service users, whilst in general representing good practice, should not be pursued indiscriminately and could not be obligatory both because an assessment is not a contractual document requiring formal acceptance and because a significant number of service users may lack the relevant mental capacity. In *R (F, J, S, R and others) v Wirral BC*,[146] McCombe J criticised the imposition of such a requirement, particularly when the 'signatories are vulnerable members of society'.

Persons unwilling to be involved in the assessment process

3.118 The issue of user involvement becomes controversial where the potential service user chooses not to participate in (or actively objects to) the assessment.

3.119 A literal interpretation of the section 47(1) duty suggests that the assessment duty is activated even when the potential service user objects

145 [2002] EWHC 2278, [2003] 1 FLR 292 at [49] – see para 24.95 below.
146 [2009] EWHC 1626 (Admin), (2009) 12 CCLR 452 at para 72.

to being assessed: strictly speaking, his or her consent is not required.[147] While he or she can refuse to take part in an assessment, he or she cannot stop the assessment taking place. Of course, in practice, an objection would generally be an end of the matter, provided the person has full mental capacity to make an informed decision on the question[148] – since, as Carnwath J observed, without some degree of co-operation the effectiveness of any assessment will be significantly impaired.[149]

3.120   The 1991 practice guidance accepts that an individual's involvement in the assessment process may be involuntary (at para 3.17) and that any individual can withdraw at any stage from active involvement. The effect of such 'wilful lack of co-operation' may be that the social services authority finds it impossible to ascertain the preferences of the user and/or carer.[150] In this respect the local government ombudsman has observed that 'before a council can conclude that it is unable to carry out an assessment due to user non-cooperation, it must try and explain to him/her the potential advantages of the process (generally in writing)'.[151] The 1991 practice guidance makes a number of further and important observations:

> 3.17 Individuals who enter voluntarily into the assessment process should also be made aware of their entitlement to withdraw at any stage. Where the assessment is on an involuntary basis, for example, as a prelude to possible compulsory admission to psychiatric hospital, it is even more important that the individuals are helped to understand, as far as they are able, the nature of the process in which they are engaged. It is less clear cut where practitioners are dealing with someone, with failing capacities, for example, relapse of a psychotic illness, where intervention has been on a voluntary basis but, at a certain threshold of risk or vulnerability, it is likely to tip over into compulsory admission. That threshold should be clearly defined in policy terms and agreed with other relevant agencies, for example, police and health authorities. All practitioners should be clear on the distinction between using assessment as an instrument of social support as opposed to social control. The former offers choices to the user while the latter imposes solutions. The one should not be allowed to shade into the other without all parties appreciating the full implications of that change.

3.121 The local government ombudsman has criticised a local authority for accepting a service user's refusal to be assessed – even though it was clear he was in considerable need and placing an unsustainable burden on his main carer. Although she accepted that a council 'cannot force services upon an unwilling person', in her opinion, such a refusal does not absolve

---

147 Para 11.2 of the practice guidance to the Carers (Recognition and Services) Act 1995 suggests that users can refuse an assessment; while this may be a statement of practice, as a matter of law it appears incorrect. All an individual can do, is not co-operate and if needs be, refuse any services which are offered.

148 Presumably the mental capacity required would need to encompass an understanding of the potential consequences of that refusal – which may for instance be an exposure to significant direct and indirect risk of harm.

149 *R v Gloucestershire CC ex p RADAR* (1997–98) 1 CCLR 476 at 282F, QBD.

150 Per Dyson J in *R v North Yorkshire CC ex p Hargreaves* (1997–98) 1 CCLR 104 at 111J, QBD.

151 Report no 02/B/03191 against Buckinghamshire CC, 5 November 2003.

it of all responsibility. The report criticised the council for not questioning whether the disabled person was in fact making an informed decision in his refusal or considering the implications for his carer. It stated that the council needed to develop a strategy to work through such a problem and referred to the fact that an intervention by the community nurse, the psychologist, and a worker from the voluntary caring organisation had proved successful in overcoming many of the problems that had led to the initial rejection of the care services.[152]

3.122   The obligation on councils not to take a refusal to be assessed as an end of the matter has been emphasised in a number of different cases and contexts.[153] *R (J) v Caerphilly CBC*[154] contains a clear expression of the public law obligation underlying the courts' approach to this question – ie the requirement for the assessor to be persistent – even though it concerns a materially different statutory regime (the CA 1989). Munby J (at para 56) stated:

> The fact that a child is uncooperative and unwilling to engage, or even refuses to engage, is no reason for the local authority not to carry out its obligations under the Act and the Regulations. After all, a disturbed child's unwillingness to engage with those who are trying to help is often merely a part of the overall problems which justified the local authority's statutory intervention in the first place. The local authority must do its best.

3.123   The public law duty to persist in the endeavour of delivering community care support services for vulnerable people even when confronted by uncooperative behaviour, is little different to that described in the above cited *Caerphilly* case. People eligible for community care services will frequently have mental health, cognitive impairment or leaning difficulties and their refusals of support may be due to misconceptions, miscomprehensions, temporary lapses and/or be contrary to their best interests. In such cases the public law duty demands perseverance. The specific issue of service refusals is considered further at para 4.54 below.

3.124   The Community Care (Delayed Discharges etc) Act 2003 obliges local authorities to complete certain assessments within set timescales (see para 4.27 below). Department of Health guidance addresses the question of where liability rests if a patient refuses to co-operate with an assessment:[155]

> If the patient is clear that they do not want the involvement of social services and that they will not accept the services put in place for them, at this stage they become responsible for themselves. Up to that point social services must use their best endeavours to perform an assessment and prepare a care plan, however limited that might be . . .

---

152 Complaint no 02/C/08690 against Sheffield City Council, 9 August 2004.
153 See eg *R v Kensington and Chelsea RLBC ex p Kujtim* [1999] 4 All ER 161, (1999) 2 CCLR 340 at 354I; *R (Patrick) v Newham LBC* (2000) 4 CCLR 48, considered further at paras 4.45 and 7.30 below and *R (WG) v Local Authority A* [2010] EWHC 2608 (Admin).
154 [2005] EWHC 586 (Admin), (2005) 8 CCLR 255.
155 *Community Care (Delayed Discharges etc) Act: Frequently asked questions on reimbursement,* 2004, Q & A 32, at www.dh.gov.uk/assetRoot/04/07/19/26/ 04071926.pdf.

The section 47(3) referral duty in relation to health and housing needs

3.125   Where the assessment discloses a possible housing or medical need, NHSCCA 1990 s47(3) obliges the authority to notify the relevant housing or health authority.[156] Section 47(3) provides:

> If at any time during the assessment of the needs of any person under subsection (1)(a) above, it appears to a local authority –
> (a) that there may be a need for the provision to that person by such Primary Care Trust or Health Authority[157] as may be determined in accordance with regulations of any services under the National Health Service Act 1977, or
> (b) that there may be a need for the provision to him of any services which fall within the functions of a local housing authority (within the meaning of the Housing Act 1985) which is not the local authority carrying out the assessment,
>
> the local authority shall notify that Primary Care Trust, Health Authority or local housing authority and invite them to assist, to such extent as is reasonable in the circumstances, in the making of the assessment; and, in making their decision as to the provision of the services needed for the person in question, the local authority shall take into account any services which are likely to be made available for him by that Primary Care Trust, Health Authority or local housing authority.

3.126   A social service failure to make a referral to the appropriate body may undermine the legality of the assessment process. In general, however, the courts have considered such cases from the public law perspective as a failure to take into account a relevant consideration (see para 26.207) rather than a breach of statutory duty. The greater the likelihood that a referral could have resulted in a different decision being reached, the more probable is it that the courts will conclude that such a failure is material. Thus in *R v Birmingham CC ex p Killigrew*[158] the point relied upon was a failure to follow the 1990 policy guidance quoted below. The applicant was profoundly disabled by multiple sclerosis and a reassessment of her needs failed to seek up-to-date medical evidence. Given the severity of

---

156   The consequent obligations on the health and housing authorities are considered below at paras 13.39 and 15.12 respectively. Although there is no duty on the notified authority to respond following notification, the service user will benefit where parallel duties are triggered.

157   Although the section has been amended (as a result of the demise of health authorities in England and Wales) to insert 'Primary Care Trusts' (National Health Service Reform and Health Care Professions Act 2002 Sch 2(2) para 56), no equivalent amendment has occurred in Wales to refer to 'Local Health Boards'. It appears, however, that this is not strictly necessary, as a result of a combination of the Health Authorities (Transfer of Functions, Staff, Property, Rights and Liabilities and Abolition) (Wales) Order 2003 SI No 813 (W98) – which transfers all functions of health authorities in Wales to the Welsh Government – and the Local Health Boards (Functions) (Wales) Regulations 2003 SI No 150 (W20) which provides (subject to exceptions) that functions that were exercised by health authorities and were transferred to the Assembly by SI No 813 (2003) are to be exercised by local health boards.

158   (2000) 3 CCLR 109.

her degenerative condition, Hooper J considered this to be a fundamental breach of the assessment obligation and accordingly quashed the resulting care plan.[159]

The NHS referral obligation

3.127   In relation to the section 47(3) obligation, the 1990 policy guidance advised as follows:

> 3.47 It is expected that, as a matter of good practice, GPs will wish to make a full contribution to assessment. It is part of the GP's terms of service to give advice to enable patients to avail themselves of services provided by a local authority.[160]

> 3.48 Where advice is needed by the local authority in the course of assessment, this should be obtained from the GP orally (eg by telephone) as far as possible. A record should be kept of the advice given. In addition to the information that only the patient's own GP can provide, local authorities may, on occasion, also require a clinical examination or an interpretation of the medical report provided by the GP. Local authorities should, therefore, be aware that GPs have a personal duty to and a relationship with their patients, and may not be best placed to act in addition as an assessor on the authority's behalf. In such circumstances local authorities may wish other practitioners to act in, this capacity.

3.128   It follows, from section 47(3), that where during the assessment process an NHS need is disclosed, the assessing authority is obliged to notify the PCT or local health board and at the same time to specify what assistance it is that the authority is requested to provide in order to facilitate the assessment. The health body is not, however, under any statutory duty to respond or co-operate.[161] A failure to respond – or failure to respond within a reasonable time or in a reasonable manner – would, however, be vulnerable to challenge as maladministration

3.129   Where the NHS responds to a section 47(3) referral, the local authority will be required to give this information substantial weight in reaching its service provision decision and in general to evidence the fact.[162] Ultimately, however, the decision on need will be for the social services authority to make and not the health body: a local authority is required to exercise independence and a misplaced belief that it is bound by a medical opinion will be vulnerable to a public law challenge.[163]

---

159   See also local government ombudsman complaint no 99/A/00988 against Southwark, 12 March 2001.
160   This obligation continues: the current GMS contract (as with the previous) requires GPs to refer (as appropriate) a 'patient for other services under [what is now the NHSA 2006/NHS(W)A 2006]' (National Health Service (General Medical Services Contracts) Regulations 2004 SI No 291 reg 15(5)(b) – see para 13.46). NHSA 2006 s254 and Sch 20 and NHS(W)A 2006 s192 and Sch 15 place substantial duties on social services for the provision of community care services – see para 9.154 below.
161   Unlike the equivalent duty under CA 1989 s27. Adult care guidance places a positive obligation on the NHS in certain situations, eg SAP policy guidance (2002) and UFSAMC 2002 (Wales).
162   But see R (Ireneschild) v Lambeth LBC [2007] EWCA Civ 2354, (2006) 9 CCLR 686.
163   R (Goldsmith) v Wandsworth LBC [2004] EWCA Civ 1170, (2004) 7 CCLR 472.

The housing authority referral obligation

3.130   Section 47(3) requires that if, during the assessment process, a housing need is disclosed, the assessing authority is obliged to notify the housing authority and at the same time to specify what assistance that authority is requested to provide in order to facilitate the assessment.

3.131   It follows that the section 47(3) duty only applies if the housing authority is a different authority – ie is not a department within the same council. Nevertheless, there is substantial guidance exhorting housing and social services departments to co-operate[164] and an administrative obligation must exist, even within unitary authorities, for such departments to work together. In *R (Wahid) v Tower Hamlets LBC*,[165] for example, Hale LJ observed that it was 'obviously good practice . . . to involve the housing department where this is part of the same local authority'. However, in *R v Lewisham LBC ex p Pinzon and Patino*[166] Laws J held that the recommendations in the circular guidance that housing and social services authorities work together does not in itself convert that obligation into a legally enforceable duty

3.132   Although the housing authority is not under any statutory duty to respond to or co-operate with a section 47(3) request,[167] separate, parallel duties under the Housing Act (HA) 1996 may well be triggered. The housing authority will be under a duty to receive applications[168] and to make enquiries under HA 1996 s184 in cases of homelessness and apparent priority need. As the application need not be in any particular form,[169] it may be argued in appropriate cases that notification of housing need amounts in itself to an application made on behalf of the assessed person.[170]

3.133   As noted above, a failure to respond to a section 47(3) referral, or failure to respond within a reasonable time or in a reasonable manner, would be vulnerable to challenge as maladministration.

The referral obligation does not extend to another local authority on the transfer of ordinary residence

3.134   *R (Buckinghamshire CC) v Kingston upon Thames*[171] concerned the lawfulness of an assessment decision of the defendant (social services) authority, made without any reference to the claimant authority, to transfer a learning disabled adult from long-term residential care in the claimant's area to a supported living arrangement there. The Court of Appeal upheld

164   See para 15.10.
165   [2002] EWCA Civ 287, (2002) 5 CCLR 239.
166   (1999) 2 CCLR 152, QBD.
167   Unlike under CA 1989 s27: see *R v Northavon DC ex p Smith* [1994] 3 WLR 403, HL.
168   *R v Camden LBC ex p Gillan* (1989) 21 HLR 114, DC.
169   *R v Chiltern DC ex p Roberts* (1990) 23 HLR 387, DC.
170   Disabled adults with insufficient mental capacity to make an application or authorise someone else to do so are not entitled to apply under Part VII of the 1996 Act – see *R v Tower Hamlets LBC ex p Begum* [1993] 2 WLR 609, (1993) 25 HLR 319, HL; however, see also *R (Patrick) v Newham LBC* (2000) 4 CCLR 48, QBD – considered at para 7.35 below.
171   [2011] EWCA Civ 457, (2011) 14 CCLR 427.

the first instance decision that there is neither a common law duty of fairness nor any duty arising under section 47(3) requiring notification, consultation or an invitation to participate in the assessment, although it was recognised that an exchange of information would be beneficial (see para 3.73 above).

3.135　　At first instance[172] Wyn Williams J held that there is no duty under section 47(3)(b) to notify a housing authority were housing benefit is going to be claimed as the duty only arises where there might be 'a need for the provision of services'. However, the defendant authority should have should have taken the 'obvious step of seeking confirmation from the local housing authority that housing benefit would be payable' before the tenancy was entered into.

The service provision decision: what needs must be satisfied by the provision of services?

3.136　　Once the authority has complied with its obligations under NHSCCA 1990 s47(1)(a) – ie it has gathered together all the data it considers necessary (reports, interviews etc) – section 47(1)(b) requires it to make a decision: to decide which of the individual's presenting 'needs' 'call for' the provision of community care services. 'Community care services' are defined by NHSCCA 1990 s46 as services which a local authority may provide or arrange to be provided under:

(a)　Part III of the National Assistance Act 1948;
(b)　section 45 of the Health Services and Public Health Act 1968;
(c)　section 254 of, and Schedule 20 to, the National Health Service Act 2006, and section 192 of, and Schedule 15 to, the National Health Service (Wales) Act 2006;
(d)　section 117 of the Mental Health Act 1983.

3.137　　NHSCCA 1990 s47(1)(b) obliges the authority to 'have regard to' the results of the section 47(1)(a) assessment, rather than obliging it to provide services to meet all the presenting needs. It is this decision that is generally referred to as the 'service provision decision'. It is of considerable importance, since it determines which community care services an individual is legally entitled to receive. It is the point at which the individual's needs are reconciled with the local resources that are available to meet such needs. As Swinton-Thomas LJ observed in the Court of Appeal decision in R v Gloucestershire CC ex p Barry:[173]

> Section 47(1)(a) provides for the provision of Community Care Services generally, the need for such services, the carrying out of an assessment and then, section 47(1)(b) gives the Local Authority a discretion as to whether to

172　[2010] EWHC 1703 (Admin) at para 72. See also para 6.28 below.
173　[1996] 4 All ER 421, (1997–98) 1 CCLR 19, CA. Although reversed by the House of Lords ([1997] 2 WLR 459, (1997–98) 1 CCLR 40, HL) these observations concerning the effect of NHSCCA 1990 s47(1) were in no way contradicted by the Lords.

provide those services. The discretion in making the decision under section 47(1)(b) arises by reason of the words 'having regard to the results of that assessment'. In making that decision they will be entitled to take into account resources.

3.138   When a decision has to be made concerning the need for services under CSDPA 1970 s2, the service provision decision under section 47(1)(b) is deemed to chime with the inherent assessment obligation under section 2. Although in theory it appears that a council deciding whether a person's 'needs call for the provision of community care services' is materially different from it 'deciding whether it is 'satisfied' it is 'necessary to meet' that person's needs, in practice the courts have determined that they are the same.

3.139   How a need is defined can be problematic, as demonstrated in the judgment of the Supreme Court in *R (McDonald) v Royal Borough of Kensington and Chelsea*.[174] The appellant, who had limited mobility, was initially assessed as needing 'assistance to use the commode at night'. However, the respondent had been proposing to replace her night time personal assistants with continence pads as a cheaper option and following two 'care plan reviews' re-cast her needs in broader terms as 'assistance with toileting', thus arguing that the re-defined need could be met through the use of night-time incontinence pads. The appellant was strongly opposed to this affront to her dignity (see paras 4.110–4.113 below for a discussion of this aspect of the case)

3.140   The majority of their Lordships were untroubled by this change in the description of what was essentially the same need, although Lord Kerr recognised that the need was 'difficulties with mobility' rather than with toileting, and accordingly decided that the appellant's needs had not in fact changed at all. However, he still managed to find the respondent had acted lawfully on the basis that the concept of needs incorporated the method of meeting them:

> On that basis, it can be said that the reviews in 2009 and 2010, although it was not their purpose, in fact involved a re-assessment of the appellant's needs and that they may now be regarded as the need to avoid having to go to the lavatory during the night. Viewed thus, the needs can be met by the provision of incontinence pads and suitable bedding. Not without misgivings, I have therefore concluded that it was open to the respondent to re-assess the appellant's needs, to re-categorise them as a need to avoid leaving bed during the night and to conclude that that need could be met by providing the appellant with the materials that would obviate the requirement to leave her bed.

3.141   This semantic debate cost the appellant her night-time care support. The dissenting opinion of Baroness Hale asserted that the decision was irrational in the *Wednesbury* sense on the basis that the need had not in fact changed and was about access not toileting *per se*:[175]

---

174   [2011] UKSC 33, (2011) 14 CCLR 341.
175   See also Richard Gordon QC (2011) *Counting the votes: a brief look at the McDonald case* (2011) 14 CCLR 337.

It seems to me that the need for help to get to the lavatory or commode is so different from the need for protection from uncontrollable bodily functions that it is irrational to confuse the two, and meet the one need in the way that is appropriate to the other. Of course, there may well be people who are persuaded that this is in fact a more convenient, comfortable and safer way of solving the problem; then it is no longer irrational to meet their need in this way.

The scope of the local authority's discretion

3.142   Although NHSCCA 1990 places responsibility on the social services authority for making the service provision decision, this does not of course mean that it is free to reach whatever decision it chooses. Social services decisions, like any public law decision, must be lawful, be reasonable, be in accordance with the evidence, must take into account all relevant factors and ignore all irrelevant ones (see para 26.207 below where these principles are further considered).

3.143   Frequently the local authority's decision is heavily influenced by the views of third parties – for instance as consultants, community nurses and occupational therapists. In such cases local authorities would need persuasive reasons to reject a clear opinion by such a professional on a matter within their area of expertise – unless of course the authority has an equally authoritative and conflicting report. The point being that there are limits to local authorities' expertise and outside these areas they may be reliant on the conclusions of third parties (but see in this respect para 3.50 above). This will also be the case in relation to certain statements by non-professionals. Carers, for instance, are experts as to what they can and cannot do – or more usually, what they are and are not prepared to do (see para 16.60 below). Likewise many of the statements made by the person being assessed will have to be accepted by social services; in some cases because these described preferences, but not always. For example, the extent of pain an individual experiences is not capable of objective calibration:

> ... medical professionals who are expert in pain do not recognise a direct link between clinical findings and pain ... As there is no direct causal link between disease or injury and pain, the only direct evidence of pain can come from the claimant.[176]

3.144   Even in those areas where a local authority is entitled to rely on its own expertise, it may still be under a duty to give reasons for rejecting the evidence or opinions of another – particularly where that evidence or opinion is well informed and of central relevance to the assessment.

Individual financial circumstances and the service provision decision

3.145   In making a service provision decision, in general an individual's financial circumstances will only be relevant to the extent that he or she may be

---

176   Social Security Commissioner's Decision CDLA 902 2004, 18 June 2004, para 15.

required to contribute towards the cost of the service.[177] It follows that the assessment of need should always precede any financial assessment.

3.146   In limited circumstances the authority is permitted to have regard to the service user's financial circumstances in determining whether it is 'necessary' to meet a presenting need. Most commonly this occurs in relation to residential care placements under National Assistance Act (NAA) 1948 s21. For the duty to be triggered under this section, the person must be in need of care and attention which is 'not otherwise' available. The courts have accepted that if a person has assets above the limits specified in the legislation, then it may be reasonable for a local authority to conclude that the support is 'otherwise available'. However, a duty to provide care home accommodation may subsist even where the subsequent financial assessment reveals that the person has capital in excess of the upper capital limit if the individual lacks the capacity to make his or her own arrangements and has no one else willing and able to make the arrangements on his or her behalf (see para 7.22).

3.147   The Prioritising Needs guidance summarises the position thus (para 71):

> An assessment of the person's ability to pay for services should therefore only take place after they have been assessed as having eligible needs. A person's ability to pay should only be used as a reason for not providing services in circumstances where a person has been assessed as needing residential accommodation, the person has the means to pay for it and if the person, or someone close to them, is capable of making the arrangements themselves.

3.148   In the unusual fact case of *R (Spink) v Wandsworth LBC*[178] the Court of Appeal held that where an application for a disabled facilities grant failed due to the applicants declining to provide details of their financial circumstances, the authority could decide that the adaptations were not 'necessary' under the CSDPA 1970 (see para 9.117).

Eligibility criteria and 'eligible needs'

3.149   Social workers need some external scale, formula or criteria in order to make consistent and sensible service provision decisions. Council treasuries also require standardised criteria in order to control overall expenditure: they have finite resources and need to ensure that these are applied equitably – to those whose needs (however, this concept is defined) are greatest.

3.150   Early guidance on eligibility criteria was provided in 1994, in what was

---

177 Some services and certain persons are exempt from charges – considered in chapters 8 and 10 below.

178 [2005] EWCA Civ 302, [2005] 1 WLR 2884, (2005) 8 CCLR 272, a finding applied in *Crofton v NHS Litigation Authority* [2007] EWCA Civ 71, [2007] 1 WLR 923, (2007) 10 CCLR 123.

termed the 'Laming Letter'.[179] It was this guidance that was central to the *Gloucestershire* proceedings[180] and its suggestion that:

> 14. Authorities can be helped in this process by defining eligibility criteria, ie a system of banding which assigns individuals to particular categories, depending on the extent of the difficulties they encounter in carrying out everyday tasks and relating the level of response to the degree of such difficulties. Any 'banding' should not, however, be rigidly applied, as account needs to be taken of individual circumstances. Such eligibility criteria should be phrased in terms of the factors identified in the assessment process.

3.151 The majority in the House of Lords in *R v Gloucestershire CC ex p Barry*[181] approved of this approach, with Lord Clyde stating as follows:[182]

> In deciding whether there is a necessity to meet the needs of the individual some criteria have to be provided. Such criteria are required both to determine whether there is a necessity at all or only, for example, a desirability, and also to assess the degree of necessity. Counsel for the respondent suggested that a criterion could be found in the values of a civilised society. But I am not persuaded that that is sufficiently precise to be of any real assistance. It is possible to draw up categories of disabilities, reflecting the variations in the gravity of such disabilities which could be experienced. Such a classification might enable comparisons to be made between persons with differing kinds and degrees of disability. But in determining the question whether in a given case the making of particular arrangements is necessary in order to meet the needs of a given individual it seems to me that a mere list of disabling conditions graded in order of severity will still leave unanswered the question at what level of disability is the stage of necessity reached. The determination of eligibility for the purposes of the statutory provision requires guidance not only on the assessment of the severity of the condition or the seriousness of the need but also on the level at which there is to be satisfaction of the necessity to make arrangements. In the framing of the criteria to be applied it seems to me that the severity of a condition may have to be to be matched against the availability of resources.

3.152 Although there are many theoretical models by which such criteria may be constructed, the Department of Health and Welsh Government have now issued detailed (and prescriptive) policy guidance that has standard-ised individual local authority eligibility criteria for community care services. These are the Prioritising Needs guidance 2010 (replacing FACS 2002 policy guidance) in England, and the UFSAMC 2002 policy guidance in Wales. The eligibility criteria sections of these two documents differ in only minor respects and both base their criteria on the issue of the poten-

---

179 CI (92) 34; although the guidance was expressed as being cancelled on 1 April 1994, Sedley J accepted that 'in the sense that it gives plainly sensible advice' its content is still relevant although not mandatory – see *R v Islington LBC ex p Rixon* (1997–98) 1 CCLR 119 at 127B, QBD.

180 *R v Gloucestershire CC ex p Barry* (1997–98) 1 CCLR 19 at 34, [1996] 4 All ER 421, CA.

181 [1997] 2 WLR 459, (1997–98) 1 CCLR 40, HL; in the context of an assessment of a person's need for services under CSDPA 1970 s2.

182 (1997–98) 1 CCLR 40, HL at 54.

tial loss of independence (and, in the English guidance, 'well-being') if no or no further support is provided.

3.153   As the Prioritising Needs guidance states (at para 44):[183]

> Councils should use the eligibility framework set out below to specify their eligibility criteria. In setting their eligibility criteria, councils should take account of their own resources, local expectations, and local costs. Councils should take account of agreements with the NHS, including those covering transfers of care and hospital discharge. They should also take account of other agreements with other agencies, as well as other local and national factors.

3.154   The evidence suggests that the introduction of nationally prescribed eligibility criteria has resulted in (or coincided with) a reduction in the number of service users who qualify for community care services.[184] Additionally CSCI found that 'an eligibility-based framework increases the likelihood of front-line staff assessing for bands and services, rather than assessing people's situations in terms of needs and risks'.[185]

3.155   The framework detailed in the Prioritising Needs guidance (at para 54) is reproduced as diagram 5 below. The equivalent framework in the Welsh guidance[186] adopts similar, though generally less demanding, phrasing. By way of example, the first descriptor of the critical band in Wales states 'life is, or could be, threatened' (as opposed to the English requirement that it 'is, or will be'); the Welsh guidance places 'abuse or neglect (self or other) have occurred or are likely to occur' in the critical band, whereas the critical band in England requires 'serious abuse or neglect has occurred or will occur'.

Diagram 5: *Prioritising Needs* guidance para 54

Critical – when

- life is, or will be, threatened; and/or
- Significant health problems have developed or will develop; and/or
- there is, or will be, little or no choice and control over vital aspects of the immediate environment; and/or
- serious abuse or neglect has occurred or will occur; and/or
- there is, or will be, an inability to carry out vital personal care or domestic routines; and/or

---

183   UFSAMC 2002, para 5.19 in Wales.

184   Between 2003 to 2006 the number of older people receiving social care services fell from 867,000 people 840,000 – despite a 3% increase in this age group – see Commission for Social Care Inspection (CSCI) (2008) *The state of social care in England 2006–07, Part one:* p18. In total terms the number of adults receiving a community care service fell by 4.7% during 2009/10, with 83,930 fewer people receiving a service (from 1.78m to 1.7m) – Care Quality Commission (2011) *The state of healthcare and adult social care in England:* an overview of key themes in care in 2009/10, HC 841.

185   Based on findings of M Henwood and B Hudson (2008) *Lost to the system? The impact of Fair Access to Care*: a report commissioned by CSCI for the production of *The state of social care in England 2006–07*, p32.

186   UFSAMC 2002, para 5.16 in Wales.

- vital involvement in work, education or learning cannot or will not be sustained; and/or
- vital social support systems and relationships cannot or will not be sustained; and/or
- vital family and other social roles and responsibilities cannot or will not be undertaken.

Substantial – when

- there is, or will be, only partial choice and control over the immediate environment; and/or
- abuse or neglect has occurred or will occur; and/or
- there is, or will be, an inability to carry out the majority of personal care or domestic routines; and/or
- involvement in many aspects of work, education or learning cannot or will not be sustained; and/or
- the majority of social support systems and relationships cannot or will not be sustained; and/or
- the majority of family and other social roles and responsibilities cannot or will not be undertaken.

Moderate – when

- there is, or will be, an inability to carry out several personal care or domestic routines; and/or
- involvement in several aspects of work, education or learning cannot or will not be sustained; and/or
- Several social support systems and relationships cannot or will not be sustained; and/or
- Several family and other social roles and responsibilities cannot or will not be undertaken.

Low – when

- there is, or will be, an inability to carry out one or two personal care or domestic routines; and/or
- involvement in one or two aspects of work, education or learning cannot or will not be sustained; and/or
- one or two social support systems and relationships cannot or will not be sustained; and/or
- one or two family and other social roles and responsibilities cannot or will not be undertaken.

3.156   Although all social services authority eligibility criteria must adopt the above framework, this does not mean that they must all come to the same service provision decisions. The guidance allows individual local authorities to decide how high on the scale an individual must be, before he or she qualifies for services. Effectively therefore the guidance sanctions a continuation of the existing local variations in eligibility for services: the so called 'postcode lottery'.[187] The extent to which this margin of discretion can lawfully extend to limiting services to those whose needs are assessed as critical is considered below (see paras 3.204–3.215 below)

3.157   One of the tenets of personalisation is early intervention and prevention. This sits uncomfortably alongside a system of service provision based on prioritising highest needs. The Prioritising Needs guidance, at paragraph 35, tries to square the circle:

> In *Cutting the Cake Fairly*,[188] CSCI identified evidence that raising eligibility thresholds without putting in place adequate preventative strategies often leads to a short term dip in the number of people eligible for social care followed soon after by a longer-term rise. Councils should therefore avoid using eligibility criteria as a way of restricting the number of people receiving any form of support to only those with the very highest needs. Rather, they should consider adopting a strong preventative approach to help avoid rising levels of need and costs at a later stage. Early interventions can also improve general community well-being and wider social inclusion.

3.158   This has led to an emphasis in England on 'universal' and 'targeted' services for those whose presenting needs do not (as yet) meet the local authority's eligibility criteria. Although the Welsh Government has chosen not to adopt the term 'personalisation', which it regards as 'too closely associated with a market-led model of consumer choice',[189] it has embraced the concept of the local authority facilitating community-based provision to fill the gaps left by narrowing eligibility criteria[190]. These options are discussed in more detail in chapter 4.

3.159   The overall process prescribed in the English and Welsh guidance accordingly follows the following sequence:

1) the local authority ascertains the extent of the individual's 'presenting needs';
2) these presenting needs are subjected to a risk analysis (risk of harm to the user and others and risks to independence and well-being);
3) these risks are then compared to the above framework categories 'critical, substantial, medium or low';
4) if the individual's 'presenting needs' fall into one or more of the categories of risk that the local authority has decided that it will provide services to meet, then the local authority must meet those needs: such needs being termed 'eligible needs'.[191]

3.160   To assist in the second stage of the above analysis, the Prioritising Needs guidance, states:

---

187   Audit Commission (1996) *Balancing the Care Equation: Progress with Community Care*, para 32 considered above at para 3.28.
188   Commission for Social Care Inspection (2008) *Cutting the cake fairly: CSCI review of eligibility criteria for social care.*
189   *Sustainable social services: a framework for action* WAG 10–11086, 2011, para 3.16.
190   *Sustainable social services: a framework for action* WAG 10–11086, 2011, para 3.22
191   Prioritising Needs guidance, para 52; UFSAMC 2002 policy guidance, para 5.14.

59. Councils should work with individuals to explore their presenting needs and identify what outcomes they would like to be able to achieve. In this way they can evaluate how the individual's presenting needs might pose risks to their independence and/or well-being, both in the immediate and longer-term. Councils should also consider with the individual any external and environmental factors that have caused, or exacerbate, the difficulties the individual is experiencing.

60. In particular councils should consider whether the individual's needs prevent the following
- Exercising choice and control;
- Health and well-being, including mental and emotional as well as physical health and well-being;
- Personal dignity and respect;
- Quality of life;
- Freedom from discrimination;
- Making a positive contribution;
- Economic well-being;
- Freedom from harm, abuse and neglect, taking wider issues of housing and community safety into account.

3.161 In Wales, in contrast, the UFSAMC 2002 policy guidance (para 5.10) defines four key factors to maintaining independence – autonomy, health and safety, managing daily routines and involvement.

3.162 In essence therefore the assessor should ask 'what are the risks to a person's independence and well-being if no services are provided'; or put another way, what would be the consequences for the individual, if services are not provided? The answer is then categorised in terms of critical, substantial, medium or low.

3.163 The Prioritising Needs guidance helpfully warns against a hierarchical or discriminatory approach to needs, which may relegate the importance of independence and social inclusion. Instead it encourages a human rights based approach (para 61):

Councils should be aware that the 'risks to independence and well-being' relate to all areas of life, and that with the exception of life-threatening circumstances or where there are serious safeguarding concerns, there is no hierarchy of needs. For example, needs relating to social inclusion and participation should be seen as just as important as needs relating to personal care issues, where the need falls within the same band. A disabled person who is facing significant obstacles in taking up education and training to support their independence and well-being should be given equal weight to an older person who is unable to perform vital personal care tasks – and vice versa. Councils should make decisions within the context of a human rights approach, considering people's needs not just in terms of physical functionality but in terms of a universal right to dignity and respect

3.164 Having identified an eligible need, the local authority must then meet it:

Once eligible needs are identified, councils should take steps to meet those needs in a way that supports the individual's aspirations and the outcomes that they want to achieve. (Support may also be provided to meet other presenting needs as a consequence of, or to facilitate, eligible needs being met.) Throughout the process of assessment, people should be supported and encouraged to think creatively about how their needs can best be met and how to achieve the fullest range of outcomes possible within the resources available to them.[192]

3.165   The community care reforms sought to challenge procrustean attitudes towards service provision – pigeon-holing disabled people into one of a dozen or so existing services. At times, however, (as above) the Prioritising Needs guidance seems to be suggesting that this can be replaced by pre-service provision pigeon-holing into only four defined categories. The importance of a wider perspective was identified in *R (Heffernan) v Sheffield City Council*[193] where Collins J expressed concern about the compartmentalisation of needs based upon a significant health problem – commenting that 'the existence of significant . . . health problems will not of itself result in any particular need, although the need to prevent development of such problems may'. Although this judgment has been the subject of criticism,[194] it is perhaps best viewed as a difficult fact case where the judge found this eligibility approach to be severely limited.

3.166   The development of the concept of an outcomes-focussed approach to both assessments and service provision, reflected in the Prioritising Needs guidance (see eg para 83 quoted at 3.101) and more widely in the literature of personalisation, encourages far greater flexibility. It represents a fundamental shift in the approach to service provision (see chapter 4). Outcomes, in this context, have been described as, 'The impacts or end results of services on a person's life. Outcomes-focussed services therefore aim to achieve the aspirations, goals and priorities identified by service users'.[195]

Consulting on and revising eligibility criteria

3.167   The formulation of eligibility criteria is a core policy function of social services authorities. The Prioritising Needs guidance directs that, councils should consult service users, carers and appropriate local organisations in formulating, reviewing and publishing their criteria.[196] It is anticipated that councils will review their criteria in line with their 'usual budget cycles'; additionally if an unforeseen financial crisis arises (for instance of the type that resulted in the *Gloucestershire* proceedings), emergency changes to the criteria may have to be instigated,[197] but in the absence of such situations, criteria should not be the subject of frequent amendments. If this were otherwise, and criteria were changed frequently, service users would have no idea from day to day where their entitlements lay – effectively comparing their need against a moving target. Such a

---

192   Prioritising Needs guidance, para 53.
193   [2004] EWHC 1377 (Admin) (2004) 7 CCLR 350 at [16].
194   See eg (2004) 14 *Journal of Community Care Law* 2.
195   C Glendinning, S Clarke, P Hare, I Kotchetkova, J Maddison and L Newbronner (2006) Adults' Services Knowledge Review 13: *Outcomes-focused services for older people*, London: Social Care Institute for Excellence, p2.
196   Prioritising Needs guidance, para 45, and UFSAMC 2002 policy guidance, para 2.17.
197   Prioritising Needs guidance, para 46 and UFSAMC 2002 policy guidance, para 5.22.

situation would give pre-eminence to short term financial issues – if not make them determinative. The issues that arise in relation to raising the bar to critical only are considered below (see paras 3.204–3.215).

Resources and the limits of eligibility criteria

3.168   In *R v Gloucestershire CC ex p Barry*[198] the House of Lords considered the legality of eligibility criteria. The case arose because the authority had its resources for community care drastically cut by an unexpected change in the size of the grant made by the Department of Health. The authority wrote to those people (about 1,500) on its lowest priority level advising them it had decided that their home care service would be reduced or withdrawn. Some of the people who were affected, who were receiving their services under CSDPA 1970 s2, sought a judicial review of the decision. Their basic argument was straightforward; their condition had not changed and so their need for services remained. How could the state of an authority's finances make their individual need no longer a 'need'? The solution adopted by the House of Lords (a majority 3:2 judgment) was that authorities can (within limits) change their eligibility criteria and if they then become more austere, they can reassess existing service users against these new criteria. If on such a reassessment it is found that they are no longer eligible for assistance, the service can be withdrawn. Accordingly it had been lawful for Gloucestershire to take into account its resources when framing its eligibility criteria, but unlawful for it to withdraw services without a prior reassessment.

3.169   The majority decision, in relation to the resource argument, has been criticised[199] and the Lords themselves have sought to restrict the impact of the decision. Subsequently, in *Re T (A Minor)*,[200] a differently constituted House of Lords held that 'resource arguments' in the *ex p Barry* decision were in large measure restricted to cases concerning CSDPA 1970 s2, the statutory construction of which the Lords held to be a 'strange one'.[201] Indeed the court found certain aspects of the majority's reasoning in *ex p Barry* to be 'with respect . . . very doubtful . . .'.[202] A similar line was taken by the Court of Appeal in *R v Sefton MBC ex p Help the Aged*[203] where the Master of the Rolls felt 'compelled' to follow the reasoning of the majority in the *ex p Barry* decision, but only to a limited degree. The Court of Appeal effectively distinguished the *ex p Barry* decision, as one peculiar to the situation under CSDPA 1970 s2. This line was also adopted by Scott Baker J in *R v Bristol City Council ex p Penfold*[204] when he rejected the

---

198   [1997] 2 WLR 459, (1997–98) 1 CCLR 40, HL.
199   See eg B Rayment, '*Ex p Barry* in the House of Lords' (1997) 2 *Judicial Review* 158 and L Clements, 'The collapsing duty' (1997) 2 *Judicial Review* 162.
200   Sub nom *R v East Sussex CC ex p Tandy* [1998] 2 WLR 884, (1997–98) 1 CCLR 352, HL.
201   (1997–98) 1 CCLR 352 at 359I, HL.
202   (1997–98) 1 CCLR 352 at 360G, HL.
203   [1997] 4 All ER 532, (1997–98) 1 CCLR 57 at 67H, CA.
204   (1997–98) 1 CCLR 315, QBD.

respondent's argument that its resource problems justified its refusal to carry out a community care assessment. It was also adopted by Dyson J in *R v Birmingham CC ex p Mohammed*[205] where he held that housing authorities were not entitled to take resources into account when deciding whether or not to approve a disabled facilities grant, in this case because of the specificity of the statutory criteria.[206]

3.170   The effect of the *Gloucestershire* and subsequent judgments is that social services authorities are entitled to take their available resources into account, when framing their general eligibility criteria. This principle is, however, subject to four significant constraints. These can be summarised as:

1) the reassessment obligation;
2) the duty to meet eligible needs;
3) resources cannot be the sole criterion;
4) the Human Rights Act (HRA) 1998 obligation.

The reassessment obligation

3.171   As noted, local authorities are entitled (within limits) to change their eligibility criteria (for instance when they have a budgetary problem – as occurred in the *Gloucestershire* case). However, when criteria are revised and made more severe, existing service users must be the subject of a full individual community care reassessment before any decision can be taken on the withdrawal of services. The logic for this requirement is two-fold: first, that the service users' circumstances may have altered since their previous assessment and so they may be eligible under the new, more austere criteria; and second, even if their needs do not satisfy the revised criteria, the criteria are not 'determinative' and so there may be special reasons why the services should continue notwithstanding.

3.172   McCowan LJ highlighted this requirement in the first instance hearing of the *Gloucestershire* case[207] when he held:

> It would certainly have been open to the Gloucestershire County Council to reassess the individual applicants as individuals, judging their current needs and taking into account all relevant factors including the resources now available and the competing needs of other disabled persons. What they were not entitled to do, but what in my judgment they in fact did, was not to re-assess at all but simply to cut the services they were providing because their resources in turn had been cut. This amounted to treating the cut in resources as the sole factor to be taken into account, and that was, in my judgment, unlawful.

205 [1999] 1 WLR 33, (1997–98) 1 CCLR 441, QBD.
206 See Housing Grants, Construction and Regeneration Act 1996 s23.
207 *R v Islington, LBC ex p McMillan, R v Gloucestershire CC ex p Mahfood, Barry, Grinham and Dartnell* (1997–98) 1 CCLR 7, DC.

The duty to meet eligible needs

3.173 The 1992 'Laming Letter'[208] stated as follows:

> 13. An authority may take into account the resources available when deciding how to respond to an individual's assessment. However, once the authority has indicated that a service should be provided to meet an individual's needs and the authority is under a legal obligation to provide it or arrange for its provision, then the service must be provided. It will not be possible for an authority to use budgeting difficulties as a basis for refusing to provide the service.

3.174 The legality of the Laming Letter advice on resources was in issue (and upheld) in the *Gloucestershire* case. McCowan LJ in the first instance hearing expressed the legal position thus:[209]

> . . . once they have decided that it is necessary to make the arrangements, they are under an absolute duty to make them. It is a duty owed to a specific individual and not a target duty. No term is to be implied that the local authority are obliged to comply with the duty only if they have the revenue to do so. In fact, once under that duty resources do not come into it.

3.175 In the House of Lords Lord Clyde reiterated this point in the following terms:[210]

> The right given to the person by section 2(1) of the Act of 1970 was a right to have the arrangements made which the local authority was satisfied were necessary to meet his needs. The duty only arises if or when the local authority is so satisfied. But when it does arise then it is clear that a shortage of resources will not excuse a failure in the performance of the duty.

3.176 Lord Clyde's approach was followed by Lord Woolf MR in *R v Sefton MBC ex p Help the Aged*[211] in relation to the duties under the NAA 1948 and is expressed by the Prioritising Needs guidance (at para 124)[212] as follows:

> Councils should plan with regards to outcomes, rather than specific services. They should consider the cost-effectiveness of support options on the merits of each case and may take their resources into account when deciding how best to achieve someone's agreed outcomes. However, this does not mean that councils can take decisions on the basis of resources alone. Once a council has decided it is necessary to meet the eligible needs

---

208 CI (92) 34; although the guidance was expressed as being cancelled on 1 April 1994, Sedley J accepted that 'in the sense that it gives plainly sensible advice' its content is still relevant although not mandatory – see *R v Islington LBC ex p Rixon* (1997–98) 1 CCLR 119 at 127B, QBD.

209 *R v Gloucestershire CC ex p Mahfood* (1997–98) 1 CCLR 7, DC; and see also *R v Kirklees MBC ex p Daykin* (1997–98) 1 CCLR 512 at 525D, QBD, where Collins J expressed the proposition in the following terms, 'once needs have been established, then they must be met and cost cannot be an excuse for failing to meet them. The manner in which they are met does not have to be the most expensive. The Council is perfectly entitled to look to see what cheapest way for them to meet the needs which are specified'.

210 [1997] 2 WLR 459 at 474G, (1997–98) 1 CCLR 40 at 54F, QBD.

211 [1997] 4 All ER 532, (1997–98) 1 CCLR 57 at 67I, CA.

212 UFSAMC 2002 policy guidance, para 5.32.

of an individual, it is under a duty to provide sufficient support to meet those needs.

3.177   The principle underlying this formulation is of fundamental importance. All local authorities have limited resources and all are required to fulfil a variety of statutory obligations. If a council could assert resource shortages as a reason for not complying with a statutory duty, this would effectively result in these duties being 'collapsed into powers' (as Richard Gordon QC argued in the *Gloucestershire* case). The resolution of this problem is achieved in the *Gloucestershire* judgment by the court holding that the duty to provide community care services only arises once a service provision decision under NHSCCA 1990 s47(1)(b) has occurred. However, once a local authority has decided that a person has 'eligible needs', these must be met irrespective of resource arguments. In *Re T (A Minor)*,[213] Lord Browne-Wilkinson dealt with this issue as follows:

> There remains the suggestion that, given the control which central Government now exercises over local authority spending, the court cannot, or at least should not, require performance of a statutory duty by a local authority which it is unable to afford . . . My Lords I believe your Lordships should resist this approach to statutory duties.

> . . . The argument is not one of insufficient resources to discharge the duty but of a preference for using the money for other purposes. To permit a local authority to avoid performing a statutory duty on the grounds that it prefers to spend the money in other ways is to downgrade a statutory duty to a discretionary power. A similar argument was put forward in the Barry case but dismissed by Lord Nicholls (at p470F–G) apparently on the ground that the complainant could control the failure of a local authority to carry out its statutory duty by showing that it was acting in a way which was Wednesbury unreasonable in failing to allocate the necessary resources. But with respect this is a very doubtful form of protection. Once the reasonableness of the actions of a local authority depends upon its decision how to apply scarce financial resources, the local authority's decision becomes extremely difficult to review. The court cannot second-guess the local authority in the way in which it spends its limited resources: see also R v Cambridge District Health Authority ex parte B [1995] 1 WLR 898, especially at p906D–F. Parliament has chosen to impose a statutory duty, as opposed to a power, requiring the local authority to do certain things. In my judgment the courts should be slow to downgrade such duties into what are, in effect, mere discretions over which the court would have very little real control. If Parliament wishes to reduce public expenditure on meeting the needs of sick children then it is up to Parliament so to provide. It is not for the courts to adjust the order of priorities as between statutory duties and statutory discretions.

3.178   It follows that once a local authority has assessed an individual as having 'eligible needs' then any failure to provide services to meet those needs will be open to legal challenge. In *R v Wigan MBC ex p Tammadge*,[214] for example, the applicant lived with her four children, three of whom had

213 [1998] 2 WLR 884, (1997–98) 1 CCLR 352 at 360, HL.
214 (1997–98) 1 CCLR 581, QBD.

severe learning disabilities. Over a considerable period of time she sought a larger property in order to be able to better provide for their needs; a complaints panel concluded this was needed, a view accepted by social services and confirmed by a multi-disciplinary meeting. However, a meeting of senior officers and members decided, however, that 'it was not appropriate to commit the authority to the purchase or adaptation of a larger property'. In quashing that decision, Forbes J held that Wigan's 'own professionally qualified staff and advisors' had concluded that that her need for larger accommodation had been established.

3.179   Once the duty had arisen in this way, it was not lawful of Wigan to refuse to perform that duty because of shortage of or limits upon its financial resources.

3.180   Many cases concerning inadequate service provision arrangements have been considered by the local government ombudsman, and are cited in the following paragraphs (see also para 3.191 below). In some cases the ombudsman recommends not insignificant sums in compensation.[215]

Waiting lists and delayed service provision decision

3.181   Rather than refusing to provide a service to meet an eligible need, councils may merely delay their decision: for instance by simple prevarication or by adopting unnecessary processes (eg continually referring the case back for further information, reports etc) or by the use of a lengthy waiting list.

3.182   In *R v South Lanarkshire Council ex p MacGregor*[216] the applicant was one of 199 people in the council's area who (due to the local authority's limited resources) were on a waiting list for a place in a nursing home, of whom 106 were in hospitals. The court (the Outer House of the Court of Session) held that the policy was unlawful, and that:

> ... once a local authority determines that an individual's needs call for a particular provision the local authority is obliged to make that provision. In particular having decided that an individual requires the provision of a permanent place in a nursing home ... a local authority could not ... refuse to make such a provision simply because it did not have the necessary resources.

3.183   The local government ombudsman has made similar findings. For example in 2001 the ombudsman upheld a complaint against Cambridgeshire that a resource-led policy that delayed the provision of residential care (once the person had been assessed as needing it) was maladministration,[217] and in a complaint against Essex[218] stated:

215 See para 26.63 below where the ombudsman's approach to compensation is considered further, and see eg, Complaint no 04/A/10159 against Southend on Sea BC, 1 September 2005 where the authority agreed to pay a total of £35,000 in compensation to a family, where it had delayed for over two years in providing adequate services for the applicant's adult son who had learning and behavioural disabilities.
216 (2000) 4 CCLR 188, (CS(OH)).
217 Complaint no 99/B/04621 against Cambridgeshire CC, 29 January 2001.
218 Complaint no 00/B/00599 against Essex CC, 3 September 2001.

The Council believes it does not have to provide a care service or funding for care immediately it has decided that it is necessary to provide the service to meet a person's assessed needs. It considers that it is acting correctly by having a waiting list on which the time a person may have to wait for resources to become available is indeterminate and depends to a significant extent on the needs and priority of other people on the waiting list and those who may come on to the list. That cannot, in my view, be correct.

Interim arrangements/physical resource shortages

3.184   The courts have reacted differently where the shortage concerns physical or human resources as opposed to financial. In such cases the courts have generally been more sympathetic to the local authority position – provided it is taking reasonable steps to resolve the problem. Thus in *R v Lambeth LBC ex p A1 and A2*[219] the Court of Appeal held that provided the authority was making a 'sincere and determined' effort to resolve the physical resource problem, it would not intervene.

3.185   However, where an authority makes no such effort, the situation will be otherwise. In *R v Islington LBC ex p Rixon*,[220] for instance, Sedley J considered that a local authority could not assess someone as needing a service (in this case a day centre placement) and then fail to provide it, merely because none was available. This reason, alone would be insufficient:

> There are two points at which, in my judgment, the respondent local authority has fallen below the requirements of the law. The first concerns the relationship of need to availability . . . [T]he local authority has, it appears, simply taken the existing unavailability of further facilities as an insuperable obstacle to any further attempt to make provision . . .

3.186   It also follows that where the first choice service is not available, in addition to demonstrating that it is taking purposeful steps to resolve the service supply problem (including if needs be, commissioning an independent specialist to help identify and secure a suitable provider or placement[221]) the local authority will be required to make alternative interim arrangements – as the Prioritising Needs guidance[222] states:

> Councils should provide support promptly once they have agreed to do so, but where waiting is unavoidable, they should ensure that alternative support is in place to meet eligible needs.

3.187   Where the delay is caused by a lack of suitable provision to meet the assessed need and the local authority can show 'no convincing evidence of reasonable efforts' to discharge its continuing statutory duty it will be acting unlawfully in breach of that duty.[223] Similarly, the local government

---

219   (1997–98) 1 CCLR 336, CA and see also *R v Islington BC ex p McMillan* (1997–98) 1 CCLR 7 at 17, QBD.

220   (1997–98) 1 CCLR 119 at 130F, QBD.

221   Complaint no 02/B/10226: against Cambridgeshire CC, 6 July 2004.

222   Para 124; UFSAMC 2002 policy guidance, para 5.35.

223   *LW: Re. Judicial Review* [2010] NIQB 62, 19 May 2010, applying a provision substantially the same as CSDPA 1970 s2.

ombudsman is prepared to investigate the causes of a delay due to alleged 'human resource' problems – such as recruitment difficulties and may not always be satisfied that these are outside a council's control.[224]

Allocation and funding panels

3.188   Many local authorities use 'panels' of various types (sometimes termed 'allocation panels', 'funding panels' or 'purchasing panels') as a means of rationing services. In effect they constitute a non-statutory 'post service provision decision' hurdle that applicants must traverse. *R v Wigan MBC ex p Tammadge*[225] (para 3.178 above) is an example: objectively the authority had made a decision that the applicant's presenting needs called for the provision of services. However, the individual officers were unable to progress this, since the local authority's procedures stated that only a panel meeting was able to make a formal decision on resource allocation; a meeting at which the assessing social worker had little or no role. This is not untypical of the procedures adopted by many local authorities. In response to judicial and ombudsmen doubts concerning the legality of these panels, some authorities have endeavoured to project these panels as 'quality control' mechanisms – namely to ensure that their social workers have completed the assessment correctly.[226] Not infrequently the panel will refer a funding application back for further analysis or paperwork to be completed. The effect of this is to create delay, which arguably is the whole point of the exercise: the protection of resources by (among other things) deferring service provision. Occasionally, however, as in *R v South Lanarkshire Council ex p MacGregor*,[227] the panel is more blatant: in that case it openly restricted access to residential care solely on the basis of the authority's budget.

3.189   Commenting upon this 'unfortunately commonplace' and 'unlawful practice' in evidence to the Joint Committee on Human Rights,[228] the charity Help the Aged explained that it persisted because:

> Individual cases are settled to avoid threatened litigation, but the widespread use of funding panels to ration care continues. Individuals

224 See eg report on complaint no 08 017 856 against Redbridge LBC, 6 August 2009, para 23 – a Special Educational Needs case concerning Occupational Therapist delays and complaint no 10008979 against Liverpool City Council, 4 April 2011, where the delay in providing support was substantially aggravated by the landlord's inaction: the LGO nonetheless found maladministration by the council in failing both to meet the assessed need in a reasonable timescale or to act once it knew of the landlord's delay.

225 (1997–98) 1 CCLR 581, QBD.

226 Many of those authorities that suggest their panels are quality control mechanisms commonly have difficulty in sustaining this argument, when their council's minutes are reviewed. Not unusually it can be shown that the panel was created as a response to a budgetary problem – rather than as a response to a concern about the quality of social workers' assessments. Indeed if this were the problem one would assume that the logical response would be to improve the quality of their training.

227 (2001) 4 CCLR 188.

228 Memorandum from Help the Aged contained in the Appendices to the Sixth Report of the Joint Committee on Human Rights, *The Case for a Human Rights Commission*, 19 March 2003. Report together with Proceedings of the Committee HL 67-I; HC 489-I.

then find themselves unable to access essential services they have been assessed as needing, thus forcing them to live in conditions which, in some cases, may be sufficiently severe as to constitute inhuman and degrading treatment within the meaning of Article 3 and potentially put their lives at risk. There is, as far as we know, no monitoring of how many people die in their homes or following emergency admission to hospital because they have been denied a service they were assessed as needing.

3.190   Panels create a fault line between the data collection phase of the assessment process and the service provision decision. In so doing they reduce a person's needs to the bare words of the assessment paperwork or to scores on a spreadsheet: they sideline (or remove completely) the assessing social worker from the decision making process and with him or her the element of discretion that is essential to any informed decision on such personal questions as the extent of human need. In effect they represent the end game in Michael Lipsky's analysis of street-level bureaucracy (see para 3.3 above), where without the knowledge of the disabled person the 'human judgment that cannot be programmed and for which machines cannot substitute' is in fact removed from the process. In *R (Goldsmith) v Wandsworth LBC*,[229] a service provision decision was overturned, inter alia, because the panel had not even had the community care assessment before it – an assessment the Court of Appeal found impressive by its thoroughness

3.191   The local government ombudsmen have considered many complaints concerning panel decisions. A frequent scenario concerns disabled people with complex needs which require potentially expensive care packages and in relation to which a social worker will have undertaken considerable research and recommended a particular care plan. The care plan is then considered by a panel and rejected – essentially the social worker being required to trim the assessment of need to fit the budget (to paraphrase Sedley J[230]) – even though no suitable alternative exists.

3.192   A 2005 ombudsman's report[231] is illustrative in this respect. It concerned the placement of a learning disabled adult in a series of inappropriate care homes. His social worker had undertaken a detailed assessment of needs and identified a suitable placement 'after a long, careful process over many months'. However, her plan was rejected by the council's Care Purchasing Panel relying on advice from an acting manager who 'barely knew' the service user (he had observed him at most on three occasions in a day centre). The alternative care package proposed proved to be unsuitable and ultimately – once the ombudsman had become involved – a suitable placement was secured. In the ombudsman's opinion:

Having correctly prepared a detailed assessment in accordance with the statutory guidance, it was wrong for the Council to dismiss all the information gathered in that process, and make a decision on the basis of

229 [2004] EWCA Civ 1170, (2004) 7 CCLR 472.
230 Sedley J referred to 'trimming the assessment of need to fit available provision' in *R v Islington LBC ex p Rixon* (1997–98) 1 CCLR 119 at 129B, QBD.
231 Complaint no 04/A/10159 against Southend on Sea BC, 1 September 2005.

[the acting manager's] assurance. The decision flew in the face of the assessment.

3.193 Even where a panel accepts that a specific care plan is required, it not infrequently defers funding, essentially to address the authority's cash flow demands (as occurred in *R v South Lanarkshire Council ex p MacGregor*[232]). A 2001 complaint against Essex[233] concerned such a practice. A council social worker had assessed the complainant's mother as in need of residential care and prepared a care plan naming an appropriate care home. This came before the 'purchasing panel' which accepted the plan, but decided that the need was not of sufficient priority to justify immediate funding and so her name was placed on a waiting list. The local government ombudsman considered that this amounted to maladministration; that there was 'no justification for the council's use of a waiting list for funding care which is otherwise available and which only comes into operation *after* the council has decided that it will provide a service to meet particular needs'.

3.194 Whilst the widespread use by local authorities of funding panels has attracted criticism, this is not to say that all 'panels' are unlawful. There is nothing inherently objectionable about a panel of social care experts being called upon to make a decision concerning the necessary elements of a complex care package (where of course it has the necessary expertise to discharge such a role). Thus in *R (Rodriguez-Bannister) v Somerset Partnership NHS and Social Care Trust*[234] the court found not unreasonable the role of a panel whose primary task was to determine the kind of accommodation that was required, 'whether residential, supported living or other', and not to make recommendations about the necessary levels of support in any particular setting.

Resources cannot be the sole criterion

3.195 Although councils are entitled to take into account the extent of their available resources when they frame their eligibility criteria, they cannot make resource availability the sole criterion: resource availability alone cannot be 'determinative'. In many situations it appears that this is precisely what allocation or funding panels do (see para 3.188 above). Likewise the application by an authority of a rigid 'costs ceiling' would have the same effect (see para 4.97 below).

3.196 In the *Gloucestershire* decision Hirst LJ (in the Court of Appeal) held that resources were 'no more than one factor in an overall assessment, where no doubt the objective needs of the individual disabled person will always be the paramount consideration'.[235] In the first instance decision McCowan LJ – when quashing the decision of the county council (to withdraw services without reassessment) – stated that this 'amounted to

232 (2001) 4 CCLR 188 – see para 3.188 above.
233 Complaint no 00/B/00599, 3 September 2001.
234 [2003] EWHC 2184 (Admin), (2004) 7 CCLR 385.
235 *R v Gloucestershire CC ex p Barry* [1996] 4 All ER 421, (1997–98) 1 CCLR 19 at 31G, QBD.

treating the cut in resources as the sole factor to be taken into account, and that was, in my judgment, unlawful'.[236]

The Human Rights Act 1998 obligation[237]

3.197 There is a point at which resource availability ceases to be a legitimate reason for refusing to provide services; or, put another way, there is a level of austerity beyond which eligibility criteria cannot venture. This aspect of the argument was articulated by McCowan LJ in the first instance *Gloucestershire* judgment,[238] when he observed:

> I should stress, however, that there will, in my judgment, be situations where a reasonable authority could only conclude that some arrangements were necessary to meet the needs of a particular disabled person and in which they could not reasonably conclude that a lack of resources provided an answer. Certain persons would be at severe physical risk if they were unable to have some practical assistance in their homes. In those situations, I cannot conceive that an authority would be held to have acted reasonably if they used shortage of resources as a reason for not being satisfied that some arrangement should be made to meet those persons' needs.

3.198 The *Gloucestershire* proceedings took place prior to the enactment of the Human Rights Act (HRA) 1998; using the language of the European Convention on Human Rights (the 'Convention') McCowan LJ was, in effect, stating that limited resources could not be used as a reason for allowing a violation of Article 3 to take place. There can be little doubt that domestic law recognises a core set of 'positive' justiciable, non-resource dependent rights – the uncertainty relates to their scope. As Lord Hoffman (speaking extra judicially) has commented:[239]

> Human rights probably include not only freedom from certain forms of state interference but also a positive obligation upon the State to provide every citizen with certain basic necessities which he requires in order to be able to function as a human being.

3.199 Arguably, therefore, there is a point at which simple decisions about the provision of community care services cross over from the realm of socio-economic rights and into the domain of those civil and political rights protected by the Convention. Although this may be an overly simplistic reading of these two categories of rights, it nevertheless serves as a useful device for considering the 'austerity' limits of eligibility criteria.

3.200 In relation to social care services, it is perhaps self evident that services could not be denied (on resource grounds) if the consequence were that the disabled person's life was at risk, or that significant health problems

---

236 *R v Gloucestershire CC ex p Mahfood* (1997–98) 1 CCLR 7 at 16I, DC.
237 For a brief review of the relevant provisions of the European Convention on Human Rights see para 27.237.
238 *R v Gloucestershire CC ex p Mahfood* (1997–98) 1 CCLR 7, DC.
239 L Hoffman, *The 'Separation of Powers'*, Annual Commercial Bar Lecture, COMBAR, 2001, unpublished transcript.

would develop or that there was a risk of serious abuse or neglect occurring. In effect, therefore, the core set of social care rights are at least those detailed in the 'critical' category of the prescribed eligibility framework (see para 3.155 above); these being risks associated with Articles 2 and 3 of the Convention.

3.201 The same could be argued in relation to Article 5. *R v Manchester City Council ex p Stennett*,[240] for instance, concerned the right of detained patients to 'free' aftercare services under Mental Health Act 1983 s117. The court accepted that in many cases patients were only discharged from their detention in psychiatric wards if they 'agreed' to move into a specialist care home. It was argued, therefore, that to require payment for this service would, in effect, be requiring a patient to pay for his or her freedom.[241] Lord Steyn found such a proposition compelling, stating:

> It can hardly be said that the mentally ill patient freely chooses such accommodation. Charging them in these circumstances may be surprising . . . If the argument of the authorities is accepted that there is a power to charge these patients such a view of the law would not be testimony to our society attaching a high value to the need to care after the exceptionally vulnerable.

3.202 It follows that a resource argument alone will seldom dispose of a claim to respect for a Convention right. In relation to the Articles 2, 3 and 5 rights, financial resource arguments will rarely if ever be relevant. Even in relation to qualified rights, such as Article 8, where the state can legitimately play the resource card, it cannot expect it to trump all others – particularly where the consequences of inaction for the applicant are serious. We separately discuss at para 4.64 below the extent to which the resource card can be played in relation to the independent living obligation and the provision of 'minimum' services – the 'dignity' principle.

3.203 However, where the Article 8 right in question is fundamental – for instance the right to a sexual relationship, then the cost impact will be subject to particular scrutiny. *A local authority v MM and KM*[242] concerned a person whose mental health problems were such that she was adjudged to lack capacity to decide where she should live, to marry or to manage her own money – but that she did have capacity to have sexual relations. The Court required the authority to make arrangements to facilitate her long term relationship with her boyfriend (a relationship that had been turbulent) and observed (para 165):

> the local authority cannot in this connection seek to avoid its positive obligations [under Article 8 of the European Convention on Human Rights] by seeking to toll the bell of scarce resources. . . . the additional financial burden which this may impose on the local authority is

240 [2002] UKHL 34, [2002] 3 WLR 584, (2002) 5 CCLR 500.
241 If a patient remains detained purely for reasons of financial expediency, it would appear that the Article 5 liability would fall on the detaining body rather than the body responsible for the delay see *R (S) v Halton BC and the Parole Board* [2008] EWHC 1982 (Admin).
242 [2007] EWHC 2003 (Fam), (2008) 11 CCLR 119. See also *Re Connor* [2004] NICA 45, (2005) 8 CCLR 328.

comparatively modest given the overall cost of its provision for MM. And the right in play here is, to repeat, too important, too precious in human terms, to be swept aside by such purely fiscal considerations.

The critical/substantial bands

3.204   A survey by Community Care magazine in September 2010 found 3 per cent of English local authorities operated a critical only threshold with several more considering following suit. 72 per cent of authorities surveyed limited services to critical and substantial bands.[243] Decisions to move to critical only have been successfully challenged, primarily on equality grounds (see paras 3.211–3.215 below), and the legal considerations are set out below.

3.205   Any analysis of this question must first acknowledge the latitude provided by some of the critical band descriptors. Local authorities may, for instance, vary widely in how they interpret:

- significant health problems;
- little or no choice and control over vital aspects of the immediate environment;
- serious abuse or neglect;
- an inability to carry out vital personal care or domestic routines.

3.206   However, some of the criteria in the 'substantial' band give a steer as to the meaning of the 'critical' band descriptions, and suggest that the bar to be crossed in order to register a critical need is a high one.[244] For instance abuse or neglect (apart from when it is 'serious') only scores a substantial rating – as does a person who is unable 'to carry out the majority of [his or her] personal care or domestic routines' or to sustain 'the majority of [his or her] social support systems and relationships'. Such an analysis suggests that the Department of Health considers it acceptable to deny support to people who are being abused and neglected, and who are unable to attend to most of their personal care needs. Such a criticism is less easily levied against the Welsh Government guidance, which (for instance) requires all abuse (not merely 'serious' abuse) to be recorded as 'critical'. The acceptance of 'non-serious' abuse flies in the face of SCIE guidance that requires commissioners of services to have a 'a zero tolerance of all forms of abuse'.[245]

3.207   In *R (A and B, X and Y) v East Sussex CC*[246] Munby J dwelt at length on the 'core value' of 'human dignity' as a component of Articles 3 and 8 of the Convention. In his opinion 'thoughtless, uncaring and uncharitable'

---

243   www.communitycare.co.uk/Articles/2010/09/15/115321/councils-to-deny-social-care-support-to-all-but-most-needy.htm
244   Indeed in *R (W) v Birmingham CC* [2011] EWHC 1147 (Admin) para 183 Walker J considered that the consequences' for disabled people of a move to 'critical only' were 'potentially devastating'.
245   SCIE, *Dignity in care: Adults' Services Practice Guide 09*, 2006, p8, accessible at www.scie.org.uk/publications/practiceguides/practiceguide09/files/pg09.pdf.
246   [2003] EWHC 167 (Admin), (2003) 6 CCLR 194 at [88].

behaviour[247] was a relevant factor in assessing the threshold at which action (or inaction) engaged Article 3. His judgment suggests that the threshold is not an excessively high one when the basic care and support needs of disabled people are being considered. In assessing whether Article 3 is engaged he considered it relevant to consider (amongst other things) 'the duration of the [lack of suitable care], its physical and mental effects . . . the sex, age and state of health of the victim'.[248]

3.208   In *R (Bernard) v Enfield LBC*[249] Sullivan J accepted that not every breach of a community care obligation would result in a breach of the Convention. However, in view of the vulnerability of the client group, he considered that Article 8 obliged councils to take positive measures 'to enable them to enjoy, so far as possible, a normal private and family life'. In the particular case he held that the council's failure to provide services had left the applicant 'housebound, confined to a shower chair for most of the day, [and] lacking privacy in the most undignified of circumstances'. It had effectively isolated her and made her a 'burden, wholly dependent upon the rest of her family' and in his opinion unquestionably violated Article 8.

3.209   An ordinary interpretation of Mrs Bernard's needs suggests that they are more likely to fall into the 'substantial' band' than the 'critical'. If correct, this means that either the critical band descriptors are too severe, or, at the very least, they do not provide a failsafe protection of human rights. Under the English Prioritising Needs guidance one of the outcomes to be particularly considered is 'personal dignity and respect',[250] this underlines the need for a human rights-based approach to determining an individual's need for support.

3.210   However, the court, in *R (Chavda) v Harrow LBC* (see para 3.211 below), declined to consider the potential violation of the applicants' human rights that would result from their future loss of eligibility for services on the ground that the argument was theoretical and premature, suggesting the claim would not crystallise until individuals had been reassessed against the revised criteria. This is a surprising decision given that the future loss of service provision was not, on the facts of this case, speculative, but relatively certain.

3.211   The courts have been more robust in their application of the public sector equality duty in this context. While equality issues will not necessarily trump resource considerations, the duty in relation to disability, formerly in Disability Discrimination Act 1995 s49A, and now consolidated by Equality Act 2010 s149, to have due regard, amongst other things, to the need to promote equality of opportunity (see para 2.32 above for a detailed analysis), is one that is recognised as imposing 'significant and onerous obligations on public bodies in the context of cuts to public

247 [2003] EWHC 167, (2003) 6 CCLR 194 at [89].
248 Here citing from the judgment of the European Court of Human Rights in *Price v UK* (2001) 34 EHRR 1285 at [24].
249 [2002] EWHC 2282 (Admin), (2002) 5 CCLR 577 at [32].
250 Para 60.

services'.[251] In *R (Chavda and others) v Harrow LBC*[252] the council decided to raise the bar for eligibility to critical only. In doing so it considered a report which referred to 'potential conflict with the DDA'. Deputy High Court Judge Mackie, held that this was not adequate to discharge the disability equality duty:

> The important reason why the laws of discrimination have moved from derision to acceptance to respect over the last three decades has been the recognition of the importance not only of respecting rights but also of doing so visibly and clearly by recording the fact. These considerations lead me to conclude that if the relevance of the important duties imposed by the Act had been adequately drawn to the attention of the decision-makers there would have been a written record of it.[253]

3.212   In *R (W) v Birmingham City Council*[254] (also concerning a decision to move to critical only) the defendant, faced with the need to make significant savings in its overall expenditure, put up a robust defence to the legal challenge which it characterised as 'a micro challenge to a macro decision' largely concerning 'petty bureaucracy, at quite a low level' (para 3 of the judgment). The case proceeded on a number of agreed principles concerning the application of the section 49A duty, arising from the body of case law and the Code of Practice, including:

- Due regard requires analysis of the relevant material with the specific statutory considerations in mind
- General awareness of the duty does not amount to the necessary due regard, being a 'substantial rigorous and open-minded approach';
- In a case where the decision may affect large numbers of vulnerable people, many of whom fall within one or more of the protected groups, the due regard necessary is very high
- In particular, decision-makers need rigorous and accurate advice and analysis from officers, not 'Panglossian' statements of what officers think members want to hear

3.213   The decision was made following a consultation exercise with two options; the first to do nothing and the second, the council's preferred option, described as 'the new offer' which included broad generalities as to the benefits of personalisation as well as the move to meet critical needs only. The equality impact needs assessment had 'identifying as potential impacts increased stress for both carers and recipients of care, basic needs being likely to go unmet, increased depression and mental illness, and a risk of abuse increasing over time – a feature being that withdrawing support for substantial needs may lead to critical needs developing'. When first produced the report was 'necessarily high level and generalised' as regards impact, but suggested that more detailed and focussed

251 See agreed legal principles set out in *R (W) v Birmingham City Council* [2011] EWHC 1147 (Admin), (2011) 14 CCLR 516.
252 [2007] EWHC 3064 (Admin), (2008) 11 CCLR 187.
253 [2007] EWHC 3064 (Admin), (2008) 11 CCLR 187 at para 40.
254 [2011] EWHC 1147 (Admin), (2011) 14 CCLR 516.

3

information would be available (para 157). By the time the decision was made no more detailed information was forthcoming. Accordingly, Walker J found it 'difficult to see how, in the circumstances of the present case, "due regard" could be paid to the matters identified in section 49A without some attempt at assessment of the practical impact on those whose needs in a particular respect fell into the "substantial" band but not into the "critical" band.' (para 176). In particular,

> The decision to consult "on broad options" required consideration of a subsidiary question whether to go beyond generalities in assessing the likely impact of the proposed course upon individuals with "substantial" needs. At the very least it seems to me that in order to pay "due regard" the Council when deciding to consult "on broad options" needed to consider whether its answer to the subsidiary question was consistent with its duty under section 49A. (para 178)

3.214 The *Birmingham* judgment is a particularly strong example of the 'anxious scrutiny' (see para 3.227 below) that courts will subject public law decisions when they believe that particularly severe consequences (in terms of fundamental human rights) will result. In this case, indeed, the court came close to arguing that a fixed belief that a resource problem meant that services had to be cut no matter how severe: 'that there was no more room for manoeuvre' (para 182) had the potential to be irrational/*Wednesbury* unreasonable (see para 3.226 below).

3.215 As a matter of public law the over-rigid application of eligibility criteria, particularly where councils have elected to limit provision to those in the high bands, is likely to amount to an unlawful fettering of the authority's discretion. For example, the statutory guidance requires attention to be given to 'how needs and risks might change over time and the likely outcome if help were not to be provided'.[255] This necessitates considering whether a current need, even though it may fall short of the eligibility bar, should nonetheless be met in order to prevent a worsening situation which will inevitably compromise the individual's independence and well-being. Similarly any analysis of the needs of a person whose condition is fluctuating must consider whether, at times of peak need, the individual meets the eligibility criteria. In the second example the support plan (see chapter 4) would reflect the variations in the intensity of support needed.

Family separation and 'locational' need

3.216 The assessment and care planning process may result in the separation of couples and/or other family members. In evidence to the Joint Committee on Human Rights, Help the Aged referred to this situation in the following terms:

> It is not uncommon for older couples to be separated against their will when the local authority says that it cannot provide sufficient care to one of them to enable them to continue living at home, and he or she must

255 Prioritising Needs guidance, para 57. See also UFSAMC, para 3.26.

instead go into residential care . . . This flagrant disregard for the Article 8 rights of older people indicates the lack of any systematic, conscious application of human rights in this area and underlines the need for a change in the culture of care planning.[256]

3.217   In what circumstances is it lawful for a local authority to conclude a care plan that has or would have the effect of separating close family members?

3.218   Before any such care plan can be proposed, an assessment must have been undertaken which considered (amongst other things) the person's important relationships. The various presenting needs would then have been graded against the four eligibility categories. Both the English and Welsh criteria describe as 'critical' a situation where 'vital social support systems and relationships cannot or will not be sustained'. An ordinary interpretation of the word 'vital' in this context would encompass the preservation of a marriage, civil partnership or common law relationship. The same may also be true for other relationships – with the factual context of each such case being crucial. Any assessment of these matters would have to ensure that full regard was had to the positive obligation under Article 8[257] of the Convention to have respect for the private and family life of the person being assessed as well as those affected by any separation. The argument may have an added dimension in relation to married partners, since Article 12 most probably enshrines a right to cohabit.[258]

3.219   By way of example, if an elderly husband has a progressive condition that means it is no longer possible for him to be cared for in his home, it may be necessary for the local authority to secure a nursing home placement for him. This in itself would not amount to a violation of Article 8 – in the sense that the authority is not actually interfering with the relationship (ie by forcibly removing the husband from the home). Whether the placement discharges the authority's positive obligations will depend upon the proportionality of the response. Assuming that it is not feasible for him to remain at home with support, the assessment must address

---

256   Memorandum from Help the Aged contained in the appendices to the Sixth Report of the Joint Committee on Human Rights, *The Case for a Human Rights Commission*, 19 March 2003. Report together with Proceedings of the Committee HL 67-I; HC 489-I. The 'widespread dread of the separation of man and wife' was also given as one reason for the 'universal' 'aversion' of the Work House – see C Booth (1894) *The Aged Poor in England and Wales* cited in P Thane *Old Age in English History*, OUP, 2000, p176.

257   Although there appear to be no directly relevant Strasbourg judgments, *Kutzner v Germany* (2002) 35 EHRR 35 at [76] stressed the positive duty to take measures to facilitate family reunification, and see also *G v E and others* [2010] EWHC 621 (Fam) (26 March 2010) where the right extended to a former foster carer now providing adult care and *A local authority v MM and KM* [2007] EWHC 2003 (Fam), (2008) 11 CCLR 119 where the Court required the authority to make arrangements to facilitate a long term relationship between the disabled person and her boyfriend observing (para 165) that 'the local authority cannot in this connection seek to avoid its positive obligations [under Article 8] by seeking to toll the bell of scarce resources'.

258   See eg *Re Jennifer Connor* [2004] NICA 45, (2005) 8 CCLR 328 at [23].

whether there is a need for the husband and wife to see each other regularly – and in normal circumstances the conclusion would be that this is a 'critical' need. In determining what is an acceptable distance between the wife's home and the care home placement, regard will have to be paid to her mobility and access to transport. If there is no suitable care home within easy reach of the wife, the local authority may have to make arrangements for the wife's transport. If, however, a suitable care home is available close by, but above the local authority's normal fees ceiling, this home may have to be funded, without top up, since the authority is merely meeting the disabled person's assessed need (and not paying for something more than is required – see para 7.111 below).

3.220　　Where there is real doubt as to whether someone can remain safely in their own home, even with a support package, there is a need for a sensitive balancing of their attachment to home and likelihood of deterioration as a result of an unwanted move on the one hand and, on the other, the risks that attach to staying put. This may arise, for example, where there is a risk of self-neglect or where an older spouse or partner providing essential care also has fragile health. A proportionate response involves the recognition that a reasonable degree of risk may be appropriate, as Munby J (as he then was) put it 'what good is it making someone safer if it merely makes them miserable?'[259]

3.221　　The importance of locational factors is not confined to assessments of married or cohabiting persons. The SAP guidance at Annex F (see above) specifically lists location as a sub-domain that must be addressed in the assessment process and the local government ombudsman has strongly suggested that a failure to address such a need (if identified as an eligible need) would amount to maladministration.[260] In *R v Sutton LBC ex p Tucker*[261] the Rubella impaired applicant's fundamental relationships were with her close family who lived in London. The local authority proposed a care home placement in Birmingham, but the family, clinicians and other experts considered that this would not be viable since she needed to be close to her family. In this case, location was therefore an assessed need and had to be met.

The written record of the assessment

3.222　There is no statutory requirement that assessments be recorded in writing, although in practice all social services authorities have standard assessment forms. These are generally completed in manuscript and then keyed into the authority's IT system. The Prioritising Needs guidance is silent on the right of service users to a copy of their assessments, although it states that a decision not to provide any help following assessment or to withdraw help following a review should be supported by written reasons

---

259　*Re MM (and adult)* [2009] 1 FLR 443, para 120 – and see also para 17.38 below.
260　Complaint no 05/C/13158 against North Yorkshire County Council, 24 July 2007.
261　(1997–98) 1 CCLR 251, QBD.

given to the individual[262] The 1991 practice guidance, however, states (at para 3.54) that a 'copy of the assessment of needs should normally be shared with the potential service user, any representative of that user and all other people who have agreed to provide a service. Except where no intervention is deemed necessary, this record will normally be combined with a written care plan.' The SAP guidance[263] is specific in this respect, stating:

> All key decisions and issues relating to assessment, eligibility and service provision should be put in writing, or other appropriate formats, and a copy given to the older person. For older people who go on to receive services, these decisions and issues will be summarised in their care plan or statement of service delivery.

3.223   Where a service user has difficulty obtaining a copy of his or her assessment and/or care plan, a formal request can be made under the Data Protection Act 1998 (see para 25.13 below).

Disputed service provision decisions

3.224   The 1990 community care reforms made social services the 'gate keepers' of the community care regime: ultimately it is the local authority that decides what a person's 'eligible needs' are and what they are not. Judges are not expert in the practice of social work and so must defer to their professional expertise – even when the decisions they reach appear harsh, provided they are arrived at lawfully.

3.225   As has been noted above (see para 3.6 above), social workers are subjected to intense scrutiny – primarily to ensure that their decisions do not place undue pressure on local authority budgets, notwithstanding the 1991 practice guidance that warns against 'trimming the assessment of need to fit available provision'.[264] On one level this is entirely reasonable, and on another it can lead to assessments being 'service' or 'budget' driven – in effect social workers being so constrained by organisational pressures that they do not assess individuals as needing services which are not available or which might exceed the available budget. The introduction of resource allocation schemes is likely to exacerbate this pressure (see chapter 4)

3.226   Given that judicial review is a blunt legal instrument and that courts are seldom prepared to consider a service provision decision '*Wednesbury*'[265] unreasonable[266] (see para 26.196 below), the question arises as to how errant authorities can be called to account – particularly if their

---

262 Prioritising Needs guidance, para 106, see also ; UFSAMC 2002 policy guidance, para 7.21.
263 SAP 2003 policy guidance annex E p19.
264 As cited in *R v Islington LBC ex p Rixon* (1997–98) 1 CCLR 119 at 129B per Sedley J, QBD.
265 *Associated Provincial Picture Houses v Wednesbury Corporation* [1948] 1 KB 223, CA.
266 Although not invariably – see eg *R v Sutton LBC ex p Tucker* (1997–98) 1 CCLR 251 at 275J, QBD.

complaints investigations are insufficiently robust or well informed to address such problems.

3.227 The evidence suggests that both the courts and ombudsmen adopt a variety of public law mechanisms to find fault with the decision-making process when they apprehend an improbably austere service provision decision. In general, the harsher the apparent service provision decision, the greater the courts/ombudsmen's insistence on 'due process' – particularly on compliance with policy and practice guidance. This approach is sometimes referred to as the anxious scrutiny test[267] (see para 26.197 below) – the more a decision engages fundamental rights, the 'more anxiously' will the courts scrutinise the procedure by which it was reached.

3.228 By way of example, *R v Birmingham CC ex p Killigrew*[268] concerned an applicant with severe disabilities whose condition (multiple sclerosis) was deteriorating. Her husband and main carer was also a disabled person. At the end of 1997 she was assessed as requiring 12 hours' continuous care each day seven days a week. The council undertook a manual handling assessment in 1998 and decided that she required two care assistants to move her, rather than the one that had previously done this. A community care reassessment then occurred, as a result of which the council proposed to reduce the day care from 12 to 3.5 hours. Hooper J held that no such reduction could occur without compliance with the 1990 policy guidance which in his view required (1) detailed reasons as to why 12 hours were no longer required and (2) up-to-date medical evidence – which the local authority had failed to obtain (1990 policy guidance, paras 3.47 onwards). The same approach can be identified in cases concerning disabled children (see chapter 23)

3.229 Where a local authority seeks to defend what appears to be a harsh or inequitable decision, the reasons it gives for the decision, as well as the process, will be scrutinised. In *R (Goldsmith) v Wandsworth LBC*[269] the court found it almost impossible to understand who in the authority had made the various decisions in issue or how they had been reached. It concluded that virtually every aspect of the council's decision making process was flawed – including its failure to share information with the applicant's daughter, its denial of her right to attend a hearing and make submissions, its failure to keep minutes at that hearing and its mistaken belief as to the evidential value of a medical opinion.

Reassessment and reviews

3.230 Councils have a general public law duty to ensure that the community care needs of service users are kept under review. As the local government ombudsman has observed:

267 See eg *R v Ministry of Defence ex p Smith* [1996] QB 517 at 554.
268 (2000) 3 CCLR 109: see also, eg, *R v Lambeth LBC ex p K* (2000) 3 CCLR 141 where the court quashed a budget driven harsh service provision decision on the basis that the council had not followed the 1990 policy guidance and had confused 'needs' and 'services'.
269 [2004] EWCA Civ 1170, (2004) 7 CCLR 472.

As an individual's need for community care services will vary over time, the duties placed on councils are continuous. Councils should therefore provide for the review of assessments and service delivery decisions.[270]

3.231   This obligation is underpinned by the Prioritising Needs guidance[271] which requires that:

The frequency of reviews should be proportionate to the circumstances of the individual but there should be an initial review within three months of help first being provided or major changes made to current support plans. Thereafter, reviews should be scheduled at least annually or more often as is necessary. Councils should also consider conducting reviews when requested to do so by the service user, their carer or service provider.

3.232   Reviews should:[272]

• Establish whether the outcomes identified in the support plan are being met through current arrangements;
• Consider whether the needs and circumstances of the service user and/or their carer(s) have changed;
• Support people to review their personal goals and consider what changes if any should be made to the support plan to better facilitate the achievement of agreed outcomes;
• Ensure that the risk assessment recorded in the care plan is up to date and identify any further action that needs to be taken to address issues relating to risk;
• Demonstrate a partnership approach across agencies and with the service user as well as their family and friends if they choose;
• Support people to strengthen their informal support networks;
• Support people to increase their productive role in their community; and
• Help determine the service user's continued eligibility for support.

3.233   The Prioritising Needs guidance requires local authorities to be flexible in how they carry out reviews, depending on the views of the individual, who must be consulted. However, the implication is that reviews should be face to face and should generally involve all relevant parties: for instance, carers; the service user's advocate; the purchasers and the providers of the care services. The outcome of reviews should be recorded in writing and shared with the service user.[273]

3.234   The local government ombudsman has stressed the importance of reviews being 'proactive and frequent' and that it will be maladministration to stick rigidly to a predetermined review cycle when changed circumstances demand an earlier review.[274] She has also stressed the need

270 Complaint no 02/B/10226 against Cambridgeshire CC, July 6 2004.
271 Prioritising Needs guidance, para 144; UFSAMC 2002 policy guidance, paras 2.54 onwards.
272 Prioritising Needs guidance, para 142; see also UFSAMC 2002 policy guidance, paras 2.44–2.51.
273 Prioritising Needs guidance, paras 142 and 145.
274 Complaint no 05/A/00880 against Essex CC, 16 January 2006, para 56 and see also complaint no 02/B/10226 against Cambridgeshire CC, 6 July 2004.

for councils to devote 'adequate resources' to this function to ensure that they adequately monitor contract performance.[275]

3.235 Where a local authority decides to reduce significantly the level of services provided as a result of a reassessment, it must provide rational and cogent reasons for this alteration[276] and before making any reduction it must provide the service user with an opportunity for the decision to be reviewed.[277] The ombudsman has commented that a social services justification for the withdrawal of services – namely the 'need to prioritise' – suggested that 'a comparative judgment was being made rather than a consideration of whether the individual's need had changed'.[278] A failure to inform carers by letter of a material change to a service user's care plan will generally constitute maladministration.[279]

3.236 Where a local authority settles a complaint by agreeing to reassess, the reassessment should do more than 'go through the motions'. In *Banks v Secretary of State for the Environment*[280] Sullivan J gave guidance on what such a review should entail, advising that one of the functions of a review procedure must be to 'give some degree of assurance' that there will be a genuine reconsideration: and that in order to dispel user suspicion, it should as far as possible involve review by another (and preferably more senior) official who has not been connected with the decision under review or given an opportunity to comment upon it.

Law Commission proposals

3.237 The Law Commission proposals for adult social care legislation[281] do not include any significant changes to the assessment duty as such. They do include proposals that:

- Assessments must focus on outcomes (goals identified by the individual) as well as needs
- There should be a duty on the Secretary of State for Health and the Welsh Assembly Ministers to make regulations prescribing the assessment process, including the circumstances in which a specialist assessment is required and the details of the eligibility criteria. Regulations may also provide for a number of other aspects of assessments including timescales, who can carry out assessments, considerations

---

275 Complaint no 03/C/17141 against Blackpool BC, 23 February 2006 and see also complaint no 01/B/00305 against Cambridgeshire CC, 9 July 2002 complaint no 05/A/00880 against Essex CC, 16 January 2006 and complaint no 05/C/6420 against Sheffield City Council, 20 February 2007.
276 *R (LB) v Newham LBC* [2004] EWHC 2503.
277 Complaint nos 02/C/14235, 02/C/15396, 02/C/15397 and 02/C/15503 against Derbyshire CC, 24 June 2004.
278 Complaint nos 02/C/14235, 02/C/15396, 02/C/15397 and 02/C/15503 against Derbyshire CC, 24 June 2004 reported at page 99 of Local Government Ombudsman Digest of Cases 2004/05.
279 Complaint no 02/B/03622 against Harrow LBC, 22 June 2004.
280 [2004] EWHC 416 (Admin): a non-community care case.
281 Law Commission (2011) *Adult Social Care*, Law Com No 326 HC 941.

to which the assessment should have regard and may specify a form of self-assessment.

- There should be an express requirement to apply the eligibility criteria with an enforceable duty to meet eligible needs
- The proposed Code of Practice should provide guidance on how self-assessment should be integrated into the assessment process and on delegation and the required degree os local authority oversight.

CHAPTER 4

The care planning process and the delivery of services

continued

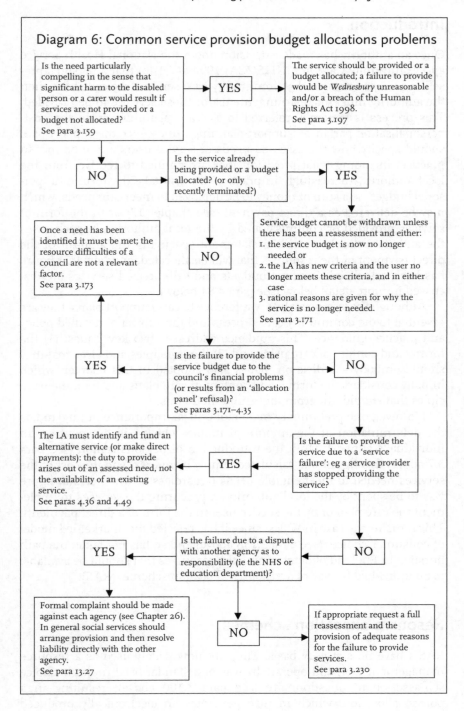

Diagram 6: Common service provision budget allocations problems

Is the need particularly compelling in the sense that significant harm to the disabled person or a carer would result if services are not provided or a budget not allocated?
See para 3.159

YES → The service should be provided or a budget allocated; a failure to provide would be *Wednesbury* unreasonable and/or a breach of the Human Rights Act 1998.
See para 3.197

NO → Is the service already being provided or a budget allocated? (or only recently terminated?) → **YES**

Service budget cannot be withdrawn unless there has been a reassessment and either:
1. the service budget is now no longer needed or
2. the LA has new criteria and the user no longer meets these criteria, and in either case
3. rational reasons are given for why the service is no longer needed.
See para 3.171

Once a need has been identified it must be met; the resource difficulties of a council are not a relevant factor.
See para 3.173

NO

YES ← Is the failure to provide the service budget due to the council's financial problems (or results from an 'allocation panel' refusal)?
See paras 3.171–4.35 → **NO**

The LA must identify and fund an alternative service (or make direct payments): the duty to provide arises out of an assessed need, not the availability of an existing service.
See paras 4.36 and 4.49

← **YES** ← Is the failure to provide the service due to a 'service failure': eg a service provider has stopped providing the service?

YES ← Is the failure due to a dispute with another agency as to responsibility (ie the NHS or education department)? ← **NO**

Formal complaint should be made against each agency (see Chapter 26). In general social services should arrange provision and then resolve liability directly with the other agency.
See para 13.27

NO

If appropriate request a full reassessment and the provision of adequate reasons for the failure to provide services.
See para 3.230

Introduction

4.1   Once an authority has made a decision under the National Health Service and Community Care Act (NHSCCA) 1990 s47(1)(b) that a person's presenting needs are such that community care services are called for, then the authority must make arrangements for those services to be provided. This process is generally referred to as 'care planning' or, in the post-personalisation parlance, 'support planning'. In essence the support plan should specify how the assessed needs of service users are to be met in practice, including what provision they are entitled to receive from the local authority. Increasingly in practice this will take the form of a 'personal budget', ie a sum of money to be deployed to meet care needs, which may be delivered as a direct payment (see chapter 12) or in the form of services provided or commissioned by the local authority. In such cases the authority should provide a statement specifying the amount of the direct payment or the resources that will be allocated, and how that figure has been calculated. Personal budgets and self-directed services are discussed in more detail below (see para 4.84 below).

4.2   Although there is no statutory reference to care/support plans, they are essential to the community care process and the subject of detailed policy and practice guidance. This guidance addresses two key issues: (1) the format and content of care plans and (2) the principles and aims that they should embody – a division that is also adopted in this chapter, which initially considers the format and content of care plans and then the principles that should underpin them, and their aims.

4.3   However, one preliminary matter, of critical importance in England, is the determination of the amount of money which will be spent on an individual's support. Until the introduction of personalisation (see para 3.7 above) this figure was calculated simply by reference to the cost of the services needed to meet eligible needs (regardless of whether that figure was to be spent by the local authority in procuring the services to implement the care plan or by the service user in the form of a direct payment). This remains the case in Wales, since it has rejected the 'market-led model of consumer choice' (see para 3.158 above) and so has not taken the path pursued in England of determining the resources that should be available to an individual by way of a 'resource allocation scheme' (RAS).

Resource allocation schemes

4.4   RAS's have no statutory basis. They are now widely used as a resource management tool, and operate by way of a standardised multiple choice self-assessment questionnaire (see para 3.100 above), resulting in a points' allocation, which in turn generates an electronically produced figure for an individual's personal budget. This figure is based often on statistical norms. At best such a RAS calculation will produce an approximate indication of the amount of money to be allocated to an individual's support package. This is generally referred to as an 'indicative amount'.

4.5   The Association of Directors of Adult Social Services (ADASS) in conjunction with Department of Health has developed a draft Common Resource Allocation Framework which includes a draft RAS and advice to support its implementation:[1] in relation to this material the Prioritising needs policy guidance advises (para 131) it 'can be voluntarily adopted by local authorities if they so choose' and that:

> While it is very unlikely that a single national RAS will be implemented across the country, given the wide variation in local circumstances, the Department of Health is committed to working with local authorities to take forward the learning from emerging systems. An evaluation of the ADASS model was published in October 2009 after the councils in the development group had used the system for six months.

4.6   The scheme is legally problematic. If the starting point is an allocation of a capped sum as a personal budget, in other words an entitlement to a given amount, then the needs-led approach which is a fundamental tenet of the current community care legal framework, frequently endorsed by the courts and ombudsmen, is critically undermined.[2]

4.7   Such a 'capped' arrangement was at the heart of the *R (JL) v London Borough of Islington*[3] proceedings, which concerned a policy of allocating points to identify a band for the provision of a personal budget (in this case to support a disabled child and her mother). Black J, in finding the process unlawful, found it:

> hard to see how a system such as this one, where points are attributed to a standard list of factors, leading to banded relief with a fixed upper limit, can be sufficiently sophisticated to amount to a genuine assessment of an individual child's needs. There will be times when, fortuitously, the needs assessed by such a system will coincide with the real needs of the family, but it is difficult to have any confidence in that occurring sufficiently frequently to justify the use of eligibility criteria on their own.

4.8   Given the significance of such RAS's in practice, the Prioritising Needs guidance has surprisingly little to say on this question, but it does affirm the primacy of ensuring that eligible needs are met: essentially that any 'indicative amount' must be a starting point for a discussion about meeting a person's eligible needs, and no more:

> Calculating what resources should be made available to individuals should not detract from a council's duty to determine eligibility following assessment and to meet eligible needs. Rather a RAS should be applied as a means of giving an approximate indication of what it may reasonably cost to meet a person's particular needs according to their individual circumstances. It is important for councils to ensure that their resource

1   The *Common Resource allocation Framework* revised version (June 2010) and associated documentation can be accessed at www.thinklocalactpersonal.org.uk/Browse/ SDSandpersonalbudgets/Resourceallocationsystems/?parent=2671&child=6376.
2   For an analysis of these concerns see L Clements 'Social Care Law Developments: A sideways look at personalisation and tightening eligibility criteria' (2011) *Elder Law Journal* Volume 1, pp 47–52.
3   [2009] EWHC 458 (Admin), (2009) 12 CCLR 322.

allocation process is sufficiently flexible to allow for someone's individual circumstances to be taken into account when determining the amount of resources he or she is allocated in a personal budget[4].

The duty to give reasons for the amount allocated

4.9   A system that is dependent on statistical norms informing the electronic allocation of personal budgets does not provide a ready means for an individual disabled person or carer to understand whether and how their assessed support needs are to be met. It is not a transparent system; in fact it is the antithesis of a personalised approach to community care.

4.10   It is unsurprising then that in *R (Savva) v Kensington and Chelsea*[5] the High Court, while accepting that there was nothing wrong in principle with a RAS scheme provided the figure it generated was simply a starting point (ie an indicative tool) rejected the local authority's argument that there was no duty to give reasons to explain how the personal budget had been arrived at in an individual case:

> . . . without being able to properly understand the use made of the RAS, the service user and anyone acting on her behalf, is left totally in the dark as to whether the monetary value of £170.45 is adequate to meet the assessed need of a 28 point score. The process of conversion made by the Panel is not explained to the service user. It should have been underpinned by an evidential base, and it was not.[6]

4.11   In moving from a service provision model of care support to an outcomes-based model (see para 3.166 above), the link to particular services to meet particular needs at a particular price is potentially lost. Thus the question of how to ascertain whether the amount of personal budget allocated will meet the eligible assessed needs of the individual has to be resolved by some consistent benchmark. For the Court of Appeal, in upholding the above first instance decision, this was unequivocally the amount and cost of services Mrs Savva had been assessed as needing:

> In many cases, the provision of adequate reasons could be achieved with reasonable brevity. In the present case, I would consider it adequate to list the required services and assumed timings (as was actually done in the FACE assessment), together with the assumed hourly cost. That would not be unduly onerous. I appreciate that some recipients require more complicated arrangements which would call for more expansive reasoning but if that is what fairness requires, it must be done.[7]

4.12   The respondent local authority in *Savva* argued that the duty to give reasons should be satisfied by notice in the decision letter that reasons would be available on request. Although Maurice Kay LJ wondered obiter whether the administrative burden for the local authority would be lessened by providing reasons only on request, he nonetheless held that:

4   Prioritising Needs guidance, para 30.
5   [2010] EWHC 414 (Admin), (2010) 13 CCLR 227.
6   [2010] EWHC 414 (Admi), (2010) 13 CCLR 227 at para 48.
7   [2010] EWCA Civ 1209, (2011) 14 CCLR 75 per Maurice Kay LJ at para 21.

It seems to me to be a matter of common sense that, in a case such as this, if a recipient is made a timely offer of the provision of reasons on request, the court would reject an application for judicial review based on a failure to provide reasons where no such request had been made (para 23).

4.13 The judicial concern for the 'administrative burden' that would be placed on councils in this context is perplexing for at least two reasons. Firstly, the opaque bureaucratic algorithms that underpin most RAS systems are entirely of councils' own making: having no basis in law, and bearing little or no resemblance to the original ideas of those propounding their use.[8] If a council decides to discharge its statutory obligation by resort to a system of labyrinthine complexity, it is difficult to see how this self imposed 'administrative burden' can then be pleaded as a reason for not explaining the process (particularly as in the *Savva* case, where on analysis, it seems the council itself was unclear as to the logic of its own process). Secondly, such concern seems to ignore the inequality of arms: a point made (in a slightly different context) by Carnwath J in *R v Gloucestershire CC ex p RADAR*,[9] concerning the adequacy of telling members of the vulnerable, poorly informed and unassertive 'community care' client group that they might request a reassessment if they wanted one:

> In some areas of law that might be an adequate response, where those affected can be assumed to be capable of looking after their own interests, and where silence in response to an offer can be treated as acceptance or acquiescence. However, that approach cannot be and is not valid in the present context.[10]

4.14 A differently constituted Court of Appeal, dealing with issues similar to those in *Savva*, decided that while there has to be a 'rational link between the needs and assessed direct payments . . . there does not have to be a finite absolute mathematical link'[11]. The Court's opinion, in *R (KM) v Cambridgeshire CC*, was that the list of services, the assumed timings with the assumed hourly costs required by the *Savva* decision (see para 4.11 above) did not necessitate such a link. The rationale for this is 'because the nature of the RAS, which it is legitimate to use as a starting point, does not admit of such a calculation or result.'[12]

4.15 This decision is difficult to reconcile with that in *Savva*, particularly as *Savva* envisaged more rather than less explanatory detail in a complex case, which KM was – a young man with musical abilities, but with complex sensory, physical and mental impairments and a learning disability, who required help with all aspects of his daily life. If *Savva* is correctly decided, then the lawfulness of a RAS-generated personal budget figure stands or falls as a result of a process of conversion from a sum of money

---

8   J Dunning (2011) 'How bureaucracy is derailing personalisation', *Community Care*, 31 May 2011 (updated 21 July 2011).
9   (1997–98) 1 CCLR 476, QBD.
10 (1997–98) 1 CCLR 476 at 482D, QBD.
11 *R (KM) v Cambridgeshire CC* [2011] EWCA Civ 682, (2011) 14 CCLR 83, per President of the Queen's Bench Division at [23].
12 *R (KM) v Cambridgeshire CC* [2011] EWCA Civ 682, (2011) 14 CCLR 83 at [24].

to a set of costed services to meet the eligible needs of the individual. That is the reality test which *Savva* required in order to fulfil the duty to give reasons and to provide sufficient transparency to local authority decision-making to meet public law requirements of fairness.

Equality issues

4.16   The RAS value of points 'scored' on the assessment questionnaire depends on local costs and, in the case of some local authorities, the financial value attributed to each point varies as between service user groups, typically with learning disabilities at the top and either older people or those with a mental illness at the bottom. It is doubtful whether such a system is compliant with equalities legislation, in particular with section 149 of the Equality Act 2010, the 'public sector equality duty' (see chapter 2).

4.17   Awarding lower value points to older people is an expression of a blanket assumption that older people's needs require fewer resources than their younger counterparts with equivalent disabling conditions. While this might be true in individual cases and could be reflected in the needs assessment, it is unlikely to be justifiable as a blanket assumption informing a policy for the allocation of resources. Local authorities devising their schemes must have regard, among other things, to eliminating discrimination and to promoting equality of opportunity.[13] The latter includes minimising disadvantage and encouraging participation in public life or in any other activity in which participation, in this case of older people, is disproportionately low.[14]

4.18   Similar arguments arise in the context of downgrading the resources available to meet the needs of people with a mental illness. Although the argument would be based on discrimination on the ground of disability as compared with others sharing the same protected characteristic (namely people with physical or learning disabilities), this would not preclude a breach of the duty (as shown in the case of *R (JL) v Islington LBC* at para 4.7 above).

4.19   If the assessment process that generates points is sufficiently thorough to ensure a comprehensive assessment then a policy that attributes the same value per point scored regardless of the generic type of disability may survive legal scrutiny.[15] However, this might not be the case if the result of such equalisation was, for example, to reduce the level of provision across the board for people with a learning disability, this group being currently the highest scorers. In *R (JL) v Islington LBC* the local authority fell foul of the disability equality duty[16] (one of the pre-cursors to

---

13   Equality Act 2010 s149 (1)(a) and (b).
14   Equality Act 2010 s149 (3)(a) and (c).
15   However, a policy of treating people who have material differences, in the same way is also capable of violating the equality principles – see eg *Thlimmenos v Greece* (2000) Application no 34369/97, (2000) 31 EHRR 411 and *Šečić v Croatia* (2007) Application no 40116/02.
16   Disability Discrimination Act 1995 s49A.

the current public equality duty) in circumstances where it revised its eligibility criteria for children's services with the express purpose of reducing provision to the most profoundly disabled children in order to redistribute funds to those with lesser impairments:

> The result of the ceiling on support might be to deprive a child of features of his support which were critical to his functioning, especially if he was particularly needy. The saving in hours may have enabled the local authority to improve the lot of another, perhaps less disabled child and secured greater equality of opportunity for him but that does not remove the disadvantage to the more disabled child.[17]

Care/support plan – format and content

4.20   The original 1990 policy guidance[18] requires that:

> Once needs have been assessed, the services to be provided or arranged and the objectives of any intervention should be agreed in the form of a care plan (at para 3.24).

and that:

> Decisions on service provision should include clear agreement about what is going to be done, by whom and by when, with clearly identified points of access to each of the relevant agencies for the service user, carers and for the care manager (at para 3.26).

4.21   The 2010 Prioritising Needs guidance (at para 121) provides greater detail, requiring support plans to be structured in such a way that they address the following eight key requirements:

> Councils should agree a written record of the support plan with the individual which should include the following:
> - A note of the eligible needs identified during assessment;
> - Agreed outcomes and how support will be organised to meet those outcomes;
> - A risk assessment including any actions to be taken to manage identified risks;
> - Contingency plans to manage emergency changes;
> - Any financial contributions the individual is assessed to pay;
> - Support which carers and others are willing and able to provide;
> - Support to be provided to address needs identified through the carers assessment, where appropriate; and
> - A review date.

4.22   In Wales, Unified and Fair System for Assessing and Managing Care (UFSAMC) 2002, sets out a fairly similar list of requirements for a 'personal plan of care' (at para 2.66):

> - A summary of the assessed needs and associated risks including how they will be managed.

17 [2009] EWHC 458 (Admin), (2009) 12 CCLR 322 per Black J at para 117.
18 *Community care in the next decade and beyond: policy guidance*, HMSO, 1990.

- Outline the contribution of family and others and address the needs that carers have in carrying out their caring role.
- The eligibility decision and basis for that decision.
- A clear statement of the objectives of providing help and care and the preferred outcomes for users.
- Details of the services to be provided together with contact details of providers.
- Record of unmet need and reason.
- Arrangements for co-ordinating and monitoring the personal plan together with contact details.
- A review date

4.23   There is further considerable guidance on care planning, both in the 1991 practice guidance and in the SAP guidance.[19]

4.24   In addition to complying with practice and policy guidance, support plans must also satisfy the demands of public law and sound administrative practice. Service users need to know, for instance, what it is that they are entitled to receive and how this decision has been reached. It follows that support plans must spell out with sufficient detail all the relevant aspects of the arrangements that are to be made – not unlike a schedule of works – such as the frequency of services,[20] the actual services that will be provided[21] and so on. As the court noted in *R (J) v Caerphilly CBC*[22] (a case concerning a disabled child – see para 23.23 below) such plans must 'to set out the operational objectives with sufficient detail – including detail of the "how, who, what and when" – to enable the care plan itself to be used as a means of checking whether or not those objectives are being met'.

4.25   Where services are not directly provided by the social services department, the details of the support plan should be spelt out in the contract with the provider as part of the service user specification. It is this detail that should be monitored as part of contract compliance in order to ensure the user receives the services that are in the support plan.[23] The move to self-directed support (see para 4.84 below) does not undermine the need for an appropriate level of specificity in the support plan.

4.26   The demands of public law were highlighted in *R v Islington LBC ex p Rixon*[24] where Sedley J accepted the respondent's submission that

---

19 See *Care Management and Assessment – a practitioners' guide*, HMSO, 1991, para 4.37; HSC 2002/001 and LAC (2002) 1 *Guidance on the Single Assessment Process for Older People*, 2002, Annexe E pp24–25, in Wales, UFSAMC, para 6.22. This more detailed guidance can be found in the 4th edition of this book paras 4.6–4.8.
20 Complaint no 03/C/16371 against Stockton-on-Tees BC, 18 January 2005.
21 *R (LH and MH) v Lambeth LBC* [2006] EWHC 1190 (Admin), (2006) 9 CCLR 515.
22 [2005] EWHC 586 (Admin), (2005) 8 CCLR 255.
23 The ombudsman has criticised councils for not ensuring that services specified in the contract have actually been provided (in two of the cases the service user died). Complaint nos 05/C/06420 against Sheffield City Council, 20 February 2007; 05/C/08592 against Liverpool City Council, 17 January 2007 and 03/C/17141 against Blackpool, 23 February 2006.
24 (1997–98) 1 CCLR 119 at 128, QBD.

'nowhere in the legislation is a care plan, by that or any other name required' and that 'a care plan is nothing more than a clerical record of what has been decided and what is planned'. In his view, however, this state of affairs:

> ... far from marginalising the care plan, places it at the centre of any scrutiny of the local authority's due discharge of its functions. As paragraph 3.24 of the [1990] policy guidance indicates, a care plan is the means by which the local authority assembles the relevant information and applies it to the statutory ends, and hence affords good evidence to any inquirer of the due discharge of its statutory duties. It cannot, however, be quashed as if it were a self-implementing document.

4.27   In this context, in *R (B) v Cornwall CC*[25] Hickinbottom observed that 'Sedley J there identifies one important purpose of a care plan, namely the application of the statutory objectives to a particular case on the basis of the information the authority have gathered'.

4.28   In assessing whether the care plan produced by the authority was fit for purpose, Sedley J paid particular regard to the local authority's obligation to 'act under'[26] the relevant policy guidance and to take into account the relevant practice guidance. When subjected to such an analysis, the care plan was deficient: in his opinion:

> The care plan ... does not comply either with the [1990] policy guidance or the [1991] practice guidance issued by central government. There has been a failure to comply with the guidance contained in paragraph 3.24 of the [1990] policy document to the effect that following assessment of need, the objectives of social services intervention as well as the services to be provided or arranged should be agreed in the form of a care plan. ...

> The care plan also fails at a number of points to comply with the [1991] practice guidance on, for example, the contents of a care plan, the specification of its objectives, the achievement of agreement on implementation on all those involved, leeway for contingencies and the identification and feeding back of assessed but still unmet need.

> In such a situation I am unable to [agree] that the failures to follow the policy guidance and practice guidance are beyond the purview of the court.

4.29   In *R v Sutton LBC ex p Tucker* Hidden J was equally critical of the council's care plan, stating:

> There are no stated overall objectives in terms of long term obligations, carers' obligations or service providers, there are no criteria for the measurement of objectives because the objectives themselves are not recorded in any care plan. There are no costings, no long term options, no residential care options considered, there are no recorded points of difference, there is no reference to unmet need and there is no reference to a next date of review.

4.30   The importance that the courts attach to policy and practice guidance in

---

25 [2009] EWHC 491 (Admin), (2009) 12 CCLR 381, para 10.
26 See para 1.49 above.
27 (1997–98) 1 CCLR 251, QBD.

this area is illustrated by the relief ordered in the *Tucker* case, which included:

> [First] an order of Mandamus to provide within 21 days a care plan which complies, as far as possible, with the [1991] practitioners' guide and with paragraph 3.25 of the [1990] policy guidance. Secondly, a declaration that the respondent has acted unlawfully and in breach of paragraphs 3.24 and 3.41[27] of the policy guidance in failing to make a service provision decision under section 47(1)(b) of the National Health Service and Community Care Act 1990, as to the long term placement of the applicant. Thirdly, a declaration that the respondent has acted unlawfully and contrary to paragraph 3.25 of the policy guidance in failing to produce a lawful care plan.

Care/support plans and 'unmet need'

4.31   The 1991 practice guidance advised that unmet need be recorded in a care plan and at the time some controversy arose as to whether the concept of 'unmet need' was lawful. Its legality (as a concept) depends, however, upon how it is defined. It is included as one component of the personal plan of care in Wales (see para 4.22 above) and the Welsh guidance[28] defines unmet need as follows:

> . . . presented needs that are not evaluated as eligible needs or where eligible needs are met but an alternative more appropriate/desirable service should ideally be available.

4.32   This explanation illustrates the difficulty, since it incorporates two distinct categories of need, namely (1) presenting needs that are not assessed as eligible needs; and (2) eligible needs that cannot be meet in the most appropriate way. To this list can be added a third, namely (3) where an eligible need does not have to be met be a local authority because it is currently being met informally – for example, by a carer. These are considered separately below.

Presenting needs that are not assessed as eligible needs

4.33   As detailed above (see para 3.91) a person may express the view that he or she has a 'need' for a variety of community care services, but on assessment the local authority may decide that these needs are not sufficiently substantial to entitle the person to such support. These are needs that do not meet the authority's eligibility criteria. On this definition therefore, unmet needs are those needs which the individual (or others) consider of

---

28   See also *R (JF) v Hackney LBC* [2010] EWHC 3130 (Admin), para 39, where Calvert-Smith J made a mandatory order requiring the production of a lawful care plan within 14 days and provision of a range of services within 28 and 56 days.

29   Which provides (among other things) that 'it is most undesirable that anyone should be admitted to, or remain in, hospital when their care could be more appropriately provided elsewhere'.

30   UFSAMC 2002 policy guidance annex 9 p101.

relevance (ie 'presenting needs') but which on assessment are not deemed sufficiently important to be 'eligible needs'.

Eligible needs the authority cannot meet in the most appropriate way

4.34 Where a presenting need is assessed as an 'eligible need' (see para 3.149 above), the authority is obliged to provide services to meet that need. If, for one reason or another, the authority finds itself unable to provide services to meet that need, it could be categorised as 'unmet' need. In certain situations this will be unlawful, but not always, since there may be a variety of reasons why the need is not being met. These include, for example, budgetary difficulties and physical or human resource shortages – which are considered separately below:

Budgetary difficulties

4.35 Once a need has been assessed as an eligible need, services must be provided to address that need. If such services are not provided because the local authority has a budgetary difficulty, this is unlawful: accordingly unmet need in this context is not permissible (see para 3.175 above). The same principle applies to direct payments and personal budgets.

Physical or human resource difficulties

4.36 In certain situations, an assessed need will not be capable of being met, not because the local authority lacks the financial resources, but simply because there is no readily available service to meet that need. Typically this will be because such a service does not exist. In such cases the court will accept that an assessed need is 'unmet' provided determined steps are being taken to resolve the problem: in essence that the local authority is doing the best that it can do.[29] Thus in *R v Sutton LBC ex p Tucker*[30] the applicant was assessed as needing a specialist facility in or around the Sutton area of London – which at that time did not exist. The local authority was not held to have acted unlawfully by not meeting the need immediately: its unlawful action lay in its failure to take prompt steps to commission the necessary services.

4.37 In a Northern Irish case, *LW: Re Judicial Review*[31], the court held that where a particular respite care facility is unavailable, a reasonable authority will take action to identify alternative provision. If due to administrative inertia this does not happen and the authority advances 'no convincing evidence of reasonable efforts' to discharge its continuing statutory duty then, whether 'viewed through the prism of an absolute (i.e.

31 See eg *R v Exeter City Council ex p Gliddon and Draper* [1985] 1 All ER 493 (a housing case) where the court held that what is suitable in the short term might not be suitable in the long term.
32 (1997–98) 1 CCLR 251, QBD.
33 [2010] NIQB 62, 19 May 2010.

unqualified) duty of provision or a duty to be measured by the criterion of reasonableness' it will be held to be in breach of its statutory duty.[32]

Eligible needs met by third parties

4.38   The third category of 'need' that could be considered to be one that is 'unmet', is one where the disabled person would suffer harm of the required level, if the support was not provided, but the support is not required from the local authority because some third party (ie a carer[33]) is currently providing the necessary support.

4.39   In this situation an eligible need exists, but it does not 'call for' a response from the authority because someone else is attending to it. Where this is the case the support plan should record it as an assessed need, rather than an unmet need, because (a) this is the case, and (b) if for some reason the third party ceased to provide the service, there needs to be a record that this need is a 'need' that would then 'call for' a local authority service response. This important point is addressed (partially) by the 2010 Prioritising Needs guidance (at para 94), which states:

> Whilst determination of an individual's need for assistance should take account of the support which carers, family members, friends and neighbours are willing and able to offer, the determination of presenting needs should identify all community care needs, regardless of whether and how they are being met. . . .

Recording unmet need

4.40   The Prioritising Needs guidance (unlike the Welsh guidance[34] and the 1991 practice guidance[35]) is coy about the requirement to record 'unmet need' on individual assessments – saying only that 'Councils should work with individuals to identify the outcomes they wish to achieve, and to identify where unmet needs are preventing the realisation of such outcomes' (para 47) and that 'information about an individual's presenting needs and related circumstances should be established and recorded' (para 52). Councils are required (para 156) to monitor 'which presenting needs are evaluated as eligible needs and which are not'. This is particularly unhelpful. In effect it means that in order to assess what 'presenting' needs are not being met, the individual (or someone on his or her behalf) will have to gain access to the file and find the relevant statement. This will then have to be compared against the care plan and a list prepared of those needs that the local authority has decided can be 'unmet'. Given that the Welsh policy guidance and the 1991 practice guidance specifically advise that unmet need should be recorded on assessments/care plans,

---

34   [2010] NIQB 62, paras 48–49.
35   In such cases, a local authority could only so decide if it had offered a carer an assessment and, if one has been undertaken, had concluded that the caring role is sustainable without such a need being met – see para 16.51 below.
36   UFSAMC 2002 policy guidance, paras 2.45, 6.22, 8.8, fn 4 p16, Annex 9 p101.
37   At para 4.32.

that recording unmet need will be relatively straight forward (if done during the assessment process) and given the bureaucratic run around that service users may have to pursue if it is not recorded – the balance of administrative fairness strongly favours it being recorded on the support plan.

4.41   It is, in addition, arguable that as a matter of sound administrative practice the recording of unmet need is an essential component of a local authority's strategic planning obligations.[36]

Confusing needs and services

4.42   In *R v Kirklees MBC ex p Daykin*[37] Collins J observed that it was 'not always easy to differentiate between what is a need and what is merely the means by which such need can be met'. The case concerned a disabled person who had been assessed as unable to manage the stairs to his council flat. Collins J considered the 'need' in this case was to be able to get into and out of his dwelling. In his opinion 'the means by which this need could be met included, among other things, the provision of a stair-lift or re-housing'. The 1991 practice guidance mirrors the statutory requirements of NHSCCA 1990 s47(1) by emphasising the importance of treating the assessment of need as a separate exercise from consideration of service response, stating (at page 14):

> It is easy to slip out of thinking 'what does this person need?' into 'what have we got that he/she could have?' The focus on need is most clearly achieved where practitioners responsible for assessment do not also carry responsibility for the delivery or management of services arising from that assessment (at para 22 of the guide's summary).[38]

4.43   The ombudsmen have also been critical of councils that are 'service led' – in the sense that they allow existing service arrangements to dictate how an individual's needs will be met – rather than seeking to meet the identified need. In a complaint concerning the failure of the authority to provide adequate respite care for a disabled child, the Public Services Ombudsman concluded:

---

38   See eg *R v Bristol CC ex p Penfold* (1997–98) 1 CCLR 315 at 322, QBD where Scott Baker J held that the duty to assess was not predicated upon the likelihood of a service being provided and the Prioritising Needs guidance (para 156) and UFSAMC 2002 policy guidance (paras 2.45, 6.22, 8.8, fn 4 p16, Annex 9 p101) which adopt the same approach, stating that the difference between presenting needs and eligible needs should be monitored, and the results used to inform service delivery, planning and commissioning.

39   (1997–98) 1 CCLR 512, QBD: see also, eg, *R v Lambeth LBC ex p K* (2000) 3 CCLR 149, QBD where the court quashed a service provision decision on the basis that the council had not followed the 1990 policy guidance and the care plan had confused 'needs' and 'services'.

40   In *R v Islington LBC ex p Rixon* (1997–98) 1 CCLR 119 at 129B, QBD Sedley J put it thus: 'The practice guidance . . . counsels against trimming the assessment of need to fit the available provision'.

I am not satisfied that the Council fully explored the commissioning of services with the private sector. Instead the Council attempted to rely on existing staff used by Children's Services whom the team manager has recognised were not specifically trained for the job. The Council had been aware of John's complex needs for some years but there was no properly directed proactive approach to recruit and train staff to meet his needs. John's assessed needs should have been met and not just made to fit in with available services which were not suitable.[39]

4.44   This approach is fundamental to a 'personalised' support plan. As the Prioritising Needs guidance puts it, 'Councils should plan with regards to outcomes, rather than specific services'[40] The term 'outcome' in this context denotes the aspirations and desired goals of the service user – focussing on what the individual seeks to achieve rather than on what he or she cannot do[41]. Assessments should be 'outcome focussed' based on the seven social care broad outcomes identified in the white paper *Our health, our care, our say: a new direction for community services.*[42]

4.45   Commonly there may be several possible services that may address an eligible need. For example, an assessment might reveal that a person who lives alone needs to be helped with many activities, such as dressing, bathing, feeding, and that there is a general need for someone to keep a watchful eye on the person to ensure there are no falls or other neglectful acts. These are all likely to be 'eligible needs' since a failure to address them could have serious consequences. The services that could meet these needs are many: home help, day centre, meals on wheels, a residential home, and so on. The support plan determines which services most appropriately meet the eligible needs. Thus, in care/support planning terminology, no one has a 'need' for a place in a day centre: what they might have is a need to be kept occupied or in a safe environment during the day. This could be met in a variety of different ways depending on the user's preference, which might be for a sitting service at home, or a direct payment or personal budget.

Delayed and/or defective care/support plans

4.46   Once an assessment has been completed, a support plan should follow without delay. If the eligible needs cannot be met immediately (because for instance there are no suitable services available), the support plan should explain how these services will be identified and procured: the drafting of the support plan should not be delayed whilst services are sought. In *R v Sutton LBC ex p Tucker*[43] the applicant had been waiting in

41   Complaint against Torfean CBC No 1712/200600588, 11 January 2008 at para 132.
42   Prioritising Needs guidance, para 124.
43   See, for instance, C Glendinning, S Clarke, P Hare, J Maddison and L Newcronner (2008) 'Progress and problems in developing outcomes-focused social care services for older people in England' in *Health and Social Care in the Community* (2008) 16 (1) 54 – 63, at 55.
44   Prioritising Needs guidance, para 60.
45   (1997–98) 1 CCLR 251, QBD.

hospital for two years without a care plan, while the local authority took inadequate steps to identify an appropriate package. In this case the court ordered that the local authority produce a care plan within 21 days – essentially spelling out how it would ensure that the applicant's care needs would be addressed without further delay. The courts have been called upon to consider very many cases of local authorities failing to provide adequate services to meet assessed needs – sometimes through delay and sometimes because the care package proved to be inappropriate. The courts' and ombudsmen's approach to such cases is also considered at paras 3.178, 3.180 and 3.227 above.

4.47 A particularly stark example concerned[44] a complainant parent who, for three years, could only keep her disabled children clean by hosing them down in the garden, strip-washing them in a downstairs toilet, or risking serious injury by getting them upstairs to a small and inadequately-equipped bathroom. During the long delay in obtaining and adapting suitable accommodation, no reasonable interim arrangements were put in place, leading to a finding of maladministration. The Local Government Ombudsman said,

> The underlying cause was ineffective management that can fairly be described as 'institutionalised indifference' – not only to the boys' needs and their mother's plight, but to the Council's duties and responsibilities.

4.48 The Prioritising Needs guidance is unequivocal:

> Councils should provide support promptly once they have agreed to do so, but where waiting is unavoidable, they should ensure that alternative support is in place to meet eligible needs[45].

Support plan breakdowns

4.49 Where a support plan is not meeting a disabled person's needs, the authority is under a duty to address the problem – the urgency of the remedial action depending in part on the severity of the situation. Where complex support packages are involved, authorities may have difficulty in making rapid and effective changes to restore the position: nevertheless a failure to take prompt and, if necessary, urgent action in such cases may amount to maladministration.[48] Where a support package is breaking down, this may be explicable in terms of the authority failing to provide appropriate services to meet the disabled person's needs, or of having failed to build in a suitable contingency arrangement.[49] This may reflect the inadequacy of the assessment on which the service provision is based (see para 3.106 above) or a failure in service provision.

4.50 Not infrequently, a support plan breakdown can occur because an existing service ceases to be available. This problem is illustrated by a 2002

46 Complaint no 07 C 03887 against Bury MBC, 14 October 2009.
47 Prioritising Needs guidance, para 124 and *UFSAMC*, para 5.35.
48 See eg report on complaint no 04/C/12489 against Oldham MBC, 7 September 2006.
49 See eg para 4.47 above.

local government ombudsman's report[50] concerning the care plan for a young adult with multiple and profound mental and physical disabilities. Her needs were assessed and provision made for her to have one weekend per month respite care in a residential unit, paid by the local authority, but provided by a charitable organisation. Several years later the family were notified that owing to funding problems the unit was closed at weekends, and the local authority, having no record of the assessment, asserted that respite at weekends was not needed. The Ombudsman upheld the complaint, stating:

> The council says that because it was not responsible for the closure of [the respite facility] it cannot be held responsible for the withdrawal of [the complainant's] provision. I do not accept this. It is the council, not [the charitable provider] which has statutory responsibility for providing for [the complainant's] needs. If [the respite facility] could not, for whatever reason, meet those needs, the council had a duty to find, in the locality, somewhere else where [the complainant] would feel equally settled and in which her parents would have confidence.

4.51   A further ombudsman's report[51] on the question of service delivery difficulties concerned a severely disabled man and his main carer, both aged over 90. He was assessed as needing help getting up and going to bed; the weekend and evening cover being provided by an agency. Because of recruitment problems the agency gave notice to the council that it proposed to withdraw its service and the council was unable to find another agency willing to provide this service unless the council would pay travel costs to the staff, above the flat rate fee for the service, and the council refused as this was against its policy. In finding a fettering of discretion and maladministration the ombudsman commented:

> It cannot be easy to arrange for home care in the rural parts of the county's area, and even the best contractual agreements must fail from time to time. But it seems to me that when a service failure occurs, the council might well have to seize any realistic opportunity to make the service good. Here it had such an opportunity. Another home care contractor offered to provide the . . . service but only if the council would pay its staff travel costs over and above the flat rate fee for providing home care. Doubtless there are many tussles between the council and its providers over such arrangements and I can understand why the council might have considered this a precedent and the thin end of the wedge, but what was that to Mr and Mrs Derwent? It seems to me that Mr Derwent's home care was entirely sacrificed to maintain the purity of the council's contractual arrangements. . . . This was a classic case of the council fettering its discretion, and was maladministration.

Breakdowns in care packages due to service user behaviour

4.52   Many service users will have behavioural difficulties which are an inextricable part of their condition. Their care plan should therefore take into

---

50   Complaint no 01/C/03521 against North Yorkshire, 19 August 2002.
51   Complaint no 99/B/00799 against Essex, 29 March 2001.

account these characteristics and in general it would be inappropriate to withdraw a service from such person because of his or her behaviour. Accordingly, the local government ombudsman has criticised a council for withdrawing respite care services from a young adult with severe learning disabilities because of a challenging outburst.[52] Although she accepted that 'sometimes brief withdrawal of provision is unavoidable in situations like this', she found that the prolonged exclusion was primarily the consequence of inadequate respite care provision services – and accordingly a failure to meet his assessed need. She recommended 'the council to adopt as a top priority the provision of a new local facility or facilities for [this client group]'.

4.53   Where, for example, a disabled person behaves offensively to home care assistants or refuses to comply with the reasonable requirements of a day centre etc, it might reach a point where the local authority cannot continue to provide a service and considers that it has discharged its duty. In deciding whether to withdraw the service, the applicant's mental health and its treatability may be relevant factors,[53] as indeed will be the authority's duties under Equality Act 2010 s15 (the 'less favourable treatment arising from disability' ground – see para 4.67 below). The impact on carers in this situation is significant. The white paper, *Valuing People* (see para 18.5 below) advises, at para 5.7

> Excluding people with learning disabilities from services if they are found to be difficult to handle or present with challenging behaviour represents a major cause of stress for carers, who may be left unsupported to cope with their son or daughter at home. This practice is unacceptable and families must not be left to cope unaided. No service should be withdrawn on these grounds without identifying alternative options and putting a suitable alternative service in place where possible. Decisions to exclude a person with learning disabilities from a service should always be referred to the Learning Disability Partnership Board, which will be responsible for the provision of alternative services in such cases, provided the person meets the eligibility criteria.

Rejection of a care package

4.54   Disabled people are entitled to refuse services,[54] either explicitly or by their behaviour. In *R v Kensington and Chelsea RLBC ex p Kujtim*,[55] for instance, Potter LJ held that the duty to provide accommodation (under National Assistance Act (NAA) 1948 s21; see para 3.123 above and para 7.29 below) can be treated as discharged if the applicant 'either unreasonably refuses to accept the accommodation provided or if, following its provision, by his conduct he manifests a persistent and unequivocal refusal to observe the reasonable requirements of the local authority in relation to the occupation of such accommodation'.

---

52 Complaint no 03/C/16371 against Stockton-on-Tees BC, 18 January 2005.
53 See *Croydon LBC v Moody* (1999) 2 CCLR 92, CA.
54 See also para 3.118 above and para 5.38 below.
55 [1999] 4 All ER 161, (1999) 2 CCLR 340, CA at 354I.

4.55   In *R v Southwark LBC ex p Khana and Karim*[56] it was alleged that Mrs Khana (the disabled party subject to the community care assessment) refused to accept the offer of a residential care home placement proposed by the local authority – and insisted upon the provision of a community based care package. In finding that the local authority had acted appropriately, Mance LJ commented:

> . . . although I do not consider that the case requires analysis in these terms, I would, if necessary, also treat Mrs Khana's refusal of the offer of residential home accommodation – the only course that would meet her assessed needs – as unreasonable in the sense intended by Potter LJ, when he was considering in *ex p Kujtim* what would discharge a local authority from any further duty for so long as such refusal was maintained.

Challenging support plans/personal budget allocation

4.56   The appropriate procedure for disputing the content of a support plan will generally be via the complaints procedures (see para 26.8 below). This may additionally include a complaint concerning the adequacy of the assessment – and particularly the needs that have been identified as 'eligible needs'. In *R (Lloyd) v Barking and Dagenham LBC*[57] the Court of Appeal held that it was not an appropriate organ to prescribe the degree of detail that should go into a support plan.

4.57   However, if the basis of the dissatisfaction with the support plan is the amount of provision made, rather than the detail of the plan, then other considerations may need to be explored. The level of service provision may be founded on an inadequate assessment of needs, for instance a failure to have regard to some key aspect such as need for support to access the wider community, and so the assessment itself may need to be reviewed. Alternatively, the resource allocation scheme may generate an indicative figure for the personal budget which is, on analysis at the support planning stage, inadequate to meet the identified eligible needs. If either of these defects cannot be otherwise resolved, they may, depending on the facts of the case, give rise to grounds for judicial review (see para 26.195 below)

Monitoring and reviewing care/support plans

4.58   Councils must not only take all reasonable steps to ensure that appropriate services are provided to satisfy the eligible needs a person is assessed as having, they must also ensure that care plans are monitored so that any problems are picked up and addressed. The Prioritising Needs guidance[58] requires that there should be an initial review of all care plans:

---

56 [2001] EWCA Civ 999, (2001) 4 CCLR 267.
57 [2001] EWCA Civ 533, (2001) 4 CCLR 196 at 205G.
58 FACS 2002 policy guidance, para 144; UFSAMC 2002 policy guidance, paras 2.54–2.51.

The frequency of reviews should be proportionate to the circumstances of the individual but there should be an initial review within three months of help first being provided or major changes made to current support plans. Thereafter, reviews should be scheduled at least annually or more often as is necessary. Councils should also consider conducting reviews when requested to do so by the service user, their carer or service provider.

4.59 The Local Government Ombudsman has made repeated criticism of local authority failures to monitor care services[59] – particularly those provided by independent agencies for whom they have private contracts. In a 2007 complaint against Liverpool City Council[60] she noted that although the one arm of the council had knowledge that the care agency was providing an unsatisfactory service, this did not stop the agency being paid by another arm of the council since the one had no input into the into the administration of the contract of the other. In her view, such a situation, placed 'the most vulnerable members of the community at serious risk' and was 'simply unacceptable and constitute[d] maladministration.' Given the vulnerability of many such service users, the ombudsman has also stressed the need for councils to monitor carefully the quality of service provision and not simply to wait for complaints: noting (in a 2011) report[61] 'I do not believe that the Council's reliance on any absence of complaint from the family during this time excuses this lack of proper attention to its statutory responsibilities.'

4.60 The Public Services Ombudsman has also expressed concerns in this area; a 2010 complaint, for example, criticising a council for failing to issue a contract default notice against a provider in a situation where the service it was providing was clearly substandard.[62]

4.61 Since review of a care plan, is at law, a 'reassessment', this question is considered at para 3.230 above.

Copies of care/support plans

4.62 As noted above, the 1991 practice guidance,[63] the Prioritising Needs guidance[64] and the SAP guidance[65] require service users to be given copies of their care plans (in the most appropriate format).

---

59 See eg complaint nos 05/C/18474 against Birmingham CC, 4 March; 2008; 05/C/06420 against Sheffield CC, 20 February 2007; 05/C/08592 against Liverpool CC, 17 January 2007; 03/C/17141 against Blackpool, 23 February 2006.
60 Complaint no 05/C/08592 against Liverpool CC, 17 January 2007, paras 30–31.
61 Complaint no 08 019 214 against Bromley LBC, 9 June 2011, para 43.
62 Complaint no 200900324 against Powys CC, 1 October 2010, paras 115–116.
63 At para 4.37.
64 At para 121; UFSAMC 2002 policy guidance, para 2.49.
65 SAP Policy Guidance 2003 annex E p24.

Key care/support planning principles

4.63   Unlike modern social welfare statutes,[66] current community care legisla-tion contains no express statement of core principles, although the Law Commission has proposed a statement of statutory principles in future adult social care legislation, based on an overarching principle that adult social care must promote or contribute to the well-being of the individual, with a presumption that the person is the best judge of their own well-being.[67] Some principles can, however, already be discerned from the government's broad policy documents and from the English and Welsh community care policy guidance. These principles are uncontroversial and have varied only slightly over the last 20 years. The declaration in the 1989 community care white paper *'Caring for people*[68] (at para 1.8) that 'promoting choice and independence underlies all the Government's pro-posals' remains true today. Neither devolution[69] nor electoral changes have altered these objectives, a point manifest in the title of the 2005 English green paper *'Independence, well-being and choice: our vision for the future of social care for adults in England'*.[70] The Coalition Government set out its 'overarching principles' in *A Vision for Adult Social Care: Capable Communities and Active Citizens*[71] While these also emphasise choice and control, they also demonstrate an acceleration of the move away from the state as the route to deliver such goals:

- Freedom: 'we want people to have the freedom to choose the services that are right for them from a vibrant plural market'
- Fairness: 'a clear, comprehensive and modern legal framework for social care'
- Responsibility: 'Social care is not solely the responsibility of the state. Communities and wider civil society must be set free to run innovative local schemes and build local networks of support'.

4.64   While the promotion of independent living and user choice are long standing and core principles underpinning the legislation, there is a third that has received less political air-time, but is nevertheless central to any analysis such as this: the issue of cost effectiveness. A final 'principle' that has come more clearly into focus over the last ten years is that of 'dignity'.[72] Although implicit in the concept of independent living, with

---

66 See eg Children Act 1989 s1 or Mental Capacity Act 2005 s1.
67 Law Commission (2011), *Adult Social Care*, Law Com No 326 HC941, Part 4 pp 17–24.
68 Secretaries of State for Health, Social Security, Wales and Scotland, *Caring for people: community care in the next decade and beyond*, Cm 849, HMSO, 1989.
69 See eg the UFSAMC 2002 policy guidance which at p6 gives as the first two 'key aims' social inclusion and independence.
70 Department of Health, March 2005: which at page 9 gave as its vision the promotion of certain principles, of which the first was the development of services 'to help maintain the independence of the individual by giving them greater choice and control over the way in which their needs are met'.
71 DH Gateway ref. 14847, Department of Health (2010).
72 Explicitly taken up by ministers with the launch of the *Dignity in care* initiative in November 2006, and echoed in *A vision for adult social care: capable communities and active citizens*, p 5 and para 4.1.

the enactment of the Human Rights Act 1998 it is a principle that now warrants analysis in its own right. Of these four 'principles' – independent living, dignity, 'choice and control' and cost effectiveness – the first two are (in jurisprudential theory at least) accorded the greater weight; however, in practice the scales appear most affected by 'cost effectiveness' (or in reality, merely 'cost'). These four principles are considered separately below.

The promotion of independent living

4.65 The promotion of independent living is a core – perhaps the core – principle underpinning the community care legislation.[73] References to independence litter the policy documents of the last 20 years and have been given quasi-statutory force in policy guidance. For instance, the basis for determining eligibility for local authority support is the extent to which 'an individual's presenting needs might pose risks to their independence. . . .'[74] The overall objectives in the current guidance on domiciliary charging are said to be 'to promote the independence and social inclusion of service users'[75] and the aim of disability-related expenditure (which is excluded from the means-test – see para 10.33 below) is 'to allow for reasonable expenditure needed for independent living by the disabled person'.[76]

4.66 The courts and ombudsmen have placed very considerable reliance upon the principle that care and support planning should promote independent living.[77] Thus in *R v Sutton LBC ex p Tucker*[78] the fact that there was an 'effective option' for the service user's discharge from long-stay care in hospital was treated as creating an obligation to act purposefully to progress this objective. In *LLBC v TG, JG and KR* McFarlane J observed that:

> Before a local authority seeks to invoke the court's powers to compel a family to place a relative in a residential care home, the court is entitled to expect that the authority will have made a genuine and reasonable attempt

---

73 This assertion has been cited with approval, see *R (B) v Cornwall County Council* [2009] EWHC 491 (Admin), (2009) 12 CCLR 381, per Higginbottom J at para 6. Curiously (and in spite of the right to independent living being enshrined in the UN Convention on the Rights of Persons with Disabilities and Independent Living – see para 4.70 below) the Law Commission considered that as a concept it was too imprecise to be expressed as a statutory principle – Law Commission (2011) *Adult Social Care*, Law Com No 326 HC941, para 4.35.

74 Prioritising Needs guidance, para 59, see also UFSAMC, for instance at 5.2.

75 Department of Health (2003) *Fairer Charging Policies for Home Care and Other Non-residential Social Services*, paras 3 and 15.

76 Department of Health (2003) *Fairer Charging Policies for Home Care and Other Non-residential Social Services*, para 44.

77 See eg *R v Islington LBC ex p Rixon* (1997–98) 1 CCLR 119 at 128, QBD, and see also Local Government Ombudsman Complaint no 07/A/01436 against Hillingdon LBC, 18 September 2008, para 31.

78 (1997–98) 1 CCLR 251 at 255H and 274H, QBD

to carry out a full assessment of the capacity of the family to meet the relative's needs in the community.[79]

The Equality Act 2010 and Independent Living

4.67   The duty to promote independent living has developed to the stage that it can be seen as a core domestic and international human rights obligation. Domestically, the Equality Act (EqA) 2010 s149[80] places a duty on all public bodies to have due regard to the need to promote equality of opportunity between disabled persons (as well as others sharing a characteristic protected by EqA 2010) and other persons. In furtherance of this duty public bodies must have particular regard to the need, inter alia, to 'encourage persons who share a relevant protected characteristic to participate in public life or in any other activity in which participation by such persons is disproportionately low' (section 149(3)(c)). The importance of this duty in the context of policies which ration services to disabled people is considered above (at paras 3.211–3.212 and 4.16–4.19 above).

4.68   The need to promote independent living through the removal of barriers which impede that goal for disabled people is also given statutory expression domestically in EqA 2010, for example, in section 20, the duty to make reasonable adjustments, including where a provision, criterion or practice puts a disabled person at a substantial disadvantage, and in Part III of EqA 2010, dealing with services and public functions.

4.69   Previous comparable duties under the Disability Discrimination Act (DDA) 1995 were considered in *R (Lunt and another) v Liverpool City Council*. In upholding the challenge to Liverpool's decision not to licence a fully wheelchair accessible form of taxi in the city, Blake J held, inter alia, that the duty to make reasonable adjustments to the taxi licensing policy in this case was 'not . . . a minimal duty, but seeks broadly to put the disabled person as far as reasonably practicable in a similar position to the ambulant user of a taxi'.[81]

The UN Convention on the Rights of Persons with Disabilities and Independent Living

4.70   Internationally, the UN Convention on the Rights of Persons with Disabilities, Article 19 declares:[82]

> States Parties to this Convention recognize the equal right of all persons with disabilities to live in the community, with choices equal to others, and shall take effective and appropriate measures to facilitate full enjoyment by persons with disabilities of this right and their full inclusion and participation in the community, including by ensuring that:

79   [2007] EWHC 2640 (Fam), [2009] 1 FLR 414 at [33].
80   Inserted by the Disability Discrimination Act 2005 s3.
81   [2009] EWHC 2356 (Admin) para 59.
82   For a general review of the provision, see C Parker and L Clements (2008) 'The UN Convention on the Rights of persons with Disabilities: a new right to Independent Living?' (2008) 4 EHRLR 508–523.

a) Persons with disabilities have the opportunity to choose their place of residence and where and with whom they live on an equal basis with others and are not obliged to live in a particular living arrangement;
b) Persons with disabilities have access to a range of in-home, residential and other community support services, including personal assistance necessary to support living and inclusion in the community, and to prevent isolation or segregation from the community;
c) Community services and facilities for the general population are available on an equal basis to persons with disabilities and are responsive to their needs.

4.71   A powerful argument can be made that the inappropriate institutionalisation of elderly and disabled people may be contrary to the European Convention on Human Rights ('the Convention') – contrary to Article 8 alone or in combination with Article 14. This is particularly the case given that the UK has accepted the right in the UN Convention on the Rights of Persons with Disabilities, Article 19 (which it ratified in June 2009[83]) and is effectively estopped from denying that such a right can be read into analogous binding conventions such as the European Convention on Human Rights (Article 8).[84]

4.72   As yet there is no decided case that addresses this question directly, although there is relevant authority for this proposition in the form of a US Supreme Court decision, *Olmstead v LC*.[85] *Olmstead* concerned the Americans with Disabilities Act 1990 which (amongst other things) proscribes discrimination in the provision of public services. Whilst there is no exactly equivalent legislation in England and Wales, Part III of the EqA 2010 (services and public functions) is sufficiently similar to permit comparison. *Olmstead* concerned a care planning regime in the state of Georgia, which skewed funding arrangements to favour institutional placements, rather than community based independent living placements.

4.73   The applicants alleged that this constituted unlawful discrimination and the majority of the Supreme Court agreed. Whilst the court emphasised that the financial resources of States' were relevant factors in determining their policies, it stressed the importance of policies being rational and fair and of the basic principle that 'unnecessary institutionalization' should be avoided if possible. In the view of the majority:

> The identification of unjustified segregation as discrimination reflects two evident judgments: Institutional placement of persons who can handle and benefit from community settings perpetuates unwarranted assumptions that persons so isolated are incapable or unworthy of participating in community life . . .;

---

83 Subject to several reservations in relation to education, freedom of movement, armed forces and social security appointees.
84 For an analysis of the enhancement effect of such interconnected Convention provisions, see L Clements and J Read, *Disabled People and the Right to Life*, Routledge, 2008 and see Article 53 of the Convention.
85 527 US 581 (1999).

and

> confinement in an institution severely diminishes the everyday life
> activities of individuals, including family relations, social contacts, work
> options, economic independence, educational advancement, and cultural
> enrichment.

4.74   The Supreme Court's acknowledgement that financial resources were of
relevance in determining the extent of the independent living obligation
raises the question of how these two community care principles,
'independence' and 'cost effectiveness', should be balanced. The issue
was addressed tangentially by the court of Appeal in *R v Southwark LBC ex
p Khana and Karim*[86] where the applicants, an elderly couple, sought
judicial review of the council's decision to meet their care needs by provision of a placement in a residential care home. The applicants wanted, for
personal and cultural reasons, to live in the community independently in
a home of their own with the support of their relatives and the statutory
services. Mance LJ, giving judgment of the Court of Appeal, held that:

> section 47 of the 1990 Act contemplate[s] an assessment by the local
> authority of a person's accommodation needs, which takes very full
> account of their wishes, including the very fundamental aim of preserving
> the independence of elderly people in the community and in their own
> homes for as long and as fully as possible. A certain degree of risk-taking is
> often acceptable, rather than compromise independence and break family
> or home links. But, where a local authority concludes, as Southwark did
> here, that 'the only way in which Mrs Khana's needs can properly be met is
> for her to go into a full time residential home', and makes a corresponding
> offer, and where this assessment and the reasonableness of the offer made
> cannot be challenged as such, then the local authority has in my judgment
> satisfied its duties under the legislation.[87]

4.75   The judgment confirms that the default position for any support plan is
the promotion of independent living and that only where the social care
authority concludes for professional (ie not solely financial) reasons that
independent living is not viable, is it reasonable for it to propound an
institutional care plan. The strong presumption in favour of independent
living (over and above financial considerations) comes additionally from
the positive obligations imposed by Article 8 of the Convention:[88] to take
action to 'the greatest extent feasible to ensure that they have access to
essential economic and social activities and to an appropriate range of
recreational and cultural activities' to ensure that their lives are not 'so
circumscribed and so isolated as to be deprived of the possibility of developing [their] personality'.[89] Such compensatory measures, as Judge Greve

---

86   [2001] EWCA Civ 999, (2001) 4 CCLR 267.
87   [2001] EWCA Civ 999, (2001) 4 CCLR 267 at 281K.
88   See, eg, the observations made by Collins J in *Gunter v South West Staffordshire PCT*
    [2005] EWHC 1894 (Admin), (2006) 9 CCLR 121 at [20].
89   Per Commissioner Bratza (as he then was) in *Botta v Italy* (1998) 26 EHRR 241 and
    cited by Munby J in *R (A, B, X and Y) v East Sussex CC* [2003] EWHC 167, (2003)
    6 CCLR 194 at [102] and see also *R (T, D and B) v Haringey LBC* [2005] EWHC 2235
    (Admin), (2006) 9 CCLR 58.

observed in *Price v UK*,[90] are fundamental to disabled people's Article 8 rights.

Choice and control

4.76 The debate about choice is not new – in the 1960's Tunstall advocated such an approach:[91]

> An old lady whose arthritis prevents her from cooking should be able to choose between having mobile meals delivered or having her home help cook them or being transported to a club or centre to eat the meals there, or a combination of the three.

4.77 Respect for service user preferences has remained central to the rhetoric accompanying all major community care policy initiatives of the last 20 years. The Coalition Government sees personalisation as central to the future of adult social care and choice is at its core:

> With choice and control, people's dignity and freedom is protected and their quality of life is enhanced. Our vision is to make sure everyone can get the personalised support they deserve.[92]

4.78 The suggestion that support goes to those who 'deserve' it, rather than those who 'need' it is at odds with the statutory framework and the eligibility scheme. However, the extent to which choice is underpinned by legislation and case law is analysed below.

4.79 'Choice' has only once been given statutory expression – in the Choice of Accommodation Directions (see para 7.103 below): all things being equal these provide a service user with the right to choose his or her care home.

4.80 The courts have distinguished between 'preferences' and 'needs'. In *R v Avon CC ex p M*[93] the applicant, because of his learning disabilities, had formed a fixed psychological attachment to a particular home which was more expensive than the alternative proposed by the local authority. A complaints panel heard uncontroverted evidence concerning his psychological needs and unanimously recommended the placement in the more expensive home. The local authority refused. Henry J, in finding for the applicant, stated as follows:

> Here, there was a clear finding by a body set up for detailed fact finding that M's needs included his psychological needs and, unless that finding could be disposed of, the authority was liable to meet those needs. Without that finding being overthrown, there were not two options before the social services committee, as the paper suggests, there was only one: to meet M's needs, including his psychological needs.

---

90 (2002) 34 EHRR 53.
91 J Tunstall, *Old and Alone*, Routledge and Kegan Paul, 1966, p296 cited in P Thane, *Old Age in English History*, OUP, 2000, pp423–424.
92 Department of Health (2010) *A vision for adult social care: capable communities and active citizens*, para 4.1.
93 (1999) 2 CCLR 185, QBD.

4.81   M's attachment to the particular home was a 'need' not a 'choice'. This point was picked up in *R v Southwark LBC ex p Khana and Karim*[94] where the applicants were demanding a care plan that the local authority considered inappropriate. The Court of Appeal dealt with the claim in the following terms:

> In some circumstances, instanced by *R v Avon CC ex p M*[95] . . . a person may have a need . . . as distinct from a preference, to reside in a particular place. Here, it seems to me that Mrs Khana . . . is in reality seeking to insist, as against Southwark, on the – no doubt strongly held – preferences or beliefs of Mrs Khana and her family as to what community services should be provided to Mrs Khana and in what way. Under the relevant legislation and guidance, Southwark must take into account Mrs Khana's and Mr Karim's beliefs and preferences, but the assessment of any needs regarding, *inter alia*, accommodation and how to provide for them rests ultimately with Southwark.[96]

4.82   However, the majority judgment of the Supreme Court in *R (McDonald) v Royal Borough of Kensington and Chelsea*[97] goes further than previous judgments of the courts in giving local authorities a wide margin of discretion in limiting choice on the basis of financial resources, even when it results in indignity to the service user. The fact that the continent but immobile appellant objected very strongly to wearing continence pads at night, finding them an affront to her dignity, did not stop the Supreme Court deciding that it was lawful for the respondent local authority to withdraw care assistance at night requiring her to wear pads instead. (For detailed discussion of this case, see paras 3.139 and 4.110–4.113 below)

4.83   The courts, therefore, treat the principle of 'user choice', not as a fundamental right, but as a relevant consideration that must be taken into account by the authority. It follows that the preferences of service user in relation to his or her support plan should (except in relation to residential care placements – for which see para 7.109 below):

1) be fully taken into account by the authority; and
2) be accommodated in the support plan, so long as the local authority does not consider it inappropriate or too expensive.

However, if an authority propounds a support plan that does not comply with the service user's preferences, the authority must:

3) give cogent reasons for so deciding and highlight those parts of the support plan where there is disagreement.[98]

94   [2001] EWCA Civ 999, (2001) 4 CCLR 267.
95   See para 3.93 above.
96   [2001] EWCA Civ 999, (2001) 4 CCLR 267 at 281H.
97   [2011] UKSC 33, (2011) 14 CCLR 341.
98   See eg *Care management and assessment – a practitioners' guide*, HMSO, 1991, para 4.37 which requires that the care plan identify any point of difference between the user, carer and care planning practitioner, and the SAP guidance (2002) annex E pp24–25 which requires that the care plan include a note on whether or not the service user has agreed the care plan, and a reason where this was not possible – the UFSAMC 2002 policy guidance contains similar obligations at para 2.44.

Choice and self-directed support

4.84 The concept of self-directed support is a central tenet of the personalisation agenda. The policy model is one in which the individual determines how to meet eligible needs based on the outcomes he or she wishes to achieve. Thus user choice takes primacy in support planning. The Prioritising Needs guidance, at para 120:

> The success of self-directed support initiatives will therefore depend upon effective support planning. This should be person-centred, exploring what is important to the individual concerned and how they can spend their personal budget to organise and create support in order to achieve their aims. In local authorities where personal budgets have not yet been implemented, choice and control should also be available to people receiving directly managed services to help identify personalised solutions to meet their outcomes. In this way, a support plan will reflect the decisions made by the individual, supported by anyone they have chosen to assist them in this planning.

4.85 Choice is assumed here to be an unalloyed good thing, and undoubtedly for many it has proved to be so. However, research has identified two limiting factors: the need for clear information as a precondition for effectively exercising choice,[99] and the fact that increased choice tends to bring with it greater uncertainty and dissatisfaction.[100]

4.86 Choice also depends on having viable options from which to choose and the Prioritising Needs guidance recognises the commissioning implications of a move from a pre-existing menu of services to a more individualised approach to support planning (para 118):

> To support the development of a more personalised social care system, effective commissioning strategies should be able to demonstrate a focus on the following key areas:
> - Diverse and innovative provision of services tailored to people's needs and aspirations and focused on outcomes. This will enable people to exercise choice and control over the types of services they want and directly shape the services that are commissioned on their behalf;
> - A greater focus on prevention, early intervention and support for self-care; and
> - Shared strategic needs assessment co-produced with local citizens and communities informing decisions across health, social care and local government. This should facilitate greater flexibility in shifting resources to where investment can have greatest impact on current and future health and well-being needs. It will also ensure the sufficient supply of care staff and services to meet known and expected demand.

99 See, for instance, K Baxter, C Glendinning, S Clarke, 'Making Informed Choices in Social Care: the importance of accessible information', *Health and Social Care in the Community*, Volume 16, No 2, March 2008, pp 197–207 (11).
100 Eg, S Iyengar and M Lepper, 'When choosing is demotivating: can one desire too much of a good thing?' (2000) *Journal of Personality and Social Psychology* 79, pp 995–1006.

Risk management/consequences of choice

4.87   One consequence of user choice is the acceptance of risk – to which a local authority of NHS body might have misgivings, believing that it is unwise and/or likely to expose the authority to a compensation claim if harm results to the user. Department of Health guidance *Independence, choice and risk: a guide to best practice in supported decision making*[101] provides a framework aimed at helping professionals to support service users to make decisions about their own lives and manage any consequent risk in relation to such choices. It endorses (at para 2.36) Health and Safety Executive guidance that describes risk management in terms of taking 'practical steps to protect people from real harm and suffering, not about bureaucratic back covering or hiding behind the legislation when a difficult decision has to be made'. Its statement of the legal position in relation to the law of negligence in such matters is concise (at para 2.26):

> an individual who has the mental capacity to make a decision, and chooses voluntarily to live with a level of risk, is entitled to do so. The law will treat that person as having consented to the risk and so there will be no breach of the duty of care by professionals or public authorities. However, the local authority remains accountable for the proper use of its public funds, and whilst the individual is entitled to live with a degree of risk, the local authority is not obliged to fund it.

4.88   Councils will, on occasions, find themselves in disagreement with disabled people and their families over what is an ideal or safe system for care arrangements – such as the use of equipment. The need in such cases is for flexibility of approach so that a solution can be reached – and a failure to do so, will constitute maladministration – particularly if it leaves the disabled person or carers without support.[102] In *R (A and B) v East Sussex CC (No 2)*,[103] a decision not to provide swimming or horse riding facilities to two young adults with complex disabilities on health and safety grounds,[104] because it would have necessitated some lifting, was held to be an unjustifiable breach of their Article 8 right to private life.

4.89   The practice guidance on NHS Continuing Healthcare[105] at para 2.3.5 refers to the Department of Health guidance *Independence, choice and risk: a guide to best practice in supported decision making*[106] and summarises its governing principle as:

---

101   Department of Health (2007) *Independence, choice and risk: a guide to supported decision making*. See also Adult Services SCIE Report 36 (2010) *Enabling risk, ensuring safety: self-directed support and personal budgets.*

102   See eg Complaint no 07/B/07665 against Luton Borough Council, 10 September 2008 para 35; and see also chapter 24 which considers the associated 'safeguarding' implications of such questions.

103   [2003] EWHC 167 (Admin), (2003) 6 CCLR 194.

104   As Munby J observed in *Re MM (an adult)* [2009] 1 FLR 443 at para 120 – 'What good is it making someone safer if it merely makes them miserable?' – see also para 17.38 below.

105   Department of Health (2010) *NHS Continuing Healthcare Practice Guidance*.

106   www.dh.gov.uk/en/Publicationsandstatistics/Publications/PublicationsPolicyAnd Guidance/DH_074773_NHS continuing healthcare practice guidance.

'*People have the right to live their lives to the full as long as that doesn't stop others from doing the same.*'

To put this principle into practice, those supporting individuals have to:

- help people have choice and control over their lives
- ecognise that making a choice can involve some risk
- respect people's rights and those of their family carers
- help people understand their responsibilities and the implications of their choices, including any risks

acknowledge that there will always be some risk, and that trying to remove it altogether can outweigh the quality of life benefits for the person

- continue existing arrangements for safeguarding people.

Cost effectiveness

Choosing between alternative care/support packages

4.90   While *ex p Khana and Karim* suggests that the promotion of 'independent living' is the principle generally to be accorded greatest weight, it is less clear as to how the balance is to be struck between 'cost effectiveness' and 'user preferences'. In general, however, if an authority is asserting resource constraints as a reason for rejecting a user's preferred option, it cannot assume that the court or ombudsman will accept these as self-evident: in such cases, as Mance LJ has observed,[107] 'any problem of resources would require to be made out by evidence, and cannot be assumed to be present'.

4.91   The assessment process may identify needs which are capable of being met by two or more alternative support packages. In such situations it is not unreasonable for the authority to consider the relative cost of each option – as the above quoted 1990 policy guidance (at para 3.25) so advises – to 'secure the most cost-effective package of services that meets the user's care needs, taking account of the user's and carers' own preferences'. However, if objectively the cheaper option does not meet an assessed need (for instance because it fails to provide for sufficiently skilled support to address the persons need, or is not in a location where he is assessed as needing to be, or separates spouses/partners against their will etc) then the local authority cannot opt for that placement – see paras 3.216–3.221 above, and cannot ask for 'top-ups' – see para 7.120 below.

4.92   Authorities are not obliged to opt for the cheapest support plan, but if the less expensive plan is favoured, a number of factors must be considered. First, if the choice concerns a care home placement, the choice of accommodation provisions may apply (see para 7.109). Secondly, if the cheaper option is within an institutional setting, it may be trumped by the 'independent living' obligation (see para 4.65 above). Finally, if in so

---

107   *R v Southwark LBC ex p Khana and Karim* [2001] EWCA Civ 999, (2001) 4 CCLR 267 at 282I; see also *Sabah Mohamoud v Greenwich LBC* January 2003 *Legal Action* 23 where impatience was expressed concerning unspecified and 'general assertions' of a similar nature (albeit in a housing context).

deciding the authority rejects a user's preferred support package, it is obliged to (a) give cogent reasons for its decision (not least because the authority may have misunderstood the costing implications[108]), and (b) be able to identify its preferred support package – in the sense that such a package must actually exist, rather than being a hypothetical alternative.[109]

4.93　　In constructing a support plan, the issue of resources (the 'cheaper option') only arises if there is objectively a real and present choice of care packages available – which was not the case in *R v Avon CC ex p M*[110] (considered above) or indeed in *R v Sutton LBC ex p Tucker*[111] which concerned a Rubella impaired applicant. The local authority favoured a home in Birmingham run by the specialist charity SENSE, but the applicant's family, clinicians and indeed the SENSE staff considered that this would not be viable since she needed to be close to her family in Sutton, where unfortunately no such facility existed. The authority balked at the cost of commissioning a purpose created unit solely for the applicant; the net result being that nothing concrete happened and she remained inappropriately placed in short term NHS accommodation. In the judicial review proceedings, the authority sought to explain their inaction by reference to the family's unreasonable refusal of a care option – namely the placement in Birmingham. Hidden J disagreed. This was not a situation where there was a choice of care plans; indeed this was a case where there was no care plan at all. In his view, the authority preference for the Birmingham placement was untenable and local placement the only option. Since there was no 'choice of care plan' the issue of resources was not relevant and the local authority had to prepare a plan to this effect.

4.94　　Another difficulty may concern the question of net versus gross costs. A care option that is more expensive in gross terms (ie to UK Plc) may be less expensive in net cost terms to the authority (because, for example, part of the cost is met by another state funding stream, or by the individuals themselves). This difficulty was identified by the Audit Commission in 1996:

> The financial incentive for authorities to use residential care remains strong. In nearly all situations it is substantially cheaper for local authorities to place people in residential care, even where there is no difference between the gross cost of residential care and care at home.[112]

4.95　In such an analysis it would presumably be unreasonable for an authority to take into account the service user's likely financial contribution. Although there appears to be no authority on this point, to permit this could have a seriously distorting influence: for instance, the net cost to an authority of placing a person with capital into residential accommodation could in many situations be nil.

108　*R (Alloway) v Bromley LBC* [2004] EWHC 2108 (Admin), (2005) 8 CCLR 61.
109　*R (LH and MH) v Lambeth LBC* [2006] EWHC 1190 (Admin), (2006) 9 CCLR 622 (in this case the choice of the parent carer).
110　(1999) 2 CCLR 185, QBD.
111　(1997–98) 1 CCLR 251, QBD.
112　*Balancing the Care Equation*, HMSO, 1996, para 40.

4.96   In similar fashion, a short term saving in provision may simply hasten greater dependency on more expensive care and support: as the 1990 policy guidance observes (at para 3.25), '[f]ailure to satisfy particular needs can result in even greater burdens on particular services, for example, where a person becomes homeless as a result of leaving inappropriate accommodation which has been provided following discharge from hospital'. The same argument is used in the Prioritising Needs guidance to promote early intervention and prevention:

> Prevention and early intervention are at the very heart of the vision for social care set out *Putting People First,* and further endorsed in the Care and Support Green Paper. *Putting People First* says that there needs to be "a locally agreed approach . . . utilising all relevant community resources, especially the voluntary sector so that prevention and early intervention and enablement become the norm." Before setting eligibility criteria for social care, councils should consider their strategy for investing in a more universal approach, which prevents or delays the need for more specialist social care interventions.

Cost ceilings

4.97   The formal or informal community care policies of many authorities include reference to a 'costs ceiling'. Not uncommonly this will take the form of a financial limit on the total weekly cost of home care services that can be put into any one household, or a maximum permitted sum on any domiciliary support package (the implication being that if the package costs more, then a residential support plan will be preferred). If the costs ceiling relates to a package of residential care, this may offend the Choice of Accommodation Directions – see para 7.109 below.

4.98   Blanket policies of this nature are likely to be unlawful, in that they would amount to a fettering of a duty (see para 27.209 below) and make resource questions determinative, rather than being 'no more than one factor in an overall assessment, where . . . the individual disabled person will always be the paramount consideration'.[113] Where such a policy would promote institutional care over non-institutional options, it would also offend the legal presumption in favour of independent living (see para 4.65 above).

4.99   Subject to these caveats, a council policy that refers to a particular costs figure as a 'guideline' rather than a fixed 'ceiling' will generally be lawful (unless the figure is entirely arbitrary). However, any such guideline must be the product of a rational and practical process that has taken into account all relevant factors – and is not an arbitrary figure dreamt up in the fog of a council meeting.[114] In her 1998 report concerning a complaint against Liverpool City Council[115] the local government ombudsman considered a council imposed financial ceiling (of £110.00 per week) on the level of domiciliary care provided, which reflected the average cost to the

---

113   Per Hirst LJ in *R v Gloucestershire CC ex p Barry* (1997–98) 1 CCLR 19 at 31G, CA.
114   Complaint nos 90/A/2675, 2075, 1705, 1228 and 1172 against Essex.
115   Complaint no 96/C/4315, 20 August 1998; (1999) 2 CCLR 128. A sum of £10,000 compensation was recommended by the ombudsman.

council for an older person in residential care. She found that in setting the limit the council had fettered its discretion since there was no evidence that it had ever exceeded the limit and that such a fees policy was unfair and unreasonably discriminated against older people (as opposed to other service users).

Cost-effectiveness and personal budgets

4.100   Debates about cost effectiveness will increasingly centre on the adequacy of the allocated personal budget to meet the assessed needs of the individual concerned. The Court of Appeal in *R (Savva) v Royal Borough of Kensington and Chelsea* was in no doubt that transparency required adequate reasoning as to how the personal budget figure was reached and that such reasons needed to be referable to the 'required services and assumed timings . . . together with the assumed hourly cost'.[116]

4.101   The subsequent decision of Judge Bidden QC in *R (KM) v Cambridgeshire County Council* rejected the contention that the Council had failed to provide an explanation of the services needed to meet the claimant's needs, which he regarded as 'a complete misunderstanding of the system of self-directed support'.[117] However, the reasoning is difficult to follow in this case as, in fact, the assessment, the basis on which the personal budget had been determined, had provided all three features – services, timings and assumed hourly costs. The system of self-directed support provides for far greater user choice in how assessed needs are to be met, but that does not undermine the dicta of the Court of Appeal that the link between the personal budget figure and the cost of provision to meet eligible needs must have sufficient specificity to achieve the necessary level of transparency in order that disabled people and their carers can understand how the personal budget figure has been reached. In the *Cambridgeshire* case, in the view of the court, this requirement had in fact been met.

Minimum services and respect/dignity

4.102   Commonly, a local authority may be able to satisfy a person's assessed needs in a variety of ways. Given that how it decides to meet the need is primarily its decision,[118] the question arises as to how austere a care package will have to be, before the courts or ombudsmen will intervene. This in turn raises the question as to the standard by which the court or ombudsman would judge 'austerity' or 'disagreeability' or whatever the measure may be.

4.103   By way of example, a local authority might assess as an 'eligible need' the person's need to access the toilet. If the problem is that the existing toilet is upstairs, and the person has mobility difficulties, this 'need' could

---

116   [2010] EWCA Civ 1209, (2011) 14 CCLR 75, para 21.
117   ]2010] EWHC 3065 (Admin), (2011) 14 CCLR 83, para 54.
118   *R v Southwark LBC ex p Khana and Karim* [2001] EWCA Civ 999, (2001) 4 CCLR 267.

be addressed by the provision of a stair lift, or the construction of a downstairs toilet or merely by the provision of a commode. Likewise a person who is unable to use their bath due to mobility problems may be assessed as needing to have help to keep clean – and this could be addressed by the provision of a wheelchair accessible shower, or a specially adapted bath or merely by an occasional 'strip/blanket' wash.

4.104   In assessing the adequacy of the service provision response, the courts and ombudsmen have sought to develop the concept of 'dignity' in the context of a state's positive obligations under Article 8 of the Convention – the duty to ensure 'respect' for individual privacy (see para 26.260 below). Accordingly the local government ombudsman has held that the ability properly to manage bathing/washing with dignity is the entitlement of everybody.[119] By this measure a policy of only doing strip washes would fail the 'dignity threshold' and amount to maladministration. In *R (Bernard) v Enfield LBC*[120] the LA's failure to act to move a wheelchair dependent claimant, mother of a family of six, to suitable accommodation left her, inter alia, unable to access the kitchen or bathroom, and forced to defecate or urinate on the floor several times a day. Sullivan J awarded damages for breach of Article 8 finding that these conditions were inimical to her family life and to her physical and psychological integrity. Providing the claimant with suitably adapted accommodation 'would have restored her dignity as a human being'

4.105   In *R (Burke) v General Medical Council and others*[121] Munby J gave an extended review of the extent to which it could be argued that the concept of human dignity is now protected by domestic law. In the analysis he cited from *Price v UK*,[122] where in her concurring opinion Judge Greve stated:

> In a civilised country like the United Kingdom, society considers it not only appropriate but a basic humane concern to try to improve and compensate for the disabilities faced by a person in the applicant's situation. In my opinion, these compensatory measures come to form part of the disabled person's physical integrity.

4.106   In his earlier judgment in *R (A, B, X and Y) v East Sussex CC and the Disability Rights Commission (No 2)*[123] Munby J had observed that the 'protection of human dignity' was a core value that the courts would protect and that in so doing this amounted to a 'solemn affirmation of the law's and of society's recognition of our humanity and of human dignity as something fundamental'.

---

119 Complaint nos 02/C/8679, 8681 and 10389 against Bolsover DC, 30 September 2003: and see also complaint no 07C03887 against Bury MBC, 14 October 2009, para 40 where the ombudsman characterised the council's inaction as 'institutional indifference' (inaction that left a mother with no option but to hose down her disabled children in the garden).
120 [2002] EWHC 2282 (Admin), (2002) 5 CCLR 577
121 [2004] EWHC 1879 (Admin), [2005] 2 WLR 431, (2004) 7 CCLR 609.
122 (2002) 34 EHRR 1285 at 1296.
123 [2003] EWHC 167 (Admin), (2003) 6 CCLR 194 at [86].

4.107   Baroness Hale of Richmond has made much the same point:[124]

human dignity is all the more important for people whose freedom of action and choice is curtailed, whether by law or by circumstances such as disability. The Convention is a living instrument . . . We need to be able to use it to promote respect for the inherent dignity of all human beings but especially those who are most vulnerable to having that dignity ignored. In reality, the niceties and technicalities with which we have to be involved in the courts should be less important than the core values which underpin the whole Convention.

4.108   Article 3(a) of the UN Convention on the Rights of Persons with Disabilities lists as its first underpinning principle "respect for inherent dignity, individual autonomy including the freedom to make one's own choices, and independence of persons". Domestically, in November 2006 the government in England launched a 'dignity in care' campaign endorsing the courts and ombudsmen's approach in this area.[125] The Commission for Social Care Inspection produced guidance on dignity in care, last updated in June 2010[126].which highlights eight key factors – choice and control, communication, eating and nutritional care, pain management, personal hygiene, practical assistance, privacy and social inclusion.

4.109   The requirement to make suitable arrangements to ensure the dignity, privacy and independence of service users applies to all persons registered with the Care Quality Commission (CQC) (essentially all service providers – see paras 7.100 and 9.20). Baroness Hale referred in the *McDonald* case to the findings of the CQCs Review of Compliance at Ipswich Hospital NHS Trust that dignity was not always sufficiently considered because people were not taken to a toilet away from their bed-space and commodes were used all the time.[127]

4.110   Given the widespread recognition of the importance of dignity in the lives of disabled and older people, the decision in *R (McDonald) v Royal Borough of Kensington and Chelsea*[128] is disappointing. The Supreme Court by a majority of 4:1 agreed with the Court of Appeal that the respondent local authority had acted lawfully in requiring a woman in her late 60s who was continent, but physically unable to access her commode unaided, to wear incontinence pads at night, rather than being provided with personal assistance to access her commode. This was of course the significantly cheaper option, which, the respondents also argued, would

---

124 'What can the human rights act do for my mental health?', the 2004 Paul Sieghart Memorial Lecture, accessible at www.bihr.org/downloads/transcipt_hale.doc. Baroness Hale used a 2002 British Institute of Human Rights report as the inspiration for her lecture – namely J Watson, *Something for Everyone: The impact of the Human Rights Act and the need for a Human Rights Commission*, British Institute of Human Rights, 2002.

125 See press release accessible at www.gnn.gov.uk/environment/fullDetail.asp? ReleaseID=241940&NewsAreaID=2&NavigatedFrom Department= False.

126 *Dignity in care, guide 15*, SCIE 2010, available at www.scie.org.uk/publications/ guides/guide15/index.asp

127 *Dignity and nutrition for older people: review of compliance Ipswich Hospital NHS Trust*, CQC, May 2011, p 8.

128 [2011] UKSC 33, (2011) 14 CCLR 341.

respect the appellant's safety and privacy. She was resolutely opposed to the proposal which she regarded as an affront on her dignity.

4.111 The appellant argued, amongst other things, that the decision interfered with her Article 8 rights. Both the human rights and disability discrimination arguments[129] were given short shrift in the leading judgment of Lord Brown. His approach to Article 8 is surprising, citing the 'margin of appreciation', a European concept enabling the Strasbourg Court to make allowances for differing domestic contexts, but not relevant to the application of the Convention in domestic courts. In finding that Article 8 is not engaged, Lord Brown relied particularly on *Anufrijeva v Southwark LBC*[130] in finding no positive duty to provide welfare support, distinguishing *R (Bernard) v Enfield LBC* (see para 4.104 above) on its facts – both because of the severity of the circumstances in the latter case and the impact on family life.

4.112 Nowhere in the judgment is there any consideration of the *East Sussex* case (see para 4.106 above) in which Munby J treated the dignity of a disabled person as a central tenet of the right to private life, nor any recognition by the majority that dignity, so closely allied with individual autonomy, must in large part be a subjective concept. Baroness Hale alluded to this, in her dissenting judgment, arguing that while supplying continence pads to people who are continent but immobile might be accepted practice (part of the respondent's case), that is not the same as obliging someone to use them against their will (para 75).

4.113 Baroness Hale, quoted Lord Lloyd in *Barry*, 'in every case, simple or complex, the need of the individual will be assessed against the standards of civilised society as we know them in the United Kingdom'. She went on to suggest that the implication of the majority judgment is that local authorities would be entitled to leave continent clients lying in their own urine and faeces both day and night, with the only constraint being how frequently it was necessary to change their pads to avoid health hazards. While the majority vociferously rejected this bold assertion, there is no doubt that the standard for dignity in the treatment of disabled and older people has been significantly undermined by the *McDonald* judgment.

Urgent cases

4.114 Where an individual's need is so pressing that there is not time even to carry out a 'fast-track' assessment (see para 3.60), a service can be provided without an assessment. NHSCCA 1990 s47(5) provides:

> Nothing in this section shall prevent a local authority from temporarily providing or arranging for the provision of community care services for any person without carrying out a prior assessment of his needs in accordance

129 Sections 21E and 49A of the Disability Discrimination Act 1995, now incorporated in similar form in the Equality Act 2010.
130 [2004] QB 1124, [2003] EWCA Civ 1406, (2003) 6 CCLR 25 (a case which concerned a failure to provide accommodation to meet the special needs of an asylum seeker and two other complaints of maladministration and delay in handling asylum claims).

with the preceding provisions of this section if, in the opinion of the authority, the condition of that person is such that he requires those services as a matter of urgency.

4.115   While an authority is not obliged by NHSCCA 1990 s47(5) to make such provision, it would be an unlawful fettering of discretion for it to reach a policy decision prohibiting the provision of any community care service without a prior assessment. 1993 guidance suggested that the power under NHSCCA 1990 s47(5) should be used sparingly[131] and the Prioritising Needs guidance advises:[132]

> Councils may provide an immediate response to those individuals who approach them, or are referred, for social care support in emergencies and crises. After this initial response, they should inform the individual that a fuller assessment will follow, and services may be withdrawn or changed as a result of this assessment.

4.116   In *R (Alloway) v Bromley LBC*[133] the applicant's urgent need for a care home placement had been delayed by the local authority's flawed assessment process. In his judgment, Crane J suggested that pending the outcome of a further reassessment, the authority could use its powers under section 47(5) to conclude a temporary placement of the applicant in order to avoid the likely hardship that would result from further delay. It follows that where an authority's delay in completing an assessment is causing hardship, it should consider using its powers under section 47(5), and a failure so to do might, in an appropriate case, amount to maladministration.

Health and safety

4.117   Specialist guidance (in relation to care home services) has been issued by the Health and Safety Executive in its booklet HS(G)220, *Health and Safety in Care Homes*.[134] The guidance details the main heads of legal responsibility to employees and residents under the Health and Safety at Work Act 1974 as well as in tort and contract. The guidance gives practical advice on the handling and reporting of incidents; occupational health; training; the working environment; kitchen, laundry and outdoor safety; as well as covering other issues such as violence to staff.

Manual handling

4.118   Of particular concern is the question of the avoidance of procedures that involve manual handling (in domiciliary and community care settings as

---

131   See eg LAC (93)2, para 17 but compare paras 21–22.
132   Para 70; UFSAMC 2002 policy guidance, para 5.36.
133   [2004] EWHC 2108 (Admin), (2005) 8 CCLR 61.
134   Health and Safety Executive (2001) *Health and safety in care homes*. HSG220. Sudbury: HSE Books. A new edition is due in 2011. The HSE also has a website that provides information about managing risks in health and social care at www.hse.gov.uk/healthservices

well as in residential care), not least because it appears that manual handling accounts for 32 per cent of all employee reported injuries in care
homes.[135]

4.119   Because of the general prevalence of such injuries throughout all types
of work environment, European Directive 90/269/EEC required all member states to take specific legislative action to reduce such injuries at work.
In consequence, the Manual Handling Operations Regulations 1992[136]
and the Management of Health and Safety at Work Regulations 1999[137]
were issued. Detailed guidance on the 1992 Regulations has been issued
by the Health and Safety Executive under reference L23.[138] Regulation 4(1)
of the 1992 Regulations (as amended) places a twofold obligation on
employers – namely (1) so far as is reasonably practicable to avoid
employees having to undertake any manual handling operations; and (2)
where this is not reasonably practicable, to assess the risks of such work,
to reduce these risks to the lowest level reasonably practicable, and to
inform employees of the risks.

4.120   As the guidance L23 states (para 16), regulation 4 establishes a clear
hierarchy of measures, namely:

(a)   Avoid hazardous manual handling operations so far as is reasonably
       practicable. This may be done by redesigning the task to avoid mov-
       ing the load or by automating or mechanising the process.
(b)   Make a suitable and sufficient assessment of any hazardous manual
       handling operations that cannot be avoided.
(c)   Reduce the risk of injury from those operations so far as is reasonably
       practicable. Where possible, mechanical assistance should be pro-
       vided, for example, a sack trolley or hoist. Where this is not reason-
       ably practicable then changes to the task, the load and the working
       environment should be explored.

4.121   The very detailed guidance given by the Health and Safety Executive is of
great practical importance, analysing the appropriate use of hoists and
other possible lifting mechanisms when moving patients. What the regulations do not do, however, is prohibit the lifting of patients. In the past it
appears that social services authorities and health bodies adopted
extremely restrictive interpretations of the regulations with the end result
that patients did not receive services (such as bathing) because it involved
some element of manual handling.

4.122   In *R (A and B) v East Sussex CC*[139] Munby J was asked to give general
guidance concerning how local authorities should seek to resolve the

---

135 Health and Safety Executive (2009) *Management of health and safety in care homes
     2009/2010,* Annex 1 LAC 79/11 HSE Books. It appears that there is no consistent
     approach to the recording residents' injuries.
136 SI No 2793.
137 SI No 3242.
138 Health and Safety Executive (2004) *Manual Handling: Manual Handling Operations
     Regulations 1992 (as amended) Guidance on Regulations* L23 (3rd edition) HSE Books.
139 [2003] EWHC 167 (Admin), (2003) 6 CCLR 194.

relative interests of disabled people – to be lifted safely and with dignity – and their paid carers – to avoid risks of injury from manual handling. By the time of the hearing the local authority had accepted that its previous inflexible 'no manual handling' policy was unlawful and had revised it. Nevertheless a dispute remained as to the application of the new policy to the needs of the applicants – two young women with profound physical and learning disabilities. In reaching his judgment, the judge not only reviewed the relevant legislation and guidance (as above) he also had regard to the relevant domestic case law, in particular *King v Sussex Ambulance NHS Trust*.[140] The case concerned an injury sustained by an ambulance man in carrying an elderly person down the stairs of a cottage. In Munby J's view the case established a principle:

> that an employee whose job is to lift people (the ambulance man) may have to accept a greater degree of risk than one who is employed to move inanimate objects (the furniture remover) and that what is reasonable (and . . . practicable) has to be evaluated having regard to the social utility of the operation and a public authority's duties to the public and to the particular member of the public who has called for the authority's help. At the same time one has to recognise, of course, that none of this can justify exposing an employee to . . . 'unacceptable risk'.

4.123   From this analysis[141] the judge concluded that there may be situations where 'some manual handling is on any view an inherent – an inescapable – feature of the very task for which those who care . . . are employed';

4.124   Munby J did not provide a definitive answer as to what degree of manual handling was required in the particular case. He gave general guidance, however, as to how the balance of interest should be struck. In his view this was not a 'situation in which the disabled person's rights "trump" those of the carer,[142] though equally . . . the carer's rights do not "trump" those of the disabled person'. There is no doubt but that such cases raise extremely challenging issues, and in difficult cases the resolution may require the installation of specialist (and expensive) equipment beyond that which has generally been sanctioned by local authorities and health bodies.

4.125   The judge gave guidance on how the assessment should be conducted and how the disabled person's wishes, feelings and preferences should be ascertained. At the end of this process, a decision had to be made:

> Once the balance has been struck, if it comes down in favour of manual handling, then the employer must take appropriate assessments and take all appropriate steps to minimise the risks that exist.

140   [2002] EWCA Civ 953, (2002) 68 BMLR 177.
141   Which included a consideration of the jurisprudence of the European Court of Human Rights and the Charter of Fundamental Rights of the European Union, Article 26.
142   In this context, see also the Public Services Ombudsman for Wales report concerning the former Cardiff Local Health Board and the former Cardiff and Vale NHS Trust case refs 200802231 and 200802232, 6 August 2010, which criticised an NHS body for failing to assess the competing risks to the patient and carer before it decided that the patient had to be cared for in hospital and not in his own home.

Manual handling and unpaid carers

4.126   In those cases where authorities are using the regulations as a reason for refusing to provide a service, they are often willing to admit that in consequence the task is carried out by a carer instead. Although such a person is not an employee for the purposes of the regulations and other health and safety at work legislation,[143] he or she is someone to whom the authority prima facie owes a duty of care (respect for, and the support of, carers being at the heart of the community care reforms). If an authority fully conversant with the good practice and knowledge engendered by the regulations stands by and allows a carer to carry out tasks it believes to be unduly hazardous for its own employees, then it may well be liable in negligence for any injuries that result (unless, perhaps, it has taken steps to inform and/or train the carer in safe lifting techniques etc). In similar vein, such action may constitute maladministration – for example, if a local authority fails to assess the competing risks to the patient and carer before making a decision based on health and safety considerations.[144]

4.127   Such health risks are foreseeable: well publicised research has shown that over 50 per cent of unpaid carers have suffered a physical injury such as a strained back since they began to care. In addition, the research reveals that caring also subjects carers to other health related problems, with over half receiving treatment for stress-related illness since becoming carers.[145]

Welfare Reform Act 2009 and the Right to Control Pilot Schemes

Services within the scheme

4.128   The Welfare Reform Act 2009 Part 2 ss38–50 make provision for the development of the personalisation programme in relation to the delivery of non-community care/Children Act/carers services (which are presently excluded by section 39(6) – although there is power to lift the exclusion on community care services – see s48). It paves the way for the introduction of pilot scheme operated by 'trailblazer sites', eight individual local authorities or local consortia, running from December 2010 to 13 December 2012. Section 38 describes the aim:

> The purpose of this Part is to enable disabled people aged 18 or over to exercise greater choice in relation to, and greater control over, the way in

---

143   Although the Health and Safety at Work etc Act 1974 3(1) places a general duty of care on employers to people not in their employment, this, however, is a penal provision – see *R (Hampstead Heath Winter Swimming Club) v Corporation of London* [2005] EWHC 713 (Admin), [2005] 1 WLR 2930.

144   The Public Services Ombudsman for Wales has also issued a report concerning the former Cardiff Local Health Board and the former Cardiff and Vale NHS Trust case refs 200802231 and 200802232 6 August 2010.

145   M Henwood, *Ignored and Invisible? Carers Experience of the NHS*, Carers National Association, 1998: cited in *Caring about Carers: A National Strategy for Carers* LASSL (99)2; and see also para 16.65 above.

which relevant services (as defined by section 39) are provided to or for them, in cases where the provision of the relevant services is a function of a relevant authority (as defined by section 40).

4.129   'Relevant services' are defined as any services (including the provision of grants or loans) 'provided to or for the benefit of a disabled person' in relation to further education, training or employment, enabling independent living, residential accommodation and, more broadly, 'enabling [the disabled person] to overcome barriers to participation in society' (s39(2)(h)).

4.130   The details of the scheme are set out in the Disabled People's Right to Control (Pilot Scheme)(England) Regulations 2010,[146] which are accompanied by Statutory and Good Practice Guidance.[147] The provisions are complex, but in summary, three funding streams constitute 'qualifying services' in the pilot scheme namely: 'Access to Work'[148] and 'Work Choice'[149] (formerly the 'Specialist Disability Employment Programme') and Supporting People (housing support, administered locally – see para 15.119 below). Where a person is receiving a qualifying service managed by the pilot programme then the regulations provide that this support can be integrated with any (a) community care support (b) Independent Living Payments (ILF) payments and (c) Disabled Facilities Grant to which the person may be entitled, so that all the support can be delivered 'seamlessly'. These supports are collectively referred to as 'Right to Control services'.[150]

4.131   The arrangements are available to disabled people over 18 who are entitled to receive a qualifying service. Such persons have little or no choice over whether or not to be part of the programme – unless they were already receiving a qualifying service before the pilot commenced: in which case they will only come within the programme if they (and the authority responsible for the service) agree that they should.

4.132   Eligible individuals must be notified in writing of what the programme entails and of the likely value of the support they will be eligible for. Once they have been advised that they are to be enrolled onto the scheme they will be subject to what are in effect, 'community care planning lookalike arrangements'. They will:

- Have a named representative to help them (eg 'a family member, friend, carer or . . . advocate – para 2.29 of the Statutory Guidance);

---

146 SI No 2862.
147 Accessible at http://odi.dwp.gov.uk/odi-projects/right-to-control-trailblazers/resources.php
148 A specialist scheme funded by the Department for Work and Pensions for which Jobcentre Plus offices are the initial point of contact. It aims to help disabled people and their employers with some of the extra costs which may arise because of the person's disability.
149 A specialist scheme funded by the Department for Work and Pensions but delivered by private providers. It aims to support disabled people in work where their needs cannot be met through other work programmes such as 'Access to Work'.
150 Which definition also includes 'qualifying services' – ie Access to Work and Work Choice funding as well as Supporting People's payments.

- Have a 'suitable person' if they lack capacity to make relevant decisions (para 2.31 of the Statutory Guidance);[151]
- Have a support plan.

Support plans

4.133 The regulations place a duty on the responsible authority to develop a support plan for the person even if s/he lacks capacity or is non-cooperative (regulation 8). The plans must include the following details:[152]

- The level of funding to which the person is entitled;
- Agreed outcomes: the Good Practice guide (chapter 2) describes an 'outcome' as 'the result or effect achieved by action'; explaining that it is 'not an individual using a service, but the increased social confidence or skills that an individual may acquire from using the service'.
- The services to be provided;
- The financial contribution to be made by the individual;
- The intervals at which the plan is to be reviewed (which must be at least yearly – and generally more frequently;

4.134 Regulations 11 and 12 provide that where outcomes have been agreed, then the responsible authority is under a duty to 'give effect to any request by [the individual] as to the manner in which any services are to be provided' and 'so far as it is reasonably practicable' to provide or secure the services agreed in the plan. Thus, although the duty is owed to the individual disabled person, its force is qualified by 'reasonable practicability'. Compliance with service user wishes is further qualified, as it is not required where (reg 11(2)):

    (b) the provision of the services in the manner requested . . .. would not secure the agreed outcomes;
    (c) the level of funding specified in the plan is not sufficient to give effect to the request.

Direct payments

4.135 The Good Practice guide emphasises that practitioners should 'avoid giving the impression that choice and control is about having a direct payment' (p15); stating that individuals may exercise this control by (p9):

- Continuing to have their existing services; or
- The relevant authority arranging for the services to be provided; or
- The making of a cash payment (ie a direct payment); or
- A combination of service provision and direct payments.

---

151 Suitable person, although mentioned on several occasions in the regulations, is not defined. It seems clear that s/he is similar to the 'suitable person' to whom a community care direct payments can be made if the service user lacks capacity (ie under Health and Social Care Act 2008 s146 – who is defined by Health and Social Care Act 2001 s57(1C) (inserted by Health and Social Care Act 2008 s146(2)) and is (if there is no LPA or deputyship order) a person who the responsible authority considers to be suitable (in this case to receive the direct payments).
152 reg 10 and para 2.20 of the Statutory Guidance.

4.136   If the individual opts for a direct payment, then the relevant rules for these payments mirror almost exactly those for community care direct payments[153] (see chapter 12). The Statutory Guidance (para 2.74), however, advises that such payments can be paid into the same bank account as has been opened by the individual for any community care direct payments or Personal Health Budget s/he may be receiving.

Right to Control and Disabled Facilities Grants

4.137   Regulation 23 and Schedule 2 provide that people resident in the pilot areas who have had an application for a DFG approved will (subject to a number of provisos) be entitled:

- to choose the contractor to undertake the works – even if that contractor was not the one whose estimate accompanied the application; and
- to receive the DFG as a direct payment.

The regulations concerning the making of a direct payment in such cases mirror closely those for community care direct payments (see chapter 12).

Community care

4.138   Trailblazer local authorities must comply with the Community Care Services: Disabled People's Choice and Control (Pilot Scheme) (England) Directions 2010.[154] The directions do not apply to people who were already in receipt of community care services, when the regulations came into effect (13 December 2010) unless the person agrees to this. For individuals who are newly assessed as being entitled to community care services, the directions require that they be informed in writing of:

- The duties that the local authority is under – by virtue both of these directions and Community Care Assessment Directions 2004;
- The availability of other Right to Control services available from the authority;
- The likely value of their personal budget – which the direction 1(5) defines as 'the amount which a pilot authority considers needs to be spent in order to meet that individual's eligible needs';[155]
- The availability of direct payments; and
- The right to complain about the actions of the trailblazer local authority.

4.139   If the individual is also entitled to other Right to Control services, the directions require that so far as is possible there is a 'seamless delivery' of

153 Ie those detailed in The Community Care, Services for Carers and Children's Services (Direct Payments) (England) Regulations 2009 SI No 1887.

154 Accessible at http://odi.dwp.gov.uk/odi-projects/right-to-control-trailblazers/resources.php.

155 Eligible needs are defined by the same direction as 'those needs, which in the pilot authority's view, call for the provision of community care services'.

these – by, for example, combining the care plans (Statutory Guidance 5.10).

The Independent Living Fund

4.140 The ILF trust Deed has been amended to refer to the Right to Control pilot areas for the period of the scheme. All existing recipients of the ILF in these areas will be given the Right to Control over the funding they receive during the period of the pilots and the ILF is contacting all relevant recipients to inform them of this.

The new language of personalisation

4.141 The Right to Control Directions represent the first legislative examples in social care law of the term 'personal budget' and the Right to Control regulations bring in the first examples in social care of 'responsibilisation' agenda – ie of disabled people having a duty to accept responsibility for their arrangements.[156] Direction 1(5) defines a personal budget in subjective terms – namely that which the 'pilot authority considers needs to be spent in order to meet that individual's eligible needs'. From the recipient's perspective such a definition is materially weaker than the more 'objective' service costed basis for the assessment of the amount of a direct payment – which must be equivalent to the authority's estimate of 'the reasonable cost of securing the provision of the service concerned'.[157]

4.142   Curiously for an initiative entitled 'Right to Control' the Regulations (reg 8) and the Statutory Guidance (para 2.19) make it clear that even if a disabled person is 'unwilling to work with the authority to develop a support plan' one will nevertheless be prepared on his or her behalf. If the regulations are to be the template for the scheme when it is rolled out nationally, it seems likely that sanctions may be imposed when a person fails to work towards the goals set out in the support plan. If so, given the seamless link with community care provision envisaged in the programme, this would represent a fundamental shift away from service provision on the basis of need to a benefits-style concept of entitlement increasingly subject to the individual continuing to 'deserve' such support.

Law Commission proposals

4.143 The recommendations in this area generally place existing requirements in statutory guidance onto a legislative footing. Proposals include:

---

156 See eg I Ferguson, (2007) ' User Choice or Privatising Risk? The Antinomies of Personalization', *British Journal of Social Work*, vol 37: 387 – 403 and L Clements 'Individual budgets and irrational exuberance' (2008) 11 CCLR 413.

157 Health and Social Care Act 2001 s57(4) and see also para 111 of the 2009 Direct Payments Guidance.

- A statutory duty on local authorities to ensure the production of a care and support plan for people with assessed eligible needs (including carers). Those assessed as falling outside the eligibility criteria should be given written reasons together with a copy of their assessment.
- Provisions requiring the Secretary of State for Health and the Welsh Assembly Ministers to make regulations prescribing the form and content of care and support plans: including that they are in writing and signed on behalf of the local authority; that they contain a summary of assessed needs, eligible needs and outcomes to be achieved; the amount of the personal budget and how the sum has been calculated; a summary of services to be provided, whether a direct payment will be provide and any financial contribution; review arrangements; and that a copy is made available to service users.
- Provisions enabling regulations to be made to require local authorities to allocate a personal budget to service users and carers, and to specify who is eligible and the circumstances in which budgets should not be allocated.
- The proposed Code of Practice should cover the delegation of production of the care and support plan and clarify self-funders' eligibility to care and support planning. It should also provide concrete examples of care and support plans.

CHAPTER 5

Assessment and planning for discharge from hospital

Introduction

5.1   The law that regulates the hospital discharge responsibilities of the NHS and social services authorities is an amalgam of statute and tort. The patient is owed a duty of care (in the tort of negligence) by both the social services authority and the relevant NHS body. In England and Wales the NHS has a statutory responsibility to provide care under the National Health Service Acts 2006 – albeit that this is a weak duty (see para 13.16 below) – and social services have responsibilities under the community care legislation to assess and provide services. Patients have in general[1] no right to remain in an NHS facility and can be discharged against their wishes – provided that the NHS and social services authorities consider that it is safe (ie have satisfied themselves that it would not be negligent – by exposing the patient to an unnecessary or involuntary risk of harm). In this respect the two bodies are subject to considerable Department of Health and Welsh Government guidance.

5.2   For a number of reasons such as the introduction of 'payment by results',[2] the dramatic decline in the number of NHS beds (see para 14.40 below) and concerns about hospital acquired infections, there is considerable pressure on hospitals to move patients from acute facilities as soon as it is safe to do so. In England, in spite of the move away from indicators and targets, delayed transfers of care remains a performance measure for national oversight.[3] Wales also has delayed transfers of care as a performance indicator and publishes statistics.[4]

5.3   In England, the introduction of the Community Care (Delayed Discharges etc) Act (CC(DD)A) 2003 saw a significant decline in the number of people in hospital recorded as subject to a 'delayed discharge'.[5] However, concerns about both delayed transfers of care and emergency readmissions have prompted the Government in England to propose

---

1   Unless they are entitled to NHS continuing healthcare support, detained under the Mental Health Act (MHA) 1983 or have been in NHS accommodation for a prolonged period – such that it might be deemed their 'home' for the purposes of European Convention on Human Rights Article 8 (see para 26.266).

2   See generally Department of Health (2011) *Payment by Results Guidance for 2011–12.* Under the programme, instead of being commissioned through block agreements, hospitals are paid for work they do – the intention being to encourage activity which should help reduce waiting lists. Since the payments are based on fixed tariffs this is also expected to reward the more efficient providers.

3   NHS Operating Framework for 2011–12. Statistics are published monthly at http://data.gov.uk/dataset/acute_and_non-acute_delayed_transfers_of_care-monthly_situation_reports

4   Published monthly available at http://wales.gov.uk/topics/statistics/headlines/health2011/110426/?lang=en

5   The records indicate that these fell from 4,147 (of whom 3,025 were over 75) in the last quarter of 2002–03 to 2,175 (of whom 1,604 were over 75) in the last quarter of 2005–06. However, some of the success of the policy may be tempered with the knowledge that in the same quarters the number of people who were readmitted as an emergency within 28 days of discharge rose from 138,773 to 198,777 – a rise from 5.5% to 7.1% of all patients discharged: see *Report of the Chief Executive to the NHS*, June 2006.

radical reform and place the responsibility for patients leaving hospital on the NHS for the first 30 days[6] – see para 5.52 below.

5.4   In most instances patients are keen to move on from a hospital ward. When a patient requires ongoing assistance either in the form of NHS or social care, establishing whether it is safe to discharge the patient, and assessing what services are needed following a hospital stay, are key to a smooth transition. In this respect the Health Select Committee's 2002 report on delayed discharges stated that the key objective was to ensure 'the right care in the right place at the right time'.[7] This objective is quoted in the guidance issued in 2010.[8]

The discharge process

5.5   In England the relationship between the NHS and social services in the discharge process is shaped by statute (namely the CC(DD)A 2003), regulations and guidance.[9] It was the coming into force of the 2003 Act in England that spurred the secretary of state, in 2004, to issue directions for the first time under National Health Service and Community Care Act (NHSCCA) 1990 s47(4) on the assessment process (see para 3.24 above).[10] In the same year directions were also issued which required the NHS to satisfy itself that a patient was not entitled to continuing NHS healthcare funding before it issued a notification under CC(DD)A 2003 s2 to social services (see para 5.29 below).[11] Both sets of directions reinforce the duty on authorities to consult with patients (and, where appropriate, their carers) and to give them information about the outcome of the assessment.

5.6   The legal obligations that arise on hospital discharge are activated by the discharge of the patient from NHS care – not his or her transfer to another NHS facility. Patients do not have the right to choose the place at which they receive NHS care.[12] The decision that they are safe to be transferred to another NHS facility is therefore primarily that of the responsible consultant and the NHS team on the receiving ward. It follows that when discussing hospital discharge, the issue is not of internal transfer but discharge from an NHS setting. A consultant's decision in conjunction with the medical team that a patient is medically fit to be transferred

---

6   According to the Department of Health about 60% of delayed transfers are attributable to the NHS and 33% to Social Care, with the remaining 7% being attributable to both. Dear colleague letter 11 May 2011 Gateway reference 16058.
7   House of Commons Health Committee, *Delayed discharges*, HC 671–1, 2002. Accessible at www.publications.parliament.uk/pa/cm200102/cmselect/cmhealth/617/617.pdf
8   Department of Health (2010) *Ready to Go?*, p4.
9   There is no present intention to bring the reimbursement provisions of the 2003 Act into force in Wales.
10 . Community Care Assessment Directions 2004 LAC (2004)24.
11   Delayed Discharges (Continuing Care) Directions 2004 which have been replaced by the Delayed Discharges (Continuing Care) Directions 2009.
12   See para 7.139.

is the *sine qua non* – the key triggering event – in the discharge planning process.[13]

5.7   When such a decision has been made and the patient has (or may have) a need for community care services, a safe discharge cannot occur until the NHS and social services are satisfied that the patient is not only (1) ready for discharge, but also (2) safe to be discharged. In essence this is therefore a twin key process. Once the system is activated, the discharge conveyor belt only starts to move when two keys have been turned; the first is primarily the responsibility of the NHS and the second, primarily (at present – see para 5.52 below) the responsibility of social services. Once the two keys have been turned and the belt is in motion, then (if the process is regulated by the CC(DD)A 2003) social services are generally unable to stop the system without incurring the possibility of reimbursing the NHS if they are the cause of any delay in the patient's discharge from hospital.

Key guidance

5.8   In England three central documents give key guidance on the process that should be followed to ensure a 'non-simple' discharge is safe. These are (1) *Ready to Go? Planning the discharge and the transfer of patients from hospital and intermediate care*;[14] (2) the safe discharge protocol *Definitions – Medical Stability and 'Safe to Transfer'*;[15] and (3) the *CC(DD)A 2003 Guidance for Implementation*[16] (referred to in the following section as the '2010 guidance', the 'safe discharge protocol' and the 'delayed discharge guidance' respectively). In terms of good practice, the 2010 guidance replaces the considerably longer guidance issued in 2003 *Pathways, process and practice*[17] and should be viewed as the core guidance shaping the basic structure, processes and the collaborations that are essential to a sympathetic and effective hospital discharge system. It contains 10 key steps for staff to follow:

1.   Start planning for discharge or transfer before or on admission.
2.   Identify whether the patient has simple or complex discharge and transfer planning needs, involving the patient and carer in decision.

13   The NHS/social services cannot (without invoking their powers under the MHA 1983) prevent patients from discharging themselves – provided they have sufficient mental capacity to make the decision (see para 17.9 below).
14   Department of Health, 2010, accessible at www.dh.gov.uk/en/ Publicationsandstatistics/Publications/PublicationsPolicyAndGuidance/DH_113950
15   Department of Health, 2003, accessible at www.dh.gov.uk/prod_consum_dh/groups/ dh_digitalassets/@dh/@en/documents/digitalasset/dh_4071848.pdf
16   *The Community Care (Delayed Discharges etc) Act 2003 Guidance for Implementation*, September 2003, HSC 2003/009: LAC (2003)21.
17   The brevity of the guidance although having the advantage of being more likely to be read by busy practitioners, nevertheless loses some of the very useful guidance issued particularly in relation to carers. The guidance though is accompanied by a number of memory sticks which may amplify some of the points lost in the main document.

3. Develop a clinical management plan for every patient within 24 hours of admission.
4. Co-ordinate the discharge or transfer of care process through effective leadership and handover of responsibilities at ward level.
5. Set an expected date of discharge or transfer within 24–48 hours of admission, and discuss with the patient and carer.
6. Review the clinical management plan with the patient each day, take any necessary action and update progress towards the discharge or transfer date.
7. Involve patients and carers so that they can make informed decisions and choices that deliver a personalised care pathway and maximise their independence.
8. Plan discharges and transfers to take place over seven days to deliver continuity of care for the patient.
9. Use a discharge checklist 24–48 hours prior to transfer.
10. Make decisions to discharge and transfer patients each day.

5.9   In Wales the guidance on hospital discharge is to be found in the relatively brief Assembly (now Welsh Government) document from 2005 *Hospital Discharge Planning Guidance*,[18] and the much longer and more informative good practice guidance *Passing the Baton* 2009.[19]

5.10   In England, good practice guidance has additionally been issued in relation to people in mental health settings[20] and regarding hospital admission and discharge of people who are homeless.[21]

Simple hospital discharges

5.11   A 'toolkit' has been issued by the Department of Health concerning 'simple' discharge procedures, entitled *Achieving timely 'simple' discharge from hospital*[22] ('the 2004 guidance'). This applies to simple discharges[23] – which it is thought make up 'at least 80% of all discharges', and are classified as cases where the patient returns to their home and does not

18 WHC (2005)35: NAFWC 17/2005 available at www.wales.nhs.uk/documents/WHC_2005_035.pdf.
19 National Leadership and Innovation Agency for Healthcare (2009) *Passing the Baton*. The guidance and associated good practice materials is at www.wales.nhs.uk/sitesplus/829/page/36467; the Welsh Government has also issued guidance on hospital discharge where this arises out of a patient exercising 'choice' under the Choice of Accommodation directions *Procedures when discharging patients to a care setting: Supplementary Guidance* WHC(2004) 066/NAFW 46/2004 -LG/ML/001/11 (see para 5.42) below.
20 Care Services Improvement Partnership (2007) *A Positive Outlook – a good practice toolkit to improve discharge from inpatient mental health care.*
21 Department for Communities and Local Government and Department of Health (2006) *Hospital Admission and Discharge: People who are homeless or living in temporary or insecure accommodation.*
22 Department of Health (2004) *Achieving timely 'simple' discharge from hospital: A toolkit for the multi-disciplinary team.*
23 Although the 2010 guidance deals with simple discharges it makes clear that this 2004 toolkit is still to be used.

require social services involvement in the form of a community care assessment. For non-simple (classified as 'complex') discharges, the 2010 guidance is the relevant document. In Wales *Passing the Baton* deals with both simple and complex discharges.

5.12   The idea behind the 2004 guidance is to implement relatively simple procedures which it appears can have a dramatic impact on freeing up beds – including discharging patients earlier in the day before the peak demand for admissions (the build-up starts in general at 7am and reaches its peak at 12.30pm); having discharge procedures operating on the same basis seven days a week; and authorising less senior medical/nursing staff to implement the process. The 2004 guidance stresses that 'patients and carers are at the centre of care and should be involved in discharge plans early in the patient's stay' and that 'discharge decisions are made following senior assessment of the patient on admission and patients and carers are informed about the expected date of discharge early in their stay'.[24]

Patient and carer involvement

5.13   The Community Care Assessment Directions (2004) have given added weight to earlier guidance regarding involving patients and carers. The directions require the local authority to 'consult the person, consider whether the person has any carers, and, where they think it appropriate, consult those carers.' Further, councils must provide information to the person and if appropriate any carers about the costs of any services they are considering providing.[25] Directions on the assessment for NHS continuing healthcare, place the same duties on the NHS to consult patients and carers, and to notify the patient of the outcome of the assessment and their right to request a review of the decision.[26]

5.14   The 2010 guidance is, however, more muted in this context than the 2003 guidance[27] which it replaced; the earlier guidance required 'the engagement and active participation of individuals and their carers as equal partners'[28] whereas the 2010 guidance speaks of the involvement of patients and carers in terms of managing their expectations.[29]

24 *Achieving Timely 'Simple' Discharges from Hospital*, 2004, p9.
25 Community Care Assessment Directions 2004, paras 2 and 4.
26 Delayed Discharges (Continuing Care) Directions 2009. These obligations are also to be found in the 2010 guidance: of the 10 key steps (see para 5.8 above) four require the involvement of the patient and carer.
27 Department of Health (2003) *Discharge from hospital: pathway, process and practice* at para 1.4.
28 An equivalent statement is still to be found at paras 22 and 24 of the Welsh Assembly circular *Hospital Discharge Planning Guidance*, 13 May 2005, WHC (2005) 035.
29 2010 guidance, p19. It is ironic that as this new guidance was being formulated the Association of Directors of Adult Services issued a report *Carers as Partners in Hospital Discharge*, pointing out the gaps between policy and practice and issuing recommendations to help improve carer recognition and make partnership a reality. Available at http://static.carers.org/files/hospital-discharge-final-version-4945.pdf

5.15   The 2010 guidance reminds practitioners that they must not to assume a carer is willing to take on or continue in a caring role (see para 16.16 below) and requires that they check the accuracy of information they are given from the patient about their relative's willingness and ability to care.[30] The 2010 guidance makes reference to the Welsh guidance *Passing the Baton*[31] which offers the following advice to practitioners:

> As part of the assessment process it is essential to consider:
> * What was the previous situation regarding the provision of informal care (who, how, when)?
> * Was it working well for both parties?
> * Has anything changed eg has the patient's condition deteriorated or have the physical, emotional or social circumstances of the carer changed?
> * Does the carer clearly understand the responsibilities they are taking on?[32]

Mental capacity

5.16   In relation to patients with limited mental capacity the 2010 guidance (page 11) stresses the need for them to have appropriate support when making decisions concerning their discharge arrangements.[33] It further states that 'where the patient cannot represent themselves, the next of kin, carer, relative or an independent mental capacity advocate (IMCA) must be involved. Their role is to represent the patient's interests, and to challenge any decision that does not appear to be in the best interest of the patient' (page 19). In contrast the Welsh practice guidance *Passing the Baton* has more detailed guidance on mental capacity issues and hospital discharge.[34]

Information/communication

5.17   In a number of investigations the Health Service Ombudsman has been critical of trusts which have failed to communicate properly with (and provide adequate information to) patients and their carers.[35] The ombudsman has stressed that where the obligation to inform is a joint one (ie shared with the social services) this does not excuse a failure by the trust to provide the information (ie it cannot assume that social services will discharge its duty).[36] The ombudsman has also criticised as

30 2010 guidance, pp 12 and 29.
31 Generally much fuller guidance than that provided in England with chapters on communicating with patients and their families, assessing the whole person, individualised care options, and legal issues.
32 *Passing the Baton*, para 3.29.
33 2010 guidance, p 11.
34 In chapter five 'Legal Issues'.
35 Complaint nos E 1631/03–04 and E 2050/02–03, both in Selected Cases for October 2003 – March 2004 which contains five cases on the question of hospital discharge. More recently the Welsh Ombudsman criticised the poor communication with the family regarding discharge *Case reference 200802248*.
36 Fifth report for session 1995–96, *Investigations of Complaints about Long-Term NHS Care*, HMSO; Complaint E.685/94–95.

inadequate the provision of general brochures to patients and situations where staff provided patients with only limited advice on their possible options.[37]

5.18   The 2010 guidance stresses the importance of effective communication with patients[38] and requires that they be provided with the provision of written information on the discharge process, noting that:

> Considerate language, well-written literature, clearly designed diagrams, simple signposting and accessible media in any format all help to complement and reinforce dialogue.[39]

Ward-based care/discharge co-ordination

5.19   Although the 2010 guidance stresses there should be a named lead discharge co-ordinator (page 25), it adds a note of caution, that at ward level 'practitioners are becoming increasingly reliant on specialist discharge teams in cases where they should be able to manage the process themselves' and that in 'today's environment it is unrealistic to expect one person to be available each day to co-ordinate care'.[40] It suggests therefore, that at ward level:

- one person has the lead for care planning each day;
- that uninterrupted time is dedicated to discharge planning, ensuring that everyone is aware of their responsibilities in the process, and that there is a named person to hand over the role to;
- that expected date of discharge should be set within 24–48 hours of admission and discussed with the patient and their family and reviewed daily with the patient;[41]
- that a discharge checklist should be completed 24–48 hours before discharge to ensure that all actions essential to a smooth discharge have been completed.[42]

Safe discharge

5.20   The 2010 guidance advises that discharge planning should commence before or on admission. The safe discharge protocol lists three key criteria for the making of the discharge decision and emphasises that they 'are not separate or sequential stages; all three should be addressed at the same time whenever possible':

1) a clinical decision has been made that the patient is ready for transfer;

37   Complaint E.672/94–95.
38   The guidance draws on the more extensive Welsh guidance *Passing the Baton* which devotes a complete chapter on communication (chapter 2).
39   2010 guidance, p 30.
40   2010 guidance, p 15.
41   2010 guidance, pp 16–18.
42   2010 guidance, p 25.

2) a multi-disciplinary team decision has been made that the patient is ready for transfer; and

3) the patient is safe to discharge/transfer.

5.21 The protocol comments that:

> In some cases we are told the process consists almost entirely of the consultant deciding a patient is medically fit for discharge, followed by referral to social services. Hence the multi-disciplinary input to the decision making process is minimal and – in extreme cases – non-existent. In addition this does not fulfil the, now legal, requirement to begin planning for discharge as soon as possible during the hospital stay.

5.22 The safe discharge protocol goes on to analyse the critical questions in relation to each of the three steps:

1) The clinical decision (ready to transfer/discharge)
   - Does the patient need to remain in an acute bed to receive intensive medical input from a consultant team?
   - Does the patient need intensive or specialist nursing, therapy or other clinical support only available in an acute setting, such as the administration of specialist drugs or intensive monitoring through the use of specialist equipment?
   - Has the patient's condition been monitored within an agreed period?
   - Is the patient's health likely to deteriorate significantly if moved elsewhere?
   - Has the patient recovered from the acute episode sufficiently to be able to return home or move to another setting?
   - Could the patient be managed at home by primary care or in a nurse or therapy led unit?

2) The multi-disciplinary team decision (ready to transfer/discharge)
   - Will the patient benefit from further acute treatment and/or rehabilitation?
   - Can rehabilitation or recuperation be provided in an alternative setting, including the patient's own home and has the team come to a decision about where the patient should be managed?
   - What are the risks of remaining in the acute bed?
   - Has the patient (and have any carers) been involved in the assessment?

3) The objective decision (safe to transfer/discharge)
   - Does the multi-disciplinary team have a clear picture of the patient's living circumstances prior to this episode and know enough to be able to make a decision that the person is safe to discharge/transfer?
   - Can the assessment be continued/completed in another setting, including the person's own home?
   - What does the patient want and expect?
   - Has the carer been consulted and what are his or her views?
   - Has a similar level of need for this patient previously been met by primary and community care services?

- Does everyone, including the patient and carer, understand the risk of transferring the patient?

5.23　Although the safe discharge protocol uses the word 'assessment' this does not appear to refer to a 'community care assessment' but merely whether the patient and carer have been involved in the multi-disciplinary decision that he or she is safe to transfer. However, CC(DD)A 2003 s4(9) and (10) clarify that assessments carried out under this Act are to be treated as done under NHSCCA 1990 s47 or, in the case of carers, under the Carers and Disabled Children Act (CDCA) 2000 ss1 or 2 (see para 16.38 below). The delayed discharge guidance at para 36 refers to this as meaning not necessarily all of the assessment and that 'assessment for discharge covers the services needed to allow the patient to move from the acute bed – a further assessment may be needed to put in place a longer term package of care or the next step, eg from intermediate care to home'. Further it specifically states that if a person is discharged to a home care package, social services 'should check the adequacy of the care package within at most two weeks of discharge. This should ensure that the patients are suitably cared for and not, for example, unable to cope or at risk of a deterioration or of readmission to hospital.'[43]

Delayed discharge payments in England

5.24　As noted below (see para 5.52) at the time of writing (September 2011) there is some doubt as to whether the charging arrangements (known as 'reimbursement') will be maintained in the medium term.

5.25　As at September 2011, however, the arrangements apply to local authorities who delay the discharge of adults who: (1) are safe to be discharged, (2) have been receiving acute medical care; and (3) are in need of community care services. A lack of capacity in a community care service (for instance the absence of any available care home places) does not exempt social services from their liability to make a payment. The provisions of the CC(DD)A 2003 are designed to synchronise with the good practice guidance; thus the service of a notice under the Act should not be seen as an event that dominates or in any way undermines the operation of good discharge planning. These provisions do not apply in Wales.[44]

Acute medical care

5.26　The reimbursement rules only apply to patients receiving 'acute medical care' – defined as 'intensive NHS funded medical treatment provided by or under the supervision of a consultant which is for a limited time after which the patient no longer benefits from that treatment'. Maternity care,

43　Hospital Discharge Implementation Guidance 2003, para 107.
44　The Welsh Government has indicated that it does not intend to implement Part I of the Act (the fining provisions) – see Health and Social Services Committee Minutes HSS(2)-11–04 (p2) 6 October 2004 at para 3.3.4.

mental healthcare,[45] palliative care, intermediate care and care provided for recuperation or rehabilitation are excluded from the definition of acute care.

The timings of the CC(DD)A 2003 notices

5.27 This NHS is required to give social services two notifications:

1) known as an assessment notification (under section 2) gives notice of the patient's possible need for services on discharge. Following this notification, social services have a minimum of three days to carry out an assessment and arrange care;

2) known as a discharge notification (under section 5) gives notice of the day on which it is proposed that the a patient will be discharged.

Reimbursement liability commences on the day after the minimum period (the third day after an assessment notification) or the day after the proposed discharge date, whichever is the later. A notification after 2pm is counted from the next day.

5.28   The technicalities of the notification are slightly involved.[46] Notifications sent on Sundays and Bank Holidays are deemed to have been sent on the following days as are notifications sent after 2pm on a Friday or after 5pm on any other day.[47] Originally it was intended that this would change so that all days were treated in the same way and no concessions made for holidays or weekends, however, as at September 2011 no changes have been made.

The CC(DD)A 2003 assessment obligations

The NHS

5.29 Before the NHS can issue the first notification (under section 2) it must:

- undertake an assessment as to whether the patient is eligible for continuing care support;[48]
- consult with the patient about involving social services (and the notification to social services must clarify the outcome of this consultation and provide certain minimum information – detailed in the regulations);[49]
- identify the patient's responsible social services authority.[50]

45 As detailed in Delayed Discharges (Mental Health Care) (England) Order 2003 SI No 2276 art 2.
46 Detailed explanations are given in guidance at http:// webarchive.nationalarchives.gov.uk/+/www.dh.gov.uk/en/Healthcare/Integrated-Care/Delayeddischarges/DH_4067268.
47 2003 Regulations, regs 10 and 11.
48 Delayed Discharges (Continuing Care) Directions 2009, direction 2.
49 The Delayed Discharges (England) Regulations 2003 reg 4.
50 HSC 2003/009: LAC (2003) 21, para 65.

5.30   Not infrequently it appears that the first time that a social services authority is aware that a trust deems a patient ready for discharge, is the receipt
of a section 2 notice. Since service of a section 2 notice starts the discharge
conveyor belt moving – a process which the social services authority is
unable to delay without paying a fine – this is contrary to the guidance.[51]
Where community care services are likely to be required on discharge, the
duty of care owed by both authorities to the patient would suggest that he
or she should not be discharged unless they both deem a discharge within
a fixed timescale to be safe and it should not be open to the NHS to act
unilaterally in this respect.

Social services

Community care assessment obligation

5.31   On receiving the section 2 notice, social services are required to undertake
an assessment of the patient's needs for community care services – and
this 'is to be treated as done' under NHSCCA 1990 s47[52] (see para 3.21
above).

Carer's assessment obligation

5.32   The assessment notification also triggers social services' obligations
under CDCA 2000[53] and in this respect the delayed discharge guidance
states:[54]

> Just as assessment for discharge need not be a full community care
> assessment, a carer's assessment related to a patient discharge may be only
> part of a full assessment which continues after the patient is discharged.
> Where the carer will be undertaking lifting, or other tasks that need
> training to ensure that the carer or patient is not put at risk, staff should
> ensure that appropriate training is provided.

The CC(DD)A reimbursement liability

5.33   To be liable for reimbursement, it must be social services provision and
only social services provision which is not available.[55] The discharge
guidance goes into considerable detail as to how responsibility can arise in
various situations – for instance when jointly commissioned care services
are delayed; where the patient receives direct payments and so on.

5.34   If social services do not have services in place by 11am of the day after
the proposed discharge date, such that the discharge cannot take place,
they are liable for a charge[56] – provided this is the sole reason for the delay.

51 Unless some collateral agreement or arrangement exists between the two bodies to
    mitigate this consequence.
52 CC(DD)A 2003 s4(9).
53 CC(DD)A 2003 s4(3).
54 HSC 2003/009: LAC (2003)21, para 47.
55 CC(DD)A 2003 s6; HSC 2003/009: LAC (2003)21, para 55.
56 CC(DD)A 2003 s6; 2003 Regulations, regs 10 and 11.

The charge, which may be increased by regulation,[57] is currently £100 per day for the majority of social services authority areas, but £120 for authorities in the Home Counties, London and the South East.[58] Liability ends when the patient is discharged[59] or the patient needs to remain in hospital for other treatment or dies.[60]

Delays to discharge caused by moving into a care home

5.35   The delayed discharge guidance states that 'it is established good practice that where possible people should not move directly from a hospital to a care home for the first time, but should have a period of time to make personal arrangements and adjust'.[61] The 2010 guidance exhorts staff to 'Always consider rehabilitation and enablement as the first options. Too many older people enter residential and nursing homes direct from acute care'.[62] Despite this advice, it remains not uncommon for patients to move permanently into care homes from an acute ward.[63]

5.36   Many patients considered to be inappropriately occupying NHS beds do so because they have been assessed as requiring a care home place and either the home of their choice has no current vacancies or the patient does not wish to move into a care home. In this respect the 2003 guidance[64] advised:

> Although *patient choice* is considered extremely important, patients who have been assessed as not requiring NHS continuing in-patient care, do not have the right to occupy, indefinitely, an NHS bed (with the exception of a very small number of cases where a patient is being placed under Part 11 of the Mental Health Act 1983). They do, however, have the right to refuse to be discharged from NHS care into a care home.

5.37   Those who on discharge will be self-funders, are not generally the responsibility of social services[65] and so will not engage their reimbursement liability. It will, however, be for social services to organise interim arrangements for those patients who are their responsibility where their choices under the Choice of Accommodation provisions (see para 7.109 below) may delay their discharge, and a failure to do so, may trigger liability for reimbursement.

57   Currently detailed in the 2003 Regulations, reg 7.
58   Known as 'Higher Rate' authorities and listed in the Schedule to the 2003 Regulations.
59   CC(DD)A 2003 s6(4)(b).
60   2003 Regulations reg 9.
61   Para 104.
62   2010 guidance, p 20.
63   In a study investigating the implementation of the reimbursement scheme, CSCI found that in some councils up to a third of older people needing council support on leaving hospital were moving into a care home. CSCI, *Leaving Hospital – the Price of Delays*, October 2004.
64   Department of Health (2003) *Pathways, Process and Practice*, para 2.2: although superseded by the 2010 guidance – which contains no equivalent statement – the extract is still valid and also to be found in the Choice of Accommodation Guidance LAC (2004) 20 para 2.5.13.
65   Unless unable to make their own arrangements and have no one else willing and able to assist them – see para 7.22 below.

5.38   The delayed discharge guidance deals with this problem as follows:

> 97. . . . [Local protocols] should make it clear that an acute bed is not an appropriate place to wait and the alternatives that will be offered. Where social services are responsible for providing services and a person's preferred home of choice is not immediately available, they should offer an interim package of care. All interim arrangements should be based solely on the patients assessed needs and sustain or improve their level of independence. If no alternative is provided which can meet the patient's needs, social services are liable for reimbursement.

> 98. Social services should take all reasonable steps to gain a patient's agreement to a care package, that is to provide a care package which the patient can be reassured will meet the needs identified and agreed in the care plan. . . .

> 99. If the patient continues to unreasonably refuse the care package offered by social services they cannot stay in a hospital bed indefinitely and will need to make their own arrangements so that they can be discharged safely. If at a later date further contact is made with social services regarding the patient, the council should re-open the care planning process, if it is satisfied that the patient's needs remain such to justify the provision of services and there is no longer reason to think that the patient will persist in refusing such services unreasonably. Councils may wish to take their own legal advice in such circumstances.

> 100. Where appropriate alternative services, which take account of the patient's views, have been offered, and active encouragement given to the patient to transfer, but they unreasonably refuse to move to the alternative, social services will not be held responsible. . . .

5.39   Although the guidance stresses that patients have the right to refuse to move into a care home[66] the trust is able (in extreme situations) to evict those who have no need for NHS care. In *Barnet Primary Care Trust v X*[67] the patient had been in a hospital ward for a prolonged period and for the previous three years he had not had any medical reason to be there. Although services to meet his social care needs were available, he was not prepared to leave. Wilkie J held that the he was not entitled to remain on the trust's premises because he was not in need of any ongoing medical or nursing treatment. In his view, the evidence was overwhelming. Since alternative arrangements had been proposed, the court considered that eviction would not violate his article 8 rights.

Where the preferred care home is full

5.40   A more frequent reason for delay is that the care home of choice is full, and the question arises as to what arrangements should then be made for the patient. The situation is generally of most concern to the statutory agencies, if the patient is in hospital awaiting discharge to such a home. The Choice of Accommodation 2004 guidance advises (para 2.5.9) as follows:

66 LAC 2004(20), para 2.5.13.
67 [2006] EWHC 787, [2006] All ER (D) 65 (Mar) and see further Stephen Cragg, 'Legislation update' (2006) *Times* 11 April.

Waiting for the preferred care home should not mean that the person's care needs are not met in the interim or that they wait in a setting unsuitable for their assessed needs, and this includes an acute hospital bed, until the most suitable or preferred accommodation becomes available. In view of the Community Care (Delayed Discharges etc.) Act 2003, councils should have contingency arrangements in place, that address the likelihood that an individual's preferred accommodation will not always be readily available. These arrangements should meet the needs of the individual and sustain or improve their level of independence. For some, the appropriate interim arrangement could be an enhanced care package at home.[68]

5.41 The (superseded) 2003 guidance advised that where a patient was waiting for a vacancy in their home of choice, that a transition or interim placement should be offered. The 2010 guidance is more laconic in this respect, merely advising that is it is acceptable to for the person to move into such a placement as long as it meets their needs.[69] However, LAC 2004 (20) contains detailed advice about interim arrangements including the possibility of an enhanced package of care at home; placing the person's name on the waiting list of the preferred accommodation and keeping them informed of progress; and not being asked for a top-up if the interim placement is more expensive.[70]

5.42 Wales has also recognised that there will be times when patients need to move into a care home from an acute ward.[71] Supplementary guidance to the Choice of Accommodation Directions[72] issued in 2011 is intended for those situations where the preferred care home does not have vacancies, and states that is must be adhered to, along with any local joint discharge protocol. It sets clear time limits for the process of discharge where the home of choice is full:

> The process of moving a person from hospital to a care home must be completed within three weeks of the date the person is assessed as being ready for discharge.[73]

5.43 Patients and families are asked to find three care homes (with vacancies likely within the next two weeks) that meet their needs and place them in an order of preference - although it recognises that in rural areas this may not be possible. Social services are tasked with making sure patients and families have all the information they need to do this as early as possible. If the patient has to move to a 'non-preferred' home as an interim measure then social services should make sure the person's name is kept on the waiting list for at least a year. Self-funders should be given the same advice, guidance and assistance as those funded by the local authority. The guidance states that 'This guidance in itself should in no circumstances

---

68 LAC 2004(20).
69 And unfortunately it gives the wrong reference to the Choice guidance.
70 LAC 2004(20) paras 2.5.9–2.5.11.
71 Although clearly states that as a general rule patients should not be discharged from an acute setting into a permanent place in a care home.
72 *Procedures when discharging patients from hospital to a care setting: Supplementary guidance to* WHC(2004) 066/NAFW 46/2004 LG/ML/001/11 June 2011.
73 Ibid para 7.

be taken as authorising the forcible removal of such a person from hospital'.[74]

Delayed discharge and ordinary residence

5.44   Difficult questions can arise concerning 'ordinary residence' since responsibility for the assessment process (and ultimately the reimbursement liability) depends upon the NHS body notifying the correct local authority – namely the one in which the patient is ordinarily resident (considered generally in chapter 6 below).[75] The delayed discharge guidance advises (para 65) that if the NHS trust serves the wrong council it will have to withdraw the notice and 'risks causing a delay in the patient's discharge, as the time allowed for the assessment and care planning process starts again for the new council'. It then states (para 67):

> ... if a council receives an assessment notification in respect of a patient who it believes is ordinarily resident elsewhere, it should inform the issuing NHS body, which should withdraw the notice if it agrees with the council's opinion. If the NHS body does not agree and the matter cannot be resolved locally and informally, the council receiving the assessment notification must proceed with assessment and care planning as if it were the responsible authority.

5.45   In such cases, if after services have been provided or reimbursement has been paid, the council which has been dealing with the case is entitled to reclaim the costs incurred in providing services or any reimbursement payments from the correct council.[76]

5.46   Disputes about ordinary residence are ultimately determined by the secretary of state in accordance with the Ordinary Residence Disputes (Community Care (Delayed Discharges etc) Act 2003) Directions 2010. If the dispute involves a Welsh council and an English council – it is the country in which the patient is located which will indicate who has responsibility for determining ordinary residence (ie either the secretary of state or the Welsh Government).

Reviews/challenges to discharge decisions

5.47   Strategic health authorities (SHAs) are required to set up disputes panels to arbitrate between social services and the primary care trusts (PCTs) over disputes as to reimbursement. These panels are not for use by patients challenging their discharge (for whom a separate process exists – see para 5.48). The panels comprise an independent chair person and a local authority and an NHS representative – both of whom must be from a different local authority/NHS body to the ones involved in the dispute.[77]

74   Ibid para 28.
75   The basic duties are detailed in the 2003 Regulations, reg 18.
76   Delayed discharge guidance, para 69 – which is largely reproduced in the 2011 Ordinary Residence Guidance (see para 6.9).
77   2003 Regulations, reg 15.

Patient's right to seek a review of a discharge decision

5.48   If patients are dissatisfied with the assessment of their needs or the proposed care package on offer after they leave hospital 'they should have access to the appropriate complaints procedure. But in the meantime they do not have the right to stay in an acute hospital bed if they no longer need that type of care and the NHS and social services will need to consider providing suitable non-acute care.'[78] In such cases it is likely that while the complaint is being dealt with other arrangements will be made; the delayed discharge guidance suggests a number of alternatives (see paras 104–106).

5.49   If there is a dispute about whether a patient should have been assessed as eligible for continuing NHS healthcare, then the review process for continuing NHS healthcare should be followed (see para 14.165 below).

Obligations following discharge

5.50   In general the normal obligations to provide services that have been assessed as being required will apply post hospital discharge. In addition the delayed discharge guidance states that if a patient is discharged home either as an interim measure or on a long-term basis, social services 'should check the adequacy of the arrangements within at most two weeks of discharge. This should ensure the patients are suitably cared for and are not, for example, unable to cope and at risk of deterioration of their condition or readmission to hospital' (para 107).

5.51   In other cases where interim arrangements have been made because the person's home of choice has no vacancies, the guidance states that councils:

> . . . should place individuals on the waiting list of their preferred accommodation and aim to move them into that accommodation as soon as possible. Information about how the waiting list is handled should be clear and the individual kept informed of progress. If the duration of the interim arrangement exceeds a reasonable time period, e.g 12 weeks, the individual should be reassessed to ensure that the interim and the preferred accommodation, are still able to meet the individual's assessed needs . . . [79]

NHS responsibilities for 30 days following discharge

5.52   In England it is proposed that from April 2012 the NHS will remain responsible for patients for 30 days following their discharge.[80] Although

---

78 HSC 2003/009: LAC (2003)21, para 96.
79 LAC (2004)20, para 2.5.10. See also para 5.42 above for the guidance in Wales.
80 The initiative stems from disquiet about a 50% increase in the 30 day emergency readmission rate (between 1999 and 2008) – see Department of Health (2011) *Payment by results guidance for 2011–12* para 54.

much of the detail about the new arrangements has not been finalised at the time of writing (September 2011) LAC DH (2010) 6 para 2, describes the new arrangements as follows:

> In future, hospitals will be responsible for arranging and paying for aftercare, including any re-ablement, for the first 30 days following discharge from hospital. 2011/12 will be a transitional year as we move towards that goal, and local arrangements will need to be in place so that the NHS supports re-ablement – further guidance on this will be issued later this year.

5.53   In preparation for this change, during 2011–12 PCTs will no longer fund hospitals for patients who are readmitted within 30 days of their discharge. The savings from this measure (together with some additional funding) are to be used by PCTs to work with providers, GPs and local authorities to improve re-ablement. It is envisaged that these services might include:

a) homecare re-ablement – primarily social care services to help people with poor physical or mental health accommodate their illness by learning or re-learning the skills necessary for daily living and regaining or maintaining their independence

b) intermediate care - time-limited, residential or community based services, in community hospitals or other settings, designed to help people make a faster and more complete recovery from illness

c) rehabilitation - medical treatment to help restore physical functioning following a hospital admission or procedure. Examples may include physiotherapy following orthopaedic surgery or speech and language therapy following a stroke

d) community health services – provided by district nurses and others

e) follow-up outpatient attendances. [81]

5.54   The duty to provide up to six weeks free intermediate care (see para 11.8) will be unaffected by the changes: accordingly an individual could receive '30 days of free NHS care followed by up to six weeks of free intermediate care.'[82] This is on the basis that:

> The NHS will provide reablement services under section 2 or 3 of the NHS Act. Services provided under section 2 or 3 of the NHS Act are not qualifying services and as such do not fall within section 15 of the 2003 Act or regulations made under section 15. To be intermediate care,[83] it must be provided under section 29 of the NAA, section 45(1) of the Health Services and Public Health Act 1983, Schedule 20 to the NHS Act 2006 or section 2 of the Carers and Disabled Children Act 2000. So, the person will get 30 days of free NHS care followed by up to six weeks of free intermediate care.

5.55   It is anticipated that medication and equipment may be included in the new programme but not pre-existing long term residential or home care

---

81 Department of Health (2011) *Payment by results guidance*, para 65.

82 Department of Health (2011) *Changes to the tariff for post-discharge support and additional funding for re-ablement in 2010–11 and future years* (annex 4).

83 Although as stated in para 5.53, the *Payment by results guidance* includes 'intermediate care' in the list of services during the 30-day period.

provided by local authorities.[84] The idea being that the NHS will be responsible for the additional services a person may need following hospital discharge.

5.56   The assumption by the NHS of responsibility for patients for the first 30 days on discharge[85] is likely to make redundant the CC(DD)A 2003 regime, although at the time of writing (September 2011) it is unclear whether equivalent measures will be applied when the patient reaches the end of the 30-day responsibility by the NHS.[86]

---

84   Department of Health (2011) *Payment by Results Guidance 2011–12*, para 67.
85   Outpatient appointments and Accident and Emergency attendances appear to be outside the scope of the new provisions.
86   If this is to occur, the definition of a 'qualifying hospital inpatient' within the Act would need to be amended.

CHAPTER 6

Ordinary residence

Establishing which geographical area is responsible for providing social care or NHS services

continued

Diagram 7: Ordinary residence

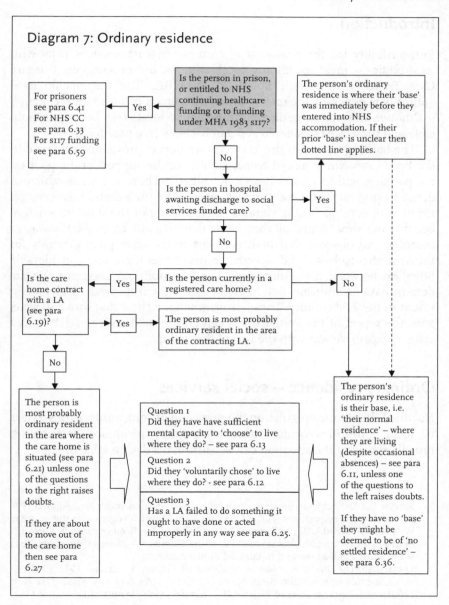

For prisoners see para 6.41
For NHS CC see para 6.33
For s117 funding see para 6.59

← Yes ← Is the person in prison, or entitled to NHS continuing healthcare funding or to funding under MHA 1983 s117?

The person's ordinary residence is where their 'base' was immediately before they entered into NHS accommodation. If their prior 'base' is unclear then dotted line applies.

No ↓

Is the person in hospital awaiting discharge to social services funded care? → Yes

No ↓

Is the care home contract with a LA (see para 6.19)? ← Yes ← Is the person currently in a registered care home? → No

Yes → The person is most probably ordinary resident in the area of the contracting LA.

No ↓

The person is most probably ordinary resident in the area where the care home is situated (see para 6.21) unless one of the questions to the right raises doubts.

If they are about to move out of the care home then see para 6.27

Question 1
Did they have have sufficient mental capacity to 'choose' to live where they do? – see para 6.13

Question 2
Did they 'voluntarily chose' to live where they do? - see para 6.12

Question 3
Has a LA failed to do something it ought to have done or acted improperly in any way see para 6.25.

The person's ordinary residence is their base, i.e. 'their normal residence' – where they are living (despite occasional absences) – see para 6.11, unless one of the questions to the left raises doubts.

If they have no 'base' they might be deemed to be of 'no settled residence' – see para 6.36.

Introduction

6.1   Responsibility for the provision of community care services rests with local bodies – most commonly, local councils, but occasionally Primary Care Trusts/Local Health Boards(PCTs/LHBs). The responsible local authority is generally the one in which the person is 'ordinarily resident'[1] – although different criteria determine which local NHS body is responsible and these are considered separately below (see para 6.72).

6.2   The baffling nature of the 'ordinary residence' provisions originate in the Poor Laws which placed responsibility for the support of the poor on the parishes within which they were 'settled'.[2] There is considerable evidence to suggest that these parishes resorted to 'underhand means to get rid of paupers',[3] including clandestine exporting of the poor into neighbouring parishes.[4] Marshall comments that 'in some cases the law was so complex and obscure that both parishes might have good grounds for thinking themselves right'[5] – with the result that there was considerable litigation between the authorities.[6] The 56 published secretary of state determinations indicate that matters have not improved to any great extent in the 21st century. These determinations show that some 60 years after the repeal of the Poor Laws it can still be said 'every parish is in a state of expensive war with the rest of the nation'.[7]

Ordinary residence – social services

6.3   Not all of the statutes regulating the provision of community care services by local authorities contain specific 'ordinary residence' restrictions: broadly speaking the situation can be summarised as in table 8.

---

1   Similar but distinct from the device of local connection used under Housing Act 1996 Part VII; in this respect, see WOC 41/93 para 20 to 21 which is guidance still in use in Wales and followed LAC (93)7 paras 16–17. LAC (93)7 has been replaced in England by 2011 guidance and makes no mention of the difference – however, the guidance in Wales must stand as relevant to England in this matter.

2   D Marshall, *The English Poor Law in the Eighteenth Century*, Routledge, 1926, p162, states that this responsibility dates 'back to 43 Eliz C.2 [*An Act for the Relief of the Poor (1601)*] and Vagrancy Laws of Richard II & Tudors' (eg the Statute of Labourers 1351 and 1388).

3   ME Rose, *English Poor Law*, David and Charles, 1971, p191 and see also J Marlow, *The Tolpuddle Martyrs*, Grafton Books, 1985, p30 where she refers to parishes smuggling their poor, one to another, to reduce the burden on the local rates. As recently as 2002 in a shocking case, a local authority not so much smuggled a young man with learning disabilities as dumped him and his suitcases on the local authority it considered should be funding him. Determination OR 1 2004.

4   Sir F M Eden, *The State of the Poor Volume 1*, 1797, Frank Cass and Co, Facsimile edition, 1966, p185.

5   Marshall (note 1 above) p169.

6   P A Fideler, *Social Welfare in Pre-Industrial England*, Palgrave, 2006, p143.

7   W Hay (1951) *Remarks on the Law Relating to the Poor with Proposals for their Better Relief and Employment* cited by N Wikeley, *Child Support Law and Policy*, Hart Publishing, 2006, p44.

Statute	Ordinary residence of direct legislative relevance	of indirect legislative relevance	of no legislative relevance	For further details see para
NAA 1948 Part III	√			6.4
HSPHA 1968 s45			√	19.22
CSDPA 1970 s2	√			9.71
HASSASSAA 1983 Sch 9			√	19.37
MHA 1983 s117	√			20.44
CA 1989 Part III	√			6.52
NHSCCA 1990 s47		√		3.80
C(RS)A 1995		√		16.32
CDCA 2000		√		6.62
HSCA 2001, ss57 and 58		√		12.7
CC(DD)A 2003	√			5.44
C(EO)A 2004		√		16.43
NHSA 2006, Sch 20 NHS(W)A 2006 Sch 15			√	9.154

Table 8: Ordinary residence and statutes

Ordinary residence and the National Assistance Act 1948

6.4   The National Assistance Act (NAA) 1948 places primary responsibility for the provision of its services (under sections 21 and 29) on the authority in which the relevant person is 'ordinarily resident'. In relation to the accommodation obligation under section 21, section 24 sets out the basic scheme by which the liable authority can be identified. Importantly, in relation to the section 21 obligation there are two so called 'deeming' provisions: situations where individuals will be 'deemed' to be ordinarily resident in a local authority area, even though they are currently residing elsewhere. The full text of section 24 is at appendix A at the end of this book.

6.5   Directions issued by the secretary of state in LAC (93)10 place a duty on local authorities to provide accommodation for the categories of person listed in NAA 1948 s21 'who are ordinarily resident in their area and other persons who are in urgent need thereof'[8] and a power to accommodate those who are not so resident. The position can be summarised as follows (table 9 below.)

8   LAC (93)10 appendix 1 para 2(1)(b).

Table 9: Residential accommodation – NAA 1948 s21		
	Ordinarily resident	**No settled residence**	**Not ordinarily resident**
P O W E R	Expectant or nursing mothers (although they may also come within the ambit of 'any other circumstance' if over 18 – see column below).	Persons aged 18 or over who by reason of age, illness, disability or any other circumstance AND are living in the authority's area when the need arises.	Persons aged 18 or over who by reason of age, illness, disability or any other circumstance AND the other authority agrees.
D U T Y	Persons aged 18 or over who by reason of age, illness, disability or any other circumstance (which includes a mental disorder of any description and alcohol or drug dependent persons).	Persons who have past or present mental health problems or for the prevention of mental health problems.	Persons aged 18 or over who by reason of age, illness, disability or any other circumstance AND who are in urgent need.

6.6   The duty to provide NAA 1948 s29 services[9] applies only to persons, who are ordinarily resident in the local authority's area, whereas a power exists to provide services for other persons.[10] There are no exceptions to these two basic requirements (eg, no exception for cases of urgency). Ordinary residence has the same meaning as in relation to NAA 1948 s21 (see para 7.37 below) with a minor exception under NAA 1948 s29(7) in relation to certain service users who are (or have been) employed in a workshop or an equivalent occupational activity promoted by the social services authority (see para 7.180 below). In *R v Berkshire CC ex p P*[11] Laws J described the arrangement of the section as follows:

> In my judgment s29(1) confers two distinct functions on local authorities; one permissive, the other mandatory. Within it the duty to make arrangements is confined to cases where the secretary of state has given a direction relating to persons ordinarily resident in the authority's area. The power to make arrangements is not so confined; it arises where the secretary of state has given his approval to arrangements being made, and his approval may be given without regard to the place of residence of any potential beneficiary.

6.7   Although from an individual's perspective it will often be academic as which authority has the responsibility for providing their care services, this will not always be so – particularly where two or more authorities are in dispute as to which is responsible: this issue is considered below. Two further problems can arise. The first concerns the administrative delay

---

9   LAC (93)10 appendix 2 para 2(1); albeit that it is only a target duty, see para 9.23.
10   *R v Berkshire CC ex p P* (1997–98) 1 CCLR 141, QBD.
11   *R v Berkshire CC ex p P* (1997–98) 1 CCLR 141, QBD at 148G.

that may occur where a person's ordinary residence changes – the delay in the new authority undertaking an assessment and providing substitute services. The second arises where the new authority has less generous eligibility criteria than the former (see para 3.156 above). In relation to these (often associated) problems it has been said that they characterise the 'worst aspects of the Poor Law system of outdoor relief . . . not least the fact that entitlement to support is lost on crossing 'parish (the local authority) boundary'.[12] Various attempts have been made to streamline the process by which one local authority hands over to another its responsibility for a person's community care services[13] and in 2011 the Law Commission announced that it was 'persuaded' that this issue required legislative attention.[14] At the time of writing (September 2011) Baroness Campbell of Surbiton has tabled a Private Members Bill – the 'Social Care Portability Bill'[15] – that seeks to address this particular problem. Until the law is clarified any person who is inconvenienced by an interruption to their care package, due to change in their ordinary residence, should consider making formal complaint that this amounts to maladministration not least because it contravenes the relevant directions[16] and guidance.[17]

6.8   The question of ordinary residence is also of importance when authority boundaries change. In *R (J and others) v Southend BC and Essex CC*[18] a number of service users had in effect become stranded when Southend became a unitary authority and ceased to be part of Essex County Council. Although initially some Essex service users continued to attend a day centre in the new unitary council area, when Southend BC decided to restrict its use to its residents, the court found no duty on Southend to assess an Essex resident prior to this decision – that responsibility lay with Essex.

Defining ordinary residence

6.9   The NAA 1948 does not define 'ordinary residence. The Department of Health has, however, issued interpretative guidance, most recently in

---

12 See eg the comments of Baroness Campbell of Surbiton, House of Lords Hansard 22 May 2008: Column GC641.
13 Eg an amendment tabled to the Bill that became the Health and Social Care Act 2008 was withdrawn on the Government undertaking to look again at this question – see comments of Baroness Thornton: House of Lords Hansard 1 July 2008 at Column 161.
14 Law Commission (2011) *Adult Social Care*, Law Com No 326, paras 10.20–10.22. See also para 6.101 below).
15 The first reading took place on 22 June 2011 in the House of Lords – the second reading has at the time of writing still to be scheduled.
16 Direction 2 of the Ordinary Residence Disputes (National Assistance Act 1945) Directions 2010.
17 See eg the 2011 guidance page 9, and para 5 page 10 which states, amongst other things that the 'provision of services should never be delayed because of uncertainty about which authority is responsible'.
18 [2005] EWHC 3457 (Admin), (2007) 10 CCLR 428.

2011[19] as *Ordinary Residence – Guidance on the identification of the ordinary residence of people in need of community care services, England.*

6.10   Although in Wales the relevant guidance dates back to 1993, (WOC 41/93[20]) since the statutory provision regulating both nations is the same, the more recent guidance issued in England will be of assistance to Welsh local authorities and advisers alike. Guidance to both England and Wales was jointly issued in 2010 in relation to settling disputes between English and Welsh authorities.[21] In contrast Scotland has enacted new legislation to clarify and update the ordinary residence provisions.[22] Guidance on the new approach to ordinary residence in Scotland is contained in CCD 3–2010.[23]

6.11   The key is in the word 'residence'; it will generally be the place where a person normally resides: where their normal residential address is to be found. The guidance states that the phrase involves questions of fact and degree, and factors such as time, intention[24] and continuity (each of which may be given different weight according to the context) have to be taken into account.[25]

6.12   The leading case on ordinary residence is the House of Lords' decision in *R v Barnet LBC ex p Shah.*[26] In Lord Scarman's judgment, in determining a person's ordinary residence, their long-term future intentions or expectations are not relevant; the test is not what is a person's real home,[27] but whether a person can show a regular, habitual mode of life in a particular place, the continuity of which has persisted despite temporary absences.[28] A person's attitude is only relevant in two respects; the residence must be voluntarily adopted, and there must be a settled purpose in living in the particular residence. 'Ordinary residence' is to be given its 'ordinary and natural meaning', namely 'a man's abode in a particular place or country which he had adopted voluntarily and for settled purposes as part of the regular order of his life for the time being, whether of short or long duration'.[29]

19 Originally issued in 2010 the guidance was further revised in April 2011 and again in July 2011 and hence is referred to by the later date.
20 *Ordinary Residence – Personal Social Services,* 26 June 1993.
21 Arrangements under section 32(4) National Assistance Act 1948 between the secretary of state and the Welsh ministers. With effect from 19 April 2010. See also para 6.68 below.
22 Adult Support and Protection (Scotland) Act 2007 s65 and Recovery of Expenditure for the Provision of Social Care Services (Scotland) Regulations 2010. Most notably these regulations ensure that the authority of ordinary residence at the time of the placement remains responsible for the funding of accommodation with support.
23 Guidance on the recovery of expenditure on accommodation and services under section 86 of the Social Work (Scotland) Act 1968 – Ordinary Residence www.scotland.gov.uk/Topics/Health/care/CrossCuttingIssues/ordresrootpage.
24 In view of the comments of Lord Scarman in *R v Barnet LBC ex p Shah* [1983] 1 All ER 226, [1983] 2 AC 309, intention must be given a restrictive interpretation.
25 English 2011 guidance para 19. WOC 41/93 para 4.
26 House of Lords [1983] 1 All ER 226: a case concerning the interpretation of 'ordinary residence' for the purposes of the Education Act 1962.
27 [1983] 1 All ER 226 at 239.
28 [1983] 1 All ER 226 at 236.
29 [1983] 1 All ER 226 at 235.

Voluntarily adopted

6.13 The question of whether a residence has been 'adopted voluntarily' raises a number of issues, particularly where the individual was unable to make that choice – through lack of sufficient mental capacity or otherwise. In *R (Mani) v Lambeth LBC*,[30] for example, the applicant had had no choice over his residence, having been 'dispersed' there by the National Asylum Seekers Support Service (see para 21.1 below). The court held that since he had been living there for six months, it was sufficiently voluntary. In doing so, the court relied on Lord Slynn's analysis in *Mohamed v Hammersmith and Fulham*,[31] that:

> . . . so long as that place where he eats and sleeps is voluntarily accepted by him, the reason why he is there rather than somewhere else does not prevent that place from being his normal residence. He may not like it, he may prefer some other place, but that place is for the relevant time the place where he normally resides.

6.14 Earlier English guidance (2010)[32] had suggested that a failed asylum seeker was not capable of having an ordinary residence for the purposes of the 1948 Act. However, this was changed in April 2011 following a determination OR 9 2010,[33] on the basis that a local authority 'has no business with the applicant's immigration status save only for the purpose of learning why the care and attention "is not otherwise available to them" as s21(1) requires'.[34] (see para 7.19 below).

6.15 There will be cases where the individual lacks sufficient mental capacity to decide where to live. *R v Waltham Forest LBC ex p Vale*[35] concerned a 28-year-old applicant with profound learning disabilities such that she was totally dependent on her parents. In these circumstances the court held that 'concepts of voluntarily adopted residence and settled purpose did not arise'. Importing principles from child care law,[36] it determined that her ordinary residence was that of her parents, not because it was her real home, but because it was her 'base'. In the 2011 guidance this is called test one.[37] The court further held that a person's ordinary residence could result after a stay in one place of only short duration; and that there was no reason why one month should be adjudged too short.

---

30 [2002] EWHC 735 (Admin), (2002) 5 CCLR 486.
31 [2001] UKHL 57, [2002] 1 AC 547, [2001] 3 WLR 1339, [2002] 1 All ER 176 para 18: a case concerning the meaning of 'normally resident' under Housing Act 1996 s199, which, however, the court held to have the same meaning as 'ordinarily resident'.
32 Department of Health (2010) *Ordinary Residence-Guidance on the identification of the ordinary residence of people in need of community care services, England* which cited *YA v Secretary of State for Health* [2009] EWCA Civ 225 at para 37 as authority for this proposition.
33 In which the Court of Appeal's approach in *R v Wandsworth LB ex p O* [2000] 4 All ER 590 was preferred.
34 See also determination OR 13 2007 regarding an overstayer.
35 (1985) *Times* 25 February, QBD.
36 See eg *In re P (GE) (an infant)* [1965] Ch 568.
37 2011 guidance para 31.

6.16   The decision was tested in *R v Redbridge LBC ex p East Sussex CC*[38] which concerned two adult male autistic twins with profound learning disabilities who were boarded at a school in East Sussex, but whose parents lived in Redbridge. Applying the principles enunciated in the *Vale* decision, the court held that the twins were at law ordinarily resident in Redbridge. Subsequently, however, the parents went to live in Nigeria. It was held that when this occurred, the twins ceased to have any settled residence and accordingly became the responsibility of East Sussex. The early (and now revoked) guidance, LAC (93)7 advised that except in cases involving persons with severe learning difficulties, 'an adult with learning disabilities should be regarded as capable of forming his own intention of where he wishes to live'.[39]

6.17   The 2011 English guidance has amplified the position regarding people who lack capacity.[40] Firstly it stresses the presumption of capacity unless established to the contrary, and the tests contained within the Mental Capacity Act. It then cautions against the above test in *Vale* as always being appropriate, as its relevance will vary depending on the ability of the person to make their own choices and the extent to which they rely on their parents. The alternative approach in *Vale* (called test two in the 2011 guidance)[41] is to consider the person's residence as if they had capacity and consider all the facts of the case, including physical presence and the nature and purpose of that presence in a particular place, as outlined in *Shah*, but without requiring the person themselves to have voluntarily adopted the residence.[42]

The 'deeming' provisions under NAA 1948 s24

6.18   Section 24 of the 1948 Act contains two so-called 'deeming' provisions: situations where a person, although resident in one area, may be 'deemed' to be resident elsewhere for the purposes of the 1948 Act. One such provision relates to persons in local authority arranged residential accommodation and the other to patients on discharge from hospital.

The 'deeming' provisions for residential accommodation

6.19   Persons provided with residential accommodation by a social services authority under section 21 of the 1948 Act, will be deemed to continue to be ordinarily resident in the area in which they were ordinarily resident immediately before the residential accommodation was provided.[43] This will be the case even if the person is in effect a 'self-funder' (see

---

38 (1993) *Times* 3 January; [1993] COD 265, QBD.
39 LAC (93)7 para 12: and see also *R v Kent CC and Salisbury and Pierre* (2000) 3 CCLR 38, QBD (at para 6.51 below).
40 2011 guidance paras 27 to 34.
41 2011 guidance para 34.
42 See OR 4 2011, OR 5 2010, OR 6 2010, OR8 2008, OR 11 2007 for cases where the secretary of state found that the parents home was the base of a person lacking capacity to decide where to live.
43 NAA 1948 s24(5).

para 6.24), but has relied upon the local authority to make the placement and contract with the care home.[44]

6.20 The 2011 English guidance gives more detail than previously on situations that have caused disputes between authorities in relation to residential accommodation, and these (broadly) engage the following questions:

Did the local authority make the residential care arrangements?

6.21 The deeming provisions will not arise where a person makes their own arrangements to move into residential care in another area (even if the local authority assists with the move provided it does not make the contract with the home).[45] The question of what constitutes making arrangements by a local authority with independent sector homes under NAA 1948 s26(2) was considered by the House of Lords in *Chief Adjudication Officer v Quinn and Gibbon*.[46] The leading judgment given by Lord Slynn held:

> . . . accommodation under section 26 must include a provision for payments to be made by a local authority to the voluntary organisation at rates determined by or under the arrangements. Subsection (2) makes it plain that this provision is an integral and necessary part of the arrangements referred to in subsection (I). If the arrangements do not include a provision to satisfy subsection (2), then residential accommodation within the meaning of Part 3 is not provided.[47]

6.22 As noted above, the guidance advises that assistance with finding a placement but falling short of making a contract does not constitute making the arrangements: taking someone to the home does not, in itself, constitute making the placement.[48]

6.23 In an unpublished determination, the secretary of state[49] found that a young man who lacked capacity and who had residential accommodation arranged for him remained the responsibility of that council after he moved to another authority in spite of an inheritance which meant he could afford to pay for his own care. Although he had a receiver to look after his finances, the council had not contacted her with a view to her making the contract with the home and there was no evidence that it expected her to do so. The invoices were sent to the council. The secretary of state found that the authority, by contacting the home in the new area, arranging a visit by the manager to see the young man and his subsequent

---

44 For instance because they wish to make use of the deferred payment arrangements or because they lack capacity to make a contract with the home and there is no one else willing and able to do so on their behalf.

45 2011 guidance, paras 72, 81 and 82 and see also determinations OR 3 1996, OR 5 2006, OR 4 2007 and OR 8 2007, OR 5 2010.

46 [1996] 1 WLR 1184, [1996] 4 All ER 72, (1997–98) 1 CCLR 529, HL.

47 This case is referred to in many determinations where a local authority contends that ordinary housing is in fact a section 21 arrangement and so the deeming provision still apply. See for instance OR 2 2008, OR 1 2009, OR 8 2010.

48 Determination OR 3 1996.

49 Determination dated 20 July 1999 (not published).

immediate transfer, and the issuing of invoices to the council by the home, amounted to 'the characteristics of an arrangement for the provision of residential accommodation under Part III of the 1948 Act'.

6.24   Where a person is placed by a local authority in another area within the 12-week property disregard (see para 8.61 below), or has agreed to a deferred payment arrangement (see para 8.81 below), then that person is the responsibility of the placing authority. Where, however, the local authority contract comes to an end after the 12-week period and the resident specifically declines a deferred payment arrangement then they cease to be the placing authority's responsibility.[50] It follows that if the resident subsequently needs support (for example, because their capital falls below the maximum threshold) they would then need to approach the authority in whose area the care home is situated. However, those who have the benefit of a deferred payment arrangement are deemed to remain ordinarily resident in the area of the placing authority.[51]

Did the local authority fail to do something that was material?

6.25   In *R (London Borough of Greenwich) v the Secretary of State*[52] Charles J considered that question of whether a local authority could avoid liability for care home fees, by failing to advise properly a resident – for example, by failing to offer a deferred payment arrangement. In his opinion if 'arrangements should have been made but had not been made', then 'the deeming provision should be applied and interpreted on the basis that they had actually been put in place by the appropriate local authority'.

6.26   The guidance picks up this point, by advising that where a local authority fails to make arrangements which it should have done, so the person was forced to make their own arrangements in another authority's area, then the person's ordinary residence would fall to be assessed at the date the person should have been provided with accommodation.[53]

Independent living and ordinary residence

6.27   The deeming provisions under section 24 of the 1948 Act only apply whilst the individual is in residential accommodation under Part III of that Act. It follows that the person's ordinary residence (for the purposes of the 1948 Act) may change if he or she moves into a non-residential care setting or the registration is changed so that the placement is no longer regarded as a 'care home' (see para 15.145 below). Many disputes between local authorities concern situations that result from such changes. In this context, the 2011 guidance advises that in such situations (ie where a person moves from a care home to independent living, or where their care

---

50   Unless of course the person does not have the capacity to enter into their own contract and there is no one willing and able to do so on the resident's behalf.
51   2011 guidance paras 84–91.
52   [2006] EWHC 2576, para 55, (2007) 10 CCLR 60.
53   2011 guidance para 74, and in relation to the failure to offer a deferred payment para 92.

home de-registers) that the key issue is whether or not the person has sufficient mental capacity to make such a decision. The position being:

- If the person who has sufficient mental capacity to agree to the changes (and on the assumption that that he or she has taken on a tenancy) the arrangement is not made under NAA 1948 s26(2) and the presumption is that the person's ordinary residence is where they are now actually living.[54]
- If, however, the person lacks the necessary mental capacity to agree to the changes Then, provided he or she has an attorney or deputy who is prepared to sign the tenancy on their behalf[55] then the person will generally acquire ordinary residence in the area where the independent living accommodation is situated.[56]

6.28   *R (Buckinghamshire CC) v Kingston upon Thames*[57] concerned a disabled person who had been placed by Kingston upon Thames Council in a care home in Buckinghamshire. After a number of years Kingston assessed that she was able to move into supported living in Buckinghamshire and arrangements were made to effect (these were dependent upon the district council making significant payments in housing benefit). Kingston considered that this move meant that Buckinghamshire became responsible by virtue of the ordinary residence rules. Buckinghamshire challenged the arrangements claiming that Kingston had a legal duty to 'act fairly' and not to have taken the action in question without notifying it. The Court rejected these arguments, although it considered it good practice for a council such as Kingston to consult with the 'host authority' in such cases so that it could 'provide the benefit of its local knowledge to the decision-making process if consulted timeously and constructively'.[58]

6.29   Although the Court considered that that there was no duty to notify a housing authority, pursuant to section 47(3)(b) of the 1990 Act (see para 3.125) where housing benefit was going to be claimed, it held that Kingston had acted unreasonably by not taking the obvious step of seeking confirmations from that authority that housing benefit would actually be payable in the event of the tenancy agreement was concluded'.[59]

6.30   In 2010 the Association of Directors of Adult Social Services (ADASS) prepared a draft a protocol by which its members could regulate the arrangements when a person's ordinary residence transferred – for example, in situations as outlined above. Although it appears that the

54 2011 guidance paras 92–101 See also determinations OR 3 2006, OR 6 2007, 7 2007, 9 2007, 10 2007, 14 2007, 3–2011.
55 The Court of Protection has issued guidance about the use of a 'single order' when authorisation is required purely to sign or terminate a tenancy. *Applications to the Court of Protection in relation to tenancy agreements.* Court of Protection 2011.
56 2011 guidance paras 102 -104. See OR 3 2010.
57 [2010] EWHC 1703 (Admin): a dismissed permission hearing which was similarly upheld on appeal: [2011] EWCA Civ 457, (2011) 14 CCLR 425.
58 [2010] EWHC 1703 (Admin) at para 58.
59 [2010] EWHC 1703 (Admin) at para 72.

protocol will not be formally adopted by member authorities, it is hoped that it will act as good practice reference document in such cases.[60]

6.31   Two additional arguments have been deployed by councils who are seeking to resist claims that a person has become ordinarily resident in their area. In *R (Manchester City Council) v St Helens Borough Council*[61] following a determination by the secretary of state[62] which established the individual's ordinary residence to be in Manchester (where she lived supported by a large care package), Manchester argued that St Helen's remained under a duty to provide care services, on the basis that St Helen's had in fact been funding that person's care for some time under section 29 of the 1948 Act, and that this duty would continue until such time as a relevant change occurred in the person's circumstances. The Court of Appeal rejected this argument: in its opinion there was no such 'customary' or other legal obligation in such cases.

6.32   In *R (Cardiff City Council) v Welsh Ministers*[63] the dispute concerned a woman with learning disabilities who had been placed and funded in residential care by Kensington and Chelsea RLBC, and the council continued to fund her care package even after she had moved out and obtained a private tenancy. When Cardiff was approached take over the funding on the basis she was ordinarily resident in that authority's area, it resisted and challenged the subsequent adverse determination by the Welsh Ministers arguing, amongst other things that notwithstanding that the person was living in an ordinary tenancy, the arrangement was still funded under section 21 of the 1948 Act (see para 7.47 where this issue is considered further). This argument was rejected, not least because for this to be the case there would have had to have been a contractual arrangement between the local authority and the landlord of the flat in question – see para 6.21 above).

The 'deeming' provisions for people formerly in NHS care

6.33   NAA 1948 s24(6) provides that where a person is in NHS care, he or she is deemed to be ordinarily resident in the area in which he or she was ordinarily resident immediately before admission as a patient. Where a person was not ordinarily resident in any area prior to admission, the responsible social services authority will be the one in whose area he or she is at that time.[64]

6.34   Until 19 April 2010 the 'deeming provisions' only applied if the person was in an NHS facility. Section 24 was amended by Health and Social Care Act 2008 s148 to cover NHS continuing healthcare funded by the NHS in independent care homes. Since that time in England and Wales the

---

60 Personal communication between an ADASS representative and the authors April 2011.

61 [2009] EWCA Civ 1348, (2010) 13 CCLR 48.

62 See OR 2 2008 – the secretary of state rejected the argument that the rented accommodation was or should have been provided under NAA 1948 s21 rather than 24-hour care under NAA 1948 s29.

63 [2009] EWHC 3684 (Admin).

64 NAA 1948 s24(3).

resident retains ordinary residence in the local authority in which they were ordinarily resident prior to being placed in a care home by the NHS. If the resident is later discharged from NHS continuing healthcare, the deeming provisions would mean that the local authority where the resident was ordinary resident immediately before being accommodated by the NHS would be responsible for funding the person's accommodation.[65]

6.35   The 2011 guidance clarifies the transitional provisions[66] for those in accommodation provided by the NHS under NHS continuing healthcare before 19 April 2010 thus:

> . . . in determining the ordinary residence of someone who went into NHS CHC accommodation on or before 18 April 2010 and continued to be there after that date, the ordinary residence rules that applied on the day they went into care should be applied – i.e. the dispute must be resolved in the light of the specific circumstances and not the deeming provisions.[67]

No settled residence

6.36   The scheme of the 1948 Act encompasses people who are without an ordinary residence – referred to as having 'no settled residence'. The 2011 English guidance suggests, however, that it should be rare for a local authority to decide that a person falls into this situation since 'it is usually possible for local authorities to decide that the person has resided in one place long enough, or has sufficiently firm intentions in relation to that place, to have acquired an ordinary residence there.'[68] In *R (Greenwich LBC) v Secretary of State for Health*[69] Charles J stressed the importance of finding an ordinary residence for individuals, where possible,[70] since local authorities are only empowered (not 'obliged') to provide services for people with no settled residence (see para 6.6). In contrast the Welsh guidance (which reflects the 1993 English guidance) makes the stronger statement that 'When a person presents him/herself to a social services authority and claims to have no settled residence or fixed abode, the authority is advised that it should normally accept responsibility.'[71]

65 Prior to the 19 April 2010 OR determinations by the secretary of state on NHS continuing healthcare cases (ie up to and including OR 04 2011) were based on the previous situation and so are not applicable to cases where a person became eligible for NHS continuing healthcare funding after that date.

66 The Health and Social Care Act 2008 (Commencement No 15, Consequential Amendments and Transitional and Savings Provisions) Order 2010 SI No 708 Part 5 articles 12(1)–(2) and (4) and SI 2010/989 art3) and The Health and Social Care Act 2008 (Commencement No 2 and Transitional Provisions) (Wales) Order 2010 SI No 989 (W98).

67 2011 guidance para 115(b). The Welsh Government has produced a note of information.

68 2011 guidance para 44; see also OR 6 2005, OR 1 2006, OR 5 2006, OR 5 2007, OR 13 2007, OR 1 2008, OR 3 2009, for determinations where the issue of no settled residence was addressed.

69 [2006] EWHC 2576, para 87, (2007) 10 CCLR 60.

70 2011 guidance para 46.

71 Welsh 1993 guidance para 20.

6.37   As a general rule, it would appear that if a person has no settled residence, his or her ordinary residence is the place where he or she is actually living (or perhaps – in extreme cases – the place where the previous night was spent).[72] Guidance accompanying the Community Care (Delayed Discharges etc) Act 2003[73] suggests that the ordinary residence of people of no fixed abode who are admitted to hospital will be determined by the postcode of the place they were at immediately prior to admission.[74] However, the 2011 guidance states that

> Where a person is not ordinarily resident in any local authority i.e. a person of "no settled residence", the 2003 Act provides that it is the local authority in which the hospital is situated that the NHS body must notify. Once notification has been received, the local authority must arrange for an assessment of the person's need for community care services to be carried out and for the provision of any services.[75]

6.38   In relation to Deprivation of Liberty Safeguards the 2011 guidance advises that:

> Where a person is not ordinarily resident in any local authority (for example, a person of "no settled residence"), the Act provides that it is the local authority in which the care home is situated that becomes the supervisory body for the purpose of granting a deprivation of liberty authorisation.[76]

Urgent need

6.39   The secretary of state's direction in LAC (93)10 places a duty on authorities to make arrangements not only for persons ordinarily resident in their area, but also for 'other persons who are in urgent need [of support services]' (see para 3.60 above).[77] Urgent need is not defined; in this context, however, it is only relevant when the person is ordinarily resident in another authority's area. It would appear therefore that the duty to persons in urgent need will almost invariably be a short-term duty, only subsisting during the currency of the urgency, and even then, only until such time as the other authority assumes responsibility. However, the 2011 guidance points out:

> On rare occasions, a person with urgent needs who has been provided with Part 3 accommodation by the local authority of the moment may be unable

---

72   In *R v Eastleigh BC ex p Betts* [1983] 2 AC 613 (which concerned a different phrase, 'normally resident') Lord Brightman suggested that 'in appropriate circumstances a single day's residence may be enough to enable a person to say that he was normally resident in the area in which he had arrived only yesterday'. It has been argued that this finding is capable of being read across into the interpretation of 'ordinary residence': see P Eccles QC, 'Ordinary Residence and Community Care: An Overview' (1999) 2 CCLR 100 at 104.

73   Note this applies to England only.

74   HSC 2003/009: LAC (2003)21 para 33. Note though that there is only a duty in relation to NAA 1948 s21 (accommodation); it is merely a power under NAA 1948 s29.

75   2011 guidance para 162.

76   2011 guidance para 171 although see para 6.50 below for when authorisation is requested prior to the person moving in to a care home.

77   LAC (93)10, para 2(1)(b), and see also NHSCCA 1990 s47(5) concerning the provision of community care services in cases of urgency.

to return to their own local authority because of a change in circumstances. In this situation, decisions relating to ordinary residence must be made on an individual basis: the local authority of the moment and the person's local authority of ordinary residence would need to consider all the facts of the case to determine whether the person's ordinary residence had changed.[78]

6.40 The situation of a person of no settled residence and in urgent need of residential accommodation has been considered in *R (S) v Lewisham LBC*[79] which held that when a person physically presents him/herself to a local authority as being in urgent need of residential accommodation, whichever authority is approached is obliged to provide the accommodation (provided it is assessed as needed).

Prisoners

6.41 The 2011 English guidance suggests where a person requires residential accommodation on release, the presumption should be that they remain ordinarily resident in the area in which they were ordinarily resident before the start of their sentence. This presumption is, however, rebuttable, for example, if the prisoner is unable to return to his/her home area, or wishes to live elsewhere. The guidance advises that if a prisoner who may need community care services expresses a wish to live in a certain area then the local authority is obliged to carry out an assessment and that the authority should initiate joint planning for prisoners at least three months before their release.[80]

Cross border placements by local authorities

6.42 Cross border placements have the potential to create considerable confusion – particularly where a person moves into independent living in Scotland having been previously placed in a care home in England by an English authority.[81] The general complexity stems from the mismatch between policy and legislation and the fact that the different residential and nursing care funding systems are devolved responsibilities. Put simply the law in this context is a mess – and given the diverging policy agendas in the four nations, it is a mess that (absent concerted action) is likely to get worse

6.43 The stated policy intention has been for English and Welsh authorities to be free to place service users in any UK nation of their choice (see para 7.107 below), however, the legislation limits the power to make placements to England and Wales. Although both Health and Social Care Act 2001 s56 and Community Care and Health (Scotland) Act 2002 s5 provide for regulations to be made to allow the placement of residents in any of the four nations (as well as the Channel Islands and the Isle of Man) as at

---

78 2011 guidance para 49.
79 (2008) EWHC 1290 (Admin) and see 2011 guidance para 50.
80 2011 guidance paras 107- 111.
81 See OR 3 2010.

the time of writing (September 2011), no such UK-wide regulations had been made.[82] Indeed the 2011 English guidance make no reference to any country other than Wales – where more formal protocols and arrangements exist.[83]

6.44   In the absence of regulations being issued the relevant guidance is contained in guidance issued jointly by Wales and England in 1993.[84] 2010 Scottish guidance[85] states:

> This guidance primarily covers **inter Scottish moves**. Section 86 of the 1968 Act, however, extends to England and Wales by virtue of section 97. This means that Scottish local authorities can recover the costs of providing or arranging care or accommodation for someone who is ordinarily resident in a local authority area in England or Wales. It also means that Scottish Ministers can determine ordinary residence disputes between a Scottish local authority and a local authority in England or Wales in relation to the costs of provision by the Scottish local authority under the 1968 Act.
>
> The Scottish Government is working with the administrations in the other parts of the UK on cross border placements and further regulations and guidance will be issued in due course. There are a number of complex issues to resolve and it may be some time before a consistent approach to cross border placements can be achieved. In the meantime Circular SWSG 6/94 on cross border placements is still in force.[86]

6.45   For those moving to Scotland and who are placed in homes in the independent sector under NAA 1948 s26, authorities are advised to arrange for the Scottish authority to contract and pay for the care home with the English/Welsh authority agreeing with the Scottish authority an appropriate financial arrangement so that the Scottish authority can recover the cost of making the arrangements net of any charges it makes on the resident.[87]

6.46   For those moving from Scotland to England/Wales, the guidance states that Scottish authorities are allowed to make placements directly for those moving into an independent residential care home but not for a nursing home. If a person wishes to move to a nursing home in England/Wales, Scottish authorities are advised to liaise with the authority to contract and pay for the care and agree appropriate financial arrangements so that the English or Welsh authority can recover the costs of making the arrangements from the Scottish authority.[88]

82 Adult Support and Protection (Scotland) Act 2007 s66 makes further provision enabling Scottish ministers to make regulations to amend the Social Work (Scotland) Act 1968 in relation to people who are placed in Scotland by an arrangement made by a local authority in any other part of the UK, Channel Isles or the Isle of Man.

83 For instance a protocol has been developed between England and Wales regarding the payment of the NHS registered nurse contribution (see para 6.91 below).

84 Department of Health/Welsh Office (1993) *The National Assistance Act 1948 (choice of accommodation) (amendment) directions 1993 amendment to the statutory direction on choice*: LAC (93)18; WOC 47/93.

85 CCD 3 2010 para 14.1 and14.2

86 This 1994 guidance is available at www.scotland.gov.uk/library/swsg/index-f/ c099.htm

87 LAC (93)18 para 7; WOC 47/93 para 8.

88 SWSG6/94, para 6.

6.47   Significant complexities arise in relation to the reimbursement obligations consequent upon the introduction of free personal care in Scotland and the advent of the NHS paying for registered nursing care in England and Wales.[89] (see para 13.109 below). In summary, Scottish authorities can arrange, but are not allowed to charge for personal and nursing care, and English and Welsh authorities can charge for personal care but are not allowed to arrange or pay for registered nurse care. In practice, however, it appears that authorities endeavour to agree an arrangement whereby residents are in the same position in respect of charges as they would have been had they remained within their home authority.[90]

6.48   Until the legislation is amended local authorities appear to lack the power to place and remain responsible for service users who wish to move to or from Scotland, Northern Ireland, the Channel Isles or the Isle of Man.

Ordinary residence and the Deprivation of Liberty Safeguards

6.49   In general the provisions in the Mental Capacity Act 2005 and the associated regulations aim to mirror the ordinary residence provisions for NAA 1948 when deciding which authority should be the supervisory body in relation to a deprivation of liberty application. Thus if a person is in a care home and is funding their own care (or has no settled residence) it will be the authority where the care home is situated that will be the authority of ordinary residence. Similarly there are deeming provisions so if the person has been placed in a care home by another authority it will be the placing authority that will be the supervisory body.[91] The 2011 guidance (paras 167–178) provides detailed information on the various permutations of responsibility that can arise in such cases, including where the detained person is supported via NHS continuing healthcare funding.

6.50   Regulations specify that where there is a dispute about the ordinary residence of the individual, the local authority which receives the request for standard authorisation must act as supervisory body until the question about the ordinary residence is determined. However, if another local authority agrees to act as supervisory body then that local authority will be the supervisory body until the question is determined. When the question

---

89   As opposed to Scotland where it is still the local authority that pays for nursing care.
90   It is implicit in the 1993 guidance that the governments intended to publish, within a short time, a clear legal framework to clarify responsibility for cross border placements. That this has not occurred means that local authorities are operating in a legal vacuum with the consequence that they believe themselves to be severely handicapped when trying to make arrangements to enable individuals to have choice as to where they live. Some of these complexities were found in determination OR 10 2010 which involved a dispute between an English and Scottish authority.
91   Paragraph 183 of Schedule A1 to the 2005 Act, apply the deeming provisions in section 24(5) and 24(6) of the NAA 1948 for the purposes of the Deprivation of Liberty Safeguards. See also 2011 guidance para 172.

has been determined then the local authority identified as the supervisory body will become the supervisory body.[92]

Ordinary residence and the Chronically Sick and Disabled Person's Act 1970

6.51   The definition of ordinary residence in the Chronically Sick and Disabled Persons Act (CSDPA) 1970 s2 is identical to that under NAA 1948 s29, and accordingly the same considerations apply.[93] Since 19 April 2010 disputes about ordinary residence in relation to CSDPA 1970 can be referred to the secretary of state or Welsh ministers.[94]

Ordinary residence and the Children Act 1989

6.52   Ordinary residence disputes are not confined to issues of social care: similar inter-authority wrangles concern such matters as the liability to maintain statements of special educational needs; the production of transition plans;[95] and the funding of costs associated with Special Guardianship Orders – and in relation to which, an exasperated Hedley J was moved to hope that 'many citizens of this state will feel a touch of shame that things could work out as they appear to have done in this case'.[96]

6.53   As a matter of principle, children are presumed to have the ordinary residence of their parents.[97] The Children Act (CA) 1989, however, adopts a different test for determining responsibility for children in need. The duty under CA 1989 s17 (to safeguard and promote the welfare of children in need)[98] and the duty under CA 1989 s20 (to accommodate) are owed by social services authorities to children 'within their area'. However, financial responsibility for certain accommodation services provided under the Act[99] rests with the local authority in whose area the child is 'ordinarily resident'. Thus a child may be ordinarily resident in local authority A but 'within the area' of local authority B. Accordingly provision is made in CA 1989 s20 (2) for local authority A to take over the responsibilities of local authority B.

---

92   Mental Capacity (Deprivation of Liberty: Standard Authorisations, Assessments and Ordinary Residence) (England) Regulations 2008 reg 18 (SI No 1858) and Mental Capacity (Deprivation of Liberty: Standard Authorisations, Assessments and Disputes about Residence) (Wales) Regulations 2009 reg 16 (SI No 783) (W69).
93   *R v Kent CC and Salisbury and Pierre* (2003) 3 CCLR 38.
94   CSDPA 1970 s2(1A) inserted by Health and Social Care Act 2008 s148(3).
95   In this respect, see for instance *R (L) v Waltham Forest LBC and Staffordshire County Council* [2007] EWHC 2060 (Admin).
96   Between Orkney Island Council and Cambridgeshire *O v L, I and Orkney Island Council* [2009] EWHC 3173 (Fam).
97   See eg *In re P (GE) (an infant)* [1965] Ch 568.
98   See para 23.4 below.
99   See CA 1989 ss20(2), 21(3), 29(7) and (9).

Within the area

6.54 A series of cases have considered the question of which authority is responsible for carrying out an assessment of children in need – and thus the true construction of the phrase 'within their area'. In *R (Stewart) v Wandsworth LBC, Hammersmith and Fulham LBC and Lambeth LBC*[100] the applicant applied to Hammersmith LBC for housing (under the homelessness provisions). Hammersmith accommodated her in a hostel in Lambeth and then determined that she was intentionally homeless and obtained a possession order against her. The applicant then requested that Hammersmith assess her children's needs under CA 1989 s17. Hammersmith refused on the basis that this was Lambeth's responsibility. Lambeth refused as did Wandsworth LBC (the children's school being within their area). The court decided that 'within their area' was simply a question of physical presence (even though that might mean that more than one authority could be under the duty to assess). Accordingly it held that Lambeth and Wandsworth were responsible but Hammersmith was not.

6.55 The decision was followed in a similar fact case, *R (M) v Barking and Dagenham LBC and Westminster LBC*[101] where the court agreed that the relevant test was physical presence. It noted that no formal guidance existed to deal with such jurisdictional problems and encouraged inter-authority co-operation in such cases:

> . . . to avoid any impression that local authorities are able to pass responsibility for a child on to another authority . . . To put it shortly, the needs should be met first and the redistribution of resources should, if necessary take place afterwards. It is also important, quite plainly, that the parents of children should not be able to cause inconvenience or extra expense by simply moving on to another local authority . . .

Ordinary residence: the Children Act/National Assistance Act interface

6.56 In *R v Lambeth LBC ex p Caddell*[102] the applicant had been placed by the respondent London borough with paid carers who lived in Kent. When he became 18 Lambeth determined that he had ceased to be their responsibility since he was no longer a child, and accordingly the ordinary residence rules under the NAA 1948 applied. Kent County Council contended, however, that Lambeth was still the responsible authority since CA 1989 s24 allowed for social services authorities to continue to provide advice and assistance to young persons who had been in care once they achieved their majority. Connell J rejected this line of argument, holding

---

100 [2001] EWHC 709 (Admin), (2001) 4 CCLR 446 and see also *R (Liverpool City Council) v Hillingdon LBC* [2008] EWHC 1702 (Admin).
101 [2002] EWHC 2663 (Admin), (2003) 6 CCLR 87.
102 [1998] 1 FLR 235.

that the duty under CA 1989 s24 was owed by the authority in whose area the young person resided, ie Kent.

6.57   CA 1989 s24 (which specifically concerns the needs of looked after children who are leaving care) has since been amended by the Children (Leaving Care) Act 2000. In effect the financial obligations imposed by the 2000 Act (particularly in the substituted sections 24A and 24B of the 1989 Act) are now the responsibility of the local authority which looked after the young person immediately before he or she left care. This responsibility extends until the age of 21 (or beyond in the case of certain education and training costs). A 2004 protocol exists for inter-authority arrangements for care leavers outside of their responsible authority.[103]

6.58   The 2011 guidance makes it clear that the 2000 Act does not extend to the provision of accommodation, and that there are times when the Children Act 1989 (as amended by the Children (Leaving Care) Act 2000) and the National Assistance Act 1948 can run in tandem. The permutations on responsibility in such cases are numerous and where disputes arise, reference should be made to the 2011 guidance (which devotes some 22 pages to young people in transition from children's services to adult services[104]).

Ordinary residence and Mental Health Act 1983 s117

6.59   The duty to provide services under Mental Health Act (MHA) 1983 s117 is a joint health and social services responsibility. MHA 1983 s117(3) stipulates that the responsible health bodies are 'the Primary Care Trust or Local Health Board and that these together with the relevant social services authority are those 'for the area in which the person concerned is resident or to which he is sent on discharge by the hospital in which he was detained'.

6.60   It might appear, therefore, that MHA 1983 s117(3) gives a choice of responsible authorities – either the health/social services authorities in whose area the person was resident at the time of admission to hospital[105] or those to which he or she is sent on discharge. The basic principle is, however, that primary responsibility rests with the local authority/PCT/ LHB in which the person was resident at the time of admission. This was clarified by Scott Baker J in *R v Mental Health Review Tribunal ex p Hall*,[106] who observed that:

---

103   LASSL (2004)20: although the protocol states that it was to be reviewed in 2005, this did not occur and (at September 2011) no new protocol had been published.

104   2011 guidance Paras 138 to 158. It is of note that of the 56 published determinations 13 are in relation to care leavers – an indication of the complexity of the legislation in this area. See ORs 1,3,4 and 6 2005, ORs 2 and 4 2006, ORs 2,3 and 5 2007, OR 5 2008, ORs 5 and 9 2009, and OR 6 2010.

105   A person does not cease to be resident in the area of an authority by reason only of his or her admission to hospital – *Fox v Stirk* [1970] 2 QB 463.

106   [1999] 3 All ER 132, (1999) 2 CCLR 361, QBD. Although the case went to the Court of Appeal – [2000] 1 WLR 1323, (1999) 2 CCLR 383 – the question of the responsible department was not argued in that court.

Section 117 does not provide for multi social services department or health authority responsibility. The words 'or to whom he is sent on discharge from Tribunal' are included simply to cater for the situation where a patient does not have a current place of residence. The sub-section does not mean that a placing authority where the patient resides suddenly ceases to be 'the local social services authority' if on discharge the Applicant is sent to a different authority'.[107]

6.61   The 2011 guidance points out that the term used in section 117 is 'resident' and that this is not the same as 'ordinarily resident' and thus the deeming provisions do not apply.[108] In *R (Hertfordshire CC) v (Hammersmith and Fulham LBC and JM,*[109] the Court of Appeal held that although it was not clear why Parliament had decided to take a different approach to ordinary residence under section 117, that is what it had done. The Court agreed with the first instance decision[110] of Mitting J, that (1) there was little or no difference in meaning between 'resident' and 'ordinarily resident' – they both connoted settled presence in a particular place other than under compulsion; and (2) that the deeming provision in section 24(5) of the NAA 1948 had no application for section 117 purposes. On this basis, therefore he held that responsibility for section 117 purposes lay with the local authority in which the person was 'resident'[111] in a care home at the time he was admitted to hospital under section 3 of the Mental Health Act 1983 (albeit he had been funded by Hammersmith and Fulham because of the deeming provisions under section 24 of the NAA 1948.)

Ordinary residence and the carers legislation

6.62   In general a carer's assessment under either the Carers (Recognition of Services) Act (C(RS)A) 1995 or Carers and Disabled Children Act (CDCA) 2000 is predicated upon a community care or Children Act assessment being undertaken (see para 16.31). Practice guidance to the CDCA 2000[112] advises that where the carer lives some distance away from the user it will be the disabled person's home authority (not the carer's) which will be responsible for the assessment and the provision of any services under the 2000 Act. The 2011 guidance reiterates this at para 127 merely adding that, 'where the carer is ordinarily resident in a different authority to the cared-for person, local authorities should work in partnership to ensure that carers' needs are properly assessed and met.'

107   This is paraphrased at para 187 of the 2011 guidance.
108   2011 guidance para 184. WOC 43/93 gives little guidance and was in any case written before the leading judgments in this area.
109   [2011] EWCA Civ 77, (2011) 14 CCLR 224, and see also *R (Sunderland City Council) v South Tyneside Council* [2011] EWHC 2355 (Admin). See para 11.92 for the Law Commission's recommendations.
110   *R (M) v Hammersmith and Fulham LBC and others* (2010) 13 CCLR 217.
111   ie *not* 'deemed' to be resident.
112   Department of Health (2000) *Carers and Disabled Children Act 2000: Carers and people with parental responsibility for disabled children: Practice Guidance* paras 24–27 and Welsh Assembly (2000) *Guidance: 2000 Act* para 4.3.

Disputed ordinary residence

6.63   Where two or more social services authorities are in dispute over a person's ordinary residence, NAA 1948 s32(3) and since 19 April 2010 CSDPA 1970 s2(1A), provide that the question is to be determined by the secretary of state or Welsh ministers. Determinations can also be sought under section 8 of the Community Care (Delayed Discharges etc.) Act 2003 (in relation to England only) and paragraph 183(3) of Schedule A1 to the Mental Capacity Act 2005 (the Deprivation of Liberty Safeguards). In England, the determination for all such disputes is regulated by directions:[113] no directions have, however, been issued in Wales.

6.64   Part five of the 2011 guidance sets out the procedures detailed in the directions, as to how disputes are to be determined. It lists the following key principles that apply in such cases:

- the key priority of local authorities should be the well-being of people who use services.
- the provision of accommodation and/or services must not be delayed[114] or otherwise adversely affected because of uncertainty over which local authority is responsible.[115]
- one local authority must accept responsibility, in accordance with the directions issued by the secretary of state, for the provision of social care services until the dispute is resolved.

6.65   A dispute arises on the first date on which one of the local authorities notifies the other in writing that it does not accept that it is liable for the provision of services (or that it be the supervisory body, or that it be issued with a notification by the NHS to undertake an assessment).[116] In relation to service provision disputes, one or other of the local authorities must agree without delay to accept responsibility pro tem and if they cannot reach agreement then the authority where the person is living or physically present must do so.[117] This requirement mirrors the view of the local government ombudsman that in such cases one authority should 'grasp the nettle' and secure the provision, before entering into protracted negotiations with the NHS on liability for the care costs.[118]

6.66   The directions stipulate that if the local authorities cannot resolve the dispute within four months the matter must be referred to the secretary of state. They then have a further 28 days to prepare and submit the application. It is expected that referrals to the secretary of state will only be as a

113   The Ordinary Residence (National Assistance Act 1948) Directions 2010; Ordinary Residence Disputes (Community Care Delayed Discharges Act 2003) Directions 2010; Ordinary Residence Disputes (Mental Capacity Act 2005) Directions 2010. Directions have not been issued in Wales and guidance on disputes is still contained in WOC 41/93.
114   Only this appears in the Welsh guidance.
115   Direction 2(1) of the The Ordinary Residence (National Assistance Act 1948) Directions 2010
116   Direction 1(3) of the Ordinary Residence (National Assistance Act 1948) Directions 2010.
117   Direction 2 (3 and 4) of the The Ordinary Residence (National Assistance Act 1948) Directions 2010.
118   Complaint no 96/C/3868 against Calderdale MBC.

last resort. The directions specify the documentation that must be submitted to the secretary of state and the guidance states that the secretary of state will endeavour to make a determination within three months of receipt of the referral.[119] In the July 2011 amendment to the guidance, authorities were informed (at para 208), 'Any local authority failing to comply with the Directions or failing to have due regard to a determination by the Secretary of State would put itself at risk of a successful legal challenge by the resident or their representative or the other local authorities to the dispute'. Determinations made by the secretary of state are published.[120]

6.67   In relation to CSDPA 1970 s2 disputes the amendments made by section 148(3) of the Health and Social Care Act 2008 do not have effect if on 19 April 2010 the question was the subject of court proceedings.[121]

Cross border disputes between England and Wales

6.68   The Health and Social Care Act 2008 s148 formalised the process for the resolution of Anglo-Welsh disputes and this has been the subject of a 2010 Department of Health/Welsh Government agreement[122] which also covers disputes regarding CSDPA 1970 s2. A similar agreement has been concluded in relation to supervising bodies under the Schedule A1 to the Mental Capacity Act 2005.[123]

6.69   Responsibility for the determination of a cross border dispute is determined by the nation in which the person is living: accordingly the secretary of state will make the determination if the person is living in England at the time the dispute is referred, the Welsh Ministers will make the determination if the person is living in Wales. In doing so they will notify each other of the referral, consult with each other and notify each other of the outcome. In cross border disputes which go to the secretary of state the 2011 guidance advises that the English local authority should comply with the Directions and the guidance so far as possible, in view of the fact that these are not applicable to the Welsh local authority. In a cross-border dispute which is being determined by the Welsh Ministers (because the person at the centre of the dispute lives in Wales), English local authorities should have regard to any guidance or Directions which

119   2011 guidance para 211.
120   Available at www.dh.gov.uk/en/Publicationsandstatistics/Publications/
      PublicationsPolicyAndGuidance/DH_113627
121   The Health and Social Care Act 2008 (Commencement No 15, Consequential
      Amendments and Transitional and Savings Provisions) Order 2010 SI No 708 Part 5
      art 12(1)-(2) and (4) and SI 2010/989 art 3) and The Health and Social Care Act 2008
      (Commencement No 2 and Transitional Provisions) (Wales) Order 2010 SI No 989
      (W98). Wales currently relies on Circular guidance WOC 41/93, Part 2 of which
      details what information should be given to Welsh Ministers.
122   Department of Health and Welsh Government (2010) *Arrangements under section
      32(4) National Assistance Act 1948 between the Secretary of State and the Welsh
      Ministers*. March 2010.
123   Department of Health and Welsh Government (2009) *Arrangements under paragraph
      183(4) of Schedule A1 to the Mental Capacity Act 2005 between the Secretary of State and
      the Welsh Ministers*.

may be issued by the Welsh Ministers in relation to the procedure for determining ordinary residence disputes.[124] The main guidance on delayed
discharges LAC (2003)21 points out that as Wales has not implemented
the Community Care (Delayed Discharges etc) Act 2003, if a resident of
Wales is delayed in an English hospital, there can be no reimbursement.

Disputed 'ordinary residence' and the Children Act 1989

6.70   Although, as noted above, there is no formal resolution process for
        inter-authority disputes as to whether or not a child is 'within their area',
        CA 1989 s30(2) provides a formal process for disputes concerning
        ordinary residence.[125] This mirrors the secretary of state process under
        NAA 1948 s32(3) (above). Where there is a dispute as to responsibility
        between two councils, one or other must accept responsibility – or they
        both will be condemned as was the case in *A v Leicester City Council*[126]
        where HHJ Farmer QC observed that:

> It is surely not beyond the wit of two local authorities with access to legal
> advice . . . to devise plans and contingencies for such situations, which
> are said not to be uncommon and perhaps to share the cost of funding
> pending the resolution of such disputes as they arise. What is not lawful,
> in my judgment, is to defer the performance of the duty of good
> parenting under the Act to the resolution of what is essentially a resource
> led dispute.

Establishing the responsible commissioner for NHS services

6.71   Entitlement to services under the National Health Service Acts 2006 is not
        in theory a local right but a 'national' one: accordingly the Acts are silent
        as to a need to establish a local connection or ordinary residence.

6.72   The framework for determining which primary care trust (PCT) or
        local health board is responsible for commissioning an individual's care is
        detailed in regulations.[127] In England it is primarily linked to registration
        with a GP, and for those who are not registered with a GP it is based on
        where they are 'usually resident'. The situation is otherwise in Wales, in
        that the responsible local health board is the one where the person is

---

124   2011 guidance para 194.
125   The Children Act 1989, s30 (as amended by the Children and Young Persons Act
      2008 Schedule 3 para 21) provides for a similar cross border dispute process to that
      under the NAA Act 1948.
126   [2009] EWHC 2351 (Admin) para 51.
127   NHS (Functions of Strategic Health Authorities and Primary Care Trusts and
      Administration Arrangements) (England) Regulations 2002 SI No 2375 as amended
      by SI Nos 2002/2548, 2003/1497, 2006/359 and 2007/559 and 2010/2649; and Local
      Health Boards (Directed Functions) (Wales) Regulations 2009 SI No 1511 (W147) and
      Health, Social Care and Well-being Strategies (Wales) Regulations 2003 SI No 154
      (W24), as amended by the Health, Social Care and Well-being Strategies (Wales)
      (Amendment) Regulations 2007 SI No 1042 (W102).

'usually resident' regardless of the address of their GP. 'Usually resident' is determined by the address the person gives to the body providing the service, or the most recent address he or she can give, or if the usual address cannot be established the patient will be treated as usually resident in the area where the person is present.[128]

6.73   Guidance in England was issued in April 2007[129] and is referred to in the subsequent paragraphs as the '2007 guidance'. In August 2011, draft guidance was published for consultation in Wales – namely *Responsible Body Guidance 2011* which it is intended will replace the 1994 'Establishment of District of Residence' guidance.[130] Although there may be some changes subsequent to this book being published, the draft guidance is referred to in this section.

6.74   The guidance makes it clear that no treatments should be refused or delayed due to uncertainty as to which PCT/LHB is responsible for funding an individual's healthcare provision. Ministers in England have specifically asked to be advised of those NHS bodies that fail to reach local resolution of any disputes between themselves or with independent providers.[131]

6.75   Currently in England PCTs[132] are responsible for commissioning hospital and community health services for patients registered with GPs associated with their PCT, and persons usually resident in their area, or resident outside the UK and present in their area who are not registered with a GP.[133] It follows that where a patient is registered with a GP the responsible PCT will generally be the one where the GP is situated rather than where the patient lives. Where a GP practice has patients resident in more than one PCT area liability will rest with the PCT in which the largest number of registered patients reside.[134]

6.76   The identification of a person's ordinary residence will only be of relevance in England where the person is not registered with a GP. Annex A of the 2007 guidance suggests that 'usually resident' should be based on the principle of the patient's perception of where he or she lives. If the patient is unable to give a current address, the address at which he or she was last resident should establish the PCT of residence. If the patient cannot give a present or most recent address, the location of the unit providing treatment (ie where the patient is 'present') should be

128 Local Health Boards (Directed Functions) (Wales) Regulations 2009 Reg 2(3).
129 Who Pays? *Establishing the Responsible Commissioner* 2007. This has been amended a number of times since it was published. The most recent version is available at www.dh.gov.uk/en/Publicationsandstatistics/Publications/PublicationsPolicyAnd-Guidance/DH_078466
130 DGM (94) 15 and DGM (93) 133.
131 2007 guidance, para 5.
132 Although see para 13.6 for the proposed changes to NHS commissioning.
133 NHS (Functions of Strategic Health Authorities and Primary Care Trusts and Administration Arrangements) (England) Regulations 2002 SI No 2375 reg 3(7).
134 2007 guidance, para 7.

considered as the district where he or she lives.[135] Similar guidance is given in Wales, namely:

> Patients <u>must not</u> be subjected to undue scrutiny when being asked for this information, or be 'led' into giving an alternative address in order to exploit any perceived financial advantage.[136]

6.77   If a patient is away from his or her normal area where he or she is registered with a GP, non-contract activity arrangements (previously known as out of area arrangements) exist to cover emergency treatments when it is not possible to get prior approval from the patient's PCT. Additionally some services are provided on an 'all-comers' basis such as accident and emergency, sexual health,[137] family planning, and NHS walk-in centres[138]. These are provided by the host PCT regardless of registration or residence. The full list of such services is provided in the 2007 guidance.

Patients who move

6.78   If a patient moves during a course of treatment, the English guidance suggests flexible solutions, which might mean that the originating PCT continues to exercise the functions on behalf of the receiving PCT for a specific time.[139]

Patients who receive fully funded NHS continuing care

6.79   Different rules apply for people who receive continuing NHS healthcare (see chapter 14) either in care homes or independent hospitals. In England, responsibility is determined by regulations.[140]

6.80   Where the placing PCT or Local Health Board arranges the care, it remains responsible for the NHS payments for the care of that placement even though the person may change GP to one in the area of the care home. However, in England if the patient requires other health services not related to the placement (for instance, in patient treatment in hospital) it will be the responsibility of the PCT where the patient is now registered. Annex C of the guidance gives more details of how this should work in practice.[141] In Wales the draft guidance merely states that the placing PCT will be responsible for funding the care home placement and secondary care services.[142]

---

135   NHS (Functions of Strategic Health Authorities and Primary Care Trusts and Administration Arrangements) (England) Regulations 2002 SI No 2375 reg 3(8).
136   Para 2.8 draft Welsh guidance, and Annex A para 5 of 2007 guidance which says patients 'should not'. . . .
137   This is also the case in Wales.
138   These are not mentioned in the Welsh draft guidance.
139   2007 guidance, para 19 – and an explanatory table is also provided at para 22: there is nothing similar in the Welsh draft guidance.
140   National Health Service (Functions of Strategic Health Authorities and Primary Care Trusts and Administrations Arrangements) (England) Regulations 2002 SI No 2375 paras (7A), (7A)(a), (7B) as amended by SI 2010/2649.
141   2007 guidance, para 89.
142   Welsh draft guidance, para 6.7.

6.81   The primary effect of the regulations in England is that where a patient receives NHS continuing healthcare funding, then regardless of the type of care home, the responsibility remains with the placing PCT.[143] In Wales the draft guidance appears to limit responsibility to placements in nursing homes, although the regulations merely refer to 'accommodation to meet continuing care needs'.[144]

6.82   In England these arrangements apply to both fully funded NHS continuing healthcare and where the NHS contribution is assessed as requiring more than just the registered nurse payment (see para 13.112 above) and there is at least one other planned service to bring about a specific outcome in relation to treatment.[145] Examples given in Annex C[146] of the guidance are physiotherapy, occupational therapy, speech and language therapy, dietetics and podiatry.

6.83   If the patient recovers sufficiently to no longer require fully funded NHS healthcare, or extra services other than registered nursing care, the resident will become the responsibility of the new PCT area.[147] The placing authority is responsible for reviews unless and until the person no longer requires the services, although it can make arrangements for the PCT where the home or hospital is to undertake reviews on its behalf.[148] It is also responsible for any increases in the care needed in the home or independent hospital if the patient's condition worsens. If the patient needs to move to another care home or independent hospital, the placing PCT remains responsible. The arrangements do not apply where a person has either independently chosen to move to a different part of the country or if the arrangement is made by social services only. However, they do apply where the placing PCT has taken the preferences of the individual on the location of the care home or independent hospital into account in making the placement.[149]

6.84   Where patients receive fully funded NHS continuing healthcare in their own home and decide to move house, they come under the normal

143 The previous regulations covered nursing homes but failed to consider cases where NHS continuing healthcare was provided in a care home that provides personal care (normally known as a residential care home). The revised guidance from 2011 makes it clear that for placements arranged from 1 December 2010 the arrangements apply regardless of whether nursing care forms part of the care package, except in cases where the only planned service is NHS-funded nursing care.
144 The draft Welsh guidance refers to continuing NHS healthcare in nursing homes. However, this is different from the wording in reg 3(a)(v) of the Local Health Boards (Directed Functions) (Wales) Regulations 2009 SI No 1511 (W147).
145 2007 guidance, para 90. This provision appears to be absent from the Welsh draft guidance.
146 2007 guidance at para 16.
147 ie the PCT area within which the patient's present GP is situated. The Welsh draft guidance does not cover where patients improve, but it would seem to follow that if this is the case and NHS continuing healthcare is no longer required that Health Board where the patient now lives (ie where the care home is) will become responsible.
148 NHS (Functions of Strategic Health Authorities and Primary Care Trusts and Administrations Arrangements) (England) Regulations 2002 SI No 2375 as amended by SI No 2006/359.
149 2007 guidance, para 8, Annex C.

rules for establishing the responsible commissioner (ie the PCT area where they are now registered with a GP or the LHB where they now live). The 2007 guidance, and Welsh draft guidance suggest[150] that there might be flexible solutions, for example, if a nursing service is already visiting the patient, an inter-authority agency agreement could be reached so that this could continue rather than subject the patient to the upheaval of staff changes.

Responsibility for NHS-funded nursing care

6.85   If the individual moves into a nursing home outside the PCT/LHB area, the registered nurse payment will become the responsibility of the PCT on whose GP list the resident is included[151] (ie normally where the home is) and in Wales the Local Health Board where the resident is now living.

6.86   Advice has been issued by the Department of Health regarding respite care in specialist facilities run by the Multiple Sclerosis Society and Vitalise (formerly known as the Winged Fellowship). As these centres take residents from all parts of the country for short periods, funding has been reallocated so that the PCTs in which the homes are situated pay for the respite care rather than the PCT where the person is registered with a GP.[152]

Cross border arrangements

6.87   England is the only country of the UK which places the responsibility on the PCT where the GP is registered, rather than where the patient is usually resident. In the case of a person living Scotland but registered with a GP in England, responsibility falls on the Scottish NHS body. For patients who are resident in England but who are registered with a GP in Wales, Northern Ireland or Scotland, responsibility lies with the English PCT where the patient is resident.[153]

6.88   In 2005 a protocol was first agreed between Wales and England for those who live in the PCTs and LHBs on the English/Welsh border.[154] This has been regularly updated[155]. In relation to these LHBs/PCTs, if a resident who lives in Wales is registered with a GP in an English PCT the health board retains legal responsibility but the English PCT is responsible on the LHB's behalf for commissioning services for that

---

150   2007 guidance, para 93, Welsh draft guidance, para 6.9.
151   Unless in England, there is some other NHS service planned for the resident (see para 6.82 above)
152   Department of Health (2009), *NHS-funded Nursing Care Practice Guide*, paras 67–88.
153   2007 guidance, para 59 and see SI 2003/1497 which amended the 2002 regulations.
154   The LHBs being the Betsi Cadwaladr University LHB, the Powys Teaching LHB and the Aneurin Bevan LHB: the PCTs being Shropshire County PCT, Herefordshire PCT, West Cheshire PCT and Gloucestershire PCT.
155   The latest is Protocol for Cross-Border Healthcare Commissioning Between the Department for Health and Social Services, Welsh Government and the Department of Health 2011–12. EH/ML/010/11.

patient.[156] If a person lives in England but is registered with a GP in Wales the PCT retains legal responsibility but the LHB in Wales will commission services on the PCT's behalf.[157]

6.89 If a patient is resident in Wales (in an area not covered by the above protocol)[158] or Northern Ireland and registered with a GP in England, both Wales/Northern Ireland and England could be deemed to be responsible. The guidance limply suggests that in such cases the health organisations should enter into discussions and negotiations locally.[159]

6.90 An agreement exists, however, between the four devolved administrations about cross border emergency treatment, when patients need immediate treatment when they are away from home.[160]

6.91 A protocol also exists between England and Wales regarding the payment of the NHS-funded nursing contribution. The English PCT where the home is based pays registered nurse payment at the English rate if the home is in England. The Welsh health board pays at the Welsh rate if the home is in Wales. The 2007 guidance points out that it is based on the default position of usual residence to ensure all patients receive the services they are assessed as needing.[161]

People not ordinarily resident in the UK and overseas visitors

6.92 Although PCTs rely on usual residence to establish whether they are responsible for commissioning services, the test for whether the NHS should provide free services for those from abroad is based on the ordinary residence test used in local authorities (see para 6.9 above). Asylum seekers who have made a formal application for refugee status are considered to be resident and so the responsible PCT is based on their GP or where they are usually resident.[162] The Welsh draft guidance gives a very truncated from of this guidance.[163]

6.93 The Government in England has promised to undertake a fundamental review of the residency conditions but in the meantime has

---

156 See SI 2009/1511 (W147).
157 See SI 2003/1497.
158 2007 guidance para 60.
159 2007 guidance, para 60.
160 Department of Health (2006) *Cross Border Emergency Treatment*, WOC (2006)066.
161 The protocol can be found at http://webarchive.nationalarchives.gov.uk/+/ www.dh.gov.uk/en/Healthcare/IntegratedCare/NHSFundedNursingCare/ DH_4000400.
162 Following judicial criticism of the then ordinary residence guidance in *YA v Secretary of State for Health* [2009] EWCA Civ 225 the Department of Health issued new guidance (that has not yet been incorporated into the 2007 guidance) – namely Department of Health letter (2 April 2009) Advice for Overseas Visitors Managers on failed asylum seekers and ordinary/lawful residence; when to provide treatment for those who are chargeable; and victims of human trafficking.
163 Para 3.7 and it does not cover the issues of those involved in human trafficking.

formalised charging arrangements for overseas visitors via consolidated regulations in effect from August 2011.[164]

Prisoners

6.94   The PCT in which the prison is situated commissions the majority of the care services for the prison population.[165] The same applies in Wales where usual residence of a prisoner is considered to be the LHB in which the prison is situated.[166] In both countries where a prisoner is transferred to hospital under Mental Health Act 1983 s47 or s48 the responsible commissioner will be the PCT/LHB that was responsible prior to imprisonment (ie where the prisoner lived or was registered with a GP). If there is no known previous address and in England if the prisoner was not registered with a GP, the usual residence will be where the offence was committed. For those from outside the UK the responsible commissioner will be the PCT/LHB where the prison is situated.[167]

People detained under the Mental Health Act 1983

6.95   If a person is detained for treatment under the Mental Health Act 1983, commissioning responsibility will lie with the PCT/LHB where the person is registered with a GP or where the person is usually resident prior to admission[168]. If these cannot be established, responsibility lies with area where the unit is providing treatment. If a patient is discharged to another area under section 117 it is the PCT/social services authority where s/he was resident before he was admitted that is responsible for section 117 services, even if s/he then registers with a new GP.[169] If the patient does not have a current residence it will be the authority where he is now placed. If a person who is subject to section 117 happens to register or be registered with a GP outside the PCT area to where s/he lives, it will be the residence of the person that decides the responsible PCT as the responsibility for provision of aftercare under section 117 is

164 Department of Health (2011) *Access to the NHS by Foreign Nationals–Government response to the consultation*, March 2011. See also National Health Service (Charges to Overseas Visitors) Regulations 2011 and see also Department of Health (2011) *Guidance on Implementing the Overseas Visitors Charging Regulations*.
165 NHS (Functions of Strategic Health Authorities and Primary Care Trusts and Administration Arrangements) (England) (Amendment) Regulations 2003 SI No 1497, and 2007 guidance para 79.
166 Welsh draft guidance para 3.19 other than HMP Parc where health services are funded by the Ministry of Justice.
167 English 2007 guidance paras 81 and 82, Welsh draft guidance paras 3.21 and 3.22. In Wales if a prisoner is detained in a medium or high security hospital the responsible body is the Welsh Health Specialised Services Committee.
168 English 2007 guidance para 84 and Welsh draft guidance para 3.17 and 18. In Wales if the patients is detained in a medium or high security hospital the responsible body is the Welsh Health Specialised Services Committee.
169 English 2007 guidance para 82. The draft Welsh guidance makes no mention of section 117.

determined solely by the area of residence of the patient, not the location of the GP.[170]

Children

6.96   Since April 2007[171] where a PCT or a local authority (or a PCT and a local authority acting jointly) arrange accommodation in an area of another PCT, the originating PCT remains responsible even where the child changes GP. When a young person who has been placed in another PCT area to meet his or her continuing healthcare needs reaches 18 years, the arrangement can be treated as being made under adult continuing care provisions. The relevant guidance notes that since the threshold for providing continuing NHS healthcare may be higher for adults than children, arrangements for a reassessment will be required, but that young people should continue to receive their healthcare on an unchanged basis pending this assessment.[172]

6.97   In Wales, since July 2007[173] responsibility for a child placed in funded accommodation rests with the LHB from which the child was placed.

Resolving disputes about who is the responsible commissioner

6.98   In England, Strategic Health Authorities (SHAs) have the responsibility for resolving disputes that threaten the delivery of services in its geographical area, although ultimately the resolution of such disputes rests with the secretary of state. Where SHAs have not been able to settle a dispute, the guidance requires that the parties submit a report to the Department of Health together with the proposed solution.[174]

6.99   The Welsh draft guidance is silent on the process of resolving disputes other than stating as a fundamental principle that 'no treatment should be refused or delayed due to uncertainty or ambiguity as to which body is responsible for funding an individual's healthcare provision.'[175] This is also a guiding principle in the English 2007 guidance.[176] Notwithstanding these fine words the Ombudsmen for Wales and England found maladministration in just such a case – where a patient with a serious and

---

170   English 2007 guidance para 86.
171   NHS (Functions of Strategic Health Authorities and Primary Care Trusts and Administration Arrangements) (England) (Amendment) Regulations 2007 SI No 559 – and see paras 30 to 38 2007 English guidance. Any arrangements made prior to April 2007 are subject to the rule that the responsible PCT is the one that funds the GP with whom the child is registered.
172   English 2007 guidance, para 38.
173   The Local Health Boards (Directed Functions) (Wales) Regulations 2009 reg 3. See also *Towards a Stable Life and Brighter Future* Welsh Assembly Government 2007.
174   English 2007 guidance, paras 8 to 11.
175   Welsh draft Guidance para 1.5.
176   See para 13.35 below regarding the duties involved in joint working which includes an obligation on NHS bodies to co-operate with each other.

deteriorating condition had been forced to fund her own treatment whilst two health bodies squabbled over funding.[177]

Reform proposals

6.100   As noted above[178] the ordinary residence rules can create barriers for disabled and older people who wish to move to the area of another authority. The Law Commission considered that 'the meaning of ordinary residence and alternative ways of determining local authority responsibility for services provision are matters for political policy and not law reform.'[179] It recommended that the inter-authority duties to co-operate be strengthened[180] – an approach that is reflected in the Welsh framework.[181]

6.101   The Law Commission did, however, recommend that there be a statutory requirement on a receiving authority to undertake an assessment when a person had a clear intention to move and that if the new support package was to be significantly different, that a clear written explanation as to the reasons for this, be provided to the service user and where appropriate the carer. It also recommended that there be a power to make regulations requiring the new authority to provide equivalent services or direct payments to those provided by the original authority until a new assessment is completed.[182]

6.102   With regard to Mental Health Act 1983 s117[183] the Law Commission has recommended that the 'concept of ordinary residence should be extended to apply to after-care services provided under section 117 of the Mental Health Act 1983. The issue of how the ordinary residence rules should be applied to section 117 should be taken forward as a general review of the policy of the Government and the Welsh Assembly Government'.[184]

6.103   In relation to the responsibilities of the NHS, the Health and Social Care Bill (as currently drafted at September 2011) proposes the abolition of PCT's and Strategic Health Authorities. They will be replaced by clinical commissioning groups and a National Commissioning Board by April 2013. It is proposed that the Bill and regulations will make clinical

---

177 Report by the Public Services Ombudsman for Wales and the Health Service Ombudsman for England of an investigation of a complaint about the Welsh Assembly Government (Health Commission Wales), Cardiff and Vale NHS Trust and Plymouth Teaching Primary Care Trust, Third Report Session 2008–2009 HC 858.

178 See para 6.7.

179 Law Commission (2011) *Adult Social Care*, Law Com No 326, para 10.11.

180 It proposes a general and enhanced duty to co-operate, and an enhanced duty would specifically apply where a services user is moving from one local authority area to another: recommendations 49 and 71(3).

181 *Sustainable Social Services for Wales – a framework for action*, WAG10–11086, para 3.5.

182 Law Commission (2011) *Adult Social Care*, Law Com No 326, Recommendation 49. This recommendation is similar to the proposals within the private members bill *Social Care Portability Bill*, which was introduced into Parliament on 23 June 2011.

183 See para 6.59 above et seq.

184 Law Commission (2011) *Adult Social Care*, Law Com No 326, Recommendation 63.

commissioning groups 'responsible for arranging emergency and urgent care services within their boundaries, and for commissioning services for any unregistered patients who live in their area – in other words, they will be responsible for their whole population, not just registered patients, except in respect of those services that the NHS Commissioning Board is responsible for.' It is expected that a significant majority of the registered patients a clinical commissioning group will be responsible for, will live within the commissioning group's boundaries.[185] It appears therefore that England might become more in line with the other countries of the UK in that responsibility will be linked to where the patient lives rather than their GP registration.

---

185   *Government response to the NHS Future Forum report.* June 2011 Para 3.45.

CHAPTER 7

Care home accommodation

continued

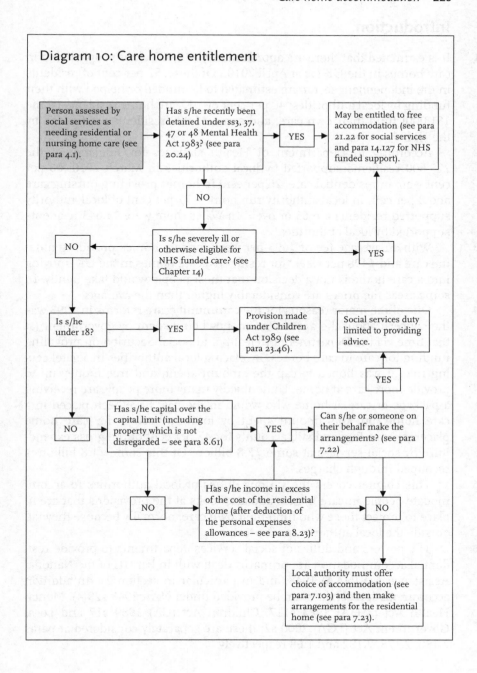

Diagram 10: Care home entitlement

Person assessed by social services as needing residential or nursing home care (see para 4.1).

Has s/he recently been detained under ss3, 37, 47 or 48 Mental Health Act 1983? (see para 20.24)

YES → May be entitled to free accommodation (see para 21.22 for social services and para 14.127 for NHS funded support).

NO

Is s/he severely ill or otherwise eligible for NHS funded care? (see Chapter 14)

NO ←   YES →

Is s/he under 18?

YES → Provision made under Children Act 1989 (see para 23.46).

Social services duty limited to providing advice.

YES

NO

Has s/he capital over the capital limit (including property which is not disregarded – see para 8.61)

YES → Can s/he or someone on their behalf make the arrangements? (see para 7.22)

NO

Has s/he income in excess of the cost of the residential home (after deduction of the personal expenses allowances – see para 8.23)?

NO

Local authority must offer choice of accommodation (see para 7.103) and then make arrangements for the residential home (see para 7.23).

Introduction

7.1   It is estimated that there are approximately 418,000 older people living in care homes in the UK (as at April 2010.) Of these, 52 per cent of residents in the independent sector are estimated to be funded or helped with their funding by local authorities; 40 per cent of UK care home residents (some 151,000) fund their own care; and some 31,000 residents are funded by the NHS.[1]

7.2   According to Department of Health statistics for England, of the 225,600 residents supported by local authorities in March 2010, 66 per cent were in residential care, 26 per cent in homes providing nursing care and 8 per cent in local authority run homes. 77 per cent of local authority supported residents are 65 or over.[2] In Wales there were 13,643 residents supported by local authorities.[3]

7.3   With an average fee of £693 per week for care homes providing nursing care and £498 per week[4] for residential care homes in the UK, moving into a care home is not a decision that most people would take lightly. In some areas the prices are considerably higher than the average.

7.4   One of the major reasons for the community care reforms in 1993 was the concern about the amount of money being spent by government (at that time via the Department of Health and Social Security) on providing funding for care in care homes. By placing local authorities in a gatekeeping role, it was hoped to cap the amount spent, and free money up to provide more care at home. Undoubtedly many more people are receiving a package of care at home who would in the past have been placed in a care home, but the amount spent by local authorities for care home placements in England still accounts for 47 per cent of the gross expenditure by social services at some £7.8 billion. Of this some £1.8 billion is recouped through charges.[5]

7.5   This chapter covers the various duties of local authorities to accommodate people in care homes and also looks at the provisions that are in place to protect those who fund their own care, normally because they fall outside the local authority means test.

7.6   The powers and duties of social services departments to provide residential accommodation are primarily dealt with in Part III of the National Assistance Act (NAA) 1948, and in particular in section 21. In addition accommodation services can be provided under NAA 1948 s29(4), Mental Health Act (MHA) 1983 s117, Children Act (CA) 1989 s17 and Local Government Act (LGA) 2000 s2; these are separately considered at paras 7.180, 7.178, 7.182 and 1.68 respectively.

1   Figures from Laing & Buisson, *Care of Elderly People UK Market Survey*, London, 2010.
2   Department of Health (2011) *Community Care Statistics 2009–2010*.
3   Welsh Government *Social Services Statistics 2009–2010*.
4   Laing & Buisson, *Care of Elderly People UK Market Survey*, London, 2010.
5   Department of Health (2011) *Personal Social Services Expenditure and Unit Costs 2009–10*.

Accommodation under National Assistance Act 1948 s21

7.7 NAA 1948 s21(1) has been much amended,[6] most recently by provisions (in section 21(1A)) that seek to exclude certain persons from abroad – and this aspect is considered further in chapter 21 and at para 7.12 below. Section 21(1) provides, however:

> (1) Subject to and in accordance with the provisions of this Part of this Act, a local authority may with the approval of the secretary of state, and to such extent as he may direct shall, make arrangements for providing—
>
> (a) residential accommodation for persons aged eighteen or over who by reason of age, illness, disability or any other circumstances are in need of care and attention which is not otherwise available to them; and
>
> (aa) residential accommodation for expectant and nursing mothers who are in need of care and attention which is not otherwise available to them.

7.8 It follows that social services authorities have no power to make any arrangements under section 21 unless and until the secretary of state has issued a direction specifying the arrangements which may be made (are 'approved') and those which must be made (are 'directed' to be made).[7] The secretary of state's most recent direction in England is found at appendix 1 to LAC (93)10[8] and came into force on 1 April 1993 (see appendix B for the full text of the direction).

7.9 NAA 1948 s21 specifies two hurdles which a person must (with one exception) surmount before being considered by a social services authority for residential accommodation under this section: the exception relates to expectant and nursing mothers, for whom the age requirement does not apply (see below). The two requirements are:

a) the person must be 18 or over and have certain characteristics (see 'client group' below), and

b) the person must be in need of care and attention which is not otherwise available.

Client group

7.10 NAA 1948 s21 lists the criteria which may cause a person to be considered in need of the necessary care and attention, namely:

Age	As under the preceding Poor Laws,[9] age is not defined by the 1948 Act. It is usually taken as a reference to

---

6 See para 7.184 below for the proposals by the Law Commission regarding NAA 1948 s21.

7 Authority to provide accommodation may, however, derive from other provisions – eg MHA 1983 s117 (see para 7.178 below) and LGA 2000 s2 (para 1.68 above).

8 WOC 35/93 in Wales; since the texts are virtually identical the English direction is referred to henceforth.

9 P Thane, *Old Age in English History*, OUP, 2000, p180.

those who have become frail as a result of the ageing process. Age is, of course, frequently accompanied by disabling conditions or illness, which are alternative qualifying conditions for the purpose of section 21.[10]

Illness   This is not defined by the NAA 1948 although by National Health Service Act (NHSA) 2006 s275/ National Health Service (Wales) Act (NHS(W)A) 2006 s206 it is defined as including mental disorder within the meaning of the MHA 1983 and any injury or disability requiring medical or dental treatment or nursing. The care and attention may be required not merely because the person is ill; it may arise in order to prevent that person becoming ill, or by way of aftercare.[11] The residential accommodation duties parallel the obligations under NHSA 2006 Sch 20 para 2/ NHS(W)A 2006 Sch 15 para 2 which enable social services authorities to provide domiciliary services for people who are or have been ill (or for the prevention of illness – see para 9.154 below).[12]

Disability   This is not qualified in NAA 1948 s21. It follows that the condition need not necessarily be substantial or permanent (unlike under section 29 – see para 7.11 below).

Expectant or nursing mothers   The secretary of state's direction specifically states that residential accommodation can be provided for expectant and nursing mothers of any age, ie irrespective of whether or not they are over 18.[13]

Any other circumstances   The secretary of state's direction[14] does not limit the potential client group entitled to services under NAA 1948 s21 (as the direction also refers to persons whose need arises as a result of any other circumstance). The direction nevertheless specifically refers to two categories of condition:

Mental disorder   Residential accommodation can be provided for persons who are or have been suffering from mental

10 The NHS has responsibilities for very frail elderly people (particularly for respite and rehabilitation services) and this obligation is considered in greater detail at para 13.56 and in relation to NHS continuing healthcare in Chapter 14 below.
11 LAC (93)10 appendix 1 para 2(5): the full text of which is at appendix B below.
12 The criterion of 'illness' was inserted into section 21 by National Health Service and Community Care Act (NHSCCA) 1990 s42(1)(a). Prior to this amendment a parallel social services accommodation obligation existed under NHSA 1977 Sch 8 para 2 which was repealed by NHSCCA 1990 Sch 10. This power to accommodate was generally used to provide accommodation for people who were able to live more independently than those accommodated under section 21, but who nevertheless required some degree of care and support. These were mostly (but not always) people under pension age (see para 8.118).
13 LAC (93)10 appendix 1 para 3.
14 LAC (93)10 appendix 1.

disorder, as well as for the purpose of the prevention of mental disorder.[15]

Alcohol or drug dependency Residential accommodation is for those actually dependent (rather than for prevention).[16] The provision of accommodation for persons who are alcohol or drug-dependent is considered in greater detail in chapter 22.

7.11 The list should be contrasted with that under NAA 1948 s29 (which deals with domiciliary services – see para 9.21). The section 29 list does not include age as a qualifying criterion and is generally more restrictive in its requirements (for instance, an impairment must substantially and permanently 'handicap' the person).

Care and attention

7.12 Accommodation under NAA 1948 s21 is only available to persons who (among other things) are in need of 'care and attention'; a phrase which is not defined in the legislation. The courts have until recently adopted a reasonably generous approach to its interpretation – based on the supposition that this too is the intention of the secretary of state.[17] Recently the interrogation of the meaning of 'care and attention' has occurred chiefly in cases concerning asylum seekers and other persons from abroad and this aspect is considered further at chapter 21 below.

7.13 The leading authority is *R (M) v Slough BC*.[18] It concerned whether an asylum seeker was the responsibility of the National Asylum Support Services (NASS) or of social services. Although HIV positive, his needs were only for medication (supplied by the NHS) and a refrigerator to store it. In allowing the council's appeal, Baroness Hale having given a succinct history of the legislation and how the 'inverted and unseemly turf war' between central and local government had come about, gave her interpretation of the need for 'care and attention' as follows (para 33):

> . . . the natural and ordinary meaning of the words 'care and attention' in this context is 'looking after'. Looking after means doing something for the person being cared for which he cannot or should not be expected to do for himself: it might be household tasks which an old person can no longer perform or can only perform with great difficulty; it might be protection from risks which a mentally disabled person cannot perceive; it might be personal care, such as feeding, washing or toileting. This is not an exhaustive list. The provision of medical care is expressly excluded.

7.14 Their Lordships also considered the tense of the legislation 'persons . . . are in need of care and attention'. They concluded that the primary focus must be on present rather than future needs, but if there is a present

15 LAC (93)10 appendix 1 para 2(3).
16 LAC (93)10 appendix 1 para 2(6).
17 *R v Westminster City Council ex p M, P, A and X* (1997–98) 1 CCLR 85 at 92D, CA.
18 [2008] UKHL 52, (2008) 11 CCLR 733.

need then authorities must be empowered to intervene before it becomes a great deal worse.[19] Lord Neuberger amplified this at para 55:

> It would seem wrong to extend a duty owed to a person who satisfies a statutory requirement to a person who currently does not satisfy the requirement simply because he will or may do so in the future. I should add that, as a matter of practicality, humanity and common sense, this cannot mean that a local authority is required to wait to act under section 21 until a person becomes seriously in need, however close and inevitable that serious need may be, and however much the authority reasonably wants to assist at once. The section must contemplate that a local authority can act, where it reasonably considers it right to do so, as soon as a person can be said to be in need of some care and attention, even to a relatively small degree.

7.15   In *R (Z) v Hillingdon LBC*[20] the Court of Appeal expressed the opinion that the extent to which the law had been modified by the *Slough* judgment had been very modest (para 18). In this case the applicant was blind and homeless and needed help with shopping and laundry and some guidance in dressing. In the view of the Court of Appeal his needs were certainly not 'de minimis' and since he needed 'others to do what he cannot do for himself to a substantial extent. A reasonable local authority was bound to find that he fell within section 21(1)(a).'

7.16   However, in *R (Nassery) v London Borough of Brent*[21] Robinson J suggested that the test in the *Slough* judgement was 'a high one: a person must need help with activities that they cannot carry out themselves or only with great difficulty'. In this case the claimant had developed mental health problems including self harming. The court upheld the local authority's decision that he was not in need of care and attention as the help he required was medical help.

7.17   This approach did not, however, find favour with the Court of Appeal in *R (SL) v Westminster City Council*.[22] In this case, the appellant, who was suffering from depression and post traumatic stress disorder, had been treated as an inpatient and then discharged. His aftercare consisted of weekly meetings with his social worker who gave advice and encouragement, and generally monitored the appellant's condition and progress. The Court of Appeal held that this amounted to care and attention that 'was not otherwise available' to him other than through the provision of accommodation by social services. In its opinion the social worker was 'doing something for the appellant which he cannot do for himself: he is monitoring his mental state so as to avoid if possible a relapse or deterioration'. The court further held that 'care and attention within the subsection is not limited to acts done by the local authority's employees or agents. . . . the subsection does not envisage any particular intensity of support in order to constitute care and attention' (para 22).

19   [2008] UKHL 52, (2008) 11 CCLR 733 at para 35.
20   [2009] EWCA Civ 1529, (2010) 13 CCLR 157 at para 19.
21   [2010] EWHC 2326 (Admin) para 69, upheld on appeal [2011] EWCA Civ 539.
22   [2011] EWCA Civ 954.

7.18   On the facts of this case, the Court of Appeal found that it would be 'absurd' to provide such a programme of assistance and support without also providing the 'obviously necessary basis of stable accommodation'. In its opinion the duty of local authorities to provide accommodation is triggered when it would not be 'reasonably practicable and efficacious' to supply the necessary services in the absence of accommodation (para 44).

'Not otherwise available to them'

7.19   The social services' obligation to provide residential accommodation only arises when the care and attention that a person needs is 'not otherwise available'. Other options may of course include a package of domiciliary care services to enable the person to remain in his or her own home, and/ or the provision of accommodation under the Housing Act 1996[23] or assistance from the NHS under its continuing care responsibilities.[24] As noted above, in *R (SL) v Westminster City Council* the Court of Appeal held that care and attention is not otherwise available 'unless it would be reasonably practicable and efficacious to supply it without the provision of accommodation' (para 38).

7.20   The interpretation of this phrase has also been considered by the House of Lords in *Steane v Chief Adjudication Officer*[25] which concerned the payment of attendance allowance to persons placed in independent residential accommodation by social services authorities but whose residential home fees were not being funded by the authority.[26] The effect of this decision was to confirm that accommodation is not being provided under NAA 1948 s21 if the resident is a 'self-funder', ie is paying for the accommodation without any support from the local authority *and* making direct payment to the home owner (see para 7.84 below). In effect, therefore, the duty on the social services authority to provide residential accommodation is one of last resort.[27]

7.21   In *R v Sefton MBC ex p Help the Aged*[28] the court accepted the proposition that local authorities did not owe a duty to provide residential

23   See chapter 15 and also para 7.59 below where this point is discussed in *R (Mooney) v Southwark LBC* [2006] EWHC 1912, (2006) 9 CCLR 670.

24   See chapter 14 below.

25   [1995] 1 WLR 1195, (1997–98) 1 CCLR 538, HL and see also *Chief Adjudication Officer v Quinn and Gibbon* [1995] 1 WLR 1184, (1997–98) 1 CCLR 529, HL.

26   Social Security (Attendance Allowance) Amendment (No 3) Regulations 1983 SI No 1741 reg 4(1)(c) provided that attendance allowance was not payable for any period during which a person is living in accommodation provided in circumstances in which the cost of the accommodation may be borne wholly or partly out of public funds. These regulations were amended by SI 2003/2259 when the 'may be borne' provisions were deleted.

27   As stated in *Adjudication Officers Guidance* para 11 (DSS 1994) concerning the payment of attendance allowance and disability living allowance. Because of the changes to the regulations since that date, this term is no longer required in the Decision Maker's Guide, but the general recognition that the duty of social services is one of 'last resort' still applies because of the requirement in NAA 1948 s21 that care and attention is 'not otherwise available' to the person.

28   (1997–98) 1 CCLR 57, CA.

accommodation under s21for 'self-funders',[29] but only in relation to persons whose means fell above the limits set out in the charging rules (see para 8.6). This issue has since been put beyond question via NAA 1948 s21(2A)[30] which stipulates that for the purposes of deciding whether care and attention are otherwise available to a person, a local authority shall disregard so much of the person's capital as does not exceed the capital limit for the purposes of NAA 1948 s22.[31] The guidance produced to accompany this statutory clarification[32] makes it clear that even if a person's capital exceeds the statutory limit, there will nevertheless be situations where the authority cannot decide that care and attention is not required (for instance because of lack of mental capacity).[33]

7.22   Once a community care assessment has been undertaken, and it is decided that care in a care home is required, a duty to provide such accommodation may rest with the local authority even where the subsequent financial assessment reveals that the person has capital in excess of the upper capital limit. In this respect LAC (98)19 advises (at para 10):

> It is the Department's view that having capital in excess of the upper limit . . . does not in itself constitute adequate access to alternative care and attention. Local authorities will wish to consider the position of those who have capital in excess of the upper limit . . . and must satisfy themselves that the individual is able to make their own arrangements, or has others who are willing and able to make arrangements for them, for appropriate care. Where there is a suitable advocate or representative (in most cases a close relative) it is the Department's view that local authorities should provide guidance and advice on the availability and appropriate level of services to meet the individual's needs. Where there is no identifiable advocate or representative to act on the individual's behalf it must be the responsibility of the LA to make the arrangements and to contract for the person's care.

7.23   The emphasis on any representative being 'willing and able' is important. It enables, for example, such a person to decline to contract with a care home directly and so benefit from the local authority's superior negotiating position in relation to care fees (which in some cases are considerably lower than the home would charge for the same services for a person making their own arrangements). In such a situation, since the care and attention is not 'otherwise available' the duty reverts to the local authority to provide or to secure the provision of the accommodation.

---

29 That is persons already in such accommodation who were paying their own fees.
30 Section 21(2A) was initially inserted by Community Care (Residential Accommodation) Act 1998 s1 and now derives from HSCA 2001 s53.
31 See para 8.39.
32 LAC (98)19; WOC 27/98 in Wales (both being 'policy guidance').
33 LAC (98)19; WOC 27/98 para 9.

Powers and duties

7.24 Certain of the accommodation obligations placed on authorities by NAA 1948 s21 are discretionary (ie, powers), whereas the majority are mandatory (ie, duties); these two categories are dealt with separately below (see para 1.21 for analysis of the nature of statutory powers and duties).

Duty

7.25 As a result of the secretary of state's direction contained in appendix 1 to circular LAC (93)10,[34] the duty to provide residential accommodation applies to all of the categories of persons described in NAA 1948 s21(1)(a), namely persons aged 18 or over who by reason of age, illness, disability or any other circumstance are in need of care and attention not otherwise available to them[35] (but subject to the asylum and immigration exceptions discussed in chapter 21). The secretary of state's direction, however, restricts the general duty to such persons who are either:

a) ordinarily resident in the social services authority's area, or
b) in urgent need of residential accommodation.

These terms are considered in greater detail in chapter 6.

7.26 Originally section 21 obliged authorities to provide temporary accommodation for persons who were homeless in circumstances that could not have been foreseen. Although the power was repealed by the Housing (Homeless Persons) Act 1977, the relic duty to provide residential accommodation for persons 'in urgent need' remains under NAA 1948 s21(1)(a). Common examples are where a person is staying with relatives outside his or her home area and the caring situation suddenly breaks down, or where a UK national returns from living abroad because he or she needs care and attention. It could also include disasters where individuals are unable to return to their local authority area. Guidance states that councils 'may' provide an immediate response in emergencies or crises to those who need social care support, but that this might be withdrawn or changed following an assessment.[36]

Mental disorder

7.27 In relation to persons who are or who have been suffering from mental disorder (or for the purpose of the prevention of mental disorder) the duty

---

34 The full text of the directions in appendix B.
35 The duty does not therefore extend to expectant or nursing mothers per se (although presumably they may nevertheless come within the ambit of 'any other circumstance').
36 Department of Health (2010) Prioritising Needs Guidance, para 70. Note the wording has changed from the Fair Access to Care guidance which stated councils *should* provide services. The original wording appears to follow the directions in LAC (93)10 more closely than the latest guidance.

to provide residential accommodation is specifically stated as including those with no settled residence who are in the authority's area.[37]

Alcoholic or drug-dependent

7.28   The secretary of state's direction specifically refers to persons who are alcoholic or drug-dependent as being persons for whom a social services authority is empowered to provide residential accommodation.[38] It would appear to follow therefore, that there is a duty to provide residential accommodation for such persons when they are ordinarily resident in the authority's area and have been assessed as needing care and attention not otherwise available to them.[39]

Discharge of the duty to accommodate

7.29   In a series of cases the courts have considered the extent to which the duty to accommodate can be deemed to have been discharged by an individual refusal: either an express refusal or one implied by his or her behaviour. In *R v Kensington and Chelsea RLBC ex p Kujtim,*[40] for example, the Court of Appeal held that the section 21 duty can be treated as discharged if the applicant 'either unreasonably refuses to accept the accommodation provided if, following its provision, by his conduct he manifests a persistent and unequivocal refusal to observe the reasonable requirements of the local authority in relation to the occupation of such accommodation'.

7.30   In *R (Patrick) v Newham LBC*[41] the applicant, who had mental health difficulties, was evicted on the grounds of neighbour nuisance. The respondent authority from whom she sought assistance decided that she was intentionally homeless and in due course evicted her from the temporary accommodation it had provided. Shortly afterwards she started sleeping rough. Lawyers wrote on her behalf, enclosing a doctor's letter confirming her significant psychiatric problems and requested urgent accommodation. The authority refused, stating that it had offered the applicant accommodation in a charitable hostel for people with mental health problems, but that she had refused this offer.

7.31   The authority sought to rely on the judgement in *Kujtim* – namely that she had unreasonably refused the accommodation offered. In rejecting this argument, Henriques J held:

---

37   LAC (93)10 appendix 1 para 2(3).
38   LAC (93)10 appendix 1 para 2(6).
39   NAA 1948 s21 sets out the full extent of the potential client group and clearly the secretary of state is unable to add new categories to the list: it follows that, since social services authorities have a potential to accommodate all of the categories of persons specified in NAA 1948 s21(1)(a), this must include persons who are alcoholic or drug dependent.
40   [1999] 4 All ER 161, (1999) 2 CCLR 340 at 354I.
41   (2001) 4 CCLR 48.

I do not myself consider that an apparent refusal of accommodation by a psychiatrically ill applicant puts an end to the respondent's continuing duty to provide Part III accommodation when she may well have been labouring under a complete misapprehension as to the nature of the accommodation.[42]

and

If the respondent sought to put an end to its section 21 duties to provide accommodation, they ought in my judgment at the very least to have ensured that the applicant was legally represented when the offer was made to her ensure not only that she understood what the offer was, both in terms of location and services offered, but also that she understood the legal consequences or potential legal consequences of refusing the offer.[43]

7.32   For the purposes of the Community Care (Delayed Discharges etc) Act 2003 the responsibility of the local authority ceases (for reimbursement purposes) where appropriate services have been offered to the patient, and despite the authority's 'active encouragement' the patient has unreasonably refused to move to take up these services (see para 5.38 above).[44]

Out of area accommodation

7.33   Not infrequently the accommodation offered by an authority in discharge of its section 21 duty is at some distance from the resident's family or home locality. There are many reasons why such an 'out of area' care home may be proposed by an authority. It may be because suitable accommodation to meet the person's needs is not available locally, especially in cases where the person needs specialised care. It may be, however, that accommodation at a price the local authority is prepared to pay is not available within a reasonable distance to enable visits from friends and family. Since individuals have a general right to choose their care home, under the 'choice of accommodation directions' (see para 7.103 below – albeit that this may require a top-up payment), in some cases a placement will be out of area through the individual's choice.

7.34   The law is silent on where individuals should be placed[45] other than that (1) they should be given choice as to where they live; and (2) that if 'locality' is an assessed need, the care plan must ensure that this need is met (see para 3.218 above). Even where locality is not an expressly 'assessed need', there must also be a strong presumption that placements will be in (or close to) ones locality. The Department of Health guidance on delayed discharges, for example, gives as an example of unreasonable

42 (2001) 4 CCLR 48 at 53D.
43 (2001) 4 CCLR 48 at 53H.
44 LAC (2003)21 annex A, *Reasonableness and adequacy of care plans.*
45 This is in contrast with housing legislation where Housing Act 1996 s208 obliges housing authorities (as far as possible) to provide accommodation in the district where the applicant resides – albeit that this is a limited right, see *R (Calgin) v Enfield LBC* [2005] EWHC 1716 (Admin), [2006] 1 All ER 112.

practice a decision by a London council to move frail older people to care homes on the south coast unless the individuals in question wished to move there.[46] Such a presumption would also follow from the House of Lords judgment in *R v Wandsworth LBC ex p Beckwith*[47] (see para 7.63 below) that councils are subject to an obligation to have sufficient residential accommodation in their area to provide for the needs of persons assessed as needing support under section 21.

Power

7.35   Social services authorities have the power (but not the duty) to provide residential accommodation for persons described in NAA 1948 s21(1)(a) and (aa) who are ordinarily resident in the area of another local authority, provided that the other authority agrees.[48]

7.36   The secretary of state's direction empowers (but does not direct) social services authorities to provide residential accommodation for expectant and nursing mothers.[49] There is not therefore a duty to accommodate such persons, although if the woman is over 17, being an 'expectant or nursing mother' would appear to be an 'other circumstance' that would therefore bring her within the ambit of NAA 1948 s21(1)(a) rather than NAA s21(1)(aa).

Ordinary residence

7.37   Section 21 is silent as to ordinary residence (unlike section 29 – see para 9.21 below). However, the secretary of state's direction limits the duty to provide accommodation to those persons who are 'ordinarily resident' in the authority, unless the need is urgent or the individual has no settled residence. If a local authority places a resident in a care home in another authority area he or she is deemed to remain ordinarily resident in the placing authority's area unless the responsibility comes to an end (for example, the individual disposes of their property and so becomes a self-funder). Ordinary residence is considered at para in chapter 6.

National Assistance Act 1948 s47: local authority's removal powers

7.38   Very occasionally local authorities use their powers to remove people to accommodation against their will. Environmental health departments have power under NAA 1948 s47 to apply to a magistrates' court for an

---

46   LAC (2003)21: HSC 2003/009 annex A.
47   [1996] 1 WLR 60, HL.
48   LAC (93)10 appendix 1 para 2(1)(a) and see NAA 1948 s24(4).
49   LAC (93)10 appendix 1 para 3.

order removing chronically sick, disabled or elderly persons to more suitable accommodation.[50]

7.39   The application for removal requires that the vulnerable person or 'some person in charge of him' be given seven days' notice of the intended application, unless the case is urgent, in which case an ex parte application is permitted to a single justice.[51]

7.40   The requirements for a removal order to be made are:

1) that the respondent is either suffering from grave, chronic disease or, being aged, infirm or physically incapacitated, is living in unsanitary conditions. Thus the 'unsanitary conditions' requirement does not apply to persons suffering from grave or chronic disease;
2) is 'unable to devote to himself and is not receiving from other persons proper care and attention'; and
3) the community physician has provided an appropriate certificate.[52]

7.41   Where the court is satisfied it can order the removal of the person concerned to a suitable hospital or other place[53] for a period of up to three months and the order can be renewed indefinitely. Inappropriate use of the provision has the clear potential to violate the European Convention on Human Rights (see para 26.252 below) and the Law Commission in its 2011 report on Adult Social Care Law advised that section 47 be repealed.[54]

National Assistance Act 1948 s48: duty to protect property

7.42   Where a person is provided with accommodation under NAA 1948 s21 or removed from his or her home by the local authority using its powers under NAA 1948 s47, section 48 obliges the authority to take steps to protect that person's property, if there is a danger of loss or damage to it and no other suitable arrangements have been made to protect it.

---

50 NAA 1948 s47 (as amended) enables a person to be detained for up to three weeks on the authority of only the most limited of medical evidence without having any prior notice of the application or right to be heard. The certifying doctors need have no particular knowledge of the detained person.
51 National Assistance (Amendment) Act 1951.
52 Essentially that he or she is satisfied that it is either in the interests of the person concerned; or for the prevention of injury to the health of, or serious nuisance to other persons; and that it is necessary to remove the person concerned from the premises in which he or she is residing. In addition, if the application is made ex parte, that it is in the interests of the person concerned that he or she be removed without delay.
53 Which hospital or other place (usually a residential or nursing home) has also been given seven days' notice of the intended application.
54 Law Commission (2011) *Adult Social Care*, Law Com No 326, HC 941, paras 9.60–9.96 and recommendation 42 and see also para 7.184 below which lists all the recommendations relating to care home accommodation).

Authorities are empowered to enter premises in order to take steps to protect property and to recover from the resident any reasonable expenses incurred in taking such action.[55]

7.43   The Law Commission in its 2011 report recognised that section 48 constituted an important safeguard where a person's property is at risk and advised that it be retained in any new legislation and that consideration be given to placing a similar duty on the NHS.[56]

The nature of residential accommodation

7.44   The duty under NAA 1948 s21 is to make arrangements for providing 'residential accommodation'. While typically this will be in a care home, the duty is not limited to the provision of such accommodation. As Hale LJ observed in *R (Wahid) v Tower Hamlets LBC*:[57]

> It can no longer be assumed that a need for care and attention can only be properly met in an institutional setting. There are people who are undoubtedly in need of care and attention for whom local authority social services authorities wish to provide residential accommodation in ordinary housing.

Ordinary housing

7.45   In *R v Newham LBC ex p Medical Foundation for the Care of Victims of Torture and others*[58] the council argued that under NAA 1948 s21 it was unlawful to provide residential accommodation in the form of simple bed and breakfast accommodation, or indeed ordinary private sector flats or houses. In rejecting this assertion, Moses J held that the word 'residential' meant no more than 'accommodation where a person lives'. In his judgment, an authority might be obliged to provide accommodation under NAA 1948 s21 notwithstanding that it had decided that the person did not need board or any other services. A similar argument was also rejected by Scott Baker J in *R v Bristol City Council ex p Penfold*[59] where he held that NAA 1948 s21 can:

> In appropriate circumstances extend to the provision of 'normal' accommodation. 'Normal' housing can be provided .. when it is the answer to a need which would otherwise have to be met by other community care services.

---

55 NAA 1948 s48(3). Any money owed as a result of protecting the person's property is recoverable as a civil debt under NAA 1948 s56.
56 Law Commission (2011) *Adult Social Care*, Law Com No 326, HC 941, paras 9.97–9.102 and recommendation 43 and see also para 7.184 below.
57 [2002] EWCA Civ 287, (2002) 5 CCLR 239 at 248D.
58 (1997–98) 1 CCLR 227, QBD.
59 (1997–98) 1 CCLR 315, QBD; see also *R v Wigan MBC ex p Tammadge* (1997–98) 1 CCLR 581 at 584A, QBD, where the respondent did not dispute that NAA 1948 s21 permitted the provision of 'normal' or 'bare accommodation, ie without any board or services.

7.46   In *ex p Penfold*, the court further held that discharge by a housing authority of its obligations under the homelessness legislation does not preclude
the need for a community care assessment. It follows therefore that a
person may be entitled to housing under the community care legislation
notwithstanding that he or she has been refused such accommodation
under the homelessness legislation. In general, however, (as was the case
in *ex p Penfold*), the mere fact that a person is entitled to a community care
assessment is no guarantee that his or her 'assessed need' will be sufficiently substantial to warrant such a service.

7.47   A series of subsequent cases confirmed the view of the High Court that
ordinary housing was capable of being provided under NAA 1948 s21.[60]
This acceptance may have been seen by some as a way of circumventing
the traditional route of obtaining publicly provided housing accommodation – most notably under the Housing Act 1996. Thus an increasing
number of applicants argued that they were entitled to more appropriate
accommodation, because this need had been referred to in their community care assessments.[61] *R (Batantu) v Islington LBC,*[62] was perhaps the
most notable of this line of cases, and concerned an applicant (who lived
in the 12th floor of a tower block) who had been assessed as needing a
ground floor property: a need that had then been referred to the housing
department. Henriques J held that the duty to accommodate lay with
social services, not the housing department; that since nine months had
elapsed since the assessment and the case was an emergency, the court
made a mandatory order to provide the accommodation.

7.48   Judicial disquiet about this trend was, however, expressed in *R (Wahid)
v Tower Hamlets LBC.*[63] The case concerned a claimant who suffered from
schizophrenia and lived in a two-bedroomed house with his wife and
eight children. His community care assessment stated that 'mental stability can only be maintained by his transfer to a more congenial and relaxed
environment'. Mr Wahid sought a judicial review to compel the provision
of appropriate accommodation. In finding that there was no duty to provide this alternative accommodation under NAA 1948 s21 (and when
giving leave) Stanley Burnton J was quoted as saying that this area of law
cried out for 'comprehensive analysis and clarification by the Court of
Appeal'.[64] This analysis and clarification was provided by the Court of
Appeal when upholding his first instance decision.[65]

7.49   Hale LJ confirmed that ordinary housing could be provided under
NAA 1948 s21 without the provision of any ancillary services, even though

60 See eg *R v Wigan MDC ex p Tammadge* (1997–98) 1 CCLR 581, QBD and *R v Kensington
    and Chelsea RLBC ex p Kujtim* (1999) 2 CCLR 340.
61 See *R v Richmond LBC ex p H* (2000) 20 July, Admin Ct, unreported. Referred to in *R
    (Batantu) v Islington LBC* (2001) 4 CCLR 445 and *R v Richmond LBC ex p T* January
    2001 *Legal Action* 28.
62 (2001) 4 CCLR 445.
63 (2001) 4 CCLR 455.
64 October 2001 *Legal Action* 17.
65 *R (Wahid) v Tower Hamlets LBC* [2002] EWCA Civ 287, (2002) 5 CCLR 239.

when originally enacted 'the kind of accommodation originally envisaged was in a residential home or hostel'. She gave as an example:

> . . . small groups of people with learning disabilities who are able to live in ordinary houses with intensive social services support; or single people with severe mental illnesses who will not receive the regular medication and community psychiatric nursing they need unless they have somewhere to live.[66]

7.50   However, the court held that the mere fact that ordinary housing could be provided under NAA 1948 s21 and that the applicant was in need of this did not mean that a duty arose under NAA 1948 s21. In the opinion of Hale LJ:

> Such care and attention as the claimant did need as a result of his illness was being met by his wife and other members of the family together with the community mental health team. He was free of hallucinations and happier than he had been for a long time. The family does have a housing problem, alleviation of which would have a beneficial effect upon the claimant's mental health. But the housing problem is the family's rather than the claimant's alone. The claimant's problem is his fragile mental health. While together they might sometimes give rise to a need for care and attention, [the social services authority] was entitled to conclude that this was not so in this case.[67]

7.51   In the court's opinion the case could be distinguished from *Batantu* since in that case it had been accepted that the family's unsatisfactory housing situation was likely to have been one of the factors which maintained the applicant's psychiatric illness;[68] and that the local authority had actually assessed the need for accommodation and the situation was urgent – whereas in *Wahid* the local authority had not assessed accommodation as being an eligible need and in the court's opinion the need was not urgent.[69]

7.52   The fact that local authorities can provide accommodation under section 21 in ordinary housing has potential implications for the so-called 'deeming provisons' under the ordinary residence rules (see para 6.27 above). In this context the Department of Health has given the following advice.

> It may be possible for a person who is a tenant of their own property still to be in receipt Part 3 accommodation, but it would be necessary for there to be contractual arrangements between the individual, the accommodation provider and the local authority which meet the requirements of section 26(3A) of the 1948 Act. In particular, the local authority would have to be the payer of default and the contractual arrangements would need to stipulate that if the individual failed to pay to the accommodation provider the amount he or she had been assessed as being able to pay in respect of

66 [2002] EWCA Civ 287, (2002) 5 CCLR 239 at 248C.
67 [2002] EWCA Civ 287, (2002) 5 CCLR 239 at 249B.
68 [2002] EWCA Civ 287, (2002) 5 CCLR 239 at 246K per Pill J.
69 *R (Wahid) v Tower Hamlets LBC* (2001) 4 CCLR 455 at 465D.

the accommodation costs (which may be the full cost), the local authority would have to pay instead and recover such payments from the individual.[70]

7.53 Where the person lacks capacity to enter into a tenancy the guidance advises that if the tenancy is entered into by a deputy or LPA it would not come under NAA 1948, s21.[71] The guidance also covers situations where the person does not have a deputy or LPA:[72]

.. the local authority may arrange the person's accommodation under section 21 of the 1948 Act and enter into a contract with the housing provider for the provision of accommodation, with reimbursement from the person as necessary. However, it should be noted that this type of accommodation would not usually be appropriate where the person requires accommodation together with nursing or personal care, as such accommodation must be provided in a registered care home.[73]

Overlapping provisions of the National Assistance Act 1948 and the Housing Act 1996

7.54 The fact that NAA 1948 s21 duties can be met by providing ordinary housing inevitably brings some overlap with the provisions of the Housing Act 1996. If an individual's need for care and attention can be met by a combination of housing and a suitable package of care it might be 'otherwise available' and so section 21 does not come into play.

7.55 A further and significant impediment to ordinary housing being made available under section 21 was identified by Hale LJ in *Wahid*, and concerned NAA 1948 s21(8), which in her opinion meant that:

Nothing in section 21 allows, let alone requires, a local social services authority to make any provision authorised or required to be made,

---

70 Department of Health (2011) *Ordinary Residence – Guidance on the identification of the ordinary residence of people in need of community care services, England* para 98 and see also Secretary of State Ordinary Residence Determinations 6/7/9/10/2007 in which cases and all subsequent determinations available on the website, the secretary of state has found that the accommodation in question was not provided under section 21 when it was in ordinary housing.

71 Ibid para 103. The guidance also suggests (scenario page 37–38) that even where the deputy is a local authority and signs the tenancy it does not convert this into a section 21 placement. The argument being that the local authority deputy is discharging separate functions when acting under the authority given by the Court of Protection: namely promoting the person's best interests by enabling greater independence of living arrangements. The guidance suggests that the situation would, however, be different if the placement is into a registered care home where the local authority has made a welfare decision that it is in the person's best interests to live there and so is required to make arrangements under section 21. In such cases the local authority would make the arrangement and the local authority finance deputy ensure that the payments were made.

72 The Court of Protection has also issued guidance about the use of a 'a single order' is when authorisation is required purely to sign or terminate a tenancy: *Applications to the Court of Protection in relation to tenancy agreements*, Court of Protection 2011.

73 The validity of tenancies executed to enable people with limited mental capacity to access higher rates of housing benefit in supported living arrangements is considered at para 15.134 below.

whether by them or by any other authority, by or under any enactment other than Part Ill of the 1948 Act. The asylum-seekers succeeded because there was no other power, let alone duty, to provide them with the care needed to sustain life and health. There is power to meet ordinary housing needs, either through the procedures for allocating social housing under Part VI of the Housing Act 1996, or through the provisions for assisting and accommodating the homeless under Part VII of that Act.

7.56   On one reading, NAA 1948 s21(8) could be interpreted as prohibiting the provision of ordinary housing (under NAA 1948 s21(1)) to anyone not specifically excluded from accessing housing under the Housing Act 1996. It is clear that this was not the Court of Appeal's interpretation. In other contexts the exclusory impact of section 21(8) has been given a limited and pragmatic interpretation.[74] In *R v North and East Devon Health Authority ex p Coughlan*,[75] for example, the Court of Appeal considered NAA 1948 s21(8) from the perspective of the provision of local authority funded nursing care (see para 14.19 below) and concluded that the section 'should not be regarded as preventing a local authority from providing any health services' – albeit that the court considered that NAA 1948 21(8) made a material distinction between NHS services and other services (such as housing).

7.57   The applicability of section 21(8) in relation to housing was considered in *R (Hughes) v Liverpool City Council*.[76] The case concerned a young man with severe mental and physical disabilities who lived with his mother in accommodation unsuitable to his needs. The property was incapable of being adapted and the local authority accepted that since 'the housing issues have remained unaddressed for a number of years . . . it has now become a crisis situation'.[77] The applicant sought a judicial review arguing that appropriate accommodation be provided under NAA 1948 s21, to which the local authority contended that section 21(8) excluded this possibility. Mitting J rejected this argument, holding that the homelessness legislation was 'not directed to cases in which a person has a requirement for specially adapted accommodation' and accordingly accommodation of this nature was not 'authorised or required' to be provided under that legislation.

7.58   While reservations have been expressed concerning the broad reasoning in the judgment,[78] the finding suggests a two stage approach, namely: (1) if the local authority secures suitably adapted accommodation for the

---

74   See eg *R (AW) v Croydon LBC* [2005] EWHC 2950, (2006) 9 CCLR 252 at [37] where (in relation to failed 'infirm destitute' asylum seekers) it was argued that section 21(8) was a bar to the provision of accommodation by a local authority since the secretary of state was empowered to provide support under Immigration and Asylum Act 1999 s4(2). However, having regard to the wording of the secretary of state's regulatory making powers under Immigration and Asylum Act 1999 s95(12) and Sch 8 paras 1 and 2(1)(b) the court determined that section 21(8) was of no relevance in such cases.

75   [2000] 2 WLR 622, (1999) 2 CCLR 285, CA.

76   [2005] EWHC 428 (Admin), (2005) 8 CCLR 243.

77   [2005] EWHC 428 (Admin), (2005) 8 CCLR 243 at [19].

78   See eg (2005) 21 *Journal of Community Care Law* 6–8.

disabled person through the use of its Housing Act 1996 powers, then section 21 is not relevant – the need for care and attention is 'otherwise available' since it can be provided via services under Chronically Sick and Disabled Persons Act 1970 s2 (see para 9.69) below); (2) if, however, suitable accommodation is not so secured, then the NAA 1948 s21 duty to provide accommodation is engaged.

7.59   This reasoning was adopted in *R (Mooney) v Southwark LBC* where the court found six reasons why in this case the NAA 1948 s21 did not apply:[79]

a)   There is a substantial gap between establishing a need for housing and triggering a duty under section 21(1). The one does not automatically follow from the other.

b)   The needs of children (which in this case were considered to be 'real and obvious') cannot trigger any duty under section 21 of the 1948 Act.

c)   The claimant's need for better accommodation was assessed as 'significant' (the penultimate category of need a scale of one to four).

d)   'Nowhere in the various assessments' was it suggested 'that the claimant had a need for care and attention by reason of her disability and that such care and attention [was] not available to her otherwise than by the provision of accommodation under section 21.'

e)   In fact the assessments concluded that there was a need for the social services (i) to provide additional support for the family, and (ii) to make a priority housing nomination under the council's housing allocation policy – which would enable her to access suitable accommodation under Part VI of the Housing Act 1996. In taking this course, social services were acting in a manner envisaged by section 47(3) of the 1990 Act.

f)   Since in this case suitable accommodation could be provided under the Housing Act 1996 this meant that section 21(8) was engaged and so the section 21 duty did not arise.

7.60   The interface between local authorities' community care and housing obligations is further considered in chapter 15 below.

Accommodation in care homes

7.61   The duty under NAA 1948 s21 is almost invariably discharged by social services authorities making arrangements for the provision accommodation in care homes. This accommodation may be provided by:

- the social services authority itself;[80] or
- another social services authority;[81] or

79   *R (Mooney) v Southwark LBC* [2006] EWHC 1912, (2006) 9 CCLR 670 at [51]–[56].
80   NAA 1948 s21(3).
81   NAA 1948 s21(3).

- a voluntary organisation;[82] or
- a private for reward provider.[83]

7.62   A key aim of the community care reforms was the promotion of a flourishing independent sector (providing services such as residential accommodation) alongside good quality public services.[84] Given this policy objective the question arose as to whether a mix of all four types of provision was essential.

7.63   In *R v Wandsworth LBC ex p Beckwith*[85] a proposal by the respondent council to close all its residential care homes for elderly people was challenged by an elderly resident on the ground that the council was under a legal duty under NAA 1948 ss21 and 26 to maintain some accommodation for the elderly under its own management. The House of Lords rejected the argument. Provided there is sufficient residential accommodation in the local authority's area, there is no requirement that any be actually provided by the authority; it can consist entirely of arrangements made with voluntary organisations or other persons. Although LAC (93)10 para 4 stated that authorities were required to maintain some public provision, this was, in the Lords' judgment 'simply wrong'.

7.64   Since the *Beckwith* judgment there has been a rapid move away from direct provision of care homes in some areas, such that by 2010, in England, only eight per cent of local authority supported residents are in local authority homes.[86] The impact of the closure of such homes on residents is considered at para 7.144.

7.65   With the greater emphasis on joint working and the freedoms contained within the NHS Act 2006 for partnership arrangements between local authorities and the NHS, some homes are now jointly owned and managed by these two bodies.[87] One such home which was owned by a NHS Trust but management of the care of residents on a day to day basis undertaken by social services was the subject of the first joint report of investigations of the Local Government Ombudsman and the Health Ombudsman.[88] There was a complaint made regarding the poor standards of care at the home, and the ombudsmen found a number or areas where there had been maladministration including the lack of proper governance arrangements which resulted in neither agreeing where overall responsibility lay in the case.

> We believe that the Trust must accept full responsibility for the conditions within the Care Home prior to the agreement coming into force in July

82 NAA 1948 s26(1).
83 NAA 1948 s26(1).
84 White Paper, *Caring for People*, Cm 849, 1989, para 1.11.
85 [1996] 1 WLR 60, HL.
86 Department of Health (2011) *Community Care Statistics* Social Services Activity 2009–2010.
87 NHSA 2006 s75/NHS(W)A 2006 s33(5). They are often still referred to as section 31 arrangements which were in the section in the Health Act 1999 which permitted such partnership arrangements.
88 Issued under The Regulatory Reform (Collaboration etc between Ombudsmen) Order 2007.

2002. The Trust was maladministrative in allowing the Care Home to deteriorate to the condition that it was in when the transfer of management took place. Thereafter the Council – having entered into the agreement – must assume the overall responsibility for the failures in the provision of the service after it took over managerial control. The Council's failure to properly apprise itself of those conditions when agreeing to take over responsibility for managing and delivering appropriate care to its residents, also amounts to maladministration.[89]

Commissioning care from the independent sector

7.66   It follows from the above analysis that the majority of local authority arranged placements in care homes are made under the provisions of NAA 1948 s26(1). In such cases the authority's commissioners negotiate with the care homes in relation to the terms and conditions (including fees). Over the years in England there has been a plethora of Department of Health guidance on commissioning practice,[90] including regular exhortations for providers and commissioners to work in partnership and develop trust. Guidance on Fairer Contracting issued by the Care Services Improvement Partnership (CSIP)[91] acknowledges that in practice relationships between providers and commissioners are not always mature and mutually sustaining, stating:

> In some instances the absence of close working relationship has lead to providers cutting costs in unsustainable ways or by failing to adequately invest in their staff or by trying to be unrealistically price-attractive and competitive. Providers may also have been complicit in bad practice in order to keep prices down and maintain contracts in order to stay in business. Conversely, local authorities have felt that some providers have sought to increase margins without fully explaining the rationale behind this, or the size or purpose of their profit. This has raised suspicions among purchasers that public money has not been well spent.

7.67   Wales has similarly developed guidance on commissioning over the years[92] and this proved pivotal in litigation concerning the level of fees and

89 Investigations into Complaint No 03/A/04618 against Buckinghamshire County Council and Complaint No HS-2608 against Oxfordshire and Buckinghamshire Mental Health Partnership Trust.

90 Department of Health (2001) *Building Capacity and Partnership in Care*, and following on from this a Better Commissioning Learning Improvement Network was set up in 2004. This in turn in 2010 became the National Market Development Forum resourced by the Putting People First Consortium and is formed of commissioners and providers from across the public, private and voluntary sectors. It has produced five briefing papers to help providers and purchasers to address the market development agenda in their area including one on Building Constructive Market Relations. www.puttingpeoplefirst.org.uk/Browse/commissioning/developing/?parent=8567&child=7959

91 CSIP (2005) *A Guide to Fairer Contracting Part 1*.

92 The Welsh Assembly Government gave guidance in respect of commissioning care services in August 2010, *Fulfilled Lives, Supportive Communities: Commissioning Framework Guidance and Good Practice* ('the 2010 Guidance'), which replaced guidance issued in March 2003, *Promoting Partnership in Care: Commissioning across Health and Social Services* ('the 2003 Guidance').

is considered at 7.71 below. Unlike English guidance Welsh guidance is issued under section 7 of the Local Authority Social Services Act 1970. The Welsh Government further propose that there should be national framework contract with care homes (where possible developed jointly with the NHS) in order to 'maximise the purchasing power of Wales'.[93]

Disputes about fee levels and contract issues

7.68   Since 1993 when local authorities took over the major role in commissioning care in care homes there have been tensions regarding the way local authorities use their negotiating power when fixing the fees they are prepared to pay. The House of Commons Health Committee noted in 2010 it is a 'common complaint of independent sector providers that they are underfunded by local authorities which relentlessly drive down contract values by capping prices below the cost of service provision and awarding contracts to the lowest bidder in a highly competitive market. This obviously constrains providers' ability to provide a quality service'.[94] The Committee noted that that in 2007–08 the average unit costs for a place in an independent sector residential care home was £420 and £467 in a nursing home whereas an objective analysis of costs suggested that the fee for a residential home outside London should be £540 a week and £670 a week for nursing home.[95] The Committee noted that the Commission for Social Care Inspection was also of the view that the major cost reduction programmes that had occurred 'were associated with lapses in quality'.[96]

7.69   The courts have, however, proved resistant to care home proprietors' claims concerning the inadequate fees they receive from local authorities[97] – suggesting that these are not so much public law issues as 'fiercely contested private law' actions.[98] Thus in *R v Cumbria CC ex p Cumbria Professional Care Ltd*[99] it was held that the council's preference for its own in-house care services and its failure to enter into block contracts with private sector respite care providers was not unlawful; did not breach its obligations under the Public Service Contract Regulations 1993[100] or EEC Directive 92/50 article 1 or its general duty to promote a 'mixed economy'

---

93   WAG10–11086 *Sustainable Social Services: A framework for Action* para 3.9.
94   House of Commons Health Committee – Third Report Social Care 2010 para 138.
95   House of Commons Health Committee – Third Report Social Care 2010 para 139.
96   House of Commons Health Committee – Third Report Social Care 2010 para 143.
97   In *Douce v Staffordshire CC* [2002] EWCA Civ 506, (2002) 5 CCLR 347 the court was prepared to consider 'arguable' that the authority's (then) regulatory functions under the Registered Homes Act 1984 could give rise to a duty of care to care home proprietors – but on the facts the claim (in tort) was rejected: see also *Yorkshire Care Developments Ltd v North Yorkshire CC* (2004) 6 August, Newcastle County Ct, Lawtel.
98   In *R v Cumbria CC ex p Cumbria Professional Care Ltd* (2000) 3 CCLR 79 at 97K per Turner J and see also *Hampshire CC v Supportways Community Services Ltd* [2006] EWCA Civ 1035, (2006) 9 CCLR 484. In *R v Cumbria CC ex p Cumbria Professional Care Ltd* (2000) 3 CCLR 79 at 97K per Turner J and see also *Hampshire CC v Supportways Community Services Ltd* [2006] EWCA Civ 1035, (2006) 9 CCLR 484.
99   (2000) 3 CCLR 79.
100 SI No 3228.

of care. In *R (Birmingham Care Consortium) v Birmingham City Council*[101] a challenge that home care fees were insufficiently high to enable residents to exercise a reasonable choice of accommodation under the NAA 1948 (Choice of Accommodation) Directions 1992 was likewise dismissed – so too was a generalised public law claim in *R v Coventry City Council ex p Coventry Heads of Independent Care Establishments and others.*[102] Likewise in *Amberley (UK) Ltd v West Sussex CC*[103] the right of a care home to unilaterally increase care home fees, in the face of local authority intransigence, was also rejected.

7.70   The courts' general position in such cases was summed up by Sullivan J in *R (S) v Birmingham City Council* (when refusing leave to seek judicial review of the fees the authority had 'agreed') in the following terms:

> . . . . the court should be very wary indeed before intervening in what are essentially private law disputes between service providers and the defendant. I accept, of course, that it is possible that there might be a public law dimension, given the claimant's interest in the service provided by Mr Langston, but this court would intervene only where it was plain not simply that there was a commercial dispute but that the defendant's conduct was unreasonable in the Wednesbury sense.[104]

7.71   A public law challenge did, however, succeed in *Forest Care Home Limited and others v Pembrokeshire County Council*[105] which concerned the methodology used by the council in arriving at the figure it was prepared to pay care home providers. The council, using an economic model, had determined the weekly fee per resident would be £390 for 2010–11 whereas the claimants considered that they would not be financially viable and would be forced to close their homes unless the fee was about £480. The court held that the approach adopted by the council in relation to the assessment of the provider's capital costs was irrational; the council had failed: (1) to consider whether any local factors militated against the use of national benchmark staffing levels; (2) to consider the adverse impact on residents of a reduction in staffing levels; (3) to take into consideration local circumstances and the possible consequences for providers and residents; and (4) to give proper consideration to the effect on the provider and/or residents of inflation[106] and changes to other costs. In the court's opinion, although the council was entitled to take into account its own

---

101 [2002] EWHC 2188 (Admin), (2002) 5 CCLR 600.
102 (1997–98) 1 CCLR 379, QBD.
103 [2011] EWCA Civ 11, (2011) 14 CCLR 178.
104 [2007] EWHC 3330 (Admin).
105 *R (Forest Care Home Limited and others) v Pembrokeshire County Council and (1) the Welsh Ministers (2) Older People's Commissioner for Wales (Interested Parties)* [2010] EWHC 3514 (Admin), (2011) 14 CCLR 103.
106 In *Tameside and Glossop Acute Services NHS Trust v Thompstone* [2008] EWCA Civ 5 (consolidated proceedings) it was held that in certain situations the annual increases in care charges should be assessed, not according to the Retail Prices Index but by reference to the wage-related index, namely 'The Annual Survey of Hours and Earnings (ASHE) for the occupational group of care assistants and home carers, produced by the Office of National Statistics (ONS)'.

financial position when exercising its discretion in these matters it was also bound to take into account and balance all other relevant factors such as the quality of the service it provided and the need to maintain stability in the care services sector. The interests and rights of residents were of particular weight in that balance.

7.72   In the judgment Hickenbottom J quoted extensively from the Welsh guidance regarding sustainability and the promotion of resident welfare and at para 143 held:

> However, when exercising its discretion in a manner which is adverse to an interested party – e.g. in this context, a provider or resident – the Council's own financial position is of course not necessarily determinative. It is bound to take into account and balance all relevant factors; and in particular it is bound to balance such matters as the quality of the service it provides and the need to maintain stability in the care services sector on the one hand, against the resources with which it has to provide that service on the other. The interests and rights of residents are of particular weight in that balance. The 2003 and now 2010 guidance makes them so, as does Article 8.

7.73   Although the equivalent English guidance (*Building Capacity*[107]) is not policy guidance (see para 1.46 above) it is in parts identical to the Welsh – in particular its statement that (para 6.2):

> Fee setting must take into account the legitimate current and future costs faced by providers as well as factors that affect these costs, and the potential for improved performance and more cost-effective ways of working. Contract prices should not be set mechanistically but should have regard to providers' costs and efficiencies, and planned outcomes for people using services, including patients.

7.74   Much of the guidance since 2001 has concentrated on the need to develop a strong market that also promotes the overall quality of life of the individual.[108] In this context the *Forest Care Home* judgment sets a benchmark for the factors to which local authorities must have proper regard when negotiating fees with care homes.

7.75   Given that some 52 per cent of care home places are commissioned or provided by local authorities (with a significantly higher percentage than this in some areas[109]) there is general concern that local authorities are, in relation to pricing, unreasonably exploiting their dominant position in the care home market.[110] This concern resulted in 2003 in an informal super-

---

107   Department of Health (2001) *Building Capacity and Partnership in Care: an agreement between the statutory and the independent social care, healthcare and housing sectors.*

108   *Prioritising need in the context of Putting People First: a whole system approach to eligibility for social care – guidance on eligibility criteria for adult social care, England 2010* para 37.

109   Laing & Buisson, *Care of Elderly People UK Market Survey 2010–11*, London, 2010.

110   In Wales there was a 2009 Memorandum of Understanding *Securing Strong Partnerships in Care* exists, aimed at delivering a 'more strategic and cost effective approach to service commissioning and contracting arrangements'. It is reported, however, that Memorandum is under strain following the *Forest Homes* judgment – see *Community Care*, 22 June 2011.

complaint under the Enterprise Act 2000.[111] The Office of Fair Trading (OFT) agreed to investigate some of the areas of the complaint, most notably consumer information, contracts and redress. However, it declined to investigate local authority fee levels on the basis that care homes are not obliged to accept the rate local authorities are prepared to pay, in combination with the duties of local authorities to provide residential care under NAA 1948, would mean that 'public authorities are unlikely to persist in setting excessively low prices for care homes residents over the medium to long term, because care homes will refuse to accept older people at such rates'.[112] Such reasoning is open to question – in that it fails to address a third possibility, namely that contract prices can be kept low and still satisfy local authority and private provider expenditure/profit objectives. This can be done by reducing the quality of care or by charging those funding their own care considerably more in order to remain viable.

7.76   If, as a result of a contractual dispute between a local authority and independent provider, notice to terminate the contract is to be given regarding a resident who lacks sufficient mental capacity to decide where he or she wishes to live, there is a requirement to convene a best interest meeting.[113] If in addition the resident is 'unbefriended' there will be a need for the local authority to appoint an independent mental capacity advocate (IMCA) (see para 17.67 below). It is indeed arguable that authorities should refer such a case to an IMCA at an earlier stage – namely when negotiations have become deadlocked: Mental Capacity Act 2005 ss35 and 39 require that an IMCA be engaged where the authority 'proposes to make arrangements' for a change in such a resident's residential accommodation.

Cost disputes and independent charitable providers

7.77   Charitable providers experience many of the same problems that other independent providers have when negotiating fee levels with local authorities. For the charitable provider, however, the problem may be less straightforward: it either accommodates an unreasonable council and undermines its viability by using its charitable resources to subsidise a public authority or it abandons the service user (even when there may be no viable or cheaper alternative care plan for him or her). As part of the negotiations such a provider would not normally feel able to serve a contract termination notice, since the very issuing of such a notice could

---

111 'Informal super-complaint on care home sector', *Which?*, December 2003. Available at www.which.co.uk/files/application/pdf/0312carehomes_scomplaint-445–55754.pdf .

112 *Response to the supercomplaint on care homes made by the Consumers Association*, OFT 703, March 2004, available at http://www.dti.gov.uk/files/file17611.pdf.

113 Seen eg in *R (W) v Croydon LBC* [2011] EWHC 696 (Admin) and *AH v Hertfordshire Partnership NHS Foundation Trust and Ealing PCT* [2011] EWHC 276 (CoP), considered further at para 17.37 below.

cause untold distress to the service user and his or her carers.[114] Unreasonable refusals (or delays) by a council to consider real costs increases born by such a provider may amount to maladministration.[115]

7.78   The view of the government is that charitable providers are entitled to full cost recovery and that statutory funders should have implemented a contractual policy of accepting the principle of full cost recovery by April 2006.[116] The Charity Commission has, however, expressed grave concern about the failure of statutory funders to implement full cost recovery contracts[117] – particularly in relation to contracts lasting over three years where research suggests that full costs recovery is less likely to occur. In 2007 advice, the Commission reinforced this view, stating:[118]

> In those circumstances where a public authority has an absolute legal duty to provide a service and no discretion over the level of service, there would have to be very clear justification in the interests of the charity for subsidising the service.

7.79   In 2009 central and local government in England published an updated 'Compact'[119] identifying (amongst other things) how they would comply with a set of principles in their dealings with the Third Sector,[120] namely *The Compact on relations between Government and the Third Sector in England*.[121] A key principle includes a commitment to avoid action which could undermine the independence of third sector organisations and to ensure that consultations complied with a minimum level of fairness (for example, that their duration would not, in general, be less than 12 weeks). The status of the Compact is uncertain, as is its applicability in any maladministration complaint.[122] As well as the national compact many

---

114 In complaint no 04/C/16195 against Birmingham City Council, 23 March 2006 the authority had advised a care provider in such a situation that she should simply abandon the service user if she was not prepared to accept the authority's payment rate – an attitude that the ombudsman considered 'extraordinary'.

115 Given the reluctance of the courts to become involved in such disputes (see para 7.69) the local government ombudsman would appear to provide the more appropriate remedy.

116 HM Treasury, *The Role of the Voluntary and Community Sector in Service Delivery: A Cross Cutting Review*, 2002, paras 6.3 and 8.1.

117 Charity Commission (2007) *Stand and Deliver: the future for charities providing public services*, RS15.

118 Charity Commission (2007) *Charities and Public Service Delivery: An introduction and overview*, CC37, para 14.

119 For a general discussion on the nature of the Compact, see J Roberts (2007) *Partners or Instruments: can the Compact guard the independence and autonomy of voluntary organisations?* Voluntary Sector Working Paper London, London School of Economics Centre for Civil Society.

120 The introduction in the updated Compact indicates that this term applies to charities, social enterprises, cooperatives, housing associations as well as 'small unfunded or modestly funded' community groups as well as 'many other organisations such as mutuals and faith groups' – Cabinet Office and Local Government Association (2009) *An introduction to the Compact*, p6 at www.thecompact.org.uk/

121 Cabinet Office and Local Government Association (2009) at www.thecompact.org.uk/

122 It would seem that the Compact should be a bench-mark for administrative practice, although where the dispute is essentially of a private contractual nature, this factor might place it outside the Ombudsmen's remit – see R Low-Beer (2009) *The Future of the 3rd Sector*, Public Law Project.

local authorities have a local compact which should reflect the national compact. In *R (Berry) v Cumbria County Council*[123] it was described as 'more than a wish list but less than a contract'. Where a local authority decides to cut its grant funding to voluntary sector organisations, there is a general duty to consult[124] in addition to the specific obligations to undertake race and disability impact assessments and since April 2011 fulfil Equality Duty obligations.[125] In Wales there is no national Compact but it appears that local compacts at council level exist.

Local authority consortia and the Competition Act 1998

7.80   The Department of Health has encouraged local authorities to co-operate and form purchasing consortia to improve the effectiveness of their commissioning role.[126] By way of example, in its advice relating to the purchase of care for drug misusers[127] it encouraged, whenever possible, joint commissioning between health, social services and other agencies, such as the probation service. It also advised on the benefits of forming consortia which could share information about needs, costs and quality, and which could pool specialist skills such as working with the prison service (para 5.3). From the purchasers' perspective, membership of a consortium enables them to impose agreed service standards and prices. From a provider perspective the benefits are that they do not have to meet different service standards from the separate purchasers. However, large consortia (such as the 29 local authority London consortia)[128] have such a dominant position that they can unbalance the market and effectively dictate contractual terms (particularly price). The guidance cautions therefore that:

> Where purchasing intentions of health and local authorities change and funding is shifted from one service provider to another, purchasers should consult with other purchasers and funders of that service, and the service provider before a decision is made, to ensure that the impact of such shifts in funding is minimised for both provider and purchaser.[129]

7.81   It is possible that unfair action by such consortia might constitute oppressive trade practices contrary to articles 101 and 102 of the Treaty on the Functioning of the European Community and more importantly,

---

123 [2007] EWHC 3144 (Admin).
124 *R (Capenhurst) v Leicester City Council* [2004] EWHC 2124 (Admin), (2004) 7 CCLR 557.
125 See eg *R (Kaur and Shah) v Ealing LBC* [2008] EWHC 2062 (Admin) and *R (Hajrula and Hamza) v London Councils* [2011] EWHC 448 (Admin).
126 Care Services Investment Programme (CSIP) (2005) *A Guide to Fairer Contracting: Part 1.*
127 Department of Health (1997) *Purchasing Effective Treatment and Care for Drug Misusers*, para 5.1.
128 Wales is proposing to do more to maximise its purchasing power by establishing a national framework contract for care homes and more commissioning undertaken on a regional basis: *Sustainable Social Services for Wales: A Framework for Action* WAG10–11086.
129 See note 127, para 5.5 and see also CSIP (2005) *A Guide to Fairer Contracting: Part 1*, p20 where similar cautionary advice is provided.

domestically contrary to Competition Act 1998 s18. Action by 'undertakings' which have the effect of distorting competition or amount to an abuse of a dominant position in the market place may violate section 18 of the 1998 Act and Articles 101 and 102 of the Treaty.

7.82   The crucial issue is whether consortia members constitute 'undertakings' within the meaning of the Treaty. It has been held that, in general, member states and local authorities, when exercising public law powers, do not constitute undertakings for the purpose of the Treaty,[130] although if the local authority or other public body is involved in a quasi-commercial activity it may come within the definition.[131] The question may become of increasing relevance if primary care trusts or clinical commissioning groups become significant members of such consortia. This may be particularly relevant given the proposals for large scale transfers of current local authority roles such as commissioning, to social enterprises or social work consortia.

7.83   The judgment of the Competition Commission Appeal Tribunal in the *Bettercare* case in 2004[132] suggested that the ambit of an 'undertaking' was wider than had hitherto been considered. But this has been called into question by a Court of First Instance decision which considered that where an organisation purchases goods, not for the purpose of offering goods and services as part of an economic activity, but in order to use them in the context of a different activity, such as an activity of a purely social nature, then it is not acting as an undertaking simply because it is a purchaser of those goods.[133] This judgment was upheld on appeal to the European Commission of Justice.[134]

Individuals who contract directly with care homes (self-funders)

7.84   Currently some 40 per cent of residents across the UK contract directly for their residential care, and in the southern home counties of England this rises to 54 per cent.[135] This may not be through choice but because their resources make them ineligible for local authority support (see para 7.21). Although such residents may have care and attention 'otherwise available'

---

130   Cases C-159 and 160/91 *Poucet v Assurances Generales de France* [1993] ECR I-637.
131   *Höfner and Elser v Macroton* [1991] ECR I-1079.
132   *Bettercare Group Limited v Director of the Office of Fair Trading* (2004) 7 CCLR 194, CCAT.
133   Case T-319/99 *Federacion Nacional de Empresas de Instrumentacion Cientifica, Medicina, Tecnica y Dental (FENIN) v Commission* [2003] ECR II-357 and Case C-264/01 *AOK Bundesverband v Ichthyol Gesellschaft Cordes* [2004] ECR I-2493.
134   Paragraphs 25–26, Case C-205/03 P [2006] ECR I-6295, [2006] 5 CMLR 559. See also *Office of Fair Trading competition in mixed markets: ensuring competitive neutrality. A Working Paper*, July 2010.
135   Laing and Buisson (2010) *Care of Elderly People, UK Market Survey 2009–10*. For England the figures are estimated to be 39.6% in residential care homes and 47.6% in nursing homes.

to them, guidance makes clear that there is still a duty to assess their needs and to offer advice about the type of care they require and information as to what services are available.[136] Welsh guidance takes this further by stating that individuals funding their own care 'should be provided with the same advice, guidance and assistance on choice as fully or partly funded individuals'.[137]

7.85   The ombudsman has found maladministration where a local authority had failed properly to assess and advise a self-funder of the type of care that was needed. A place in a nursing home was found although in fact the requisite level of care could have been provided in a residential care home. As the resident had been self-funding this involved substantial excess payments being made.[138]

7.86   Lack of information to self-funders was the cause of maladministration in another local government ombudsman's finding, where a relative was merely told that social services would contribute towards a resident's care if the private care insurance plan he proposed to purchase did not meet the full fees. The authority did not explain that this would only be up to a maximum rate. As the nursing home chosen was more expensive than the local authority 'maximum rate', the family were asked to make a top-up. Had they been advised of this at the outset, they might have chosen a different investment plan. The ombudsman considered that the information given was too general to be of use, and that the council should have been clear as to the approximate level of support that would have been available.[139]

7.87   It will not always be the case that a person prefers the local authority to be involved. A personal injury claimant is entitled to seek damages for future care and accommodation costs and therefore entitled to opt for self-funding in preference to reliance on local authority provision.[140]

7.88   Concern about the parlous position of those funding their own care has prompted several critical reports. In its 2008 report on the state of social care in England, the Commission for Social Care Inspection described such residents as 'People lost to the system'. A study for the report found people funding their own care to be disadvantaged and at risk of being fast tracked into residential care without an exploration of other options. Indeed none of the people questioned in the study funding their own arrangements had experienced a needs assessment prior to moving into a home.[141] In spite of exhortations from successive

---

136   LAC (1998)19 para 8 and also Department of Health, Prioritising Needs Guidance, paras 71 and 104–111.

137   NAFWC 46 (2004) para 8.1.

138   Complaint nos 00/C/03176 and 00/C/05525, against Nottingham CC and Nottingham City Council, 22 January 2002: the recommendation was for repayment of the excess fees amounting to almost £7,000 and in addition for £16,584 to cover the expenses of the attorney in dealing with the complaint.

139   Complaint no 05/B/12629 against Wiltshire CC, 30 April 2007.

140   *Peters (by her litigation friend Susan Mary Miles) v East Midlands Strategic Health Authority and others* [2009] EWCA Civ 145, (2009) 12 CCLR 299. See para 8.52 in relation to personal injury claims and charging

141   CSCI (2008). *The State of Social Care in England 2006–07.*

governments (most recently in the *Vision for Social Care*,[142]) that councils should undertake assessments and provide guidance for all people who need care regardless of how it is to be funded, it is clear that this is not happening in many areas.[143] In a recent study the experience of those funding their own care was that:

> 'Almost nobody identified social services as a source of information and advice, and people who *did* have contact with the council had a negative experience that focused solely on their financial status rather than their need for care and support'.[144]

7.89   Local authorities are not alone in failing to provide self-funders with appropriate support and information. A 2005 OFT report of its Market Study[145] made a number of recommendations regarding the need for better information and redress for residents as consumers.[146] The study found in a mystery shopping exercise that it was difficult to get fee information even with prompting, and 66 per cent of the 152 contracts scrutinised had more than one fee related term that the OFT considered was potentially unfair and 6 per cent had no fee related terms. In a separate earlier exercise the OFT had already scrutinised the contracts of ten of the larger providers and received undertakings that they would change their contracts to comply with the Unfair Terms in Consumer Contracts Regulations 1999.[147] The OFT also issued guidance to advisers and the public on what might constitute an unfair term in care homes.[148]

7.90   In 2006, in response to the OFT report amended regulations were issued[149] to require the provision of information in the service user's guide (issued by a care home) about the fees payable[150] and the arrangements for paying such fees; the arrangements for charging and paying for any additional services; and a statement of whether services, terms and conditions and fees vary according to the source of funding for a person's care. Although the evidence suggests that this obligation was routinely

---

142 Department of Health (2010) *Vision for Adult Social Care: Capable Communities and Active Citizens,* Department of Health, and see also *Think Local, Act Personal: Next Steps for Transforming Adult Social Care,* Putting People First, published 4 November 2010.

143 A British Association of Social Work manager suggested that this failure was due to the staff shortages – stating that if 'councils started giving self-funders full assessments and guidance' the consequence would be increased workloads and a 'need more social workers and care managers', *Community Care* 23 February 2011.

144 *Journeys without maps* p 49. Part II of *People who Pay for Care.* Putting People First 2011.

145 In response to a supercomplaint brought by *Which?* (see para 7.75).

146 Office of Fair Trading (2005) *Care homes for older people: a market study,* OFT780.

147 Details about the homes can be found in a press release issued in March 2005 at www.oft.gov.uk/news/press/2005/51–05.

148 *Guidance on unfair terms in care home contracts,* OFT, October 2003.

149 Care Standards Act 2000 (Establishments and Agencies) (Miscellaneous Amendments) Regulations 2006 SI No 1493.

150 In the case of nursing homes, the information about the total fees payable had to relate to the fee before any contribution from the NHS is taken into account.

flouted[151] it is of concern, given that care homes often charge those funding their own care considerably more than the fees negotiated by local authorities, that the duty to inform about the existence of such differential fee arrangements has disappeared in the new regulatory regime in England (and the revocation of the 2006 regulations[152] see para 7.94 below).

7.91   Wales did not amend its regulations in the light of the OFT report. Regulation 5A of the Care Homes (Wales) Regulations 2002[153] requires providers to provide a fees statement that must include a statement of the fees payable in respect of accommodation and food; nursing; personal care. Where the NHS is making a payment for the registered nursing care, the provider must then provide the service user with a statement as to the date and amount of the payment.

7.92   The Law Commission in its 2011 report recommended that direct payments be extended to cover residential accommodation.[154] If this is enacted there could be many more people contracting directly with care homes (albeit using public funding to do so) in effect in part replicating the pre 1993 system whereby funding was given to the individual by the then DHSS.

Self-funders who have complaints

7.93   If a resident who is funding their own care has a complaint about the service provided by the care home they can use the complaints procedure that all registered providers are required to have under the Health and Social Care Act (HSCA) 2008 in England, and Care Standards Act 2000 in Wales. As a general rule neither the Care Quality Commission in England nor the Care and Social Services Inspectorate in Wales are able to review the outcome of such a complaint, since they have no statutory duties or powers to investigate complaints. However, from the 1 October 2010 in England (but not Wales) any self funding resident who is dissatisfied with the outcome of their care home complaint can ask the Local Government Ombudsman to investigate as their powers have been amended to cover this function.[155]

---

151   A survey of 50 homes in March 2007 found that two in five packs sent by homes failed to mention fees, only two out of 43 packs received included the latest inspection report, and only eight homes sent an example of their contract – see 'Care essentials', *Which?* June 2007.

152   The 2006 regulations were revoked by the Health and Social Care Act 2008 (Commencement No 16, Transitory and Transitional Provisions) Order 2010 SI No 807.

153   Inserted by The Care Homes (Wales) (Amendment No 2) Regulations 2003.

154   Law Commission (2011) *Adult Social Care*, Law Com No 326, HC 941, Recommendation 35.

155   Local Government Act 1974 ss 34A–34T, inserted by HSCA 2008 Sch 5 – see para 26.116 below).

The regulation of care homes

7.94   Where the provider or manager of a care home is carrying out a 'regulated activity' the provider or manager must be registered under the HSCA 2008 in England. Most of the provisions are now governed by regulations that came into force in October 2010.[156] In this context, a regulated activity is 'the provision of accommodation together with nursing or personal care' for which the provider must be registered.[157] Where the provider provides 'accommodation for persons who require nursing or personal care' or accommodation and nursing or personal care in the further education sector' they will not need to register additionally for the activity of 'personal care' within that service. Providers and managers have to show that they will comply with all the essential standards of quality and safety for each regulated activity provided at each location.[158]

7.95   In Wales the Care Standards Act (CSA) 2000 still applies to homes carrying out personal or nursing care.[159] Personal care is not defined in the CSA 2000, although section 121(3) states that the expression 'does not include any prescribed activity' and section 121(9) states that the care that is provided must include 'assistance with bodily functions (eg toileting, eating) where such assistance is required'. Welsh Government[160] guidance on the 2000 Act currently defines personal care as care requiring:

- assistance with bodily functions such as feeding, bathing, and toileting;
- care which falls just short of assistance with bodily functions, but still involving physical and intimate touching, including activities such as helping a person get out of a bath and helping him or her to get dressed.

7.96   In contrast in England personal care is defined for the purpose of whether it is a regulated activity as:

  (a) physical assistance given to a person in connection with –
      (i) eating or drinking (including the administration of parenteral nutrition),

---

156 The Care Quality Commission (Registration) Regulations 2009 SI No 3112 and the Health and Social Care Act 2008 (Regulated Activities) Regulations 2010 SI No 781.
157 Health and Social Care Act 2008 (Regulated Activities) Regulations 2010 SI No 781 reg 2. It follows therefore that (as under the Care Standards Act 2000) where accommodation is disaggregated from the provision of care, then the provider is not undertaking the regulated activity of providing accommodation with personal or nursing care: see for instance *R (Cardiff City Council) v Welsh Ministers* [2009] EWHC 3684 (Admin) 3 June 2009; see also para 15.145 where deregistration is further considered.
158 CQC (2010) *Guidance about Compliance: essential standards of quality and safety. What providers should do to comply with the section 20 regulations under the Health and Social Care Act 2008.*
159 With associated Regulations the Care Homes (Wales) Regulations 2002 SI No 324 (W37) as amended.
160 *Clarification of the registration requirements for supported housing and extra care schemes under the Care Standards Act 2000 guidance*, August 2002. See also para 15.151 for CQC 2011 guidance on what constitutes regulated activities for supported living schemes.

     (ii) toileting (including in relation to the process of menstruation),
     (iii) washing or bathing,
     (iv) dressing,
     (v) oral care, or
     (vi) the care of skin, hair and nails (with the exception of nail care
          provided by a chiropodist or podiatrist); or
(b) the prompting, together with supervision, of a person, in relation
to the performance of any of the activities listed in paragraph (a),
where that person is unable to make a decision for themselves in
relation to performing such an activity without such prompting and
supervision.

7.97   In England if a care home offers nursing care, the proprietor or manager will almost invariably need to be registered for the regulated activity of 'Treatment of disease, disorder or injury'.[161] In Wales the regulatory body has power when issuing a certificate of registration to impose conditions, including the categories of person that the home can accommodate – for instance authorising the accommodation of people requiring nursing care.[162] The current terminology therefore for what formerly was called a nursing home is a 'care home with nursing'. It is of course legally possible for nursing to be provided at a care home that just provides personal care if, for example, the nursing care is provided by the NHS district nursing services.[163]

7.98   The bodies responsible for the registration, regulation and inspection of care homes are the Care Quality Commission in England (CQC) and the Care and Social Services Inspectorate in Wales (CSSIW).

Standards

7.99   In England the Care Quality Commission (CQC) has, by virtue of HSCA 2008 s3 the following objectives:

    (1) to protect and promote the health, safety and welfare of people who use health and social care services.
    (2) to perform its functions for the general purpose of encouraging—
        (a) the improvement of health and social care services,
        (b) the provision of health and social care services in a way that focuses on the needs and experiences of people who use those services, and
        (c) the efficient and effective use of resources in the provision of health and social care services.

7.100 Pursuant to its statutory duty under HSCA 2008 s23(1) the CQC has produced guidance for providers of health and adult social care, to help them comply with the regulatory framework that governs their activities.

---

161 Nursing care is defined in the Care Quality Commission (Regulated Activities) Regulations 2010 and mirrors section 49(2) of the Health and Social Care Act 2001: see para 13.110.

162 National Care Standards Commission (Registration) Regulations 2001 SI No 3969 reg 9(f).

163 *R (Goldsmith) v Wandsworth LBC* [2004] EWCA Civ 1170, (2004) 7 CCLR 472.

The guidance, *Essential standards of quality and safety,*[164] is substantial, applies to all forms of regulated activity and addresses the following areas: involvement and information; personalised care, treatment and support; safeguarding and safety; suitability of staffing; quality and management; suitability of management. For each of these areas, expected 'outcomes' have been developed, along with a series of 'prompts'. Although not mandatory, for compliance purposes providers and managers must be able to demonstrate that they have been taken into account.[165]

7.101　　CSA 2000 s23 gives power to the Welsh Government to publish 'national minimum standards' which the CSSIW must take into account when making their decisions. These standards form the basis for judgments made by the CSSIW regarding registration and the imposition of conditions for registration, variation of any conditions and enforcement of compliance with the CSA 2000 and associated regulations, including proceedings for cancellation of registration or prosecution. The Welsh Government has published national minimum standards for care homes for older people and separately for care homes for younger adults, which in effect flesh out the basic requirement of the regulations. In February 2011 CSSIW began a review of Regulation.[166]

7.102　　Care homes are also inspected by the Health and Safety executive which issued guidance covering both England and Wales in 2009[167]

Choice of accommodation

7.103　The NAA 1948 (Choice of Accommodation) Directions 1992 constitute one of the few examples of genuine choice that individuals have in relation to their community care services. In general service users' wishes and preferences must be taken into account – but not necessarily satisfied. However, when they are engaged, the directions give service users a legal right to choose the setting of their residential care.[168]

7.104　　The 1992 directions have been amended[169] as a result of the deferred

164　CQC (2010) *Guidance about compliance: essential standards of quality and safety. What providers should do to comply with the section 20 regulations under the Health and Social Care Act 2008.*

165　Health and Social Care Act 2008 (Regulated Activities) Regulations 2010 SI No 781 and the Care Quality Commission (Registration) Regulations 2009 SI No 3112 reg 26.

166　CSSIW Annual Report 2009–2010 p18.

167　Health and Safety Executive, *Health and safety in care homes*, HSG 220, HSE Books. A new edition is due out in 2011. The HSE also has a website that provides information about managing risks in health and social care at www.hsegov.uk/healthservices.

168　This does not extend to the right to choose to remain at home. However, the Ombudsman has stated in a Complaint No 07/A/01436 against Hillingdon LBC, 18 September 2008, that a council had no right to disregard the client's wishes to remain at home and promoting independent living should not be lightly disregarded.

169　Department of Health (2004) *LAC (2004) 20: Guidance on National Assistance Act 1948 (Choice of Accommodation) Directions 1992 and National Assistance (Residential Accommodation) (Additional Payments and Assessment Of Resources) (Amendment) (England) Regulations 2001* and National Assembly for Wales (2004) Guidance on National Assistance Act 1948 (Choice of Accommodation) Directions 1993 NAFWC 46/2004.

payments scheme[170] (see para 8.81 below) and new guidance on the amended directions was issued in 2004 (referred to in the following section as the '2004 guidance'[171]): a copy of the directions and guidance is at appendix B of this text.

7.105   Once a social services authority has assessed a person as eligible for accommodation under NAA 1948 s21, it is then obliged to make arrangements to accommodate that person in a care home of his or her choice provided that the conditions specified in direction 3 of the NAA 1948 (Choice of Accommodation) Directions 1992 (as amended) are satisfied. The conditions are:

• the preferred accommodation appears to the authority to be suitable[172] in relation to the person's needs as assessed by it;
• the cost of making the arrangements at the preferred accommodation would not require the authority to pay more than it would usually expect to pay having regard to the assessed needs (in this context, however, a local authority cannot reject a care home on cost grounds before a viable alternative has been identified[173]);
• the preferred accommodation is available; and
• the persons in charge of the preferred accommodation will provide it subject to the authority's usual terms and conditions, having regard to the nature of the accommodation, for providing accommodation for such a person under NAA 1948 Part III.

7.106   In *R (S) v Leicester City Council*[174] it was held that the Choice of Accommodation Directions do not require a service user to live in the most suitable accommodation that is available. So long as the service user's preferred accommodation is suitable to meet his or her needs, it should not matter that another residential placement would provide a better range of services – and a residential placement is not unsuitable merely because it is located some distance from the funding authority.

7.107   The preferred accommodation must be in England, Wales or Scotland.[175] HSCA 2001 s56 provides regulatory powers to the secretary of state to make provision for cross border placements by local authorities in Scotland, Northern Ireland, the Channel Islands and the Isle of Man,

170 Direction 4 of the 1992 Directions was repealed by the NAA 1948 (Choice of Accommodation) (Amendment) (England) Directions 2001. The revised text of relevance to 'Preferred accommodation outside local authority's usual limit' is now found in the National Assistance (Residential Accommodation) (Additional Payments and Assessment of Resources) (Amendment) (England) Regulations 2001 SI No 3441. The guidance accompanying the 1992 Directions was revised as a result of LAC (2001)29. The revised directions, the 2001 regulations and the revised guidance are contained in appendix B.
171 LAC (2004)20, NAFWC 46/2004.
172 Accommodation will not necessarily be unsuitable simply because it fails to conform with the authority's preferred model of provision – see 2004 guidance para 3.5.2.
173 *R (Alloway) v Bromley LBC* [2004] EWHC 2108 (Admin), (2004) 8 CCLR 61.
174 *R (S) v Leicester City Council* [2004] EWHC 533 (Admin), (2004) 7 CCLR 254.
175 NAA 1948 (Choice of Accommodation) Directions 1992 direction 2, extended to Scotland by NAA 1948 (Choice of Accommodation) (Amendment) Directions 1993. See LAC (93)18 and WOC 47/93 in relation to the 1993 Scottish amendment. See also para 16.42 for more details about cross border placements and 'ordinary residence'.

however, at the time of writing (September 2011) no such regulations had
been made. It is possible that the restriction of funded accommodation
to Great Britain could be vulnerable to an EU law challenge, since, on
the face of it, it appears to be an unreasonable restriction on the free
movement of services.[176]

7.108   There is a duty on social services authorities to explain to residents and
prospective residents (and their carers) their rights under the direction.[177]
Any failure in this regard would amount to maladministration as would
be a policy of requiring service users or their carers to find accommodation at an acceptable cost to the authority.[178]

More expensive accommodation

7.109   Where a person's preferred accommodation is more expensive than the
accommodation proposed by the authority, then he or she may nevertheless require the authority to support him or her in that accommodation,
provided either:

a)   a third party agrees to top up the difference *and* that third party can
reasonably be expected to pay the sum for the duration of the proposed placement[179] (in this category the directions exclude residents
from topping up their own fees[180] and also residents' spouses if a
liable relative payment has been sought[181]);

b)   the resident is subject to the 12-weeks property disregard – during
which the resident can top up his or her own fees (see para 8.61
below); or

c)   the resident has entered into a deferred payment scheme with the
local authority under HSCA 2001 s53 — in which case the resident
can top up his/her own fees (see para 8.81 below).

7.110   The amount of top-up is calculated as the difference between:

a)   the cost which the authority would usually expect to pay for the
accommodation having regard to the person's assessed need; and

b)   the full standard rate for the accommodation.[182]

176   See eg article 56 of the Treaty on the Functioning of the European Community which
prohibits restrictions on the freedom to provide services within the Community. A
reported case challenging the discriminatory impact of the restriction in Great
Britain on access to care home accommodation ((1996) Independent 4 March) was –
it appears – withdrawn as a result of the death of the applicant- by analogy, see *R
(Watts) v Bedford PCT* [2004] EWCA Civ 166, (2004) 77 BMLR 26.
177   2004 guidance para 7.1 (9.1 in Welsh guidance).
178   Complaint no 97/A/3218 against Merton LBC, 25 October 1999.
179   2004 guidance para 3.5.4 (4.2 in Welsh guidance).
180   This exclusion was confirmed in *R v East Sussex CC ex p Ward* (2000) 3 CCLR 132.
181   Since 1 October 2001 a resident's spouse making a payment cannot enter into a
topping up agreement (National Assistance (Residential Accommodation)
(Additional Payments and Assessment of Resources) (Amendment) (England)
Regulations 2001 reg 4 and 2004 guidance para 3.5.10). In practice this has no effect
given the abolition of the liable relative rules – see para 8.125. Note this provision
regarding spouses topping up is absent in Wales.
182   LAC (2001)29 Annex 1 para 10; as specified in NAA 1948 s22(2) or pursuant to
section 26(2) and (4) of that Act.

7.111 The 2004 guidance emphasises that it is the cost the council would usually have expected to pay for someone with the individual's assessed need that must be used for comparative purposes.[183] While the Choice of Accommodation Directions enable an individual to opt for more expensive accommodation (and to enter into a topping up agreement) this only applies if the usual cost figure used by the authority would genuinely secure the person a placement in a less expensive home which met his or her assessed needs (including in certain situations psychological needs).[184] The English 2004 guidance gives detail as to how councils should set their prices including having due regard to the actual costs of providing care and other local factors. They must not set arbitrary ceilings on the amount they would pay, and residents and relatives should not routinely be required to make up the difference between what the local authority will pay and the actual cost of the home. It further reminds councils that costs may vary depending on the type of care.[185]

7.112 It follows that local authorities should give individuals information about their usual funding 'limits' for care homes. The ombudsman has found maladministration in a case where (amongst other failings) the council failed to give the residents' son and information about homes in the area with vacancies that would meet his mother's needs at its usual cost. In ignorance, he identified a care home above the usual limit and was left liable for a substantial third party contribution.[186]

7.113 The English guidance[187] makes clear that if an individual wishes to exercise choice and the home is more expensive, this has to be a genuine choice:

> Individual residents should not be asked to pay more towards their accommodation because of market inadequacies or commissioning failures. Where an individual has not expressed a preference for more expensive accommodation, but there are not, for whatever reason, sufficient places available at a given time at the council's usual costs to meet the assessed care needs of supported residents, the council should make a placement in more expensive accommodation. In these circumstances neither the resident nor a third party should be asked to contribute more than the resident would normally be expected to contribute and councils should make up the cost difference between the resident's assessed contribution and the accommodation's fees. Only when an individual has expressed a preference for more expensive accommodation than a council would usually expect to pay, can a third party or the resident be asked for a top up (see paragraph 3.1).[188]

---

183 2004 guidance para 3.5.5 (this is not made so explicit in the Welsh guidance which merely refers to being more than it would 'expect to pay').

184 *R v Avon CC ex p M* [1994] 2 FCR 259, QBD.

185 2004 guidance paras 2.5.4–2.5.8.

186 Complaint No 09 005 944 against Bristol City Council, June 2011 See also complaint against Wiltshire County Council No 05B12629, April 2007 detailed in para 7.86 above.

187 The Welsh guidance is far less expansive on this subject.

188 2004 guidance para 2.5.5.

7.114   Both the English and Welsh 2004 guidance reflect that the preferred accommodation may be outside the council's area and that 'because costs vary from area to area, if in order to meet a resident's assessed needs it is necessary to place an individual in another area at a higher rate than the funding council's usual costs, the placing council should meet the additional costs itself'.[189]

7.115   In spite of the guidance clearly explaining the responsibilities of local authorities in relation to enabling genuine choice there is concern about widespread disregard by councils of the directions and guidance. A 2005 OFT Market Study report[190] found that between 30 and 35 per cent of local authority residents were relying on top-ups, and that 40 per cent of the authorities surveyed suspected that more top-ups were being paid than they knew about.[191] The report found a general lack of information in local authority leaflets about top-ups, and also found that some could lead residents and their relatives to believe, mistakenly, that top-ups were required before a care home place could be found. The OFT recommended that local authority leaflets should make it clear that third party top-ups do not need to be secured in order to find a care home place suitable to the person's needs.

7.116   In 2008 the Welsh Government issued a guidance letter to local authorities reminding them of their responsibilities and of the 2004 guidance. It drew particular attention to a local government ombudsman report (see para 7.137 below) and advised that the CSSIW would undertake a thematic study on the operation of top-ups.[192] The outcome of this study was published in 2010. Of the care homes responding 40% charged a top-up, with variations around the country. Of providers charging top-ups 68% negotiated them directly with the third party, although only 27% had a contract solely between the care home and the third-party. The majority of providers responding regarded third party top-ups as covering the shortfall of the local authority rate and the cost of running a home.

> In 88 per cent of responses from our survey providers stated that they charged third party payments to make up the difference between the costs of them providing the care and the rate the local authority paid them. There were no benefits to the service users. In only 12 per cent of cases did providers state that this charge was for increased services or facilities.[193]

7.117   Authorities in England were reminded in 2009 'when making arrangements for residential care for an individual under the 1948 Act, a council is responsible for the full cost of that accommodation. Therefore, where a council places someone in more expensive accommodation, it must contract to pay the accommodation's fees in full. The resident's or third

---

189   2004 guidance, para 2.4 (para 3.3 in Welsh guidance).
190   Office of Fair Trading (2005) *Care homes for older people: a market study*, OFT780.
191   A further study of 10 councils in 2007 by the Commission for Social Care Inspection *A Fair Contract with Older People?* found 5% to 75% of homes councils dealt with charged a top-up.
192   Letter dated 27 February 2008
193   CSSIW (2010) *Third party payments for care home fees in Wales: Report of a national review by CSSIW.*

party's contribution will be treated as part of the resident's income for charging purposes and the council will be able to recover it in that way.' Even if by agreement the third party make their payment direct to the home, the council is still liable for the full cost of the accommodation.[194] Some local authorities have contracts that debar care homes from making separate contracts with third parties outside of the contract with the local authority for a local authority funded resident.[195]

7.118   One aspect of the *Forest Care Home* proceedings[196] (see para 7.71) concerned the legality of the care home seeking top-up payments. The care home contracts specifically required local authority agreement to any funding arrangement that arose out of a resident exercising choice over the use of any service. In the court's opinion this precluded any such payment without the council's approval and that:

> . . . The claimants appeared intent on breaching their contracts with the Council by soliciting contributions from third parties without the Council's consent. In the circumstances, the Council were entitled to prevent such a breach of contract in the manner of the modest steps that they took. (Para 151.)

7.119   The modest steps taken by the council was to send its own letters to the next of kin and others responsible for residents asking them to contact the Council if such a request was made.

Challenging top-up payments

7.120   The need for a third party top-up payment can be challenged in two ways. The first route is via the assessment. The local government ombudsman has stressed that since councils have discretion to exceed the normal amount that they are willing to contribute to the costs of residential care, they must have regard to the particular circumstances of each case.[197] If the prospective resident has needs which can only be met in homes that are more expensive than the local authority would generally pay, this should be met by the local authority. In assessing such needs the authority must take into account all needs including the psychological and social needs of the resident (see para 4.80 above).

7.121   The second way a top-up payment can be challenged arises where the authority has imposed an arbitrary costs ceiling. In such cases the authority must be able to show that there are homes in the area with vacancies at the designated price. In this respect the press release which accompanied the 2004 English guidance put the position with some force:

---

194 LAC (DH) 2009(3).
195 The CSSIW study found in Wales 20% of providers had contracts with local authorities that restricted the amount and frequency of review of third party top-ups.
196 *R ((1) Forest Care Home Limited, (2) Mavalon Limited, (3) Woodhill Care Limited) v Pembrokeshire County Council and (1) the Welsh Ministers (2) Older People's Commissioner for Wales (Interested Parties)* [2010] EWHC 3514 (Admin), (2011) 14 CCLR 103.
197 Complaint no 97/A/3218 against Merton LBC, 25 October 1999.

Councils should not request top-up payments from either residents or their families simply because they have failed to agree fees that reflect the actual costs of care with providers. It is totally unacceptable for residents or their relatives to pick up the tab, week in, week out, as a result of poor commissioning practice by councils.

7.122   It follows that if local authorities are not able to show a choice of homes at their normal price they could be open to challenge for setting arbitrary ceilings. The Welsh guidance implies there should be at least three homes to choose from.[198]

Where the preferred care home is full

7.123   Not infrequently the care home of choice will be full, and the question arises as to what arrangements should then be made for the service user. The situation is generally of most concern to the statutory agencies, if the patient is in hospital awaiting discharge. Detailed guidance has been issued in relation to choice of accommodation and hospital discharge (see para 5.40).[199] The 2004 guidance states at para 2.5.9 as follows:

> Waiting for the preferred care home should not mean that the person's care needs are not met in the interim or that they wait in a setting unsuitable for their assessed needs, and this includes an acute hospital bed, until the most suitable or preferred accommodation becomes available. In view of the Community Care (Delayed Discharges etc.) Act 2003, councils should have contingency arrangements in place, that address the likelihood that an individual's preferred accommodation will not always be readily available. These arrangements should meet the needs of the individual and sustain or improve their level of independence. For some, the appropriate interim arrangement could be an enhanced care package at home.[200]

7.124   If interim arrangements in another care home are made, councils should place the individual on the waiting list of their preferred home and they should be kept informed of progress. If the temporary accommodation is more expensive than the authority would normally pay, councils should make up the cost difference.[201] If a person later chooses to remain at a home even if a place at his or her preferred home becomes available, 'upon making the choice to remain in that home, a third party or the resident could be approached for the total difference between the two

198 National Assembly for Wales (2004) *Guidance on: National Assistance Act 1948 (Choice of Accommodation) Directions 1993* NAFWC 46/2004 para 3.12.
199 The Welsh Government has issued supplementary guidance to the Choice of Accommodation Directions – *Procedures when discharging patients from hospital to a care setting.* LG/ML/001/11 June 2011 for people being discharged from hospital. Because of delays in discharge of patients where the home of choice is not available the guidance has set a time limit of three weeks between the time the person is considered ready for discharge and placement in a care home. If none of the homes of choice have vacancies within the two week period the local authority will find a suitable home to meet the patient's needs on an interim basis (see 5.42 for further details).
200 Similar wording is in the Welsh 2004 guidance at para 3.11.
201 2004 guidance paras 2.5.10 and 2.5.11 (Welsh guidance has similar wording).

rates'.[202] It is arguable that any top-up should not apply until the person has expressly stated that he or she chooses to stay in the interim home and not move to the preferred accommodation.

Residents already in care homes

7.125 The right to exercise choice over accommodation extends not only to prospective residents, but also to existing residents who wish to move to different or more expensive accommodation.[203]

7.126 Conversely (and more frequently) residents may wish to stay in the home in which they have lived for some time. However, residents who were funding their own care but now have to apply to the local authority for help towards the fees, may be requested to move if it is more expensive than the local authority would generally pay for that level of assessed need. The wording in the guidance on this subject is significantly different in England and Wales. The English guidance states at para 4.1:

> Should a self-funder who is resident in a care home that is more expensive than a council would usually expect to pay later becomes the responsibility of the council due to diminishing funds, this may result in the resident having to move to other accommodation, unless after an assessment of need, it is shown that the assessed needs can only be met in the current accommodation.

7.127 The Welsh guidance in contrast states at para 5.1:

> Their needs should be assessed using the Unified Assessment Process. Any such individual who wishes to remain in more expensive accommodation than that usually funded by the local authority may seek to do so on the same basis as anyone about to enter residential care for the first time. The individual should not be asked for a top-up or be expected to move from the care home if the assessment process has identified that a move to alternative accommodation poses a risk to the individual's care and well being.

7.128 The Welsh guidance is to be preferred since it makes clear (unlike the English guidance) that a risk assessment of moving the person should be part of the assessment. Where residents have lived in a home for some time, both the risk of moving them and whether this would be detrimental to their social and psychological needs should be taken into account. In addition the local authority would need to be able to show that there are other homes in the area that would be able to meet the person's needs at the price the authority is prepared to pay. These questions should all be satisfied before any question is raised either about the person moving or a third party top-up being requested.

7.129 Not infrequently top-ups start to be required from existing residents because local authority fee ceilings increase at a lower rate than the fees of

---

202 2004 guidance para 2.5.14. The Welsh 2004 guidance para 3.19 states that the 'local authority would need to require the resident or third party to agree to pay the difference in the costs'.
203 2004 guidance para 4.1 (England) and 5.1 (Wales).

the care homes. In such cases the resident has not chosen to move into more expensive accommodation; instead the home has become more expensive than the local authority is prepared to pay. If the resident has lived at the home for a long period and it is his or her settled environment and/or to move would cause severe distress or harm to health – then the assessment would most probably conclude that there is an 'assessed need' to remain. In such a scenario, there could be no requirement to 'top up' since the placement would be the only one that could meet the resident's need (and top ups are only payable when an alternative and cheaper placement exists).

7.130   The guidance is silent on this question, but such residents can rely on the requirement (noted above) that there be (a) a proper assessment of the risk of moving including the needs to remain near family and friends[204] and (b) that alternative suitable homes are available to meet the needs of the resident at the local authority price.

7.131   If, as frequently happens, the home approaches the family directly for the additional top-up sum, the local authority should be informed so it is aware that this is happening, since local authority contracts with care homes should prohibit such an arrangement. If, however, any top up is agreed, the contract should in general be made via the local authority even if the third party pays the home directly, so that full liability remains with the local authority- see 7.117 above.

Payments of top-ups

7.132   Councils are advised that persons making top-up payments will need to demonstrate that they will be able to meet the payment for the duration of the arrangements.[205] In *R (Daniel) v Leeds City Council*[206] Richards J held (when refusing permission for a judicial review) that a local authority was entitled to refuse to enter into a top-up arrangement because it had doubts as to whether the third party would, in fact, pay the top-ups.[207]

7.133   Authorities are advised to have a written agreement with the resident, third party and the person providing the accommodation when they seek to exercise their right to use more expensive accommodation. In particular it should be made clear from the outset that:[208]

- failure to keep up top-up payments may result in the resident having to move to other accommodation, unless, after an assessment of need, it is shown that assessed needs can only be met in the current accommodation. In these circumstances councils should make up the cost difference between the resident's assessed contribution and the accommodation's fees. Where resident's top-ups are being made against the value of property subject to a deferred payments agreement,

---

204   See 3.219.
205   2004 guidance para 3.5.4 (Welsh guidance para 4.9).
206   [2004] EWHC 562 (Admin).
207   (2004) 12 *Community Care Law* 8.
208   LAC (2001)29 Annex 1 para 13.

a council will have assured itself from the outset that top-up payments are viable and recoverable when the home is sold;

- an increase in the resident's income will not necessarily lessen the need for a top-up contribution, since the resident's own income will be subject to charging by the council in the normal way;
- a rise in the accommodation's fees will not automatically be shared equally between council, resident (if making a top-up), and third party.[209]

7.134 The local government ombudsman has stressed the importance of councils having a consistent charging policy for top-ups and criticised a top-up scheme whereby the amount by which a relative had to supplement a home care fee varied depending upon the year in which the person became a resident (because the council had adopted differing 'standard' care home rates for differing years).[210]

More expensive accommodation and Mental Health Act 1983 s117

7.135 Although the choice of accommodation rules do not apply to accommodation provided under MHA 1983 s117 (see para 20.25 below), there appears to be nothing in principle to suggest topping-up is not permitted by service users (or third parties on their behalf) in relation to such services. The Law Commission has recommended[211] that any new legislation should contain regulation making powers to enable the right of choice of accommodation/the making of additional payments to extend to residents accommodated under section 117.

7.136 In many cases a care home placement under section 117 will be one that a resident must accept or risk not being discharged from formal detention under the 1983 Act. It follows that any interference with a person's choice in such a situation would engage Article 8 of the European Convention on Human Rights (private and family life) and require justification. Put in the alternative, any interpretation of what is permitted under section 117 in terms of service provision should, so far as possible, avoid an interference with the Article 8 right. Given that section 117 is capable of being interpreted so as to allow top-ups, this interpretation would seem to be preferred in the absence of compelling statutory prohibitions to the contrary. In practice what might occur is that the aftercare meeting would agree that a residential home package (with certain specified facilities) would meet the detained patient's needs. If, however, he or she wished to have more than this, there would seem no reason why he or she could not contract directly with the home to pay for the additional facilities.

7.137 The local government ombudsman has criticised a local authority that refused to permit a top-up under section 117, for not properly taking into

209 See chapter 8.
210 Complaint no 03/C/02451 against Bolton MBC, 10 March 2004.
211 Law Commission (2011) *Adult Social Care*, Law Com No 326, HC 941, Recommendation 61.

account the impact that this would have on the service user – and indeed saw nothing obviously wrong with such a 'top-up' arrangement, advising that:[212]

> In the absence of specific guidance or case law on the subject of 'top-up' payments related to section 117 aftercare, local authorities need to take care when reaching decisions on individual cases. A council should be able to show that it has: considered all relevant factors including the particular circumstances of the individual case; reached a reasoned decision without undue delay; and considered any representations that it receives with an open mind. If this can be shown, I would be unlikely to criticise a council or find maladministration.[213]

7.138   In the case of section 117 placements, the need for residential care will generally be linked to the person's mental health difficulties.[214] It is therefore important to establish that the local authority price offered to the care home reflects in full the assessed needs of that particular person, rather than the general price it is prepared to pay for people with mental health problems.

NHS-funded care home placements

7.139   Although patients in NHS-funded care homes do not have a statutory right of choice; it is expected that before any placement there will be 'considerable consultation with the patient and his or her family and [hospitals should] take account of the patient's wishes'.[215] Additionally, it has been argued that the effect of principle 4 of the NHS Constitution (see para 13.31 below) that 'NHS services must reflect the needs and preferences of patients, their families and their carers' means that PCTs should fund care home accommodation of choice unless they are able to provided good reasons to the contrary.[216]

7.140   The problem of patients having to move care home once they are funded by the NHS was mentioned in the Health Select Committee report on continuing care. In its response the government stated that:

> . . . the risks (both physical and emotional) of moving that resident should be fully considered before the decision is made to move him/her. However, the Department cannot say that continuing care should always be provided in the care home where the individual is currently resident, since this would constrain the NHS's responsibility to provide appropriate care (the

---

212   Complaint no 04/B/01280 against York City Council, 31 January 2006.
213   Complaint no 05/C/13158 against North Yorkshire County Council 24 July 2007.
214   In Complaint no 06/B/O7542 against Poole Borough Council, 5 September 2007 the Ombudsman found against the authority on the grounds that it appeared to have considered that as the need for residential care had been triggered by the illness of her carer the section 117 could be lifted. In addition it had used moving out of the area to be in a home with her husband near her son, which the ombudsman considered not be a justification for lifting section 117.
215   Statement of the Minister for Health, John Bowis, to Health Committee, recorded at para 79 of *First Report into Long-Term Care*, HMSO, 1995.
216   See K Ashton and J Gould, community care update, June 2009 *Legal Action* 11–16.

care home may not be able to provide the type of care needed) and manage its finances.[217]

7.141　In this context, the 2010 NHS Continuing Healthcare practice guidance[218] refers to 2009 guidance[219] concerning NHS patients who wish to pay for additional private care and advises (amongst other things) that:

- The care plan should set out the services to be funded and/or provided by the NHS. It may also identify services to be provided by other organisations such as LAs but the NHS element of the care should always be clearly identified. Any care which would normally have provided in the course of good NHS practice should continue to be offered free of charge on the NHS.
- Where an individual advises that they wish to purchase additional private care or services, PCTs should discuss the matter with the individual to seek to identify the reasons for this. If the individual advises that they have concerns that the existing care package is not sufficient or not appropriate to meet their needs, PCTs should offer to review the care package in order to identify whether a different package would more appropriately meet the individual's assessed needs.

7.142　The 2010 practice guidance gives various examples (including where a self funder (or someone previously LA funded who was topping up) becomes entitled to NHS continuing healthcare and a move to less expensive accommodation would involve a significant risk to health and well being) and advises (at para 11.16) that:

> it will not usually be permissible for individuals to pay for higher-cost services and/or accommodation (as distinct from purchasing additional services). However, there may be circumstances where the PCT should consider the case for paying a higher-than usual cost.[220]

7.143　The Welsh 2010 guidance[221] has little to say about choice other than whilst 'there is currently no legal obligation on the NHS to offer choice of treatment or healthcare, it improved the individual's experience, dignity and respect and increases the opportunity to make shared and sustainable decisions' (para 7.15).

217　*Response to the Health Select Committee Report on Continuing Care*, Cm 6650, June 2005.
218　Department of Health (2010) *NHS Continuing Healthcare Practice Guidance*, para 11.15.
219　Department of Health (2009) *Guidance on NHS patients who wish to pay for additional private care* at www.dh.gov.uk/en/Publicationsandstatistics/Publications/PublicationsPolicyAndGuidance/DH_096428
220　See also para 14.149 below.
221　Welsh Assembly Government (2010) *Continuing NHS Healthcare: the National Framework for Implementation in Wales*, Welsh Assembly Government Circular EH/ML 018/10.

Closure of care homes

7.144　The closure of care homes, in particular for older people, has proved to be one of the more controversial effects of the community care changes. The period 1990–95 saw a 25 per cent reduction in the number of local authority homes in England (amounting to almost 40,000 fewer residents). As at March 2010 only 18,000 people were resident in local authority care homes in England.[222] In some cases this fall is due to care homes being transferred to the independent sector rather than closed. In other cases, due to reconfiguring services, some local authority homes have closed in order to concentrate resources on sheltered or extra care housing. In April 2010 there were 382,000 residents in independent sector homes across the UK.[223]

7.145　Care homes can close or change their status[224] for a number of reasons, but whatever the cause, it often results in anxiety and distress for the resident and their family – particularly if as a result he or she has to move.[225]

7.146　In relation to the closure of long-stay NHS accommodation, there is an obligation on health bodies to consult with patients and their representative bodies (including overview and scrutiny committees),[226] and (in Wales) the community health council.[227] Registered social landlords are also subject to a duty to consult when contemplating the closure of a supported living scheme, as well as ensuring that suitable alternative accommodation is secured for tenants.[228]

222　Department of Health (2011) *Community Care Statistics: Social Services Activity 2009–2010.*

223　Laing and Buisson, *Care of Elderly People:Market Survey 2010–2011.*

224　Eg by de-registration see para 15.145.

225　See Association of Directors of Adult Social Care (2011)*Achieving closure: good practice in supporting older people during residential care closures available at www.dh.gov.uk/en/ Publicationsandstatistics/Publications/PublicationsPolicyAndGuidance/DH_128733*

226　NHSA 2006 s242/NHS(W)A s183 as amended by the Local Government and Public Involvement in Health Act 2007 and subsequent Department of Health (2003) guidance, *Strengthening accountability involving patients and the public,* February 2003 and *Overview and scrutiny of health – guidance,* July 2003, and *Real Involvement* October 2008. Local Involvement Networks have also had a role in supporting public involvement in commissioning and provision decisions and scrutinising health and social care. It appears that these functions will be taken over by local 'healthwatch' and further there will be greater flexibility in the way overview and scrutiny is undertaken, and health over view and scrutiny will go to local authorities: Health and Social Care Bill 2010.

227　Community Health Councils (Constitution, Membership and Procedure) (Wales) Regulations 2010 SI No 288 reg 27. See also *R v North East Devon Health Authority ex p Pow* (1997–98) 1 CCLR 280, QBD and *R v North East Devon Health Authority ex p Coughlan* (1999) 2 CCLR 285 considered at paras 13.19 and 26.266 below.

228　Under the Housing Act 1985 landlords must consult secure tenants and take account of their views in 'matters of housing management' and the Housing Corporation (in its Regulatory Code) requires all registered landlords to meet similar requirements and offers good practice advice.

Guidance

7.147 In England there is no national Government guidance for local authorities on the process of managing home closures.[229] However, in response to an particular incident regarding the closure of an NHS facility, health service guidance on the 'transfer of frail elderly patients to other long stay settings' (HSC 1998/048) was issued in 1998. Although primarily aimed at NHS bodies, the circular was copied to all directors of social services in England, and has formed the basis of many protocols developed by local authorities.[230]

7.148 The guidance provides checklists of steps to be taken during the closure process and emphasises the importance of consultation at all stages. A key part of any strategy should be a 'project plan ... which is flexible enough to adapt to changing circumstances'. Authorities should set up a steering group to see the whole project through, with a project manager, a patient transfer co-ordinator, a key worker who works at the hospital and knows the patient and his or her needs and will liaise with the patient and relatives or carers as well as with staff in the receiving care setting. Contingency plans must be prepared for all aspects of the project and the vital importance of information sharing (both between all professionals and with patients and carers) is stressed.

7.149 The guidance advises against winter and weekend transfers and suggests that whenever possible groups of friends should be moved together. There should be a named staff member authorised to postpone or cancel the transfer of any individual should this become necessary – even if this means that the patient has to be moved within the hospital.

7.150 In contrast the Welsh Assembly Government has issued policy guidance to both local authorities and Local Health Boards which reminds them of their various statutory duties and requires them to set up a Home Operations Support Group (HOSG) to focus upon co-ordination and management of the transfer of service users from the registered care home. The guidance is practical and detailed – requiring individual relocation plans and stressing the importance of comprehensive needs assessments of all residents (including self-funders).[231]

Challenging home closures

7.151 The courts have indicated that they consider home closure decisions to be an area where litigation should be avoided if at all possible. In *Cowl and*

---

229 Although see footnote 225 above regarding recent ADASS guidance.
230 Many local authorities do, however, have protocols – see J Williams and A Netten, *Guidelines for the Closure of Care Homes: Prevalence and Content of Local Government Protocols*, PSSRU discussion paper 1861/2, 2003, available at www.pssru.ac.uk/pdf/dp1861_2.pdf.
231 Welsh Assembly Government (2009) *Statutory guidance on escalating concern with, and closures of, care homes providing services for adults.*

others v Plymouth City Council[232] the Court of Appeal spoke of the heavy obligation on lawyers in such disputes to resort to litigation only it is really unavoidable, and in *R (Lloyd) v Barking and Dagenham LBC*[233] the Court of Appeal held that it was not an appropriate organ to prescribe the amount of consultation to be carried out with a resident's advisers. Courts are similarly reluctant to investigate the closure of community care facilities – see *R (Bishop) v Bromley LBC*[234] (a case concerning a day centre see para 8.22 below) where the court reaffirmed the Court of Appeal's view in *Coughlan* that it was only in exceptional circumstances that a comprehensive multi-disciplinary assessment would be required before a decision could be taken to close such a facility. Increasingly it appears that judicial review challenges to care home closures are being rejected at the permission stage (see for instance *R (Lindley) v Tameside MBC*[235] and *R (Grabham and others) v Northamptonshire CC*.[236]

7.152   The numerous challenges that have been mounted to local authority and NHS decisions to close care homes have raised many different public law arguments which can be broadly categorised under the following five general headings.

Promises for life

7.153   Not infrequently existing residents assert that they were given a promise – or at least formal or informal assurances – that on moving to the particular home, they would be able to remain there for the rest of their lives. Moving into a care home is a very major step for many people, and often taken at a time when they are frail and uncertain about the wisdom of giving up their independence. Such explicit or implicit assurances can be pivotal in the making of these crucial decisions.

7.154   *R v North and East Devon Health Authority ex p Coughlan*[237] concerned such a promise. The Court of Appeal took as its starting point that the health authority could break its promise 'if, and only if, an overriding public interest required it' (at para 52). Having considered the reasons advanced by the health authority (essentially budgetary) the court undertook an extensive review of the public law principles underlying the concept of legitimate expectation (see para 26.217) and considered that such expectations can fall into three broad categories:

　　1)　where the public authority need only bear in mind its assurance when reaching a decision;

232 [2001] EWCA Civ 1935, [2002] 1 WLR 803, (2002) 5 CCLR 42 at 49B. Views reiterated by Maurice Kay J in *R (Dudley, Whitbread and others) v East Sussex CC* [2003] EWHC 1093 (Admin).
233 [2001] EWCA Civ 533, (2001) 4 CCLR 196 at 205G.
234 [2006] EWHC 2148 (Admin), (2006) 9 CCLR 635.
235 [2006] EWHC 2296 (Admin).
236 [2006] EWHC 3292 (Admin).
237 [2000] 2 WLR 622, (1999) 2 CCLR 285.

2) where the assurance was such as to require the authority to follow a particular procedural course in its decision making process (for instance consulting the relevant parties);

3) where the assurance was so specific that it gave rise to substantive rights – in which case the court must determine 'whether to frustrate the expectation is so unfair that to take a new and different course will amount to an abuse of power'.

7.155   The court considered that the *Coughlan* case fell into the third category, and after weighing up the competing questions it held:

> 89. We have no hesitation in concluding that the decision to move Miss Coughlan against her will and in breach of the Health Authority's own promise was in the circumstances unfair. It was unfair because it frustrated her legitimate expectation of having a home for life in Mardon House. There was no overriding public interest which justified it. In drawing the balance of conflicting interests the court will not only accept the policy change without demur but will pay the closest attention to the assessment made by the public body itself. Here, however, as we have already indicated, the Health Authority failed to weigh the conflicting interests correctly. . . .

7.156   What counts as overriding public interest justifying closure where home for life promises have been made was the main issue in *CH and MH v Sutton and Merton PCT*.[238] A previous judicial review on the promise for life had been successful in 2000 (see para 26.216 below) but in 2004 it was proposed again that the hospital be closed as it was considered to be in the residents' 'best interests . . . to re-provide services that enable residents to live in small groups in everyday settings'. Evidence from the assessments raised questions about whether a move would be in the best interests of a number of patients. The court found that the question as to whether there is an overriding public interest is one the court needs to resolve actively rather than measure from a distance, and patients were entitled to challenge whether the closure was in their best interests and the court must determine this for itself on the evidence.[239]

7.157   Although not concerned with a closure of a specific establishment, the issue of an individual's best interests in the context of the 'campus closure' policy (see para 18.24 below) has been considered by the Court of Protection. The case concerned a proposal to move a resident from a rural residential care setting (in which he had been for many years) to a flat in an urban area. Notwithstanding that this new placement carried the label

238 [2004] EWHC 2984 (Admin), (2005) 8 CCLR 5.
239 The difficulty in assessing whether or not closure of such facilities is in the best interests of the applicants who are seeking to stop the closure was brought into sharp relief in this case. The facility concerned was subsequently the subject of a report by the Healthcare Commission (*Investigation into the service for people with learning disabilities provided by Sutton and Merton Primary Care Trust*, January 2007) which was requested after a series of serious incidents including allegations of physical and sexual abuse.

of 'independent living', the Court of Protection[240] considered that it was not in his best interests, holding that :

> These residents are not an anomaly simply because they are among the few remaining recipients of this style of social care. They might better be seen as a good example of the kind of personal planning that lies at the heart of the philosophy of care in the community. Otherwise, an unintended consequence of national policy may be to sacrifice the interests of vulnerable and unusual people like AH.

7.158 The courts will in general only accept that a promise for life has been made when 'convincing' evidence is advanced by the applicant of a 'clear and unequivocal assurance'.[241] The assurance should, however, be viewed from the perspective of the resident – the test being 'what would the ordinary resident think that the [statement in question] was trying to convey'.[242]

Failure to consult properly

7.159 *R v Devon CC ex p Baker and Durham CC ex p Curtis and others*[243] concerned the proposed closure of residential homes in Devon and in Durham. The Court of Appeal held that (in respect of the procedure followed by Durham County Council) the decision to close a particular home was unlawful; the council had failed to consult the residents properly. The court approved the proposition that consultation contained four elements,[244] namely:

> First, that consultation must be at a time when proposals are still at a formative stage. Second, that the proposer must give sufficient reasons for any proposal to permit of intelligent consideration and response. Third, that adequate time must be given for consideration and response and, finally, fourth, that the product of consultation must be conscientiously taken into account in finalising any statutory proposals.

7.160 The consultation process must include a statement setting out the relevant context for the proposals under consideration – for instance that some residents may have been promised a home for life. Although a failure to refer to such key topics may not vitiate the consultation process,

240 *AH v Hertfordshire Partnership NHS Foundation Trust and Ealing Primary Care Trust* [2011] EWHC 276 (CoP), (2011) 14 CCLR 301 at para 80: at para 2 the court observed that 'It is of importance that the NHS trust that is responsible for SRS has no plan to discontinue the service in the foreseeable future. Had the real issue been the continuation of the service rather than the interests of its individual occupants, the appropriate jurisdiction would have been judicial review and not the Court of Protection'.

241 *R (Phillips and Rowe) v Walsall MBC* [2001] EWHC 789 (Admin), (2001) 5 CCLR 383 at 387D; and see also *R (Lloyd) v Barking and Dagenham LBC* [2001] EWCA Civ 533, (2001) 4 CCLR 196.

242 *R (Bodimeade) v Camden LBC* [2001] EWHC 271 (Admin), (2001) 4 CCLR 246 at 255H.

243 [1995] 1 All ER 72 at 91, CA.

244 These elements were first propounded in *R v Brent LBC ex p Gunning* (1986) 84 LGR 168 and adopted by the Court of Appeal in *R v North and East Devon Health Authority ex p Coughlan* [2000] 2 WLR 622, (1999) 2 CCLR 285, CA at [108].

it may render the decision making process vulnerable to challenge on the basis of having omitted a relevant consideration.[245] Consultation will be held to be inadequate if the residents are not given the true reason for the closure, and for why one home was favoured to remain open rather than another.[246]

7.161   The court also approved the proposition that if a resident is to be transferred from one home to another (for whatever reason), he or she must be consulted over his or her removal from the existing home as well as over the home to which he or she is to be transferred.[247]

7.162   Provided the key stages of the consultation process are followed and the product of the consultation 'conscientiously taken into account',[248] the court will 'not strain to find technical defects which will make the obligations imposed on local authorities unworkable'.[249] The courts will also be slow to add additional obligations, for instance that a proposal could only be adopted (after consultation) if it enjoyed 'consensus or the agreement or consensus of the consultees'.[250] Whether or not there is a duty to 're-consult' if new issues emerge during the consultation process will depend upon the facts of a given case,[251] but in general there is 'no duty to consult further on [an] amended proposal which had itself emerged from the consultation process'.[252] Even if in the early stages the consultation process is problematic, and the process of consultation 'challenging', such flaws may not, when viewed as part of the overall process, inevitably invalidate the consultation.[253] The consultation duty is further considered at para 26.220 below.

Failure properly to assess existing residents

7.163   In *Coughlan* it was argued that prior to consulting on the closure of her nursing facility there should have been a multi-disciplinary assessment of her individual needs and a risk assessment of the effects of moving her to new accommodation;[254] the argument being that if her needs were incapable of being met elsewhere then closure of the facility would not have been possible.

245   *R v Merton, Sutton and Wandsworth Health Authority ex p Perry and others* (2000) 3 CCLR 378, QBD at [112].
246   *R (Madden) v Bury MBC* [2002] EWHC 1882, (2002) 5 CCLR 622.
247   [1995] 1 All ER 72 at 86.
248   *R v North and East Devon Health Authority ex p Coughlan* [2000] 2 WLR 622, (1999) 2 CCLR 285, CA at [108].
249   *R (Smith) v East Kent NHS Hospital Trust* [2002] EWHC 2640 (Admin), (2003) 6 CCLR 251 at 276C.
250   [2002] EWHC 2640 (Admin), (2003) 6 CCLR 251 at 267C.
251   [2002] EWHC 2640 (Admin), (2003) 6 CCLR 251 at 271F.
252   *R v Islington LBC ex p East* [1996] ELR 74 at 88 cited with approval by Silber J in *Smith v East Kent NHS Hospital Trust* [2002] EWHC 2640 (Admin), (2002) 6 CCLR 251 at 266H.
253   *R (Grabham) v Northamptonshire CC* [2006] EWHC 3292 (Admin).
254   *R v North and East Devon Health Authority ex p Coughlan* [2000] 2 WLR 622, (1999) 2 CCLR 285, CA at [94]: 'as required both by the guidance in both HSG(95)8 (paras 17–20) and HSC 1998/048 and also by the general obligation to take all relevant factors into account in making the closure decision'.

7.164   The health authority denied that such an obligation existed, arguing that under the relevant guidance (HSG 1998/048 – see para 7.147) it was only after a closure decision that the detailed transfer procedures (set out in the 1998 guidance) applied and that it was:

> . . . impracticable and unrealistic in the vast majority of cases to carry out the assessments and to identify alternative placements prior to a closure decision, let alone prior to consultation on a proposed closure. Funds for the development of alternative facilities might only become available after the closure decision is taken; only then would the range of alternative available placements become clear; large closure programmes might take years to implement, in which case assessments and alternative facilities considered at the time of consultation or closure would change over time; and in practice the necessary co-operation of individual patients for effective assessments and alternative placements might be more difficult to obtain before rather than after a final decision has been taken on closure.[255]

7.165 On the facts of this particular case (and in view of its other findings against the health authority) the court considered that it was unnecessary to rule separately in the legality of the health authorities' actions in this regard.

7.166   However, *R v Merton, Sutton and Wandsworth Health Authority ex p Perry and others*[256] concerned a decision to close a long stay hospital and provide alternative community-based replacement services for over a hundred long stay residents who had profound learning disabilities, and physical impairments such as lack of mobility, incontinence and eating problems. Some of the residents who challenged the closure decision had been at the facility for almost 30 years. They argued (among other things) that they had not had a full assessment of their needs prior to the consultation on closure, and the health authority responded by citing the Court of Appeal's judgment in *Coughlan* that a failure to undertake such an assessment did not necessarily render the process unlawful. Jackson J found in favour of the residents, stating:[257]

> It should be remembered that Miss Coughlan was not a person with learning disabilities. The government guidance which is applicable in the present case, but which was not applicable in Coughlan, is HSG(92)42. This circular states on page 2 as follows:
>
> > The large majority of people with learning disabilities not living with their families can be cared for in residential accommodation arranged through the relevant social services authority. There are, however, likely to be a small number of people with severe or profound learning disabilities and physical, sensory or psychiatric conditions who need long term residential care in a health setting. Where this seems to be the case a multi-professional assessment and consultation with parents or carers are necessary to determine whether the services they need can only be provided by the NHS or whether other alternatives would be more appropriate and cost effective.

---

255 HSG 1998/048. para 98.
256 (2000) 3 CCLR 378, 31 July 2000, QBD.
257 (2000) 3 CCLR 378, 31 July 2000, QBD at [91]–[93].

The residents of Orchard Hill, whose problems are far greater than those of the average person with learning disability, require a detailed assessment of the kind set out in HSG(92)42 before any decision can be taken about moving them out of NHS care.

7.167 In the absence of special factors, such as existed in the *Merton, Sutton and Wandsworth* proceedings, it would appear that as a general principle specialist assessments (such as specifically addressing the psychological and risk impacts of a relocation) are 'not necessary or appropriate when making decision on closure'.[258]

Failure to consider relevant matters

7.168 In *R (Dudley, Whitbread and others) v East Sussex CC*[259] the claimant argued that the authority had reached its closure decision without considering relevant guidance, including (1) a report prepared at the request of Plymouth City Council[260] following *Cowl and others v Plymouth City Council*[261] and (2) Department of Health guidance concerning *The transfer of frail older NHS patients to other long stay settings*, HSG 1998/048 (see para 7.147 above). In relation to the former the court held that notwithstanding the eminence of the report's author, Plymouth did not have the authority to promulgate guidelines for the world at large and so the material was not something to which East Sussex had to have regard. In relation to HSG 1998/048, since it was specifically NHS guidance and not addressed to social services (although it had been copied to them) it was again not something to which the authority had to have regard. If, however, there was a best interests declaration that it would be a risk to move the person, this would be a relevant consideration that had to be addressed in relation to closure.

Human Rights Act 1998

7.169 Many home closure cases have invoked the provisions of the Human Rights Act (HRA) 1998. With the enactment of HSCA 2008 s145 independent sector care homes are (when providing care under NAA 1948 s21) also subject to the provisions of the 1998 Act.[262]

---

258 *R (Phillips and Rowe) v Walsall MBC* [2001] EWHC 789 (Admin), (2001) 5 CCLR 383 at 387J; see, however, *R (B) v Worcestershire County Council* [2009] EWHC 2915 (Admin), (2010) 13 CCLR 13 – considered further at para 9.90 below.
259 [2003] EWHC 1093 (Admin).
260 *Report and Findings of the Extraordinary Complaints Panel – Closure of Granby Way Residential Care Home for Older People, Plymouth – November 2002* (2002) 6 CCLR 393 and see also D Latham, *Scrutiny Inquiry into Care Homes, Gloucestershire County Council*, June 2003, accessible at www.gloucestershire.gov.uk/index.cfm?articleid=4397; *Guidelines for the Closure of Care Homes for Older People*.
261 [2001] EWCA Civ 1935, [2002] 1 WLR 803, (2002) 5 CCLR 42.
262 This is of course not restricted to matters such as home closures but covers all aspects of care see para 26.237.

Article 2

7.170   The relocation of institutionalised older people to a new residence may have a dramatic effect on their mental health and life expectancy.[263] Although the research evidence is mixed,[264] adverse publicity concerning the deaths[265] of older people following such relocations add to the general concern about the consequences of home closures. Closure decisions engage the public authority's common law duty of care to the residents. Courts will be prepared to take action where there is 'any firm evidence' that the closure may shorten a resident's life.[266]

7.171   In *R (Dudley, Whitbread and others) v East Sussex CC*[267] a closure decision was challenged on (among others) human rights grounds. Maurice Kay J accepted that Article 2 of the Convention (the right to life) had been given 'an extended meaning', observing:

> As was said by the Strasbourg Court in *Osman v UK* [1998] 29 EHRR 245 at paragraph 115:

> Article 2 of the Convention may also imply in certain well-defined circumstances a positive obligation on the authorities to take preventative operational measures to protect an individual whose life is at risk.

> Although the risk in that case was of criminal acts, the principle is not so limited. However, the evidence does not point to a breach of Article 2 in this case. No particularised medical evidence has been filed showing that the life of any particular resident is seriously at risk. What the claimant needs to establish is that 'the authorities did not do all that could reasonably be expected of them to avoid a real and immediate risk to life of which they have or ought to have knowledge' – see *Osman*. The claimants have not established that in this case.

Article 3

7.172   Again in *R (Dudley, Whitbread and others) v East Sussex CC*[268] Maurice Kay J assessed the submissions concerning a violation of Article 3 of the Convention in the following terms:

263   See eg (1994) *Times* 7 July, 'Elderly patients die within weeks of transfer'; J M Mallick and T W Whipple, 'Validity of the nursing diagnosis of relocation stress syndrome' (2000) 49(2) *Nursing Research* 97–100; J A Thorson and R E Davis, 'Relocation of the institutionalised aged' (2000) 56(1) *Journal of Clinical Psychology* 131–138; A A McKinney and V Melby, 'Relocation stress in critical care: a review of the literature' *Journal of Clinical Nursing* 149–157.
264   *Guidelines for the Closure of Care Homes for Older People* (note 230 above). See also *R (Thomas) v Havering LBC; R (W) v Coventry City Council* (2008) EWHC 2300 (Admin) where HHJ Pelling QC, in refusing leave observed that whilst medical evidence established, at most, that in some studies geriatric relocation resulted in an increased mortality, in other studies it had not: that different people reacted in different ways, and a sensitively handled move was less likely to result in any increase in mortality – and see also *R (Turner) v Southampton CC* [2009] EWCA Civ 1290.
265   Violet Townsend, 10 June 2003, http://news.bbc.co.uk/1/hi/england/gloucestershire/2978234.stm and Winifred Humphrey, 8 July 2003, http://news.bbc.co.uk/1/hi/england/kent/3054264.stm.
266   *R (Watts) v Wolverhampton City Council* [2009] EWCA Civ 1168 at para 18.
267   [2003] EWHC 1093 (Admin) at [27]–[33].
268   [2003] EWHC 1093 (Admin) at [27]–[33].

The issue here is whether the closure decision crosses the threshold of the minimum level of severity required which depends on the circumstances of the particular case. . . . the threshold is simply not reached in this case – see, for example, *R v North West Lancashire Health Authority ex p A* [2000] 1 WLR 977 at pages 1000 to 1001, per Buxton LJ:

> Article 3 of the ECHR addresses positive conduct by public officials of a high degree of seriousness and opprobrium. It has never been applied to merely policy decisions on the allocation of resources, such as the present case is concerned with. That is clear not only from the terms of Article 3 itself, and the lack of any suggestion in any of the authorities that it could apply in a case even remotely like the present, but also from the explanation of the breach of Article 3 that has been given by the Convention organs. Thus in *Tyrer v UK* [1978] 2 EHHR 1, a case concerned with corporal punishment, the Strasbourg Court held, at paragraphs 30 and 35 of its judgment that:
>
> > in order for a punishment to be 'degrading' and in breach of Article 3, the humiliation or debasement involved must attain a particular level . . . the court finds that the applicant was subjected to a punishment in which the element of humiliation attained the level inherent in the notion of 'degrading' punishment.
>
> More generally, the Strasbourg Commission has on a number of occasions stressed the degree of seriousness of the conduct that article 3 addresses. For instance, the Commission said in *East African Asian v United Kingdom* [1973] 3 EHRR 76, 81, paragraph 195:
>
> > The Commission finally recalls its own statement in the first *Greek* case (1969) 12 YB Eur Conv HR 1 that treatment of an individual may be said to be degrading in the sense of Article 3 'if it grossly humiliates him before others or drives him to act against his will or conscience' . . . the word 'grossly' indicates that Article 3 is only concerned with 'degrading treatment' which reaches a certain level of severity.
>
> These strong statements clearly demonstrate, if demonstration were needed, that to attempt to bring the present case under Article 3 not only strains language and common sense, but also, and even more seriously, trivialises that Article in relation to the very important values that it in truth protects.

In my judgment, the same considerations apply to the present case.

Article 8

7.173 The Court of Appeal in *ex p Coughlan*[269] considered the finding of the first instance judge that Miss Coughlan's rights under Article 8 of the Convention had been violated, in the following terms:[270]

> Miss Coughlan views the possible loss of her accommodation in Mardon House as life-threatening. While this may be putting the reality too high, we can readily see why it seems so to her; and we accept, on what is

269 [2000] 2 WLR 622, (1999) 2 CCLR 285, CA.
270 [2000] 2 WLR 622, (1999) 2 CCLR 285, CA at [92]–[93].

effectively uncontested evidence, that an enforced move of this kind will be emotionally devastating and seriously anti-therapeutic.

The judge was entitled to treat this as a case where the Health Authority's conduct was in breach of article 8 and was not justified by the provisions of article 8(2). Mardon House is, in the circumstances described, Miss Coughlan's home. It has been that since 1993. It was promised to be just that for the rest of her life. It is not suggested that it is not her home or that she has a home elsewhere or that she has done anything to justify depriving her of her home at Mardon House.

7.174   In *R (Madden) v Bury MBC*[271] Richards J held that in such cases Article 8 was engaged and in consequence there needed to be:

... a clear recognition of the interests at stake under article 8 and of the matters relied on by way of justification of an interference with those interests, with an appropriate balancing exercise to ensure that the principle of proportionality is observed. This can be done on a relatively generalised basis looking at the interests of residents as a whole and does not, in the absence of special circumstances, require an individualised balancing exercise by reference to an assessment of the needs of each individual resident. The detailed individual assessment can follow. It may well be that in a situation of this kind, the balancing exercise does not need to be elaborate, and that its outcome is reasonably predictable, especially given the existence of what are plainly substantial public interest considerations in favour of closure.

The fact remains that the point needs to be addressed. There is no evidence in this case that is was addressed .... Thus there was a failure to consider article 8; a failure to reach a proper assessment that the admitted interference with the rights of residents under article 8 was justified. In my judgment that amounts to a further and independent reason for upholding the decision to be unlawful.

7.175   In *R (Dudley, Whitbread and others) v East Sussex CC*,[272] however, Maurice Kay J was satisfied (on the facts of this case) that any interference with Article 8 could be justified,[273] stating:

I am prepared to assume, without deciding, that Article 8 is engaged. That may be a generous assumption in a case which does not have the *Coughlan* element of a particular home for life, and when the Council will be finding alternative accommodation for the residents. The issue then becomes justification under Article 8(2). In my judgment, the Council has clearly established justification. It is relevant that the East Sussex area contains a higher proportion of residents aged 65-plus than any other local authority. It has also been 'zero' rated by the Audit Commission which restricts the level of finance available. That is not a matter for congratulation, but it highlights the circumstances in which the Council was carrying out its review of residential care homes. These are plainly relevant considerations

---

271 [2002] EWHC 1882 (Admin), (2002) 5 CCLR 622 at 636–637.
272 [2003] EWHC 1093 (Admin) at [27]–[33].
273 See also *R (Lloyd) v Barking and Dagenham LBC* [2001] EWCA Civ 533, (2001) 4 CCLR 196, another disputed home closure case where the Court of Appeal upheld the first instance judge's finding that arguments under Article 8 added 'nothing to the case'.

as the Council seeks the most effective ways of fulfilling its various statutory responsibilities within existing financial constraints. It is hardly surprising that it was anxious not to lose the prospect of a £1 million grant from central government. The court is slow to interfere with decisions which 'involve a balance of competing claims on the public purse in the allocation of economic resources', see Neill LJ in *R v CICB ex p P* [1995] 1 WLR 845 at 857. This has been reaffirmed in home closure cases since the coming into force of the Human Rights Act. In *R (Phillips and Rowe) v Walsall MBC* [2001] ECHR Admin 789, Lightman J said, paragraph 11:

> I may add that if (contrary to my view) a move such as is presently contemplated could possibly constitute an interference with a fundamental right under Article 8, it would surely be justified as required for the economic well-being of the Council and of those in need of its services. Resources of public authorities are notoriously limited and it must be a matter for elected authorities such as the Council to have leeway in how they are husbanded and applied.

7.176 In *R (Goldsmith) v Wandsworth LBC*[274] the Court of Appeal noted:

> It is not in dispute that a change to a strange environment for a person of the Appellant's frailty could have serious if not fatal consequences. The proportionality of the response is, therefore, of the utmost importance. In my judgment it is not good enough for Wandsworth, after the institution of proceedings, to produce evidence that this was a factor in its mind when it made the decision (whenever that was). In my judgment, the court has to look at the decision at the time it was made and at the manner in which it was communicated to the person or persons affected by it.

Residential accommodation services and the NHS overlap

7.177 Both social services authorities and the NHS have obligations to care for people who are disabled, ill or who have learning difficulties. In the context of care home accommodation, however, the overlap takes three forms:

1) the duty on the NHS to deliver specific services to persons in care homes (both private residents and those where the accommodation is secured by the local authority) and this issue is considered at para 13.98 below;
2) the duty on the NHS to make registered nursing care contributions under HSCA 2001 s49, which is considered at para 13.109 below;
3) the duty on the NHS to pay for the care home fees as part of an NHS continuing healthcare package – which is considered in Chapter 14.

274 [2004] EWCA Civ 1170, (2004) 7 CCLR 472.

Accommodation under Mental Health Act 1983 s117

7.178   The duty to provide accommodation (and other community care services) under MHA 1983 s117 is a separate community care service to the duty under NAA 1948 s21.[275] The duty only arises in respect of persons who have been detained under MHA 1983 s3,[276] or admitted to a hospital under one of the criminal provisions (ie section 37[277] or transferred to a hospital under a transfer direction made under section 47 or 48[278] – see para 20.24 below) and then cease to be detained and leave hospital.

7.179   The duty to provide accommodation under MHA 1983 s117 only arises after the patient has been assessed as requiring this service. Accommodation provided under MHA 1983 s117 differs from the service under NAA 1948 s21 in that authorities are not permitted to charge for this service. MHA 1983 s117 services are considered at para 20.25 below.

Accommodation under National Assistance Act 1948 s29(4)(c)

7.180   NAA 1948 s29(4) empowers social services authorities (subject to direction by the secretary of state) to provide hostel accommodation for disabled people engaged in workshops provided by the authority under that section. The secretary of state's direction empowers (but does not oblige) authorities to provide such facilities.[279]

7.181   The provision of workshop activities is considered at para 9.54 below. The effect of NAA 1948 s29(4A) is to make the hostel accommodation so provided subject to the same charging provisions as apply to residential accommodation services under NAA 1948 s21 (see para 8.6 below).

Accommodation under Children Act 1989 s17

7.182   Children Act 1989 s17 requires social services authorities to safeguard and promote the welfare of children in need in their area; this includes the provision of an almost unlimited range of services, of which accommodation (in a care home or ordinary rented dwelling) may be one. The duties owed to children in need (including disabled children) are considered at para 23.4 below.

275   NHSCCA 1990 s46(3).
276   Admission to hospital for treatment of a mental disorder.
277   A hospital order made in criminal proceedings.
278   Transfer to hospital of a prisoner suffering from a mental disorder.
279   LAC (93)10 appendix 2 para 2(4) – the text of which is at appendix B to this text.

Accommodation under Health and Social Care Act 2001

7.183 A curious and probably unusual funding arrangement was found to exist in *Amberley (UK) Ltd v West Sussex CC*.[280] The local authority had became responsible for paying the fees for certain residents in 2002 (known as resident's with 'Preserved Rights') whose obligations to pay fees consti- tuted 'existing arrangements' within the HSCA 2001 s50(6) – such that the residents liability became the liability of the local authority. Prior to April 1993 many residents had their fees paid via Income Support and for those who were in care homes at April 1993 this payment arrangement was preserved. On the 8 April 2002, however, the preserved rights arrangement was abolished, and responsibility for funding such residents passed to local authorities via HSCA 2001 ss 50–52. Local authorities were required undertake community care assessments of these residents and thereafter to fund their care under the normal community care regime – ie under NAA 1948 s21. Pending assessment and agreement on funding (which would include agreeing a fee with the care home) HSCA 2001 s50 provided that the contract would pass to the local authority. It appears that some local authorities (including West Sussex) never formalised their arrangements for such residents – and so they remained accommodated under section 50 of the 2001 Act. This has many consequences, not least that these residents are not being provided with 'community care services' within the meaning of section 46 of the NHS Community Care Act 1990 (see para 1.2 above).

Law Commission proposals

7.184 The Law Commission[281] has put forward a number of proposals relating to the provision of residential care, which have been mentioned briefly at relevant points of this chapter. In summary the recommendations comprise:

- NAA 1948 s21, should be retained and, ideally within the adult social care statute, as a long-stop legal duty, available only to those who fall below the local authority eligibility criteria: Recommendation 18.
- Direct payments should be extended to cover residential accommoda- tion: Recommendation 35.
- A regulation-making power should be introduced to enable the sec- retary of state and Welsh Government to require or authorise local authorities to accommodate a person at the place of their choice within England and Wales and to allow for the making of additional

---

280 [2011] EWCA Civ 11, (2011) 14 CCLR 178.
281 Law Commission (2011) *Adult Social Care*, Law Com No 326, HC 941.

payments: Recommendation 36 – and that this should extend to MHA 1983 s117 residents: Recommendations 61 and 62.

- The compulsory removal power under NAA 1948 s47 should be repealed: Recommendation 42.
- Local authorities should be required to protect property when a person is admitted to hospital or residential care: Recommendation 43.

Local authority charges for accommodation

continued

Diagram 11: Charging for care home accommodation

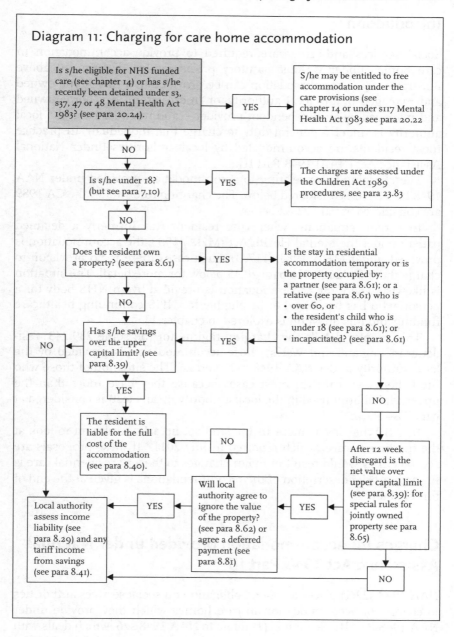

Introduction

8.1   Social services authorities are required to provide accommodation in care homes under various statutory provisions, as diagram 10 above illustrates. Such accommodation can be provided in a care home owned and managed by the local authority, or (more often) in a home owned and managed by an independent provider – and in either case, the local authority is under a general duty to charge that individual.[1] In practice most residents are accommodated by local authorities under National Assistance Act (NAA) 1948 Part III.

8.2   The charging rules relating to accommodation provided under NAA 1948 Part III are considered below. The charging rules under the CA 1989 are considered at para 23.82 below.

8.3   In certain situations, where the resident was formerly a detained patient under the Mental Health Act (MHA) 1983, the accommodation is provided under MHA 1983 s117. In such cases there is no provision to charge the individual. See para 20.45 below for more detail. The situation is likewise where the accommodation is provided by an NHS body for a person who has been held to be eligible for NHS continuing healthcare funding and this question is explored in chapter 14.

8.4   This chapter details the charging regime for the some 239,243[2] residents in England and Wales whose accommodation is provided by the local authority under NAA 1948 ss21 and 26. The situation of those who fund their own care (in most cases because they have more than the upper capital limit used in the local authority means test) is considered at para 7.84 above.

8.5   In 2010 the Government in England set up a Commission to look at the funding of care, which reported in July 2011.[3] If these proposals are accepted they would result in major changes to the way residential care is funded. A brief description of the recommendations is given at the end of this chapter.

Charges for accommodation provided under National Assistance Act 1948 Part III

8.6   NAA 1948 s22(1) places a general obligation on social services authorities to charge for accommodation in care homes which they provide under NAA 1948 Part III. Section 22(1) refers to NAA 1948 s26, which deals with the charging situation where the authority has provided residential accommodation in an independent home. The only exceptions to the

1   By virtue of s26(1A)(b) the person running the home has to be registered under the Health and Social Care Act 2008 in England or the home has to be registered under the Care Standards Act 2000 in Wales.

2   As at March 2010 – Figures taken from Social Services Activity Report (England) April 2011 and Assessments and Social Services for Adults (Wales) September 2010.

3   *Fairer Care Funding: The Report of the Commission on Funding of Care and Support*, July 2011.

obligation to charge are during the first eight weeks of a stay, or if it is part of a package of intermediate care (see chapter 11).[4]

8.7   NAA 1948 s22(2) stipulates that the maximum charge for such accommodation shall be fixed by the local authority but that this must be the full cost to the authority of providing that accommodation.[5]

8.8   Section 22(3) requires that the charging provisions be means-tested, and section 22(4) directs that every resident must be allowed to retain a minimum weekly personal allowance. The amount is laid down each year by regulation and is the same for each resident whether in a social services authority-run home or an independent sector home (see para 8.23 for details of the allowance).

8.9   Most importantly, however, NAA 1948 s22(5) stipulates that the way the means-tested charging system operates is to be specified in separate regulations made by the secretary of state. The principal regulations in this respect are the National Assistance (Assessment of Resources) Regulations 1992,[6] which are the subject of regular amendments. Detailed guidance has been issued on the interpretation of the National Assistance (Assessment of Resources) Regulations 1992 (subsequently referred to in this section as the AOR Regulations 1992). The guidance, known as CRAG (Charging for Residential Accommodation Guide), is issued separately by the Department of Health and the Welsh Assembly Government.[7] The CRAG guidance specifically National Assistance (Assessment of Resources) Regulations 1992 states that it is 'policy guidance' for the purposes of Local Authority Social Services Act 1970 s7(1). It is therefore guidance which local authorities must follow in all but the most exceptional of circumstances.[8]

8.10   Where a resident requires assistance in paying for their care home, the authority is obliged to assess that person's ability to pay by reference to the AOR Regulations 1992 and to CRAG. If, having carried out such an assessment, the authority is satisfied that the resident is unable to pay the full amount the authority must decide on the basis of the assessment what the person's contribution should be. If the resident refuses to co-operate

4   Local authorities are not obliged to charge for periods of accommodation of less than eight weeks, NAA 1948 s22(5A), see para 8.121 below. In most instances local authorities use this provision when providing respite care. As a result of Community Care (Delayed Discharges etc) Act (CC(DD)A) 2003 ss15 and 16 and the Community Care (Delayed Discharges etc) Act (Qualifying Services) (England) Regulations 2003 SI No 1196 intermediate care services are to be provided free of charge.

5   This is known as the 'standard rate' and for local authority homes is the full cost to the authority of providing such accommodation, and for independent homes the full cost to the authority for purchasing the care under contract with the care home. (NAA 1948 ss22(2) and 26(2)).

6   SI No 2977 as amended.

7   Up to date versions of CRAG are available on the Department of Health website along with LAC (DH) 2011(1) and the Welsh Government website along with WAGC 010/2011. Much of the National Assistance (Assessment of Resources) 1992 Regulations directly refers to the Income Support (General) Regulations 1987. Reference should be made to specialist texts for an analysis of the interplay between these differing regimes – see eg Child Poverty Action Group, *Paying for Care Handbook* and Disability Alliance, *Disability Rights Handbook*. Both are updated regularly.

8   See para 1.46 above for consideration of 'policy guidance'.

with the financial assessment, the authority will usually charge the full standard rate.

8.11   In this chapter where the paragraph numbers differ between the English and Welsh version of CRAG this will be made clear and both numbers given. The details given below are those applying as at September 2011.

Paying the assessed charge

8.12   Residents can pay their assessed charge direct to the local authority. However, NAA 1948 s26(3A) provides that where residents have been placed by local authorities in independent sector homes (and where the resident, the authority and the organisation or person managing the home *all* agree), the resident may pay the assessed charge direct to the home with the authority paying the remainder.[9] CRAG reminds authorities that residents should be offered choice over the way they pay, and the authority remains responsible for the full fee and it is not good practice to expect the home to recover any debt which is the responsibility of the local authority to recover.[10]

8.13   The local government ombudsman has criticised a council for asking a residents' son to pay his father's contribution directly to the care home without attempting to explain the legal position that it retained contractual responsibility and legal liability to the care provider for the full costs of the care. Neither did it explain that the son was not obliged to agree on his father's behalf to pay the care provider direct.[11]

8.14   CRAG suggests that the advantage of paying the assessed charge direct to the home is not only administrative convenience; it may also enable the resident to have a direct contractual relationship with the home owner (rather than having to rely on the authority's agreement). However, such a relationship can be problematical if care homes use it as a device to claim top-ups directly from the resident or their relatives without the local authority being aware of this.[12] It is arguable that local authorities, as part of their duty of care, should have a clause in their contract in order to protect residents and relatives from being approached directly for top-ups in such a way.[13]

8.15   In the current situation of some homes charging those who make their own contracts (self-funders) more than the amount agreed with local

9   This provision was introduced in 1993 as an 'administrative easement' when benefits were paid by order book and is now largely redundant.
10   CRAG paras 1.030 and 1.031 (England), paras 1.024 and 1.024 (Wales).
11   Complaint No 08 019 214 against the London Borough of Bromley, 9 June 2011.
12   The Office of Fair Trading, in its study of the care home market (see para 7.115 above) found that 40% of local authorities responding to the survey suspected top-ups were requested which they did not know about outside of the local authority contract.
13   As indeed was the case in *R (Forest Care Home Ltd and ors) v Pembrokeshire CC* [2010] EWHC 3514 (Admin), (2011) 14 CCLR 103 where the court found that the homes would have been in breach of contract had they obtained third party top-ups from relatives (para 151).

authorities, it can be of benefit for these individuals to have the local authority contract with the home, and for the authority to pay the home the gross amount. Such residents can then take advantage of the negotiating power of the local authority in setting the fee to be paid, although of course the resident will pay a full contribution to the local authority. Such arrangements will most commonly arise where residents lack the capacity to make their own contract with the home and no one else is willing and able to do so on their behalf. In such cases the responsibility for providing accommodation remains with the local authority (see para 7.22 above). The general obligation on local authorities to maintain client confidentiality would mean that councils should not disclose a resident's contributions (or the absence of them) to a care home without the resident's permission.

8.16   A further advantage of the local authority paying the gross fee is that defaults in contributions can be speedily picked up and investigated. Where a three way arrangement exists the authority still remains liable to the home owner for any arrears, should the resident fail to pay the home as agreed. Nevertheless there can be delays where the home is being paid directly either by the resident or his or her representative, as commonly the home tries to resolve the problem with them first (during which significant arrears may accrue).

Preliminary financial advice

8.17   CRAG obliges authorities to ensure that residents are given a clear explanation (usually in writing) of how their assessed contribution has been calculated and why this figure may change. Such fluctuations are particularly common in the first few weeks of admission because, for instance, of the effect of benefit pay-days on income support/pension credit or the withdrawal of attendance allowance CRAG para 1.019 (para 1.016 Wales).

8.18   There have been several local government ombudsman reports concerning local authority failures to provide information: for example, where a council failed to mention that the resident would need to make a contribution, in addition to that being paid by his son (who had agreed to make a third party top-up of £75 per week).[14]

8.19   Guidance issued under the Community Care (Residential Accommodation) Act 1998[15] – LAC (98)19 – requires local authorities to have in place procedures to ensure that when the net capital of a resident (who is self-funding) reduces below the upper capital limit (see para 8.39 below), they undertake an assessment and if necessary step in and take over funding arrangements to ensure that the resident is not forced to use capital below the upper capital limit (other than the tariff income from that capital in England). It follows that a failure to provide appropriate

14 Case H3 in Digest of Cases 2005–06 (case reference confidential): as part of the settlement the council agreed to waive the care home charges of nearly £3,000 and pay the legal costs incurred.
15 Repealed and re-enacted by HSCA 2001 s53 and Sch 6.

advice in such cases could amount to maladministration and may render the authority liable to reimburse the 'spent down' monies.[16]

8.20   Similar advice is provided in LAC (2000)11 and LAC (2001)25[17] which states (para 25):

> . . . once a council is aware of the resident's circumstances, any undue delay in undertaking an assessment and providing accommodation if necessary would mean that the council has not met its statutory obligations. Consequently, the council could be liable to reimburse the resident for any payment he has made for the accommodation which should have been met by the council pursuant to its duties.

8.21   There is no requirement to specify the assessed charge in the contract with the home. As stated above, if the local authority has the contract with the home, and is paying the gross fee, it is not a relevant matter for the home. If in such a situation the authority gave information about the assessed charge to the home without the consent of the resident, it would be a breach of the duty of confidentiality.

The treatment of income

8.22   Part II of the AOR Regulations 1992 contains the procedure by which a resident's income (earned and unearned) is assessed for charging purposes; the provisions adopt many of the same rules used in the assessment of income for income support[18] and are the subject of detailed guidance in sections 8 and 9 of CRAG. A major difference between the two assessment regimes is that the income taken into account for CRAG purposes is that of the resident' alone. Under NAA 1948 authorities have no power to assess a couple (whether or not married or in a civil partnership) according to their joint resources. Each person entering residential care should be assessed according to his or her individual means (CRAG para 4.001).

Personal expenses allowance (PEA)

8.23   The basis of the charging provisions is that residents are required to pay all of their assessed income, which is based on net income less any disregarded income (above the PEA) towards the charge for the residential accommodation: 'The personal expense allowance is intended to enable residents to have money to spend as they wish' (CRAG para 5.004 (para 5.001 Wales)). The minimum amount of the personal expenses allowance

16 Equally the Welsh Ombudsman was critical of the delay in providing funding of a resident who needed to move from a care home to a nursing home following a period in hospital, thus delaying the individual's discharge. The authority was operating a waiting list which was unlawful, and had failed to meet the individual's needs in a reasonable time: *Case reference 200801935 Welsh Ombudsman Casebook Aug 2010*.
17 Similar wording is in Welsh circular NAFWC 11–01.
18 Under the Income Support (General) Regulations 1987 SI No 1967.

is stipulated each year in regulations,[19] although by virtue of NAA 1948 s22(4) there is power to allow a different amount from that prescribed for personal expenses in special circumstances (see below).

8.24   For about the last ten years councils and providers have been reminded the PEA should not be expected to be used for items that should be provided within the local authority contract. The guidance for 2011 is no exception.

> The PEA is intended to allow residents to have monies for personal use. Councils, providers of accommodation and residents are again reminded that the PEA should not need to be spent on aspects of board, lodging and care that have been contracted for by the council and/or assessed as necessary to meet individuals' needs by the council or the NHS. Councils should therefore ensure that an individual resident's need for continence supplies or chiropody is fully reflected in their care plan. Neither councils nor providers have the authority to require residents to spend their PEA in particular ways and, as such, should not do so. Pressure of any kind to the contrary is extremely poor practice.[20]

8.25   CRAG expands on this stating that it is up to residents to decide how they spend their PEA and residents are not precluded from buying extra services that are genuinely additional to those assessed as necessary by the council or NHS.[21]

8.26   The weekly allowance for the period April 2011–March 2012 is £22.60 in England and in Wales is £23.00.

Discretion to allow different amounts of personal expense allowance

8.27   Under NAA 1948 s22(4) authorities have the power in 'special circumstances' to allow a different amount from that prescribed for personal expenses. CRAG reminds authorities that this could 'be particularly important for residents where certain activities or services, although not specifically included in their care plan, can nevertheless contribute significantly to optimum independence and well-being'.[22] It then gives various examples at para 5.008 (para 5.007 Wales) where it may be appropriate for an authority to allow a resident to retain a higher amount, including:

- where a person in residential accommodation has a dependent child, the authority should consider the needs of the child in setting the personal allowance;

---

19 The regulations for 2011–2012 are National Assistance (Sums for Personal Requirements) (Amendment) (England) Regulations 2011 SI No 724. The equivalent Welsh regulations are The National Assistance (Assessment of Resources and Sums for Personal Requirements) (Amendment) (Wales) Regulations 2011 SI No 708 (W110).
20 LAC (DH) 2011(1) para 4 and in CRAG at para 5.005. Similar wording is contained in WAGC 010–2011 para 4 and in CRAG at para 5.002 Wales.
21 CRAG para 5.006, para 5.003 Wales.
22 CRAG para 5.006, para 5.003 Wales. Although it could be argued that such activities or services should have been included in any care plan which is based on an assessment of risk to independence or well-being.

- where a person temporarily in residential accommodation receives income support/pension credit including an amount for a partner who remains at home;
- where the resident is the main recipient of an unmarried couple's overall income, the authority can use its discretion to increase the resident's personal expenses allowance in special circumstances to enable the resident to pass some of that income to the partner remaining at home (see also para 8.35 below);
- where someone does not qualify as a 'less dependent' resident because his or her care home accommodation provides board and so cannot be assessed under the rules relating to 'less dependent' residents (see para 8.118 below). In such cases the local authority can increase the personal expenses allowance if it considers that this could enable the resident to lead a more independent life, for example, if he or she is working;
- where the resident is responsible for a property that has been disregarded, for example, because the stay is temporary (see para 8.124 below), the local authority should consider increasing the allowance to meet any resultant costs. In such cases the authority should disregard any reasonable housing related expenditure (CRAG para 3.019 (para 3.013 Wales)).

8.28   The above examples are illustrative, not exhaustive. Accordingly in any case where a resident is experiencing hardship or their well-being is affected, an application can be made for an increase in the allowance. This may be because the lack of income means that he or she is unable to live as independent a life as possible (for instance being unable to take part in community activities or attend family gatherings etc) or for any other reason. Such a claim would be made by way of a request for a review (see para 8.126 below). In any such request it would be relevant for the local authority to have regard to any health and well-being strategy[23] and to their equality duties: on the basis that they apply to all people within its area, including care home residents.

Income disregards

8.29   In general income is taken into account in full. The situation can, however, be briefly summarised as follows:

Income taken into account in full

8.30   Most income is taken into account in full. This includes, for instance, net earnings,[24] most social security benefits,[25] annuity income, pensions, trust income etc (CRAG paras 8.005–8.021). Attendance allowance/disability

---

23   Health, social care and well-being strategies in Wales.
24   Subject to a £5 or £20 disregard; see CRAG paras 9.017–9.018, paras 9.019–9.020 Wales.
25   Provision exists, however, to disregard housing benefit that continues to be paid during a 'notice period'.

living allowance (care component) is taken into account in full if the resident is a permanent resident, but disregarded if the stay is temporary. However, these benefits normally cease to be paid after four weeks if a resident is funded by the local authority (although if the resident will later be paying the authority back- for instance they have a deferred payment agreement – it will continue to be paid.)

8.31   Payments to Equitable Life with profit holders to compensate for their relative loss as a consequence of regulatory failure,[26] will be made either as a lump sum or as a regular payment on an annual basis. In both cases they will be taken fully into account for charging purposes.[27]

Income partly disregarded

8.32   Some income is partly ignored, for instance £10 of certain war pensions, half of occupational and private pensions in certain circumstances (see para 8.35 below) and modest amounts of the income from lodgers/ sub-letting are ignored (CRAG paras 8.035–8.036 (paras 8.030–8.031 Wales)).

8.33   A specific disregard of income exists for people aged 65 and over called a 'savings disregard'. The pension credit scheme provides a minimum income guarantee for people aged over the qualifying age for a pension. In addition, people aged 65 and over can benefit from 'savings credit' which is designed to reward those who have made provision for their old age through second pensions or similar savings. In order to reflect in part the rules that are in the pension credit scheme, a 'savings disregard' was introduced for people aged 65 and over in 2003. The disregard applies to income and savings that count, within the pension credit scheme, towards the 'savings credit'. A resident who actually receives the 'savings credit' within his or her pension credit receives up to a maximum 'savings disregard' of (for April 2011–March 2012) £5.75 for a single person and £8.60 for a couple. So, for example, if the resident receives only £4.45 actual 'savings credit' it would be this figure that is disregarded. If he or she happens to receive a 'savings credit' above £5.75 (as a single person) he or she would still only have £5.75 of this figure disregarded. Individuals whose income is such that it takes them above the pension credit 'savings credit' level are still entitled to have £5.75 of their income disregarded (CRAG para 8.025 (para 8.023 Wales)).

8.34   Temporary residents who continue to have commitments for their home are allowed such disregards on their income as appear reasonable. CRAG suggests that this would include interest charges on loans for repairs for improvements to the dwelling, services charges, insurance premiums, and water rates. The list is not exhaustive (CRAG para 3.019 (para 3.013 Wales)).

---

26 This disregard was announced in the comprehensive spending review 2010: HM Treasury (2010) *Spending Review 2010* Cm 7942, p73.
27 LAC (DH) (2011)1, WAGC 010–2011 paras 11 and 12.

Occupational and personal pensions

8.35   Where the resident has an occupational, personal pension or payment from a retirement annuity contract and has a spouse or civil partner who is not living in the same residential home, 50 per cent of the amount should be disregarded, providing the resident is actually paying such a sum over to the spouse or civil partner. In cases where there is an unmarried partner the use of the 'discretion' to increase the personal expenses allowance detailed at para 8.27 above should be considered (CRAG para 8.027 (para 8.023B Wales)). State pensions including additional state pensions are not disregarded in this way but are counted in full.

Income fully disregarded

8.36   Some income is fully disregarded. Examples include disability living allowance mobility component (and mobility supplement),[28] disability living allowance care/attendance allowance for temporary residents (these cease in any event after four weeks if a resident is helped with funding by the local authority and is not going to be paying the funding back), Christmas bonus payments, the winter fuel payment, and war widows' and widowers' special payments and certain charitable and voluntary payments[29] (CRAG para 8.042 (para 8.037 Wales) gives the full list).

8.37   The following income from personal injury payments is disregarded:

- Payments from a trust whose funds are derived from a payment made in consequence of any personal injury.
- Payments under an annuity purchased pursuant to any agreement or court order to make payments in consequence of personal injury, or from funds derived from a payment, in consequence of any personal injury.
- Payments received by virtue of any agreement or court order to make payments to the resident in consequence of any personal injury (CRAG 10.028 (para 10.027 Wales)).

The treatment of capital

8.38   Part III of the AOR Regulations 1992 deals with the way a resident's capital is calculated for charging purposes. These differ in a number of respects from those that apply for income support and pension credit purposes, particularly in respect of the maximum permissible sums and the disregards. Capital is widely defined for care home charging purposes, and includes all land and buildings (unless disregarded – see below). It

---

28 Proposals were made by the Coalition Government to end payments of the mobility component to care home residents who are funded by local authorities from 2012 on the grounds that mobility needs are part of assessed needs and therefore met by local authorities. This has now been put back (it appears until 2013–14) but it will still be considered in the wider review of disability living allowance as a 'personal independence payment'.

29 Note that this provision came into effect from 2008 in England and 2011 in Wales. See WAGC 010–2011, para 7.

also includes savings, shares, bonds and the like (CRAG para 6.002 provides a list that is not exhaustive).

Capital limits

8.39 The capital limits are generally increased each year although in England there was no increase in 2011. Between April 2011 and March 2012, in England the upper limit was £23,250 (above which fees have to be paid in full) and the lower limit was £14,250 (above which a 'tariff income is calculated – see para 8.41 below). Wales in contrast has only one limit to capital which for this period was £22,500.

8.40 For so long as the resident's assessed capital exceeds the upper limit, he or she is not entitled to receive financial assistance from the local authority in respect of the payment of care home fees. In most cases this means that the resident will make his or her own arrangements with the care home (see para 7.84 above). If the resident moves into a local authority home or lacks the capacity to contract with an independent care home (see para 7.22 above), the local authority will be responsible for providing the accommodation. In such cases, however, the resident will be liable to pay the full cost to the local authority. (See para 8.81 below for situations where the local authority funds on an interim basis until funds are accessed.)

8.41 In England capital between the upper and lower limits is taken into account by attributing a 'tariff income' of £1.00 per week for each £250 (or part of £250) above the lower limit. Thus if a resident in England has £15,130 capital, a tariff income of £4.00 per week is taken into account as income. The English CRAG explains that where tariff income is taken into account, actual interest earned is not to be treated as income to avoid double counting. If actual interest is not drawn and increases the value of the capital, it will be taken into account as capital in future reassessment (para 6.009).

8.42 In Wales no income is assumed to accrue on capital below £22,500 and Welsh authorities have been reminded that below that limit 'authorities should not ask residents to contribute to their care costs from their capital resources'.[30] This has been the subject of a technical amendment to the regulations that 'no resident is liable to contribute from capital'[31] below the capital limit which clarifies that any real income in the form of interest also must not be taken into account, although presumably as in England if actual interest is not drawn and increases the value of capital it will be taken into account as capital in future assessments if it has taken the resident above the capital limit.

Capital disregards

8.43 Some capital is taken into account in full and some is disregarded indefinitely or for a fixed period. The treatment of the former home is covered

30 WAGC 010–2011 para 5.
31 AOR Regulations 1992 (Wales) reg 20(A).

at paras 8.61 to 8.80 below. Full details of the disregards are contained in Sch 4 to the Regulations and at chapter 6 of CRAG.

Capital taken into account in full

8.44   Most capital is taken into account including capital held abroad (where the transfer is not prohibited, in which case it may have a lower value)[32]or capital that is not immediately realisable – such as premium bonds or National Savings Certificates.[33] The surrender value of investment bonds (unless there is a life assurance element) is also taken into account.[34] Where capital (other than land) is held jointly, it is divided equally by the number of joint owners. If the account is split so that the resident is in possession of his or her actual share, that amount is then used in the calculation.[35]

Capital disregarded indefinitely

8.45   This includes the surrender value of an insurance policy or annuity; the value of any payment made from the social fund; personal possessions (as long as they were not purchased with the intention of reducing capital to avoid charges); payments 'in kind' from a charity; student loans; the value of funds held in trust or administered by a court which derive from a personal injury payment (see para 8.52 below); payments from the Macfarlane, Eileen trusts, the MFET Ltd, the Skipton fund, the London Bombings charitable relief fund. (See CRAG para 6.030 (para 6.028 Wales) for the full list). In 2011 a new charitable trust is to be set up to make payments for those infected by hepatitis C or HIV through contaminated blood – and payments from this source will be disregarded.[36]

Capital disregarded for 26 weeks or longer

8.46   This includes business assets where the resident intends to take up work again (if the resident is planning to dispose of the business asset it will be disregarded for a 'reasonable period'); money acquired for repairs to the resident's home; and capital from the former home if it is intended to buy another property.[37]

Capital disregarded for 52 weeks

8.47   This includes arrears of most benefits (although as they cover specific periods they are normally treated as income) and payments and refunds for dental or optical treatment and travel expenses.[38]

32 CRAG para 6.028, para 6.026 Wales.
33 CRAG para 6.029, para 6.027 Wales.
34 CRAG para 6.004, para 6.002A Wales. In England there has been a consultation on whether investment bonds which contain an element of life assurance should be taken into account. There was also consultation on whether to disregard pre paid funeral plans. However, at the time of writing (September 2011) no firm proposals have been made regarding any changes.
35 CRAG para 6.013 (para 6.010 Wales).
36 LAC (DH) (2011)1 and WAGC 010–2011 para 9 and 10.
37 CRAG para 6.032, para 6.029 Wales.
38 CRAG para 6.033, para 6.030 Wales.

Capital disregarded for two years

8.48   This includes payments made to relatives of CJD victims.[39]

Couples

8.49   As with income, the authority is only permitted to take into account the capital of the resident. CRAG is explicit on this point, stating:

> The LA has no power to assess a couple, or civil partners according to their joint resources. Each person entering residential care should be assessed according to their individual means, (para 4.001).

8.50   If the capital of a couple is in a joint account,[40] there will be a presumption that it is owned in equal shares, thus if the account is held by the resident and his or her partner it will be presumed that half of it is owned by the resident (CRAG para 6.013 (para 6.010 Wales)). For some couples it is advisable to split the account in order to avoid spending down more than necessary. For example, if a couple jointly own £56,500, if they leave it in a joint account they would need to spend down to £46,500 in England (ie spend £10,000) before the resident qualifies for help. Whereas if they split their account to £28,250 in each account, the resident will receive help after spending £5000.

Trust funds

8.51   Section 10 of CRAG advises on the question of the assessment of trust funds[41] from which a resident may benefit. In general the capital value where there is an absolute trust is taken into account, but if the trust deed directs that the beneficiary is to receive an income from the capital, then the capital is disregarded but the payments made taken into account. The capital value of a discretionary trust is disregarded and as any payment from a discretionary trust is a voluntary payment this should also be disregarded (see para 8.36 above). CRAG advises that certain minimum information be obtained in all such cases, and accordingly parties should ensure this is made available – even if satisfied that the trust monies ought ultimately be disregarded for means testing purposes.

Personal injury trusts

8.52   In respect of personal injury trusts, revised regulations came into effect in England in 2008[42] and in Wales in 2011.[43] Sch 4 para 10A to the Regulations stipulate that where a personal injury payment is made which has

---

39   CRAG para 6.034, para 6.030A Wales.
40   Different rules apply in relation to jointly owned interests in land – see para 8.65 below.
41   Other than payments from those trusts which have to be disregarded see para 8.37 above.
42   National Assistance (Sums for Personal Requirements and Assessment of Resources) Amendment (England) Regulations 2008 SI No 593 reg 6(a).
43   National Assistance (Assessment of Resources and Sums for Personal Requirements) (Amendment) (Wales) Regulations 2011 SI No 708 reg 6(a).

not been put into a trust it must be disregarded for up to 52 weeks as long and it does not contain a specifically identified element for care. Where there is an element for care then that element is taken into account during this time. Once any payment (even if it includes a payment for care) has been placed in a personal injury trust (or is held by the court or can only be disposed of by court order or direction) it will be disregarded (CRAG para 10.026 and 10.027 (paras 10.025 and 10.026 Wales)).

8.53   There is a general concern by local authorities that apart from this limited change, no charges can be made for the local authority provision of care against personal injury awards.[44] The concern being that claimants may benefit from 'double recovery' and that insurers may gain where local authority residential care is to be provided, by paying reduced damages: in effect, the public purse being used to subsidise the 'tortfeasor'.

8.54   This issue has been the subject of considerable litigation. The cases concern the difficulty of predicting the future care needs of an individual as well as the suitability of the care arrangements that would be made by a local authority. The Court of Appeal in *Sowden v Lodge; Crookdake v Drury*[45] has held that *if* the statutory provision of care and accommodation is capable of meeting the reasonable requirements of the individuals, the liability for this element does not fall on the insurers. In this case Pill LJ stressed the importance of:

> . . . placing before the court cogent evidence as to how the regimes proposed by the parties for the care and accommodation of claimants will operate . . . Whatever is proposed should be particularised and costed in the schedule, or counter-schedule, of damages (para 85).

8.55   The sense of injustice about public subsidy of such settlements was expressed by Longmore LJ in the same case, in the following terms:

> It might be thought that it would be more appropriate for legislation to provide that both National Health Trusts and local authorities could recover the costs of medical expenses and care respectively from the tortfeasor as the Law Commission recommended (at any rate in relation to medical expenses) in 1999 (para 89).

> Some judges also have an instinctive feeling that if no award for care is made at all, on the basis that it will be provided free by local authorities, the defendant and his insurers will have received an undeserved windfall (para 92).

8.56   Given the recent trend towards greater rights for disabled people to have their care needs met in more independent living situations, it might be considered dangerous to make assumptions that a disabled person will

---

44 This issue was the subject of consultation in England in 2010. The proposal is to allow local authorities to take into account any payment made for care, regardless of where it is held. Although the consultation ended in June 2010, at the time of writing September 2011 there has been no further information about the outcome.

45 [2004] EWCA Civ 1370, [2005] 1 WLR 2129. In relation to *Sowden*, the Court of Appeal held that the claimant should remain in residential care funded by her local authority but that the personal injuries award should include an element to top up the provision. In relation to *Crookdake*, the state provision could not be said to meet the claimant's reasonable requirements and so the personal injury award was made to include the private provision of care costs.

remain in a care home setting for the rest of his or her life, or that the charging regimes will remain unaltered: a point made by the Court of Appeal in *Crofton v NHS Litigation Authority*[46] in the following terms:

> It is by no means far-fetched to suggest that, at some time in the future, the ministerial policy of ring-fencing personal injury damages and/or the Council's approach to that policy will change. (para 108)

8.57 In relation to persons living in non-residential care settings, the prospect of accurately predicating future funding and charging regimes would appear to be no less daunting – given that these may change as a result of both national and local policy decisions[47] (see para 10.28 below where this issue is considered).

8.58 As with other cases regarding the interplay between the awards of damages and local authority responsibilities to provide care and their charging regimes, the Court of Appeal in *Crofton* expressed 'dismay at the complexity and labyrinthine nature of the relevant legislation and guidance, as well as (in some respects) its obscurity' (para 111).

8.59 In *Peters v East Midlands SHA, Halstead and Nottingham City Council*[48] the Court of Appeal approved a mechanism designed to limit the potential for 'double recovery' by a claimant. It held that where a person's affairs were being administered by the Court of Protection (ie via a deputy) the personal injury award could include an order prohibiting the claimant or the deputy from applying for publicly funded assistance under the NAA without further order from the Court. The Court of Protection has held that (notwithstanding the public policy argument to the contrary) the *Peters* provisions are not capable of being applied retrospectively.[49]

8.60 It should be noted that arrangements arising out of personal injury awards constitute a specific exception to the deprivation rules (see para 8.86 below) permitting the awards to be placed in a trust for the benefit of the resident.[50]

The treatment of property

8.61 In general the capital value of a property or former home is taken into account in full (less 10 per cent for disposal costs – CRAG para 6.014 (para 6.011 Wales)); there are, however, a number of circumstances in which it must be disregarded. These are:

a) The value of a resident's home is disregarded for the first 12 weeks of a permanent stay in a care home as a resident provided with care by the local authority under NAA 1948 s21. There had been some confusion about the position of people who were already permanently in a

---

46 [2007] EWCA Civ 71, (2007) 10 CCLR 123.
47 A point accepted by Tomlinson J in *Freeman v Lockett* [2006] EWHC 102.
48 *Peters v East Midlands SHA, Halstead and Nottingham CC* [2009] EWCA Civ 145, (2009) 12 CCLR 299.
49 See *In the matter of Mark Reeves* No 99328848, judgment 5 January 2010 available at www.7br.co.uk/uploads/court-of-protection-judgment-mark-reeves.pdf.
50 AOR Regulations 1992, reg 25(1)a.

care home having been funding themselves, who approach the local authority for funding after 12 weeks. This was clarified by the Department of Health in 2010[51] and CRAG now explains the situation thus:

> The disregard applies irrespective of whether the resident was already in a care home as a self-funder before being provided with Part 3 accommodation. This is because the legislation defines 'resident' in this context as a person who is provided with accommodation under Part 3 of the 1948 Act or a prospective resident (a person for whom accommodation is proposed to be provided under Part 3 of the 1948 Act) (CRAG para 7.006 (para 7.003B Wales)).

b) The value of a dwelling normally occupied by a resident as his or her home should be ignored if his or her stay in a care home is temporary; and

- he or she intends to return to that dwelling, and the dwelling is still available to him or her; or
- he or she is taking reasonable steps to dispose of the property in order to acquire another more suitable property for the resident to return to.

If the resident's stay is initially thought to be permanent but turns out to be only temporary, the dwelling should be treated as if the stay had been temporary from the outset (CRAG para 7.002). Regulation 2(1) of the AOR Regulations 1992 allows an authority to regard a person's stay as temporary if it is likely to last for any period not exceeding 52 weeks, or, in exceptional circumstances, is unlikely to exceed that period substantially.

c) Where the resident no longer occupies a dwelling as his or her home, its value should be disregarded where it is occupied in whole or in part by:

- the resident's partner or former partner or civil partner[52] (except where the resident is estranged or divorced from the former partner – unless a lone parent);[53] or
- a relative[54] of the resident or member of his or her family (ie,

---

51 LAC (DH) (2009)3 para 19.

52 This need not therefore be a 'spouse' but could include an unmarried couple living together as husband and wife. It follows (although it is not clear in CRAG) that if a same sex couple are living together as if they were civil partners, the property would have to be disregarded. For instance if a same sex couple have either decided not to register as civil partners, or have not done so because by the time the legislation came into force one of the partners was no longer, through lack of capacity, able to consent to registration, they should be in no worse position than heterosexual partners who never married.

53 See para 8.88 below for what happens if a spouse or civil partner wishes to move from the disregarded property, but still needs funds from the proceeds to buy somewhere else.

54 'Relative' is specified as including: parents, parents-in-law, sons, sons-in-law, daughters, daughters-in-law, step-parents, step-sons, step-daughters, brothers, sisters, grandparents, grandchildren, uncles, aunts, nephews, nieces and the spouse, civil partner or unmarried partner of any except the last five (CRAG para 7.007 (para 7.004 Wales)). The relevant point here is that this is an *inclusive* definition rather than an exclusive one.

another person for whom the resident is treated as responsible) who:

i) is aged 60[55] or over, or

ii) is aged under 18 and is a child whom the resident is liable to maintain, or

iii) is incapacitated.[56]

In cases where the relative is living in the property at the time the resident moves into a care home, and later reaches the age of 60, or becomes incapacitated, the mandatory disregard should apply from the date the relative reaches 60 or becomes incapacitated (if the property has not already been disregarded under the discretionary provisions described at para 8.62 below).

More difficult is the situation where a relative in the above categories moves into the property as his or her home after the resident has moved into a care home. It is likely that a court determining a case concerning such a situation would be heavily influenced by its particular facts, although its interpretation may well be guided by principles of public policy – namely that the aim of the AOR Regulations 1992 appears to be to protect from homelessness, certain people living in the property when the owner is institutionalised and not to protect people who use the exemption as a means of acquiring a benefit at public expense. It may be that in certain situations, where there is a perceived exploitation of the exemption, the question of a deprivation of assets may be considered[57] (see para 8.86 below).

The ombudsman has found maladministration in a case where a property was not disregarded in spite of the mental health problems of the daughter who lived in it, and considered that in all likelihood

55 The age at which the disregard applies is currently not being increased in line with the qualifying age for pensions. This was explained in LAC (DH) 2010(2) as 'raising the relatives property disregard from 60 to 65 would result in properties, that would have been disregarded under the current AOR regulations, being taken into account and, possibly, having to be sold to pay for residential care, forcing the relative to move.' Para 12. No such explanation was given in any Welsh circular but the age of the disregard for relatives remains at 60 years. Note also that the property will be disregarded whatever the age of the partner – the regulations were amended in 2010 to put this beyond doubt and bring the regulations in line with policy and practice. See LAC (DH) (2010)2 and WAGC 014/2010.

56 The meaning of 'incapacitated' is not defined by the Regulations, but CRAG suggests that it includes a person receiving (or whose incapacity is sufficient to that required to qualify for) one of the following: 'incapacity benefit, severe disablement allowance, disability living allowance, attendance allowance, constant attendance allowance, or an analogous benefit'. Again this is an inclusive rather than an exclusive definition (CRAG para 7.009 (para 7.005 Wales)).

57 It is uncertain how far such an argument could be taken. First the resident still owns the property, thus raising the question of whether he has 'deprived' himself of it. Second, the AOR Regulations 1992 merely state that capital is disregarded if 'it is occupied in whole or in part' by the relatives specified 'as their home'. They do not specify 'continuing to occupy' which by implication would mean that they were living in the home before the resident moved to residential care. Absent the word 'continue' and given the present tense of the words 'is occupied' it is thus arguable that where a relative moves into the resident's home with the resident's permission, the property should be disregarded from that date if the relative is in one of the above categories.

being told the house had to be sold played a key part in her breakdown.[58]

d) Where the resident has acquired property which he or she intends eventually to occupy as his or her home, the value should be disregarded for up to 26 weeks from the date the resident first takes steps to take up occupation, or such longer period as is considered reasonable (CRAG para 7.010 (para 7.006 Wales)); Regulations Sch 4 para 16).

8.62   In addition local authorities importantly have an overall discretion to disregard the capital value of premises, in which a third party lives where they consider it reasonable to do so.[59] Paragraph 7.011 of CRAG (para 7.007 Wales) suggests that:

> LAs will have to balance the use of this discretion with the need to ensure that residents with assets are not maintained at public expense. It may be reasonable, for example, to disregard a dwelling's value where it is the sole residence of someone who has given up their own home in order to care for the resident, or someone who is an elderly companion of the resident particularly if they have given up their own home. These are only examples and not exhaustive.

8.63   CRAG further cautions authorities 'to consider the intention behind the occupation of the premises by the third party (eg, whether it was to care for the resident or whether it was in anticipation of avoiding the inclusion of the property in the financial assessment) . . . The timing of the move into the property by the third party and the prognosis of the resident at that time will also be relevant.' (CRAG para 7.012 (para 7.008 Wales).

8.64   It appears that local authorities vary widely in their use of this power to disregard property. A freedom of information request established that 46 per cent of councils did not use this power at all in 2007–08. Even among those that did use this power there was huge variation in how often it was used. The rate of use per 100 admissions varied from 0.2 times to 15.6 times.[60]

Joint beneficial ownership of property

8.65   The AOR Regulations 1992 and CRAG[61] deal with the approach to be adopted in order to value property which is the subject of joint beneficial ownership. The general rule is that where a resident jointly owns property (ie, he or she has the right to receive some of the proceeds of a sale) the resident's share is valued as the amount that that interest would realise if it were sold to a willing buyer. From this figure a further 10 per cent is deducted (for the costs of sale etc) as is the amount of any encumbrance secured on the resident's share.

---

58   Case H1 2005–06 Digest of cases (case reference confidential).
59   AOR Regulations 1992 Sch 4 para 18.
60   Conservative Party Press Release 28 January 2009.
61   AOR Regulations 1992 reg 27(2) and CRAG paras 7.012–7.016.

Establishing beneficial interest

8.66   In some cases, prior to any valuation of jointly owned property it is necessary to establish who might have beneficial interest in the property. This is particularly relevant in 'right to buy' cases where not uncommonly, although the property is in the name of the resident (who at the time the property was bought was the council tenant entitled to the statutory discount), other relatives have funded the purchase or paid the mortgage. In *Kelly v Hammersmith and Fulham LBC*[62] the resident had purchased her council house but her daughter had funded the entire purchase costs and mortgage repayments. The court nevertheless held that the local authority was entitled to maintain a caution on the property in the mother's name for outstanding residential home fees because the daughter was unable to adduce sufficient evidence to show that her mother had no beneficial interest in the property, in particular because of the £50,000 discount.

8.67   In *Brighton and Hove City Council v Audus*[63] the court came to a different conclusion: namely that the purchasing relative had an overriding interest. In this case he had paid the purchase price on the understanding that he had ownership of the flat, but had postponed his rights to live in the property, and had met all the costs of the home whilst the elderly couple lived in the home rent free. In effect the nephew was the legal owner and therefore the local authority could not recoup the fees by way of a legal charge. In *Nottingham City Council v Beresford*[64] (a decision of the Adjudicator to the Land Registry) the house was purchased with a 60 per cent 'right to buy' discount and subject to an oral agreement: that the resident's children would pay all of the mortgage payments and maintain the property; that the property would be held on trust for the children in equal shares; and that the resident would live rent free for as long as she wished and was able to do so. When she moved into residential care the local authority sought to register a legal charge as the property was in her sole name. On the evidence, the Adjudicator was satisfied that a constructive trust existed in favour of the children.

8.68   A trust was also found to exist in *Campbell v Griffin*,[65] where a long term lodger, who had provided care over a number of years to an elderly couple prior to their moving into a care home, was held in consequence to have acquired an equitable interest in the property. Rather than providing him with the right to remain in the property, the court found entitlement to £35,000 from the proceeds of sale of the property, albeit that this claim ranked above the charge on the property placed by the council for unpaid care home fees.

---

62   [2004] EWHC 435 (Admin), (2004) 7 CCLR 542.
63   [2009] EWHC 340 (Ch).
64   [2011] EWLandRA 2010_0577, 30 March 2011 – see (2011) 74 *Journal of Community Care Law* 8.
65   [2001] EWCA Civ 990.

Valuation of jointly owned property

8.69   Regulation 27 of the AOR Regulations 1992 provides that:

> (2) Where a resident and one or more other persons are beneficially
> entitled in possession to any interest in land –
> (a) the resident's share shall be valued at an amount equal to the price
> which his interest in possession would realise if it were sold to a
> willing buyer. . . .; and
> (b) the value of his interest so calculated shall be treated as if it were
> actual capital.

8.70   CRAG points out that the value of the resident's interest in a jointly
owned property will be governed by:

a)   the resident's ability to reassign the beneficial interest to somebody
else; and

b)   there being a market, ie, the interest being such as to attract a willing
buyer for the interest.

8.71   CRAG suggests that in most cases there is unlikely to be any legal
impediment preventing a joint beneficial interest in a property being
reassigned. But the likelihood of there being a willing buyer will depend
on the conditions in which the joint beneficial interest has arisen. It goes
on to advise (CRAG para 7.012 (para 7.015 Wales)) that where an interest
in property is beneficially shared between relatives:

> . . . the value of the resident's interest will be heavily influenced by the
> possibility of a market amongst his or her fellow beneficiaries. If no other
> relative is willing to buy the resident's interest, it is highly unlikely that any
> 'outsider' would be willing to buy into the property unless the financial
> advantages far outweighed the risks and limitations involved. The value of
> the interest, even to a willing buyer, could in such circumstances effectively
> be nil. If the local authority is unsure about the resident's share, or their
> valuation is disputed by the resident, again professional valuation should
> be obtained . . .

8.72   CRAG provides local authorities with further advice (including the
'example' below) as to what action they should take in such situations
(CRAG para 7.014A (para 7.015A Wales):

> If ownership is disputed and a resident's interest is alleged to be less than
> seems apparent from the initial information, the local authority will need
> written evidence on any beneficial interest the resident, or other parties
> possess. Such evidence may include the person's understanding of events,
> including why and how the property came to be in the resident's name or
> possession. Where it is contended that the interest in the property is held
> for someone else, the local authority should require evidence of the
> arrangement, the origin of the arrangement and the intentions for its
> future use. The law of equity may operate to resolve doubts about beneficial
> ownership, by deciding what is reasonable by reference to the original
> intentions behind a person's action, rather than applying the strict letter of
> the law.

Example
The resident has a beneficial interest in a property worth £60,000. He shares the interest with two relatives. After deductions for an outstanding mortgage, the residual value is £30,000. One relative would be willing to buy the resident's interest for £5,000. Although the value of the resident's share of the property may be £10,000, if the property as a whole had been sold, the value of just his share is £5,000 as this is the sum he could obtain from a willing buyer. The resident's actual capital would be £4,500 because a further 10 percent would be deducted from the value of his share to cover the cost of transferring the interest to the buyer.

8.73   If a local authority disputes a valuation in such a case, CRAG advises that a professional valuation be obtained (CRAG para 7.020 (para 7.015 Wales)). A failure to do this may constitute maladministration.[66] Further it has been stressed in England that disputes should be resolved quickly with councils obtaining an independent valuation and seeking to agree a valuation within the 12-week disregard period.[67]

8.74   Anecdotal evidence suggests that some local authorities are disinclined to follow the above guidance, when a jointly owned property falls to be valued. It appears that these councils value on the basis of a sale of the whole property on the open market – rather than on the basis a sale of the resident's share to a willing buyer. As a matter of principle, it would appear inappropriate that it be left for the individual to have to challenge such a valuation, as in many cases they or their families may not understand the potential difference between these two approaches.

8.75   It has been suggested that the assertion in CRAG that it may be 'highly unlikely that any 'outsider' would be willing to buy' in such cases (see para 8.71 above), is open to challenge for two reasons, namely:

1) that almost invariably there will be a willing buyer, on the grounds that a reasonably informed buyer would be aware that after purchase he or she will have rights as a co-owner, which include the right to apply to the court for a sale; and/or

2) that authorities could offer themselves as the willing buyer

8.76   When a co-owner seeks to enforce a sale of property (under Trusts of Land and Appointment of Trustees Act 1996 s14) the court is required to have regard to a number of factors, including (under section 15(1)):

(a) the intentions of the person or persons (if any) who created the trust,
(b) the purposes for which the property subject to the trust is held,

8.77   It follows that where the property was purchased to provide a home for the joint owners, it would seem unlikely that a sale could be forced.[68] In this context, in *Chief Adjudication Officer v Palfrey*[69] (a case concerning the

---

66   Complaint no 03/C/09384 against Lincolnshire CC, 28 June 2004.
67   LAC (DH) (2010) 2 para 21.
68   See *Bull v Bull* [1955] 1 QB 234 concerning a son claiming possession of property bought jointly with his mother and which was subsequently registered in his name only. The claim failed as his mother was in occupation of the home and thus the purpose of the acquisition subsisted.
69   [1995] 11 LS Gaz R 39, (1995) *Times* 17 February.

valuation of a value of a property which is lived in by one of the joint owners and the other had moved into a care home) Hobhouse LJ in observed:

> Where the capital asset is a jointly owned dwelling house held for the purpose of accommodating the joint owners and that purpose is subsisting, there is nothing obscure or abstruse in the conclusion that the amount of capital which the applicant's joint possession of that dwelling house represents may fall, for the time being, to be quantified in a nominal amount.

8.78   The position may, however, be otherwise, where the original purpose was not to provide a home for the joint owner – for example, where the joint ownership has arisen because children have inherited half of the property on the death of one parent and then the other parent moves into a care home. In such a situation Mummery LJ in *Wilkinson v CAO*[70] considered that *Palfrey* was not a relevant authority and that a sale could be enforced at market value.

8.79   Any valuation of a joint share for charging purposes must therefore take account of these factors. Although CRAG gives no indication as to how local authorities should instruct an independent valuer, useful advice on this question can be found in the *Decision Maker's Guide.*[71]

8.80   The suggestion that a local authority could offer to buy the property itself, although superficially attractive to local authorities, is doubtful. It is of course problematic that the only reason for offering to buy the property is to give it a value. The fundamental difficulty with such an approach is that it still requires that a market value be established, and it is arguable that there is no value because there is no competing bidder.

Charges to enable the sale of property to be deferred

8.81   Health and Social Care Act (HSCA) 2001 ss53–55 introduced a 'deferred payments' scheme which enables a resident to enter into an agreement with the local authority whereby the value of his or her main home is disregarded when deciding whether or not that person needs 'care and attention which is not otherwise available'. In effect the council then pays the resident's care home fees (including any top-up' – see para 7.109 above) and recovers these payments from the sale of the property, normally after the resident's death. The scheme was implemented in England in 2001 and in Wales in 2003[72] and is the subject of guidance[73] that explains that its aim is to:

---

70 [2000] EWCA Civ 88.
71 Department for Work and Pensions (2011) *Decision Maker's Guide* Vol 5 chapter 29 paras 29642–29647.
72 National Assistance (Residential Accommodation) (Relevant Contributions) (England) Regulations 2001 SI No 3069; National Assistance (Residential Accommodation) (Additional Payments, Relevant Contributions and Assessment of Resources) (Wales) Regulations 2003 SI No 391; National Assistance (Residential Accommodation) (Disregarding of Resources) (Wales) Regulations 2003 SI No 969.
73 LAC (2001)25 and LAC (2001)29 in England; NAFWC 21/2003 in Wales.

... allow people with property, but without income and other assets sufficient to meet their full assessed contribution, to have a legal charge placed on their property to meet any shortfall. Hence people will be able to keep their homes on admission to residential care and for the duration of the deferred payments agreement.

8.82 The Department of Health was sufficiently concerned about the low take up of deferred payments by local authorities that in 2002 it reminded them that they are expected to have a deferred payments scheme in place and that they 'could be challenged if they did not consider exercising their discretion to offer deferred payments in individual cases'.[74] More recently in 2009[75] as result of concern about the credit crisis and the problems of selling properties the guidance accompanying CRAG stated 'Health Ministers expect councils to offer deferred payment agreements in appropriate cases and draw deferred payments arrangements to the attention of prospective residents.'[76] In Wales there is a duty under the National Assistance Deferred Payment Directions 2003 on local authorities to draw attention to and offer deferred payments arrangements to all eligible, or prospective, residents. Guidance to remind authorities of their duties was also issued in Wales in 2009.[77]

8.83 The local government ombudsman has held it be maladministration for a local authority not to have introduced a deferred payment scheme.[78] Maladministration was also found where a council did not offer a deferred payment. Had it done so it would have been possible to avoid selling the resident's house until after he had died, which would have increased in value significantly.[79] Such a facility can be particularly valuable whilst a resident is appealing a refusal of NHS continuing healthcare funding – and CRAG now makes a specific point on this, requiring that 'Local Authorities should liaise with PCT's to provide appropriate information to patients, and make every effort to ensure that residents who are appealing against refusal of CHC funding are made aware of the scheme' (CRAG para 7.025 (para 7.020 Wales)).

8.84 The procedure for implementing a deferred payment arrangement is described by CRAG at para 7.024 (para 7.019 Wales) which includes reference to a pro forma legal agreement (in respect of the legal charge – revised to take account of the Land Registration Act 2002) that councils may wish to use in such cases. At para 7.025 (para 7.020 Wales) it contrasts such agreements with charges imposed under Health and Social

---

74 LAC (2002)15 which drew attention to CI (2002)12 in which this was first stated.

75 A freedom of information request in 2009 established that 20 per cent of councils did not use this power at all in 2007–08. Even among those using this power there was huge variation in how often it was used. The rate of use per 100 admissions varied from 0.2 times to 40.9 times. Conservative Party Press Release 2009

76 LAC (DH) (2009) 3.

77 WAGC11/2009.

78 Complaint no 04/C/04804 against Manchester City Council, 31 March 2005.

79 See Health Service and Parliamentary Ombudsman, *Report on retrospective continuing care funding and redress*, 2007, Annex A (see para 14.189). The council agreed to pay the lost value – amounting to £20,000.

Services and Social Security Adjudications Act (HASSASSAA) 1983 s22 (see para 8.114 below) in the following terms:

> Councils should bear in mind that deferred payments under section 55 of the Health and Social Care Act 2001 are distinct from the pursuit of debt through section 22 of HASSASSA 1983 . . . Deferred payments should be offered when individuals are willing to pay their assessed contribution but do not wish to do so immediately. Section 22 of HASSASSA applies to situations where residents are unwilling to pay their assessed contribution, either now or in the future, and a debt arises

Property owned but rented to tenants

8.85   CRAG provides (CRAG para 7.023 (para 7.018 Wales)) that where a resident owns property, the value of which takes the resident's total capital above the upper capital limit, and the property is rented to tenants, the resident will be assessed as able to pay the standard charge for the accommodation (because of the level of capital). In such a situation the local authority may deem the resident to be a 'self-funder' or require him or her to pay the rental income (along with any other income) to it in order to reduce the accruing debt. In cases where no deferred payment arrangement has been agreed (see para 8.81 above) authorities may choose to place a legal charge on the property and wait until the tenant dies before enforcing payment of the accrued debt (plus interest from the date of death) against the estate,[80] but they are not obliged to take this course (see para ? below).

Deprivation of capital

8.86   Regulation 25(1) of the AOR Regulations 1992 provides that:

> A resident may be treated as possessing actual capital of which he has deprived himself for the purpose of decreasing the amount that he may be liable to pay for his accommodation except –
>
> (a)   where that capital is derived from a payment made in consequence of any personal injury and is placed on trust for the benefit of the resident; or
>
> (b)   to the extent that the capital which he is treated as possessing is reduced in accordance with regulation 26 [the diminishing notional capital rule – see para 8.94 below]; or
>
> (c)   any sum to which paragraph 44(a) or 45(a) of Schedule 10 to the Income Support Regulations[81] (disregard of compensation for personal injuries which is administered by the Court) refers.

---

80   See HASSASSAA 1983 ss22 and 24.
81   The Income Support (General) Regulations 1987 SI No 1967 which provide for the disregard of capital where such sum derives from (a) an award of damages for a personal injury to that person; or (b) compensation for the death of one or both parents where the person concerned is under the age of 18. Note, however, that since October 2006 changes to the income support regulations mean that regs 44(a) and 45(a) have been altered and are now contained in regs 44(1)a and 45(1)a.

8.87 In seeking to determine whether a deprivation has occurred, para 10 of LAC (98)8 advised as follows:

> Much information can be verified by reference to recent documentation provided by the client such as bank statements and building society account books. Authorities should also make use of information available to them from other departments within the authority or District Councils to verify client details, for example council tax benefit and housing records. They should also, as appropriate and with the consent of the client, undertake checks with other agencies such as the Social security office, banks and private pension firms. Obviously it is not necessary for all information to be verified, and it is for authorities themselves to determine the extent and circumstances for verifying information.

Purpose of disposal

8.88 CRAG explains (CRAG paras 6.062 et seq (para 6.057 Wales)) the impact of the rule in AOR Regulations 1992 reg 25(1) – that where an authority feels that a resident has deliberately deprived him/herself of a capital asset in order to reduce the accommodation charge it may treat the resident as still possessing the asset. CRAG at paras 6.068 and 9, (paras 6.062 and 6.063 Wales), provides further guidance in the following terms:

> There may be more than one purpose for disposing of a capital asset, only one of which is to avoid a charge for accommodation. Avoiding the charge need not be the resident's main motive but it must be a **significant** one.

> If, for example, a person has used capital to repay a debt, careful consideration should be given to whether there was a need for the debt to be repaid at that time. If it seems unreasonable for the resident to have repaid that debt at that time, it may be that the purpose was to avoid a charge for accommodation.

> *Examples (the figures are different in the Welsh examples)*

> [1] A person moves into residential accommodation and has a 50% interest in property which continues to be occupied by his spouse or civil partner. The LA ignore the value of the resident's share in property while the spouse or civil partner lives there but the spouse or civil partner decides to move to smaller accommodation and so sells the former home. At the time the property is sold, the resident's 50% share of the proceeds could be taken into account in the charging assessment but, in order to enable the spouse or civil partner to purchase the smaller property, the resident makes part of his share of the proceeds from the sale available to the spouse or civil partner. In these circumstances, in the Department's view, it would not be reasonable to treat the resident as having deprived himself of capital in order to reduce his residential accommodation charge.

> [2] A person has £24,000 in the bank. He is about to move permanently to a residential care home, and before doing so, pays off £3,500 outstanding on a loan for home improvements. It would be reasonable in these circumstances not to treat him as having deprived himself of the £3,500 deliberately in order to reduce his residential accommodation charge.

[3] A resident has £18,000 in a building society. Two weeks before entering the home, he bought a car for £10,500, which he gave to his son on entering the home. If the resident knew he was to be admitted permanently to a residential care home at the time he bought the car, it would be reasonable to treat this as deliberate deprivation. However, all the circumstances must be taken into account. If he was admitted as an emergency and had no reason to think he would not be in a position to drive the car at the time he bought it, it would not be reasonable to treat it as deliberate deprivation.

Timing of the disposal

8.89   The length of time between the disposal and the application for financial assistance will generally be relevant; the longer the time between the disposal of an asset and a person's liability for accommodation charges, the less likely it is that the obtaining of the financial advantage was a foreseeable consequence of the transaction. CRAG states at para 6.070 (para 6.064 Wales):

> The timing of the disposal should be taken into account when considering the purpose of the disposal. It would be unreasonable to decide that a resident had disposed of an asset in order to reduce his charge for accommodation when the disposal took place at a time when he was fit and healthy and could not have foreseen the need for a move to residential accommodation.

8.90   The leading judgment concerning a deprivation under regulation 25 is that of the Scottish Court of Session (Extra Division) in *Yule v South Lanarkshire Council*[82] where it was held that a local authority was entitled to take account of the value of an elderly woman's home transferred to her daughter over 18 months before the woman entered residential care. The court held that there was no time limit on local authorities when deciding whether a person had deprived him/herself of assets for the purposes of avoiding residential care fees.

8.91   Richards J relied upon the following extract from the *Yule* judgment in the subsequent case of *R (Beeson) v Dorset CC*:[83]

> The process of assessment, therefore begins with the requirement for the resident or prospective resident to provide information to the local authority from which the local authority can be satisfied that he is unable to pay the standard charge for the accommodation. The local authority cannot be so satisfied if the capital, both actual and notional, exceeds the specified sum. In determining the matter of notional capital, the local authority can only proceed upon the material which is available to them either from their own sources or upon that material as supplemented by material from the applicant and from such other sources as the local authority can reasonably be expected to apply to. We agree with counsel for the petitioner that in considering whether there is notional capital to be added to the actual capital of an applicant, the local authority must look to the information

---

82 (2001) 4 CCLR 383 (CS (ED)).
83 The extract from the *Yule* judgment is at (2001) 4 CCLR 383 at 395–396 and is cited in the *Beeson* judgment at [2001] EWHC 986 (Admin), (2002) 5 CCLR 5 at [9].

before them to determine whether a purpose to the effect specified in the regulations can be deduced. But in our opinion, this is not a matter of onus of proof. Rather, before the local authority can reach such a view, it must have material before it from which it can be reasonably inferred that the deprivation of capital took place deliberately and with a purpose of the nature specified. The local authority cannot look into the mind of the person making the disposition of capital or of others who may be concerned in the transaction. It can only look at the nature of the disposal within the context of the time at which and the circumstances in which that disposal took place

. . . [W]e do not consider . . . that it is necessary that the claimant should know of 'the' capital limit above which, in terms of the relevant regulations applicable at the time, the local authority is bound to refuse the application, if it is a reasonable inference, looking to the transaction in the whole surrounding circumstances relating to the applicant, that it must have been a purpose of the transaction to avoid having to pay any charges in the event of becoming a resident in residential accommodation provided by the local authority. In this respect we consider that the 1992 Regulations have to be looked at in a different light to those concerned with provision for income related benefits, not least because the purpose of the individual may have formed possibly some time ahead of the prospect that he or she might require to enter such residential accommodation . . .

8.92   The *Beeson* proceedings concerned a challenge to a decision that the resident had deprived himself of his house for the purpose of decreasing his liability for residential care fees. Mr Beeson senior transferred his house to his son by deed of gift, his stated reason being that he wished to ensure his son had a home if he needed it following the breakdown of his marriage. He then continued to live in the house for two years before finally being assessed by the council as being in need of residential care. His wish had been to live at home as long as possible and to die there. He returned home after several spells in hospital and received home care. At the time of the transfer, social services had not mentioned the possibility of residential care being required, but the council took the view that residential care was an inevitability and that this was the motive in making the transfer and accordingly it treated the house as notional capital for the purposes of regulation 25.

8.93   The Court of Appeal[84] upheld the first instance decision of Richards J concerning the relevant test for disposals of assets, as stated in *Yule v South Lanarkshire*. Richards J held that the local authority had shown no evidence that Mr Beeson had transferred the property with the intention of reducing his potential liability for care home charges – indeed the evidence was the other way. The council's decision was therefore quashed and had to be reconsidered.

84   *R (Beeson) v Dorset CC* [2002] EWCA Civ 1812, (2003) 6 CCLR 5.

Diminishing notional capital rule

8.94   Where a resident is deemed to possess notional capital (such that he or she is deemed liable to pay some or all of the standard rate for the residential accommodation), the diminishing notional capital rule means that over time he or she may nevertheless qualify for financial assistance from the authority in meeting the accommodation charges. Regulation 26 provides that where a resident has been assessed as having notional capital, that capital will have to be reduced each week by the difference between the rate which the resident is paying for the accommodation and the rate he or she would have paid if he or she was not treated as possessing the notional capital. CRAG gives the following example of the workings of such a calculation although the figures are different in Wales (CRAG para 6.074 (para 6.068 Wales)):

> A resident is assessed as having notional capital of £20,000 plus actual capital of £6,000. This results in him having to pay the standard charge for the cost of the accommodation e.g. £400. If he did not possess the notional capital, his capital would not affect his ability to pay for the accommodation so, based on an income of £120.60 and a personal allowance of, for example, £22.60 he would be assessed as paying a charge of £98. The notional capital should be reduced by £302 per week i.e. the difference between the sum he has to pay because of the notional capital (£400) and the charge he would have had to pay if the notional capital did not exist (£98).

Local authority responses to deliberate deprivations

8.95   If a authority believes that a resident has disposed of capital in order to reduce the charge payable, it will have to decide whether to treat the resident as having the capital (notional capital) and assess the charge payable accordingly. It will then have to decide what if any action it should take. Although few cases come to the courts, there is evidence that local authorities are taking a more robust approach when deprivation is considered to have taken place.

8.96   CRAG advises that there are two options, namely (CRAG para 6.073 (para 6.067 Wales)):

a)   to recover the assessed charge from the resident; or

b)   if the resident is unable to pay the assessed charge, to use the provisions of HASSASSAA 1983 s21 to transfer liability to the recipient of the asset for that part of the charges assessed as a result of the notional capital (see para 8.104 below).

8.97   In addition to their enforcement powers under HASSASSAA 1983 s21 authorities are able in certain situations to use powers provided by the Insolvency Act 1986. These options are considered below.

8.98   Local authorities would also appear to have a further response where it is believed that a deliberate deprivation has occurred. If the authority believes that in consequence the resident has notional capital in excess of the upper capital limit it may decide that it need not provide or fund the accommodation at all. Whether this is a lawful response will almost certainly depend upon the context of any particular case – although if the resident has sufficient mental capacity to make the arrangement, then it may well be that the local authority has no continuing obligation (see in this respect para 7.21 above). However, if he or she lacks the necessary capacity the situation may be otherwise. In *Robertson v Fife Council*[85] the House of Lords had to construe the Scottish legislation on this issue – which although similar is in key respects materially different from that in England.[86] Fife Council had assessed an applicant as having notional capital above the upper limit and then had refused to provide assistance on the above basis (that no continuing obligation existed under NAA 1948 s21). The House of Lords rejected this, holding:

> The assessment of need and decisions as to whether they call for the provision of any of the community care services comes first. The assessment of means, and the requirement to pay what a person can afford, comes afterwards.

8.99　A persuasive argument exists that the opposite conclusion would have been reached had the case been determined according to the legislative regime in England/Wales: namely that a person with full capacity who had notional capital above the upper limit might be owed no duty under NAA 1948 s21. This was referred to by the Court of Appeal in the *Beeson* judgment, where it was noted (but the question not determined) that it had been argued:

> That different amendments to the 1948 Act as between England and Scotland made all the difference; and if it had been an English appeal *Robertson* would have been decided the other way.[87]

8.100　However, if a person no longer has access to the amount assessed as notional capital (perhaps because the person to whom the funds have been transferred has spent them) and has been assessed as in need of care

---

85 [2002] UKHL 35 at [53], (2002) 5 CCLR 543 at 558G.
86 The material difference between the two legislative frameworks being that unlike the situation in England and Wales – where the duty to assess is separate from the 'community care service' provision obligation – in Scotland the two functions are combined (in the Social Work (Scotland) Act 1968). The key provisions of the 1968 Act are (1) section 12(1) (which is broadly equivalent to a hybrid version of NAA 1948 s21/ s29 and CA 1989 s17) which places a general duty on local authorities to promote social welfare by making a variety of services available including residential (but not nursing care); (2) section 12A (which in broadly the same wording as NHSCCA 1990 s47(1) creates the assessment obligation); and (3) section 13A which has no English/ Welsh equivalent, and which creates a specific duty to provide nursing home accommodation, where a person has been assessed as needing it. Neither this obligation (nor that under section 12(1) above) is subject to a proviso (as in England/ Wales under section 21) that the duty only arises 'if the need for care and attention is not otherwise available'. Mrs Robertson was in need of nursing home accommodation.
87 *R (Beeson) v Dorset CC* [2001] EWHC 986 (Admin), (2002) 5 CCLR 5 at 22D; see also in this respect *Ellis v Chief Adjudication Officer* [1998] FLR 184.

in a care home, it is arguable that a duty will still arise to provide accommodation.

Enforcement powers

8.101   If the local authority decides to take action to recover the disposed property (or the proceeds of sale) it has a number of statutory provisions available to assist.

8.102   The Court of Appeal has held that in any enforcement proceedings the respondent is, as a general principle, entitled to plead a public law breach by the local authority as one of its grounds for resisting a claim (for instance a failure to follow CRAG or other guidance etc).[88]

8.103   Where the resident has transferred assets to other parties with the purpose of avoiding or reducing his or her liability for charges, the options available to the authority will depend, in part, on when the transfer occurred.

Transfers within six months requiring local authority help with funding in a care home

8.104   HASSASSAA 1983 s21(1) provides:

> (1) Subject to the following provisions of this section, where –
>   (a) a person avails himself of Part III accommodation; and
>   (b) that person knowingly and with the intention of avoiding charges for the accommodation –
>   (i) has transferred any asset to which this section applies to some other person or persons not more than six months before the date on which he begins to reside in such accommodation; or
>   (ii) transfers any such asset to some other person or persons while residing in the accommodation; and
>
>   (c) either –
>   (i) the consideration for the transfer is less than the value of the asset; or
>   (ii) there is no consideration for the transfer,
>   the person or persons to whom the asset is transferred by the person availing himself of the accommodation shall be liable to pay the local authority providing the accommodation or arranging for its provision the difference between the amount assessed as due to be paid for the accommodation by the person availing himself of it and the amount which the local authority receive from him for it.

8.105   The effect of HASSASSAA 1983 s21 is that where a resident has transferred any asset to a third party at less than its full value, the authority can take enforcement proceedings against the third party if:

a)   the transfer took place no more than six months before the resident entered local authority funded care home accommodation, and

---

88   *Derbyshire CC v Akrill* [2005] EWCA Civ 308, (2005) 8 CCLR 173 and see also *Rhondda Cynon Taff CBC v Watkins* [2003] EWCA Civ 129, [2003] 1 WLR 1864.

b)   the authority can establish that the transfer was effected 'knowingly and with the intention of avoiding charges for the accommodation'.

8.106   Although section 21 is differently worded to the notional capital rule under regulation 25 of the Regulations ('knowingly and with the intention of' rather than 'for the purpose of'), it is doubtful whether any practical differences of interpretation emerge from the two phrases; where a deprivation of capital is assessed as having occurred, it would seem that this is also sufficient for the purposes of section 21.

Transfers over six months before requiring help with funding in a care home

8.107   If an authority has determined that:

a)   a resident has notional capital,˙ and
b)   the notional capital asset was transferred to a third party more than six months before the resident took up residence and required help with funding in the care home, and
c)   in order to recover its charges (or payments made on the resident's behalf) it needs to take proceedings to set aside the disposition of the notional capital asset,

the authority has the option of using the enforcement procedures under the Insolvency Act 1986 by which the court is empowered in certain situations to set aside such transfers and restore the position to what it would have been if the resident had not entered into the transaction.

8.108   By virtue of Insolvency Act 1986 s339, where an individual is adjudged bankrupt and he or she has entered into a transaction at an undervalue, the trustee in bankruptcy may (subject to the following time limits) apply to the court for an order restoring the position to what it would have been had the transaction not occurred.[89] The relevant time limits are computed backwards from the day of presentation of the bankruptcy petition and are, in general:

5 years   if the individual was insolvent[90] at the time of the transaction, or became insolvent in consequence of the transaction; or

2 years   if the above criteria do not apply.

8.109   By virtue of Insolvency Act 1986 s423, where the court is satisfied that an individual entered into a transaction (amongst other things) at an under-

89   The details given here are a simplified account of the actual provisions; 'transactions at an undervalue' are defined by Insolvency Act 1986 s339 and are contrasted with 'preferences' (section 340), for which slightly different rules apply.
90   Insolvency Act 1986 s341(3) states that an individual is insolvent if he or she is unable to pay his or her debts as they fall due, or the value of his or her assets is less than the amount of his or her liabilities, taking into account contingent and prospective liabilities. Section 341(2) creates a rebuttable presumption that an individual is insolvent where he or she enters into a transaction at an undervalue with an associate – see section 435.

value for the purpose of putting assets beyond the reach of a creditor or future creditor, it may make such order as it thinks fit (including an order restoring the position to what it would have been had the transaction not been entered into).

8.110   The powers available to the court under section 423 are without time limit and are exercisable without the need for bankruptcy proceedings[91] (or for the individual in question to be insolvent). In *Midland Bank v Wyatt*[92] the court held that for the purposes of section 423 proof of dishonesty was not a requirement, 'merely proof of avoidance of creditors whether they be existing or future creditors'; that the judge had to be 'fully satisfied as to the true nature or object of the transaction'; and that:

> . . . if the purpose of the transaction can be shown to put assets beyond the reach of future creditors, s423 will apply whether or not the transferor was about to enter into a hazardous business . . . . It is a question of proof of intention or purpose underlying the transaction. Clearly, the more hazardous the business being contemplated is, the more readily the court will be satisfied of the intention of the settlor or transferor.

8.111   The breadth of section 423 has been explained thus:

> While the burden of proof remains on the applicant, establishing the necessary purpose should be less difficult to achieve than proving intent to defraud under the previous law . . . The inclusion of persons who 'may at some time claim' against the debtor envisages potential future creditors who, individually unknown to the debtor at the time of the transaction, become victims of a risky business enterprise against the consequences of failure of which the debtor seeks to protect himself at the outset. In extending the purposes of present or future claimants, the ambit of the section is made very wide . . .[93]

8.112   Where the resident has transferred the capital asset using a firm or business which specifically markets schemes designed to avoid the value of the asset being taken into account for residential fee purposes, this may, perversely, be used as evidence to establish the purpose behind the transaction.[94]

8.113   In *Derbyshire CC v Akrill*[95] the local authority's claim included a claim under Insolvency Act 1986 s423 for an order that the house be retransferred to the deceased's estate. In this case the deceased had completed various transactions including a gift and leaseback of the house in which he had been living, and a declaration of solvency whilst in hospital following several strokes and a few weeks before moving into a care home. Although the case was remitted back to the county court to resolve, it was

---

91   See generally *Midland Bank v Wyatt* [1995] 1 FLR 697.
92   [1995] 1 FLR 697.
93   Berry et al, *Personal Insolvency*, Butterworths, 1993: an analysis largely vindicated by the subsequent case law – see eg *Hill v Spread Trustee Co Ltd* [2006] EWCA Civ 542, [2007] 1 WLR 2404 and *Curtis v Pulbrook* [2011] EWHC 167 (Ch).
94   See the Law Society Practice Note, *Making Gifts of Assets*, July 2009 and see also *Barclays Bank v Eustice* [1995] 1 WLR 1238, CA.
95   *Derbyshire CC v Akrill* [2005] EWCA Civ 308, (2005) 8 CCLR 173.

held that section 423 could be used to set aside a gift of property in such situations, where the purpose was to put property beyond the reach of the authority.

Registering of a charge or caution on any interest in land which the resident may have (under HASSASSAA 1983 s22)[96]

8.114   Where a resident fails to pay an assessed charge for accommodation and has a beneficial interest in land, HASSASSAA1983 s22 enables the local authority to create a charge in its favour on that land.[97] CRAG advises that where a local authority is contemplating taking such a step, it should advise the resident to consult a solicitor about the procedure. Any charge so registered does not carry interest until the resident's death, when section 24 of the 1983 Act provides for interest from that date 'at a reasonable rate' (determined by the local authority). Whilst local authorities have no statutory power to charge interest[98] there would appear to be nothing to prevent them suing on the accumulated arrears since such a judgment debt would normally then carry interest at the statutory rate.

8.115   Section 22 empowers, but does not oblige, local authorities to place charges on property. In certain situations authorities may consider that the possession of a valuable asset (such as a house) is such that the resident has no need of assistance, if he/she has been offered a deferred payment agreement but has refused. The basis for this view being that the resident has capital in excess of the upper capital limit (ie the value of the house) and accordingly is able to pay his or her own way (by for instance, raising a commercial loan secured on the property, pending its sale). The authority could then determine that the care and attention is 'otherwise available' and refuse to provide temporary financial support and to register a charge under HASSASSAA 1983 s22.

8.116   As section 22 is phrased in discretionary terms, authorities are in principle entitled, where the circumstances allow, to take such a course. Whether such a decision is reasonable in any particular situation will depend upon the relevant facts. In general, a suggestion that a person take out a commercial loan (or obtain a home's agreement to defer payment until the sale of a property) assumes (at a minimum);

- the need for accommodation does not arise in an emergency (ie there is sufficient time to arrange a loan); and
- that the person has sufficient mental capacity and experience to arrange such a loan; and
- that in all the circumstances, the taking of a commercial loan is something that it would be reasonable for the resident to do.

96 For guidance on the application of section 22 see CRAG Annex D.
97 If the land is jointly owned, CRAG advises that the local authority cannot create a charge, but can register a caution (CRAG Annex D para 3.5).
98 CRAG Annex D para 3A specifically states that the general powers under Local Government Act 1972 s111 cannot be used for this purpose.

8.117   The ombudsman held that it was maladministration for a local authority to fail to inform the home owner properly when it imposes such a charge.[99]

Less dependent residents

8.118   For the purposes of the charging rules[100] 'less dependent' means:

> . . . a resident who is in, or for whom accommodation is proposed to be provided in, premises which are not an establishment which is carried on or managed by a person who is registered under Part II of the Care Standards Act 2000.[101]

8.119   Regulation 5 of the AOR Regulations 1992 allows local authorities not to apply the rules for calculating income and capital if they consider it reasonable in the circumstance not to do so. It is recognised that, for some people, leaving just the personal expenses allowance (see para 8.23 above) would hamper the acquisition of independent living skills (such as purchasing their own food and paying for their expenses or travel to work), often with a view to eventually living independently in the community. Where ordinary housing (see para 7.45 above) is provided under NAA 1948 s21 it would of course make little sense to apply the charging rules as if the person were in a care home.

8.120   Regulation 5 accordingly enables authorities to continue to treat 'less dependent' residents differently where they consider it reasonable in the circumstances to do so. It enables authorities to disregard the resources of such residents, taking into account:

- the resident's commitments, ie, costs of necessities such as food, fuel, and clothing,
- the degree of the resident's independence, ie, the extent to which he or she should be encouraged to take on expenditure commitments, and
- whether he or she needs a greater incentive to become more independent, eg, he or she may be encouraged to take on paid employment if most or all of the earnings are disregarded.

Temporary residents

8.121   The definition of a temporary resident is a resident whose stay is unlikely to exceed 52 weeks, or, in exceptional circumstances, is unlikely to substantially exceed 52 weeks. CRAG advises decisions on the temporary or permanent status of a resident must have been agreed with the resident

---

99   Complaint no 04/C/04804 against Manchester City Council, 31 March 2005.
100 AOR Regulations 1992 reg 2(1).
101 The wording in the English AOR Regulations 1992 has not yet been changed to refer to the Health and Social Care Act 2008. In Wales of course the relevant Act is still the Care Standards Act 2000.

and/or their representative and included in the written care plan[102] (CRAG para 3.005 (para 3.002 Wales)).

8.122   As noted above (para 8.6 above) residents placed in care home accommodation as part of a programme of intermediate care are entitled to that service free of charge. Additionally, NAA 1948 s22(5A) stipulates that authorities are not obliged to apply the charging rules for the first eight weeks of a stay[103] – and many temporary residents and those going into a home for respite care will stay for less than eight weeks. The subsection provides:

> If they think fit, an authority managing premises in which accommodation is provided for a person shall have power on each occasion when they provide accommodation for him, irrespective of his means, to limit to such amount as appears to them reasonable for him to pay the payments required from him for his accommodation during a period commencing when they begin to provide the accommodation for him and ending not more than eight weeks after that.

8.123   CRAG advises that where the authority decides to make an assessment of ability to pay, it should do so on the normal charging basis. Where it decides not to make such an assessment, it is able to charge such amount as it considers reasonable for the resident to pay (CRAG para 3.008 (para 3.007 Wales)).

8.124   Additional disregards are allowed for temporary residents (including the disregard of the home) in order to enable them to keep more income to carry on running the home. These are explained at paras 3.013–3.022 (paras 3.013–3.016 Wales), the main ones being for a range of housing costs and a disregard on attendance allowance and disability living allowance.

Liable relatives

8.125   NAA 1948 ss42 and 43, under which local authorities could pursue spouses of residents for payments towards care costs were repealed in 2009.[104]

Challenging charges

8.126   Complaints about the level of charges levied by an authority are subject to the usual social services complaints procedures; see chapter 26. However,

---

102 Although it is recognised that someone who moves in on a permanent basis may improve and in such cases should be treated as if temporary.

103 Recently the position of those using their direct payments to pay for residential care for periods of up to 4 weeks (see para 12.37) has been put on a similar footing – the local authority can charge what it considers a reasonable charge – The Community Care Services for Carers and Children's Services (Direct Payments) (England) (Amendment) Regulations 2010, SI No 221.

104 Via Health and Social Care Act 2008 s147.

many local authorities have a separate procedure for appeals against the amount being charged. While such a process may be sensible, it cannot of course disqualify or limit a service user's right to make a complaint under the standard local authority's complaints procedure.

Proposals for changes to the funding and charging for care

8.127   The latest in what is becoming an increasingly long line[105] of proposals to ensure a sustainable but fairer system of funding and charging in England was published in July 2011. Known as the Dilnot Commission it has put forward a number of recommendations, many of which relate to paying for care in care homes. The main proposals in the report *Fairer Care Funding*[106] are:

- To place a cap on the amount a person would pay for care over a lifetime at a suggested figure of £35,000. Contributions would count towards this cap based on an assessment by social services that a person has substantial needs,[107] and the amount social services considered necessary to meet that need. Contributions would count for both domiciliary and residential care.
- For residential care only, for those who cannot afford the full cost, the capital limits should rise to £100,000 from the current £23,250 with tariff income still being assumed from £14,250. The personal expenses allowance will remain although it is suggested consideration be given to raising it.
- The £35,000 cap does not include the general living costs in a care homes, but it is proposed that the Government should fix a standard amount for these costs at £7000 to £10,000 per year.
- As a minimum there should be an extension to the deferred payment scheme so that it is a full universal offer across the country. In making this change local authorities should be allowed to charge interest.
- People whose disability starts before they are 40 years will get free care and if a person needs care between 40 and 65 there would be an increasing rate to have to pay towards the cap depending on when care needs started.

8.128   At the time of writing (September 2011) it is not known how far the Government might agree to these proposals. A Department of Health Press release has stated:[108]

105 Such as Royal Commission on Long Term Care (1999) *With Respect to Old Age* Cm 4192-I. D Wanless (2006) *Securing Good Care for Older People*, King's Fund: followed by the previous Government's consultation and white paper: HM Government (2010) *Building the National Care Service* CM 7854.

106 Commission on Funding of Care and Support (2011) *Fairer Care Funding: the report of the commission on funding of care and support* (the 'Dilnot' Report) at www.dilnotcommission.dh.gov.uk/2011/07/04/commission-report/.

107 This level is proposed 'in the short term' based on the fact most local authorities now only fund care at substantial level.

108 Department of Health (2011) *Creating a fair and sustainable care and support system*, press release July 2011.

The Government will consider each recommendation carefully to test whether it meets the wider objectives for reform, including increased personalisation, choice and quality, closer integration of health and social care and greater prevention and early intervention. The Commission recognises that implementing its reforms would have significant costs, which the Government will need to consider against other calls on constrained resources. Reform of care and support is not only about funding. The Government wants to create a social care system that offers people and their carers choice and personalised, high quality care. We will be engaging with the care sector over the autumn to develop and refine our priorities and plans for action, bearing in mind the financial context. Following this engagement, we will publish a White Paper on wider social care issues next spring, and a progress report on funding reform.

Domiciliary and community based services

continued

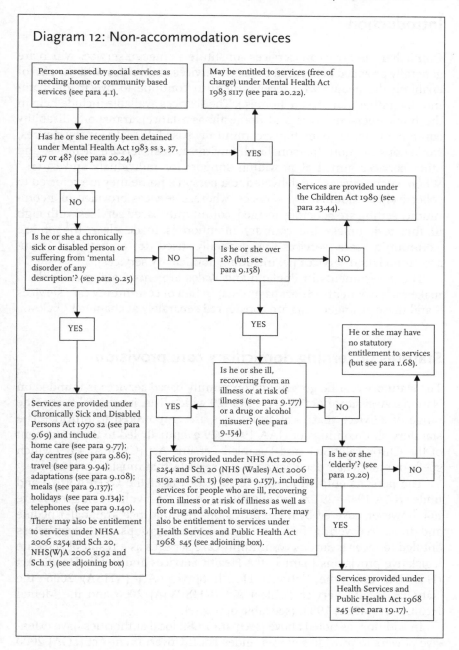

Diagram 12: Non-accommodation services

Person assessed by social services as needing home or community based services (see para 4.1).

May be entitled to services (free of charge) under Mental Health Act 1983 s117 (see para 20.22).

Has he or she recently been detained under Mental Health Act 1983 ss 3, 37, 47 or 48? (see para 20.24)

YES

NO

Services are provided under the Children Act 1989 (see para 23.44).

Is he or she a chronically sick or disabled person or suffering from 'mental disorder of any description'? (see para 9.25)

NO

Is he or she over 18? (but see para 9.158)

NO

YES

YES

He or she may have no statutory entitlement to services (but see para 1.68).

Is he or she ill, recovering from an illness or at risk of illness (see para 9.177) or a drug or alcohol misuser? (see para 9.154)

YES

NO

Services are provided under Chronically Sick and Disabled Persons Act 1970 s2 (see para 9.69) and include home care (see para 9.77); day centres (see para 9.86); travel (see para 9.94); adaptations (see para 9.108); meals (see para 9.137); holidays (see para 9.134); telephones (see para 9.140).

There may also be entitlement to services under NHSA 2006 s254 and Sch 20, NHS(W)A 2006 s192 and Sch 15 (see adjoining box)

Services provided under NHS Act 2006 s254 and Sch 20 (NHS (Wales) Act 2006 s192 and Sch 15) (see para 9.157), including services for people who are ill, recovering from illness or at risk of illness as well as for drug and alcohol misusers. There may also be entitlement to services under Health Services and Public Health Act 1968 s45 (see adjoining box).

Is he or she 'elderly'? (see para 19.20)

NO

YES

Services provided under Health Services and Public Health Act 1968 s45 (see para 19.17).

Introduction

9.1   Domiciliary and day care services constitute a range of services which are generally provided or secured by social services authorities with the aim of enabling the people who receive them to continue to live in the community (rather than in care homes). The services available include help in the home (personal care and domestic assistance); transport; disability equipment; home adaptations; community based day care (in day centres, workshops or more 'personalised' environments); leisure facilities; and other services aimed at providing support for individuals and carers.[1] Where such services are delivered to a person's home they are referred to collectively as 'domiciliary' services, whereas services provided in a community setting are generally termed 'community based services', although in this text, unless the contrary intention is made clear, the phrase 'community care services' is generally used to embrace all non-accommodation services (ie, including domiciliary services).

9.2   The governments in England and Wales are encouraging councils to make cash payments (direct payments) in lieu of community care services – and these arrangements are considered separately at chapter 12 below.

Statutes governing domiciliary care provision

9.3   The statutory regime governing community based services is founded on National Assistance Act (NAA) 1948 s29 which lists, in general terms, the range of services that local authorities are empowered to provide. The statutory shortcomings of NAA 1948 s29 eventually led to the enactment of the Chronically Sick and Disabled Persons Act (CSDPA) 1970 which spells out in greater detail some of the services that must be provided.

9.4   The persons entitled to receive services under the CSDPA 1970 and under NAA 1948 s29 are broadly the same. Certain vulnerable groups are not, however, covered by these provisions (for instance, frail older people and those recovering from an illness). Such groups are nevertheless entitled to receive various community care services as a result of separate legislative provisions (namely the Health Services and Public Health Act (HSPHA) 1968, the National Health Service Act (NHSA) 2006, the National Health Service (Wales) Act (NHS(W)A) 2006 and the Mental Health Act (MHA) 1983) (see table opposite).

9.5   In addition, as noted above (see para 1.68), local authorities have extensive powers to provide services under Local Government Act (LGA) 2000 s2 to promote (amongst other things) 'social well being' and, under the 'Supporting People' programme (to the extent that this still exists in England – see para 15.119 below), to provide housing-related support services. The NHS too, has power to provide a range of community based services,

---

1   See white paper *Caring for People: Community Care in the Next Decade and Beyond*, Cm 849, 1990, para 3.61.

NAA 1948 s29	See para 9.21 below	Disabled (including older people who are disabled) people and those with a mental disorder
CSDPA 1970 s2	See para 9.69 below	
HSPHA 1968 s45	See para 19.17 below	Older people
NHSA 2006 Sch 20 and NHS(W)A 2006 Sch 15	See para 9.154 below	Disabled and ill people
MHA 1983 s117	See para 20.22 below	Certain people with a mental disorder

for persons eligible for continuing care funding and for reducing the risks of a person becoming unwell.[2]

9.6　Although limited steps have been taken to harmonise these disparate statutory provisions, they still retain distinctive features – often incongruous and frequently overlapping.

9.7　With the enactment of the Children Act (CA) 1989, an attempt was made to make separate provision for disabled children; accordingly community based services for children are now primarily governed by CA 1989 Part III and CSDPA 1970 s2. The CA 1989 amended NAA 1948 ss21 and 29 so that in general services under these sections are not available to children. Accordingly the community care statutes are often considered to be restricted to providing services for adults. There are, however, exceptions to this rule (most significantly, services under NHSA 2006 Sch 20 para 3 are available for adult or child alike).

9.8　The National Health Service and Community Care Act (NHSCCA) 1990 Part III made a further attempt to introduce some logical structure into the various community care statutes; section 46(3) defining (for the purposes of the Act) 'community care services' as being services under:

- NAA 1948 Part III;
- HSPHA 1968 s45;
- NHSA 2006 s254 and Sch 20;
- NHS(W)A s192 and Sch 15;
- MHA 1983 s117.

9.9　While the NHSCCA 1990 s46 makes no direct reference to services provided under CSDPA 1970 s2, the Court of Appeal has, however, determined that services under section 2 are (when provided for adults) 'community care services' notwithstanding this omission. The particular difficulties caused by the wording of CSDPA 1970 s2 in this respect are considered in detail at para 9.141 below. Contradictions and inconsistencies of this kind run like fault lines through the community care

---

2　See also Department of Health (2007) *Commissioning Framework for Health and Wellbeing* which offers a number of suggestions as to the flexibility with which NHS funds can be used to avoid hospital admission or prevent illness.

legislation, which has been well described as a set of sometimes incomprehensible and frequently incompatible principles. Nowhere is this statement truer than in relation to domiciliary and community based services; these services have developed erratically since the war, first by way of cautious general provisions (eg, NAA 1948 s29), and subsequently by way of more idealistic and specific rights (such as those provided by CSDPA 1970 s2). Fundamental contradictions have emerged between these statutes, as a result of both poor and hurried drafting and the absence of any coherent policy underlying the provision of community care. In 2011 the Law Commission reported[3] on the need for codification of the law in this field and proposed that the current wide ranging list of services that come within the definition of 'community care services' be replaced by a simple list – namely: (1) residential accommodation; (2) community and home-based services; (3) advice, social work, counselling and advocacy services; and (4) financial or any other assistance.

9.10   Each of the various community care statutes entitles similar (but not identical) client groups to similar (but not identical) services. An analysis of these statutory provisions could therefore either focus on client groups or the services they deliver. Given the substantial overlap between the client groups covered by each statute and the overwhelming legal and practical importance of NAA 1948 s29 and CSDPA 1970 s2, this chapter will focus on the legal entitlements that derive from these two so called 'major provisions'. These two provisions apply to people who are disabled, or chronically sick or who have a mental disorder (including a learning disability) of any description. The final section of this chapter considers NHSA 2006 Sch 20/NHS(W)A 2006 Sch 15. Although the social care obligations created by the NHS Acts 2006 are in practice of primary legal relevance to drug and alcohol misusers, these provisions encompass many other potential service users (including disabled people) and accordingly more conveniently fall to be considered in this general chapter.

9.11   The remaining community care statutory provisions, namely HSPHA 1968 s45 (which applies only to frail older people) and MHA 1983 s117 (which applies only to certain formerly detained psychiatric patients) are considered separately in the chapters addressing these specific client groups (namely chapters 19 and 20).

9.12   In general the statutory provisions that authorise or require councils to provide community care services, do so in such a way that the authority has the power to provide the services itself or to make arrangements for the service to be provided by a third party. By way of example, NAA 1948 s30 enables a local authority to provide services under section 29 via 'any voluntary organisation[4] or any person carrying on, professionally or by way of trade or business, activities which consist of or include the provision of services'. In addition Local Government (Contracts) Act 1997 s1 in

3   Law Commission (2011) *Adult Social Care*, Law Com No 326, HC 941, Recommendation 28.
4   NAA 1948 s64 defines a voluntary organisation as 'a body the activities of which are carried on otherwise than for profit, but does not include any public or local authority' – see *R (A and B) v East Sussex CC* [2002] EWHC 2771 (Admin), (2003) 6 CCLR 177.

general terms permits councils to contract with third parties to discharge functions of this nature.

9.13 The mere fact that the local authority has commissioned such a third party to provide care to meet the assessed needs of a person, does not absolve the council of its duties to ensure that the care is actually delivered. The local authority duty is to ensure that the assistance provided is 'adequate and effective' and to 'act reasonably'.[5] Thus if the commissioned service is 'inadequate, inconsistent and subject to rapid fluctuation' such that 'a complaint of gravity and substance' arises, it will amount to breach of statutory duty.[6] It follows that it will be maladministration if there are inadequate mechanisms in place to monitor effectively contracts with care agencies[7] and resolve promptly the problem of poor service these provide.[8]

Regulation of domiciliary care services

9.14 The system of care standards regulation for care homes (considered at para 7.94 above) applies with some modification in relation to the provision of domiciliary care services. In England the Health and Social Care Act (HSCA) 2008 creates the framework for the regulation of care services, with the detail fleshed out in regulations[9] and guidance.[10] The Act requires all providers of a regulated service to be registered with the Care Quality Commission (CQC).

9.15 In England HSCA 2008 s8(2) defines a regulated activity as 'any activity which involves, or is connected with, the provision of health or social care' and section 9(3) defines 'social care' widely: as comprising 'all forms of personal care and other practical assistance provided for individuals who by reason of age, illness, disability, pregnancy, childbirth, dependence on alcohol or drugs, or any other similar circumstances, are in need of such care or other assistance'. The relevant regulations[11] stipulate that (subject to exceptions) a regulated activity includes the 'provision of personal care for persons who, by reason of old age, illness or disability are unable to provide it for themselves, and which is provided in a place

---

5   *R (LW) v Belfast Health and SC Trust* [2010] NIQB 62, 19 May 2010 at para 38.
6   *R (LW) v Belfast Health and SC Trust* [2010] NIQB 62, 19 May 2010 at para 46, but see *R v Islington LBC ex p McMillan* (1997–98)1 CCLR 7, QBD at 17 where the court considered the local authority had acted reasonably; that the service delivery failings were comparatively minor; and due to staff leave and staff sickness.
7   Complaint no 05/C/06420 against Sheffield City Council, 20 February 2007.
8   See eg complaint no 05/C/08592 against Liverpool City Council, 17 January 2007; no 07/A/01436 against Hillingdon LBC, 18 September 2008; no 09 005 944 against Bristol City Council, 13 June 2011; and no 08 019 214 against Bromley LBC, 9 June 2011.
9   The Care Quality Commission (Registration) Regulations 2009 SI No 3112 and the Health and Social Care Act 2008 (Regulated Activities) Regulations 2010 SI No 781.
10   See in particular, Care Quality Commission (2010) *Guidance about compliance: essential standards of quality and safety.*
11   Health and Social Care Act 2008 (Regulated Activities) Regulations 2010 SI No 3112 Sch 1 para 1.

where those persons are living at the time the care is provided' and 'personal care' in this context is defined as:[12]

  (a) physical assistance given to a person in connection with –
      (i) eating or drinking (including the administration of parenteral nutrition),
      (ii) toileting (including in relation to the process of menstruation),
      (iii) washing or bathing,
      (iv) dressing,
      (v) oral care, or
      (vi) the care of skin, hair and nails (with the exception of nail care provided by a chiropodist or podiatrist); or
  (b) the prompting, together with supervision, of a person, in relation to the performance of any of the activities listed in paragraph (a), where that person is unable to make a decision for themselves in relation to performing such an activity without such prompting and supervision.

9.16   The material exceptions include[13] care provided 'in the course of a family[14] or personal relationship[15] for 'no commercial consideration' and care provided in relation to children – for which the relevant registration authority is Her Majesty's Chief Inspector of Education, Children's Services and Skills (Ofsted) and the relevant statute the Care Standards Act 2000. Distinct provisions apply in relation to adult placement schemes and these are considered at para 15.128 below.

9.17   In Wales the Care Standards Act (CSA) 2000 creates the framework for the regulation of care services, again with the detail fleshed out in regulations[16] and guidance.[17] Personal care is not defined in the CSA 2000, although section 121(3) states that the expression 'does not include any prescribed activity' and section 121(9) states that the care that is provided must include 'assistance with bodily functions (eg toileting, eating) where such assistance is required'. Welsh Assembly[18] guidance on the 2000 Act defines personal care as care requiring:

  • assistance with bodily functions such as feeding, bathing, and toileting;
  • care which falls just short of assistance with bodily functions, but still involving physical and intimate touching.

---

12 Health and Social Care Act 2008 (Regulated Activities) Regulations 2010 SI No 781 reg 2.
13 Health and Social Care Act 2008 (Regulated Activities) Regulations 2010 SI No 781 Sch 2 para 1(1).
14 This includes a 'relationship between two persons who (a) live in the same household; and (b) treat each other as though they were members of the same family: Sch 2 para 1(2).
15 This includes 'a relationship between or among friends': Sch 2 para 1(3).
16 The Care Homes (Wales) Regulations 2002 SI No 324 (W37) as amended and the Domiciliary Care Agencies (Wales) Regulations 2004 SI No 219 (W23).
17 See eg Welsh Government (2004) *National Minimum Standards for Domiciliary Care Agencies in Wales.*
18 Welsh Assembly Government (2004) *National Minimum Standards for Domiciliary Care Agencies in Wales* piv: earlier guidance (*Clarification of the Registration Requirements for Supported Housing and Extra Care Schemes under the Care Standards Act 2000 Guidance,* (August 2002) added ' including activities such as helping a person get out of a bath and helping him or her to get dressed'.

9.18   CSA 2000 s4 defines a 'domiciliary care agency' as:

> An undertaking[19] which consists of or includes arranging the provision of personal care in their own homes for persons who by reason of illness, infirmity or disability are unable to provide it for themselves without assistance.

9.19   The requirement to register as a domiciliary agency with the Care and Social Services Inspectorate in Wales (CSSIW) is limited to undertakings that provide care to persons who are 'unable to provide [the personal care] for themselves' – a narrower requirement than for the registration of care homes.[20]

Standards

9.20   The standards imposed on domiciliary care providers in England and Wales mirror those that apply for care homes – for which reference should be made to para 7.99 above. In England the key guidance issued by the CQC is *Essential standards of quality and safety*[21] and in Wales the key guidance issued by the National Assembly 2004 *National Minimum Standards for Domiciliary Care Agencies.*[22] In February 2011 CSSIW began a review of regulation.[23]

Services under National Assistance Act 1948 s29

9.21   The cross-heading to NAA 1948 s29 reveals the profound change in terminology (if not social attitude) that has occurred in the last 60 years – describing the content of the section as 'Welfare arrangements for blind, deaf, dumb and crippled persons, etc'. The amended text of NAA 1948 s29(1) now reads as follows:

> 29(1) A local authority may, with the approval of the secretary of state, and to such extent as he may direct in relation to persons ordinarily resident in the area of the local authority shall, make arrangements for promoting the welfare of persons to whom this section applies, that is to say persons aged eighteen or over who are blind, deaf or dumb or who suffer from mental disorder of any description, and other persons aged eighteen or over who are substantially and permanently handicapped by illness, injury, or congenital deformity or such other disabilities as may be prescribed by the Minister.

9.22   As with NAA 1948 s21 (see para 7.8), it follows that social services authorities have no power to make any arrangements for the promotion of

19 Widely defined in CSA 2000 s121(2).
20 Minister of State, Department of Health (Mr John Hutton) HC Standing Committee G, 4 July 2000.
21 CQC (2010) *Guidance about Compliance: essential standards of quality and safety. What providers should do to comply with the section 20 regulations under the Health and Social Care Act 2008.*
22 Welsh Government (2004) *National Minimum Standards for Domiciliary Care Agencies in Wales.*
23 CSSIW Annual Report 2009–2010 p18.

anyone's welfare under this section unless and until the secretary of state has issued a direction specifying the arrangements which may be made (are 'approved') and those which must be made (are 'directed' to be made). The secretary of state's most recent direction in respect of NAA 1948 s29 is found at appendix 2 to LAC (93)10[24] and came into force on 1 April 1993 (the full text of the direction is in appendix B below).

9.23   The nature of the duty created by section 29 is uncertain. It was suggested in *R v Islington LBC ex p Rixon*[25] that it was a 'target' duty rather than a duty owed to a specific individual (see para 1.23). However, in *R v Kensington and Chelsea RLBC ex p Kujtim*[26] the Court of Appeal indicated that it had difficulty in following the logic of this particular argument. More recently, in *R (Hughes) v Liverpool City Council*[27] Mitting J held that the section 29 duty crystallised into a specific law duty subsequent to an assessment under section 47 of the 1990 Act and in this respect was indistinguishable from the duty created by NAA 1948 s21. In most cases the nature of the duty will be academic, since the section 29 functions are duplicated by those in CSDPA s2: and the section 2 duties are universally accepted as being specific law duties.

18 or over and ordinarily resident

9.24   Section 29 services are only available if they promote the welfare[28] of persons who are 18 or over. The duty to provide section 29 services[29] applies only to persons who are ordinarily resident in the local authority's area, whereas a power exists to provide services for other persons[30] (ordinary residence is considered in chapter 6 above).

Disabled people – statutory definition

9.25   The definition provided in NAA 1948 s29(1) of the persons who may potentially qualify for its services, comprises:

> ... persons ... who are blind, deaf or dumb or who suffer from mental disorder of any description, and other persons aged eighteen or over who are substantially and permanently handicapped by illness, injury, or congenital deformity or such other disabilities as may be prescribed by the Minister.

9.26   People who fall within this definition are entitled to services, not only under NAA 1948 s29 but also under CSDPA 1970 s2. It is this definition

---

24 WOC 35/93 in Wales.
25 (1997–98) 1 CCLR 119 at 131H, QBD.
26 [1999] 4 All ER 161, (1999) 2 CCLR 340, CA at 353J – where Potter LJ admitted to finding difficulty in following the arguments of Sedley J.
27 [2005] EWHC 428 (Admin), (2005) 8 CCLR 243 at [26].
28 It would appear from the wording of NAA 1948 s29(1) that the service need not be provided *to* the disabled person. It is at least arguable that a service provided to a carer may be an 'arrangement which promotes the welfare of the disabled person'.
29 LAC (93)10 appendix 2 para 2(1); albeit that it is only a target duty, see para 1.23 above.
30 *R v Berkshire CC ex p P* (1997–98) 1 CCLR 141, QBD.

(with amendment as to age alone) that was also adopted in CA 1989 s17(11) (see para 23.6). NAA 1948 s29 does not, however, permit the provision of services to people whose need arises by virtue of age alone – ie because their age has made them frail.[31] The social care needs of this group are addressed by HSPHA 1968 s45 which is considered at para 19.17 below.

9.27   In order to be eligible for any of the services available under NAA 1948 s29, a person must be within the above definition. The list should be contrasted with that under NAA 1948 s21 (see para 7.10 above) which is less restrictive, including such groups as frail elderly people, expectant mothers and disabled persons (without having to establish that their 'handicap' is either permanent or substantial).[32]

9.28   As noted above (para 2.3) NAA 1948 s29 places a duty on social services authorities to maintain registers of people in their area who may be entitled to its services. The test, however, of whether a person qualifies for services under NAA 1948 s29 is independent of whether or not he or she is on a particular authority's register – ie registration is not a prerequisite to obtaining assistance.[33]

Blind

9.29   Although NAA 1948 s29 makes no reference to partially sighted people, previous guidance[34] confirms that the phrase 'other persons who are substantially and permanently handicapped' covers such persons.

9.30   Social services authorities have well established procedures for determining whether a visually impaired person is blind or partially sighted and thus whether the terms of NAA 1948 s29(1) – and registration – apply. The procedure is initiated by a hospital eye clinic completing the relevant form – a certificate of vision impairment (CVI)[35] – which certifies that the person is severely sight impaired or sight impaired. When signed by a consultant ophthalmologist, the CVI is the formal notification required for section 29 registration purposes. Circular guidance advises that the effective date of registration should be the same as that of certification.[36]

---

31 The omission of reference to older people in section 29 list was the subject of considerable discussion (see generally R Means and R Smith, *From Poor Law to Community Care*, Policy Press, 1998 at pp266–269). The widening of local authority duties/powers to provide certain services for older people, as a result to the National Assistance (Amendment) Act 1962 (see para 19.16 below) was, however, considered insufficient to remedy this failing. Ultimately, rather than amend 29, equivalent provision was made in Health Services and Public Health Act 1968 ss 13 and 45 (see para 19.17 below).

32 It has been suggested that there was no systematic thought given to the nature of the groups to be covered by Part III of the 1948 Act, or indeed the services it was to provide: that it was essentially a social services 'tidying-up' exercise of what was left after Beveridge's major health and social security reforms – see R Means and R Smith, *From Poor Law to Community* Care, Policy Press, 1998 at p111.

33 LAC (93)10 appendix 4 para 3. See also para 2.3 above in regard to registration.

34 LAC 13/74 para 11(i).

35 Details of the arrangements are provided on the Department of Health website under the heading 'Identification and notification of sight loss'.

36 LAC (93)10 appendix 4 para 6.

The guidance further recommends that social services authorities have separate sections in their register for each of the groups of persons to whom NAA 1948 s29 applies (ie, that blind and partially sighted persons be separately recorded).[37]

9.31   Concern has been expressed by the local government ombudsman about delays in the assessment of people who have suffered sight loss and about inadequate referral arrangements between the NHS and social services.[38] The Department of Health has sought to improve the co-ordination of services for such persons, with the development of a website containing key information on service arrangements[39] and the distribution of a joint Chief Inspector Social Services Inspectorate/NHS Executive letter 'Identifying and Assessing People With Sensory Impairment' in October 2000.[40] In addition the Association of Directors of Social Services in 2002 took steps to establish a national standard for services in this field with the publication of *Progress in Sight: national standards of social care for visually impaired adults*.[41] Amongst other things this states that 'the waiting time for an assessment should be closely monitored to ensure that it is not more than four weeks from the date of referral'.[42]

9.32   Longstanding concern exists about the failure of some social services authorities properly to assess the needs of people with visual impairments, such that they 'slip into ill-health and premature dependency'.[43] The personalisation programme in England has the potential to exacerbate this problem, given that the rehabilitation workers who specialise in this field are predominantly employed by local authorities and it is not immediately obvious how their services could be delivered via a spot purchasing system of crude personal budgets: many of the supports they provide involve the provision of low cost but important items[44] which substantially enhance independence and reduce risk – and no less problematic would be the simple commodification of their support and training roles.[45]

---

37   LAC (93)10 appendix 4 para 9.
38   Complaint no 02/C/03831 against Stockport MBC, 28 August 2003.
39   Accessible at www.dh.gov.uk/PolicyandGuidance/HealthandSocialCareTopics/ Optical/fs/en.
40   www.dh.gov.uk/en/Publicationsandstatistics/Lettersandcirculars/ Dearcolleagueletters/DH_4008252.
41   Association of Directors of Social Services, October 2002 now largely superseded by RNIB (2008) *Good practice in sight* (a collaborative publication with the ADASS and Department of Health endorsement).
42   *Progress in Sight: national standards of social care for visually impaired adults*, para 11.2 – the four-week period being the limit recommended by the Social Services Inspectorate in its report *A sharper focus: inspection of services for adults who are visually impaired or blind*, Department of Health, 1998.
43   RNIB (2005) *Facing FACS: Applying the eligibility criteria in 'Fair access to care services' to adults with sight problems*.
44   Eg tactile/high visibility markers to aid access to appliance settings; electronic reading aids and access technology; liquid level indicators: white canes or support sticks; talking clocks/watches to enable access and orientation etc.
45   Eg in developing daily living, mobility, orientation and independence skills; training in using specialist equipment, in developing communication skills (eg Braille, moon ec); advising on low vision strategies etc.

Deaf

9.33 Although NAA 1948 s29 makes no specific reference to people with impaired hearing, previous guidance[46] confirms that the phrase 'other persons who are substantially and permanently handicapped' covers persons who are hard of hearing.

9.34 There are no formal examination procedures for determining whether a person is deaf for the purposes of NAA 1948 s29.[47] Social services authorities are advised that all persons who suffer from a disabling loss of hearing should be regarded as being deaf for the purposes of section 29.[48] The guidance suggests, however, that this single class should be subdivided into three categories:[49]

Deaf without speech:	Those who have no useful hearing and those whose normal method of communication is by signs, finger spelling or writing.
Deaf with speech:	Those who (even with a hearing aid) have little or no useful hearing but whose normal method of communication is by speech and lip-reading.
Hard-of-hearing:	Those who (with or without a hearing aid) have some useful hearing and whose normal method of communication is by speech, listening and lip-reading.

9.35 The guidance in LAC (93)10 appendix 4 annex 2 makes a number of general statements concerning the importance the government attaches to services for deaf people; these statements are directed principally at the training and duties of specialist social workers in this field rather than being specific statements about the type of services to be provided.

Deafblind

9.36 The Department of Health has issued policy guidance (2009)[50] concerning the assessment and care planning needs of people who are deafblind, which requires local authorities to:

- identify, contact and record all such persons in their area;
- ensure that assessments are undertaken by people with specific skills concerning this impairment;
- ensure that services are appropriate (which may mean that they are not 'mainstream' or aimed primarily at blind people or deaf people);
- ensure that deafblind people are able to access specifically trained one-to-one support workers where necessary;
- provide information about services in accessible ways; and

---

46 LAC 13/74 para 11(i); see also LAC (93)10 appendix 4 para 7.
47 LAC (93)10 appendix 4 para 7.
48 LAC (93)10 appendix 4 annex 2 para 2.
49 LAC (93)10 appendix 4 annex 2 para 2.
50 Department of Health (2009) *Social Care for Deafblind Children and Adults* LAC(DH)(2009)6.

- ensure that overall responsibility for deafblind services lies within the specific remit of a member of senior management.

9.37   In Wales 2001 National Assembly policy guidance has been augmented by particularly detailed (2008) practice guidance[51] – which places similar emphasis on the importance of the above factors.

Dumb

9.38   The guidance gives no advice as to the criteria for determining whether or not a person with limited speech comes within the scope of NAA 1948 s29 (other than by reference to persons who are 'deaf without speech' – see above). By implication, however, persons who have little or no useful speech must come within the scope of the phrase 'substantially and permanently handicapped'.[52]

Mental disorder of any description

9.39   Persons suffering from a mental disorder of any description (ie, within the ambit of MHA 1983 s1) are included in the NAA 1948 s29 client group.[53] However, as is detailed below, NAA 1948 s29 services cannot be provided to a person if the same service has been 'required' to be provided under the NHSA 2006 or the NHS(W)A 2006.[54] The relevant part of the NHS Acts 2006 (and the secretary of state's direction issued under them) has been so drafted that NAA 1948 s29 services are generally of little relevance to persons suffering from a mental disorder. The importance, however, of including such persons within section 29 is that they are thereby included and eligible for services under CSDPA 1970 s2. Persons who suffer from a mental disorder are entitled to community care services under NHSA 2006 Sch 20 and NHS(W)A 2006 Sch 15 and/or under MHA 1983 s117 (see para 9.173 and para 20.22 respectively) in addition to CSDPA 1970 s2.[55]

9.40   It would appear that Autism,[56] when diagnosed, must now be accepted as a mental disorder and so included within the section 29 definition and as must be attention deficit disorders[57] – and that any difference in treatment

51   National Assembly for Wales (2001) Circular No 10/01 *Social Care for Deafblind Children and Adults* (policy guidance) and WAG (2008) *Moving Forward: services to deafblind people* practice guidance.
52   See LAC 13/74 para 11(i) and LAC (93)10 appendix 4 annex 2 para 2.
53   LAC (93)10 appendix 4 para 14.
54   NAA 1948 s29(6); see para 9.65.
55   LAC (93)10 appendix 4 para 13 incorrectly states that such services are generally provided under HSPHA 1968 s12 – this section had been repealed and reference should have been made to the then NHSA 1977 Sch 8 (although since CSDPA 1970 s2 applies to persons suffering from a mental disorder of any description, arguably this section is of greater importance).
56   See (by analogy) eg the decision of Social Security Commissioner Jacobs, 13 November 2007: CDLA 2288 2007.
57   See eg L S Goldman and others, 'Diagnosis and treatment of attention-deficit/ hyperactivity disorder in children and adolescents' (1998) *Journal of the American Medical Association* 279 (14): 1100–1107 which concluded that there was little evidence of misdiagnosis of ADHD.

by a local authority of persons with these conditions will have the potential to constitute unlawful discrimination contrary to the Equality Act 2010, s15.[58] Whereas all the other potential service users under NAA 1948 s29 (and/or CSDPA 1970 s2) are persons whose 'handicap' is permanent and substantial, this is not, however, a requirement for persons suffering from a mental disorder.

Substantially and permanently handicapped

9.41   Circular guidance[59] states:

> It has not proved possible to give precise guidance on the interpretation of the phrase 'substantially and permanently handicapped'. However, as hitherto, authorities are asked to give a wide interpretation to the term 'substantial', which the Department fully recognises must always take full account of individual circumstances. With regard to the term 'permanent', authorities will also wish to interpret this sufficiently flexibly to ensure that they do not feel inhibited from giving help under s29 in cases where they are uncertain of the likely duration of the condition.

'Illness, injury, or congenital deformity or such other disabilities as may be prescribed by the Minister'

9.42   To qualify for services under NAA 1948 s29 a person who is substantially and permanently handicapped must be so by virtue of an illness, an injury, or congenital deformity; no further disabilities have been pre-scribed by the minister. Section 29 provides for no definition of illness although it is not unreasonable to assume that it would have the same meaning as that provided by NHSA 2006 s275(1)/NHS(W)A 2006 s206(1), namely as including mental disorder within the meaning of the MHA 1983 and any injury or disability requiring medical or dental treatment or nursing. Persons who are disabled as a result of an illness or congenital deformity will not be entitled to receive NAA 1948 s29 services where those services are required under the NHS Acts 2006.[60] It is undecided as to whether substantial and permanent handicap resulting from drug or alcohol misuse can be defined as arising out of illness or injury so as to qualify the person for NAA 1948 s29 services; in practice domiciliary services to such persons will generally be delivered under the NHS Acts 2006 (and are considered at para 9.154).

Services

9.43   NAA 1948 s29 leaves to the secretary of state the power to determine the type of domiciliary services which can be provided by local authorities; the only limitations being:

---

58   See eg *Governing Body of X School v SP and others* [2008] EWHC 389 (Admin).
59   LAC (93)10 appendix 4 para 8.
60   NAA 1948 s29(6).

a)   that the purpose of the services must be the promotion of the welfare of the NAA 1948 s29 client group;[61]

b)   by virtue of NAA 1948 s29(6)(a) that the direct payment of money to service users is not permitted under section 29 (except if a payment for their work or produce). However, the impact of this restriction has largely been neutered by the direct payments legislation see chapter 12 below); and

c)   by virtue of NAA 1948 s29(6)(b) no accommodation or services can be provided under section 29 if the accommodation or services have been 'required' to be provided under the NHS Acts 2006.[62]

9.44   Although NAA 1948 s29(4) contains an illustrative list of the type of services that may be made available, the Act leaves to the secretary of state the power to decide what services must and what services may be provided. The text of section 29(4) is provided in appendix A.

9.45   The secretary of state's most recent directions in respect of section 29 services were issued as appendix 2 to LAC (93)10[63] in March 1993. The directions distinguish between services[64] which a social services department *may* provide (ie, has a power to provide – generally known as an 'approval') and those which it *must* provide (ie, is under a duty to provide).

Services which social services departments have a duty to provide

9.46   As noted above, the duty on social services departments to provide services under NAA 1948 s29 is restricted to persons who are ordinarily resident in the authority's area. The services being:

Social work service, advice and support

9.47   Social services authorities are required to 'provide a social work service and such advice and support as may be needed for people in their own homes or elsewhere'.[65] This duty is complemented by Local Authority Social Services Act 1970 s6(6) which obliges local authorities to provide 'adequate staff for assisting' the director of social services in the exercise of his or her functions.[66] 'Advice and support' would cover such services as welfare rights advice and counselling.[67] Previous circular guidance[68]

---

61   A person's welfare may, however, be promoted by providing a service to a third party (eg, a carer).

62   The provision of accommodation is, however, specifically excluded from NHSA 2006 Sch 20 para 2(11) and NHS(W)A 2006 Sch 15 para 2(11). For an analysis of section 29(6)(b) see L Clements and P Bowen, 'NHS continuing care and independent living' (2007) 10 CCLR 343–351.

63   The full text of which is at appendix B below. The directions were issued in Wales as WOC 35/93.

64   The local authority may provide the services alone, or in conjunction with another authority or by employing an independent or private provider: see NAA 1948 s30 and LAC (93)10 appendix 2 paras 3 and 4.

65   LAC (93)10 appendix 2 para 2(1)(a).

66   See para 1.8 above.

67   Complaint no 05/A/00880 against Essex CC, 16 January 2006.

68   DHSS circular 13/74 para 11(ii) – cancelled by LAC (93)10.

advised that the provision of advice and support would frequently necessitate offering advice and other help to the families of the disabled person; and that authorities should bear in mind the part which voluntary workers can play in delivering this service. Welfare rights advice has often been considered as a core local authority activity,[69] sometimes working in joint teams with the Department for Work and Pensions or other advice agencies.[70] Such advice and support is required when (for example) charges are being assessed for non-residential care services (see para 10.13 below). The NHS is also empowered to provide advice and assistance in relation to access to state benefits for its service users, under section 3(1)(e) of the NHS Acts 2006.[71]

Social rehabilitation or adjustment to disability

9.48   Social services authorities are required 'to provide, whether at centres or elsewhere, facilities for social rehabilitation and adjustment to disability including assistance in overcoming limitations of mobility or communication'.[72] These services will generally be provided for a short or medium-term period covering the disabled person's rehabilitation or adjustment to his or her disability. The reference to 'social' rehabilitation makes the point that medical rehabilitation is either a service to be provided by social services under NHSA 2006 Sch 20/NHS(W)A 2006 Sch 15 (and thus excluded from provision under NAA 1948 s29)[73] or is one which should be provided by the NHS. The bundle of services referred to in this category covers, in many cases, services for which there is an overlapping responsibility between the NHS and the social services authority. These include 'intermediate care' (see chapter 11) and occupational therapy which depending upon its context and purpose may be a social services responsibility (eg in determining whether home adaptations for a disabled person are necessary and appropriate – see para 15.66 below); an NHS responsibility if it is primarily medical in its purpose (and so provided pursuant to the NHS Acts 2006) or indeed an educational responsibility, if for example provided pursuant to a special educational needs statement.[74]

---

69 Local authorities have a variety of powers to fund advice groups. Where a decision is taken to cease such support, it will need to comply with the principles of public law, including proper consultation and an equality impact assessment. In *R (Hajrula) v London Councils* [2011] EWHC 448 (Admin) para 69, Calvert-Smith J considered that, in relation to the public sector equality duty (see para 2.32 below) where a cut impacted on a vulnerable group the obligation to have 'due regard' to its impact was 'very high'.

70 A recent example being the trailblazer pilot sites established under the Disabled People's Right to Control (Pilot Scheme) (England) Regulations 2010 SI No 2862 – see para 4.138 above.

71 *R (Keating) v Cardiff Local Health Board* [2005] EWCA Civ 847, [2006] 1 WLR 159, (2005) 8 CCLR 504 – see para 13.13 below.

72 LAC (93)10 appendix 2 para 2(1)(a).

73 NAA 1948 s29(6)(b).

74 See eg *Bromley LBC v SENT* (1999) 2 CCLR 239, [1999] ELR 260 and the report on complaint no 08 017 856 against Redbridge LBC, 6 August 2009.

9.49   The direction, in respect of these services, subsumes (and extends) the services referred to in NAA 1948 s29(4)(b), which merely refers to arrangements for 'giving persons instruction in their own homes or elsewhere in methods of overcoming the effects of their disabilities'.

Information for disabled people

9.50   Social services authorities are required to make arrangements 'for informing persons to whom [section 29] relates of the services available for them [under section 29]'.[75] The extent and nature of this duty is considered at para 2.42 above.

Day centres and other facilities

9.51   Social services authorities are required 'to provide, whether at centres or elsewhere, facilities for occupational, social, cultural and recreational activities and, where appropriate, the making of payments to persons for work undertaken by them'.[76] These services include the day centre in its various forms, workshops, recreational and educational activities, as well as art, sport, drama sessions and so on. In relation to people with learning disabilities (in particular) there has been a long standing central government aim of reduce reliance on day centres and workshops.[77] Accordingly in *R (J and others) v Southend BC and Essex CC*[78] (a case challenging the closure of a day centre) Newman J observed:

> It is plain that the underlying reason for the closure of the M Centre is to comply with Government policy and that policy itself is designed to foster the autonomy of the learning disabled, to ensure services are provided to them and that they are not set apart from the community. It is a situation in which the policy itself is driving towards what could be regarded as an aspect of private life which it is seen will be enhanced by these measures.

9.52   Desirable as it is, in general, to provide services that do not 'set apart from the community' people with learning disabilities, such an approach is not a universal panacea. In *AH v Hertfordshire Partnership NHS Foundation Trust and others*[79] the Court of Protection noted that for the individual in question the local authority's proposal to move him out of a relatively segregated unit constituted, in some respects the antithesis of person centred planning or 'personalisation': that for him community living did not hold benefits – and that 'facing up to these realities does not in any way diminish or demean [him], but values and respects him for who he is.' In the opinion of Jackson J (para 80):

---

75 LAC (93)10 appendix 2 para 2(1)(2) and NAA 1948 s29(4)(g).
76 LAC (93)10 appendix 2 para 2(1)(c).
77 Secretary of State for Health (2001) *Valuing People: a new strategy for learning disability for the 21st Century*, Cm 5086, March 2001, paras 4.7 and 7.21.
78 *R (J and others) v Southend BC and Essex CC* [2005] EWHC 3457 (Admin), (2007) 10 CCLR 407.
79 [2011] EWHC 276 (CoP), (2011) 14 CCLR 301.

guideline policies cannot be treated as universal solutions, nor should initiatives designed to personalise care and promote choice be applied to the opposite effect. . . . . These residents are not an anomaly simply because they are among the few remaining recipients of this style of social care. They might better be seen as a good example of the kind of personal planning that lies at the heart of the philosophy of care in the community.

9.53 The direction, in respect of day care services, overlaps with the workshop services referred to in NAA 1948 s29(4)(c) and subsumes (and extends) the services referred to in section 29(4)(f) which merely refers to arrangements for 'providing such persons with recreational facilities in their own homes or elsewhere'. In most cases services of this nature will in fact be provided to the eligible NAA 1948 s29 service user via CSDPA 1970 s2(1)(c) (see para 9.85 below).

Workshop and workshop hostel services

9.54 The provision of facilities for occupational activities often takes the form of a local authority workshop which provides employment (paid or otherwise) for particular user groups – frequently people with learning disabilities. In addition to the power to pay users employed in the workshops,[80] social services authorities are specifically empowered to help such persons dispose of the products of their work. The use of workshops continues the tradition of the segregated workhouse of the pre-welfare state. In the early post-war years many such workshops were former poor-law workhouses which continued to be devoted to menial mechanical tasks. Almost all such workshops have been closed in the last decade, with the current focus on enabling disabled people to access mainstream work using social security support – such as the Access to Work schemes.[81]

9.55 The social services authorities' duty to provide workshops is coupled with the power to provide hostel accommodation (including board and other services, amenities and requisites)[82] for those engaged in the workshop or other occupational activity under NAA 1948 s29(4). Section 29(4A) applies the same charging rules for the provision of such accommodation as apply to residential accommodation provided under NAA 1948 s21 (see para 8.6 above).

Services which social services departments have power to provide

9.56 The directions[83] give social services authorities the discretion to provide the following services (regardless of the potential service user's ordinary residence).

---

80 LAC (93)10 appendix 2 para 2(1)(c) contains an express power for local authorities to pay disabled persons who undertake work in workshops.
81 See Department for Work and Pensions (2011) *Getting in, staying in and getting on: disability employment support fit for the future*, a report by Liz Sayce Cm 8081.
82 NAA 1948 s29(4)(c) and LAC (93)10 appendix 2 para 2(4).
83 LAC (93)10 appendix 2 paras 2(3) and (4).

Holiday homes

9.57　The discretion to provide holiday homes under NAA 1948 s29 should be contrasted with the duty under CSDPA 1970 s2(1)(f) to facilitate the taking of a holiday (see para 9.134 below).

Free or subsidised travel

9.58　'Provide free or subsidised travel for all or any persons who do not otherwise qualify for travel concessions, but only in respect of travel arrangements for which concessions are available.' Travel concessions are dealt with under the Transport Act 1985 s93 as amended[84] and is more fully considered below at para 9.94 below. Under the 1985 Act the persons concerned must be:

a)　over their state retirement age;[85] or
b)　under 16; or
c)　aged 16–18 undergoing full-time education; or
d)　blind; or
e)　suffering from any disability or injury which, in the opinion of the authority, seriously impairs their ability to walk.

9.59　All disabled people and pensioners are entitled to free off peak bus travel.

Assistance in finding accommodation

9.60　'Assist a person in finding accommodation which will enable him or her to take advantage of any arrangements made under s29(1) of the Act.' The power to provide such assistance mirrors that approved for older people under DHSS circular 19/71 para 4 (see para 19.21 below).

Subsidy of warden costs

9.61　'Contribute to the cost of employing a warden on welfare functions in warden assisted housing schemes.' The power to provide such assistance mirrors that approved for older people under DHSS circular 19/71 para 4 (see para 19.21 below).

Warden services

9.62　'Provide warden services for occupiers of private housing.' The power to provide such assistance mirrors that approved for older people under DHSS circular 19/71 para 4 (see para 19.21 below).

84　See also Greater London Authority Act 1999 s151, the Travel Concessions (Eligibility) Act 2002 and the Transport for London (Consequential Provisions) Order 2003 SI No 1615.
85　Travel Concessions (Eligibility) Act 2002 and see The Travel Concessions (Eligibility)(England) Order 2010 SI No 459.

Information on disability services

9.63 The power under section 29 to provide information services for disabled people[86] has been subsumed into the wider duty set out in CSDPA 1970 s1 (see para 2.43 above).

Direct payments to service users under NAA 1948 s29

9.64 Although section 29(6)(a) prohibits authorities from making cash payments (under section 29) to service users to enable them to procure their own care,[87] its impact has been largely neutralised by Health and Social Care Act 2001 s57 which is considered at para 12.7 below.

Section 29(6)(b) and the NHS overlap

9.65 NAA 1948 s29(6)(b) excludes services being provided under section 29 where such services 'are required to be provided' under the NHS Acts 2006.

9.66 The use of the word 'required' suggests that it is only where there is a duty to provide the service under the 2006 Acts that the provision must be under those statutes rather than under NAA 1948 s29. A consideration of the similar exclusionary provision which exists in relation to accommodation services under NAA 1948 s21[88] supports this interpretation. The section 21(8) prohibition is more severe, since it proscribes services that are 'authorised or required' to be provided under the 2006 Acts and was considered by the Court of Appeal in *R v North East Devon Health Authority ex p Coughlan*[89] (see also para 7.55 above and 14.8 below). Amending the relevant part of the judgment (para 29) to accommodate the slightly different wording of NAA 1948 s29(6)(b),[90] the court's interpretation would appear to be as follows:

> The subsection should not be regarded as preventing a local authority from providing any health services. The subsection's prohibitive effect is limited to those health services which, in fact, [been] . . . required to be provided under the [NHS Acts 2006]. Such health services would not therefore include services which the secretary of state legitimately decided under section 3(1) of the [NHS Acts 2006] it was not necessary for the NHS to provide . . . The true effect is to emphasise that [the NAA 1948] provision, . . . is secondary to [the NHS Acts 2006] provision.

9.67 The fact that NAA 1948 s29(6)(b) may require certain services to be provided under the NHS Acts 2006, does not in itself exclude social services responsibility for the provision of such services, since such authorities also have functions under the NHS Acts 2006 – see para 9.154 below.

---

86 NAA 1948 s29(4)(a) and LAC (93)10 appendix 2 para 2(4).
87 This provision is mirrored in NHSA 2006 Sch 20 para 2(2) and NHS(W)A 2006 Sch 15 para 2(2) (see para 9.172 below).
88 NAA 1948 s21(8); although this subsection prohibits social services from providing any services which are '*authorised or* required' to be provided under the NHSA 2006.
89 [2000] 2 WLR 622, (1999) 2 CCLR 285, CA.
90 That is by excluding reference to the phrase '*authorised or*'.

9.68　　In *R v Gloucestershire CC ex p Mahfood*[91] the council sought to argue that a further consequence flowed from NAA 1948 s29(6)(b). The argument hinged on whether or not services provided by virtue of CSDPA 1970 s2 are NAA 1948 s29 services or free-standing CSDPA 1970 s2 services.[92] This general question is considered in greater detail at para 9.141. In the context of NAA 1948 s29(6)(b), McCowan LJ disposed of the respondent counsel's submissions as follows:

> His argument was that it is a pre-condition of the duty under section 2 of the 1970 Act that the local authority has power to provide the service under section 29 of the 1948 Act. If there is no power under section 29 there can be no duty under section 2. But section 29(6) of the 1948 Act positively provides that there is no power to exercise certain functions, in particular those which involve services which have to be provided under the National Health Service Act 1977.[93] There is a duty to provide home helps for the aged and handicapped, but it is a duty under the 1977 Act. Therefore, the power to provide the service is excluded and home help services could not lawfully have been provided to Mr Mahfood and Mr Barry under section 2 of the 1970 Act.
>
> The submission is an unattractive one because it would follow that if the local authority was satisfied by reason of the fact that general arrangements had not been made for the home help, it would have no power and thus no duty to make these arrangements. The short answer to the point, however, is that section 29(6) of the 1948 Act merely states 'nothing in the foregoing provisions of this section shall authorise or require'. What is authorising the local authority to make arrangements under section 2 is section 2. Thus the provisions which authorise the local authority to meet the needs of a disabled person if those needs are not being otherwise met are section 2 itself.[94]

Services under Chronically Sick and Disabled Persons Act 1970 s2

9.69　　The CSDPA 1970, sponsored by Alf Morris MP, was the first of a distinguished line of private members' bills in this field[95] and represents an early marker in the continuing struggle by disabled people for full civil rights. Writing 25 years after its enactment, Alf Morris commented:

> It seems incredible and outrageous now, but from 1945–1964, there was not one debate in the Commons on disability. Westminster and Whitehall

91　(1997–98) 1 CCLR 7, QBD.
92　The respondent did not pursue this argument in the Court of Appeal or the House of Lords.
93　The material provisions in the 1977 Act have been transposed in identical terms into the NHS Acts 2006 – see para 13.8.
94　(1997–98) 1 CCLR 7 at 16K, QBD.
95　The Disabled Persons (Services, Consultation and Representation) Act 1986 was promoted by Tom Clarke MP, the Carers (Recognition and Services) Act 1995 was promoted by Malcolm Wicks MP and the Carers (Equal Opportunities) Act 2004 was promoted by Dr Hywel Francis MP.

always had more pressing things to do than respond to the claims of people with disabilities. No-one even knew how many disabled people there were in Britain. They were treated not so much as second-class citizens, more as non-people: seen or heard only by families or, if they were in institutions, by those who controlled their lives.[96]

9.70 The speed with which the Act was drafted resulted in ambiguities which have frustrated its interpretation, most significantly the extent to which CSDPA 1970 s2 is distinct from NAA 1948 s29; this question is considered in greater detail below. The underlying purpose of section 2 was undoubtedly to convert the vaguely worded, generally discretionary services under section 29 into a set of specific services to which individual disabled people had an enforceable right. The full text of CSDPA 1970 s2(1) is provided at appendix A below.

'Ordinarily resident'

9.71 Section 2 services are only available to persons who are ordinarily resident in the local authority's area. Ordinary residence has the same meaning as it does under NAA 1948 s24 and is subject to the same statutory procedure for resolving inter-authority disputes on this question (as under NAA 1948 s32(3)[97] – see para 6.63 above.

Client group

9.72 CSDPA 1970 s2 services are available to both disabled children and disabled adults (unlike services under NAA 1948 s29, which are only available to disabled adults). Section 2 requires social services authorities to make arrangements 'for that person' – whereas NAA 1948 s29 speaks of the need to make arrangements to 'promote the welfare' of a class of people. It follows therefore that services under CSDPA 1970 s2 must only be provided to the disabled person, whereas it is arguable that NAA 1948 s29 services can be provided to third parties so long as they thereby 'promote the welfare' of the person in question.[98]

Disabled adults

9.73 Section 2 services are available to the same group of adult persons as specified in NAA 1948 s29, namely persons aged 18 or over who are blind, deaf, dumb or who suffer from mental disorder of any description, and other persons aged 18 or over who are substantially and permanently handicapped by illness, injury, or congenital deformity (see para 9.25 where these terms are considered).

---

96 DW Issues, June 1995.
97 CSDPA s2(1A) inserted by Health and Social Care Act 2008 s148.
98 A person's welfare may be promoted by providing a service to a third party (eg, a carer).

Disabled children

9.74   By virtue of CSDPA 1970 s28A, section 2 services are additionally available to disabled children within the meaning of CA 1989 s17(11), namely a child who is 'blind, deaf, dumb or suffers from mental disorder of any kind or is substantially and permanently handicapped by illness, injury or congenital deformity'. It will be seen that the CA 1989 follows the wording used in NAA 1948 s29, and accordingly the comments made in this following section in respect of the adult client group apply equally to disabled children.

9.75   While the CA 1989 itself makes provision for a wide range of services for disabled children (considered at para 23.44 below), in general, if the service is capable of being provided under both Acts, then it will (as a matter of law) be provided under the CSDPA 1970.[99]

Services

9.76   As already noted (see para 3.177 above), once a social services authority has carried out an assessment of the needs of a disabled person and decided that the provision of services under CSDPA 1970 s2 is necessary in order to meet that person's needs, the authority is under an specific duty to provide that service.[100] The services detailed in section 2 (a 'strange list' in Lord Browne-Wilkinson's opinion[101]) are described below.

Practical assistance in the home

9.77   Means and Smith[102] chart the historical development of the home help service from its first statutory mentions in the Maternity and Child Welfare Act 1918 and the Public Health Act 1936 and its expansion during the World War II[103] (due in part to the mass discharge of frail and ill older people from hospital at that time) and the early involvement of the Women's Voluntary Service due to wartime labour shortages. Since the Beveridge reforms a parallel duty to provide such support has existed in the NHS legislation – eg the NHS Act 1946 s29[104] in very similar terms to that appears in the NHS Acts 2006 (see para 9.82 below).

9.78   Section 2(1)(a) of the 1970 Act speaks not of 'home help' but of the provision of 'practical assistance' in the home – which encompasses a wide range of services. It has for instance been suggested that the phrase

---

99   *R v Bexley LBC ex p B* (2000) 3 CCLR 15, see para 9.150 below where this question is considered further.

100   *R v Gloucestershire CC ex p Mahfood* (1997–98) 1 CCLR 7, QBD.

101   *R v East Sussex County Council, ex p Tandy* [1998] 2 WLR 884, [1998] AC 714 at 748.

102   R Means and R Smith (1998) *From Poor Law to Community* Care, Policy Press, 1998, pp81–92.

103   Defence (General Regulations) 1939 Regulation 68E and Ministry of Heath Circular 179/44 'Domestic help'.

104   For 'households where such help is required owing to the presence of any person who is ill, lying-in, an expectant mother, mentally defective, aged or a child not over compulsory school age'.

encompasses the provision of some disabled facilities[105] although these are traditionally considered to be covered by section 2(1)(e) (see para 9.105 below). Although it is possible to divide such services into two broad categories – those primarily concerned with the maintenance of the home (eg, house cleaning, ironing, decorating etc) and those primarily concerned with the personal care of the disabled person (eg, help with getting out of and into bed, dressing, cooking, laundry, a sitting service etc), it would be a mistake to suggest that the first category is of less importance than the second.[106] Nevertheless many (if not most) social services departments operate a rigid policy of not providing the former services under CSDPA 1970 s2. Such a policy is not merely a fettering of their duty; it is also contrary to good practice, in that it is 'needs' that are prioritised under the community care regime, not services. While it may follow that a need for personal care will generally be of higher priority than a need to live in a clean and safe environment, this will not always be the case.[107]

9.79   The local government ombudsman has held it to be maladministration for a council to have criteria which stipulate that no domestic assistance can be provided – unless accompanied by a need for personal care,[108] and guidance to the Carers and Disabled Children Act 2000 emphasises this point:[109]

> . . . local authorities that have decided not to provide or commission certain services as community care services – such as shopping only, cleaning only, or other low-level services – should review their positions. Such services, if targeted purposively, can be of genuine assistance in sustaining the caring relationship, and be cost effective.

9.80   Notwithstanding the value accorded to home help by disabled and elderly people, and their carers, there has been a steady decline in the number of households receiving this support: falling from 528,500 in 1992 to 337,000

---

105   Department for Communities and Local Government, Department for Education and Skills and the Department of Health (2006) *Delivering Housing Adaptations for Disabled People: a good practice guide*, para 2.6.
106   Despite help with housework and other domestic tasks being highly valued and important 'pro active' support services, in practice social services do not consider these to be a priority – see eg T Ware (et al) 'Commissioning care services for older people in England: the view from care managers, users and carers', (2003) *Ageing and Society*, no 23, pp 411–428; H Clark (et al) *That bit of help: the high value of low level preventative services for older people*, Policy Press, 1998; J Francis and A Netten 'Raising the quality of home care: a study of service users' views', (2004) *Social Policy and Administration*, no 38, pp290–305 (cited in C Glendinning et al *Social Care Institute for Excellence Adults' Services Knowledge Review 13: outcomes-focused services for older people*, Policy Press, 2006 at para 1.4.4.
107   See for instance Complaint no 09 013 172 against Worcestershire County Council, 6 July 2011.
108   Complaint no 01/C/17519 against Salford CC, 11 December 2003.
109   Department of Health (2001) *Practitioners guide to carers' assessments under the Carers and Disabled Children Act 2000*, para 80.

in 2010[110] and the proportion is now low by international standards.[111] All too often the home help that is provided, comes in inappropriately short, 'undignified and unsafe' timeslots (for example 15 minutes)[112] provided by the independent sector.[113]

9.81   Not only have some authorities adopted arbitrary and unlawful policies of not providing domestic assistance, many have also restricted their bathing support services assistance to cases where there is an identified medical need: essentially requiring the disabled person to produce a doctor's letter verifying that such a medical need exists. The local government ombudsman has declared it to be maladministration for a local authority to have such a policy – to suggest that bathing is not an essential activity. Some authorities have attempted to circumvent their duty to provide bathing assistance by suggesting that the 'service response' to a person's 'need to clean' might be a strip wash rather than a bath. In this respect, the ombudsman has further held that the ability properly to manage bathing/ washing with dignity is the entitlement of everybody[114] – see also para 4.102 above.

9.82   There is appreciable overlap between the duty under CSDPA 1970 s2(1)(a) and that under NHSA 2006 Sch 20 para 3, which places a duty on social services authorities to provide home help for households where such help is required owing to the presence of a person who is suffering from illness, lying in, an expectant mother, aged, or 'handicapped' as a result of having suffered from illness or by congenital deformity (see para 9.178 below).The main differences between these two provisions are:

a)   The NHS Acts 2006 service is available to a wider client group (ie, the 'handicap' need not be permanent or substantial: expectant mothers, the temporarily ill and the elderly are covered), but it does not cover persons 'handicapped' as a result of injury.

b)   The service under the NHS Acts 2006 is generally regarded as a target duty, whereas the duty under CSDPA 1970 s2 can create an individual right to the service (see para 1.25 above).

c)   The NHS Acts 2006 service is provided to 'households' (ie, a direct beneficiary might be the carer), whereas the CSDPA 1970 s2 service can only be provided to the disabled person (ie, a carer could only be an indirect beneficiary).

d)   The NHS Acts 2006 use the phrase 'home help' whereas CSDPA

---

110   NHS Information Centre (2011) *Adult Social Care Statistics: Community Care Statistics 2009–10: Social Services Activity Report, England*, Table 4.1, p42. Although there had been an increase between 2004 and 2008 in the actual amount of home care provided (ie more intensive support to fewer people) reflecting the fall in residents supported in care homes, this too has dropped – falling 8% in the year to 2009–10 (ibid p43).

111   Commission for Social Care Inspection (CSCI) (2006) *Time to Care? An overview of home care services for older people in England*, 2006, p4.

112   *Time to Care? An overview of home care services for older people in England*, 2006.

113   *Time to Care? An overview of home care services for older people in England*, 2006 – the proportion of home care purchased from independent sector increased from 2% in 1992 to more than 73% in 2005.

114   Complaint nos 02/C/8679, 8681 and 10389 against Bolsover DC, 30 September 2003.

1970 s2(1)(a) refers to 'practical assistance' in the home – although it is difficult to see whether anything of significance can be discerned from this difference.

9.83　In *R (T, D and B) v Haringey LBC*[115] the court held that the concept of 'practical assistance' within the meaning of section 2 could not cover the provision of services akin to medical treatment (in this case the replacement of oesophageal feeding tubes (see para 14.29 below) even where this service was not being undertaken by a qualified nurse.

The provision of a wireless, television, library, etc

9.84　The service described by CSDPA 1970 s2(1)(b) consists of the social services authority actually providing (or helping with the acquisition of) equipment to satisfy a recreational need. The items referred to (ie wireless, television, library or similar recreational facilities) are illustrative not exhaustive, and presumably equipment such as a personal computer, iPod or similar system could also be provided under section 2(1)(b). Whether or not this provision enables a local authority also to provide aids that facilitate the use of such equipment (such as a sound loop or audio-headphone for people with impaired hearing) would appear questionable, since (unlike section 2(1)(h)) there is no additional reference to 'special equipment necessary to enable him to use' the wireless, TV library etc. Such equipment could, however, be provided pursuant to the duty under NAA 1948 s29 (see para 9.42 above), namely the duty to provide 'facilities for social rehabilitation and adjustment to disability including assistance in overcoming limitations of mobility or communication'.[116]

The provision of recreational/educational facilities

9.85　CSDPA 1970 s2(1)(c) requires social services authorities to provide two separate types of service, namely:

Recreational facilities

9.86　This service is complementary to the home-based service detailed in CSDPA 1970 s2(1)(a) above, and must be provided outside the person's home. Included within this provision are traditional day centres and 'drop-in' clubs as well as such recreational activities as outings and so on.

9.87　It is government policy to require local authorities to develop more positive activities for disabled people (particularly people with learning disabilities[117]) than those traditionally provided by day centres. This policy initiative (which is noted at para 9.48 above and considered further at para 18.22 below) has resulted in a number of challenges to the closure of

115 [2005] EWHC 2235 (Admin), (2006) 9 CCLR 58.
116 LAC (93)10 appendix 2 para 2(1)(b).
117 See eg Secretary of State for Health (2001) *Valuing People: A New Strategy for Learning Disability for the 21st Century*, Cm 5086, March 2001, paras 4.7 and 7.21.

such centres and these actions (in the context of care homes) are considered at para 7.144 above.

9.88   In *R v Haringey LBC ex p Norton*[118] the council, when carrying out its assessment, only considered its obligation to provide 'personal care needs' rather than other needs such as social, recreational and leisure needs (such as those available under section 2(1)(c)). The court held this to be unlawful; the assessment had to investigate all potential needs (see para 3.88 above).

9.89   Where a person's assessment identifies a need that could be met by services under section 2(1)(c)) – for instance in a day centre –that need must be met. If the appropriate centre is full, merely placing that person's name on the waiting list is likely to be an inadequate response (unless the wait is known to be reasonably short). This situation was considered by Sedley J in *R v Islington LBC ex p Rixon*[119] where he held:

> The duty owed to the applicant personally by virtue of section 2(1) of the Chronically Sick and Disabled Persons Act 1970 includes the provision of recreational facilities outside the home to an extent which Islington accepts is greater than the care plan provides for. But the local authority has, it appears, simply taken existing unavailability of further facilities as an insuperable obstacle to any further attempt to make provision. The lack of a day care centre has been treated, however reluctantly, as a complete answer to the question of provision for Jonathan's needs. As McCowan LJ explained in the *Gloucestershire* case, the section 2(1) exercise is needs-led and not resource-led. To say this is not to ignore the existing resources either in terms of regular voluntary care in the home or in budgetary terms. These, however, are balancing and not blocking factors.

For further consideration of waiting lists, see para 3.181 above.

9.90   It follows that if a person's care arrangements are being met, satisfactorily, at a particular day centre, then that day centre cannot be closed without the council having undertaken a 'detailed analysis'[120] to satisfy itself that the needs can be met elsewhere. In most situations there is no set choreography that has to be followed between a proposal to close a day centre and the care planning for those attending. Generally what occurs will be characterised (in the words of Stadlen J in *R (B) v Worcestershire County Council*[121]) as:

> a multi-staged decision-making process [where] it is not possible at the first stage of the process or of closure to identify where the people will go, what their needs will be and whether those places will satisfy their needs.

Stadlen J accepted,[122] however, that in cases where service users have high level and very specific needs the care planning and the closure proposals

---

118   (1997–98) 1 CCLR 168, QBD.
119   (1997–98) 1 CCLR 119 at 126D, QBD.
120   See *R (B) v Worcestershire County Council* [2009] EWHC 2915 (Admin), (2010) 13 CCLR 13 at paras 76, 86 and 104.
121   [2009] EWHC 2915 (Admin), (2010) 13 CCLR 13 at para 85.
122   [2009] EWHC 2915 (Admin), (2010) 13 CCLR 13

may have to be linked – for example if the authority was not sure that it could meet the disabled person's assessed needs at an alternative placement.

Educational facilities

9.91 The educational service required in this case may be either home-based or otherwise. The wording of section 2(1)(c) suggests that the service provided by the authority consists of enabling the disabled person to have access[123] to an (already existing) educational facility – rather than the provision of the educational facility itself and case law confirms that the s2 duty does not require the provision of 'purely education facilities'.[124] Potentially, however, the scope of the educational obligation is wide. In particular the subsection appears to enable the provision of:

a) services for which there is an overlapping NHS responsibility (eg, communication assistance via speech synthesisers, speech therapy, hearing and writing aids etc); and

b) services to support disabled (adult) students. In *R(M) v Birmingham City Council*[125] for example Cranston J considered that it would include personal care assistance at the educational facility as well as escorted travel to and from it – and potentially it could include the provision of additional facilities at the institution. LAC (93)12[126] gives specific guidance on the these responsibilities, and in particular stresses that CSDPA 1970 s2(1)(c) covers funding the personal care requirements of such students so as to enable them to pursue their studies (even if those studies are undertaken outside the local authority's area). The relevant part of the circular states as follows:

> 9. Social services departments have been reminded of their duty under s2(1)(c) of the Chronically Sick and Disabled Persons Act 1970 to make arrangements for assisting a disabled person who is ordinarily resident in their area in taking advantage of educational facilities available to him/her, (even where provision is made outside that local authority's area), if they are satisfied that it is necessary in order to meet that person's needs. Such assistance might, in appropriate cases include the funding by the local authority of the personal care required to enable the student in question to pursue his/her studies. It is, of course, for the authority to decide, in each case, what the individual's needs are, and how they are to be met.

123 In such cases there will be a complimentary duty on the educational establishment to make reasonable adjustments under the Equality Act 2010 – for consideration of this question, see S Broach, L Clements and J Read, *Disabled Children: a legal handbook*, Legal Action Group, 2010 at chapter 9 (free to view at www.ncb.org.uk/cdc/resources/legal_handbook.aspx.
124 Per Jowitt J, in *R v Further Education Funding Council and Bradford MBC ex p Parkinson* (1996) *Times* 31 October.
125 [2009] EWHC 688 (Admin).
126 See paras 9–11.

10. Disabled students attending higher education courses may be eligible to receive up to three Disabled Students Allowances[127] from the local education authority, as part of their mandatory award. These allowances are for a non-medical helper, major items of special equipment, or minor items such as tapes or braille paper. They are aimed at helping students with costs related to their course, and are not intended to meet other costs arising from their disability which would have to be met irrespective of whether or not they were in a course. For those attending further education courses, similar support may be provided at the discretion of the LEA.

11 There may be occasions where the social services department is asked to consider the provision of additional care support for an individual who will receive a Disabled Students Allowance or discretionary support from the LEA. It will, therefore, be appropriate in some circumstances for the support for an individual's personal care needs to be provided jointly by the SSD and the LEA.

9.92   The judgment in *R v Islington LBC ex p Rixon* also considered the interplay between the duties owed under CSDPA 1970 s2(1)(c) and the general duty under Education Act 1944 s41[128] which obliges education authorities to secure adequate further education facilities for (amongst others) adults who have learning difficulties. Sedley J considered that for persons with the gravest learning difficulties the section 41 duty might be met by the provision of facilities under CSDPA 1970 s2. He suggested, however, that if this was the case, the appropriate remedy for an alleged breach of the section 41 duty was (in the first instance) via the secretary of state's default powers under the Act (default powers are further considered at para 26.231 below).

9.93   Although children with Special Educational Needs cease to benefit from Part IV of the Education Act 1996 on adulthood, the Learning and Skills Act 2000 s139A (section 140 in Wales) provides some continuity, by requiring that all young people with statements of SEN have a learning difficulty assessment in their final year of school (and providing councils with a power to assess those without such a statement).[129]

---

127 The criteria for Disabled Students Allowances have been revised (see the Education (Student Support) Regulations 2009 as amended by the Education (Student Support) Regulations 2009 (Amendment) Regulations 2010) and for the current guidance on Disabled Students' Allowances see *Disabled Students' Allowances. Higher Education Student Finance in England 2011/12 Academic Year* at www.assist-tech.co.uk/ DSA1112.html#mozTocId464912 and generally see K Grehan, *Life, not numbers a report into the experiences of disabled students in higher education using personal care packages,* NUS, 2010.

128 As substituted by Further and Higher Education Act 1992 s11. See also DFE circular 1/93 *The Further and Higher Education Act 1992 Guidance* (WOC 15/93 in Wales) and *Duties and Powers: The Law Governing the Provision of Further Education to Students with Learning Difficulties and/or Disabilities,* HMSO, 1996.

129 Department for Children, Schools and Families (2010) *Supporting young people with learning difficulties to participate and progress – incorporating guidance on learning difficulty assessments* at para 3.4 and see also *R (Alloway) v Bromley LBC* [2008] EWHC 2449 (Admin). For analysis of local authority obligations under the 2010 Act – see S Broach, L Clements and J Read, *Disabled Children: a legal handbook,* Legal Action Group, 2010 at chapter 10 (free to view at www.ncb.org.uk/cdc/resources/ legal_handbook.aspx).

Travel and other assistance

9.94 CSDPA 1970 s2(1)(d) concerns the provision of travel assistance or facilities to enable a disabled person to travel from his or her home in order to participate in any community based services provided under CSDPA 1970 s2 and NAA 1948 s29.[130] In relation to services not provided under section 29, but which are of a similar nature, the local authority has a discretion to provide assistance under section 2(1)(d) ('with the approval of the authority').

9.95 Where a local authority has assessed a person as needing community based services provided under the 1970 or 1948 Acts, it must consider the transport needs, to access these services. It cannot assume that a carer is willing or able to provide this (see para 16.60 below) and, as noted below, cannot assume that a person is able to fund this service themselves – for example through the use of their mobility allowance. The care plan must therefore address this question and a failure to provide for an appropriate and flexible arrangement will amount to maladministration.[131]

9.96 While social services authorities are empowered (but not obliged) to charge for such transport services[132] (see para 10.39 below), in assessing a person's ability to pay, his or her mobility component of disability living allowance (DLA) (if received) must be ignored.[133] It remains, however, a moot point as to whether a local authority could determine that a person did not have a need for transport under section 2(1)(d) because he or she was in receipt of the DLA mobility component. A blanket policy of this nature would, of course, amount to a fettering of the council's duty. Even in individual cases, such a decision may be unreasonable, since a person's need to be compensated for limitations of mobility covers a wide range of situations and expenses (eg additional car use expenses, taxi costs, wheelchair servicing and repair costs, the travel costs of an escort and so on): in such circumstances, for a council to expect a disabled person to use his or her mobility allowance solely (or predominantly) to offset its liability under section 2(1)(d) would seem unreasonable.

9.97 The Welsh Ombudsman has found maladministration where a local authority refused to provide transport to a day centre for a new service user because she was in receipt of the DLA mobility component. This did not apply to existing service users. Systematic maladministration was found on the basis there was an absence of any policy framework and no written guidelines on the eligibility of clients who could use local authority run transport.[134]

9.98 In general, where transport is required in order that a disabled child attend a school specified in a special educational needs statement, it will

---

130 Travel assistance under NAA 1948 s29 is considered at para 9.58 above.
131 Complaint no 07C03887 against Bury MBC, 14 October 2009 paras 27 and 45.
132 Although in Wales there is no longer any power to charge for transport to services see para 10.40 below.
133 Social Security Contributions and Benefits Act 1992 s73(14).
134 Complaint no B2004/0180 against Newport City Council, 31 August 2006.

be for the education department to provide this.[135] Occasionally a disabled parent may be unable get a non-disabled child to school – or to some other location – because the parent's impairment renders him or her unable to undertake this task. In such cases, there is often agreement as to the need for transport, but a dispute as to whether this is the responsibility of the adult social services or of the children's services department. This question is considered at para 3.44 below – however, as a general rule the need should be deemed to be a need of the disabled adult (a need to discharge a usual parenting role) and accordingly addressed in the parent's community care assessment.

9.99   The application of any transport policy affecting disabled and older people, engages the Equality Act 2010. It follows that all such polices must be considered from the perspective of the authority's public sector equality duty (s149 – see para 2.32 above). Accordingly a failure at a general level to consider this duty when making changes to such a policy will constitute maladministration,[136] as will such a failure on an individual level – for example a failure by a council to provide appropriate home transport for a disabled child after attending an after-school club.[137] Regardless of any equality obligations, it will of course be maladministration to change a transport arrangement (eg changing the provider of this service) without discussing this with the service user.[138]

Blue Badge Scheme

9.100   CSDPA 1970 s21 (as subsequently amended) requires motor vehicle badges to be made available for the benefit of disabled people and for regulations to be issued concerning the operation of this scheme, now known as the Blue Badge Scheme. As at March 2010 it was estimated that there were over 2.55 million such badges across England.[139]

9.101   The detail of the scheme is set out in regulations in both England[140] and Wales;[141] and in 2008 guidance was also issued in England.[142] As a result of amendments made in 2007 the English scheme provides for two categories of person who may be issued with a badge: the first, being

135 This may even be the case where the statement provides that 'the mother [is] to be responsible for transport to and from the school at her own expense', see *R v Havering LBC ex p K* (1997) *Times* 18 November.

136 See the local government ombudsman report concerning complaints against seven councils commencing no 07B15825 against Havant Borough Council, 28 September 2009.

137 *Bedfordshire County Council v D* [2009] EWCA Civ 6789.

138 Summary of a report issued under section 21 of the Public Services Ombudsman (Wales) Act 2005, Case Number: 200900664 (2010).

139 Blue Badge Scheme Statistics *Statistical Release*. November 2010, Department for Transport.

140 The Disabled Persons (Badges for Motor Vehicles) (England) Regulations 2000 SI No 682, as amended – principally by the Disabled Persons (Badges for Motor Vehicles) (England) (Amendment) Regulations 2007 SI No 2531.

141 The Disabled Persons (Badges For Motor Vehicles) (Wales) Regulations 2000 SI No 1786 (W).

142 Department for Transport (2008) *The Blue Badge Scheme Local Authority Guidance (England)*.

persons who are referred to as 'eligible without further assessment'. These are people more than two years old who:

- receive the Higher Rate of the Mobility Component of the Disability Living Allowance; and/or
- are registered blind; and/or
- receive a War Pensioner's Mobility Supplement.

On furnishing the relevant proof of these qualifying factors, applicants in this category are eligible for a badge.

9.102   The second category comprises persons whose eligibility depends upon an assessment, and these are persons who:

- drive a vehicle regularly, have a severe disability in both arms, and are unable to operate, or have considerable difficulty in operating, all or some types of parking meter; and/or
- are over two years of age and are unable to walk or have very considerable difficulty in walking because of a permanent and substantial disability.
- Are under the age of two and:
  - have a condition that requires that they be always accompanied by bulky medical equipment which cannot be carried around with the child without great difficulty; and/or
  - have a condition that requires that they must always be kept near a motor vehicle so that they can, if necessary, be treated for that condition in the vehicle or taken quickly in the vehicle to a place where they can be so treated.

9.103   Applicants who are refused a badge are entitled to appeal – and it will be maladministration to fail to advise of this entitlement.[143] Although local authorities are entitled to charge £2 for processing Blue Badge applications, they are advised[144] not to claim it, since it costs substantially more than this to collect and process this sum. In 2011 the Department for Transport published a proposals for reform of the scheme,[145] which include permitting councils to increase the processing charge (from in 2012).

9.104   In Wales the scheme operates along similar (but not identical) lines,[146] and reforms are being considered[147] that would align the Welsh arrangements more closely with those in England.

---

143 Complaint no 09 009 572 against Redbridge LBC, 11 August 2010.
144 Department of Health (2006) *Care Services Efficiency Programme 'Blue Badge Initiative' Report*, para 2.5.
145 Department for Transport (2011) *Reform of the Blue Badge Scheme* at www2.dft.gov.uk/ transportforyou/access/bluebadge/reform/index.html
146 Eg the scheme does not (at July 2011) cover children under the age of 3 or people with severe disabilities in both arms who drive a vehicle and are unable to operate or have difficulty in operating parking meters or pay and display equipment.
147 See WAG (2010) *A Modern Blue Badge Scheme for Wales: Action Plan for key stakeholders January 2010* at http://wales.gov.uk/docs/det/publications/ 100712bluebadgeactionplanen.pdf

Home adaptations and disabled facilities

9.105   CSDPA 1970 s2 (1)(e) reads as follows:

> The provision of assistance for that person in arranging for the carrying out of any works of adaptation in his home or the provision of any additional facilities designed to secure his greater safety, comfort or convenience.

9.106   Section 2(1)(e) is in two parts; one concerned with adaptations (ie, significant works, possibly of a structural nature) and the other with the provision of additional facilities (ie, works involving the provision of fixtures and fittings and equipment). As noted above (para 9.78 above) it has been suggested that section 2(1)(a) may also require the provision of certain disabled facilities.

9.107   In relation to 'additional facilities' the duty on the authority is to provide these ('the provision of'), whereas in relation to adaptations the duty is stated as being the 'provision of assistance . . . in arranging for the carrying out of'. Whether the difference in wording is legally significant is not clear. On the face of it, the 'provision of assistance;' might mean no more than assistance in finding a suitable architect or builder or assistance with a grant application form. The guidance in relation to disabled facilities grants suggests, however, that the duty is more substantial, namely a duty to ensure that appropriate works are carried out including, for instance, the provision of financial assistance.

Adaptations

9.108   The social services obligation under CSDPA 1970 s2(1)(e) to assist in arranging works of adaptation is a specific duty and arises once an assessment has concluded that it is necessary for this service to be provided. In legislative terms it is distinct from the responsibility born by the housing authority[148] under Housing Grants, Construction and Regeneration Act (HGCRA) 1996 Part I to provide (subject to a means test[149]) disabled facilities grants (DFGs) for such works. The procedures for securing such grants are considered in detail at para 15.27 below. Unfortunately, however, the manner in which authorities discharge these two responsibilities often results in considerable confusion and delay and has resulted in numerous complaints to the local government ombudsman.

Interface with the disabled facilities grant obligation

9.109   The suggestion has been made that since the duty under the 1970 Act only arises where the authority is satisfied its assistance is 'necessary', that this duty does not in general arise (if at all) until after a DFG application has been determined.[150] This is an unattractive argument for a number of reasons, not least the very different nature of the two obligations. By way

---

148   Notwithstanding that the two authorities will frequently be one and the same.
149   The means test for DFGs depends upon the financial resources of the disabled person and his or her partner.See para 15.96 below.
150   See *R (Fay) v Essex CC* [2004] EWHC 879 (Admin) at [28].

of example, the HGCRA 1996 permits a delay of six months in the payment of a grant (see para 15.101 below). Given that the need for adaptations is often urgent and the fact that the section 2(1)(e) duty has no such deferment proviso, it would arguably be unlawful for a social services authority to refuse to assess a person's needs for an adaptation under the 1970 Act on the ground that it was possible that at some time in the future that a DFG may be awarded.

9.110   Although the relationship between the duties under the 1996 and 1970 Acts is best characterised as one of overlapping and complementary responsibilities, the existence of the two provisions has in practice created a pretext for considerable administrative delay.[151]

9.111   In general, social services in assessing a need for assistance under section 2(1)(e) will require that an application be made to the housing authority for a DFG. At this stage, the applicant is likely to be told that an occupational therapist will have to undertake an assessment of the need for which there may be a lengthy waiting list. The problem of chronic delay in this context is well documented and, notwithstanding many critical reports from the local government ombudsman, persists.

9.112   When such delay occurs and the grant is being processed by a separate council (ie a district council) the appropriate response from the social services authority will be to assist the disabled person in resolving the problem – by actively intervening in the process if needs be. Such delay, however, does not of itself absolve the social services authority of its separate responsibility under CSDPA 1970 s2(1)(e): indeed it is maladministration for a council to fail to appreciate that it has a duty under the 1970 Act to provide adaptations, separate from the obligation to process DFGs.[152] This point was emphasised in circular LAC (90)7,[153] which referred to the social services department as the 'lead body', and (as noted below) states that its duty to act remains regardless of the housing authority's actions.[154]

9.113   Typically home adaptations concern such matters as stair lifts, ground-floor extensions, doorway widening, ramps and wheelchair accessible showers. Unlike under HGCRA 1996 Part I (considered at para 15.63 below), the 1970 Act imposes no requirement that work be either 'appropriate' or 'reasonable and practicable'. All the 1970 statute requires is that the social services authority be satisfied that the works are necessary in order to meet the needs of the disabled person (by securing his or her greater safety, comfort or convenience).

9.114   Department of Health guidance, LAC (90)7, illustrates this difference of approach (at paras 15–17 and also at para 58):

---

151 See paras 9.121 and 15.113 for a general analysis of the ombudsman's comments on such delay.
152 Complaint no 05/C/13157 against Leeds City Council, 20 November 2007.
153 At para 14. LAC (90)7 was issued jointly as Department of the Environment circular 10/90. While DoE circular 10/90 has been withdrawn (and superseded by new guidance circular 17/96), LAC (90)7 remains in force (see DoE 4/98 and LASSL (99)21).
154 LAC (90)7 para 15.

15. The existing responsibilities of [social service's authorities] under s2 of the CSDP Act are unchanged. In cases of their duty to make arrangements for home adaptations, under s2(1)(e), the responsibility will, in many instances, be effectively discharged on their behalf by the housing authority, by the giving of a disabled facilities grant. However, the [social services authority's] duty to act remains, and they may be called upon to meet this duty in two ways. The first is where the needs as assessed by the [social services] authority exceed the scope for provision by the housing authority under s114(3) of the 1989 [Local Government and Housing] Act[155] and where the authority decline to use their discretionary powers under s114(4). If the [social services] authority deem the need to be established, then it will be their responsibility in these circumstances to make arrangements for this need to be met under s2 of the CSDP Act.

16. Such a responsibility might arise when for instance the [social services] authority considers there is need related to the individual's social needs that demands a greater level of provision than is required for the disability alone, and where the housing authority chooses not to exercise its discretionary powers. This may occur, for example, where the size of a bedroom for a disabled child is required to be greater than is necessary for sleeping, because it needs to fulfil the role of bed/sitting room to provide more independent social space.

17. The second instance where *the [social services] authority may find they have a continuing duty to provide assistance concerns cases where a disabled person asks the [social services] authority for financial assistance, under section 2(1)(e) of the CSDP Act, with that part of the costs of an adaptation which he is expected to finance himself in the light of the test of resources for the disabled facilities grant. On occasion, this could be as much as the total costs of the adaptation. In such cases, the [social services] authority still has a duty to assist.*[156] However, in order to maintain consistency with the new arrangements for disabled facilities grants, the [social services] authority may wish to use their existing powers to charge for their services (under section 17 of the [Health and Social Services and Social Security Adjudications] Act 1983) to recover the full cost of any assistance given, provided that they consider that the client is able to afford to repay this. In examining the question of financial assistance, [social services] authorities are recommended to bear in mind that the amount of grant approved will have been calculated on the basis of a test of resources (described in more detail in paragraphs 64 and 65 and Appendix II below). [Social services] authorities should not try to make their own separate assessment of what a grant applicant is expected to pay; but they might consider whether, in their opinion, the meeting of those costs would cause hardship.[157] The method of charging or of recovery of costs is for the [social services] authority to decide; but alternatives which might be considered include loans, with or

155 Now Housing Grants, Construction and Regeneration Act 1996 Part 1 – see para 15.33 below.

156 This section in italics (emphasis added) has been the subject of adverse comment by Richards J – see para 15.105 below.

157 Charging for domiciliary services is considered in detail at chapter 10. The reference to 'hardship' in the circular is unhelpful: Health and Social Services and Social Security Adjudications Act (HASSASSAA) 1983 s17 merely requires that the disabled person satisfy the authority that his or her means are insufficient for it to be reasonably practicable for him or her to pay for the service – in this respect see in particular para 10.8 below.

without interest, possibly secured in either case by a charge on the property[158] or the placing of a charge on the property for a set period.

9.115 Similar advice was given in now revoked circular guidance 17/96 issued by the Department of the Environment (see para 15.38 below), namely:

Role of the social services authority to assist with adaptations
5. Social services authorities' responsibilities under s2 Chronically Sick and Disabled Persons Act 1970 to make arrangements for home adaptations are not affected by the grants legislation. Where an application for DFG has been made, those authorities may be called upon to meet this duty in two ways:
(a) where the assessed needs of a disabled person exceeds the scope for provision by the housing authority under section 23 of the 1996 Act; and
(b) where an applicant for DFG has difficulty in meeting is assessed contribution determined by the means test and seeks financial assistance from the authority.

6. In such cases, where the social services authority determine that the need has been established, it remains their duty to assist even where the local housing authority either refuse or are unable to approve the application. Social services authorities may also consider using their powers under section 17 of the Health and Social Services and Social Security Adjudications Act 1983 to charge for their services where appropriate.

9.116 Where a DFG is inadequate to cover the full cost of the necessary works, the social services authority can make up the shortfall by way of support under section 2(1)(e) and/or the housing authority can assist using its powers under the Regulatory Reform (Housing Assistance) (England and Wales) Order 2002 (see para 15.85 below). In either situation the relevant council can impose conditions on such a 'top-up' payment. In *R (BG) v Medway Council*[159] the High Court held that it was not unreasonable for a local authority in a case such as this to make the payment by way of a loan secured as a 20 year legal charge on the home which would not be repayable, unless the disabled person ceased to reside at the property during that period and that any amount repayable would be subject to interest. In this case the authority had agreed that in the event of repayment being required it would have regard to the family's personal and financial circumstances and would not act unreasonably by insisting repayment immediately or on terms that would result in financial hardship.

9.117 Where a DFG application is not completed or fails on financial grounds and it is not unreasonable for the authority to believe that the applicant may have sufficient resources to fund the adaptations, the authority may be entitled to refuse to provide support under the 1970 Act on the ground that its support was not 'necessary'. Such a situation arose

---

158 Such a charge could presumably only be secured on the property with the owner's consent as neither HASSASSAA 1983 s17, nor the Welsh Charging Measure 2010 empower authorities to create such charges (unlike section 22).
159 [2005] EWHC 1932 (Admin), (2005) 8 CCLR 448.

in *R (Spink) v Wandsworth BC*[160] where the applicants argued unsuccessfully that having decided that the adaptations were required, the authority was obliged to provide them under the 1970 Act. In the High Court[161] held that in deciding whether it was *necessary* to provide a service to meet an assessed need a local authority could have regard to the applicant's resources 'when deciding under section 2 of the 1970 Act whether it is necessary for it to make arrangements to meet the claimant children's needs' (at para 50).

9.118   Accordingly, Wandsworth was entitled to take into account the parents' financial resources when deciding whether it was necessary for them to fund the works of adaptation. This interpretation differed from guidance in LAC (90)7 which advised:

> ... the welfare authority may find they have a continuing duty to provide assistance concerns cases where a disabled person asks the welfare authority for financial assistance, under section 2(1)(e) of the CSDP Act, with that part of the costs of an adaptation which he is expected to finance himself in the light of the test of resources for the disabled facilities grant. On occasion, this could be as much as the total costs of the adaptation. In such cases, the welfare authority still has a duty to assist.

9.119   The judge held that to a limited degree this advice was incorrect, stating:

> It pays insufficient attention to the second stage of the analysis under section 2, namely the decision whether it is 'necessary' for the local social services authority to make arrangements to meet the relevant needs. In any event, in so far as it states that an authority is under a duty to make such arrangements irrespective of whether the disabled person (or, by implication, the parent of a disabled child) has the resources to meet the needs, I take the view that the circular is wrong.

9.120   The approach adopted by the courts in *Spink* was followed in *Freeman v Lockett*[162] where Tomlinson J stated (in the context of a personal injuries damages assessment) that it 'might be said that it is unnecessary [for a local authority to provide adaptations for] . . . a person who has received an award of damages calculated so as to cater for all his or her foreseeable needs in a reasonable manner, at any rate for so long as the award can be seen to be fulfilling that purpose'.

Delay

9.121   As noted above, the local authority duty under the 1970 Act to assist with adaptations is all too frequently associated with unreasonable delay. In assessing whether this is unlawful or constitutes maladministration, it is necessary to consider separately the statutory obligations under the CSDPA 1970 s2 and the HGCRA 1996 Part I. In relation to the duty under CSDPA 1970 s2, the principles relevant to the assessment and provision

---

160 [2005] EWCA Civ 302, (2005) 8 CCLR 272.
161 [2004] EWHC 2314 (Admin), [2005] 1 WLR 258, affirmed on appeal – [2005] EWCA Civ 302, (2005) 8 CCLR 272.
162 [2006] EWHC 102 (QB).

of services timetable (under NHSCCA 1990 s47) apply – see para 3.181 above. The assessment will generally require specialist involvement and this may result in delay. The local government ombudsman has produced a number of reports on this issue.[163] A 1991[164] report for example dealt with a situation where the complainant had (among other things) waited nine months for an occupational therapist's (OT) assessment. In finding maladministration, the report noted:

> The Council say that they suffered from a shortage of OTs during 1989; while I recognise that this is a national problem, nevertheless the Council still retain their responsibility to assess their client's needs. If sufficient OTs are not available, they may need to find another way of assessing those needs.

9.122　The finding in this case does not of course mean that delays of less than nine months are acceptable: indeed the ombudsman has suggested that for even complex assessments, the time from an OT referral to the completion of his or her report would not exceed 3 months.[165] The finding means, however, that any council, knowing that the use of OTs for an assessment will cause a substantial delay, is guilty of maladministration when it opts to use OTs (ie, it is maladministration the moment such a procedure is adopted).

9.123　Unlike the CSDPA 1970, HGCRA 1996 s36 allows for the delayed payment of a DFG – up to a maximum of 12 months following the date of the application. The issue of delay in relation to DFGs is considered further at para 15.101 below.

Equipment and additional facilities

9.124　CSDPA 1970 s2(1)(e) also covers the provision of 'additional facilities' designed to secure the disabled person's greater safety, comfort or convenience. This includes all manner of fittings and gadgets such as handrails, alarm systems, hoists, movable baths, adapted switches and handles, and so on.

9.125　The importance of the provision of appropriate equipment in promoting the independence and quality of disabled peoples' lives has been emphasised in much guidance and its speedy provision is an England performance indicator.[166] The *National Service Framework for Older People*,[167] for instance, at para 2.48 advises that:

- services should take a preventive approach, recognising that effective equipment provision (including for people with moderate disabilities) is likely to:

163　See para 26.111 below where the ombudsman's role is considered.
164　Complaint no 90/C/0336 against Redbridge LBC, 3 October 1991.
165　Complaint no 07/A/11108 against Surrey County Council, 11 November 2008.
166　Indicator AO/D54 (2006–07): the percentage of items of equipment and adaptations delivered within seven working days – see para 2.16 above.
167　See para 19.3 below.

- help older people to maintain their independence and live at home
- slow down deterioration in function and consequent loss of confidence and self-esteem
- prevent accidents
- prevent pressure sore damage
- support and better protect the health of carers
- services should be timely and resolve the frequently long delays which inhibit older people's discharge from hospital, or their safety and confidence in coping at home.[168]

9.126   In 2000 and 2002 the Audit Commission published highly critical reports on the state of public provision of equipment for disabled people.[169] The 2002 report found that equipment services were in a parlous state; that users reported 'long delays for equipment of dubious quality'. Its recommendation of a substantial overhaul of the service led to a government initiative to establish integrated 'community equipment services' where both NHS and social services equipment could be accessed at a single point. Each integrated community equipment service is required to meet the following criteria:[171]

- Revenue funding from pooled health and social services contributions using Health Act 1999 flexibilities.
- A single operational manager for the service.[170]
- A board to advise the manager, whose members include representatives of stakeholder organisations.
- Unified stock.

9.127   The guidance accompanying this initiative[172] defined community equipment as follows:

> Community equipment is equipment for home nursing usually provided by the NHS, such as pressure relief mattresses and commodes, and equipment for daily living such as shower chairs and raised toilet seats, usually provided by local authorities. It also includes, but is not limited to:
> • Minor adaptations, such as grab rails, lever taps and improved domestic lighting.
> • Ancillary equipment for people with sensory impairments, such as liquid level indicators, hearing loops, assistive listening devices and flashing doorbells.

---

168 This final point is given considerable emphasis in the now superseded NHS hospital discharge guidance, *Discharge from hospital: pathway, process and practice*, Department of Health, February 2003, appendix 5.3.1 pp71–72 (see also para 5.8 below).

169 *Fully Equipped: The Provision of Equipment to Older or Disabled People by the NHS and Social Services in England and Wales*, 29 March 2000 and *Fully Equipped 2002 – Assisting Independence*, 27 June 2002. Concern about the quality of equipment provision remain: in 2009 one of the performance indicators introduced by the Department of Health initiative *Transforming Community Services* – indicator 21 Department of Health (2009) *Transforming Community Services Quality Framework: Guidance for Community Services*.

170 Now NHSA 2006 s75/NHS(W)A 2006 s33.

171 *Community Equipment Services* HSC 2001/008; LAC (2001)13 para 8.

172 LAC (2001)13 para 7.

- Communication aids for people with speech impairments.
- Wheelchairs for short term loan, but not those for permanent wheelchair users, as these are prescribed and funded by different NHS services.[173]
- Telecare equipment such as fall alarms, gas escape alarms and health state monitoring for people who are vulnerable.

9.128 The above guidance makes plain that the provision of some forms of equipment may be construed as joint social services/NHS responsibility. Similarly, some forms of equipment can be viewed as a joint social services/housing authority responsibility. Circular LAC (90)7 seeks to clarify this question (at para 19):

> ... equipment which can be installed and removed with little or no structural modification to the dwelling should usually be considered the responsibility of the [social services] authority. However, items such as stair lifts and through-floor lifts, which are designed to facilitate access into or around the dwelling would, in the view of the Secretaries of State, be eligible for disabled facilities grant. With items such as electric hoists, it is suggested that any structural modification of the property – such as strengthened joists or modified lintels – could be grant aidable under the disabled facilities grant, but that the hoisting equipment itself should be the responsibility of the [social services] authority.

9.129 In Wales the relevant guidance, *Fulfilled Lives, Supportive Communities* (2009)[174] noted that community equipment services were 'in need of urgent modernisation' and that the current arrangements meant that resources being wasted and poor and unsafe practices existed. It advises that Local Health Boards and local authorities put in place formal agreements under NHS(W)A 2006 s33 (see para 13.127) covering pooled funding arrangements for equipment for daily living, home nursing equipment, and equipment for disabled children.

Minor adaptations under £1,000

9.130 In England, minor adaptations costing less than £1,000 should be provided free of charge by virtue of regulations made under the Community Care (Delayed Discharges etc) Act (CC(DD)A) 2003 ss15 and 16.[175]

9.131   Many minor adaptations are relatively routine and straightforward and do not, therefore, require the input of an occupational therapist before being approved and provided. The College of Occupational Therapists has produced an excellent two volume guide which identifies a range of minor adaptations for which there is a clear consensus that initial assessment by

---

173 See para 13.76 below concerning the provision of permanent wheelchairs.
174 WAG (2009) *Fulfilled Lives, Supportive Communities. Guidelines for Developing and Integrating Community Equipment Services in Wales.*
175 Community Care (Delayed Discharges etc) Act (Qualifying Services) (England) Regulations 2003 SI No 1196 and see also Department for Communities and Local Government (2006) *Delivering Housing Adaptations for Disabled People: a good practice guide*, para 2.26 – and see para 15.71 below.

an OT is generally not required (such as grab and hand rails, threshold ramps and drop kerbs, kitchen and bathroom taps and handles).[176]

Reform

9.132   In 2007 the government in England investigated the possibility of a 'retail solution'[177] to the way equipment is provided: essentially that social services and the NHS would issue users with a 'prescription' that could be exchanged for free equipment at an approved/accredited retailer. Although it appears that this programme has now been accorded a lower priority in 2010, a Department of Health led team – the Transforming Community Equipment Services team – established a 'detailed imple-mentation pathway' for such a scheme (by both NHS bodies and local authorities) together with a national catalogue and proposed tariff for Simple Aids to Daily Living.[178]

9.133   There is evidence that some authorities no longer stock 'small items of equipment' in their stores, and instead signpost those in need, to where such items can be purchased. The legality of such approach will depend upon what is meant by a 'small item'; the procedure by which this policy decision was reached; and the extent to which it is applied as a 'blanket policy'. In principle, such policies would appear questionable given that the basic requirement is that such equipment 'be provided free of charge'[179] and the Department of Health 2010 policy guidance advises that 'councils should not assume that low-level needs will always be equated with low-level services or that complex or critical needs will always require complex, costly services in response'.[180]

Holidays

> Facilitating the taking of holidays by that person, whether at holiday homes or otherwise and whether provided under arrangements made by the authority or otherwise.

9.134   The power of social services authorities to provide holiday homes under NAA 1948 s29 (see para 9.57) is complemented by the duty under CSDPA 1970 s2(1)(f) to facilitate the taking of holidays by disabled

---

176 College of Occupational Therapists, *Minor Adaptations Without Delay: A Practical Guide and Technical Specifications for Housing Associations*, 2002, accessible at www.housingcorp.gov.uk/server/show/ConWebDoc.7502.

177 Care Services Improvement Partnership (2007) *Community Equipment – a vision for the future*, CSIP Transforming Community Equipment and Wheelchair Services programme.

178 See the 'TCES national catalogue of equipment for independent daily living' at www.national-catalogue.org/smartassist/nationalcatalogue.

179 Department for Communities and Local Government (2006) *Delivering Housing Adaptations for Disabled People: a good practice guide*, para 2.26 – and see para 15.71 below.

180 Department of Health (2010) *Prioritising need in the context of Putting People First: a whole system approach to eligibility for social care. Guidance on Eligibility Criteria for Adult Social Care, England 2010* para 62.

persons: conceivably this might extend to the purchase of a caravan.[181] In *R v Ealing LBC ex p Leaman*[182] the council refused to consider a request made by the applicant for financial assistance in taking a privately arranged holiday – on the ground that it would only grant such assistance which it itself had arranged or sponsored. In quashing the council's decision Mann J held that:

> The effect of the general policy adumbrated by the council is, in my judgement, to excise the words 'or otherwise' where they second occur in section 2(1)(f). Accordingly, the London Borough were wrong in declining to consider any application which the Applicant might have made for assistance with his private holiday. Whether, having regard to a proper consideration of a person's needs, those needs required the making of a grant to a private holiday is an entirely different question. It is a question wholly within the province of the local authority. However, it was quite wrong for them to deprive themselves of the opportunity of asking that question.[183]

9.135　Holidays can amount to a form of respite care for carers – where they have a need for a break and it is not possible or desirable for the disabled person not to accompany them.[184] In such cases, the local authority may be able to fund the carer's holiday costs as a carers service under the Carers and Disabled Children Act 2000 (see para 16.92 below). In some cases, however, an authority will have to fund the full cost of the holiday under the 1970 Act (and not merely the additional costs attributable to the user's impairment), where for instance the carer's attendance is necessary (for instance as an escort) as was the case in *R v North Yorkshire CC ex p Hargreaves (No 2)*.[185]

9.136　　It is arguable that most community care assessments should identify a need for an annual holiday – it is something recognised as a 'need' by a large majority of the population. Such a need may be all the more important for disabled people to give them a break from the routine and exhaustion of living and caring for themselves. In *R (B) v Cornwall County Council*[186] the court was prepared to accept that holiday expenses could be included as a disability related expenditure for domiciliary care charging purposes (see para 10.34 below) and the it would seem a reasonable presumption that, in appropriate cases, a care plan will have a holiday component. This was accepted as the case for care home residents (when

---

181　ADASS (2009) *Personalisation and the law: Implementing Putting People First in the current legal framework* p15.

182　(1984) *Times* 10 February, QBD.

183　From pp4–5 of the transcript of the judgment.

184　However, in *R (JL) v Islington LBC* [2009] EWHC 458 (Admin) it was held in general terms that overnight respite care accommodation for a disabled person alone could not normally be classed as a 'holiday' for the purposes of section 2(1)(f) of the 1970 Act (para 98).

185　(1997–98) 1 CCLR 331, QBD.

186　*R (B) v Cornwall County Council and Brendon Trust* (interested party) [2009] EWHC 491(Admin) upheld on appeal: [2010] EWCA Civ 55, (2010) 13 CCLR 117.

national minimum standards were first produced for such services[187] –
Standard 14, para 14.4 of which stated:

> Service users in long-term placements have as part of the basic contract
> price the option of a minimum seven-day annual holiday outside the home,
> which they help choose and plan.

Meals

The provision of meals for that person whether in his home or elsewhere.

9.137   CSDPA 1970 s2(1)(g) covers the provision of meals at day centres (or
indeed anywhere) as well as meals in the disabled person's home such as
meals-on-wheels. The equivalent service for the elderly is governed by
HSPHA 1968 s45 (see para 19.17 below).

9.138   The origins of meals services (like home help services) owes much to
the conditions created by the Second World War and the mass discharge
of frail and ill older people from hospital (see para 9.77 below). Means and
Smith[188] describe the *ad hoc* development of services for older people by
voluntary sector groups during this period with the WRVS emerging
as the dominant player. The NAA 1948 continued this role[189] as well as
providing that a funding power (in relation to meals) should also be
available to district councils (a power now found in HASSASSAA 1983
Sch 9 Part II para 1 see para 9.177 below). The 1948 Act only empowered
local authority provision of meals via the funding of a voluntary sector
organisation (under section 31) but this restriction was removed by the
National Assistance Act 1948 (Amendment) Act 1962.[190]

9.139   There is a material difference the provision of a personal assistant to
help a disabled person prepare their meal (which is addressed by s2(1)(a))
and the provision of a meal (which is covered by s2(1)(g)). Which is provided, should depend upon the assessed need, rather than (for example)
the financial implication for the authority.[191] Supporting a disabled people
in the preparation of their own meals will be a service that is more likely to
promote their ability to live independently than the mere provision of a
cooked meal and may also address user choice.

---

187   Department of Health (2003) *Care Homes for Adults (18–65) and supplementary
      standards for care homes accommodating young people aged 16 and 17: national
      minimum standards care homes regulations* – though such standards [in England] have
      now been withdrawn – see para 7.94 above and in Wales see the Care Standards
      Inspectorate for Wales (2002) *National minimum standards for care homes for younger
      adults*, accessible at www.csiw.wales.gov.uk/docs/yng_adult_stands_e.pdf
188   R Means and R Smith, *From Poor Law to Community Care*, Policy Press, 1998,
      pp92–97.
189   Section 31 by empowered local authorities to make contributions 'to any voluntary
      sector organisation whose activities consist in or include the provision of recreation
      or meals for old people'.
190   These provisions were (save in relation to district councils – see para 9.177 below,
      HASSASSA 1983) in turn repealed by the Health Services and Public Health Act
      1968 (see para 19.17 below) and the 1968 provision (s13) was itself repealed by the
      NHS Act 1977.
191   Many councils impose a flat rate charge for meals (see para 10.13 below): a person on
      a low income may therefore be exempt from charging 'home help' but required to
      pay a not insignificant sum for their 'meals on wheels service'.

Telephone and ancillary equipment

> The provision for that person of, or assistance to that person in obtaining, a telephone and any special equipment necessary to enable him to use a telephone.

9.140　　CSDPA 1970 s2(1)(h) may 'cover the installation of a telephone line as well as the provision of an appropriate handset, loud telephone bell (or a flashing visual or vibrating signal), amplifiers, inductive couplers for personal hearing aids and visual transmission machines such as minicoms, faxes and possibly modems for computer email transmission etc.

Chronically Sick and Disabled Persons Act 1970 s2 and National Assistance Act 1948 s29

9.141　The rapid drafting[192] of CSDPA 1970 s2 has led to considerable confusion as to its status. The section commences with the clause '[w]here a local authority having functions under section 29 of the National Assistance Act 1948 are satisfied . . . ' and concludes 'it shall be the duty of that authority to make those arrangements in exercise of their functions under the said section 29'. It is not surprising therefore that CSDPA 1970 s2 has been considered as an extension to NAA 1948 s29 – to the extent that services identified under CSDPA 1970 s2 are in fact NAA 1948 s29 services: ie delivered as 'arrangements in exercise of . . . s29'.

9.142　　In the courts' view it is for this reason that CSDPA 1970 s2 services are not specifically listed as 'community care services' in National Health Service and Community Care Act (NHSCCA) 1990 s46 – since the reference in section 46 to services under NAA 1948 Part III includes CSDPA 1970 s2 services.[193] However, and conversely, when statutory provisions make specific reference to section 2 in addition to section 29, the courts have generally explained this in terms of *ex abundante cautela*[194] (from an abundance of caution).

9.143　　It follows that the assessment duty under NHSCCA 1990 s47(1) will require consideration of whether services under CSDPA 1970 s2 are 'called' for (see para 3.136 above), notwithstanding the absence of specific reference to this provision. This was explained by Collins J in *R v Kirklees MBC ex p Daykin*[195] in the following terms:

> . . . section 47 and section 2 go hand in hand. Parliament may in other Acts have specifically mentioned section 2 but that was for the purposes of those Acts and no doubt for the avoidance of any doubt. It seems to me quite

---

192　For a description of the speed with which the bill was drafted see *Be it Enacted*, RADAR, 1995 and see also the introduction paras I.17–I.19 above. Unfortunately there is nothing in the *Hansard* reports on the passage of the bill through Parliament to elucidate the confusing references to section 29.

193　Hansard (HC) Standing Committee E, cols 1055 et seq, 15 February 1990.

194　*R v Powys CC ex p Hambidge* (1997–98) 1 CCLR 182 at 189D, QBD, per Popplewell J.

195　(1997–98) 1 CCLR 512 at 525A, QBD.

clear that in the context of section 2 and section 47 the definition of 'community care services' is apt to include the services provided under section 2.

9.144   This interpretation of the status of CSDPA 1970 s2 adult care services must now be considered as settled law. It is probably the 'best fix' that can be achieved in terms of reconciling these two radically different statutes – both in terms of their origins and their philosophical outlook – and in terms of their relations with the other community care statutes.

9.145   However, having accepted that CSDPA 1970 s2 services are essentially a specifically enforceable species of services provided under the generic umbrella of NAA 1948 s29, certain collateral interpretative difficulties arise. For example NHSCCA 1990 s47(2) appears to create a different assessment procedure for CSDPA 1970 s2 services to those under the NHSCCA 1990 s46 community care statutes. As noted above (see para 3.18 above) the explanation advanced for this difference of treatment by the Department of Health (namely that section 47(2) assessments are required to be 'comprehensive') was rejected by Carnwath J in *R v Gloucestershire CC ex p RADAR*.[196]

9.146   A similar incongruity was exposed in *R v Gloucestershire CC ex p Mahfood*.[197] Here the respondent argued that if CSDPA 1970 s2 services were provided under NAA 1948 s29 it followed that a home help service could not be provided under CSDPA 1970 s2 notwithstanding that section 2(1)(a) is concerned with precisely such a service. The argument turned upon NAA 1948 s29(6), which prohibits services being provided under section 29 if they can be provided under the NHS Acts 2006. The 2006 Acts make provision for a home help service.[198] The argument, as already noted (para 9.68 above), was described as 'unattractive' by McCowan LJ.[199]

9.147   In *R v Powys CC ex p Hambidge*[200] the point in issue was the ability of local authorities to charge for services provided under CSDPA 1970 s2 notwithstanding that the provision that authorises charges to be levied for non-accommodation services (Health and Social Services and Social Security Adjudication Act (HASSASSAA) 1983 s17 – see para 10.5 below below) made no reference to services under CSDPA 1970 s2. The Court of Appeal accepted the view of the Department of Health that section 2 services 'are arranged by local authorities in exercise of their functions under s29 of the 1948 Act'[201] – and since HASSASSAA 1983 s17 refers to NAA 1948 s29 services, that was sufficient authority for charges to be levied.

196   (1997–98) 1 CCLR 476, QBD.
197   (1997–98) 1 CCLR 7, QBD.
198   This aspect is also considered at para 9.178 below.
199   (1997–98) 1 CCLR 7 at 17C, QBD.
200   (1997–98) 1 CCLR 458, CA, QBD.
201   Footnote 2 to the SSI advice note on non-accommodation charges, January 1994.

Chronically Sick and Disabled Persons Act 1970 s2 and the Children Act 1989

9.148 An additional difficulty stems from the differences between the CSDPA 1970 s2 and NAA 1948 s29 client groups. CSDPA 1970 s28A[202] provides that:

> This Act applies with respect to disabled children in relation to whom the local authority have functions under Part III of the Children Act 1989 as it applies in relation to persons to whom section 29 of the National Assistance Act 1948 applies.

9.149 Accordingly the CSDPA 1970 s2 client group includes all disabled people, whereas NAA 1948 s29 applies only to disabled people over 18 years of age. It follows that children's services provided under CSDPA 1970 s2 cannot be provided 'in exercise of . . . functions under . . . s29'.

9.150 In *R v Bexley LBC ex p B*[203] (see para 23.44 below) the respondent council sought to argue (amongst other things) that home care services provided to a disabled child were provided under the CA 1989 rather than under CSDPA 1970 s2. Latham J rejected the argument, holding that such services were provided under section 2 itself.[204]

9.151 Although the *Bexley* decision is authority for the fact that community based services provided to disabled children are generally provided under CSDPA 1970 s2, it did not address the question of whether or not they were delivered under the generic CA 1989 Part III umbrella. The question is of importance since, if they are, it would entitle local authorities to charge for such services (in pursuance of their powers under CA 1989 s29 – see para 23.78 below). The provenance of the section 2 duty in relation to disabled children was settled by the Court of Appeal in *R (Spink) v Wandsworth LBC*.[205] In the court's opinion:

> 34. . . . section 2 of the 1970 Act expressly provided that local authorities were to comply with their obligations under that section in the exercise of their functions under section 29 of the 1948 Act '*notwithstanding anything in any scheme made by the authority under section 29*'. Just as the secretary of state might be able to impose a duty on local authorities, enforceable by individuals, to exercise their functions under section 29, so section 2 of the 1970 Act could impose a similar duty.

> 35. Once this is appreciated, there is no difficulty in interpreting sections 2 and 28A of the 1970 Act as requiring local authorities to comply with the requirements of section 2, in so far as these apply to children, by the exercise of their functions under Part III of the Children Act, of which section 17 is particularly relevant.

---

202 Inserted by CA 1989 s108(5), Sch 13 para 27.
203 (2000) 3 CCLR 15, 31 July 1995, QBD.
204 (2000) 3 CCLR 15 at 23C, 31 July 1995, QBD.
205 [2004] EWHC 2314 (Admin), [2005] 1 WLR 258 at [34]–[35].

9.152   It follows, that in relation to disabled children, section 2 should be read as follows:

> Where a local authority having functions under Part III Children Act 1989 are satisfied in the case of a disabled child . . . it shall be the duty of that authority to make those arrangements in exercise of their functions under the said Part III.

9.153   Statutory recognition of the distinctiveness of CSDPA 1970 s2 services and services under the CA 1989 is found in Carers (Recognition and Services) Act 1989 s1(2)(a). This provision only applies when 'a local authority assess the needs of a disabled child for the purposes of the CA 1989 Part III or s2 of the CSDPA 1970'.

Services under the National Health Services Acts 2006

9.154   Most disabled people receive their domiciliary/community based services from social services authorities under CSDPA 1970 s2. These services, however, are only available to people who are 'substantially and permanently handicapped'[206] or who 'suffer from a mental disorder of any description'. Section 2 services are not therefore available to persons whose impairment is not 'permanent,' notwithstanding that it may be substantial. Domiciliary and community based services for such persons are generally provided by social services pursuant to duties under NHSA 2006 s254 and Sch 20 and NHS(W)A 2006 s192 and Sch 15. Frequently the persons covered by these provisions are referred to as 'ill people';[207] ie people who have a substantial impairment as a result of an accident or severe illness, but whose prognosis is that they will make a full recovery (and will not therefore be 'permanently handicapped'). The Acts, however, also cover services for a wider client group including older people, expectant mothers, drug and alcohol misusers as well as disabled people.

9.155   In discussing the provision of care services for ill people, one enters the minefield that marks the medical/social divide; a subject considered further in chapter 14. The NHS Acts 2006 attempt to demarcate the duties of the NHS and the social services authorities. Sections 1–3 of these Acts spell out the general nature of the NHS obligation in relation to disease prevention, the care and after-care of ill people. NHSA 2006 s254 (NHS(W)A 2006 s192) then outlines the services which are the responsibility of the social services authorities – these being amplified in NHSA 2006 Sch 20 (NHS(W)A 2006 Sch 15). NHSA 2006 s82 contains a requirement of co-operation between health and social care service providers (see para 13.35 below).

---

206   See para 9.25 above.
207   NHSA 2006 s275(1)/ NHS(W)A 2006 s206(1) defines illness as including mental disorder within the meaning of the MHA 1983 and any injury or disability requiring medical or dental treatment or nursing.

9.156   The text of NHSA 2006 s254(1) and Sch 20 paras 1–3[208] is set out in appendix A below.

Client group

9.157   The Act requires social services authorities to provide a variety of services for a diverse client group, certain services being restricted to particular client groups. There is no requirement that the persons be ordinarily resident within the social services authority's area.

9.158   The potential client group is wide, in that services can be provided for any adult in order to prevent illness – to which everyone is, of course, vulnerable. The provision of home help under NHSA 2006 Sch 20 para 3 has no age restriction on the person whose need triggers the service (ie, it applies to children as well as adults). It should also be noted that the provision of home helps is specified as being for the benefit of the 'household', rather than merely for the qualifying individual within the home.

9.159   NHSA 2006 Sch 20/ NHS(W)A 2006 Sch 15 paras 1 and 2 are subject to directions issued by the secretary of state (presently LAC (93)10 appendix 3[209] – see appendix B below where the full text of the directions is provided).

Mothers

9.160   The client group is restricted to 'expectant and nursing mothers (of any age)'.[210] The services available are without restriction, save only that the provision of accommodation is not permitted. The accommodation needs of such mothers are covered by NAA 1948 s21(1)(aa) (see para). It is difficult, however, to view this category (and that below of 'mothers lying in') as anything other than a historical anomaly. Either deriving from a 1948 concern about the dangers of child birth and the need for mothers to 'lie in' and rest prior to the birth – or perhaps more probably a throwback to Poor Law Amendment Act 1834 s62 which led to the prohibition of 'outdoor relief' for able-bodied persons and their families, and for whom relief would only be available in harsh workhouses. It has been argued that this put women in particular in an impossible position – forcing them to decide whether they were women or workers[211] – and hence the importance of being classified as an expectant or nursing mother for relief purposes.

208   The text of NHS(W)A 2006 s192 and Sch 15 is in all material terms the same save only that it contains no equivalent of Sch 15 para 3: the omission is because the definition of 'local authority' in NHSA 2006 s275 encompasses Welsh as well as English authorities and so there is no need for para 3 to be replicated in the NHS(W)A 2006.
209   WOC 35/93 in Wales: by virtue of National Health Service (Consequential Provisions) Act 2006 s4 and Sch 2 para 1(2), directions issued in relation to the NHSA 1977 continue and apply with equal effect to the consequent provisions in the NHS Acts 2006.
210   LAC (93)10 appendix 3.
211   See M Levine-Clark 'Engendering relief: women, ablebodiedness, and the new poor law in early Victorian England' (2000) 11(4) *Journal of Women's History* 107–130.

The ill

9.161   NHSA 2006 s275(1)/NHS(W)A 2006 s206(1) defines illness as including mental disorder within the meaning of MHA 1983 and any injury or disability requiring medical or dental treatment or nursing. Persons who are alcoholic or drug-dependent are specifically included.[212] Services can also be provided for the purpose of preventing illness and for the after-care of persons who have been so suffering; the client group is therefore limited only by the size of the adult population.

9.162   The client group is generally restricted to persons aged 18 or over.[213] The exception to this general rule is that home help and laundry services (under para 3) are available to ill adults or children alike.

Mothers lying-in

9.163   At first sight it might appear incongruous that separate reference be made to mothers 'lying-in' (literally, 'being in childbed'), when nursing mothers are already included as a category (see para 9.160 above). The reason for this is related to the different services available. Where the need exists, there is a duty to provide home help for mothers lying in, whereas the other services available to expectant and nursing mothers are discretionary. The mother may be of any age (ie, over or under 18).

The aged

9.164   No definition is provided for 'aged'.[214] The overlap with the corresponding provision under HSPHA 1968 s45 (see para 19.17 below) is presumably explained on the basis that (where need for home help is assessed) section 45 services are discretionary whereas the NHS provision is obligatory.

The handicapped

9.165   The 'handicapped' person may be of any age (ie, over or under 18) and there is no requirement that the 'handicap' be either substantial or permanent (unlike the requirement in NAA 1948 s29 – see para 9.41 above); it must, however, result from either illness or congenital deformity. Those whose impairment results from injury are therefore excluded (NAA 1948 s29 covers this category if the consequent impairment is both permanent and substantial). The apparent lacuna is, however, largely academic – the definition of illness in the NHS Acts 2006 (as detailed above) includes an injury which requires medical or dental treatment or nursing – and the Acts cover the provision of services for the after-care of such persons.

---

212 LAC (93)10 appendix 3 para 3(g); see chapter 22 below where services for alcohol and drug misusers are considered in greater detail.

213 NHSA 2006 Sch 20 (NHS(W)A 2006 Sch 15) para 2(10).

214 See NAA 1948 s21, where no definition is given of 'age' and likewise HSPHA 1968 s45, which uses the phrase 'old people' – dealt with at paras 7.10 above and 19.20 below respectively.

Excluded groups

9.166　The effect of NHSA 2006 Sch 20 (NHS(W)A 2006 Sch 15) para 2(6) is to exclude from services people who are asylum seekers and are in need of community care services solely on account of being 'destitute' (see para 21.14 above).

Services

9.167　Before the implementation of the NHSCCA 1990, the services that could be provided under NHSA 1977 Sch 8 included the provision of accommodation. The NHSCCA 1990 by amendment[215] removed this power, and all social services authority community care accommodation obligations for adults (with the exception of their joint MHA 1983 s 117 obligations, see para 20.22 below) are now dealt with under the NAA 1948.[216]

9.168　NHSA 2006 Sch 20 paras 1–3 (NHS(W)A 2006 Sch 15 paras 1–2) deal with three separate services:

Paragraph 1　Services for expectant and nursing mothers;
Paragraph 2　Services for the prevention of illness, and the care and after-care of sufferers;
Paragraph 3　Home help and laundry services.

9.169　Paragraphs 1 and 2 follow the traditional community care drafting convention; they do not authorise the provision of any services but leave to the secretary of state the power to specify in directions what services may and what services must be provided. The most recent directions in this respect were issued on 17 March 1993 as LAC (93)10 appendix 3.[217] Although these pre-date the NHS Acts 2006, by virtue of National Health Service (Consequential Provisions) Act 2006 s4 and Sch 2 para 1(2) they apply with equal effect to the consequent provisions in the NHS Acts 2006.

9.170　Paragraph 3 is not, however, subject to directions, being a free-standing statutory provision. These three categories of services are dealt with separately below.

Services for expectant and nursing mothers

9.171　The directions merely state[218] that 'the secretary of state approves the making of arrangements ... for the care of expectant and nursing mothers (of any age) other than the provision of accommodation for them'.[219] For mothers under the age of 18 there is of course an overlapping responsibility under CA 1989 Part III (if the mother or child are considered to be 'in need' – see para 23.5). No circular or other guidance has

---

215　NHSCCA 1990 Sch 9 para 18(4).
216　NAA 1948 s21 as amended by NHSCCA 1990 s42 (see LAC (93)10 para 6) – and the provision of certain hostel accommodation under NAA 1948 s29 – see para 7.180.
217　WOC 35/93 in Wales.
218　LAC (93)10 appendix 3 para 2.
219　Accommodation services being covered by NAA 1948 s21(1)(aa).

been issued concerning the nature or extent of these services – they remain at the discretion of the social services authority. There is no reason why the service provided by the social services authority should not include the giving of assistance in kind or, in exceptional circumstances, in cash.[220] The only restrictions (which follow from the actual wording of the direction) are that the service must be a 'care' service and that the service must be for the care of the mother (ie, not for the infant or anyone else in the household).

Services for the prevention of illness etc

9.172   Detailed directions have been issued in relation to the range of services that can be provided for the prevention of illness and the care and after-care of those who have been ill (see appendix B for the full text). While the directions oblige social services authorities to provide services for the prevention of mental disorder (or for the care of persons who have been suffering from mental disorder) they leave the provision of services for the alleviation of 'non-mental disorder' to the discretion of the social services authority. These two services are therefore dealt with separately below. The services are, in both cases, only available to adults and (subject to the specific exceptions detailed below) may not include the payment of money to the service user (although the availability of direct payments for such services, under the Health and Social Care Act 2001, has in large measure neutered this prohibition – see chapter 12 below).

The duty to provide services to alleviate mental disorder

9.173   The secretary of state's directions oblige social services authorities to make domiciliary care arrangements (detailed in items a) and b) below) for the purpose of preventing mental disorder, as well as for persons who are or who have been suffering from mental disorder[221] (see appendix B for full text). The directed services are the provision of:

a)   centres (including training centres and day centres) or other facilities (including domiciliary facilities), whether in premises managed by the local authority or otherwise, for training or occupation of such persons, including the payment of persons engaged in suitable work at the 'centres or other facilities';[222]

b)   social work and related services to help in the identification, diagnosis, assessment and social treatment of mental disorder and to provide social work support and other domiciliary and care services to people living in their own homes and elsewhere.

---

220   The general prohibition on making payment to service users under the community care legislation does not apply in this case; compare NAA 1948 s29(6)(a) and NHSA 2006 Sch 20 (NHS(W)A 2006 Sch 15) para 2(4) and also compare CA 1989 s17(6).

221   LAC (93)10 appendix 3 para 3(2).

222   LAC (93) 10 appendix 3 para 3(3)(b) – but subject to NHSA 2006 Sch 20 (NHS(W)A 2006 Sch 15) para 2(5), which provides that the amount of such remuneration shall be limited to payment of such persons' occasional personal expenses if their work would not normally be remunerated.

9.174   The directions would appear to be so widely drafted as to cover most of the commonly encountered domiciliary care services, ie, day centres, drop-in centres, educational, occupational and recreational facilities, transport, meals, home helps and so on. Accommodation services are, however, specifically excluded by NHSA 2006 Sch 20 (NHS(W)A 2006 Sch 15) para 2(11).

9.175   The directions additionally require local authorities to appoint sufficient social workers in their area to act as approved social workers for the purposes of the MHA 1983 and to make arrangements to enable them to exercise their guardianship functions under that Act.

9.176   As has been noted above (see para 9.65), NAA 1948 s29(6)(b) excludes services being provided under section 29 where such services are 'required to be provided' under the NHS Acts 2006. The inclusion of the phrase 'mental disorder of any description' within NAA 1948 s29 and in the secretary of state's direction relating to services under NHSA 2006 Sch 20 (NHS(W)A 2006 Sch 15) would tend to suggest that NAA 1948 s29 is of limited relevance to persons suffering from a mental disorder. It is, however, unlikely that this exclusion applies to services under CSDPA 1970 s2 (for the reasons stated by McCowan LJ noted at para 9.68 above). The tortuous relationship between the almost irreconcilable provisions in these Acts is so unsatisfactory, that only primary legislation can lead to a rational resolution.

The power to provide services to alleviate 'illness'

9.177   The secretary of state's direction empowers (but does not oblige) social services authorities to make the domiciliary care arrangements detailed below. In each case the service can only be provided for the purpose of either preventing illness, or for the care or after-care of a person suffering or recovering from an illness. The directed services are the provision of:

a)   Centres or other facilities for training such persons or for keeping them suitably occupied (and the equipment and maintenance of such centres), together with any other ancillary or supplemental services for such persons.[223] The services provided by a social services authority may include the payment of 'persons engaged in suitable work at the centres or other facilities'.[224] The equivalent services for disabled people (under CSDPA 1970 s2) are considered at para 9.85 above and for elderly people (under HSPHA 1968 s45) at para 19.26 below.

b)   Meals at the centres referred to in a) above, or at other facilities (including domiciliary facilities) and meals-on-wheels for housebound people, provided they are not available under HSPHA 1968 s45(1)[225] or from a district council under HASSASSAA 1983 Sch 9

---

223   LAC (93)10 appendix 3 paras 3(1)(a) and (b).
224   See note 80 above.
225   See para 19.26 below.

Part II para 1.[226] The equivalent services for disabled people (under the CSDPA 1970) are considered at para 9.137 above and for elderly people (under the HSPHA 1968) at para 19.26 below.

c) Social services (including advice and support) for the purposes of preventing the impairment of physical or mental health of adults in families where such impairment is likely, and for the purposes of preventing the break-up of such families, or for assisting in their rehabilitation; the equivalent services for disabled people (under NAA 1948 s29) are considered at para 9.47 above.

d) Night-sitter services. Such a service is a specific form of 'practical assistance within the home' (as covered by CSDPA 1970 s2(1)(a)) and 'home help' (as covered by NHSA 2006 Sch 20 para 3 – see below). The inclusion of specific reference to this service is therefore probably unnecessary.

e) Recuperative holidays. CSDPA 1970 s2(1)(f) covers holidays for disabled people (see para 9.134 above) and NAA 1948 s29 enables authorities to provide holiday homes (see para 9.57 above).

f) Facilities for social and recreational activities; this is an equivalent power to the duty under CSDPA 1970 s2(1)(c) (see para 9.86 above) and under HSPHA 1968 s45 (see para 19.26 below).

g) Services specifically for persons who are alcoholic or drug-dependent. Such services are considered separately in chapter 22.

Home help and laundry services

Home help

9.178 NHSA 2006 Sch 20 para 3 requires social services authorities to provide[227] a home help service for households where such help is required owing to the presence of a person who is suffering from illness, lying-in, or is an expectant mother, aged, or handicapped as a result of having suffered from illness or by congenital deformity.[228] The potential extent of the service, as well as the overlap (and differences) between this provision and that under CSDPA 1970 s2(1)(a) has been noted above. The NHSA 2006 home help service, unlike the 1970 Act service, can be provided for the benefit of 'the household' rather being restricted to the disabled service user's needs.

---

226 The paragraph empowers a district council to make arrangements (or to employ a suitable voluntary organisation to make these arrangements) for providing meals and recreation for old people in their homes or elsewhere, see para 19.37 below.

227 Although the provision is not found in NHS(W)A 2006 this is because the definition of 'local authority' in NHSA 2006 s275 encompasses Welsh as well as English authorities. The services may either be provided by the authority or arranged by the authority but provided by another authority, a voluntary organisation or private person – see LAC (93)10 appendix 3 para 4.

228 The power was included in the NHS Act 1946 s29 in similar terms – namely for 'households where such help is required owing to the presence of any person who is ill, lying-in, an expectant mother, mentally defective, aged or a child not over compulsory school age'.

Laundry service

9.179 Social services authorities are empowered (but not obliged) to provide[229] a laundry service for households where they assess it as being required owing to the presence of a person who is suffering from illness, or lying-in, an expectant mother, aged, or handicapped as a result of having suffered from illness or by congenital deformity. Laundry services can therefore be provided in any situation where the Act enables the provision of home help; they are not, however, dependent on the household actually receiving that home help service.

9.180 The NHS has overlapping responsibilities for laundry services, particularly as a consequence of incontinence (see para 13.84 below) or the involvement of the district nursing services or as part of a continuing care package (see para 14.135 below).

229 See para 9.3 above.

CHAPTER 10

Charges for non-accommodation services

continued

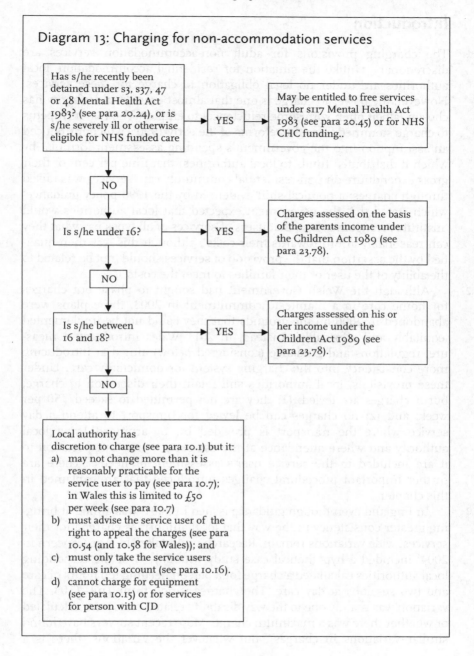

Diagram 13: Charging for non-accommodation services

Has s/he recently been detained under s3, s37, 47 or 48 Mental Health Act 1983? (see para 20.24), or is s/he severely ill or otherwise eligible for NHS funded care

YES → May be entitled to free services under s117 Mental Health Act 1983 (see para 20.45) or for NHS CHC funding..

NO

Is s/he under 16?

YES → Charges assessed on the basis of the parents income under the Children Act 1989 (see para 23.78).

NO

Is s/he between 16 and 18?

YES → Charges assessed on his or her income under the Children Act 1989 (see para 23.78).

NO

Local authority has discretion to charge (see para 10.1) but it:
a) may not change more than it is reasonably practicable for the service user to pay (see para 10.7); in Wales this is limited to £50 per week (see para 10.7)
b) must advise the service user of the right to appeal the charges (see para 10.54 (and 10.58 for Wales)); and
c) must only take the service users means into account (see para 10.16).
d) cannot charge for equipment (see para 10.15) or for services for person with CJD

Introduction

10.1   The charging provisions for adult non-accommodation services are discretionary. Unlike the situation for residential accommodation, local authorities are under no legal obligation to charge for these services. However, the power to charge is one that almost every local authority has chosen (albeit often with some reluctance) to employ. The major impetus to charge stemmed from the reforms of the early 1990's which introduced an assumption into the government's spending assessment formula (by which it distributed funds to local authorities) that nine per cent of their gross expenditure on non-residential community care services was raised through charges: a political shift evidenced by the 1990 policy guidance[1] which stated that the government expected that local authorities would 'institute arrangements so that users of services of all types pay what they can reasonably afford towards their costs', although this was then qualified by the assertion that the provision of services should 'not be related to the ability of the user or their families to meet the costs'.

10.2   Although the Welsh Government had sought to phase out charges for home care in a manifesto commitment in 2003, these plans were abandoned in 2006 on the grounds that they could not be implemented 'equitably and affordably'. Instead, in 2011 Wales introduced a measure, regulations and guidance (considered below) aimed at introducing more consistency into the charging system for domiciliary care. Under these provisions, local authorities still retain their discretion to charge, but if charges are levied: (1) they are not permitted to exceed £50 per week; and (2) no charges can be levied for transport to attend a day service where the transport is provided by, or arranged by, a local authority and where attendance at the day service and transportation to it are included in the service user's assessment of needs.[2] There are further important procedural changes introduced that are explained in this chapter.

10.3   In England even though guidance issued in 2001[3] was aimed at bringing greater consistency in the way that local authorities charged for their services, wide variations remain. Research undertaken by Age Concern in 2004[4] included a hypothetical case study whereby 65 of the responding local authorities calculated a charge for a person needing ten hours of care and two sessions at day care. The charges varied from £nil–£103. The variation was mainly due to the way disability related costs were calculated or whether there was a maximum charge. More recent surveys have found similar variations in charges.[5] But whatever the variations, there is a

1   *Community Care in the Next Decade and Beyond: Policy Guidance*, 1990, para 3.31.
2   The Social Care Charges (Means Assessment and Determination of Charges) (Wales) Regulations 2011 reg 5(2) – maximum weekly charge and reg 4(2) – transport.
3   *Fairer Charging Policies for Home Care and other Non-Residential Social Services*, issued by the Department of Health in 2001(see para 10.1).
4   P Thompson and D Mathew, *Fair Enough?* Age Concern England, April 2004.
5   *Which?* 20 January 2011. www.which.co.uk/news/2011/01/home-care-charges-lottery-revealed-by-which-242460/

general trend to increase charges, for example by removing any subsidy in hourly charging rates and/or by removing maximum weekly charge that might have existed.

10.4   There is general disquiet about the current system[6] and the perverse incentives it can produce, either for authorities to place people in residential care if they can then access funds through sale of the resident's former home, or where charges act as a disincentive for people to get the care they need until they reach a crisis. This latter point was made in a joint report by the All Party Parliamentary Groups on Primary Care and Public Health and Social Care[7] which concluded that 'the level of charges for domiciliary social care is very unpopular with service users and acts as a deterrent from using such services for those with income above entitlement to free provision. This often leads to earlier use of more expensive institutional care.' In England major new proposals regarding the funding and paying of care have been proposed by the 'Commission on Funding of Care and Support'[8] and these (in so far as they relate to domiciliary care) are listed at the end of this chapter.

The statutory framework for charges

10.5   In England there is no statutorily defined procedure for assessing non-accommodation charges. The discretionary power to charge for certain non-accommodation services derives from Health and Social Services and Social Security Adjudications Act (HASSASSAA) 1983 s17. In Wales from April 2011 the discretionary power derives from the Social Care Charging (Wales) Measure 2010:[9] referred to as the 'Welsh charging measure' in this

---

6   See eg *Securing Good Care for Older People – Wanless Social Care Review*, King's Fund, March 2006.
7   Report of Joint Inquiry by the Primary Care and Public Health and Social Care All Party Parliamentary Groups, *Our health, our care, our say*, November 2006, p33.
8   Commission on Funding of Care and Support (2011) *Fairer Care Funding: The Report of the Commission on Funding of Care and Support* (the 'Dilnot' Report).
9   HASSASSAA 1983 s17 has been amended by the Welsh charging measure to relate to England only, other than when short term respite residential care is provided by a Welsh authority under Carers and Disabled Children Act 2000 s2, when the authority may recover such charge (if any) for it as they consider reasonable. The exclusion of carers services in the form of residential care from the charging regime under the Measure presumably arises because the National Assembly's relevant legislative competence was restricted to making laws about charges for non-residential care services. That legislative competence order expressly stated that it did 'not include charges and payments for residential care': see the National Assembly for Wales (Legislative Competence) (Social Welfare) Order 2008 (SI No 1785) and the National Assembly for Wales (Legislative Competence) (Social Welfare and Other Fields) Order 2008 (SI No 3132). The effect is that for such a service the charging restrictions in the Measure do not apply so that, subject to Welsh Government statutory guidance, a charge in excess of £50 may be imposed. Where respite care is arranged under NAA 1948 s21 it comes under the charging regime for residential care which also includes special provisions for charges for short residential periods (ie under eight weeks) – see para 8.122.

chapter. There is also now a statutorily defined procedure laid down in regulations in Wales.[10] Separate charging provisions relate to services provided under Children Act (CA) 1989 Part III, and these are considered at para 23.78.

10.6 HASSASSAA 1983 s17[11] as amended by the Welsh charging measure is produced at appendix A). The effect of section 17 and the Welsh charging measure[12] is that local authorities can recover reasonable charges for services provided or arranged under

(a) section 29 of the National Assistance Act 1948 (welfare arrangements for disabled persons);

(b) section 45(1) of the Health Services and Public Health Act 1968 (welfare of old people);

(c) schedule 20 to the National Health Service Act 2006 or Schedule 15 to the National Health Service (Wales) Act 2006.

(d) section 8 of the Residential Homes Act 1980[13] (meals and recreation for old people); and

(e) paragraph 1 of Part II of Schedule 9 to this Act, other than the provision of services for which payment may be required under section 22 or 26 of the National Assistance Act 1948.

(f) section 2 of the Carers and Disabled Children Act 2000.

Not reasonably practicable

10.7 HASSASSAA 1983 s17 enables local authorities to make reasonable charges for non-residential services, but also requires that they have procedures for reducing or waiving the charge where it is not '*reasonably practicable*' for the user to pay the full charge. Section 7 of the Welsh charging measure has similar provisions. The framework to help local authorities decide what is reasonable is now contained in policy and practice guidance in England and by regulations in Wales (which in Wales, include being subject to a maximum charge of £50 per week[14]).

---

10 The Social Care Charges (Means Assessment and Determination of Charges) (Wales) Regulations 2011 SI No 962; The Social Care Charges (Direct Payments) (Means Assessment and Determination of Reimbursement or Contribution) (Wales) Regulations 2011 SI No 963 and The Social Care Charges (Review of Charging Decisions) (Wales) Regulations 2011 SI No 964.

11 The power was formerly to be found under NAA 1948 s29(5) which provided that '[a] local authority may recover from persons availing themselves of any service provided under this Section such charges (if any) as, having regard to the cost of the service, the authority may determine, whether generally or in the circumstances of any particular case'.

12 Section 1(1) of the Welsh charging measure uses the words 'A local authority in Wales which provides, or makes arrangements for the provision of, a chargeable service may (but does not have to) impose a reasonable charge for the service'.

13 Repealed by HASSASSAA 1983 s30, Sch 10 Part I. This provision is not mentioned in the Welsh charging measure as a chargeable service.

14 Reg 5 of the Social Care Charges (Means Assessment and Determination of Charges) (Wales) Regulations 2011. As this maximum reasonable charge is set without reference to a person's means it follows that the £50 maximum is the most a person would have to pay even if they have capital above the capital limits used in the assessment of means to establish what a person can afford to pay below that amount.

10.8   The local government ombudsman has held it to be maladministration for an authority to adopt a charging policy which only permits exceptions if users provide 'proof of hardship'[15] since this is a materially more severe criterion than 'not reasonably practicable'. Likewise in *R v Calderdale DC ex p Houghton*[16] the local authority conceded that its procedures for assessing the reasonableness of its charges were unreasonably demanding: they required that applicants establish that their expenditure was so exceptional that it was not reasonable for the authority to charge the full amount.

10.9   The ombudsman has further held that where a claimant had produced evidence that her expenditure exceeds her income, the authority cannot insist on her paying the full charge without providing cogent reasons why it considers her able to pay the amount claimed.[17]

10.10   In *Avon CC v Hooper*[18] (an unusual fact case) the Court of Appeal considered the interpretation of 'reasonably practicable to pay'. Hobhouse LJ considered the interpretation of section 17(3) in the following terms:[19]

> If the local authority decides to charge and is acting reasonably [under section 17(1)] . . . the person availing himself of the service has . . . to satisfy the authority under subsection (3) that his means are insufficient for it to be reasonably practicable for him to pay the amount which he would otherwise be obliged to pay. It is for the recipient of the service to discharge this burden of persuasion. He must show that he has insufficient means. The time at which he has to do this is the time when the local authority is seeking to charge him for the services. If his means have been reduced, as might be the case with a business man whose business had run into difficulties after his being injured, the reduction in his means is something upon which he would be entitled to rely as making it impracticable for him to pay, even though at an earlier date he might have been better off. The consideration under subsection (3) (b) is the practical one: are his means such that it is not reasonably practicable for him to pay?

> This also bears on the alternative argument . . . that only cash should be taken into account. This is too narrow a reading of subsection (3). As a matter of the ordinary use of English, the word 'means' refers to the financial resources of a person: his assets, his sources of income, his liabilities and expenses. If he has a realisable asset, that is part of his means; he has the means to pay. The subject matter of paragraph (b) is the practicability of his paying. If he has an asset which he can reasonably be expected to realise and which will (after taking into account any other relevant factor) enable him to pay, his means make it practicable for him to pay.

> Where the person has a right to be indemnified by another against the cost of the service, he has the means to pay. He can enforce his right and make the payment. There is nothing in any part of section 17 which suggests that it is intended that subsection (3) should have the effect of relieving those

15   Complaint nos 99/C/02509 and 02624 against Gateshead, 28 February 2001.
16   Unreported but see (1999) 2 CCLR 119.
17   Complaint nos 99/C/02509 and 02624 against Gateshead, 28 February 2001.
18   [1997] 1 WLR 1605, (1997–98) 1 CCLR 366, 22 February 1996, CA.
19   [1997] 1 WLR 1605, (1997–98) 1 CCLR 366 at 371E–K, 22 February 1996, CA.

liable to indemnify the recipient of the service for the cost of the service from their liability. On the contrary, it is clear that the intention of the section is to enable the local authority to recover the cost save when it is unreasonable that it should do so or impracticable for the recipient to pay.

Policy guidance: England

10.11   Until 2001 no national policy guidance on non-accommodation charges existed, with the result that very wide disparities existed in the charges levied by social services authorities. In its white paper '*Modernising Social Services*[20] the then government acknowledged these local variations and committed itself to establish greater consistency and fairness.[21] This was realised in November 2001 with the publication by the Department of Health of *Fairer Charging Policies for Home Care and other non-residential Social Services*[22] under Local Authority Social Services Act (LASSA) 1970 s7). The current guidance in England was issued as an update in September 2003 (to reflect the introduction of the pension credit)[23] and is referred to in this chapter as the '2003 policy guidance'.

Regulations and policy guidance: Wales

10.12   Previous Welsh policy guidance has now been superseded by the Welsh charging measure and regulations, for which new policy guidance was issued in 2011 as *Introducing More Consistency in Local Authorities' Charging for Non-Residential Social Services*.[24] In the succeeding sections, references to regulations will be to the Social Care Charges (Means Assessment and Determination of Charges) (Wales) Regulations 2011 (unless otherwise stated). The policy guidance will be referred to as the Welsh 2011 guidance. Where the Welsh regulations and policy differ from the English policy, this will be noted in the text.

The charging regime in England and Wales

10.13   The key principles in both England and Wales can be summarised as follows:

1) Councils are not obliged to charge for non-residential social services.
2) Flat-rate charges are acceptable only in limited circumstances (for instance where they are a substitute for ordinary living costs – such as

---

20 Cm 4169, 1998.
21 Ibid, para 2.31.
22 LAC (2001)32.
23 Accessible at www.dh.gov.uk/en/Publicationsandstatistics/Publications/ PublicationsPolicyAndGuidance/DH_4117930.
24 Welsh Government (2011) *Introducing More Consistency in Local Authorities' Charging for Non-Residential Social Services* WAG10–12408 April 2011.

for meals on wheels or meals at a day centre).[25] In Wales the guidance also suggests laundry services could be charged at a flat rate.[26]

3) Net incomes should not be reduced below basic income support/ employment and support levels or the guarantee credit of pension credit, plus a buffer of 25 per cent (35 per cent in Wales[27]); 'basic levels' of income support includes the personal allowance and all premiums, but it 'need not include the Severe Disability Premium' (para 18).[28]

4) In England councils are advised to consider and specifically consult on the need to set a maximum charge,[29] (in Wales the Welsh Government has imposed a maximum charge of £50).

5) Where disability benefits are taken into account as income in assessing ability to pay a charge, councils should assess the individual user's disability-related expenditure with the overall aim 'to allow for reasonable expenditure needed for independent living';[30] councils should specifically consult on the need to assess disability-related expenditure for other users. It is not acceptable to make a charge on disability benefits without assessing the reasonableness of doing so for each user[31]. In Wales councils must ensure that all service users have a disability expenditure disregard of 10 per cent of the 'basic' level of the appropriate benefit.[32] If service users have expenditure above this amount, they should be encouraged to give details of this during the assessment so that it can be based on their individual expenditure.

6) Councils should ensure that comprehensive benefits advice is provided to all users at the time of a charge assessment. Councils have a responsibility to seek to maximise the incomes of users, where they would be entitled to benefits, particularly where the user is asked to pay a charge.[33]

7) Where councils take into account capital, as a minimum, the same savings limits as for residential care charges should be applied. Councils are free to operate more generous rules. In addition the main home of the person must be disregarded.[34]

25 2003 policy guidance para 80.
26 Flat rate charges are exempt from the requirement in the regulations to undertake a means assessment (reg 13), and are also excluded from the maximum charge of £50 so that a person could be charged the flat rate for say meals on top if they are paying the maximum £50 charge (reg 5.4). See also paras 43–46 and 49 of Welsh 2011 guidance. Authorities are told 'it is not acceptable for authorities to set flat rate charges for other services as a way of potentially avoiding the duties placed upon them by the Measure and the regulations': para 45.
27 Reg 15 (2) and Welsh 2011 guidance para 79.
28 Because the buffer is based on benefits which are paid at different rates according to age, it leads to large differences between what younger disabled people and older people are able to keep. A few authorities try to avoid this potential age discrimination by using the more generous pension credit rates for younger people.
29 2003 policy guidance para 17.
30 2003 policy guidance para 44.
31 2003 policy guidance para 3.
32 Reg 15(2)(iii) and Welsh 2011 guidance para 54.
33 2003 policy guidance para 3. The Welsh 2011 guidance also states that councils should offer benefits advice: paras 108 and 109.
34 2003 policy guidance paras 57–59. Reg 14 and Welsh 2011 guidance para 69.

8) 'To ensure that disabled people and their carers, who wish to do so, are able to enter and progress in work', earnings (including tax credits) are disregarded in charge assessments.[35]

9) Any savings credit paid under the pension credit arrangements is disregarded.[36]

Practice guidance

10.14   In England there is also practice guidance concerning the home care charging policy issued by the Department of Health with the Department for Work and Pensions in 2002.[37] The notable points in this guidance include:

- It favours the creation of a specialist service, separating financial assessment from assessment of care needs (para 27); these financial assessments should normally be carried out by personal interview in the user's own home.

- Users who may be entitled to benefits which would bring them within charging, may be given an 'interim assessment' so that the local authority has the option of backdating the charge assessment against any backdated benefits award: however, the guidance notes that this is 'an issue for local policy' (para 35).

- Spending not incurred (ie for needs that the person would ideally like to satisfy) should not be allowed (para 36). However, where disability benefit has been newly awarded, an assessment should be capable of review to take account of the likelihood of the disabled person increasing his or her disability related expenditure due to the higher level of income (para 37).

- Research informing the practice guidance (undertaken in Torbay in 1999/2000) showed that 34 per cent of those assessed had disability related expenditure above £40 per week, and 49 per cent above £30 (para 44).

- Para 46 provides a detailed list of typical disability related expenditure, and how local authorities might cost this including:
  - community alarm;
  - private care arrangements, including respite care. In *R (Stephenson) v Stockton-on-Tees BC*[38] the Court of Appeal held that it was unlawful for a local authority to apply inflexibly a general rule that payments made to family members for help with personal care were not deemed to be 'disability related expenditure';

35   2003 policy guidance para 72. Reg 14(4) and Welsh 2011 guidance para 69.
36   2003 policy guidance para 27. Reg 14(4) and Welsh 2011 guidance para 69.
37   Department of Health and Department for Work and Pensions (2002) *Fairer Charging Policies for Home Care and other Non-residential Social Services Practice Guidance*: this is now only available in the archive section of the DH website, although it does not appear to have been superseded – contrary to the statement on the webarchive – see http://webarchive.nationalarchives.gov.uk/+/www.dh.gov.uk/en/Publicationsand-statistics/Publications/PublicationsPolicyAndGuidance/DH_4005701.
38   [2005] EWCA Civ 960, (2005) 8 CCLR 517.

- specialist washing powders;
- laundry;
- specialist diets;
- clothing/footwear;
- additional bedding (eg because of incontinence);
- extra heating or water (standard rates suggested for heating; and councils must ignore winter fuel/cold weather payments);
- garden maintenance;
- cleaning or domestic help – the cost of private cleaning services should be allowed when they are not provided through social services, and 'consideration should be given to higher needs for cleaning as a consequence of disability and the needs of carers';
- purchase, maintenance and repair of disability related equipment;
- personal assistance costs – eg paying for the meals or transport costs for personal assistants or carers;
- other transport costs 'over and above the Mobility Component of DLA';
- it may be reasonable for a council not to allow costs where a reasonable alternative *is available* at lesser cost.
- Information about how to complain should be available as a matter of routine (para 64).

Services that must be provided free

10.15   Certain non-accommodation services must be provided free of charge, and these include:

- services under MHA 1983 s117 (see para 20.45 below);
- intermediate care services in England[39] (see chapter 11);
- in England[40], community equipment, and in the case of minor adaptations where the cost is £1,000 or less including the cost of buying and fitting.[41] Councils retain the discretion to charge if a minor adaptation

39   In England this is established by Community Care (Delayed Discharges etc) Act (CC(DD)A) 2003 s15 and the subsequent regulations SI 2003 No 1196. In Wales the Charging Measure and Regulations are silent on the matter of intermediate care although there is reference to 'any regulations made by Welsh Ministers under section 16 of the Community Care Delayed Discharges Act 2003'. The Welsh 2011 guidance at para 117 refers to previous guidance NAFWC 05/02 relating to targeted free home care for six weeks and at para 118 that authorities will need to ensure that their charging policies should achieve the general aims of promoting independence.

40   Equipment is not currently listed in the regulations in Wales as being a free service although see footnote above regarding possible regulations in the future. Para 54 of the Welsh 2011 guidance specifically mentions equipment as a disability related expenditure. However, information from the Welsh Government is that currently no local authority charges for equipment (private correspondence with the authors, 17 May 2011).

41   It is often mistakenly believed that equipment is only free if it is £1,000 or less. However, the Community Care (Delayed Discharges etc) Act (Qualifying Services) (England) Regulations 2003 only define an *adaptation* as minor if the cost of making the adaptation is £1,000 or less.

costs more than £1,000. The guidance[42] is silent on the position when a number of minor adaptations are required simultaneously which together cost more than £1,000 for the buying and fitting. It is arguable that each should count as a minor adaptation of less than £1,000 and so be free of charge. See para 9.109 above for details on the interface between adaptations under Chronically Sick and Disabled Persons Act (CSDPA) 1970 s2 and the housing provisions for disabled facilities grants (DFGs);

- services provided to persons suffering from any form of Creuzfeldt Jakob Disease (CJD);[43]
- in Wales the provision of transport to attend a day service where the transport is provided by a local authority and where attendance at the day service and the provision of transport to enable such attendance are included as part of the service user's assessment of needs;[44]
- where a person's means have been assessed the same or lower than the prescribed amount within the guidance (or regulations in Wales)[45]
- advice about the availability of services or assessment including the assessment of community care needs.[46] Councils also cannot include in the cost of the service, the associated costs of the purchasing function or the costs of operating the charging system.[47] In Wales regulations specify that there must be no charge for information about charges or for the provision of a statement of information about charges.[48]

Assessable income and assets

10.16   HASSASSAA 1983 s17(3) directs local authority attention to the question of whether a service user's means are sufficient for it to be reasonably practicable for him or her to pay for the service.[49] It follows that the question concerns the service user's means alone. The 2003 policy guidance reinforces this stating:

> 62. Section 17 of the HASSASSA Act 1983 envisages that councils will have regard only to an individual user's means in assessing ability to pay a charge.

42   LAC (2003)14.
43   2003 policy guidance para 75. In Wales reg 41(1) specifies that the person must that the person with CJD must have been clinically diagnosed by a registered practitioner.
44   Reg 4(2)(a) and Welsh 2011 guidance para 32.
45   Para 19 2003 policy guidance. Reg 4(1)(c).
46   2003 policy guidance para 8.
47   2003 policy guidance para 77.
48   Welsh Charging Measure s10 and reg 4(2).
49   The Social Care Charges (Direct Payments) (Means Assessment and Determination of Reimbursement or Contribution) (Wales) Regulations 2011 SI No 963 reg 2 defines a service user 'as an adult who had been offered or is receiving a service provided by the local authority'.

63. This will mean that parents and other members of an adult user's family cannot be required to pay the charges, except in certain legal circumstances, for example, where a family member may be managing the user's own resources.[50]

10.17 There will be situations where assets belonging to the service user are in fact held in the name of a third party, such as under a power of attorney, deputyship or a simple trust arrangement. In such cases the assets, although administered by a third party can be taken into account in the means test. In this respect the guidance advises:

> Councils may wish to consider in individual cases whether a user's means may include resources not held in that person's name, but to which the user has a legal entitlement. The most likely instances of this kind will arise in relation to married or unmarried couples. In some circumstances, the user may have a legal right to a share in the value of an asset, for example a bank account, even if it is not in his or her name. In some circumstances, statutory provisions provide such a right. In other circumstances, what are known as 'equitable principles' may apply to give such a right, for example where there is an unwritten agreement between partners that they both own a property or an asset, even though the title is in only one of their names. If the council has some reason to believe that the user does have means other than those initially disclosed, a request may reasonably be made for the user to arrange for the partner to disclose his or relevant resources. If there is no such disclosure, the council may consider that it is not satisfied that the user has insufficient means to pay the charge for the service. It will be for the council to consider each case in the light of their own legal advice.[51]

Couples

10.18 Although the law is clear: that it is the service user's means and these means alone that can be taken into account for charging purposes, the above advice illustrates that in certain situations this may not be entirely straightforward. However, if it suspected that a partner has assets owned by the service user, the local authority would need to provide the evidence for this belief, before seeking disclosure of that person's means. The service user may not, of course, be in a position to insist that the partner disclose his or her assets.

10.19 In some cases it will be in the interests of the partner to disclose his or her financial circumstances – for example where the service user who owns the majority of the income or assets, and thus a charge based purely on these (which assumed the partner was paying for half of the households outgoings) could leave the couple in financial difficulties.[52] The National Association of Finance Officers has issued its own advice which many local authorities appear to follow which suggests that couples should be given the option of a single or a joint assessment and can then choose the assessment that is most beneficial to them.

50 Virtually identical wording is used in Welsh 2011 guidance para 86.
51 2003 policy guidance para 64 and Welsh 2011 guidance para 87.
52 See 2003 policy guidance para 65 and Welsh 2011 guidance para 88.

10.20   Research in 2004[53] found that while nearly all authorities did not take the partner's income into account (or only did so in order to maximise the couple's income) six authorities stated they would charge the full cost if the partner refused to disclose his or her income and a further 11 authorities said they would do so in some cases. Some assessment forms (seen as part of the research) asked a partner to give information but gave no reasons as to why this was being requested; others did not ask for partners' resources at all. A hypothetical case study revealed that within those few authorities which charged against the partner there was considerable variation in what aspects of the partners' resources were taken into account. Some took the income only, one took the capital only and some took both.

10.21   Given the variation in practice on this issue, it is perhaps surprising that little case law exists concerning decisions to charge against a partner's resources, although this may be attributable to cases/complaints being settled at an early stage.[54]

Assessment of income

10.22   Certain income is excluded from the charging calculation. This includes any earnings, tax credits, any pension credit savings credit (see para 8.33 above) and any income received from the Independent Living Fund.[55] Para 72 of the 2003 policy guidance advises that 'earnings' should have the same meaning as in the Charging for Residential Accommodation Guide (CRAG) – which at para 9.001 defines 'earnings' in terms of 'any remuneration or profit derived from employment' and at para 9.002 specifically excludes as earnings income from (among other things) any occupational pension. The Welsh regulations (reg 14(4)(a)) link the definition of earnings to the Housing Benefit Regulations.[56]

10.23   Although disability living allowance (DLA) (care component) and attendance allowance can be taken into account, this is only in relation to services provided for the time of day for which the allowance is paid. In *R v Coventry City Council ex p Carton*[57] the local authority changed its non-residential care charges so that there was no automatic disregard for the night component of higher rate DLA for service users receiving day care only. The court held that it was irrational, unlawful and unfair for the

53 P Thompson and D Mathew, *Fair Enough?* Age Concern England, April 2004.
54 In *R (Fay) v Essex CC* [2004] EWHC 879 (Admin) the High Court held that it was unnecessary on the facts, to determine this question and *R (Spink) v Wandsworth LBC* [2005] EWCA Civ 302, (2005) 8 CCLR 272 is an unusual fact case which concerned non-disclosure by parents of their means in relation to the needs of their disabled children.
55 2003 policy guidance para 74. The Welsh regulations specify a full disregard of any payment received by a service user which is referred to in paragraph 24 of Schedule 3 to the 1992 Regulations (sums to be disregarded in the calculation of income other than earnings) which cover such payments as the MacFarlane Trust, the Eileen Trust, the ILF – basically those listed as disregarded in CRAG, see para 8.36.
56 Housing Benefit Regulations 2006 SI No 213 regs 35 and 37.
57 (2001) 4 CCLR 41, QBD.

council to apply a charging policy which treated as income available for day care, sums of DLA paid in respect of night care.[58]

10.24   In addition the mobility component of DLA must be disregarded.[59] The Welsh Ombudsman has found maladministration where a new service user was told she could not use the transport to a day centre because she was in receipt of DLA mobility component. This did not apply to existing service users. She therefore had to use taxis and found this too expensive. Systematic maladministration was found on the basis there was an absence of any policy framework and no written guidelines on the eligibility of clients who could use local authority run transport.[60] See para 10.40 below, for new rules in relation to transport to day services for Wales.

Assessment of capital

10.25   The 2003 policy guidance para 59 state that as a minimum councils should use the upper capital limit as set out in CRAG (see para 8.39 above). Regulations and guidance give the same effect in Wales.[61] Local authorities can have more generous capital limits if they wish. The value of the home cannot be taken into account, but apart from that, in England councils are advised that 'other forms of capital may be taken into account as set out in CRAG'.[62] This then begs the question of how far local authorities should follow guidance that operates under a different legislative regime. In *Crofton v NHS Litigation Authority*[63] Dyson LJ held as follows:

> Section VIII 'includes the minimum requirements for treatment of savings' (paragraph 57). There is no difference between 'savings' and 'capital'. That is clear from the first sentence of paragraph 57 viz: 'Councils may take account of a user's savings or *other capital*' (emphasis added). Paragraph 59 states unequivocally that the main residence occupied by the user should not be taken into account. The sentence continues: 'but other forms of capital may be taken into account, as set out in CRAG'. This wording is not happily expressed. But in our view it means that the CRAG rules for determining what capital should be taken into account are imported in their entirety, on the footing that local authorities have a discretion to treat a person's capital more generously. It follows that, if CRAG stipulates that certain items of capital are to be disregarded, then the Fairer Charging Policy requires the local authority to exercise its discretion in the same way.

10.26   This view may be helpful in ensuring that items not mentioned in the 2003 policy guidance should be disregarded – for instance payments

---

58 See 2003 policy guidance paras 35–43 and Welsh 2011 guidance paras 83–85 in relation to AA and DLA and day and night care.
59 Social Security Contributions and Benefits Act 1992 s73(14) requires this benefit to be disregarded in any charging scheme – see the 2003 policy guidance at para 30 and Welsh 2011 guidance para 77. See also para 9.96 above, where this question is also considered.
60 Complaint no B2004/0180 against Newport City Council, August 2006.
61 Reg 14(2)(a) and Welsh 2011 guidance para 70.
62 2003 policy guidance para 59.
63 [2007] EWCA Civ 71, [2007] 1 WLR 923, (2007) 10 CCLR 123.

made in relation to people who have been infected with Hepatitis C as a result of NHS treatment with blood or blood products (see para 8.45 above). The question must remain about guidance setting a framework for establishing the reasonableness of charges under HASSASSAA 1983 s17, by reference to CRAG which operates under a separate regulatory regime – namely NAA 1948 s22. This could be contentious; for example, if an authority considered that a person had deprived him/herself of capital and sought to argue that he or she had 'notional capital' for the purposes of setting the charge for non-residential care. It is arguable that in the absence of an enabling legislative provision, local authorities have no power under HASSASSAA 1983 s17 to deal with a suspected deprivation of capital in this way (see para 8.86 above). Local authorities should therefore keep the discretionary nature of the section 17 power at the forefront of their decision processes: that in every case the decision on charging be based upon whether it is reasonably practicable for the person to pay, and only pray in aid the CRAG guidance when it does not conflict with this overriding requirement.

10.27   In Wales reg 14(2) requires that (other than the disregard of the services user's main residence, and the overriding discretion to be more generous) capital must be calculated in accordance with National Assistance (Assessment of Resources) Regulations 1992 Part 3. It follows that reg 25 (which concerns deprivation of capital and notional capital) is part of the legislative framework for non-residential charging in Wales. However, how there must be limits to which this provision can be applied, since (as in England) the overriding requirement of the Welsh measure and regulations is that the decision is based on what it is reasonably practicable for the person to pay.

Personal injury payments and domiciliary care charges

10.28   As for residential care (see para 8.54 above) there have been a number of cases relating to whether payments for care costs should be included in a personal injury award if local authorities are not able to charge against them. In the Court of Appeal case *Crofton v NHS Litigation Authority*,[64] referring to an earlier case where another claimant wanted to set up care in her own home via a direct payment, May LJ in relation to the capital award commented:

> 93. In *Freeman v Lockett*, Tomlinson J decided that there should be no reduction in the claimant's damages to reflect the possibility of direct payments by the local authority. A sufficient basis for his decision was his finding that, provided that no deduction on account of the possible receipt of state or local authority funding was made from her award of damages, the claimant would withdraw her application for funding; she wanted to rely exclusively on private funding for her care.
>
> 94. But he would in any event have refused to make any reduction in the claimant's damages on account of direct payments for other reasons. He

64   [2007] EWCA Civ 71, [2007] 1 WLR 923, (2007) 10 CCLR 123.

said that there was no principled basis on which the court could estimate what funding the claimant could reliably expect to receive from the local authority for the rest of her life. The court 'does not speculate unnecessarily or in an unprincipled manner . . . I cannot understand how it can be appropriate to impose upon the Claimant the unnecessary risk that funding from an alternative source may cease or be reduced rather than simply to order the provision of the fund in its entirety' (paragraph 35).

95. In making these observations, Tomlinson J was influenced by the fragility of the policy from which the right to receive direct payments derived. He said that 'in the ordinary way, the regime pursuant to which direct payments are made for domiciliary care is very much more vulnerable to adjustment in order to save costs than is the direct provision of residential care' (paragraph 38).

96. We would accept that there may be cases where the possibility of a claimant receiving direct payments is so uncertain that they should be disregarded altogether in the assessment of damages. It will depend on the facts of the particular case. But if the court finds that a claimant will receive direct payments for at least a certain period of time and possibly for much longer, it seems to us that this finding must be taken into account in the assessment. In such a case, the correct way to reflect the uncertainties to which Tomlinson J referred is to discount the multiplier.

10.29 Although the court was able to be certain that the capital from the award would be disregarded in the case of domiciliary care because of the link in the 2003 policy guidance to CRAG (see para 10.25 above), it was far from clear how income derived from the capital would be treated in the discretionary regime of HASSASSAA 1983 s17. Referring to para 22 of the 2003 policy guidance the court reflected:

But it seems to us unlikely that the phrase 'other income' is intended to include investment income. The words in brackets 'usually disability-related benefits' and the reference to the explanation in the next section (which is headed 'Treatment of disability-related benefits') strongly suggest that paragraph 22 is not intended to apply to investment income. But whether there is a lacuna or paragraph 22 does apply, the treatment of investment income is a matter for the discretion of the local authority, untrammelled by any guidance in the Fairer Charging Policy as to how it should be exercised. The question arises, therefore, how in the exercise of its discretion the Council would treat income derived from the claimant's damages. (para 84)

10.30 The court concluded that it could not decide whether the income derived from an award of damages would affect the amount of direct payment the council would make to the claimant. The same difficulties would apply to care provided or arranged by the council. The case was remitted back for a further hearing with the comment:

110. In view of the difficulty of the relevant legislation and guidance, the size of the care costs and the fact that the claimant will need care for the rest of his life, we think that it would be highly desirable if the Council were joined as a party to the proceedings.

111. We cannot conclude this judgment without expressing our dismay at the complexity and labyrinthine nature of the relevant legislation and

guidance, as well as (in some respects) its obscurity. Social security law should be clear and accessible. The tortuous analysis in the earlier part of this judgment shows that it is neither.

10.31　It would seem that unless the 2003 policy guidance is made clearer as to the treatment of income or parliament decides whether the cost for care in damages cases should fall on the public purse or the tortfeasor, the question of the treatment of damages awards is likely to remain problematic.

10.32　The Welsh regulations in relation to income do not link directly with the National Assistance (Assessment of Resources) Regs 1992 other than in relation to disregards for payment made under or by the Macfarlane Trust, the Macfarlane (Special Payments) Trust, the Macfarlane (Special Payments) (No 2) Trust, the Fund, the Eileen Trust, MFET Limited or the Independent Living Fund (2006)[65] and there is no mention of the treatment of income from personal injury awards in either the regulations or the guidance. However, given the overriding maximum charge of £50 per week applies equally to people who have been awarded personal injury payments and others who have capital above the capital limits, this question may be less contentious in Wales.

Expenditure and costs

Disability related expenditure

10.33　The 2003 policy guidance is clear that authorities must take account of disability related expenditure if they take disability related benefits into account. Local authorities have a degree of discretion as to what expenditure they take into account, and variations are wide.[66] The Welsh regulations specify that the disability related expenditure must be no less than 10% of the basic amount of the relevant benefit.[67] The advantage of the Welsh approach is that all users will have a token amount recognised without having to face intrusive questions and prove expenditure. Whether this amount has been set high enough to enable most users to accept it without a further individual assessment is questionable. The Welsh 2011 guidance at para 54 encourages authorities to invite services users to give information about disability related expenditure at an early stage in the assessment 'to ensure that any disability related expenditure a service user may have, which goes beyond the basic contribution towards this allowed for by the Disability Related Expenditure Disregard, is properly taken account of in any means assessment undertaken'.

10.34　In *R (B) v Cornwall County Council*[68] the claimant's initial means test assessment concluded that there should be no charge because of the high

65　Reg 14(4).
66　In one of the case studies in *Fair Enough?* the amount allowed by local authorities for a list of disability related expenditure ranged from £4.09–£70.38.
67　Reg 15.
68　*R (B) v Cornwall County Council and Brendon Trust* (interested party) [2009] EWHC 491 (Admin), (2009) 12 CCLR 681 upheld on appeal [2010] EWCA Civ 55, (2010) 13 CCLR 117.

level of disability expenditure. A paper review by the council then determined that some items of expenditure should not have been classed as disability related and that other items should not have been included due to the lack of sufficient supporting evidence – such that a charge was payable of £68.50 per week. The court held the authority had acted unlawfully in failing to consult with the claimant and his family as required under the Community Care Assessment Directions (see para 3.24 above); that there was evidence in the care plan to justify the level of expenditure; that the authority had failed to offer the family opportunity to provide the necessary evidence; and that the authority had been over rigid in its application of its guidance. The court further considered that holiday expenses could be included as a disability related expenditure – including the consequent extra expenses of carers required

Capital expenditure and equipment repairs

10.35　It is in general not unlawful for a local authority to adopt a policy that purchase of a capital item (for instance an electrical reclining bed) should be amortised over the life of the item – ie if the item costs £1,800 and the local authority consider it to have a life of ten years – then this would equate to a weekly disability related expenditure of £3.46. However, it is unlikely that it would be reasonable to adopt the same approach to the repair costs for such equipment.[69]

Housing costs

10.36　The guidance[70] explains that income should be assessed as net of housing costs less any housing benefit or council tax benefit. It adds that councils might wish to consider other costs such as home insurance and water charges. Thus even in a fairly straightforward case of a home owner without a mortgage, variations can exist between authorities.[71]

10.37　　The 2003 policy guidance and the Welsh 2011 guidance are silent on the position of housing costs where service users are living with their families. Most often this is where disabled adults live with their parents, or older people with adult children. Practice appears to vary as to whether any housing costs are allowed for either a contribution towards council tax or rent. If the family are charging for housing costs it would be unreasonable for a local authority not to allow these, given that housing costs are always considered to be a priority in any debt situation. On the basis that charges should be designed so that they do not undermine the independence and social inclusion of service users[72] it is arguable the amount allowed for rent and other housing costs in such cases should be set at a level based on what the person would pay for equivalent accommodation

---

69　*R (Stephenson) v Stockton-on-Tees BC* [2004] EWHC 2228 (Admin), (2004) 7 CCLR 459.
70　2003 policy guidance para 21 and Welsh 2011 guidance para 98
71　P Thompson and D Mathew, *Fair Enough?* Age Concern England, April 2004. The case study showed a range from £11.02–£32.55 being allowed as housing costs.
72　2003 policy guidance para 3 (Welsh 2011 guidance para 26).

on a shared basis if it did not happen to be owned or rented by the person's family, and his or her proportion of council tax.

10.38   Clearly there is no duty on families to provide support in such cases – the 'liable family' rule (which required families to support disabled adult members) was abolished by the National Assistance Act 1948 s1. Even if the family does not charge a specific rent it is arguable that at the very least local authorities should consider making an allowance based on the non-dependent deduction for housing and council tax benefit, in recognition of the fact that adults are expected to contribute towards their housing costs.[73] As a general principle, local authorities should not rely on relatives (who are often the carers) to subsidise service users further, by not leaving the user enough money to make a contribution to household expenses.

Costs of transport to services

10.39   The 2003 policy guidance warns councils against flat rate charges other than for meals where it is argued that the service user would have to pay for food in any case. However, it is not uncommon for local authorities to have a similar flat rate charge for transport to and from services such as day care. In part this is to avoid having to conduct lengthy financial assessments on people whose only service is for day care (which in some councils is still free). As transport to the day care service will have been assessed as part of the service user's needs, it should not be charged in isolation, but be part of the whole cost of the care package. Service users should only pay for transport if they can afford to do so according to the local authority policy. Adding a flat rate charge for transport to the service is in effect adding an extra charge to the individual over and above that which he or she has been assessed as being able to pay.

10.40   In Wales since April 2011 the regulations preclude charges for transport to day services where the transport is provided by a local authority and where attendance at the day service and the provision of transport to enable such attendance are included as part of the service user's assessment of needs.[74]

Local charging schemes: the duty to consult

10.41   HASSASSAA 1983 s17(1) requires local authorities to set a rate that they consider 'reasonable'. This necessarily requires the consideration of a variety of factors – including the views of service users. Although in Wales

---

73   Although many service users do not work, and may well be on the type of benefit that would in reality preclude a non-dependent deduction for housing benefit, it could be argued, for the purposes of an allowance against charges, that housing costs should be set at least to an equivalent of non- dependent deduction amounts based on the earned income levels which increase as income levels rise. For instance individuals with an income of £120–£180 per week are expected to contribute £21.55 towards rent and £5.70 towards council tax rising on a sliding scale to £60.60 (rent) and £8.60 (council tax) if their income is £387 or more per week.

74   Reg 4(2)(a) and Welsh 2011 guidance para 32.

the maximum charges is set by the Welsh assembly other aspects of and any changes to the local charging policy should be consulted upon.[75]

10.42 As a matter of public law, consultation will be required before any significant changes are made to a charging regime;[76] a point emphasised by the 2003 policy guidance, which makes several references to consultation including:

- Consultation is one of the guiding principles and '[w]here changes in charging policies would result in significant increases in charges for some users, this should be specifically explained and considered as part of the consultation' (paras 98 and 99);
- Users should be specifically consulted on whether and how to set an overriding maximum charge (para 17);
- Consultation should be used to establish what is a reasonable level of charge and the government expects all the issues that the guidance addresses to be explained to users and carers as part of the consultation (para 80(i) and (xi)).

10.43 The local government ombudsman has been critical of charging schemes that have been introduced without proper consultation.[77] The manner of consultation also came under severe criticism by the ombudsman in a case where it was found to have been inadequate, extremely difficult to understand, complex and unfocused, and where the results were not reported back to the council's cabinet. In this case the ombudsman observed:

'There is little point in a consultation exercise unless you tell the consultees what you are consulting them on. To say that it might prejudice the decision if consultees were told the proposals is as absurd as informing neighbours that a planning application has been received but that they cannot know what the application is for as it might prejudice the decision of the Planning Committee.'[78]

10.44 In *R (Domb) v Hammersmith and Fulham LBC*[79] the Court of Appeal found that in reintroducing charges for community care services, it was not unreasonable for the council to limit its consultation as to whether it should reintroduce charges or to raise eligibility criteria (once a decision had been made to cut council tax). There had been careful consultation and the disability discrimination duty had been sufficiently considered by the council. However, Sedley J expressed his misgivings that the appeal had to be conducted on a debatable premise – that the prior decision of the local authority that council tax was to be cut by three per cent had to be implemented thus:[80]

75 Welsh 2011 guidance para 39.
76 *R v Coventry City Council ex p Carton* (2001) 4 CCLR 41.
77 Complaint no 91A/3782 against Greenwich LBC (1993) and see also Complaint nos 02/C/14235, 02/C/15396, 02/C/15397 and 02/C/15503 against Derbyshire CC, 24 June 2004.
78 Complaint no 05/C/08648 against Oldham MBC, 29 January 2007.
79 [2009] EWCA Civ 941.
80 [2009] EWCA Civ 941 at para 80 – and see also para 2.35 above.

The object of this exercise was the sacrifice of free home care on the altar of a council tax reduction for which there was no legal requirement. The only real issue was how it was to be accomplished. As Rix LJ indicates, and as I respectfully agree, there is at the back of this a major question of public law: can a local authority, by tying its own fiscal hands for electoral ends, rely on the consequent budgetary deficit to modify its performance of its statutory duties? But it is not the issue before this court.

The assessment process and information about charges: England

10.45   The 1990 policy guidance makes it clear 'the assessment of means should, therefore, follow the assessment of need and decisions about service provision' (at para 3.31). The 'binding' 2003 policy guidance likewise places the assessment of the ability to pay *after* the service needs decision has been made. However, it stresses that information about charges should be given to a service user promptly.

> Once a person's care needs have been assessed and a decision has been made about the care to be provided, an assessment of ability to pay charges should be carried out promptly, and written information about any charges assessed as payable, and how they have been calculated, should be communicated promptly. This should normally be done before sending a first bill. Charges should not be made for any period before an assessment of charges has been communicated to the user, although this may be unavoidable where the user has not co-operated with the assessment. A first bill for a charge for a lengthy past period can cause needless anxiety. Any increase in charges should also be notified and no increased charge made for a period before the notification.[81]

10.46   The Prioritising Need guidance 2010 is clear at para 71 stating:

> Once an individual's needs, and those of their carer(s) where appropriate, have been assessed and a decision made about the support to be provided, an assessment of the individual's ability to pay charges should be carried out promptly, and written information about any charges or contributions payable, and how they have been calculated, should be communicated to the individual. This means that once a person has been identified as having an eligible need, councils should take steps to ensure that those needs are met, regardless of the person's ability to contribute to the cost of these services. An assessment of the person's ability to pay for services should therefore only take place after they have been assessed as having eligible needs. A person's ability to pay should only be used as a reason for not providing services in circumstances where a person has been assessed as needing residential accommodation, the person has the means to pay for it and if the person, or someone close to them, is capable of making the arrangements themselves.[82]

---

81   2003 policy guidance para 96.
82   Department of Health (2010) *Prioritising Need in the Context of Putting People First.*

10.47   Whilst the onus is on service users to provide the necessary information in order that the amount of the charge can be reviewed,[83] there is a concomitant obligation on the authority to ensure that it gives clients accurate information about the charges they will face and information as to how they can challenge those charges if they believe that they are unreasonable. Guidance issued by the Social Services Inspectorate in January 1994 (ostensibly as advice to its own officers – the '1994 SSI guidance') at para 28 stipulated:

> Good practice requires that users should be given an accurate indication of the charges that they will incur before they are required to commit themselves to a particular care plan. Only exceptional circumstances can justify not doing so. They also should be given a written statement of their financial liability at the earliest opportunity, with access to advice and explanation as required.

10.48   Local authorities are under great pressure from the government to find efficiencies in times of budget cuts. A section within the Department of Health tasked with helping local authorities in this endeavour has investigated the financial assessment process for domiciliary services. It found that financial assessments were often not completed until services had been in place for about six weeks, and calculated that this might result in a loss to an authority of between £300,000–£500,000 per annum. It considered that the problem is caused by councils 'delaying the financial assessment until the needs assessment is complete' and suggests that this arises because of a desire not to waste a financial staff visit. It fails, however, to have regard to the binding policy guidance that requires financial assessments to follow needs assessments, and accordingly there must be doubt as to the lawfulness of its advice: the advice being 'to trigger the financial assessment from the first exchange at the contact centre. Staff will establish that the customer has eligible needs and ask about their financial circumstances, before booking the visit.'[84]

The assessment process and information about charges: Wales

10.49   The Welsh measure brought into effect a number of changes to the process of assessment and information that must be provided in relation to domiciliary care charges. The main change is that under the Welsh charging measure s4 the local authority must[85] invite a person who is

---

83   If a service user refuses to co-operate with the financial assessment, the authority will in general be entitled to charge the full standard rate.

84   Care Services Efficiency Delivery Programme, *Initiative 003 Effective Financial Assessment*. Available at www.csed.dh.gov.uk/_library/Resources/CSED/ CSEDProduct/Effective_Financial_Assessment.pdf – the paper makes it clear that it is merely an initiative which councils are not obliged to follow.

85   This duty to invite the person to request a means test applies even where the only service provided is a flat rate charge. However, reg 13 states that the local authority is not under a duty to assess in such cases.

being offered a chargeable service (see para 10.6 above) to request a means test.[86] This implies that the decision to offer the services must come before the invitation to request a means test. Regulations specify that the information in the invitation must be in writing and must include:

(a) the services that are being offered to, or provided for, the service user for which a charge is being considered;

(b) its charging policy, which must include the following—

   (i) its policy in relation to which, if any, of the services it provides are subject to a charge,

   (ii) details of the standard charge which may be imposed in relation to any such service,

   (iii) details of any service for which a flat-rate charge is imposed, and

   (iv) details of the maximum reasonable charge for services that may be imposed in accordance with regulation 5, or the maximum reasonable charge that the local authority applies, where that charge is lower;

(c) its means assessment process;

(d) its procedure for dealing with a means assessment for a service user who receives only services for which a flat-rate charge is imposed;

(e) the information and documentation that a service user is required to provide in order that an assessment of the service user's means can be undertaken;

(f) the time, as specified in regulation 8, within which a service user is required to supply the information and documentation referred to in sub-paragraph (e);

(g) the format in which it will accept the information and documentation referred to in sub-paragraph (e);

(h) any home visiting facility that it provides within its area;

(i) the consequences of failing to respond to the invitation in accordance with sub-paragraph (f);

(j) the named individuals within the authority whom a service user should contact should that person require additional information or assistance in respect of any of the processes attendant upon the issue of the invitation;

(k) a service user's right to appoint a third party to assist, or to act on his or her behalf, in respect of all or part of the means assessment process; and

(l) the contact details of any organisation in its area which provides support or assistance of the type referred to in sub-paragraph (k).[87]

10.50   The time scale for the service user to respond to the invitation is 15 working days (although this can be extended).[88] The Welsh 2011 guidance suggests it will be good practice to remind the services user shortly before the 15 days are up and take the opportunity of establishing whether the

---

86 It is surprising that neither the regulations nor the guidance appear to cover the situation of those who lack capacity to respond to an invitation for a means-test other than where there is a representative appointed by the user, or an attorney or deputy. This could lead to a situation where a person could be charged the maximum charge because they do not have the mental capacity to respond to the invitation and they have no one who is acting as a representative.

87 Reg 7.

88 Regs 8 and 9.

individual is having difficulty in gathering the information needed.[89] The service user can appoint a representative. If the service user fails to respond to the invitation then the local authority can impose the standard charge subject to the maximum charge of £50 per week (plus any flat rate charge).[90]

10.51 The authority need not undertake an assessment where a previous assessment and determination of a charge for the service received already exists and the authority reasonably considers that there has been no relevant change in the service or financial means of the service user to warrant a new assessment.[91]

10.52 The regulations also offer transitional provisions to the effect that those whose charge is below £50 per week at the date of change continue to be charged at that rate unless they ask for a reassessment. Those whose charge was above £50 should have had their charge reduced to £50 per week on 11 April 2011 without a reassessment.[92]

10.53 Where a person is being charged for services then a statement which gives full information of the services provided, the standard charge for those services, how the individual's charge was calculated, and the right to challenge the charge must be provided within 21 days of the decision to impose or alter the charge.[93] The authority may not impose (or alter) a charge until the date the statement is provided.[94] The Welsh 2011 guidance suggests that where a service fluctuates frequently – that the information in the statement should explain this, ie 'the fluctuating level of the given service that the service user is to receive with the charge that would relate to each fluctuation of that service.' However, it cautions that this is only for frequent fluctuations and where service levels change periodically or the service itself changes then the full statement must be completed.[95]

Challenging the assessed charge: England

10.54 Where a service user wishes to challenge a non-accommodation charge, in England, the usual procedure will be to pursue the matter through the local authority's complaints procedures (see chapter 26). Although many authorities have ad hoc informal appeals processes, these do not override the ability to use the complaints process.

89 Welsh 2011 guidance para 54.
90 Reg 10. It is most likely that those who have capital above the capital limit or a very high income will opt not to respond to the invitation and merely pay the £50 per week. Service users can also withdraw from the means assessment but again will be subject to the standard charge or the maximum charge of £50 whichever is less.
91 Welsh charging measure s5(5) and Welsh 2011 guidance para 65.
92 Regs 17–20 although it is likely that as the provisions were introduced in April at a time when local authorities tend to reassess individuals due to changes in income, that most authorities will have reassessed services users against the new provisions.
93 Welsh charging measure s10 and Welsh 2011 guidance para 105.
94 Reg 16 (and reg 19 of Social Care Charges (Direct Payments) (Means Assessment and Determination of Reimbursement or Contribution) (Wales) Regulations 2011 SI No 763 in relation to contributions for direct payments).
95 Welsh 2011 guidance para 106.

10.55   The local government ombudsman has emphasised that service users should be given clear information as to the criteria for having charges reduced or waived, and of their right to a hearing before an appeal panel if their initial challenge was unsuccessful. He has also stressed the need for panel decisions to be as consistent as possible and that clear reasons for their decisions should be given so that appellants can then decide whether or not to pursue the matter further.[96]

10.56   At any hearing, the panel will need to bear in mind that an authority's power to reduce or waive charges is not limited to a consideration of the service user's financial means. As the authority has an overall discretion whether or not to levy any charges, it must retain discretion to waive or reduce charges on any ground. Such an overall discretion might be used where, for instance, the service user lacked mental capacity and the services were therefore being put in without consent, or where the service user is at risk of serious and immediate harm if the services are not provided, but refuses to have the services if he or she is charged for them.

10.57   The 2003 policy guidance at para 102 refers councils to the 1996 *Good Practice Handbook* of the former Association of County Councils/Association of Metropolitan Authorities in relation to making reviews accessible to users and ensuring consistency of decisions. This states (at p29) that 'the principle that service users should be enabled to seek independent advice and advocacy is one which needs to underpin any charging policy or procedure'. The ombudsman has specifically criticised the lack of proper advocacy assistance to appellants during the appeals process.[97] The ombudsman has also been critical of the lack of clear references to a right of appeal in decision letters that are sent to users.[98]

Challenging the assessed charge: Wales

10.58   The Welsh charging measure and regulations have introduced a review process as 'Ministers wished to introduce a consistent, relatively simple process whereby service users could have authorities review charging decisions made at an early stage, before they became complaints to an authority which may eventually end up being considered under an authority's formal complaints procedure.'[99]

10.59   In brief service users or direct payment recipients have the right to request a review, orally or in writing, of the charge or contribution. Regulation 3(2) stipulates

---

96 Complaint nos 90/A/2675, 90/A/2075, 90/A/1705, 90/A/1228 and 90/A/1172 against Essex CC (1990).
97 Complaint nos 98/C/0911, 98/C/1166, 98/C/1975, 98/C/1977 and 98/C/1978 against Stockton-on Tees BC, 29 July 1999.
98 Complaint nos 02/C/14235, 02/C/15396, 02/C/15397 and 02/C/15503 against Derbyshire CC, 24 June 2004.
99 Welsh 2011 guidance para 119. This has been done via The Social Care Charges (Review of Charging Decisions) (Wales) Regulations 2011. Section 17 of the Welsh 2011 guidance covers in detail the review process that should be followed.

A request may relate to (but is not limited to) the following circumstances–
(a) a local authority having not complied with any of the duties imposed upon it by the Measure or by regulations made under it;
(b) a local authority having not correctly applied its own charging policy in imposing a charge, or determining a reimbursement or contribution;
(c) an error having been made in the calculation of the charge, reimbursement or contribution;
(d) a charge having been imposed for a service that has not at any time been provided to the requester;
(e) the requester's financial circumstances having changed since the charge, reimbursement or contribution was calculated;
(f) a requester considering that they do not have the financial means to pay the charge, reimbursement or contribution as to do so would cause them financial hardship.

10.60 On receiving the request for a review the authority must appoint a person to deal with the matter, and acknowledge the receipt of the request within five working days. Where the person is in receipt of direct payments they will be paid gross during the time of the review. If the requester wishes to have a home visit the authority must provide one.[100] The time limits for the individual to provide further documentation, if this is reasonably required, is 15 days (which can be extended).[101]

10.61 Once the information is provided the local authority must make a decision within 10 working days and send a statement to the requester giving reasons for the decision and information about the complaints process. If the authority cannot meet the deadline it must send information stating why it cannot do so and the date by which it will make a decision.[102]

10.62 The guidance states the local authority need to take account of any wider 'financial hardship' a service user may have as a result of their impairment, condition or personal circumstances.[103] If the decision results in an amendment of the charge, reimbursement or contribution, the authority must also send the service user a revised statement of that charge, as required by section 10 of the Charging Measure and regulation 19 of the Direct Payments Regulations.[104]

The consequences of non-payment

10.63 Where the community care service is provided by the authority in consequence of a statutory duty (for instance under CSDPA 1970 s2), the service cannot as a matter of law be withdrawn merely because the service user is refusing to pay for it. The ombudsman has held, accordingly, that it

---

100 Social Care Charges (Review of Charging Decisions) (Wales) Regulations 2011 reg 7.
101 Social Care Charges (Review of Charging Decisions) (Wales) Regulations 2011 reg 8.
102 Social Care Charges (Review of Charging Decisions) (Wales) Regulations 2011 reg 9.
103 Welsh 2011 guidance para 142 where examples are given.
104 Welsh 2011 guidance para 137.

is maladministration to allow a person to terminate his or her care services due to an inability to pay for them, without advising that social services cannot withdraw services for non-payment;[105] and for the council to take such action without first informing the service user of his or her right to challenge the charge.[106]

10.64   The policy guidance states:

> Once someone has been assessed as needing a service, that service should not be withdrawn because the user refuses to pay the charge. The council should continue to provide the service, while pursuing the debt, if necessary through the civil courts.[107]

10.65   HASSASSAA s17(4) and s1(5) of the Welsh measure state that any charge levied 'may, without prejudice to any other method of recovery, be recovered summarily as a civil debt'. The use of the phrase 'summarily as a civil debt' is generally taken as a reference to Magistrates' Courts Act 1980 s58(1). In principle it appears undesirable that such a procedure (normally reserved for the collection of overdue local taxes such as council tax) be used to collect such monies. A far more appropriate course would be the use of the small claims system in the county courts. It is unclear whether local authorities are able to use this option, although, as the magistrates' procedure is expressed as being 'without prejudice to any other method', it would in principle appear to be a possibility.[108]

10.66   The advantage of the county court process is that the case will be considered by a judge familiar with such civil concepts as lack of mental capacity and its legal consequences (a problem which is frequently an issue with frail service users) and the civil courts have greater expertise in determining realistic debt repayment arrangements. Where a local authority seeks to enforce charges through a county court action, the court is permitted to review the reasonableness of the original charging decision and the reasons given for its refusal to waive the charges[109] – and if the reasons for not waiving the charges are irrational at public law, then the county court is entitled to refuse the application.[110]

Charging for direct payments and personal budgets

10.67   The policy intention underlying the charging for direct payments and personal budgets (more generally considered at para 12.50) is that

---

105   Complaint no 99/C/1983 against Durham, 9 October 2000.
106   Complaint nos 02/C/14235, 02/C/15396, 02/C/15397 and 02/C/15503 against Derbyshire CC, 24 June 2004.
107   2003 policy guidance para 97, similar wording is in Welsh 2011 guidance para 116.
108   In *Avon CC v Hooper* [1997] 1 WLR 1605, (1997–98) 1 CCLR 366 the proceedings took place in the High Court and the jurisdictional issue does not appear to have been raised.
109   *Wandsworth LBC v Winder* [1985] UKHL 2, [1985] 1 AC 461.
110   As did HHJ Hawkesworth QC in *City of Bradford MDC v Matthews* (2002) BD No 108518, 9 October 2002.

recipients should be subject to the same regime as that which applies to other service users. Accordingly the 2003 policy guidance (at para 87) advises:

> In considering whether, and if so how, to ask an individual to make a financial contribution to the cost of their care package, councils should treat people receiving direct payments as they would have treated them under the council's charging policy, if those people were receiving the equivalent services. Charges should be assessed and made in all respects in accordance with this guidance.

10.68 In Wales the Welsh charging measure s12(3) stipulates that reimbursements or contributions should be subject to equivalent conditions to those that apply in relation to charges for services. Accordingly the Social Care Charges (Direct Payments) (Means Assessment and Determination of Reimbursement or Contribution) (Wales) Regulations 2011 contain provisions that are virtually identical to the regulations described above in relation to people who do not receive direct payments, and the Welsh 2011 guidance uses the term 'service user' to cover those who receive direct payments.[111]

10.69 In England[112] the relevant regulations[113] have the effect of creating a materially different regime for direct payments, since it requires the authority to have 'regard to the prescribed person's means'. It obliges the authority, therefore, to undertake a means assessment, which it is not required to do for service users who are not receiving direct payments. This difference in treatment applies, notwithstanding that in 2010 the regulations were amended,[114] to overcome the obligation to undertake a means test for recipients of direct payments when the recipient used their direct payment to purchase residential care.[115] The amendment was effected specifically in order to put direct payment recipients on the same footing as those whose residential care is provided or arranged by the local authority, namely that the authority can charge a reasonable amount for up to eight weeks without having to apply the mandatory means test for residential care.[116] The same provisions apply in Wales, to enable the

---

111 Welsh 2011 guidance paras 7–8.
112 In Wales, the Community Care, Services for Carers and Children's Services (Direct Payments) (Wales) Regulations 2011 SI No 831 (W125) reg 10 covers charging in similar terms although linking it to the Welsh charging measure and the Social Care Charges (Direct Payments) (Means Assessment and Determination of Reimbursement or Contribution) (Wales) Regulations 2011.
113 Community Care, Services for Carers and Children's Services (Direct Payments) (England) Regulations 2009 SI No 1887 reg 9 as amended by the Community Care, Services for Carers and Children's Services (Direct Payments) (England) (Amendment) Regulations 2010 SI No 2246.
114 The Community Care, Services for Carers and Children's Services (Direct Payments) (England) (Amendment) Regulations 2010 SI No 2246 reg 2 which amended the Community Care, Services for Carers and Children's Services (Direct Payments) (England) Regulations 2009 SI No1887 reg 9.
115 See para 12.37 for the limited ability to use direct payments for residential care.
116 See also Department of Health (2010) *Fairer Contributions Guidance* para 7.2(b).

authority to charge a reasonable amount when a direct payment is used for purchasing residential care.[117]

10.70 England has issued guidance in relation to contributions to personal budgets. This guidance does not make any changes to individual charges as charges for direct payments and personal budgets are still subject to HASSASSAA 1983 and the 2003 policy guidance. The *Fairer Contributions Guidance*[118] which came into effect in March 2010 is guidance to local authorities on how to set a 'chargeable amount' when services are not provided or arranged, but based on an amount calculated through a resource allocation system (see para 4.4). Where authorities do not provide any subsidised or free services the maximum chargeable amount could be the full cost (ie 100%) of the amount a person is calculated as needing, to meet their assessed needs – although in general the actual charge to the individual will be less depending on the means-test under *Fairer Charging*.[119]

10.71 Para 2.12 of the guidance advises that where authorities provide subsidised or free services and 'a portion of the personal budget is going to be deployed on such services from the council or on their equivalent services via direct payments it would be fair to exclude their value from any portion of the personal budget to which a percentage is applied.' The guidance gives as its aim, to ensure that individuals are not be disadvantaged by having a personal budget or direct payment and so do not miss out on free or subsidised services. The guidance explains the calculation thus:

> 2.14. In determining the chargeable amount, councils should separately calculate:
>
> 1) any chargeable amount for that part of the personal budget which is to be spent on services which, or the equivalent of which, are not subsidised when provided by the council, ensuring that non-personal budget holders are not treated less favourably than the budget holder and
>
> 2) any chargeable amount for that part of the personal budget which is to be spent on services which, or the equivalent of which, are subsidised services when provided by the council (based on the council's charging policy).
>
> 2.15. These two figures added together will give the maximum possible contribution to the personal budget that the person might be asked to make, subject to any lower locally set maximum contribution and the person's available income.[120]

10.72 The guidance further reminds authorities that no charges must be made for equipment and after care services and that:

---

117 Reg 10(8) of the Community Care, Services for Carers and Children's Services (Direct Payments) (Wales) Regulations 2011 SI No 831 (W125).
118 Department of Health (2010) *Fairer Contributions Guidance 2010: calculating an individual's contribution to their personal budget.*
119 Para 2.4.
120 However, many authorities are moving away from providing free or subsidised services.

Care must therefore be taken to exclude from charging any portion of a personal budget that is to be spent on these items or services. Similarly, a personal budget holder should not be expected to make a financial contribution towards advice about the availability of services or for assessment, including assessment of community care needs. Ongoing support such as payroll services could be subject to a contribution.[121]

Services not directly provided by the social services authority

NHS services

10.73 While the principles of charging for community care services are relatively straightforward in relation to services provided by a social services authority, they become more complex in the case of jointly supplied services, such as those provided by a jointly funded NHS/social services arrangement. In this respect the 2003 policy guidance advises:[122]

Use of powers to transfer funds
88. Local councils and health authorities may jointly commission social care services under section 28A of the NHS Act 1977.[123] The details of any charges should be devised with advice from the local council's own lawyers. The council may recover from users up to the full cost of the social care service, even though the NHS may have met some or all of the cost of the social care service. Local councils must, however, bear in mind that section 17 of the HASSASSA Act 1983 is not a provision designed to enable them to raise general revenue. If a council purchases social care and a health authority purchases healthcare services from the same provider, then charges to users may only be made for the social care element. Any services for which the NHS has underlying responsibility are automatically free at the point of use,[124] in whatever setting they are provided and whichever agencies provide or commission the service in practice.

Health Act 1999 Partnerships[125]
89. The Health Act 1999 did not alter the local authority powers to charge in the event of a partnership arrangement. In agreeing partnership arrangements, agencies will have to consider how best to manage charging (where local councils charge for services) and how to clarify the difference between charged-for and non-charged for services. There is no intention to increase or expand charging arrangements through the Partnership

---

121 Para 7.1: it is arguable that contributions should only be required for pay roll services if these have been included within the personal budget otherwise the payments for pay roll services would leave a personal budget recipient with less money than required to meet their assessed needs.

122 The same guidance was in the previous Welsh guidance at paras 76–78, but the Welsh 2011 guidance is silent on the subject.

123 Now NHSA 2006 s256; NHS(W)A 2006 s194.

124 Other than services for which specific charging powers exist, such as NHS prescription charges.

125 These provisions are now to be found in NHSA 2006 ss75–76 and 256–257/ NHS(W)A 2006 ss33–34 and 194–196.

Arrangements. In entering into an arrangement, the partners will need to agree on the approach to be taken on charging.

90. Partners will need to bear in mind that, where charging is retained, the arrangements will need to be carefully explained to users of services, to avoid any misunderstanding that NHS services are being charged for, especially when an NHS Trust is providing a service, part of which is being charged for. It will be critical that charging arrangements are properly explained at the outset of the assessment process. See section XIX below. The existing charging review or appeals mechanisms should be made clear to the user.

Mental Health Act 1983 services

10.74   Authorities are only empowered to charge for the community care services listed in HASSASSAA 1983 s17(2). This list does not mention the MHA 1983 and accordingly the 2003 policy guidance reminds authorities that they must not charge for MHA 1983 s117 services.[126] The Welsh regulations specify that charges cannot be imposed for after-care services.[127] It is, however, silent on the question of charging for guardianship under MHA 1983 s7. This is considered in detail at para 20.52 below.

Supporting People services

10.75   In England the 'Supporting People' grant support (which was formerly aid under Local Government Act 2000, s93) was withdrawn in April 2011 (see para 15.122 below). The monies formerly allocated under this grant are now paid as part of the local authority 'Formula Grant'. As we discuss at para 15.22 below, there is considerable uncertainty as to the basis for continuing payments made to individuals of what was formerly supporting people's monies. Arguably the provisions for making charges for such services[128] (and the circumstances where there is relief from such charges) still subsist, or at the very least create a legitimate expectation amongst service users that they will continue to be applied until such time as a new charging scheme is implemented (and presumably such an initiative would require prior consultation with those liable to be affected).

10.76   In practice, it appears that the 2003 supporting people's charging guidance is still being adhered to by a number of local authorities. This provides that short term services of less than two years should be free of charge, and individuals who receive housing benefit should receive supporting people services free of charge. Local authorities can use the 2003 policy guidance for *Fairer Charging* to establish the level of charge for people who are not in receipt of housing benefit.[129] The Welsh 2011

---

126   2003 policy guidance para 7, Welsh 2011 guidance para 10.
127   The Social Care Charges (Means Assessment and Determination of Charges) (Wales) Regulations 2011 SI No 962 (W136) reg 4(1)(b) and Welsh 2011 guidance para 32.
128   Local Authorities (Charges for Specified Welfare Services) (England) Regulations 2003 SI No 907 as amended.
129   Office of Deputy Prime Minister (ODPM) (2003) *Supporting People Guidance*, para 43.

guidance makes it clear that Supporting People Services are not within the Welsh Charging Measure and directs local authorities with queries about them to the Housing Directorate of the assembly Government.[130] The Welsh guidance[131] that was issued in relation to charging for supporting people's services in Wales still refers to *Fairer Charging* which no longer exists.

Charging for Chronically Sick and Disabled Persons Act 1970 s2 services

10.77   Notwithstanding that CSDPA 1970 s2 services are not listed in HASSASSAA 1983 s17(2), or the Welsh charging measure, the 1994 SSI guidance advised that charges could be recovered for services provided under that section, as 'these services are arranged by local authorities in exercise of their functions under s29 of the 1948 Act'. This advice was upheld by the Court of Appeal, in *R v Powys CC ex p Hambidge*.[132] The relationship between CSDPA 1970 s2 and NAA 1948 s29 is, however, a difficult one. While the Court of Appeal decision confirmed that local authorities are acting lawfully when they charge adults for the services they provide under CSDPA 1970 s2, the judgment did not address the problem of the different client groups covered by the two sections. If services, assessed as being necessary under section 2, are actually provided 'in exercise of functions under section 29', the question arose as to the authority for providing disabled children with such services since section 29 only applies to persons aged 18 or over. This question was resolved in *R (Spink) v Wandsworth LBC*[133] where the Court of Appeal held that charges could be recovered for services provided under section 2 for disabled children, as these services were arranged by local authorities in exercise of their functions under CA 1989 s17 (for which charges can be levied – see para 23.78).

Possible changes to charges

10.78   The Law Commission has recommended that a regulation-making power should be introduced to enable the secretary of state and Welsh ministers to require or authorise local authorities to charge for residential and non-residential services, or to establish a framework for services. The existing regulations-making power, which enables services to be provided free of charge should be maintained and as a minimum the current services that must be provided free of charge should be included in the regulations.[134]

130   Welsh 2011 guidance para 110.
131   *Charging and assessment for recipients of Supporting Peoples Services*, Welsh Assembly Government 2003.
132   (1997–98) 1 CCLR 458, CA.
133   [2004] EWHC 2314 (Admin), [2005] 1 WLR 258.
134   *Adult Social Care*, Law Com No 326. Recommendations 37 and 39.

10.79   The Commission on Funding of Care and Support has made a number of recommendations regarding the way care should be funded and paid for in the future. Those recommendations relating to residential care are listed in chapter 8. The main proposals in the report *Fairer Care Funding*[135] in relation to domiciliary charging are:

- To place a cap on the amount a person would pay for care over a lifetime at a suggested figure of £35,000. Contributions would count towards this cap based on an assessment by social services that a person has substantial needs,[136] and the amount social services considered necessary to meet that need. Contributions would count for both domiciliary and residential care.
- People whose disability starts before they are 40 years will get free care and if a person needs care between 40 and 65 there would be an increasing rate to have to pay towards the cap depending on when care needs started.
- Everyone would be entitled to universal disability benefits (which will also support people in addressing lower care and support needs).
- As a potential further change a rationalisation of housing assets to create a level playing field between domiciliary and residential care and the way housing is treated. To support such change a universal deferred payments scheme would need to be in place.
- Another potential further change would be to introduce a taper (suggested at 65%) into the way income is counted above the minimum threshold of IS/PC plus 25%

10.80   At the time of writing, September 2011, it is not known how far the Government might agree to these proposals. A White Paper on wider social care issues is due early 2012 together with a progress report on funding reform.[137]

---

135 Commission on Funding of Care and Support (2011) *Fairer Care Funding: the report of the commission on funding of care and support* (the 'Dilnot' Report).
136 This level is proposed 'in the short term' based on the fact most local authorities now only fund care at substantial level.
137 Department of Health (2011) *Creating a fair and sustainable care and support system*, press release, July 2011.

Intermediate care and re-ablement

Introduction

11.1   Intermediate care (also referred to in this chapter as 're-ablement') is the product of the previous government's response to the Royal Commission for Long Term Care's report *With Respect to Old Age*.[1] Rather than meet the proposal to fund free personal care, the English government decided to invest £900 million between 2001–2004 into 'new intermediate care and related services to promote independence and improve quality of care for older people'.[2] The initial programme was not underpinned by legislation, but was shaped by statutory guidance[3] that sought to build on health and social services' legislative joint working obligations – with the aim of improving rehabilitation services as well as services that helped avoid unnecessary hospital admissions.

11.2   Although the current English scheme is governed by brief regulations (the '2003 regulations'[4]) the detail is provided by non-statutory 'best practice' guidance (the '2009 guidance')[5] which was augmented by charging specific guidance[6] issued as a result of concerns that some authorities were improperly making charges for this service. Councils were advised to review their arrangements and satisfy themselves that they were not wrongly charging, and to make refunds in appropriate cases. A similar (but less detailed scheme) operates in Wales, albeit that it is subject only to Welsh Government guidance.[7]

11.3   The intermediate care initiative is aimed at freeing up acute hospital beds and promoting the independence of older people. It provides intensive short term support services to prevent unnecessary admissions and facilitate earlier discharge, either back home or via 'step-down' community hospital/care home facilities.[8]

11.4   Although the provision of intermediate care services will often satisfy a patient's needs for rehabilitation and recuperation, this will not always be the case. Given the time limited nature of the service, it will frequently be only a first stage of a programme – for which the NHS may have full responsibility.[9]

1   Cm 4192–01, March 1999.
2   Department of Health (2000) *NHS Plan: The Plan for Investment and Reform*, Cm 4818–1, para 7.4.
3   LAC (2001)1/HSC 2001/01 issued under LASSA 1970 s7: now superseded by Department of Health (2009) *Intermediate Care – Halfway Home: updated guidance for the NHS and local authorities.*
4   Community Care (Delayed Discharges etc.) Act (Qualifying Services) (England) Regulations 2003 SI No 1196.
5   Department of Health (2009) *Intermediate Care – Halfway Home: updated guidance for the NHS and local authorities.*
6   LAC (DH) 2010 (6).
7   National Assembly for Wales (2002) *Intermediate Care Guidance* WHC (2002) 128 NAFWC 43/02.
8   The Department of Health has produced a model contract for use when contracting with independent sector care homes for intermediate care – see Department of Health (2001) *A guide to contracting for intermediate care services.*
9   See in this respect, comments in para 11.8 and chapter 14 below.

11.5   It appears that the majority of people using intermediate care are older people, with over half being over 85 years of age[10] and that while the programme has clear benefits for many patients, it is questionable whether short term intermediate care is effective in meeting the needs of older people with more severe cognitive problems or of those who are suffering from depression.[11]

11.6   A 2002 Nuffield Foundation Research Report suggests that this failure can be attributed to inadequate assessment, skills shortages, cash limits, inadequate home support and the timescale of six weeks being inappropriate for many people with mental health needs. It appears that because of this skills (or 'attitude') deficit many people with dementia are deteriorating, through inappropriate care, in acute settings such that they are not being enabled to maximise their coping skills and to return to community based situations.[12] The 2009 guidance stresses the importance of intermediate care services being inclusive of people with mental health needs and that 'those with dementia may need an extended period of intermediate care while a physical condition stabilises'.[13]

11.7   The Welsh Government has stated that re-ablement will be at the heart of its approach to social care, and that re-ablement services will be provided across Wales, planned and commissioned on a regional basis led jointly by social services and the NHS.[14]

Definition

11.8   The 2003 regulations[15] define intermediate care as a 'service which consists of a structured programme of care provided for a limited period of time to assist a person to maintain or regain the ability to live in his home' which 'is required to be provided free of charge to any person to whom it is provided for any period up to and including six weeks'.

11.9   The 2009 guidance describes intermediate care as a service that:

- is targeted at people who would otherwise face unnecessarily prolonged hospital stays or inappropriate admission to acute in-patient care, long term residential care, or continuing NHS in-patient care;
- is provided on the basis of a comprehensive assessment, resulting in a structured individual care plan that involves active therapy, treatment or opportunity for recovery;
- has a planned outcome of maximising independence and typically enabling patient/users to resume living at home;

10 Institute of Health Sciences and Public Health Research (2005) *An Evaluation of Intermediate Care for Older People Final Report – 2005*, University of Leeds.
11 Institute of Health Sciences and Public Health Research (2005) *An Evaluation of Intermediate Care for Older People Final Report – 2005*, University of Leeds.
12 Nuffield Institute for Health (2002) *Meeting Mental Health Needs in Intermediate Care.*
13 Department of Health (2009) *Intermediate Care – Halfway Home: updated guidance for the NHS and local authorities*, p4.
14 *Sustainable Social Services A Framework for Action:* WAG 10 - 11086
15 Community Care (Delayed Discharges etc) Act (Qualifying Services) (England) Regulations 2003 SI No 1196 regs 2 and 4.

- is time-limited, normally no longer than six weeks and frequently as little as 1–2 weeks or less; and
- involves cross-professional working, with a single assessment framework, single professional records and shared protocols.[16]

11.10   The 2009 guidance stresses inclusion of adults of all ages including young people managing transition to adulthood, people with dementia, flexibility over the length of the time limited period, integration with mainstream health and social care, timely access to specialist support, and governance and quality. In particular it suggests that intermediate care could also form part of a pathway for end of life care if there were specific goals for the individual and carer(s) that could be addressed in a time limited period. It gives as an example 'enabling someone to move back home, establishing a suitable environment and routine, setting up a care package and helping carers to develop the skills they might need'.[17]

11.11   In line with current policy on helping people to remain in their homes, the 2009 guidance stresses the importance of considering those who might be facing admission to residential care, and that they 'should be given the opportunity to benefit from rehabilitation and recuperation and their needs to be assessed in a setting other than an acute ward. They should not be transferred directly to long-term residential care from an acute hospital ward unless there are exceptional circumstances.' The exceptional circumstances might include those who have already completed a period of specialist rehabilitation; those judged to have had sufficient previous attempts at being supported at home and those for whom a period in residential intermediate care followed by another move is judged likely to be distressing.[18]

Service models

11.12   For planning purposes, intermediate care can be categorised into various service models, which are identified in 2009 guidance as:

- rapid response teams to prevent avoidable admission to hospital for patients referred from GPs, A&E or other sources, with short-term care and support in their own home;
- acute care at home from specialist teams, including some treatment such as administration of intravenous antibiotics;
- residential rehabilitation in a setting such as a residential care home or community hospital, for people who do not need 24-hour consultant-led medical care but need a short period of therapy and rehabilitation, ranging from one to about six weeks;
- supported discharge in a patient's own home, with nursing and/or therapeutic support, and home care support and community equipment where necessary, to allow rehabilitation and recovery at

16 The Welsh guidance is practically identical at para 11.
17 Department of Health (2009) *Intermediate Care – Halfway Home: updated guidance for the NHS and local authorities*, p5.
18 Department of Health (2009) *Intermediate Care – Halfway Home: updated guidance for the NHS and local authorities*, p4.

home. The arrangements may work well in specialist accommodation such as extra care housing;

- day rehabilitation for a limited period in a day hospital or day centre, possibly in conjunction with other forms of intermediate care support.

11.13 The Welsh guidance does not specifically list these as being service models for intermediate care, but suggests a similar list in the glossary at Annex 1.

11.14 The 2009 guidance also reminds authorities that sheltered or extra care housing can be part of intermediate care, and that telecare, rapid care and repair services also enable people to move back home.

Charging

11.15 In England the 2003 regulations have put beyond doubt that intermediate care is free for any period up to and including six weeks.[19] Although no equivalent regulations exist in Wales, the guidance states that intermediate care should be free of charge.[20] However, the latest Welsh guidance on charging for non-residential services, reminds local authorities of what it calls 'previous' guidance namely NAFWC 05/02 which had the overall aim of providing up to 6 weeks free homecare, and just states that authorities will 'need to ensure that their charging policies support their own local arrangements to achieve the general aims.'[21]

11.16 A problem remains, because different localities describe intermediate care in different ways, and the potential exists therefore, for it not to be free purely because it is not described as intermediate care.[22]

11.17 It also appears that on occasions the intermediate care team is unable (due to resource constraints) to take on new work, such that patients may be referred elsewhere. In such cases, the mere fact that the service is not being provided by the intermediate care team, should not be used as a reason for charges to be levied. This view has been strengthened by the functional approach taken by the 2009 guidance (see para 11.12 above).

19 Community Care (Delayed Discharges etc.) Act (Qualifying Services) (England) Regulations 2003 SI No 1196 reg 4(2).
20 NAFWC 43/2002 para 22.
21 *Introducing More Consistency in Local Authorities' Charging for Non-Residential Social Services*: WAG10–12408 paras 117 and 118.
22 The terms intermediate care, rehabilitation and re-ablement tend to be used interchangeably. It is of interest that had the Personal Care at Home Act 2010 been enacted (the present government has stated it will not be) the draft regulations proposed a definition of re-ablement as a 'service which consists of a structured programme of care provided for a limited period of time to assist a person to maintain or regain the ability to live at home.' It would have replaced the definition of intermediate care in the 2003 regulations and become the definition for re-ablement. The Care Services Efficiency Delivery programme has produce a document that purports to explain the subtle difference between intermediate care and re-ablement see Department of Health (2010) *Intermediate Care and Home Care Re-ablement: What's in a Name?* Care Services Efficiency Delivery: Homecare Re-ablement Toolkit 2010.

11.18   In England for patients who have been discharged from hospital, it is planned that their care should always be free for the first 30 days as it will be provided by the NHS acute trusts from April 2012. The aim of this initiative is to reduce the growing numbers of emergency readmissions to hospital. 'Making hospitals responsible for a patient's ongoing care after discharge will create more joined-up working between hospitals and community services and may be supported by the developments in re-ablement and post-discharge support. This will improve quality and per-formance and shift the focus to the outcome for the patient.'[23] This is described in more detail in para 5.52 above. It has provisionally been clarified that once the NHS takes responsibility for the first 30 days a person could get '30 days of free NHS care followed by up to six weeks of free intermediate care.'[24]

---

23 Revision to the Department of Health Operating Framework of the NHS in England 2010/11 para 31.
24 Department of Health (2011) *Changes to the tariff for post-discharge support and additional funding for re-ablement in 2010–11 and future years*, annex 3. Although final guidance on the 30-day post discharge arrangements has still to be published.

CHAPTER 12

Direct payments and the Independent Living Fund

continued

Introduction

12.1 Direct payments are a different way by which local authorities (and in certain situations the NHS) can discharge their community care responsibilities. Having assessed a need, social services can satisfy that need not by the provision of care services but by the payment of cash to the service user or someone on his or her behalf. Historically such an arrangement was not possible: although the principal social care statutes provided social services with flexibility as to how they discharged their obligations, they almost invariably prohibited the payment of cash directly to the service user.[1]

12.2 The inability of service users to make their own care arrangements was frequently seen as disabling and disempowering.[2] In addition research suggested that the making of direct payments could result in much improved user satisfaction, and indeed cost savings to local authorities.[3] Kestenbaum, for instance, drew attention to the high value placed by service users on choice and control and that in general this could not be provided by local authorities:

> It is not simply a matter of resource levels, though these are significant. As important are the qualities that any large-scale service providing organisation would find hard to deliver: choice of care assistant, flexibility, consistency, control of times and tasks, etc.[4]

12.3 As a consequence of this pressure for reform a number of direct payment options have been developed over the last 25 years. Initially these consisted of 'indirect' or 'third party schemes' whereby the local authority paid the cash to an intermediary who then brokered the care arrangements that the service user required. 1988 saw the development of the first 'Independent Living Fund' which specifically allowed for direct payments to a restricted group of disabled people from a fund set up by the Department of Social Security rather than via local authorities. In 1996 the provisions of the Community Care (Direct Payments) Act (CC(DP)A) 1996 brought the possibility of direct payments by social services to almost all adult disabled people.[5] The 1996 Act was augmented by the Carers and Disabled Children Act (CDCA) 2000 which extended[6] direct payments to certain carers and parents of disabled children. These developments have

1 See eg National Assistance Act (NAA) 1948 s29(6)(a) and National Health Service Act (NHSA) 2006 Sch 20 para 2(4)/National Health Service (Wales) Act (NHS(W)A) 2006 Sch 15 para 2(4). Although Children Act (CA) 1989 s17(6) (prior to its amendment by the Carers and Disabled Children Act (CDCA) 2000) permitted the payment of cash, this was only in 'in exceptional circumstances' (section 17(6) has now been amended by the Children and Young Persons Act 2008 s24 to omit the words 'in exceptional circumstances'.
2 See eg J Morris, *Independent lives: community care and disabled people*, Macmillan, 1993.
3 See eg K Kestenbaum, *Independent living: a review,* Joseph Rowntree Foundation, 1996.
4 K Kestenbaum, *Independent living: a review,* Joseph Rowntree Foundation, 1996, p77.
5 Although older people had to wait until 2000 before they could be make use of direct payments.
6 By amendment to the CA 1989 – inserting section 17A.

now been superseded by the provisions of Health and Social Care Act (HSCA) 2001 ss57–58.

12.4   Notwithstanding the perceived benefits of the direct payments scheme, local authorities incur not inconsiderable costs in providing support for direct payment service users and in the training of staff. A 2006 Audit Commission study suggested that these costs generally outweighed potential savings in transferring administrative responsibilities to direct payment recipients,[7] although 2009 research has suggested that such payments may be cost neutral, but that the 'opportunity costs savings' are appreciable.[8]

12.5   The Department of Health has, since the enactment of the 2001 reforms, placed considerable pressure on councils to increase the number of individuals receiving such support. Initially the target numbers were expressed as 'crucial performance indicators',[9] although they have since been subsumed into targets that have been set for the implementation of the personalisation programme (see para 3.7). The 2010 social services *Vision for Adult Social Care* in England,[10] maintained this drive with the requirement that authorities 'provide personal budgets, preferably as direct payments, to everyone eligible' by April 2013. In April 2011 the Department of Health announced that intention to issue directions to ensure that 'a full and open discussion about direct payments' took place with all service users.[11]

12.6   There has been a linear increase in number of people receiving direct payments in England – rising from 24,000 users in 2004–05 to 107,000 in 2009–10, when there were, however, a total of 1.46 million people receiving community based services.[12] The numbers do not disclose the whole picture, in that the total spend on such payments for 2008/09 (the most recent data at the time of writing) amounted to £605 million – only 4% of overall gross spend on adult care by councils. The data also discloses the wide variation in the types of people seeking these payments – such that although 9.5% of all adults aged 18–64 receiving community-based or carers services received direct payments, for those aged 65 and over the figure was only 3.6%.[13]

---

7   Audit Commission, *Choosing well*, 2006.
8   T Stainton, S Boyce and C Phillips, 'Independence pays: a cost and resource analysis of direct payments in two local authorities', (2009) *Disability and Society*, Vol 24, No 2, March 2009, pp161–172.
9   In England the number of direct payment arrangements in any particular authority has been included as a Key Threshold criterion, see www.csci.gov.uk/care_provider/councils/paf/performance_indicator_definiti/2006–07_pis.aspx
10   Department of Health (2010) *A vision for adult social care: capable communities and active citizens* para 4.9.
11   Department of Health Press Release 13 April 2011. http://nds.coi.gov.uk/Content/detail.aspx?NewsAreaId=2&ReleaseID=419164&SubjectId=2
12   NHS Information Centre (2011) *Community Care Statistics 2009–10: Social Services Activity Report, England* p9 at www.ic.nhs.uk/webfiles/publications/009_Social_Care/carestats0910asrfinal/Community_Care_Statistics_200910_Social_Services_Activity_Report_England.pdf.
13   Care Quality Commission (2010) *The state of healthcare and adult social care in England: key themes and quality of services in 2009*, HC 343, p30.

Direct payments and the Health and Social Care Act 2001

12.7 The power to provide direct payments under the CC(DP)A 1996 and those deriving from the CDCA 2000 have now been superseded in England and Wales by the provisions of HSCA 2001 ss57–58.

12.8 Section 57 of the 2001 Act provides the secretary of state in England and the Welsh Government with regulatory making powers to enable direct payments to be made to persons for whom a local authority has decided to provide services as a result of an assessment under either National Health Service and Community Care Act (NHSCCA) 1990 s47 or CDCA 2000 s2. Section 58 of the 2001 Act amends the Children Act (CA) 1989 s17A and provides the secretary of state in England and the Welsh Government[14] with regulatory making powers to enable direct payments to be made when, as a result of an assessment under CA 1989 s17, the authority has decided that services should be provided. In such a case, the payment may be made either to the person with parental responsibility for a disabled child, or to a disabled person with parental responsibility for a child[15] or to a disabled child aged 16 or 17. The 2001 Act additionally repealed the relevant parts of the 1996 Act[16] (and those deriving from the CDCA 2000).

12.9 The 2001 Act's delegated powers have been used in England[17] and Wales[18] and regulations issued (the 'regulations') which provide that individuals can insist upon a direct payment in certain situations. The central criteria being:

- the person consents to the making of a direct payment (or a suitable third part receives them on behalf of a person who lacks capacity to consent to the payment);
- that payments can only be made to persons who appear to be capable of managing a direct payment alone or with 'such assistance as may be available to him';
- the person is entitled to services under the community care legislation or the Carers and Disabled Children Act (CDCA) 2000 or (in the case of a parent of a child in need) the CA 1989;
- the person is not a proscribed person (effectively someone with an addiction problem who is subject to certain court orders);
- the local authority is satisfied that the person's needs for the relevant

---

14 The Welsh Government has power to legislate about direct payments – The National Assembly for Wales (Legislative Competence) (Social Welfare) Order 2009 SI No 3010.

15 See para 3.44 above.

16 HSCA 2001 s67 and Sch 6.

17 The Community Care, Services for Carers and Children's Services (Direct Payments) (England) Regulations 2009 SI No 1887.

18 The Community Care, Services for Carers and Children's Services (Direct Payments) (Wales) Regulations 2011 SI No 831 (W125). It appears that these regulations have drafting errors and will be amended/replaced – see http://wales.gov.uk/publications/accessinfo/drnewhomepage/drlegislation/2011/drftdirectpaymntregs/?lang=en

service can be met by securing the provision of it by means of a direct payment (or in the case of a child in need — that his/her welfare will be safeguarded and promoted by securing it by the provision of it by means of the direct payment);

12.10   In addition to the regulations, (2009) practice guidance has been issued by the Department of Health[19] and (2004) policy guidance by the Welsh Assembly.[20] The Welsh Government is consulting on revised policy and practice guidance[21] and in the following section this April 2010 guidance and the English 2009 guidance is collectively referred to as the 'guidance'. The relevant paragraph numbers of the Welsh guidance are cited in the footnotes and where the guidance differs materially, this difference is addressed in the text.

The obligation to make direct payments

12.11   Individuals are not assessed for direct payments. The direct payment scheme is integral to the assessment and care planning process and such payments are not available unless and until the appropriate assessment has been undertaken; ie either a community care assessment or an assessment under CA 1989 or under CDCA 2000. However, once a local authority has decided that services are to be provided, then (unless one of the below detailed exemptions apply – see paras 12.13 and 12.37) it can be required to provide direct payments in lieu of services: the relevant regulations being phrased in mandatory terms.[22] It follows that it is unlawful for a local authority to have a policy of refusing direct payments for certain services (ie services it can provide 'in house'[23] or via a block contracted service[24]) or of requiring reasons to be given by a potential recipient of direct payments as to why he or she wishes this facility.[25]

12.12   In practice, such an obligation can create budgetary difficulties for local authorities – especially where their expenditure on services is committed to block contracts or to the funding of 'in-house' services. In such situations, a requirement by an individual to switch to a direct payment may create additional expenditure, since the authority will remain liable (at least in the short term) to fund the service no longer required. However, given that much of the governmental pressure to increase the number of people receiving direct payments stems from a desire to see a reconfiguration of service provision, both the Department of Health and

19   Department of Health (2009) *Guidance on direct payments for community care, services for carers and children's services England.*
20   Welsh Assembly Government (2004) *Direct Payments Guidance Community Care, Services for Carers and Children's Services (Direct Payments) Guidance Wales.*
21   Welsh Assembly Government (2010) *Community Care Direct Payments 2010*, April 2011.
22   English Regulations reg 7; Welsh Regulations reg 8.
23   Complaint no 08 005 202 against Kent CC, 18 May 2009, para 39.
24   Complaint no 06/A/08746 against Ealing LBC, 7 May 2008.
25   Public Service Ombudsman (Wales) Complaint no B2004/0707/S/370 against Swansea City Council, 22 February 2007, para 75.

the Welsh Government guidance states that internal authority budgeting arrangements cannot be used to stifle such arrangements.[26]

Service users who are excluded

12.13   The Regulations list those service users who are prohibited from receiving direct payments.[27] The list comprises persons who are subject to certain court orders or controls arising out of their drug and/or alcohol dependencies (eg being subject to a drug rehabilitation or alcohol treatment requirement).

Service users for whom a discretion exists

12.14   Prior to the coming into force of the current regulations in England and in Wales, service users who were subject to compulsory measures under the Mental Health Act 1983 and similar legislation were prohibited from receiving direct payments. These exclusions have largely been removed – and in consequence, as the guidance advises:[28]

> It is expected that, in most cases, people subject to mental health legislation will now enjoy exactly the same rights to direct payments as anyone else. However, in a few cases, councils will have a power (but not a duty) to make direct payments to such people.

12.15   There remains, however, a difference in treatment for some service users who are subject to controls under mental health related legislation – most obviously the Mental Health Act 1983 (for example under section 8, as a result of a guardianship order or under 17B as a result of community treatment order – or persons on section 17 leave). The full list of the relevant statutory provisions is detailed in the second schedule to both the English and Welsh regulations. For persons subject to these controls, councils have a power, but not a duty to provide direct payments.

Consent

12.16   HSCA 2001 s57 and CA 1989 s17A require direct payments to be made only where the proposed recipient consents to such an arrangement. This brings with it the notion of 'informed consent' and the issue of sufficient mental capacity (considered below) as well as the important principle that an individual can refuse to have such a payment in which respect the guidance[29] stresses that:

> A person does not have to accept direct payments; if they wish, they can choose instead to receive services that are provided or arranged by the

26   Para 23 of the (now) superseded 2003 English Guidance and para 2.5 of the Welsh guidance.
27   Schedule 1 to the English Regulations and Schedule 1of the Welsh Regulations.
28   Para 208 of the English guidance and paras 6.51 and 6.52 of the Welsh guidance.
29   Para 15: para 4.36 of the Welsh guidance makes clear that if 'a person does not agree to direct payments, the local authority remains responsible for arranging the care and support they are assessed as needing.'

council. In this respect, the individual is still exercising choice over how their support is delivered. Individuals eligible for care and support should not be unfairly influenced in their choices one way or the other.

12.17   It appears that some councils are putting disabled and older people under considerable pressure to agree to a direct payment: either as a mechanism to avoid commissioning difficult care packages or as a way of hitting their central government targets. Essentially service users are told that the only way their care needs can be met, is if they accept a direct payment and make the arrangement themselves. In such a situation direct payments become disabling rather than enabling, placing a further and unwelcome obligation on the service user. Such an approach not only constitutes maladministration, but it also calls into question the notion of whether the requisite 'consent' is genuine and freely given.

12.18   In *P (MP) v Hackney LBC*[30] Andrew Nicol QC did not find it necessary to decide whether there was a requirement for a service user to give reasons for refusing a direct payment. However, since the legislation is clear – that payments cannot be made without consent and the community care statutes create a specifically enforceable duty to provide services – it must follow that there is no need for a potential recipient of direct payments to give any reason for refusal.

12.19   As a result of the reforms introduced by the HSCA 2008 s146 it is now possible to pay a suitable third party, where the service user lacks capacity to consent to the making of a direct payment – and this mechanism is considered further below.

Mental capacity and direct payments

12.20   An outline of the law concerning mental capacity is provided at chapter 17 below. However, whether or not a person has sufficient mental capacity to consent to a direct payment will depend in part on the use to which the direct payment is put. A person may have sufficient mental capacity to manage certain direct payments but not others. For instance, a direct payment to pay for meals might require very little capacity, whereas a direct payment used to employ a care assistant would generally require significantly more capacity – since employment responsibilities bring with them a number of significant legal consequences. Although such a service user might have assistance in managing the PAYE arrangements, the drafting of the employment contract and the overseeing of the care assistant's training needs, ultimately if the arrangement broke down it would be the service user's name on the unfair dismissal complaint. It is difficult to see how it could be argued that a person could have capacity to enter into a contract of employment but lack capacity to represent him/ herself in any consequent employment proceedings.

12.21   In *South Lanarkshire Council v Smith and others*[31] the Scottish Employment Appeal Tribunal heard a complaint concerning unfair dismissal by a

30 [2007] EWHC 1365 (Admin) para 39.
31 19 January 2000, unreported.

care assistant ostensibly employed by two service users, one of whom had significant learning disabilities. The employment arrangements were put in train by the local authority and a brokerage intermediary – but the contract of employment specified the two service users as the employer. The care assistant named the local authority as one of her employers and the Appeal Tribunal agreed. It was, however, at pains to emphasise that this was an unusual case. Lord Johnstone in his judgment noted that 'we would not for a moment seek to suggest that disabled persons cannot be an employer, particularly over someone caring for them'.

Guidance on capacity

12.22   The guidance advises councils 'should not make blanket assumptions that whole groups of people will or will not be capable of managing direct payments. A council cannot make direct payments if it cannot be satisfied that the potential beneficiary is capable of managing the payments, by themselves or with available assistance. However, very many people will be able to do so, particularly if they have access to help and support.'[32] It continues:[33]

> If a council is concerned that a person who wishes to receive direct payments may not be able to manage the payments, the council should ensure that it takes into account and subsequently records all relevant factors before making a decision not to make direct payments. These decisions may need to involve professional staff who are trained to assess capability and help people make decisions, and who should consider:
> • the person's understanding of direct payments, including the actions required on their part;
> • whether the person understands the implications of taking or not taking on direct payments;
> • what help is available to the person;
> • what kind of support the person might need to achieve their identified outcomes; and
> • what arrangements the person would make to obtain this support.

12.23   In this context, the guidance provides further helpful advice[34] on issues such as the use of a nominee to manage day to day finances, the development of a trust to take on employment responsibilities and approaches where the service user has an episodic condition that could result in fluctuating levels of mental capacity.

People who lack capacity to consent to direct payments

12.24   HSCA 2001 s57(1A)[35] enables local authorities to make direct payments where the disabled adult lacks capacity. The rules, which are detailed in

---

32 Para 69 of the English guidance and para 3.22 of the Welsh guidance.
33 Para 71 of the English guidance and para 3.24 of the Welsh guidance.
34 Para 73–77 of the English guidance and para 3.26 of the Welsh guidance.
35 Inserted by HSCA 2008 s146.

the relevant English and Welsh Regulations (and expressed diagrammatically at Diagram 14 below) provide in general terms, that:

1.   If the person does not have a Court of Protection appointed 'deputy' or a Lasting Power of Attorney (LPA), the authority will have discretion to decide whether a third party is suitable to be a recipient of direct payments.

2.   However, if the person does have a deputy or LPA then the arrangement will depend upon whether the LPA or deputy has authority to make 'decisions about securing the provision of a community care service'[36] (known as a 'surrogate'[37]): if they have this power, they can veto the making of a direct payment; but failing this the local authority, if it wishes to make a direct payment, must give the LPA or deputy (in this case known as a 'representative'[38]) first refusal on being the recipient of the payment.

12.25   Where a local authority proposes to make a direct payment in relation to an adult who lacks the requisite mental capacity, the regulations[39] require that the authority:

- consults with family and friends, in accordance with the duty under the Mental Capacity Act 1983 s4 (see para 17.34 below);
- obtains an enhanced Criminal Records Certificate (unless the payment is to a family member or friend);

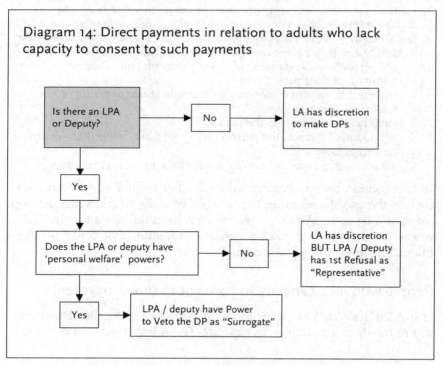

Diagram 14: Direct payments in relation to adults who lack capacity to consent to such payments

Is there an LPA or Deputy? → No → LA has discretion to make DPs

Yes ↓

Does the LPA or deputy have 'personal welfare' powers? → No → LA has discretion BUT LPA / Deputy has 1st Refusal as "Representative"

Yes ↓

LPA / deputy have Power to Veto the DP as "Surrogate"

36   Reg 5 of the English Regulations; reg 6 of the Welsh Regulations.
37   HSCA 2001 s57(5C).
38   HSCA 2001 s57(5B) and English Regulations reg 6; Welsh Regulations reg 7.
39   English Regulations reg 8; Welsh Regulations reg 9. See also Welsh Direct Payments 'Suitable Person' Guidance, April 2011.

- be satisfied :
  a) that the person's community care needs can be met by a direct payment; and
  b) that the recipient of the direct payment will act in best interests of the service user; and;
  c) that in all the circumstances, a direct payment would be appropriate.

The provision of assistance in managing the direct payment

12.26 The Regulations[40] (but not the 2001 or 1989 Acts) specify that direct payments can only be made to persons who appear to the authority 'to be capable of managing' the payment by themselves 'or with such assistance as may be available' to them.

12.27 It is not only people with limited mental capacity that are likely to benefit from assistance in the managing of a direct payment, and the guidance[41] stresses the importance of councils providing support – particularly from user led organisations/local centres for independent living since (as the guidance states) the 'experience of existing recipients of direct payments is that they find it easier to seek advice from someone who is independent of their local council.' The guidance provides an illustrative list of the practical support that can be provided to direct payment recipients:[42]

- a list of local provider agencies or available personal assistants;
- support and advice in setting up and maintaining a direct payment scheme, including financial management;
- help for people to draft advertisements, job descriptions and contracts;
- help in explaining the safeguards needed in the employment of people to work with children or adults;
- rooms for interviews and assistance with interviewing;
- an address for responses to advertisements;
- support and advice about the legal responsibilities of being an employer;
- support and advice about being a good manager of staff;
- support and advice about issues of religion and ethnicity;
- information about income tax and National Insurance;
- a payroll service;
- advice on health and safety issues, including moving and handling;
- regular training, for example on assertiveness or budgeting skills;
- some emergency cover support;
- signposting to other services such as welfare benefits and advocacy; and
- advice about user-controlled trusts.

40 Regs 2, 4 and 8 of the English Regulations and regs 3, 5 and 9 of the Welsh Regulations.
41 Paras 33–37 of the English guidance and paras 2.6–2.14 of the Welsh guidance.
42 Para 37 of the English guidance and para 2.10 of the Welsh guidance.

12.28   Many councils provide 'brokerage services' of this kind by funding an independent living support scheme or an independent company. By emphasising the importance of such support, the guidance puts councils on notice that without them direct payment recipients are likely to experience particular difficulties. Given the existence of a duty of care and the foreseeability of difficulties, it may follow, that councils who fail to provide adequate support services become vulnerable to a complaint of maladministration, where for instance a direct payment recipient incurs liability (eg due to a payroll or unfair dismissal problem) which might have been avoided if general assistance of this nature had been available.

The assessed need will be met by the direct payment

12.29   The Regulations[43] stipulate that a direct payment can only be made where the authority is satisfied 'that the person's need for the relevant service can be met by securing the provision of it by means of a direct payment' – or in the case of a disabled child, that his or her welfare 'will be safeguarded and promoted by securing the provision of it by the means of the direct payment'.

12.30   Given that the policy underpinning the 2001 reforms was to make mandatory the previous discretionary entitlements to direct payments, it would appear to follow that:

   1)   there must be a presumption (most probably a 'strong' presumption):
      a)   that service users will be able to satisfy their assessed needs if they receive a direct payment; and
      b)   that persons with parental responsibility will, if they receive direct payments, use them to safeguard and promote the interests of the relevant disabled child(ren); and
   2)   that if a local authority is of a contrary view it will be obliged to provide cogent reasons for its opinion.

Excluded service providers

12.31   Recipients of a direct payment are subject to few restrictions as to who they engage in delivering their services. They are, for instance, exempted from the key requirements of the Safeguarding Vulnerable Groups Act 2006: section 6(5) of which excludes from the definition of 'a regulated activity provider' private arrangements made by individuals.[44]

12.32   The Regulations,[45] however, restrict the ability of the recipients of direct payments to use the monies to purchase care services from their close relatives or partners. They provide that direct payments cannot (subject to the proviso listed below) be used to purchase services from:

43   English Regulations reg 7(2); Welsh Regulations reg 8(2).
44   Regulatory power exists for the government to require local authorities to 'inform direct payment recipients of their right to receive information under the new Vetting and Barring Scheme' – Safeguarding Vulnerable Groups Act 2006 s30(8) and see para 129 of the English guidance and para 5.26 Welsh draft guidance.
45   Reg 11 of the English Regulations and reg 12 of the Welsh Regulations.

a) the direct payment recipient's spouse or civil partner;

b) anyone who lives with the direct payment recipient 'as if their spouse or civil partner (ie in a common law relationship);

c) anyone living in the same household as the direct payment recipient who is also his/her:

(i) parent or parent-in-law (or their spouse or civil law or common law partner);

(ii) son or daughter (or their spouse or civil law or common law partner);[46]

(iii) son-in-law or daughter-in-law (or their spouse or civil law or common law partner);[47]

(iv) stepson or stepdaughter (or their spouse or civil law or common law partner);

(v) brother or sister (or their spouse or civil law or common law partner);

(vi) aunt or uncle(or their spouse or civil law or common law partner); or

(vii) grandparent (or their spouse or civil law or common law partner).

12.33 The Regulations[48] provide, however, that a direct payment recipient can purchase services from one of the above excluded service providers if the social services authority is 'satisfied that securing the service from such a person is necessary . . . to meet satisfactorily the prescribed person's need for that service'. Where, however, the payment is made to the parent of a disabled child, payments can be made to 'live-in' close relatives provided the social services authority 'is satisfied that securing the service from such a person is necessary . . . for promoting the welfare of the child . . .'.[49] There is, however, no statutory restriction on the direct payment recipient paying any other relation to provide care.

12.34 The guidance explains[50] that there may be occasions when the council decides that it is necessary for the suitable person to use the direct payments to secure services from a member of the family of the person lacking capacity. However, such situations are likely to be exceptional[51] and

---

46 This exclusion does not apply in the case of a person mentioned in section 17A(2)(c) of the 1989 Act, namely 'a disabled child aged 16 or 17, and a local authority . . . have decided for the purposes of section 17 that the child's needs (or, if he is such a disabled child, his needs) call for the provision by them of a service in exercise of functions conferred on them under that section' – reg 11(3) of the English regulations and reg 12(3) of the Welsh regulations.

47 This exclusion does not apply in the case of a person mentioned in section 17A(2)(c) of the 1989 Act (see footnote above).

48 Welsh Regulations reg 12(1); English Regulations reg 11(1).

49 Welsh Regulations reg 12(1); English Regulations reg 11(1). Paying relatives is not a novel development: Elizabethan Poor Laws parish officers 'commonly' paid 'needy close relatives, to care for the mentally or physically sick, disabled, and aged poor' – see P Thane, *Old Age in English History*, Oxford University Press, 2000, p109.

50 At para 197 of the English guidance and at para 6.41 of the Welsh guidance.

51 The situation need not in fact be 'exceptional': the regulations speak only of the authority being satisfied that the payment is necessary – see by analogy *R (Ross) v West Sussex PCT* [2008] EWHC 2252 (Admin), (2008) 11 CCLR 787 and *R (M) (Claimant) v Independent Appeal Panel of Haringey* [2009] EWHC 2427 (Admin) at para 27.

the council should be satisfied at all times that arrangements are made in the best interests of the person lacking capacity.

12.35   In England the Department of Health has encouraged the use of direct payments to pay close relatives, with the Minister issuing a press release stating:[52]

> some councils say they are confused over the rules governing how individuals can use their direct payments to pay close relatives. We're reminding councils that there is no legal restriction on individuals using their direct payment to pay close relatives who don't live with them . . . [and that] . . . in exceptional circumstances, people can also use their direct payment to pay a relative who lives with them, if they and their local council decide this is the only satisfactory way of meeting their care needs

12.36   Relatives who are employed under a direct payment arrangement may cease to be entitled to an assessment and services under the carers' legislation,[53] since these rights only relate to carers who do not provide 'the care in question . . . by virtue of a contract of employment . . .'. If, however, the relative provides additional (and substantial) care over and above that to which the payment relates, the entitlement to an assessment/services would remain.

Excluded services

Residential care

12.37   Direct payments cannot be used to purchase prolonged periods of residential care. Regulation 13 of the English Regulations (regulation 14 of the Welsh) caps the amount of residential accommodation that can be funded by direct payments to a maximum of four consecutive weeks in any period of 12 months: the important word being 'consecutive'. The guidance[54] clarifies the scope and purpose of this prohibition, as well as the method for calculation – which the English guidance explains as follows:

> 103. For example, someone might have one week of residential care every six weeks. Because each week in residential care is more than four weeks apart, they are not added together. The cumulative total is only one week and the four-week limit is never reached. Another person might have three weeks in residential care, two weeks at home and then another week in residential care. The two episodes of residential care are less than four weeks apart and so they are added together making four weeks in total. The person cannot use their direct payments to purchase any more residential care within a 12-month period.

---

52 Department of Health press release, 26 January 2004 at www.info.doh.gov.uk/doh/intpress.nsf/page/2004–0028?OpenDocument.
53 See para 16.21; carers may also cease to be entitled to social security in the form of the Carers Allowance.
54 Paras 101–105 of the English guidance and paras 4.19–4.20 of the Welsh guidance.

12.38   A person living full time in a residential care home is able to receive direct payments in relation to non-residential care services – for instance a day care service or 'to try out independent living arrangements before making a commitment to moving out of their care home'.[55]

12.39   In *R (M) v Suffolk County Council*[56] Charles J held that the above restriction did not mean that a person in residential care could not receive direct payments. The case concerned a 17-year-old with learning disabilities at a special school. He considered that anyone in such care had three categories of expense, namely (a) education, (b) social care and practical care, and (c) basic residence and that the prohibitory regulation did not in principle preclude direct payments to cover that portion of the overall fees that related to social care and practical care (at para 23). This is a slightly surprising conclusion and possibly one that should be limited to the particular facts of the case.

12.40   The Law Commission in its 2011 Report on Adult Social Care law reform recommended that direct payments should be extended to cover residential accommodation.[57]

Local authority in-house services

12.41   Previous guidance[58] stated that direct payments cannot be used to purchase a service from a local authority (ie an in-house local authority provided service), explaining that this restriction exists because legally local authorities are not permitted to sell their services. Both the present English and the Welsh guidance are silent on this question although it would appear on balance that such a restriction continues to be valid. There must, however, be a slight question as to whether this prohibition still remains at law, in view of the wide powers now available to local authorities, for instance under Local Government Act (LGA) 2000 s2[59] (see para 1.68 above).

The amount of the payment

12.42   HSCA 2001 s57(4) requires that direct payments must be calculated on the basis of the 'reasonable cost of securing the provision of the service concerned'. In *R (KM) v Cambridgeshire County Council*[60] the Court of Appeal held that that whilst there had to be a rational link between the

---

55   At para 106 of the English guidance and para 4.22 of the draft Welsh guidance.
56   [2006] EWHC 2366 (Admin).
57   Law Commission in its report *Adult Social Care*, Law Com No 326 HC941, recommendation 35.
58   Department of Health LAC (2000)1 para 32 and Welsh Assembly Government (2004) Direct Payments Guidance Community Care, Services for Carers and Children's Services (Direct Payments) Guidance Wales para 95.
59   While LGA 2000 s3(2) provides that section 2 powers cannot be used to 'raise money', it is questionable whether this prohibits councils recouping costs of providing a service – particularly where the authority will have paid the user the necessary monies in the first place.
60   [2011] EWCA Civ 682, (2011) 14 CCLR 83 at [23].

needs and the amount of the proposed direct payment 'there does not need to be a finite absolute mathematical link'.

12.43   The legislation permits payments to be paid gross or net of any charge the local authority deems it is reasonably practicable for the service user to pay.[61] In deciding whether to make a direct payment gross or net (ie having deducted the assessed charge) the guidance advises that authorities 'should take into account the views of users . . . allowing sufficient flexibility to respond to individual circumstances'.[62]

12.44   The guidance picks up the statutory requirement that the payment must be 'equivalent to the reasonable cost of securing' the assessed needs, advising that:

> the direct payments should be sufficient to enable the recipient lawfully to secure a service of a standard that the council considers is reasonable to fulfil the needs for the service to which the payments relate. There is no limit on the maximum or minimum amount of direct payment either in the amount of care it is intended to purchase or on the value of the direct payment.

12.45   In some cases the calculation of the appropriate amount of a direct payment may be complex. Advice on how this should be done is given in the guidance and in specialist 2007 guidelines produced by the Chartered Institute of Public Finance and Accountancy (CIPFA) for local authorities[63]. The guidance[64] comments:

> 111. It is up to the council to decide on the amount of direct payments. However, the direct payments legislation provides that it must be equivalent to the council's estimate of the reasonable cost of securing the provision of the service concerned, subject to any contribution from the recipient. This means that the direct payments should be sufficient to enable the recipient lawfully to secure a service of a standard that the council considers is reasonable to fulfil the needs for the service to which the payments relate. There is no limit on the maximum or minimum amount of direct payment either in the amount of care it is intended to purchase or on the value of the direct payment.
>
> . . .
>
> 114. In estimating the reasonable cost of securing the support required,

61 HSCA 2001 s57(3)(b) and reg 9 of the English Regulations and reg 10 of the Welsh Regulations.
62 Para 120 of the English guidance and para 4.39 of the Welsh guidance.
63 'Chartered Institute of Public Finance and Accountancy (CIPFA) (2007), *Direct Payments and Individual Budgets: Managing the Finances.* London: CIPFA. The 2007 guide is only available for purchase from CIPFA, although the Department of Health website at www.personalhealthbudgets.dh.gov.uk/Topics/latest/Resource/?cid=8260 links to the freely available Scottish Government equivalent guide CIPFA (2009) *Self Directed Support: Direct Payments A Guide for Local Authority Finance Managers.* London: CIPFA, prepared for the Scottish Government: accessible at www.cipfa.org.uk/scotland/download/Direct_Payments_A_Guide_for_Local_ Authority_Finance_Managers_Final.pdf] which it states 'covers much of the same ground'
64 Paras 111–118 of the English guidance and paras 4.31–4.32 of the draft Welsh guidance.

councils should include associated costs that are necessarily incurred in securing provision, without which the service could not be provided or could not lawfully be provided. The particular costs involved will vary depending on the way in which the service is secured, but such costs might include recruitment costs, National Insurance, statutory holiday pay, sick pay, maternity pay, employers' liability insurance, public liability insurance and VAT. Some councils have found it helpful to include a one-off start-up fund within the direct payments to meet these costs as well as other forms of support that might be required, such as brokerage, payroll services and Criminal Records Bureau checks on employees.

12.46 The Personal Social Services Research Unit (PSSRU) has expressed concern about the process by which direct payment rates are calculated. This normally results in the authority deducting their direct and indirect overheads such that average direct payment rates 'are almost universally lower than the costs of contracted home care, the main service for which direct payments substitutes'. In the PSSRU's opinion, by setting rates at a level below market value for any form of care other than that of recruiting a personal assistant, the opportunities of direct payments are likely to be reduced.[65] Conversely, however, a 2006 Audit Commission study suggests that in order for direct payment schemes to be cost neutral (ie no more expensive than the local authority providing or commissioning the service), councils should reduce the value of payments below the sum they paid for comparable levels of care.[66]

12.47 Most local authorities have standard rates for the more common services for which a direct payment is required, for instance an hourly rate for day care. Occasionally there are alternative rates, depending upon whether the service user employs a care assistant directly or uses an agency: with the agency rate being higher. Such an arrangement would of course address some of the concerns raised by the PSSRU above. It would also enable service users to have direct payments who did not wish to employ a care assistant but preferred to purchase agency services. Provided such an arrangement was no more expensive than the cost that the authority would bear if it was responsible for the service provision arrangements, it would appear that a service user could insist on such an option.

12.48 The rate proposed by the authority may be insufficient to cover the cost of the services required, for instance because no suitable care assistant or agency can be identified that is prepared to provide the service at that rate. In such cases the service user can challenge the rate through the complaints process. In this respect the CIPFA 1998 guidance[67] advised:

> 87. There may be cases where an individual thinks that the total value of the direct payment should be greater than the local authority proposes,

65 V Davey (2006) *Direct Payment Rates in England*, PSSRU, Kent University at www.pssru.ac.uk/uc/uc2006contents.htm#contents

66 Audit Commission (2006) *Choosing well: analysing the costs and benefits of choice in local public services.*

67 CIPFA (1998) *Community Care (Direct Payments) Act 1996: accounting and financial management guidelines and Welsh guidance* para 4.36.

and/or that his or her contribution or the amount they are asked to pay by way of reimbursement should be less than the council proposes. Where these cases cannot be resolved through discussion, local authorities should advise the individual that he or she can pursue the matter through the authority's complaints procedure.

88. A local authority should give individuals as much notice as possible of the value of a direct payment, and the contribution or repayment they will be expected to make to the cost of their care package. This should be done before the payment begins, or its level is changed, to provide the opportunity for any dispute over the level to be resolved before the payment begins or the change takes effect. If that is not possible, whilst any complaint is being considered, individuals may choose either to manage on the amount of direct payments being offered or refuse to accept the direct payments. If a person does not agree to a direct payment, the authority remains responsible for providing or arranging the provision of the services they are assessed as needing.

Frequency of payments

12.49 Local authorities must agree with the service user the frequency of payments – ensuring that they are in a position to pay for services when payment is due. The guidance advises that it may also be necessary to 'set up procedures for making additional payments in emergencies, for example, if needs change or regular payments go astray' and should ensure that recipients clearly understand these arrangements.[68] The guidance advises that payments can be made such that the recipient accumulates a reserve, namely:[69]

> The flexibility inherent in direct payments means that individuals can adjust the amount they use from week to week and 'bank' any spare money to use as and when extra needs arise (this might be particularly helpful for people with long-term and fluctuating conditions). As long as overall the payments are being used to achieve the outcomes agreed in the care plan, the actual pattern of support does not need to be predetermined.

Charges for direct payments

12.50 Although, as noted above, direct payments can be paid gross, they will in general be paid 'net' – ie after the council has deducted the sum it would have charged the recipient had the service been provided or commissioned by the council. In this context, the regulations require that any charge be an amount (if any) that it is reasonably practicable for the individual to pay.[70] Whilst the policy intention appeared to be that local authority charges would be the same for individuals regardless of whether their assessed needs were met by way of a direct payment or by the local

---

68 Para 122 of the English guidance and para 4.52 of the Welsh guidance.
69 Para 123 of the English guidance and para 4.53 of the Welsh guidance.
70 English Regulations reg 9(2); Welsh Regulations reg 10(2).

authority services commissioned by the local authority,[71] the regulations in fact make it mandatory for councils to undertake a means assessment – whereas the legislation relating to the assessment of charges for local authority commissioned non-residential services is expressed as a discretion. Although such a difference in treatment appears to be without rational basis, it is clearly not an oversight, since a not dissimilar anomaly (concerning people using direct payments for short periods of residential care) has been addressed by amendment (see para 10.69 where this question is further considered).

Direct payments and social security

12.51   The relevant social security regulations require 'any payment' made under the direct payments legislation to be disregarded for benefits purposes.[72] This does not, however, apply to carers who are paid using these payments – since the disregard does not apply to 'earnings'.[73] In such cases a carer could, however, still benefit from the means-tested benefits earnings disregard (though modest) and it has also been suggested that, in certain cases the problem could be avoided by the local authority making the direct payment to the carer under the carers legislation[74] (see para 16.100 below).

The obligations upon the recipient of direct payments

12.52   The recipient of the direct payment must ensure that it is spent on services to meet the assessed need. In relation to the monitoring and auditing of the payments the guidance advises that 'monitoring arrangements should be consistent both with the requirement for the council to be satisfied that the person's needs can and will be met, and with the aim of promoting and increasing choice and independence'.[75] It continues:[76]

> 221.   Councils should focus on achieving agreed outcomes, rather than on the service being delivered in a certain way. The council should discuss with individuals what steps it intends to take to fulfil its responsibilities, and may also wish to discuss how it might support them in securing quality care that meets their needs in the way best suited to them. The council should be prepared to consider variations to what it proposes.

> 222.   Councils should aim to ensure that the information that the direct payment recipient is asked to provide is straightforward and the least onerous possible, consistent with monitoring requirements. Guidance

---

71   See Department of Health (2003) *Fairer Charging Policies for Home Care and Other Non-residential Social Services* para 86 and Welsh Government (2011) *Introducing More Consistency in Local Authorities' Charging for Non-Residential Social Services Guidance for Local Authorities* WAG 10–12408: para 7, p2.
72   Income Support (General) Regulations 1987 SI No 1967 Sch 9 para 58; Jobseeker's Allowance Regulations 1996 SI No 207 Sch 7 para 56; Housing Benefit Regulations 2006 SI No 213 Sch 5 para 57.
73   See *Casewell v Secretary of State for Work and Pensions* [2008] EWCA Civ 524.
74   See commentary in the June 2008 *Journal of Community Care law* Issue 49.
75   English guidance para 220; Welsh guidance para 7.1.
76   English guidance paras 221–222; similar wording is in Welsh guidance paras 7.2–7.3.

from the Chartered Institute of Public Finance and Accountancy (CIPFA) provides more advice about risk management and proportionate monitoring.

12.53   Recipients are generally required to open a single bank account into which only direct payment and Independent Living Fund money (and other money related to personal assistance) is paid. In certain situations it may be necessary for the account to be in a nominee's name if the service user has problems opening an account (because of, for instance, a bad credit rating) – although a local authority cannot insist on such an inter-mediary arrangement.[77] CIPFA guidance draws attention to the use of Payment Cards in such cases – which it suggests have many additional benefits.[78] A 2006 exchange of letters between the Department of Health and the British Bankers Association has endeavoured to clarify (and resolve) some common banking problems encountered by service users such as difficulties in proving their identity and being unable through disability to sign cheques.[79]

12.54   Direct payment users are legally responsible for the services they purchase with the monies they receive from social services. It follows that in respect of any problem they encounter with the service they purchase, they cannot make complaint to social services, although they can seek the authority's assistance. In this context the guidance advises:[80]

> 237. Councils should make people aware that they should plan for the unexpected and discuss with each person what arrangements they will make for emergencies, to ensure that the person receives the care they need when the usual arrangements break down (e.g. through the sickness of one of the person's personal assistants). The council will need to be prepared to respond in these circumstances just as it would with any other person using a service. It may decide to step in and arrange services where this is necessary to meet its responsibilities. The council could also explore other ways of providing assistance to enable the person to continue to manage their own care using direct payments, particularly if the difficulty is temporary or unforeseen.

> 238. Councils may also wish to make people aware that, in planning for the unexpected, they might consider giving someone a lasting power of attorney to manage their affairs relating to personal welfare, in the event that they lose capacity and are unable to do so themselves. This person, for example a close relative or friend already involved in the provision of their care, could then continue to manage the direct payments to purchase services on their behalf.

---

77   *H and L v A City Council* [2011] EWCA Civ 403, (2011) 14 CCLR 381, paras 86–87.
78   CIPFA (2009) *Self Directed Support: Direct Payments A Guide for Local Authority Finance Managers* London CIPFA: www.cipfa.org.uk/scotland/download/ Direct_Payments_A_Guide_for_Local_Authority_Finance_Managers_Final.pdf at paras 5.4 – 5.8.
79   Accessible at www.dh.gov.uk/en/Publicationsandstatistics/Lettersandcirculars/ Dearcolleagueletters/DH_063742.
80   Para 237–239 of the English guidance and paras 8.2–8.3 of the Welsh guidance.

Repayment and discontinuance

12.55 The Regulations provide authorities with the power to seek repayment of a direct payment[81] if they are satisfied that it has not been used to secure the provision of the service to which it relates (or that the person has not met any condition that the council has properly imposed). The guidance advises that[82]:

> ... Councils should bear in mind that repayment should be aimed at recovering money that has been diverted from the purpose for which it was intended or that has simply not been spent at all, or where services have been obtained from someone who is ineligible to provide them. It should not be used to penalise honest mistakes, nor should repayment be sought where the individual has been the victim of fraud.

> 246. Councils are able to seek repayment where a suitable person has been responsible for managing direct payments on behalf of someone lacking capacity if they are satisfied that:

> - the suitable person has not used the direct payments to secure the services for which they were intended; or
> - the suitable person has not met a condition properly imposed by the council.

> In such situations, councils should seek repayment from the suitable person, not the person lacking capacity for whose care and support the direct payments were made. Before commencing the making of direct payments to a suitable person, therefore, councils should inform the suitable person from the outset of their responsibilities for ensuring appropriate use of the money.

> 247. A council should be satisfied, before it begins to make payments, that the potential recipient of that payment understands all of the conditions that they will be required to meet. The council should also discuss with potential recipients of direct payments the circumstances in which it might wish to consider seeking repayment. Councils may wish to take into account hardship considerations in deciding whether to seek repayments. Councils should also bear in mind that there might be legitimate reasons for unspent funds. There may be outstanding legal liabilities necessitating a direct payment recipient to build up an apparent surplus (for example to pay their employees' quarterly PAYE, or to pay outstanding bills from a care agency).

12.56 The Regulations additionally provide that a council shall cease making direct payments if considers that the person is no longer capable of managing the direct payment (or of managing it with help) unless (1) the 'incapability' is reasonably expected to be temporary; and (2) a third party is prepared to accept and manage the payments; and (3) any care assistant (or other care provider) agrees to accept payment from this third party.[83]

12.57 Where a local authority does decide to terminate a direct payment due to 'very serious concerns' over the use of the funds then there is no

---

81 English Regulations reg 15; Welsh Regulations reg 16.
82 Para 245–247 of the English guidance and similar wording is at paras 8.10–8.13 of the Welsh guidance.
83 Regulation 17 of the English Regulations and regulation 18 of the Welsh Regulations.

obligation that it maintain the same funding as before – provided the court is satisfied that the level of services that had been previously assessed as required had been maintained.[84]

Equipment/adaptations

12.58   Direct payments can be used to purchase equipment or pay for adaptations or fixtures/fittings assessed as being required by the disabled person.[85] They cannot, however, be used to pay for services or equipment for which the authority is not responsible, for example services that the NHS provides, and the guidance also makes clear that they are not a substitute for a disabled facilities grant for major property adaptations.[86]

12.59   Local authorities may be reluctant to make direct payments for the purchase of equipment, even though equipment in England is exempt from charging (see para 10.15) because of a concern that it might thereby cease to be available for 're-use'. Many authorities recycle the majority of their equipment, recovering and redeploying it when no longer required by a particular service user. The guidance makes clear that direct payments may not conflict with this practice, stating:[87]

109. When making direct payments, councils will need to satisfy themselves that the person's eligible needs will be met by their own arrangements. In the case of direct payments for the purchase of items of equipment, councils will wish to ensure that the direct payment recipient is adequately supported by specialist expertise. This is particularly true in the case of major items, when advice may be needed to ensure that the equipment purchased is safe and appropriate.

110. Where a council makes a direct payment for equipment, it needs to clarify with the individual at the outset where ownership lies as well as who has responsibility for ongoing care and maintenance (just as it should where it arranges for the provision of equipment itself). A council will need to consider what conditions, if any, should be attached to the direct payment when it is used to purchase equipment, for example concerning what will happen to the equipment if it is no longer required by the individual. Equipment can also be purchased as part of making a package cost-effective, for example supplying pagers or mobile phones to personal assistants.

84   See *TG and AH v North Somerset District Council*, unreported, 1 July 2011. The payments had been made under a third party arrangement (see para 12.70 below) to the disabled person's trustees. The court accepted that there it was arguable that the revised care plan may have failed to meet all the assessed needs, but considered this failure to be 'de minimis': ie minimal.
85   One-off payments for equipment appear to be relatively common – see V Davey et al *Direct Payments: a national survey of direct payments policy and practice* Personal Social Services Research Unit London School of Economics and Political Science (2007) p52 at www.pssru.ac.uk/pdf/dprla.pdf.
86   English guidance para 108 and para 4.26 of the Welsh guidance.
87   English guidance paras 109–110 and paras 4.27–4.29 of the Welsh guidance.

Contractual and employment issues

12.60 It appears that local authority direct payments budgets are largely expended on significant packages of care, involving 10 or more hours of personal care each week.[88] The assumption appears to be that many, if not most, of these will involve the disabled person employing one or more care support workers.

12.61 The general position at law – that the funding local authority will not be responsible for the service secured by a recipient of a direct payment – also applies when the payment is used to employ a care assistant. The employee's well-being and employment rights are the responsibility of their employer, not the funding council. In this context, a number of commentators have suggested that such personal assistants may be at a significant disadvantage: for example that their rates of pay are generally lower than that of other home care workers; that they lack training and external support and in general have no pension provision or awareness of their right to sickness pay.[89] Other research has suggested that direct payment assistants are more likely to have concerns about what they consider to be aspects of emotional blackmail[90] connected with their work including a feeling that they are being required to undertake tasks they feel inappropriate.[91]

12.62 From the direct payment recipient's perspective, however, there is sometimes a perception that the local authority is seeking to impose inappropriate conditions on the way they discharge their role as employer. Although the regulations permit the imposition of conditions on the making of direct payments,[92] they are subject to significant limits. In *H and L v A City Council*[93] the council sought to impose a condition that the payment went into a managed account over which the local authority retained control, rather than directly to the disabled person. In finding such an arrangement to be unlawful, Munby LJ held that the legal right to impose a condition could not be used 'to destroy the very essence of the right'. In so doing, he cited with approval the English guidance that:[94]

88 One-off payments for equipment appear to be relatively common – see V Davey et al *Direct Payments: A National Survey of Direct Payments Policy and Practice* Personal Social Services Research Unit London School of Economics and Political Science (2007) chapter 5 at www.pssru.ac.uk/pdf/dprla.pdf.

89 J Leece , 'Direct Payments and the experience of personal assistants', (2008) *Community Care,* November 2008, issue 27, pp 32–33 and see also J Leece, 'Paying the Piper and Calling the Tune: Power and the Direct Payment Relationship', (2008) *British Journal of Social Work* 1–19.

90 C Ungerson, 'Whose empowerment and independence? A cross-national perspective on 'cash for care' schemes' (2004) *Ageing and Society,* 24(2) pp189–212.

91 C Glendinning, S Halliwell, S Jacobs, K Rummery and J Tyrer, *Buying Independence: Using Direct Payments to Integrate Health and Social Services,* Policy Press, 2000.

92 Regulation 11(4) of the English Regulations and regulation 12(4) of the Welsh Regulations.

93 [2011] EWCA Civ 403, (2011) 14 CCLR 381, paras 86–87.

94 English guidance para 92 and para 4.8 of the Welsh guidance.

Councils may set reasonable conditions on the direct payments, but need to bear in mind when doing so that the aim of direct payments is to give people more choice and control over their support and how it is delivered. For example, individual choice and control would not be delivered were a condition to be set that someone who receives direct payments might only use certain providers. Conditions should be proportionate and no more extensive, in terms or number, than is reasonably necessary. Councils should also avoid setting up disproportionately intensive monitoring procedures. Financial payments should not begin until the recipient has agreed to any conditions that the council considers are necessary in connection with the direct payments. In order to avoid delays for people requiring support, councils should take all reasonable steps to resolve issues about conditions in a timely manner.

12.63   An area where some local authorities have sought to impose significant conditions, concerns the way that the disabled person's manual handling needs should be undertaken. In relation to this matter (which is also considered at para 4.118 above) the guidance gives the following advice:[95]

Health and Safety

132. . . . As a general principle, councils should avoid laying down health and safety policies for individual direct payment recipients. Individuals should accept that they have a responsibility for their own health and safety, including the assessment and management of risk. They should be encouraged to develop strategies on lifting and handling and other tasks, both in the home and outside it where lifting equipment, for example, may not be available.

133. . . . councils will wish to take appropriate steps to satisfy themselves that recipients and potential recipients are aware of the health and safety issues that affect them as individuals, anyone they employ, and anyone else affected by the manner in which their support is delivered.

134. . . . councils should give the recipients and potential recipients the results of any risk assessments that were carried out as part of the initial assessment or support plan. This allows the individual to share the assessment with the care agency or the employee who provides the service. They can therefore take reasonable steps to minimise the risks to the health and safety of any staff they employ. (The recipient or potential recipient has a common law duty of care towards the person they employ.) . . .

12.64   The guidance seeks to tread the delicate line between ensuring that recipients of a direct payment are made aware of their daunting legal responsibilities as an employer and yet not letting this information dampen their enthusiasm for taking on such a role: advising that this information should not be given 'in such a way as to put off the recipient, for example by overstressing the extent and complexity of these responsibilities, but neither should the council fail to make recipients aware of what is involved'.[96] The guidance further advises:[97]

95   English guidance paras 132–134 and paras 5.7–5.10 of the Welsh guidance.
96   English guidance para 140 and para 5.16 of the Welsh guidance.
97   English guidance paras 138–139 and paras 5.13–5.15 of the Welsh guidance.

138. Individuals should be made aware of their legal responsibilities in terms of providing written details of the main terms of the employment contract within two months of commencement of the employment. The essential terms that must be provided include, for example:

- the date on which employment commenced;
- hours of work;
- particulars of remuneration (which must meet the national minimum wage);
- place of work;
- job title;
- whether the job is fixed-term or permanent;
- statutory entitlement to sick pay and annual leave;
- pension scheme provision (where appropriate); and
- notice requirements.

Any changes to the terms must also be notified in the same way.

139. If support services are provided, councils may wish to include a payroll service, which will take responsibility for administering wages, tax and National Insurance for the direct payment recipient. A written contract between the employer and the employee will help ensure that the parties have the same understanding about the terms of employment and statutory disciplinary and grievance procedures. Helpful guidance on employment law issues is also available from websites such as www.direct.gov.uk and www.businesslink.gov.uk

12.65 The employment obligations of direct payment recipients may be of particular complexity if the employed person is to care for a disabled child or disabled young person. Detailed guidance exists on this process[98] including advice concerning checks under the Protection of Children Act 1999 via the Criminal Records Bureau (CRB).

Transition into adulthood

12.66 Direct payments can be paid to the parents of a disabled child until the child becomes 18. At that age, the payment must either pass to the young person or cease or be paid to a third party (eg under HSCA 2001 s57(1A) if she or he lacks the requisite mental capacity – see para 12.24 above). CA 1989 s17A(2) provides for direct payments to be paid to disabled young persons' at the age of 16. This enables them (if they chose) as part of their transition to adulthood, 'to take control of part or all of the direct payment that have to date been managed by the person with parental responsibility. This can allow them to gain experience of managing direct payments in a gradual way prior to reaching adulthood'.[99] The guidance further advises that:[100]

---

98   Paras 143–151 of the English guidance and paras 5.18–5.22 of the Welsh guidance.
99   Para 176 of the English guidance and para 6.18 of the Welsh guidance.
100 Para 178–180 of the English guidance and paras 6.20–6.22 of the Welsh guidance.

178. Some disabled 16- and 17-year-olds may have previous experience of direct payments because their parents are receiving them to meet the family's needs. However, many disabled 16- and 17-year-olds' parents will have been receiving services direct from their council.

179. A way to develop a young person's ability to manage the direct payments can be to put in place transitional arrangements, initially set up with the young person managing only a proportion of their support with direct payments. This proportion could increase as the young person matures, with the objective of full management of the support package at age 18.

180. Young disabled people may receive assistance with managing the direct payments, just as any other direct payment recipient may do. Where that assistance takes the form of a user-controlled trust or similar arrangement, it should be set up in the knowledge of the views of those people with parental responsibility. Their ability to express their views should not be undermined by the arrangement.

12.67   The guidance advises on the need for support for young people taking on direct payments, not least the importance preparing for the transition to adult services.[101] It also addresses the question of young person/parent conflict advising that if the council believes that the 16/17 year old is able to manage the direct payments with appropriate support, and that such a payment safeguards and promotes his or her welfare 'then it has a duty to make the payments'.[102]

Carers

12.68   The CDCA 2000 s2(2) makes provision for social services to provide services to carers (aged 16 or over) which in their opinion 'help the carer care for the person cared for'. As a matter of law, however, respite care is not a service under the 2000 Act (see para 16.93 below). The type of assistance available under the 2000 Act includes such services as relaxation therapy/ counselling; mobile phones; trips/holidays/special events for carers; driving lessons; travel assistance; training and the like.

12.69   Where a local authority has decided that such a service should be made available, the carer can require it to be provided by way of a direct payment.

Independent user trusts (IUTs) and third party payments

Social services IUTs

12.70   Prior to the implementation of CC(DP)A 1996 social services departments were (with few exceptions) subject to a specific prohibition against

---

101   Para 40 of the English guidance and para 2.13 of the draft Welsh guidance.
102   Para 46 of the English guidance and para 2.17 of the draft Welsh guidance.

making payments of cash to disabled people, in lieu of services.[103] They were, however, permitted by NAA 1948 s30 to pay third parties (such as independent home care service providers) that had undertaken to deliver the assessed services. A number of authorities accordingly developed 'third party' schemes whereby they made payments to an intermediary (typically a trust fund or brokerage scheme) which then worked closely with the disabled person in the purchasing of his or her care. Such schemes gave the disabled person effective control over the purchasing of care services and also provided assistance with the administrative obligations inherent in any employment situation (recruitment and appointment of carers, employment contracts, grievance procedures, PAYE, etc).

12.71   Although the 1996 and 2001 Acts have materially relaxed the restrictions on direct payments, there remain a number of instances whereby third party schemes are still of value: most notably where the service user lacks the necessary mental capacity to manage the payments – even with assistance – and where the potential recipient is eligible for NHS continuing healthcare funding (see para 14.150). A failure to consider the use of an IUT, may in certain situations constitute maladministration.[104]

12.72   With the passing of the 1996 Act, questions were raised as to whether third party schemes continued to be lawful (despite government assurances[105]). This question was settled in *R (A and B) v East Sussex CC (No 1)*[106] which concerned a local authority payment to a specially created independent trust (known as a 'user independent trust') whose sole purpose was then to arrange the care of two young women with profound physical and learning disabilities. The trust in this case was a company limited by guarantee.

12.73   The applicants argued, amongst other things, that NAA 1948 s30 permitted such payments, since it provides that:

> A local authority may, in accordance with arrangements made under section 29 of this Act, employ as their agent for the purposes of that section any voluntary organisation or any person carrying on, professionally or by way of trade or business, activities which consist of or include the provision of services for any of the persons to whom section 29 above applies, being an organisation or person appearing to the authority to be capable of providing the service to which the arrangements apply.

12.74   Section 64 defines a 'voluntary organisation' as 'a body the activities of which are carried on otherwise than for profit, but does not include any public or local authority'. Munby J concluded that the trust in question

---

103   See eg NAA 1948 s29(6)(a), NHSA 2006 Sch 20 para 2(2)(a) and NHS(W)A 2006 Sch 15 para 2(2)(a).
104   Report by the Public Services Ombudsman for Wales on an Investigation into a Complaint no 200801373 against Powys County Council, 7 July 2010.
105   Asked to confirm that the 'new possibilities created by the' 1996 Act would not affect the status of existing third-party schemes, the minister, John Bowis, stated that 'schemes that are in place now should not be affected. We are not seeking to undermine such schemes', HC Debates col 380, 6 March 1996.
106   [2002] EWHC 2771 (Admin), (2003) 6 CCLR 177.

came within this definition and that it followed, therefore, that such a third party scheme was compatible with the legal requirements of NAA 1948 s29. Had this not been the case, he expressed himself satisfied that the scheme would have been lawful in any event by virtue of both the LGA 1972 s111 and LGA 2000 s2.

12.75   In England the Care Quality Commission has advised that in general Independent Living Trusts – if set up solely for the support of a specified disabled user (or siblings) – will not require to be registered as a domiciliary care agency (see para 9.14 above).[107] The Care and Social Services Inspectorate Wales has also confirmed that it adopts a similar position.[108]

12.76   *Trusting Independence* is an excellent guide to independent living trusts, available from Values into Action.[109]

NHS IUTs

12.77   As noted below (para 12.86) it has been held that NHS Acts 2006 as originally enacted, do not permit the NHS to make direct payments to patients. Whilst this omission has been addressed by the Health Act 2009, at the time of writing (September 2011) not all PCTs have the power to make such payments – and there are no plans for this power to be extended to Wales. This legislative gap creates difficulties for a number of people, not least those receiving direct payments from social services, who are then adjudged to be eligible for NHS continuing healthcare funding (see para 14.149 below). IUTs represent one mechanism mitigating this problem.

12.78   In *Gunter v SW Staffordshire PCT*[110] Collins J held that there was nothing in principle in the NHS Acts to preclude a PCT (or by inference a LHB) from making direct payments to an IUT which would then arrange for the healthcare needs of the profoundly disabled 21 year old applicant, stating:

> 26. It seems to me that Parliament has deliberately given very wide powers to Primary Care Trusts to enable them to do what in any given circumstances seem to them to achieve the necessary provision of services. I have no doubt that this could involve the use of a voluntary organisation such as an IUT as the supplier. There seems to me to be no difference in principle between an IUT set up specially for a small number of persons or an individual and a nursing or other agency so far as the defendants are concerned. It would obviously be necessary for a member of the defendants to be a trustee so as to ensure that money was properly and prudently spent.

12.79   It is arguable that Collins J's comments concerning the governance arrangements are an 'aside' in the sense that these were not central to the

---

107 See Care Quality Commission Guidance on 'Direct Payment support schemes'
108 Personal communication with authors, 29 July 2011.
109 A Holman and C Bewley, *Trusting independence: a practical guide to independent living trusts*, 2001, published by Values into Action: www.viauk.org.
110 [2005] EWHC 1894 (Admin), (2006) 9 CCLR 12.

proceedings and not (it appears) the subject of specific argument. With respect, whilst the trustees in such a scheme would need to ensure financial accountability, proper co-ordination, sound clinical governance and so on, there would appear to be no overarching legal imperative that (for example) a PCT member would need to be a trustee in every such scheme.

12.80   *Using independent user trusts to manage personal health budgets*[111] is an excellent guide to NHS funded IUTs and can be accessed via the In Control website at www.in-control.org.uk/

Taxation and IUTs

12.81   Trust and taxation law is a complex area, and outside the scope of this text. Many trusts are subject to taxation disadvantages compared to most individuals: for example, the trust rates of income tax can be equivalent to the highest rates of income tax paid by individuals; trusts may not benefit from the annual personal allowance enjoyed by most individuals, and so on. When considering the development of a trust, expert advice should be sought, especially where a trust might hold any significant assets and/or receive non-direct payment income. The pitfalls of not taking such advice were highlighted in *Pitt v Holt*[112] where the a discretionary trust had been created which gave rise to a very large unanticipated and largely avoidable tax liability. As the Court of Appeal noted it 'would have been easy to create the settlement in a way which did not have these tax consequences'.

12.82   Subject to the above caveat, what follows should be taken as a general guide designed to identify some of the key issues – but in every case, independent advice should be obtained, not least because this is an area of law that is particularly subject to change.

12.83   In a number of respects Independent User Trusts may be able to avoid some of the adverse aspects of the trust taxation regime since direct payment income from a local authority or the NHS should not normally be deemed taxable income, so the only taxable income of the trust normally will be a small amount of interest earned on sums deposited in the trust's bank or building society account. Likewise capital gains tax may not be a problem if the trust is not acquiring and disposing of chargeable assets.

12.84   It appears likely that IUTs should be able to benefit from specific rules on trusts created to safeguard certain 'vulnerable persons', including 'disabled persons'.[113] Guidance on these trusts can be obtained from the HM Revenue and Customs website.[114] To take advantage of these rules the trust

---

111 J Fitzgerald, *Using independent user trusts to manage personal health budgets*, Mitchell James Ltd, 2011 at www.in-control.org.uk/what-we-do/staying-in-control-health/news/new-paper-personal-health-budgets-and-independent-user-trusts.aspx
112 [2011] EWCA Civ 197.
113 Finance Act 2005, Part 2, chapter 4. Section 38 provides that a disabled person is (a) a person who by reason of mental disorder is incapable of administering his property or managing his affairs or (b) a person in receipt of attendance allowance or the highest or middle rate of the care component of disability living allowance.
114 www.hmrc.gov.uk/trusts/types/vulnerable.htm

must be a qualifying one and the trustees will need to make a vulnerable person election. Under the rules, the income tax liability of the trustees will be reduced to the same amount that would have been paid by the beneficiary had the income been earned by the beneficiary rather than by the trust. In other words the beneficiary's own annual allowance can be used (to the extent that it is not used on other income that the beneficiary receives) and the beneficiary's own income tax rates will apply. For capital gains tax purposes, if the trustees do actually dispose of a chargeable asset, the beneficiary's annual exemption can be used instead of the smaller trustees' annual exemption.

12.85   A vulnerable person election does not have the same impact for inheritance tax purposes, although it appears likely that the beneficiary of the trust will be regarded as having a right to the income of the trust (and thus, for inheritance tax purposes, an 'interest in possession'). This would mean that if the beneficiary died whilst the trust was still in existence, the value of the trust property might be aggregated with the value of his or her estate when calculating whether inheritance tax is payable. However, the sums involved are often not likely to exceed the threshold at which inheritance tax becomes payable (the basic threshold at September 2011 being £325,000).

NHS and direct payments

12.86   The HSCA 2001 s57, makes no provision for direct payments to be made in relation to NHS responsibilities and in *R (Harrison) v Secretary of State for Health*[115] relying heavily on statutory construction the High Court held that there was no power in the NHS Acts 2006 (as originally enacted) to make direct payments to patients (notwithstanding that there was nothing in the Acts to say they could not be made).[116]

12.87   The absence of such a power has caused problems for a number of service users and one mechanism for overcoming them is considered above (para 12.77), namely the use of IUTs. Another possible mechanism is the use of the powers in the 2006 Acts which enable health bodies to make funding transfers to local authorities, and this is considered at para 13.122 below. In England, however, the enactment of the Health Act 2009 has initiated a process which may result in all health bodies having the power to make such payments.

---

115   [2009] EWHC 574 (Admin), (2009) 12 CCLR 93.

116   An appeal in this case became academic and was withdrawn when the day before it was listed for hearing the Health Act (Commencement No 1) Order 2010 brought the material provisions of the Health Act 2009 into force. At the same time separate proceedings (*R (Garnham) v Secretary of State for Health and Islington PCT* (No C1/2009/0802) concerning the powers of PCTs to make indirect payments by transferring funds to social services via NHSA 2006 s256 (NHSWA 2006 s194 (see para 13.125 below)) were adjourned. For analysis of this complex question see L Clements and P Bowen 'NHS Continuing care and independent living' (2007) 10 CCLR 343 at 350.

Direct payments and the Health Act 2009

12.88 An early official proposal to extend the idea of personal budgets to the health sector came with the publication of Lord Darzi's final report 'High quality care for all' in 2008,[117] in which the English government undertook to 'explore the potential of personal budgets, to give individual patients greater control over the services they receive and the providers from which they receive services.' (para 42).

12.89 In 2009 the Department of Health published its proposals 'Personal health budgets: first steps' in which it proposed healthcare direct payments similar to those in social care, stating (at para 48) that it was 'seeking powers in the Health Bill (currently before Parliament) to allow direct payments to be tested in the pilots, and, if successful, introduced more widely'.

12.90 The Health Act 2009 s11 (which inserted NHS Act 2006 s12A) empowers PCTs to make direct payments to patients along similar lines to those paid by social services. As at July 2011 over half of all PCTs were participating in the personal health budgets programme of which 29 had the power to make direct payments and/or children in transition payments.[118] The Act provides for the detail of the scheme (including the process by which PCTs can become pilot sites[119]) to be spelled out in regulations which have been published and came into effect in June 2010.[120] The regulations create a parallel regime for such payments to that which operates in social services departments. The most significant difference between the two regimes, being that, unlike the social services scheme, the NHS scheme is discretionary.

12.91 As with the social services scheme, certain patients (listed in the schedule to the regulations) are excluded, namely people who are subject to certain specific criminal court orders or controls arising out of their a drug and/or alcohol dependencies (eg being subject to a drug rehabilitation of alcohol treatment requirement).

12.92 Regulation 7 defines the primary group for whom direct payments can be made as persons 16 or over who are not specifically excluded and who have capacity to consent and do consent. Payments can, however, be made in relation to children and people who lack the necessary capacity: the procedure for making such payments is detailed in regulations 8 and 9 which requires agreement from the person's 'representative'[121] (where one exists) and for the payment to be made to a person nominated by the representative or the PCT.

---

117 Secretary of State for Health (2008) *High Quality Care For All: NHS Next Stage Review Final Report* CM 7432.
118 Details can be accessed at the Department of Health 'personal health budgets' website at www.personalhealthbudgets.dh.gov.uk/About/aboutPilots/
119 Now detailed in the National Health Service (Direct Payments) Regulations 2010 SI No 1000 Part 2.
120 National Health Service (Direct Payments) Regulations 2010 SI No 1000.
121 Regulation 1 defines a representative in essence as either the person's LPA/deputy with personal welfare powers, or in the case of a child, the person with parental responsibility for that child.

12.93   Regulation 10 provides for a range of persons to be consulted before a decision is made as to whether a direct payment should be made, together with the provision of written reasons if a decision not to make a payment is made (regulation 10(10)). If a payment is agreed, then detailed care planning criteria must be addressed (listed in regulation 11) which include specific regard to the risks associated with the proposed care plan and the PCT being satisfied that the patient's health needs can be met by the specified services and that the direct payments are sufficient to provide for the full cost of each of these services. The regulations stipulate that the payment being made into a designated account and additionally cover such matters as support and advice; the imposition of conditions; repayment and recovery and so on.

12.94   It appears that there are no current proposals (as at September 2011) to legislate for NHS direct payments in Wales or for the launch of any formal personal health budget pilots.

The Independent Living Fund

12.95   The Independent Living Fund (ILF) was established by the Department of Health and Social Security in 1988 as an independent trust to provide a weekly payment to approximately 300 severely disabled people who would have suffered significant financial loss as a result of the abolition of supplementary benefits 'additional requirements' payments in that year.[122] Initially the ILF was intended to be temporary but its expenditure grew from £1.1m in 1988–89 to £359.2m in 2011.[123] The fund is financed by the government, but administered by independent trustees.

12.96   The original trust was wound up in 1993 as part of the community care reforms, with the fund monies being transferred to local authorities via the special transitional grant. However, the payments that were being made to disabled people at the time it was wound up were preserved and paid from what was known as the Independent Living (Extension) Fund.

12.97   In 1993, a new fund, known as the Independent Living (1993) Fund, was created for new applicants and in 2007 both funds were replaced by the Independent Living (2006) Fund. The new fund differentiates between the former users of the Extension Fund – for whom a maximum award of £815 per week is permitted – and all other users for whom the maximum award is £475 per week (and for whom a local authority contribution of between £200 and £340 worth of services or cash payment is required depending on when the ILF funding commenced).

12.98   In June 2010 the ILF closed for all new applications and in December 2010 the Government announced[124] the permanent closure of the scheme

---

122 R Means and R Smith, *Community Care Policy and Practice*, Macmillan, 1994.
123 M Gheera, *Independent Living Fund*, House of Commons Library briefing SN/SP/ 5633 7 January 2011.
124 Written Ministerial Statement 13 December 2010, Department for Work and Pensions *Independent Living Fund*, Parliamentary Under-Secretary of State for Work and Pensions (Maria Miller MP).

on the grounds that it was 'financially unsustainable'. It confirmed that existing recipients would be fully protect 'throughout this Parliament' and indicated that the decision as to what to do with the scheme would be taken following the publication in July 2011 of the Report of the Commission on the Funding of Care and Support (the 'Dilnot Report' – see para 10.78).

12.99   Disabled people who are already receiving payments from the ILF will, therefore, continue to receive these payments until a successor arrangement is approved. If their care needs change, then any additional need will fall to be addressed by the contributing local authority undertaking a reassessment and if needs be, providing for the extra support. Where, however, a recipient of ILF support is adjudged to be eligible for NHS Continuing healthcare funding, then as a general rule,[125] all ILF payments will cease.

12.100   Whilst the eligibility criteria for ILF support are now largely academic, they can be accessed at the ILF's website at www.dwp.gov.uk/ilf/

---

125 In exceptional circumstances the ILF may be prepared to fund the cost of 'domestic duties' for claimants who had been funded under the Extension Fund – see ILF policy circular 27/07, 10 June 2010 at www.dwp.gov.uk/docs/continuing-health-care.pdf.

NHS general responsibilities for services

continued

Introduction

13.1   At no time since the formation of the NHS has there been a clear separation between its responsibilities for healthcare and those of the local authorities for social care services. As we note at para 1.12 above, the creation of the NHS in 1948 did not initially wrest responsibility for health services from local authorities, and the present division of responsibilities between social services and the NHS has developed largely as a consequence of subsequent legislation.

13.2   Until 1990, successive governments sought, by simultaneous amendment[1] of the community care and NHS legislation, to transfer most health functions from local authorities to specific NHS bodies. During this period, however, perceptions as to what was a 'health function' changed. In consequence the NHS tended to concentrate upon the provision of acute healthcare and sought to shed its responsibilities for the long term healthcare needs of individuals.

13.3   During the 1980s responsibility for people who would formerly have been resident in a long stay mental hospital or geriatric ward was in large measure transferred to the social security budget, leading to a substantial increase in the number of private residential and nursing homes. Accordingly the legislative changes of the last 25 years have been dominated by the tripartite tension between these three agencies. The National Health Service and Community Care Act (NHSCCA) 1990 radically altered the respective responsibilities of the Department of Health and Social Security (as the Department for Work and Pensions was then called) and local authorities, but left virtually unchanged the interface between the NHS and local authorities. In contrast, however, the most recent reforms of the NHS have sought to redraw the relationship between the NHS and local authorities.

13.4   This chapter concentrates on the non-acute services for which the NHS is responsible: it does not cover the NHS responsibilities for hospital provision for acute care, nor the ever changing structure of the NHS which is outlined in chapter 1 (para 1.13 above).

13.5   This chapter first considers the legislation, and then the general services which the NHS provides in the community and to care homes. It then covers the specific duties on health bodies to meet the registered nursing needs of nursing home residents. Chapter 14 turns to the vexed question of when the NHS is responsible for the full cost of a patient's health and social care needs under what is termed NHS continuing healthcare funding: it is the chapter that takes us to the heart of the health and social care divide.

---

1   The NHS Act 1946 and the National Assistance Act (NAA) 1948 came into force on the same day; as did the Health Services and Public Health Act 1968 and the Local Authority Social Services Act (LASSA) 1970; as did the Local Government Act 1972 and the NHS Reorganisation Act 1973.

Reform

13.6   At the time of writing (September 2011) proposals contained in the Health and Social Care Bill are before parliament to effect fundamental change to aspects of the NHS. The proposals are controversial and have been the subject of amendment. Given the uncertainty over the future shape of the Bill and the timescale for implementation, the Bill is not further considered in this edition. However, it does appear likely that during 2013 PCTs will be abolished and their functions replaced by clinical commissioning groups, and that Strategic Health Authorities (SHAs) will also be abolished and replaced by the NHS Commissioning Board. Although the NHS Commissioning Board is still subject to parliamentary approval it is proposed that SHAs are reduced to four regional centres from October 2011 pending the Board's creation.

13.7   It is inevitable that the coming years will see major changes to the structure of the NHS, not least because it is currently charged under the 'Quality, Innovation, Productivity and Prevention' (QIPP)[2] scheme with identifying £15–£20 billion of efficiency savings by the end of 2013/14.

The National Health Service Acts 2006

13.8   The National Health Service was created by the enactment of the NHS Act 1946. The 1946 Act was replaced in 1977 by the NHS Act of that year, which consolidated the changes that had occurred in the intervening years. In 2006 a further codification occurred with the repeal of the 1977 Act. This was replaced by two principal Acts: the NHS Act (NHSA) 2006 and the NHS (Wales) Act (NHS(W)A) 2006. A third Act, the NHS (Consequential Provisions) Act 2006, addressed technical drafting requirements that attended the codification. The decision to have two principal Acts is an expression of the extent to which devolution has created a distinct legal regime for the health service in Wales. However, it is a mistake to consider the NHSA 2006 as an English statute. Although it was possible in most places to 'split' the provisions of the 1977 Act into two separate statutes, in drafting terms this was not feasible in relation to certain cross-cutting obligations. Accordingly by default these common provisions appear in the NHSA 2006 together with 1977 provisions which were not devolved to the Welsh Government.[3] By way of example, the duty on NHS bodies to co-operate with local authorities (being a duty that could require co-operation between an English local authority and a Welsh NHS body) is not found in the NHS(W)A 2006. Instead it is found in NHSA 2006 s82 which when read with NHS(W)A 2006 ss28(6) and 275(1) makes it clear that the duty encompasses local health boards (LHBs) and Welsh NHS trusts. Likewise NHSA 2006 Sch 20 para 3, which requires social services authorities to provide home help support (see para 9.178), has no equivalent in the Welsh Act because the definition of 'local authority' in NHSA 2006 s275 covers Welsh as well as English authorities.

The core health service obligation

13.9 The general NHS duty is to be found in section 1 of both the NHSA 2006 and the NHS(W)A 2006. The wording of section 1 in both Acts is identical, save only that the Welsh Act substitutes for the 'secretary of state' the words 'Welsh Ministers' and for 'England' the word 'Wales'. NHSA 2006 s1 provides:

> 1 (1) The secretary of state must continue the promotion in England of a comprehensive health service designed to secure improvement –
>   (a) in the physical and mental health of the people of England, and
>   (b) in the prevention, diagnosis and treatment of illness.[4]
> (2) The secretary of state must for that purpose provide or secure the provision of services in accordance with this Act.
> (3) The services so provided must be free of charge except in so far as the making and recovery of charges is expressly provided for by or under any enactment, whenever passed.

13.10 NHSA 2006 s2(1) confers wide ranging powers in England[5] on the secretary of state to provide such services as are appropriate, namely:

> **Secretary of state's general power**
> 2 (1) The secretary of state may –
>   (a) provide such services as he considers appropriate for the purpose of discharging any duty imposed on him by this Act, and
>   (b) do anything else which is calculated to facilitate, or is conducive or incidental to, the discharge of such a duty.

13.11 NHSA 2006 s3 then sets out those general services which it is the secretary of state's duty in England[6] to provide – to such extent as s/he considers necessary – to meet all reasonable requirements. Most of the services that may be described as hospital and community health services are included under this section.[7]

13.12 Section 3(1) provides:

> **Secretary of state's duty as to provision of certain services**
> 3 (1) The secretary of state must provide throughout England, to such extent as he considers necessary to meet all reasonable requirements –
>   (a) hospital accommodation,
>   (b) other accommodation for the purpose of any service provided under this Act,

---

4   NHS Act 2006 s275(1) and NHS (Wales) Act 2006 s 206, define 'illness' as including 'any mental disorder of the mind and any injury or disability requiring medical or dental treatment or nursing'.
5   In NHS(W)A 2006 the text is identical save that 'Welsh Ministers' is substituted for 'secretary of state' and the word 'they' for 'him'.
6   In NHS(W)A 2006 the text is identical save that 'Welsh Ministers' is substituted for 'secretary of state' and the word 'they' for 'he'.
7   By virtue of section 3(1A) there is power to secure these services from outside England and Wales.

(c) medical, dental, ophthalmic, nursing and ambulance services,
(d) such other services or facilities for the care of pregnant women, women who are breastfeeding and young children as he considers are appropriate as part of the health service,
(e) such other services or facilities for the prevention of illness, the care of persons suffering from illness and the after-care of persons who have suffered from illness as he considers are appropriate as part of the health service,
(f) such other services or facilities as are required for the diagnosis and treatment of illness.

13.13   In *R (Keating) v Cardiff Local Health Board*[8] the Court of Appeal held that the word 'facilities' in section 3(1)(e) included not only the accommodation, plant and other means by which health services were provided, but also the personnel who actually provided the services. Accordingly, a LHB had the power to fund a project providing a service of advice and assistance in relation to access to state benefits for those with mental health problems (see para 9.47 above).

13.14   The responsibility for the actual provision of services under the NHS Acts 2006 is in general terms delegated to NHS trusts. Trusts are semi-autonomous bodies set up to assume responsibility for the ownership and management of hospitals or other establishments or facilities. NHS trusts do not receive funding in the way that primary care trusts (PCTs) or LHBs do, but rather through obtaining contracts for their services from PCTs/LHBs.[9]

13.15   NHSA 2006 s8 empowers the secretary of state to issue directions to NHS bodies and in turn section 15 empowers strategic health authorities (SHAs) to direct PCTs. In Wales the Welsh ministers' principal powers of direction are found at NHS(W)A 2006 s12 (for LHBs) and s19 (for NHS Trusts). There is no provision in the 2006 NHS Acts concerning the power to issue general guidance[10] akin to that in Local Authority Social Services Act (LASSA) 1970 s7(1) (see para 1.44 above for an analysis of the status of directions and guidance) and para 1.64 regarding NHS guidance.

The duty to promote a 'comprehensive' health service

13.16   In contrast to the detailed legislative duties laid upon social services authorities, the NHS's statutory duties under sections 1 and 3 are general and indeterminate: 'target duties' in the language of public law (see para

---

8   [2005] EWCA Civ 847, [2006] 1 WLR 159, (2005) 8 CCLR 504.
9   NHS contracts are dealt with in NHSA 2006 s9 and NHS(W)A 2006 s7. Essentially such contracts are not legally enforceable but are subject to arbitration by the secretary of state/Welsh Government. For details of the contracting and commissioning responsibilities of PCTs, see generally www.pcc.nhs.uk/commissioning. See also the Department of Health (2008) *Commissioning for Quality and Innovation (CQUIN) Payment framework* at www.institute.nhs.uk/world_class_commissioning/pct_portal/cquin.html
10 NHS(W)A 2006 s40(7) does, however, contain a general power enabling the Welsh ministers to issue guidance in relation to health and well-being strategies.

1.26 above). Accordingly the courts have been reluctant to disturb NHS administrative decisions where these general public law duties are involved. In *R v Cambridge Health Authority ex p B*[11] the decision in question concerned 'the life of a young patient'. At first instance Laws J criticised the authority's justification for its decision not to fund any further chemotherapy treatment for the child as consisting 'only of grave and well-rounded generalities', stating that:

> . . . where the question is whether the life of a 10-year-old child might be saved, however slim a chance, the responsible authority . . . must do more than toll the bell of tight resources . . . they must explain the priorities that have led them to decline to fund the treatment.

13.17 The Court of Appeal felt unable to sustain this line, holding instead:

> Difficult and agonising judgements have to be made as to how a limited budget is best allocated to the maximum advantage of the maximum number of patients. That is not a judgement which the court can make . . . It is not something that a health authority . . . can be fairly criticised for not advancing before the court . . .
>
> It would be totally unrealistic to require the authority to come to court with its accounts and seek to demonstrate that if this treatment were provided for B then there would be a patient, C, who would have to go without treatment. No major authority could run its financial affairs in a way which would permit such a demonstration.

13.18 The *ex p B* decision should not be seen as an abrogation by the court of its duty to scrutinise 'anxiously' questions which engage fundamental human rights (see para 26.237 below). In the case the court heard evidence of the lengths to which the health authority had gone to weigh up the likelihood of the treatment being successful, the adverse effects of the treatment and had consulted with the family. The court accepted that it was a bona fide decision taken on an individual basis and supported by respected professional opinion. In such cases, where the key consideration is expertise that the court does not possess, even with the enactment of the Human Rights Act 1998,[12] the court will inevitably hesitate to substitute its opinions. The situation will, however, be otherwise where the issue concerns questions of law or logic, or where an NHS body is seeking to provide a service that does not properly meet the person's needs – or subjects the person to inappropriate institutionalisation.[13]

13.19 Health bodies must, therefore, comply with the law, respect fundamental human rights and ensure that their decisions are reached in accordance with established public law principles. They must not, for

---

11 [1995] 1 WLR 898, CA.
12 In *R (Watts) v Bedford PCT* [2003] EWHC 2228 (Admin), (2003) 6 CCLR 566 Munby J reviewed the domestic and Strasbourg jurisprudence concerning the public law obligations to provide healthcare services. He concluded that notwithstanding the enactment of the Human Rights Act 1998, section 1 remained a 'target' duty (see para 1.26); see also *R (Watts) v Bedford PCT* [2004] EWCA Civ 166, (2004) 77 BMLR 26.
13 See eg *Gunter v South Western Staffordshire PCT* [2005] EWHC 1894 (Admin), (2006) 9 CCLR 121 at [19]–[20]. See also para 4.71 below.

instance: ignore circular guidance;[14] violate European Union law;[15] operate an irrational[16] or a perverse policy;[17] fetter their discretion to fund the treatment;[18] fail to consult before reaching certain decisions; or refuse funding due to the patient's financial circumstances.[19]

13.20   Sections 1 and 3, the 'core NHS provisions', were subjected to considerable scrutiny by the Court of Appeal in *R v North and East Devon Health Authority ex p Coughlan*.[20] There the court noted (at para 22) that:

> Section 1(1) does not place a duty on the secretary of state to provide a comprehensive health service. His duty is 'to continue to promote' such a service. In addition the services which he is required to provide have to be provided 'in accordance with this Act.'[21]

and (at para 23):

> . . . the secretary of state's section 3 duty is subject to two different qualifications. First of all there is the initial qualification that his obligation is limited to providing the services identified to the extent that he considers that they are *necessary* to meet *all reasonable requirements* . . .[22]

and

> 24. The first qualification placed on the duty contained in section 3 makes it clear that there is scope for the secretary of state to exercise a degree of judgment as to the circumstances in which he will provide the services, including nursing services referred to in the section. He does not automatically have to meet *all* nursing requirements. In certain circumstances he can exercise his judgment and legitimately decline to provide nursing services. He need not provide nursing services if he does not consider they are reasonably required or necessary to meet a reasonable requirement.
>
> 25. When exercising his judgment he has to bear in mind the comprehensive service which he is under a duty to promote as set out in section 1. However, as long as he pays due regard to that duty, the fact that the service will not be comprehensive does not mean that he is necessarily contravening either section 1 or section 3. The truth is that, while he has the duty to continue to promote a comprehensive free health service and he must never, in making a decision under section 3, disregard that duty, a comprehensive health service may never, for human, financial and other resource reasons, be achievable. Recent history has demonstrated that the

14 *R v North Derbyshire Health Authority ex p Fisher* (1997–98) 1 CCLR 150, QBD.
15 *R (Watts) v Bedford PCT* [2004] EWCA Civ 166, (2004) 77 BMLR 26.
16 *R (Rogers) v Swindon NHS PCT* [2006] EWCA Civ 392, [2006] 1 WLR 2649, (2006) 9 CCLR 451 but see also *R (Condliff) v North Staffordshire PCT* [2011] EWCA Civ 910.
17 *R (Ross) v West Sussex Primary Care Trust* [2008] EWHC 2252 (Admin), (2008) 11 CCLR 787.
18 *R v North West Lancashire Health Authority ex p A* [2000] 1 WLR 977, (1999) 2 CCLR 419, CA.
19 *R (Booker) v NHS Oldham and Directline Insurance Plc* [2010] EWHC 2593 (Admin), (2011) 14 CCLR 315.
20 [2000] 2 WLR 622, (1999) 2 CCLR 285, CA. The case concerned the NHSA 1977 but the context of sections 1 and 3 in that Act and in the 2006 Acts is identical.
21 (1999) 2 CCLR 285, CA at para 22.
22 (1999) 2 CCLR 285, CA at para 23.

pace of developments as to what is possible by way of medical treatment, coupled with the ever increasing expectations of the public, mean that the resources of the NHS are and are likely to continue, at least in the foreseeable future, to be insufficient to meet demand.

26. In exercising his judgment the secretary of state is entitled to take into account the resources available to him and the demands on those resources. In *R v Secretary of State for Social Services and Ors ex parte Hincks* [1980] 1 BMLR 93 the Court of Appeal held that section 3(1) of the Health Act does not impose an absolute duty to provide the specified services. The secretary of state is entitled to have regard to the resources made available to him under current government economic policy.

13.21   Where a health body decides to fund a care package in such a way that it has an adverse impact on a Convention right, that decision will not be immune from court or ombudsman scrutiny. In *Gunter v South Western Staffordshire PCT*[23] the applicant wished to remain in her own home rather than be placed in an institutional setting by the PCT (which accepted continuing care responsibility for her). Collins J considered this to be a 'very important' consideration which had to 'be given due weight in deciding on her future' since to remove her from her home would 'interfere with her right to respect for her family life'.

13.22   In respect of the PCT's argument that it would be less expensive to provide the care in an institutional setting, the judge observed:

> I do not regard evidence of what benefits could accrue from the expenditure of sums which could be saved in providing a less costly package for Rachel as helpful. It is obvious that Health Authorities never have enough money to provide the level of services which would be ideal, but that cannot mean that someone such as Rachel should receive care which does not properly meet her needs.

13.23   In his opinion:

> The interference with family life is obvious and so must be justified as proportionate. Cost is a factor which can properly be taken into account. But the evidence of the improvement in Rachel's condition, the obvious quality of life within her family environment and her expressed views that she does not want to move are all important factors which suggest that to remove her from her home will require clear justification.

NHS Constitution

13.24   The Health Act 2009 s2 obliges every NHS body in England, when performing their NHS functions,[24] to have regard to the NHS Constitution. The duty also extends to everyone (including subcontractors) who

---

23   [2005] EWHC 1894 (Admin), (2006) 9 CCLR 121.
24   Defined in Health Act 2009 s2(3) as 'any function under an enactment which is a function concerned with, or connected to, the provision, commissioning or regulation of NHS.'

'provides NHS services under a contract, agreement or arrangements' or under the NHSA 2006 s12(1).[25]

13.25   The preamble to the NHS Constitution (2010)[26] states:

> This Constitution establishes the principles and values of the NHS in England. It sets out rights to which patients, public and staff are entitled, and pledges which the NHS is committed to achieve, together with responsibilities which the public, patients and staff owe to one another to ensure that the NHS operates fairly and effectively. All NHS bodies and private and third sector providers supplying NHS services are required by law to take account of this Constitution in their decisions and actions.

13.26   The constitution is built around seven key principles, which in summary comprise:

1. The NHS provides a comprehensive service, available to all irrespective of gender, race, disability, age, sexual orientation, religion or belief. It has a duty to each and every individual that it serves and must respect their human rights. . . .
2. Access to NHS services is based on clinical need, not an individual's ability to pay. . . .
3. The NHS aspires to the highest standards of excellence and professionalism – in the provision of high-quality care that is safe, effective and focused on patient experience; . . .
4. NHS services must reflect the needs and preferences of patients, their families and their carers. Patients, with their families and carers, where appropriate, will be involved in and consulted on all decisions about their care and treatment.
5. The NHS works across organisational boundaries and in partnership with other organisations in the interest of patients, local communities and the wider population. . . . The NHS is committed to working jointly with local authorities and a wide range of other private, public and third sector organisations at national and local level to provide and deliver improvements in health and well-being.
6. The NHS is committed to providing best value for taxpayers' money and the most effective, fair and sustainable use of finite resources. . . .
7. The NHS is accountable to the public, communities and patients that it serves. . . . The system of responsibility and accountability for taking decisions in the NHS should be transparent and clear to the public, patients and staff. . . .

13.27   Accompanying the Constitution is a substantial handbook 'designed to give NHS staff and patients all the information they need about the NHS Constitution for England'.[27]

13.28   In *R (Booker) v NHS Oldham and Directline Insurance Plc*[28] a PCT's decision to refuse funding for a patient was scrutinised by reference to

---

25 Which enables the secretary of state to arrange for services to be provided by any person or body – eg a commercial or a voluntary organisation etc.
26 Department of Health (2010) *The NHS Constitution*.
27 Department of Health (2010) *The Handbook to the NHS Constitution*.
28 [2010] EWHC 2593 (Admin), (2011) 14 CCLR 315 at [27].

(amongst other things) the Constitution, and in finding the practice to be unlawful, the court placed considerable reliance on principle 2 (that access to NHS services is based on clinical need, not an individual's ability to pay).

13.29   The Health Services Ombudsman has signalled that she intends to use the Constitution as a benchmark in her investigations (together with the *'Ombudsman's Principles'* – see para 26.152 below). In a 2011 report[29] reference is made to the need for the Constitution's principles to be seen in their wider contexts, embracing as they do 'the principles of human rights – fairness, respect, equality, dignity and autonomy'. The report's concluded (page 10) that the 'NHS must close the gap between the promise of care and compassion outlined in its Constitution': that 'every member of staff, no matter what their job, has a role to play in making the commitments of the Constitution a felt reality for patients'.

13.30   It has been argued[30] that the mandatory nature of the statutory obligation to 'have regard to' may well be interpreted by the courts as requiring NHS bodies to act in line with the Constitution, unless they have articulated good reasons for not doing so.

Choice

13.31   The Constitution's emphasis on 'choice' has attracted considerable analysis.[31] Although the seven underpinning principles do not mention this word (talking instead of reflecting individual 'needs and preferences', and of people being 'involved in and consulted on' relevant decisions) section 2a asserts the individual right: (1) to choose a GP practice, (2) to express a preference for using a particular doctor within that GP practice; and (3) to make choices about one's NHS care and to information to support these choices. To bolster these 'rights', in 2009 the Department of Health issued directions[32] and best practice guidance on the 'right to choice'.[33] Direction 2 places a qualified duty on PCTs to ensure that patients requiring an elective referral[34] for which the trust is responsible, are able to choose any clinically appropriate secondary care provider for their first outpatient appointment. The directions also place an obligation on PCTs to (amongst

---

29 Health Service Commissioner (2011) *Care and compassion?* Report of the Health Service Ombudsman on ten investigations into NHS care of older people. Fourth report of the Health Service Commissioner for England Session 2010–2011 HC 778, p9.

30 K Ashton and J Gould, Community care law update, June 2009 *Legal Action* 11–16.

31 See eg, K Ashton and J Gould, Community care law update, June 2009 *Legal Action* 11–16; D Wolfe and R Logan, 'Public law and the provision of healthcare', (2009) *Judicial Review*, 14(2), pp210–223; and S Farg and A Chapman, 'Who cares wins?', (2010) NLJ, 160(7417), pp671–672.

32 Department of Health, Primary Care Trust Choice of Secondary Care Provider Directions 2009.

33 Department of Health (2009) *Implementation of the right to choice and information set out in the NHS Constitution.*

34 Defined in direction 2(4) as a referral by a 'general medical practitioner, dental practitioner or optometrist to a secondary care provider'.

other things) publicise the availability of the right to makes such choices. Ashton and Gould[35] suggest that one aspect of this right will be to create a general expectation that PCTs will fund care home placements of choice unless the health body has provided good reasons for not doing so see para 14.129 below on choice and NHS continuing healthcare.

The medical/social divide

13.32   The conflict between health and social care is not a new one. What is a social need and what is a medical need is an intractable problem. In general (but see para 14.142 below) it is only of practical importance to community care service users because a service provided by the NHS is generally free at the point of need, whereas a service provided by the social services department is generally subject to a means-tested charge. Help with bathing is therefore free if provided in a person's home by the district nurse (or NHS auxiliary), whereas if provided by a social services care assistant it may be subject to a charge. The argument is repeated in a hundred different ways with such items and services as walking sticks, hoists, commodes, speech therapy, chiropody, medication prompting and toenail cutting.

13.33   Exhortations to organisations, professionals and other service providers to work together more closely and effectively, litter the policy landscape: yet the reality is all too often a jumble of services factionalised by professional culture, organisational boundaries and by tiers of governance.[36] Lymberry[37] for example has pointed to the differences of power and culture between health and social services authorities as being a key factor in this continuing failure, together with the 'inherently competitive nature of professions jostling for territory in the same areas of activity'. He like many researchers in this field concludes that 'these issues cannot be resolved unless they are properly understood; a rhetorical appeal to the unmitigated benefits of 'partnership' alone will not produce more effective joint working'.

35   See note 30 above.
36   A Webb, 'Co-ordination: A problem in public sector management', (1991) 19(4) *Policy and Politics* 229–241; quoted in R Means and R Smith, *Community Care*, Macmillan, 1994. There has been considerable criticism of successive governments' concentration upon creating administrative joint planning structures, on creating coterminosity, and other organisational devices to promote joint working. The research evidence suggested, however, that 'where mutual trust has existed between senior officers from health and local authorities, the relationship has appeared to be far more important than joint planning machinery', R Davidson and S Hunter, *Community Care in Practice*, Batsford, 1994; see also L Clements and P Smith, *A 'Snapshot' Survey of Social Services' Responses to the Continuing Care Needs of Older People in Wales* (1999).
37   M Lymbery, 'United we stand? Partnership working in health and social care and the role of social work in services for older people', (2006) 36(7) *British Journal of Social Work* 1119.

The duty to co-operate

13.34 There are a number of statutory duties on local authorities and health bodies to work together constructively. These fall into three broad categories, namely:

1) the obligation to co-operate at the strategic level, ie in the preparation of plans for the improvement of the health of the general population – these are analysed at para 2.24 above;
2) the obligation on a general day-to-day level requiring co-operation in the delivery of services to individuals who are disabled, elderly or ill – these are considered below;
3) the obligation to co-operate under the Mental Health Act (MHA) 1983 – which is considered at para 20.31 above.

Statutory duties to co-operate under the NHS Act 2006

13.35 NHSA 2006 s72 places a duty on all NHS bodies to co-operate with each other in exercising their functions and s82 provides that:

> In exercising their respective functions NHS bodies (on the one hand) and local authorities (on the other) must co-operate with one another in order to secure and advance the health and welfare of the people of England and Wales.

13.36 The section 82 duty (as with the section 72 duty) is a cross border obligation extending to all English and Welsh health bodies and local authorities. This extensive obligation derives from an amendment made by HA 1999 s27. The notes of guidance to the 1999 Act explained that the purpose of the amendment was to extend the duty of partnership in order to:

> ... secure and advance the health and welfare of the people of England and Wales, to cover Primary Care Trusts and NHS trusts as well as Health Authorities and Special Health Authorities. This recognises the need to work in partnership in commissioning and delivering care, as well as at the strategic planning level. Welfare is used in its wide general sense and is designed to cover functions relating to social services, education, housing and the environment.

13.37 The section 72 duty requires, as noted above, NHS bodies to cooperate with each other and (like the section 82 duty) is augmented by principle 5 of the NHS Constitution (considered at para 13.24 above). Accordingly if two or more health bodies are in a funding dispute, it will be maladministration[38] if they fail to consider one of them funding the patient on an interim basis until the matter had been resolved and in all the circumstances to take a flexible approach to the needs of patients. A 2007 Welsh

---

38 Report by the Public Services Ombudsman for Wales and the Health Service Ombudsman for England of an investigation of a complaint about the Welsh Assembly Government (Health Commission Wales), Cardiff and Vale NHS Trust and Plymouth Teaching Primary Care Trust, Third Report, Session 2008–2009, HC 858.

Ombudsman's report[39] concerned such a case. The complainant required a specialist profiling bed and a specialised seating system, but there was a dispute between two trusts as to which should fund this equipment. The Ombudsman, in finding maladministration, considered that the relevant LHB should have taken responsibility as an interim measure, pending the resolution of the dispute between the various NHS bodies.[40]

13.38   Where a community care service user suffers as a result of an inter-agency dispute, it is generally appropriate for complaints to be made against each authority primarily on the basis that they have failed to 'work together' in violation of their specific statutory obligations. The local government ombudsman has repeatedly criticised authorities for failing to provide services whilst they squabbled over their respective obligations. A 1996 ombudsman complaint, for example, concerned the failure of a health authority and social services department to co-operate. Although the ombudsman considered that the health authority's involvement had been 'reluctant, if not unhelpful', she nevertheless found the social services authority guilty of maladministration. In her opinion, having accepted that a need existed, social services should have 'grasped the nettle' and secured the provision, before entering into protracted negotiations with the NHS on liability for the care costs.[41]

Additional specific duties to co-operate

13.39   During the community care assessment process a specific duty to co-operate arises if the assessor considers that there 'may be a need' for NHS input. The duty, under NHSCCA 1990 s47(3) is considered at para 3.125 above. A similar, but more extensive, duty exists in relation to patients detained under section 3 or one of the criminal provisions of the MHA 1983. The aftercare duty, under section 117 of the 1983 Act, is considered at para 20.25 below.

13.40   Certain patients who are being discharged from hospital care in England are the subject of the Community Care (Delayed Discharges etc) Act (CC(DD)A) 2003 and for them a duty to co-operate between the NHS and social services arises although the obligations are largely one way – on the social services to facilitate a discharge. The duty is considered at para 5.27 above.

13.41   In relation to children's services Children Act (CA) 1989 s27 provides children's services departments with significant powers to request assistance from (among other agencies) the NHS. This power has been augmented by CA 2004 s10 (s25 in Wales).

---

39 Public Services Ombudsman for Wales Complaint against Bro Morgannwg NHS Trust, Cardiff and Vale NHS Trust, Vale of Glamorgan Council and Vale of Glamorgan Local Health Board case ref 200501955, 200600591 and 20070064, 28 November 2007 – see pages 28 and 30.
40 See chapter 6 for details about establishing the responsible commissioner.
41 Complaint no 96/C/3868 against Calderdale MBC.

General duties to provide NHS services in the community and to care homes

13.42 The NHS general duty to promote a comprehensive health service requires a range of services in the community and elsewhere. All people within the UK have a right to these services – regardless of where they are living. These services include of course access to primary care such as that provided by GPs and dentists as well as the full range of services such as physiotherapy, occupational therapy, chiropody, district nursing and community nursing and general ophthalmic services etc.

13.43 2009 English guidance[42] gives examples of the range of health services which PCTs are expected to provide, stating that the list 'includes but is not limited to':

- primary healthcare;
- assessment involving doctors and registered nurses;
- rehabilitation and recovery (where this forms part of an overall package of NHS care as distinct from intermediate care);
- respite healthcare;
- community health services;
- specialist support for healthcare needs;
- palliative care and end of life healthcare.

13.44 Earlier 2001 English guidance[43] and existing Welsh guidance[44] lists, in addition to the above, equipment and specialist transport, which are clearly NHS responsibilities, and are considered further below (see para 13.92 below).

General practitioner services

13.45 NHSA 2006 s84 (NHS(W)A 2006 s42) empowers PCTs (LHBs in Wales) to arrange with medical practitioners to provide personal medical services for all persons in their area who wish to take advantage of the arrangements. These services are described as 'general medical services'. As with hospital services, it is not the PCT/LHB itself which provides the service; instead, it enters into separate statutory arrangements with independent practitioners for the provision of those services. GPs are not therefore employees of the PCT/LHB, but independent professionals who undertake to provide general medical services in accordance a general medical services contract,[45] the terms of which are prescribed by regulations –

---

42 Department of Health, *The National Framework for NHS Continuing Healthcare and NHS Funded Nursing Care*, 2009, para 104 and the NHS Continuing Healthcare (Responsibilities) Directions 2009 – see para 14.42 below.

43 Department of Health guidance LAC (2001)18 *Continuing Care: NHS and Local Councils' responsibilities* para 16, now superseded by the 2009 National Framework.

44 *Continuing NHS Healthcare* paras 7.18 and 7.20, Welsh Government 2010.

45 At the time of writing (September 2011) the most recent GP contract can be accessed at www.dh.gov.uk/en/Publicationsandstatistics/Publications/PublicationsPolicyAnd Guidance/DH_116299 .

currently the National Health Service (General Medical Services Contracts) Regulations 2004[46] as amended.[47]

13.46   Longstanding concern exists as to the general performance of GPs in
fulfilling their community care obligations: primarily the responsibility of
ensuring that people in need of community care services are provided
with the necessary assistance to obtain them.[48] Regulation 15(5)(b) of the
2004 Regulations requires that GPs refer (as appropriate) patients 'for
other services under [what is now the NHSA 2006 and NHS(W)A 2006]'.
As noted at para 9.154 above, NHSA 2006 s254 and Sch 20 (NHS(W)A
2006 s192 and Sch 15) place substantial duties on social services authorities. It follows that GPs are contractually obliged to make appropriate
referrals to social services where it appears that a patient may be entitled
to community care services. In those cases where the patient lacks mental
capacity or it is otherwise unlikely that he or she will respond to such advice
or referral, there will frequently be an equivalent duty owed to the patient's
carer and this obligation is considered further at para 16.102 below.

13.47   Disquiet also exists about the difficulty of some care home residents
accessing GP services[49] and the failure of GPs to make appropriate referrals for NHS continuing care assessments. Guidance in relation to the
former has been issued via the Department of Health website.[50] Although
there has been no specific guidance to address the latter, PCTs are
required to ensure that an appropriate assessment is carried out in all
cases where it appears there may be a need for continuing care services.
GPs should therefore be aware of the eligibility criteria for NHS continuing healthcare and make the appropriate referrals if when visiting patients
they consider they meet that criteria see para 14.76 below.

GPs' obligation to prescribe drugs and appliances

13.48   The obligation on GPs to render general medical services for their
patients brings with it a need to prescribe. This requirement is addressed
by the 2004 Regulations[51] which provide:

> Subject to paragraphs 42 and 43, a prescriber shall order any drugs,
> medicines or appliances which are needed for the treatment of any patient
> who is receiving treatment under the contract by issuing to that patient a
> prescription form or a repeatable prescription and such a prescription form
> or repeatable prescription shall not be used in any other circumstances.

46   National Health Service (General Medical Services Contracts) (Wales) Regulations
2004 SI No 478 (W48).
47   See eg The National Health Service (General Medical Services Contracts) (Prescription
of Drugs etc.) (Amendment) Regulations 2010 SI No 2389.
48   See eg EL (96)8 para 11.
49   C Glendinning et al, 'A survey of access to medical services in nursing and residential
homes in England' (2002) 52 *British Journal of General Practice* 545.
50   See Department of Health (2007) *NHS-funded nursing care: guide to care home managers
on GP services for residents.* at http://webarchive.nationalarchives.gov.uk/+/
www.dh.gov.uk/en/Healthcare/IntegratedCare/NHSfundednursingcare/
DH_4000392
51   NHS (General Medical Services Contracts) Regulations 2004 SI No 291 Sch 6 para 39;
National Health Service (General Medical Services Contracts) (Wales) Regulations
2004 SI No 478 (W48).

13.49   The responsibility for prescribing and the administration of prescription medicines, brings with it the question of whether the whole process is an NHS function and if so whether charges can be levied by social services, when what it is arguably fulfilling an agency role in this process.

13.50   The administration of prescription medication stems from a doctor's decision that the patient needs to take that medication. From this decision flows the concomitant obligation on the NHS to ensure that the drugs are correctly administered (eg as to the frequency, quantity, and circumstances etc); that records of when the drugs are taken are maintained (if the patient is unable to do this) and that contra indications or adverse reactions to the medication are closely monitored and the regime kept under appropriate review.[52] All of these 'control' functions would appear to be the responsibility of the NHS – even though there may be no need for every aspect to be undertaken by an NHS employee (provided that appropriate training, guidance and back up support is available). If this is so, the lawfulness of a social services authority levying charges to a service user for its role in this process, is open to question. It is arguable that the authority (which must be incurring substantial expense in fulfilling this role) should instead be seeking payment from the health body, for discharging this health function on its behalf (eg under NHSA 2006 s256 – see para 13.125 below).

13.51   The combined effect of: (1) an increasing population of older and disabled people, shorter patient hospital stays, fewer NHS hospital beds and the decline in the number of district nurses;[53] and (2) the general policy of local authorities of restricting care support those with the most acute need (ie within the critical and substantial bands) has been that social services home care support is increasingly being provided to a cohort of service users who need a high level of assistance to take their medication (although they do not meet the criteria for NHS continuing healthcare funding for 'Drug Therapies and Medication' – see para 14.104 below).

13.52   Paragraph 39 of the 2004 Regulations additionally enables GPs to prescribe 'appliances'; ie medical aids, dressings, pads etc as well as basic equipment to help overcome the effects of disability. In relation to disability equipment there is frequently an overlap of responsibility with the local social services department's community care duties. It is therefore common practice for health and social services to arrange joint equipment stores which can be accessed by both social services and the relevant NHS trust (see para 9.128).

13.53   The appliances which a GP can prescribe are detailed in a list known as

---

52 It appears, eg to be not uncommon for care assistants to pick up errors on Medication Administration Records (MAR charts) requiring liaison with the pharmacy to clarify and correct the error and to ensure that the correct chart and medication is provided (sometimes urgently) to the service user.

53 The number of qualified District Nurses fell by 23% between 1996 and 2006 – a trend that appears to be continuing – see Queen's Nursing Institute (2010) *Position Statement* London: QNI; and Queen's Nursing Institute (2010) *District nurse is becoming an endangered species.* Press Release 26 March 2010 at www.qni.org.uk/news_events/2010_press_releases

the Drug Tariff[54] at Part IX. The lists enable GPs to provide a range of general items. Where more specialist equipment is needed, this may be obtained via a hospital consultant (see below).

13.54   The appliance list in the Drug Tariff includes such items as:

- stoma and some incontinence care equipment (see also para 13.84 below where PCT/LHB responsibility for incontinence supplies is considered);
- elastic hosiery, dressings, bandages, trusses etc;
- respiratory equipment (including oxygen cylinders and oxygen concentrators);
- chiropody appliances. GPs can refer patients to NHS chiropodists and consultants for more specialist equipment. PCTs/LHBs must also ensure that adequate chiropody services are available to residents placed by social services in care home accommodation (see para 8.24 below).

GPs' obligation to provide statements of fitness for work

13.55   GPs have an important role in providing certificates for a variety of purposes, including establishing whether the patient is fit for work. Accordingly NHS (General Medical Services Contracts) Regulations 2004 reg 21 provides that GPs are required to issue free of charge to their patients (or their personal representatives) any medical certificate which is reasonably required for certain specified purposes; these being set out in column 1 of Schedule 4 to the 2004 Regulations.

Rehabilitation and recovery services

13.56   There is considerable guidance directed at the NHS stressing the importance of the provision of after-care services where they help promote independent living.[55] Nowadays the term rehabilitation is linked with reablement which is discussed in more detail in chapter 5. It is defined as:

> A programme of therapy and re-enablement designed to maximise independence and minimise the effects of disability.[56]

13.57   If, with the assistance of rehabilitation or respite services, a patient can live independently in the community, resources should be devoted towards this end.[57] In the Government's *Vision for Social Care* effective rehabilitation is seen as an essential element for the NHS 'Quality, Innov-

---

54 A copy of the Electronic Drug Tariff compiled by the NHS Business Services Authority NHS Prescription Services can be viewed at www.ppa.org.uk/edt/July_2011/mindex.htm.

55 See for instance Department of Health *Transforming Rehabilitation Services: Best Practice Guidance* available at www.dh.gov.uk/en/Publicationsandstatistics/Publications/PublicationsPolicyAndGuidance/DH_124178

56 Department of Health (2009) *The National Framework NHS Continuing Healthcare and NHS-funded Nursing Care*.

57 The Audit Commission noted, however, that '[r]ehabilitation is currently advocated by many as the "missing factor" in the care of elderly people. What is clear is that many health authorities lack basic knowledge about the rehabilitation services for older people in their area', *Coming of Age*, Audit Commission, 1997.

ation, Productivity and Prevention' programme see para 13.7 above.⁵⁸ 1995 guidance⁵⁹ suggested that 'the existence of good rehabilitation services and well developed community health services and social care support may lessen, although not eliminate, the need for continuing inpatient care'.⁶⁰ The importance of developing rehabilitation and recovery services was described as a 'crucial priority' in EL (96)89.⁶¹ The 1995 guidance required health authorities to take full account of the need for services:

> ... to promote the effective recovery and rehabilitation of patients after acute treatment so as to maximise the chances of the successful implementation of long-term care plans. This is particularly important for older people who may need a longer period to reach their full potential for recovery and to regain confidence. Local policies should guard against the risk of premature discharge in terms of poorer experiences for patients and increased levels of readmissions.

13.58   Follow-up guidance in February 1996 on the local eligibility criteria (EL (96)8) expressed concern over certain rehabilitation and recovery criteria, stating (at para 16) that they would be unduly 'restrictive if they limit NHS responsibility for rehabilitation to post-acute care and do not take account of responsibilities to contribute to longer-term rehabilitative care' and again cautioned against the use of restrictive time limits.

13.59   The reference to 'longer-term' rehabilitative care is of importance and is echoed by the 1995 guidance in relation to respite services (see para 13.63 below). Health bodies were required to provide rehabilitation services for persons with chronic conditions, as well as acute needs. In general this obligation is not fulfilled; while the NHS provides rehabilitation following an acute episode, such as a stroke, hip operation or accident, such services are not commonly available to people with chronic conditions such as Parkinson's disease. 'Active rehabilitation' for such patients can improve their ability to cope with daily living skills and so prolong their ability to live in the community and relieve some of the pressure on their carers.

National Service Framework for Long-term Conditions

13.60   The *National Service Framework (NSF) for Long-term Conditions*⁶² places considerable emphasis on the importance of appropriate rehabilitation support. Although the weight that should be accorded to the NSF is uncertain (see para 1.61), it is clearly a benchmark of service provision and best practice against which the performance of health bodies should be

58 Department of Health (2010) *Vision for adult social care: capable communities and active citizens.*
59 LAC (95)5: HSG (95)8, *NHS responsibilities for meeting continuing health care needs* (WOC 16/95 and WHC (95)7 in Wales). Similar guidance is in the 2009 framework in England and the 2011 framework in Wales which stress the need to consider rehabilitation throughout.
60 HSG (95)8, Annex A p14.
61 Para 6; and this emphasis was underscored by its inclusion in the NHS Priorities and Planning guidance of 1996/97 and 1997/98.
62 Department of Health, March 2005.

assessed by disabled people and their carers. Para 16 explains what is meant by a long-term condition, namely one that is primarily neurological in origin[63] and 'results from disease of, injury or damage to the body's nervous system (ie the brain, spinal cord and/or their peripheral nerve connections) which will affect the individual and their family in one way or another for the rest of their life'. Para 17 then explains:

> 17. Long-term neurological conditions can be broadly categorised as follows:
> - **Sudden onset conditions**, for example acquired brain injury or spinal cord injury, followed by a partial recovery. (Note: stroke for all ages is covered in the NSF for Older People);
> - **intermittent and unpredictable conditions**, for example epilepsy, certain types of headache or early multiple sclerosis, where relapses and remissions lead to marked variation in the care needed;
> - **progressive conditions**, for example motor neurone disease, Parkinson's disease or later stages of multiple sclerosis, where progressive deterioration in neurological function leads to increasing dependence on help and care from others. For some conditions (eg motor neurone disease) deterioration can be rapid. (Note: dementia for all ages is covered in the NSF for Older People);
> - **stable neurological conditions, but with changing needs due to development or ageing**, for example postpolio syndrome or cerebral palsy in adults.

13.61   At the heart of the NSF are the 11 quality requirements which must be fully implemented by 2015, three of which (standards 4, 5 and 6) specifically relate to rehabilitation support, namely:

4. Early and specialist rehabilitation;

5. Community rehabilitation and support;

6. Vocational rehabilitation.

Intermediate care

13.62   The intermediate care initiative is aimed at freeing up acute hospital beds and promoting the independence of older people. It is a time limited service, normally for no more than six weeks, and is considered further at chapter 11. Although the provision of intermediate care services will often satisfy a patient's needs for rehabilitation and recuperation, this will not always be the case. Given the time limited nature of the service, it will frequently be only a first stage of a programme. If at the end of a period a patient has not fully recovered, it may be that he or she can no longer receive rehabilitation support from the intermediate care team. This does not of course mean that NHS responsibility for rehabilitation has come to an end – merely that the specialised input of the intermediate care team is no longer appropriate. A similar situation arises in some areas where the

---

63   Para 4 states, however, that although this NSF focuses on people with neurological conditions, much of the guidance it offers can apply to anyone living with a long-term condition.

intermediate team is unable to provide a full service to all patients due to excessive demand. Again, in such cases, the duty remains with the NHS, notwithstanding that the intermediate care team is unable to field it.

Respite services

13.63   In *R (T, D and B) v Haringey LBC*[64] the High Court held that the provision of respite care was capable of being a core NHS responsibility, a fact that has been repeatedly emphasised by NHS guidance.

13.64   The most recent guidance – the 2009 *National Framework for NHS Continuing Healthcare*[65] includes respite healthcare within the 'range of services that the NHS is expected to arrange and fund' (apart from NHS-funded nursing care). However, the now superseded 1995 guidance[66] was more expansive and required the then health authorities to 'arrange and fund an adequate level of such care' and gave three examples of the type of patient who ought to be able to access NHS funded respite services, namely:

- people who have complex or intense healthcare needs and will require specialist medical or nursing supervision or assessment during a period of respite care;
- people who during a period of respite care require or could benefit from active rehabilitation; and
- people who are receiving a package of palliative care in their own homes but where they or their carer need a period of respite care.

13.65   The above reference to 'active rehabilitation' is directed towards the needs of people whose condition is chronic rather than acute. By providing such persons with regular periods of respite care where they also receive such services as intensive physiotherapy, speech and occupational therapy, the NHS can prolong their ability to live independently in the community and reduce the pressure on their carers.

13.66   Follow up guidance in 1996[67] advised that NHS eligibility criteria would in general be too restrictive if confined to the above three examples, suggesting that the criteria should cover other contingencies, such as 'where carers have been providing a level of healthcare which is not reasonably available in a residential setting'. It is likely that all such respite care provided by the NHS should be fully funded and so free at the point of use.

13.67   In 2001 the above guidance was, in England, consolidated[68] with the updated guidance advising (at para 25) that although local councils would

64 [2005] EWHC 2235 (Admin), (2006) 9 CCLR 58.
65 Department of Health (2009) *The National Framework for NHS Continuing Healthcare and NHS Funded Nursing Care*, para 104.
66 LAC (95)5: HSG (95)8 *NHS Responsibilities for Meeting Continuing Healthcare Needs* (WOC 16/95 and WHC (95)7 in Wales).
67 EL (96)8 para 16.
68 Department of Health (2001) *Continuing Care: NHS and Local Councils' responsibilities* guidance LAC (2001)18.

'usually have the lead responsibility for arranging and funding respite care' nevertheless 'the NHS also has important responsibilities for respite healthcare, including people who, during a period of respite care, require or could benefit from rehabilitation (which may include a package of intermediate care)'. The 2001 guidance has now been replaced by the 2009 Framework.

13.68   In Wales the absence of guidance concerning the nature and quality of NHS funded respite care services[69] has been highlighted by independent research[70] and in 2011 was the subject of a Welsh Government consultation document.[71]

13.69   The *NSF for Long-term Conditions*[72] addresses respite care in the context of it being a shared obligation of the NHS and social services and highlights the importance of 'appropriate respite care at home or in specialised settings', noting that 'respite care is a key factor in enabling care to be provided at home over a long period'.

Palliative healthcare

13.70   The World Health Organization definition of palliative healthcare[73] (which is accepted by the Department of Health[74]) is:

> The active holistic care of patients with advanced, progressive illness. Management of pain and other symptoms and provision of psychological, social and spiritual support is paramount. The goal of palliative care is achievement of the best quality of life for patients and their families.

13.71   Palliative care should be distinguished from the care of end of life care which is defined as:[75]

> Care that helps all those with advanced, progressive, incurable illness to live as well as possible until they die. It enables the supportive and palliative care needs of both patient and family to be identified and met throughout the last phase of life and into bereavement. It includes management of pain and other symptoms, and provision of psychological, social, spiritual and practical support.

13.72   The 1995 guidance[76] required health authorities to fund palliative health

---

69   Like the English 2009 Framework, the latest guidance in Wales the *National Framework for Continuing NHS Healthcare* 2010 merely lists respite care as part of a range of services – para 7.3.

70   LE Wales (2010) *Respite Care in Wales* para 11, at http://wales.gov.uk/docs/dhss/consultation/110315reporten.pdf at para 11.

71   Welsh Assembly Government (2011) WAG11–11254, *Consultation Document Review of Respite Care in Wales*.

72   Department of Health, March 2005, p47 para 6. See para 13.60 above.

73   World Health Organization (2002) *National Cancer Control Programmes: policies and guidelines*.

74   See National Institute for Clinical Excellence (2004) *Improving Supportive and Palliative Care for Adults with Cancer* p20.

75   Department of Health (2008) *End of Life Care Strategy – promoting high quality care for all adults at the end of life*, para 3.6.

76   LAC (95)5: HSG (95)8 *NHS Responsibilities for Meeting Continuing Healthcare Needs*, p15 (WOC 16/95 and WHC (95)7 in Wales) building on earlier English guidance – see eg EL (93)14 Annex C paras 10–14 and HSG (92)50.

care in a range of settings, including as an inpatient, in a care homes and patients own homes. Concern about the inadequate level of support led the Department of Health remind health authorities that eligibility criteria which applied time limits for palliative care would be inappropriate: that such care should be provided by the NHS purely on the basis of clinical need.[77]

13.73 This concern led in 2004 to a critical report from the House of Commons Select Committee[78] which characterised the system for providing palliative care for terminally ill patients as unfair, 'abhorrent' and leading to 'unseemly arguments about who should pay for different elements of a care package [which could result in] inexcusable delays and poor practice that is anything but patient-centred'.

13.74 One result of this disquiet was the publication in 2008 of the government's End of Life Care Strategy[79] which committed significant resources[80] and required PCTs (amongst other things) to improve coordination of their palliative care services; provide round the clock home care services; improve ambulance transport services for people near the end of life; provide additional specialist palliative care outreach services to provide advice and care for non-cancer patients; to increase input into care homes and community hospitals; and to improve education and training of existing staff in care homes, hospitals and the community.

13.75 In July 2011 an independent review commissioned by the secretary of state for health in England was published concerning the reform of the support and funding regime of patients with palliative needs.[81] The NHS has additional responsibilities for patients entering a terminal phase of their illness and these are considered at paras 14.60 and 14.157 below.

Wheelchairs

13.76 It is estimated that there are 1.2 million wheelchair users in England (almost 70% of whom are over 60[82]), of which over 800,000 are regular users of NHS wheelchair services – with still more needing to use the service for a time limited period only.[83] In Wales, there are almost 80,000 wheelchair users known to the NHS.[84]

---

77 EL (96)8, para 16.
78 House of Commons Health Committee Fourth Report of Session 2003–04, *Palliative Care, Volume 1*, HC 454-I, at www.publications.parliament.uk/pa/cm200304/cmselect/cmhealth/454/454.pdf.
79 Department of Health (2008) *End of Life Care Strategy – promoting high quality care for all adults at the end of life.*
80 Ibid, para 28.
81 Palliative Care Funding Review (2011) *Funding the Right Care and Support for Everyone Creating a Fair and Transparent Funding System.* The Final Report of the Palliative Care Funding Review. http://palliativecarefunding.org.uk/
82 Department of Health (2010) *Local innovations in wheelchair and seating services: Best Practice Guidance.*
83 Department of Health/CSIP (2006) *Out and about: Wheelchairs as part of a whole-systems approach to independence*, p5.
84 Welsh Assembly Government (2010) Health, Well-being and Local Government Committee: Ministerial Evidence session HWLG(3)-04–10-p4: 4 March 2010.

13.77   It appears that the service provided by the NHS has for many years been far from satisfactory not least due to 'inequitable variations in prescribing, management structures, staffing, criteria, funding, costs and levels of services' and the lack of any national minimum standards.[85] Over the last 25 years a steady stream of critical reports concerning the inadequacies of the NHS wheelchair services have emerged[86] and the evidence suggests that the service continues to leave much to be desired.[87] In 2010, for example the Minister accepted that it was 'quite common for people to wait months for a wheelchair, and not uncommon for them to wait years for a powered wheelchair' and that '57% of wheelchair budgets currently go on back-office costs'.[88]

13.78   Delay in the provision of a wheelchair may amount to maladministration particularly where it results in prolonged use of inadequate equipment or potential harm to carers.[89]

13.79   Wheelchairs are seen as a facility or service provided by the NHS under section 3 of the 2006 Acts[90] and are the subject of brief Department of Health guidance issued in 1996[91] (when electrically powered indoor/outdoor wheelchairs (EPIOCs) and vouchers (in England only) became available for severely disabled people through the NHS) and 2004 good practice guidance.[92] Individual can also obtain a powered wheelchair (or a scooter) through the Motability Scheme by surrendering their high rate mobility component of DLA.

13.80   Wheelchairs may be obtained from NHS trusts for temporary use on discharge from hospital,[93] and residential care homes are expected to pro-

85 See *National standards for wheelchair services: final consultation draft document*, 2003, at www.wheelchairmanagers.nhs.uk/servicestandards.doc.
86 See for example I McColl, *Review of artificial limb and appliance centre services*, DHSS, 1986; *National Prosthetic and Wheelchair Services Report 1993–1996* (the Holderness report), College of Occupational Therapists; Audit Commission, *Fully equipped: the provision of equipment to older or disabled people by the NHS and social services in England and Wales*, 2000; Audit Commission, *Fully equipped 2002: assisting independence*, 2002; Department of Health (2002) *Evaluation of the Powered Wheelchair and Voucher System 2000*; emPower, *NHS Wheelchair and Seating Services Mapping Project: final report*, Limbless Association, 2004; Prime Minister's Strategy Unit, *Improving the life chances of disabled people*, 2005; and N Sharma with J Morrison, *Don't push me around! Disabled children's experiences of wheelchair services in the UK*, 2006.
87 See eg Muscular Dystrophy Campaign (2010) *Get Moving – the case for effective Wheelchair Services*.
88 HC Hansard, 28 Jun 2010: Column 693: The Minister of State, Department of Health (Mr Paul Burstow).
89 See eg NHS Ombudsman (2011) *Listening and Learning: a Review of Complaint Handling by the NHS in England 2009/10* p28 at http://nhsreport.ombudsman.org.uk/ where the recommendation was for a compensation payment by the PCT of £5,000.
90 Department of Health/CSIP (2006) *Out and about: Wheelchairs as part of a whole-systems approach to independence*, p30.
91 Department of Health (1996) *Powered indoor/outdoor wheelchairs for severely disabled people* HSG (96)34 and Department of Health (1996) *The wheelchair voucher scheme* HSG(96)53.
92 Department of Health (2004) *Improving Services for Wheelchair Users and Carers: Good Practice Guide*.
93 It appears that in practice many trusts fail to provide wheelchairs in such situations, relying on separate PCT commissioning (eg, from the local Red Cross) or via a joint equipment store (see para 9.126).

vide wheelchairs for occasional use[94] – but for regular use they should access the same wheelchair services as disabled people living independently.[95] It appears that not infrequently the provision of wheelchairs for nursing home residents is unsatisfactory.[96] In such situations, where a resident is disadvantaged, the difference in treatment could be challenged as unjustified discrimination in relation to goods and services: when the difference stems from the location of the care, rather than individual need.[97]

13.81   The assessment of need for, and the provision of, wheelchairs (and wheelchair cushions etc) is in practice undertaken by local NHS wheelchair services in England, and in Wales by the Artificial Limb and Appliance Service.[98] The assessment is undertaken by a specialist, usually an occupational therapist, physiotherapist or consultant who will then identify the most suitable wheelchair. If the disabled person has difficulty using a manual wheelchair the trust can supply an electric model, including one for outdoor use if appropriate.[99] The NHS in England additionally operates a 'wheelchair voucher scheme' that gives users the option of purchasing from an independent supplier or from the wheelchair service. In either case the user can top up the voucher cost (which covers only the cost of a 'standard' wheelchair to meet the user's needs – ie not an EPIOC) to enable a more expensive model to be acquired. However, if the chair is purchased from an independent supplier it is owned by the user who is responsible for its maintenance and repair, whereas if the 'wheelchair services' option is chosen, the trust retains ownership but is also responsible for its maintenance.[100]

13.82   Since 1996 funding has been available for the provision of EPIOCs, although targeted on 'more severely disabled users (including children) who could benefit from them to enjoy enhanced levels of independent mobility inside and outside their home'.[101] The suggested

94   Department of Health (2003) *Discharge from hospital: pathway, process and practice*, para 5.3.1. Although this guidance has now been superseded by, Department of Health (2010) *Ready to Go* which does not mention wheelchairs.
95   Department of Health (2001) *Community Equipment Services*, HSC 2001/008: LAC (2001)13, which at para 7 makes clear that although community equipment services may provide wheelchairs for short term loan, the service is not for permanent wheelchair users, 'as these are prescribed and funded by different NHS services'.
96   The misunderstanding may have arisen due to a flawed interpretation of former Department of Health guidance (2003) (*Discharge from hospital: pathway, process and practice*, para 5.3.1 – see note 94 above) which stated that nursing homes should provide 'some standard items of equipment for anyone needing them and for the safety of staff'.
97   In this respect, see also Department of Health (2001) *Guidance on free nursing care in nursing homes* HSC 2001/17: LAC (2001)26, p8 para 9 which states that PCTs should ensure that care home residents should have access to the full range of specialist NHS support that is available in other care settings including 'aids to mobility'.
98   Which operates from three centres, namely Cardiff, Swansea and Wrexham.
99   HSG (96)34.
100 HSG (96)53.
101 As a general rule, once an individual receives an EPIOC, the manual wheelchair should also be retained as a back up.

(1996) criteria for such wheelchairs being that the severely disabled person is:[102]

- unable to propel a manual chair outdoors;
- able to benefit from the chair through increased mobility leading to improved quality of life;
- able to handle the chair safely.

Research has, however, suggested that these criteria exclude significant numbers of potential beneficiaries.[103]

13.83   A 2006 Department of Health report concerning wheelchair provision[104] advised that social services authorities could, in appropriate cases, consider using their powers under Carers (Equal Opportunities) Act 2004 s3 (see para 16.106) to 'request that the NHS provide a certain type of wheelchair (perhaps one more expensive than usual) in order not only to meet the needs of the disabled person, but also to make life easier for the carer'. The 2006 report also suggests that a wheelchair could be provided by social services under the community care legislation[105] (presumably under Chronically Sick and Disabled Persons Act 1970 s2).

Continence services

13.84   Continence services, despite their significant cost,[106] frequently appear to be of poor quality. A 2006 report[107] expressed concern over the reduced availability of specialist nurses, the continued inadequate assessment of incontinence and the over emphasis on the use of pads rather than less expensive preventative measures which gave greater dignity to users. A 2010 report commissioned by the Department of Health's Healthcare Quality Improvement Partnership[108] concluded that (page 6):

---

102 Department of Health (1996) *Powered indoor/outdoor wheelchairs for severely disabled people*, HSG (96)34.

103 Department of Health funded research undertaken by the York Health Economics Consortium (2000) *The Evaluation of the Powered Wheelchair and Voucher Scheme Initiatives.*

104 Department of Health/CSIP (2006) *Out and about: wheelchairs as part of a whole-systems approach to independence*, p30.

105 Department of Health/CSIP (2006) *Out and about: wheelchairs as part of a whole-systems approach to independence*, p15 Case Study E.

106 The annual cost of these services to the NHS in 2004 was estimated to be in the region of £743 million per year: D A Turner, C Shaw, C W McGrowther et al 'The cost of clinically significant urinary storage symptoms for community dwelling adults in the UK' (2004) 93(9) *BJU International* 1246–1252. A National Institute for Health and Clinical Excellence guide (2008) *Faecal continence service for the management of faecal incontinence in adults* made the important point, that it was not only the cost that was of concern – that the failure of the current service represents a 'missed opportunity to assess, treat and reduce the numbers of incontinent people' (pp4–5).

107 Royal College of Physicians (2006) *National Audit of Continence Care For Older People.*

108 Royal College of Physicians (2010) *National Audit of Continence Care Combined Organisational and Clinical Report.*

The great majority of continence services are poorly integrated across acute, medical, surgical, primary, care home and community settings, resulting in disjointed care for patients and carers.

The way continence services are presently commissioned means that:
- those providing the care are not included in the process of commissioning
- many services are not set up to provide joined-up care across healthcare boundaries
- most lack a designated lead whose responsibility it is to organise, develop and improve the delivery of continence care to patients
- users almost never contribute to service planning or evaluation

13.85 Since April 2004 continence supplies in England and Wales[109] should be provided free of charge by PCTs/LHBs in all settings.[110] The English 2001 guidance[111] stated that 'PCTs are responsible for arranging . . . the provision of nursing advice, eg continence advice and stoma care' and at para 29 that it is their responsibility to provide 'continence pads and equipment and nursing aids'. The revised 2009 *NHS Funded nursing care practice guidance*[112] now advises as follows:

> 50. Residents of care homes, including those providing nursing care, should have access to professional advice about the promotion of continence. See *Good Practice in Continence Services.*[113]

> 51. As well as prevention and advice services, the continence service should also include the provision of continence products, subject to a full assessment of an individual's needs. Continence products or payments should be made available by the NHS to care homes for residents who are also receiving NHS-funded nursing care, if required.

13.86 Detailed practice guidance has additionally been issued in England concerning the organisation and range of continence services that should be made available.[114]

13.87 The nature and quantity of continence supplies made available will depend upon an individual assessment of need in every case. The evidence suggests[115] that despite the need for continence pads to be available on the basis of clinical need, that the majority of PCTs operate a fixed

---

109 Welsh Government (2004) NHS Funded Nursing Care in care homes Guidance 2004: NAFWC 25/2004 / WHC (2004)024 para 59 of which states that (from April 2004) 'the NHS will fund the cost of necessary continence products for all care home residents assessed as requiring care by a registered nurse. This funding is included in NHS Funded Nursing Care NHS Funded Nursing Care . . . . Residents should not have to pay for continence supplies for which the NHS is responsible.

110 Prior to 2001 in England and 2004 in Wales people in nursing homes were not provided with incontinence supplies by the NHS.

111 LAC (2001)18, para 23.

112 Department of Health (2009) *NHS-funded nursing care practice guide* (revised) paras 50–51.

113 Department of Health (2000) *Good Practice in Continence Services* PL CNO (2000)2 and the accompanying 45-page guidance of the same title.

114 Ibid.

115 Royal College of Physicians (2006) *National Audit of Continence Care For Older People*, which found that almost 75% of PCTs had maximum number of pads policy.

policy which stipulates a maximum number that can be provided over a specified period. A 2010 report[116] found that contrary to the stated policy of most PCTs (that provision of continence products was based on clinical need) 66% of them imposed a limit on provision. Such policies are contrary to the guidance, fetter the authorities' discretion and, where individual hardship results, constitute maladministration.

Chiropody, speech therapy and physiotherapy

13.88   The NHS is responsible for the provision of such services as physiotherapy, speech and language therapy and chiropody[117] for all people in need of such services regardless of whether they are living independently or in a care home. To this list, 2001 guidance[118] in England added occupational therapy, dietetics and podiatry.[119]

13.89   Cutbacks to chiropody services have been widespread over recent years. In many areas toe nail cutting services have been withdrawn and increasingly chiropody services are only available to people with specific conditions such as diabetes.

13.90   As a result of many people in care homes having to pay for chiropody services, guidance has reminded local authorities that residents should not be expected to use their personal expenses allowance for items that have been assessed as necessary to meet their needs by the council or the NHS: the guidance further reminds authorities that the care plans of residents must fully reflect their incontinence and chiropody needs.[120]

Transport

13.91   The 2006 English White Paper[121] committed the government to extending eligibility for two NHS transport schemes, namely:

116   Royal College of Physicians (2010) *National Audit of Continence Care Combined Organisational and Clinical Report*, p33, table 40.

117   LAC (92)24, para 2 and see also Department of Health (1993) *NHS Responsibilities for Meeting Continuing Health Care Needs* LAC (95)5: HSG (95)8; WOC 16/95 and WHC (95)7 in Wales.

118   LAC (2001)18, paras 23 and 29. The Welsh 2004 guidance NAFWC 41/2004 similarly lists 'therapies, diatetics and podiatry' in annex B para 2. Although the English 2001 guidance is now superseded (see para 14.38) and the 2009 guidance does not mention these services, absent an announcement to the contrary it is inconceivable that the policy intention (or indeed legal obligation) that the NHS provide this range of services, does not remain.

119   See also Department of Health (2011) *GP consortia: What Allied Health Professionals (AHPs) can do for you* at http://healthandcare.dh.gov.uk/allied-health-professionals/ where such practitioners are referred to as 'Allied Health Professionals', which it states includes additionally dietitians, occupational therapists, orthoptists, orthotists, prosthetists, paramedics, diagnostic radiographers, therapeutic radiographers, art therapists, dramatherapists and music therapists.

120   The latest *Charging for Residential Care Guide* in England (see para 8.24 above) mentions the need for chiropody services to be fully reflected in the care plan at para 5.005 (para 5.002 Wales).

121   Department of Health (2006) *Our health, our care, our say: a new direction for community services*, White Paper: Cm 6737, 2006, paras 6.67–6.68.

- the patient transport service (PTS), which had traditionally provided only for transport to and from hospital. The commitment was to extend this to cover transport for health services which were delivered in a community setting; and
- the healthcare travel costs scheme (HTCS) for patients on low incomes.

Patient transport service (PTS)

13.92 Guidance on the revised PTS scheme was issued in 2007,[122] including updated performance standards for emergency and urgent ambulances. In relation to non-emergency transport services, the decision as to a patient's eligibility is determined (para 10) 'either by a healthcare professional or by non-clinically qualified staff who are both clinically supervised and/or working within locally agreed protocols or guidelines, and employed by the NHS or working under contract for the NHS'. Eligible patients are those (para 8):

- Where the medical condition of the patient is such that they require the skills or support of PTS staff on/after the journey and/or where it would be detrimental to the patient's condition or recovery if they were to travel by other means.
- Where the patient's medical condition impacts on their mobility to such an extent that they would be unable to access healthcare and/ or it would be detrimental to the patient's condition or recovery to travel by other means.
- Recognised as a parent or guardian where children are being conveyed.

13.93 The scheme also provides for the transport of a patient's escort or carer where (para 9):

their particular skills and/or support are needed e.g. this might be appropriate for those accompanying a person with a physical or mental incapacity, vulnerable adults or to act as a translator.

Healthcare Travel Costs Scheme (HTCS)

13.94 Guidance on the revised HTCS scheme was issued in 2010.[123] The scheme is underpinned by regulations[124] and applies to all PCTs, NHS trusts and NHS Foundation Trusts. It provides for patients on low incomes or receiving specific qualifying benefits to be reimbursed in full or in part for the costs incurred in some journey that are made in order to receive certain NHS services. The eligible 'NHS travel expenses' are defined in the

---

122 Department of Health (2007) *Eligibility Criteria for Patient Transport Services: Best Practice Guidance*.

123 Department of Health (2010) *Healthcare Travel Costs Scheme: Instructions and guidance for the NHS*.

124 The National Health Service (Travel Expenses and Remission of Charges) Regulations 2003 SI No 2382 as extensively amended – most recently (at September 2011) by the National Health Service (Travel Expenses and Remission of Charges) Amendment Regulations 2010 SI No 620.

regulations,[125] which the guidance explains are travel expenses that a person necessarily incurs:

1) in attending any place in the UK for the provision of any services under the National Health Service Act 2006 ('the 2006 Act') (except primary medical or primary dental services) which are provided pursuant to a referral by a doctor or dentist (and which are not provided at the same visit and on the same premises as the primary medical services which lead to a referral for such services), or

2) in travelling to a port in Great Britain for the purpose of travelling abroad in order to receive services provided pursuant to arrangements made under section 12 of, or paragraph 18 of Schedule 4 to, the 2006 Act (i.e. arrangements for the provision of services made by a PCT or NHS trust).

13.95   The guidance explains (p.11) the effect of the eligibility criteria which are to be applied, namely that:

1) The patient must be:
   a) in receipt of one of the qualifying benefits or allowances specified in the 2003 Regulations (or in certain cases be a member of the same family as a person receiving a qualifying benefit or allowance), or
   b) be named on a NHS Low Income Scheme certificate HC2 or HC3 (or in certain cases be a member of the same family as a person named on a NHS Low Income Scheme certificate).
2) The journey undertaken must be made to receive services under the National Health Service Act 2006, which are not primary medical or primary dental care services, for which the patient has been referred by a doctor or dentist ;
3) Where a doctor or dentist has provided the primary medical or primary dental services which lead to the referral for non-primary care services, those services must be provided on a different visit or involve an additional journey to the premises where the primary medical or primary dental services which lead to that referral were provided.

13.96   The permitted travel costs are calculated on the basis of the cheapest form of transport appropriate to the patient and should be 'reasonable', taking into account that patient's personal circumstances. The guidance goes into considerable detail as to the factors that should be taken into account in determining what is reasonable and the application of the means testing criteria.

13.97   Similar arrangements exist in Wales, concerning the provision of non-emergency transport[126] (on which the outcome of a 2010 review is pending[127]) and for assistance with travel costs.[128]

---

125 Reg 3 of the amended 2003 Regulations.
126 See Welsh Assembly Government (2007) *Non-Emergency Patient Transport Eligibility Criteria* WHC (2007) 005.
127 Welsh Assembly Government (2010) *The Griffiths' Review – Non-Emergency Patient Transport in Wales.*
128 Welsh Assembly Government (2010) *Help with health costs Are you entitled to help with health costs?* HC11W.

NHS specialist or intensive services for people in care homes

13.98　It is a basic tenet of the NHS that all medical and nursing services are provided free at the point of need. Whilst this principle is curtailed in so far as it applies to the needs of residents in nursing homes not funded by the NHS, the limitation only applies to the non-registered nursing[129] needs of such residents.

13.99　The respective responsibilities of the NHS and social services authorities in this area have been the subject of successive guidance. LAC (92)24 advised, at para 2:

> 2. Local authority contracts for independent sector residential care should not include provision of any service which it is the responsibility of the NHS to provide. It will continue to be the responsibility of the NHS to provide where necessary community health services to residents of LA and independent residential care homes on the same basis as to people in their own homes. These services include the provision of district nursing and other specialist nursing services (eg, incontinence advice) as well as the provision, where necessary, of incontinence and nursing aids, physiotherapy, speech and language therapy and chiropody. Where such services are provided they must be free of charge to people in independent sector homes as well as to residents of local authority Part III homes.

13.100　1995 guidance[130] clarified this distinction in the following terms:

> Some people who will be appropriately placed by social services in nursing homes, as their permanent home, may still require some regular access to specialist medical, nursing or other community health services. This will also apply to people who have arranged and are funding their own care. This may include occasional continuing specialist medical advice or treatment, specialist palliative care, specialist nursing care such as incontinence advice, stoma care or diabetic advice or community health services such as physiotherapy, speech therapy and language therapy and chiropody. It should also include specialist medical or nursing equipment (for instance specialist feeding equipment) not available on prescription and normally only available through hospitals . . .

> Assessment procedures and arrangements for purchasing care should take account of such needs and details should be identified in individual care plans. In such cases the NHS can either provide such services directly or contract with the home to provide the additional services required. Such additional services should be free at the point of delivery.

13.101　LAC (92)24 defined what was meant by 'specialist nursing' as 'primarily continence advice and stoma care, but also other specialist nursing such as diabetic liaison and other community health services (primarily physiotherapy, speech and language therapy and chiropody'.

129　The NHS is responsible for all nursing care provided by a registered nurse, or nursing care planned, supervised and/or delegated by a registered nurse (even if actually undertaken by a non-registered nurse) – see para 13.109 below.

130　Department of Health (1995) *NHS Responsibilities for Meeting Continuing Health Care Needs* LAC (95)5: HSG (95)8: WOC 16/95 and WHC (95)7 in Wales.

13.102   In relation to English NHS services for care home residents, the range of general health services described in 2009 *National Framework for NHS Continuing Healthcare*[131] (see para 13.43 above) should also be made available.

Specialist medical equipment in care homes

13.103 The joint responsibilities of social services and the NHS for the community equipment services is considered at para 9.126 above. However, the issue of 'specialist medical and nursing' equipment can cause problems. In general, however, a care home providing nursing only has to provide the general equipment which is a prerequisite for its registration. Thus if a patient is in need of equipment which is not part of the basic registration requirement, it may be argued that this is therefore 'specialist' in the sense that it ought to be funded by the NHS.[132] The Health Service Ombudsman has, for instance, investigated a complaint[133] concerning an elderly nursing home resident who had to be fed by means of a gastric tube. Although the liquid feed was supplied on prescription she was required to pay for the tubes through which the feed was delivered (at £25 per week). The health authority accepted that this was incorrect and refunded the cost of the tubes.

13.104   The above formulation is, however, slightly circular, since the English care standards regulations[134] oblige regulated providers to 'ensure that equipment[135] is available in sufficient quantities in order to ensure the safety of service users and meet their assessed needs'. Clearly a care home should not take a patient until such time as it has the necessary equipment – and this begs the question of whether it or the NHS body is responsible for its provision.

---

131 Department of Health (2009) *The National Framework for NHS Continuing Healthcare and NHS-funded Nursing Care*: July 2009 (revised), para 104. There is no equivalent list in the 2010 Welsh Framework (see para 14.40 below) although at para 7.3 it advises that 'a range of services may be required to support individuals (whether or not they are eligible for CHC) including, reablement, rehabilitation, palliative care, respite care etc.'

132 Para 5.3.1 of the 2003 Discharge from hospital: pathway, process and practice guidance which has now been superseded (see para 5.8) states that 'care homes providing nursing care are expected to have, as part of the facilities they provide, some standard items of equipment for anyone needing them and for the safety of staff. These should include hoists, wheelchairs for occasional use, bath and shower seats and fixed items such as grab rails. All other items of equipment to meet the needs of an individual should be, or should have been, provided to them on the same basis as if they were living in a private house, applying the same eligibility criteria'.

133 Case no E.985/94, p61 Selected Investigations April–September 1996.

134 The Health and Social Care Act 2008 (Regulated Activities) Regulations 2010 SI No 781, reg 16.

135 Regulation 16(4) states that 'equipment' includes a medical device; and that a 'medical device' has the same meaning as in the Medical Devices Regulations 2002 SI No 618.

13.105   The revised 2009 *NHS Funded nursing care practice guidance*[136] advises (at para 49) that where a care home resident requires equipment to meet their care needs, 'there are several routes by which this may be provided':

a) The care home may be required to provide certain equipment as part of regulatory standards or as part of its contract with the PCT. Further details of the regulatory standards can be found on the Care Quality Commission's website at www.cqc.org.uk.

b) Individuals who are entitled to NHS-funded nursing care have an entitlement – on the same basis as other patients – to joint equipment services. PCTs and LAs should ensure that the availability to those in receipt of NHS-funded nursing care is taken into account in the planning, commissioning and funding arrangements for these services.

c) Some individuals will require bespoke equipment (or other non-bespoke equipment that is not available through routes (a) and (b) above) to meet specific assessed needs identified in their care plan. PCTs and (where relevant) LAs should make appropriate arrangements to meet these needs.

13.106 Guidance has been issued concerning the provision of such equipment through joint community equipment stores[137] (see para 9.126). Department of Health circular HSC 2001/17: LAC (2001)26[138] additionally made the following comments concerning specialist equipment:

8. For the majority of care home residents, much of the equipment necessary for their care will be available in the care home. Equipment is also available on prescription from a GP or a prescribing nurse. Details are contained in the Drug Tariff. This covers a range of appliances, including stoma and incontinence appliances, as well as the domiciliary oxygen therapy service.

9. Care home residents should have access to the full range of specialist NHS support that is available in other care settings and to people receiving care at home. In addition to equipment that is provided or secured by the care home in accordance with the minimum standards, the NHS should also consider whether there is a need to provide residents with access to dietary advice, as well as to the full range of available community equipment services, including pressure redistributing equipment, aids to mobility, and communication aids, etc that are available in other settings. Specialist equipment needs for individual use should be specified in the assessment and subsequent care plan, together with the arrangements for getting the equipment in place, and any aftercare that may be necessary. Residents should have access to other NHS services, such as the wheelchair service, and staff working for the NHS should be responsible for assessing them.

136 Department of Health (2009) *NHS-funded Nursing Care Practice Guide* (revised) 2009 Best Practice Guidance paras 50–51.
137 Department of Health (2001) *Community equipment services* HSC 2001/008: LAC (2001)13.
138 Department of Health (2001) *Guidance on free nursing care in nursing homes.* Although this guidance has been discontinued as a result of the new free nursing care guidance (see para 13.111 below), its advice in this respect would appear to remain valid, not least because it is cited frequently in the (extant) guidance *Community Equipment in Care Homes* (cited below).

13.107   LAC 2003 (7): HSC 2003/006[139] states at para 30:

> Where the NHS has determined that the individual requires a particular piece of equipment, it should ensure either that the care home provides it; or provide it on a temporary basis until the care home is able to provide it; or provide it to the individual as long as they need it. It would be unreasonable to expect care homes to provide items of equipment, that by the nature of the design size and weight requirements, need to be specially tailored to meet the individual's needs and would not be capable of being used by other care home residents.

13.108   One approach to the difficulty in distinguishing between standard items, that should be provided by the care home, and items to be funded by the PCT/LHB was suggested in 2004 non-statutory guidance:[140]

> If a significant number of people use a particular item of equipment in a particular care home it is more likely to be for the care home to provide. If it is for a single user as part of a specific agreed care plan, then it is more likely for health or social services to be the provider even though some of these items may not always be called 'specialist'.

NHS payments for registered nursing care in nursing homes

13.109   In 1999 the Royal Commission on long term care published its report *With Respect to Old Age*[141] recommending that personal care and nursing services should be provided free of charge to all persons assessed as being in need of these services (regardless of whether they were living in the community, a care home or a hospital). The government in England felt unable to accept the full recommendations and opted instead only to extend (free at the point of need) funding to cover the registered nursing care costs of residents in nursing homes.[142]

13.110   The policy proposal was brought into effect in England and Wales via Health and Social Care Act (HSCA) 2001 s49 which makes it unlawful for a local authority to provide nursing 'by a registered nurse'. Section 49 provides:

---

139   Department of Health (2000) *Good practice in continence services*, April 2000.
140   Department of Health (2004) *Community equipment and care homes: integrating community equipment services*. It states that it does not create new guidance, nor resolve contradictions that may occur from the application or interpretation of existing or future government guidance, nor does it necessarily represent the views of the Department of Health.
141   Royal Commission on Long-Term Care, (1999) *With Respect to Old Age: Long-Term Care – Rights and Responsibilities*, Cm 4192.
142   Announced in Department of Health, *The NHS Plan*, July 2000, para 15.181 and enacted as HSCA 2001 s49.

49(1) Nothing in the enactments relating to the provision of community care services[143] shall authorise or require a local authority, in or in connection with the provision of any such services, to –

(a) provide for any person, or

(b) arrange for any person to be provided with, nursing care by a registered nurse.

(2) In this section 'nursing care by a registered nurse' means any services provided by a registered nurse and involving –

(a) the provision of care, or

(b) the planning, supervision or delegation of the provision of care, other than any services which, having regard to their nature and the circumstances in which they are provided, do not need to be provided by a registered nurse.

13.111 In England the operation of the scheme created by section 49 is regulated by directions issued in 2007 and 2009[144] and by statutory[145] and practice guidance.[146] In Wales a similar scheme applies, with directions[147] and guidance[148] issued in 2004.

13.112 In both England and Wales all nursing home residents (regardless of whether self funding or supported by social services) are provided with an assessment by their PCT/LHB, which determines their eligibility to a payment in relation to their nursing care needs (known as the NHS funded nursing care, in England and the registered nurse contribution (RNCC) in Wales.[149] In England, direction 2(5) of the 2007 Directions (as amended) provides that where the PCT determines that the person has a need for nursing care and wishes to receive this care then the PCT is required to pay to the care home a 'flat rate' payment in respect of that person's nursing care'.[150]

13.113 In England as at July 2011 the 'flat rate' RNCC amounted to £108.70 per week and in Wales it amounted to £119.66 per week. Some patients

---

143 In *R (T, D and B) v Haringey LBC* [2005] EWHC 2235 (Admin), (2006) 9 CCLR 58 the section 49 prohibition was found only to apply to adults. This arises out of the wording of section 49 which prohibits registered nursing care being provided pursuant to local authorities' community care functions under NHSCCA 1990 s46 which do not include CA 1989.

144 The NHS (Nursing Care in Residential Accommodation) (England) Directions 2007 as amended by The National Health Service (Nursing Care in Residential Accommodation) (Amendment) (England) Directions 2009.

145 The guidance is to be found in annex D of Department of Health (2009) *The National Framework for NHS Continuing Healthcare and NHS-funded Nursing Care* (revised).

146 Department of Health (2009) *NHS-funded Nursing Care Practice Guide* (revised).

147 National Health Service (Nursing Care in Residential Accommodation) (Wales) Directions 2004.

148 NHS Funded Nursing Care in care homes Guidance 2004: NAFWC 25/2004 / WHC (2004)024.

149 In England pursuant to direction 2 of the amended 2007 Directions: such an assessment can only be undertaken when the PCT has determined that the resident is not eligible for NHS Continuing healthcare funding (direction 2(2) of the 2007 Directions and Annex D to the 2009 guidance: in Wales see para 46 of the 2004 guidance.

150 In Wales direction 2 of the 2004 Directions speak not of the LHB making of a payment but of providing the resident with 'such nursing care as appears' to the LHB to be 'appropriate' – although in practice this is done by the making of a flat rate payment.

in England (who were resident in a nursing home prior to October 2007) may be receiving a higher payment – by virtue of having a preserved entitlement to 'high band' funding (considered below) and this, at September 2011 amounted to £149.60 per week. Patients in all care settings also have the right to a full range of primary, community, secondary and other health services,[151] including continence care supplies (see para 13.84 above) and provision of such products or payments must be in addition to the payment for NHS-funded nursing care.[152]

13.114   Prior to October 2007 in England three bands existed,[153] namely 'high', 'medium' and 'low' and a different contribution was made by the PCT in relation to each (as at April 2007, these amounted to £139, £87 or £40 per week, although flexibility existed to pay a higher rate than the £139). Unfortunately the guidance[154] detailing the criteria for an award of the high band was found to be more demanding in terms of a resident's healthcare needs, than the Court of Appeal had been in determining eligibility for NHS continuing healthcare funding in *R v North and East Devon Health Authority ex p Coughlan*.[155] This error was confirmed by Charles J in *R (Grogan) v Bexley NHS Care Trust and others*.[156] In response to this judgment the government decided to abolish the banding system (which had not operated in Wales) and opt for a single flat rate payment. However, residents at the date of this change (October 2007) who were on the higher rate, were given transitional protection[157] (direction 4 of the 2007 directions). Their entitlement to the higher rate continues until:[158]

a) on review, it is determined that they no longer have any need for nursing care;
b) on review, it is determined that their needs have changed, so that under the previous three-band system, they would have moved onto the medium or low bands. In this situation, the individual should be moved onto the single rate;
c) they are no longer resident in a care home that provides nursing care;
d) they become eligible for NHS continuing healthcare; or
e) they die.

---

151 See Department of Health (2009) *NHS-funded Nursing Care Practice Guide (revised)*, paras 41–51.
152 See Department of Health (2009) *NHS-funded Nursing Care Practice Guide (revised)*, para 51.
153 Detailed in Department of Health (2001) *NHS Funded Nursing Care Practice Guide and Workbook*.
154 Detailed in Department of Health (2001) *NHS Funded Nursing Care Practice Guide and Workbook*.
155 *R v North and East Devon Health Authority ex p Coughlan* [2000] 2 WLR 622, (1999) 2 CCLR 285.
156 [2006] EWHC 44 (Admin), (2006) 9 CCLR 188, para 61.
157 It follows therefore that such people who are still transitionally protected at the higher rate may well qualify for NHS Continuing Healthcare.
158 Direction 4 of the 2007 Direction, and see also para 12 of Department of Health (2009) *NHS-funded Nursing Care Practice Guide (revised) 2009*.

Section 49 and its interface with continuing care

13.115 It could argued that with the advent of section 49, continuing healthcare responsibilities came to an end, since the section provided a clear demarcation between the respective responsibilities of the NHS and social services. This is not the case. The obligation under section 49 is entirely separate. As the explanatory note accompanying the section made clear – its purpose was to remove:

> local authorities' functions to purchase nursing care by a registered nurse under community care legislation. This is intended to strengthen the incentives for the NHS to ensure effective rehabilitation after acute illness or injury. It is estimated that around 35,000 people who are currently paying for their nursing care will receive free nursing care through the NHS.

13.116 Earlier (now superseded) 2001 English guidance[159] was explicit about the distinction between section 49 payments and continuing care:

> *Relationship with Continuing Care*
>
> Nothing in this guidance changes the duties of HA's to arrange and fully fund services for people whose primary needs are for healthcare rather than for accommodation and personal care.

13.117 The English 2009 continuing healthcare guidance makes this important point in the following terms:[160]

> In all cases, individuals should be considered for eligibility for NHS continuing healthcare before a decision is reached about the need for NHS-funded nursing care (NHS-funded nursing care provided by registered nurses) in residential accommodation.

Payments during absences

13.118 The 2009 practice guidance[161] adopts a pragmatic approach to payments whilst a resident is temporarily in hospital. It suggests that in order to secure a place in the home 'PCTs will want to consider' paying a retainer equivalent to the value of the payment for NHS-funded nursing care. It points out that custom and practice has been for local authorities to agree to pay the full fee for a set period of time (usually six weeks).[162]

---

159 Department of Health (2001) HSC (2001)17: LAC (2001)26 *Guidance on Free Nursing Care in Nursing Homes* appendix 6.

160 Department of Health (2009) *The National Framework for NHS Continuing Healthcare and NHS-funded Nursing Care* (revised) annex D para 1 and reiterated throughout the Department of Health (2009) *NHS-funded Nursing Care Practice Guide (revised) Best Practice Guidance.* In similar terms, the Welsh 2004 guidance states (para 32): 'NHS Funded Nursing Care is different from, and not a substitute for, continuing NHS healthcare. . . . In carrying out an assessment, the first consideration should always be the extent to which the identified needs may meet the criteria for continuing NHS healthcare'.

161 Department of Health (2009) *NHS-funded Nursing Care Practice Guide (revised)* paras 69–71.

162 There is similar but not identical guidance in Wales: 2004 guidance para 38. The implication is that a retainer can be paid for up to six weeks during a period of hospital admission.

Responsible commissioner

13.119 The responsibility for the funding of HSCA 2001 s49 payments to nursing home residents is based on the usual rules of each country for establishing the responsible commissioner (ie in England it is generally based on the PCT of the GP with whom the person is registered, and in Wales it is based on the LHB where the home is situated.) This question (including the cross border protocols have been developed to deal with the differing amounts paid by England and Wales) is considered further at para 6.91 above.

Reviews of the payment of NHS-funded nursing care

13.120 The guidance states that reviews should take place within three months of admission to a care home and annually thereafter (or more often should the resident's circumstances warrant it).[163]

13.121   If a person is dissatisfied with the outcome of a decision relating to their eligibility for NHS-funded nursing care, then the procedure for challenge is the same as under the NHS continuing healthcare provisions, and is considered at para 14.166 below.[164]

Budget sharing arrangements

13.122 The gap between the political rhetoric urging joint working and the organisational imperatives of the health bodies and councils, has been noted above (see para 13.33 above). Lymbery, citing Means and Smith's[165] view that the 'Berlin Wall' that exists between the two services is in large measure a creation of successive governments, argues that 'to imply that organizations or professions are responsible for this is disingenuous at best or duplicitous at worst'.[166]

13.123   Since the creation of the health service, attempts have been made to span this organisational divide by amending the successive NHS Acts to provide legal mechanisms that can be used, if and when there is a common desire to collaborate. These provisions inevitably come with complex governance requirements,[167] which derive from the macro distinction (in

163 Department of Health (2009) *NHS-funded Nursing Care Practice Guide (revised) 2009* paras 52–55; Welsh 2004 guidance appendix 3 para 3.19. The 2007 guidance, by integrating the determination of nursing payments into the general framework for NHS continuing healthcare, also places the same timescales for reviews, namely three months following the initial decision and then at least one a year.

164 Department of Health (2009) *NHS-funded Nursing Care Practice Guide (revised)* paras 56–60.

165 R Means and R Smith *From Poor Law to Community Care,* 2nd edn, Policy Press (1998) and R Means, H Morbey and R Smith, *From Community Care to Market Care?* Policy Press, 2002.

166 M Lymbery 'United we Stand? Partnership Working in Health and Social Care and the Role of Social Work in Services for Older People' *British Journal of Social Work* (2006) 36 1120.

167 See eg Audit Commission (2008) *Clarifying joint financing arrangements: a briefing paper for health bodies and local authorities*; and Audit Commission (2009) *Working better together? Managing local strategic partnerships.*

budgetary terms) between the two organisations: the 'free at the point of need' NHS and the 'means tested' social care service. Accountability is an additional material distinction: unlike local health bodies, local authorities rely on local taxes (council tax) for which their elected politicians are answerable. A cost shunt of £1 million from the local NHS to social services (a not uncommon occurrence in relation to NHS continuing healthcare decisions – see para 14.7 below) is equivalent to 1% of council tax in an average council area.

13.124   Historically the ability of the NHS and social services authorities to pool budgets, or transfer resources from one to another was severely curtailed. In consequence it was argued that innovation had been stifled and 'cost shunting' between authorities encouraged.[168] This situation was relaxed as a consequence of HA 1999 ss29–31, which enabled health bodies and social services to enter into a wide range of 'partnership arrangements'. These provisions are now to be found in NHSA 2006 ss75–76 and 256–257.[169]

13.125   NHSA 2006 ss256–257[170] enable SHAs and PCTs to make payments to local authorities in respect of any local authority function that is 'health-related', and section 76[171] provides a reciprocal power for local authorities to make payments to SHAs or PCTs in relation to 'prescribed functions'. Regulations[172] made under this section have defined 'prescribed functions' widely,[173] excluding only such matters as 'surgery, radiotherapy, termination of pregnancies, endoscopy, [certain] laser treatments and other invasive treatments'.[174]

13.126   In relation to people with learning disabilities in English long stay NHS accommodation, a major structural transfer of this kind has occurred as a result of a 2007 Department of Health initiative – the *Valuing People Now: From Progress to Transformation* – and this is considered further at para 18.23 below.

Section 75 partnerships arrangements

13.127 NHSA 2006 s75[175] allows NHS bodies and local authorities to pool their resources, delegate functions and transfer resources from one party to

168 Department of Health (1998) *Partnership in Action*, discussion paper, September 1998.
169 NHS(W)A 2006 ss33–34 and ss194–196.
170 NHS(W)A 2006 ss194–196 provides LHBs with the same powers.
171 NHS(W)A 2006 s34 provides local authorities with the same powers to make payments to LHBs.
172 NHS (Payments by Local Authorities to NHS Bodies) (Prescribed Functions) Regulations 2000 SI No 618 and NHS (Payments by Local Authorities to Health Authorities) (Prescribed Functions) (Wales) Regulations 2001 SI No 1543 (W108). Both regulations have been amended and both continue to be valid by virtue of NHS (Consequential Provisions) Act 2006 s4 and Sch 2 para 1(2).
173 Including services under the NHS Acts 2006 ss2 and 3(1) as well as functions under MHA 1983 ss25A–25H and 117.
174 NHS (Payments by Local Authorities to NHS Bodies) (Prescribed Functions) Regulations 2000 SI No 618 reg 2 and NHS (Payments by Local Authorities to Health Authorities) (Prescribed Functions) (Wales) Regulations 2001 SI No 1543 (W108) reg 2.
175 NHS(W)A 2006 s33.

another and enable a single provider to provide both health and local authority services. Such arrangements derive from provisions in the Health Act 2009, s31 and were therefore formerly referred to as 'section 31 agreements'. Section 75, in effect permits:

- **Pooled fund arrangements:** where authorities pool resources so that they will effectively 'lose their health and local authority identity', allowing staff from either agency to develop packages of care suited to particular individuals irrespective of whether health or local authority money is used.
- **Delegation of functions – lead commissioning:** where PCTs and local authorities delegate functions to one another (including the secondment or transfer of staff). In the case of health and social care this enables one of the partner bodies to commission all mental health or learning disability services locally.
- **Delegation of functions – integrated provision:** this consists of the provision of health and local authority services from a single managed provider. The arrangement can be used in conjunction with lead commissioning and pooled fund arrangements.

13.128   As with the budget sharing regulations above, most NHS functions can be the subject of partnership arrangements (with the same exceptions – see para 13.125 above).[176] Likewise a wide range of social services functions can be the subject of partnership arrangements – including in England (but not Wales) charging for care home accommodation under the National Assistance Act 1948 and for non-accommodation community care services.[177] NHSA 2006 s75(5)[178] provides that any partnership arrangements made under section 75 will not affect the liability of the NHS body or the local authority for the exercise of its functions. Liability remains, therefore, with the body primarily responsible for the discharge of the function (ie the body with this responsibility prior to the partnership arrangement). Guidance on these arrangements was issued in England in 2000.[179]

13.129   The most common pooled budget arrangements involve local authorities taking the lead role as commissioners of learning disability services

---

176 NHS Bodies and Local Authorities Partnership Arrangements Regulations 2000 SI No 617 and National Health Service Bodies and Local Authorities Partnership Arrangements (Wales) Regulations 2000 SI No 2993 (W193), which Regulations continue to be valid by virtue of NHS (Consequential Provisions) Act 2006 s4 and Sch 2 para 1(2).

177 NHS Bodies and Local Authorities Partnership Arrangements (Amendment) (England) Regulations 2003 SI No 629, which regulations continue to be valid by virtue of the NHS (Consequential Provisions) Act 2006 s4 and Sch 2 para 1(2).

178 NHS(W)A 2006 s33(5).

179 Department of Health (2000) *Implementation Of Health Act Partnership Arrangements* HSC 2000/010 / LAC (2000)9 accompanied by guidance on 'The Health Act section 31 Partnership Arrangements'. As at September 2011 the website note to this guidance (bearing the date August 2008) states that it is 'being reviewed for amendment in the light of changes in legislation in the NHS Act 2006. It is expected that, apart from a few areas such as VAT advice, amendments will largely be about changing titles and references.'

and health bodies taking the lead role as commissioners of mental health services.

Dowry payments and post dowry arrangements

13.130   Prior to the HA 1999 amendments, budget transfers were only permitted one way – from NHS bodies to local authorities, housing associations and certain other bodies in respect of personal social services, education for disabled people and housing. Detailed guidance[180] and directions[181] were issued in relation to these payments. These provisions permitted various schemes, including an arrangement known as 'dowry' payments.

13.131   Dowry payments were used to facilitate the transfer of patients from long-stay hospitals into the community. They involved a lump-sum payment or annual payment to a local authority taking over the patient's care; the amount of the lump-sum or annual payment and the length of time for which annual payments were to be made being negotiated by the respective authorities. In this context HSG (95)45 advised:[182]

> . . . in respect of people being discharged from long stay institutions, the NHS is responsible for negotiating arrangements with local authorities, including any appropriate transfer of resources which assist the local authority meeting the community care needs of such people and of their successors who may otherwise have entered the institution.

13.132   The relevance of such arrangements (or more precisely the lack of these) was spelt out in 1992 guidance[183] which stated that:

> Where residential care arrangements in the community for a person who was formerly a patient in a long-stay hospital appear to be breaking down . . . then the LA . . . should take the lead in seeing that the appropriate arrangements are secured . . . Where no agreement has been made between the DHA responsible for the hospital care before discharge and the LA about respective responsibilities, the HA should assist the LA . . . and if the resecuring or reprovisioning of care leads the LA to incur additional expenditure, the HA will be expected to use its powers under s28A to assist the LA to fund the care.

---

180   LAC (92)17, HSG (92)43 and HSG (95)45.
181   Directions under NHSA 1977 s28A being contained as annex C to HSG (92)43.
182   Department of Health (1995) *Arrangements between health authorities and NHS Trusts and private and voluntary sector organisations for the provision of community care Services* HSG (95)45 annex, para 4.1. The circular was cancelled by the much criticised (see para 14.25 below) Department of Health (2001) *Continuing Care: NHS and Local Councils' responsibilities* HSC 2001/015: LAC (2001)18 Annex A which was, however, silent on this question. The 2001 circular has now been superseded by Department of Health (2009) *The National Framework for NHS Continuing Healthcare and NHS Funded Nursing Care* which (as noted at para 14.55 below) places considerable emphasis on the importance of neither the PCT or local authority unilaterally withdrawing from a funding arrangement.
183   LAC (92)17: HSG (92)43, annex A para 10. This circular was 'superseded' by Department of Health (2000) *Commencement of sections 29 and 30 of the Health Act, 1999* HSC 2000/011: LAC 2000/10 which although silent on this specific issue, is framed in terms of local authority / health body agreements on funding and funding transfers.

13.133 Despite the emphasis on a joint agreement between health and social care bodies for any funding transfer (collective or individual) this is not always found in practice.[184] In the past decades, health bodies have often transferred responsibility for individuals or groups of individuals to third parties: for example to independent supported living schemes or by the misuse of arrangements under Health Services and Public Health Services Act 1968 s64 (see below). The health bodies have gained financially from such transactions, by essentially transferring the cost of supporting the individual to another public budget (eg the housing benefit and/or supporting peoples' budgets). With the demise or curtailment of these funding streams the care arrangements for some of these individuals are breaking down: individuals for whom no funding agreement has been secured from social services. In such cases there remains considerable weight to the above advice (not least from a public accounting perspective) – namely that 'if the resecuring or reprovisioning of care leads the LA to incur additional expenditure' the health body would be expected to use its powers under what is now NHSA 2006 ss256–257.[185]

13.134   It would appear that there has been a consistent government view on this question. The first NHS continuing healthcare guidance in 1995[186] advised that where 'either health or local authorities are proposing a significant change in the pattern of services which will impact on the resources of the other agencies for providing care, they must seek the agreement of the other agency.' The current English[187] 2009 guidance states that 'neither the PCT nor the LA should unilaterally withdraw from funding of an existing package without appropriate reassessment and agreement by the other body that it accepts funding responsibility'.[188]

Section 64 agreements[189]

13.135 Although NHSA 2006 ss256–257[190] are the appropriate statutory provisions by which a health body transfers to a social services authority its responsibility for patients who are capable of being supported through the

184 In some cases, it appears that although agreements have been reached concerning a patient or a cohort of patients, these have not been evidenced in writing (or the written agreement has expired). In such cases, significant problems can result when there is a change in the status quo – eg if there is an increase in the service costs or of the needs of a particular individual.
185 NHS(W)A 2006 ss194–196.
186 LAC (95)5: HSG (95)8 *NHS Responsibilities for Meeting Continuing Healthcare Needs*: WOC 16/95 and WHC (95)7 in Wales para 36.
187 Welsh Assembly Government (2010) *Continuing NHS Healthcare: The National Framework for Implementation in Wales* at para 8.15.
188 Department of Health (2009) *The National Framework for NHS Continuing Healthcare and NHS Funded Nursing Care* para 144. Similar wording is at para 8.15 of the Welsh National Framework 2011.
189 Under Health Services and Public Health Services Act 1968 s64. For details of the section 64 grant replacement scheme – see Department of Health (2009) *Third Sector Investment Programme Innovation Excellence and Service Development Fund 2010–11.*
190 NHS(W)A 2006 ss194–196.

community care regime, it appears that in the past, a number of health authorities and PCTs have inappropriately sought to use their powers under Health Services and Public Health Act 1968 s64. This improper use was highlighted by the Department of Health in a 2003 report.[191]

13.136   Section 64 of the 1968 Act gives the secretary of state powers to make grants to voluntary and community sector organisations. These can be made nationally (from the 'General Scheme') although most frequently they are made locally, for which the use of section 64 has been delegated to PCTs. There is no requirement to report on the use made of section 64, and, as the Department of Health report makes clear, it does not in fact hold any information about the grants that have been awarded.

13.137   The 2003 report describes how PCTs (and indeed the Department of Health) have been using section 64 inappropriately. Instead of making grants under this provision, they entered into service level agreements with voluntary and community sector organisations. As the report states (para 10), the 'distinction between a grant and a contract for the provision of a service is clear'. The report also explains that the appropriate mechanism for a PCT to enter into a contract for services, is to use its powers under what is now NHSA 2006 s12[192] or to transfer the money to social services via what is now NHSA 2006 ss256–257.[193] The importance of the latter arrangement is that, in order to do so, the PCT (or the Health Authority before it) would have had to have obtained social services' agreement to it discharging the (hitherto) NHS function. In the absence of such an agreement the function remains with the NHS – if for example the voluntary/community sector organisation withdraws from the contract. This has occurred on a number of occasions in the recent past, due to the schemes becoming uneconomic due to the reconfiguration of Supporting People's monies (see para 15.119 below).

191 Department of Health (2003) *Report of a review group established to examine the use of the power to make grants under Section 64 of the Health Services and Public Health Act 1968.*
192 NHS(W)A 2006 s10.
193 NHS(W)A 2006 ss194–196.

CHAPTER 14

NHS continuing healthcare responsibilities

continued

Introduction

14.1   This chapter considers the interface between the NHS's responsibilities for social care support under the NHS Acts 2006 and the responsibilities of social services authorities under the community care legislation. At some point individuals, because they have become so unwell, may move across the interface – from the means tested social services system to the 'free at the point of need' NHS system. In crossing the interface one moves from a detailed community care statutory regime into a system regulated by largely aspirational legislation and guidance of questionable quality. In many respects such people are crossing from a system shaped by its Poor Law origins to a regime infused with the idealistic principles of the Attlee government – principles that come at a cost that no government has been able or willing to fund fully.

14.2   Governments are not the only bodies with a financial interest in the line at which healthcare/social care divide is drawn. For many individuals, entitlement to fully funded NHS healthcare is of great significance, particularly if living in a care home. As at March 2010 the average weekly nursing home fee amounted to £693 per week – and of course in some areas, particularly London and the Home Counties, fees are considerably higher.

14.3   Since its introduction in England on 1 October 2007, the National Framework appears to have resulted in a significant increase in the numbers of people qualifying for NHS Continuing Care – from 27,822 at the end of September 2007 to 53,246 in March 2011, although the rising numbers appear now to have somewhat plateaued. The profound impact of the Court of Appeal's 1999 judgment in *R v North and East Devon Health Authority ex p Coughlan*[1] can be seen when it is realised at that time just 18,000[2] individuals were in receipt of NHS continuing care.

14.4   Since 1995 the debate concerning continuing healthcare responsibilities has been dominated by criticism of the relevant Department of Health guidance. The 1995 guidance was shown to be inadequate in *Coughlan* and the replacement 2001 guidance was rejected as unfit for purpose by the Health Service Ombudsman, the High Court, the Health Select Committee and many other commentators. A similar fate befell the Department of Health's 2001 Registered Nursing Care guidance[3] (see para 13.114 above) as a result of the judgment in *R (Grogan) v Bexley NHS Care Trust and others*.[4] To lose one set of guidance might be regarded as a misfortune but lose three looks like carelessness or perhaps more accurately an internal problem within the Department of Health that somehow frustrated its normally assured legal analysis.

14.5   This chapter considers the legal position as of September 2011. For the legal position prior to 1 October 2007 in England (or in August 2010 in

---

1   *R v North and East Devon Health Authority ex p Coughlan* [2000] 2 WLR 622, (1999) 2 CCLR 285, CA.
2   Laing & Buisson, *Market Survey* 2000.
3   HSC (2001)17: LAC (2001)26 *Guidance on free nursing care in nursing homes.*
4   [2006] EWHC 44 (Admin), (2006) 9 CCLR 188.

Wales) reference should be made to the third and fourth editions of this text which explain in detail the situation prior to the introduction of a single national framework and decision support tool (and provide a more detailed analysis of the critical reports of the Health Service Ombudsman and the Health Select Committee that have proved to be formative in shaping and developing policy in this area).

14.6   Wales has worked to a national framework and decision support tool from 16 August 2010 and has chosen to call it Continuing NHS Healthcare. The English term NHS continuing healthcare (or NHS CHC) will be used throughout.

Historical and legal context of the health and social care divide

14.7   The debate over continuing healthcare responsibilities is not new. Means, Morbey and Smith[5] chart the organisational tensions that have existed over the health/social care divide since the formation of the NHS in 1948. They conclude that these have been characterised by a failure of the NHS to invest in community health services or to transfer significant resources to social services (p85). They describe how the conflict has generally been expressed in debates over what is healthcare and what is social care. Guidance issued in 1957[6] on the relative responsibilities of local authorities and the NHS shows how far the demarcation line has shifted since that time;[7] a point emphasised by a number of academic commentators who have suggested that the NHS has been particularly effective at shifting its responsibilities to social services.[8]

14.8   Pivotal to an understanding of the health social services divide is the interaction between NHS Act (NHSA) 2006 ss1 and 3[9] (see para 13.9 above) and National Assistance Act (NAA) 1948 s21(1) and (8).[10]

14.9   NAA 1948 s21(1) places a duty on social services authorities to provide residential accommodation for (amongst others) elderly ill and disabled people. However, section 21(8) contains a caveat, namely:

> Nothing in this section shall authorise or require a local authority to make any provision authorised or required to be made (whether by that or by any other authority) by or under any enactment not contained in this Part of

5   R Means, H Morbey and R Smith, *From Community Care to Market Care?* Policy Press, 2002.

6   The 'Boucher report', cited in Means, Morbey and Smith (see note 5 above) p78.

7   Suggesting eg that the NHS should provide care for 'the chronic bedfast who may need little or no medical treatment, but who do require prolonged nursing care over months or years'.

8   See eg, J Lewis, 'Older people and the health-social care boundary in the UK: Half a century of hidden policy conflict' (2001) *Social Policy and Administration* 35(4) pp343–59.

9   Which are materially unchanged since 1948: the 1948 and 1946 Acts came into force on the same day – 5 July 1948.

10 Section 29 provisions are dealt with at para 9.43 above.

this Act, or authorised or required to be provided under the [NHS Acts 2006].

14.10 In simple terms section 21(8) means that it is unlawful for social services to provide a service that could be provided by the NHS (but see para 14.142 below). The full implications of this provision, however, had to wait until 1999 when the Court of Appeal delivered its judgment in *R v North and East Devon Health Authority ex p Coughlan*[11] – discussed in detail below.

14.11 Although the demarcation of the health/social care boundary has changed considerably over the years since 1948, legally there has been no material diminution in the scope of the NHS's continuing healthcare responsibilities since that time. In both England and Wales there has been no amendment to the primary statutory obligation (albeit that the duty is now to be found in the consolidated 2006 Acts). There has been no ministerial statement, no direction by the secretary of state or any other kind of announcement to the effect that the entitlement to continuing healthcare has been curtailed. Indeed in 2007 the then Care Minister was reported as having accepted that Primary Care Trusts (PCTs) had 'reneged on their responsibilities for funding continuing care and shunted costs on to councils'.[12]

14.12 The material changes have been in terms of demography, policy and funding arrangements. In relation to the latter two factors, the most significant concerned the availability in 1979 of supplementary benefit payments (later income support) to cover the cost of private nursing home accommodation. This situation led to the closure of many NHS continuing care wards, with the patients being transferred to privately run nursing homes funded by the social security budget. The strain on this budget resulted in targeted action against NHS bodies deemed to be inappropriately exploiting the situation (most notably in *White v CAO*[13]) and ultimately in the wholesale reform of the community care system (see above) showed the robust stance taken in cases where it was felt that the NHS was using the benefits system.

14.13 On 1 April 1993 social services authorities became the 'gate keepers' for such community placements. This led to a general, but incorrect, assumption that the NHS no longer had the same responsibility for funding long-term care. The fact that social services authorities were (for the first time) empowered to make payments towards the cost of independent nursing home placements also encouraged the view that the NHS was no

---

11 *R v North and East Devon Health Authority ex p Coughlan* [2000] 2 WLR 622, (1999) 2 CCLR 285, CA.
12 February 2007 *Community Care* 22–28 p8.
13 *White v Chief Adjudication Officer* (Social Security Decision R(S) 8/85; (1993) *Times*, August 2) where the court held that patients transferred to a nursing home under a contract with the NHS body, remained the responsibility of the NHS as they were deemed to be in a 'hospital or similar institution'; and see also the Tribunal of Commissioners Decision R(DLA) 2/06, CDLA/3161/2003 27 July 2005 where the Tribunal, in finding against the NHS body, criticised it for believing that it was 'legitimate to make every effort to minimise its proper liabilities under the 1977 Act by seeking to transfer them to a budget of another limb of Government through a wholly artificial scheme'.

longer an agency responsible for making similar payments. In fact, the responsibility for the care of persons in need of nursing home accommodation is an overlapping one between the two services.

14.14   The 1980s were characterised by a rapid closure of long-term beds[14] and an increase in inheritable wealth. By the early 1990s many individuals found that when they became chronically ill and needed care outside their own home, they had to pay for this in a nursing home – whereas previously such people had received it free in a long-stay NHS bed. They and their carers accordingly paid substantial sums to private nursing homes (not infrequently having to sell their former family home[15]) in situations where previously the care would have been provided without charge by the NHS.

14.15   It is this aspect that came prominently to the fore with the publication by the Health Service Commissioner of a highly critical report into a hospital discharge by the Leeds Health Authority in 1994.[16] The complaint concerned a 55-year-old man who had had a stroke which rendered him with little or no physical or mental capacity (details of his condition are contained in table 17 below). In spite of considerable health needs – albeit that he was stable and needed no 'active treatment' – the patient was discharged to a nursing home where he had to pay for his care. A complaint concerning the payment was upheld by the ombudsman who found that 'the failure to make available long-term care within the NHS for this patient was unreasonable and constitutes a failure in the service provided by the Health Authority' (para 22).

14.16   The ombudsman was so concerned about the situation disclosed by the Leeds complaint that he took the exceptional step of having his report separately published. In response, the government undertook to issue guidance, indicating:

> If in the light of the guidance, some health authorities are found to have reduced their capacity to secure continuing care too far – as clearly happened in the case dealt with by the Health Service Commissioner – then they will have to take action to close the gap.[17]

---

14   Between 1983 and 1993 there was a 30% (17,000) reduction in the number of long-term geriatric and psychogeriatric NHS beds (T Harding et al, *Options for long-term care*, HMSO, 1996, p8) and between 1988 and 2001 a loss of 50,600 such beds; see House of Commons Health Committee, *Delayed Discharges: Third Report of Session 2001–02 Volume 1*, HC 617-I, 2002, p35.

15   In 2006 it was estimated that about 40,000 people sell their homes each year to pay for their care home fees, of which a conservative estimate suggests that between 120 and 640 should have had their fees funded by the NHS – M Henwood, *Self-funding of long-term care and potential for injustice*, background paper prepared for BBC Panorama, 2006.

16   Health Service Commissioner Second Report for Session 1993–94; Case no E62/93–94: see table 17 below for a brief description of his condition.

17   Virginia Bottomley, Secretary of State for Health, 4 November 1994.

1995–2010: guidance, case law[18] and complaints

1995 Guidance

14.17 In February 1995, as a consequence of the Health Service Ombudsman's 'Leeds report',[19]continuing care guidance was published in England and Wales as a first step towards defining with greater precision the boundaries between the responsibilities of the NHS and social services authorities for continuing care.[20] The guidance required every health authority to prepare and publish local 'continuing healthcare statements' which spelt out which patients would be entitled to free continuing healthcare funded by the NHS. As part of this process the government also announced procedures that enabled patients to challenge their discharge from in-patient hospital care.[21]

14.18 Although in 1996 the Department of Health issued follow-up guidance to improve the quality of continuing healthcare statements,[22] the evidence suggests that the 1995 guidance was misapplied by health authorities and that the Department of Health was inactive in policing individual health authority continuing care statements.[23]

The Coughlan judgment

14.19 In 1999 the Court of Appeal delivered its judgment in *R v North and East Devon Health Authority ex p Coughlan*.[24] It reinforced the finding of the Health Service Commissioner in the Leeds health authority complaint, that entitlement to NHS continuing healthcare support arose, not merely when a patient's healthcare needs were complex, but also when they were substantial – the so called 'quality/quantity' criteria (see below).

14.20 The Court of Appeal held that social services could only lawfully fund low-level nursing care – low in terms of its quality and quantity. The court expressed this as follows (at [30]):

> (d) There can be no precise legal line drawn between those nursing

18 As can be seen from the cases cited the courts have been robust – however, there is some evidence that they may be losing enthusiasm for judicial review application in this field – and prepared to give health bodies the benefit of the doubt when construing less than perfect criteria – see eg *R (Green) v South West Strategic Health Authority and others)* [2008] EWHC 2576 (Admin).
19 At para 3 it states that the guidance 'addresses a number of concerns raised in the report made last year by the Health Service Ombudsman'.
20 LAC (95)5: HSG (95)8 *NHS Responsibilities for Meeting Continuing Health Care Needs*: WOC 16/95 and WHC (95)7 in Wales.
21 LAC (95)17: HSG (95)39.
22 See eg EL (96)8 and EL (96)89.
23 Indeed the evidence suggests the contrary – as the Health Service Ombudsman noted in her Second Report for Session 2002–03 *NHS funding for long term care*, HC 399, 2003, para 21: 'My enquiries so far have revealed one letter (in case E.814/00–01) sent out from a regional office of the Department of Health to health authorities following the 1999 guidance, which could justifiably have been read as a mandate to do the bare minimum'.
24 [2000] 2 WLR 622, (1999) 2 CCLR 285, CA.

services which are and those which are not capable of being treated as included in such a package of care services.

(e) The distinction between those services which can and cannot be so provided is one of degree which in a borderline case will depend on a careful appraisal of the facts of the individual case. However, as a very general indication as to where the line is to be drawn, it can be said that if the nursing services are:

- merely incidental or ancillary to the provision of the accommodation which a local authority is under a duty to provide to the category of persons to whom section 21 refers; and
- of a nature which it can be expected that an authority whose primary responsibility is to provide social services can be expected to provide, then they can be provided under section 21.

It will be appreciated that the first part of the test is focusing on the overall quantity of the services and the second part on the quality of the services provided.

14.21   Additionally the court emphasised that the setting of a person's care was not determinative of eligibility for continuing healthcare funding. In its view, 'where the primary need is a health need, then the responsibility is that of the NHS, even when the individual has been placed in a home by a local authority' (at [31]) and 'the fact that a case does not qualify for in-patient treatment in a hospital does not mean that the person concerned should not be a NHS responsibility' (at [41]).

14.22   In relation to the specific eligibility criteria of North and East Devon Health Authority the Court of Appeal stated (para 48):

However, the eligibility criteria cannot place a responsibility on the local authority which goes beyond the terms of section 21. This is what these criteria do. Cases where the healthcare element goes far beyond what the section permits were being placed upon the local authority as a result of the rigorous limits placed on what services can be considered to be NHS care services. That this is the position is confirmed by the result of the assessment of Miss Coughlan and her fellow occupants. Their disabilities are of a scale which are beyond the scope of local authority services.

14.23   It is perhaps in this respect that the *Coughlan* case is most remarkable. Pamela Coughlan has a C-5/6 complete spinal cord injury. As a consequence she is doubly incontinent, requires regular catheterisation and has partial paralysis in the respiratory tract (although she is able to breathe without artificial support – details of her condition are at table 17 below). However, in many respects, Pamela Coughlan's nursing needs are comparatively modest (when compared with many residents of nursing homes). She leads a relatively autonomous life, being able to study, campaign and to use her electric wheelchair. Nevertheless when applying the court's 'quality /quantity' formulation, it concluded that her needs were 'wholly different category' (para 118) to that which a social services authority could fund.

14.24   The continuing care policies of North and East Devon Health Authority were, it appears, not unusual. A 1999 Royal College of Nursing report *Rationing by Stealth*, suggested that the continuing care policies of over 90 per cent of health authorities were equally deficient.

Continuing care guidance following the Coughlan judgment

14.25   The Department of Health took two years to issue further guidance (HSC 2001/015: LAC (2001)18). This guidance has been the subject of robust criticism by the High Court[25] and the Health Service Commissioner, most particularly in her special report on continuing NHS healthcare.[26] The need for a special report stemmed from the large number of complaints that the Commissioner had received on this issue (as had been the case with her predecessor in 1994[27]). She was trenchant in her criticism of the Department of Health's failure to provide clear guidance in conformity with the Court of Appeal's judgment in *Coughlan*. The guidance in 2001 could be viewed as an attempt to blunt the impact of the *Coughlan* judgment – to use guidance in effect to frustrate the law, something that has of course a reasonable pedigree.[28]. Although the 2001 guidance had been subject to so much criticism, the Welsh Assembly Government issued similar guidance in 2004.[29]

14.26   The ombudsman has since 2003 issued further reports expressing concern about the processes PCTs and strategic health authorities (SHAs) were adopting to remedy their past failures[30] and relating to restitution and the level of interest that should be paid. In addition she has given written and oral evidence to the Health Select Committee.[31]

Pointon and the Health Service Ombudsman's report

14.27   A further individual report of note relates to the home care provided to a man suffering from Alzheimer's disease by his wife and care assistants, known as the *Pointon* case. The Health Service Ombudsman held that the fact that Mr Pointon was receiving (what was in effect) nursing care from his wife, did not mean he could not qualify for continuing healthcare; that the health bodies had failed to take into account his severe psychological problems and the special skills it takes to nurse someone with dementia; that the assessment tools used by the NHS were skewed in favour of physical and acute care; and the fact that Mr Pointon needed care at home

---

25   *R (Grogan) v Bexley NHS Care Trust and others* [2006] EWHC 44 (Admin), (2006) 9 CCLR 188 – see para 14.32 below.

26   Health Service Ombudsman's Second Report for Session 2002–03 *NHS funding for long term care*, HC 399, 2003, para 38.

27   While it appears that Sir William Reid as Health Service Ombudsman in 1994 had had about 20 such complaints, Ann Abrahams the current Health Service Ombudsman had had over 3,000 complaints at the time of her 2003 report and over 4,000 at the time of her 2004 report.

28   See eg *R v Secretary of State for Health ex p Pfizer Ltd* (1999) 2 CCLR 270, QBD.

29   WHC (2004)54: NAFWC 41/2004 which apart from a note to address the findings in *Grogan* (see para 14.32 below) WHC (2006) 046: NAFWC 32/2006 has been the guidance followed in Wales until 2010.

30   As a result the ombudsman has issued checklists for PCTs to follow.

31   *NHS funding for long term care – follow-up report*, HC 144, 2004–05; Memorandum by the Health Services Ombudsman for England to the Health Select Committee inquiry into NHS continuing care; *Retrospective Continuing Care Funding and Redress*, HC 386, 2006–07. All available at www.ombudsman.org.uk.

– rather than in a nursing care home – was not material to the question of continuing healthcare responsibility.[32]

14.28   The *Pointon* report is of considerable importance, being a clear example of entitlement to continuing healthcare funding where (1) the nature of the healthcare need was not for acute medical support but for nursing of a quality that could manage his psychologically challenging behaviour and (2) the need arose from someone living in the community and not a residential care setting. Mr Pointon was also receiving care from untrained assistants and his wife, and this too is sometimes used as an inappropriate reason for refusing entitlement to continuing healthcare. This (as the following *Haringey* case illustrates) is an irrelevant factor. What is of key importance is what a person needs – not what he or she is receiving.[33]

R (T, D and B) v Haringey LBC

14.29   *R (T, D and B) v Haringey LBC*[34] concerned a three-year-old child who had a complex medical condition which required – among other things – a tracheostomy (a tube in the throat) which needed regular suctioning and was replaced each week by a nurse. If it was not suctioned there was a severe risk of death or serious brain damage within a very short time. Although children who have tracheostomies are often discharged from hospital and cared for at home, their parents are trained to carry out the daily routines and cope with the emergencies that may arise. In the *Haringey* case the care was primarily being provided by the child's mother – but nevertheless the court held that it was of a nature that social services could not provide.

14.30   In the opinion of Ouseley J the *Coughlan* criteria applied with equal force to children, regardless of the fact that the social services care regime would have been regulated by the Children Act 1989 and not the NAA 1948 (see para 7.56 above). In his opinion the decisive factors were the 'scale and type of nursing care' and the purpose of the care – in this case it was 'designed to deal with the continuing medical consequences of an operation, which if not met will give rise to urgent or immediate medical needs'. Ouseley J additionally addressed the central dilemma of the case, namely the different public law entitlements provided by the social care statutes and the NHS Acts: the former creating specifically enforceable duties and the latter 'target duties' (see para 1.23 above). The judge accepted that in principle there could be an entitlement gap – essentially that a person could cease to be eligible for social care support because his or her need fell above the limits of what social care could provide (ie the section 21(8) cut off) but have needs below that which the Department of Health/Welsh Government had specified as necessary to qualify for NHS continuing care support, ie the 'primary health need' requirement.

32   Case no E.22/02/02–03 Funding for Long Term Care (the *Pointon* case).
33   A point stressed at para 49 of the English 2009 Framework Guidance (see para 14.38 below) and para 4.4 of the Welsh 2010 Framework Guidance.
34   [2005] EWHC 2235 (Admin), (2006) 9 CCLR 58.

R (Grogan) v Bexley NHS Care Trust

14.31 The question of the 'gap' in entitlement identified in the *Haringey* judgment was addressed directly in *R (Grogan) v Bexley NHS Care Trust and others*.[35] In essence Charles J held that the section 21(8) 'limits of social care' test was the crucial determinant. The reason for this conclusion was straightforward. The 'limits of social care' test is statutory in origin (ie section 21(8)) and had been authoritatively interpreted by the Court of Appeal in *Coughlan*. On the other hand the 'primary health need' test is a policy construct developed by the secretary of state. While it is the secretary of state's entitlement under the NHS Acts to propound such a policy, she could not (by guidance) undermine the statutory regime. Since the secretary of state (and the Welsh Government) had made unequivocal statements that there must be no gap in entitlement, then in Charles J's opinion the only way of resolving this dilemma (short of statutory amendment) was for the NHS to drop the policy 'bar' to the height set by the Court of Appeal in *Coughlan* when defining the limits of social care support.

14.32 Like the ombudsman, Charles J was critical of the Department of Health's 2001 guidance, in particular (at [66]):

i) the absence of a clear, distinct and early expression of the test and approach to be applied, and thus of the test or approach, against which the relevance and effect of the qualitative and quantitative criteria and factors listed in the Guidance have to be assessed, and

ii) . . . the absence of an explanation that the Primary Health Need Approach is to be applied to achieve the result that all nursing care (including RNCC) is merely (a) incidental or ancillary to the provision of the accommodation which a local authority is under a duty to provide, and (b) of a nature which prior to the enactment of s49 Health and Social Care Act (HSCA) 2001 it could have been expected that an authority whose primary responsibility is to provide social services could have been expected to provide, and could thus have been lawfully provided by a local authority (see *Coughlan*).

And (at [67]) the lack of:

. . . sensibly drafted guidance as to the provision of Continuing NHS Healthcare should inevitably include a clear and distinct expression of the overall test to be applied and thus the test to which the factors identified were relevant.

14.33 In the opinion of Charles J, the guidance used by Bexley NHS Trust failed to explain how relevant factors, such as the quantity and/or quality of a patient's care needs, should be weighted – with the consequence that a decision-maker was left to 'drift on a sea of factors without guidance as to the test or tests he should apply to assess and weigh (in the words of the criteria) the nature or complexity or intensity or unpredictability and the impact on an individual's health needs in determining the category into which the relevant person falls'.

---

35 [2006] EWHC 44 (Admin), (2006) 9 CCLR 188.

14.34   The *Grogan* judgment additionally addressed the incongruity between the continuing healthcare criteria and the registered nursing care contribution (RNCC) criteria (see para 13.114 above).

2006 Guidance

14.35   As a consequence of the findings in this case the Department of Health issued interim guidance revising the RNCC banding (see para 13.114 above) and advising health bodies and local authorities to work together to ensure that service users do not fall into a 'gap' between services.[36] The guidance additionally committed the government in England to the introduction of a single national framework for continuing healthcare entitlement.

14.36   With the judicial rejection of the 2001 guidance, new guidance was issued in 2007 and a commitment made to divert modest resources to pay for the cost of the additional patients expected to qualify for NHS continuing healthcare as a consequence.[37]

14.37   Whether the English 2009 and Welsh 2010 Frameworks and in particular their Decision Support Tools constitute an adequate response to the *Coughlan* judgment is debatable. It appears, for example, that Ms Coughlan herself would have difficulty qualifying for NHS continuing healthcare funding under the new regimes (see para 14.69 below). Since guidance cannot trump the law – it follows that the English and Welsh Frameworks must be interpreted in a way that ensures that, not only would Ms Coughlan qualify under the new regime, but that they apply the principles propounded in the key judgments to all persons who might be eligible for such support.

The current National Framework and directions

14.38   In June 2007 a new *National Framework for NHS Continuing Healthcare and NHS funded Nursing Care in England*[38] was issued by the Department of Health accompanied by a 'decision support tool'[39] designed to provide a fair and effective way of establishing individual entitlement to continuing healthcare. With the publication of these two documents the 2001 guidance[40] was cancelled. The implementation materials accompanying the new Framework emphasised that it was a clean break with what had gone before and the local authorities and PCTs would need to 'think and act differently' and that the expectation was that the new policy would result in 'more people [being] eligible for full funding'.[41]

---

36 Issued on 3 March 2006, *Action following the Grogan judgment*. This guidance has now been superseded by the framework guidance.
37 Estimated to be £219 million in the first year, based on the assumption that 5,500 more people would qualify for NHS continuing healthcare: Department of Health (2007) *Regulatory Impact Assessment Final*.
38 Department of Health, *The National Framework for NHS Continuing Healthcare and NHS funded Nursing Care in England*, 2007 and 2009.
39 Department of Health, *Decision-Support Tool for NHS Continuing Healthcare*, 1 July 2007 and July 2009.
40 HSC 2001/015: LAC (2001)18.
41 Department of Health (2007) *Resource pack: PowerPoint Introduction Module 1: slide 7.*

14.39   The Department of Health undertook to evaluate and consult on the effectiveness of the 2007 reforms and to make any changes that were considered necessary. In consequence, minor changes were made to the key documents which took effect in 1 October 2009. Since the publication of the revised framework in 2009, the Department of Health has published a practice guide,[42] and where this adds significantly to the framework guidance it is mentioned below.

14.40   People living in Wales had to wait until August 2010[43] when a not dissimilar national framework and Decision Support Tool was published. Until that time Wales was working to its 2004 guidance (see fourth edition of this text). Differences between the Welsh and English frameworks will be highlighted in this chapter. There is no equivalent practice guidance in Wales. However, although in some cases the process and wording of the framework and DST is different in Wales, the qualifying criteria must be the same, in that it should be no more difficult or easy to access NHS continuing care in either country given that the same legislation and case law applies: accordingly analysis of the English materials should be of direct relevance to practitioners in Wales and vice versa.

14.41   Currently PCTs[44] (and in Wales local health boards (LHBs)) are responsible for ensuring consistency in the application of the national policy, promoting awareness of the policy, as well as ensuring it is properly implemented and applied.[45] SHAs and HBs continue to have their general overview function of 'ensuring local systems operate effectively and deliver improved performance'.[46]

Directions

14.42 In England (but not in Wales) directions were issued 2007 and revised in 2009 to underpin the national framework, to both the NHS under NHSA 2006 and to social services under Local Authority Social Services Act (LASSA) 1970 s7.[47] The 2009 Responsibilities Directions require PCTs to:

42 Department of Health, April 2010.
43 EH/ML 018/10 Welsh Assembly Government Circular 018/2010.
44 However, this may well change under the provisions of the Health and Social Care Bill in which it is proposed to abolish PCT's and Strategic Health Authorities. See para 13.6 above.
45 Which includes maintaining good practice, providing training, identifying and acting on issues in the provision of NHS continuing healthcare, and informing commissioning arrangements both on a strategic and individual basis – Framework guidance para 166 in England and para 13.2 in Wales.
46 Framework guidance, para 168 in England and para 13.2 in Wales.
47 The NHS Continuing Healthcare (Responsibilities) Directions 2009 (described in this chapter as the 2009 Responsibilities Directions). At the same time the Delayed Discharges (Continuing Care) Directions 2009 were issued to NHS bodies regarding their responsibilities to undertake assessments for NHS continuing healthcare where a person is about to be discharged from hospital – these are discussed at para5.29. The 2007 Directions have been amended in relation to the NHS payments for the registered nursing care contribution in care homes providing nursing which are discussed in para 13.111 above.

- take reasonable steps to ensure that an assessment for NHS continuing healthcare is carried out in all cases where it appears there may be a need for such care, or where an individual already receiving NHS continuing healthcare may no longer be eligible for such care (direction 2(2));
- undertake assessments for NHS continuing healthcare prior to an assessment for NHS funded nursing care (direction 2(3));
- use the NHS continuing healthcare checklist (see para 14.6.7 below) if the PCT wishes to use an initial screening process to decide if such an assessment is needed, (direction 2(4));
- ensure that a multi-disciplinary team undertakes an assessment to inform a decision as to a person's eligibility for NHS continuing healthcare and following that assessment ensure the decision support tool (see para 14.78 below) is completed to inform the decision as to whether the person has a primary health need, and if they have, then the PCT must decide that the person is eligible for NHS continuing healthcare (directions 2(5 and 6);
- consider, when deciding if the person has a primary health need, whether nursing or other health services are more than incidental or ancillary to accommodation which social services . . . or of a nature beyond which a social services authority whose primary responsibility is to provide social services could be expected to provide, and if in totality they are above this level, then the PCT must decide that the person has a primary health need (direction 2(7));
- decide that the person is eligible for NHS continuing healthcare (where an appropriate clinician has completed the Fast Track Pathway Tool), and notify the person (or someone acting on their behalf) of that decision (directions 2 (8)(9) and (10)) (see para 14.60 below);
- inform the person in writing and give reasons for the decision, and if they are not considered eligible for NHS continuing healthcare inform the person (or someone acting on their behalf) of the circumstance and manner in which they can apply for a review if they are dissatisfied with the procedure followed or the application of the criterion in relation to the decision (directions 2 (11 and 12);
- consult (as far as reasonably practicable) with the relevant social services department before making a decision about eligibility for NHS continuing healthcare and the social services department is required as far as practicable to provide advice and assistance to the PCT and use any information from an assessment pursuant to NHS and Community Care Act (NHSCCA) 1990 s47 to provide such advice and assistance (direction 3).

14.43   There are no equivalent directions relating to NHS continuing healthcare in Wales.

Definition of NHS continuing healthcare

14.44 The 2009 Responsibilities Directions define continuing healthcare as a 'package of care arranged and funded solely by the health service for a person aged 18 or over to meet physical or mental health needs which have arisen as a result of illness': (Direction 1(2)). In Wales the 2010 framework guidance defines it as 'A complete package of ongoing care arranged and funded solely by the NHS, where it has been assessed that the individual's primary need is a health need' (para 2.1).

The current framework and the health/social care divide

The 'primary health need' vs 'limits of social care' assessments

14.45 The 2009 Framework guidance is, in large measure, high-quality guidance that faithfully implements the principles articulated by the Court of Appeal in its *Coughlan* judgment: this cannot, however, be said of its associated documents – materially the Decision Support Tool and the Checklist (discussed below). Adherence to the framework (and the practice guidance in England) should result in greater transparency in the decision-making process than has been the case in the past.[48]

14.46 Notwithstanding its positive contribution to the NHS continuing healthcare determination process, the Framework does have certain shortcomings, one of which is its continued reliance on a number of concepts that were not thought to be of overarching value by the Court of Appeal in *Coughlan*: concepts such as a 'primary health need' and the 'nature, intensity, complexity and unpredictability' of a health need. These have been criticised as unnecessarily complicating the assessment process[49] and as the Framework acknowledges (at para 15) do not appear in the legislation. Ultimately, however, the guidance accepts (at paras 26 and 28) that these concepts can (and should) be equated with the court's 'quality/quantity' test as the defining issue in identifying the section 21(8) boundary.

14.47 The 2009 framework guidance states (in terms) that a 'primary health need' arises where a person has exceeded the limits of the social care responsibility. This acceptance is important and is contained at para 26, which provides:

---

48 M Henwood, *Continuing Health Care: review, revision and restitution*, 2004. This review found that poor quality of documentation and of assessment data featured throughout the sites. Sometimes this was simply a reflection of the passage of time, more often it was indicative of a lack of base line assessments, failure to continue any care management, and a casual disregard for the importance of record keeping (p8).

49 See eg Law Society, *National Framework for NHS Continuing Healthcare and NHS-funded Nursing Care in England Comments by the Law Society of England and Wales*, 2006, where they were described as 'elusive, overlapping and likely to confuse'.

There should be no gap in the provision of care. People should not find themselves in a situation where neither the NHS nor the relevant LA (subject to the person meeting the relevant means test and having needs that fall within the appropriate local Fair Access to Care bandings) will fund care, either separately or together. Therefore, the 'primary health need' test should be applied, so that a decision of ineligibility for NHS continuing healthcare is only possible where, taken as a whole, the nursing or other health services required by the individual:

a) are no more than incidental or ancillary to the provision of accommodation which LA social services are, or would be but for a person's means, under a duty to provide; and

b) are not of a nature beyond which an LA whose primary responsibility it is to provide social services could be expected to provide.

14.48   This is in contrast to the Welsh 2010 framework which states that the 'sole criterion for eligibility for CHC is whether there is a primary health need' (para 4.1). Although the *Coughlan* quality/quantity test is mentioned in the description of the *Coughlan* judgment, the Welsh 2010 framework does not link the limits eligibility for NHS continuing healthcare in terms of the limits of social services responsibilities as clearly as the English guidance. Instead it relies on establishing eligibility with reference to the terms nature, intensity, complexity and unpredictability (para 4.2).

14.49   The English framework guidance also retains the references to the terms nature, intensity, complexity and unpredictability[50] which first appeared in the 1995 guidance. The English framework guidance attempts (at para 28) to link these four indicators with the quantity/quality test preferred by the Court of Appeal in *Coughlan*. It suggests that use of the decision support tool along with practitioner's own experience and professional judgement 'should enable them to apply the primary health need test in practice in a way which is consistent with the limits on what can lawfully be provided by a local authority, in accordance with the *Coughlan* and *Grogan* judgments' (para 31). This aspect is again missing in the Welsh 2010 framework.

Assessment and the framework

14.50   The framework guidance contains detailed guidance and a number of helpful statements on the assessment process, most notably:

- 'The process of assessment and decision-making should be person-centred. This means placing the individual, his or her perception of his or her support needs and preferred models of support at the heart of the assessment and care-planning process' (para 33) (para 5.1 Welsh framework).

- 'Assessments . . . should be organised so that the individual being

50   '[B]eing predictably unpredictable' should never be used as a reason for *not* giving NHS continuing healthcare – Department of Health (2007), *A National Framework for NHS Continuing Healthcare and NHS-Funded Nursing Care in England: Response to Consultation*, p13.

assessed and their representative understand the process, and receive advice and information that will maximise their ability to participate in informed decisions about their future care' (para 35). (Similar wording is at para 5.4 Welsh framework.)

- ... 'the individual's informed consent should be obtained before the start of the process of determining eligibility for NHS continuing healthcare' (para 36) ... If there is a concern that the individual does not have capacity to give consent, this should be determined in accordance with the Mental Capacity Act 2005 and associated code of practice (para39)......If the person lacks the capacity either to refuse to or to consent a 'best interests' decision should be taken (and recorded) as to whether or not to proceed with an eligibility assessment for NHS continuing healthcare. Those making this decision should bear in mind the expectation that everyone potentially eligible for NHS continuing healthcare should have the opportunity to be considered for eligibility (para 41). Similar wording to the above is in the Welsh framework at paras 6.1–6.5.
- PCT's should ensure that individuals are made aware of local advocacy and other services that may be able to offer advice and support (para 44) (para 6.22 in the Welsh framework contains similar wording).
- Local authorities should not allow an individual's financial circumstances to affect a decision to participate in a joint assessment (para 73). The Welsh framework states that involving social services colleagues is 'essential' (para 5.17).

14.51   An important statement regarding assessment is that: 'The decision-making rationale should not marginalise a need because it is successfully managed: well managed needs are still needs' (para 47).[51] In effect – 'you ignore the individual's actual situation with the benefit of the course of treatment and consider her as if she was not having the treatment and the impairment was completely unchecked.'[52] The Welsh framework (para 4.5) also recognises the 'fact that somebody has a health need that is well managed does not mean that it should be disregarded in the assessment'. This is a principle is of great importance. Many patients who have challenging behaviour or a severe risks of falls or an inability to adhere to a complex medication regime, will often stabilise in well-managed care regimes, and their aggression, their falls and their chaotic medication taking cease to be a problem. This may not be because their health needs have ceased – but merely a reflection of the regime they are under. As the Framework guidance states, it is only if the regime has 'permanently reduced or removed an ongoing need will this have a bearing on NHS continuing healthcare eligibility'.

51   *R (Booker) v NHS Oldham and Directline Insurance Plc* [2010] EWHC 2593 (Admin), (2011) 14 CCLR 315. It was argued unsuccessfully that para 47 of the Framework guidance could also be interpreted as abnegating NHS responsibility where a package of care was well managed as a result of a self-funding arrangement.
52   Per Lord Rodger of Earlsferry in *SCA Packaging Ltd v Boyle* [2009] UKHL 37 at para 27 – by analogy since the case concerned the Disability Discrimination Act 1995.

14.52   Para 49 of the English Framework (with similar wording at paragraph 4.4 of the Welsh framework) also provides an invaluable checklist of unacceptable reasons for declining entitlement to NHS continuing health-care funding – all of which derive directly from the observations of the Court of Appeal in its *Coughlan* judgment. It states:

> The reasons given for a decision on eligibility should not be based on:
> - the person's diagnosis;
> - the setting of care;
> - the ability of the care provider to manage care;
> - the use (or not) of NHS-employed staff to provide care;
> - the need for/presence of 'specialist staff' in care delivery;
> - the fact that a need is well managed;
> - the existence of other NHS-funded care; or
> - any other input-related (rather than needs-related) rationale.

14.53   PCTs and LHBs are reminded that assessment may need to be delayed to ensure the individuals' needs are accurately reflected and time has been given for rehabilitation:

> It should always be borne in mind that assessment of eligibility that takes place in an acute hospital may not always reflect an individual's capacity to maximise their potential. (Para 56) . . . In order to address this issue, and ensure unnecessary stays on acute wards are avoided, there should be consideration whether the provision of further NHS- funded services is appropriate . . . In such situations, assessment of eligibility for NHS continuing healthcare should usually be deferred until an accurate assessment of future needs can be made. The interim services (or appropriate alternative interim services if needs change) should continue in place until the determination of eligibility for NHS continuing healthcare has taken place (para 57. There is similar wording in the Welsh framework para 5.24).

14.54   In England this is likely to change from April 2012 when NHS acute trusts take responsibility for patients for the first 30 days following an inpatient stay in hospital. The Department of Health has stated that the expectation will be that assessment for NHS continuing healthcare eligibility should, at the earliest, usually take place within the 30-day period as part of assessment and care planning for future care and support needs beyond that time. At that point there should be further investigation of whether a further period of rehabilitation is needed – funded by the NHS. 'The key issue is that, where assessment for continuing healthcare has been deferred, it is the PCT rather than social care that is responsible for funding such services whether or not they are re-ablement services.'[53]

14.55   On the question of reassessments that NHS continuing healthcare is no longer required, the guidance make the following important statement:

> Neither the PCT nor the LA should unilaterally withdraw from an existing funding arrangement without a joint reassessment of the individual and

---

53 Department of Health, *Post-Discharge Support and additional funding for re-ablement*, appendix 5, Dear Colleague Letter, January 2011.

without first consulting one another and the individual about the proposed change of arrangement. Alternative funding agreements should first be agreed and put into effect. Any proposed change should be put in writing to the individual by the organisation that is proposing to make such a change. If agreement cannot be reached upon the proposed change, the local disputes procedures should be invoked and current funding arrangements should remain in place until the dispute has been resolved (para 143).

14.56 Similar wording is at para 8.15 in the Welsh Framework. This approach has been considered by the Welsh Ombudsman who found to do so without a thorough reassessment and (if appropriate) invoking its inter-authority dispute arbitration procedures would be maladministration – indeed 'wholly wrong, and totally unreasonable'.[54]

14.57 Furthermore the decision support tool (DST) has a space for the individual's views of his or her care needs and whether they consider that the multi-disciplinary assessment accurately reflects their needs (p12). In addition it must be noted whether the individual or their representative contributed to the assessment of needs (and if they were not involved a record made of whether or not they were invited or whether they declined to participate (p13)) and a space for a note on the views of the individual on the completion of the DST and whether they agree with the domain levels selected, and if they disagree reasons for this should be recorded (p40). Similar statements are also in the Welsh DST.

Individuals who refuse to be assessed for NHS continuing healthcare

14.58 As we note below, certain individuals are prejudiced by an award of NHS continuing healthcare funding – most obviously persons who prior to the award were receiving direct payments from a social services authority (see para 14.149 below). In such cases the individual might, quite naturally refuse to co-operate with the assessment process. Whilst this is of course their right, it remains a moot point as to whether they can actually stop the assessment taking place. The theoretical legal position being that if a social services authority believes a person to have a primary healthcare need above the NAA 1948 s21(8) line, then it may be unlawful for that authority to continue to fund that person. The framework guidance (para 38) (para 6.14 in the Welsh framework with similar wording) puts the position as follows:

> If an individual does not consent to assessment of eligibility to NHS continuing healthcare, the potential effect this will have on the ability of the NHS and the LA to provide appropriate services should be carefully explained to them.

14.59 The Welsh framework (para 6.15) further states that a consequence of

54 The Public Services Ombudsman for Wales Complaint against Cardiff LHB reference 2007/01329, 29 March 2009, para 32.

such a refusal would be that the NHS cannot become responsible for arranging and funding the patient's entire care package and that the NHS and the local authority might share the responsibility for package. This must be a debatable – if not a highly questionable – interpretation of the law. If a patient is above the section 21(8) line, then social services cannot fund. However, the logic for the argument – that the NHS cannot be responsible for a person in such a situation who refuses an assessment – is not (with respect) immediately obvious. The English framework is to be preferred, since it makes clear that the fact that an individual has declined an assessment does not of itself mean that a local authority has any additional responsibility it would have had to meet their needs over and above if consent had been given (para 38).[55] Arguably the practice guidance provides the most compelling legal analysis, which is predicated on the assumption that a refusal to be consent to the assessment process might nevertheless result in a determination of NHS continuing health-care entitlement. It states (para 2.4.1) that in such a case 'the NHS has responsibility for funding the support necessary to meet their assessed health and social care needs'.

Fast track pathway tool

14.60   The fast track pathway tool has been introduced in England only (see para 14.66 below for Wales) for individuals with a rapidly deteriorating condition which may be entering a terminal phase. The tool enables fast tracking and to bypass the checklist tool and the DST for immediate provision of NHS continuing healthcare. This might be where the person wishes to return home to die or to allow appropriate end of life support to be arranged. In such cases the rate of deterioration would bring the patient within the 'primary health needs' requirement and the framework guidance provides for the use of a fast track. This aspect of the framework has been considerably changed in England by the 2009 review. The responsibilities directions (directions 2(8) and (9): see para 14.42) stipulate that where an 'appropriate clinician' has decided that an individual has a primary health need arising from a rapidly deteriorating condition which is entering a terminal phase and has completed the fast track pathway tool, the PCT must on receipt of the fast track pathway tool decide that the person is eligible for NHS continuing healthcare.

14.61   An appropriate clinician is defined in the 2009 Responsibility Directions (Direction 2(13)(a)) as:

   . . . a person who is –

   (i)   responsible for the diagnosis, treatment or care of the person in respect of whom a Fast Track Pathway Tool is being completed,

---

55 The principle would appear to be the same as for a community care assessment – that a person (or their parent) can decline to participate in an assessment but they cannot stop the assessment taking place. Of course if he or she refuses to participate, it may be that the NHS will conclude that there is insufficient evidence to establish full entitlement to NHS continuing healthcare funding.

(ii)   diagnosing, or providing treatment or care to, that person under the 2006 Act, and

(iii)   a registered nurse or is included in the register maintained under section 2 of the Medical Act 1983.

14.62   The framework guidance amplifies this by stating 'the clinician should have an appropriate level of knowledge or experience on whether the individual has a rapidly deteriorating condition that may be entering a terminal phase, and an increasing level of dependency'.[56] It can also include clinicians employed in the voluntary sector, such as hospices, who are offering services pursuant to the NHS Act 2006.

14.63   Although the tool requires that the clinicians provide a prognosis, it states that 'strict time limits that base eligibility on some specified expected length of life remaining should not be imposed'.[57] This is amplified in the practice guidance:

> 'The phrase 'rapidly deteriorating' in the Tool should not be interpreted narrowly as only meaning an anticipated specific or short time frame of life remaining. Similarly the phrase 'may be entering a terminal phase' is not intended to be restrictive to only those situations where death is imminent. Also, someone may currently be demonstrating few symptoms yet the nature of the condition is such that it is clear that rapid deterioration is to be expected before the next planned review. It may therefore be appropriate to use the Fast Track Pathway Tool now in anticipation of those needs arising and agreeing the responsibilities and actions to be taken once they arise, or to plan an early review date to reconsider the situation.'[58]

14.64   Any necessary evidence should be included together with a care plan developed as part of the end of life care pathway that describes the immediate needs to be met and the patient's preferences.[59] Where a recommendation is made for an urgent package of care via the fast-track process this should be accepted and acted upon immediately by the PCT.[60] Only 'exceptionally' can it be questioned by the PCT, and in such cases it should 'urgently ask the relevant clinician to clarify the nature of the person's needs and the reason for the use of the fast track pathway tool'.[61]

14.65   The framework guidance reminds PCTs (at para 89) that careful decision-making is essential to avoid undue distress that might result from moving in and out of continuing care within a very short period of time. It further stresses that although the DST asks practitioners to document observed and likely deterioration, this should not be used as a means of circumventing the use of the fast track pathway tool when individuals satisfy the criteria for its use.[62]

14.66   Although the Welsh framework does not have a fast track tool or any 'directions' to LHBs, the Welsh framework requires that a similar fast

56   Framework guidance England para 85.
57   Framework guidance England para 87.
58   Practice guidance para 5.7.
59   Fast track pathway tool para 6.
60   Framework guidance England para 88.
61   Practice guidance para 5.9.
62   Framework guidance England para 91.

track system be developed by LHBs to that in England. Guidance to this effect is provided at paras 5.49–5.56 of the Welsh framework. This requires that LHBs put in place a fast track process that reduces the amount of information required, the time taken to gather information and reduce timescales for making a decision for those individuals who require 'fast tracking' – albeit that sufficient information must be obtained to support the need for fast tracking and for the decision makers to agree a package of care. The guidance defines 'appropriate clinicians' as in England, and exhortations about not imposing strict time limits are made. Where a recommendation is made for an urgent package of care by an appropriate clinician through the fast track process, this should be accepted and actioned immediately by the LHB.

The NHS continuing healthcare checklist[63]

14.67   Originally called a screening tool (which is what it is) a checklist tool in England has been designed to help practitioners identify people who need a full assessment for NHS continuing healthcare. The checklist is based on the DST. The 2009 Directions[64] require that if any PCT or NHS body wishes to use an initial screening process it must complete and use the checklist to inform the decision and inform the person in writing of the outcome of the decision whether to carry out an assessment for NHS continuing healthcare. The practice guidance states that it 'is not necessary to complete a checklist in every case provided PCTs take reasonable steps to ensure that individuals are assessed for NHS continuing healthcare in all cases where it appears to them that there may be a need for such care.'[65]

14.68   The practice guidance states that the checklist has been designed to give 'a low threshold for passage through to the full eligibility consideration process' (para 10.2). The checklist, however, replicates the 12 domains of the DST, albeit that they have only three levels: A, B or C representing the descriptors of high, medium and low in the decision support tool. The checklist guidance advises that a full assessment for NHS continuing healthcare is required if there are:

- two or more domains selected in column A;
- five of more domains selected in column B, or one selected in column A and four in column B; or
- one domain selected in column A (for any domain carrying a priority level) with any number of selections in the other two columns

14.69   The shortcomings of the checklist are laid bare, when it is appreciated that Pamela Coughlan would probably only score one A and two Bs – ie that if applied mechanistically it would screen out a person whom the Court of

---

63   Department of Health (2009) *The NHS Continuing Healthcare Checklist.*
64   This requirement is in both the 2009 Responsibilities Directions (direction 2(4)) and the Delayed Discharge (Continuing Care) Directions 2009 (direction 2(4)).
65   Practice guidance para 6.2.

Appeal considered unquestionably entitled to NHS continuing healthcare (see para 14.22 above). Since the checklist cannot undermine the law, it is important that the checklist guidance (para 20) is paid especial attention – namely that there may also be circumstances where a full assessment is considered necessary even though the individual does not apparently meet the indicated threshold.[66] Arguably this caveat is insufficiently robust, given that the screening tool may be used by a wide range of staff who might be unfamiliar with the *Coughlan* judgment.

14.70　　The framework guidance and the checklist guidance stress the importance of informing individuals that completing the checklist is not an indication of the likelihood that an individual will necessarily be determined as being eligible for NHS continuing healthcare.[67] However, 2007 advice by the Association of Directors of Adult Social Services and the Local Government Association[68] to local authorities on the application of the framework and associated documents observed that (p5):

> Any individual who 'crosses' the Checklist threshold but is ultimately deemed not to be eligible for NHS Continuing Healthcare is still likely to have their care jointly funded/provided by the LA and PCT.

14.71　The checklist can be completed by a range of professionals – the guidance suggests nurse, doctor, other qualified healthcare professional or social worker. There appears to be no reason therefore why the checklist could not be completed by suitable care home staff at their regular reviews of residents' needs as a guide as to whether a referral should be made for NHS continuing healthcare. Patients or relatives may want to use it to prompt themselves as to whether a full assessment should be requested. The guidance on the checklist states that the aim is to allow a variety of people in a variety of settings to refer individuals for a full assessment for NHS continuing healthcare. It is for each organisation to decide for itself which are the most appropriate staff to participate in the completion of the checklist.[69] The practice guidance suggests 'in general this should include all staff involved in assessing or reviewing individuals' needs as part of their day-to-day work'.[70]

14.72　　In an acute hospital setting, the framework advises that the checklist should not be completed until the individual's needs on discharge are clear.[71] It should then be used as part of the process of discharge and if it indicates a need for a full assessment, a decision may be made at this point (and recorded) first to provide other services and then to carry out a full assessment at a later stage. This full consideration should be completed in the most appropriate setting once it is possible to make a

---

66　Checklist para 20.
67　Framework guidance para 61. Checklist guidance para 8.
68　Association of Directors of Adult Social Services and the Local Government Association (2007) *Commentary and Advice for Local Authorities on The National Framework for NHS Continuing Healthcare and NHS-funded Nursing Care*, October 2007.
69　Checklist para 3.
70　Practice guidance para 6.3.
71　Framework guidance para 60.

reasonable judgment about an individual's ongoing needs. In the interim the PCT retains responsibility for funding appropriate care (para 64).[72]

14.73   From October 2009 individuals who are screened out of an assessment are no longer entitled to request a review of that decision using the Strategic Health Authority review panel. Instead the framework guidance now states:

> Where the outcome is not to proceed to full assessment of eligibility, the written decision should also contain details of the individual's right to ask the PCT to reconsider the decision. The PCT should give such requests due consideration, taking account of all the information available, including additional information from the individual or carer. A clear and written response should be given to the individual and (where appropriate) their representative, as soon as is reasonably practicable. The response should also give details of the individual's rights under the NHS complaints procedure.[73]

14.74   The Welsh 2010 guidance contains no equivalent checklist. Instead the framework advises (unhelpfully) that assessments for NHS continuing healthcare should be placed within the context of the 'Creating a Unified and Fair System for Assessing and Managing Care' (National Assembly for Wales 2002)[74] which, it states, 'provides the basis for determining the types and levels of assessment that will be appropriate in particular circumstances'.[75] The decision on what types of assessment are required may be made by any number of people involved in a person's care: this may include the multi-disciplinary team in the hospital; social workers and community nurses; and/or primary care staff.[76] If the outcome of the enquiry/contact assessment is that a referral for a full consideration for CHC is unnecessary, the decision and the reasons should be communicated clearly to the individual, and their carers or representatives where appropriate, and recorded in the individual's notes. If the individuals or their carers request a full assessment, the LHB must give this due consideration taking into account all the information available, including any additional information from the patient or their carer.[77]

14.75   The Welsh framework is silent on what should happen if the LHB considers the person ineligible for a full assessment of their need for NHS continuing healthcare. It is clear that if they have had a full assessment then they can apply to the LHB for an independent review.[78] The

---

72 See also para 5.54 above.
73 Framework guidance England para 66. This change is a matter of concern as it may be less likely that the individual will succeed in overturning the decision, or persuading the PCT to review the decision using the complaints procedure. It was likely that rather than go to the lengths of convening a panel, that PCTs decided it was easier to complete the full MDT assessment.
74 National Assembly for Wales (2002) *Creating a Unified and Fair System for Assessing and Managing Care* – see para 3.30 above.
75 Welsh Framework Guidance para 5.6.
76 Welsh Framework Guidance para 5.8.
77 Welsh Framework Guidance para 5.37.
78 Welsh Framework Guidance para 11.8.

assumption must be that as in England the individual could use the complaints process if he or she is are dissatisfied that they have not been given the opportunity of a full assessment. Individuals in the position might find it helpful to refer to the English checklist in order to challenge assumptions that may have been made about the person's condition.

The role of general practitioners in NHS continuing healthcare

14.76 The directions oblige PCTs (and guidance obliges LHBs) to take reasonable steps to ensure that an assessment for NHS continuing healthcare is carried out in all cases where it appears there may be a need for such care. However, one group of professionals who may have the most contact with an individual, are not directly employed by the NHS, namely general practitioners (GPs). There has been some concern expressed about the failure of GPs to make appropriate referrals for NHS continuing care assessments. The fact that PCTs have the duty to ensure assessment, it follows that GPs should be expected to be aware of the eligibility criteria for NHS continuing healthcare and make the appropriate referrals when visiting patients who they consider meet that criteria.

14.77 Further the contract to which GPs work with the NHS includes the requirement of referral of patients to other services under the NHS Act and liaison with other healthcare professionals where appropriate.[79] It is therefore arguable that GPs who fail to refer patients for an NHS continuing healthcare assessment where it would be appropriate for them to do so are in breach of their contract. There is particular concern in relation to individuals in care homes, whose condition may well have worsened, or indeed have reached a terminal phase, but do not require hospitalisation as their care can be best dealt with within the care home.

The decision support tool

14.78 As noted above, in England the PCTs and local authorities are required, when assessing entitlement to NHS continuing healthcare funding, to use the DST published by the Department of Health in 2009[80] and in Wales LHBs and local authorities are required to use a similar document, which appeared in the 2010 framework.[81]

14.79 There are severe limitations in using standardised assessment tools of this nature to assess patient entitlement. Such tools tend to require micro-measurement of various factors which are then combined to produce a determination or presumption for or against qualification. Such tools, while they have their uses, are clearly open to considerable criticism. Most obviously they cannot say where the line between NHS and social services responsibility lies.

---

79 Paras 47 and 46 of the Standard General Medical Services Contract.
80 Department of Health (2009) *Decision-Support Tool for NHS Continuing Healthcare*.
81 Welsh Assembly Government (2010) *Continuing NHS Healthcare: The National Framework for Implementation in Wales* EH/ML 018/10 Welsh Assembly Government Circular 015/2010.

14.80   Additionally, standardised assessment tools seek to render empirical a process that has been legally (not scientifically) determined and may depend upon highly subjective factors (eg patient perceptions of pain – see para 14.104 below). The choice of the individual factors to be measured and the range of scores available for these factors is also a subjective process. The Health Service Ombudsman's report on the *Pointon*[82] complaint was, for instance, critical of the tools adopted by the relevant PCT as they were 'skewed in favour of physical and acute care' and did not take into account the patient's significant psychological problems. Criticism has also been levelled at the use of tools, on the ground that they could inhibit communication with patients and their carers – and thereby sideline crucial user information from the decision-making process.[83]

14.81   Nevertheless in order to try to overcome some of the criticisms about variable decision making, a standard DST was introduced in England in 2007 and revised in 2009, and in Wales in 2010. Whilst there are many similarities between the tools used in Wales and England there are some significant differences, which will be highlighted in the following paragraphs. In both countries the DST is used following a comprehensive multi-disciplinary assessment. An individual (or individuals) should be identified to co-ordinate and take responsibility for the whole process until the decision is made and a care plan written.[84]

14.82   As noted in para 14.42 above, the DST must be completed by a multi-disciplinary team (MDT). The English 2009 Responsibility Directions direction 2(13)(c) defined this as comprising at least 'two professionals who are from different healthcare professions, or one professional who is from a healthcare profession and one person who is responsible for assessing individuals for community care services under section 47 of the National Health Service and Community Care Act 1990'. The Welsh Framework (annex 1) defines it as 'usually' comprising members from 'both health and social care backgrounds' and should include those who have an up-to-date knowledge of the individual's needs, potential and inspirations (*sic*.)'

14.83   The DST comprises 12 care domains, all of which must be completed by the multi-disciplinary team: there is space in each domain for the reasons why a particular level ('No Need'; 'Low'; 'Moderate'; 'High', 'Severe'; or, 'Priority') is appropriate. The tables (reproduced as tables 15 and 16 summarise the domains, from which it can be seen that not all have a 'Priority' or 'Severe' category. It can also be seen there are some significant differences between England and Wales. The tables have been

---

82   Case no E.22/02/02–03 Funding for Long Term Care (the *Pointon* case).

83   See eg G Huby et al 'Planning older people's discharge from acute hospital care: linking risk management and patient participation in decision-making' (2004) 6(2) *Health, Risk and Society* 115–132 who found that standardised assessment tools inhibited communication because they did not afford older people the opportunity to put any results into context for staff – cited in Social Care Institute for Excellence, *Using qualitative research in systematic reviews: older people's views of hospital discharge*, February 2006, p36.

84   Framework guidance para 67 England, para 9 Wales.

taken from the English DST. There is no equivalent table in the Welsh DST (which also describes only 11 defined domains with an additional twelfth domain) but the English table has been adapted to reflect the Welsh domains and levels of need.

Table 15: Division of levels of need in the different care domains England

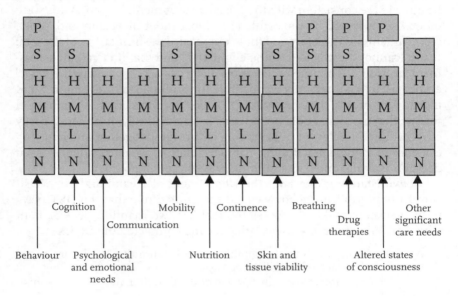

Table 16: Division of levels of need in the different care domains Wales

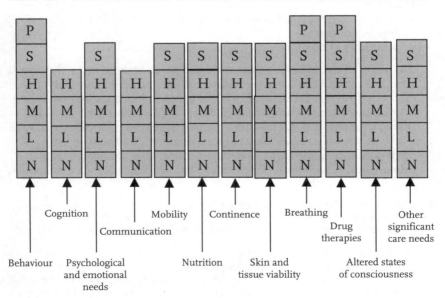

14.84   The decision support tool is considered at para 14.90 below, but crucial to its application is an appreciation of (a) its status and (b) its shortcomings.

14.85   The DST guidance is merely guidance, albeit that its use is mandated by direction 2(5)(a) of the 2009 Responsibilities Directions. It is, however, only a 'tool' and like many such tools, requires skilled use. It has been designed to ensure that decisions on entitlement to NHS continuing healthcare are consistent with the *Coughlan* judgment: indeed, if this were otherwise, it would be unlawful. The Department of Health and Welsh Government has therefore sought to emphasise the limitations of the tool: that it 'cannot directly determine eligibility'[85] and that it is 'not an assessment in itself.'[86] The implementation materials accompanying the DST[87] emphasised that it was 'not a substitute for professional judgement'[88] and that it was not 'A decision MAKING tool' (capitals in the original). It follows that the tool should not be used mechanistically: it is merely a way of recording the relevant information, of 'bringing together and applying evidence in a single practical format to facilitate consistent evidence-based decision making' on NHS continuing healthcare eligibility.[89]

14.86   Notwithstanding that both the Department of Health and the Welsh Government explicitly acknowledged the limited role that the DST plays in the decision 'making' process the tool has two manifest defects, both of which derive from the advice[90] that having completed the DST:

> A clear recommendation of eligibility to NHS continuing healthcare would be expected in each of the following cases:
> * A level of **priority** needs in any one of the four domains that carry this level
> * A total of two or more incidences of identified **severe** needs across all care domains.
>
> If there is:
> * One domain recorded as severe, together with needs in a number of other domains, or
> * a number of domains with **high** and/or **moderate** needs,
>
> **this may well also indicate a primary health need.** In these cases, the overall need, the interactions between needs in different care domains, and the evidence from risk assessments, should be taken into account in deciding whether a recommendation of eligibility to NHS continuing healthcare should be made. It is not possible to equate a number of incidences of one level with a number of incidences of another level, for example 'two moderates equals one high'. The judgement whether someone has a primary health need must be based on what the evidence indicates about

85 DST para 6 and Welsh framework guidance para K15.
86 DST para 2 and Welsh framework guidance para 5.27.
87 Department of Health (2007) Resource pack: PowerPoint Introduction Module 1: slide 19.
88 Welsh framework guidance para K15.
89 DST para 2 and Welsh framework guidance para 2.
90 The quoted material comes from the Department of Health DST at para 32. The Welsh framework guidance adopts this wording (at para 31) save only that it fails to remind LHBs of the need to consider the limits of local authority responsibility.

the nature and/or complexity and/or intensity and/or unpredictability of the individual's needs. MDT's are reminded of the need to consider the limits of local authority responsibility when making a Primary Health Need recommendation (see paragraph 26 of the National Framework for Continuing Healthcare).

33. If need in all domains are recorded '**no need**', this would indicate ineligibility. Where all domains are recorded as '**low need**', this would be unlikely to indicate eligibility. However, because low needs can add to the overall picture and alter the impact that other needs have on the individual, all domains should be completed.

14.87   The above advice creates the impression that the recording of a 'severe' in any one domain would of itself place the person below the line identified by the Court of Appeal in *Coughlan*. Likewise it creates the impression of a presumption, that in the absence of a 'priority' or two 'severe' needs being recorded, that the person will not be entitled to NHS continuing health-care funding. Analysis of what is required to score a 'severe' reveals how unrealistically high this band has been placed. No doubt this was done by those drafting the document out of fear of 'opening the flood gates' but this error bears a strong resemblance to that identified by Charles J in *R (Grogan) v Bexley NHS Care Trust and others*[91] concerning the 2003 Regis-tered Nursing Care bands: namely that the top band, which logic demanded should be below the limit set by *Coughlan*, had been placed well above it. It is arguable that the same criticism arises with the DST: that the severe band is well above the limit set by *Coughlan* – particularly (as Charles J noted) the decision of the Court of Appeal was that the care she needed was well outside the limits of what could be lawfully provided by a local authority.

14.88   Examples of the unrealistically high requirements for a 'severe' score are outlined below – but include the fact that (for example) (1) a person cannot 'take food and drink by mouth, intervention inappropriate or impossible' and (2) has open wounds/pressure ulcers that are 'not responding to treatment' or wounds/pressure ulcers that include 'necro-sis extending to underlying bone'. In either case it seems manifestly absurd to suggest that prima facie entitlement to NHS continuing health-care funding does not arise where a person whose condition is destined to result in their death by starvation within a few days or which consists of such severe wounds that their bone is actually visible. Equally bizarre is the suggestion that, in relation to breathing difficulties, an appropriate indicator for when a person has traversed the NAA 1948 s21(8) line, is where he or she is incapable of breathing 'independently' and 'requires invasive mechanical ventilation'. To suggest that 'being on a ventilator' is a useful indicator of when the person has traversed the section 21(8) line is, with respect, an absurdity.

14.89   Equally problematic is that, although the Court of Appeal considered that Ms Coughlan's condition was of a 'wholly different category'[92] to that

91   [2006] EWHC 44 (Admin), (2006) 9 CCLR 188 para 61 (see para 13.114 above).
92   *R v North and East Devon Health Authority ex p Coughlan* [2000] 2 WLR 622, (1999) 2 CCLR 285 at [118], CA.

for which social services could provide services, a mechanistic application of the DST suggests that (at very best) she is a borderline/non-qualifying patient – and as a consequence a number of PCTs have inappropriately rejected people with equally severe spinal injuries (and consequent healthcare needs).[93]

The decision support tool domains

14.90   Whilst a detailed analysis of the 12 individual DST domains is beyond the scope of this book, brief comment is made below, particularly in relation to those cases considered by the courts and the ombudsman.

14.91   **Behaviour domain** – this domain contains a 'priority' band – a finding for which would (if the DST is used mechanistically) create the expectation of eligibility for NHS continuing healthcare. In interpreting this provision (as with all DST descriptors) it is necessary to bear in mind the Framework advice (para 47), that 'well managed needs are still needs'. It follows that the person being assessed need not be exhibiting the requisite 'challenging behaviour', but merely that this would resurface if the care regime were removed. It is also essential that any interpretation of the descriptor be consistent with the NHS Ombudsman's findings in the *Pointon* complaint (Health Service Commissioner, 2004). In that case she concluded that Mr Pointon was eligible for NHS continuing healthcare funding on the basis of his challenging behaviour – which was managed in the family home by his wife and a rota of part-time care assistants. Mr Pointon suffered from the advanced stage of dementia characterised by mood changes and behavioural disturbance, although by the time of the decision the NHS ombudsman noted that the severe behavioural problems, which had characterised his illness (during the earlier stage of dementia), had diminished.

14.92   The Welsh DST makes specific reference to potential overlap between its mental health domain and this domain – and this is considered below.

14.93   **Cognition domain** – the cognition domain does not contain a 'priority' band, only a 'severe' and in Wales only up to a 'high' band. The DST cautions against the 'double counting' of symptoms (para 26 England and para 25 Wales), advising that where a 'condition could be reflected in more than one domain' it should be so recorded, but the fact that there is duplication 'should be recorded' and considered in the multi-disciplinary team's final recommendation. In general, however, duplication will be rare. What has to be asked in such cases is whether two conditions always co-exist. Thus a person with severe cognition difficulties does not always have severe behavioural difficulties (and vice versa) and so in this context, there would be no duplication.

14.94   **Psychological and emotional needs/mental health** – this domain is

---

93   Personal communication with the Spinal Injuries Association.

described differently in England and in Wales. In Wales it is described as the mental health domain, which highlights the omission of a specific domain for this healthcare condition in the English DST – and suggesting that (as the NHS Ombudsman observed in the *Pointon* complaint (see para 14.27 above) that there is a tendency for such descriptors to favour of physical and acute care over care that addresses psychological and mental health needs.

14.95   The Welsh descriptor has a severe category that is not present in the English, namely:

> Significant changes in mental health which manifests in extremely challenging unstable, unpredictable and repetitive behaviour over 24 hours on a prolonged basis. Requires the continual intervention of specialist healthcare professionals over and above what can be provided by core NHS services. High risk of suicide.

14.96   The Welsh guidance advises that to 'avoid double weighting, if the individual presents with behavioural concerns that are primarily to do with their emotional or mental health, this should be reflected in domain 3 rather than domain 1. On the face of it this leads to the absurd result that if their behaviour problems are not related to a mental health problem they could be in the priority category of need, but if their similar behaviour problems are linked to their mental health difficulties they would only be categorised as severe: irrational as this appears to be, it would only have a practical impact if the DST was used mechanistically as a decision 'making' tool – which it is not (see para 14.85 above).

14.97   **Communication domain** – although this domain has a maximum score of 'high', there will be situations where this fails to reflect the gravity of the problem. For example, if an inability to communicate is associated with significant or severe unexplained medical problems. These might, for example be due to the patient experiencing extreme pain which he or she cannot communicate. Such a combination, etc should therefore be detailed in the blank (final) box 12 of the DST.

14.98   **Mobility domain** – this domain does not contain a 'priority' band, only a 'severe'. The Court of Appeal's assessment in *Coughlan* is of direct relevance to this domain, given that a restricted interpretation of the severe descriptor might otherwise suggest that it excludes someone with Pamela Coughlan's impairments. Given the court's finding that her needs were well outside what could be provided by social services (ie that she was unquestionably entitled to NHS continuing healthcare funding) it serves as a further example of the importance of not applying the DST mechanistically as a decision 'making' tool.

14.99   **Nutrition, food and drink domain** – the nutrition domain does not contain a 'priority' band, only a 'severe', and as noted above is an example of how unreasonably high the Department of Health and the Welsh Government are endeavouring to place the qualifying bar for NHS continuing healthcare. In 2003 the NHS Ombudsman reported on a complaint concerning the refusal of NHS continuing healthcare funding for a patient who had had several strokes, as a result of which she had no speech or comprehension and was unable to swallow and required feeding by a PEG tube[94]. The ombudsman concluded that no health body could 'reasonably conclude that her need for nursing care was merely incidental or ancillary to the provision of accommodation or of a nature one could expect Social Services to provide'. Notwithstanding this trenchant criticism, the DST only accords a 'high' band to persons who have 'problems relating to a feeding device (for example PEG) that require skilled assessment and review.' The fact that the severe category is only available to those who are in the English case, destined to die of starvation,[95] and, in the Welsh case, would normally be an in-patient would appear to be something that the Court of Appeal in *Coughlan* would have found incomprehensible.

14.100   **Continence** – in England this domain only has a high level of need for those whose continence care is problematic and requires skilled intervention. But since the management of urinary catheters, double incontinence and, chronic urinary tract infection are only considered to be moderate needs, the high band is set remarkably high. The Welsh descriptor appears to set the high band even higher requiring qualified staff and specialists such as stoma nurses. This in spite of it being established by the ombudsman in the *Pointon* case and in the framework that eligibility is not determined by the characteristics of the person who provides the care or the provision of specialist staff.[96] Further the Welsh descriptor sets its severe domain at bowel management and skilled intervention that is required at least daily to prevent life-threatening situations. The fact that without such care a person would be likely to die makes it incomprehensible that it should not give an automatic entitlement to NHs continuing healthcare.

14.101   **Skin (including tissue viability) domain** – the skin domain is, as noted above, a further example of how inappropriately high the Department of Health and the Welsh Government are endeavouring to pitch the qualifying bar for NHS continuing healthcare funding – ie that the severe category requires, in essence that there be severe open wounds/pressure ulcers that are not responding to treatment or severe wounds/pressure ulcers that include necrosis extending to underlying bone (ie the bone is actually visible). Wales has further specified that a tissue viability nurse is required for the monitoring and assessment.

14.102   **Breathing domain** – as noted above, the breathing domain is perhaps the ultimate example of the questionableness of the line at which the Department of Health and the Welsh Government seek to draw the section 21(8) boundary – requiring as it does for the 'priority' band – that the patient, not only be 'unable to breathe independently' but also that he or she 'requires invasive mechanical ventilation' – in essence that the

94   Complaint concerning the Wigan and Bolton Health Authority and Bolton Hospitals NHS Trust Case no E.420/00–01 in the Health Service Ombudsman's Second Report for Session 2002–03 NHS funding for long term care, HC 399, 2003 – see para 14.111, table 17 below.

95   The severe band describes patients who are unable to take food and drink by mouth, and either require ongoing skilled professional intervention or monitoring of artificial means of meeting nutritional requirements, eg IV fluids, or such intervention is inappropriate or impossible.

96   Para 4.4 Welsh framework guidance.

patient is on a ventilator. This gives the impression that NHS continuing healthcare funding is only available to those whose conditions are of an exceptional order of gravity.

14.103   The severe band requires 'difficulty in breathing, even through a tracheotomy, which requires suction to maintain airway or demonstrates severe breathing difficulties at rest, in spite of medical therapy.' The Welsh DST adds an even higher bar by requiring 'regular suction by a qualified nurse' which appears to contradict Welsh Framework advice (see para 14.52 above). In 2005 the High Court considered a claim[97] concerning a child with a tracheotomy (a tube in the throat) which needed suctioning about three times a night and replacing once a week. The child lived at home and her mother had been trained by the hospital to make the daily routines and cope with the emergencies that might arise. Mr Justice Ouseley considered that these functions were indicative of a primary health need – and that to suggest otherwise would be 'to provide an impermissibly wide interpretation, creating obligations on a social services authority which are far too broad'. It would indeed be difficult to find many people who could disagree with this view – and yet given that such a need would only register as a 'severe' on the English breathing domain, absent other needs, the DST (if used mechanistically) would indicate no automatic entitlement to NHS continuing healthcare funding.

14.104   **Drug therapies** – although the domain contains a 'priority' it requires some very fine (arguably impossible) differences to be identified by the assessors. For example, to, in effect, distinguish between a person's untreatable 'severe recurrent or constant pain' and their 'unremitting and overwhelming pain': the former being accorded a 'severe' scoring and the latter a 'priority'. Since there is no independent way of measuring pain[98] it is difficult to see how such an exercise can be objectively accomplished and, in any event, it is difficult to understand how a person whose condition consists of living with untreatable 'severe recurrent or constant pain' should not be considered, prima facie, to have a primary healthcare need.

14.105   **Altered states of consciousness (ASC)** – although the English DST accords a person in a coma a 'priority' score, in Wales this only amounts to a 'severe'. If the line between priority and severe is seen as the important by the Welsh Government as indicative of entitlement to NHS continuing healthcare funding – it does defy common sense to suggest that being in a coma, of itself, does not constitute prima facie entitlement to NHS continuing healthcare funding. To express this as a 'severe' does nothing other than telegraph to LHBs and councils that the bar to qualifying for NHS funding is exceedingly high – and very substantially higher than indicated by the Court of Appeal in *Coughlan*. The domain also includes 'ASC that occur on most days, do not respond to preventative treatment,

97   *R (T, D and B) v Haringey LBC* [2005] EWHC 2235 (Admin), (2006) 9 CCLR 58 – see para 14.29 below.

98   See eg Social Security Commissioner's Decision no CDLA 902 2004, 18 June 2004 which at para 15 found that 'medical professionals who are expert in pain do not recognise a direct link between clinical findings and pain [accordingly authorities state that] . . . there is no direct causal link between disease or injury and pain, the only direct evidence of pain can come from the claimant'.

and result in a severe risk of harm' – and this could of course include (for example) people subject to brittle diabetes or constant epileptic fits.

14.106   **Blank box** – the blank (12th) box is of importance, since it is in this box that the factors (and combinations of factors) not properly recognised by the other 11 domains should be described. It is in this box that reference should also be made to the factors and cases that have been used by the courts and the NHS ombudsman as of relevance: above all it is in this box that issues of professional judgment taking into account all such factors should be detailed.

Decided cases as comparators

14.107   Given the patent shortcomings of the English and Welsh DSTs it is important to have regard to the findings of the court and the NHS ombudsman: to appreciate that the framework guidance and the DST cannot trump court decisions and that both the Department of Health and the Welsh Government have sought to emphasise the limitations of the DST and that it is not to be used prescriptively (para 77 of English framework and 5.35 of Welsh framework).

14.108   Whilst practitioners might use the DST as a method of gathering all the information, they need to be careful that the application of the criteria of the DST does not conflict with the findings of the courts or NHS ombudsman. The courts, the NHS ombudsman and the government in England have found it helpful to cite decisions when seeking to determine a 'benchmark' that signifies eligibility for NHS continuing healthcare funding. For example Virginia Bottomley, Secretary of State for Health in 1994, specifically referred to the care needs of the patient at the centre of the Leeds complaint as a benchmark for funding;[99] the Health Service Commissioner compared the nursing care needs for the patient in the complaint concerning Wigan and Bolton Health Authority to those of Pamela Coughlan;[100] as did Mr Justice Charles in the *Grogan*[101] proceedings. Table 17 below provides a resume of the care needs of some of the patients whose cases have been reported.

14.109   The English Framework guidance (para 79) requires that practitioners should be aware of these cases, although it warns against drawing generalisations from the limited information about those cases, adding that, 'is no substitute for a careful and detailed assessment of the needs of the individual whose eligibility is in question'.

14.110   Although it is undoubtedly the case that there is no substitute for a careful appraisal of the facts in individual cases, the reality is that the

---

99   Department of Health press release of 4 November 1994 and the Department of Health in its guidance EL (96)8 at para 16.

100   See eg the comments of the Health Service Commissioner in her 2003 report concerning Wigan and Bolton Health Authority and Bolton Hospitals NHS Trust Case no E.420/00–01, Second Report for Session 2002–03, *NHS funding for long term care*, HC 399.

101   *R (Grogan) v Bexley NHS Care Trust and others* [2006] EWHC 44 (Admin), (2006) 9 CCLR 188.

Court of Appeal in its *Coughlan* judgment provided considerable detail about her healthcare needs and concluded that these were 'well outside' the limits of social care. The primary point of reference must therefore be to this judgment and to the criteria the court advanced (see para 14.19 above) The fact that the courts, the NHS ombudsman and the government have used this and other findings as benchmarks means that they are of great importance – particularly when trying to ensure that the use of the DST does not result in conflicting outcomes. As the English (2010) practice guidance reminds PCTs.

> Where the outcomes of the individual care domains do not obviously indicate a primary health need (e.g. a priority level in one domain or severe levels in two domains being found), but the MDT is using professional judgement to recommend that the individual does nonetheless have a primary health need, it is important to ensure that the rationale for this is clear in the recommendation (para 8.10).

14.111 The guidance in the DST (para 22) and the Welsh Framework (Annex 6 para 21) and practice guidance (para 8.8) suggest that where members of the MDT do not agree on the level, or there is difficulty in placing the individual in one or other of the levels, then the MDT should choose the higher of the levels and record any significant differences of opinion. The practice guidance further indicates that where an individual has concerns about the level they have been placed at, 'these should be fully considered by reviewing the evidence provided, and if areas of disagreement remain, recorded in the relevant parts of the DST (para 8.9).

Table 17:   Resume of patients involved in continuing care disputes

Leeds Ombudsman Report Case no E.62/93–94, January 1994

A man suffered a brain haemorrhage and was admitted to a neuro-surgical ward . . . He received surgery but did not fully recover. He was incontinent, unable to walk, communicate or feed himself. He also had a kidney tumour, cataracts and occasional epileptic fits, for which he received drug treatment. After 20 months in hospital he was in a stable condition but still required full time nursing care. His condition had reached the stage where active treatment was no longer required but he was still in need of substantial nursing care, which could not be provided at home and which would continue to be needed for the rest of his life (para 22 of report).

The importance of this assessment was emphasised in NHS guidance EL (96)8 which (at para 16) criticised continuing care statements which placed an 'over-reliance on the needs of a patient for specialist medical supervision in determining eligibility for continuing in-patient care' and specifically referred to the fact that this was not considered by the ombudsman in the Leeds case as an acceptable basis for withdrawing NHS support.

Continued

R v North and East Devon Health Authority ex p Coughlan

Miss Coughlan was grievously injured in a road traffic accident in 1971. She is tetraplegic; doubly incontinent; requiring regular catheterisation; partially paralysed in the respiratory tract, with consequent difficulty in breathing; and subject not only to the attendant problems of immobility but to recurrent headaches caused by an associated neurological condition (para 3 of judgment).

Wigan and Bolton Health Authority and Bolton Hospitals NHS Trust Case no E.420/00–01[102]

Mrs N had suffered several strokes, as a result of which she had no speech or comprehension and was unable to swallow, requiring feeding by PEG tube (a tube which allows feeding directly into the stomach). Mrs N was being treated as an in-patient in the Trust's stroke unit and was discharged to a nursing home (para 1, p24).

The Health Services Commissioner concluded (para 30, p32): 'I cannot see that any authority could reasonably conclude that her need for nursing care was merely incidental or ancillary to the provision of accommodation or of a nature one could expect Social Services to provide (paragraph 15). It seems clear to me that she, like Miss Coughlan, needed services of a wholly different kind.' (In essence the ombudsman had found the decision *Wednesbury* unreasonable.)

Dorset Health Authority and Dorset HealthCare NHS Trust Case no E.208/99–00[103]

Mr X suffered from Alzheimer's disease and was admitted to a nursing home (p11 para 1), allegedly receiving services very similar to Miss Coughlan's (p20 para 23).

The Health Services Commissioner concluded (at para 26, p21): 'I . . . recommend that the . . . Authority should, with colleague organisations, determine whether there were any patients (including Mr X senior) who were wrongly refused funding for continuing care, and make the necessary arrangements for reimbursing the costs they incurred unnecessarily . . . Mr X senior suffered a degenerative condition, so he was more likely to be eligible for funding as time went by.'

Berkshire Health Authority Case no E.814/00–01[104]

Mrs Z, a 90-year-old admitted to a hospital suffering with vascular dementia (para 1, p35) and in need of 'all help with daily living, except

continued

102　From the Health Service Ombudsman's Second Report for Session 2002–03 *NHS funding for long term care*, HC 399, 2003.

103　*NHS funding for long term care*, HC 399, 2003.

104　*NHS funding for long term care*, HC 399, 2003.

feeding' and resistant to help and needing supervision if she was to take the medication she needed (para 12 p38).

The Health Services Commissioner concluded (at para 39, p46): 'It is certainly very possible (but not entirely certain) that, if appropriate criteria had been applied, Mrs Z would have qualified for fully funded care.'

Birmingham Health Authority Case no E.1626/01–02[105]

Mrs R, a 90-year-old admitted to hospital following a severe stroke, which had left her immobile, incontinent, and confused (and unlikely that her condition would change) (para 1, p49).

The Health Services Commissioner concluded (at para 23, p54): 'Had Mrs R been assessed against criteria which were in line with the then guidance and the Coughlan judgment, she might (though it is not possible to be certain) have been deemed eligible for NHS funding for her nursing home care.'

Complaint against the former Shropshire Health Authority Case no E.5/02–03[106]

Mrs F has Alzheimer's Disease and in June 2000 was assessed by a consultant psychiatrist as needing specialist elderly mentally ill (EMI) care. A nursing assessment in November 2000 noted that she required full assistance with all her personal tasks including washing, dressing, feeding and toiletting. She was also doubly incontinent, was dependent upon others for her safety, and could only mobilise with assistance.

The ombudsman was advised by her independent clinical assessor that Mrs F required significant nursing care and it was debatable whether that could properly be regarded as merely incidental or ancillary to the accommodation which Mrs F also needed. The ombudsman upheld the complaint.

Complaint against the former Shropshire Health Authority Case no E.2119/01[107]

Mr C suffered a severe stroke and the clinical assessment found that he was unable to manage any aspect of personal care independently. The notes recorded that he had an in-dwelling urinary catheter, occasional faecal incontinence (largely avoided by regular toiletting by hoist transfer to commode/toilet); that he required to be fed soft pureed diet

continued

---

105 *NHS funding for long term care*, HC 399, 2003.
106 Health Service Ombudsman's Fifth Report for the Session 2002–03, HC 787, 2003.
107 Health Service Ombudsman's Fifth Report for the Session 2002–03, HC 787, 2003.

with thickened oral fluids; that he had a PEG Gastrostomy tube in place, used to administer additional fluids overnight if necessary; that a hoist was used for all transfers; that all pressure areas remained intact with repositioning two hourly; that communication was by eye contact and head movement; that he could not speak.

The ombudsman's specialist assessor concluded that from the information provided Mr C's needs were primarily health needs.

Complaint against Cambridgeshire Health Authority and PCT (the *Pointon* case)[108]

Mr P is severely disabled with dementia and unable to look after himself. His wife cared for him at home. She took a break one week in five but had to pay more than £400 for the substitute care assistant, because the NHS would not pay, because Mrs P was not a qualified nurse (and could not therefore be offering nursing care). It was held that the fact that Mr P was receiving (what was in effect) nursing care from his wife, did not mean he could not qualify for continuing healthcare; that the health bodies had failed to take into account his severe psychological problems and the special skills it takes to nurse someone with dementia; that the assessment tools used by the NHS were skewed in favour of physical and acute care; the fact that Mr P needed care at home – rather than in a nursing care home – was not material to the question of continuing healthcare responsibility.

R (T, D and B) v Haringey LBC [109]

This concerned a patient who required – amongst other things – a tracheostomy (a tube in the throat). The tube needed suctioning regularly and replacing about once a week. If the tube was not suctioned the patient could die within minutes. Patients in this condition could be cared for at home if their carers are trained to make the daily routines and cope with the emergencies that may arise. The judge held that care of this type could not be provided by local authorities – that it was an NHS responsibility. In his opinion the decisive factors were the 'scale and type of nursing care' and the purpose of the care – in this case it was 'designed to deal with the continuing medical consequences of an operation, which if not met would give rise to urgent or immediate medical needs. The advice on management is provided by a hospital: the training is provided by the medically qualified.'

108   Case no E.22/02/02–03 Funding for Long Term Care (the *Pointon* case).
109   [2005] EWHC 2235 (Admin), (2006) 9 CCLR 58.

The funding decision

14.112 The final decision on funding is for the PCT or LHB. The framework guidance recognises that many PCTs use panels but cautions against their use as a gate keeping function or as a financial monitor.

> Only in exceptional circumstances and for clearly articulated reasons, should the multi-disciplinary team's recommendation not be followed. A decision to overturn the recommendation should never be made by one person acting unilaterally (para 80).

> PCTs may ask a multi-disciplinary team to carry out further work on a Decision Support Tool if it is not completed fully or if there is a significant lack of consistency between the evidence recorded in the Decision Support Tool and the recommendation made. However, PCTs should not refer a case back, or decide not to accept a recommendation, simply because the multi-disciplinary team has made a recommendation that differs from the one that those who are involved in making the final decision would have made, based on the same evidence (para 81).

14.113 In the above context, the Department of Health has reportedly advised that the word 'exceptional' 'means exactly what it says on the tin, there must be something truly exceptional. If more than 1% of MDT recommendations are not being followed then something is wrong: exceptional circumstances means that there is something 'truly unusual'.[110]

14.114 The framework guidance reminds PCTs and LHBs, that the final eligibility decision should be independent of budgetary constraints, and so finance officers should not be part of a decision-making panel (para 82): similar wording to the above appears in the Welsh framework at paras 5.39–5.41.

14.115 What appears to be happening in practice is that the PCT (often through a 'panel') is using the device of seeking 'further evidence' or 'corroborating documentation' as a way of delaying and ultimately refusing entitlement for funding – even though the multi-disciplinary team completing the DST may have made a recommendation in favour of NHS funding. A complaint investigated by the Public Services Ombudsman for Wales[111] is relevant in this context. The LHB's panel's delayed making a decision on the pretext of seeking additional assessments and evidence – although eventually it refused NHS funding. The Ombudsman considered this to be 'perverse' and suggested and that the Panel 'appeared to be trying to avoid making a decision'. He emphasised that since the multi-disciplinary team had made a clear recommendation in favour of eligibility for funding this should have been approved without demur by Panel.

14.116 Where an individual or a local authority is faced by what appears to be such obstructive behaviour, it may be appropriate to seek an early

---

110 Personal communication with the authors from participants at a Department of Health Stakeholders meeting 1 July 2010.

111 Public Services Ombudsman for Wales report on a Complaint No 200800779 against Carmarthenshire Local Health Board, 15 December 2009.

escalation of the review (or dispute resolution) process (see para 14.181 below). It could also be argued that:

- Where the missing evidence is evidence that should be provided by the NHS, that (in its absence) there is a presumption in favour of NHS funding.
- Where the evidence is effectively to show that a condition is only stable because it is 'well managed' that it is for the NHS to demonstrate a change has occurred which would enable the regime to be removed without a regression of the patients (to argue otherwise is to require, in effect, proof of a negative[112]).
- That the only additional evidence required by a panel must be genuinely 'material' and not of a merely bureaucratic or 'diagnostic' nature.[113]

Timescales for making the decision

14.117 The English framework allows 28 days for the PCT to make a decision from the time of receipt of the checklist.[114] It suggests that in acute settings the time should be considerably less if a patient is ready for discharge. Where there are valid and unavoidable reasons for the process taking longer, timescales should be clearly communicated to the person and (where appropriate) their carers and/or representatives.

14.118   The Welsh framework is even less robust in this respect, and suggests that, subject to exceptional circumstances, the 'time taken for assessments and agreeing a care package may vary but should be completed in six to eight weeks from initial trigger to agreeing a care package' (para 5.45). The care co-ordinator is required, however, to ensure that timescales, decisions and rationales relating to eligibility are transparent from the outset for individuals, carers, family and staff (para 5.46).

14.119   In 2010 the Department of Health[115] issued Refunds Guidance setting out the approaches to be taken by PCTs and local authorities when a decision is awaited on eligibility for NHS continuing healthcare (or there is a dispute following a decision see paras 14.165–14.184 below).

14.120   The refunds guidance explains the respective responsibilities for providing services during these periods and for refunding the costs of services provided. It covers three situations:

a)   Where there is a need for health or community care services to be provided to an individual during the period in which a decision on

---

112 Where a care regime requires ongoing care management – the care provider should, however, be required to keep records to identify what daily precautionary/anticipatory care is being provided and what would occur if this were withdrawn.

113 See para 14.52 above – citing para 47 of the English Framework, para 4.5 of the Welsh Framework.

114 Para 84: an extension on the previous framework which only allowed 14 days.

115 Department of Health (2010) *NHS Continuing Healthcare Refunds Guidance.*

eligibility for NHS continuing healthcare is awaited, in a case that does not involve hospital discharge:[116]

- any package already existing should continue, unless there is urgent need for adjustment;
- if services are provided by a local authority, but some health services are needed in the interim which are not within the power for a local authority to provide, the PCT should consider its responsibilities to provide them prior to a decision being made on NHS continuing healthcare;
- if the individual is not getting either a local authority or PCT package but is awaiting a decision on NHS continuing healthcare, if the person needs community care services the local authority should assess and if necessary provide services urgently in advance of an assessment. Likewise if the local authority identifies health needs the PCT should consider its responsibilities pending a decision. The local authority and PCT should jointly agree actions to be taken until the outcome of the decision making process is known. No individual should be left without appropriate support.

b) Where a PCT has unjustifiably taken longer than 28 days to reach a decision on eligibility for NHS continuing healthcare:

- PCTs have 28 days to reach a decision from receipt of the checklist or other notification of potential eligibility for NHS continuing healthcare;
- if it takes longer than this and the delay was not outside of the PCT's control the individual or local authority should be refunded from the 29th day;
- the local authority should be refunded the gross amount and then pay back the individual any contributions he or she made. In the case of a person who has funded their own care, the PCT should make an ex gratia payment:

c) Where, as a result of an individual disputing an NHS continuing healthcare eligibility decision, a PCT has revised its decision:

- the decision remains in effect until the PCT revises its decision;
- if the local authority has funded in the interim the PCT should refund gross to the local authority which should refund any contributions made by the individual;
- if the individual has funded themselves in the interim an ex gratia payment should be considered.

14.121 Where an individual disputes a PCT decision on whether to provide redress to them or disputes the amount of redress payable this should be considered by the PCT through the NHS complaints process.

---

116 The guidance fails to explain what should happen if the person is to be discharged from hospital on the grounds that this is covered in the framework in paras 56, 57 and 64, namely that the NHS remains responsible for any interim package of care prior to a decision being made.

14.122   There is no equivalent guidance in Wales regarding the position of individuals whilst awaiting a decision on continuing healthcare which could take up to eight weeks.

Care planning for NHS continuing healthcare

14.123 Both the English and Welsh frameworks contain guidance concerning care planning and provision once an eligibility decision has been made. It reminds LHBs/PCTs that NHS commissioning includes an ongoing case management role in addition to regular reviews. The ultimate responsibility for arranging and monitoring the services required to meet the needs of those who qualify for NHS continuing healthcare rests with PCT/LHB commissioners.[117]

14.124   Although the PCT is not bound by the views of the local authority as to what services the individual needs, its contribution to the assessment will be important in identifying the individual's needs and the options for meeting them.[118]

14.125   In England the 2010 practice guidance (section 11) contains useful detail about aspects of commissioning services and care planning with a strong emphasis on personalisation, agreeing outcomes and choice and control. It reminds PCTs that in the context of NHS continuing healthcare, case management necessarily entails management of the whole package, not just the healthcare aspects (para 11.4) and where the care plan includes access to non-NHS services, for example, leisure services, that the arrangements for these services must also be sustained and seen to be working effectively. It also reminds PCTs that those receiving NHS continuing healthcare continue to be entitled to access the full range of primary, community, secondary and other health services, and that these should be set out clearly in the contract between the provider and the PCT. (para 11.5).[119] The ombudsman in Wales[120] has also emphasised that the NHS is obliged to meet the person's *full* healthcare needs (in the particular case, this included a substantial package of speech, language, occupational and physiotherapy). This is reflected at para 9.19 in the Welsh Framework.

14.126   The practice guidance makes it clear the starting point for agreeing the package and the setting where NHS continuing healthcare services are to be provided should be the individual's preferences (para 11.7). Where this is more expensive, any cost comparison has to be on the basis of the genuine costs of alternative models and should take into account human rights considerations. In cases where the person wants to be supported in

---

117 Framework guidance paras 95 and 96 (paras 7.1 and 7.2 Wales).

118 Framework guidance para 100 (there is wording to a similar effect in the Welsh framework at para 7.5).

119 The Department of Health has published standard contracts for the NHS and care homes for 2011.

120 Public Services Ombudsman for Wales Report on a Complaint No 200800779 against Carmarthenshire Local Health Board, 15 December 2009.

their own home, the actual costs of doing this should be identified on the basis of the individual's assessed needs and agreed desired outcomes, and that cost has to be balanced against other factors in the individual case, such as an individual's desire to continue to live in a family environment (and in this respect the practice guidance refers to the *Gunter* judgment[121]).

Care packages in care homes

14.127 It is likely the majority of cases, when an individual is entitled to NHS continuing healthcare, the care package will be arranged in a nursing home as the most suitable way of meeting care needs. The care should be arranged using the principles of care planning described above, with the care home being clear about the outcomes desired and the need to deliver care in a person centred manner. Individuals in residential care homes may also be entitled to NHS continuing healthcare, for example, where they require palliative care and wish to remain in their residential care home, or for those who require specifically trained staff (eg a specialist home for patients with Alzheimer's disease where the care is provided by non-nursing staff[122]). The National Framework makes it clear that NHS continuing healthcare cannot be determined by setting.[123]

14.128   Concern has been expressed about PCTs seeking to move residents in residential care homes (following an assessment of eligibility for NHS Continuing Healthcare funding) into nursing homes – for example, where the 'fast track pathway' tool has identified the person as entering the final phase of their lives. In response to this concern, the Department of Health has issued guidance stating that 'there is nothing within the regulatory framework, which would prevent a person in receipt of NHS continuing healthcare remaining within a Care Home (Personal Care)'.[124]

Top-ups

14.129   A contentious issue in relation to care packages in care homes arises when an individual wants to move into (or is currently living in) a home that is more expensive than the PCT or HB considers necessary to meet their health needs. There is no specific right to choose an NHS-funded home in the same way as there is for local authority residents to 'top-up' within the Choice of Accommodation Directions (see para 7.103). This issue was raised in the case of *R (on the application of S) v Dudley PCT.*[125] In this case when the PCT accepted responsibility for NHS continuing

---

121 *Rachel Gunter v SW Staffordshire Primary Care Trust* [2005] EWHC 1894 (Admin), (2006) 9 CCLR 121. See also para 13.21.

122 There appears, eg, to be no material difference between the situation of care being provided by personal care staff and that of Mr Pointon who was being cared for at home – see para 14.27 above.

123 Framework guidance para 47 (para 4.4 Wales).

124 Department of Health (2008) *Joint Statement re: NHS Continuing Healthcare Funding for End of Life Care within Care Homes.*

125 [2009] EWHC 1780 (Admin).

healthcare it wanted the applicant to move to a cheaper facility within the same site as the home he had chosen. The court did not find it unlawful to top-up hotel type costs, noting that:

> ... it has always been the case within the National Health Service that those who wish to enjoy what are known in National Health Service jargon as 'hotel-type services', may do so at their own cost. Thus, ever since the foundation of the National Health Service there have been available within National Health Service hospitals enhanced facilities, such as individual rooms, available to patient who are willing to pay for such facilities, but the principle has always been, and remains, subject to exceptions recently canvassed in relation to drugs administered to those with life-threatening illnesses, that healthcare services are provided free.

> By reference to what is on any view a fairly fine line, the defendant is thus able to provide free continuing healthcare while at the same time accepting that additional contributions can be made for facilities that may meet non-healthcare needs (paras 21 and 22).

14.130 In this context, the practice guidance advises that unless 'it is possible separately to identify and deliver the NHS-funded elements of the service, it will not usually be permissible for individuals to pay for higher-cost services and/or accommodation (as distinct from purchasing additional services)'. The guidance then stresses the need for PCTs to liaise with the individual as to why he or she wishes to pay for higher than usual accommodation and to consider paying higher than usual costs where a need is identified for clinical reasons. It follows that top-up payments should only be made where the individual is genuinely opting for something over and above that which the NHS is responsible for providing, and such cases should be rare.

14.131   In cases where the individual is already in a care home which charges higher fees than the PCT would normally consider necessary, the 2010 practice guidance advises:

> ... PCTs should consider whether there are reasons why they should meet the full cost of the care package, notwithstanding that it is at a higher rate, such as that the frailty, mental health needs or other relevant needs of the individual mean that a move to other accommodation could involve significant risk to their health and well-being (para 11.6).

14.132   The same paragraph in the practice guidance further reminds PCTs of the need to consider paying higher costs if the placement is in a more expensive area, and if it is close to family members who play an active role in the life of the individual, or if the individual has lived in the home for many years and it would be significantly detrimental to move them.

> Where a PCT determines that circumstances do not justify them funding an existing higher cost placement or services that they have inherited responsibility for, any decisions on moves to other accommodation or changes in care provider should be taken in full consultation with the individual concerned and put in writing with reasons given. Advocacy support should be provided where this is appropriate. Where an individual become entitled to NHS continuing healthcare and has an existing high-cost care package PCTs should consider funding the full cost of the existing

higher-cost package until a decision is made on whether to meet the higher cost package on an ongoing basis or to arrange an alternative placement (para 11.6.)

14.133 An individual can use the complaints process if he or she wishes to challenge a decision not to pay the higher cost. The practice guidance suggests a transition care plan should be developed. The PCT should keep in regular liaison with the new provider and with the individual during the initial weeks of the new services to ensure that the transition has proceeded successfully and to ensure that any issues that have arisen are being appropriately addressed.

14.134 Although this advice is contained in English guidance there seems no reason why it should not also be good practice in Wales. The Welsh framework says little about choice other than while there is no legal obligation to offer choice it improves the individual's experience, results in improved outcomes and that 'every effort should be made therefore to enable the person to participate in decision about how and where their care needs are to be met' (paras 7.15 and 7.16 Welsh framework).

Care packages in community settings

14.135 It is now well established that NHS continuing healthcare can be provided in an individual's own home. In a 2003 complaint investigated by the Health Service Commissioner[126] she criticised an authority whose continuing healthcare statement had the effect of requiring 'on-site medical provision' (ie hospital based) in order to qualify for full NHS funding. The *Haringey* and *Pointon* cases (see paras 14.29 and 14.27 above) likewise further clarified the position that NHS continuing healthcare could be provided in people's own homes and that the fact that Mr Pointon's care was provided by non-health staff did not preclude his needs from being health needs. The framework guidance states:

> NHS Continuing Healthcare may be provided by PCTs in any setting (including, but not limited to, a care home, hospice or the person's own home). Eligibility for NHS Continuing Healthcare is therefore not determined or influenced either by the setting where the care is provided or by the characteristics of the person who delivers the care.[127]

14.136 Whereas it is clear in a care home that the NHS funds the full cost and so relatively straightforward, it is more difficult to delineate what should be within the NHS continuing healthcare plan and thus funded by the NHS when a person receives care in their own home. The framework in Wales states somewhat starkly:

> Where CHC is provided in a person's own home, it means that the NHS funds all the care that is required to meet their assessed health and social

126 Berkshire Health Authority Case no E.814/00–01; Second Report for Session 2002–03 *NHS funding for long term care*, HC 399, 2003.
127 Para 47 (the Welsh framework guidance also provides that continuing care can be in any setting).

care needs to the extent that this is considered appropriate as part of the health service. This does not include the cost of accommodation, food or general household support' (para K10).

14.137   In England the practice guidance gives rather more helpful indications about what should be included in a care package for a person at home:

> Where someone is assessed as eligible for NHS continuing healthcare but chooses to live in their own home in order to enjoy a greater level of independence, the expectation in the Framework is that the PCT would remain financially responsible for all health and personal care services and associated social care services to support assessed health and social care needs and identified outcomes for that person, e.g. equipment provision, routine and incontinence laundry, daily domestic tasks such as food preparation, shopping, washing up, bed-making, support to access community facilities, etc. (including additional support needs for the individual whilst the carer has a break) (para 11.8).

14.138   The practice guidance also takes account of the needs of carers, stating:

> When a PCT decides to support a home-based package where the involvement of a family member/friend is an integral part of the care plan then the PCT should give consideration to meeting any training needs that the carer may have to carry out this role. In particular, the PCT may need to provide additional support to care for the individual whilst the carer(s) has a break from his/her caring responsibilities and will need to assure carers of the availability of this support when required. Consideration should also be given to referral for a separate carer's assessment by the relevant LA. PCTs have been allocated funding to support carers by DH and through their strategic commissioning they should consider how this funding can best be used to support carers of people eligible for NHS continuing healthcare (para 11.9).

14.139   In relation to equipment both the framework and the practice guidance remind PCT's that individuals in receipt of NHS continuing healthcare should be able to access equipment in the same way as anyone else. Where individuals require bespoke equipment necessary to meet specific assessed needs within the care plan PCTs and LHBs should make appropriate arrangements to meet these needs.[128]

14.140   There is less clarity regarding adaptations. The practice guidance in England[129] refers to the possibility of disabled facilities grants (DFGs – which for adults are means tested), but reminds PCT's that they (along with housing authorities and social services) have discretionary powers to provide additional support where appropriate. 'PCTs should consider having clear arrangements with partners setting out how the adaptation needs of those entitled to NHS continuing healthcare should be met, including referral processes and funding responsibilities.' The practice guidance goes on to remind PCTs of their responsibilities and powers to

---

128   Para 111 of the English framework guidance and para 11.4 of the practice guidance (para 9.21 Welsh framework guidance).
129   Also at para 11.4.

meet housing related needs of those patients entitled to NHS continuing healthcare.[130]

14.141 The Local Government ombudsman found maladministration in a case where a profoundly disabled woman whose care package was funded by the NHS under continuing healthcare, was confined to bed in one room of her house for two years longer than necessary. The ombudsman criticised the council's failure recognise its legal duties to the woman under Chronically Sick and Disabled Person's Act (CSDPA) 1970 s2, its failure to have any direct social work contact with the family for 15 months, and its handling of her DFG application.[131]

Social services responsibilities

14.142 Whilst there is general acceptance that the duties of social services do not end if a person is entitled to NHS continuing healthcare at home, there is some disagreement as to the extent of these continuing obligations. In the fourth edition of this book (paras 14.113–14.119) aspects of this issue were considered. This concerns the scope of the exclusionary effect of NAA 1948 s21(8), which it appears is limited to people in residential accommodation and to services provided 'in connection with' such accommodation. Although still of legal interest, it is arguable that in England this discussion is no longer pressing, since the effect of the NHS Continuing Healthcare Responsibilities Directions[132] (as discussed above) and the judgment in *R (Harrison) v Secretary of State for Health and others*[133] has been to provide (in large measure) a clean demarcation of responsibilities between the health and social services agencies. For those interested in the analysis, reference should be made to fourth edition of this book.[134]

14.143 The difficulty over ascertaining the scope and implications of the NAA 1948 s21(8) exclusion is acknowledged in both the English and Welsh frameworks (paras 19 and 3.8 respectively):

> LAs also have the function of providing services under section 29 of the National Assistance Act 1948 (which includes functions under section 2 of the Chronically Sick and Disabled Persons Act 1970). Section 29(6)(b) of the National Assistance Act 1948 only prohibits LAs from providing services under section 29 which are 'required' to be provided under the National Health Service Act 2006 so excludes only those services which must, as a matter of law, be provided under the National Health Service Act 2006.

14.144 And at para 101 the English framework guidance further advises:

130 Namely the general responsibility under NHSA 2006 s3(e), the power to make payments to housing bodies, etc under NHSA 2006 ss256 and 257, the general power to make payments to local authorities, and the wider partnership agreements under NHSA 2006 s75.
131 Complaint No 05/C/13157 Leeds City Council, 20 November 2007.
132 Directions 1, 2(6) and 2(7) in particular.
133 [2009] EWHC 574 (Admin).
134 And see also L Clements and P Bowen, 'NHS Continuing Care and independent living' (2007) 10 CCLR 343–351.

The LA is, however, not prevented from providing services, subject to the limits outlined in paragraphs 16–21. Indeed in some cases, individual arrangements may have to be reached between LAs and PCTs with respect to the provision of services. This may be particularly relevant where the person is to be cared for in a community setting.

14.145   In contrast the Welsh framework guidance (para 7.4) leaves the situation much more open (arguably too open), stating:

> As indicated earlier in this Framework, while the overall responsibility for the care provision for those individuals who are eligible for CHC will lie with the LHB there will be ways in which other agencies, such as (but not only) social services may become involved, for example:
> * Through ongoing responsibilities for meeting related needs, such as those of carers.
> * Through ongoing social work services.
> * Through agreed delegated responsibility for purchasing or providing care.
> * Through agreed delegated or shared responsibility for providing ongoing assessment and/or care management.
> * Through locally developed joint service provision.
> * Through their housing, education and leisure services responsibilities, local authorities have a corporate role in enabling people to have fulfilling lifestyles and to participate in and contribute to the wider community.
> * Through the provision of equipment.

14.146   The guidance confirms the Department of Health and the Welsh Government, view that notwithstanding a determination of entitlement to NHS continuing healthcare support, social services' duty to assess under the National Health Service and Community Care Act (NHSCCA) 1990 can still arise[135]: a view that the Department of Health has reiterated elsewhere (see para 3.79). Indeed the framework guidance states that the assessment of the local authority under section 47 will be important in identifying the individual's needs and options available to people qualifying for NHs continuing healthcare.[136]

14.147   In England the practice guidance elaborates on the responsibilities of local authorities thus:

> Whilst LAs and PCTs have some overlapping powers and responsibilities in relation to supporting individuals eligible for NHS continuing healthcare in their own home, a reasonable division of responsibility should be negotiated locally. In doing this PCTs should be mindful that their responsibility under NHS continuing healthcare involves meeting both health and social care needs based on those identified through the MDT assessment. Therefore, whilst LAs and PCTs have overlapping powers, in determining responsibilities in an individual case, PCTs should first consider whether the responsibility to meet a specific need lies with them as part of their NHS continuing healthcare responsibilities. LAs

---

135   *R v Bristol City Council ex p Penfold* (1997–98) 1 CCLR 315, QBD.
136   Framework guidance para 100 (similar wording is at para 7.5 of the Welsh framework guidance)

should be mindful of the types of support that they may provide in such situations (para 11.4).

14.148 The guidance at para 11.8 lists the types of additional care that it might be appropriate for local authorities to address such as assistance with property adaptation, support with essential parenting activities, support to access other community facilities, carer support services that may include additional general domestic support, or any appropriate service that is specifically required to enable the carer to maintain his or her caring responsibilities.

Direct payments

14.149 A difficulty for those receiving direct payments from social services is that, for them, a finding of eligibility for NHS continuing healthcare funding can result in the loss of their direct payments.

14.150 In *R (Harrison) v Secretary of State for Health and others*,[137] relying heavily on statutory construction the High Court held that there was no power in the NHS Acts to make direct payments. However, on a separate, but closely linked, question in *Gunter v SW Staffordshire PCT*[138] Collins J held that there was nothing in principle in the NHS Acts to preclude a PCT (and by implication a HB) making direct payments to an Independent User Trust (IUT) which would then use the funds to procure the person's health and social care needs, stating:

> 26. It seems to me that Parliament has deliberately given very wide powers to Primary Care Trusts to enable them to do what in any given circumstances seem to them to achieve the necessary provision of services. I have no doubt that this could involve the use of a voluntary organisation such as an IUT as the supplier. There seems to me to be no difference in principle between an IUT set up specially for a small number of persons or an individual and a nursing or other agency so far as the defendants are concerned.

14.150 The English framework guidance stresses that PCTs should use their very broad commissioning powers to try to avoid continuity problems, stating:

> PCTs should commission services using models that maximise personalisation and individual control and that reflect the individual's preferences, as far as possible. It is particularly important that this approach should be taken when an individual who was previously in receipt of an LA direct payment begins to receive NHS continuing healthcare; otherwise they may experience a loss of the control they had previously exercised over their care.
>
> PCTs and LAs should operate person-centred commissioning and procurement arrangements, so that unnecessary changes of provider or of care package do not take place purely because the responsible commissioner has changed from a PCT to an LA (or vice versa).

137 [2009] EWHC 574 (Admin).
138 [2005] EWHC 1894 (Admin), (2006) 9 CCLR 121.

The above approaches apply both to NHS continuing healthcare and to the NHS elements of a joint package.[139]

14.152 It follows that although there is the potential for a 'gap' to arise when a person transits from social services to NHS continuing healthcare responsibility, it is the responsibility of the NHS body to ensure that care planning continuity remains despite the transfer of commissioning and funding responsibility. The NHS body must have full regard to the local authority community care assessment, and in an unusual situation where it disagreed with the assessed needs – should provide cogent reasons for its disagreement.

14.153 The above-cited Framework guidance is particularly important, given that there is evidence that the NHS is more rigid in the care arrangements it is prepared to put in place for those who become eligible for NHS Continuing Healthcare funding. The Public Services Ombudsman for Wales, for example, in a 2010 report[140] noted that:

> ... this is one of a number of reports that I have issued which has high-lighted the difficulties which can be caused when the responsibility for someone's care transfers from social services to the NHS. Care provided by the NHS has traditionally been less flexible and allows patients and their carers less control than care provided and funded by social services and the ILF. I therefore intend to draw this report to the attention of the Director General of the Department for Health and Social Services.

14.154 It is regrettable that this report was published too late for consideration within the Welsh framework, which merely states at paragraph 7.17:

> The risks and benefits to the individual of a change of location or support(including funding) should be considered carefully by the MDT before any move or change is confirmed.

14.155 Section 12A of the NHS Act 2006[141] empowers PCTs to make direct payments to patients along similar lines to those paid by social services. In June 2010 the government in England announced that this power would be piloted in eight regions, with seven having power to make direct payments and/or children in transition payments.[142] The Act provides for the detail of the scheme to be spelled out in regulations, which have been published and came into effect in June 2010.[143] The full list of pilot sites was published in December 2010[144] and many of the sites are piloting the

---

139 Paras 135–144: see also para 3.204 above which covers issues such as locational need, not separating couples, and taking into account a person's preferences when packages have differential costs.

140 Public Services Ombudsman for Wales report concerning the former Cardiff Local Health Board and the former Cardiff and Vale NHS Trust ref: 200802231 and 200802232, 6 August 2010, at para 171.

141 Inserted by the Health Act 2009 s11.

142 The areas on occasions extending to more than one PCT – the areas being Doncaster PCT, Eastern and Coastal Kent PCT, Central London (Hammersmith and Fulham PCT, Kensington and Chelsea PCT and Westminster PCT) Islington PCT, Oxford PCT and Somerset PCT.

143 The National Health Service (Direct Payments) Regulations 2010 SI No 1000.

144 Available at www.dh.gov.uk/en/Healthcare/Personalhealthbudgets/DH_109426.

use of personal health budgets for NHS continuing healthcare. The pilot sites will be evaluated in the summer of 2012 (with a potential extension time of up to a maximum of five years for piloting).[145] Notwithstanding this the government is committed to:

> . . . to expanding the use of personal budgets for service users. As set out in *Equity and excellence: Liberating the NHS*, this includes continuing and developing the personal health budget pilot programme, both extending existing sites and encouraging proposals for additional sites in 2011/12. The learning from the pilot programme will inform wider rollout in 2012. Personal budgets will allow greater integration between health and social care at the level of the individual and give people more choice and control over their care.[146]

14.156 The 2010 practice guidance in England (paras 11.10–11.14) expands on personal health budgets, giving details about notional health budgets held by the PCT and personal health budgets held by a third party. At present there is no indication that Wales intends to introduce personal health budgets. NHS direct payments are further considered at para 14.149 above.

Palliative care and end of life care

14.157 Palliative care and end of life care have different meanings. The World Health Organization definition of palliative care is 'the total active care of patients whose disease is not responsive to curative treatment . . .'. The Department of Health defines the 'terminally ill' as people with an active and progressive disease for which curative treatment is not possible or not appropriate and whose death can reasonably be expected within 12 months.[147]

14.158 The Fast Track Pathway Tool (see para 14.60 above) is designed to ensure that disputes and delay are avoided concerning the care of people in need of palliative and end of life care. In this context, the Framework guidance advises (paras 87–90) that 'strict time limits that base eligibility on some specified expected length of life remaining should not be imposed' and that where the Tool has being applied for someone expected to die in the very near future, 'particular attention' should be paid to 'whether it is appropriate for the PCT to continue to take responsibility for the care package until the end of life'.

14.159 Considerable concern has been expressed about the patchy nature of PCT acceptance of responsibility for patients who require palliative care, and whose prognosis is that they are likely to die in the near future.[148] In

145 Regulation 4(a) of the NHS (Direct Payments) Regulations 2010 SI No 1000.
146 The operating framework for NHS 2011/12.
147 EL (93)14 Annex F; in contrast, for the purposes of social security legislation a person has a terminal illness if it is a 'progressive disease and his death in consequence of that disease can be reasonably be expected within 6 months' – Social Security Contributions and Benefits Act 1992 s66.
148 See eg, House of Commons Health Committee Fourth Report of Session 2003–04 on Palliative Care, Volume 1, HC 454-I, accessible at www.publications.parliament.uk/pa/cm200304/cmselect/cmhealth/454/454.pdf.

response[149] the previous government outlined plans as to how it proposed to make the option of dying at home a reality – not least by requiring PCTs to accept responsibility for 'unscheduled care' (ie 24-hour care and support at home).[150] One aspect of this commitment has been reflected in the strengthened advice given in the Framework guidance concerning such care. At para 29, for example, the guidance stresses the importance of taking into account likely (rather than present) deterioration in a condition. It then provides four examples, including:

- If an individual has a rapidly deteriorating condition that may be entering a terminal phase, he or she may need NHS continuing healthcare funding to enable their needs to be met urgently (eg to allow them to go home to die or appropriate end of life support to be put in place). This would be a primary health need because of the rate of deterioration. In all cases where an individual has such needs, consideration should be given to use of the Fast Track Pathway Tool, as set out in paragraphs 85–94.
- Even when an individual does not satisfy the criteria for use of the Fast Track Pathway Tool, one or more of the characteristics listed in paragraph 28 may well apply to those people approaching the end of their lives, and eligibility should always be considered.

14.160 The guidance requires (at para 30) that the 'principles of the national End of Life Care Strategy[151] should be reflected in all NHS continuing healthcare cases that involve individuals with an end of life condition' and highlights (paras 93–94) the importance of integrated care planning, 'person-centred commissioning and procurement' and of taking into account 'patient preferences, including those set out in advance care plans' in such cases. The 2010 practice guidance stresses that where a patient is in hospital a care package should be in place within 48 hours.[152]

Reviews

14.161 The framework guidance states that cases should be reviewed after three months following the initial eligibility decision and at least yearly thereafter.[153] The Welsh framework requires an initial review of the care plan within six weeks and that where there is an obvious deterioration in the person's circumstances a review should be carried out within two weeks.[154] When reviewing the NHS-funded nursing care (see para 13.109

---

149 Secretary of State for Health, *Government Response to House of Commons Health Committee Report on Palliative Care: Fourth Report of Session 2003–04*, Cm 6327, 2004.
150 *Palliative Care Funding Review: finding the right care and support for everyone*, July 2011 has called for access to 24/7 support in every clinical commissioning group.
151 www.dh.gov.uk/en/Publicationsandstatistics/Publications/PublicationsPolicyAnd-Guidance/ DH_086277
152 Para 5.11.
153 Framework guidance para 138.
154 Welsh framework guidance para 8.2.

above) potential eligibility for NHS continuing healthcare should always be considered.

14.162 As stated above, of considerable importance is the framework guidance requirement that:

> ... neither the NHS nor an LA should unilaterally withdraw from an existing funding arrangement without a joint reassessment of the individual, and without first consulting one another and the individual about the proposed change of arrangement. Any proposed change should be put in writing to the individual by the organisation that is proposing to make such a change. If agreement cannot be reached on the proposed change, the local disputes procedure should be invoked, and current funding arrangements should remain in place until the dispute has been resolved.[155]

14.163 The Welsh framework is unusually more expansive than the English framework on the subject of reviews, stressing as it does the need to communicate review timescales to the individual verbally and in writing; offering the individual the opportunity to re assess their own needs and be offered support in doing so; considering whether a further carer's assessment is necessary; and care providers contributing information to the review.[156]

14.164 The Department of Health seeks in the framework guidance to restrict successful claims for NHS continuing healthcare being backdated prior to October 2007, at para 142:

> Assuming that the previous decision under the old system was properly taken (ie the criteria at the time were lawful, the criteria were properly applied, there were sound reasons for the decision taken and the process was properly documented) – this should not entitle the person to be reimbursed from the date they were previously refused NHS continuing healthcare. However, if their needs have not changed, it should be considered whether their funding should be back-dated to the implementation date of the National Framework (ie October 2007).

Disputing an NHS continuing healthcare decision

14.165 Challenges to NHS continuing healthcare decisions take two possible forms:

- Challenges (including requests for reviews) by the individual or their representative in relation to the process or decisions made.
- Disputes between a PCT and a local authority regarding eligibility.

Challenges by individuals

14.166 The 2009 Responsibilities Directions detail the procedure for reviewing NHS continuing healthcare decisions. There is a similar review system in Wales described in annex 4 of the Welsh framework.

155 Framework guidance para 143 (Welsh framework guidance para 8.15).
156 Welsh framework guidance para 8.3–8.6.

14.167   Direction 4(2) provides for reviews to be instigated by 'someone acting on a person's behalf'. The English framework (para 17) advises that this role may be undertaken by a relative, carer or advocate acting on the individual's behalf. The 2010 practice guidance (para 2.3.1) additionally stresses the importance of having advocates/representatives in the review process.

14.168   One alteration that occurred with the 2009 amendments to the framework concerned individuals screened out of assessment by the checklist. They are no longer able to seek a review of this decision, but now only have recourse to the NHS complaints procedure (see para 26.6 below above).

14.169   The review process consists of two stages: local resolution, followed by a further review by a SHA panel. The framework guidance offers the following on the local resolution procedures:

> Each PCT should agree a local review process, including timescales, which is made publicly available; a copy should be sent to anybody who requests a review of a decision. The local review process may include referral of the case to another PCT for consideration or advice, in order to provide greater patient confidence in the impartiality of the decision making (para 152).

14.170   No time limits for local resolution are prescribed and it is this that often causes delay. The directions attempt to ensure a more speedy process by stating that a person may apply to a SHA for a review where he or she 'has been unable to resolve the matter through any local dispute resolution procedure where the use of such a procedure would not have caused undue delay' (direction 4 (2(b)(ii)).

14.171   Once local resolution has been exhausted the case should be referred to the SHA's independent review panel (IRP), which will consider the case and make recommendations to the PCT. The key tasks of the panel are to assess whether the PCT has correctly applied the *National Framework for NHS Continuing Healthcare or NHS funded nursing care*, and has followed the processes set out in the guidance.[157]

14.172   The framework guidance (at paras 154 et seq) gives key principles that should be followed by the IRP regarding evidence gathering, involvement of the individual/carer and giving them opportunity to input at all stages, recording of the panel and clear and evidence based written decisions. Annex E of the framework guidance outlines the purpose and scope of the review panel. The Welsh framework contains similar guidance.

14.173   The review procedure does not apply if individuals or their families wish to challenge the content of the eligibility criteria, the type or location of any NHS funded care, the content of any alternative package or their treatment by any of the services they are receiving. This should be dealt with through the usual NHS complaints procedure (see para 26.6 below.)

14.174   Individuals must be informed of their right to use the review procedure and advocates should be provided where this supports the

---

157   Framework guidance para 148.

individual through the review process. There should be a designated individual in each SHA to maintain the review procedure, and each SHA must identify clear time frames for the process, which should be made explicit especially to individuals and carers.[158] In contrast the Welsh framework stipulates each LHB should aim to ensure that the review procedure is completed within two weeks of the request being received (once any action to resolve the case informally has been completed).[159]

14.175   The chair of the IRP should be selected by open recruitment. The appointment of representatives of PCTs and local councils will be on the basis of nomination of those organisations. Panels are open for key parties to put their views in writing or to attend. An individual may have a representative to speak on his or her behalf if he or she chooses. If the IRP needs independent clinical advice such arrangements should avoid any obvious conflict of interest between the individual clinicians giving the advice and the organisation from which the individual has been receiving care. If a SHA decides in very exceptional circumstances to reject an IRP recommendation, it should put in writing to the individual and the chairman of the panel its reasons for so doing. In all cases the SHA must communicate in writing to the individual the outcome of the review with reasons.

14.176   If the individual is still aggrieved the case should be referred to the Health Service Ombudsman in England or the Public Services ombudsman, in Wales.

Funding pending a review

14.177 The 2009 English guidance instituted a major change in what happens whilst a case is being reviewed. All previous guidance had stipulated that no existing package of care should be withdrawn pending a review. The latest guidance states in annex E paragragh 12:

> No individual should be left without appropriate support while they await the outcome of the review. The eligibility decision that has been made is effective while the independent review is awaited . . . Further guidance on responsibilities whilst awaiting the outcome of a request for an independent review will be issued later in 2009.

14.178 This guidance, issued as the Refunds Guidance in 2010, reiterates the position that when 'a PCT has made a decision on NHS CHC eligibility, that decision remains in effect until the PCT revises the decision' (para 14). If as a result of the review the decision is revised PCTs are advised that they:

---

158   This aspect of the guidance is different from the 2001 guidance regarding reviews which stated: '[e]ach Health authority should aim to ensure that the review procedure is completed within two week of the request being received. This period starts once any action to resolve the case informally has been completed, and should be extended only in exceptional circumstances.' The 2009 Responsibilities Directions merely state at directkion 4(7) that notice about the decision must be given as soon as reasonably practicable.

159   Welsh framework guidance annex 5 para A 5.5.

... should consider making an ex-gratia payment to the individual. . . . this
is a recognition that the original decision, or the process leading up to
the decision, was incorrect. An ex-gratia payment would be to remedy any
injustice or hardship suffered by the individual as a result of the incorrect
decision, and would be made using the PCT's powers under section 2(1)(b)
and paragraph 15(1) of Schedule 3 to the 2006 Act (para 17).

14.179   Where a local authority has funded an individual who is challenging the
decision of the PCT the advice is that the PCT should consider refunding
the local authority the costs of the care package. This should be based on
the gross care package costs that the LA has incurred until the date that
the revised decision comes into effect. The PCT could use its powers
under section 256 of the 2006 Act to make such payments. The local
authority should refund any financial contributions made to it by the
individual in the light of the fact that it has been refunded on a gross
basis.[160] See para 14.189 below, regarding offering deferred payments
whilst an NHS continuing healthcare decision is being challenged.

14.180   The Welsh framework in contrast stipulates that 'While the review
procedure is being conducted any existing care package, whether hospital
care or community health services, should not be withdrawn until the
outcome of the review is known (annex 5 para A 5.12).

Disputes between PCTs and social services

14.181   *R (St Helen's BC) v Manchester PCT and another*[161] concerned a disputed
decision in 2006 as to entitlement to NHS continuing healthcare funding.
The Court of Appeal held that the decision as to who was entitled to NHS
continuing healthcare funding at that time rested with the PCT/LHB. The
court considered that the PCT was the primary decision maker when it
came to determining whether a person has a primary healthcare need
and reached this conclusion on the basis that the PCT had followed a
highly structured statutory process in compliance with the relevant directions (the Continuing Care (National Health Service Responsibilities)
Directions 2004) and that was effectively the end of the matter. May LJ
stated (para 37), however, that the judgment did not necessarily have any
bearing on the scheme created by the National Framework (which did not
apply when the dispute arose). Since that time the 2004 Directions have
been repealed and replaced by the NHS Continuing Healthcare
(Responsibilities) Directions 2009, direction 3(4) of which requires local
authorities and PCTs to have a dispute resolution procedure as to any
disagreement over eligibility for NHS continuing healthcare. In relation
to this the 2009 Framework (at para 161) states that: 'PCTs and LAs in
each local area should agree a local disputes resolution process to resolve
cases where there is a dispute between NHS bodies, or between an LA and
a PCT, about eligibility for NHS continuing healthcare and/or about the
apportionment of funding in joint funded care/support packages.' It

160 Refunds Guidance paras 15 and 16.
161 [2008] EWCA Civ 931, (2008) 11 CCLR 774.

follows that, provided the PCT or the local authority invoke their local disputes process in a timely way, then this is the process by which disputes about such matters are now resolved.

14.182 The requirement that inter-authority dispute resolution processes be developed/invoked is amplified in the Framework at para 161, in the following terms:

> . . . Disputes should not delay the provision of the care package, and the protocol should make clear how funding will be provided pending resolution of the dispute. Where disputes relate to LAs and PCTs in different geographical areas, the relevant LA and PCT should agree a dispute resolution process to ensure resolution in a robust and timely manner. This should include agreement on how funding will be provided during the dispute, and arrangements for reimbursement to the agencies involved once the dispute is resolved.[162]

14.183 The guidance further suggests (para 161) that such disputes protocols could operate in a similar way the panels established under the Community Care (Delayed Discharges etc) Act 2003.

14.184 The refunds guidance stresses the needs for the process to be more than simply a form of further discussion, but should include 'an identified mechanism for final resolution, such as referring the case to another PCT and LA and agreeing to accept their recommendation' (para 18).

Reviews of cases prior to the National Framework

14.185 In any case where a person wishes to have a review of a NHS continuing healthcare decision made in England prior to 1 October 2007 (when the National Framework was introduced) or in Wales 16 August 2010, it will be necessary to be aware of the guidance and the eligibility criteria that applied at the time the decision was made. In England this will be the 2001 guidance along with the particular policy of the NHS body concerned and advice issued in 2006 following the *Grogan* judgment,[163] and in Wales guidance issued in 2004, 2006 and 2007.[164] Details of this guidance can be found in the fourth edition of this book.

14.186 The Department of Health issued a letter in 2007[165] aiming to close requests for reviews of eligibility decisions made before April 2004 or which involve a period of time falling mainly before April 2004 not previously challenged. Such cases could be raised until 30 November 2007. Unless there are exceptional circumstances new cases involving decisions made prior to April 2004 will be returned with an explanation of why they cannot be examined. In Wales a similar notification was issued in July

---

162 The Welsh framework guidance contains the same wording at para 11.2.
163 HSC2001/15 and LAC2001(18).
164 WHC (2004)54 and NAFWC 41/2004 (Guidance), NAFWC 41a/2004 (CHC Framework), WHC (2006)046 and NAFWC 32/2006, WHC (2007)083.
165 Closing the continuing care retrospective review process. Dear colleague letter, 31 July 2007.

2009 (and effect in December 2009) in relation to claims arising wholly before April 2003.[166]

Redress

14.187   The protracted nature of many of the reviews that have been undertaken since 2003 and the backdating of NHS continuing healthcare responsibilities has raised the issue about the financial losses that have been suffered by complainants. Even in more recent cases since the introduction of the National Framework it can take a considerable period to resolve cases that are appealed to the Health Service Ombudsman.

14.188   In 2007 a special report was issued by the Parliamentary Ombudsman and the Health Service Ombudsman. The Parliamentary Ombudsman found that there was maladministration in the Department of Health's decision making and communication of its approach to recompense for wrongly denied continuing care funding. The department had advised the NHS to pay recompense based on the principle of restitution for only those monies paid out in care fees. This approach discouraged PCTs from considering full redress, including, for example, redress for claimed financial loss for premature sale of a property or inconvenience and distress that individuals had suffered in making unnecessary difficult decisions about how to fund care.

14.189   In the same report the Health Service Ombudsman found no maladministration on the part of an NHS trust, in a case where a house had been sold when it need not have been if the NHS continuing healthcare decision had been correctly made, since this was due to the Department of Health's 'unclear and inconsistent' guidance. In this case the local government ombudsman had already considered the complaint that no deferred payment (see para 8.8.1 above) had been offered to the family – since this would have avoided the necessity of selling the property pending the outcome of the NHS challenge.[167] As a result of the 2007 special report the Department of Health issued guidance to remind PCTs of their responsibilities concerning maladministration and redress; to remind them that they are empowered to make ex gratia payments where appropriate; to advise them how to calculate interest payments for redress; and to remind them about the powers of local authorities regarding deferred payment agreements.[168]

14.190   The court has also scrutinised the question of interest and found that the award of interest should be 'tailor made to each case'.[169] It agreed that no account should be taken of payments made to the claimant by third parties (such as the benefits paid by the Department for Work and Pensions) in deciding the rate of interest payable. The court changed its provisional decision that the applicant should receive interest at the retail

---

166   Issued on 30 July 2009.
167   *Retrospective Continuing Care Funding and Redress*, February 2007.
168   Department of Health (2007) *NHS Continuing Healthcare; Continuing Care Redress*.
169   *R v Kemp and Denbighshire Health Board* [2006] EWHC 1339 (Admin).

price index rate and ordered that he should receive interest at the (higher) court rate.

14.191   In England the Refunds guidance refers to Treasury guidance 'Managing Public Money'.[170] This sets out that, where public services organisations have caused injustice or hardship, they should consider providing remedies that, as far as reasonably possible, restore the wronged party to the position that they would have been in, had matters been carried out correctly.[171]

Impact on social security benefits

14.192 The Department for Work and Pensions and Department of Health guidance issued guidance in 2004[172] concerning the impact on social security benefits of a decision that a person is eligible for NHS continuing healthcare support. In care homes residents will generally be treated as hospital inpatients for benefit purposes, from the date the PCT made a formal entitlement decision – provided the care home concerned is a 'similar institution to a hospital' – and payments made to refund patients for the period during which they were wrongly charged for their care do not retrospectively turn these claimants into hospital inpatients for that period (ie provided the resident notifies the Department for Work and Pensions of the funding, there should be no overpayment).

14.193   As a consequence of changes to the rules governing entitlement to benefits while a hospital in-patient there are fewer problems about what happens to benefits if NHS continuing healthcare payments are made.

14.194   For people who live at home, benefits are not affected by NHS continuing care payments. However, any Independent Living Fund payment will stop.

Patients covered by NHS continuing healthcare guidance

14.195 The framework guidance in both England and Wales applies only to adults and states that '[t]he actual services provided as part of that package should be seen in the wider context of best practice and services development for each client group'.[173]

Children

14.196 In relation to children the framework guidance was published prior to the publication in March 2010 of the National Framework for Children and

---

170 HM Treasury (2009) *Managing Public Money*.
171 Ibid. annex 4 at para 4.14.4.
172 The Department for Work and Pensions guidance was a Decision Makers Guide memo 08/04 but no longer appears on the website.
173 Framework guidance para 8.

Young People's Continuing Care. In Wales the framework guidance states that a separate policy for those less than 18 years of age will be issued later.[174] At the time of writing (September 2011) no guidance has been produced on children in Wales.

14.197   In *R (T, D and B) v Haringey LBC*[175] the High Court indicated that it considered the *Coughlan* principles applied to children as to adults. The *Haringey* case was unusual in that the applicant was arguing that the child was not the responsibility of the NHS and accordingly there was limited argument on the question. It is at least arguable that social services have no power whatsoever to fund any nursing home provision for disabled children. It appears that in no legislation concerning local authority responsibilities for children are they permitted to fund any nursing care. This is different for adults (as the court noted in *Coughlan*) since NAA 1948 s26(1B) did make limited reference to nursing care (now in NAA 1948 s26(1A) and (1C)).

14.198   Space does not permit an extensive discussion of the framework for children which is materially different from that of adults.[176] The adult framework at para 119 (para 9.7 Welsh Framework) states that: 'the legislation and the respective responsibilities of the NHS, social care and other services are different in child and adult services. The term 'continuing care' also has different meanings in child and adult services.' Unfortunately the children's framework in England pays little attention to the legal complexities of the differences between the Children Act 1989 and the NAA 1948, and fails to acknowledge, that the NHS Acts make no distinction as to age – so that, as a matter of law, the responsibilities of the NHS are arguably the same as for adults.

14.199   Although the children's framework follows some of the adult framework, namely the use of a DST with similar care domains to adults, the main difference is within the definition in section 1.1.

> A continuing care package will be required when a child or young person has needs arising from disability, accident or illness that cannot be met by existing universal or specialist services alone . . .
>
> Continuing care is organised differently for children and young people than for adults. Continuing care for adults is governed by the National Framework for NHS Continuing Healthcare and NHS-funded Nursing Care. That framework gives guidance on putting in place complete packages of care where an adult has been assessed as having a primary health need. It means that the provision of all their resulting care needs, whether at home or in a care home, is the responsibility of the NHS.
>
> However, childhood and youth is a period of rapidly changing physical, intellectual and emotional maturation alongside social and educational development. All children of compulsory school age (5 to 16) should receive suitable education, either by regular attendance at school or

---

174   Welsh framework guidance Para 9.6.
175   [2005] EWHC 2235 (Admin), (2006) 9 CCLR 58.
176   See, however, S Broach, L Clements and J Read, *Disabled Children: a legal handbook*, Legal Action Group, 2010.

through other arrangements. There may also be social care needs. Most care for children and young people is provided by families at home, and maintaining relationships between the child or young person, their family and other carers, and professionals, is a particularly important aspect.

This means that a wider range of agencies is likely to be involved in the case of a child or young person with continuing care needs than in the case of an adult. Children and young people's continuing care needs are best addressed holistically by all the agencies that are involved in providing them with public services or care: predominantly health, social care and education. It is likely that a continuing care package will include a range of services commissioned by PCTs, local authority children's services and sometimes others.

14.200   It appears therefore that if a child is eligible for continuing care, the PCT will be responsible for leading the commissioning process, and involving other agencies, but not wholly funding the package. All partners are responsible for funding their own contributions to the continuing care package in line with their statutory functions.[177] It is unclear how this new framework will assist in cases where there is a dispute (such as in the *Haringey* case) about whether services fall within the scope of social services, or of the NHS.

14.201   The development of a distinct framework for children has the potential to exacerbate the service provision difficulties faced by disabled children on their transition into adulthood. The framework guidance addresses this issue at paras 118 to 132 (paras 9.6–9.13 of the Welsh guidance which has virtually identical wording in relation to LHBs). The main points are:

- PCTs should ensure that adult NHS continuing healthcare is appropriately represented at all transition planning meetings to do with individual young people whose needs suggest that there may be potential eligibility.
- PCTs should be notified by children's continuing care teams when the child reaches 14 years, with a formal referral for screening at 16 years.
- At the age of 17, eligibility for adult NHS continuing healthcare should be determined in principle by the relevant PCT using the adult framework, so that, wherever applicable, effective packages of care can be commissioned in time for the individual's 18th birthday.
- Where a young person receives support via a placement outside the PCT's area, it is important, at an early stage in the transition planning process, to establish who the responsible commissioner presently is, and whether this could potentially change. A dispute or lack of clarity over commissioner responsibilities must not result in a lack of appropriate input into the transition process.
- The key aim is to ensure that a consistent package of support is provided during the years before and after the transition to adulthood. The nature of the package may change because the young person's needs or circumstances change. However, it should not change simply

177   Para 15 Children's framework.

because of the move from children's to adult services or because of a switch in the organisation with commissioning or funding responsibilities. Where change is necessary, it should be carried out in a phased manner, in full consultation with the young person. No services or funding should be withdrawn unless a full assessment has been carried out of the need for adult health and social care services, including the funding responsibilities.

Learning disability services and NHS continuing healthcare

14.202   Circular guidance HSG (92)43 and LAC (92)17 has referred to the historically anomalous position of people with learning difficulties; essentially that although for many their needs are primarily social, historically the NHS has provided for people with learning difficulties and therefore the NHS has received the funding for the continuing care needs of such people. Thus the 1992 guidance states that:

> . . . it is well recognised that many people (ie people with learning difficulties) traditionally cared for in long-stay hospitals are predominantly in need of social care, and should be cared for in the community. In order to support in the community ex long-stay patients and people who might in earlier times have been cared for in long-stay hospitals, health finance may be spent on social services rather than on health services.

14.203   Until the large scale closure of the large NHS hospitals specifically catering for people with learning disabilities, one-fifth of people with severe or profound learning disabilities received their care services from the NHS.[178] The 1992 guidance advocated, therefore, not only that the NHS transfer monies to social services for the present support of such persons (and their successors[179]) but also that it should develop new and innovative services to meet the social (as opposed to health) needs of such persons. The 2006 white paper *Our Health, Our Care, Our Say*[180] and the 2007 *Valuing People Now* strategy[181] sought to close NHS campuses for people with learning disabilities and, as a result, by September 2010 only 534 remained in such settings.[182]

14.204   The *Valuing People Now* 2009 programme,[183] transferred responsibility for the funding and commissioning of social care for adults with learning disabilities from the NHS to local government. The change in funding and commissioning responsibility took effect from April 2009. It was agreed that, for the remaining years of the current spending review, 2009–10 and 2010–11, transfers would be carried out locally (ie based on the

---

178   LAC (92)15.
179   HSG (92)43: LAC (92)17.
180   Department of Health (2006) *Our Health, Our Care, Our Say,* Cm 6737, para 4.91.
181   Department of Health (2007) *Valuing People Now: From progress to transformation:* section 8.
182   Department of Health (2010) *Valuing People Now: summary report.*
183   Department of Health (2009) *Valuing People Now: a new three-year strategy for people with learning disabilities.*

actual local spend) and reported to the Department of Health. From 2011–12 this funding will be transferred centrally from the NHS budget to social care and issued to councils as part of a Department of Health specific grant, the Learning Disability and Health Reform Grant. The redistribution will not occur, however, where the health and social services bodies have entered into NHSA 2006 s75 pooled budget arrangements (to the extent of those arrangements) – see para 13.127 above.

14.205 Para 110 of the Framework guidance advises that individuals for whom a dowry or other payment has been made by a health body to a local authority to facilitate their transfer out of long-stay NHS care are not automatically to be assumed as eligible for NHS continuing healthcare. However, it also notes that where the care needs of such person's change:

> it will be important for the PCT to first check whether there is clarity in such agreements on whether or not they cover responsibilities to meet such needs. If the additional needs fall outside the agreement, PCTs must consider their responsibilities to meet them, in terms both of a PCT's general responsibilities and potential eligibility for NHS continuing healthcare. PCTs should also have arrangements in place for the transfer to the relevant LA of commissioning and funding responsibilities for social care services for people with learning disabilities.

14.206 Many people with learning disabilities will still qualify directly for NHS continuing healthcare funding on the general ground that as a consequence of their healthcare needs, the care they require is neither incidental or ancillary to the provision of social services nor of a nature such that an authority whose primary responsibility is to provide social services can be expected to provide. A learning disability comes within the definition of 'illness' in both NHSA 2006 (s275(1)) and the NHS(W)A 2006 (s206(1)) and where, for example, this is characterised by challenging behaviour of a severity or frequency or unpredictability that presents an immediate and serious risk to self or others, then, as the NHS Ombudsman determined in the *Pointon* complaint[184] (and the DST notes in its 'behavioural domain), then eligibility for NHS continuing healthcare funding could be expected. Such an expectation will also arise where the behaviour in question is no longer manifest, because the person is in a well managed regime – but would re-present, if that regime were withdrawn (see para 14.151 above).

14.207 In contrast the Welsh framework suggests that: 'Challenging behaviour may be caused by a number of factors including biological, social, environmental, and psychological or as a means of communication. Therefore, the task of meeting the needs of people with complex behavioural needs may need to be owned by a wide variety of agencies, services and professionals' (para 9.18).

---

184 Case no E.22/02/02–03 Funding for Long Term Care (the *Pointon* case) where the Health Service Ombudsman emphasised that the assessment must take into account a person's psychological problems and the special skills it takes to care for such people, even if the care is not in fact provided by healthcare staff – see para 14.27.

Mental health services and NHS continuing healthcare

14.208   The current joint[185] nature of the duty under MHA 1983 s 117 (see para 20.31 below) has created tensions, since it is arguable that a patient could fall within the entitlement criteria for both regimes. To a large extent it is probably immaterial to most individuals as in either case the care will be free, but the question is of considerable budgetary relevance to health and social services bodies since section 117 services are a joint responsibility. The framework guidance seems to maintain a studied naivety to this point, stating merely that because section 117 services are free and constitute a free standing duty 'it is not therefore necessary to assess eligibility for NHS Continuing Healthcare if all the services in question are to be provided as after-care under section 117'.[186] It goes on to state:

> However, a person in receipt of after-care services under section 117 may also have needs for continuing care that are not related to their mental disorder and that may not fall within the scope of section 117. An obvious example would be a person who was already receiving continuing care in relation to physical health problems before they were detained under the 1983 Act and whose physical health problems remain on discharge. Where such needs exist, it may be necessary to carry out an assessment for NHS continuing healthcare that looks at whether the individual has a primary health need on the basis of the needs arising from their physical problems. Any mental health after-care needs that fall within section 117 responsibilities would not be taken into account in considering NHS continuing healthcare eligibility in such circumstances.[187]

14.209   The last sentence of the above advice is arguably too simplistic as it does not consider occasions where there is a complex interplay between the mental health of the person and their physical needs. To ignore the mental health needs of the individual just because he or she falls under section 117 would seem to skew the normal decision making in establishing a primary health need in such cases.

14.210   It is clearly of importance that the health and social services bodies have a protocol as to how they determine their respective contributions to such packages – and it could be that a sensible approach would be that the division could logically be determined by social services taking responsibility for those individuals who were primarily in need of social support and the NHS taking responsibility for those whose primary need was for healthcare – ie the same as under the NHS continuing healthcare provisions.[188] The practice guidance suggests:

---

185   See para 20.33 below for the proposed changes to Mental Health Act 1983 s117 within the Health and Social Care bill.

186   Framework guidance para 115 (para 9.4 of the Welsh framework guidance).

187   Framework guidance para 116 (similar wording can be found at para 9.4 in the Welsh framework guidance).

188   An approach suggested in the guidance issued by the Association of Directors of Adult Social Services (ADASS) and the Local Government Association (2007) *Commentary and Advice for Local Authorities on The National Framework for NHS Continuing Healthcare and NHS-funded Nursing Care* at para 6a.

It is preferable for a PCT to have separate budgets for funding section 117 and NHS continuing healthcare. Where they are funded from the same budget they still continue to be distinct and separate entitlements (para 4.13).

14.211 The inter-relationship between section 117 services and NHS continuing healthcare is considered further at para 20.47 below.

Reforms that could affect NHS continuing healthcare

14.212 The current government has made no indications that it will reform the current system of NHS continuing healthcare. This was clarified in a written answer 17 May 2011.

It is anticipated that there will be no changes to the sections of the framework covering the eligibility criteria for continuing healthcare. However, the sections covering the statutory powers of primary care trusts and strategic health authorities will be rewritten to reflect the proposed reforms which will move these powers to general practitioner consortia and the NHS Commissioning Board respectively.[189]

14.213 The latter point reflects the provisions in the Health and Social Care Bill to abolish PCTs and Strategic Health Authorities, which are to be replaced by clinical commissioning groups (previously GP consortia) and the NHS Commissioning Board. The presumption is that clinical commissioning groups will take the responsibilities of the current PCTs and will be the decision-making body for NHS continuing healthcare, and that the NHS Commissioning Board (which is likely to have a regional presence) will take on the responsibilities for the independent reviews.

14.214 The Law Commission when looking at adult social care reform has made several recommendations in relation to NHS continuing health-care, namely:

- the existing prohibitions on the provision of healthcare should be retained[190] but the wording should be reviewed and where appropriate simplified;
- where possible NHS guidance and directions should always distinguish between legal powers and duties;
- the prohibition should include a clear statement to the effect that the range of powers and duties given to the NHS are those set out in regulations and guidance issued under the NHS Acts 2006;
- the quantity and quality test should be set out in statute law;
- the secretary of state and Welsh ministers should be given a power to establish in regulations an eligibility framework and what combination of needs would make a person eligible for NHS continuing healthcare.[191]

---

189 House of Commons Written Answers 17 May 2011.
190 See eg the prohibitions NAA 1948 s21(8) and s29(6).
191 Law Commission *Adult Social Care* Law Com no 326, Recommendation 51.

CHAPTER 15

Housing and community care

continued

Introduction

15.1   Appropriate housing has been described as 'the basic requirement – the foundation – of community care'.[1] Such a view recognises not merely the increased acknowledgment of the right to 'independent living' (see para 4.65 above) but also the practical everyday benefits that suitable housing can provide for people in need of community care services. As the Audit Commission has noted:[2]

> . . . it is not simply the provision of a roof over people's heads that makes housing's contribution so important, it is the personal support to help vulnerable people cope with everyday living – for example, negotiating the complexities of rent payments or resolving problems with water, gas and electricity suppliers – that makes the difference between life in the community and institutionalisation.[3]

15.2   This chapter is concerned with the general obligations on housing authorities in relation to matters that impinge upon community care support services – including those that may arise in eviction proceedings; in relation to the provision of disabled facilities grants and accommodation for homeless people who have community care needs. It additionally considers the discreet questions of services provided under the 'Supporting People' and the 'Adult Placement' regulatory regimes, and supported living arrangements in general which are aimed at helping people have more choice in their accommodation arrangements.

15.3   Since appropriate accommodation is a fundamental theme in relation to almost all community care services, many aspects of the housing contribution to community care are also considered elsewhere in this book, most notably the provision of residential care accommodation (which may comprise nothing more than a simple tenancy), which is considered at para 7.45 above and home adaptations under the Chronically Sick and Disabled Persons Act (CSDPA) 1970 s2(1)(e) are considered at para 9.105 above.

Responsibilities of housing authorities

15.4   Housing authorities, in meeting their responsibilities under Housing Act (HA) 1985 s8 (to consider housing conditions and provision in their area), are required, by CSDPA 1970 s3, to have specific regard to the special

---

1   P Arnold et al, *Community Care: the housing dimension,* Joseph Rowntree Foundation, 1993; see also P Arnold and D Page, *Housing and Community Care,* University of Humberside, 1992 and *Think Local, Act Personal,* 2011 at www.thinklocalactpersonal.org.uk/_library/Resources/Personalisation/TLAP/THINK_LOCAL_ACT_PERSONAL_5_4_11.pdf
2   Audit Commission (1998) *Home Alone: the housing aspects of community care,* para 7.
3   A survey of Directors of Adult Services revealed that over half of those responding had taken on responsibility for housing services, and suggests that the importance of housing in the well-being of a community is now being recognised more clearly (*Community Care,* 4 April 2007).

needs of chronically sick and disabled persons. In this respect 2006 good practice guidance[4] issued to housing authorities stresses the importance of aspiring 'for the social inclusion of all their citizens' and the general need 'to design in access and accept a corporate responsibility for countering disabling environments'. The promotion of independent living is clearly as much a goal for housing authorities as it is for social services authorities (see para 4.65 above).

15.5   Housing authorities must, in the framing of their allocation schemes – which determine who is to have priority for housing – give reasonable preference to people who need to move on medical or welfare grounds including grounds relating to a disability.[5] In *R (Ireneschild) v Lambeth LBC*[6] the High Court considered the relationship between a housing needs assessment undertaken by the housing department (to ascertain the applicant's priority for rehousing) and a community care assessment considering that person's need for accommodation under National Assistance Act (NAA) 1948 s21. In the opinion of Lloyd Jones J the two assessments had 'entirely different' foci. The fact that the housing assessment indicated an urgent need for rehousing did not mean that section 21 accommodation had to be provided. However, the housing needs assessment was a material (and possibly a 'compelling') consideration to be taken into account in the community care assessment. This finding was approved by the Court of Appeal.

Eviction

15.6   The community care needs of disadvantaged people will not infrequently come to the notice of the courts by way of possession proceedings founded upon their failure to pay rent or their behaviour. In such cases the courts have power to adjourn to enable an urgent assessment of needs to be carried out. Such an assessment will inevitably involve the social services department liaising with the housing authority under National Health Service and Community Care Act (NHSCCA) 1990 s47(3) (see para 3.125 above). The courts have wide powers to adjourn possession proceedings in secure and assured tenancy cases;[7] however, in assured shorthold cases judges will generally need to rely on the power they have to adjourn under the Civil Procedure Rules (CPR) 3.1 and 3. 2 in furtherance of the over-riding objective in CPR 1.1 to enable the court to deal with the case 'justly'. In *Manchester City Council v Pinnock*[8] the Supreme court accepted that in all possession proceedings there was scope for the courts

---

4   *Delivering housing adaptations for disabled people: a good practice guide,* June 2006, issued by the Department for Communities and Local Government in conjunction with the Departments for Education and Skills and for Health.
5   HA 1996 s167(2)(d) as amended by HA 2004 s223; see also Housing Act 2004 (Commencement No 2) (England) Order 2005 SI No 1120.
6   [2006] EWHC 2354 (Admin), (2006) 9 CCLR 686.
7   HA 1985 s85 and HA 1988 s9.
8   [2010] UKSC 45, [2011] 1 All ER 285.

to consider the proportionality of such action, for the purposes of Article 8 European Convention on Human Rights, and that (para 64):

> ... proportionality is more likely to be a relevant issue 'in respect of occupants who are vulnerable as a result of mental illness, physical or learning disability, poor health or frailty', and that 'the issue may also require the local authority to explain why they are not securing alternative accommodation in such cases'.

15.7   *Barber v Croydon LBC*[9] concerned a decision by the council to seek possession proceedings against a person with learning disabilities and a personality disorder who, in an isolated incident, swore, kicked and spat at a caretaker. The Court of Appeal held that this was a decision that no local authority could reasonably have taken, not least because it had failed to consult the specialist agencies, consider alternatives and pay proper regard to an expert report that the behaviour was a manifestation of the tenant's mental disorder. The local government ombudsman has come to similar conclusions in possession proceedings involving disabled people.[10]

15.8   A decision to commence possession proceedings will engage the public sector equality duty[11] (see para 2.32 above) and any question as to the tenant's mental capacity to litigate must be resolved before the possession proceedings hearing takes place.[12]

15.9   Section 15 of the Equality Act 2010 makes it discriminatory if the discriminator:

- treats the person unfavourably because of something arising 'in consequence of' his or her disability; and
- cannot show that the treatment is 'a proportionate means of achieving a legitimate aim'.

15.10   It follows that if action is being taken against a tenant because of his or her actions (or inactions) and these can reasonably be said to arise in consequence of his or her disability (which is known to the person taking the action) – then the onus will be on that person to show that the action is 'a proportionate means of achieving a legitimate aim'. In doing this it will generally be necessary to show that the person taking the action: (1) has adopted as flexible a policy as is reasonable in the situation; (2) has attempted to help the tenant modify his or her behaviour – or the consequences of that behaviour; and (3) that the action is the least discriminatory way of achieving the legitimate aim.

---

9   [2010] EWCA Civ 51, (2010) *Times*, 24 March; see also *Carmarthenshire County Council v Lewis* [2010] EWCA Civ 1567.

10   See eg complaint no 05/C/04684 against Kirklees MC, 28 February 2007 where a failure to make proper enquiries before taking legal action was held to constitute maladministration and Complaint no 03/A/14278 against Southend-on-Sea BC, 27 June 2005 where the authority instituted possession proceedings based on arrears that had arisen due to the authority's failure to take into account the claimant's mental illness when processing his housing benefit claims.

11   *Barnsley MBC v Norton* [2011] EWCA Civ 834.

12   *Carmarthenshire County Council v Lewis* [2010] EWCA Civ 1567.

15.11   Where a person is evicted because of his or her disability related conduct, the social services authority will have a duty to that person under the
community care legislation. However, in *R v Kensington and Chelsea RLBC
ex p Kujtim*[13] the Court of Appeal held that the duty to provide accommodation under NAA 1948 s21 can be treated as discharged if the applicant 'either unreasonably refuses to accept the accommodation provided
or if, following its provision, by his conduct he manifests a persistent and
unequivocal refusal to observe the reasonable requirements of the local
authority in relation to the occupation of such accommodation' (see para
4.54 above).

Collaboration and joint working

15.12   Housing and social services authorities are under a variety of statutory
duties to co-operate in the community care planning and assessment
processes – most obviously under NHSCCA 1990 s47(3) (see para 3.125
above[14]). The duty to co-operate has been reinforced by joint guidance
issued by the Department of Health and the Department of Environment
in 1992,[15] which includes the following advice:

> 16. Social services authorities and housing should construct an individual's
> care plan with the objective of preserving or restoring non-institutional
> living as far as possible, and of securing the most appropriate and cost-
> effective package of care, housing and other services that meets the
> person's future needs. For some people the most appropriate package of
> care will be in a nursing or residential home, but in many cases this will be
> achieved by bringing in domiciliary support and making any necessary
> adaptations to the individual's existing home. The balance between these
> should be considered carefully. For example, where expensive or disruptive
> adaptations or improvements are being considered it may be more cost-
> effective to provide domiciliary care and support together with more minor
> works. In other cases adaptations or improvements (eg to help people
> bathe or cook by themselves) may reduce or obviate the need for
> domiciliary support . . .
>
> 19. The new proposals will require effective relationships to be established
> and built upon between all parties involved. The aim should be to provide a
> seamless service for clients, with a mutual recognition of all authorities'
> responsibilities. This will require all the relevant agencies, including
> housing, health and social services authorities, to put an emphasis on
> discussion, understanding and agreement in the planning of services,
> rather than unilateral decision making. Joint working will be important to

13 [1999] 4 All ER 161, (1999) 2 CCLR 340, CA at 354I.
14 As noted at para 3.130 above, in *R (Buckinghamshire CC) v Kingston upon Thames*
    [2011] EWCA Civ 457, (2011) 14 CCLR 425 the Court of Appeal held that s47(3) did
    not impose either a common law duty of fairness nor any duty arising under requiring
    notification, consultation or an invitation to participate in the assessment, although in
    the particular case it was held that the social services authority should have sought
    confirmation from the housing authority concerning housing benefit eligibility.
15 *Housing and Community Care* LAC (92)12/DOE Circular 10/92.

maximise the use of existing resources. Administrative systems will need to be developed, perhaps including joint planning structures, in order to monitor and plan effective use of services. Authorities may wish to set up pilot projects. In taking forward their role in community care, housing authorities in particular should have regard to the points made in the annex to this circular [which amongst other things expands upon what 'joint working' is likely to entail].

15.13 A duty on housing authorities to co-operate with social services is mirrored by the duty under HA 1996 s213(1) which requires social services to co-operate to the extent that 'is reasonable in the circumstances' where its assistance is sought by a housing authority in relation to the discharge of its duties under the 1996 Act.

15.14 Similar advice is given in relation to the process of housing renewal, with central government guidance[16] to local authorities stressing the need for integrated working with all agencies:[17]

> 2.11. Housing, Social Service Departments and the National Health Service (NHS) are delivering increasingly integrated services for vulnerable households that recognise the benefits of enabling people to stay in their own homes wherever possible. Poor housing can be a barrier for older and disabled people, contributing to immobility, social exclusion, ill health and depression. Renewal policies can contribute by facilitating hospital discharge and preventing hospitalisation, and by enabling people to live in secure, safe, well-maintained, warm and suitable housing.

Joint working

15.15 Homelessness Act 2002 s3 requires all housing authorities to have a homelessness strategy that seeks to prevent homelessness, to secure that sufficient accommodation is available for people in their district who are or may become homeless, and that there is satisfactory provision of support for people who are or are at risk of homelessness. The social services authority must assist with the development of these strategies and the English 2006 Homelessness Code of Guidance for Local Authorities[18] stresses the need for housing authorities to:

> 8. . . . ensure that all organisations, within all sectors, whose work can help to prevent homelessness and/or meet the needs of homeless people in their district are involved in the strategy. This will need to include not just

---

16 ODPM circular 05/2003 *Housing Renewal*.

17 As a result of the Regulatory Reform (Housing Assistance) (England and Wales) Order 2002 SI No 1860 (RRO) (see para 15.66 below) local authorities have a new wide-ranging power to provide assistance for housing renewal, and much of the former prescriptive legislation concerning renewal grants has been repealed (with the exception of disabled facilities grants (DFG)).

18 Department for Communities and Local Government (2006) *Homelessness Code of Guidance for Local Authorities*: July 2006 and in Wales see Welsh Assembly Government (2003) *Code of guidance for local authorities on allocation of accommodation and homelessness* – para 8.13. At the time of writing (September 2011) the Welsh Government is consulting on a revised code – see http://wales.gov.uk/consultations/housingcommunity/codehomelessness/?lang=en

housing providers (such as housing associations and private landlords) but also other statutory bodies such as social services, the probation service, the health service and the wide range of organisations in the private and voluntary sectors whose work helps prevent homelessness or meet the needs of people who have experienced homelessness.

9. Housing authorities will also need to give careful consideration to the scope for joint working between social services and the many other key players in the district who are working to meet the needs of people who are homeless or have experienced homelessness.

15.16   At para 5.6 it gives examples of the collaborative working envisaged, for instance:

- establishment of a multi-agency forum for key practitioners and providers to share knowledge, information, ideas and complementary practices;
- clear links between the homelessness strategy and other key strategies such as Supporting People, and the NHS Local Delivery Plan;
- protocols for the referral of clients between services and sharing information between services – for example, a joint protocol between hospital-based social workers and housing officers to address the housing needs of patients to be discharged from hospital;
- joint consideration of the needs of homeless people by housing and social services authorities under Part 7 of the Children Act 1989 and community care legislation;
- establishment of formal links with other services – for example with those provided by voluntary and community sector organisations.

15.17   At para 5.14 the guidance specifically refers to local authority powers under Local Government Act (LGA) 2000 s2 (see para 1.68 above) suggesting that these provide substantial opportunity for 'cross-boundary partnership working with other authorities and partners, such as the health and social services sectors'. In relation to healthcare, this will be of particular relevance in the context of hospital discharge, for which specific guidance in England, has as its 'over arching aim' to 'ensure that no one is discharged from hospital to the streets or inappropriate accommodation'.[19] In Wales the *Passing the Baton* guidance (see para 5.9 above)[20] states that it is 'not acceptable to simply discharge a homeless person with instructions to attend their local housing office. Adequate provision must be in place for someone recovering from a hospital admission'.

19   Department for Communities and Local Government and Department of Health (2006) *Hospital admission and discharge: people who are homeless or living in temporary or insecure accommodation.*
20   National Leadership and Innovation Agency for Healthcare (2009) *Passing the Baton* at para 3.26: the guidance indicates that further guidance is being developed in this issue.

Housing homeless persons overlap

15.18 The obligation to house homeless persons originated as NAA 1948 s21(1)(b), being a power to provide temporary accommodation for persons who were homeless in circumstances that could not have been foreseen. The power was repealed by the Housing (Homeless Persons) Act 1977, although the relic duty to provide residential accommodation for persons 'in urgent need' remains under NAA 1948 s21(1)(a) (see para 7.26). Likewise in relation to the needs of 'children in need' the Children Act 1989 empowers social services authorities to provide ordinary housing in appropriate circumstances (see para 24.58 below).

15.19 Disabled, elderly or ill people may, however, also come within the scope of the homelessness provisions of HA 1996 Part VII since it provides that:

1) a person is homeless for the purposes of the Act if he or she has no accommodation which 'it would be reasonable for' him or her to occupy[21] (HA 1996 s175(3)); and

2) a person is considered in priority need if he or she 'is vulnerable as a result of old age, mental illness or handicap or physical disability or other special reason, or is a person with whom such a person resides or might reasonably be expected to reside' (HA 1996 s189(1)(c)).[22]

15.20 Once a person is found to be homeless for the purposes of the 1996 Act (and to be in priority need and not intentionally homeless) the housing authority is under a duty to secure that suitable accommodation[23] is available for occupation by the applicant (section 193), and (by virtue of section 176) 'any other person who normally resides with him as a member of his family, or any other person who might reasonably be expected to reside with him'.

15.21 In *Sharif v Camden LBC*[24] the local authority accepted that the applicant (who cared for her disabled father and her younger school age sister) was homeless and entitled to be accommodated under the 1996 Act. It purported to satisfy this duty by offering two separate flats: one for her and her sister and the other for her father (the flats were separate but on the same floor of the building). The Court of Appeal held that this was not a lawful discharge of the council's duty: the accommodation had to enable them to live 'together with' one another – and not in separate units.

---

21 HA 1996 s175(3); which section 176 qualifies by stipulating that accommodation shall be treated as available for a person's occupation only if it is available for occupation by him or her together with any other person who normally resides with him or her as a member of the family, or any other person who might reasonably be expected to reside with him or her – see eg *Sharif v Camden LBC* [2011] EWCA Civ 463.

22 As a cautionary note, see *Ortiz v City of Westminster* (1995) 27 HLR 364, CA.

23 A person may have to remain in less than perfect accommodation for a short period, but in the opinion of the House of Lords 'one cannot overlook the fact that Parliament has imposed on [councils] clear duties to the homeless, including those occupying unsuitable accommodation': see *Birmingham City Council v Ali* [2009] UKHL 36, [2009] 4 All ER 161, [2009] 1 WLR 1506.

24 [2011] EWCA Civ 463.

15.22   In *Boreh v Ealing LBC*[25] the homeless (wheelchair using) applicant was also entitled to the full housing duty under 1996 Act. The council offered her accommodation, which although not suitable, could (the council asserted) be adapted. The court held that this might be an acceptable discharge of the duty, provided the necessary adaptations were clearly stated in the offer and subject to 'assurances that the applicant could fairly regard as certain, binding and enforceable' (para 27). The proposals did not, however, explain how the applicant could access the property, since the front door was inaccessible (although it might have been possible for her to access via a side alleyway and rear patio doors). In the court's view, however, access through a front door is generally an essential requirement for a property to be suitable – stating (para 37) 'that a proper regard for Mrs Boreh's comings and goings in the ordinary course of her occupation of the house required that she should be able to access it via the front door'.

15.23   The relationship between the housing authority homelessness obligations under (what is now) HA 1996 Part VII and the community care obligations of social services authorities was considered in 1992 guidance in the following terms:

> 3. Housing authorities should bear in mind their duties under the homelessness legislation to secure accommodation for applicant households who are unintentionally homeless and in priority need. Section 59(1) of the Housing Act 1985[26] defines priority need categories as including families with dependent children, households containing a pregnant woman, or people who are vulnerable through old age, mental illness or handicap or other special reasons.

> 4. Paragraph 6.11 of the Homelessness Code of Guidance (Third Edition) sets out the procedures to be followed in the case of those recently discharged, or about to be discharged, from psychiatric or learning difficulty (mental handicap) hospitals. In such cases, if the housing authority sees the need, they should establish whether the local social services authority has been involved and give consideration to referring cases for assessment if this seems appropriate.[27]

15.24   This advice has been given statutory effect via Homelessness Act 2002 s1(2) which requires social services authorities to assist housing authorities in the formulation of their homelessness strategies. This obligation is explained in the 2006 English[28] Homelessness Code of Guidance as follows:

---

25   [2008] EWCA Civ 1176.
26   Now HA 1996 s189(1).
27   Department of Health and Department of Environment (2002) *Housing and Community Care*. LAC (92)12 Annex para 3–4.
28   Department for Communities and Local Government (2006) *Homelessness Code of Guidance for Local Authorities*: July 2006 and in Wales – see Welsh Assembly Government (2003) *Code of Guidance for Local Authorities on Allocation of Accommodation and Homelessness* – see eg para 8.13, 8.57 and 10.3. At the time of writing (September 2011) the Welsh Government is consulting on a revised Code – see http://wales.gov.uk/consultations/housingcommunity/codehomelessness/?lang=en

1.6. In non-unitary districts, where the social services authority and the housing authority are different authorities, section 1(2) of the 2002 Act requires the social services authority to give the housing authority such assistance as may be reasonably required in carrying out a homelessness review and formulating and publishing a homelessness strategy. **Since a number of people who are homeless or at risk of homelessness will require social services support, it is unlikely that it would be possible for a housing authority to formulate an effective homelessness strategy without assistance from the social services authority. It will be necessary therefore in all cases for housing authorities to seek assistance from the social services authority.**[29] In unitary authorities the authority will need to ensure that the social services department assists the housing department in carrying out a homelessness review and formulating and publishing a homelessness strategy.

15.25 Para 10.13 of the 2006 Code advises that the critical test of vulnerability for applicant is:[30]

> . . . whether, when homeless, the applicant would be less able to fend for him/herself than an ordinary homeless person so that he or she would suffer injury or detriment, in circumstances where a less vulnerable person would be able to cope without harmful effects.

15.26 The guidance then provides advice in relation to the specific classes of people deemed to be 'vulnerable'[31] and in so doing stresses the importance of 'close co-operation between housing authorities, social services authorities and mental health agencies' (including undertaking, where appropriate, joint assessments). The guidance highlights the need to consider information from all relevant sources, for example from medical professionals and current providers of care and support: of keeping 'an open mind' and avoiding 'blanket policies that assume that particular groups of applicants will, or will not, be vulnerable'.

Disabled facilities grants

15.27 Disabled facilities grants (DFGs) are grants paid towards the cost of building works which are necessary in order to meet the needs of a disabled occupant. The housing authority is responsible for the administration and payment of the grant, although the original application may be instigated (and referred to it) by a social services authority as part of the community care or Children Act assessment process. Grants are subject to a means test for disabled adults (see para 15.96 below). It appears that in England, about 35,000 DFG awards are made each year[32] and that substantial

---

29 Emphasis as in the original code.
30 In Wales, at para 14.11 of the 2003 Code. See also *R v Camden LBC ex p Pereira* (1998) 31 HLR 317 and *Osmani v Camden LBC* [2004] EWCA Civ 1706, [2005] HLR 22.
31 Paras 10.15–10.32 of the English 2006 guidance and paras 14.12–14.25 of the 2003 Welsh Code.
32 Department for Communities and Local Government (2008) *Disabled Facilities Grant – the package of changes to modernise the programme*, p8.

numbers of disabled people continue to live in unsuitably adapted accommodation.[33]

15.28　The relevant guidance recognises that the obligation to facilitate adaptations for disabled people extends beyond the mere detail of the specific statutory regime, since the underlying purpose is 'to modify disabling environments in order to restore or enable independent living, privacy, confidence and dignity for individuals and their families'.[34] While the precise extent of the 'right to independent living' is uncertain (see para 4.62 above), it is undoubtedly the case that a gross failure by a public authority to discharge its responsibilities in this respect will engage article 8 of the European Convention on Human Rights ('the Convention').

15.29　*R (Bernard) v Enfield LBC*[35] concerned a disabled applicant and her family, who through the local authority's failure to assess her community care needs properly, and then to provide the necessary adaptations, had been forced to live in 'deplorable conditions' for over 20 months. The court considered that the council's failure to act on its assessments had the effect of condemning the applicant and her family to live in conditions which made it virtually impossible for them to have any meaningful private or family life and accordingly found a violation of article 8 of the Convention.

15.30　The Local Government Ombudsman has taken a similar line with delayed DFGs; concluding a 2008 report with the following finding:

> I have considered whether her rights under Article 8 . . . were engaged and I conclude they were, given the common goal was for Joanna to live at home, and enjoy the benefits of family life. The greater a person's disability, the greater is the need to give proper and timely consideration to that person's basic rights and, what concerns me most, the values and principles underlying those rights – such as dignity, equality, fairness and respect.
>
> If the Council had properly considered Joanna's case, with her human rights clearly in mind, she would not have been denied the full enjoyment of her home and family life in the way described in this report. A proper consideration of human rights issues and values would have led to an improvement in Joanna's and her mother's lives.[36]

15.31　Evidence of systemic failing in the processing and award of DFGs and the related works, can be found from the disproportionate number of local government ombudsman reports published concerning this subject. Reports that have not pulled punches – for example describing council

---

33　C Greenhalgh and E Gore, *Disability Review 2009*, Leonard Cheshire Disability, cited in C Wood and E Grant (2010) *Destination Unknown*. Demos, p52 – which suggests, eg that almost half of homes occupied by disabled people who are privately renting, are unsuitable.

34　*Delivering housing adaptations for disabled people: a good practice guide*, June 2006, jointly issued by the Department for Communities and Local Government, Department for Education and Skills and the Department of Health, at para 1.6.

35　[2002] EWHC 2282 (Admin), (2002) 5 CCLR 577.

36　Complaint no 07/A/11108 against Surrey County Council, 11 November 2008, paras 48–49.

behaviour as 'appalling'; 'impenetrable, insensitive and disrespectful';[37] constituting 'institutionalised indifference'; 'breathtaking insensitivity';[38] and which 'beggars belief'.[39] Reports which frequently conclude with recommendations that thousands of pounds be paid in compensation as well as, for example, the commissioning of a report as to 'capacity of senior managers in the relevant services to provide leadership' and to respond to 'front line concerns about service failures and pressures'.[40] The position also appears to be far from perfect in Wales.[41]

15.32   The Local Government Ombudsman has additionally stressed the importance of councils ensuring that their local policies concerning the award of DFGs have been subjected to a full impact review under (what is now) Equality Act 2010 s149 (see para 2.32 above).[42]

Statutory regime

15.33   The relevant statutory provision regulating the availability of DFGs is Housing Grants, Construction and Regeneration Act (HGCRA) 1996 Part I, section 23 of which provides:

> *Disabled facilities grants: purposes for which grant must or may be given.*
> 23.–(1) The purposes for which an application for a grant must be approved, subject to the provisions of this Chapter, are the following –
>   (a) facilitating access by the disabled occupant to and from –
>   (i) the dwelling, qualifying houseboat or caravan, or
>   (ii) the building in which the dwelling or, as the case may be, flat is situated;
>   (b) making –
>   (i) the dwelling, qualifying houseboat or caravan, or
>   (ii) the building,
>   safe for the disabled occupant and other persons residing with him;
>   (c) facilitating access by the disabled occupant to a room used or usable as the principal family room;
>   (d) facilitating access by the disabled occupant to, or providing for the disabled occupant, a room used or usable for sleeping;
>   (e) facilitating access by the disabled occupant to, or providing for the disabled occupant, a room in which there is a lavatory, or facilitating the use by the disabled occupant of such a facility;
>   (f) facilitating access by the disabled occupant to, or providing for the disabled occupant, a room in which there is a bath or shower (or both), or facilitating the use by the disabled occupant of such a facility;

---

37 Complaint no 07 C 05809 against Kirklees, 26 June 2008 paras 47 and 50.
38 Complaint no 07C03887 against Bury MBC, 14 October 2009 paras 40 and 43.
39 Complaint no 07/B/07665 against Luton Borough Council, 10 September 2008 para 37.
40 Complaint no 07C03887 against Bury MBC, 14 October 2009 paras 49.
41 See C Jones (2005) *Review of housing adaptations including disabled Facilities Grants – Wales*, National Assembly for Wales.
42 Confidential Report of which a résumé appears in the Digest of Cases 2008/09 Section F, Housing, at p2.

(g) facilitating access by the disabled occupant to, or providing for the disabled occupant, a room in which there is a washhand basin, or facilitating the use by the disabled occupant of such a facility;

(h) facilitating the preparation and cooking of food by the disabled occupant;

(i) improving any heating system in the dwelling, qualifying houseboat or caravan to meet the needs of the disabled occupant or, if there is no existing heating system there or any such system is unsuitable for use by the disabled occupant, providing a heating system suitable to meet his needs;

(j) facilitating the use by the disabled occupant of a source of power, light or heat by altering the position of one or more means of access to or control of that source or by providing additional means of control;

(k) facilitating access and movement by the disabled occupant around the dwelling, qualifying houseboat or caravan in order to enable him to care for a person who is normally resident there and is in need of such care;

(l) such other purposes as may be specified by order of the secretary of state.

. . .

(3) If in the opinion of the local housing authority the relevant works are more or less extensive than is necessary to achieve any of the purposes set out in subsection (1), they may, with the consent of the applicant, treat the application as varied so that the relevant works are limited to or, as the case may be, include such works as seem to the authority to be necessary for that purpose.

15.34   The provisions of the 1996 Act are fleshed out by regulations, principally the Housing Renewal Grants Regulations 1996 (regularly updated in both England and Wales) and separate regulations dealing with such matters as the maximum amount of the grant,[43] the prescribed forms to be used for the application process.

15.35   The secretary of state in England and the Welsh Government have used their powers under section 23(1)(l) of the 1996 Act[44] to extend the purposes for which an application for a grant must be approved, to include:

1)   facilitating access to and from a garden[45] by a disabled occupant; or

2)   making access to a garden safe for a disabled occupant.

15.36   DFGs are only available where a disabled person has been assessed as needing the relevant adaptations. It follows that there is a clear overlap with the responsibilities owed by social services authorities to disabled people who are assessed as needing assistance with adaptations under CSDPA 1970 s2. Since the duty under the CSDPA 1970 only arises where

---

43 See eg the Disabled Facilities Grants (Maximum Amounts and Additional Purposes) (England) Order 2008 SI No 1189 and the Disabled Facilities Grants (Maximum Amounts and Additional Purposes) (Wales) Order 2008 SI No 2370 (W 205).

44 Ibid, order 3 in each case.

45 Ibid, order 3(3) in each case defines a garden as (amongst other things) including a balcony, a yard, outhouse or land adjacent to a mooring.

the authority is satisfied that its assistance is necessary, it is arguable that this duty does not in general arise (if at all) until after a DRG application has been determined.[46]

NHS powers

15.37 NHS bodies have extensive statutory powers to transfer monies to social services (discussed at para 13.122 above) and the guidance advises[47] that these can be used to facilitate housing adaptation, particularly if in so doing it 'releases beds by expediting discharge'. It cautions, however, that patients 'should not be discharged without either an adaptation in place or appropriate interim arrangements already in place'. The NHS has, of course, the power to fund or jointly fund adaptations where the need is health related – for example a disabled person with severe cellulites who requires frequent washing for hygiene purpose or an immobile patient who requires a ceiling track rail in his home before being discharged from hospital.

Guidance

15.38 Detailed 'non-statutory' good practice guidance on the scheme has been issued by the Department for Communities and Local Government[48] as *Delivering Housing Adaptations for Disabled People: A Good Practice Guide* (June 2006): this is referred to in this section as the 'practice guidance', and references to paragraphs in the following section are references to paragraphs of this guidance unless otherwise stated. In Wales relatively brief guidance was issued in 2002 and the equivalent paragraphs (where they exist) are cited in the footnotes that follow.[49]

15.39   The local government ombudsman has used the English Good Practice guidance (and the timescale targets it provides – see para 15.115, table 18 below) as the benchmark for maladministration determinations and stressed the importance of 'all officers dealing with DFG applications' being trained in its use.[50] The following extracts have, in particular, been

46 See *R (Fay) v Essex CC* [2004] EWHC 879 (Admin) at [28], but see also para 9.97 above.
47 Department for Communities and Local Government (2006) *Delivering housing adaptations for disabled people: a good practice guide*, June 2006 para 5.26 and 5.24 and National Assembly for Wales (2002) *Housing Renewal Guidance* NAFWC 20/02 paras 30 and 34.
48 Department for Communities and Local Government, *Delivering housing adaptations for disabled people: a good practice guide*, June 2006, para 1.14 explains that it replaces the previous guidance contained in annex I of Department of Environment circular 17/96 annex I and states that it should be read in conjunction with Office of Deputy Prime Minister circular 05/2003 (and, in particular, chapter 4 of that Circular) which is primarily concerned with the impact of the RRO – see para 15.85 below.
49 National Assembly for Wales (2002) *Housing Renewal Guidance* NAFWC 20/02 annex D. The guidance is primarily concerned with the implementation of the RRO (see para 15.66 below) and only contains relatively brief advice concerning DFGs, which largely replicates previous advice in annex I of WOC 59/96.
50 See egComplaint no 07/C/01269 against Lincoln CC and 07/C/09724 against West Lindsey DC, 14 October 2009 and Complaint no 07C03887 against Bury MBC, 14 October 2009.

cited as evidence of the way councils should approach the processing of such grants.[51]

> . . . The starting point and continuing focus of those seeking to provide an adaptation service should be the needs experienced and identified by the disabled person and his or her carers. . .The process that delivers an adaptation should be one of partnership in which the person and carer experiencing the disabling environment are the key partners. The appropriateness and acceptability of the adaptation outcome should be measured by the extent to which it meets the needs identified by that disabled person sensitively, efficiently and cost-effectively (para 1.8).

> . . . There should be a corporate responsibility, binding on all partners to ensure that the adaptation is delivered sensitively, is fit for the purpose identified by the end user and within a time-frame that is made explicit from the outset (para 1.9).

> It has long been recognized as crucial to involve disabled people in the assessment of their own needs and today it is appropriate. . .to argue for the primacy of the disabled persons perspective above all others. This is because the disabled person is the expert on his/her needs and should be carefully listened to by the relevant professionals . . . (para 5.3)

> The experience and expertise of professionals is clearly also of great importance but combining these with the views of the disabled person should enable an inclusive and sustainable solution to be developed within the constraints of time, funding and other resources (para 5.5).

> It is important to keep the disabled person and his carers informed about progress (and problems) at all stages in the provision of service. Lack of information is widely recognized as one of the main sources of client . . . dissatisfaction.' An authority should: 'ensure that there is regular contact with the disabled person and their representatives rather than waiting to be approached [and] . . . provide accurate and clear information on timescales, waiting lists and other sources of help (para 3.20).

15.40   As has been noted above (para 9.108), there is considerable overlap between the duties of the housing authority to process these grants, and the duties owed by social services authorities to facilitate such adaptations. Unfortunately this complex interplay of duties has not been simplified by the existence of separate guidance from the Department of Health on the social services responsibilities, as LAC (90)7.[52]

Reform

15.41   The government in England is (at September 2011) piloting proposals to enable people entitled to a DFG to receive this as a direct payment and also to choose the contractor to undertake the works – even if that

---

51   Complaint no 07/C/01269 against Lincoln CC and 07/C/09724 against West Lindsey DC, 14 October 2009 paras 7–9.
52   LAC (90)7 was issued jointly as Department of the Environment Circular 10/90. While DoE Circular 10/90 has been withdrawn LAC (90)7 appears to remain in force (see DoE 4/98 and LASSL (99)21).

contractor was not the one whose estimate accompanied the application. This initiative is considered further at para 4.137 above.

Eligibility

Disability

15.42 The grant is only payable in respect of disabled occupants; ie, persons who are 'substantially and permanently handicapped' within the meaning of NAA 1948 s29 (see para 9.25 above). It is not therefore available for persons whose need arises solely through age or a temporary non-mental illness.[53]

Main residence

15.43 HGCRA 1996 ss21(2)(b) and 22(2)(b) provide that DFGs are only available to disabled people who live (or intend to live) in the accommodation as their only or main residence.[54]

15.44 Where a disabled child has parents who are separated and the child lives for part of the time with both parents, arrangements may need to be made to provide for adaptations at both locations. A mandatory DFG is, however, only available at the 'main residence' of the disabled occupant (annex B para 50 of the practice guidance). It follows that if a community care assessment determines that adaptations are required at the other location, this may trigger a duty under CSDPA 1970 to facilitate those adaptations – see para 9.108 above.

Tenants

15.45 All disabled owner-occupiers, tenants (council, housing association[55] and private) and licensees[56] are eligible to apply for disabled facilities grants as are landlords on behalf of disabled tenants. The practice guidance advises:[57]

> 3.21 Access to assistance in the provision of adaptations should not depend upon the tenure of the disabled person. A local authority may determine that it will fund adaptations in property within its own ownership other than through the DFG mechanism. However, this should not result in a worse service to their occupants than that received by applicants who live in

---

53 Housing authorities have a general power under article 3 of the RRO to give discretionary assistance in such cases, in any form (eg grant, loan or equity release) for adaptations. This power replaces the previous 'discretionary' grant schemes that operated prior to the RRO – see para 15.85 below.

54 Annex B paras 42–47 of the practice guidance and Annex D para 42 of the Welsh guidance.

55 A failure by a council to appreciate that housing association tenants are able to apply for a DFG, will constitute maladministration – see complaint no 09 001 059 against Lewes District Council, 6 April 2010.

56 HGCRA 1996 s19(5) extends eligibility for a DFG to a range of licensees, eg secure or introductory tenants who are licensees, agricultural workers, and service employees such as publicans.

57 *Delivering housing adaptations for disabled people: a good practice guide*, 2006, para 3.21.

other tenures. This applies both to the level of support received and the time taken to provide a service.

15.46 Accordingly any material difference in treatment of council and non-council tenants may constitute maladministration.[58]

15.47 In certain cases councils may have an agreement with a housing provider that it will be responsible for facilitating the necessary adaptations (eg where former council housing stock has been passed to a registered social landlord). However, this agreement cannot 'trump' the statutory duty: a point made clear in the practice guidance para 29):

> The obligation to provide DFGs to eligible applicants for eligible work (subject to the test of the applicant's resources) is primary, absolute and remains irrespective of whether other assistance is provided by a social services authority or other body such as an RSL.

15.48 The local government ombudsman has found maladministration in such a case,[59] where a disabled person was advised by his landlord (with whom the council had an adaptations protocol) that the necessary adaptations would be delayed by at least two years. Instead of the council intervening and securing the necessary works, it failed to take any action, seeking to rely rigidly on the protocol.

15.49 The local government ombudsman has highlighted a problem with the DFG scheme in that it only applies to existing tenants (HGCRA 1996 s24(2)).[60] Accordingly where it is proposed that a disabled person move to a new tenancy and that tenancy be adapted prior to the move, in order to obtain the grant it will be necessary to take on the new tenancy. During this period the applicant will bear the cost of two tenancies. It follows that there is a need for such works to be done as quickly as possible and without any unnecessary delays.[61]

15.50 Where the tenant is the applicant for the DFG the consent of the landlord of the property will be required. The practice guidance advises that the authority should make every effort to secure this approval 'and in appropriate circumstances authorities should be prepared to assure the landlord that if requested by him they will "make good" when a tenant no longer requires the adaptation' (para 6.3). The Equality Act 2010 Part 4 places significant obligations on landlords in such situations – not least the section 36 duty to make reasonable adjustments (including to 'common parts') – which is fleshed out in Schedule 4 to the Act.

58 See the report and further report on complaint no 99/B/00012 against North Warwickshire DC, 15 May 2000 and 30 November 2000 respectively.
59 Complaint no 10 008 979 against Liverpool City Council, 4 April 2011.
60 In *R v Bradford MDC ex p Pickering* (2001) 33 HLR 38, Munby J held that a purchaser under an (uncompleted) rental purchase agreement had a sufficient 'owner's interest' for the purposes the grant.
61 Complaint no 00/C/19154 against Birmingham, 19 March 2002.

Caravans, mobile homes and houseboats

15.51 The DFG scheme was extended in 2003[62] to persons living in mobile homes and houseboats. However, only mobile home owners living in a 'qualifying park home' were covered, ie people on a protected site within the meaning of the Mobile Homes Act 1983. As a result of representations made concerning the discriminatory effect of this measure (Gypsies living on local authority sites did not come within the scope of the provision) the scheme was amended by HA 2004 s224 which substituted references to 'park homes' in the 1996 Act with the term 'caravans' and likewise the references to 'pitch' with references to 'land'.

15.52 Section 19(1)(c) of the 1996 Act now provides that DFGs are available where 'the applicant is an occupier (alone or jointly with others) of a qualifying houseboat or a caravan and, in the case of a caravan, that at the time the application was made the caravan was stationed on land within the authority's area'.[63]

Five years' occupancy requirement

15.53 Grants are payable subject to a requirement that the disabled person lives (or intends to live) in the accommodation as his or her only or main residence throughout the grant condition period 'or for such shorter period as his health and other relevant circumstances permit'.[64] HGCRA 1996 s44(3)(a) provides that 'the "grant condition period" means the period of five years, or such other period as the secretary of state may by order specify or as may be imposed by the local housing authority with the consent of the secretary of state, beginning with the certified date' and section 44(3)(b) states that 'the "certified date" means the date certified by the local housing authority as the date on which the execution of the eligible works is completed to its satisfaction'.

15.54 In relation to this question, the practice guidance advises as follows:

> 6.7 Where it appears to the person carrying out the assessment, or the person evaluating the application for grant, that the applicant may not continue to occupy the adapted property for a period of five years or more they should consider the circumstances. If the reason for suspecting this is a prognosis of a deteriorating condition or possible imminent death of the applicant, this should not be a reason for withholding or delaying grant approval. This is the case whether or not the prognosis is known to the disabled person, their family or carer.

15.55 In this context, earlier advice in the guide is relevant, namely:

> 5.22 Assessment and recommendation should seek sensitively to provide for the progress of the illness which may be difficult to predict. A relatively limited period in which a particular adaptation is appropriate should not be regarded as a sufficient reason for delaying or withholding its provision.

---

62 By virtue of an amendment to HCGRA 1996 s23 via RRO art 2.
63 Although this provision came into effect on 18 January 2005, the 2006 practice guidance on DFGs still persists in using the term 'park home'.
64 HCGRA 1996 ss21(2)(b) and 22(2)(b).

15.56   However, para 29 of annex B to the practice guidance qualifies this advice, stating that 'where an applicant's prognosis implies that degeneration in the short term will occur, then this should be taken into account when considering the eligible works'.

Maximum grant

15.57   The maximum mandatory grant is currently £30,000 in England[65] and £36,000 in Wales,[66] although local authorities are empowered to make higher awards. Special rules apply for minor adaptations under £1,000 (see para 15.58 below). In England the government in 2007 undertook to keep the maximum grant figure under review 'with the aim of increasing to £50,000 in stages'.[67] Where an adaptation is assessed as costing more than the grant maximum, various options exist to cover the excess, including the housing authority providing additional sums by exercising its discretionary powers (see para 15.85 below) and/or the social services authority paying for the excess. A council's failure to inform an applicant that costs exceeding the maximum amount are discretionary (although see para 9.114 below) may constitute maladministration, as will be a fixed policy of not funding above the maximum sum.[68]

Adaptations under £1,000

15.58   Community Care (Delayed Discharges etc) Act (CC(DD)A) 2003 ss15 and 16 provide for 'qualifying services' to be exempt from any charge in England and Wales (respectively). Regulations have been issued in England[69] which stipulate that qualifying services for the purposes of section 15(1) are intermediate care and community equipment (aids and minor adaptations) services. Regulation 2 then defines 'community equipment (aids and minor adaptations) service' as consisting of:

> the provision of an aid, or a minor adaptation to property, for the purposes of assisting with nursing at home or aiding daily living; and, for the purposes of this paragraph, an adaptation is 'minor' if the cost of making the adaptation is £1000 or less;

It follows that there is no cost limit on the value of the equipment provided under this provision: the cost limit (of £1,000) only applies to minor adaptations.

---

65   Disabled Facilities Grants (Maximum Amounts and Additional Purposes) (England) Order 2008 SI No 1189 order 2.

66   Disabled Facilities Grants (Maximum Amounts and Additional Purposes) (Wales) Order 2008 SI No 2370 (W 205) order 2.

67   Department for Communities and Local Government (2007) *Disabled Facilities Grant Programme: the Government's proposals to improve programme delivery*, January, para 31a.

68   Complaint no 07/B/07346 against Walsall Metropolitan Borough Council, 17 June 2008 para 23–24.

69   Community Care (Delayed Discharges etc) Act (Qualifying Services) (England) Regulations 2003 SI No 1196 reg 3 – see also the good practice guidance at para 2.26.

15.59   Early guidance to the CC(DD)A 2003 advised that 'all community equipment for older people (eg aids and minor adaptations) will be provided within seven days'.[70]

15.60   Concern has been expressed about an increasing number of people needing aids and adaptations being directed, inappropriately, by social services authorities to the Social Fund. In a 2009 report the Commissioners[71] highlighted the primary responsibility of such authorities for the provision of this support and commented critically on the fact that in a number of cases social services had not conducted a proper assessment of need; had fettered their discretion by stating that they did not provide help with, for example, electrically operated adjustable beds or chairs; and had purported to discharge their statutory duties not by meeting the need but by referring the disabled person to the Social Fund. In the Commissioners' opinion it was 'unacceptable that people who are often in desperate situations and with urgent needs find themselves passed between their local authority and the Social Fund' and that it was vital that the Secretary of State for Work and Pensions and the Secretary of State for Communities and Local Government took action to resolve this situation.

Role of the housing authority

15.61   The housing authority is responsible for the administration of the disabled facilities grant, through all stages from initial enquiry (or referral by the social services authority) to post-completion approval. This requirement stems from HGCRA 1996 s24(3):

> A local housing authority shall not approve an application for a grant unless they are satisfied –
> (a) that the relevant works are necessary and appropriate to meet the needs of the disabled occupant, and
> (b) that it is reasonable and practicable to carry out the relevant works having regard to the age and condition of –
>   (i) the dwelling, qualifying houseboat or caravan, or
>   (ii) the building.
>
> In considering the matters mentioned in paragraph (a) a local housing authority which is not itself a social services authority shall consult the social services authority.

15.62   Although the HGCRA 1996 specifically requires housing authorities to consult with social services authorities over whether the proposed works are necessary and appropriate, it is nevertheless for housing authorities to decide in any particular case whether or not to approve a grant: they are not bound to follow the social services authority's advice (annex B para 34

---

70 Department of Health (2003) *Discharge from hospital: pathway, process and practice,* 2003, para 2.3 – now 'superseded by 2010 guidance which is silent on this question – see para 5.8 above.

71 Independent Review Service for the Social Fund (2009) *The Social Fund Commissioner's Annual Report 2008/2009* pp53–54.

of the guidance). Provided the housing authority has considered all the facts and has acted rationally, the court is unlikely to interfere with that decision.[72] Where, however, a dispute arises between the occupational therapist's view and that of the grants officer about what work is 'necessary and appropriate', it will be maladministration for the authority not to have a means of resolving this conflict.[73]

Reasonable and practicable

15.63   HGCRA 1996 s24(3)(b) charges the housing authority with the duty of deciding whether it is reasonable and practicable to carry out the proposed adaptation works. In making its assessment, a housing authority is specifically required to have regard to the age and condition of the dwelling or building. While section 24(4) permits grants to be made even where on completion of the works the property would remain unfit for human habitation, the guidance advises as to the alternatives that should be investigated by the housing and social services departments if the final 'unfitness' of the property is considered to render the proposed works unreasonable and impractical.[74] In determining whether the work is reasonable and practicable, the guidance refers to other relevant considerations, including the architectural and structural characteristics of the property, conservation considerations, the practicalities of carrying out work on properties with difficult or limited access (such as steep flights of steps or narrow doorways, etc) and the impact on other occupants of the proposed works[75] (annex B para 37 of the practice guidance).

More suitable alternative accommodation

15.64   On occasions a housing authority may have misgivings about approving a DFG on the basis that it would be more cost-effective if the disabled person moved to different accommodation. It is unclear as to whether the existence of such an alternative would constitute lawful reasons for refusing a grant – if the proposed adaptations were in every other respect 'reasonable and practicable' and 'necessary and appropriate'. Much would no doubt turn on the context of the individual case and the extent to which 'what is reasonable' would encompass a consideration of other alternatives which might appear 'more reasonable'.

---

72 *R (L) v Leeds City Council* [2010] EWHC 3324 (Admin).

73 Complaint no 05/C/13157 against Leeds City Council, 20 November 2007

74 Annex B para 36 of the practice guidance; annex D para 39–40 Welsh guidance: including urging the disabled person to seek other assistance (if available) to make the property fit; considering whether a reduced level of adaptations to the property would be viable; and considering re-housing in more suitable accommodation: in which respect the guidance advises that this 'would make sense if major expenditure on adaptations could be avoided and a suitably adapted house was available'.

75 That is, if the works would lead to substantial disruption to other tenants (eg the noise of an air-compressor, in *R v Kirklees MBC ex p Daykin* (1997–98) 1 CCLR 512, QBD or alternatively be of indirect benefit to neighbours as in *R v Kirklees MBC ex p Good* (1997–98) 1 CCLR 506, QBD.

15.65   The practice guidance, however, advises that 'where major adaptations are required and it is difficult to provide a cost-effective solution in a client's existing home, then the possibility of moving elsewhere, either into a local authority or registered social landlord (RSL) dwelling, or a more suitable dwelling in the private sector should be considered' (para 6.15). Without addressing the question of what would occur if the applicant was unwilling to consider this option, it considers the process that would need to be followed if he or she were willing to consider a move. These would include 'close liaison with local authority or RSL housing management staff' and the use of the authority's powers under the Regulatory Reform (Housing Assistance) (England and Wales) Order 2002 (see para 15.85 below) if a move to another private sector home is a possibility – including helping with the purchase and adaptation of a new property either within or outside the authority's area.

Necessary and appropriate

15.66   In deciding whether the proposed works are necessary and appropriate to meet the needs of the disabled occupant, HGCRA 1996 s24 requires housing authorities, which are not themselves social services authorities, to consult the relevant social services authority on the adaptation needs of disabled people.

15.67   The consideration of what 'meets' the assessed needs of a disabled person may include consideration of any alternative way of meeting the need. Thus in *R v Kirklees MBC ex p Daykin*[76] (a case concerning CSDPA 1970 s2) the disabled person was assessed as needing to be able to get into and out of his council flat. Collins J held that it was reasonable for the authority to decide that this need could either be met by the provision of a stair lift, or by re-housing, and for it to take into account the respective costs of both options, in deciding which was to be preferred.

15.68   *R (B) v Calderdale MBC*[77] the Court of Appeal considered the interplay between HGCRA 1996 s23 and s24(3), commenting as follows:

> 28. . . . What . . . the local authority has . . . failed to do . . . [is] to separate the s24(3) question from the s23(1) question, and to answer it in the light of the fact that the claimant has established his grant-eligibility in principle under [section 23(1)]. The council must now decide whether it is satisfied that a loft conversion is necessary and appropriate to meet D's particular needs, which include the need not to harm his brother. This is a matter for the council's considered judgment. Unless it is so satisfied it cannot pay the grant.
>
> 29. One has no wish to be critical of non-lawyers who have to apply this difficult and sensitive legislation not in the calm of a courtroom but in the course of a pressured day's work in the office. But one straightforward guideline is that s23(1) and s24(3) should be applied sequentially. A lot of the difficulty in the present case arose from decision-makers running the

76   (1997–98) 1 CCLR 512, QBD.
77   [2004] EWCA Civ 134, [2004] 1 WLR 2017.

two together. S23(1) is a gateway provision. S24(3) is a control for those applications which get through the gateway. In a suitable case, no doubt, it may be legitimate to decide that, even assuming that the application passes the s23(1) threshold, the work cannot be regarded as necessary or as appropriate. But that too is sequential reasoning. What is not permissible is to decide the s23(1) issue by reference to the s24(3) criteria.

15.69   The fact that the statutory duty to consult only exists where the housing authority is not itself a social services authority, does not mean that a similar level of co-operation is not required in unitary authorities. The local government ombudsman has found maladministration where, although the housing and social services sections were within the same Directorate their actions were characterised by 'inadequate communication, a lack of co-ordination, inattention and inactivity'.[78]

15.70   When undertaking its assessment, the social services authority will generally rely on an assessment by an occupational therapist. Such assessments should, as a general rule, look at all the relevant needs of the disabled person and it may constitute maladministration (particularly in complex cases) if they merely confine themselves to matters that can be funded by a DFG.[79]

Grant-eligible works

Mandatory grants

15.71   Section 23(1) of the 1996 Act details the purposes for which mandatory grants may be awarded – principally to facilitate access and provision. As detailed above, these are primarily for the purpose of:

- facilitating a disabled person's access to:
  - the dwelling;
  - a room usable as the principal family room, or for sleeping in;
  - a WC, bath, shower, etc (or the provision of a room for these facilities);
- facilitating the preparation of food by the disabled person;
- improving/providing a heating system to meet the disabled person's needs;
- facilitating the disabled person's use of a source of power;
- facilitating access and movement around the home to enable the disabled person to care for someone dependent upon him or her;
- making the dwelling safe for the disabled person and others residing with him or her.
- facilitating the disabled person's access to and from a garden; or
- making access to a garden safe for the disabled person.

15.72   The duty is not a 'resource' dependent duty (see para 1.23 above); thus in

---

78   Complaint no 07C03887 against Bury MBC, 14 October 2009, para 38.
79   Complaint no 07/A/11108 against Surrey County Council, 11 November 2008.

R v Birmingham CC ex p Taj Mohammed[80] Dyson J held that housing authorities were not entitled to take resources into account when deciding whether or not to approve a DFG. It follows that it will be maladministration for the responsible authority not to allocate sufficient funds to 'meet the demand for DFGs'.[81]

15.73   Works eligible for grant support will generally be within a dwelling but may in certain situations be elsewhere, for instance, in the common parts of a building containing flats (annex B para 31 of the guidance) or in relation to accessing the garden. Such works can be conveniently grouped as follows.

Making the dwelling safe

15.74   Section 23(1)(b) allows a grant to be given for adaptations to make a property safe for the disabled person and other persons residing with him or her. The practice guidance[82] explains that works under this heading may include 'adaptations designed to minimise the risk of danger where a disabled person has behavioural problems which causes him to act in a boisterous or violent manner damaging the house, himself and perhaps other people'. It may also include enhanced alarm systems for people with hearing difficulties (annex B para 19 of the practice guidance).

15.75   In *R (B) v Calderdale MBC*[83] Sedley LJ (at [24]) considered that a grant to make a dwelling safe (under HGCRA 1996 s23(1)(b)) required that:

> . . . the proposed works must be such as to minimise the material risk, that is to say to reduce it so far as is reasonably practicable, assuming that it cannot be eliminated.

Facilitating access and provision

15.76   Annex B para 16 of the practice guidance explains that this includes works which remove or help overcome any obstacles which prevent the disabled person from moving freely into and around the dwelling and enjoying the use of the dwelling and the facilities or amenities within it. In particular this includes works which enable the disabled person to prepare and cook food as well as facilitating access to and from the dwelling and to the following:

- the principal family room;
- a room used for sleeping (or providing such a room);
- a room in which there is a lavatory, a bath or shower and a washbasin (or providing such a room).

---

80 (1997–98) 1 CCLR 441, QBD.
81 Complaint no 07/C/01269 against Lincoln CC and 07/C/09724 against West Lindsey DC, 14 October 2009 para 34.
82 Annex B para 18 and annex D para 11 of the Welsh guidance.
83 [2004] EWCA Civ 134, [2004] 1 WLR 2017.

Room usable for sleeping

15.77   The practice guidance[84] advises that the building of a new room 'usable for sleeping' should only be grant funded if the housing authority is satisfied that the adaptation of an existing room (or access to that room) is not a suitable option. It states, however, that where the disabled person shares a bedroom, grant funding may be given to provide a room of sufficient size 'so that the normal sleeping arrangements can be maintained'.

Bathroom

15.78   The practice guidance[85] explains that the Act separates the provision of a lavatory and washing, bathing and showering facilities, in order to clarify that a grant support is available to ensure that the disabled person has access to each of these facilities (as well as facilitating their use). The local government ombudsman considers that DFG grants officers should not expect disabled persons and their families to give up a family room in order to make way for a ground floor shower/toilet[86] and has stressed the fundamental importance disabled people being able properly to manage bathing/washing with dignity[87] – see para 4.104 above.

Facilitating preparation and cooking of food

15.79   Eligible works under this heading include the rearrangement or enlargement of a kitchen to ease manoeuvrability of a wheelchair, and specially modified or designed storage units, gas, electricity and plumbing installations to enable the disabled person to use these facilities independently. The practice guidance[88] advises, however, that a full adaptation of a kitchen would not generally be appropriate where most of the cooking and preparation is done by another household member.

Heating, lighting and power

15.80   The guidance[89] advises that although grant support may be made in order to provide (or improve, or replace) a heating system, this should only extend to rooms normally used by the disabled person and central heating should only be funded 'where the well-being and mobility of the disabled person would be otherwise adversely affected'. Works in relation to lighting and power may include the relocation of power points and the provision of suitably adapted controls.

---

84 Annex B para 21 and annex D para 14 of the Welsh guidance.
85 Annex B para 22 and annex D para 15 of the Welsh guidance.
86 Complaint no 05/C/13157 against Leeds City Council, 20 November 2007.
87 Complaint nos 02/C/8679, 02/C/8681 and 02/C/10389 against Bolsover DC, 30 September 2003.
88 Annex B paras 23–24 and annex D paras 16–17 of the Welsh guidance.
89 Annex B paras 25–26 and annex D paras 18–19 of the Welsh guidance.

Safe access to a garden

15.81   As noted above, in 2008 the English and Welsh governments issued orders[90] extending the scope of the mandatory grants regime to cover:

- facilitating the disabled person's access to and from a garden; or
- making access to a garden safe for the disabled person.

15.82   Order 3(3) of the relevant Orders in each case defines a garden as (amongst other things) including a balcony, a yard, outhouse or land adjacent to a mooring. The Welsh guidance includes specific mention that works within the definition of 'making the dwelling safe' would also include the 'construction or erection of external fencing may also be required to assist on the management of individual behavioural problems and the prevention of self-harm or risk' (annex D para 13). A garden fence could also be provided as a Children Act 1989 service or as a service under the Carers Act 2000 (see para 16.98 below).

Dependent residents

15.83   Grant support is available to cover work which improves a disabled person's access and movement around a dwelling in order to care for another person who normally resides there (HGCRA 1996 s23(1)(k)). The practice guidance[91] makes it clear that the dependent being cared for need not be a disabled person and need not be a relation.

Sensory impaired disabled people

15.84   Mandatory grants are available to meet the adaptation needs of disabled people whose needs 'are less obvious such as those with sight or hearing impairment'.[92] The guidance gives the following example:

> . . . partially sighted people may require an enhanced form of lighting of a particular kind in the dwelling to enable them to carry out every day tasks and activities in the home. Such works may be required to facilitate access into and around the home and for such purposes as the preparation and cooking of food, to improve the ability to use sources of power or to provide greater safety of the disabled occupant. Works for these purposes qualify for mandatory grant under section 23(1). Where safety is an issue, the works could qualify under subsection (1)(b).

Discretionary grants

15.85   Prior to July 2003, the HGCRA 1996 provided for discretionary grants (under section 23(2)) to be made in certain situations. Although this provision has been repealed, it has been replaced with a wide ranging power

---

90 Disabled Facilities Grants (Maximum Amounts and Additional Purposes) (England) Order 2008 SI No 1189, order 3; and the Disabled Facilities Grants (Maximum Amounts and Additional Purposes) (Wales) Order 2008 SI No 2370 (W205) order 3.
91 Annex B para 27 and annex D para 20 in the Welsh guidance.
92 Annex B para 28 and annex D para 21 in the Welsh guidance.

under article 3 of the RRO which enables housing authorities to give discretionary assistance, in any form, for adaptations or other housing purposes. The financial assistance can also be provided indirectly to the disabled person through a third party and may be paid in addition, or as an alternative to the grant, and there is no restriction on the amount of assistance that may be given. English guidance on the RRO was issued by the Office of Deputy Prime Minister as circular 05/2003.[93]

15.86   The practice guidance[94] gives examples of the type of assistance that can be provided under the RRO powers:

- to provide small-scale adaptations to either fulfil needs not covered by mandatory DFGs or, by avoiding the procedural complexities of mandatory DFGs, to deliver a much quicker remedy for urgent adaptations;
- to provide top-up assistance to mandatory DFG where the local authority takes the view that the amount of assistance available under DFG is insufficient to meet the needs of the disabled person and their family; and
- to assist with the acquisition of other accommodation (whether within or outside the authority's area) where the authority is satisfied that this will benefit the occupant at least as much as improving or adapting his existing accommodation.

15.87   Para 6.18 of the practice guidance advises that the RRO powers could additionally be used where an authority considers that the statutory means test is 'biting particularly harshly in a particular case'.

15.88   Assistance provided under the RRO may be in any form deemed appropriate by the authority – for instance, as an outright grant or as a loan or by way of an equity release. In this context the guidance advises:[95]

> 6.22 The greater funding flexibility now opened up by the new RRO powers is also encouraging local housing authorities to consider alternatives to supporting disabled persons through grant assistance. For example, Houseproud[96] is a partnership between a number of local authorities and the Home Improvement Trust to provide advice and financial help to disabled people for housing adaptations and repairs. This is done by the provision of affordable loans and for those over 75 an equity release policy is available. Again such policies do not affect a persons right to mandatory DFG and a loan of this type can be used as an additional form of assistance if the applicant for a DFG is assessed as having to make a contribution towards the costs of the works.
>
> 6.23 More generally local authorities should consider whether any adaptations assistance provided under the RRO powers always needs to be in the form of grant. For example, assistance to fund works in excess of [the

93 Office of Deputy Prime Minister circular 05/2003 *Housing Renewal*: in Wales as the National Assembly for Wales (2002) *Housing Renewal Guidance* NAFWC 20/02.
94 Para 2.24; annex D para 63 in the Welsh guidance.
95 See also para 4 of the Welsh guidance.
96 See www.houseproud.org.uk.

maximum grant] or to help with the applicants assessed contribution could be met through some form of loan or equity release scheme.[97]

15.89 The existence of this discretionary power allied with the public sector equality duty may, in appropriate situations, be such as to create a substantial obligation on a council to facilitate necessary works – or at the very least to provide cogent reasons why this is not possible.[98]

Ineligibility for grant and the social services overlap

15.90 Cases arise where the social services authority assesses a need for an adaptation, but the housing authority refuses or is unable to approve the grant. This may occur because the works in question do not come under the mandatory scheme, or because the housing authority does not consider the proposed works to be reasonable or practicable or because the applicant fails the means test. In addition it may be that the proposed works will cost significantly more than the maximum grant (see para 15.57 above). In such situations the failure of the DFG application does not absolve the social services authority of its duty to meet an assessed need under CSDPA 1970 s2 (a point emphasised at para 2.6 of the practice guidance). The practice guidance states at para 6.19 that 'social services funding streams can also be legitimately utilised to increase the overall resource to fund an adaptation' since 'by definition, adaptations increase independence'. This advice is further and amplified at para 2.8 in the following terms:

> Social Service authorities may discharge their duties by the direct provision of equipment or adaptations, by providing loan finance to a disabled person to enable them to purchase these facilities, or by providing a grant to cover or contribute to the costs of provision. They may make charges for their services, where appropriate, using their powers under section 17 of the *Health and Social Services and Social Security Adjudications Act 1983*. They have a duty to ensure that the assistance required by disabled people is secured. This includes those cases where the help needed goes beyond what is available through DFG, or where a DFG is not available for any reason, or where a disabled person cannot raise their assessed contribution.

15.91 It is maladministration for a local authority to fail to appreciate that it has a duty under section 2 of the 1970 Act to provide adaptations – separate from the obligation to process DFGs.[99] The social services authority obligations under CSDPA 1970 s2 in relation to adaptations and other facilities are considered at para 9.93 above.

15.92 In *R (BG) v Medway Council*[100] the High Court held that it was not

---

97 Similar considerations will apply where the top-up grant support is paid under CSDPA 1970 s2 – see para 9.108 above.
98 Complaint no 07 C 05809 against Kirklees MBC, 26 June 2008 at para 50.
99 Complaint no 05/C/13157 against Leeds City Council, 20 November 2007, and see also complaint no 10 008 979 against Liverpool City Council, 4 April 2011.
100 [2005] EWHC 1932 (Admin), (2005) 8 CCLR 448.

unreasonable for an authority to impose conditions on a grant that it made under CSDPA 1970 s2 to cover the shortfall in the monies awarded under a DFG. The 'top-up' loan in question was to be secured by way of a 20-year legal charge on the home – which would not be repayable, unless the disabled person ceased to reside at the property during the 20-year period, and any amount repayable would be subject to interest. The authority, however, undertook that in the event of repayment being required it would have regard to the family's personal and financial circumstances and would not act unreasonably by insisting on repayment immediately or on terms that would result in financial hardship.

Fixtures and fittings

15.93   While DFGs are available to cover (among other things) adaptations to the fabric of a building, questions do arise as to whether items such as specialist equipment come within the scheme. The 2006 practice guidance is largely silent upon this question, whereas the previous (now revoked) guidance[101] gave some steer as to how the line should be drawn. Since that guidance suggests a workable approach to such problems, its advice would appear to remain pertinent notwithstanding that it no longer has any formal authority. It advises:

> 7.6.1 Under arrangements agreed between the Secretaries of State for Health and the Environment, help with equipment which can be easily installed and removed with little or no modification to the dwelling, is normally the responsibility of the social services authority under its responsibilities under the 1970 Act with larger adaptations requiring structural modification of a dwelling normally coming within the scope of a disabled facilities grant. However, it is for housing authorities and social services authorities between them to decide how the particular adaptation needs of a disabled person should be funded. In taking such decisions authorities should not forget that the needs of the disabled occupant are paramount within the framework of what can be offered.

> 7.6.2 Close cooperation between the respective authorities is vital to ensure that those requiring help in paying for works for essential adaptations to meet their special needs, are given the most efficient and effective support.

15.94   Additional advice in the (revoked) guidance, at annex I states:

> 7. It is for housing authorities and social services authorities between them to decide how particular adaptations should be funded either through CSDPA 1970 or through a DFG.

> 8. However, since DFGs were introduced in 1990 under the Local Government and Housing Act 1989, it has been common practice that equipment which can be installed and removed fairly easily with little or no structural modification of the dwelling is normally the responsibility of the social services authority.

> 9. For larger items such as stairlifts and through floor lifts which require

101   Department of the Environment guidance circular 17/96.

such structural works to the property, help is normally provided by housing authorities through DFG. However, some routine installations may not involve structural work. To ensure that such adaptations are progressed quickly, the respective authorities should jointly agree a standard line on the installation of lifts which will apply unless there are exceptional circumstances. Authorities will wish to include arrangements for routine servicing, maintenance, removal and possible re-use.

Equipment service costs

15.95　The practice guidance advises (para 8.1) that where items of equipment have been installed (such as stair and through-floor lifts, ceiling hoists, etc) which will need 'regular servicing and provision made for repair in cases of failure' then it is:

> . . . good practice for these arrangements, covering the likely service life of the equipment, to be secured by the local authority at the time of installation. The cost of securing services by way of extended guarantee or service contract, when met by a single payment on commissioning, should be included in the calculation of any grant payable.

Means testing of disabled facilities grants

15.96　HGCRA 1996 s30 provides that eligibility for a DFG is subject to a means test. Only the financial circumstances of the disabled occupant,[102] his or her spouse or civil partner[103] or co-habiting partner are assessed and not other members of the household. If the DFG is required in order to enable a spouse or civil partner to return to his or her home and that person's absence is likely to exceed 52 weeks, his or her financial circumstances alone may be relevant.[104] Applications for a disabled person under the age of 19 no longer require a means test.

15.97　The details of the means test are determined by regulations[105] and are relatively complex, although in many instances the calculation adopts housing benefit principles; thus the value of a person's savings is determined in the same way as for housing benefit and a tariff income is applied to any capital in excess of £6,000 (there is no upper capital limit). Unlike housing benefit, however, there are no deductions for 'non-dependents'. There is also an extra premium to reflect housing costs.[106]

15.98　The net income of each assessed person is taken into account,

---

102　The disabled occupant may or may not be the applicant.
103　It is at least arguable that estranged spouses living in the premises may not, however, be members of the same 'household' – see *R (Fay) v Essex CC* [2004] EWHC 879 (Admin) at [15].
104　Housing Renewal Grant Regulations 1996 SI No 2890 reg 9(2)(b) and see also local government ombudsman complaint no 05/B/06334 against Stafford BC, 20 July 2006.
105　The Housing Renewal Grants Regulations which are subject to annual amendment in England and separately in Wales.
106　For more detail and regularly updated information on the DFG means test see *Disability Rights Handbook*, 36th edn, Disability Alliance, 2011.

although for grant purposes the income of those on income support or income-based jobseeker's allowance/joint jobseeker's allowance is deemed to be nil.

15.99   Various allowances and premiums are included in the calculation (relating to such matters as dependent children, lone parenthood, disability and old age) as are certain income disregards.

15.100   Where the total income equals or is below the applicable allowances and premiums (the 'threshold'), the applicant will be entitled to a grant equivalent to the full cost of the approved works, or the maximum DFG sum whichever is less. However, where the total income exceeds the threshold, the grant is reduced pro rata based on a notional 'loan generation factor' – which represents the payments that would have to be made on a loan taken out for the sum repayable over ten years for an owner occupier or five years for a tenant.

Timescales, delay and grant deferment

15.101   HGCRA 1996 s34 requires housing authorities to approve or refuse a grant application as soon as reasonably practicable and in any event not later than six months after the date of application. By section 36 the actual payment of the grant may be delayed until a date not more than 12 months following the date of the application.

15.102   Section 36 provides the only statutory flexibility local authorities have in the managing of the cost implications of the grant: a grant, as noted above, payable as a consequence of a non-resource dependent duty.[107] Notwithstanding the mandatory nature of this obligation, local authorities routinely adopt all manner of extra-statutory impediments to frustrate the expeditious processing of grant applications. Since the statutory clock only starts ticking once a completed application has been submitted to the housing authority, a common tactic is to delay the pre-application assessment process, by creating inappropriate administrative hurdles[108] and by delaying the preliminary assessments, for instance, by claiming a shortage of assessors.[109] Disappointingly, the government, and to a degree the local

---

107   *R v Birmingham CC ex p Taj Mohammed* (1997–98) 1 CCLR 441, QBD – (see para 15.72 above).

108   See eg complaint no 02/C/04897 against Morpeth BC and Northumberland CC, 27 November 2003 where the ombudsman criticised a process which required an applicant to queue twice – once for the social services input and then again for the housing authority determination.

109   For very many years local authorities have claimed that a shortage of occupational therapists (OTs) has rendered it impossible for them to undertake timely assessments. In complaint no 90/C/0336, 3 October 1991 the local government ombudsman, in holding that a wait of nine months for an OT assessment amounted to maladministration, observed that if insufficient OTs were available, authorities should find other way of assessing the needs. This advice is reinforced by the practice guidance which encourages (at para 5.11) the use of 'other staff' to carry out assessments for minor adaptations – such as 'Care Managers and those undertaking assessment for Home Care services' who may be well placed to carry out assessments for minor adaptations.

government ombudsman,[110] have been less than robust in challenging such behaviour – appearing to sympathise more with local authority cash flow difficulties than compliance with the law or the often dreadful circumstances endured by disabled people as they wait for vital works.

15.103   A government assurance that it was to strengthen its advice to local authorities to ensure that grants were only delayed in 'exceptional circumstances' has not been honoured – nor has its view that 'waiting times for any adaptation of more than 250 working days, from the point of initial inquiry to completion, are unacceptable'[111] been given any substance in guidance. Indeed the previous Department of Environment guidance[112] which contained a number of specific and important statements concerning delay – for instance, that 'local authorities should not use pre-application tests as a way of delaying applications or avoiding their statutory duty to process applications within six months'[113] and that the power to defer payment for up to 12 months from the date of application 'should be used only in exceptional circumstances and not where the applicant would suffer undue hardship'[114] – has been revoked and replaced by the comparatively anodyne 2006 practice guidance (see para 15.38 above) in which neither of the above statements are to be found.

15.104   The practice guidance does, however, provide target timescales for the completion of the various stages of the DFG process and the local government ombudsman[115] has placed considerable reliance in these – for example that for a grant of £5,000, there should be a maximum target time of 52 weeks from the initial enquiry about services to completion of adaptations work; and that even complex assessments, the time from an OT referral to the completion of his or her report should not exceed three months.[116]

15.105   While the courts have not as yet been called upon to consider the legality of the widespread use by local authorities of rationing mechanisms, this may be due to cases of this nature being settled at an early stage by local authorities. In *Qazi v Waltham Forest LBC*[117] Richards J dismissed a private law claim which alleged that the authority had deliberately delayed the processing of grant applications and failed to explain clearly

---

110   Eg in a 2009 report where mention is made of excessive delay (in excess of a year) and yet no reference made to the underlying statutory illegality of this – see Complaint no 07/C/01269 against Lincoln CC and 07/C/09724 against West Lindsey DC, 14 October 2009 para 44; however, maladministration was found where a local authority delayed by four months a financial assessment – see complaint no 05/C/13157 against Leeds City Council, 20 November 2007.

111   HC Debates col 696, 27 January 2003, Parliamentary Under-Secretary of State, Office of the Deputy Prime Minister (Mr Tony McNulty).

112   Department of the Environment guidance circular 17/96.

113   Department of the Environment guidance circular 17/96, annex I para 45.

114   Department of the Environment guidance circular 17/96, para 7.5.4.

115   Complaint no 07/A/11108 against Surrey County Council 11 November 2008, para 10 and see eg Complaint no 06/C/16349 against Sheffield City Council 26 June 2008 para 46.

116   Complaint no 07/A/11108 against Surrey County Council 11 November 2008

117   (1999) 32 HLR. 689, a case based upon an allegation of misfeasance in public office and negligent misstatement.

the status of applications – namely that they were not 'pending applications' (to which the mandatory timescales in the Act applied) but merely 'enquiries'. While the judgment addressed the specific private law issues in the case, the judge observed that 'it is plainly arguable that the scheme operated by the defendant was unlawful' and that:

> Notwithstanding the difficulties that the 1989 Act[118] created for local authorities, with their limited resources, I confess to a degree of surprise that systems of this kind received approval in principle, as I am told, from the Local Government Commissioner. Had an application been made at the time to challenge the system by way of judicial review, there must be a good chance that it would have been successful or at the very least that leave would have been granted.

15.106　Where hardship is being caused by the delayed processing of a grant, social services authorities should be pressed to facilitate the works via their underpinning duties under CSDPA 1970 s2 (see above) and, if it be the case, requiring that the works be completed urgently and without the delay occasioned by a full community care assessment.

15.107　　Where the maladministration (for example, delay in implementing adaptations or in failing to honour promises to take action) is attributable to a social housing provider and not a local authority – then it may be possible to complain to the Housing Ombudsman Service.[119] The Housing Ombudsman is able to undertake investigations and to make compensation recommendations in much the same way as the local government ombudsman.[120]

Priority cases and interim arrangements

15.108　The practice guidance in England[121] accepts that in processing DFG applications local authorities will prioritise some applications over others. It advises (at para 4.8) that although most such schemes depend upon an assessment of medical risk these should be 'broadened to reflect the social model of disability' and (at para 5.21) that particular attention need be paid to people with deteriorating conditions where the response 'should be as fast as possible' with consideration being given 'to expedited procedures and interim solutions where some measure of delay is inevitable'.

15.109　　The need for expedition is often particularly acute in relation to people being discharged from hospital. Para 5.24 of the practice guidance stresses that 'patients should not be discharged without either an adaptation in place or appropriate interim arrangements already in place'. Its

---

118　The case concerned the Local Government and Housing Act 1989 under which DFGs were payable at the time. The material parts of the Act are now found in the 1996 Act.

119　Housing Ombudsman Service, 81 Aldwych, London, WC2B 4HN. Tel: 0300 111 300, www.housing-ombudsman.org.uk/contactus.aspx

120　See eg complaint reference 200901278 – Adaptations, Repairs, 30 July 2010 – a complaint that involved delayed adaptations and where the ombudsman awarded compensation for the social landlord's failure to communicate, lack of co-ordination and the lack of timeliness in completing the work.

121　The Welsh guidance contains similar advice at annex D paras 34–35.

assertion (at para 5.40) that it 'is not acceptable that the disabled person and carers should be left for a period of weeks or months without such interim help' has been forcefully endorsed by the local government ombudsman.[122]

15.110 In order to meet their statutory duties local authorities must inevitably undertake a strategic assessment of need and then set aside an adequate budget to ensure that the need is met.[123] An inevitable corollary of this duty is, as stated in the guidance (paras 3.13–3.14), that 'budgets, cashflow and workload arrangements should ensure that there is equity in outcomes regardless of when in the year the first approach is made'.

15.111 The guidance advises that the measurement of the target time for the completion of assessment should begin at the point at which a priority is assigned and that this must be done within two working days of the receipt of an enquiry or referral (para 4.9) and that the applicant must be advised of this and given an explanation of (among other things) the local authority's criteria for its priorities and the likely timescale for the completion of the assessment.

15.112 Any social welfare system of this nature must endeavour to prioritise those whose needs are most urgent while ensuring that all potential applicants are dealt with expeditiously and in accordance with the law. Inevitably there is potential for conflict, since a clear prioritisation process is only one part of a fair and legal scheme. A poorly resourced system might have an admirable prioritisation process – but in practice might only progress the applications of those in most urgent need. Although the local government ombudsmen have long accepted (and indeed advocated for) local authority DFG prioritisation procedures,[124] this approach was questioned by the High Court (as noted above – see para 15.105) in *Qazi v Waltham Forest LBC.*[125]

15.113 In the last decade, the ombudsmen appear to be developing a more consistent approach on this question – namely that provided all grants are processed expeditiously, such an arrangement is to be encouraged. The problem is, however, that there is evidence to suggest that the focus on prioritisation arrangements has led to a neglect of the severe and widespread problem of chronic delay for non-priority applicants – whose need may still be very substantial.

---

122 Complaint no 06/C/16349 against Sheffield City Council, 26 June 2008. In this case the delay was such that the disabled person and his family put in place the adaptations, before the grant was finalised: the ombudsman noted that the council had reimbursed this expenditure (over £14,000) and paid £2,000 compensation for 'the indignity, inconvenience and distress that he experienced and his time and trouble in pursuing his complaint'.

123 It is maladministration for an authority not to allocate sufficient funds to 'meet the demand for DFGs' – see complaint no 07/C/01269 against Lincoln CC and 07/C/09724 against West Lindsey DC, 14 October 2009 para 34.

124 See eg complaint no 04/C/12312 against West Lancashire DC, 9 June 2005, complaint no 02/C/04897 against Morpeth BC and Northumberland CC, 27 November 2003; and complaint no 04/C/12312 against West Lancashire DC, 9 June 2005.

125 (1999) 32 HLR 689, a case based upon an allegation of misfeasance in public office and negligent misstatement.

15.114   The local government ombudsman's concern about chronic delay and the importance of having reasonable time targets for the completion of works, is evidenced in a 2002 report in which it was stated that she did 'not accept that lack of resources is an acceptable reason for excessive delays in helping people whose need have been clearly assessed and accepted' and that she 'would generally regard any delay beyond six months as unjustified'.[126] Likewise in a 2006 report[127] the ombudsman stated:

> It seems to me that eight months is an unreasonable length of time for a disabled person to have to wait for a request for adaptations to be properly assessed; and then to wait a further six months for the relatively minor adaptations recommended to be carried out . . . In my view, a process taking 14 months should have taken no longer than six months to complete.

15.115   The practice guidance advises that in the setting of target times for the processing of DFGs local authorities should estimate the complete process (ie including the period prior to the formal application). It then provides (at page 54) a table (Table 18 below) to illustrate 'a possible approach to time targeting, setting out possible target times for each stage from the initial enquiry about services, which may or may not result in a DFG, to completion of adaptations work' (at para 9.3). As noted above (see para 15.39) the local government ombudsman has used these timescale targets as the benchmark for maladministration determinations.

Interim arrangements

15.116   In many, if not most, cases there will be a delay between the identification of a need for adaptations and the completion of the works. Local authorities have an obligation, not only to process the DFG application with expedition, but also to ameliorate – to the extent that they are able – the hardship experienced by the disabled person (and all others affected) by any delay and by the works, if they are extensive and if they severely disrupt ordinary living arrangements. In this respect the practice guidance advises that (para 5.40):

> It is not acceptable that the disabled person and carers should be left for a period of weeks or months without such interim help when the timescale for the provision of an adaptation is foreseen to be lengthy. In addition to the problems an absence of interim measures may cause for the disabled person and for carers, it may result in additional costs for Health and Social Care authorities.

15.117   In relation to the disruption caused by building works the advice is as follows:

> 5.43 . . . where the period of significant disruption is expected to be only a few days then the disabled person may be able to stay with friends or

---

126   Complaint nos 02/C/8679, 02/C/8681 and 02/C/10389 against Bolsover DC, 30 September 2003.
127   Complaint no 05/B/00246 against Croydon LBC, 24 July 2006 para 37.

Table 18:   Disabled Facilities Grants

INDICATIVE TIME TARGETS (working days)	Priority ranking in Assessment		
	High	Medium	Low
Referral to allocation/response (including screening, prioritisation and preliminary test of resources form issued)	2	2	2
(NB where complex needs are identified some time may elapse before the need for adaptation is clarified and the process proceeds)			
Assessment carried out within:	3	15	40
Recommendation and report prepared and forwarded	2	5	5
Notice to disabled person of recommendation and application form issued	2	2	2
Home visits to assist in completion of form, measure up and consult on proposals	5	15	30
Preparation of schedule and drawings	10	20	30
Second home visit to confirm proposals	5	15	30
Issue specification to contractors, concurrently seek confirmation of title, etc	3	5	5
Await return of tenders, concurrently seek completion of full test of resources	30	30	30
Evaluate tenders, calculate and check DFG, issue confirmation of DFG	3	5	5
Date to start not exceeding	10	30	60

Time on site will depend upon the size and complexity of works but allow 5 days per £5,000 value for general building work, less when value includes major items of equipment such as stairlifts:

For average DFG of £5,000:	5	5	5
Inspection on completion	1	2	5
Secure guarantees and documentation, advise on repair and maintenance, consult disabled person on satisfaction, consider any remaining needs	2	5	10
TOTALS	**83**	**151**	**259**

family, or take a holiday. The social services and the housing authority should consider meeting all or part of the costs arising from such arrangements.

5.44 Where more prolonged disruption is unavoidable then a temporary move to other accommodation should be considered. An RSL or the local authority housing service may have appropriate stock available. Arranging such a temporary move is a complex and difficult business in which practical and financial support should be available where the disabled person requests it.

15.118 The local government has considered complaints where councils have failed to make suitable interim arrangements. In a 2009 report, a delay in processing a DFG meant that the family were without suitable bathing assistance. A proposal that the bathing take place on an interim basis at a nearby Day Centre was turned down by the panel (see para 3.188) – a decision found to be maladministration by the ombudsman. A 2008 report came to a similar finding where the disabled person had to spend an extended period in a residential placement – the costs of which the ombudsman recommended be reimbursed to the disabled person.[128]

Supporting People programme

15.119   In 2003, in an effort to streamline the housing benefit scheme, the costs attributable to various housing support services required by vulnerable people, were transferred to a separate budget – the 'Supporting People programme'. People who needed these support services ceased to be eligible for enhanced rates of housing benefit, but sought instead assistance with the costs from the Supporting People administering authority – essentially the social services authority in whose area they lived.

15.120   The statutory basis for the Supporting People programme is LGA 2000 s93. Section 93 authorises the secretary of state and the Welsh Government to pay grants to local authorities towards expenditure incurred by them 'in providing, or contributing to the provision of, such welfare services' as the secretary of state/Welsh Government determine or 'in connection with any such welfare services'. Section 93 empowers the secretary of state/Welsh Government to issue guidance and directions and to set terms and conditions for the award of grant support.

15.121   The Supporting People programme in England (which has now been effectively annulled) was previously underpinned by a regulations, directions, formal grant conditions and guidance – details of which are to be found in the fourth edition of this book, paras 15.99–15.111.

15.122   The specific section 93 scheme was, however, withdrawn in England in April 2011 and the monies formerly paid under this grant to social services authorities, are now paid as part of the standard formula grant. The funds are no longer ring-fenced and the recipient authorities would appear to have a wide discretion over how they are spent. The speed with which this grant has disappeared has resulted in a degree of confusion – for example, it is still cited as a qualifying benefit for the purposes of the Disabled People's Rights to Control (Pilot Scheme) (England) Regulations 2010 (see para 4.128 above). A particular difficulty relates to the status of such support that disabled and older people are continuing to receive. Is it now to be deemed a community care support services (although previously such support was explicitly outside the community care scheme) or possibly a Local Government Act 2000, s2 well-being payment (see para 1.68 above)? No guidance on this question had been issued as at September 2011 – particularly as to what, if any, charges can be levied for the support payments that are made with these funds. This issue is further considered at para 10.75 above.

---

128   Complaint no 07/B/07346 against Walsall Metropolitan Borough Council, 17 June 2008 para 25 and 28.

15.123 In Wales, the statutory scheme still operates and is governed by detailed 2010 guidance[129] which requires that the Supporting People Revenue Grant be used to prevent certain vulnerable people from becoming homeless or requiring residential institutional services. The categories of person for whom the payments can be made are:

- Women fleeing domestic violence
- Men fleeing domestic violence
- People with learning difficulties
- People with mental health problems
- People suffering from alcohol dependency
- People suffering from drug dependency
- Refugees
- People with physical disabilities who require support
- Young single homeless who require support and young people leaving care
- Ex-offenders
- People who are homeless or potentially homeless and in need of support
- People with chronic illness including AIDS, AIDS-related conditions or who are HIV positive
- Vulnerable single parents who require support.

15.124 Specific (2003) guidance[130] on charging for such support is considered at para 10.75 above.

Adult placements or shared lives schemes

15.125 Adult placements or 'shared lives schemes' are frequently likened to fostering arrangements. They involve a provider (often, but not always, a local authority) placing a vulnerable and disabled adult in the care (and frequently the home) of an approved adult placement carer. Most commonly the disabled person has learning disabilities but the scheme is not limited in this respect and can provide for people with physical disabilities, mental health issues or drug/alcohol problems. It appears that there are about 10,000 adult placement schemes in England[131] and about 234 in Wales.[132]

15.126 The purpose of such an arrangement is to enable the person to live as independently and to have as normal a life in the community as is possible. Placements may be long term or as a transitional arrangement. Before any placement the disabled person must have been assessed under the community care legislation and the placement must be deemed an appropriate care plan to meet the person's assessed needs.

129 Welsh Assembly Government (2010) *Supporting People Revenue Grant: the grant conditions and criteria.*
130 Welsh Assembly Government (2003) *Supporting People in Wales: charging and financial assessment for recipients of supporting people services.*
131 NAPPS (2010) *The shared life of my choice* at www.naaps.co.uk.
132 Care and Social Services Inspectorate Wales (2008) *Adult Placement Schemes 2007–08.*

15.127   Adult placement carers are self employed and in Wales can care for a maximum, at any one time, of two adults.[133] Although there is no longer an equivalent maximum number in England, in practice the limit of three adults (imposed by the previous legislative regime[134]) remains, since such schemes can benefit from simplified regulatory arrangements concerning houses in multiple occupation, taxation, fire/health and safety as well as dedicated insurance facilities.[135]

Statutory and regulatory regime

15.128   As with all care standards regulation (see paras 7.101 and 9.14 above) adult placement schemes are subject to distinct regimes in England and Wales. In England the Health and Social Care Act 2008 (Regulated Activities) Regulations 2010 reg 2 defines an 'adult placement scheme' as:

> . . . a scheme carried on (whether or not for profit) by a local authority or other person for the purposes of –
>
> (a) recruiting and training adult placement carers;
> (b) making arrangements for the placing of service users with adult placement carers; and
> (c) supporting and monitoring placements; . . .

and an 'adult placement carer' is defined as an individual who, under the terms of a carer agreement, provides, or intends to provide, personal care for service users together with, where necessary, accommodation in the individual's home. Such schemes need register only for the regulated activity 'personal care' even though they provide accommodation since they are specifically exempted in this latter respect by Schedule 1 para 2 (a) of the 2010 Regulations. As with all registrations under the HSCA 2008 regime – the care services must meet the same standards as any other provider (see para 9.20 above).

15.129   In England adult placement schemes are required to adhere to the Care Quality Commission's (CQC) 'Essential standards of quality and safety'[136] that apply to all care providers as well as the Good Practice Guide jointly published by the CQC and the shared lives provider organisation NAPPS.[137] In Wales National Minimum Standards for Adult Placement Schemes have been published[138] in accordance with Care Standards Act 2000 s23.

133   Adult Placement Schemes (Wales) Regulations 2004 SI No 1756 (W188) reg 2.
134   Adult Placement Schemes (England) Regulations 2004 SI No 2071 reg 2.
135   See Care Quality Commission (2010) *Shared Lives Schemes: joint statement by cqc and NAAPS* and supporting notes, p5 and generally NAPPS (2011) *Homeshare Good Practice Guide*, 3rd edition at www.naaps.co.uk.
136   Care Quality Commission (2010) *Guidance about compliance: essential standards of quality and safety.*
137   NAPPS (2011) *Homeshare Good Practice Guide*, 3rd edition at www.naaps.co.uk/ and see Care Quality Commission (2010) *Shared Lives Schemes: Joint statement by CQC and NAAPS and supporting notes.*
138   Care and Social Services Inspectorate Wales (2004) *National minimum standards for adult placement schemes.*

15.130   In Wales adult placement schemes are subject to regulations[139] made under the Care Standards Act 2000, The regulations provide for the control and conduct of such schemes – including such matters as the fitness of the persons carrying on and managing a scheme and the terms and conditions upon which a person can be placed, the monitoring and review of such placements.

15.131   The Welsh Regulations (reg 2) defines an 'adult placement scheme' as:

> . . . a scheme under which arrangements are made or proposed to be made for not more than two adults to be accommodated and provided with personal care in the home of a person who is not their relative; . . .

and an 'adult placement carer' is defined as 'a person in whose home an adult is or may be accommodated and provided with personal care under an adult placement agreement entered into or proposed to be entered into by the carer'.

15.132   Since it is the scheme that is registered (in both England and Wales) and not the placement, it means that disabled people in such placements are not subject to the 'ordinary residence' 'deeming rules' under NAA 1948 s24 (see para 6.18 above) and neither are they subject to the residential charging rules, but can claim benefits and are charged for their care as if they were living in their own home (see below).

Charging

15.133   Disabled people in an adult placement can be charged for their accommodation in the normal way – and apply for housing benefit to help with such costs.[140] Their care support services are subject to the standard charging rules applying to all non-domiciliary care services –these are considered at chapter 10, above.

Supported living

15.134   Supported living is a generic term that has come to describe arrangements whereby a local authority secures a package of care together with accommodation for a disabled, elderly or ill person. However, because of the way the arrangements are made (the delivery of care being separated at an organisational level, from the provision of accommodation[141]), the

---

139   Adult Placement Schemes (Wales) Regulations 2004 SI No 1756 (W188).
140   Almost invariably, such schemes will not, however, qualify as exempt accommodation for housing benefit purposes – see Upper Tribunal decision [2009] UKUT 12 (AAC) and para 15.139 below.
141   The Care Standards Act 2000 s3(2) (which applies in Wales) requires establishments to be registered if they provide accommodation 'together with nursing or personal care'; and in England in general the provision of residential accommodation, 'together with nursing or personal care' is a regulated activity under Health and Social Care Act 2008 (Regulated Activities) Regulations 2010 SI No 781 Sch 1 para 2 – see para 15.145 below.

accommodation is not deemed to be a registered care home and so does not have to be registered as such under the relevant legislation.

15.135   Apart from the laudable goal of maximising user independence, local authorities have a number of reasons for promoting such schemes, not least government targets and local finances. A department of health performance indicator places emphasis on councils spending that less than 40 per cent of their overall adult social care budget on 'residential care'[142] and the social security system places a greater burden on local finances for service users living in residential care accommodation than it does for those living 'independently'. In practice, authorities can improve local finances and their 'performance ratings' simply by changing the status of someone's accommodation – for instance by encouraging the home to 'deregister' (see para 15.145 below).

15.136   Such a change may result in no greater independence for the service user and in certain situations it may result in less security and indeed an inferior support package. It follows that local authority activity to promote 'supported living' packages is not necessarily synonymous with the promotion of independent living.

15.137   Key elements of 'supported living' arrangements include:

1) **Non-residential care**
   The service user does not live in a residential care home ie is not funded under NAA 1948, s21. In certain situations this has involved deregistration of care homes and this question is addressed at para 15.145 below. It follows that the local authority social services support provided under the arrangement will be delivered as a domiciliary care package – most probably under CSDPA 1970 s2 (see para 9.76 above).

2) **Tenancy rights**
   Frequently the former care home resident is granted an assured tenancy of the property he or she occupies, in order to attract housing benefit for the rental component and 'supporting people' funding for housing related support (see para 15.119 below). On occasions there may be questions as to whether the service user has sufficient mental capacity to enter into a tenancy[143] and this question is considered further at para 17.26. The courts and the Care Quality Commission have made it clear that the mere fact that a person has a tenancy agreement, does not in itself mean that it is not a residential care home for registration purposes (see para 15.152 below).

3) **Mixed funding streams**
   A wide range of funding streams may be attracted by such an arrangement. These may include, in addition to social security and disability related benefits for the service user, Independent Living Fund

---

142 Department of Health (2009) *Use of resources in adult social care – a guide for local authorities*, p6.

143 It appears that if the landlord is aware of the incapacity (to enter into a tenancy) at the time the tenancy is entered into, this has the effect of creating a valid (but voidable) contract – voidable by the tenant – and so housing benefit is payable for such an arrangement. See decision of Social Security Commissioner Mesher, CH/2121/2006, 13 November 2006 analysed in *Social Care Law Today*, Issue 47, May 2007.

support (prior to December 2010) and in appropriate cases funding via NHSA 2006 ss256–257[144] in cases where the NHS and social services agree to joint funding arrangement (see para 13.122 above).

The mix of benefits and grants that are attracted by supported living arrangements has the benefit in many cases of increasing the overall amount of funding available for an individual package (and decreasing the local authority contribution). It has dangers, however, since some of the funding streams are insecure – as has proved to be the case with the supported living grant (see para 15.119 above) and the Independent Living Fund (see para 12.95 above) – and even those that may endure, may see changes to their qualifying criteria. In this respect, housing benefit entitlement changes have caused significant difficulties for some such schemes – and this question is considered at para 15.139 below).

4) **Ordinary residence**

Determination of a person's ordinary residence is considered at chapter 6 above. Particular difficulties can arise where a supported living arrangement involves a service user placed outside the area of the funding authority. If the initial placement is in a registered care home, the service user's ordinary residence is deemed by NAA 1948 s24(5) to be that of the placing authority and not the host authority and accordingly the placing authority retains financial responsibility. If, however, the care home deregisters or the service user moves into ordinary (ie non-registered) accommodation, in principle the ordinary residence changes and crystallises with the host authority – evidenced by the *R (Buckinghamshire CC) v Kingston upon Thames*[145] proceedings – considered at para 6.28 above.

15.138 Disabled people in supported living schemes can be charged for their care support in the normal way – ie subject to the standard charging rules applying to all non-domiciliary care services. These are considered at chapter 10, above. Guidance has been issued (jointly with the Department of Health) concerning charges for such schemes.[146]

Housing benefit and independent living schemes

15.139 A key factor in many supported living schemes is their ability to access higher rates of housing benefit. Such payments are only made in relation to 'exempt accommodation' for certain vulnerable groups, for which the entitlement criteria were highlighted in what has come to be known as the *Turnbull decision*.[147] In 2008 the Department of Work and Pensions issued

---

144 NHS(W)A 2006 ss194–196 provide LHBs with the same powers.
145 [2011] EWCA Civ 457, (2011) 14 CCLR 425: at first instance as [2010] EWHC 1703 (Admin).
146 See Housing Learning and Improvement Network (2010) *Charging in extra care housing* at www.housinglin.org.uk/Topics/type/resource/?cid=7337&.
147 The decision of the Social Security Commissioner Charles Turnbull, CH/423/2006, 19 June 2006 (generally known as the 'Turnbull decision').

helpful guidance on this question, which summarises a number of the relevant commissioners' decisions.[148]

15.140   To be exempt accommodation,[149] it must be provided by a:

- non-metropolitan county council in England;
- housing association (as defined in Housing Associations Act 1985 s1(1));
- registered charity (as defined in Charities Act 2006 Part 1), or
- voluntary organisation (as defined in Housing Benefit Regulations 2006 SI No 213 – reg 2(1)

15.141   The landlord must be providing care, support or supervision, which must be 'more than minimal' – ie which 'goes beyond that which is normally provided by a housing provider'. This may, however, include the carrying out of repairs and maintenance to accommodation which goes beyond 'ordinary housing management' – for example, a higher level of repairs caused by residents with challenging behaviour or installing a bath lift, or providing specialist non-slip flooring.[150] Although the care/support must be provided by 'or on behalf of'[151] the landlord, it does not have to be the main provider of the person's care.

15.142   The scheme must not be a 'sham' – ie one 'contrived to take advantage' of this particular exemption.

15.143   Although exempt accommodation is not subject to the 'local reference rent' restrictions, a housing authority is not obliged to pay the full amount claimed if it considers that there is suitable alternative accommodation available for the particular claimant and to which it would be reasonable for that person to move to.[152]

15.144   The amount of housing benefit paid may include costs to cover communal charges (such as the cleaning of communal areas) where the accommodation is deemed to be 'sheltered accommodation'.[153] The Upper Tribunal has held that 'sheltered accommodation' is a reasonably wide concept and not (for example, restricted to warden controlled accommodation or accommodation with an alarm system).[154]

---

148 Department for Work and Pensions (2008) *Guidance to Local Authorities on dealing with claims from those living in supported accommodation* at www.dwp.gov.uk/docs/ a22–2008.pdf.

149 Housing Benefit and Council Tax Benefit (Consequential Provisions) Regulations 2006 SI No 217 Sch 3 para 4(10).

150 *Chorley BC v IT* [2009] UKUT 107 (AAC) 12 June 2009 – see analysis (2009) *Journal of Community Care Law* Issue 59 Sept 2009 p11.

151 See the 'Turnbull decision' (above) CH/423/2006 and *R (S) v Social Security Commissioner and others* [2009] EWHC 2221 (Admin).

152 In such cases, however, the onus is on the authority to establish these facts –see CH/ 3528–3560/2007 considered at p23 of the DWP guide.

153 Housing Benefit Regulations 2006 SI No 213 Sch 1(5).

154 *JB v Oxford City Council* [2011] UKUT 136 (AAC) see (2011) *Journal of Community Care Law* issue 74 June 2011 p14.

Deregistration

15.145 As noted above, over the last decade a number of residential care homes have sought to change their registration status (in England with what is now the 'Care Quality Commission' and in Wales with the Care and Social Services Inspectorate Wales) so that they are no longer a 'care home' in the sense of being an establishment that provides both accommodation and social care. In order to achieve this change, they have sought to separate the provision of accommodation from the provision of care.[155] A consequence of this alteration is that the accommodation is deemed not to be 'residential accommodation' and so not subject to a general exclusion for housing benefit purposes[156] and also eligible for 'supporting people's funding'.[157]

15.146 Where a care home seeks to deregister, it must consult with its residents – and in certain situations an independent mental capacity advocate (see para 17.67 below) should be instructed.[158] The same obligation applies where a registered social landlord is contemplating the closure of a supported living scheme.[159]

15.147 The mere fact that accommodation and care services are provided by separate legal entities (as may happen in 'supported housing' schemes for instance) does not in itself mean that the unit is not required to be registered as a care home (or in England as a provider of residential accommodation, 'together with' personal care' – see para 7.94 above).

15.148 In *Alternative Futures Ltd v National Care Standards Commission*[160] the Care Standards Tribunal held that whether an establishment was a 'care home' for the purposes of the Care Standards Act 2000, was, in borderline cases, a difficult question for which no single factor could be considered determinative. Thus the fact that the care and accommodation were provided by separate companies was not conclusive (especially if these

---

155 The Care Standards Act 2000 s3(2) (which applies in Wales) requires establishments to be registered if they provide accommodation 'together with nursing or personal care'; and in England in general the provision of residential accommodation, 'together with nursing or personal care' is a regulated activity under Health and Social Care Act 2008 (Regulated Activities) Regulations 2010 SI No 781 Sch 1 para 2.

156 But see the Housing Benefit Regulations 2006 SI No 213 reg 7.

157 Research suggests that the rapid expansion of supported living schemes, following the sudden availability of supporting people monies may have 'diluted the meaning' of 'supported living' – such that some were 'little different from the registered care homes they had replaced' see R Fyson, B Tarleton and L Ward (2007) *The impact of the Supporting People programme in adults with learning disabilities*, Joseph Rowntree Foundation.

158 The Code of Practice to the Mental Capacity Act 2005 para 10.54 – see para 17.3 below: see also Social Care Institute for Excellence (SCIE) *Good practice guidance for the commissioning and monitoring of Independent Mental Capacity Advocate (IMCA) Services* SCIE 31 – deregistering services at www.scie.org.uk/publications/guides/guide39/services/index.asp

159 Under the Housing Act 1985 landlords must consult secure tenants and take account of their views in 'matters of housing management' and the Housing Corporation (in its Regulatory Code) requires all registered landlords to meet similar requirements and offers good practice advice.

160 (2004) 7 CCLR 171.

services remained closely co-ordinated) nor was the level of personal care provided,[161] nor was the provision of tenancies to the residents, nor the fact that the residents had 'person centred' care plans.

15.149   In the tribunal's view an important factor was that of choice – that it was necessary for the provider to demonstrate that service users were genuinely able to choose who provided their personal care.

15.150   The tribunal's decision was the subject of an unsuccessful judicial review by some of the care home residents. In the High Court[162] Mitting J upheld the decision but questioned whether the reliance on user choice was a relevant question, commenting that 'it was unnecessary for it to go on to consider, let alone hold to be decisive, the absence of choice by residents when entering into the new arrangements'.[163] The Court of Appeal[164] concurred. It agreed that 'establishment' need not have a technical meaning and could include a situation where different agencies provided the accommodation and care services – and that there was nothing in principle to exclude the provision of accommodation by way of a tenancy.[165] In the court's view:

> The crucial consideration is whether the establishment provides the accommodation together with nursing or personal care. That is essentially a question of fact which does not arise in the present case as the appellants accepted for the purposes of the appeal that Housing and Futures, together with each house, were an establishment. The establishment of a lessor and lessee relationship can be an indicator of a situation where an establishment does not provide both the accommodation and the care, but cannot be determinative.[166]

15.151   The CQC has issued 2011 guidance concerning the registration of supported living schemes under the Health and Social Care Act 2008.[167] It defines (at page 5) such schemes in the following terms:

> Where people live in their own home and receive care and/or support in order to promote their independence. If there is genuine separation between the care and the accommodation, the care they receive is regulated by CQC, but the accommodation is not. The support that people receive is

---

161   As the tribunal noted, 'the level of personal care is not on its own the determining factor. We agree . . . that s 121(9) must not be read to mean that where bodily assistance is provided or required then registration as a care home is required'.

162   *R (Moore) v Care Standards Tribunal and National Care Standards Commission* [2004] EWHC 2481 (Admin), (2005) 8 CCLR 91.

163   *R (Moore) v Care Standards Tribunal and National Care Standards Commission* [2004] EWHC 2481 (Admin), (2005) 8 CCLR 91 at [34].

164   *Moore v Care Standards Tribunal and Commission for Social Care Inspection* [2005] EWCA Civ 627, [2005] 1 WLR 2979, (2005) 8 CCLR 354.

165   The existence of tenancies was contested in the appeal although the court expressed reservations about the possibility of tenancies in the present case – see *Moore v Care Standards Tribunal and Commission for Social Care Inspection* [2005] EWCA Civ 627, [2005] 1 WLR 2979, (2005) 8 CCLR 354 at [10]–[11].

166   *Moore v Care Standards Tribunal and Commission for Social Care Inspection* [2005] EWCA Civ 627, [2005] 1 WLR 2979, (2005) 8 CCLR 354 at [21].

167   Care Quality Commission (2011) *Supported living schemes: regulated activities for which the provider may need to register: guidance for providers* PoC1C 100832.

often continuous and tailored to their individual needs. It aims to enable the person to be as autonomous and independent as possible, and usually involves social support rather than medical care.

15.152 The guidance at pages 7–8 provides the following advice as to the approach that the Commission takes to registration in such cases:

8. What factors may be indicative of accommodation being provided 'together with' care?

There are a number of possible indicators to be taken into consideration in making a judgement about whether the accommodation and care are provided together. The indicators below are not conclusive in their own right and it is important to consider the whole picture. They will not all be applicable in every case.

- The provider of the care and the accommodation is the same legal entity, with no clear separation between the provision of the two elements.
- (Note, however, that although the accommodation and care have to be provided together to satisfy the regulated activity definition, this does not have to be by the same company or individual. There may be different legal entities involved, for example different companies within the same group, or organisations that are otherwise unrelated but work together in some way to provide the service given. The facts surrounding how the entities function in practice to provide the service are what is important and this will need to be examined in each case.)
- Any tendering process undertaken did not permit different unconnected organisations to tender for the care and for the accommodation.
- The two functions of care and accommodation are provided literally 'together', that is, wholly joined and relying on each other. They could be different legal entities, or different arms of a social landlord, but there is significant connection or coordination between the two.
- There is mutual reliance or coordination between the two functions.
- Receiving accommodation is dependent on receiving care from the accommodation provider or an associated company body, and vice versa.
- Accommodation is dependent on the receipt of care from a given care provider, with no element of choice on the part of the person using the service.
- People using the service do not hold genuine and valid tenancy agreements.

9. If people have a tenancy agreement, does this mean the service is not providing care and accommodation together?

No, even if people using the service do hold genuine and valid tenancy agreements, this in itself does not mean that the accommodation and care is not being provided together. It will depend on the overall picture of accommodation and care provision.

- The terms of the tenancy, the extent to which the rights of occupation may be linked to the care, or a care provider, will be important. It may also indicate that the tenancy is not independent of the care provider.

- In some cases, there may be one contract that covers the care and accommodation or one over-arching framework agreement or contract (such as a management agreement which covers the sharing of landlord and/or care functions). You should consider whether the terms of the agreement mean that the accommodation and personal care are provided as one service.

CHAPTER 16

Carers

continued

Diagram 19: The rights of carers

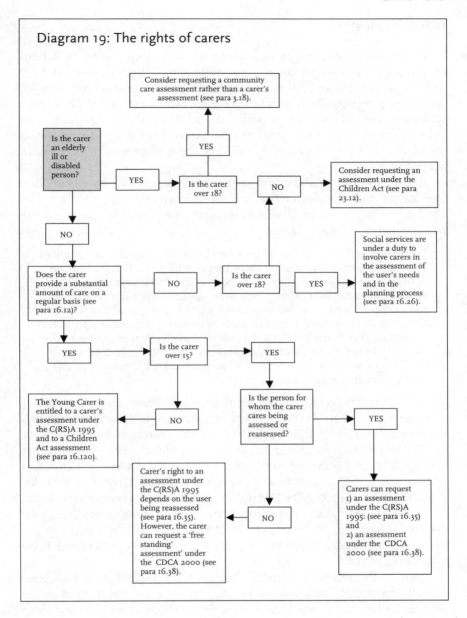

Introduction

16.1   The 2001 census reveals that there are nearly six million 'carers' in Britain of whom 1.25 million provide care for more than 50 hours a week, and 1.9 million for more than 20 hours. Roughly half of all carers combine work with caring responsibilities, while 174,995 carers are under 18. Caring varies between ethnic groups, with Bangladeshi and Pakistani men and women three times more likely to be carers than their British white counterparts.[1] Providing care has left 55 per cent of carers with significant health problems.[2]

16.2   A key objective of the community care reforms was to ensure that 'service providers made practical support for carers a high priority'.[3] The 1989 white paper[4] emphasised the crucial role played by carers in the provision of community care:

> The reality is that most care is provided by family, friends and neighbours. The majority of carers take on these responsibilities willingly, but the Government recognises that many need help to be able to manage what can become a heavy burden. Their lives can be made much easier if the right support is there at the right time, and a key responsibility of statutory service providers should be to do all they can to assist and support carers. Helping carers to maintain their valuable contribution to the spectrum of care is both right and a sound investment. Help may take the form of providing advice and support as well as practical services such as day, domiciliary and respite care.[5]

16.3   Since 1986 carers have attracted significant legislative attention. Initially as a passing reference in the Disabled Persons (Services, Consultation and Representation) Act (DP(SCR)A) 1986 and then through a series of carer specific statutes, originating as private members' bills – the Carers (Recognition and Services) Act (C(RS)A) 1995, the Carers and Disabled Children Act (CDCA) 2000 and the Carers (Equal Opportunities) Act (C(EO)A) 2004. Since 2004 the rights of carers are, increasingly, being addressed in general statutes whose focus is wider than carers caring for disabled, elderly or ill people: relevant examples of this trend are the Work and Families Act 2006 and the Childcare Act 2006, both of which are considered below.

16.4   Prior to the enactment of C(EO)A 2004 the Carers' Acts had been directly concerned with sustaining the caring role: ensuring that the services received by the disabled person were sufficient to enable the carer to maintain a caring role. The 2004 Act adopted a different approach seeking to address the social exclusion experienced by many carers (in

---

1   *Who cares wins, statistical analysis of the Census*, Carers UK, 2001. See also *Half a million voices: improving support for BAME carers*, Carers UK, 2011.
2   Research reported in *Missed opportunities: the impact of new rights for carers*, Carers UK, 2003.
3   *Caring for People*, Cm 849, 1989, para 1.11.
4   *Caring for People*, Cm 849, 1989, para 1.11.
5   *Caring for People*, Cm 849, 1989, para 2.3.

effect 'by association' with disabled people). It focussed on opportunities to work, to study and to engage in a life beyond caring.

16.5   One reflection of the growing recognition of the importance of carers has been the development of National Carers' Strategies in England[6] and Wales[7] to determine the national policy agenda for carers. The coalition government has identified the following priorities for the next three to four years:

- Supporting those with caring responsibilities to identify themselves as carers at an early stage, recognising the value of their contribution and involving them from the outset both in designing local care provision and in planning individual care packages.
- Enabling those with caring responsibilities to fulfil their educational and employment potential.
- Personalised support both for carers and those they support, enabling them to have a family and community life.
- Supporting carers to remain mentally and physically well.[8]

At the time of writing the Welsh Assembly Government is carrying out a review of its carers' strategy.

16.6   The coalition government sees carers as embodying 'the spirit of the big society' and thus, 'Supporting carers' well-being is therefore in all our interests. There are key issues – employment, support, respite – that carers are likely to face in their caring role'.[9] However, the significant reduction in public sector resources and the increasing reliance on 'social capital' for the delivery of social care (see para 3.7 above) will inevitably shift more caring responsibilities onto informal carers. There is an inherent tension between shrinking resources and tightened eligibility criteria on the one hand and the laudable aim for carers to achieve greater autonomy on the other. This conflict is thrown into sharp relief by the findings of a study by Leeds University and Carers UK into carers and employment:

> Caring should not end a carer's career, damage their education, put their ability to acquire skills and training at risk, or force them to give up work. Although most working carers in the CES study felt they had support from their family and friends in combining work and care, and about half considered their employer was 'carer-friendly', only a minority (about a quarter) believed they had adequate support from formal services – even though 42% were paying privately for these. Very few were getting carer's breaks or respite services, and a large minority felt poorly informed about available support. Many stressed that they were keen to continue in work – yet more than a third had considered giving up because of their caring role[10].

6   In England, HM Government (2008) *Carers at the heart of 21st century families and communities*, updated by the coalition government in HM Government (2010) *Recognised, valued and supported: next steps for the carers strategy*.
7   In Wales, *Carers strategy action plan 2007*.
8   *Recognised, valued and supported* (note 6 above), p6.
9   *Recognised, valued and supported* (note 6 above), p3.
10   S Yeandle and L Buckner *Carers, employment and services: time for a new social contract?* Carers UK and University of Leeds, 2007.

Statutory overview

16.7   Of the three Acts that deal directly with the needs of carers, C(RS)A 1995 contains the core statutory responsibilities. It introduced the concept of a 'carer's assessment'. The CDCA 2000 extended the rights of carers, to include the right to support services, and for these services to be made available by way of direct payments and 'vouchers'. The C(EO)A 2004 extended the obligations in relation to assessments, by: (1) introducing a statutory obligation on social services to inform carers of their rights, and (2) by requiring that carer's assessments consider whether the carer works or wishes to work and/or is undertaking, or wishes to undertake, education, training or any leisure activity.

Guidance

16.8   Guidance has been issued in relation to all three carers Acts. Policy and practice guidance was issued concerning C(RS)A 1995 in England[11] and Wales[12] (in identical terms). A number of volumes of guidance were issued concerning CDCA 2000, both in England and in Wales.[13] The policy guidance for CDCA 2000 has, in England, been consolidated (see below) but the English practice guidance[14] remains relevant.[15] In addition guidance has been issued in both England and Wales (in very similar terms) concerning the carer's assessment process.[16]

16.9   In 2004 combined policy guidance was issued by the Department of Health concerning both CDCA 2000 and C(EO)A 2004. In addition, practice guidance on C(EO)A 2004 was issued by the Social Care Institute for Excellence (SCIE).[17] In Wales no guidance on this Act has been issued, although in anticipation of the implementation of the Act an additional

---

11   *Carers (Recognition and Services) Act 1995: Policy guidance and practice guidance* LAC (96)7.

12   *Carers (Recognition and Services) Act 1995 Guidance* WOC 16/96: WHC (96)21.

13   Comprising in England (1) *Carers and Disabled Children Act 2000: carers and people with parental responsibility for disabled children: policy guidance*; (2) *Carers and Disabled Children Act 2000: carers and people with parental responsibility for disabled children: practice guidance*; (3) *Practitioners guide to carers' assessments under the Carers and Disabled Children Act 2000*; (4) *Carers and Disabled Children Act 2000: direct payments for young people: policy guidance and practice guidance*; (5) *Carers and Disabled Children Act 2000: practice guidance on the provisions of the Act as they affect disabled 16- and 17-year-old young people*; and in Wales (1) *Guidance 2000 Act*; and (2) *Practitioners guide to carers' assessment*.

14   Department of Health (2001) *Carers and Disabled Children Act 2000: practice guidance.*

15   The English practice guidance is similar (but slightly more extensive) than the Welsh policy guidance – namely Welsh Assembly (2001) *Guidance 2000 Act.*

16   Department of Health (2001) *Practitioners guide to carers' assessments under the Carers and Disabled Children Act 2000*, and Welsh Assembly (2001) *Practitioners guide to carers' assessment*, 2001.

17   *SCIE practice guide 5: implementing the Carers (Equal Opportunities) Act 2004.* The guidance is updated (most recently in October 2005). It has the status of Department of Health practice guidance: see statement by Liam Byrne, Parliamentary under Secretary of State for Care Services, HC Debates col 722W, 11 July 2005.

annex (12) to the Unified Assessment Process was issued to strengthen the practice obligations in Wales to provide separate carer's assessments.

Carer – definition

16.10 There is no single definition of a 'carer' although its use in this text excludes persons who are under a contract of employment to provide the care. National Health Service and Community Care Act (NHSCCA) 1990 s46(3) defines a private carer (for the purposes of strategic planning – see above) as:

> . . . a person who is not employed to provide the care in question by any body in the exercise of its function under any enactment.

16.11 Such a definition includes non-resident carers and makes no stipulation as to the age of the carer or the quantity or quality of care provided. In general any reference to a 'carer' (unless the context shows otherwise) must therefore be to such a heterogeneous group; indeed the 1990 policy guidance makes clear that the term may encompass 'families, friends and neighbours'.[18] The common denominator for such carers is that they all provide some 'service', even though this might be, for instance, in the form of advocacy or emotional support, rather than a personal care service of the kind delivered by a social services authority.

Defining 'substantial' and 'regular'

16.12 The carers Acts use, but do not define the phrase, 'substantial and regular care'. The Department of Health has elsewhere given advice on the interpretation of the word 'substantial' and advised that it should be given a 'wide interpretation' which takes 'full account of individual circumstances'.[19]

16.13 The English combined policy guidance[20] states:

> The process of assessing the impact of the caring role on the carer, and thus whether the care provided is regular and substantial, is based on a consideration of two dimensions:
> * key factors relevant to sustaining the chosen caring role,
> * extent of the risk to the sustainability of that role.
> Any such judgement should recognise that it is not only the time spent caring that has an impact on carers. For some, such as those caring for disabled children or adults with learning disabilities, the caring role can have the additional impact of being a life long commitment. Others, for example people caring for those with mental health problems or some neurological conditions, may have responsibilities that are not necessarily based on physical tasks and the caring role may be sporadic or preventative

---

18 1990 policy guidance para 3.28.
19 LAC (93)10 appendix 4 para 8: see para 9.35 above.
20 At paras 48–49 and the Welsh policy guidance to the 2000 Act at para 4.11.

in nature. The carer may not be physically or practically caring at all times, but may still be anxious or stressed waiting for, or trying to prevent, the next crisis. In addition, caring responsibilities may conflict with other family responsibilities such as parenting or holding down a job. Any assessment of the carer's need for support has to look at the impact of the whole caring situation.

16.14   It follows that what is 'substantial' has both a subjective and objective element and is primarily concerned with the impact that the caring role has on the individual carer.

16.15   It appears that the word 'regular' adds little to the qualifying require-ments, since 'regular' should be distinguished from 'frequent': merely connoting an event which recurs or is repeated at fixed times or uniform intervals.[21] The practice guidance to C(RS)A 1995[22] points out that:

> Some users with mental health or substance misuse problems or with conditions such as neurological disorders, dementia, cancer or HIV/AIDS will have care needs which vary over time but may present regular and substantial burdens for carers.

Thus 'regular', in the caring context, does not necessarily imply a uniform pattern. In practice, it appears simply to mean an ongoing caring responsibility.

Defining 'intending to provide'

16.16   A carer may be entitled to a carer's assessment even if not presently fulfilling a caring role, provided the authority is satisfied that he or she is intending to provide a substantial amount of care on a regular basis. The intent underlying this provision was explained by the policy guidance to C(RS)A 1995 (at para 16):

> By including carers both providing or intending to provide care, the Act covers those carers who are about to take on substantial and regular caring tasks for someone who has just become, or is becoming, disabled through accident or physical or mental ill health. Local and health authorities will need to ensure that hospital discharge procedures take account of the provisions of the Act and that carers are involved once planning discharge starts.

16.17   The provision (although not restricted to such cases) is of particular relevance to the carers of people who are about to be discharged from hospital. The English guidance on the hospital discharge process, *Ready to go: planning the discharge and the transfer of patients from hospital and intermediate care*, contains substantial advice concerning the involvement of carers, and is considered at para 5.8 above.

21   *Shorter Oxford English Dictionary.*
22   LAC (96)7 para 7; WOC 16/96 and WHC (96)21 in Wales.

Disputes as to whether a carer provides 'substantial' amounts of care

16.18   In practice, there should be little need for an authority to dispute whether a carer is providing regular and substantial care. The policy guidance implies a low threshold, emphasising as it does the importance of the carer's subjective experience of caring. Additionally, while authorities are under a duty to undertake assessments of carers who provide regular and substantial care, they have a power to assess carers even if their caring responsibilities are not deemed 'substantial' (under Local Government Act 2000 s2 if needs be – see para 1.68 above).

16.19   Not infrequently a local authority will be unable to decide upon the extent of a carer's responsibilities without undertaking such an assessment. Where there is uncertainty an assessment should take place. The local government ombudsman has been highly critical of a local authority that refused to undertake a carer's assessment in such circumstances, commenting:[23]

> It should also have been obvious to the Council that a carer's assessment was necessary in order to see (a) how much support [the carer] could reasonably be expected to provide for his brother without placing his own health at unacceptable risk; and (b) what practical help could be provided to [the carer] with respite from his caring responsibilities.

Employed and volunteer carers

16.20   The carers Acts do not give rights to persons who provide the care by virtue of a contract of employment or as volunteers for a voluntary organisation.[24] This restriction does not exclude carers who are in receipt of carer's allowance[25] or similar social security benefits, but care assistants employed by a home care service (whether private or public) will be excluded as may be foster carers of disabled children.

16.21   If a disabled person uses a community care direct payment (see para 12.20 below) to employ his or her (previously unpaid) carer, this might seem to disentitle that person to an assessment and services under the carers legislation. If, however, the carer provides additional (and substantial) care over and above that to which the payment relates, the entitlement to an assessment/services would remain, since the restriction only relates to carers who provide 'the care in question ... by virtue of a contract of employment'. The care in question will only amount to the eligible unmet needs of the disabled person, almost inevitably significantly less than the carer provides.

---

23   Complaint no 02/C/08690 against Sheffield City Council, 9 August 2004.
24   C(RS)A 1995 s1(3) and CDCA 2000 s1(3).
25   A taxable, non-contributory benefit for people aged 16 or over caring for more than 35 hours a week for someone who is getting attendance allowance or the middle/higher rate care component of disability living allowance.

Carers' involvement in community care assessments

16.22   As well as a specific duty to assess on request carers who provide substantial care on a regular basis, local authorities have obligations to carers during the assessment of a disabled person.

16.23   The Disabled Persons (Services, Consultation and Representation) Act 1986 s8(1)[26] provides that where:

(a) a disabled person is living at home and receiving a substantial amount of care on a regular basis from another person (who is not a person employed to provide such care by any body in the exercise of its functions under any enactment), and

(b) it falls to a local authority to decide whether the disabled person's needs call for the provision by them of any services for him under any of the welfare enactments,

the local authority shall, in deciding that question, have regard to the ability of that person to continue to provide such care on a regular basis.

16.24   Thus, whether or not a carer's assessment takes place, any service provision decision concerning a disabled person must be informed by and take into account the continuing ability of the carer to provide care. This applies whether or not a carer's assessment takes place and is not dependent on a request by the carer.

16.25   The Community Care Directions 2004, direction 2 requires that when undertaking a community care assessment, social services must:

• consider whether the person has any carers and, if so, also consult them if the authority 'thinks it appropriate'; and

• take all reasonable steps to reach agreement with the person and, where they think it appropriate, any carers of that person, on the community care services which they are considering providing to meet his or her needs.

16.26   This duty to involve carers, is not limited to carers who provide substantial care on a regular basis. Guidance issued concurrently with the Directions makes the point that the involvement of carers in the assessment process ensures that 'a realistic account' is taken of the carer's continuing ability to provide care and the sustainability of the caring role.[27] In cases where the disabled person lacks capacity to make some or all of the necessary decisions, the obligation to involve carers before a care plan is finalised, is in general better characterised as a duty.[28] If it is felt to be inappropriate to

---

26   This subsection of the Act came into force on 1 April 1987; subsections (2) and (3) are still not in force.

27   Department of Health (2004) *The Community Care Assessment Directions* LAC(2004)24 para 2.2.

28   See eg *R (W) v Croydon LBC* [2011] EWHC 696 (Admin) where the court considered that the obligation to undertake such consultation arose under, not only the Community Care Assessment Directions (direction 2), the NAA 1948 (Choice of Accommodation Directions); the Department of Health's 2010 policy guidance *Prioritising need in the context of Putting People First* as well as under the Mental Capacity Act 2005 s4 – see para 17.36).

involve a carer, the guidance states that there should be a record kept evidencing the active consideration of carer involvement and the reasons for deciding not to involve the carer in the assessment process.

16.27 The requirements of the Directions, as elaborated in the Guidance, and read together with extensive references to engagement with carers both in statutory guidance[29] and in the Code of Practice under the Mental Health Act 1983 (see paras 16.132–16.134 below) arguably give rise to a rebuttal presumption in favour of involving carers in the assessment and support planning of the disabled people for whom they provide care.

16.28 Local authorities have duties both towards carers and cared for, and decisions made in either case will almost inevitably affect both. As Dame Philippa Russell, Chair, Standing Commission on Carers, put it:

> Historically there has often been too much of a divide between the user and the carer, whereas the physical and emotional well-being of both are inextricably linked[30].

16.29 Best practice guidance[31] specifically focussing on carers and personalisation has identified the potential cost in terms of the health and well-being of both carer and cared for if the duty to consult carers in community care assessments is overlooked:

> Too often, carers have experienced a lack of co-ordination between the assessment of need for the person they support and both their own role in meeting that person's needs, and the support they might need in order to maintain that role. At best this is unnecessarily time consuming and wasteful of resources, and at worst it can lead to inaccurate assessments of individual needs for support and mistaken assumptions about the willingness and ability of carers to provide levels of care, which can have a detrimental effect on the health and well-being of all concerned.

16.30 The importance of the views and expertise of carers also underpins national carer strategies (16.5), which recognise carers as expert partners in care:

> Yet so many carers of all ages have developed an expert knowledge of the condition of the person they are supporting and have a close understanding of that person's own aspirations and needs. Involving carers in planning and designing hospital discharge arrangements and individual care packages is common sense as they are key partners in ensuring effective delivery of care at home.[32]

---

29 E.g Department of Health (2010) *Prioritising need in the context of Putting People First: a whole system approach to eligibility for social care.*
30 Quoted in the introduction to Department of Health (2010) *Carers and personalisation: improving outcomes.*
31 Department of Health (2010) *Carers and personalisation: improving outcomes,* p7.
32 *Recognised valued and supported* (see fn 6 above) para 1.9.

624   *Community care and the law / chapter 16*

Carers' assessments

16.31   As noted above, carers who provide (or intend to provide) a substantial amount of care on a regular basis have additional rights during the assessment process, most particularly the right to a separate carer's assessment. These additional rights are considered in the context of the three primary Acts, namely C(RS)A 1995, CDCA 2000 and C(EO)A 2004. The duty to assess qualifying carers is a duty owed to all carers, irrespective of the age of the carer or the age of the person for whom they care (and so, for example, encompasses parent carers and young carers – see below) and is a duty to ensure that the assessments are updated as needs change.[33]

Carers' assessments and the Carers (Recognition and Services) Act 1995

16.32   The C(RS)A 1995 originated as a private member's bill[34] aimed at securing for carers recognition of their central importance as providers of community care services. This recognition is provided by requiring the social services authority (if so requested) to carry out a separate assessment of the carer at the same time as it assesses the person for whom the care is provided. The right of a carer to an 'assessment' under C(RS)A 1995 is to be contrasted with the situation under DP(SCR)A 1986 (see para 16.23) which merely requires the social services authority to 'have regard to' the carer's ability. The C(RS)A 1995 is however misnamed, in that there is only one service it provides for carers, namely an assessment.[35]

16.33   Section 1(1) of the Act is aimed at carers (of whatever age) who care for adults and section 1(2) at carers (of whatever age)[36] who care for disabled children.

16.34   Carers, in order to be eligible for an assessment under the Act, must, in addition to the substantial/regular and unpaid requirements:

1) request the assessment (considered further at para 16.43 below); and
2) have their assessment in conjunction with the service user's assessment.

16.35   It follows that there is no free-standing right to a carer's assessment under C(RS)A 1995: such an assessment must coincide with the disabled person's community care or Children Act (CA) 1989 assessment. This had the potential to cause problems – if, for instance, the disabled person refused an assessment. Such difficulties have, however, been resolved by

---

33   See eg complaint no 05/C/11921 against Trafford MBC, 26 July 2007 where a failure to review an out of date carers assessment was held to constitute maladministration.
34   Sponsored by Malcolm Wicks MP.
35   Local Authority Social Services Act 1970 Sch 1 was amended to include the assessment under C(RS)A 1995 s1 as a social services authority function.
36   It would include young carers, for example, if caring for disabled siblings etc.

CDCA 2000 which makes provision for free-standing assessments in such cases (see below).

16.36   In large measure the combined effect of C(RS)A 1995 and CDCA 2000 is to create a unified assessment duty although in some contexts the C(RS)A 1995 remains the primary provision – not least for carers under the age of 16, whose needs are not addressed by CDCA 2000. It also has an important function in highlighting the importance of carers' needs being addressed through the provision of additional support services for the cared for person.

Carers' assessments and the Carers and Disabled Children Act 2000

16.37 In 1999 the Department of Health published its first national strategy for carers[37] in which it acknowledged that the then legislation prevented carers receiving help in their own right. It undertook 'when Parliamentary time allowed' to rectify this situation, and to ensure that:

> Individual carers . . . have greater flexibility and choice . . . [via] . . . direct payments or credit scheme arrangements to enable them – with the consent of the person needing care – to arrange for services to be given to them in a way that was useful and at a time and a form that was appropriate.

16.38 These undertakings were discharged with the enactment of CDCA 2000. The Act has the same restrictions as C(RS)A 1995 in relation to substantial/regular (see para 16.11 above) and paid carers (para 16.19 above) and by section 1 entitles qualifying carers aged 16 or over who care for another person aged 18 or over to an assessment of their need for services (under section 2). The right to an assessment exists even where the person cared for has refused a community care assessment or community care services following the assessment. Section 2 provides for services for such carers (see para 16.86), section 3 provides for respite vouchers (see para 16.92) and section 6 provides for an assessment of the needs of people with parental responsibility for disabled children.

16.39   The CDCA 2000 uses much of the same terminology as C(RS)A 1995 and in many respects duplicates its provisions (for instance CDCA 2000 s6 and C(RS)A 1995 s1(2)). Given the substantial overlap, the following review of the carer's assessment duty combines analysis of these two Acts and the impact that C(EO)A 2004 has had upon them both.

---

37 Department of Health (1999) *Caring about Carers: A national strategy for carers.* LASSL (99)2, chapter 6 paras 12–14.

The carer's assessment duty

Preliminary questions

Referral protocols

16.40   The English policy guidance to CDCA 2000[38] attempted to deal with the problem of how a local authority could determine whether a carer was actually providing regular and substantial care if the disabled person had refused to co-operate or agree to an assessment, and advised that 'referral protocols' be developed. Paragraph 21 of the practice guidance explained that:

> Such a form would record that in the opinion of a professional, GP, voluntary sector worker, carers' group representative etc that the carer being referred was a substantial and regular carer within the terms of the Act and local eligibility criteria.

16.41   Paragraph 21 additionally contains a simple pro forma example. It is difficult to understand the logic for such a bureaucratic approach to the problem. A radical solution might be simply to trust carers who ask for assistance in such situations and who confirm that their caring role is both regular and substantial (see also para 16.12 above).

Boundary problems

16.42   The English practice guidance to CDCA 2000[39] gives guidance on boundary problems where the carer lives some distance away from the user. It advises that in general it will be the disabled person's 'home authority' (not the carer's) which will be responsible for the assessment and the provision of any services under the Act.

The carer must request the assessment

16.43   The local authority duty to undertake a carer's assessment under C(RS)A 1995 and/or CDCA 2000 is only triggered once a carer has requested that one take place. This is in contrast to a community care assessment which is triggered not by a request but 'by the appearance of need' (see para 3.69 above). The evidence[40] suggested that many carers were not being made aware of their assessment rights by local authorities and accordingly

---

38   At paras 11–13: the Welsh guidance only makes brief reference to this issue, at para 3.3.3.
39   At paras 24–27; para 4.3 of the Welsh guidance.
40   A research study by Carers UK (2003) *Missed opportunities: The impact of new rights for carers* suggested that almost half of qualifying carers were not advised of their right to an assessment when the person they care for is being assessed. This evidence was reinforced by a Department of Health (Social Services Inspectorate) (2003) study *Independence Matters*, para 5.25, p33 which confirmed that carers 'were not consistently offered a separate assessment of their needs' and see also para 19 of the combined policy guidance under the 2000 and 2004 Acts.

C(EO)A 2004 s1 (through amendment to C(RS)A 1995 and CDCA 2000[41]) now places a duty on social services authorities to inform carers of their right to request a carer's assessment. This duty arises when the social services department is either:

1) carrying out a community care or Children Act assessment of a disabled person; or is

2) contemplating undertaking such an assessment.[42]

16.44 The duty does not arise, however, if the carer has recently been informed of the right in another context,[43] for instance a carer's assessment has recently been undertaken or the carer has had a shortened assessment as part of a hospital discharge of the person for whom he or she cares.[44]

16.45   The guidance requires that authorities should make the information available in 'minority languages and a variety of formats'.[45] It encourages authorities to build upon the statutory duty to advise of the right to an assessment by providing more extensive information services for carers.[46]

Delegation of carers' assessments

16.46 The duty to assess under the carers Acts is a social services function which cannot be delegated unless (and relatively unusually) the authority has entered into a formal partnership arrangement with an NHS body under NHS Act 2006 s75.[47] The general position is explained by the combined policy guidance under CDCA 2000 and C(EO)A 2004 (at para 45):

> A local authority may contract with another body to carry out part of the assessment process on its behalf, for example interviewing the carer, researching possible assistance, preparing a report and even making a recommendation. However, as an assessment is a statutory function of the local authority it will have to make the final decision about whether or not to provide services itself. It is not enough for the local authority to simply check on a complete or partial basis the outcomes of another organisation's assessments.

16.47 The Localism Bill, if enacted, may enable local authorities to delegate functions, including the carrying out of carers' assessments (see para 3.51).

The setting and format of the assessment

16.48 Guidance under both C(RS)A 1995 and CDCA 2000 has emphasised the importance of carers having the opportunity to have their assessments

---

41 By amending C(RS)A 1995 s1 (by inserting a new section 2B) and by amending CDCA 2000 s6 (by inserting a new section 6A).

42 But has not as yet completed one (eg because the disabled person is refusing to co-operate with the assessment).

43 CDCA 2000 s6A.

44 Community Care (Delayed Discharges etc) Act 2003 s4(3) – see para 5.37 above.

45 Para 20 of the combined policy guidance under the 2000 and 2004 Acts.

46 See eg L Clements, *Carers and their rights: the law relating to carers*, 4th edition, Carers UK, 2010, para 4.5.

47 NHS (Wales) Act 2006 s33: or in England if it is a 'pilot scheme' under the Contracting Out (Local Authorities Social Services Functions) (England) Order 2011 SI No 1568.

in private – ie away from the disabled person, if the carer so chooses. The guidance states that 'the assessment should listen to what [carers] are saying and offer an opportunity for private discussion in which carers can candidly express their views'.[48] The CDCA 2000 guidance takes this right further by advising that in order that the carer have an opportunity to opt for a confidential meeting, the assessor is advised to make arrangements for the assessment 'over the phone, and away from the home or while the cared for person is out'.[49]

Advocacy/support

16.49   The guidance advises that carers should be made aware that they can have a friend or advocate present at their assessment.[50]

The carer's assessment process

16.50   A carer's assessment differs markedly from a community care assessment. Under NHSCCA 1990 s47(1) the object of a user's assessment is to identify that person's need for community care services. The object of a C(RS)A 1995 carer's assessment is to identify his or her 'ability to provide and to continue to provide care' (section 1(1) and (2)); thus sustainability is the primary focus of the carer's assessment process. Additionally, however, the assessment may reveal a need by the carer for services in his or her own right. In such cases these can be provided either: (1) under CDCA 2000 s2 if the carer is 16 or older and caring for someone aged 18 or over; or (2) under CA 1989 s17 in the case of a young carer aged under 16 or someone with parental responsibility for a disabled child. The process by which such an assessment provides benefits to the carer is outlined in the example below.

The carer's assessment process – general outline

When a community care assessment (or Children Act assessment of a disabled child) is being undertaken and there is a carer providing or intending to providing on a regular basis a substantial amount of care, he or she may request an assessment. The process should then proceed as follows:

1) The information about the 'presenting needs' of the disabled person should be gathered in the normal way – ie all those needs that he or she (and those close to him or her) identifies as well as those identified by the assessor (see para 3.89 above).

continued

---

48   Para 9.1 – Practice guidance LAC (96)7 and WOC 16/96 and WHC (96)21 in Wales.
49   *Carers and Disabled Children Act 2000: practice guidance* para 59 and the Welsh Assembly policy guidance *Guidance 2000 Act* para 3.11.
50   *Carers and Disabled Children Act 2000: practice guidance* para 60 and the Welsh Assembly policy guidance *Guidance 2000 Act* para 3.1.

> 2) Before the assessor decides which of these various needs 'call for the provision' of services by the local authority, the carer should have his or her assessment.
>
> 3) The carer's assessment analyses the sustainability of the caring role – primarily whether the carer is willing and able to carry on caring and/or providing the same level of care. The risks to sustainability can include health risks to the carer, his or her wishes to remain in work or return to work or undertake training, education or leisure activities, etc.
>
> 4) Once the assessor has completed the carer's assessment, he or she will then be in a position to decide what services should be provided to the disabled person and (if needs be) what services might be provided to the carer (ie services under CDCA 2000 or CA 1989).
>
> 5) The assessor should then draw up a support plan explaining how the disabled person's needs will be met (ie by identifying the provision the local authority will make) and how the carer's needs will be met (either by providing additional services to the disabled person, eg respite care) and/or (more unusually) by providing services to the carer.

16.51 The C(RS)A 1995 and CDCA 2000 enable the secretary of state to issue directions as to the manner in which a carer's assessment is to be carried out.[51] As at August 2011 no such direction had been issued.

16.52 The policy guidance accompanying C(RS)A 1995 gives limited and general advice on the form such assessments should take (at paras 21–25), whereas slightly more detail is provided in the practice guidance[52] including:

> 9.1 The assessment is not a test for the carer. It should not be prescriptive but recognise the carer's knowledge and expertise. The assessment should listen to what they are saying and offer an opportunity for private discussion in which carers can candidly express their views.

16.53 Guidance under CDCA 2000 provides significantly more assistance in detailing the key attributes and approach of a carer's assessment.[53] This, for instance, stresses that an 'assessment is not a process for its own sake' and should 'not be a bureaucratic process based on ticking boxes'[54] and that the presumption is that assessments will be 'face-to-face'.[55]

---

51 C(RS)A 1995 s1(4) and CDCA 2000 ss1(4) and 6(3); mirroring NHSCCA 1990 s47(4).
52 For adult carers at paras 9–11 and for young carers at para 16.
53 Department of Health (2001) *Practitioners guide to carers' assessments under the Carers and Disabled Children Act 2000* and Welsh Assembly (2001) *Practitioners guide to Carers' Assessment*.
54 *Carers and Disabled Children Act 2000: practice guidance* para 47.
55 *Carers and Disabled Children Act 2000: practice guidance* para 61.

16.54   Specific guidance exists in both England and Wales[56] concerning the assessment process, emphasising that it should 'focus on outcomes the carer would want to see help them in their caring roles and maintain their health and well-being'.[57]

16.55   Notwithstanding the above guidance, a number of councils have developed self assessment forms for carers which fail to emphasise several key issues, including: that carers have a right to a 'face-to-face' assessment; that this should be in private (ie away from the person cared for); that there must be no assumption that the carer is willing or able to provide or continue to provide care; and that the outcome of a carer's assessment will generally be a changed/improved care package for the disabled person (rather than being limited to, for instance, a 'carers personal budget' (see para 3.8 above).

Carer's assessment – key issues

16.56   The law requires that carer's assessments address two distinct questions, namely:

1) The sustainability of the caring relationship. The assessment must assess the carer's 'ability to provide and to continue to provide care' for the person cared for.[58]

2) The work education and leisure needs of the carer. The assessment must specifically consider whether the carer (a) works or wishes to work; and (b) is undertaking, or wishes to undertake, education, training or any leisure activity.[59]

Sustainability

16.57   The C(RS)A 1995 requires an assessment of the carer's 'ability to provide and to continue to provide care'. As noted above the practice guidance to CDCA 2000 advised that:[60]

> In any given situation, the test that a practitioner should apply will relate to the impact of the caring role on the individual carer. In particular the practitioner will need to address the following questions.
> • Is the caring role sustainable?
> • How great is the risk of the caring role becoming unsustainable?

16.58   The English practice guidance to the CDCA 2000 suggests that in determining what is 'sustainable', four crucial dimensions of the carer's experience should be considered, namely:

56 Department of Health (2001) *Practitioners guide to carers' assessments under the Carers and Disabled Children Act 2000* and Welsh Assembly (2001) *Practitioners guide to carers' assessment*.
57 *Practitioners guide to carers' assessments under the Carers and Disabled Children Act 2000* para 29 and para 3.6 of the Welsh guidance.
58 C(RS)A 1995 s1.
59 C(EO)A 2004 s2.
60 *Carers and Disabled Children Act 2000: practice guidance* para 68.

- autonomy,
- health and safety,
- managing daily routines, and
- involvement.

16.59 These four domains derived from community care assessment eligibility guidance.[61] Although this approach has been dropped from the current English prioritising needs guidance both in relation to carers and disabled people[62], the 2000 English practice guidance to CDCA 2000 remains current. Thus the domains are one suggested approach to determining sustainability, local authorities have a discretion as to how they approach this task. The following section considers each of these domains.

Autonomy/choice

16.60 Coercion and compulsion have no place in the language that describes caring relationships. While parents have responsibilities towards their children and spouses are liable to maintain each other, the law recognises that it is impossible to compel one individual to provide care for another. Good practice therefore dictates that carers should have the right to choose the nature and the extent of their caring responsibilities. Ultimately if a failure of care occurs, the state has a positive obligation to provide support.

16.61 The practice guidance to CDCA 2000[63] explains that the concept of autonomy (in the context of caring relationships):

> . . . describes the carer's freedom to choose the nature of the tasks they will perform and how much time they will give to their caring role. It is dependent on recognition of their role and an agreed sense of shared responsibility between the local councils and the carer/s.

16.62 The practice guidance to C(RS)A 1995[64] described the proposition in the following terms:

> In assessing the carer's ability to care or continue to care, care managers should not assume a willingness by the carer to continue caring, or continue to provide the same level of support. They will wish to bear in mind the distinction between caring about someone and caring for them. Many carers continue to care deeply about a person even though their ability to care for them may change.

16.63 The choice available to carers should relate not only to the quantity of care they provide but also the quality or type of the caring roles they are prepared to assume. As the practice guidance to C(RS)A 1995[65] explains:

---

61 Department of Health (2001) *Fair access to care services guidance on eligibility criteria,* para 40 and see also Welsh Assembly (2002) *Creating a unified and fair system for assessing and managing care,* para 2.36.

62 Department of Health (2010) *Prioritising need in the context of Putting People First: a whole system approach to eligibility for social care,* see paras 97–103.

63 *Carers and Disabled Children Act 2000: practice guidance* para 69.

64 LAC (96)7 para 9.8; WOC 16/96 and WHC (96)21 in Wales.

65 LAC (96)7 para 9.3; WOC 16/96 and WHC (96)21 in Wales. For adult carers at paras 9–11.

... it is important that care managers do not make assumptions about carers' willingness to undertake the range of caring tasks, particularly those related to intimate personal care. This is highlighted in a discussion of spouse carers[66] which emphasises the difficulties faced by some husbands or wives when their ability to cope with changed behaviour or personality and/or tasks involving physical intimacy is taken for granted ...

16.64   The practice guidance to CDCA 2000[67] describes 'an extensive loss of autonomy' as a 'critical risk' for a carer – ie one that demands a response by the local authority. Such a situation would arise where the carer believed that he or she was essentially trapped, having no choice over the caring commitments and that no adequate support or respite was available. Such an extensive loss of autonomy would require a response from the social services department to the extent that it enabled the carer to recover a belief that he or she had 'freedom to choose the nature of the tasks they will perform and how much time they will give to their caring role'.[68]

Health and safety

16.65   The practice guidance to CDCA 2000 (para 69) describes the importance of assessments addressing the health and safety impacts on carers, in the following terms:

> Here the issues of risk to the carer's own health of maintaining their caring role at its current level must be looked at in view of their own age and other commitments. For example, cover may need to be provided in such a way as to allow the carer to attend medical and dental appointments as and when they need. Suitable equipment may need to be installed to aid the carer in providing intimate support to the person they care for. Issues may need to be discussed around the safety of the carer from harm caused by the person cared for. Harm can be caused intentionally or unintentionally.

16.66   There is substantial evidence to suggest significant caring responsibilities can be harmful. A Princess Royal Trust for Carers' report[69] found that:

- 85% of carers had found that caring had an adverse impact on their health, with particularly high-risk groups including those who looked after people with serious or mental and physical illnesses, and long-term carers;
- caring had been to the detriment of the mental well-being of almost 90% of carers;
- over 40% said their physical well-being had been affected by caring.

---

66 K Atkin, 'Similarities and differences between informal carers' in *Carers: research and practice*, HMSO, 1992.
67 *Carers and Disabled Children Act 2000: practice guidance* para 70 – and see table 20 below.
68 *Carers and Disabled Children Act 2000: practice guidance* para 69.
69 Princess Royal Trust for Carers, *Carers speak out project: report on findings and recommendations*, October 2002.

16.67 A similar study by Carers UK[70] found that:

- 55% of carers reported they had significant health problems;
- 43% reported they had sought medical treatment for depression, stress or anxiety since becoming a carer (these problems were particularly apparent in young carers and carers looking after mentally ill people).

16.68 The practice guidance to CDCA 2000[71] describes 'the development of major health problems' as a 'critical risk' for a carer, ie one that demands a response by the local authority. Such a situation would arise not merely when a carer had been diagnosed as suffering from a serious illness, but also where a link had been established between an illness and the carer's caring responsibilities (ie chronic stress and anxiety in a carer who already had high blood pressure or a history of stress related illnesses).

16.69 In addition to addressing the negative impact that caring may have on a carer's health, a local authority may have a general duty of care to a carer – a question that is considered separately at para 4.126 above.

Managing daily routines and 'involvement'

16.70 Carer's assessments should address the extent to which caring responsibilities interfere with the ability of carers 'to manage their daily routines' as well as the extent to which they inhibit the freedom of carers 'to maintain relationships, employment, interests and other commitments alongside their caring responsibilities'.[72] In this context the practice guidance to CDCA 2000[73] states that a critical risk includes 'an inability to look after one's own domestic needs and other daily routines; a risk to employment or other responsibilities; a risk to significant social support systems or relationships'.

16.71 This categorisation of 'critical' is of importance, being an explicit statement by the Department of Health that a risk to a carer's employment or a 'significant relationship' is one that demands action from the statutory authorities. Thus if a carer feels compelled to give up full time work, or is at risk of losing a significant relationship because of his or her caring responsibilities, this risk should result in a positive intervention by the local authority to secure support services and ensure that the caring responsibilities do not jeopardise the employment or the relationship.[74]

---

70 Carers UK (2003) *Missed opportunities: the impact of new rights for carers.*
71 *Carers and Disabled Children Act 2000: practice guidance* para 70 and reiterated in the 2010 *Prioritising need* policy guidance – see para 16.87 below) – and see also table 20 below.
72 *Carers and Disabled Children Act 2000: practice guidance* para 69.
73 *Carers and Disabled Children Act 2000: practice guidance* para 70 – and see table 20 below.
74 *SCIE practice guide 5: implementing the Carers (Equal Opportunities) Act 2004*, p5, citing L Clements, *Carers and their rights: the law relating to carers*, Carers UK, 2005. Carers UK approves the assertion that 'identification of a critical risk in a Carers' Act assessment triggers a local authority obligation to make an appropriate response to address this risk'.

Employment, training, education and leisure activities

16.72 The above categorisation of a risk to employment or other responsibilities as a 'critical risk' has been reinforced by further specific guidance and subsequently by statute. In respect of the former, the practice guidance to CDCA 2000 develops the theme in the following terms:

> 35. Carers should be supported to stay in work, or to return to work, where this is what they want to do. The local council should therefore:
> - identify links with partner agencies to ensure carers assessed have access to good quality information on training and other support to build confidence prior to returning to work
> - make sure that the Welfare to Work Joint Investment Plan cross-refers to the multi-agency carers' strategy and state where the local council's policy on carers and employment is addressed
> - audit services to identify how well they support carers through providing flexible and reliable packages of care which allow carers to continue to work
> - remember that if involvement in employment is or will be at risk this constitutes a critical risk to the sustainability of the caring role . . .

16.73 Statutory reinforcement to this right has come via C(EO)A 2004 s2, which places a duty on local authorities when undertaking a carer's assessment specifically to consider whether the carer:

i) works or wishes to work;
ii) is undertaking, or wishes to undertake, education, training or any leisure activity.

16.74 During the reading of the bill (that became the 2004 Act), the minister expressed the government's intention in relation to this provision, stating:[75]

> We want carers who wish to work to have the right to work. For those carers who wish to take part in education, we want that to be built in to the care plans that are put together for the person for whom they are caring. We want them to have the opportunity to engage in leisure activities, to the extent that I feel that it would be appropriate that if a carer wanted to take part in a physical fitness or aerobics class in the evening, the care plan should be adapted to ensure that the person could be cared for while the carer went out to engage in such activity.

16.75 Relying heavily on the obligations created by C(EO)A 2004, the Welsh Ombudsman[76] has held it be maladministration for a local authority to assert that 'childcare was the responsibility of the parents, whether or not children have a disability' and for the authority to fail to provide appropriate support to a parent of a disabled child who wished to pursue his university studies. In the ombudsman's opinion there was an obligation

---

75 Parliamentary Under-Secretary of State for Health (Dr Stephen Ladyman): Standing Committee C, col 7, 10 March 2004.
76 Public Service Ombudsman (Wales) Complaint no B2004/0707/S/370 against Swansea City Council, 22 February 2007 – see in particular paras 78, 133 and 137.

on the local authority to ensure that the parent was not 'disadvantaged in pursuit of education/training any more than other parents'.

Carers' employment rights

16.76 An extended analysis of the employment rights of carers is outside the scope of this book[77], but in summary, they include the following:

Emergency leave employment rights

16.77 Carers have limited rights to take (unpaid) time off work to care for a dependant. This right is found in Employment Rights Act 1996 s57A(1)[78] which provides:

> **57A(1)** An employee is entitled to be permitted by his employer to take a reasonable amount of time off during the employee's working hours in order to take action which is necessary –
> (a) to provide assistance on an occasion when a dependant falls ill, gives birth or is injured or assaulted
> (b) to make arrangements for the provision of care for a dependant who is ill or injured,
> (c) in consequence of the death of a dependant,
> (d) because of the unexpected disruption or termination of arrangements for the care of a dependant, or
> (e) to deal with an incident which involves a child of the employee and which occurs unexpectedly in a period during which an educational establishment which the child attends is responsible for him.

16.78 'Dependant' is defined widely in relation to persons who live in the same household[79] and there is a general obligation upon carers who take such time off work, to tell the employer the reason for the absence as soon as practicable and how long the absence is likely to last.[80] In relation to the situations detailed in subsections (a)–(c) above, the event which requires the carer to take time off need not be 'unexpected'. Any time off work claimed as a result of this statutory provision is to be taken as unpaid leave.

Flexible working rights

16.79 Parents with children under six, or disabled children under 18, who have worked for their employer for at least 26 weeks have the right to apply for flexible working arrangements.[81] This right was extended by Work and

---

77 For more detailed information see L Clements *Carers and their rights: the law relating to carers*, 4th edn, Carers UK, 2010, para 4.51–4.73.
78 Inserted by Employment Relations Act 1999 s8 and Sch 4 Part II.
79 Employment Rights Act (ERA) 1996 s57A(3).
80 ERA 1996, s57A(2).
81 Employment Act 2002 s47 (which amended ERA 1996).
   primarily by way of the insertion of a new Part 8A into that Act) and see generally the Department of Trade and Industry guidance (2003) *Flexible Working: the right to request and the duty to consider*.

Families Act 2006 s12[82] to cover other carers. The procedure for requesting flexible working rights is governed by detailed regulations[83] which require that the employee submits a carefully considered application.[84] The employer is then required to follow a set procedure to ensure the request is considered seriously: a refusal is only permitted where there is a recognised business ground for doing so.

16.80   The Regulations[85] define a 'carer' for the purposes of the 2006 Act as an employee who is or expects to be caring who:

1) is married to, or the partner (including a civil partner) of the employee; or
2) is a relative of the employee; or
3) falls into neither category i) nor ii), but lives at the same address as the employee.

16.81   Relative is defined widely[86] and the regulations do not require in addition a level of care that has to be provided by such a carer, in order to qualify for the permissive right (to request flexible working rights). In the government's view 'defining a level of care would be extremely complex'; would be 'unlikely to make matters any clearer'; and might deter some people from applying for flexible working if they felt that the definition did not cover their exact circumstances.[87]

16.82   It has been argued that an unjustified refusal to allow a woman flexible working rights may amount to unlawful sex discrimination since such a practice would disadvantage women more than men, because more women than men take primary responsibility for child care and are disadvantaged by having to work longer hours and (in relation to women caring for adults) more women of working age are carers of adults than men.[88]

82 Amending ERA 1996 s80F.
83 Flexible Working (Eligibility, Complaints and Remedies) Regulations 2002 SI No 3236 as amended by Flexible Working (Eligibility, Complaints and Remedies) (Amendment) Regulations 2006 SI No 3314 and Flexible Working (Eligibility, Complaints and Remedies) (Amendment) Regulations 2007 SI No 1184.
84 The Department for Employment and Learning has produced a leaflet which provides a detailed explanation of the process, its timescales and the application form – *ER 36 Flexible working: a guide for employers and employees*, and ACAS has produced two guidance notes: (1) *Advice leaflet – the right to apply for flexible working, a short guide for employers, working parents and carers* and (2) a more detailed guidance note, *Flexible working and work-life balance*.
85 Flexible Working (Eligibility, Complaints and Remedies) Regulations 2002 reg 3B.
86 Ibid, reg 2 (as amended).
87 Department of Trade and Industry, *Draft flexible working: regulations summary of responses and Government Response to the 2006 consultation*, 2006.
88 See C Palmer, 'New rights at work for parents and carers from April 2007' April 2007 *Legal Action* 33–35 at 35.

Unpaid parental leave[89]

16.83 People who have been employed by their employer for over 12 months and who have responsibility for a child born on or after 15 December 1999 are entitled to unpaid parental leave of up to 13 weeks for children under five or 18 weeks for a disabled child. The leave can usually be taken for up to four weeks a year. In the case of a disabled child the leave can be taken as a day or multiples of a day or, for children under five, in weekly blocks.

Discrimination by association

16.84 In *Coleman v Law*[90] the parent of a disabled child claimed constructive dismissal on grounds of disability in that she had been treated less favourably than other parents of non-disabled children. The case was referred to the European Court of Justice which ruled that the protection of the Equal Treatment Framework Directive 2000/78/EC from direct discrimination and harassment extends to employees who are associated with disabled people, but who are not disabled themselves. After unsuccessful appeals by her former employers, Sharon Coleman's case was eventually settled in her favour.

16.85 The concept of discrimination by association with someone who has a characteristic protected by equalities legislation is now incorporated in domestic statute law by the Equality Act 2010.

Section 13 Direct discrimination:

(1) A person (A) discriminates against another (B) if, because of a protected characteristic, A treats B less favourably than A treats or would treat others.

16.86 The change in the language of the prohibition on direct discrimination to less favourable treatment *because of* a protected characteristic means that the person alleging discrimination no longer needs to have that characteristic themselves. This opens up the possibility of carers being able to argue that they have been subject to discrimination by association with, say, a disabled person or an older person. The principle of discrimination by association with a protected characteristic extends to harassment (section 26) and to the public sector equality duty (section 149[91]).

Eligibility criteria and carer's assessments

16.87 The practice guidance to CDCA 2000 (para 70) advises local authorities to grade the 'extent of risk to the sustainability of the caring role' into

---

89 These derive from the Maternity and Parental Leave etc Regulations 1999 SI No 3312 and Maternity and Parental Leave (Amendment) Regulations 2001 SI No 4010 in exercise of powers under the ERA 1996 as amended by the Employment Relations Act 1999 implementing (among other things) the provisions of Council Directive 92/85/EEC and the Framework Agreement on Parental Leave annexed to Council Directive 96/34/EC.

90 Case C-303/06; EAT decisions [2007] IRLR 88 and [2008] IRLR 722.

91 See L Clements, E Holzhausen and J Bangs, *The Equality Act 2010 and Carers*, Carers UK, 2010.

one of four categories, namely 'critical, substantial, moderate and low' and provides descriptors for these four bands in a table, which is reproduced below. The grading system is a formal determination of:

> ... the degree to which a carer's ability to sustain that role is compromised or threatened either in the present or in the foreseeable future by the absence of appropriate support.

This approach to determining eligibility for support for carers is now affirmed in the statutory prioritising needs guidance.[92]

16.88   Although the grading system is modelled on that which regulates community care assessments the consequences of a categorisation are different. If a disabled person is assessed as having a 'critical' need, this means that the local authority is under a duty to make services available to meet that need. However, a categorisation of critical (and arguably 'substantial') in relation to the caring relationship does not mean that the local authority is under a duty to make services available to the carer – since there is no duty under CDCA 2000 to provide services (merely a 'power').

16.89   However, as a matter of public law, the categorising of a risk to the sustainability of a caring role as 'critical' brings with it an obligation on the authority to secure support services and ensure that this state of affairs does not continue (or come to pass). Although in such a situation the local authority is not obliged to provide the carer with services, it is obliged to act. It has the choice therefore of providing the necessary support either to the carer by way of a service under CDCA 2000 or by way of additional support to the disabled person by provision of a community care service. The bottom line, however, is that the identification of a critical risk (at the very least) in a carer's assessment triggers a local authority obligation to make an appropriate response to address this risk.[93] This proposition has been expressed by the Commission for Social Care Inspection in the following terms:[94]

> ... there is a duty to address carers' eligible needs but discretion about whether to meet these through carers services or community care services – however, some practitioners appear to think [incorrectly] the discretion is about whether to help carers.

---

92   Department of Health (2010) *Prioritising need in the context of Putting People First policy guidance* para 99.

93   *SCIE practice guide 5: implementing the Carers (Equal Opportunities) Act 2004*, p5, citing L Clements *Carers and their rights: the law relating to carers*, Carers UK (2005). Carers UK approves the assertion that 'identification of a critical risk in a Carers' Act assessment triggers a local authority obligation to make an appropriate response to address this risk'.

94   Commission for Social Care Inspection (2008) *Cutting the cake fairly: CSCI review of eligibility criteria for social care*, para 3.22.

Table 20:   Carers: eligibilty criteria

CRITICAL

Critical risk to sustainability of the caring role arises when:

- their life may be threatened;
- major health problems have developed or will develop;
- there is, or will be, an extensive loss of autonomy for the carer in decisions about the nature of tasks they will perform and how much time they will give to their caring role;
- there is, or will be, an inability to look after their own domestic needs and other daily routines while sustaining their caring role;
- involvement in employment or other responsibilities is, or will be, at risk;
- many significant social support systems and relationships are, or will be, at risk.

SUBSTANTIAL

Substantial risk to sustainability of the caring role arises when:

- significant health problems have developed or will develop;
- there is, or will be, some significant loss of autonomy for the carer in decisions about the nature of tasks they will perform and how much time they will give to their caring role;
- there is, or will be, an inability to look after some of their own domestic needs and other daily routines while sustaining their caring role;
- involvement in some significant aspects of employment or other responsibilities is, or will be, at risk;
- some significant social support systems and relationships are, or will be, at risk.

MODERATE

Moderate risk to sustainability of the caring role arises when:

- there is, or will be, some loss of autonomy for the carer in decisions about the nature of tasks they will perform and how much time they will give to their caring role;
- there is, or will be, some inability to look after their own domestic needs and other daily routines while sustaining their caring role;
- several social support systems and relationships are, or will be, at risk.

LOW

Low risk to sustainability of the caring role arises when:

- there is, or will be, some inability to carry out one or two domestic tasks while sustaining their caring role;
- one or two social support systems and relationships are, or will be, at risk.

Support services for carers

16.90   Although a carer's assessment may have many outcomes, its legislative purpose is to provide information that enables the social services department to decide what additional services or support should be provided:

- to the disabled person;[95] and/or
- to the carer.[96]

16.91   If these services are provided to the disabled person, they will be provided under the community care or Children Act legislation. However, if the services are required by the carer, ordinarily they will be provided either under CDCA 2000 s2 or under CA 1989.

Respite/short break care

16.92   Research and consultation has repeatedly identified the availability of breaks from their caring role as one of the highest priorities for carers[97]. Funding streams have been directed towards this, particularly by way of implementation of the National Carers' Strategy,[98] although research suggests that the funding may not have been used for its intended purpose. There is also evidence that authorities can be insufficiently imaginative and persistent[99] in developing suitable short breaks care packages and have inadequate arrangements for certain groups – for example for people with dementia.[100]

16.93   In general terms respite (or short break) care services are services provided to a disabled person which enable the carer to take a break from his or her caring responsibilities. In other words, respite care support is legally a community care service[101] or service under CA 1989 and not a

---

95   These services can be provided either under the community care legislation – generally where the disabled person is over 18 – or under CA 1989 s17 if the disabled person is under 18.

96   Services can be provided to carers aged 16 or over caring for someone 18 or over under CDCA 2000 s2 or under CA 1989 s17 if the disabled person is under 18.

97   See, for instance, the key messages from the response to the coalition government's consultation on the carers' strategy, *Recognised, valued and supported: next steps for the carers' strategy*, DH November 2010 p.6 and the findings and recommendations from *Respite care in Wales: final report to Welsh Assembly Government*, LE Wales December 2010

98   Including £100 million to PCTs in England to increase support for carers in 2010/11 in November 2010 the Minister announced a further £400 million for this purpose over the next four years,

99   See Public services Ombudsman for Wales report on complaint 1712/200600588 against Torfean CBC 11 January 2008 where it was held that the authority had failed to fully explore with the private sector the recruitment of staff with skills to address the disabled person's complex needs.

100   See for example, Department of Health/Care Services Improvement Partnership (2008) *Creative models of short breaks (respite care) for people with dementia*, Department of Health.

101   Eg as 'practical assistance in the home' (eg a 'sitting service') under Chronically Sick and Disabled Persons Act 1970 s2 or as a short period in residential care under National Assistance Act 1948 s21.

service provided under CDCA 2000. This state of affairs has been explained in the following terms:[102]

> People who care may be assessed as needing a break from their caring role. This need will be clearly recorded on their own assessment documentation.
>
> The person they care for will then be assessed for the additional support that they will need to allow their usual carer to take a break. This need will be recorded on their assessment documentation. The additional service remains a community care service delivered to the cared for person, not a carer service under this Act.

16.94 Since respite care services are technically (ie as a matter of law) community care services rather than services provided under the Carers' Acts, it follows that once a disabled person has been assessed as needing respite care, the local authority is legally obliged to provide services to meet this need.[103] The only exception is where the care is required for a disabled child and which can only[104] be provided by way of a residential placement. In such a case the care generally falls to be provided under Children Act 1989 s17, a target duty (see para 23.49 below).

16.95 Nevertheless, a Northern Irish case, *LW: Re Judicial Review*[105] considering both domiciliary arrangements under parallel provisions to the Chronically Sick and Disabled Persons Act (CSDPA) 1970 and residential respite pursuant to a similar target duty,[106] concluded that where a need for respite care has been identified adequate, effective and reasonable[107] steps must be taken to ensure it is provided. If a particular respite care facility is unavailable, then a reasonable authority will take action to identify alternative provision. If due to administrative inertia this does not happen and the authority advances 'no convincing evidence of reasonable efforts' to discharge its continuing statutory duty then, whether 'viewed through the prism of an absolute (ie unqualified) duty of provision or a duty to be measured by the criterion of reasonableness' it will be held to be in breach of its statutory duty.[108]

16.96 Although respite care will be recorded as a service on the disabled person's support plan there is no reason why the 'break' that the carer enjoys as a consequence should not be recorded as a 'service to the carer': ie the carer's support plan recording that he or she has been given a

---

102 Department of Health, 'Questions and Answers' briefing to the 2000 Act, question 7.
103 See eg *R (Hughes) v Liverpool City Council* [2005] EWHC 428 (Admin), (2005) 8 CCLR 243 at [33]–[34].
104 If the respite care is capable of being provided as a home or community based service (eg a sitting service under CSDPA 1970 s2) then there will be a duty on the local authority to 'take a proactive approach' to this need and if necessary recruit and train the appropriate staff – rather than merely seeking to fit the need into an available services which may not be suitable – see Public services Ombudsman for Wales report on complaint no 1712/200600588 against Torfean CBC 11 January 2008 at para 132.
105 [2010] NIQB 62, 19 May 2010.
106 Health and Social Services (NI) Order 1972 art 15.
107 *LW: Re Judicial Review*, para 38.
108 *LW: Re Judicial Review*, paras 48–49.

'break'.[109] Equally, the funding source for such breaks may derive from budgets specifically allocated for expenditure to support carers, and local authorities have a discretion under the Health and Social Services and Social Security Adjudication Act 1983 (see para 10.7 above) to opt not to charge for services which benefit carers

Respite care and voucher schemes

16.97   CDCA 2000 ss3 and 7 provide for local authority social services departments to run short break voucher schemes. Voucher schemes are designed to offer flexibility in the timing of carers' breaks and choice in the way services are delivered to disabled people while their usual carer is taking a break. Regulations[110] made under CDCA 2000 s3 and guidance[111] have been issued in England. It would appear that with the increased use of direct payments and the development of personal budgets (see para 3.8 above) there has been a corresponding decline in the number of local authority short breaks voucher schemes.

Carers' services under the Carers and Disabled Children Act 2000

16.98   CDCA 2000 s2 enables social services departments to provide services to carers following a carer's assessment. The Act does not define what is a carers' service other than to stipulate that a carers' service can be anything that could 'help the carer care for the person cared for'.[112] It follows that the range of services capable of being provided under section 2 is wide, given that anything that promotes a carer's sense of personal well-being is likely to help him or her 'care for the person cared for'. The only specific limitation, is that (in general) a service to a carer under the CDCA 2000 cannot involve any intimate care of the person for whom he or she cares. This question is considered separately below (para 16.113 below).

16.99   The guidance gives examples of the type of services that could be provided to carers, including:

Examples in the CDCA 2000 practice guidance
- Trips (such as holidays or on special events);
- driving lessons;
- travel assistance (including for instance help with taxi fares);
- training;

---

109   This was the approach adopted by the Commission for Social Care Inspection in its performance indicator guidance which required authorities to record the number of 'breaks services' that they had provided for carers – see CSCI (20045) PAF Guidance Book PAF C62.
110   Carers and Disabled Children (Vouchers) (England) Regulations 2003 SI No 1216.
111   Department of Health (2003) *Carers and Disabled Children's Act 2000 – vouchers for short-term breaks: policy and practice guidance.*
112   CDCA 2000 s2(2)(b).

- laundry;
- gardening;
- help with housework.

Examples given in the combined policy guidance under CDCA 2000 and C(EO)A 2004
- Driving lessons, moving and handling classes, a mobile phone, taxis to work to maximise the carer's time, or a short holiday for the carer to enable them to have time to themselves (para 65).

Examples given in the C(EO)A 2004 practice guidance
- A computer for a carer who could not access computer services from the local library because he felt unable to leave the person he cared for;
- repairs/insurance costs for a car, where transport is crucial to the caring role;
- entry phone with audio/video system where the carer lives in a two storey house and has mobility problems;
- £500 contribution to a flight for a grandmother to come from another country and care for a woman with MS.

Direct payments

16.100 Health and Social Care Act 2001 s57 enables carers to receive direct payments in lieu of services (see generally para 12.9 above). Thus if a carer is assessed as needing a service such as driving lessons or relaxation therapy and the authority decides that it will provide this support, the carer has the right to have the assistance provided as a direct payment.

16.101 As well as being able to receive direct payments for carers' services, carers often play a major role in the administration of direct payments for the support of the cared for person. This may be formalised where the disabled person lacks mental capacity to manage a direct payment even with all the available help; carers are likely to be the obvious choice to take on the role of 'suitable person' to receive the direct payment in many cases. In other cases carers often play a significant role in managing direct payments for community care support. Research indicates that carers are more likely than not to have positive experiences of direct payments,[113] nevertheless, in common with all aspects of the caring role, support should not be taken for granted. Practice guidance on improving outcomes for carers includes this 'key practice point':[114]

> No assumptions are made about the willingness or ability of carers to take on responsibilities of managing the money, employing staff, procuring support or services etc. and there is a range of good support options available to assist with this.

---

113 See *Choice or Chore – carers' experience of direct payments*, Carers UK, November 2008.
114 Department of Health (2010) *Carers and personalisation: improving outcomes*, p24.

NHS responsibilities for carers

16.102   Neither C(RS)A 1995 nor CDCA 2000 place any obligation on the NHS to address the support needs of carers. The policy guidance to the C(RS)A 1995 advised (at para 29) that local authorities should 'review with NHS commissioning agencies and NHS providers how they might best be involved in the carer's assessment', and that:

> 30. Primary care staff, including GPs and community nurses through their contact with users and carers, are in a good position to notice signs of stress, difficulty or rapidly deteriorating health particularly in carers. The provisions of the Act will help primary care staff to meet the medical and nursing needs of their patients who are carers. When making a referral for a user's assessment they should be able to inform the carer that they may also have a right to request an assessment and will be well-placed to encourage patients whom they consider will benefit most to take up the opportunity. Social services departments should make sure that primary care staff have relevant information about social services criteria and know who to contact to make a referral. GPs nurses and other members of multi-disciplinary teams may be able to assist in an assessment of a carer's ability to provide and continue to provide care.

16.103   The evolving carers' strategies in both England and Wales (see para 16.5 above) acknowledge the need for more effective inter-agency working alongside recognition of carers as 'expert partners' in this context. One of the aims of the Welsh refocused carers' strategy in 2007 was to ensure 'better constructive engagement with carers as key partners in the policy and delivery of both health and social services'.[115] Progress in this area is slow, as exemplified by the responses to the 2010 review of the English strategy. A key messages was that 'carers can often feel excluded by clinicians – both health and social care professions should respect, inform and involve carers more as expert partners in care'.[116]

16.104   Specific statutory duties towards carers are notably absent from NHS legislation. However, there is an increasing acknowledgement in guidance of the importance of working in partnership with carers. For instance the National Treatment Agency for Substance Misuse (a special health authority) has issued detailed guidance on supporting and involving carers.[117] The guidance relating to hospital discharge arrangements contains substantial reference to the importance of ensuring that carers' needs and concerns are addressed, and is considered separately at para 5.13 above.

NHS operating framework

16.105   During the transition towards the coalition government's proposals for reforming health and social care (see para 13.6 above) the 2010 NHS Operating Framework set out the direction of travel measurable through a

---

115   Welsh Assembly Government (2010) *Carers' strategy for Wales: action plan 2007*, p7.
116   Department of Health (2010) *Recognised, valued and supported: next steps for the carers' strategy*, p6.
117   *Supporting and involving carers*, NTA, September 2006.

range of indicators. One of the new indicators for 2011 being 'carers' breaks' – to be delivered by PCTs and monitored by SHAs:

> It has not always been apparent how funding to support carers has been used in each PCT. The Spending Review has made available additional funding in PCT baselines to support the provision of breaks for carers. PCTs should pool budgets with local authorities to provide carers' breaks, as far as possible, via direct payments or personal health budgets. For 2011/12, PCTs should agree policies, plans and budgets to support carers with local authorities and local carers' organisations, and make them available to local people.[118]

Importantly this requires greater transparency by PCTs in relation to spending on carers' support measures.

The duty to co-operate under the Carers (Equal Opportunities) Act 2004

16.106 CEOA 2004 s3 reinforces the general duty of the NHS and local authorities to co-operate under NHS Act 2006 s82 (see para 13.35 above). It provides:

- that a local authority may request another authority or health body[119] to assist it in planning the provision of services to carers and persons being cared for. The other body is then required to give 'due consideration' to such a request; and
- that where a local authority forms the view that a carer's ability to provide care might be enhanced by the provision of services by another authority or health body it may request that other body to provide the service, to which request the other body must give due consideration.

16.107 In the light of this statutory obligation the combined policy guidance under CDCA 2000 and C(EO)A 2004 advises (at para 33) that social services and their local NHS partners:

> . . . develop a multi-agency carers strategy . . . [and] . . . ensure that agreed protocols are in place for support from partner organisations in providing support to carers. This sort of process may also help to embed carers' needs in other local strategies, for example, welfare to work, joint investment plans, hospital discharge plans and life-long learning strategies.

and explains (at para 36) that:

> . . . due consideration means . . . an NHS organisation could not refuse to consider any request made to them in relation to the provision of lifting and handling support for carers . . . In demonstrating that due consideration has been given, it would be reasonable to expect public

---

118 Department of Health (2010) *The Operating framework for the NHS in England 2011–12*, para 4.22.
119 Being either 'another local authority, an education authority, a housing authority or a Special Health Authority, a Local Health Board, a Primary Care Trust, an NHS Trust or NHS foundation trust'.

authorities to document the decision taken in relation to requests, along with the reasons for that decision.

16.108 A 2006 Department of Health report[120] has given as an example of this power, the possibility of a social services authority requesting 'that the NHS provide a certain type of wheelchair (perhaps one more expensive than usual) in order not only to meet the needs of the disabled person, but also to make life easier for the carer'.

Carers Strategies (Wales) Measure 2010

16.109 Once in force this Measure will enable the Welsh ministers to regulate to require local authorities and health bodies to work together and to consult with carers in order to prepare, publish and implement local carers' strategies.

16.110 The draft regulations[121] designate local health boards (LHBs) as the lead authority, but require the participation of local authorities, and the strategy must set out how each body will work together to achieve the aims set out in section 2(1) of the Measure, namely:

a) to provide appropriate information and advice to carers,

b) to ensure that, where it falls to an authority to decide what services (if any) are to be provided to or for a carer or the person cared for, the carer is consulted before that decision is made, and

c) to ensure that each authority consults carers before it makes decisions of a general nature regarding the provision of services to or for carers and the persons they care for.

16.111 Appropriate information and advice is usefully elaborated in the draft regulations, as is consultation. For example, information prescribed as appropriate includes: information about medical conditions, medication and side effects; information to assist young carers; information on the availability of, entitlement to and sources of support; information on crisis support and how to access it, and information on programmes to assist carers to carry out their caring role safely and effectively in a range of specified areas. The implementation of the Measure will also be supported by guidance.[122]

NHS continuing care

16.112 At para 14.142 above we consider the residual duties of social services authorities in cases where it has been determined that a person is entitled to NHS continuing care. Without explaining the legal basis of its opinion, the Department of Health has also advised[123] that carers do not lose their

---

120   Department of Health/Care Services Improvement Partnership (2006) *Out and about: wheelchairs as part of a whole-systems approach to independence*, p30.

121   The Carer Strategies (Wales) Regulations 2011.

122   See http://wales.gov.uk/consultations/healthsocialcare/carers/?lang=en

123   Department of Health (2009) *The National Framework for NHS Continuing Healthcare and NHS Funded Nursing Care*, para 45.

entitlement to an assessment when the person for whom they care is entitled to NHS continuing care (see para 14.148 above).

Carer/service user conflict

16.113 Department of Health guidance[124] and other publications[125] give general advice as to appropriate local authority responses where there is (or may be) conflict between carers and the persons for whom they care. However, CDCA 2000 s2(3) contains a provision designed to get around the problem of a disabled person who refuses services that would be of benefit to his or her carer. It states that a service, although provided to the carer:

(a) may take the form of a service delivered to the person cared for if it is one which, if provided to him instead of to the carer, could fall within community care services and they both agree it is to be so delivered; but

(b) if a service is delivered to the person cared for it may not, except in prescribed circumstances, include anything of an intimate nature.

16.114 This arrangement is explained by the English practice guidance to CDCA 2000 by reference to an example, which is reproduced below.

Jim is a substantial and regular carer for his mother Elsie who is frail and in the early stages of dementia. She is often incontinent. Elsie lives round the corner from Jim. Jim does all his mother's laundry.

There are various ways the local council may be able to help Jim:

a) Elsie is eligible for community care support. If Elsie agrees to be assessed by social services, then a cleaning and laundry service could be provided as a **community care service** and delivered to her. Elsie would be the person financially assessed for any charges.

b) If Elsie refuses to be assessed by social services (although she would be eligible for community care services) Jim could ask for a carers' assessment. The local council could agree to provide, as a carer's service, a cleaning and laundry service at Elsie's house. The local council would need to be satisfied that Elsie is prepared to tolerate the visits from these services. It turns out that so long as they don't bother her, Elsie will tolerate them. Social services arrange to pick the laundry up when Jim is at Elsie's home. This is a **carer's service provided for the carer (Jim), delivered to the cared for person (Elsie).**

Continued

---

124 LAC (2004)24 *Guidance accompanying the Community Care Directions 2004*, paras 2.3–2.5.

125 See eg L Clements, *Carers and their rights: the law relating to carers*, 4th edn, Carers UK, 2010, chapter 9.

Jim would be liable for any charge as the service is provided to help him in his caring role. Jim and the care manager hope that Elsie will get used to people other than Jim coming round and may subsequently change her mind about being assessed and helped by social services.

c) If Jim decides that the easiest way for him to cope with all this extra laundry is for him to have a new washing machine installed at his own home, he could then discuss with the care manager the provision of a direct payment so that he can buy one. This would then be **a carers' service provided for the carer (Jim), delivered to the carer (Jim).** Jim would again be the person financially assessed in relation to any charges.

16.115   Accordingly certain care services, that would otherwise be construed as community care services, may be deemed to be services under CDCA 2000. Such services can only be delivered to the carer, if:

- they could be a community care service;
- both the disabled person and the carer agree to them being provided to the carer; and
- the services are not of an intimate nature (except in prescribed circumstances).

16.116   In respect of these services the English policy guidance to CDCA 2000 (at para 25) states:

Cared for people may not be forced to accept services they do not wish to receive. However, in some circumstances they may accept a level of contact with social services that helps the person who cares for them. A cared for person who has refused an assessment may agree to the delivery of a non-intimate sitting service provided as a carer's service to give their usual carer a short break.

16.117   Regulations[126] define the meaning of 'intimate care' – stipulating that a service is deemed to be of an 'intimate' nature if it involves physical contact such as 'lifting, washing, grooming, feeding, dressing, bathing or toileting the person cared for'. Such service cannot be provided to the cared for person under CDCA 2000 s2(3) except in 'prescribed circumstances'. The Regulations[127] clarify the scope of 'prescribed circumstances' as where (essentially):

a)   the person cared for agrees to the intimate care; or

b)   in an emergency (which is likely to cause the cared for person serious personal harm) either:

---

126   Carers (Services) and Direct Payments (Amendment) (England) Regulations 2001 SI No 441 reg 2(1) and in Wales the Carers (Services) and Direct Payments (Amendment) (Wales) Regulations 2001 SI No 2186 (W150).

127   SI No 441, reg 2(2) and see also para 28 of the 2001 policy guidance (para 2.3 of the Welsh guidance).

   – the cared for person is unable to consent; or

   – he or she does not consent but the intimate care is necessary to alleviate the imminent risk of serious personal harm.

16.118 Despite the best efforts of the CDCA Act 2000, the fundamental principle that a competent person cannot be compelled to receive a service (save for specific provisions of the Mental Health Act 1983 outside the scope of this text), can leave carers anxious and shouldering significant caring responsibilities sometimes unrecognised by the cared for person. Even when the carer and the local authority agree that the cared for person needs and is eligible for service provision, the law is clear:

> If, as the evidence overwhelmingly suggests, the only reason Mr Woods is not getting the 20 hours of care and support the defendant has assessed he ought to be getting is because Mr Woods has refused to allow the Defendant to provide it, there is no prospect of a successful claim in judicial review.[128]

16.119 Such a refusal by the service user does not negate the right of the carer to an assessment (see para 16.38) nor does it absolve the local authority from its duty to develop a strategy to enable 'successful interaction' with the disabled person – possibly by involving third parties (such as voluntary sector group) so that reasons for the refusal are overcome.[129] In such cases, however, the statutory duty on the local authority is to support the carer through an assessment and if it so decides, to then consider its power to provide services directly to the carer. This underlines the importance of proactively informing carers of their entitlement to assessment when the cared for person is refusing to engage with the local authority.[130]

Young carers

16.120 Carers who are under the age of 18 are generally referred to as 'young carers'. Statistics from the 2001 census indicate that there were at that time some 175,000 young carers in the UK. The C(RS)A 1995 and C(EO)A 2004 apply to all carers irrespective of their age. In addition to the benefit of a carer's assessment under C(RS)A 1995, young carers may be entitled to services in their own right, under the Children Act (CA) 1989. In general it will be more appropriate for a young carer to be assessed under the 1989 Act. In this respect the combined policy guidance under CDCA 2000 and C(EO)A 2004 states (at para 10):

> Children (anyone aged under 18) who are carers should be routinely assessed under the Children Act 1989. As a matter of law they could be assessed under the 1995 Act but that would not be expected, nor would it be

---

128 *R (Woods) v Rochdale MBC* [2009] EWHC 323 (Admin) at para 46.

129 See eg, complaint no 02/C/08690 against Sheffield City Council, 9 August 2004, para 133.

130 See, for instance, *Implementing the Carers (Equal Opportunities) Act 2004*, SCIE Guide 9, updated August 2007, p25.

in line with the Children Act 1989 guidance. Nevertheless, whichever of these Acts they were assessed under, the new obligation to consider a young carer's wish to work or undertake education, training or leisure would still apply . . .

16.121 While the CA 1989 may be the general assessment route for young carers, this will not always be the case. The obligations under C(RS)A 1995 specifically encompass the needs of young carers because it is recognised that some adult services have, in the past, failed this group. The C(RS)A 1995 obliges adult services to ensure that children and young people looking after an adult are not left with unreasonable caring responsibilities.

Young carers and the Carers (Recognition and Services) Act 1995

16.122 Young carers, if they are providing or intending to provide a substantial amount of care on a regular basis, are entitled to an assessment under the C(RS)A 1995. Although this is primarily directed at establishing their ability to provide and continue to provide care (the continuation of which will generally be inappropriate), it must additionally address (by virtue of C(EO)A 2004 s2) not only their desire to work (for example, if a 15-year-old wanted to take up a paper round[131]) but also whether they wish to undertake, education, training or any leisure activity.

16.123   As a result of amendments made by CA 2004,[132] any assessment of a young carer must, among other things:

a) ascertain the child's wishes and feelings regarding the provision of such services as the local authority is proposing to make available; and

b) give due consideration (having regard to his or her age and understanding) to such wishes and feelings of the child as it has been able to ascertain.

Young carers and the Children Act 1989

16.124 There is no legislation which specifically refers to young carers. Guidance concerning young carers has, however, been issued by the Department of Health[133] and the Social Services Inspectorate in England (SSI).[134] The SSI guidance adopts a definition of a 'young carer' as 'a child or young person who is carrying out significant caring tasks and assuming a level of responsibility for another person, which would usually be taken by an adult'. Such duties as are owed to young carers by a social services

---

131 Para 10 of the combined policy guidance under the 2000 and 2004 Acts.
132 CA 1989 s17(4A) (inserted by CA 2004 s53).
133 Department of Health, Social Services Inspectorate (1998) *Young carers: making a start.*
134 Guidance letter CI (95)12.

authority are primarily contained in CA 1989 as clarified by guidance issued by the Department of Health[135]/Welsh Assembly.[136]

16.125   For a child to benefit from help under CA 1989, it is necessary for him or her to come within the definition of a 'child in need'. CA 1989 s17(10) defines a child to be 'in need' if:

(a) he is unlikely to achieve or maintain, or to have the opportunity of achieving or maintaining, a reasonable standard of health or development without the provision for him of services by a local authority . . .; or

(b) his health or development is likely to be significantly impaired, or further impaired, without the provision for him of such services; or

(c) he is disabled.

16.126 The policy guidance under C(RS)A 1995 (at para 14) refers to, and adopts the SSI guidance,[137] stating:

. . . many young people carry out a level of caring responsibilities which prevents them from enjoying normal social opportunities and from achieving full school attendance. Many young carers with significant caring responsibilities should therefore be seen as children in need.[138]

16.127 A key determinant therefore is whether the young carer's caring responsibilities are 'significant'. In this respect the practice guidance to C(RS)A 1995 (at para 15.2) stressed that young carers should not be expected to carry out 'inappropriate' levels of caring. It follows that when undertaking a community care assessment of a disabled or ill parent, the local authority must ensure that support mechanisms are put in place to prevent a young carer undertaking unreasonable caring responsibilities – or indeed suffering in any other inappropriate way. The general duties under CA 1989 s17 are considered at para 23.46 below.[139]

16.128   The policy guidance concerning the assessment of young carers issued by the Department of Health and the Welsh Assembly[140] states (among other things):

Assessing the Needs of Young Carers
3.61 A group of children whose needs are increasingly more clearly recognised are young carers for example those who assume important

---

135 Principally Department of Health (2000) *Framework for the Assessment of Children in Need and their Families*, and two volumes of guidance issued under CA 1989 of relevance to young carers – Volume 2: *Family Support* and Volume 6: *Children with Disabilities* (both 1991).

136 Department of Health (2000) *Framework for the Assessment of Children in Need and their Families*.

137 Guidance letter CI (95)12 annex A para 1.1.

138 See also para 2.4 of Volume 2: *Family Support* (note 135 above) which emphasises that 'the definition of "need" in the Act is deliberately wide to reinforce the emphasis on preventive support and services to families'.

139 See also J Richards and M Waites, *Working together to support disabled parents*, SCIE adults' services resource guide 9, August 2007

140 Department of Health (2004) *Framework for the Assessment of Children in Need and their Families* and Welsh Assembly, *Framework for the Assessment of Children in Need and their Families*, 2001; the cited extract appears at para 3.65 of the Welsh guidance.

caring responsibilities for parents and siblings. Some children care for parents who are disabled, physically or mentally ill, others for parents dependent on alcohol or involved in drug misuse . . .

3.62 An assessment of family circumstances is essential. Young carers should not be expected to carry inappropriate levels of caring which have an adverse impact on their development and life chances. It should not be assumed that children should take on similar levels of caring responsibilities as adults. Services should be provided to parents to enhance their ability to fulfil their parenting responsibilities. There may be differences of view between children and parents about appropriate levels of care. Such differences may be out in the open or concealed. The resolution of such tensions will require good quality joint work between adult and children's social services as well as co-operation from schools and healthcare workers. This work should include direct work with the young carer to understand his or her perspective and opinions. The young person who is a primary carer of his or her parent or sibling may have a good understanding of the family's functioning and needs which should be incorporated into the assessment.

3.63 Young carers can receive help from both local and health authorities. Where a child is providing a substantial amount of care on a regular basis for a parent, the child will be entitled to an assessment of their ability to care under section 1(1) of the *Carers (Recognition and Services) Act 1995* and the local authority must take that assessment into account in deciding what community care services to provide for the parent. Many young carers are not aware that they can ask for such an assessment. In addition, consideration must be given as to whether a young carer is a child in need under the Children Act 1989. The central issue is whether a child's welfare or development might suffer if support is not provided to the child or family. As part of the *National Strategy for Carers,*[141] local authorities should take steps to identify children with additional family burdens. Services should be provided to promote the health and development of young carers while not undermining the parent.

Parent carers

16.129 People with parental responsibility for a disabled child (ie a person aged under 18) are entitled (if their caring role is substantial) to an assessment under C(RS)A 1995 s1(2) and under CDCA 2000 s6. It is self-evident that most parent carers provide a 'substantial amount of care on a regular basis'. Neither C(RS)A 1995 nor CDCA 2000 include a stipulation (found in social security law) that the care provided to the disabled child must (for instance) be 'substantially in excess of the normal requirements of persons of his age'.[142]

16.130   Parent carers have a right to a separate assessment under the 1995 and 2000 Acts in addition to their needs being fully addressed in their child's Children Act assessment. In general, however, this should not be neces-

---

141   Department of Health (1999) *Caring about carers: a national strategy for carers.*
142   See eg Social Security Contributions and Benefits Act 1992 s72(6).

sary, provided the local authority fully addresses the parent's employment, training, education, leisure and other needs. As the combined policy guidance under CDCA 2000 and C(EO)A 2004 advises (at para 71):

> Following the passage of the 2004 Act, the assessment should take account of the parent's ability to provide or continue to provide care for the child and consideration of whether they work, or undertake any education, training or leisure activity or wish to do so. This means that local authorities have a duty to ask carers about these activities and take their wishes into account when planning the care package.

16.131 The risk of an integrated assessment process is that the needs of the parent carer are not adequately recognised. In *JR 30 (HN, a minor) Re Judicial Review*[143] the court observed:

> What the Trust has done in this case has been to relegate the carer's position as something inferior or secondary to that of the autistic child . . . this was an incorrect approach to carer assessments. In taking this approach the Trust failed to recognise that the needs of the carer, the child and indeed the family are interlinked. This is clear from an examination of the language, structure and clear statutory purpose of the legislative provisions.

16.132 The court held that there was an 'unconditional statutory obligation' to carry out a carer's assessment when requested so to do – within a reasonable period of time. Similarly, the LGO has found maladministration where a local authority focussed disproportionately on the educational needs of a particularly disruptive autistic child without giving adequate weight to the social needs of the whole family, which, in the circumstances of the case, would have required separate assessments of the needs of the parents as carers as well as the child and his sister as children in need.[144]

16.133 The legal obligation on a local authority to respond to critical carer need (see para 16.82 above) applies equally to parent carers. In *R (LH and MH) v Lambeth LBC*[145] the local authority accepted that the applicant's son's behaviour was having an adverse affect on her health, emotionally, mentally and physically: that she was 'depressed and at the end of her tether, crying all the time and only just coping'. However, the care plan for the son failed to explain how his mother's needs would be addressed. The court declared that the authority was in breach of its assessment obligations under CA 1989 (to the child) and under C(RS)A 1995 and CDCA 2000 (for the mother).

16.134 Parent carers (like all other qualifying carers) have the right to have their employment, training, education and leisure aspirations addressed.

143 [2010] NIQB 86 (3 December 2010) considered article 18A of the Children (Northern Ireland) Order 1995 which is in material terms, indistinguishable from Carers (Recognition and Services) Act 1995 s1(2), together with other provisions which mirror those set out in section 17 of the Children Act 1989.
144 Complaint No 07B04696 and 07B10996 against Croydon LBC, 16 September 2009.
145 [2006] EWHC 1190 (Admin), (2006) 9 CCLR 622.

The English practice guidance to the CDCA 2000 highlights the importance of providing such assistance, stating (at para 36):

> People with parental responsibility for disabled children will also benefit
> from joining or re-joining the workforce. Such carers often face difficulties
> re-entering the workforce because of lack of suitable child-care services.
> Many parents of disabled children would like to return to work and, if they
> were able to do so, would benefit socially and emotionally as well as
> financially.

16.135   The policy guidance to C(EO)A 2004 amplifies this point, stating:

> . . . the assessment should take account of the parent's ability to provide or
> continue to provide care for the child and consideration of whether they
> work, or undertake any education, training or leisure activity or wish to do
> so. This means that local authorities have a duty to ask carers about these
> activities and take their wishes into account when planning the care
> package. For example, the package may provide the possibility of freeing
> some leisure time for the carer and for other children in the family through
> a structured playtime with the disabled child, while social services provides
> services to run the house. The local authority must take assessments
> carried out under section 6 of the 2000 Act into account when deciding
> what services, if any, to provide under section 17 of the Children Act 1989.

16.136   The Childcare Act 2006 requires English and Welsh councils (sections 6
and 22) to secure, 'so far as is reasonably practicable', sufficient child care
to meet the requirements of parents in their area who require child care in
order to work or to undertake training or education to prepare for work. In
relation to disabled children, the obligation extends to child care facilities
up to 1 September after their 18th birthday. In determining whether the
provision of child care is sufficient, councils must have regard to (among
other things) the needs of parents for child care that is eligible for the
child care element of the working tax credit, and for child care that is
suitable for disabled children.

Short breaks for parent carers

16.137   Section 25 of the Children and Young Persons Act 2008 amends paragraph 6 of Schedule 2 of the Children Act 1989 (Provision for disabled
children) to impose a duty, to be performed in accordance with regulations, on local authorities to provide breaks 'to assist individuals who
provide care for such children to continue to do so, or to do so more
effectively, by giving them breaks from caring'. English regulations made
under paragraph 6[146] limit the scope of carer in this context to a parent or
person with parental responsibility. In the performance of this duty the
local authority must have regard to the needs of carers who would be
unable to continue to provide care without breaks given to them; and
those who would be able to provide care to their disabled child more
effectively with breaks to allow them to:

---

146   The Breaks for Carers of Disabled Children Regulations 2011 SI No 707. The Welsh
Government has yet to publish regulations to implement this provision.

(i) undertake education, training or any regular leisure activity,
(ii) meet the needs of other children in the family more effectively, or
(iii) carry out day to day tasks which they must perform in order to run their household.[147]

16.138 The duty is to provide, so far as is reasonably practicable, a range of services; and, under paragraph 4(2) of the Regulations:

In particular, the local authority must provide, as appropriate, a range of—

a) day-time care in the homes of disabled children or elsewhere,
b) overnight care in the homes of disabled children or elsewhere,
c) educational or leisure activities for disabled children outside their homes, and
d) services available to assist carers in the evenings, at weekends and during the school holidays

16.139 Additionally local authorities must publish a 'short breaks services statement' by 1 October 2011, and subsequently keep the statement under review. There is a duty to consult carers ('to have regard to the views of carers in their area'). The statement must include the range of services provided, how they are designed to meet carers' needs in their area and any eligibility criteria for accessing the services.[148]

Carers of mental health service users

16.140 People with mental health problems are entitled to a community care assessment, in common with other disabled people. In some cases, however, they are entitled to additional assistance, under the 'Care Programme Approach' (CPA) (considered separately at para 21.7 below). The rights of persons subject to the CPA have been detailed in English and Welsh *National Service Frameworks for Mental Health*[149] and their carers identified as entitled to certain specified rights. The English framework states:

Standard 6 – Caring about carers

All individuals who provide regular and substantial care for a person on CPA should:
• have an assessment of their caring, physical and mental health needs,
• repeated on at least an annual basis,
• have their own written care plan, which is given to them and implemented in discussion with them.

---

147 The Breaks for Carers of Disabled Children Regulations 2011 SI No 707 para 3.
148 The Breaks for Carers of Disabled Children Regulations 2011 SI No 707 para 5.
149 Department of Health (1999) *A National Service Framework for Mental Health: modern standards and service models.* In Wales the equivalent NSF is Welsh Assembly (2005) *Raising the Standard: the revised adult mental health national service framework and an action plan for Wales,* para 1.4 of which states that the relevant Standard (Standard 2) concerning carer participation is under 'review'.

16.141 The rights under Standard 6 are in addition to the basic rights to which all carers of people with a mental health problem are entitled. Thus if the person cared for is not receiving care from the specialist psychiatric services, his or her carer will be entitled to an assessment under C(RS)A 1995 and CDCA 2000 (if providing or intending to provide regular and substantial care).

16.142   The rationale behind Standard 6 is explained in the following terms:[150]

> Carers play a vital role in helping to look after service users of mental health services, particularly those with severe mental illness. Providing help, advice and services to carers can be one of the best ways of helping people with mental health problems. While caring can be rewarding, the strains and responsibilities of caring can also have an impact on carers' own mental and physical health. These needs must be addressed by health and social services.

16.143 Standard 6 contains detailed guidance on what action should be taken to support the carer.[151] It requires social services to draw up a care plan and agree it with the carer and at the same time to take into account his or her health needs. The plan should be in writing and reviewed at least annually and its contents should be communicated to the GP and primary care team. The carer's care plan should include:

- information about the mental health needs of the person for whom he or she is caring, including information about medication and any side-effects which can be predicted, and support services available;
- action to meet defined contingencies;
- information on what to do and who to contact in a crisis;
- what will be provided to meet the carer's own mental and physical health needs, and how it will be provided;
- action needed to secure advice on income, housing, educational and employment matters;
- arrangements for short-term breaks;
- arrangements for social support, including access to carers' support groups;
- information about appeals or complaints procedures.

Involving carers in mental health decisions

16.144 The current code of practice under the Mental Health Act 1983 reflects the approach of the Community Care Assessment Directions (see para 3.24 above) in establishing a rebuttable presumption that carers will be centrally involved in decision-making in relation to functions carried out under MHA 1983. One of the four guiding principles, the participation principle, includes the following:

> The involvement of carers, family members and other people who have an interest in the patient's welfare should be encouraged (unless there are particular reasons to the contrary) and their views taken seriously.

150 Ibid, p69.
151 Ibid, p72.

16.145 Many patients discharged or on leave from hospital will be subject to the Care Programme Approach (CPA) (see para 20.7). Some key elements in the English CPA guidance highlight a range of carer concerns:

- Significant reliance of carers or own caring responsibilities are both characteristics indicating a level of complexity of need to bring a patient within the narrowed scope of the CPA.[152]
- Carers, as well as patients, should be involved in a thorough risk assessment before a decision is made to bring a CPA to an end.[153]
- Outcomes should be explicitly agreed with carers as well as service users at the outset of the care plan.[154]
- Recognising the impact of mental illness on all aspects of the life of the care giver, the guidance stresses the need to inform and advise carers, including young carers, of their right to their own assessment and support plan, and that this process should be coordinated with the mental health assessment.[155]

16.146 Particular issues arise for carers of patients subject to community treatment orders or on leave from hospital where the cared for person is subject to conditions, the breach of which can lead to recall to hospital, putting carers potentially in the invidious position of policing compliance. The MHA Code of Practice (see para 20.28 below) recognises that carers and relatives are typically in much more frequent contact with the patient than professionals, even under well-run care plans.[156] Accordingly in the context of a community treatment order:

> Particular attention should be paid to carers and relatives when they raise a concern that the patient is not complying with the conditions or that the patient's mental health appears to be deteriorating. The team responsible for the patient needs to give due weight to those concerns and any requests made by the carers or relatives in deciding what action to take.[157]

16.147 In deciding whether to grant leave from hospital under MHA 1983 s17, the Code suggests that engagement with the carer may amount to a pre-condition to a grant of leave:

> If patients do not consent to carers or other people who would normally be involved in their care being consulted about their leave, responsible clinicians should reconsider whether or not it is safe and appropriate to grant leave.[158]

---

152 Department of Health (2008) *Refocusing the care programme approach*, p13.
153 Department of Health (2008) *Refocusing the care programme approach*, p15.
154 Department of Health (2008) *Refocusing the care programme approach*, p20.
155 Department of Health (2008) *Refocusing the care programme approach*, p25.
156 Code of Practice, para 25.46.
157 Code of Practice, para 25.46.
158 Code of Practice, para 21.20.

Law Commission proposals

16.148 The Law Commission proposals for adult social care legislation (see para 3.237 above) will incorporate carer legislation and include the following recommendations:

- a single duty to assess a carer, which would apply to all carers who are *providing or intending to provide care to another person*, and not just those *providing a substantial amount of care on a regular basis*. The assessment would be triggered where a carer appears to have, or will have upon commencing the caring role, needs that could be met by the provision of carers' services or by the provision of services to the cared-for person.
- A proposal that local authorities should be required to use a mandatory national eligibility framework in exercising their power to provide services to carers. In effect, this would mean the introduction of a duty to provide carers' services, since authorities would be required to provide services to those who fall within its eligibility criteria.[159]

159 Law Commission (2010) *Adult Social Care: outline of our proposed adult social care statute*, Law Com 24.

CHAPTER 17

Mental capacity

Introduction

17.1   Not infrequently questions are raised as to the extent of a community care service user's mental capacity to make decisions. In this chapter we provide a brief guide to key principles and procedures that regulate this branch of the law. We do not seek, however, to emulate the many excellent and extensive guides concerning the law of mental capacity, to which reference should be made for a more detailed understanding of the law in this field. We additionally consider issues of capacity elsewhere in this text, for instance, in relation to the community care assessment process (see para 3.113 above), hospital discharges (see para 5.16 above), direct payments (see para 12.20 above), and access to personal information (see para 25.17 below).

Overview

17.2   The law regulating mental capacity has been developed by many centuries of court decisions which have established various principles to be applied in individual cases. The law, like this chapter, can be divided into two broad sections: (1) the legal rules that are used to determine whether an individual has sufficient mental capacity to make a particular decision, and (2) the legal rules that are applied when a decision has to be made on behalf of someone who has been held to lack the requisite mental capacity to make the decision.

17.3   The law relating to this field (in so far as it applies to persons aged 16 or over[1]) is governed by the Mental Capacity Act (MCA) 2005, which at section 42 provides for the publication of a code of practice ('the Code') and reference to this Code[2] is made in the section that follows. The Code provides an excellent starting point for the understanding of the law in this field. Section 42 of the Act sets out categories of people who are placed under a duty 'to have regard' to the Code, namely:

- People working in a professional capacity (for example, a social worker who is arranging for a person lacking capacity to move into a supported living arrangement);
- People who are receiving payment for work in relation to a person without capacity (for example, a care assistant working in a residential care home for people with learning disabilities);
- Anyone who is an attorney of a Lasting Power of Attorney, a deputy appointed by the Court of Protection, an Independent Mental Capacity Advocate or who is carrying out research approved in accordance with the Act (these terms are considered below).

---

1   For a brief analysis of the law relating to persons under 16 – see S Broach, L Clements and J Read, *Disabled Children: a legal handbook*, LAG, 2010, paras 5.83–5.90.
2   Department of Constitutional Affairs (2007) *Mental Capacity Act 2005 Code of Practice*, accessible at www.dca.gov.uk/menincap/legis.htm#codeofpractice.

17.4 As the Code explains (p2) such persons 'must be aware' of its contents 'when acting or making decisions on behalf of someone who lacks capacity to make a decision for themselves' and (at p5) that a 'failure to comply with the Code can be used in evidence before a court or tribunal in any civil or criminal proceedings'.

17.5 Section 1 of the Act details five key principles that must be considered whenever a decision has to be made either concerning a person's capacity to make a decision, or their best interests, namely:

- A person must be assumed to have capacity unless it is established that he or she lacks capacity.
- A person is not to be treated as unable to make a decision unless all practicable steps to help him or her to do so have been taken without success.
- A person is not to be treated as unable to make a decision merely because he or she makes an unwise decision.
- An act done, or decision made, under this Act for or on behalf of a person who lacks capacity must be done, or made, in his or her best interests.
- Before the act is done, or the decision is made, regard must be had to whether the purpose for which it is needed can be as effectively achieved in a way that is less restrictive of the person's rights and freedom of action.

17.6 The following section considers – first, the underpinning legal provisions and concepts of relevance to determinations as to whether a person has sufficient mental capacity to make a particular decision; and second the law, policy and good practice that applies in situations where a person is adjudged to lack the necessary capacity to make a particular decision.

The determination of capacity

17.7 In seeking to determine whether a person has sufficient mental capacity to make a particular decision, it is useful to bear in mind the following principles/concepts:

1) Presumption of capacity.
2) A functional question – what is it that has to be decided?
3) Understanding the consequences of acting/not acting.
4) An ability to rationalise/weigh up the information.
5) An appreciation that there is a problem – upon which advice is required.
6) Ultimately a legal not a medical question.

Presumption of capacity

17.8 MCA 2005 s1(2) creates, for people aged 16 over, a presumption of capacity, that 'a person must be assumed to have capacity unless it is established that he lacks capacity'. The fact that (for instance) a person has been diagnosed as having advanced dementia or has been described as having severe learning disabilities or has been detained under the Mental Health Act (MHA) 1983 does not affect this presumption. In the absence of proof to the contrary, such a person is assumed to retain his or her capacity to make informed decisions. The standard of proof is 'the balance of probabilities'.

Functional test

17.9   Whether, as a matter of law, a person has sufficient mental capacity to make a decision depends upon the decision that has to be made. Thus a person may have sufficient mental capacity to buy a chair but insufficient to purchase a house. In the former case the issue is straightforward whereas in the latter the size and implications of the transaction (including the legal responsibilities of a home owner) demand a greater comprehension. In *A local authority v MM*[3] for example, the court adjudged the principal party to have capacity to consent to sexual relations but not to have capacity to litigate, to manage her finances, to decide where and with whom she should live or to decide with whom she should have contact. MCA 2005 s2(1) provides therefore that (for the purposes of the Act):

> . . . a person lacks capacity in relation to a matter if at the material time he is unable to make a decision for himself in relation to the matter because of an impairment of, or a disturbance in the functioning of, the mind or brain.

17.10   The 'matter' specific nature of the test means that it is not normally sufficient (for instance) to state that a person is 'incapable of handling money' without clarifying exactly how much money: someone may not have the capacity to manage an inheritance of £250,000 but may be quite capable of handing a small weekly allowance. Likewise a person might have sufficient mental capacity to manage a direct payment – which enabled him or her to retain a home care agency to provide the care – but insufficient capacity to be an employer (see para 12.20 above).

Understanding the consequences

17.11   While a person may be unable to make a decision about a matter because of (for instance) its size and complexity, it is also necessary to have regard to the potential consequences of the decision. Ultimately a person can decide to take action which may result in their death – for instance to require the ventilator that is keeping them alive to be switched off (as occurred in *B v NHS Hospital Trust*[4]). To make a life and death decision, however, one requires considerably more mental capacity than to decide, for instance, what clothes to wear or television programme to watch. Accordingly a gravely ill person who is unable to care for him or herself, will require more capacity to discharge him or herself from hospital

---

3   *Re MM, Local Authority X v MM* [2007] EWHC 2003 (Fam), (2008) 11 CCLR 119, [2008] 3 FCR 788.
4   [2002] EWHC 429 (Fam), [2002] 2 All ER 449.

(where no home care may immediately be available) than a person for whom a premature hospital discharge had no such risks. Ultimately, however, if a person understands the consequences of the decision and is capable of 'weighing up' the risks (see below), he or she can decide to take the action regardless of whether the professionals concerned think it sensible. In this respect MCA 2005 s1(4) specifically states that a person is not to be treated as unable to make a decision merely because the decision is an unwise one.

Ability to rationalise

17.12　Infrequently a person may understand the consequences of a decision, but because of a mental block (for instance, an extreme phobia or incontrollable obsessional and compulsive disorder) be mentally powerless to act on that understanding. *Re MB (Caesarean Section),*[5] for instance, concerned a patient whose life was believed to be in severe danger unless she delivered her baby by caesarean section. MB understood the danger, but refused the operation because she had an absolute phobia of needles and was incapable of agreeing to anything that might involve her being injected. The Court of Appeal held that this inability to apply any rationality to the information meant that she lacked capacity to decide on the treatment in question. MCA 2005 s3(1) adopts the court's approach and provides:

> . . . a person is unable to make a decision for himself if he is unable –
> (a) to understand the information relevant to the decision,
> (b) to retain that information,
> (c) to use or weigh that information as part of the process of making the decision, or
> (d) to communicate his decision (whether by talking, using sign language or any other means).

17.13　Section 3(1) requires, therefore, the ability to understand and retain relevant information for sufficiently long to make the decision. Thus if a person has a short-term memory problem, as long as the relevant information is understood at the time the decision is made, the fact that it is then forgotten may not mean there is a lack of capacity (see also in this respect section 3(3)). Information need only be retained if it is relevant. Accordingly a person with dementia who is demanding to be discharged from hospital may lack capacity to make this decision if unable to remember that the reason for the admission was his or her severely neglected state.

17.14　　In an extreme situation, an obsessional refusal to consider certain factors, due, for instance, to an 'autistic spectrum disorder' may result in the person being unable to 'weigh' all the relevant factors. *RT and LT v A Local Authority*[6] is such a case, where the court held that the young adult

5　[1997] 2 FLR 426, [1997] FCR 541, (1998) 38 BMLR 175.
6　[2010] EWCA 1910 (Fam).

who was so refusing (although having only a mild learning disability) lacked the necessary capacity to decide where she should live.

17.15   Section 3(1)(d) raises an additional ground, namely the problem that arises where a person is incapable of communicating intelligibly (or at all) and a decision has to be taken on his or her behalf. A person may suffer from 'locked in syndrome', for instance – namely he or she appears to be in a coma and incapacitated, but in fact is aware of what is going on but completely unable to communicate, even by blinking an eye. Alternatively the person may be able to communicate, but what is said or done may make no sense to anyone involved in his or her care. In such cases (provided all practicable steps to help the person communicate have been taken without success – section 1(3)) he or she may be deemed to lack capacity. Obviously what is practicable may depend on the urgency of the situation.

Understanding there is a problem

17.16   The legal test of capacity thus focuses on the issue of understanding and not the ability to make prudent or wise decisions,[7] or indeed the ability to comprehend personally the fine detail of the choice or question in issue. In many situations the fact that a person is aware that he or she has a problem, may be sufficient to establish capacity to make that decision.

17.17   *White v Fell*[8] concerned the capacity of a disabled person to agree settlement terms in court proceedings. Boreham J considered that the assessment of capacity should be construed in a common sense way and observed:

> I have no doubt that the plaintiff is quite incapable of managing unaided a large sum of money such as the sort of sum that would be appropriate compensation for her injuries. That, however, is not conclusive. Few people have the capacity to manage all their affairs unaided . . . It may be that she would have chosen, and would choose now, not to take advice, but that is not the question. The question is: is she capable of doing so? To have that capacity she requires first the insight and understanding of the fact that she has a problem in respect of which she needs advice . . . Secondly, having identified the problem, it will be necessary for her to seek an appropriate adviser and to instruct him with sufficient clarity to enable him to understand the problem and to advise her appropriately . . . Finally, she needs sufficient mental capacity to understand and to make decisions based upon, or otherwise give effect to, such advice as she may receive.

17.18   In the judge's opinion it followed that:

> . . . the court should only take over the individual's function of decision making when it is shown on the balance of probabilities that such person does not have the capacity sufficiently to understand, absorb and retain information (including advice) relevant to the matters in question

7   *Masterman-Lister v Jewell* [2002] EWCA Civ 1889, [2003] WLR 1511, (2004) 7 CCLR 5 at [46].

8   12 November 1987, unreported, cited in *Masterman-Lister v Jewell* [2002] EWCA Civ 1889, [2003] 1 WLR 1511, (2004) 7 CCLR 5 at [18]–[20].

sufficiently to enable him or her to make decisions based upon such information.

17.19 In many situations a person may be aware that he or she does not understand something – for instance, that he or she is having difficulty adding up or remembering the value of certain coins. The fact that he or she is aware of the problem is an indication that he or she has capacity – because he or she can then seek help. If the person has a learning disability, this might mean that an advocate could help him or her to learn what can and cannot be purchased with certain coins or who to ask when having to make payments. Such a state of affairs is indeed little different to many normally intelligent people not understanding (for example) the terms of a consumer credit agreement.

Ultimately a legal not a medical test

17.20 Where in court proceedings the extent of a person's mental capacity is in issue, medical evidence will generally be sought: ultimately, however, the decision is a legal one.[9] In this respect, the senior judge of the Court of Protection has observed that[10] 'although the court attaches a great deal of weight to the evidence of a registered medical practitioner on questions of incapacity, it does not automatically prefer medical opinion to lay opinion'.

17.21 *Re K (Enduring Powers of Attorney)*[11] illustrates the medical/legal distinction in this area. The case concerned a refusal by the Court of Protection to register an enduring power of attorney.[12] Shortly after the power was signed, the attorney applied for its registration, which was refused on the basis that the short period between the signing and the attempted registration suggested that the person lacked mental capacity at the time the document was signed. Allowing the appeal Hoffmann J held that there was no logical reason why a person who understood that something needed to be done, but who lacked the requisite understanding to do it personally, should not confer on another the power to do what needs to be done.[13] Accordingly a person may have insufficient mental capacity to manage his or her affairs, but have sufficient capacity to delegate this function to an attorney.

17.22 It follows that medical evidence may be of limited value unless it is demonstrated that the expert is aware of the relevant legal test for capacity: what exactly it is that the person is required to comprehend. The courts have given guidance on a large range of capacity decisions (eg the capacity

9 *Masterman-Lister v Jewell* [2002] EWCA Civ 1889, [2003] WLR 1511, (2004) 7 CCLR 5 at [34] and *Richmond v Richmond* (1914) 111 LT 273 at 274.
10 D Lush, *Elderly Clients*, Jordans, 1996, p38.
11 [1988] Ch 310.
12 Now replaced by Lasting Powers of Attorney (property and affairs) – see para 17.51 below: these authorised the attorney to make financial decisions on behalf of a donor who lacked the requisite capacity, but only when the EPA had been registered.
13 [1988] Ch 310 at pp315B–C; see also Chadwick LJ in *Masterman-Lister v Jewell* [2002] EWCA Civ 1889, [2003] WLR 1511, (2004) 7 CCLR 5 at [83].

to make a will;[14] to revoke a will;[15] to have sexual relations;[16] to make a gift;[17] to litigate; to consent to medical treatment – and so on) and guidance on the relevant criteria has been given by the British Medical Association and the Law Society.[18] In this context, two issues of importance for community care planning purposes, include the capacity required to decide where to live and the capacity required to enter into a tenancy agreement.

Capacity to decide where to live

17.23   There has been no case that has clearly identified the capacity a person requires in order to consent to live in a particular place – or to choose where to live. In *JE v DE and Surrey CC*[19] the court was of the view that DE (aged 76) lacked capacity to decide where he should live. He was described in the following terms (para 80):

> A major stroke in 2003 left him blind and with significant short-term memory impairment. He is disorientated and needs assistance with all the activities of daily living. He needs a guide when walking. Although he suffers from dementia he is able to express his wishes and feelings with some clarity and force, though expert evidence suggests that he has a psychological dependence on others which is greater than that arising from his physical disabilities, so there is room for debate as to just how genuinely independent his expressions of wish actually are.

17.24   In *Newham LBC v BS and S*[20] the court's considered that the principal party did not have capacity to decide where she should live and who should provide care for her. Her moderate/severe learning disability and its consequences was described by the court as follows:

> She has a poor attention span and her level of comprehension and cognitive function is extremely limited. Her understanding of events is dependent on contextual and situational cues. S also has no concept of time nor has the ability of recall of events that may have occurred in the past. S is not in a position to express her views as a consequence of limitation in her communication skills and learning disability, which is a permanent condition. As such, she is unable to comprehend and retain any information material to decisions about her future. Neither is she capable of evaluating the positive and negative aspects

17.25   In *RT and LT v A Local Authority*[21] (see para 17.14 above) although the person concerned had only a mild learning disability, a symptom of her autistic spectrum disorder was that she was only able to look at a problem

---

14   See eg, *Banks v Goodfellow* (1870) LR 5 QB 549, *Sharp v Adam* [2005] EWHC 1806 (Ch); and *Kostic v Chaplin* [2007] EWHC 2298 (Ch).
15   *Re Sabatinin* (1970) 114 SJ 35.
16   *Re MM, Local Authority X v MM* [2007] EWHC 2003 (Fam), (2008) 11 CCLR 119, [2008] 3 FCR 788.
17   *Re Beaney* [1978] 2 All ER 595.
18   P Letts (ed) *Assessment of Mental Capacity: a practical guide for doctors and lawyers*, 3rd edn, Law Society (a joint BMA/Law Society publication) 2010.
19   [2006] EWHC 3459 (Fam), (2007) 10 CCLR 149.
20   [2003] EWHC 1909 (Fam), (2004) 7 CCLR 132.
21   [2010] EWHC 1910 (Fam), (2010) 13 CCLR 580.

from one perspective – particularly if it ran counter to her pre-formed views, or did not support her wishes. She was adamant that she wanted to return to live with her parents and shut off all considerations to the contrary. In the court's opinion, this meant that she was not able to weigh information in the balance – and so as a consequence, lacked the capacity to decide where to live.

Capacity and tenancies

17.26 As we note above (para 15.137 above) a number of supported living schemes are predicated on the disabled person accessing housing benefit – and this has, in turn, raised questions as to the mental capacity a person requires in order to enter into a tenancy agreement.

17.27 Guidance on this question has been issued by the Court of Protection[22] and by the Department of Health.[23] The Court of Protection guidance advises that were the person lacks capacity to sign a tenancy agreement, then if that person already has a court appointed deputy (see below) 'the deputy can terminate or enter into a tenancy agreement without further authorisation from the court'. If, however, there is no deputy, and the only issue concerns the signing of a tenancy, then this can be done by a single order and the procedure for this is explained in the guidance note.

17.28 In *G v (1) E and (2) A local authority and (3) F*[24] the court held to be invalid a purported tenancy allegedly entered into on behalf of an adult with severe learning disabilities. The court's reasons for so determining, included the fact that:

- the disabled person lacked capacity to enter into any such agreement;
- the document was signed by the landlord on behalf of the disabled person;
- the disabled person did not have exclusive possession of his room – staff had unrestricted access to it and so it failed the tenancy test, set out in *Street v Mountford*.[25]

17.29 A number of cases raising the validity of tenancies entered into on behalf of people with limited mental capacity, have arisen in the context of housing benefit claims. In *Wychavon District Council v EM*[26] the Upper Tribunal rejected the claim for housing benefit on the basis that:

A tenancy agreement requires two parties – the landlord and the tenant. Here the claimant was not, and was incapable of being, a party to any agreement. Regardless of her capacity to consent, she could not and did not communicate any agreement to the tenancy and I infer that she could

---

22 Court of Protection (2011) *Guidance on tenancy agreements.*
23 Department of Health (2007) Housing Learning and Improvement Network, *Housing provision and the Mental Capacity Act 2005: factsheet No 20.*
24 [2010] EWHC 621 (COP).
25 [1985] 1 AC 809.
26 [2011] UKUT 144 (AAC).

never have been asked to. There simply was no such agreement, and therefore no liability to pay rent.

17.30   The *Wychavon* judgment has been questioned[27] on two grounds. The first is that it failed to consider a relevant Social Security Commissioner decision[28] which drew a distinction between voidable and void contracts – suggesting that even if a person lacked the requisite capacity to enter into a tenancy agreement – this merely rendered it voidable. Accordingly where the landlord was aware of the capacity difficulty and did not seek to avoid the tenancy, housing benefit could still be paid. The second ground on which the judgment has been questioned concerns MCA 2005 s7 pursuant to which contracts for the supply of 'necessary goods or services' can create a liability on behalf of the person lacking capacity.

Best interests

17.31   Where a decision needs to be made in respect of a person who lacks the requisite mental capacity, the law requires that the decision be based upon the concept of 'best interests'. This is an unfortunate phrase since in common usage it connotes simply 'what is best for the person' – ie an objective analysis. However, at law it also contains a subjective component – namely 'what would the person have done if she or he had the necessary capacity' (ie standing in the person's shoes and trying to make the decision she or he would have made).

17.32   The 'best interests' to be served by the intervention are, of course, those of the incapacitated person's alone. Thus in *Re Y (Mental Incapacity: Bone Marrow Transplant)*[29] the court held that the fact that the donation of bone marrow by a mentally incompetent woman to her sister would save the sister's life, was not relevant unless as a result of that donation the best interests of the donor were served.

17.33   In *Re MB (Caesarean Section)*[30] the Court of Appeal held that a patient's best interests were not confined to her medical best interests and in *Re A (Medical Treatment: Male Sterilisation)*[31] the High Court considered that they could encompass medical, emotional and all other welfare issues.

17.34   MCA 2005 s4(1)–(7) provides:

> **Best interests**
> (1) In determining for the purposes of this Act what is in a person's best interests, the person making the determination must not make it merely on the basis of –
>   (a) the person's age or appearance, or
>   (b) a condition of his, or an aspect of his behaviour, which might lead others to make unjustified assumptions about what might be in his best interests.

27 See analysis in (2011) 74 *Journal of Community Care Law* 13.
28 Decision CH 2121 2006 of Commissioner Mesher.
29 [1997] 2 WLR 556.
30 [1997] 2 FLR 426, [1997] FCR 541, (1998) 38 BMLR 175.
31 (2000) 53 BMLR 66 at 72.

(2) The person making the determination must consider all the relevant circumstances and, in particular, take the following steps.

(3) He must consider –
  (a) whether it is likely that the person will at some time have capacity in relation to the matter in question, and
  (b) if it appears likely that he will, when that is likely to be.

(4) He must, so far as reasonably practicable, permit and encourage the person to participate, or to improve his ability to participate, as fully as possible in any act done for him and any decision affecting him.

(5) Where the determination relates to life-sustaining treatment he must not, in considering whether the treatment is in the best interests of the person concerned, be motivated by a desire to bring about his death.

(6) He must consider, so far as is reasonably ascertainable –
  (a) the person's past and present wishes and feelings (and, in particular, any relevant written statement made by him when he had capacity),
  (b) the beliefs and values that would be likely to influence his decision if he had capacity, and
  (c) the other factors that he would be likely to consider if he were able to do so.

(7) He must take into account, if it is practicable and appropriate to consult them, the views of –
  (a) anyone named by the person as someone to be consulted on the matter in question or on matters of that kind,
  (b) anyone engaged in caring for the person or interested in his welfare,
  (c) any donee of a lasting power of attorney granted by the person, and
  (d) any deputy appointed for the person by the court,
  as to what would be in the person's best interests and, in particular, as to the matters mentioned in subsection (6).

17.35 The Act does not, therefore, define best interests – for instance in terms of explaining whether the principle of 'doing what the person would have done (had they capacity)' trumps the principle of 'doing what is objectively considered best for them'. It merely lays down a process, at the end of which the decision maker is presumed to be able to form a reasonable belief as to what decision would be in the person's best interests. In doing this the decision-maker will (following the key steps in section 4) need to consider:

1) Whether the decision is really necessary – or if it could be put off. This may be of particular relevance for a person thought likely to recover capacity in the near future – for instance someone who has had a stroke, but is recovering or someone with fluctuating capacity. In such cases it might be in the person's best interest to delay any decision.

2) The present views of the incapacitated person – these are of great importance even if they are not ultimately determinative.

3) The person's past views – these are of primary relevance when ascertaining 'what they would have done' had they not lost capacity.

4) The views of significant others: ie 'anyone engaged in caring for the person or interested in his welfare'. This will of course include family, friends, carers (paid and unpaid), professionals and so on. The aim is

to ascertain from the relevant third parties (a) what they think the person would have done had he or she not lost capacity as well as (b) what they objectively think would be the best decision for that person. In certain situations, if there are no family or friends available – an Independent Mental Capacity Advocate may need to be appointed (see para 17.67 below).

17.36   *R (W) v Croydon LBC*[32] illustrates the vital importance that courts attach to the section 4 process being observed by practitioners. In this case the council decided in principle to move a young adult (who lacked capacity to decide where to live) from his placement and convened a best interests meeting with his parents to discuss this. It did not, however, alert the parents to the fact that it had formed a very strong view that the placement was unsuitable (in part because of its cost – almost £5,000 per week). The court held that this process was unlawful: that the parents (and the service provider) should have been informed and been involved at a much earlier time (when the assessments were being undertaken) and given time to consider and make representations on the proposals – as the council would then have had the benefit of the material the parents had produced.

17.37   In assessing a person's 'best interests' for the purposes of section 4, the decision maker – or the best interests meeting[33] – will often have to draw up a 'balance sheet'[34] listing the potential benefits and 'dis-benefits' that may result from the various choices available. This process is further considered at para 24.92 below. In *AH v Hertfordshire Partnership NHS Foundation Trust and Ealing PCT*[35] (a case concerning the proposed change of the address of a learning disable adult – considered at para 9.52 above) the court was highly critical of the respondent PCT and local authority for failing to undertake 'a baseline balance-sheet exercise about whether it was' in his best interests to move – and noted that that they had not been able 'to identify a single dependable benefit arising from the proposed move'.

17.38   The 'balance sheet' approach to best interests decision making, does not mean that it is designed to avoid 'risk'. In *Re MM*[36] Munby J observed:

> The fact is that all life involves risk, and the young, the elderly and the vulnerable, are exposed to additional risks and to risks they are less well equipped than others to cope with . . . Physical health and safety can sometimes be bought at too high a price in happiness and emotional welfare. The emphasis must be on sensible risk appraisal, not striving to avoid all risk, whatever the price, but instead seeking a proper balance and being willing to tolerate manageable or acceptable risks as the price

32 [2011] EWHC 696 (Admin).
33 Valuable advice as to the procedures to be followed at a 'best interests' meeting are provided in T Joyce, *Best Interests Guidance on adults who lack capacity to make decisions for themselves [England and Wales]*, The British Psychological Society, 2007, funded by Department of Health.
34 *Re A (Medical Treatment: Male Sterilisation)* [2000] 1 FLR 549 at 560F–560H.
35 [2011] EWHC 276 (CoP), (2011) 14 CCLR 301.
36 *Re MM, Local Authority X v MM* [2007] EWHC 2003 (Fam), [2008] 3 FCR 788.

appropriately to be paid in order to achieve some other good – in particular to achieve the vital good of the elderly or vulnerable person's happiness. What good is it making someone safer if it merely makes them miserable?[37]

'Necessity' and 'section 5 acts'

17.39   MCA 2005 s5 endeavours to convert the common law principle of necessity into statutory language. It does this by stipulating that if:

1) a person (eg a carer) 'acts in connection with the care or treatment of' someone believed to lack capacity; and
2) the person (eg a carer) has formed a reasonable belief as to:
   a) the person's lack of capacity; and
   b) the person's best interests,
3) then the person (eg the carer) will not be liable for that action – provided it is something that the incapacitated person could have consented to had he or she capacity.

17.40   Accordingly if a consultant in a hospital casualty ward is confronted by an unconscious patient who is haemorrhaging she might have a reasonable belief that (a) the person lacks capacity to consent to medical treatment; and (b) that to operate would be in the person's best interests. Since people can consent to medical treatment, in such a case the consultant could not be sued/prosecuted for assault. However, if she was negligent in her treatment, section 5 would provide no defence because negligence is not something to which one can consent. Such acts are known as 'section 5 acts' and of course may be performed by a range of people on any one day. The key requirements are that the person acts in connection with the care or treatment of another person and that the person carrying out the act has formed a reasonable belief as to the incapacitated person's lack of capacity and their best interests.

17.41   The Code of Practice (at para 6.5) suggests that the following actions might be covered by section 5:

Personal care
- helping with washing, dressing or personal hygiene
- helping with eating and drinking
- helping with communication
- helping with mobility (moving around)
- helping someone take part in education, social or leisure activities
- going into a person's home to drop off shopping or to see if they are alright
- doing the shopping or buying necessary goods with the person's money
- arranging household services (for example, arranging repairs or maintenance for gas and electricity supplies)
- providing services that help around the home (such as homecare or meals on wheels)

37   *Re MM (an adult)* [2009] 1 FLR 443, per Munby J at [120].

- undertaking actions related to community care services (for example, day care, residential accommodation or nursing care) . . .[38]
- helping someone to move home (including moving property and clearing the former home).

Healthcare and treatment
- carrying out diagnostic examinations and tests (to identify an illness, condition or other problem)
- providing professional medical, dental and similar treatment
- giving medication
- taking someone to hospital for assessment or treatment
- providing nursing care (whether in hospital or in the community)
- carrying out any other necessary medical procedures (for example, taking a blood sample) or therapies (for example, physiotherapy or chiropody)
- providing care in an emergency.

Paying for goods and services

17.42   Section 5 will also sanction the use of the money of incapacitated adults to pay for necessary goods and services when this is believed to be in the person's best interests. In such situations there will be no requirement for a lasting power of attorney or other Court of Protection order. What is 'necessary' for an individual depends in part upon his or her wealth and expectations, as the Code advises:

> 6.58. 'Necessary' means something that is suitable to the person's condition in life (their place in society, rather than any mental or physical condition) and their actual requirements when the goods or services are provided (section 7(2)). The aim is to make sure that people can enjoy a similar standard of living and way of life to those they had before lacking capacity. For example, if a person who now lacks capacity previously chose to buy expensive designer clothes, these are still necessary goods – as long as they can still afford them. But they would not be necessary for a person who always wore cheap clothes, no matter how wealthy they were.

Restraint

17.43   It is outside the scope of this text to consider the detailed MCA 2005 provisions that are capable of authorising the detention of a person – known as the Deprivation of Liberty Safeguards (DoLS). However, in summary, the Act draws a crucial distinction between placing restrictions on a person's liberty and depriving them of their liberty. This fine line is crucial, since 'restrictions' are permitted under the Act, without the need

---

38   In certain situations these changes may require external sanction – for instance, the commissioning of a report by an Independent Mental Capacity Advocate – see para 17.70 below.

for compliance with any formal authorisation procedures, whereas such procedures are mandatory in relation to any 'deprivation'.

17.44   The distinction is made clear in section 6, which places limitations on certain section 5 acts: materially in relation to 'restraint', which is defined as the use or threat of force where the incapacitated person is resisting, and secondly on any restriction of liberty of movement (eg pulling someone away from the road, putting a seat belt on someone in a car or administering sedatives in order to undertake treatment).

17.45   Restraint can only be used when:

1) the person restraining reasonably believes it is necessary to prevent harm to the incapacitated person; and
2) it is proportionate both to:
   a) the likelihood of the harm; and
   b) the seriousness of the harm; and
3) it does not constitute detention under Article 5(1) of the European Convention on Human Rights ('the Convention').

17.46 The Code of Practice (paras 6.40–6.53) contains an analysis of the principles involved when assessing the extent and reasonableness of any restraint including:

> 6.44. Anybody considering using restraint must have objective reasons to justify that restraint is necessary. They must be able to show that the person being cared for is likely to suffer harm unless proportionate restraint is used. A carer or professional must not use restraint just so that they can do something more easily. If restraint is necessary to prevent harm to the person who lacks capacity, it must be the minimum amount of force for the shortest time possible.

17.47 Although the Act permits reasonable restraint, it does not permit action which would amount to a deprivation of liberty for the purposes of Article 5(1) of the Convention (without there being in place a valid order or authorisation permitting this deprivation – see below).

17.48   *G v E, a local authority and F*[39] concerned a 19-year-old with severe learning disabilities with significant (albeit intermittent) challenging behaviour. For the purposes of the proceedings it was accepted that he lacked the necessary capacity to make the decisions in issue in the case. He had lived for a number of years with his former foster parent, in (what became) an adult placement. Due to local authority concerns about the adult placement carer the young man was removed to a private placement run by specialised company, where he was provided with 2:1 care. Reviewing the facts, the court held that this amounted to a deprivation of liberty – not a mere 'restriction' of his liberty, since (para 78):

> Staff at [the Centre] exercise . . . complete control over E's care and movements, and over assessments, treatment, contacts and residence. . . . the concrete situation is that E is currently confined to [the Centre] except when he is escorted to school or on visits or activities, and has no space or

---

39 [2010] EWHC 621 (Fam).

possession that is private or safe from interference or examination. [He] . . . is unable to maintain social contacts because of restrictions placed on access to other people, including family members, and a decision has been made by the local authority that he will not be released into the care of others, or permitted to live elsewhere, unless such a move is considered appropriate. In assessing whether he is at liberty, it is also important to note that E has been prescribed Haloperidol, a neuroleptic medication, to reduce his agitation and more challenging behaviour. He has no control over the administration of that medication.

Deprivation of Liberty Safeguards (DoLS)

17.49   As noted above, it is outside the scope of this book to consider in detail the MCA 2005 Deprivation of Liberty Safeguards (DoLS). In addition to scholarly works on this complex body of law[40] reference should be made to the *Mental Capacity Act 2005: Deprivation of Liberty Safeguards – Code of Practice* (jointly published by the Department of Health and the Welsh Assembly Government) that supplements the main Mental Capacity Act 2005 Code of Practice.[41] The Act (as a result of its amendment by the Mental Health Act 2007) permits the detention of an adult who is believed to lack sufficient mental capacity to decide where to live, where:

1) It has been authorised by Schedule A1 of the 2005 Act; or
2) It is necessary (under section 4B) to enable 'life sustaining treatment'; or
3) It is has been authorised by court under section 16(2)(a) of the 2005 Act.

17.50   In the absence of authority to detain under the above provisions or under any other enactment (for example MHA 1983) the deprivation of the liberty of an adult lacking capacity will be unlawful. It follows that where there is any doubt, legal advice is essential and the question must be addressed with speed. The DoLS Code of Practice (para 2.5) suggests that the following principles are relevant in determining whether a person may be deprived of their liberty:

- Restraint is used, including sedation, to admit a person to an institution where that person is resisting admission.
- Staff exercise complete and effective control over the care and movement of a person for a significant period.
- Staff exercise control over assessments, treatment, contacts and residence.
- A decision has been taken by the institution that the person will not be released into the care of others, or permitted to live elsewhere, unless the staff in the institution consider it appropriate.
- A request by carers for a person to be discharged to their care is refused.

40 See P Fennell, *Mental health law and practice,* 2nd edn, Jordans, 2011 – and R Jones, *Mental Health Act manual,* 13th edn, Sweet and Maxwell, 2011.
41 Accessible at www.dh.gov.uk/en/Publicationsandstatistics/Publications/ PublicationsPolicyAndGuidance/DH_085476

- The person is unable to maintain social contacts because of restrictions placed on their access to other people.
- The person loses autonomy because they are under continuous supervision and control.

Lasting powers of attorney

17.51   MCA 2005 ss9–14 enable individuals to grant lasting powers of attorney' (LPA) to persons they chose. Two types of LPA exist: one that enables the attorney to make financial decisions on the person's behalf (known as a 'property and affairs' LPA) and the other (known as a 'personal welfare' LPA) enables the attorney to make decisions concerning personal welfare matters (including healthcare and consent to medical treatment). A separate form must be completed to create each and (if desired) different attorneys may be appointed to take these different types of decision.

17.52   Financial LPAs can be used both before and after the donor loses capacity, according to the donor's wishes. However, personal welfare LPAs can only be used when the donor lacks capacity to make a particular personal welfare decision.

Personal welfare lasting powers of attorney

17.53   The Code (at para 7.21) provides advice concerning the scope of personal welfare LPAs:

> LPAs can be used to appoint attorneys to make decisions about personal welfare, which can include healthcare and medical treatment decisions. Personal welfare LPAs might include decisions about:
> - where the donor should live and who they should live with
> - the donor's day-to-day care, including diet and dress
> - who the donor may have contact with
> - consenting to or refusing medical examination and treatment on the donor's behalf
> - arrangements needed for the donor to be given medical, dental or optical treatment
> - assessments for and provision of community care services
> - whether the donor should take part in social activities, leisure activities, education or training
> - the donor's personal correspondence and papers
> - rights of access to personal information about the donor, or
> - complaints about the donor's care or treatment.

17.54   The Code (at para 7.27) explains that even where an LPA includes healthcare decisions, attorneys do not have the right to consent to or refuse treatment in situations where:

- **the donor has capacity to make the particular healthcare decision (section 11(7)(a))**
  An attorney has no decision-making power if the donor can make their own treatment decisions.

- **the donor has made an advance decision to refuse the proposed treatment (section 11(7)(b))**
  An attorney cannot consent to treatment if the donor has made a valid and applicable advance decision to refuse a specific treatment (see chapter 9). But if the donor made an LPA after the advance decision, and gave the attorney the right to consent to or refuse the treatment, the attorney can choose not to follow the advance decision.
- **a decision relates to life-sustaining treatment (section 11(7)(c))**
  An attorney has no power to consent to or refuse life-sustaining treatment, unless the LPA document expressly authorises this . . .
- **the donor is detained under the Mental Health Act (section 28)**
  An attorney cannot consent to or refuse treatment for a mental disorder for a patient detained under the Mental Health Act 1983.

Property and affairs lasting powers of attorney

17.55   A property and affairs LPA can limit the powers of the attorney to certain acts, although if unrestricted, a general property and affairs LPA would cover actions such as those listed below (extracted from para 7.36 of the Code):

- buying or selling property
- opening, closing or operating any bank, building society or other account
- giving access to the donor's financial information
- claiming, receiving and using (on the donor's behalf) all benefits, pensions, allowances and rebates (unless the Department for Work and Pensions has already appointed someone and everyone is happy for this to continue)
- receiving any income, inheritance or other entitlement on behalf of the donor
- dealing with the donor's tax affairs
- paying the donor's mortgage, rent and household expenses
- insuring, maintaining and repairing the donor's property
- investing the donor's savings
- making limited gifts on the donor's behalf
- paying for private medical care and residential care or nursing home fees
- applying for any entitlement to funding for NHS care, social care or adaptations
- using the donor's money to buy a vehicle or any equipment or other help they need
- repaying interest and capital on any loan taken out by the donor.

Court of Protection powers and deputies

17.56 The Court of Protection (now governed by MCA 2005 ss45–61) although based in London, has a regional presence, sitting in Birmingham, Bristol, Cardiff, Manchester, Preston and Newcastle. Sections 15–21 detail the powers of the court, which includes the power to make declarations and the power to appoint deputies to make substitute decisions about personal welfare matters as well as issues concerning the property and affairs of persons lacking capacity.

17.57 Section 20 sets a number of limitations on the powers of deputies. They cannot make decisions prohibiting a person from having contact with the adult lacking capacity or to direct a person responsible for the healthcare of the person lacking capacity to allow a different person to take over the healthcare: such decisions must be made by the court.

Social security appointees

17.58 Social security claimants are able to nominate a person to collect their benefits for them when they are unable, due to illness or other circumstances, to collect the benefits personally. In such cases the person collecting the benefit is simply acting as an 'agent' for the claimant. Such agency arrangements can, however, only occur in respect of claimants who have the requisite mental capacity to manage their social security monies.

17.59 Social Security (Claims and Payments) Regulations 1987[42] reg 33 allows for an appointee to be appointed where the claimant is 'unable for the time being to act'. Guidance suggests that persons are unable to act if they 'do not have the mental ability to understand and control their own affairs, for example because of senility or mentally illness'.

17.60 The Department for Work and Pensions is the responsible authority for the appointment, supervision and revocation of appointeeships. The appointee is personally responsible for ensuring that the social security monies are applied in the patient's interests.[43]

17.61 Concern has been expressed about the lack of protection for people who are the subject of an appointeeship order,[44] including the lack of any adequate appeal provision. At present all that an individual can do in such cases is to request that the secretary of state exercise his or her discretion to revoke such an order. The absence of formal appeal rights would appear to contravene Article 6(1) of the European Convention on Human Rights – a point tacitly acknowledge by the government when on ratifying the UN Convention on the Rights of Persons with Disabilities (see para 4.70 above) it entered a reservation to Article 12.4 (safeguards for substituted

---

42 SI No 1968.
43 See CIS/12022/96 which concerned an appointee's failure to notify the DSS about an increase in the disabled person's savings; the consequent overpayment was held to be recoverable from the appointee in addition to the claimant.
44 See eg Parliamentary Ombudsman annual report Session 2002–2003 (5th report) case reference C1560/02.

decision making) – on the basis that the Department for Work and Pensions was 'working to establish a proportionate system of review to address this issue'.

Advance decisions (ADs) to refuse treatment

17.62   MCA 2005 ss24–26 put on a limited statutory basis 'living wills'; particularly ADs to refuse treatment, advance decisions (ADs) to refuse treatment. These can only be made by persons 18 or over who have capacity. The Act does not impose any particular formalities concerning the format of ADs to refuse treatment or the procedures involved in making an AD, except for decisions relating to life-sustaining treatment. Although ADs concerning the refusal of other types of treatment may be written or oral, para 9.19 of the Code provides a checklist of information that it would be helpful to find in any written statement, namely:

- full details of the person making the advance decision, including date of birth, home address and any distinguishing features (in case healthcare professionals need to identify an unconscious person, for example)
- the name and address of the person's GP and whether they have a copy of the document
- a statement that the document should be used if the person ever lacks capacity to make treatment decisions
- a clear statement of the decision, the treatment to be refused and the circumstances in which the decision will apply
- the date the document was written (or reviewed)
- the person's signature (or the signature of someone the person has asked to sign on their behalf and in their presence)
- the signature of the person witnessing the signature, if there is one (or a statement directing somebody to sign on the person's behalf).

Advance decisions to refuse life-sustaining treatment

17.63   MCA 2005 s25 imposes strict formalities concerning ADs refusing life-sustaining treatment. Paragraph 9.24 of the Code of Practice lists the requirements for a valid AD refusing life-sustaining treatment:

- They must be put in writing. If the person is unable to write, someone else should write it down for them. For example, a family member can write down the decision on their behalf, or a healthcare professional can record it in the person's healthcare notes.
- The person must sign the advance decision. If they are unable to sign, they can direct someone to sign on their behalf in their presence.
- The person making the decision must sign in the presence of a witness to the signature. The witness must then sign the document in the presence of the person making the advance decision. If the person making the advance decision is unable to sign, the witness can witness them directing someone else to sign on their behalf. The witness must

then sign to indicate that they have witnessed the nominated person signing the document in front of the person making the advance decision.

- The advance decision must include a clear, specific written statement from the person making the advance decision that the advance decision is to apply to the specific treatment even if life is at risk.
- If this statement is made at a different time or in a separate document to the advance decision, the person making the advance decision (or someone they have directed to sign) must sign it in the presence of a witness, who must also sign it.

17.64 Section 4(10) defines life-sustaining treatment as treatment which a person providing healthcare regards as necessary to sustain life. The Code at para 9.25 explains that whether a treatment is 'life sustaining' or not depends not only on the type of treatment, but also on the particular circumstances in which it may be prescribed – for example 'in some situations antibiotics may be life-sustaining, but in others they can be used to treat conditions that do not threaten life'.

17.65 An AD may not refuse measures that are necessary to keep a patient comfortable, sometimes called basic or essential care – eg warmth, shelter, action to keep a person clean. The Code explains at para 9.28 that this also includes the offer 'of food and water by mouth' – but that an AD 'can refuse artificial nutrition and hydration'.

17.66 An AD will not apply where the person who created it has not lost his or her capacity to make the decision;[45] or if it is defective, eg the person lacked capacity when he or she created it;[46] or it relates to life sustaining treatment and does not comply with the above detailed formalities; or if there is evidence to believe that the person may have changed his or her mind since creating it;[47] or if the treatment in issue is not covered (or was not anticipated) by the AD.[48]

Independent mental capacity advocate service

17.67 The role of the independent mental capacity advocate (IMCA) service and the powers and duties of individual advocates stem from MCA 2005 ss35–41, and are fleshed out in regulations[49] and are the subject of

45   See eg *Re C (Adult Refusal of Medical Treatment)* [1994] 1 WLR 290.
46   See eg *NHS Trust v T* [2004] EWHC 1279 (Fam), [2005] 1 All ER 387, (2005) 8 CCLR 38.
47   MCA 2005 s25(2)(c): 'has done anything else clearly inconsistent with the advance decision remaining his fixed decision' – and see eg *HE v A Hospital NHS Trust* [2003] EWHC 1017 (Fam), [2003] 2 FLR 408.
48   MCA 2005 s25(4) lists various examples, namely that treatment is not the treatment specified in the AD, or any circumstances specified in the AD are absent, or there are reasonable grounds for believing that circumstances exist which the person creating the AD did not anticipate at the time of the AD and which would have affected the decision.
49   Mental Capacity Act 2005 (Independent Mental Capacity Advocate) (General) Regulations 2006 SI No 1832; Mental Capacity Act 2005 (Independent Mental Capacity Advocate) (Expansion of Role) Regulations 2006 SI No 2883; Mental Capacity Act 2005 (Independent Mental Capacity Advocate) (Wales) Regulations 2007 SI No 852 (W77).

detailed guidance in chapter 10 of the Code of Practice. IMCAs also have a role in relation to the DoLS procedures, but these are not addressed in this

17.68   The IMCA's role is to support and represent the person who lacks capacity, and when acting in this role the IMCA has the right to see relevant healthcare and social care records.[50] The local authority/NHS is obliged to take into account the IMCA's comments and findings as part of their decision-making process. An IMCA must be independent of the decision-maker and must support and represent the incapacitated person to identify and promote his or her best interests.

17.69   MCA 2005 ss35–41 require (save in cases of emergency)[51] that an IMCA must be instructed to prepare a report on behalf of people lacking capacity who have no one else to support them – ie no family or friends[52] (other than paid staff), whenever:

- an NHS body is proposing to provide (or withhold) serious medical treatment,[53] or
- an NHS body or local authority is proposing to arrange accommodation (or a change of accommodation) in hospital or a care home, and
  - the person will stay in hospital longer than 28 days, or
  - the person will stay in the care home for more than eight weeks.

17.70   The Code explains (at paras 10.51–10.58) that the obligation to instruct an IMCA in relation to a change of accommodation decision arises where accommodation is provided or arranged by the NHS, or the local authority or under MHA 1983 s117. This includes placements:

- by the NHS of a person in a hospital or a decision to move the person to another hospital for any period in excess of 28 days; or
- by the NHS and/or a local authority in a care home or its equivalent[54] for what is likely to be longer than eight weeks.

17.71   The local authority obligation only arises, however, where it has assessed the person under NHS and Community Care Act 1990 s47(1) and has decided it has a duty to accommodate the person under the community

50 MCA 2005 s35(6)(b).
51 MCA 2005 ss37(4) and 39(4)(b). In such cases the Code of Practice (para 10.24) requires that where the decision concerned a move of accommodation, the local authority must appoint an IMCA as soon as possible afterwards. In relation to serious medical treatment, para 10.46 of the Code states that an IMCA will be required for any serious treatment that follows the emergency treatment.
52 A financial LPA or a financial attorney does not count, when deciding whether there is support available to the person lacking capacity – MHA 2007 Sch 9 (which amends MCA 2005 ss38–39).
53 Para 10.45 of the Code states that it is impossible to set out all types of procedures that may amount to 'serious medical treatment', but by way of illustration suggests chemotherapy, ECT, sterilisation, major surgery (such as open-heart surgery or brain/neuro-surgery), major amputations, treatments which will result in permanent loss of hearing or sight, the withholding or stopping artificial nutrition and hydration, and termination of pregnancy.
54 Which para 10.11 of the Code states would include a care home, nursing home, ordinary and sheltered housing, housing association or other registered social housing or private sector housing provided by a local authority or hostel accommodation.

care legislation. The role of the IMCA in such an accommodation decision may be of some complexity where the person is in hospital but ordinarily resident in another authority.[55]

17.72   In addition to the mandatory grounds for the appointment of an IMCA, Regulations[56] provide that one may be instructed to support someone who lacks capacity to make decisions concerning:

- care reviews, where no one else is available to be consulted;[57]
- adult protection cases, whether or not family, friends or others are involved.[58]

17.73   Where, after providing his or her report, an IMCA disagrees with the NHS or local authority decision and this cannot be resolved by discussion, the IMCA is empowered to make a formal complaint challenging a decision.[59]

17.74   The Code makes clear (at paras 10.37–10.39) that an IMCA can pursue a complaint as far as the relevant ombudsman if needed. In particularly serious or urgent cases, an IMCA may seek permission to refer a case to the Court of Protection or even for a judicial review, having first sought the assistance of the Official Solicitor.

55 A 2006 evaluation of the IMCA service found that the average time taken to complete a case was 65 days involving a total of seven hours, plus two hours travelling: see M Redley et al *The evaluation of the pilot independent mental capacity advocacy service*, Department of Health, 2006.
56 Mental Capacity Act 2005 (Independent Mental Capacity Advocate) (Expansion of Role) Regulations 2006 regs 3 and 4.
57 Code of Practice para 10.62.
58 Code of Practice para 10.66.
59 Mental Capacity Act 2005 (Independent Mental Capacity Advocate) (General) Regulations 2006 reg 7 provides that the IMCA 'has the same rights to challenge the decision as he would have if he were a person (other than an IMCA) engaged in caring for P or interested in his welfare'.

Learning disability and autism: policy and services

684   *Community care and the law / chapter 18*

Introduction

18.1   Estimates as to the number of people in England with a learning disability
vary from about 1 million[1] to 1.5 million.[2] In 2008 there were about
177,000 adults who were users of learning disability services in England
(and an estimated 10,830 people in Wales[3]), most of whom had a severe or
profound learning disability.[4] Whereas the average life expectancy of a
person with learning disabilities was estimated to be less than 20 years of
age in 1930,[5] today even for someone with severe learning disabilities it is
almost 60 and for a person with mild learning disabilities it is indistinguishable from that for all persons.[6]

18.2   Expenditure on adults with a learning disability represents one of
the fastest growing budgets in social care amounting to £4.0 billion in
2009–10 (only more is spent on older people) and represents 24 per cent of
gross expenditure by social services.[7] During this period council spending
on learning disability services increased by 10 per cent;[8] with the unit cost
of providing residential and nursing care to adults with learning disabilities increasing by 8 per cent to an average in 2009–10 of £1,218 per
week.[9]

18.3   People with learning disabilities come within the definition of a 'disabled person' (see para 9.33 above) for the purposes of the primary community care statutes (ie National Assistance Act (NAA) 1948 and Chronically Sick and Disabled Persons Act (CSDPA) 1970 s21) as well as the
Equality Act 2010 s6. It follows that they have an equal right to services
under these statutes and that any difference in treatment, based upon a
categorisation of 'learning disability', will require justification under the
2010 Act.

18.4   The service provision needs of people with learning disabilities are
such that in a number of situations policy and practice guidance singles
them out for specific mention. This can be seen, for instance, in relation
to the obligations on the NHS to fund long term support arrangements
(see para 14.202 above) and in relation to the 'less dependent residents'

1   E Emerson and C Hatton, *People with learning disabilities in England,* Centre for
    Disability Research, Lancaster University, 2008.
2   Department of Health (2001) *Valuing people: a new strategy for learning disability for the
    21st Century,* Cm 5086, p2.
3   Welsh Assembly Government (2007) *Statement on policy and practice for adults with a
    learning disability* (policy guidance), p15.
4   E Emerson and C Hatton, *People with learning disabilities in England* Lancaster: Centre
    for Disability Research, Lancaster University, 2008.
5   T Holland, *Mental capital and well-being: making the most of ourselves in the 21st century,*
    The Government Office for Science, Foresight Mental Capital and Well-being Project.
6   A M Bittles et al, 'The influence of intellectual disability on life expectancy' (2002)
    The Journals of Gerontology Series A: Biological Sciences and Medical Sciences 57(7)
    pp470–472.
7   The Health and Social Care Information Centre (2010) *Personal social services
    expenditure and unit costs England 2009–10,* p7
8   Department of Health (2010) *Valuing people now: the delivery plan 2010–2011* 'Making it
    happen for everyone', para 3.1.
9   The Health and Social Care Information Centre (2011) *Personal social services
    expenditure and unit costs England 2009–010,* p16.

provisions that apply to some people with learning disabilities receiving services under NAA 1948 s21 (see para 8.118).

18.5   In 2001 the Department of Health published the white paper *Valuing people: a new strategy for learning disability for the 21st century*[10] which promised a number of new policy initiatives concerning the rights of people with learning disabilities and undertook to ensure that four key principles would underpin all new proposals: 'Rights, Independence, Choice and Inclusion'.

18.6   In large measure the white paper sought to ensure that existing schemes were sensitive to the needs of people with learning disabilities. It additionally committed the government to take measures to increase the potential for people with learning disabilities to benefit from direct payments, and to improve their access to advocacy services. In relation to direct payments the subsequent guidance has emphasised the policy aim of increasing take up from this client group (see para 12.22 above), and much of the research concerning personal budgets (see para 3.8 above) has focused on its potential for people with learning disabilities. In addition changes to the direct payment regulations now make it possible for a 'suitable person' to receive a direct payment on behalf of a person who lacks the capacity to consent to having a direct payment (see para 12.20 above)

18.7   The white paper proposed the development within each local authority area of learning disability partnership boards whose responsibility it would be to implement the adult aspects of the programme. Policy guidance in 2001[11] outlined the composition and responsibilities of these boards. This has since been followed up by more detailed practice guidance on implementation.[12]

18.8   In 2008 the Joint Committee on Human Rights[13] expressed its concern that the *Valuing People* programme appeared to have had limited 'impact in Government departments other than the Department of Health or the wider public sector'; and that implementation by local authorities and individual service providers had 'been so patchy'. In response, in 2010 the Department of Health published a 'three year strategy for people with learning disabilities' entitled Valuing People Now,[14] following which it commissioned what has become a highly influential report by Professor

10 Cm 5086, March 2001.
11 Department of Health (2001) *Valuing people: a new strategy for learning disability for the 21st Century: Implementation Guidance* HSC 2001/016: LAC(2001)23 (policy guidance for the purposes of Local Authority Social Services Act 1970 s7) (see para 1.46 above).
12 See Department of Health (2001) *Planning with people towards person centred approaches – guidance for partnership boards* and Department of Health (2008) *Health action planning and health facilitation for people with learning disabilities: good practice guidance*, p36.
13 Joint Committee on Human Rights (2008) *A life like any other? Human rights of adults with learning disabilities* HL 40-I/HC 73-I, para 104.
14 See eg Department of Health (2009) *Valuing people now: a new three-year strategy for people with learning disabilities*.

Mansell (the 'Mansell report'[15]) concerning the support needs of adults with profound intellectual and multiple disabilities. Subsequently, in 2010 the Department published its 'delivery plan' for such services.[16]

Wales

18.9   In Wales the Welsh Office's 1983 *All Wales strategy for the development of services for mentally handicapped people* remains the underpinning policy, as updated in 2007 by 'Revised Guidance'.[17] In 1999 a Learning Disability Implementation Advisory Group (LDIAG) was charged with the preparation of a draft framework of services designed to promote the interests of people with learning disabilities along similar lines to that proposed by the Department of Health's white paper *Valuing People*. A 2001 report from the Advisory Group *Fulfilling the promises*[18] was adopted in principle by the Assembly Government and a new LDIAG commissioned to take the policy forwards. The Assembly in 2004 issued *Service principles, service responses*: as with *Valuing People* it advocated such matters as 'person-centred' approaches to individual planning, adequate advocacy support, joint working partnership in planning and community living.[19] In 2007 follow up policy guidance was published[20] and this represents the key policy document. In 2010, the Welsh Government issued *Local community living – accommodation and support for adults with a learning disability* (Circular 008/2010) which provides important guidance about the size, scale, location and mix of individuals in commissioned accommodation. In 2011 it published detailed guidelines for the development of commissioning strategies to support adults with learning disabilities in the community.[21]

Definition and IQ

18.10   *Valuing People* does not attempt an exhaustive definition of what constitutes a learning disability, but at para 1.5 states that it includes the presence of:

- A significantly reduced ability to understand new or complex information, to learn new skills (impaired intelligence), with;

---

15   J Mansell, (2010) *Raising our sights: services for adults with profound intellectual and multiple disabilities*, Department of Health.
16   Department of Health (2010) *Valuing people now: the delivery plan 2010–2011 'making it happen for everyone'*.
17   The original 1983 Strategy is not accessible on the internet.
18   LDIAG, *Fulfilling the promises*, 2001.
19   Welsh Assembly (2004) *Section 7 guidance on service principles and service responses for adults and older persons with a learning disability*.
20   Welsh Assembly Government (2007) *Statement on policy and practice for adults with a learning disability* (policy guidance).
21   Welsh Assembly Government (2011) *Practice guidance on developing a commissioning strategy for people with a learning disability*.

- a reduced ability to cope independently (impaired social functioning);
- which started before adulthood, with a lasting effect on development.

18.11 At para 1.6 it goes on to caution against overreliance on IQ scores. Not infrequently, however, some local authorities do define learning disability in such terms – typically having a score of less than 70 or 75. There has been substantial criticism of such an approach[22] and reliance on this fact alone could not be considered a rational way of approaching the community care assessment duty.

18.12 Although the Department of Health's definition includes many people with (amongst other conditions) autism, it would not cover someone with a higher level autistic spectrum disorder who may be of average or even above average intelligence – such as some people with Asperger's syndrome.[23] However, this does not mean that such a person is not 'disabled' within the meaning of the community care legislation or the Children Act (CA) 1989 or indeed the Equality Act 2010.[24] The definition of 'disabled' under NAA 1948 s29 and CA 1989 s17(11) includes persons with a 'mental disorder of any kind' from which it follows that a person with a condition such Asperger's Syndrome who had an above average IQ would still be entitled to community care services if an assessment revealed an eligible need (see in this respect para 9.40 above).

Person-centred planning/self directed support

18.13 A key phrase emerging from the white paper is that of a 'person-centred approach' to the needs of people with learning disabilities to enable them 'to have as much choice and control as possible over their lives'. This phrase is being superseded in the context of the personalisation programme by a similar idea, namely 'self-directed support' (see para 3.8 above).

18.14 The need for such an approach is explained in at para 4.1 of the white paper in the following terms:

> People with learning disabilities currently have little control over their own lives, though almost all, including the most severely disabled, are capable of making choices and expressing their views and preferences. The current problems are:
> - Services have been too slow to recognise that people with learning disabilities have rights like other citizens;
> - Provision of advocacy services is patchy;
> - People with learning disabilities have little involvement in decision making;

---

22 There is an extensive literature on this question, but see eg D Francis et al, 'Defining learning and language disabilities' (1996) 27 *Language, Speech, and Hearing Services in Schools* 132–143; and L Siegel 'IQ is irrelevant to the definition of learning disabilities' (1989) 22(8) *The Journal of Learning Disabilities* 469–478, 486.
23 *Valuing People* para 1.6.
24 See eg *Dunham v Ashford Windows* [2005] IRLR 608, EAT.

- Few people with learning disabilities receive direct payments;
- People with learning disabilities and their families are not central to the planning process;
- Not enough effort to communicate with people with learning disabilities in accessible ways.

18.15 Follow-up 2001 practice guidance[25] stipulated that the development of a person-centred approach in organisational cultures and practice was a priority for partnership boards who were required to produce a framework for implementation of this approach by April 2002. The guidance defined 'person centred planning' as (page 2):

> . . . a *process* for continual listening and learning, focussed on what is important to someone now and for the future, and acting upon this in alliance with family and friends. This listening and learning is used to understand a person's capacities and choices. Person centred planning is a basis for problem solving and negotiation to mobilise the resources necessary to pursue the person's aspirations. These resources may be obtained from a person's personal network, from service agencies or from a range of non-specialist and non-service sources.

18.16 Although it has now become common to refer to the care plans for people with learning disabilities as 'person centred plans', this is a misnomer. As the 2001 guidance explains (page 4):

> Person centred planning is not the same as assessment and care planning under section 47 of the NHS and Community Care Act (1990). Assessment and care planning should, however, be undertaken using person centred *approaches* and is greatly assisted by person centred planning undertaken independently of it. Where services are required, formal assessment might well be triggered by person centred planning. [Neither is it] the same as reviews of service provision. Person centred planning should, however, make a significant contribution to reviews, ensuring that they are based on what matters to a person from their own perspective.

Autism Act 2009

18.17 The Autism Act 2009 originated as a private members bill, promoted by Cheryl Gillan MP. It requires the secretary of state to publish an 'autism strategy' for meeting the needs of adults in England with autistic spectrum conditions by improving the provision of relevant services to such adults by local authorities, NHS bodies and NHS foundation trusts. The first strategy was published in 2010[26] and lists actions necessary to improve health, social care and other public services for people with autism (including action improve employment and staff training). It emphasises (amongst other things) the need for staff training; clear pro-

25 Department of Health (2001) *Planning with people towards person centred approaches – guidance for partnership boards.*
26 Department of Health (2010) *Fulfilling and rewarding lives – an adult autism strategy for England.*

cedures and 'pathways' to enable speedy diagnosis; and the fact that people with autism have a right to a community care assessments even if they have average or above average IQ. Further guidance followed in 2010[27] concerning the adjustments that the strategy required to existing programmes and practices (ie increasing awareness and understanding of autism among frontline professionals and improving access to the services and work) without creating a new architecture of specific obligations.

18.18   Section 2 of the Act requires guidance to be issued to health and social care bodies (see para 1.66 above) which the Act specifies (section 2(5)) 'must in particular include' guidance about:

a)   the provision of relevant services for the purpose of diagnosing autistic spectrum conditions in adults;

b)   the identification of adults with such conditions;

c)   the assessment of the needs of adults with such conditions for relevant services;

d)   planning in relation to the provision of relevant services to persons with autistic spectrum conditions as they move from being children to adults;

e)   other planning in relation to the provision of relevant services to adults with autistic spectrum conditions;

f)   the training of staff who provide relevant services to adults with such conditions;

g)   local arrangements for leadership in relation to the provision of relevant services to adults with such conditions.

18.19   Guidance in compliance with section 2 was issued in 2010[28] focusing on key areas where is was thought that health and social care bodies could practically change the way they support adults with autism – namely: (1) by increasing understanding of autism amongst staff; (2) by strengthening diagnosis and assessment of needs; (3) by improving transition support for young people with autism; and (4) by ensuring adults with autism are included within local service planning.

18.20   Although the Act is expressed as applying to both England and Wales (section 6) it only places obligations on the secretary of state in England.

Service reconfigurations

18.21   The 2001 *Valuing People* white paper sought to address the severe social exclusion experienced by many people with learning disabilities by endeavouring (among other things) to bring about service reconfigurations including (para 4.19) a requirement that local bodies make 'significant progress' in relation to the reduction in the use of large day centres.

27   Department of Health (2010) *Towards 'fulfilling and rewarding lives: the first year delivery plan for adults with autism in England.*

28   Department of Health (2010) *Implementing 'fulfilling and rewarding lives: Statutory guidance for local authorities and NHS organisations to support implementation of the autism strategy.*

In the government's opinion (at para 1.18) some of these offered little more than 'warehousing'. Authorities were to replace these services with flexible and individual support, the white paper stating:

> 7.25 These problems will be addressed through a five year programme to support local councils in modernising their day services. Our aim will be to ensure that the resources currently committed to day centres are focused on providing people with learning disabilities with new opportunities to lead full and purposeful lives. Securing the active involvement of people with learning disabilities and their families in redesigning services will be essential to the success of the programme. The Government recognises that, for many families, day centres have provided essential respite from the day to day demands of caring. The services that replace them must result in improvements for both users and their families. The needs of people with profound or complex disabilities will be carefully considered as part of the modernisation programme.

18.22 The last decade has witnessed the closure of very many day centres, and not infrequently users and carers have questioned whether the replacement provision has proved to be an 'improvement'. Challenges to such closures have resulted in limited litigation (see, for example, paras 7.151 and 9.87 above). As a general rule, the courts have required, not only evidence that the authority has addressed the community care impact on individual users of the closure, but also (where they lack the necessary mental capacity to choose their care support) that a best interests assessment has been undertaken (see para 17.31 above). A 2011 judgment[29] illustrates the importance of such an assessment, since it ensures that an individual's well-being is not sacrificed on the twin alters of dogma and budgetary advantage – or as the court expressed it: 'guideline policies cannot be treated as universal solutions, nor should initiatives designed to personalise care and promote choice be applied to the opposite effect.'

NHS learning disability funding transfer

18.23 In 2007 the government in England announced its intention[30] to transfer funding for all learning disability social care services from the NHS to local government. The amount to be transferred by each PCT to their respective local authority was to be calculated upon that PCT's expenditure in 2007/8 with the final transfer taking effect from 1 April 2009 and in April 2011 the actual allocations being made directly from the Department of Health to local authorities.[31]

---

29 *AH v Hertfordshire Partnership NHS Foundation Trust and Ealing PCT* [2011] EWHC 276 (CoP) para 80 – and see also para 9.52 above.
30 Department of Health (2007) *Valuing People Now: from progress to transformation,* para 1.4.3.
31 Department of Health (2008) Letter Gateway Reference: 9906 *Valuing people now: transfer of the responsibility for the commissioning of social care for adults with a learning disability from the NHS to local government and transfer of the appropriate funding.*

18.24   The transfer proved to be a complex and contentious operation[32] and follow up guidance in 2009[33] addressed a number of difficult issues. These included (1) the so-called 'campus closure' programme, namely that all NHS facilities/campuses accommodating people with learning disabilities were to be closed[34] by the end of 2010 with their running costs being transferred in advance of the closure to the relevant local authority; and (2) attempts by some PCTs to reduce their funding transfer to councils by deciding that some residents in fact qualified for NHS continuing healthcare funding (and so remained a PCT responsibility) and then proposing to deduct the cost of those residents from the amount for transfer. The guidance advised that this was unacceptable.

Exclusions from services

18.25   The local government ombudsman has criticised councils that have excluded disabled people from services because of their challenging behaviour – where that behaviour was part and parcel of their condition (see para 4.52 above). In so doing the ombudsman has cited[35] with approval the following reference in the white paper:

> Excluding people with learning disabilities from services if they are found to be difficult to handle or present with challenging behaviour represents a major source of stress for carers, who may be left unsupported to cope with their son or daughter at home. This practice is unacceptable and families must not be left to cope unaided. No service should be withdrawn on these grounds without identifying alternative options and putting a suitable alternative service in place where possible. Decisions to exclude a person with learning disabilities from a service should always be referred to the Learning Disability Partnership Board, which will be responsible for the provision of alternative services in such cases . . .[36]

18.26   A 2004 ombudsman's complaint[37] concerned a young man with challenging behaviour associated with his autism. The council, largely for resource reasons, placed him in insufficiently supportive accommodation on his transition from schooling. His mother was strongly opposed to the placement, but her views were not properly heeded. In the ombudsman's view the council ignored her objections 'and attempted to force on the family its [placement] decision'. In so doing 'it ignored both the principles

---

32 See eg V Pitt (2010) 'Progress report on *Valuing People Now*', *Community Care*, 15 January 2010.
33 Department of Health (2009) Letter 17 December 2009 to PCT/LA LD. Commissioners: *Transfer of commissioning and funding of social care for adults with learning disabilities from the NHS to local government.*
34 A commitment made by the government in Department of Health (2006) *Our health, our care, our say: a new direction for community services* Cm 6737, para 4.90.
35 Complaint no 03/C/16371 against Stockton-on-Tees BC, 18 January 2005 para 13.
36 Department of Health (2001) *Valuing People* para 5.7 and see also HSC 2001/016: LAC (2001)23 paras 37 and 38.
37 Complaint no 02/C/17068 against Bolton MBC, 30 November 2004.

of the white paper *Valuing People* and the impracticality of trying to integrate [the young man] successfully into a placement his mother (to whom he is very close) did not accept'.

18.27   The council, because of its failure to undertake a proper assessment, underestimated how extreme his response to change could be and failed to take into account how severely challenging his behaviour became when he was under stress. His behaviour became so violent that he was eventually detained under MHA 1983 s3 and remained in a locked psychiatric ward for 18 months. The ombudsman concluded that this was because 'the Council failed to fund an appropriate alternative placement'. In her opinion, although the 'decision to detain him was lawful, [he] was only in this situation because of the failure by the Council to make proper provision to meet his needs'. She considered that there was 'no excuse for the Council's failure to anticipate the level of violence and destructive behaviour of which [he was] capable when faced with sudden change or social situations that he finds difficult or frightening'. The report recommended a total of £30,000 compensation be paid.

18.28   At para 24.71 below, further consideration is given to situations where the courts and ombudsmen have held the actions of local authorities to have been heavy handed: situations in which the comments of Munby LJ in *A Local Authority v A (A Child)* [38] are apt: that the council should not forget that it 'is the servant of those in need of its support and assistance, not their master'.

Advocacy and learning disability services

18.29   The Disabled Persons (Services, Consultation and Representation) Act 1986 ss1 and 2 entitle all disabled people who were being assessed to have an 'authorised representative'. Although this provision remains on the statute book – successive governments have failed to bring it into force. In 1991 the then secretary of state observed that (in the context of the community care reforms) the government had 'decided not to implement these sections' since it believed that they would 'carry the danger of diverting resources into complex administrative arrangements at the expense of services' but undertook to 'review the situation'. [39]

18.30   The Law Commission, in its 2011 report [40] detailed the many policy documents in England and Wales that presupposed the presence of advocates as well as the few statutory references – including the duty to appoint an Independent Mental Capacity Advocate in limited situations (see para 17.67 above). Noting that many of those responding to the consultation exercise had stressed the essential role for advocates in 'helping

---

38 [2010] EWHC 978 (Fam) para 52.
39 Virginia Bottomley MP, *Hansard* HC Debates Written Answers to Questions for 22 March 1991, Col 253.
40 Law Commission (2011) *Adult Social Care*, Law Com No 326 HC941, paras 12.2–12.9.

people to enforce their rights, secure access to justice and obtain an effective remedy' it recommended that the right to advocacy contained in the 1986 Act be retained in any codified statute with a power for the secretary of state and Welsh ministers 'to implement the right and modify it to bring it into line with modern understandings' (recommendation 72).

18.31 Despite the general absence of any underpinning legal duty to provide an advocacy service, such services exist in most parts of England and Wales and have many different names and functions.[41] Broadly, however, they can be divided into the following two general categories.

Citizen advocacy

18.32 Citizen advocacy involves 'developing a longer term relationship with the disabled person'.[42] It is a form of advocacy where: 'an ordinary citizen develops a relationship with another person who risks social exclusion or other unfair treatment because of a handicap. As the relationship develops, the advocate chooses ways to understand, respond to, and represent the other person's interests as if they were the advocate's own.'[43]

Crisis advocacy

18.33 Crisis advocacy is generally concerned with short-term interventions, most commonly in relation to a dispute or complaint. The following sections are primarily concerned with the provision of this form of advocacy support.

18.34 While the white paper[44] acknowledged that effective advocacy, including self-advocacy, had the ability to transform the lives of people with learning disabilities, it cautioned that:

... both citizen advocacy and self-advocacy are unevenly developed across the country. Barriers to future development include: insecure funding; limited support for local groups; and potential for conflicts of interest with statutory agencies who provide funding. This must change.

18.35 In order to address the problem it committed the government to the (long-term) aim of 'developing a range of independent advocacy services available in each area so that people with learning disabilities can choose the one which best meets their needs' (para 4.9) and to establish 'a National Citizen Advocacy Network and to promote self-advocacy, both in partnership with the voluntary sector', the aim being to ensure the establishment of at least one citizen advocacy group in each local authority area. Advocacy arrangements were accordingly made a high priority for the

41 For a review of the role of advocacy see R Henderson and M Pochin, *A Right Result?* Policy Press, 2001.
42 See eg A Dunning, *Citizen advocacy with older people: a code of good practice*, CPA, 1995.
43 See B Sang and J O'Brien, *Advocacy: the United Kingdom and American experiences*, King's Fund Project paper no 51, 1984, p27.
44 Department of Health (2001) *Valuing People* para 4.7.

new learning disability partnership boards.[45] In its 2005 review[46] the Department of Health referred to its continuing (indirect) funding of advocacy services[47] although it expressed concern (at para 4.1.7) that much local authority 'advocacy funding is short-term, which makes it difficult for advocacy organisations to plan for the future' and recommended that 'councils and other funders need to find ways of providing more secure funding'.

45   See LAC (2001)23 para 27.
46   Department of Health (2005) *The story so far . . . Valuing People: a new strategy for learning disability for the 21st century.*
47   Ibid, para 2.4.4, that through its Learning Disability Development Fund £40 million (2005–06) is provided which 'has made a real difference' in particular 'for advocacy and person centred planning'.

Older people: policy and services

Introduction

19.1   The proportion of people aged 65 and over is growing – from 17 per cent in 2010 to an estimated 23 per cent by 2035. But the fastest growth is in the number of people aged 85 and over, reaching 1.4 million in 2010. By 2035 the number of people aged 85 and over is projected to be 2.5 times larger than in 2010, reaching 3.6 million and accounting for 5 per cent of the total population.[1]

19.2   In 2006 almost 45 per cent of both the NHS's and social services' budgets was spent on people over the age of 65.[2] About 1.46 million people in England received community based services from the local authority in 2009–10 of which 65 per cent were 65 and over and of the 225,600 residents supported in care homes 77 per cent were aged 65 or over.[3] In terms of social services care home expenditure alone, this equates to approximately £9.4 billion per annum with over £1.9 billion being recouped in charges:[4] charges, however, fall unequally – one in 10 people, at age 65, face future lifetime care costs of more than £100,000.[5]

19.3   In response to the social and healthcare challenges posed by an ageing population, the government in England published in 2001 a *National Service Framework for Older People* (NSF).[6] The NSF sets out eight key standards, providing in each case guidance on the local action required to ensure these are implemented – with detailed timescales and 'milestones to ensure progress, with performance measures to support performance improvement'. The eight standards are as follows:

1) *Rooting out age discrimination*
   NHS services will be provided, regardless of age, on the basis of clinical need alone. Social care services will not use age in their eligibility criteria or policies, to restrict access to available services.

2) *Person-centred care*
   NHS and social care services treat older people as individuals and enable them to make choices about their own care. This is achieved through the single assessment process, integrated commissioning arrangements and integrated provision of services, including community equipment and continence services.

3) *Intermediate care*
   Older people will have access to a new range of intermediate care

---

1   Office of National Statistics (2011) *Ageing* at www.statistics.gov.uk/cci/nugget.asp?id=949

2   Commission for Healthcare Audit and Inspection (2006) *Living well in later life: A review of progress against the National Service Framework for Older People*, p5.

3   Information Centre (2011) *Community Care Statistics: social services activity report England 2009–10.*

4   Information Centre (2011) *Personal social services expenditure and unit costs England, 2009–10.*

5   Commission on Funding of Care and Support (2011) *Fairer care funding: the report of the commission on funding of care and support* (the 'Dilnot' Report) p12.

6   See para 1.61 above: in Wales the equivalent initiative is Welsh Assembly Government (2003) *The strategy for older people in Wales.*

services at home or in designated care settings, to promote their independence by providing enhanced services from the NHS and councils to prevent unnecessary hospital admission and effective rehabilitation services to enable early discharge from hospital and to prevent premature or unnecessary admission to long-term residential care.

4) *General hospital care*

Older people's care in hospital is delivered through appropriate specialist care and by hospital staff who have the right set of skills to meet their needs.

5) *Stroke*

The NHS will take action to prevent strokes, working in partnership with other agencies where appropriate. People who are thought to have had a stroke have access to diagnostic services, are treated appropriately by a specialist stroke service, and subsequently, with their carers, participate in a multidisciplinary programme of secondary prevention and rehabilitation.

6) *Falls*

The NHS, working in partnership with councils, takes action to prevent falls and reduce resultant fractures or other injuries in their populations of older people. Older people who have fallen receive effective treatment and, with their carers, receive advice on prevention through a specialised falls service.

7) *Mental health in older people*

Older people who have mental health problems have access to integrated mental health services, provided by the NHS and councils to ensure effective diagnosis, treatment and support, for them and for their carers.

8) *The promotion of health and active life in older age*

The health and well-being of older people is promoted through a co-ordinated programme of action led by the NHS with support from councils.

19.4   Despite the policy aim in the first standard, of rooting out age discrimination and ensuring that age is not an element in 'eligibility criteria or policies' – the reality is that the eligibility criteria of virtually every local authority are predicated on age.[7] For example, many council's have different rules for direct payments for older people or limits (general or rigid) on the amount of domiciliary care that an older person is entitled to before a care home placement would be expected (limits that are not imposed for younger disabled people). At present such criteria would constitute maladministration, in that they directly contradict the NSF. It is proposed, however, that in 2012 the prohibition of age discrimination under the Equality Act 2010, be extended to (amongst others) the health and social care sectors, and that there be 'no specific health and social care

7   See eg I Carruthers and J Ormondroyd (2009) *Achieving age equality in health and social care*, Secretary of State for Health, para 5.27.

exceptions to the ban on age discrimination – any age-based practices by the NHS and social care should be objectively justified'.[8]

Older people and the single assessment process

19.5   Key Standard 2 (above) of the 2001 NSF committed the government to improve the assessment process for older people – particularly to reduce the number of times they had to tell their story to different professionals and be subject to multiple assessments within the NHS and social care, stating at para 2.29:

> All older people should receive good assessment which is matched to their individual circumstances. Some older people will benefit from a fuller assessment across a number of areas or domains . . . and some may need more detailed assessment of one, or a few, specialist areas. The single assessment process should be designed to identify all of their needs. For the older person, it will also mean far less duplication and worry – the fuller assessment can be carried out by one front-line professional and where other professionals need to be involved to provide specialist assessment this will be arranged for the older person, to provide a seamless service.

19.6   Although in theory the single assessment process (SAP) is operational throughout England, the evidence suggests that the assessment process for older people still leaves much to be desired. In 2006, for instance, a joint report by the Commission for Social Care Inspection, the Healthcare Commission and the Audit Commission expressed the need for a 'change of culture' of the assessment process, and the need to move away from:

> . . . services being service-led to being person centred, so that older people have a central role not only in designing their care with the combination and type of service that most suits them, but also in planning the range of services that are available to all older people.[9]

19.7   Guidance[10] on the SAP has been issued to health and social services bodies and requires that they have fully integrated commissioning arrangements and integrated provision of services including community services and continence services.

19.8   Apart from the insistence on a joint health/social services assessment process, the SAP guidance is in many respects a gloss on the previous *Fair Access to Care Services* (FACS) guidance, now the Prioritising need guidance[11] and reference should be made to chapter 3 where this guidance is further considered. Such assessments cannot in fact be 'unified' in the

8   Equalities Office (2011) *Equality Act 2010: banning age discrimination in services, public functions and associations A consultation on proposed exceptions to the ban*, para 5.41.
9   Commission for Healthcare Audit and Inspection (2006) *Living well in later life: a review of progress against the national service framework for older people*, p9.
10   In particular HSC 2002/001: LAC (2002)1 *Guidance on the single assessment process for older people*, January 2002. The guidance is also considered at para 3.35 above.
11   Department of Health (2010) *Prioritising need in the context of Putting People First: a whole system approach to eligibility for social care. Guidance on eligibility criteria for adult social care, England 2010.*

legal sense, unless the agencies have entered into formal partnership arrangements under National Health Service Act (NHSA) 2006 s75[12] (see para 13.127 above).

Wales

19.9 In Wales the Unified and Fair System for Assessing and Managing Care (UFSAMC) 2002 policy guidance[13] (see para 3.30 above) constitutes the equivalent guidance (ie effectively a combined FACS and SAP document).

Commissioner for older people (Wales)

19.10 In Wales, a commissioner for older people has been appointed to ensure that the interests of older people in Wales, who are aged 60 or more, are safeguarded and promoted.[14] The commissioner has undertaken a number of investigations and published a variety of reports – for example in 2011 *Dignified care,*[15] which concluded that the 'treatment of some older people in Welsh hospitals is shamefully inadequate'.

SAP and the care programme approach

19.11 Severe misgivings have been expressed about the quality of older persons' mental health services compared with the equivalent services provided for young persons: that the 'division between mental health services for adults of working age and older people has resulted in the development of an unfair system'.[16]

19.12 The Department of Health has issued a clarification note[17] concerning the interface between these two assessment regimes (the care programme approach (CPA) process is considered at para 20.7 below). The guidance advises:

- The CPA should be applied to older people with severe mental illness due to schizophrenia or other psychoses. The assessment of their needs should be based on the SAP for older people.
- SAP, plus critical aspects of CPA, should be applied to other older people with severe functional or organic mental health problems, who were they younger would be provided for under CPA.
- When individuals subject to CPA reach old age, switches to SAP are not inevitable, and should only be made in the best interests of individuals and the continuity of their care.

---

12 NHS (Wales) Act 2006; (NHS(W)A) 2006 s33.
13 Welsh Assembly (2002) *The unified and fair system for assessing and managing care.*
14 Pursuant to the Commissioner for Older People (Wales) Act 2006 and the Commissioner for Older People in Wales Regulations 2007 SI No 398 (W44).
15 Older People's Commissioner for Wales (2011) *Dignified care? The experiences of older people in hospital in Wales.*
16 Commission for Healthcare, Audit and Inspection (2006) *Living well in later life: a review of progress against the national service framework for older people,* p7.
17 Department of Health (2002) *Care management for older people with serious mental health problems.*

Advocacy and older people

19.13   Increasing attention is being given to the important role that advocacy services can fulfil in ensuring that the needs of older people are properly addressed. In this respect the SAP guidance advises:[18]

> Agencies should consider at the earliest opportunity whether older people might need, or benefit, from the assistance of advocates, interpreters and translators, and specific communication equipment, during the assessment process and subsequent aspects of care planning and service delivery. Where such a need exists, councils should either arrange for this support or facilitate access to it.
>
> As emphasised in the NSF for Older People, the contribution of trained bi- or multi-lingual co-workers can be important in this regard. It is the Department of Health's view that translation and interpretation is best provided by accredited professionals. The role of an advocate is a specialism in its own right, and should ideally be provided by professionals who are independent of both statutory agencies and the older person.

Community care services for older people

19.14   As noted above (para 1.19), the community care legislation divides service users into three discreet (but largely artificial) categories: namely older people; disabled people; and ill people. Not infrequently an individual will straddle all three categories – for instance, an older person with dementia. However, for some people, the need for services arises not because of illness or disability, but merely because the ageing process has made them frail – for instance, through muscle wastage. Although such persons are entitled to accommodation services under National Assistance Act (NAA) 1948 s21 (see para 7.10), they are not eligible for domiciliary or community based services under NAA 1948 s29 or Chronically Sick and Disabled Persons Act (CSDPA) 1970 s2 – because they do not fall within the definition of a disabled person for the purposes of these sections (see para 9.20). Such persons are, however, entitled to care services under Health Services and Public Health Act (HSPHA) 1968 s45.

19.15   The statutory duty to provide support provision for older people and the role of the 1968 Act is a matter of significant historical interest. Means and Smith,[19] in particular, detail the dreadful treatment of older people during the first part of World War II, with the eviction of profoundly sick elderly people from hospital (a total of 140,000 patients were discharged in just two days[20]) and the repeated hostile official references to them 'as if

---

18   Department of Health (2002) *Guidance on the single assessment process for older people*, HSC 2002/001: LAC (2002)1 annex pp19–20.
19   R Means and R Smith, *From Poor Law to Community Care*, Policy Press, 1998, chapter 2.
20   R Means and R Smith, *From Poor Law to Community Care*, Policy Press, 1998, p21.

they lacked value as human beings'.[21] They explain[22] how this action later resulted in the involvement of the charitable sector in providing services, such as a home meals service (see para 9.138 above) as well as the development of many of the services we now collectively refer to as domiciliary care.

19.16 The omission of reference to older people in NAA 1948, s29 list (see para 9.26 above) was the subject of considerable discussion[23] which led to the widening of local authority powers to provide certain services for older people, as a result the National Assistance (Amendment) Act 1962. This was, however, considered an insufficient statutory response and ultimately, rather than amend 29, equivalent provision was made in HSPHA 1968 ss13 and 45. Section 13 can claim to be one of the first provisions aimed at the support of carers, since it provided for social care support for 'households' (though now repealed and found as NHSA 2006 Sch 20 para 3 – see para 9.178 above) and for which guidance[24] stressed that this meant that 'authorities who until now have felt unable, for example, to assist relatives caring single handed for elderly people may now find advantage in the reconsideration of how to accommodate this need'.[25]

Care services under Health Services and Public Health Act 1968 s45

19.17 Section 45 of the 1968 Act provides:

(1) A local authority may with the approval of the secretary of state, and to such extent as he may direct, shall make arrangements for promoting the welfare of old people.

19.18 Section 45 is drafted to the same pattern as NAA 1948 s29 (see para 9.43 above), in that it does not require the provision of any services but leaves to the secretary of state the power to specify in directions what services may and what services must be provided.

19.19 The only (and current) directions that have been issued are contained in DHSS circular 19/71 (see below). The circular explains (at para 3) that the purpose of HSPHA 1968 s45 is to enable authorities to make approved arrangements for the elderly who are not substantially and permanently handicapped, and thus to promote the welfare of the elderly generally and so far as possible to prevent or postpone personal deterioration or breakdown.

21 R Means and R Smith, *From Poor Law to Community Care*, Policy Press, 1998, p51.
22 R Means and R Smith, *From Poor Law to Community Care*, Policy Press, 1998, chapter 3.
23 R Means and R Smith, *From Poor Law to Community Care*, Policy Press, 1998, pp266–269.
24 *Help in the home: section 13 Health Services and Public Health Act*, DHSS Circular 53/71.
25 Cited in R Means and R Smith, *From Poor Law to Community Care*, Policy Press, 1998 at p242.

Client group

Old people

19.20   HSPHA 1968 s45 services are specific to old people. The phrase 'old people' is not defined, and probably needs no definition. If a person requires domiciliary services for any reason other than the fact that age has made him or her frail, other statutory provisions exist to enable that service to be provided.[26]

19.21   However, the circular guidance suggested that in the early days of the power (ie, post April 1971):

> . . . it might prove desirable to start by identifying the needs of certain groups of the elderly who seem likely to be particularly vulnerable, eg, (a) elderly people, especially the more elderly, who are housebound or living alone or recently bereaved or about to be discharged from hospital, and (b) other persons over, say, 75 living in the community, particularly where there are high concentrations of very elderly people in particular districts.[27]

Ordinarily resident

19.22   Neither the Act nor the directions restrict HSPHA 1968 s45 services to persons 'ordinarily resident' in the local authority's area. This again is not strictly necessary, in that the directions have been limited to authorising (but not directing) the provision of such services. Accordingly social services authorities are entitled to reach a general policy decision (without fettering their individual discretion) to limit the use of their powers to elderly persons ordinarily resident within their area.

Services under Health Services and Public Health Act 1968 s45

19.23   The statutory framework for the provision of services under HSPHA 1968 s45 is similar to that under NAA 1948 s29. As with NAA 1948 s29, section 45 leaves to the secretary of state the power to determine the type of domiciliary services which can be provided. Section 45 services are subject to three basic limitations, namely:

1) that the purpose of the service must be the promotion of the welfare of elderly people;[28]
2) by virtue of section 45(4)(a) that the direct payment of money to 'old people' is not permitted (except if a payment for their 'work in accordance with the arrangements'). As noted, however, this restriction is

26 That is, under NAA 1948 s29, CSDPA 1970 s2, NHSA 2006 Sch 20, NHS(W)A 2006 Sch 15 or Mental Health Act 1983 s117.
27 DHSS circular 19/71 para 7.
28 The wording of HSPHA 1968 s45 is such that the service need not be provided *to* the disabled person; ie, a service provided to a carer may be 'an arrangement which promotes the welfare of an elderly person'.

now academic as a consequence of the direct payments legislation (see chapter 12 above); and

3) by virtue of section 45(4)(b) that no accommodation or services can be provided under section 45 if the accommodation or services could be provided under the NHS Acts 2006.[29]

19.24 The secretary of state's only direction in respect of HSPHA 1968 s45 services was issued in DHSS circular 19/71 para 4, in March 1971. Although the wording of section 45 would allow the directions to place social services authorities under a duty to provide certain services, the directions merely empower the provision of the specified services, without creating any obligation.

19.25 The directions give social services authorities the discretion to provide[30] the services specified below. Authorities may provide services over and above those actually specified in the directions if they first obtain the secretary of state's specific approval.[31] Given the wide powers now available under Local Government Act 2000 s2 (see para 1.68 above), such a provision would now appear to be redundant.

'Meals and recreation in the home or elsewhere'

19.26 The guidance suggests that:

> ... many of the elderly who are mobile or who can be transported will require social centres providing meals and opportunities for occupation as well as companionship and recreation. For the housebound and the frailer elderly meals-on-wheels will also need to be developed.[32]

19.27 The services available under this direction include the provision of 'recreation'. This would include day centres, outings, the provision of a television in the home and so on. District councils are empowered to provide similar services by virtue of Health and Social Services and Social Security Adjudications Act (HASSASSAA) 1983 Sch 9 (see para 19.37 below). The equivalent services for disabled people (under CSDPA 1970 s2(1)(g) and (c) respectively) are considered at paras 9.137 and 9.51 above, and for people who are, or have been, ill, under the NHS Acts 2006, at para 9.712 above.

Information on elderly services

19.28 'To inform the elderly of services available to them and to identify elderly people in need of services.' The guidance cautions against attempts to develop a comprehensive register of elderly people.[33] It emphasises, however, that:

29 See para 14.142 above and see also para 9.65 where a similar exclusion applies to NAA 1948 s29.
30 The local authority may provide the services alone, or by employing independent or private providers – see HSPHA 1968 s45(3) and DHSS circular 19/71 paras 5(b), 7 and 11 et seq.
31 DHSS circular 19/71 para 4.
32 DHSS circular 19/71 para 10.
33 DHSS circular 19/71 para 6(a).

... good services together with wide and continuing publicity about them are a pre-requisite of any scheme for finding out needs. The elderly and those who know of them cannot be expected to come forward if they do not know of any reason for doing so.[34]

19.29   The more specific duty to inform under CSDPA 1970 s1 is considered at para 2.24 above.

Travel assistance to participate in section 45 services

19.30   'To provide facilities or assistance in travelling to and from the home for the purpose of participating in services provided by the authority or similar services.' The equivalent duty under the CSDPA 1970 is dealt with at para 9.94 above.

Assistance in finding boarding accommodation

19.31   'To assist in finding suitable households for boarding elderly persons.' Social services authorities are given the power to provide this service (and those detailed in paras 19.32 and 19.33 below) to meet the needs of elderly people, similar to the powers approved for disabled people under NAA 1948 s29 in LAC (93)10 appendix 2 para 3 (see para 9.60 below).

Social work support and advice

19.32   'To provide visiting and advisory services and social work support.' The guidance suggests that social visiting services should be given high priority and that they should be co-ordinated by local authorities but largely undertaken by voluntary workers or others after suitable preparatory training.[35]

Home help and home adaptations

19.33   'To provide practical assistance in the home, including assistance in the carrying out of any additional facilities designed to secure the greater safety, comfort or convenience.' The guidance states that 'home-help, including laundry services and other aids to independent living, should probably be high on any priority list'.[36] The equivalent (and more substantial) duties to provide such services under CSDPA 1970 s2 and under NHSA 2006 Sch 20 para 3 (home helps only) are dealt with at paras 9.77 and 9.178 respectively.

Subsidy of warden costs

19.34   'To contribute towards the cost of employing a warden on welfare functions in warden-assisted housing schemes.' Social services authorities are given the power to provide this service to meet the needs of elderly people,

---

34   DHSS circular 19/71 para 6(b).
35   DHSS circular 19/71 para 10; and see also para 9.41 where the equivalent service under NAA 1948 s29 is considered.
36   DHSS circular 19/71 para 10.

similar to the powers approved for disabled people under NAA 1948 s29 in LAC (93)10 appendix 2 para 3 (see para 9.54).

Warden services

19.35 'To provide warden services for occupiers of private housing.' Social services authorities are given the power to provide this service to meet the needs of elderly people, similar to the powers approved for disabled people under NAA 1948 s29 in LAC (93)10 appendix 2 para 3 (see para 9.62 above).

Excluded groups

19.36 The effect of Immigration and Asylum Act 1999 s117, by amending section 45, is to exclude from services older people who are asylum seekers and are in need of community care services solely on account of being 'destitute'[37] (see para 21.13 below).

Care services under Health and Social Services and Social Security Adjudications Act 1983 Sch 9

19.37 HASSASSAA 1983 s29 and Sch 9 Part II make provision for district councils to provide 'meals and recreation for old people' (see para 9.138 above). Schedule 9 para 1 states:

> A district council or Welsh county council or county borough council shall have power to make such arrangements as they may from time to time determine for providing meals and recreation for old people in their homes or elsewhere and may employ as their agent for the purpose of this paragraph any voluntary organisation whose activities consist in or include the provision of meals or recreation for old people.

19.38 In order to achieve these objectives Schedule 9 para 2 empowers such authorities to contribute to the funds of voluntary organisations, and to permit them to use their premises or furniture, vehicles or equipment (gift or loan or otherwise). Paragraph 3 provides the secretary of state with regulation making powers – which have not as yet been exercised.

19.39 It appears that these powers are generally exercised by district councils in collaboration with social services authorities in respect of supported accommodation arrangements. The partnership arrangements under NHSA 2006 s75[38] (see para 13.127 above), enable payments to be made by health bodies to district councils in relation to such arrangements.[39]

---

37 Section 45(4A) as inserted by Immigration and Asylum Act 1999 s117.
38 NHS(W)A 2006 s33.
39 Health Act 1999 s31(8).

CHAPTER 20

Mental health: policy and services

Introduction

20.1   Mental ill health in the UK is the largest single cause of disability and represents up to 23 per cent of the total burden of ill health.[1] At least one in four people will experience a mental health problem at some point in their life[2] and at any one time, approximately one in six people of working age have a mental health problem (most often anxiety or depression) and one in 250 will have a psychotic illness such as schizophrenia or bipolar affective disorder.[3]

20.2   People who have a mental disorder of any description are entitled to the full range of community care services: including accommodation under the National Assistance Act (NAA) 1948, and non-accommodation services under NAA 1948 s29, Chronically Sick and Disabled Persons Act (CSDPA) 1970 s2, and the NHS Acts 2006. The definition of 'disabled' under NAA 1948 s29 and Children Act (CA) 1989 s17(11) includes persons with a 'mental disorder of any [description/kind]'. It follows that a person with even a transient mental health problem is entitled to a community care assessment and services if the assessment reveals an eligible need. Certain persons with mental health difficulties are entitled to distinct community care services under MHA 1983 s117 and this service regime is considered at para 20.22 below.

National service framework for mental health

20.3   In order to address the social and mental health needs of working age adults up to 65, in 1999 the government in England published a *National service framework (NSF) for mental health*.[4] The NSF was has been reviewed[5] and a number of its principles widened to cover people of all ages – most importantly in the 2011 Mental Health Strategy.[6] The role and status of NSFs are considered at para 1.61 above. In Wales an equivalent NSF was published in 2002 and updated in 2005.[7]

---

1   Department of Health (2011) *No health without mental health: a cross-government mental health outcomes strategy for people of all ages*, p10.
2   Department of Health (2011) *No health without mental health: a cross-government mental health outcomes strategy for people of all ages*, p8.
3   Department of Health (1999) *A national service framework for mental health: modern standards and service models*, p1.
4   Department of Health (1999) *A national service framework for mental health: modern standards and service models*.
5   Department of Health (2004) *A National Service Framework for Mental Health – five years on*.
6   Department of Health (2011) *No health without mental health: a cross-government mental health outcomes strategy for people of all ages* – which supersedes Department of Health (2009) *New horizons: a shared vision for mental health*.
7   Welsh Assembly Government (2005) *Raising the standard: the revised adult mental health national service framework and an action plan for Wales*.

20.4   The English NSF[8] set out seven key standards, providing in each case detailed guidance on the local action required to ensure these are implemented – with timescales and 'milestones to ensure progress, with performance measures to support performance improvement'. The seven English standards are as follows:

1) *Mental health promotion*
   Health and social services should:
   - promote mental health for all, working with individuals and communities,
   - combat discrimination against individuals and groups with mental health problems, and promote their social inclusion.

2) *Primary care and access to services*
   Any service user who contacts their primary healthcare team with a common mental health problem should:
   - have their mental health needs identified and assessed,
   - be offered effective treatments, including referral to specialist services for further assessment, treatment and care if they require it.

3) *Primary care and access to services*
   Any individual with a common mental health problem should:
   - be able to make contact round the clock with the local services necessary to meet their needs and receive adequate care,
   - be able to use NHS Direct, as it develops, for first-level advice and referral on to specialist helplines or to local services.

4) *Effective services for people with severe mental illness*
   All mental health service users on the Care Programme Approach (CPA) should:
   - receive care which optimises engagement, prevents or anticipates crisis, and reduces risk,
   - have a copy of a written care plan which:
     - includes the action to be taken in a crisis by service users, their carers, and their care co-ordinators
     - advises the GP how they should respond if the service user needs additional help
     - is regularly reviewed by the care co-ordinator
     - be able to access services 24 hours a day, 365 days a year.

5) *Effective services for people with severe mental illness*
   Each service user who is assessed as requiring a period of care away from their home should have:
   - timely access to an appropriate hospital bed or alternative bed or place, which is:

8   The Welsh NSF (ibid) has eight standards, namely (1) promoting social inclusion, (2) empowerment and support of service users and carers, (3) promotion of opportunities for a normal pattern of daily life, (4) providing and commissioning equitable, accessible services, (5 and 6) delivering responsive, comprehensive services, (7) effective client assessment and care pathways and (8) ensuring a well-staffed, skilled and supported workforce.

- in the least restrictive environment consistent with the need to protect them and the public
- as close to home as possible
- a copy of a written after care plan agreed on discharge, which sets out the care and rehabilitation to be provided, identifies the care co-ordinator, and specifies the action to be taken in a crisis.

6) *Caring about carers*
All individuals who provide regular and substantial care for a person on CPA should:
- have an assessment of their caring, physical and mental health needs, repeated on at least an annual basis,
- have their own written care plan, which is given to them and implemented in discussion with them.

7) *Preventing suicide*
Local health and social care communities should prevent suicides by:
- promoting mental health for all, working with individuals and communities (standard one),
- delivering high quality primary mental healthcare (standard two),
- ensuring that anyone with a mental health problem can contact local services via the primary care team, a helpline or an A&E department (standard three),
- ensuring that individuals with severe and enduring mental illness have a care plan which meets their specific needs, including access to services round the clock (standard four),
- providing safe hospital accommodation for individuals who need it (standard five),
- enabling individuals caring for someone with severe mental illness to receive the support which they need to continue to care (standard six).

and in addition:
- supporting local prison staff in preventing suicides among prisoners,
- ensuring that staff are competent to assess the risk of suicide among individuals at greatest risk,
- developing local systems for suicide audit to learn lessons and take any necessary action.

Assessment and care planning for mental health service users

20.5   Standard two of the NSF concerns the right of mental health service users to a needs' assessment and standard three entitles them to 'round the clock' access to the local services necessary to meet their needs and to receive adequate care. Standard four elaborates upon the rights of mental health service users to be assessed using the care programme approach (CPA, considered below).

20.6   As noted above, people with mental health problems are eligible to receive community care services and, if under 18, services under the CA 1989. In addition, however, many adults of working age in contact with the secondary mental health system are entitled to an integrated health and social care assessment: the CPA.

The care programme approach

20.7   The CPA was introduced by the joint health/social services circular HC (90)23: LASSL (90)11. Health authorities were given lead responsibility for implementing the policy although there was an obligation on health and social services authorities to reach formal and detailed inter-agency agreements to ensure its full implementation.[9] The Department of Health has consistently stressed the importance it attaches to the CPA, which has been subject to revisions[10] culminating with the current 2008 guidance.[11] In many respects the CPA can be viewed as a specialised community care assessment – and the relationship between these two process is considered at para 20.16 below.

20.8   Similar guidance was issued in Wales in 2003,[12] which was updated in 2004[13] and in 2010 with 'interim' guidance.[14] In Wales the intention is that the CPA is integrated into the community care assessment process (the unified assessment process – see para 3.30 above). Wales has (unlike in England) a two-tiered CPA system (mirroring the English system prior to 2008) and the lower tier the 'standard CPA', is considered at 20.14 below. The upper tier of the Welsh CPA – the 'enhanced CPA – is, however, little different from the English CPA, which is considered below.

The CPA in England

20.9   The 2008 CPA applies to persons who are entitled to support from secondary mental health services and 'who have complex characteristics'. There is no specific intervention under the MHA 1983, that triggers entitlement although anyone subject to a Community Treatment or Guardianship Order (under MHA 1983 s17A and s7 respectively) will be

9   Department of Health (1995) *Social services departments and the care programme approach: an SSI inspection report,* para 4.3.11.
10 See Department of Health (1994) *Guidance on the discharge of mentally disordered people and their continuing care in the community,* HSG (94)27: LASSL (94)4; Department of Health (1996) *Audit pack for monitoring the care programme approach,* and Department of Health (1999) *Effective care co-ordination in mental health services: modernising the care programme approach – a policy booklet.*
11 Department of Health (2008) *Refocusing the care programme approach: policy and positive practice guidance.*
12 Welsh Assembly Government (2003) *Mental health policy wales implementation guidance: the care programme approach for mental health service users.*
13 Welsh Assembly Government (2004) *Adult mental health services: stronger in partnership.*
14 Welsh Assembly Government (2010) *Delivering the care programme approach in Wales: interim policy implementation guidance.*

subject to the 2008 CPA regime unless for 'reasons . . . clearly documented in care records' it is not considered appropriate.[15]

20.10   People in contact with secondary mental health services will be subject to the 2008 CPA if one or more of the following factors are considered to be relevant to their situation:[16]

- Severe mental disorder (including personality disorder) with high degree of clinical complexity;
- Current or potential risk(s), including:
  ○ Suicide, self harm, harm to others (including history of offending)
  ○ Relapse history requiring urgent response
  ○ Self neglect/non concordance with treatment plan
  ○ Vulnerable adult; adult/child protection, eg,
    ▪ exploitation, eg, financial/sexual
    ▪ financial difficulties related to mental illness
    ▪ disinhibition
    ▪ physical/emotional abuse
    ▪ cognitive impairment
    ▪ child protection issues;
- Current or significant history of severe distress/instability or disengagement;
- Presence of non-physical co-morbidity, eg, substance/alcohol/prescription drugs misuse, learning disability;
- Multiple service provision from different agencies, including: housing, physical care, employment, criminal justice, voluntary agencies;
- Currently/recently detained under Mental Health Act or referred to crisis/home treatment team;
- Significant reliance on carer(s) or has own significant caring responsibilities;
- Experiencing disadvantage or difficulty as a result of:
  ○ Parenting responsibilities
  ○ Physical health problems/disability
  ○ Unsettled accommodation/housing issues
  ○ Employment issues when mentally ill
  ○ Significant impairment of function due to mental illness
  ○ Ethnicity (eg, immigration status; race/cultural issues; language difficulties; religious practices); sexuality or gender issues.

20.11   Notwithstanding the above list of individuals qualifying for CPA, the evidence suggested that some key groups were not 'being identified consistently and that services are sometimes failing to provide the support they need'.[17] Accordingly the 2008 guidance creates a presumption that the following categories of person (in contact with secondary mental health services) will qualify for the CPA 'unless a thorough assessment of need and risks shows otherwise':[18]

15   2008 CPA guidance pp14–15.
16   2008 CPA guidance table 2.
17   2008 CPA guidance p14.
18   2008 CPA guidance p14.

- who have parenting responsibilities
- who have significant caring responsibilities
- with a dual diagnosis (substance misuse)
- with a history of violence or self harm
- who are in unsettled accommodation.

20.12 At every formal CPA review, consideration must be given as to whether the support provided as part of the CPA intervention is still needed. However, the 2008 guidance cautions against withdrawing support prematurely and distinguishes between CPA support and other services (eg community care support services – see para 20.19 below). CPA support can only be withdrawn after a formal review which satisfies the requirements of the guidance – including the production of a care plan detailing who is to take over day to day responsibility and which contains 'a clear statement about the action to take, and who to contact, in the event of relapse or change with a potential negative impact on that person's mental well-being'.[19]

The CPA in Wales

20.13 The CPA guidance in Wales provides for a very similar scheme – to that described in paras 20.9–20.12 above. In Wales this level of support is known as the 'enhanced' CPA. Wales, however, retains a lower tier of support, known as the 'standard CPA'. At the time of writing (September 2011) the CPA guidance in Wales is 'interim' – as a result (in part) of the adoption of the Mental Health (Wales) Measure 2010.[20] The Measure is expected to have a phased commencement during 2012 with Parts 2 and 3 (assessment, care and treatment planning and care coordination within secondary mental health services) commencing in June 2012 and Part 1 (concerning local primary mental health support services) in October 2012. In 2010 the Welsh government issued interim updating CPA guidance[21] to local health boards (LHBs) and local authorities and this is the principle guidance, although reference is necessary in parts to the earlier 2003 and 2004 guidance.[22]

The standard CPA

20.14 The 2010 Welsh interim CPA guidance at para 171 suggests that 'service users covered by the Standard Care Programme Approach will be likely to':

---

19   2008 CPA guidance p15.
20   For analysis of the Measure – see P Fennell, *Mental health law and practice*, 2nd edn, Jordans, 2011.
21   Welsh Assembly Government (2010) *Delivering the care programme approach in Wales: interim policy implementation guidance.*
22   Welsh Assembly Government (2003) *Mental health policy Wales implementation guidance: the care programme approach for mental health service users* and Welsh Assembly Government (2004) *Adult mental health services: stronger in partnership.*

- require the support or intervention of one agency or one discipline or require low key support from more than one agency or discipline;
- be more able to self-manage their mental health;
- have an informal support network;
- pose little danger to themselves and/or others;
- be more likely to maintain contact with services.

20.15　The 2010 guidance explains (para 38) that individuals subject to the standard CPA will benefit from the five key components of CPA (namely assessment; planning of care and treatment; delivery of care and treatment; monitoring and review; and discharge) and that (para 40):

> Each service user will have a care coordinator appointed for them, who will be responsible for ensuring these five components are delivered. The care coordinator is central to the effective delivery of the CPA: they are responsible for ensuring a care and treatment plan is developed and delivered, and where necessary reviewed and revised. They are also responsible for coordinating the care which is delivered (both by themselves and others), and for keeping in touch with the service user . . .

CPA and community care assessments

20.16　The relationship between the administrative obligation on joint NHS/ social services teams to prepare CPA assessments and the social services statutory duty to undertake community care assessments under National Health Service and Community Care Act (NHSCCA) 1990 s47 has on occasions been misunderstood.

20.17　In a number of respects the CPA can be considered to be a formalised community care assessment and care planning process. However, in some respects it is distinct – for example, it is capable of being undertaken by an NHS employee and is largely directed at providing care coordination – via an expert key worker or 'care co-ordinator'.[23] Those subject to the CPA have a right to a level of support which goes beyond the core entitlement of any community care service user, notably a right to:

- a comprehensive multi-disciplinary, multi-agency assessment covering the full range of needs;
- a comprehensive formal written care plan, including a risk and safety/ contingency/crisis plan;
- on-going review, formal multi-disciplinary, multi-agency review at least once a year but generally more frequently; and
- increased advocacy support.

20.18　Once a person is no longer in need of the level of intensive support provided by the CPA, she or he may still require on-going support from

---

23　Page 36 of the 2008 CPA guidance describes who can be the care co-ordinator, and states that it 'should usually be taken by the person who is best placed to oversee care management and resource allocation and can be of any discipline depending on capability and capacity'.

health and social services. As the 2008 English CPA guidance states (p15):

> ... it is important that service users and their carers are reassured that when the support provided by ... CPA is no longer needed that this will not remove their entitlement to receive any services for which they continue to be eligible and need, either from the NHS, local council, or other services

20.19 The interplay between the obligations under the CPA and the community care legislation was considered in *R (HP and KP) v Islington LBC*.[24] The case concerned a patient being cared for by his family at home. He was assessed by the psychiatric services as suffering from a form of depression and at risk of severe neglect and 'vulnerable to deterioration in his mental state particularly if he stops taking his medication'. He was, however, considered not to have a 'severe and enduring mental illness' and deemed ineligible for CPA support. In view of this finding the local authority determined that he was not eligible for 'community care provision'. In quashing this decision, Munby J held that the authority had misunderstood the relationship between the CPA and the duty to assess under section 47(1). The fact that the patient lacked a 'severe and enduring mental illness ... was not determinative of whether he nonetheless had a need for generic health or social services community care'.[25] Accordingly, in the judge's opinion:

> In my judgment, Islington's demonstrable and serious error in its whole approach to the fundamental underlying questions must, in the circumstances, invalidate both parts of the process.[26] In my judgment there has never been a proper and comprehensive Community Care assessment of Mr P, only a CPA assessment. The process in relation to the Community Care assessment must start again.

20.20 It will be maladministration to fail to undertake an expeditious community care assessment in circumstances where a compulsorily detained patient cannot be discharged until it has been completed.[27]

CPA and the single assessment process

20.21 Guidance on the interface between the CPA and the single assessment process (SAP) is provided in a 2002 Department of Health clarification note[28] and is considered further at para 19.11 above.

---

24 [2004] EWHC 7 (Admin), (2005) 82 BMLR 113.
25 [2004] EWHC 7 (Admin), (2005) 82 BMLR 113 at [37].
26 The first being to undertake a 'needs assessment' and the second to arrive at a 'service provision decision' – see [2004] EWHC 7 (Admin), (2005) 82 BMLR 113 at [38].
27 Complaint no 04/B/01280 against York City Council, 31 January 2006.
28 Department of Health (2002) *Care management for older people with serious mental health problems*.

Services under Mental Health Act 1983 s117

20.22   Most non-accommodation services that authorities provide for people with a mental health difficulty are delivered under CSDPA 1970 s2. These services are available to persons 'who suffer from a mental disorder of any description'.[29] Likewise, most accommodation services that authorities provide for people with a mental health difficulty are delivered under NAA 1948 s21.

20.23   Only a small minority of people who receive community care services are entitled to their services under MHA 1983 s117. For such people, however, as section 117 creates specifically enforceable individual rights to a wide range of services, the availability of these services under other Acts is in reality academic. From a service user's perspective, the receipt of services under MHA 1983 s117 has the added advantage that social services authorities are not empowered to charge for them (see para 20.45).

20.24   The full text of MHA 1983 s117 (as amended) is provided at appendix A to this book. The section places a joint responsibility on the NHS (ie a PCT or LHB) and social services to provide 'after-care' services for persons who are in hospital as a result of being detained/transferred/admitted under MHA 1983 s3,[30] s37,[31] s45A,[32] s47[33] or s48[34] – 'and then cease to be detained and (whether or not immediately after so ceasing) leave hospital'.

The nature of the section 117 duty

20.25   The duty to provide after care services under MHA 1983 s117 crystallises when the person 'ceases to be detained'. The nature of the duty under section 117, and the meaning of the phrase 'ceases to be detained' has been considered in a number of diverse fact cases, including by the Court of Appeal in *R (K) v Camden and Islington Health Authority*[35] and the House of Lords in *R (IH) v Secretary of State for the Home Department and others*.[36] From these decisions, it appears that the section 117 duty:

---

29   In addition services are also available under the NHS Acts 2006 for (amongst others) persons who are, or have been, suffering from an illness (see para 9.172 above).
30   Where a patient is admitted for treatment (as opposed to being admitted under MHA 1983 s2 for assessment).
31   Where a patient is detained by a criminal court after being convicted of a serious criminal offence and the court being satisfied (amongst other things) that at the time of conviction the offender was suffering from a mental disorder.
32   An order (subject to certain provisos) made by a Crown Court when sentencing a person who has a mental disorder which makes it appropriate that he or she be detained in a specified hospital.
33   Persons serving a sentence of imprisonment for whom the secretary of state is satisfied (among other things) that they are suffering from a mental disorder and should in consequences be removed and detained in a hospital.
34   As for section 47 above, save only it applies to persons who, although detained, are not serving a sentence of imprisonment (eg, they are on remand pending trial, are civil prisoners or being detained under the Immigration Act 1971).
35   [2001] EWCA Civ 240, [2001] 3 WLR 553, (2001) 4 CCLR 170.
36   [2003] UKHL 59, [2003] 3 WLR 1278, (2004) 7 CCLR 147.

1) only arises on the patient's discharge from hospital although the NHS body has the power to take preparatory steps prior to discharge.[37] In *R (B) v Camden LBC and others*[38] Stanley Burnton J held that no express duty to take steps to secure after-care services arose until the health/social services authorities were informed of the discharge of a detainee (see para 3.70 above);

2) in so far as it relates to the provision of ordinary social care services, there is a specific duty (see para 1.25 above) to ensure that these services are made available;[39]

3) in so far as it relates to the provision of personal/professional services (most notably by the NHS in the form of securing a psychiatrist prepared to accept responsibility for the patient on discharge into the community), the duty is merely to 'use its best endeavours to procure' the services it deems necessary (or those specified by a mental health review tribunal).[40]

20.26 MHA 1983 s117 services are also available to patients on MHA 1983 s17 leave.[41] Section 17 provides that a 'responsible clinician' may authorise leave of absence to patients detained under Part II of the Act (ie under non-criminal detention). This entitlement arises because section 117 services are available to persons who are detained under (amongst others) section 3 and then 'cease to be detained and (whether or not immediately after so ceasing) leave hospital'. A person can therefore be entitled to section 117 services even though still formally detained under section 3, since the crucial question is whether or not he or she is physically detained in a hospital rather than legally 'liable to be detained' under MHA 1983 s3.

Services

20.27 Section 117 places no restriction upon the type of services that can be provided.[42] The courts have held that although a wide range of services can be provided under section 117, they are restricted to those services necessary to meet a need arising from a person's mental disorder.[43] In *Clunis v*

---

37 *R (K) v Camden and Islington Health Authority* [2001] EWCA Civ 240, [2001] 3 WLR 553, (2001) 4 CCLR 170 at [20].

38 [2005] EWHC 1366 (Admin), (2005) 8 CCLR 422 at [66]–[67].

39 *R v Ealing District Health Authority ex p Fox* [1993] 1 WLR 373, QBD.

40 *R (IH) v Secretary of State for the Home Department and others* [2003] UKHL 59, [2003] 3 WLR 1278, (2004) 7 CCLR 147 at para 29; and see also in this regard *R (K) v Camden and Islington Health Authority* [2001] EWCA Civ 240, [2001] 3 WLR 553, (2001) 4 CCLR 170.

41 This entitlement, which is noted in the English and Welsh Codes of Practice to the Mental Health Act 1983 (paras 21.25 and 31.5 respectively) was confirmed by Sullivan J in *R v Richmond LBC and others ex p Watson and others* (1999) 2 CCLR 402, QBD; see also para 20.36 below.

42 In co-operation with the relevant voluntary agencies – MHA 1983 s117(2).

43 See for example, *R (Mwanza) v Greenwich LBC and Bromley LBC* [2010] EWHC 1462 (Admin), (2010) 13 CCLR 454, paras 66 and 79.

Camden and Islington Health Authority,[44] Beldam LJ considered that the services available under section 117:

> . . . would normally include social work, support in helping the ex-patient with problems of employment, accommodation or family relationships, the provision of domiciliary services and the use of day centre and residential facilities.

20.28   Only limited guidance on the nature and extent of section 117 services has been issued.[45] 1996 guidance advised that they might include 'appropriate daytime activities, accommodation, treatment, personal and practical support, 24-hour emergency cover and assistance in welfare rights and financial advice' as well as 'support for informal carers'. The English Code of Practice to MHA 1983[46] advises that the user's care plan should identify various needs, including: daytime activities or employment; appropriate accommodation; counselling and personal support; and assistance in welfare rights and managing finances and notes that:

> 27.4 Services provided under section 117 can include services provided directly by PCTs or LSSAs as well as services they commission from other providers.
>
> 27.5 After-care is a vital component in patients' overall treatment and care. As well as meeting their immediate needs for health and social care, after-care should aim to support them in regaining or enhancing their skills, or learning new skills, in order to cope with life outside hospital

20.29   The Welsh Code of Practice to MHA 1983[47] advises that:

> After-care services are provided to meet an assessed need arising from the patient's mental disorder and are aimed at reducing the likelihood of the patient being readmitted to hospital for treatment for that disorder. Services will therefore normally include treatment for mental disorder, social work support to help the patient with problems of employment, accommodation or family relationships, the provision of domiciliary services and the use of day centre and residential facilities. Administration of medication for mental disorder, and its subsequent monitoring, will often be a key part of an after-care plan.

20.30   Although the courts have confirmed that the section 117 duty includes the provision of accommodation,[48] this has been in the context of accommodation with care support. In *R (Mwanza) v Greenwich LBC and Bromley LBC*[49] Hickinbottom J was not prepared to rule that the provision of 'bare accommodation' (ie a tenancy and nothing else) could not be provided under section 117 – but in his view this would only be possible very exceptionally, noting:

---

44   [1998] 1 WLR 902, (1997–98) 1 CCLR 215 at 225G, CA.
45   Department of Health (1996) *Guidance on supervised discharge (after-care under supervision) and related provisions* LAC (96)8: HSG (96)11 para 18.
46   Department of Health (2008) *Code of Practice: Mental Health Act 1983*, para 27.13.
47   Welsh Assembly Government (2008) *Mental Health Act 1983: Code of Practice for Wales* at para 31.20.
48   See for eg *R (B) v Lambeth* [2006] EWHC 2362 (Admin), (2007) 10 CCLR 84.
49   [2010] EWHC 1462 (Admin) at para 77.

it simply cannot have been the intention of Parliament to have required local authorities (let alone health authorities), free of charge, to provide a roof over the head of former section 3 patients so long as they simply required housing

A joint health/social services duty

20.31 In *R v Mental Health Review Tribunal ex p Hall*[50] the Divisional Court held that the duty to provide aftercare services under MHA 1983 s117(2) was jointly shared by the health and social services authority in which the patient was resident at the time he or she was detained. It is therefore up to individual health bodies and social services authorities to decide among themselves how they will discharge these joint responsibilities. Although the Department of Health has advised health and social services authorities to develop local policies clarifying their respective responsibilities,[51] it appears that in practice this is something that has been neglected.

20.32 Many patients entitled to section 117 services have healthcare needs which could also qualify them for NHS continuing healthcare funding and the interface between these responsibilities is considered at para 14.208 above and para 20.47 below.

Reform

20.33 At the time of writing (September 2011) the Health and Social Care Bill (2011) cl 32 proposes the transfer to clinical care groups of the NHS's duty to provide section 117 after-care (currently with PCTs). If enacted as currently drafted, the bill would amend section 117(2) to enable a consortium or social services authority to terminate aftercare (ie to take away the requirement that this be a joint decision). It would also (via a new subsection (2E)) restrict the power of consortia, to only commission health services as part of aftercare under section 117. This would constitute a radical departure, since at present (as with their NHS continuing healthcare responsibilities) the PCTs can have responsibility under section 117 for all a person's health and social care needs.

The duration of the duty

20.34 The services provided under MHA 1983 s117 must continue to be supplied until the authorities are satisfied that the former patient is no longer in need of them. In this context, the English 2008 Code of Practice states:[52]

---

50 [2000] 1 WLR 1323, (1999) 2 CCLR 383, DC.
51 Department of Health (2003) *After-care under the Mental Health Act 1983: section 117 after-care services* HSC 2000/003: LAC (2000)3.
52 Department of Health (2008) *Code of Practice: Mental Health Act 1983*, para 27.19: similar advice is found Welsh Assembly Government (2008) *Mental Health Act 1983: Code of Practice for Wales* at para 31.13. The Codes have been held to be strong policy guidance (see para 1.56 above) that should be followed unless in an individual case there is a good reason for departing from it – see *Munjaz v Mersey Care NHS Trust and others* [2003] EWCA Civ 1036, [2003] 3 WLR 1505, (2003) 74 BMLR 178.

The duty to provide after-care services exists until both the PCT and the LSSA are satisfied that the patient no longer requires them. The circumstances in which it is appropriate to end section 117 after-care will vary from person to person and according to the nature of the services being provided. The most clear-cut circumstance in which after-care will end is where the person's mental health has improved to a point where they no longer need services because of their mental disorder. But if these services include, for example, care in a specialist residential setting, the arrangements for their move to more appropriate.

20.35   2000 guidance issued by the Department of Health[53] expressed the position thus:

Aftercare provision under section 117 does not have to continue indefinitely. It is for the responsible health and social services authorities to decide in each case when aftercare provided under section 117 should end, taking account of the patient's needs at the time. It is for the authority responsible for providing particular services to take the lead in deciding when those services are no longer required. The patient, his/her carer and other agencies should always be consulted.

20.36   In *R v Richmond LBC and others ex p Watson and others*[54] (a case concerning the lawfulness of charging for services under MHA 1983 s117 – see para 20.45 below), Sullivan J held that aftercare provision under section 117 does not have to continue indefinitely, although it must continue until such time as the health body and the local authority are satisfied that the individual is no longer in need of such services.

20.37   In his judgment he considered the following question: 'What are the local authorities' duties under MHA 1983 s117 towards a person, who because of old age, illness or other circumstances, has been provided with residential accommodation under NAA 1948 s21, then becomes mentally unwell, is detained under MHA 1983 s3, is discharged from hospital and returns to his or her former accommodation as part of their after-care package?' He held:

I can see no reason why such a person should be in any worse position than the patient who has not previously been provided with accommodation under s21. On leaving hospital, the local authority will owe them a duty under s117. There may be cases where, in due course there will be no more need for after care services for the person's mental condition' but he or she will still need social services provision for other needs, for example, physical disability. Such cases will have to be examined individually on their facts, through the assessment process provided for by s47. In a case . . . where the illness is dementia, it is difficult to see how such a situation could arise.

20.38   The question of the lawfulness of the discharge of section 117 responsibilities was central to the case of *R (Mwanza) v Greenwich LBC and*

---

53 Department of Health (2000) *After-care under the Mental Health Act 1983: section 117 After-Care Services* HSC 2000/003: LAC (2000)3: para 4.
54 (1999) 2 CCLR 402, QBD.
55 [2010] EWHC 1462 (Admin).

Bromley LBC.[55] The applicant had been detained under section 3 in September 2000 and was discharged from section and from hospital in January 2001. A brief care plan was prepared by the community mental health team (CMHT) and in the following six months home visits and out-patients appointments ensued. His condition fluctuated but by July 2001 the view was that his condition had much improved and in November, due to his failure to engage with the CMHT, his GP was advised that he was to be discharged from the CMHT's allocated cases. The file was then closed and he made no further contact with the CMHT until mid-2009 when, for reasons connected with his immigration status (see para 21.42 below) he argued that his entitlement to section 117 support subsisted

20.39   In the court's opinion the 2001 decision by the CMHT to discharge its section 117 responsibilities was a lawful decision, based upon a proper conclusion that he was no longer in need of such aftercare services. Effectively, the court considered that if the responsible local authority and NHS body decide that a person is no longer in need of aftercare services and no longer receiving such services, then provided the decision is made at a properly constituted meeting the court will not look too closely at the merits of the decision (ie limiting its remit to administrative law review). In the proceedings it was argued that *R v London Borough of Richmond ex p Watson*[56] was authority for the proposition that a person could not be discharged from section 117 lawfully without a prior community care assessment being undertaken. The court sidestepped this argument on the basis of the evidential difficulties in establishing exactly what had occurred, due to the delay in this case (ie between 2001 and the launch of the judicial proceedings). The local government ombudsman has, however, held that as a general rule such an assessment is mandatory: that any decision that a person no longer needs aftercare should only be taken following a multi-disciplinary meeting of those involved in a person's care and who understand his or her needs; and a formal reassessment of need. Not only does the ombudsman require that correct procedures have been followed, he also requires sight of adequate documentation to support any assertions to this effect.[57]

20.40   The local government ombudsman has considered the reasonableness of a purported discharge of section 117 responsibilities in a complaint against Clwyd.[58] The facts were that the resident had been detained under MHA 1983 s3 from which she was discharged and eventually moved to an elderly mentally ill nursing home. Steps were then taken by the local authority to assess her liability for residential care charges and in due course the authority placed a charge on her home.

20.41   After the authority's power to levy such charges was questioned, the hospital consultant met with the relevant social worker and purported to

---

56 (1999) 2 CCLR 402, QBD.
57 Complaint no 06/B/07542 against Poole Borough Council 5 September 2007.
58 Dated 19 September 1997, see (1997–98) 1 CCLR 546; and see also Report no 98/B/ 0341 from the English local government ombudsman against Wiltshire where a similar finding was made coupled with a recommendation that the cases of other people who might have had to pay for services inappropriately also be reviewed.

discharge the section 117 aftecare: neither the resident or her daughter were aware of the discharge meeting or decision.

20.42   The local government ombudsman considered all these matters, but in particular the decision to discharge the MHA 1983 s117 arrangements. In his decision he held:

1)   The council had a duty to provide aftercare services at no cost to the resident from the moment she was discharged from hospital until such time as it was satisfied that she was no longer in need of such services.

2)   In deciding that she no longer needed after-care under MHA 1983 s117 the council had failed to address the relevant question which was whether she needed and whether she continued to need aftercare services. The ombudsman concluded that if the council had asked itself the relevant question, it would have had to conclude that she was in need of the specialist care provided at a home for the elderly mentally infirm.

3)   The ombudsman concluded that the council's maladministration had been exacerbated by a number of factors including its failure to take account of the daughter's views before ceasing to provide aftercare services under MHA 1983 s117.

20.43   The local government ombudsman has also held it to be maladministration to discharge a person from section 117 aftercare merely because she had 'settled' in a residential care home – where if that home were withdrawn, the resident would be at risk of admission to hospital.[59] In this respect the English 2008 Code of Practice cautions against the discharge of section 117 support even where the after-care arrangements have proved to be successful and the 'the patient is now well settled in the community' since he or she 'may still continue to need aftercare services, for example to prevent a relapse or further deterioration in their condition'.[60]

District or area of residence

20.44   MHA 1983 s117(3) provides that services under that section are the responsibility of the social services/health body for the area in which 'the person concerned is resident or to which he is sent on discharge by the hospital in which he was detained'. The question of ordinary residence under section 117 is considered further at para 6.59 above.

Charging for Mental Health Act 1983 s117 services

20.45   In *R v Manchester City Council ex p Stennett and others*[61] the House of Lords held that it was unlawful for local authorities to charge for services under MHA 1983 s117. Although the judgment confirmed the consistent view

---

59   Complaint no. 06/B/16774 against Bath and North East Somerset Council, 12 December 2007.

60   Department of Health (2008) *Code of Practice: Mental Health Act 1983*, paras 27.20–27.21.

61   [2002] UKHL 34, [2002] 3 WLR 584, (2002) 5 CCLR 500.

of the Department of Health,[62] many local authorities had hitherto been charging for such services and accordingly a substantial number of claims were then made for reimbursement – many of which came to the notice of the local government ombudsman. Accordingly in July 2003 a special report was issued by the three English local government ombudsmen,[63] the key advice therein being summarised as follows (p5):

> That, in general, social services authorities (SSAs) should not carry out retrospective assessments purporting to remove a person from section 117 aftercare as from an earlier date.
> - That SSAs should review any retrospective assessments that have so far been made.
> - That, for the next 12 months at least, complaints made about previous assessments to end section 117 aftercare should not be rejected by SSAs as out of time.
> - That where previous assessments to end section 117 aftercare were not properly made, then restitution will generally be appropriate until a proper assessment is devised.
> - That people who have paid for section 117 aftercare should receive financial restitution with interest.
> - That SSAs should now put mechanisms in place to identify those persons improperly charged, or improperly deprived of financial assistance, and establish arrangements for reimbursing them or their estates.
> - That no generally applicable cut-off date should be used when calculating repayments. Cases where such cut-off dates have been applied should be reviewed.

20.46 While it is clearly established that service users cannot be charged for section 117 services, it is less clear whether a resident receiving section 117 support can 'top up' the care home fees to purchase a service more expensive than the assessed need requires. This question is considered further at para 7.135 above.

Section 117 and NHS continuing healthcare

20.47 We consider at chapter 14 above the responsibilities of the NHS for the care of people who are so unwell that they are entitled to NHS continuing healthcare funding (see specifically para 14.208). Many of these individuals may have mental health problems. Where such a person was formerly detained under MHA 1983 s3 or one of the criminal provisions,

62 See eg LAC (2000)3 *After-care under the Mental Health Act 1983: section 117 after-care services.*

63 The Local Government Ombudsmen (2003) *Special Report: Advice and guidance on the funding of aftercare under section 117 of the Mental Health Act 1983* LGO 604 (07/03) London: The Commission for Local Administration in England: the report contains copies of the key reports: Clwyd, 19 September 1997, (1997–98) 1 CCLR 546; Wiltshire County Council, 14 December 1999, (2000) 3 CCLR 60; and Leicestershire, 25 October 2001; C00/B/08307.

the question arises as to whether his or her entitlement to services derives from section 117 or under the NHS continuing healthcare regime.

20.48   While the Assembly in Wales has suggested that in certain situations the NHS continuing healthcare funding responsibility may 'trump' the section 117 duty,[64] the Department of Health has indicated otherwise, stating:[65]

> Under section 117 of the Mental Health Act 1983 ('section 117'), PCTs and LAs have a duty to provide after-care services to individuals who have been detained under certain provisions of the Mental Health Act 1983, until such time as they are satisfied that the person is no longer in need of such services. Section 117 is a freestanding duty, and guidance[66] advises PCTs and LAs to have in place local policies detailing their respective responsibilities

20.49   The Department of Health is certainly correct in stating that section 117 is a free-standing service provision obligation. This in itself does not mean that the NHS continuing health care obligation is irrelevant. The duty to provide services under NAA 1948 s29 is a free-standing obligation but in certain situations it is trumped by the overlapping duty under CSDPA 1970 s2.

20.50   At present there is no decided case-law to determine the issue but the following considerations would need to be addressed in order to decide this point.

1) To what extent is the NHS continuing healthcare obligation seen to trump other service provision duties? This was seen to occur in *Coughlan*[67] in relation to the duty under NAA 1948 s21 and in *R (T, D and B) v Haringey LBC*[68] in relation to CA 1989 s17 duty – where Ouseley J thought that this was a principle of general application (see para 14.29 above). Since section 117 services are but one example of the community care services listed in NHSCCA 1990 s46(3) (see para 3.136 above), this might suggest that it should be subject to such a general principle.

2) What liability is triggered as a result of an aftercare meeting preceding a patient's discharge? It seems unlikely that it is to provide all services that are required by the patient – since the guidance suggests that this does not include care provided by an unpaid carer and in *Mwanza* it was been held that as a general rule it would not include ordinary housing services. If this is the case, it might be argued that the duty is to provide those services which would not otherwise arise – ie the

---

64 Welsh Assembly Government (2004) *NHS responsibilities for meeting continuing NHS Healthcare needs* WHC (2004)54: NAFWC 41/2004 at p6 para 14(iii).

65 Department of Health (2009) *The national framework for NHS continuing healthcare and NHS funded nursing care*, para 113.

66 Department of Health (2003) *After-care under the Mental Health Act 1983: section 117 after-care services* HSC 2000/003: LAC (2000)3.

67 *R v North and East Devon Health Authority ex p Coughlan* [2000] 2 WLR 622, (1999) 2 CCLR 285.

68 [2005] EWHC 2235 (Admin), (2006) 9 CCLR 58.

shortfall. If this is the case, it could be argued that the NHS continuing healthcare obligation arises before the section 117 obligation.

3) Is it relevant that the Health and Social Care Act 2001 s49 restriction treats section 117 services in the same way as it does other community care provisions (see para 13.110 above)? If section 117 creates an entirely separate regime outside the usual NHS/social services for-malities, it is arguable that section 49 would not have included explicit reference to such services.

4) Is it anomalous that the NHS can have less responsibility in financial terms for a patient who has been forcibly detained in a psychiatric unit than for one who has not?

5) What is the weight to be given to the (now superseded) 2004 Welsh Assembly Continuing Care Guidance,[69] which stated that an individual will qualify for NHS continuing healthcare if (among other things) he or she is 'detained in accordance with Section 17 of the Mental Health Act'? As noted at para 20.26 above, patients on section 17 leave come within the ambit of section 117.

6) Is the comment of Otton LJ in *Richmond BC v Watson, Stennett and others*[70] determinative? In his opinion the section 117 duty was one that 'reduces the opportunity of [health and social services] authorities to try to pass the buck and as a result [make] no proper provision'. In his opinion 'the language of section 117 ensures a seamless provision . . . permitting cross-funding of community care services between the two authorities'.

20.51 While the above analysis suggests that the demarcation of responsibilities under the two regimes is by no means clear, it would suggest that section 117 creates a distinct funding regime to that of NHS continuing health-care (so long as the section 117 responsibility endures). If such a con-clusion is correct, it does not answer the question of how the NHS and social services should apportion their respective liabilities. Arguably the division could logically be determined by social services taking responsi-bility for those individuals who were primarily in need of social support and the NHS taking responsibility for those whose primary need was for healthcare – ie the same as under the NHS continuing healthcare provisions (see para 14.210 above where this question is considered further).

69 Welsh Assembly Government (2004) *NHS responsibilities for meeting continuing NHS Healthcare needs* WHC (2004)54: NAFWC 41/2004 at p6 para 14(iii).
70 [2000] 3 WLR 1127, (2000) 3 CCLR 276, CA.

Charging and guardianship under Mental Health Act 1983 s7

20.52   MHA 1983 ss7–9 provide for the making of guardianship orders and for the powers of guardians (considered further at para 24.38 below). The 1983 Act does not, however, authorise or require the provision of any services in connection with the guardianship. Accordingly where residential or domiciliary care services are provided for a person the subject of a guardianship order, an issue arises as to the provenance of this power/ duty. From the perspective of that person, the question is particularly relevant when a local authority seeks to charge for the accommodation or care service.

20.53   If the service is provided under a separate statutory provision (ie NAA 1948 s21, CSDPA 1970 s2, MHA 1983 s117, etc), the default charging position is reasonably clear. However, it could be argued that the support is provided under the 1983 Act itself, although silent on this question. There are a number of reasons for believing that this might be the case, not least that as a general rule a statutory provision authorising a local authority to take specific action must, if it does not contain an explicit procedure for effecting this action, be implied to contain such a power. The MHA 1983 not only contains no explicit power to provide accommodation or domiciliary care services (other than for those to whom section 117 applies) it also contains no explicit power to charge. This situation is in contrast, for example, to that under NAA 1948 s47 (see para 7.38 above) where subsection (9) provides a clear statement of the power to charge, and the basis for this power.

20.54   The argument as to an implied power could derive from (for example) Local Government Act 1972 s111 which provides that local authorities are to have the power to do anything that is 'necessary and properly required for carrying into effect the undertaking and works which the Act had expressly sanctioned'. Section 111 would therefore constitute the authority for the provision of accommodation or domiciliary care in such a case – but not for the imposing of any charge.[71]

20.55   Although it could be suggested there is no need to 'imply' such a power (since alternative provisions exist under the community care legislation) there would appear to be at least two reasons why such an argument may be incorrect. The first is a human rights interpretative argument (see paras 20.56–20.59 below) and the second is practical. The practical difficulty stems from the problem of what would occur if a person subject to a guardianship residence condition did not satisfy the statutory requirements for support under NAA 1948 s21 – because for instance, being wealthy and having full mental capacity he or she refused to pay for their accommodation, or because, although meeting the criteria under section 7 (eg accommodation required in order to protect 'other

71   See eg *McCarthy and Stone (Developments) Ltd v Richmond upon Thames RLBC* [1992] 2 AC 48, [1991] 4 All ER 897.

persons') she or he did not meet the eligibility criteria for community care services (see para 3.149 above).

20.56   The Northern Irish charging rules prohibit charges being levied for accommodation provided to residents subject to guardianship[72] and the Department of Health in 1995 expressed the opinion[73] that the right to free services under MHA 1983 s117 also applies to guardianship. Nevertheless an argument exists that charges might in certain situations be unconscionable. Persons subject to guardianship may have no choice but to live at a specified address, and while this may not amount to detention (see para 17.50 above) it is clearly a significant restriction on their liberty and engages Article 8 of the European Convention on Human Rights (right to respect for private life and home – see para 26.260 below). If the state is requiring them to live in more expensive accommodation (a registered care or nursing home rather than rented accommodation), the added requirement that they pay the additional cost could again be articulate in the language of Article 8.[74]

20.57   Some support for this line of reasoning is provided by the comments of Lord Steyn in *R v Manchester City Council ex p Stennett and others*[75] where he referred with approval (at [14]) to the observations by Buxton LJ in the Court of Appeal[76] that not charging service users under section 117 was not anomalous since they constituted:

> . . . an identifiable and exceptionally vulnerable class. To their inherent vulnerability they add the burden, and the responsibility for the medical and social service authorities, of having been compulsorily detained. It is entirely proper that special provision should be made for them to receive after-care, and it would be surprising, rather than the reverse, if they were

72 Department of Health, Social Services and Public Safety (Northern Ireland) (2011) *Charging for Residential Accommodation Guide (CRAG)*, 2011, provides at para 1.005A that: 'Trusts should not charge for aftercare services, which can include residential care, provided under Article 18 of the Mental Health (NI) Order 1986. 'Aftercare' includes the provision of accommodation for persons who are subject of a guardianship order that requires them to reside at a place other than a hospital. Therefore the Health and Personal Social Services (Assessment of Resources) Regulations (Northern Ireland) 1993 do not apply and the Trust cannot charge a person for the residential accommodation in which he resides whilst subject to guardianship under the 1986 Order.'

73 In a letter of 18 January 1995 to Oldham Social Services. The letter states that: 'until recently it had been assumed that local authorities could use an implied power to charge based upon s111 Local Government Act 1972, if they wished to charge for any services where they had no express power to charge. Following the decision in *R v Richmond LBC ex p McCarthy* [1992] 2 AC 48, it is now clear that this is not the case . . .'

74 It would appear at least arguable, that the absence of any general discretion to waive/ disapply charges for residential accommodation under the National Assistance (Assessment of Resources) Regulations 1992 SI No 2977 (considered at para 8.9 above) may render them incompatible with the Convention. Pending such a determination, it may be that local authorities should use the powers they have, to minimise their charges in appropriate cases: eg, to raise the detained persons' personal expenses allowance to such a level that no charge arises (see para 8.27 above).

75 [2002] UKHL 34, [2002] 3 WLR 584, (2002) 5 CCLR 500.

76 *Richmond LBC v Watson, Stennett and others* [2000] 3 WLR 1127, (2000) 3 CCLR 276, CA.

required to pay for what is essentially a health-related form of care and treatment.

20.58   Lord Steyn then referred to the situation of patients discharged into residential care under section 117 and observed (at [15]) that in relation to such accommodation and care, it:

> . . . can hardly be said that the mentally ill patient freely chooses such accommodation. Charging them in these circumstances may be surprising. Moreover, under section 73 of the 1983 Act in respect of restricted patients . . . the tribunal is empowered to impose conditions of discharge upon the patient with which the patient is obliged to comply, eg in respect of residence and treatment . . . Plainly in such cases the patients do not voluntarily avail themselves of the after-care services. If the argument of the authorities is accepted that there is a power to charge these patients such a view of the law would not be testimony to our society attaching a high value to the need to care after the exceptionally vulnerable.

20.59   In a number of respects it could be argued that this analysis also has force for patients required to reside in a care home under conditions of a guardianship order.

CHAPTER 21

Asylum seekers and other overseas nationals

Diagram 21: Eligibility of current and former asylum seekers for asylum support and community care (other than unaccompanied minors)

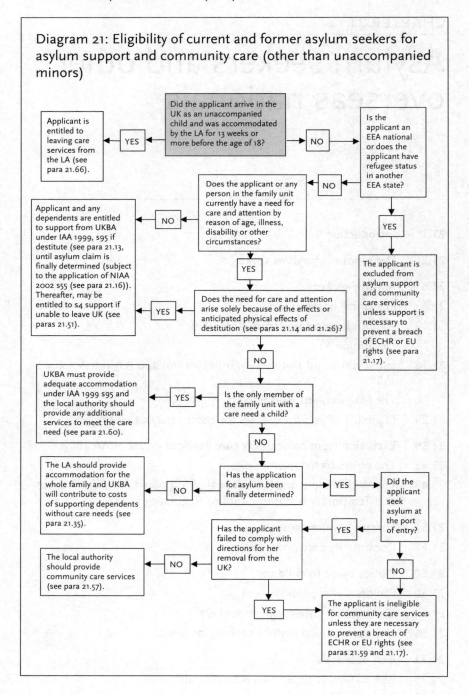

Introduction

21.1 This chapter deals with the community care support available to asylum seekers and to other overseas nationals in the UK who, for whatever reason, are unable to access social welfare assistance (public housing support and welfare benefits). Constant legislative change over the course of the last two decades and the consequent case law has made the subject exceedingly complex and on occasions brought the higher courts to the point of exasperation. In order, therefore, to make the subject comprehensible it is necessary to commence with a review of the relevant history and of the key definitions.

Definitions – 'asylum seeker'

21.2 In loose terms an asylum seeker is someone who has applied for asylum in the UK and whose application remains pending (either before the secretary of state or at appeal). The statutory definition, however, is set out in Immigration and Asylum Act (IAA) 1999 s94(1) which defines an 'asylum seeker' as:

> . . . a person who is not under 18 and has made a claim for asylum which has been recorded by the secretary of state but which has not been determined.

21.3 Section 94 also clarifies the meaning of a claim for asylum, namely:

> . . . a claim that it would be contrary to the United Kingdom's obligations under the Refugee Convention, or under Article 3 of the Human Rights Convention, for the claimant to be removed from, or required to leave, the United Kingdom.

21.4 Asylum seekers within this definition are, in general, entitled to accommodation and financial support while in the UK. The key question which this chapter considers in relation to this group is as to the circumstances when they are entitled to local authority support under community care provisions, and when they are entitled to support from the UK Border Agency (UKBA) under IAA 1999. This question is important because where accommodation is provided by UKBA, it is offered on a strictly no-choice basis, normally outside London and the South East, and in very basic accommodation. Thus the ability of asylum seekers with community care needs to secure accommodation and support from the local authority under the National Assistance Act (NAA) 1948 can be critical to their ability to remain in their local area with their existing support networks. Moreover, the standard of accommodation provided by UKBA is such that the delivery of social care within that accommodation can be problematic.[1] Diagram 21 summarises the availability of community care and asylum support for asylum seekers and their families (other than unaccompanied children).

---

1 See the concerns expressed by the Law Commission (2011) *Adult Social Care* Law Com No 326 HC941, para 6.26.

21.6   This chapter also considers the related questions of the availability of community care provision and other support for the following groups:

- people who were, but are no longer, asylum seekers within the definition above ('former asylum seekers');
- children – both unaccompanied children and children who are present in the UK with their families;
- EEA nationals;
- victims of domestic violence subject to a 'no recourse to public funds' condition.

Asylum seekers

Historical background[2]

21.6   Until 6 February 1996 asylum seekers were entitled to means tested benefits and housing through the homeless provisions.[3] However, from that date applicants who applied for asylum 'in country' rather than 'at port' (ie those who claimed after they had entered the UK rather than on their arrival) were excluded from social welfare benefits and homelessness assistance. This change was brought about by virtue of Asylum and Immigration Act 1996 ss9 and 11. Subsequently IAA 1999 s115 extended the disentitlement of benefits from late-claiming asylum seekers to almost all those subject to immigration control.

21.7   The 1999 Act envisaged that the majority of asylum seekers would become the responsibility of a new designated body, namely the National Asylum Support Service (NASS[4]). However, persons who had made a claim for asylum on arrival ('at port') in the UK on or before the introduction of the IAA 1999[5] continued to be entitled to means tested benefits.[6]

---

2   For a detailed and authoritative description of the history of community care for persons from abroad, see the speech of Baroness Hale in *R (M) v Slough BC* [2008] UKHL 52, [2008] 1 WLR 1808, at [7]–[29].

3   Housing Act 1996 Part VII.

4   In March 2007 asylum cases were transferred to a new regime known as New Asylum Model or 'NAM'. NAM was designed to be a more efficient and streamlined approach to processing and deciding asylum claims. A key feature of NAM is that asylum claims are dealt with by one single named case owner. In addition to changes to the asylum process, NASS as an organisation ceased to exist and NAM case owners now deal with all asylum support decisions for asylum seekers who initially sought asylum in or after March 2007. A 'legacy' team was put in place to deal with cases where the application for asylum was originally made before March 2007, known as the Case Resolution Directorate (CRD). In such cases, CRD caseworkers dealt with applications for support. In April 2011, outstanding 'unresolved' legacy cases were transferred to a new Case Assurance and Audit Unit (CAAU) and responsibility for applications for support from this group in most cases to the UKBA's North West Immigration Teams in Liverpool. CAAU is only intended to exist for two years from April 2011. Given this complexity, reference will be made in this chapter to the UK Border Agency (UKBA) as the decision-making body for asylum support questions, and support under IAA 1999 (whether under ss4, 95 or 98) as 'UKBA support'.

5   Which came into force on 2 October 2000.

6   Social Security (Immigration and Asylum) Consequential Amendment Regulations 2000 SI No 636 reg 12(4).

These people (known as the '2000 Transitional Protected' cases) retained their entitlement to benefits until the first negative decision on their asylum claim[7] (after which time they fell to be supported by UKBA).

21.8   As a consequence of the 1996 removal of benefit entitlement from in-country asylum applicants, a number of asylum seekers became destitute and sought assistance under NAA 1948 s21(1)(a) on the basis that they came within the 'any other circumstance' category (see para 7.7 above) and were thus entitled to residential accommodation from the local authority. In *R v Hammersmith LBC ex p M*[8] their claims succeeded, albeit that the Court of Appeal stressed that section 21 was not a 'safety net' provision 'on which anyone who is short of money and/or short of accommodation can rely'.[9]

21.9   The *Hammersmith* judgment caused not inconsiderable financial problems for a number of local authorities. A 1998 government white paper described the position thus:[10]

> The Court of Appeal judgment . . . meant that, without warning or preparation, local authority social services departments were presented with a burden which is quite inappropriate, which has become increasingly intolerable and which is unsustainable in the long term, especially in London, where the pressure on accommodation and disruption to other services has been particularly acute.

21.10   The *Hammersmith* judgment has come to be seen as a landmark decision, since when many aspects of asylum and immigration law have become inextricably intertwined with community care law. As the case law has developed, parliament has responded with new Acts and regulations such that the system is today complex to a degree bordering on the Kafkaesque and so lacking in any obvious logic that it has prompted judicial exasperation – as occurred, for example, in *R (AW and others) v Croydon LBC*,[11] where Laws LJ observed:

> In the course of this judgment we have used the term 'paper chase', and have done so advisedly. This important area of the law governs the use of scarce public resources in a difficult and sensitive field. We have already referred . . . to the pressing and uneven burden borne by some local authorities. One part of the overall scheme has had to be litigated in the House of Lords. Now this part, closely related, has had to be litigated in this court. No doubt there are great pressures on the legislators. But the distribution of responsibility which is at the core of this case could surely have been provided much more clearly and simply.[12]

---

7   Social Security (Immigration and Asylum) Consequential Amendment Regulations 2000 SI No 636 regs 2 and 12.
8   This being a consolidated appeal, comprising *R v Hammersmith LBC ex p M; R v Lambeth LBC ex p P and X and R v Westminster City Council ex p A* (1997–98) 1 CCLR 85, QBD.
9   (1997–98) 1 CCLR 85 at 94K.
10   Home Office (1998) *Fairer, faster and firmer – a modern approach to immigration and asylum*, Cm 4018, para 8.14, cited by Lord Hoffman in *Westminster CC v NASS* [2002] UKHL 38, [2002] 1 WLR 2956, (2002) 5 CCLR 511 at 519C.
11   [2007] EWCA Civ 266 at [55], (2007) *Times* 11 May.
12   Judgment at [55].

21.11   This chapter treads a difficult line. It seeks to focus on the rights to community care support of people who are non-UK nationals and either seeking asylum or unlawfully in the UK or for some other reason have restricted rights to such services. It is difficult, however, to focus on this question without straying occasionally into the more general area of immigration law. Of necessity, however, we have had to limit these incursions severely, and a reader wishing to understand these issues in further detail should refer to a specialist text on the subject.[13]

Asylum support under the IAA 1999

21.12   Following the *Hammersmith* judgment, the government announced its intention to amend the NAA 1948[14] to:

> ... make clear that social services departments should not carry the burden of looking after healthy and able bodied asylum seekers. This role will fall to the new national support machinery.

21.13   The vehicle for this change was IAA 1999 Part VI, which inserted section 21(1A) into the 1948 Act to exclude support for 'able bodied' asylum seekers. Support for such persons is now provided for by the UKBA.[15] On first applying for asylum support, asylum seekers who appear to be destitute[16] are entitled to 'Initial' or 'Emergency' accommodation provided under IAA 1999 s98 until a decision is reached on the person's claim for 'full asylum support' under IAA 1999 s95. Full UKBA support can include accommodation and financial support but, unlike community care services, accommodation under s95 is almost always provided away from London and the South East (in accordance with the government's policy to disperse those reliant on this support away from these areas). An applicant for UKBA support who has access to available accommodation but not the means to meet his or her other essential living needs, can apply for subsistence only support.

Destitution

21.14   Destitution is a key concept in the determination of entitlement to UKBA support[17] and is defined in IAA 1999 s95(3) as follows:

13   See eg S Wilman and S Knafler, *Support for Asylum Seekers and other Migrants: a guide to legal and welfare rights*, 3rd edn, Legal Action Group, 2009; and Joint Council for Welfare Immigrants (2006) *Immigration Nationality and Refugee Handbook*, JCWI, 2006.
14   Home Office (1998) *Fairer, faster and firmer – a modern approach to immigration and asylum*, Cm 4018, para 8.23.
15   See note 4 above. Community care services under the Health Services and Public Health Act 1968 and the NHS Acts 2006 are also excluded – see paras 9.166 and 19.36 above.
16   There is some irony in the reappearance of the word 'destitute' into the 1948 Act, since its drafters considered that the omission of any reference to the notion of destitution was one of its greatest achievements– see comments of Mrs Braddock MP, *Hansard* HC Debates 24 November 1947 on the National Assistance Bill para 1631.
17   This definition applies to both section 95 support and to section 4 support (see further para 21.51 below).

For the purposes of this section, a person is destitute if –

(a) he does not have adequate accommodation or any means of obtaining it (whether or not his other essential living needs are met), or

(b) he has adequate accommodation or the means of obtaining it, but cannot meet his other essential living needs.

21.15 The Asylum Support Regulations 2000[18] set out what UKBA caseworkers must consider when assessing whether an applicant is destitute. The whole family's circumstances must be considered in assessing whether any individual member is destitute (regulations 6 and 12), and when assessing an applicant's resources account must be taken of any other support which the person might reasonably be expected to have during the prescribed period (regulation 6(4)). For the purposes of an initial application for support, the prescribed period is 14 days' essential living needs. Where other support is 'available', UKBA support can be denied: a point of importance in situations where an asylum seeker might be seeking community care support.[19]

Late claims and Nationality, Immigration and Asylum Act 2002 s55

21.16 In order to qualify for UKBA s95 support, asylum seekers are expected to show that they claimed asylum 'as soon as reasonably practicable' after their arrival in the UK. Failure to do so can result in support being refused (NIAA 2002 s55(1)). Applicants cannot be excluded under section 55 if they have dependent children under the age of 18 (section 55(5)(b) and (c)) or if to do so would result in a breach of their human rights (section 55(5)(a)).

The human rights exemption

21.17 In *R (Adam, Limbuela and Tesema) v Secretary of State for the Home Department*[20] the House of Lords sought to identify the point at which deprivation becomes so grave that the state is obliged to intervene and provide support. The Lords held that an asylum seeker would be at risk of suffering degrading treatment (contrary to Article 3 of the European Convention on Human Rights ('the Convention')) if he, with 'no alternative sources of support, unable to support himself, is, by the deliberate action of the state, denied shelter, food or the most basic necessities of life'.[21] The state therefore had a duty to provide support when:[22]

---

18 SI No 704 as amended. This contains the detailed rules concerning UKBA support, and in addition the UKBA has produced Asylum Support Policy Bulletins which set out the internal guidance that UKBA caseworkers should follow when making support decisions; these are available on the UKBA website at www.ukba.homeoffice.gov.uk/policyandlaw/guidance/asylumsuppbull/

19 See para 21.21 below.

20 [2005] UKHL 66, [2005] 3 WLR 1014, (2006) 9 CCLR 30.

21 [2005] UKHL 66, [2005] 3 WLR 1014, (2006) 9 CCLR 30 at [7].

22 [2005] UKHL 66, [2005] 3 WLR 1014, (2006) 9 CCLR 30 at [8].

. . . it appears on a fair and objective assessment of all relevant facts and circumstances that an individual applicant faces an imminent prospect of serious suffering caused or materially aggravated by denial of shelter, food or the most basic necessities of life. Many factors may affect that judgment, including age, gender, mental and physical health and condition, any facilities or sources of support available to the applicant, the weather and time of year and the period for which the applicant has already suffered or is likely to continue to suffer privation.

21.18   While it was not possible to 'formulate any simple test applicable in all cases' the court considered that the potential breach of Article 3 would require that a person be supported if the person was:

. . . obliged to sleep in the street, save perhaps for a short and foreseeably finite period, or was seriously hungry, or unable to satisfy the most basic requirements of hygiene.

21.19   Baroness Hale in her judgment (at [78]) did come close to providing a simple test – essentially arguing that 'cashlessness + rooflessness = inhuman and degrading treatment'.[23]

21.20   In *MSS v Belgium and Greece*,[24] the Grand Chamber of the European Court of Human Rights affirmed that while Article 3 did not impose a general obligation to house the homeless, given the particular vulnerability of asylum seekers and the positive obligations to provide material reception conditions imposed by EU law,[25] a failure to provide any accommodation or support at all to asylum seekers could violate the prohibition on inhuman and degrading treatment in Article 3.[26]

21.21   The current position is, therefore, that on receiving a section 55 'refusal of support decision' an asylum seeker must show that he or she or a dependant is facing an imminent prospect of serious suffering caused, or materially aggravated, by denial of shelter, food or the most basic necessities of life, and that a failure to support will result in a breach of their rights under Article 3. They must be able to point to evidence that they have sought charitable support and that this is either not available or has been exhausted.

21.22   In practice, since the decision in *Limbuela*, UKBA will normally only apply section 55 to those who are applying for subsistence only support,

23   See in this regard the commentary in A Mackenzie, 'Case analysis: *R v Secretary of State for the Home Department ex p Adam, Limbuela and Tesema*' [2006] EHRLR 67–73.
24   Application no 30696/09, judgment of 21 January 2011.
25   Specifically, Directive 2003/9 on minimum standards for the reception of asylum seekers.
26   Paras 249–264. The court upheld the applicant's claim that conditions in Greece did breach Article 3, observing that: 'the Greek authorities have not had due regard to the applicant's vulnerability as an asylum seeker and must be held responsible, because of their inaction, for the situation in which he has found himself for several months, living in the street, with no resources or access to sanitary facilities, and without any means of providing for his essential needs. The Court . . . considers that such living conditions, combined with the prolonged uncertainty in which he has remained and the total lack of any prospects of his situation improving, have attained the level of severity required to fall within the scope of Article 3 of the Convention' (para 263).

ie those who have accommodation available to them but are unable to meet their other essential living needs, the rationale for this being that such cases are less likely to be able to demonstrate the necessary level of suffering because they will have a roof over their heads. There have been serious delays in the making of section 55 decisions in such cases, leaving applicants with no form of support for weeks or months, although steps have been taken recently to address these issues.

21.23   This jurisprudence is essential to an assessment of whether support is necessary to prevent a breach of a person's human rights, which is also the critical question in relation to people excluded from community care services under Nationality, Immigration and Asylum Act (NIAA) 2002, s54 and Sch 3, discussed at para 21.43 below. It requires a consideration of whether such persons may be expected to leave the country in order to avoid a breach of their ECHR rights (in the case of current asylum seekers, this is unlikely to be a possibility, but it is more relevant in the case of former asylum seekers and other migrants), as well as whether their circumstances in the UK are such that they are likely to be exposed to inhuman or degrading treatment. That consideration requires attention to be paid to the individual characteristics of the person concerned, and the threshold will more readily be crossed in the case of a child, or of a person suffering from mental or physical illness or disability.

Eligibility of asylum seekers for community care services

21.24   At the same time as introducing the national system of asylum support under IAA 1999 Part VI, in order to achieve the aim of excluding able-bodied asylum seekers from section 21 support, amendments were made to the community care legislation[27] (including NAA 1948 s21) by IAA 1999 s116, which inserted into NAA 1948 s21 a new subsection (1A), namely:

> (1A) A person [subject to immigration control, including asylum seekers] may not be provided with residential accommodation under subsection (1)(a) if his need for care and attention has arisen solely –
> (a) because he is destitute; or
> (b) because of the physical effects, or anticipated physical effects, of his being destitute.

21.25   The 1999 amendment to section 21 did not, however, achieve its objective of relieving social services authorities from the bulk of their obligations to asylum seekers.[28] As Lord Hoffman noted in *Westminster CC v NASS*[29] (hereafter the 2002 *Westminster* case):

---

27   See also para 7.7 above.
28   The close connection between this amendment and asylum policy was recognised by the Law Commission in its consultation and report on Adult Social Care, in which, despite concerns expressed by many consultees about the negative impact of the 'destitution plus' test on asylum seekers' health, it made no recommendation about reform of this test, recognising it was a matter of asylum policy rather than legal reform (Report no 326, 10 May 2011, paras 11.34, 11.37).
29   [2002] UKHL 38, [2002] 1 WLR 2956, (2002) 5 CCLR 511 at 519E.

29. What may have escaped notice in the aftermath of *ex p M*[30] was that the 1996 Act had brought into the scope of section 21 of the 1948 Act two distinct classes of asylum seekers who would not have been entitled to Part III accommodation if the 1996 Act had not excluded them from the normal social security system. The first class were the able bodied asylum seekers who qualified solely because, being destitute, they were already or were likely to become in need of care and attention. This was the class highlighted in *ex p M*. I shall call them 'the able bodied destitute', who came within section 21 solely because they were destitute. The second class were asylum seekers who had some infirmity which required the local social services to provide them with care and attention, but who would not ordinarily have needed to be provided with accommodation under section 21 because it was available in other ways, for example, under the homelessness legislation. They would not have come within the section 21 duty because they would not have satisfied the third condition which I have quoted from the judgment of Hale LJ in *Wahid's* case[31] . . .

21.26   The problem highlighted by Lord Hoffman was that use of the word 'solely' in amended NAA 1948 s21(1A) had the effect of only excluding the 'able bodied' destitute. The second class (which he referred to as the 'infirm destitute') were able to claim assistance from social services authorities under NAA 1948 s21, not 'solely' because of their destitution, but additionally because of their infirmity. And since they had access to such assistance they were excluded from the IAA 1999 scheme by virtue of the Asylum Support Regulations 2000 reg 6(4)(b)[32] which requires the UKBA in deciding whether an asylum seeker is destitute to take into account any other support which was, or could reasonably be expected to be, available to the asylum seeker. Lord Hoffman accordingly held:

> The present case has been argued throughout on the footing that [the applicant] has a need for care and attention which has not arisen solely because she is destitute but also (and largely) because she is ill. It is also common ground that she has no access to any accommodation in which she can receive care and attention other than by virtue of section 21 or under Part VI of the 1999 Act. The first question for your Lordships is whether in those circumstances she comes prima facie within section 21(1)(a) and, if so, the second is whether she is excluded by section 21(1A). In my opinion, the answers to these questions are yes and no respectively. The third question is whether the existence of a duty under section 21 excludes [the applicant] from consideration for asylum support. Again, in agreement with the Court of Appeal, I think that the answer is yes.[33]

21.27   In the 2002 *Westminster* case, regard was had to two earlier consolidated appeals, *R v Wandsworth LBC ex p O* and *R v Leicester CC ex p Bhikha*[34] in

---

30 This being a consolidated appeal, comprising *R v Hammersmith LBC ex p M; R v Lambeth LBC ex p P and X* and *R v Westminster City Council ex p A* (1997–98) 1 CCLR 85, QBD.
31 Namely that 'the care and attention which is needed must not be available otherwise than by the provision of accommodation under section 21': *R (Wahid) v Tower Hamlets LBC* [2002] EWCA Civ 287, (2002) 5 CCLR 239 at 247H – see para 7.44 above.
32 SI No 704.
33 [2002] UKHL 38, [2002] 1 WLR 2956, (2002) 5 CCLR 511 at [49].
34 [2000] 1 WLR 2539, (2000) 3 CCLR 237, CA.

which the local authorities argued that the insertion of subsection (1A) into section 21 made the claimants ineligible under that section. In the leading judgment Simon Brown LJ (as he then was)[35] adopted the applicants' construction of section 21, namely:

> ... that if an applicant's need for care and attention is to any material extent made more acute by some circumstance other than the mere lack of accommodation and funds, then, despite being subject to immigration control, he qualifies for assistance.

21.28 In this respect, Simon Brown LJ observed that:

> The word 'solely' in the new section is a strong one and its purpose there seems to me evident. Assistance under the Act of 1948 is, it need hardly be emphasised, the last refuge for the destitute. If there are to be immigrant beggars on our streets, then let them at least not be old, ill or disabled.

21.29 In *R (M) v Slough BC*,[36] he[37] said:

> If, however, that state of need has been accelerated by some pre-existing disability or infirmity – not of itself sufficient to give rise to a need for care and attention but such as to cause a faster deterioration to that state and perhaps to make the need once it arises that much more acute – then for my part, consistently with the views I expressed in the earlier cases, I would not regard such a person as excluded under section 21(1A).[38]

21.30 It follows that an applicant, in order to cross the NAA 1948 s21(1A) threshold, must establish that he or she is a person whose need for care and attention does not arise solely because of destitution or its physical, or anticipated physical effects. This requirement is commonly referred to as the 'destitution plus test'.

21.31 The *ex p O* and *ex p Bhikha* decisions were followed in *R (Mani) v Lambeth LBC*.[39] The question in *Mani* was whether a local authority has a duty to provide residential accommodation for a destitute asylum seeker who suffers a disability which, of itself, gives rise to a need for care and attention which falls short of calling for the provision of residential accommodation. The decision of the court was that it did, consistent with the *dicta* of Lord Brown in *R (M) v Slough BC* (see para 21.29 above).

21.32 This line of case law, culminating in the 2002 *Westminster* case, established that where an asylum seeker does satisfy the destitution plus test, the responsibility for financially supporting and accommodating that person lies with the local authority, rather than with UKBA.

---

35 [2000] 1 WLR 2539, (2000) 3 CCLR 237 at 2548D–2549B.
36 [2008] 1 WLR 1808.
37 By this stage, sitting in the House of Lords as Lord Brown.
38 At 1822F; Baroness Hale, who had also been party to the decision in *ex p O* in the Court of Appeal, commented that the Court of Appeal had not appreciated that the effect of the Asylum Support Regulations 2000 was that any asylum seeker who was eligible for section 21 accommodation would not be eligible for UKBA support; she said the court had 'assumed that the new national asylum support scheme would provide for destitute asylum seekers even if they were especially vulnerable, if the care and attention they needed could be provided for them in the accommodation provided by the new scheme' (at 1817F).
39 [2002] EWHC 735 (Admin), (2002) 5 CCLR 486.

21.33   An important consequence of this is that where an asylum seeker falls within section 21(1)(a) and is not excluded by section 21(1A) the fact that his community care needs are not 'such as necessarily to call for the provision of residential accommodation' does not mean that the local authority is entitled to meet those needs by way of services under NAA 1948 s29 and Chronically Sick and Disabled Persons Act 1970 s2(1).[40] UKBA support under IAA 1999 s95 is residual, and a local authority is not entitled to refuse to accommodate under section 21 on the ground that it could simply provide services to the claimant while he was accommodated by UKBA, or on the ground that a claimant's only need for 'care and attention' which is not medical care is a need which can be met by the provision of accommodation and subsistence by UKBA, provided always that his or her need for care and attention is made more acute by some factor other than destitution, or the actual or anticipated physical effects of destitution.[41] As noted at para 7.17 above, in *R (SL) v Westminster City Council*[42] the Court of Appeal held that section 21(1)(a) did not envisage any particular intensity of support in order to constitute 'care and attention' that 'was not otherwise available' – and this could consist (as in this case) of weekly counselling /monitoring meetings: where the social worker was 'doing something for the appellant which he cannot do for himself'.

21.34   The important role played by section 21 in providing for 'people who need care and attention, which could be provided in their own homes, if they had them'[43] was recognised by the Law Commission in its May 2011 report on adult social care. The need to ensure that people in need of care and attention, including particularly asylum seekers, were not left homeless simply because their need fell below that which would engage the Law Commission's proposed new eligibility criteria, was one of the justifications for proposing the retention of section 21 despite the otherwise wholesale reform of adult social care law proposed by the Law Commission.[44]

21.35   In order to qualify for support under NAA 1948 s21, asylum seekers must therefore satisfy the following criteria:

1) That they are not excluded from support under section 21 by virtue of Nationality, Immigration and Asylum Act (NIAA) 2002 Sch 3 (see

---

40   *R (Z) v Hillingdon LBC* [2009] EWCA Civ 1529 at [18].
41   *R (Pajaziti) v Lewisham LBC* [2007] EWCA Civ 1351; although note that Lewisham effectively conceded that the claimants' need for 'shelter and warmth in residential accommodation' was a need for care and attention within the meaning of section 21(1)(a): it is doubtful whether this concession could survive the construction of section 21(1)(a) by the House of Lords in *R (M) v Slough BC*, but that does not affect the validity of the Court's construction of section 21(1A). However, note that UKBA's Policy Bulletin 82 on Asylum Seekers with Care Needs points out that no duty will arise under section 21(1)(a) if the person's other needs can be met otherwise than through the provision of accommodation by the local authority, such as by a friend or family member providing the care and attention in UKBA accommodation (para 4.2).
42   [2011] EWCA Civ 954.
43   *R (M) v Slough BC* [2008] UKHL 52, [2008] 1 WLR 1808 at [30].
44   Law Commission (2011) *Adult Social Care,* Law Com No 326 HC941, paras 6.18–6.32 and Recommendation 18.

para 21.41 below). For most asylum seekers this is straightforward as they are not excluded from community care provisions under Schedule 3.[45]

2) That they are in need of 'care and attention' by reason of old age, illness, disability or any other circumstances.

3) That the care and attention which they need is not otherwise available to them. In *R (M) v Slough BC*,[46] the House of Lords emphasised that it was the 'care and attention' which must not be otherwise available under section 21(1)(a), rather than the residential accommodation.

4) That they pass the 'destitution plus test' under section 21(1A). As outlined above, this proviso has been interpreted[47] to mean that their need for care and attention is to any material extent made more acute by some factor other than destitution or the effects or anticipated physical effects of destitution.

5) That they do not have support otherwise available in accordance with NAA 1948 s21(1). The potential availability of UKBA support is to be disregarded because, by virtue of regulation 6(4) of the Asylum Support Regulations 2000, a person who is entitled to accommodation under NAA 1948 s21 is not entitled to asylum support because he is not destitute.[48]

21.36   Since the 2002 *Westminster* case the courts have been asked to consider what illness or level of infirmity would satisfy the destitution plus test. Accordingly in *R (M) v Slough BC*[49] the Court of Appeal held that an HIV positive asylum seeker had to be accommodated by the authority: that he satisfied the 'destitution plus' test even though he was not suffering symptoms and his condition was stable. However, that decision was reversed in the House of Lords, which held that the 'need for care and attention' in section 21(1)(a) of the 1948 Act, while not limited to a need for nursing or personal care, required that a person needed 'looking after', and that a person whose only needs were for medication (which was provided by the NHS), a refrigerator in which to store it and regular appointments with a doctor could not be said to need 'looking after'.[50] The fact that M's condition may deteriorate in the future did not mean that he presently had a need for care and attention.[51] Accordingly, the House did not find it necessary (or indeed possible) to consider whether M's need for care and attention arose 'solely' from his destitution.

---

45   The only exception being EEA nationals or persons who already have refugee status in another EEA state.

46   [2008] UKHL 52, [2008] 1 WLR 1808.

47   Consolidated appeals as *R v Wandsworth LBC ex p O and R v Leicester City Council ex p Bhikha* [2000] 1 WLR 2539, (2000) 3 CCLR 237.

48   *Westminster City Council v NASS* [2002] UKHL 38, [2002] 1 WLR 2956, (2002) 5 CCLR 511; but note the discussion at paras 21.60–21.62 below of the position of families where some but not all members of the family would qualify for community care provision under NAA 1948 s21.

49   [2006] EWCA Civ 655, (2006) 9 CCLR 438.

50   *R (M) v Slough BC* [2008] UKHL 52, [2008] 1 WLR 1808; see para 7.13 above.

51   Baroness Hale at [35]–[36]; Lord Neuberger at [55] and [65].

21.37   'Destitution plus' status may also arise through mental health difficulties.[52] In *R (PB) v Haringey LBC*[53] the court considered that if the applicant's depression arose from factors other than just destitution,[54] it cannot be said that destitution and its physical effects are the sole cause. In *R (Pajaziti) v LB Lewisham*,[55] the claimants' mental health problems made their need for 'shelter and warmth' more acute, and accordingly it did not arise *solely* from their destitution.[56]

21.38   UKBA's Asylum Support Policy Bulletin on 'Asylum Seekers with Care Needs'[57] advises that in 'clear and urgent cases',[58] Immigration Officers or UKBA screening officers should refer asylum applicants with care needs directly to the local authority; in all other cases, applicants should first be dispersed and any community care assessments (CCA) carried out in the dispersal area.[59] The policy suggests that where a CCA has been commenced in emergency accommodation or an induction centre but not completed, the assumption should be that the asylum seeker will be dispersed and a new CCA commenced by the new local authority. UKBA will not therefore ordinarily accept the fact that there is a CCA in progress as a 'reasonable excuse' for failing to travel to the dispersal accommodation.[60]

Exclusion from community care services under NIAA 2002

21.39   Before considering the position of former asylum seekers and other migrants, it is necessary to refer to the provisions of the NIAA 2002 which exclude certain categories of migrant from community care services. The NIAA 2002 was a response, in part, to the perceived failure of the IAA 1999 to deter sufficient numbers of unlawful immigrants and asylum seekers from entering the UK. In addition it sought to deal with what the government termed 'entitlement shopping' – namely 'individuals who move to the UK for the sole or main purpose of accessing residential

---

52   Where entitlement to Mental Health Act (MHA) 1983 s117 support exists, there is no prohibition in the provision of such community care support.
53   [2006] EWHC 2255 (Admin), (2007) 10 CCLR 99 at [49]–[50].
54   PB's anxieties were largely attributable to her fragile mental health and her concern about her children who were subject to care proceedings.
55   [2007] EWCA Civ 1351.
56   Although as noted above (footnote 41), it is doubtful whether the authority's concession that a need for 'shelter and warmth' was a need for 'care and attention' within section 21(1)(a) would be made following *R (M) v Slough BC*.
57   UKBA (2009) *Policy Bulletin 82, Version 3.0*, as amended 18 September 2009.
58   Defined as cases where 'an asylum seeker's need for care and attention is immediately obvious . . . , and they have an urgent need for services' (para 8.1).
59   Paras 3.4–3.5; see also 6.2 and section 8. This guidance applies to single adults only; see para 21.60 below for the policy in relation to families with children. In relation to families with adult dependents but no children, the policy expresses an expectation that the local authority will support close relatives as well as the person with care needs, although they are not under a duty to do so, and indicates that otherwise UKBA will seek to accommodate the dependent adults as close as possible to the person with care needs (paras 9.1–9.3).
60   Paras 6.3–6.4.

accommodation and other services in preference to similar services in the EEA[61] country of origin'.[62]

21.40   The NIAA 2002 does not change the law concerning social services responsibilities to asylum seekers (whose claims have not been determined), although (as discussed above) section 55 did materially change the obligations of the UKBA to asylum seekers who failed to make their asylum claim 'as soon as reasonably practicable' after their arrival in the UK.[63] It did, however, significantly alter the position in respect of former asylum seekers and a number of other categories of migrant.

21.41   NIAA 2002 s54 and Sch 3 prohibit local authorities from providing community care services in general, services under Children Act (CA) 1989 s17 (except for minors) and services under Local Government Act (LGA) 2000 s2 for:

- individuals with refugee status in other EEA countries;
- citizens of other EEA countries;
- former asylum seekers who have not co-operated with removal directions;[64] and
- individuals who are unlawfully in the UK and who are not asylum seekers.[65]

21.42   As noted above, these exclusions do not apply to *current* asylum seekers (save where they are EEA nationals or have refugee status in another EEA state), and nor do they exclude entitlement to care under MHA 1983 s117.

The rights-based exemption

21.43   As with NIAA 2002 s55 (para 21.16 above), there is a human rights exemption, ie the prohibition does not apply where support is necessary to prevent a breach of a person's ECHR rights and also an exception where the provision of support is necessary to prevent a breach of a person's EU Treaty rights.

21.44   As noted above, the jurisprudence on the human rights exemption to section 55 will be relevant to the equivalent exemption under Schedule 3. However, in section 55 cases it will be assumed that applicants cannot avoid being exposed to inhuman and degrading treatment by leaving the

---

61   European Economic Area – this consists of the EU countries together with Iceland, Liechtenstein, Norway and Switzerland.

62   Department of Health (2003) *Section 54 of the Nationality, Immigration and Asylum Act 2002 and community care and other social services for adults from the EEA living in the UK: Note of Clarification* para 4, accessible at www.dh.gov.uk/prod_consum_dh/idcplg?IdcService=GET_FILE&dID=4171&Rendition=Web

63   NIAA 2002 s55.

64   Note that where there are dependent children who were supported with the main applicant before his application for asylum was refused, the asylum seeker continues to be eligible for section 95 support while he remains in UK, and will only be covered by Schedule 3 if the secretary of state certifies that he has failed to take reasonable steps to leave the UK.

65   The exclusions also apply to people who are dependents of the above, unless they are British citizens or children.

UK because by definition they will have an extant (first) asylum claim. Community care support may, however, also be necessary to avoid a breach of individuals' Convention rights either (a) pending their departure from the UK if they are taking reasonable steps to leave or (b) where it would be unreasonable to expect the person to leave the UK in order to avoid being exposed to the degrading treatment which is likely to follow from any extended period of destitution and street homelessness, following *Limbuela* and *MSS*.[66] The additional issue that arises in respect of exclusion from community care services under Schedule 3 is thus whether it is possible or reasonable to expect the applicant to immediately leave the UK, and the extent to which the local authority should investigate that issue for itself.

21.45   In the case of former asylum seekers who have made a 'fresh asylum claim' (ie further representations to UKBA that their removal would breach the Refugee Convention or Article 3 ECHR), then support should be regarded as necessary to prevent a breach of their Convention rights pending consideration of that claim by UKBA. The local authority should not attempt to assess the fresh asylum claim for itself, although it may refuse to provide community care services if the representations were merely repetitious or manifestly unfounded.[67]

21.46   Although some earlier cases had adopted a more conservative approach where a claim to remain in the UK was founded on Article 8[68] grounds,[69] the correct approach is now set out in the decision of the Court of Appeal in *R (Clue) v Birmingham City Council*,[70] which was concerned with the availability of accommodation and services under CA 1989 s17 to an overstayer and her children who would otherwise have been on the street. Dyson LJ held that the local authority had to consider a series of questions:

1) First, it must consider whether the person concerned is excluded from support by NIAA 2002, Sch 3, save to the extent that it is necessary to prevent a breach of his Convention rights.[71]

2) Next, it must consider whether the person has available to them any other source of accommodation and support, so that withholding assistance would not in any event result in a breach of Convention rights.[72]

3) Third, and only if the answer to the second question is that the person would otherwise be destitute, it must consider whether there is 'an

---

66   See paras 21.17 and 21.20 above.
67   *R (AW) v Croydon* [2005] EWHC 2950 (Admin); this part of the judgment of Lloyd Jones J was not appealed to the Court of Appeal.
68   Article 8 protects the right to respect for private and family life and has been interpreted as entitling a person to resist removal from the UK where that would result in a substantial interference with his family life with one or more persons with a right to remain in the UK, or where he has established a 'private' life through a long period of residence, particularly if he came to the UK as a child.
69   See *R (Grant) v Lambeth LBC* [2004] EWCA Civ 1711, [2005] 1 WLR 1781 and *R (Kimani) v Lambeth LBC* [2003] EWCA Civ 1150, [2004] 1 WLR 272, both of which were distinguished and not overruled by *Clue*.
70   [2010] EWCA Civ 460, [2011] 1 WLR 99, (2010) 13 CCLR 276.
71   Judgment at [54].
72   Judgment at [54]–[55].

impediment' to the person returning to his country of origin.[73] If the impediment is 'practical in nature', such as an inability to pay for flights, the local authority might legitimately arrange transport: *R (Grant) v Lambeth LBC*.[74]

4) If, however, there is a 'legal impediment' to return, in the form of a claim that return would itself breach Convention rights, the local authority must first consider whether the person has made an application to UKBA for leave to remain which 'expressly or implicitly raises grounds under the Convention'.[75] If so, and if support is otherwise necessary to prevent a breach of Convention rights, the local authority may only refuse to provide support if the application is 'not "obviously hopeless or abusive"' which would include applicants which are 'merely a repetition of an application which has already been rejected'.[76] It may not have regard to its financial resources.[77] It is the responsibility of the UKBA to decide applications for leave to remain in the UK and local authorities are not permitted to usurp that responsibility by making it impossible for the person concerned to remain in the UK.[78] UKBA accepted it should prioritise consideration of applications for leave to remain from families who were being supported by local authorities.[79]

5) If no application has in fact been made to the UKBA, or none is pending, then the local authority must consider for itself whether the applicant's circumstances engage the ECHR and, in an Article 8 case, is 'entitled to have regard to the calls of others on its budget in deciding whether an interference with a person's Article 8 rights would be justified and proportionate within the meaning of Article 8.2'.[80]

21.47 This approach was applied to a claim under NAA 1948 s21 in *R (Mwanza) v Greenwich LBC and Bromley LBC*,[81] Hickinbottom J considered it to be 'well-settled' law that where an immigration application was outstanding, 'claims for section 21 support should only be dismissed if such an immigration claim is manifestly unfounded or not "obviously hopeless or abusive"'.[82] In the case before him he held that the claimant had not established that he had any pending application for leave to remain and that any potential Article 8 claim (none having in fact been advanced) was 'unarguable', so that the local authority was prohibited by section 54 and Schedule 3 from providing support to the claimant and his family.

21.48 In a case in which there is no practical or legal impediment to the applicant returning to their country of origin to avoid a breach of their ECHR rights, support will not be 'necessary to prevent a breach of a person's

73 Judgment at [55].
74 [2005] 1 WLR 1781; *Clue* at [56].
75 Judgment at [53] and [60].
76 Judgment at [66].
77 Judgment at [72].
78 Judgment at [63]–[66].
79 Judgment at [84].
80 Judgment at [73].
81 [2010] EWHC 1462 (Admin).
82 Para [47].

rights'. In *R (Kimani) v Lambeth LBC*,[83] the Court of Appeal rejected Ms Kimani's case that as she would not return to her own country, Kenya, the refusal of the local authority to provide accommodation and support for her and her 10-year-old son would inevitably lead to breaches of their rights under Articles 3 and 8 ECHR (because of the likelihood that if she was homeless, her son would be taken into care). The Court of Appeal held that any interference in their rights would not be the result of the refusal of support, but rather of her unreasonable refusal to leave the UK.[84]

The Withholding and Withdrawal of Support (Travel Assistance and Temporary Accommodation) Regulations 2002

21.49   As well as the rights-based exemptions, paragraphs 8–10 of NIAA 2002 Sch 3 and the Withholding and Withdrawal of Support (Travel Assistance and Temporary Accommodation Regulations (WWS Regs) 2002[85] create very limited powers for local authorities to:

- make travel arrangements for people who are excluded because they are EEA nationals or EEA refugees, to enable them to leave the UK;[86]
- provide accommodation for such people pending their departure from the UK;[87]
- provide accommodation for people who are excluded because they are in breach of immigration law, but who have not failed to comply with removal directions.[88]

Accommodation can only be provided in either case if the person has a dependent child.[89]

21.50   Local authorities are required to comply with guidance issued by the Secretary of State for the Home Department[90] in providing support and making travel arrangements under these provisions. In *R (M) v Islington LBC*,[91] the Court of Appeal considered the impact of that guidance[92] in a case involving a mother who was ineligible for CA 1989 services because she was unlawfully present in the UK, having stayed beyond the expiry of her visa. The guidance stated that it would be 'preferable' for accommodation to be provided only for 10 days in such a case. The Court of Appeal

---

83   [2003] EWCA Civ 1150, [2004] 1 WLR 272.
84   Note that in *Clue*, the court distinguished *Kimani* on the grounds that Ms Kimani's appeal against the refusal of an EEA residence card could be pursued from Kenya, whereas Ms Clue's application for leave to remain on Article 8 grounds would in all probability be treated as having lapsed if she left the UK.
85   SI No 3078.
86   Para 8 of Sch 3.
87   Para 9 of Sch 3.
88   Para 10 of Sch 3.
89   Para 9(2) and 10(2) of Sch 3.
90   WWS Regulations (2002), reg 4 (4).
91   [2004] EWCA Civ 235.
92   The guidance at that time being Home Office (2002) *Guidance to assist authorities to determine whether to make travel arrangements/grant temporary short-term accommodation*.

held that the local authority was entitled – and indeed, on the facts of the case, bound – to provide accommodation for longer than ten days in circumstances where the UKBA had not yet issued directions for M's removal from the UK. It was unreasonable to withdraw accommodation because M had not been removed from the UK after ten days, when that was a matter entirely outside the control of both M and the local authority.

Former asylum seekers

21.51   Asylum seekers whose applications for asylum have been refused and finally determined (ie appeal rights exhausted) are expected to leave the UK. However, there are some former asylum seekers who are destitute and unable to leave the UK immediately due to circumstances beyond their control. In such cases they can be provided with support under IAA 1999 s4(2).[93] Section 4 support (previously commonly known as 'hard case support') was intended as a limited and temporary form of support for people who are expected to leave the UK within a short period of time. Many former asylum seekers, however, find themselves supported under section 4 for indefinite periods.

21.52   In order to obtain support, the applicant must show that he or she is destitute. The definition of destitution for section 4 purposes is the same as in IAA 1999 s95(3) (see para 21.14 above). It can be particularly difficult to demonstrate destitution to the satisfaction of UKBA if a former asylum seeker has been without UKBA support for any significant period and a very detailed account will be required of how the applicant has maintained him or herself and any dependents in that period, and why he or she cannot continue to do so.[94]

21.53   Former asylum seekers requesting support under section 4 must also meet the eligibility criteria in the relevant regulations.[95] Broadly speaking, these limit support to situations where it would not be reasonable to expect the former asylum seeker to immediately leave the UK. They include cases where the person is taking reasonable steps to leave the UK but cannot do so immediately, such as where travel documentation needs to be obtained,[96] where there is a medical impediment to travel,[97] and a

93   As amended by NIAA 2002 s49.
94   For a critique of the application of this test by UKBA to applications under section 4, see Asylum Support Appeals Project, *No credibility: UKBA decision making and section 4 support*, 26 April 2011.
95   Immigration and Asylum (Provision of Accommodation to Failed Asylum Seekers) Regulations 2005 SI No 930 reg 3.
96   Reg 3(2)(a); current UKBA policy severely limits the time for which support will ordinarily be provided in these cases notwithstanding that it can in some cases take months or years to obtain travel documentation.
97   Reg 3(2)(b); note that this is very limited in its application and will only apply where a person is physically *unable* to travel. It also applies to pregnant women in the late stages of pregnancy and those with new-born children – UKBA policy is currently not to normally grant support until six weeks before the estimated date of delivery (EDD) and to withdraw it once the baby is six weeks old. However, the First-Tier Tribunal (Asylum Support) has upheld appeals on grounds of pregnancy earlier than six weeks before the EDD.

catch-all provision allowing support to be provided where there would otherwise be a breach of the person's ECHR rights.[98] This latter provision most commonly arises where the former asylum seeker has made a fresh claim for asylum which is still under consideration by UKBA, but in light of *Limbuela*,[99] it would cover any situation where it would be unreasonable to expect the applicant to leave the UK to avoid the breach of his or her Article 3 rights which would arise if he or she were left destitute and street homeless for any significant period.

21.54   Section 4 support is circumscribed by the statutory term 'facilities for the accommodation of a person'. What can be provided under section 4 must be linked to the accommodation being provided. There is thus no provision within the relevant regulations for support to be provided as cash,[100] and it is ordinarily provided by way of accommodation and a payment card pre-loaded each week.[101] This inevitably causes problems, in particular in terms of clothing, telephone calls and travel.[102]

21.55   The Immigration, Asylum and Nationality Act 2006 s43 alleviated the situation somewhat by amending IAA 1999 s4 to allow the Secretary of State for the Home Department to make regulations allowing for the provision of facilities and services. These are the Immigration and Asylum (Provision of Services or Facilities) Regulations 2007,[103] and they allow for additional support to be provided to pay for travel for necessary healthcare treatment or to register a birth,[104] birth certificates,[105] telephone calls and correspondence for limited purposes,[106] additional support for pregnant women and young children[107] and other exceptional specific needs.[108] It is of course possible, in the case of a former asylum seeker with a child, for a request to be made to the local authority for an assessment and services under CA 1989 s17 (see para 23.12 below)[109] for items that section 4 cannot provide.

98   Reg 3(2)(e). The other two classes are where the secretary of state has declared that there is no viable route of return to a given country (Reg 3(2)(c)) – in practice extremely unlikely – and where the applicant has been granted permission to apply for judicial review (Reg 3(2)(d)). In *R (NS) Somalia v First Tier Tribunal (Social Entitlement Chamber)* [2009] EWHC 3819 (Admin), the Administrative Court held that a person who was claiming judicial review but did not yet have permission was likely to qualify for support under Reg 3(2)(e).

99   [2005] UKHL 66, [2005] 3 WLR 1014, (2006) 9 CCLR 30; see paras 21.17 above.

100   Immigration and Asylum (Provision of Accommodation to Failed Asylum Seekers) Regulations 2005 SI No 930.

101   At the time of writing, the weekly rate of support was £35.39 per person. For single adults, any amount over £5 could not be carried over to the following week. As at 10 February 2011, the shops in which the payment card could be used were Tesco, Asda, Boots, Peacocks, Sainsbury's, the Co-operative and Morrisons; see www.ukba.homeoffice.gov.uk/sitecontent/documents/asylum/vouchers.pdf

102   See *R (AW (Kenya)) v Secretary of State for the Home Department* [2006] EWHC 3147 (Admin).

103   SI No 3627.

104   SI No 3627 reg3.

105   SI No 3627 reg 4.

106   SI No 3627 reg 5.

107   SI No 3627 regs 6–8.

108   SI No 3627 reg 9.

109   NIAA 2002 Sch 3 does not prevent services being provided to a child.

21.56   One of the most problematic issues which the limitation of IAA 1999, s4 support to 'facilities for accommodation' creates is that, given the impermissibility of providing support to meet essential living needs without also providing accommodation, families where some family members are not eligible for section 4 support (for example, because they are British or otherwise have permission to reside in the UK) may not be accommodated together. In *R (MK and Others) v Secretary of State for the Home Department*,[110] the Court of Appeal affirmed that the Secretary of State for the Home Department was not entitled under section 4 to provide subsistence support without also taking some responsibility for the provision of accommodation, and was accordingly entitled to have a general policy of only providing support under target contracts: section 4 is not a provision aimed at alleviating destitution, but at providing accommodation to those who are unable to leave the UK. However, the Court of Appeal did not rule out that Article 8 might, in some circumstances, require the provision of accommodation for a family together.

Community care provision

21.57   As with asylum seekers, former asylum seekers who satisfy the 'destitution plus' test are the responsibility of local authority social services departments under NAA 1948 s21, subject to NIAA 2002 Sch 3. In *R (AW) v Croydon LBC*[111] the Court of Appeal held that vulnerable former asylum seekers whose human rights call for accommodation are to have that accommodation provided by local authorities, and not by UKBA.[112] Laws LJ observed that there was 'nothing to show that the legislature intended to distribute responsibility for the support of failed asylum-seekers between central and local government in a radically different manner from the arrangements which ... were made in relation to asylum seekers'.[113] For social care purposes the law divides former asylum seekers into two distinct categories.

21.58   The first category is comprised of those asylum seekers who claimed asylum as soon as they arrived in the UK ('at port'). They will normally have been granted temporary admission to enter the UK which means they are in the UK lawfully.[114] As they are lawfully present, they remain entitled to local authority support until such time as formal steps to remove them from the UK are not complied with. If a former asylum seeker fails to comply with removal directions (by which in this context we mean directions given to a carrier such as a ship or aeroplane) at any time, they are excluded from community care services by virtue of NIAA 2002 Sch 3.[115]

---

110 [2011] EWCA Civ 671.
111 [2007] EWCA Civ 266, [2007] 1 WLR 3168, (2007) 10 CCLR 225.
112 Since the definition of 'destitution' for IAA 1999 s4 purposes is the same as that under IAA 1999 s95, which, as discussed above, requires the UKBA to take account of any other support which is, or might reasonably be expected to be, available. A person who is entitled to community care is thus unlikely to be destitute.
113 [2007] EWCA Civ 266, [2007] 1 WLR 3168, (2007) 10 CCLR 225 at [54].
114 NIAA 2002 s11 and British Nationality Act (BNA) 1981 s50A(6).
115 Subject to the human rights exemption discussed below.

21.59   Former asylum seekers who did not claim at port are in the UK in breach of immigration law. They are excluded by NIAA 2002 Sch 3 and can only receive community care assistance if support is necessary to avoid a breach of their Convention rights. In consequence, former asylum seekers who claimed asylum 'at port' ordinarily remain eligible for section 21 accommodation even after their claim for asylum has been refused, whereas those who did not claim 'at port' cease to be eligible for section 21 accommodation once their claims for asylum have been finally determined, unless support is required to prevent a breach of their Convention rights.[116]

Duties owed to children[117]

Children of asylum seekers

21.60   As noted above, IAA 1999 s95 empowers the secretary of state (through the UKBA) to provide support for adult asylum seekers who are destitute or likely to become destitute. However, by IAA 1999 s122, there is a duty on UKBA to support destitute asylum seekers with dependent children, and, in particular, under section 122(3), to make available 'adequate accommodation for the child'. In *R (A) v NASS and Waltham Forest LBC*[118] the court held that the accommodation of asylum seeking families with disabled children was the sole responsibility of NASS (now the UKBA), although in discharging this duty it could seek assistance from a local authority under IAA 1999 s100 (and in such cases the authority must assist so far as is 'reasonable in the circumstances').

21.61   UKBA's policy is to refer families with children with a clear care need to the local authority for an assessment to be carried out and any necessary services to be provided in addition to UKBA support.[119] The policy also makes clear that accommodation provided by UKBA to a family which includes a child with care needs must be 'adequate' for the needs of that child, and that the duty to ensure the accommodation is adequate is a

---

116   For an example of a case where the provision of section 21 accommodation was held not to be necessary to prevent a breach of the claimant's human rights because he could return to his own country, his appeal against removal on Article 3 grounds having been dismissed by the Asylum and Immigration Tribunal, see *R (N) v Coventry City Council* [2008] EWHC 2786 (Admin). Note that in that case the local authority had offered to 'assist the claimant in directing him to free air services to his country of origin and to accommodate him to a period of 14 days . . . whilst arrangements are made' (at [51]).

117   For a more detailed consideration of the entitlement of migrant children and their families to services under Children Act 1989 Part III, see I Wise, S Broach, C Gallagher, A Pickup, B Silverstone and A Suterwalla, *Children in Need: local authority support for children and families*, Legal Action Group, 2011, chapter 6.

118   [2003] EWCA Civ 1473, [2004] 1 WLR 752, (2003) 6 CCLR 538 – see also *R (O) v Haringey LBC* [2003] EWHC 2798 (Admin) where it was held that the NASS had responsibility even where there were disabled adult family members.

119   Policy Bulletin 82, para 9.4.

continuing one.[120] However, in assessing whether accommodation is adequate, UKBA is entitled to take account of the length of time for which the family is likely to be in the accommodation (the assumption being that it will be short-term given the aim of resolving asylum claims quickly), and of the availability of accommodation in different areas. The fact that a dependent child has a care need will not normally be regarded as a reason not to disperse a family providing those needs can be met in the dispersal area.[121]

21.62   In *R (O) v Haringey LBC and Secretary of State for the Home Department*[122] the facts were reversed in that it was the mother who was disabled, not the children. In that case the Court of Appeal held that the local authority owed the mother a duty under NAA 1948 s21, but this did not extend to accommodating her children, for whom NASS was responsible under IAA 1999 s122(5).[123] On a practical level the court suggested that the local authority should accommodate the whole family, with NASS making a financial contribution to cover the cost of accommodating the children.[124] This suggestion is reflected in UKBA's policy guidance, which states that UKBA will contribute 'the full subsistence rate for a child of that age and a contribution towards accommodation costs', but not any additional costs which arise from the adult's care needs.[125]

Children of former asylum seekers

21.63   IAA 1999 s122 only applies to asylum seekers. The case of former asylum seekers is materially different since there is no free-standing obligation or power enabling UKBA to accommodate or fund the child of a former asylum seeker. However, where the family included a dependent child under the age of 18 before the asylum claim was finally determined, they do not cease to be 'asylum seekers' for support purposes until the child turns 18 or both the parent and child leave the UK.[126]

21.64   Where the local authority is supporting an adult former asylum seeker under NAA 1948 s21 it also falls to the local authority to support the children under CA 1989 s17. This is because a person who has ceased to be an asylum seeker is not entitled to be considered for support under IAA 1999 s95 and therefore the provisions under section 122 do not apply. The power to accommodate dependents of a former asylum seeker is found in section 4(2) and only exists where there is a power to accommodate the adult former asylum seeker. Unlike with asylum seekers, the local social services authority in this situation is not precluded from

---

120   Policy Bulletin 82, paras 9.2, 9.4–9.6.
121   Policy Bulletin 82, paras 9.3, 9.7.
122   [2004] EWCA Civ 535, (2004) 7 CCLR 310.
123   They are to be treated as 'destitute' by virtue of Asylum Support Regulations 2000 regs 6 and 12 even though living with their mother.
124   These authorities are reflected in the guidance in UKBA Policy Bulletin 82 (paras 3.7–3.9).
125   Policy Bulletin 82, paras 10.1–10.5.
126   IAA 1999 s94(5).

providing support under CA 1989 s17 (subject to the provisions of NIAA 2002 s 54 and Sch 3).

21.65   In *R (VC) v Newcastle City Council*, heard in April 2011, the Divisional Court was asked to consider whether a family with children who may have been eligible for support under IAA 1999 s4 were primarily the responsibility of UKBA or of the local authority. In the case in question, the local authority had been supporting the family under section 17, but terminated that support on the basis that the family could apply to UKBA for section 4 support. At the time of writing, the judgment was not yet available.

Unaccompanied asylum seeking children

21.66   The UKBA defines an unaccompanied asylum seeking child as:

> ... an individual who is under 18 and applying for asylum in his/her own right; and is separated from both parents and not being cared for by an adult who by law or custom has responsibility to do so.[127]

21.67   CA 1989 s 20(1) provides that the local authority shall:

> ... provide accommodation for a child in need who requires it as a result of there being no-one with parental responsibility for him; being lost or abandoned or the person caring for him has been prevented (whether or not permanently and for whatever reason) from providing him with suitable accommodation or care.

21.68   The duty of the local authority under section 20 applies in relation to a child in need 'within their area' (see para 6.54 above). The duty of accommodating and supporting unaccompanied asylum seeking children therefore falls to the local authority within whose area the child is residing or has just arrived.

21.69   If the local authority disputes the claimed age of the applicant, it has the power to conduct a detailed age assessment.[128] Following the judgment of the Supreme Court in *R (A) v Croydon*,[129] if there is any dispute about the age of the applicant following the local authority's assessment, the matter will be determined as a question of precedent fact by the court on an application for judicial review. In *R (FZ) v Croydon*,[130] the Court of Appeal indicated that all such judicial review claims should be transferred to the Upper Tribunal (Immigration and Asylum Chamber) under Senior Courts Act 1981 s31A(3).[131]

21.70   Just as in the case of any other person leaving care, when a UASC turns 18, the local authority may owe them obligations as a former rele-

127 *Planning better outcomes and support for unaccompanied asylum seeking children*, IND Consultation Paper, February 2007.
128 *B v Merton LBC* [2003] EWHC 1689 (Admin), [2003] 4 All ER 280, (2003) 6 CCLR 457.
129 [2009] UKSC 8, [2009] 1 WLR 2557.
130 [2011] EWCA Civ 59, [2011] HLR 22.
131 Inserted by Tribunals, Courts and Enforcement Act 2007 s19. For a more detailed discussion of the age assessment process and challenges to it following *R (A) v Croydon*, see I Wise, S Broach, C Gallagher, A Pickup, B Silverstone and A Suterwalla, *Children in Need: local authority support for children and families*, Legal Action Group, 2011, chapter 3.

vant child if they have accrued sufficient looked after time (see para 23.26 below). If the young person has been granted leave to remain, their position is likely to be identical to that of any other young person.[132] As for those who are still asylum seekers or are former asylum seekers, in *R (SO) v Barking and Dagenham LBC*,[133] the Court of Appeal held that in deciding whether to provide accommodation to a care leaver who is a former relevant child under CA 1989 s23C(4)(c), the local authority is not entitled to take account of the availability of UKBA support. Thus responsibility for the accommodation and subsistence of former relevant children remains with the local authority.[134]

EEA nationals

21.71 The EEA consists of 30 countries, made up of the EU states together with Norway, Iceland and Liechtenstein.[135]

21.72 Under the Treaty of Rome 1959 (and subsequent treaties and legislation) citizens of these states enjoy various rights of free movement within the territory of the EEA. These rights are set out in various European directives and regulations.[136]

21.73 Free movement benefits not only citizens of the member states but also certain of their family members (whatever the nationality of the family member) and confers rights of residence and various associated rights and entitlements (eg to social assistance and benefits entitlements). These rights vary, however, according to the nationality and economic status of the citizen in question. The most extensive rights are enjoyed by nationals of the 18 states who were members of the EEA prior to 1 May 2004 (the so-called pre-enlargement states) as well as nationals of Cyprus and Malta.[137] Until 30 April 2011, more limited rights were in general enjoyed by nationals of eight of the countries that joined the EU on 1 May 2004 (the so-called A8 countries[138]), although those restrictions were removed with

---

132 Provided that the grant of leave to remain is still current, it will ordinarily carry no restriction on recourse to public funds. If it has expired but an application for further leave to remain was made before expiry, and that application or any appeal is still pending, Immigration Act 1971 s3C means that leave is statutorily extended with the same conditions.

133 [2010] EWCA Civ 1101, [2011] HLR 4.

134 This judgment changes the position as set out in the previous edition of this work and reflected in the UKBA Asylum Support Policy Bulletin 29 'Transition at Age 18', which suggests that in the case of asylum seekers, such young people will remain in local authority accommodation, but that the costs of their accommodation and subsistence will be met by UKBA.

135 The full list of EEA states is Austria, Belgium, Denmark, Finland, France, Germany, Greece, Holland, Ireland, Italy, Luxembourg, Portugal, Spain, Sweden, the UK, Norway, Iceland, Liechtenstein, Cyprus, Malta, Czech Republic, Estonia, Hungary, Latvia, Lithuania, Poland, Slovakia, Slovenia, Bulgaria and Romania.

136 Of which the most important are EC/1612/68 and EC/2004/38.

137 Rights of free movement also apply to citizens of Switzerland.

138 Czech Republic, Estonia, Hungary, Latvia, Lithuania, Poland, Slovakia and Slovenia.

effect from 1 May 2011, and nationals of the A8 countries now have full free movement rights.[139]

21.74   Restrictions continue to apply to nationals of the two countries that joined on 1 January 2007 (Romania and Bulgaria, known as the A2 countries). The restrictions affect access to the labour market for nationals of these countries and have consequential limitations on their access to social assistance (welfare benefits and housing assistance). The restrictions have always been far more extensive for A2 nationals than for A8 nationals.

EEA nationals other than A2 nationals[140]

21.75   The key concept in EEA law for the purposes of this text is that of the 'qualified person' as defined in the Immigration (European Economic Area) Regulations 2006.[141] An EEA national (other than an A2 national) is qualified if he or she is:

- a worker;[142]
- a work seeker;
- a self-employed person or a service provider;
- a student;
- economically self-sufficient.

21.76   A qualified EEA national has an entitlement to reside in the UK 'without the requirement for leave to remain under the Immigration Act 1971 for as long as he remains a qualified person'.[143] Such persons are said to enjoy 'full free movement rights' and have unrestricted access to the UK labour market.

21.77   Qualified EEA nationals are not excluded from social welfare assistance (housing and welfare benefits) under IAA 1999 s115 and thus should

139 The Accession (Immigration and Worker Registration) (Revocation, Savings and Consequential Provisions) Regulations 2011 SI No 544.

140 Note that prior to 1 May 2011, A8 nationals also had more limited rights; their position prior to that date is not considered further here and readers are referred to earlier editions of this work, or to S Wilman and S Knafler, *Support for Asylum Seekers and Other Migrants*, Legal Action Group, 2009, chapter 2.

141 SI No 1003.

142 This definition includes workers temporarily unfit for work through illness or accident or pregnancy and childbirth.

143 *Barnet LBC v Ismail and Abdi* [2006] EWCA Civ 383, [2006] 1 WLR 2771 clarified that an EEA national who is not a qualified person does not have a right to reside and is subject to immigration control. However, note that certain persons have a right to reside as a matter of EU law even though they are not qualified persons within the terms of the Regulations; this includes so-called *Chen* parents (the parents of EU citizen children who are resident in an EU state) and parents or carers of the children of former qualified persons who are in education (under Article 12 of Regulation 1612/68 EEC) – see *Teixeira v Lambeth LBC* (C-480/08) [2010] HLR 32 and *Ibrahim v Harrow LBC* (C-310/08) [2010] HLR 31. The domestic courts have rejected any suggestion that the Treaty on the Functioning of the European Union (TFEU) creates any wider right of residence for a non-economically active EU national who is not self-sufficient – *Abdirahman v Secretary of State for Works and Pensions* [2007] EWCA Civ 657, [2008] 1 WLR 254; *Kaczmarek v Secretary of State for Work and Pensions* [2008] EWCA Civ 1310, [2009] PTSR 897.

not normally need to access community care provisions. However, EEA nationals who are not qualified have no access to social assistance provisions (with the exception of contributory benefits). The consequence is that on facing destitution, these EEA nationals frequently turn to the local social services authority for assistance. However, EEA nationals are excluded from most community care provision under NIAA 2002 s54 and Sch 3.[144]

21.78   As previously noted, the prohibition in NIAA 2002 s54 against social services providing care services does not apply where a failure to provide assistance would constitute a breach of the person's Convention rights. This applies equally where failure to provide services would breach a person's rights under an EU Treaty. The Department of Health considers that the EU exception will mean that:

> EEA nationals who work or have worked in the UK, their families, self-employed and former self-employed EEA nationals, and students should be provided with social care services by councils if they are eligible for such care in order to protect their freedom of movement. They are entitled on the same basis as UK nationals.[145]

A2 nationals

21.79   Nationals of the 'A2' countries (Bulgaria and Romania) are subject to the Worker Authorisation Scheme which came into effect on 1 January 2007. The restrictions imposed on A2 nationals under this scheme are more extensive than those which were imposed on A8 nationals under the Worker Registration Scheme prior to 1 May 2011.

21.80   In general A2 workers are required to obtain work authorisation from the Home Office before taking up employment.[146] A2 nationals are entitled to 'in-work benefits' during their 12-month period of authorised work and acquire full movement rights after 12 months' lawful employment. Note, however, that these restrictions only apply to 'workers' and not to self-employed persons, students or those who are self-sufficient.

21.81   A2 job seekers do not have a right to reside. They are thus excluded from most benefits, and like other EEA nationals they are also excluded from community care services by NIAA 2002 Sch 3, but will not be able to rely on their EU law rights to non-discrimination because they do not have a right to reside in the UK.

Domestic violence

21.82   A difficult situation can arise in relation to foreign spouses of British or settled persons where the foreign spouse has suffered domestic violence

---

144 Indeed this was, as noted above (para 21.39), one of the objects of the legislation.
145 *Note of clarification* (footnote 62 above) para 13.
146 The details of the scheme are involved and beyond the scope of this text, however, for further details, see *Immigration Nationality and Refugee Handbook*, JCWI, 2006.

and as a consequence needs social services support and accommodation. More commonly than not, the foreign spouse is the wife and she has fled before being granted indefinite leave to remain[147] or after her spousal visa has expired.[148]

21.83   Provided the foreign national spouse is in the UK on a spouse visa, she will have express permission to work but there will be a prohibition on recourse to public funds. When the violence causes the spouse to flee, she may turn to the local authority social services department for assistance. Frequently there are children, meaning that the wife's ability to work is impaired (not least that she will not be able to claim tax credits for her child care costs) or she may have been prevented from learning sufficient English to be able to communicate effectively enough to work.

21.84   A spouse in the UK on a visa is not precluded from support under community care provisions by NIAA 2002 Sch 3. Unfortunately, many women who have experienced domestic violence have also had their husbands refuse to put in an extension application, such that they are then in the UK unlawfully, having overstayed. 'Overstayers' are precluded from community care provisions unless support is required to prevent a breach of their Convention rights.

21.85   Where there are children who are dependent on the foreign spouse, she may turn to the local authority for support under CA 1989 s17. Children are not excluded from support by NIAA 2002 Sch 3, regardless of their immigration status and the local authority will have a duty to assess their needs under CA 1989 s17 and a power to provide services. Local authorities are able to accommodate the parent together with the children under section 17(6) but in practical terms unless there is some legitimate impediment to the parent and children leaving the UK together (such as, for example, that the children still have regular contact with their other parent), local authorities will often offer to accommodate the children only under CA 1989 s20. In *R (G) v Barnet LBC*,[149] the House of Lords held that local authorities were in general entitled to have a policy of not accommodating families together under section 17, but instead offering to accommodate the children if necessary under section 20, subject to assessment of the individual child's needs and Article 8 considerations.[150] There is thus in practice little distinction between the position of overstayers, who must show that support is necessary to prevent a breach of their ECHR rights, and those with leave to remain, where

---

147 A grant of indefinite leave to remain attracts full recourse to public funds.

148 Ordinarily, the spouse of a British citizen or a person with indefinite leave to remain in the UK will be granted an initial probationary period of two years' leave to remain; if the marriage is subsisting at the end of that period and the spouse can be maintained and accommodated without recourse to public funds, indefinite leave to remain will ordinarily be granted.

149 [2003] UKHL 57, [2004] 2 AC 208.

150 For more detailed consideration of this decision, its relationship with *Clue* and the power or duty of local authorities to provide accommodation under section 17(6) to families of children in need, see I Wise, S Broach, C Gallagher, A Pickup, B Silverstone and A Suterwalla, *Children in Need: local authority support for children and families*, Legal Action Group, 2011, paras 6.31–6.40.

the local authority has a wide discretion whether to provide support to the parents, likely be amenable to challenge in practice only where the refusal of support would breach the authority's obligations under HRA 1998 s6.

21.86 Where there are no children it is less likely that the foreign spouse will be able to access community care services as domestic violence itself does not satisfy the destitution plus test for services under NAA 1948 s21. The destitution is said to result from the domestic violence but the domestic violence is not a need for care and attention over and above destitution. In such a situation, in *R (Khan) v Oxfordshire CC*[151] it was decided that domestic violence was the cause of destitution only and the need for care and attention arose solely from the destitution. However, the court considered that in some circumstances, in addition to causing destitution, domestic violence could make the need for care and attention more acute. When faced with such a case, careful consideration should be given to establish whether there are any additional circumstances which create a section 21 need. Examples might include physical or mental injury caused by the domestic violence.

21.87 In late 2009, the Home Office established and funded a pilot project with Eaves Housing to provide accommodation and subsistence for women whose marriages had broken down during their initial two-year probationary period of their spousal visa, along with any dependent children.[152] Accommodation and subsistence is provided for an initial 20 working days to enable an application for indefinite leave to remain under the Home Office's domestic violence rule to be submitted and, providing the application is submitted within that period, a further 20 working days is provided during which time it is expected that UKBA will make a decision whether or not to grant ILR. At the time of writing, the government's intention was that this scheme would run until April 2012, at which point a more permanent solution would be introduced,[153] likely to involve the grant of a short period of leave to remain without any restriction on access to public funds to enable access to mainstream housing and benefits while an application for ILR is made and considered.[154]

---

151 [2004] EWCA Civ 309, (2004) 7 CCLR 215: see also para 1.69 above.
152 For details of the programme, known as the Sojourner Project, see www.eaveshousing.co.uk/
153 See Home Office announcement 'Victims of domestic violence without indefinite leave to remain' at www.homeoffice.gov.uk/crime/violence-against-women-girls/domestic-violence-rule/
154 See announcement (2011) 'Sojourner project long term solution' at www.welshwomensaid.org/news/35323.html.

CHAPTER 22

Drug, alcohol and HIV/AIDS services

Introduction

22.1   This chapter considers the community care responsibilities for people with HIV/AIDS and for those who misuse drugs and alcohol. The analysis takes the form of an overview, since the needs of these distinct groups are frequently addressed by specialist agencies or within the mainstream NHS.

22.2   We commence by reviewing the community care responsibilities for drug and alcohol misusers, and at para 22.44 below the obligations towards people with HIV/AIDS.

22.3   In the UK it is thought that over 3 million adults use an illicit drug each year of which in England, about 320,000 have a heroin and/or crack cocaine addiction. It is estimated that of the 1.6 million people in the UK with 'alcohol dependence' about a third of these face challenges similar to those dependent on drugs and need support to help them recover. The social and economic costs associated with drug misuse are thought to be in the region of £15.4 billion a year and the equivalent costs for alcohol in the region of £18–25 billion a year (of which the cost to the NHS alone is estimated at £2.7 billion a year).[1]

Drug and alcohol misuse policy framework

22.4   In 1998 the government published a strategy paper *Tackling drugs to build a better britain*[2] in order to co-ordinate its 'combating misuse' policies. The policy was revised in 2002 and in 2006 when the aim was to target those considered to have a serious drug problem, the 50 per cent who were not in treatment.

22.5   Although the strategy has not achieved its aim of doubling the number of people in treatment, the numbers have increased (from 125,000 people in 2003/04[3] to over 190,000 people in 2011[4]).The most recent English strategy (2010) retains the commitment to providing treatment, but additionally aims by 2014 'to break the cycle of dependence on drugs and alcohol' by (1) reducing demand; (2) restricting supply; and (3) building recovery in communities.

22.6   The service provision strategy in England is co-ordinated via the National Treatment Agency for Substance Misuse (NTA), a special health authority created in 2001[5] to improve the availability, capacity and effectiveness of treatment for drug misuse. The NTA issues policy and practice guidance and distributes funding (via its nine regional offices) to local drug partnerships, generally in the form of drug action and alcohol teams (referred to below as 'DATs') comprising representatives of the local

---

1   Home Office (2010) *Drug Strategy 2010* pp5–7.
2   Department of Health (1998) *Tackling drugs to build a better britain: the government's ten-year strategy for tackling drugs misuse,* Cm 3945.
3   Department of Health and Home Office (2006) *Models of care for treatment of adult drug misusers,* para 2.3.
4   National Treatment Agency for Substance Misuse (2011) statistics at www.nta.nhs.uk/facts.aspx.
5   National Treatment Agency (Establishment and Constitution) Order 2001 SI No 713.

agencies involved in tackling the misuse of drugs, including primary care trusts, the local authority, police, and probation. It is the responsibility of DATs to provide drug misusers with access to advice and information, needle exchanges, and counselling.

22.7   A number of similar alcohol misuse policy initiatives have occurred in parallel with these programmes, including the 2004 *Alcohol harm reduction strategy for England*[6] and the 2006 Department of Health guidance *Models of care for alcohol misusers* (hereafter referred to as the *Models of care (alcohol misuse)*).[7] These are considered further below.

Wales

22.8   The following sections provide an overview of substance misuse policies in England. It will be seen that there are two similar policy documents, one directed at alcohol misuse and the other at drug misuse, and both entitled 'Models of care'.[8] In Wales a combined policy document exists that closely mirrors these two documents (and which adopts similar terminology including the differing levels of assessment and tiers of service response). The guidance, *Substance misuse treatment framework for Wales*,[9] comprises five separate chapters, namely: (1) Service framework for residential rehabilitation; (2) Service framework for community prescribing; (3) Service framework for inpatient treatment; (4) Service framework to meet the needs of people with co-occurring substance misuse and mental health problems; and (5) Needle exchange service framework.

22.9   Given the similarity between the Welsh and English policy initiatives, the following analysis is limited to the English guidance.

Community care provision for drug and alcohol misusers

22.10   As detailed below (paras 22.34 and 22.37) persons who are alcoholic and/ or drug dependent are explicitly identified as being entitled to residential[10] and non-residential[11] community care services. The 1991 white paper *Health of the nation*[12] and the 1990 policy guidance[13] both confirmed that

6   Cabinet Office (2004) *Alcohol harm reduction strategy for England.*
7   Department of Health National Treatment Agency for Substance Misuse (2006) *Models of care for alcohol misusers.*
8   Department of Health National Treatment Agency for Substance Misuse (2006) *Models of care for alcohol misusers.*
9   Welsh Assembly Government (2004) *Substance misuse treatment framework for Wales.*
10   Under National Assistance Act 1948 s21 pursuant to direction 2(6) contained within LAC (93)10 appendix 1.
11   Under the NHS Act 2006 Sch 20/NHS (Wales) Act 2006 Sch 15 pursuant to direction 3(3)(g) contained within LAC (93)10 appendix 3. Although the Directions pre-date the NHS Acts 2006, by virtue of National Health Service (Consequential Provisions) Act 2006 s4 and Sch 2 para 1(2) they apply with equal effect to the consequent provisions in the NHS Acts 2006.
12   Department of Health (1991) *The health of the nation*, Cm 1523 – see eg paras D.17– D.18.
13   Department of Health (1990) *Community care in the next decade and beyond: policy guidance* – see para 1.51 above

an important objective of the community care reforms was to ensure that services were available to those whose need for them arose by reason of alcohol or drug misuse. The 1990 policy guidance (at para 8.4) emphasised the point thus:

> The Government attaches a high priority[14] to tackling the problems associated with the misuse of alcohol and drugs, and to ensuring the provision of a comprehensive network of services for alcohol and drug misusers.

22.11 In similar vein, guidance on the housing/community care interface LAC (92)12 stated:

> Housing authorities will need to be aware that for some clients, such as alcohol and drug misusers, their care plan may include a planned progression from some form of residential care to a more independent lifestyle, possibly away from their original area of residence.[15]

22.12 The principal social services circular guidance concerning services for drug and alcohol misusers remains LAC (93)2, which stresses the special circumstances surrounding the provision of services for this client group, and in particular comments:

> 12. Addressing the needs of people with alcohol and drug problems will present a particular challenge to LAs. The aim must be to respond effectively and to offer a programme of care that will help the misuser make positive changes to his or her life. LAs will need to bear in mind that people who misuse alcohol and drugs may:
> - present to LAs with problems other than alcohol and/or drug misuse. LAs will need to ensure that the possibility of alcohol and drug misuse is covered in essential procedures;
> - have particularly complex needs including urgent workplace or family crises or difficulties with child care, which may not have been revealed to LA services;
> - move between areas frequently, and a significant proportion will have no settled residence or be living away from their area of ordinary residence;
> - self-refer to agencies which are not in their home area, both because of their transient lifestyle and for therapeutic reasons, and many will need urgent help;
> - avoid contact with statutory services; drug misusers in particular may be reluctant to become involved with statutory agencies because of the illegal nature of their drug-related activities;
> - need to be provided with services several times before they succeed in controlling their alcohol or drug misuse;
> - require residential treatment and rehabilitation as a positive treatment choice;
> - sometimes behave unpredictably and may not fit easily into assessment and care management systems designed to meet the needs of other client groups.

---

14 The point was also made in the white paper Home Office (1995) *Tackling drugs together: a strategy for England 1995–1998*. Cm 2846, para B.55.
15 At para 2 of the annex to the circular.

Assessment procedures

22.13 At para 3.71 above reference is made to the difficulties that some prisoners can experience in obtaining a community care assessment. However, once an assessment is being undertaken the key guidance in relation to drug treatment strategies *Models of care (drug misuse)* [16] advises that the relevant professionals adopt three broad levels of assessment, each of which incorporates a risk assessment that addresses (at para 4.5):

- risk of suicide or self-harm;
- risks associated with substance use (such as overdose);
- risk of harm to others (including harm to treatment staff, harm to children and domestic violence);
- risk of harm from others (including domestic violence);
- risk of self-neglect.

22.14 The three levels of assessment are:

1) **Screening assessment** (at para 4.1). These are brief assessments that seek to establish whether there is a drug and alcohol problem, what other related problems exist, and whether there is an immediate risk for the client. The assessment will identify whether there is a need to refer on to drug treatment services and the urgency of the referral.

2) **Triage** [17] **assessment** (at para 4.2). These are usually undertaken when the misuser makes contact with the specialist drug treatment services. The assessment seeks to determine the seriousness and urgency of the problems, the most appropriate treatment and the person's motivation to engage in treatment, current risk factors and the urgency of need to access treatment. The assessment will generally include 'an initial care plan' (para 4.3).

3) **Comprehensive assessment** (at para 4.4). These are targeted at drug misusers with 'more complex needs and those who will require structured drug treatment interventions'. Comprehensive assessments will be an ongoing process rather than a single event and may have input from various professionals, such as doctors (for prescribing expertise) and psychologists.

22.15 The *Models of care (alcohol misuse)* [18] guidance adopts the same terminology and requires the same three broad levels of assessment, which (with the necessary changes) require the same content and level of analysis.

22.16 Circular LAC (93)2 makes a number of important points concerning the need for authorities to adopt flexible assessment procedures in relation to people who misuse alcohol or drugs, and the related need in many cases to develop a close working relationship with the probation services.

---

16 Department of Health and Home Office (2006) *Models of care for treatment of adult drug misusers.*

17 A process for sorting people based on their need for, or likely benefit from, treatment (from the French 'trier' – to sort).

18 Department of Health National Treatment Agency for Substance Misuse (2006) *Models of care for alcohol misusers*, para 2.3 onwards.

13. People with serious and urgent alcohol and/or drug problems are likely to need a rapid response because of crises and to capture fluctuating motivation. Serious deterioration which may carry social, legal and care implications may ensue if there is delay before assessment or if assessment procedures are prolonged.

Eligibility for assessment

14. LAs should ensure that any criteria they may develop governing eligibility for assessment are sensitive to the circumstances of alcohol and drug misusers. As with all other user groups, the LA should have criteria for determining the level of assessment that is appropriate to the severity or complexity of the need. LAs should ensure that:

- arrangements have been agreed with all the agencies in their area to which misusers are likely to present for help, which will enable those agencies to initiate assessment procedures where in their view they are indicated;
- arrangements are in place to facilitate the assessment of a person by another authority where that person is ordinarily resident in that other authority's area, for example by agreeing with another LA to undertake an assessment on that authority's behalf;
- individuals who are of no settled residence are not excluded from assessment by means of eligibility criteria which require duration of residence. The Department proposes to issue guidance to LAs in 1993 about the resolution of disputes and the procedures to be adopted in the last resort where disputes cannot be resolved between the authorities concerned.[19] Disputes about ordinary residence should not prevent people receiving the care they need.

Adapting assessment to the special needs of alcohol and drug misusers

15. LAs will need to ensure that their assessment systems take full account of the different ways in which alcohol and drug misusers present for services, their different characteristics and their particular needs:

- standard LA assessment procedures and documentation should include consideration of substance misuse.
- LA staff will need to be able to identify the indications of substance misuse so that specialist agencies can be involved where appropriate.

Rapid assessment procedures ('fast-track' assessment)

16. There are a range of organisations and professionals who deal frequently with alcohol and drug misusers. A great many of the services, including virtually all residential services, are provided by the independent sector. There is, therefore, within the independent sector, a substantial reservoir of experienced professionals with skills to undertake assessment in this field. LAs should consider involving independent sector agencies in the assessment process. Practice guidance issued by the Department of Health Social Services Inspectorate[20] emphasises the importance of training to equip those people within LAs who undertake assessment with the necessary knowledge and skills. Policy guidance issued by the Department, 'Community care in the next decade and beyond'[21] states

---

19 This was effected via LAC (93)7 Part II, now superseded by 2011 guidance see para 6.9 above.

20 Department of Health (1991) *Care management and assessment: a practitioners' guide*, see para 3.22 above.

21 Referred to in this text as the 1990 policy guidance; see paras 1.51 and 3.115 above.

that where a specialist service – for example a drug and alcohol service – is provided by an independent agency under arrangements with a social services department, it will be possible to include assessment of needs in relation to such services in contract arrangements. In these circumstances LAs will need to ensure that the specialist agency is aware of other potential needs for which LAs have a responsibility.

17. Residential placements should not normally take place without a comprehensive needs assessment. Where assessment is contracted to an independent specialist agency, decisions to commit resources and ultimate responsibility for the assessment remains with the LA.

18. Because many alcohol and drug misusers present or are referred to services outside their area of ordinary residence LAs are encouraged to work together to identify systems so that they can feel confident about committing resources on the basis of an assessment undertaken in another LA. This may be facilitated by the development of standard and agreed assessment procedures and forms and networks of named responsible officers within LAs.

19. The Department is encouraging local authority associations to work with the independent sector to establish rapid assessment procedures for alcohol and drug misusers and good practice guidance in out of area referrals which they can commend to local authorities.

20. Individual LAs and independent service providers should, together, ensure that rapid assessment procedures meet the needs of alcohol and drug misusers. In order to do so LAs and providers may want to determine the pattern of referrals of their residents/clients in order to establish contact and set up appropriate arrangements where regular flows exist. LAs and independent sector service providers will together wish to have regard to the Department's study examining good practice in care management and assessment for alcohol and drug misusers which will be available to local authorities shortly.

Emergency action
21. LAs need to be aware that alcohol and drug misusers may sometimes be in such urgent need that residential care will need to be provided immediately. 'The Care Management and Assessment' practice guidance issued by the Department of Health covers the arrangements for urgent admission to both residential and nursing home care.[22]

22. LAs may contract with a provider to offer an emergency direct access service for people in urgent need, with assessment and a decision about longer term treatment following as soon as practicable. LAs may wish to contract with a voluntary organisation to provide direct access to residential care without assessment in these circumstances. In such cases of urgent need the area of ordinary residence of the person should not be a consideration.[23]

Out of area referrals
23. Because of the transient lifestyles of a significant proportion of drug and alcohol misusers LAs will be involved in negotiations about area of

22 Department of Health (1991) *Care management and assessment: a practitioners' guide* para 4.45 for nursing homes and para 4.97 for residential homes.
23 National Assistance Act (NAA) 1948 s24(3).

ordinary residence for people with alcohol and drug misuse problems to a greater extent than for others. Where people are ordinarily resident in the area of the LA undertaking the assessment, there may be therapeutic benefit in referring people to a residential service away from the area in which they are experiencing their alcohol and drug problems. LAs are reminded that the statutory direction on choice[24] of residential accommodation advises that people assessed as needing residential care should be able to exercise choice over the place where they receive that care. LAs should ensure that resources can be identified for out of area placements.

24. LAs should ensure that there are arrangements in place for responding to the following types of out of area referrals:
- where people are ordinarily resident outside the area of the LA undertaking the assessment, there will be a need to liaise with the LA in the area of ordinary residence to establish responsibility for funding the care package;
- where people are ordinarily resident outside the area of the LA but are in urgent need of residential care;[25]
- here it is impossible to identify a person's area of ordinary residence; in these circumstances the LA where they present for services should assume responsibility for arranging and providing the necessary services.[26]

Probation service
25. Some alcohol and/or drug misusing clients of the Probation Service will continue to seek access to residential and non-residential care, and LAs should liaise with probation services to ensure that these needs can be considered within the community care arrangements. Attention should be given to establishing joint assessment or common assessment procedures, such as those LAs have developed with other client groups. LAs will also need to be aware that there may be requests for resources to provide residential and non-residential care for persons whose alcohol or drug misuse comes to light through offending, appearance in court and/or involvement with probation services. LAs are reminded that the Criminal Justice Act 1991 which came into force on 1 October 1992 emphasises that it is preferable for offenders who misuse alcohol or drugs to be dealt with in the community rather than in custody.[27]

22.17   In this respect, the strategy paper, *Tackling drugs to build a better britain*[28] also highlighted the crucial role of inter-disciplinary working (particularly between health, social services, housing, education and employment services).

24 NAA 1948 (Choice of Accommodation) Directions 1992; see para 7.103 above and appendix B.
25 NAA 1948 s24(3)(b).
26 NAA 1948 ss24(3)(a) and 32.
27 See Powers of Criminal Courts Act 1973 Sch 1A.
28 Cm 3945, 1998, p23.

The provision and commissioning of services

22.18 Although the statutory responsibility for the provision of heath and social care services for drug and alcohol misusers rests with the NHS and social services authorities, in practice the assessment and service provision functions are discharged by DATs.

22.19 Every DAT should have access to a range of services to cater for the assessed needs of misusers. These services are detailed in *Models of care (drug misuse)*.[29] Although the precise nature of the guidance is unclear, its predecessor guidance stated that it was to have a 'similar status to a national service framework'.[30] The guidance anticipates that a person may receive a number of different forms of treatment at the same time – for example, someone may be receiving counselling as well as medication, or a sequence of treatment, for example, as a hospital inpatient for a detoxification programme, followed by a residential rehabilitation service.

22.20 *Models of care (drug misuse)* provides general advice on the care planning process (at chapter 5), outlining the format and contents of care plans. More detailed guidance on the care process has also been issued.[31] *Models of care (drug misuse)* envisages care plans as being not merely descriptive of the care package that is to be provided, but also an 'agreement on a plan of action between the client and service provider' (para 5.3.2). Care plans should be 'brief and readily understood by all parties involved' and explicitly identify the roles of specific individuals and services in the delivery of the care plan. Considerable emphasis is placed on the need to sustain and retain the service user during the early phases of treatment and for there to be a key worker in this context (paras 5.3.3– 5.3.4).

22.21 Care plans should address four key domains, in order to identify goals by which progress can be measured. The domains are:

- drug and alcohol misuse;
- health (physical and psychological);
- offending;
- social functioning (including housing, employment and relationships).

22.22 *Models of care (drug misuse)* requires that DATs ensure that users have access to four 'tiers' of service. The 2006 guidance requires 'far greater emphasis' to be given to reducing drug-related harm (para 3.2.1) and seeks to expand the commissioning of Tier 4 services (specialist

---

29 Department of Health and Home Office (2006) *Models of care for treatment of adult drug misusers.*

30 Department of Health (2002) *Models of care for treatment of adult drug misusers; Framework for developing local systems of effective drug misuse treatment in England*, para 2.1.

31 National Treatment Agency for Substance Misuse (2006) *Care planning practice guide.*

residential services) which it considers to be 'crucial' and to have been (in comparative terms) neglected. A 2007 report[32] makes the same point:

> One major weakness in the existing array of treatment options is in the provision of services involving residential care. Residential rehabilitation has been found to be generally more effective than treatment in the community where 'effective' is taken to mean enabling people to become drug-free.[33] . . . In recent years, as the treatment system has developed, the residential rehabilitation sector has been neglected in favour of maintenance prescribing and other services at the Tier 3 level, delivered in the community. At present it can accommodate no more than 5 per cent of all the people in drugs treatment.

and

> Moreover, even if there were a system in place for making referrals to residential rehabilitation, as often as not the funding is not there to pay for them. Drug rehabilitation has tended to come, like other forms of residential care, out of the community care budgets of local authorities' social services departments and it therefore competes with all the other demands on these overstretched budgets.

22.23 *Models of care (drug misuse)* advises that in commissioning care packages, greater emphasis should be given to 'effective and well-co-ordinated' drug-related aftercare provision and that Supporting People funding should be considered in tandem with other funding streams (para 3.7).

22.24 *Models of care (drug misuse)* at p20 onwards describes the four tiers of intervention that must be commissioned and provided locally. It recommends that these be in a range of settings and that local systems should 'allow for some flexibility in how interventions are provided, with the crucial factors being the patterns of local need and whether a service provider is competent to provide a particular drug treatment intervention' (para 3.8). The four tiers are summarised as follows:

Tier 1 Drug-related information and advice, screening and referral to specialised drug treatment services.

This level of support will usually be provided in general healthcare settings (where the main focus is not drug treatment, eg liver units, antenatal wards, Accident and Emergency and pharmacies), as well in social services, education or criminal justice settings. As a minimum, commissioners must ensure that the following services are available:
- drug treatment screening and assessment;
- referral to specialised drug treatment;
- drug advice and information;
- partnership or 'shared care' working with specialised drug treatment services to provide specific drug treatment interventions for drug misusers.

32 Royal Society for the Encouragement of Arts, Manufactures and Commerce (2007) *Drugs facing facts* pp199–200.
33 M Gossop (2004) 'Developments in the treatment of drug problems' in P Bean and T Nemitz (eds), *Drug treatment: what works?* Routledge, 2004.

Tier 2 Assessment, referral to structured drug treatment, brief psychosocial interventions, harm reduction interventions (including needle exchange) and after-care.

This level of support will generally be provided by specialised drug treatment services or in hospital – however they may be provided in outreach services, in primary care settings, in pharmacies, criminal justice settings and so on.

As a minimum commissioners must ensure that the following services are available:
- triage assessment and referral for structured drug treatment;
- drug interventions;
- interventions to reduce harm and risk due to blood-borne viruses including dedicated needle exchanges;
- interventions to minimise the risk of overdose and diversion of prescribed drugs;
- brief psychosocial interventions for drug and alcohol misuse;
- brief interventions for specific target groups including high-risk and other priority groups;
- drug-related support for clients seeking abstinence;
- drug-related after-care support for those who have left care-planned structured treatment;
- liaison and support for generic providers of Tier 1 interventions;
- outreach services to engage clients into treatment and to re-engage people who have dropped out of treatment;
- a range of the above interventions for drug-misusing offenders.

Tier 3 Community-based specialised drug assessment and co-ordinated care planned treatment and drug specialist liaison.

This level of support will generally be provided by the same range of providers as Tier 2 interventions above.

As a minimum commissioners must ensure that the following services are available:
- comprehensive drug misuse assessment;
- care planning, co-ordination and review for all in structured treatment, often with regular keyworking sessions as standard practice;
- community care assessment and case management for drug misusers;
- harm reduction activities as integral to care-planned treatment;
- a range of prescribing interventions[34] as part of a package of care including: prescribing for stabilisation and oral opioid maintenance prescribing; community based detoxification; injectable maintenance prescribing, and a range of prescribing interventions to prevent relapse and ameliorate drug and alcohol-related conditions;
- a range of structured evidence-based psychosocial interventions to assist individuals to make changes in drug and alcohol using behaviour;
- structured day programmes and care-planned day care;
- liaison services for acute medical and psychiatric health services (eg pregnancy, mental health and hepatitis services);

34 In compliance with Department of Health (2007) *Drug misuse and dependence – UK guidelines on clinical management*, known as 'the clinical guidelines'.

- liaison services for social care services (eg social services (child protection and community care teams), housing, homelessness);
- a range of the above interventions for drug-misusing offenders.

Tier 4 Specialised drug treatment (including inpatient drug detoxification and stabilisation) 'care planned and care coordinated to ensure continuity of care and aftercare'.

This level of support will generally be provided in specialist settings such as residential substance misuse units or wards, specialist inpatient detoxification beds or specialist addiction units attached to residential rehabilitation units, step programmes, residential rehabilitation or halfway houses which may be located away from their area of residence and drug misusing networks.

As a minimum commissioners must ensure that the following services are available:

- inpatient specialist drug and alcohol assessment, stabilisation, and detoxification/assisted withdrawal services;
- a range of drug and alcohol residential rehabilitation units to suit the needs of different service users;
- a range of drug halfway houses or supportive accommodation for drug misusers;
- residential drug and alcohol crisis intervention units (in larger urban areas);
- inpatient detoxification/assisted withdrawal provision, directly attached to residential rehabilitation units for suitable individuals;
- provision for special groups for which a need is identified (eg for drug-using pregnant women, drug users with liver problems, drug users with severe and enduring mental illness);
- a range of the above interventions for drug-misusing offenders.

22.25 *Models of care (alcohol misuse)* [35] adopts a similar four tiered service provision response requirement, which are, in brief:

Tier 1. The provision of alcohol-related information and advice; screening; simple brief interventions; and referral. At this stage the intervention is aimed at identifying hazardous, harmful and dependent drinkers; providing information on sensible drinking; simple brief interventions to reduce alcohol-related harm; and referral of those with alcohol dependence or harm for more intensive interventions.

Tier 2. Open access, non-care-planned, alcohol-specific interventions: at this stage interventions include the provision of open access facilities and outreach services that provide alcohol-specific advice, information and support; extended brief interventions to help alcohol misusers reduce alcohol-related harm; and assessment and referral of those with more serious alcohol-related problems for care-planned treatment.

Tier 3. Community-based, structured, care-planned alcohol treatment: at this stage interventions include providing community-based specialised alcohol misuse assessments, and alcohol treatment that is care co-ordinated and care-planned.

---

35 Department of Health National Treatment Agency for Substance Misuse (2006) *Models of care for alcohol misusers*, pp20–23.

Tier 4. Specialist inpatient treatment and residential rehabilitation: at this stage interventions include the provision of residential, specialised alcohol treatment services which are care-planned and co-ordinated to ensure continuity of care and after-care.

Service user failure

22.26 Drug and alcohol services can be expensive, and the guidance (LAC (93)2 para 11) states, 'there is a comparatively rapid turnover' of such service users in residential accommodation due in part to the relatively high 'failure rate' experienced by people trying to rid themselves of an addiction. The NTA endorses this advice – that relapses are to be expected and planned for, stating that 'most drug misusers relapse and need to return to treatment a number of times before getting their habit under control'. It notes, however, that 'around 50 per cent of those who do complete a comprehensive treatment programme are still drug-free after five years'.[36]

22.27 The importance of this factor was also stressed in *Purchasing effective treatment and care for drug misusers*[37] which stated (at para 1.7):

> Drug misusers suffer relapses, and may need several periods of treatment before they achieve the ultimate aim of 'abstinence'. 'Instant' cures are relatively rare, partly because drug misuse is closely associated with many other problems. These include unemployment, family break up, homelessness and crime. Tackling drug misuse effectively may therefore involve a range of interventions by several agencies, for people at different stages of their drug misusing careers. If these are not properly co-ordinated resources will be wasted.

22.28 *Models of care (drug misuse)* refers to US evidence (at para 3.9.1) that suggests that:

> . . . an average time in treatment for someone with a heroin or crack dependence problem is five to seven years, with some heroin users requiring indefinite maintenance on substitute opioids. Evidence also tells us that service users gain cumulative benefit from a series of treatment episodes. However, the biggest improvements in client outcomes are likely to be made in the first six years of treatment.

22.29 In similar vein *Models of care (alcohol misuse)*[38] advises that alcohol dependence is recognised to be a commonly recurring condition and that individuals:

> . . . may require a number of episodes of treatment before they reach their goals, which in relation to their drinking behaviour are likely to be either lower-risk drinking or abstinence. Some more 'entrenched' or recurrent alcohol misusers with severe dependence, and who may have other problems, may not reach their drinking goals or other goals in a particular

---

36 NTA 'background' briefing statement at www.nta.nhs.uk.
37 Department of Health (1997) *Purchasing effective treatment and care for drug misusers guidance on commissioning better services for people with drug related problems*, Health Promotion Division, Drugs Services Team.
38 Department of Health National Treatment Agency for Substance Misuse (2006) *Models of care for alcohol misusers*, para 2.5.

episode of care. Treatment interventions may, in some cases, need to be carried out over extended periods, or individuals may benefit from multiple treatment episodes.

NHS obligations

22.30   The effects of alcohol/drug misuse can be life-threatening and frequently require specialist medical and nursing interventions. The NHS has a clear responsibility in this field, although it is, in relation to such matters as rehabilitation and recovery, an overlapping responsibility with social services authorities. LAC (93)2 confirms (para 7) that: 'the new community care arrangements do not affect health authorities' responsibilities for funding the healthcare element of any alcohol and drug service. LAs will need to consider and draw up agreements with health authorities covering arrangements for funding treatment and rehabilitation services for people with alcohol and/or drug problems.'

22.31   The white paper *Tackling drugs together*,[39] in referring to the role of healthcare services stated (para B.49):

> The Government's aim is to provide a comprehensive range and choice of local services to help drug misusers give up drugs and maintain abstinence. Such services also promote better health and reduce the risks of drug misuse, including infections associated with sharing injecting equipment such as HIV and hepatitis. These services include residential detoxification and rehabilitation, community drug dependency services, needle and syringe exchange schemes, advice and counselling, and after-care and support services. Facilities are provided by both statutory and independent agencies. General practitioners are also encouraged to address the needs of drug misusers. Guidelines on clinical management, *Drug Misuse and Dependence*[40] were issued to all doctors in 1991. Guidelines for the clinical management of substance misusers in police custody[41] were issued in March 1995.

22.32   EL (95)114 required health authorities to review and report on their arrangements for 'shared care' of drug misusers. The outcome of this review and advice on general health authority commissioning is contained in *Purchasing effective treatment and care for drug misusers*, appendix C to which lists a number of specific health services that ought to be available for drug misusers. These include hospital drug detoxification units,[42] providing urgent assessment and acute care as well as support, counselling and rehabilitation; methadone reduction programmes; hospital out-patient and community-based clinics; and general counselling; as well as

---

39   Home Office (1995) *Tackling drugs together: a strategy for England 1995–1998*, Cm 2846.
40   Department of Health (1991) – now superseded by Department of Health (2007) *Drug misuse and dependence – UK guidelines on clinical management.*
41   Department of Health (1995) *Substance misuse detainees in police custody: guidelines on clinical management.*
42   Or through specialist nursing home facilities.

GP training and encouragement to 'identify drug misuse, promote harm minimisation and where appropriate refer to specialist services'. The publication expressed particular concern about failures of co-ordination between health and local authorities such that there were 'long waits for detoxification', noting that this may mean that drug misusers lose their motivation to continue with treatment (para 8.5).

22.33   The above guidance has now been augmented by 2006 guidance on the commissioning of in-patient and residential rehabilitation drug and alcohol treatment interventions[43] and the extensive 2007 clinical guidelines.[44]

Social services obligations

Accommodation

22.34   As noted above (para 22.10) the duty to provide residential care or nursing home accommodation under NAA 1948 s21 specifically includes a duty towards persons who are 'alcoholic or drug-dependent'.[45] The duties under NAA 1948 s21 are considered in detail in chapter 7. Specific guidance has been issued concerning the commissioning of residential services.[46]

22.35   The role of residential care facilities is the subject of guidance in LAC (93)2, which states:

> 10. Residential services are an important component of overall service provision for alcohol and drug misusers and have developed as a national network. There are many LAs without such an alcohol or drug service in their area. Residential services offer a number of different treatment approaches, and LAs will need to ensure that people are referred to a service best suited to their needs. LAs can obtain information about the network of residential service provision in publications from two national voluntary organisations, Alcohol Concern and SCODA.[47]

> 11. The length of treatment programmes in a residential setting varies between three and eighteen months. The comparatively rapid turnover of alcohol and drug clients in residential care mean that places will begin to become vacant on a relatively large scale after 1 April 1993. LAs will need to address issues of assessment and care management for these people now so that they are ready from 1 April 1993 to provide new applicants with the care they need.[48]

43 Department of Health and Home Office (2006) *Initial guide for the commissioning of in-patient and residential rehabilitation drug and alcohol treatment interventions as part of treatment systems*.

44 In compliance with Department of Health (2007) *Drug misuse and dependence – UK guidelines on clinical management*, known as 'the clinical guidelines'.

45 LAC (93)10 appendix 1 para 2(6).

46 Department of Health and Home Office (2005) *Initial guide for the commissioning of in-patient and residential rehabilitation drug and alcohol treatment interventions as part of treatment systems*.

47 Standing Conference on Drug Abuse, Waterbridge House, 32–36 Loman Street, London SE1 0EE. Tel: 020 7928 9500.

48 LAC (93)2 was issued in January 1993.

22.36   A Social Services Inspectorate report *Residential care for people with drug/ alcohol problems*, 1994, made the following general comments concerning the accommodation needs of such people:

- Drug/alcohol misusers often have a range of problems which may contribute to, or be exacerbated by, substance misuse; residential care is only one part of a continuum of services.
- Residential care may be the preferred option most appropriate to meet individual need for one of the following reasons:
  - the service user may need 'time out' from an environment which is not conducive to cessation of drug/alcohol misuse;
  - the service user many have a number of complex and inter-related problems which can be addressed only in a residential environment.
- A primary and major need of people, in other client groups, requiring residential care is usually for supervised accommodation; for drug/ alcohol misusers, accommodation is often only one of a range of needs which require intensive support.
- The characteristics and needs of drug/alcohol misusers are different in some ways from those of other client groups who require residential care because they are unable, or do not feel able, to live independently in their home environment. Many drug/alcohol misusers are in their early adult years and residential care is required as an appropriate temporary environment in which to provide intensive therapeutic care as well as physical and social care. Residential care is rarely provided for drug/alcohol misusers as a permanent home.

Non-accommodation obligations

22.37   As noted above (para 22.10), services under NHS Act (NHSA) 2006 Sch 20 and NHS (Wales) Act (NHS(W)A) 2006 Sch 15 are specifically available for persons who are 'alcoholic or drug-dependent' and these services are considered at para 9.176 above.

22.38   The description of possible arrangements which can be made under NHSA 2006 Sch 20 (NHS(W)A 2006 Sch 15) is so widely drafted as to be capable of encompassing virtually all the traditional domiciliary and community care services. The inclusion in the directions (appendix 3 to LAC(93)10) of a separate category of potential service 'specifically for persons who are alcoholic or drug-dependent', is clearly designed to ensure that authorities are empowered to provide all the relevant services which may be required by alcohol or drug misusers. The 1990 policy guidance (at para 8.6) states that the range of services local authorities will need to consider 'include prevention and harm minimisation, advice and counselling, day care and residential rehabilitation'.[49]

49   SCODA (1997) *New options: changing residential and social care for drug users* (see note 47 above).

22.39   *Purchasing effective treatment and care for drug misusers*[50] gives commissioning advice on various community and residential based services, including outreach programmes and structured day care.[51] However, it emphasises the central part played by counselling (both structured and general) in all drug misuse treatments (para 8.6) and the 'evidence that residential rehabilitation programmes can effectively help many drug misusers, particularly with chaotic lifestyles and severe problems related to their misuse' (para 8.5).

Dual diagnosis

22.40   Between a third to a half of people with severe mental health problems have substance misuse related problems.[52] In order to avoid such persons being 'shuttled between services, with a corresponding loss of continuity of care', attempts have been made to ensure that specialist mental health services and specialist substance abuse services co-operate closely.

22.41   The key 'good practice guideline' in this domain is a Department of Health publication *Mental health policy implementation guide dual diagnosis good practice guide 2002*, which has been augmented by 2006 guidance[53] concerning the assessment and clinical management of such patients who are in psychiatric inpatient or day care settings. The 2002 guidance seeks to better integrate working between the specialist agencies – rather than create a separate organisation for 'dual diagnosis' users. In relation to the policy that should inform specialist units working in these fields, it summarises the key points of its advice thus:

- Mainstream mental health services have a responsibility to address the needs of people with a dual diagnosis.
- Where they exist, specialist teams of dual diagnosis workers should provide support to mainstream mental health services.
- All staff in assertive outreach must be trained and equipped to work with dual diagnosis.
- Adequate numbers of staff in crisis resolution and early intervention teams, community mental health teams (CMHTs) and inpatient settings must also be so trained.
- They must be able to link up with each other and with specialist advice and support, including from drug and alcohol agencies.
- All local health and social care economies must map need including for those in prison.

50 Department of Health (1997) *Purchasing effective treatment and care for drug misusers guidance on commissioning better services for people with drug related problems*, Health Promotion Division, Drugs Services Team.
51 See also SCODA (1996) *Structured day programmes: new options in community care for drug misusers.*
52 Department of Health (2002), *Mental health policy implementation guide dual diagnosis good practice Guide*, para 1.3.1.
53 Department of Health (2006) *Dual diagnosis in mental health inpatient and day hospital settings. Guidance on the assessment and management of patients in mental health inpatient and day hospital settings who have mental ill-health and substance use problems.*

- Project teams must be set up and must agree a local plan to meet need which must contain an agreed local focused definition, care pathways/care coordination protocols and clinical governance guidelines.
- All clients must be on the care programme approach (CPA) and must have a full risk assessment regardless of their location within services.
- LITs should take the lead in implementing these guidelines ensuring that commissioning is coordinated across PCTs and DATs.

22.42   It summarises the key points of its advice, concerning assessment and treatment approaches in the following terms:

- Assessment of substance misuse forms an integral part of standard assessment procedures for mental health problems.
- Services need to develop routine screening procedures and, where substance misuse is identified, the nature and severity of that misuse and its associated risks should be assessed.
- An awareness of specific groups for whom these dual conditions generate specific needs must inform the assessment process.
- Treatments should be staged according to an individual's readiness for change and engagement with services.
- Staff should avoid prematurely pushing clients towards abstinence but adopt a harm reduction approach.
- An optimistic and longitudinal perspective regarding the substance misuse problem and its treatment are necessary.
- A flexible and adaptive therapeutic response is important for the integrated management of these dual conditions.
- Attention must be paid to social networks of clients, to meaningful daytime activity and to sound pharmacological management.

22.43   In Wales there appears to be no specific equivalent guidance, although 2010 advice to community mental health teams[54] states that:

> For those individuals with a dual diagnosis of substance misuse and mental disorder, where the primary issue is the mental disorder, mental health services will take the lead, but work closely with the substance misuse team who should continue to provide support.

People with HIV/AIDS

22.44   It appears that about 63,500 adults were living with HIV in the UK at the end of 2005, of whom 20,100 (32 per cent) were unaware of their infection. In 2005, there were about 7,450 new diagnoses of HIV. While the number of new HIV diagnoses is increasing (almost doubling in the five years to 2005), the number of AIDS diagnoses and deaths in HIV-infected individuals has declined (largely due to effective drug combination

54   Welsh Assembly Government (2010) *The role of community mental health teams in delivering community mental health services: interim policy implementation guidance and standards*, p12.

therapy introduced in 1996), with 730 reports of AIDS and 503 deaths during 2005.[55]

22.45 In contrast to the requirements of people who abuse alcohol or drugs, the needs of people with HIV or AIDS are not specifically mentioned in the community care legislation or directions. However, people with HIV/AIDS are potential (or actual) community care users and therefore entitled to an assessment and, where appropriate, services. In general residential care or nursing home accommodation will be provided by social services departments under NAA 1948 s21 (see chapter 7 above) and by health authorities under the continuing care obligations (see chapter 14 above). Para 21.36 above considers the particular problems faced by some HIV positive asylum seekers and other overseas nationals in accessing community care services.

22.46 In relation to non-accommodation services, the social services obligation under Chronically Sick and Disabled Persons Act (CSDPA) 1970 s2 is owed to people who are already 'substantially and permanently handicapped'. These services are therefore only likely to be available for people who have developed the AIDS symptoms. In contrast the social services duties under NHSA 2006 Sch 20 (NHS(W)A 2006 Sch 15) are owed to people who have an illness (whether or not it is has already resulted in them becoming permanently and substantially handicapped) or people who are recovering from an illness or in order to prevent illness. These services, which are of primary relevance to people with HIV who have not yet developed the AIDS symptoms, are considered in detail at para 9.137 above.

22.47 The Department of Health[56] has published guidance and issued a number of circulars concerning the social care needs of people with HIV infection and AIDS, including:

1) *HIV infection – The working interface between voluntary organisations and social services departments*, 1992.
2) *Children and HIV – guidance for local authorities*, 1992.
3) *The health and social care of people with HIV infection and AIDS – Findings and good practice recommendations from research funded by the DoH 1986–1992*, 1993.
4) *Women and HIV*, 1993.
5) *Inspection of local authority services for people affected by HIV/AIDS: overview*, 1994.
6) *Implementing caring for people: caring for people with HIV and AIDS*, 1994.
7) *Support grant for social services for people with HIV/AIDS* LAC (DH) (2007)5.
8) *Better prevention; better services; better sexual health: the national strategy for sexual health and HIV implementation action plan*, June 2002.

---

55 Office for National Statistics, *HIV and AIDS*, 2007, at www.statistics.gov.uk/cci/nugget.asp?id=654.
56 There does not appear to be any community care-specific AIDS/HIV guidance issued by the Welsh Assembly.

CHAPTER 23

Children Act 1989 duties to children in need

Introduction

23.1   There are about 950,000 disabled children in the UK.[1] The evidence suggests that these numbers are increasing, particularly in relation to children with autistic spectrum and attention deficit disorders as well as low birthweight babies (and those with severe and complex disorders) who are surviving and being cared for at home. It is estimated that there are perhaps 6,000 technologically dependent children in the UK.[2]

23.2   This chapter reviews the social care service provision entitlements of disabled children, although frequently this is done by cross reference to other chapters where the particular issue is capable of being addressed in a context that is not age specific. The community care rights of disabled parents are considered at para 3.44 above.

Disabled children and the Children Act 1989

23.3   The Children Act (CA) 1989 is widely regarded as a statute that both radically reformed and simplified child care law in England and Wales. While this is objectively correct in relation to child protection proceedings, it is much more debatable in relation to the provision of services for disabled children. Indeed, in this respect the Act complicated matters, creating new rights and duties which apply alongside and overlap those of the pre-existing legislation.[3] As a consequence disabled children and their carers have rights to child and family support services under the CA 1989 and under the community care and carers' legislation.[4] In general, however, it will be appropriate for disabled children to be assessed under the CA 1989 regime – even if the services that are subsequently provided derive from another statute.

Disabled child – definition

23.4   CA 1989 s17(1) places a general duty on social services authorities to safeguard and promote the interests of children 'in need' and in furtherance of this duty they are empowered to provide a wide range of services.

---

1   C Blackburn, N Spencer and J Read, 'Prevalence of childhood disability and the characteristics and circumstances of disabled children in the UK: secondary analysis of the Family Resouces Survey', (2010) *BMC Pediatrics*, 10:21.

2   See generally, S Broach, L Clements and J Read, *Disabled children: a legal handbook*, Legal Action Group, 2010 para 1.25 onwards.

3   The difficulties for disabled children created by the CA 1989 (and particularly the problems at 'transition' – see para 23.66 below) have been exacerbated by the creation in England of separate children's services departments pursuant to CA 2004 – see in this context, L Clements, 'Respite or short breaks care and disabled children' (2008) *Seen and Heard* vol 18(4), pp23–31.

4   Disabled children have rights to services under the community care legislation (eg NHSA 2006 Sch 20 para 3 which contains no restriction on the age of the service user – see para 9.178 above). As a consequence they are entitled to be assessed under National Health Service Community Care Act (NHSCCA) 1990 s47.

23.5 CA 1989 s17(10) provides that a child shall be taken to be 'in need' if:

(a) he is unlikely to achieve or maintain, or to have the opportunity of achieving or maintaining, a reasonable standard of health or development without the provision for him of services by a local authority . . . ; or

(b) his health or development is likely to be significantly impaired, or further impaired, without the provision for him of such services; or

(c) he is disabled.

23.6 The definition of a disabled child (which closely follows the definition of a disabled adult in National Assistance Act (NAA) 1948 s29 – see para 9.25 above) is contained in CA 1989 s17(11), namely:

For the purposes of this Part, a child is disabled if he is blind, deaf or dumb or suffers from mental disorder of any kind or is substantially and permanently handicapped by illness, injury or congenital deformity or such other disability as may be prescribed; and in this Part –

'development' means physical, intellectual, emotional, social or behavioural development; and

'health' means physical or mental health.

23.7 By including reference to a 'mental disorder of any kind' the legislation defines disability in broad terms. As noted at para 9.40 above (in relation to the 1948 Act) autism[5] must now be accepted as a mental disorder and so included within the definition, as well as a person with Asperger's Syndrome (even if they have an above average IQ) or an attention deficit disorder (ADD).[6] Even where there has been no formal diagnosis to confirm that a child has a particular disorder, they may be deemed to be 'in need' by virtue of section 17(10)(a) and/or (b).

23.8 Many children's services departments discharge their various responsibilities through specialist social work teams – for instance, a 'child protection team', a 'disabled children's team' and so on. Not infrequently a disabled children's' team will have terms of reference that exclude certain children, for instance those with Asperger's syndrome or ADD. Authorities are, in general, free to make these organisational arrangements provided they ensure that the needs of all disabled children are addressed and do not fall between the terms of reference of the various teams. It would be maladministration (and potentially unlawful action under the Equality Act 2010 s15[7]) if organisational arrangements of this nature resulted in the needs of some disabled children being treated less favourably.

---

5 See (by analogy) eg the decision of Social Security Commissioner Jacobs 13 November 2007: CDLA 2288 2007.

6 See eg L S Goldman and others, 'Diagnosis and treatment of attention-deficit/ hyperactivity disorder in children and adolescents', (1998) *Journal of the American Medical Association* 279 (14): 1100–1107 which concluded that there was little evidence of misdiagnosis of ADD.

7 See eg *Governing Body of X School v SP and others* [2008] EWHC 389 (Admin).

23.9   Having identified the potential recipients of assistance under section 17, the Act then follows a similar route to the community care legislation, namely that access to support services is in general dependent upon a needs assessment.

Disabled children's register

23.10   Social services departments are, by virtue of CA 1989 Sch 2 para 2 obliged to keep a register of children with disabilities, as part of their duty to safeguard and promote the interests of disabled children. Volume 6 of the original (1991) *Children Act guidance (children with disabilities)*[8] stressed (para 4.2) that although registration was a voluntary procedure, it could 'contribute positively to coherent planning of service provision for children with disabilities' and that:

> 4.3 SSDs . . . will need to liaise with their education and health counterparts to achieve an understanding of disability which permits early identification; which facilitates joint working; which encourages parents to agree to registration and which is meaningful in terms of planning services for the children in question and children in general. The creation of a joint register of children with disabilities between health, education and social services would greatly facilitate collaboration in identification and a co-ordinated provision of services under the Act . . .

> 4.4 Whichever agency is the first to identify a child as having a disability whether it is the [local education authority] LEA, SSD or child health services they should initiate discussions with the parents about services or procedures which might be beneficial to the child and family. This should include an explanation of what other agencies can provide and information about the register. The registration of children with disabilities will be effective and productive only if parents and children are regarded as partners in the assessment process and as experts in their own right, from whom professionals may have much to learn.

23.11   CA 2004 s12 made provision for the creation of an information database (largely directed at child protection concerns). In consequence, a major database was constructed (known as ContactPoint) underpinned by a detailed regulatory framework.[9] Although the regulations remain in operation (as at September 2011) the Coalition Government has indicated that it proposes to abandon this initiative.

The assessment of children in need

23.12   There is no explicit duty to assess under the CA 1989 equivalent to that found in NHS and Community Care Act (NHSCCA) 1990 s47. In *R (G) v*

---

8   Department of Health (1991) *The Children Act 1989: guidance and regulation, volume 6, Children with Disabilities.*

9   See the Children Act 2004 Information Database (England) Regulations 2007 SI No 2182 and the Children Act 2004 Information Database (England) (Amendment) Regulations 2010 SI No 1213.

Barnet LBC[10] the majority of the House of Lords accepted that as a matter of public law, such a duty did exist.[11] This view is buttressed by the existence of substantial policy guidance, which places assessments at the centre of the duty to 'safeguard and promote', stating (amongst other things) that the 'effectiveness with which a child's needs are assessed will be key to the effectiveness of subsequent actions and services and, ultimately, to the outcomes for the child'[12].

23.13　Additionally, disabled children are entitled, not only to services under the Chronically Sick and Disabled Persons Act (CSDPA) 1970 s2 but also to services under NHSA 2006 Sch 20 para 3[13] (see para 9.178 above). In relation to the 1970 Act, the Department of Health considers that it contains a duty to assess (see para 3.13 above) and in relation to the 2006 Act, there is a statutory duty to assess, since such services are 'community care services' (see para 3.136 above).

23.14　The original CA 1989 policy guidance[14] concerning assessments' states as follows:

> 2.7　Good practice requires that the assessment of need should be undertaken in an open way and should involve those caring for the child, the child and other significant persons. Families with a child in need, whether the need results from family difficulties or the child's circumstances, have the right to receive sympathetic support and sensitive intervention in their family's life . . .
>
> 2.8　In making an assessment, the local authority should take account of the particular needs of the child – that is in relation to health, development, disability, education, religious persuasion, racial origin, cultural and linguistic background, the degree (if any) to which these needs are being met by existing services to the family or the child and which agencies' services are best suited to the child's needs.

Guidance on assessment

23.15　The two key guidance documents in England concerning the CA 1989 assessment process are the 2000 *Framework for assessing children in need*

10　[2003] UKHL 57, [2003] 3 WLR 1194, (2003) 6 CCLR 500. Lord Scott (also part of the majority) was of the opinion that at the very least it was 'implicit in this provision that the local authority will assess the actual needs of a child in need whenever it appears necessary to do so' – at [117].

11　Lord Nicholls at para 32 (with whom Lord Steyn agreed); Lord Hope at para 77 (with whom Lord Millett agreed), with only Lord Scott at para 116 suggesting that there was only a duty 'whenever it appears necessary to do so'.

12　Department of Health, Department for Education and Employment and Home Office (2000) *Framework for assessing children in need and their families* (policy guidance), p viii; Welsh Assembly Government (2001) *Framework for assessing children in need and their families*, p viii.

13　The NHSA 2006 Sch 20 para 3 contains no restriction on the age of the service user – see para 9.178 above and footnote 4 above.

14　Department of Health (1991) *The Children Act 1989: guidance, volume 2, Family Support*, para 2.7.

and their Families policy guidance[15] and practice guidance[16] issued by the Department of Health. Very similar policy and practice guidance has been issued in Wales[17] and the following section refers to the English framework guidance.

23.16   The policy guidance requires assessors to look at the needs of disabled children in the context of the whole family and local community and details three domains, each with a number of 'dimensions':[18]

1) Domain A: child's developmental needs
   - health
   - education
   - emotional and behavioural development
   - identity
   - family and social relationships
   - social presentation
   - self-care skills.
2) Domain B: parenting capacity
   - basic care
   - ensuring safety
   - emotional warmth
   - stimulation
   - guidance and boundaries
   - stability.
3) Domain C: family and environmental factors
   - family history and functioning
   - wider family
   - housing
   - employment
   - income
   - family's social integration
   - community resources.

23.17   The practice guidance takes the view that practitioners need to start by assuming that disabled children have the same basic needs as all children, but because they are living with impairments some may require additional support, assistance and intervention (at para 3.6). Considerable emphasis is placed upon social factors which restrict and disable. The guidance requires that the needs, capacities and opinions of all family members, including the disabled child, are taken into account.

23.18   The English and Welsh policy guidance describes the social services

15 Department of Health, Department for Education and Employment and Home Office (2000) *Framework for assessing children in need and their families* (policy guidance).
16 Department of Health (2000) *Assessing children in need and their families: practice guidance.* The practice guidance contains detailed material on the way in which the framework should be applied to disabled children and their families.
17 Welsh Assembly Government (2001) *Framework for assessing children in need and their families*; Welsh Assembly Government (2001) *Assessing children in need and their families: practice guidance.*
18 Page 17: the domains are set out graphically as sides to a triangle, with the child in the centre.

response to an initial contact or a referral requesting help as 'critically important' (para 3.3) and lays down a timetable for the assessment process, in the following terms:

3.8 There is an expectation that **within one working day** of a referral being received or new information coming to or from within a social services department about an open case, there will be a decision about what response is required. A referral is defined as a request for services to be provided by the social services department. The response may include no action, but that is itself a decision and should be made promptly and recorded. The referrer should be informed of the decision and its rationale, as well as the parents or caregivers and the child, if appropriate.

3.9 A decision to gather more information constitutes an initial assessment. An initial assessment is defined as a brief assessment of each child referred to social services with a request for services to be provided. This should be undertaken **within a maximum of [7/10][19] working days** but could be very brief depending on the child's circumstances. It should address the dimensions of the Assessment Framework, determining whether the child is in need, the nature of any services required, from where and within what timescales, and whether a further, more detailed core assessment should be undertaken. An initial assessment is deemed to have commenced at the point of referral to the social services department or when new information on an open case indicates an initial assessment should be repeated. All staff responding to referrals and undertaking initial assessments should address the dimensions which constitute the Assessment Framework . . .

3.10 Depending on the child's circumstances, an initial assessment may include some or all of the following:
- interviews with child and family members, as appropriate;
- involvement of other agencies in gathering and providing information, as appropriate;
- consultation with supervisor/manager;
- record of initial analysis;
- decisions on further action/no action;
- record of decisions/rationale with family/agencies;
- informing other agencies of the decisions;
- statement to the family of decisions made and, if a child is in need, the plan for providing support.

As part of any initial assessment, the child should be seen. This includes observation and talking with the child in an age appropriate manner . . .

3.11 A core assessment is defined as an in-depth assessment which addresses the central or most important aspects of the needs of a child and the capacity of his or her parents or caregivers to respond appropriately to these needs within the wider family and community context. While this assessment is led by social services, it will invariably involve other agencies or independent professionals, who will either provide information they

19 The original guidance stated seven working days and this remains the case in Wales. In England this has been increased to ten working days – see Department for Children, Schools and Families (2010) *Working together to safeguard children*, para 5.38.

hold about the child or parents, contribute specialist knowledge or advice to social services or undertake specialist assessments. Specific assessments of the child and/or family members may have already been undertaken prior to referral to the social services department. The findings from these should inform this assessment. At the conclusion of this phase of assessment, there should be an analysis of the findings which will provide an understanding of the child's circumstances and inform planning, case objectives and the nature of service provision. The timescale for completion of the core assessment is a **maximum of 35 working days**. A core assessment is deemed to have commenced at the point the initial assessment ended, or a strategy discussion decided to initiate enquiries under s47, or new information obtained on an open case indicates a core assessment should be undertaken. Where specialist assessments have been commissioned by social services from other agencies or independent professionals, it is recognised that they will not necessarily be completed within the 35 working day period. Appropriate services should be provided whilst awaiting the completion of the specialist assessment.

23.19   In *R (AB and SB) v Nottingham City Council*[20] Richards J described the assessment process detailed in the policy guidance in the following terms:

> There should be a systematic assessment of needs which takes into account the three domains (child's developmental needs, parenting capacity, family and environmental factors) and involves collaboration between all relevant agencies so as to achieve a full understanding of the child in his or her family and community context. It is important, moreover, to be clear about the three-stage process: identification of needs, production of a care plan, and provision of the identified services. It seems to me that where an authority follows a path that does not involve the preparation of a core assessment as such, it must nevertheless adopt a similarly systematic approach with a view to achievement of the same objectives. Failure to do so without good cause will constitute an impermissible departure from the guidance.

23.20   The *Nottingham* case concerned a child with learning disabilities and behavioural problems for whom the local authority had sought an anti-social behaviour order under the Crime and Disorder Act 1998. It was argued on his behalf that no such order could be made where the authority had failed properly to assess the child's needs under CA 1989.[21] The court agreed and made mandatory order that the council carryout a full assessment in compliance with the framework, within 35 working days. In the judge's opinion, the council had 'concentrated unduly on the anti-social behaviour order proceedings and insufficiently on the discharge of its duty, in particular under section 17 of the Children Act' and that the

20   [2001] EWHC 235 (Admin), (2001) 4 CCLR 294 at 306G–I. See also *R (J) v Newham LBC* [2001] EWHC (Admin) 992, (2002) 5 CCLR 302 where a similar mandatory order to undertake a CA 1989 assessment was made.
21   See also *R (M) v Sheffield Magistrates' Court* [2004] EWHC 1830 (Admin), [2005] 1 FLR 81 where it was held that a conflict of interest would arise when a local authority sought an anti-social behaviour order in relation to a child in its care, and accordingly special safeguards should apply in such proceedings, and see also *R (K) v Manchester City Council* [2006] EWHC 3164 (Admin), (2007) 10 CCLR 87.

young man's behavioural problems could not excuse the council's 'failure to comply with the section 17 duty'.

23.21   Given the mandatory phrasing of the framework as to time (a 'maximum of 35 working days') the ombudsman has held it to be mal-administration not to complete a core assessment within this timescale.[22]

23.22   As we note below (para 23.36) the *Framework for Assessing Children in Need and their Families* guidance is conceptually a child protection tool – predicated on the need to 'intervene' rather than of providing support to families in terms of eligibility assessments and services. For this reason, many social workers do not progress disabled children's assessments to the 'core assessment' stage, choosing instead to address a less formalised assessment process – such as the 'Common Assessment Framework' (CAF)[23] – an English assessment process designed to be used by those practitioners who come into contact with children (be they working for a children's services department or not). In many localities, a completed CAF form is a route to accessing services – and as such it is seen by some as flexible and lacking in the formality of the *Framework for assessing children in need* process. The problem with such an approach is not merely that it is in conflict with the policy guidance (which in many cases will require the preparation of a core assessment) but it can further marginalise disabled children and their families and entrench professional belief that the *Framework for assessing children in need* is reserved for the core business of the department – namely child protection.

Care plans

23.23   As with community care assessments, assessments of the needs of disabled children (where it is decided that support is required) must culminate in the preparation of a care plan. The plan must not be merely 'descriptive': it must contain a 'clear identification of needs . . . what [is] to be done about them, by whom and by when':[24] it must 'to set out the operational objectives with sufficient detail – including detail of the "how, who, what and when" – to enable the care plan itself to be used as a means of checking whether or not those objectives are being met'.[25] For further analysis of the role of care plans, see para 4.20 above.

22 Public Services Ombudsman for Wales Report concerning a complaint against Merthyr Tydfil CBC, 25 May 2006, para 108.
23 Department for Children, Schools and Families (2006) *Common assessment framework* (CAF), and see also Department for Children, Schools and Families (2010) *Working together to safeguard children*.
24 *R (AB and SB) v Nottingham City Council* [2001] EWHC Admin 235, [2001] 3 FCR 350, para 43 and see also *R (J) v Caerphilly CBC* [2005] EWHC 586 (Admin), (2005) 8 CCLR 255 at para 44 and *R(B) v Barnet LBC* [2009] EWHC 2842 (Admin) para 26.
25 *R (J) v Caerphilly CBC* [2005] EWHC 586 (Admin).

Children (Leaving Care) Act 2000

23.24   The Children (Leaving Care) Act 2000 implemented proposals first detailed in the Department of Health 1999 consultation document *Me, survive, out there? – new arrangements for young people living in, and leaving care* published designed to improve the life chances of young people living in and leaving local authority care. The Act (which has been amended) places duties on social services authorities to provide support for children who have been accommodated – to a level equivalent to that which children who have not been in care might in general expect from their parents. Guidance under the Act has been issued in both England and Wales.[26]

23.25   The main purpose of the 2000 Act is to help young people who have been looked after by a local authority move from care into living independently in as stable a fashion as possible. Its provisions have been buttressed by additional measures in Children and Young Persons Act 2008, Part 2.[27] Both of these Acts seeks to promote the wellbeing of children who are or who have been accommodated by local authorities. In legislative terms this is achieved by amendment to the CA 1989: principally section 22 and Schedule 2. The resulting scheme has become complex – if not very complex. Although a detailed analysis of this system lies outside the scope of this text, the general scheme is described in the following section and in the table 22 which follows – this is a summary of a set of tables that appear in the English 2010 guidance.[28]

23.26   The scheme contains two broad categories of young people who qualify for support. The first being young people who remain looked after and for whom plans need to be made to support them when they leave care. These are known as 'eligible children' and for which distinct guidance and regulations exist in England.[29] The second broad category includes young people who have ceased to be looked after, and these are referred to in the legislation as 'relevant' and 'former relevant' children, and for whom separate regulations and guidance exist in

---

26   Department for Education (2010) *The Children Act 1989 guidance and regulations Volume 3: planning transition to adulthood for care leavers including The Care Leavers (England) Regulations*, Department for Education (2010) *The Children Act 1989 guidance and regulations 2010 Volume 2: care planning, placement and case review* and Welsh Assembly Government (2001) *Children Leaving Care Act Guidance*.

27   At the time of writing (September 2011) the 2008 Act's amendments have not come into force in Wales (with the exception of the introduction of bursaries – see Children Act 1989 (Higher Education Bursary) (Wales) Regulations 2011 SI No 823. When the remaining provisions come into force, it is expected that revised guidance will follow.

28   Department for Education (2010) *The Children Act 1989 guidance and regulations Volume 3: planning transition to adulthood for care leavers including the Care Leavers (England) Regulations*: p.5–9.

29   Care Planning, Placement and Case Review (England) Regulations 2010 SI No 959, and Department for Education (2010) *The Children Act 1989 guidance and regulations Volume 3: planning transition to adulthood for care leavers including the Care Leavers (England) Regulations*.

England.[30] In Wales, at the time of writing (September 2011) a single set of guidance and regulations exist for all categories of young people who qualify for support under the scheme.[31]

Table 22 Young persons entitled to care leaving support	
Definitions	**Main statutory obligations of LA**
Eligible child is a child who is:[32] a) looked after, b) aged 16 or 17, and c) has been looked after by a local authority for a period of 13 weeks, or periods amounting in total to 13 weeks, which began after she/he reached 14 and ended after she/he reached 16.	The LA has the same obligations for such a child as for all looked after children and in addition, it must:[33] 1) Prepare an assessment of the child's needs while looked after and after they cease to be looked after; 2) Prepare a pathway plan and keep it under regular review 3) Appoint a personal adviser
Relevant child is a child who is:[34] a) not looked after, b) aged 16 or 17, and c) was either (i) before she/he last ceased to be looked after, an eligible child or[35] (ii) when 16 was detained (i.e. on remand or hospital) and before this was looked after by a LA for at least 13 weeks after the age of 14. Or[36] Although formerly looked after, has lived for six months with someone with parental responsibility or who has had a residence order and the living arrangements break down.	The LA must:[37] 1) Take reasonable steps to keep in touch; 2) Prepare an assessment of the child's needs; 3) Prepare a pathway plan and keep it under regular review; 4) Appoint a personal adviser; 5) Safeguard and promote the child's welfare by maintaining them, providing or maintaining them in suitable accommodation and providing assistance in order to meet their needs in relation to education, training or employment as provided for in the pathway plan.

Continued

---

30 Care Leavers (England) Regulations 2010 SI No 2571, Department for Education (2010) *The Children Act 1989 Guidance and Regulations 2010 Volume 2: care planning, placement and case review.*
31 Children (Leaving Care) (Wales) Regulations 2001 SI No 2189 (W151), Welsh Assembly Government (2001) *Children Leaving Care Act Guidance.*
32 CA 1989 Sch 2 para 19B and the Care Planning, Placement and Case Review (England) Regulations 2010 SI No 959 reg 40.
33 CA 1989 Sch 2 para 19B (4) and (5) and the Care Planning, Placement and Case Review (England) Regulations 2010 SI No 959 regs 42, 43 and 44.
34 CA 1989 s23A(2).
35 The Care Leavers (England) Regulations 2010 SI No 2571 reg 3.
36 The Care Leavers (England) Regulations 2010 SI No 2571 reg 3.
37 CA 1989 ss23B(1), 23B(3)(a), 23E(1D), 23B(2), 23B(8) and the Care Leavers (England) Regulations 2010 SI No 2571 regs 4–9 inclusive.

Definitions	Main statutory obligations of LA
Former relevant child is a child who is:[38] a) aged 18 or above, and either b) has been a relevant child and would be one if under 18, or c) immediately before she/he ceased to be looked after at age 18, was an eligible child.	The LA must:[39] 1) Take reasonable steps to keep in touch and to re-establish contact if lost; 2) To keep the pathway plan under regular review 3) To continue with the personal adviser; 4) If their welfare requires it, to provide financial assistance including certain accommodation expenses; 5) If the welfare and educational needs require it, provide certain financial assistance for education; 6) If pursing higher education in accordance with the pathway plan, to pay a higher education bursary;[40] Duties continue until the child is 21 or if the pathway plan includes education beyond their 21st birthday – for so long as this is pursued.
Former relevant child pursuing further education or training is a child:[41] a) who is aged under 25, b) for whom the duties to keep in touch, to maintain a pathway plan and personal adviser and to assist financially no longer apply, and c) who has informed the LA that she/he wants to pursue education or training.	The LA must:[42] 1) appoint a personal adviser 2) assess their needs to determine what assistance (if any) it would be appropriate for them to provide 3) prepare a pathway plan; 4) to the extent the person's educational or training needs require it, provide financial assistance

Continued

---

38 CA 1989 s23C(1).
39 CA 1989 ss23C(2), 23C(3)(b), 23C(3)(a), s23C(4)(a), 23B(1), 23C(4)(b), 23B(2), 23C(5A), 23C(2), 23C(3), 23C(4)(b); the Children Act 1989 (Higher Education Bursary) (England) Regulations 2009 SI No 2274 and the Care Leavers (England) Regulations 2010 SI No 2571 regs 7 and 8.
40 Children Act 1989 (Higher Education Bursary) (England) Regulations 2009 SI No 2274, and Children Act 1989 (Higher Education Bursary) (Wales) Regulations 2011 SI No 823.
41 CA 1989 s23CA(1)
42 CA 1989 ss23CA(2), 23CA(3)(a), 23CA(3)(b), 23CA(4) and the Care Leavers (England) Regulations 2010 SI No 2571 regs 4–6 inclusive.

A person qualifying for advice and assistance is:[43]	The LA must consider whether the following help is needed:[44]
a) aged at least 16 but is under 21, b) is subject to a special guardianship order (or was when they reached 18) and was looked after before the making of that order, or c) at any time after reaching 16, but while still a child was looked after, accommodated or fostered (but is no longer).	1) to advise, befriend and give assistance, 2) to give financial assistance including (in certain situations) assistance in relation to securing vacation accommodation.

23.27 As detailed in table 22 above, an 'eligible' child is one who is shortly to stop being 'looked after' as they approach 18.[45] For such a qualifying young person the local authority is required to:

1) Undertake an assessment of their needs with a view to determining what advice, assistance and support it would be appropriate to provide:
   a) while the local authority is still looking after them; and
   b) after the local authority has ceased to look after them,
   and then to prepare a pathway plan for them.[46] The assessment should be completed not more than three months after the child reaches the age of 16.[47]

2) Prepare a written statement describing the manner in which their needs would be assessed. The content of these statements is specified in the regulations and must include, for instance, the complaints process and the name of the person responsible for conducting the assessment.

3) Appoint a personal adviser who is responsible for (among other things) the co-ordination of services – including ensuring that the person leaving care makes use of such services. In *R (J) v Caerphilly CBC*[48] the High Court held that it was essential that the personal adviser was independent of the authority and was not the person responsible for the preparation of the assessment or the pathway plan.

23.28 'Relevant' children are aged 16 and 17 who would have been 'eligible' before they ceased being 'looked after'.[49] The local authority duties include:

1) to 'keep in touch' with such care leavers, until aged 21 and beyond in some cases;

43 CA 1989, s24.
44 CA 1989 ss24(5), 24A, 24B, 24A(2), 24A(3) and 24(B).
45 CA 1989 Sch 2 para 19B(2).
46 CA 1989 Sch 2 para 19B(4).
47 Care Planning, Placement and Case Review (England) Regulations 2010 SI No 959 reg 42; Children (Leaving Care) (Wales) Regulations 2001 SI No 2189 (W151) reg 7.
48 [2005] EWHC 586 (Admin), (2005) 8 CCLR 255 at [30] and see also *R (A) v Lambeth LBC* [2010] EWHC 1652 (Admin).
49 CA 1989 s23A.

2) to prepare 'pathway plans'. These plans take over from the child's existing care plan and run at least until the age of 21, covering education, training, career plans and support needs. Such plans will be subject to review every six months. The legislation and guidance[50] identify these plans as 'pivotal to the process whereby children and young people map out their future'.[51]

23.29   The courts have been robust in requiring that the pathway plans are practical and properly constructed: that they have a clear sense of their 'ultimate direction' and contain the 'necessary detail' and 'urgency'.[52] In *R (P) v Newham LBC*[53] a local authority was held to have acted unlawfully by failing to provide a personal pathway plan before the severely disabled child in care turned 19 years. It was irrelevant that the local authority had started an alternative process which it believed to be more appropriate – namely a transitional plan. As Ouseley J observed, 'whatever the merits of that process may be and however well it may be done, it is not one which meets the requirements of the statute'.

The child's perspective

23.30   The policy guidance requires social services departments to 'develop clear assessment procedures for children in need . . . which take account of the child's and family's needs and preferences, racial and ethnic origins, their culture, religion and any special needs relating to the circumstances of individual families'.[54] The importance of involving children in the assessment process is emphasised in the policy guidance at para 3.41 which stresses that:

> . . . direct work with children is an essential part of assessment, as well as recognising their rights to be involved and consulted about matters which affect their lives. This applies all children, including disabled children. Communicating with some disabled children requires more preparation, sometimes more time and on occasions specialist expertise, and consultation with those closest to the child. For example, for children with communication difficulties it may be necessary to use alternatives to speech such as signs, symbols facial expression, eye pointing, objects if reference or drawing.

23.31   A failure properly to involve a disabled child in their assessment (even if there are profound communication or behavioural problems[55]) may well

50   CA 1989 s23(3)(b); Care Leavers (England) Regulations 2010 SI No 2571 reg 6 Department for Education (2010) *The Children Act 1989 guidance and regulations Volume 3: planning transition to adulthood for care leavers including The Care Leavers (England) Regulations* para 3.4; and Welsh Assembly, *Children Leaving Care Act Guidance*, 2001, para 7.2.
51   See also *R (J) v Caerphilly CBC* [2005] EWHC 586 (Admin), (2005) 8 CCLR 255.
52   *R (C) v Lambeth LBC* (2008) [2008] EWHC 1230 (Admin), para 36.
53   [2004] EWHC 2210 (Admin), (2004) 7 CCLR 553.
54   Department of Health (1991) *The Children Act 1989 guidance and regulations volume 6, 'Children with Disabilities'*, para 5.1.
55   *R (J) v Caerphilly CBC* [2005] EWHC 586 (Admin), (2005) 8 CCLR 255.

result in a court holding the procedure unlawful.[56] *CD v Anglesey CC*,[57] for example, concerned a 15-year-old wheelchair user with quadriplegic cerebral palsy. Her mother was unwell and felt unable to care for her daughter full-time, even with substantial social services funded support. Accordingly, when aged five, a respite placement was found for her daughter and legally therefore she became a 'looked after child' under CA 1989 s20.

23.32 The daughter developed a very strong bond with her respite foster carers even though, as she grew older, their home became increasingly unsuitable. The authority decided that the placement should end and that she should return to live with her mother, who opposed this alteration and sought a judicial review (acting as her daughter's litigation friend).

23.33 The authority failed to assist with adaptations to the foster carers' home and (against the advice of an independent social worker it had commissioned) decided that they should be deregistered.

23.34 Legally, the daughter was a child in need, under CA 1989 s17(1), to whom the authority owed a duty to promote her welfare and, so far as is consistent with that duty, to promote her upbringing by her family, by providing a range and level of services appropriate to her needs. As a disabled child, by virtue of section 17(2) and Schedule 2(6) the authority was obliged to provide services designed to minimise the effect upon her of her disabilities and to give her the opportunity to lead a life which was as normal as possible. As a 'looked after' child, by section 23(8), the local authority was obliged (so far as reasonably practicable) to secure that the accommodation was not unsuitable for her particular needs. In addition under section 20(6) there was a duty to ascertain her wishes regarding such provision and give due consideration to them having regard to her age and understanding.

23.35 The court held the local authority's actions to be unlawful. In particular it had failed to give due consideration to the child's wishes, had failed to take account of her mother's inability to provide full time care when formulating a care plan and had acted unlawfully in deregistering the child's foster carers on the pretext that their home was unsuitable without giving due consideration to the child's needs.

Disabled children's services and the service provision decision

23.36 As with community care assessments, entitlement to services under the CA 1989 depends upon the assessment disclosing sufficient evidence to prompt a service response. However, unlike the community care assessment process the guidance lays down no standard procedure for establishing who is eligible for support services. It is in this respect that the policy and practice guidance are particularly weak. The policy guidance fails because it is, in reality, dominated by the notion of child protection:

---

56 *R v North Yorkshire CC ex p Hargreaves* (1997–98) 1 CCLR 105.
57 [2004] EWHC 1635 (Admin), (2004) 7 CCLR 589.

accordingly its advice on responses to identified needs (at chapter 4) leans heavily in the direction of family interventions. The practice guidance, although specifically directed at the needs of disabled children, is also disappointing when it comes to service responses and is silent on the assessment of eligibility.

23.37   It is difficult to envisage how a consistent policy of responding to assessed needs can be implemented without some agreement as to what constitutes eligible needs. Unfortunately the guidance lays down no clear guidelines – indeed it has even been suggested that use of eligibility criteria in relation to children's services may be inappropriate: Lord Laming for example in his Victoria Climbié Inquiry Report said as follows:

> 1.53 The use of eligibility criteria to restrict access to services is not found either in legislation or in guidance, and its ill-founded application is not something I support. Only after a child and his or her home circumstances have been assessed can such criteria be justified in determining the suitability of a referral, the degree of risk, and the urgency of the response.
>
> 1.54 Local government in this country should be at the forefront of organisations serving the public. Sadly, little I heard persuades me that this is so. Many of the procedures that I heard about seemed to me to be self-serving – supporting the needs of the organisation, rather than the public they are set up to serve.[58]

23.38   Lord Laming was presumably concerned, not so much about the notion of deciding who should and who should not receive support services, but rather about the use of inappropriate and rigid criteria to make this determination. In practice, authorities have to decide and in so doing require – whatever one might like to call it – a formula or scale by which they can prioritise those in most need and devote resources to those for whom the resources can have the most positive impact.

23.39   Local authorities do, in practice, have such prioritisation procedures for disabled children's services, although they are not infrequently inadequate, poorly publicised and formulated with little or no consultation. It appears that in many cases, access to support services is measured largely by assessing the imminence of family breakdown.[59] Thus if it is imminent or has occurred, resources can be accessed, but not otherwise. Clearly such criteria cater for the needs of children suffering abuse or neglect but are likely to be inappropriate for many families with disabled children or young carers. In practice such policies deny support to families until such time as they fall into (or are at severe risk of falling into) the child protection regime: effectively therefore they cater, not for CA 1989 Part III (provision of services for children and their families) but for Part VI (child protection).

---

58 Lord Laming (2003) *The Victoria Climbié Inquiry: Report of an Inquiry*, Cm 5730.
59 It has been suggested that in some authorities 'children have to be virtually on the edge of child protection to be considered "in need"' – see M Garboden 'It's hard to prove need' in *Community Care* 29 October 2009, p20 quoting Cathy Ashley, chief executive of the Family Rights Group.

23.40   As a minimum, local authority eligibility criteria should be: published – ie accessible and comprehensible to disabled children and their families; should have been the subject of a consultation which took into account the equality duties under the Equality Act 2010 (see para 2.32 above); be rational (in the sense of prioritising those in most need and directing resources to where they can have the most positive impact); comply with the law and government guidance; and be flexible in their application. There is, however, (as Black J observed in *R (JL) v Islington LBC*[60]) a 'pressing need' for government guidance on eligibility criteria in this area.

23.41   Once all the relevant evidence concerning the needs of the child and his or her family have been identified, the authority must make a rational decision as to which (if any) of these needs require to be met by the provision of support services. The decision will have to take into account the consequences of not providing services – be it harm or impaired development of the child (development including physical, intellectual, emotional, social and behavioural – section 17(11)) as well as the consequences for the family – in terms of their needs (for instance to work, or undertake education, training and leisure activities – see para 16.72) and also their ability to sustain the caring relationship. If the family support cannot be sustained without services (including respite provision) the child is likely to suffer significant harm.

23.42   In *R (Spink) v Wandsworth BC*[61] the Court of Appeal held that in deciding whether services were required, a local authority could (in the somewhat unusual facts of the case) take into consideration the financial situation of the parents.

23.43   Following an assessment, a wide spectrum of services can be made available to disabled children. These services may be home, community or institutionally based and may derive from a variety of legislative provisions, although the primary statutes are CSDPA 1970 and CA 1989.

Services for disabled children under the Chronically Sick and Disabled Persons Act 1970

23.44   As noted at para 9.148 above, by virtue of CSDPA 1970 s28A, services under section 2 of the 1970 Act are available to disabled children. In *R v Bexley LBC ex p B*[62] the court held that if there was a choice of providing services under the 1970 Act or under CA 1989 s17, then the duty under the 1970 Act effectively trumped the 1989 duty (see para 9.150 above) – not least because the duty under the 1970 Act is a specific law duty whereas the duty under section 17 is almost certainly a target duty (see para 1.23 above).

23.45   It follows that once an authority is satisfied that it is necessary to provide a service under the 1970 Act, then it is under a specifically

---

60 [2009] EWHC 458 (Admin), (2009) 12 CCLR 322.
61 [2005] EWCA Civ 302, [2005] 1 WLR 2884, (2005) 8 CCLR 272.
62 (2000) 3 CCLR 15.

enforceable duty to do so. The range of services under the 1970 Act is considered at para 9.76 above.

Services for children in need under the Children Act 1989

23.46   Once a child has been accepted as being 'in need', and that need identified by an assessment or otherwise, the CA 1989 specifies that a range of support services be made available. Section 17(1) provides:

> It shall be the general duty of every local authority (in addition to the other duties imposed on them by this Part) –
> (a) to safeguard and promote the welfare of children within their area who are in need; and
> (b) so far as is consistent with that duty, to promote the upbringing of such children by their families,
>
> by providing a range of services appropriate to those children's needs.

23.47   Section 17(2) refers to additional specific duties under Part I of Schedule 2 to the Act, which comprise:

> *Para 6 – Provision for disabled children*
> (1) Every local authority shall provide services designed –
> (a) to minimise the effect on disabled children within their area of their disabilities; and
> (b) to give such children the opportunity to lead lives which are as normal as possible; and
> (c) to assist individuals who provide care for such children to continue to do so, or to do so more effectively, by giving them breaks from caring.
>
> (2) The duty imposed by sub-paragraph (1)(c) shall be performed in accordance with regulations[63] made by the appropriate national authority.

> *Para 8 – Provision for children living with their families*
> Every local authority shall make such provision as they consider appropriate for the following services to be available with respect to children in need within their area while they are living with their families –
> (a) advice, guidance and counselling;
> (b) occupational, social, cultural, or recreational activities;
> (c) home help (which may include laundry facilities);
> (d) facilities for, or assistance with, travelling to and from home for the purpose of taking advantage of any other service provided under this Act or of any similar service;
> (e) assistance to enable the child concerned and his family to have a holiday.

23.48   The guidance to the CA 1989 conveniently summarises the breadth of powers available to social services authorities in such cases:[64]

---

63 Breaks for Carers of Disabled Children Regulations 2011 SI No 707 – see para 23.55 below.
64 Department of Health (1991) *The Children Act 1989 guidance and regulations Volume 6*, 'Children with disabilities', para 3.3.

This general duty is supported by other specific duties and powers such as the facilitation of 'the provision by others, including in particular voluntary organisations of services' (section 17(5) and Schedule 2). These provisions encourage SSDs to provide day and domiciliary services, guidance and counselling, respite care and a range of other services as a means of supporting children in need (including children with disabilities) within their families. The Act recognises that sometimes a child can only be helped by providing services for other members of his family (section 17(3)) 'if it [the service] is provided with a view to safeguarding or promoting the child's welfare' . . . The SSD may make such arrangements as they see fit for any person to provide services and support 'may include giving assistance in kind, or in exceptional circumstances in cash' (section 17(6)[65]). However, where it is the SSD's view that a child's welfare is adequately provided for and no unmet need exists, they need not act.

23.49   In *R (G) v Barnet LBC and others*[66] (which involved a number of consolidated appeals) the House of Lords had to determine (among other things) whether the obligation to provide services under the 1989 Act was a target or specific law duty. The case was unusual in that the CA 1989 service sought by the appellants was the provision of housing. In a split 3:2 judgment, the majority held that although there was an obligation under the CA 1989 to provide accommodation (once it had been identified in an assessment as a 'need'), this was a target duty rather than a specific law duty (see para 1.23 above). The thrust of the judgment in relation to the target nature of the section 17 duty was applied in *R (T, D and B) v Haringey LBC*[67] where the court held that the service provision arrangements under Schedule 2(5) to the Act were also target in nature: that the section 17(1) duty:

> . . . left substantial matters to the discretion of the local authority . . . which could not lead to an enforceable duty towards an affected individual.

23.50   The rationale underpinning the *Barnet LBC* decision is not easy to comprehend and has been the subject of criticism. It can also lead to absurd outcomes – not least that disabled children in certain situations have inferior rights to social care support than do disabled adults. In practice, however, the judgment is likely to have only a limited legal impact on the rights of disabled children to services. This arises, principally, from the fact that most of the support services required by disabled children and their families will derive from the broad list of services specified in CSDPA 1970 s2. In a few situations the service may not be capable of being met by the 1970 Act – for instance respite care to be delivered in a residential setting, and this service is considered at para 23.57 below.

23.51   The *Barnet* decision creates two conceptual problems. The first being to distinguish between the needs of a disabled child that are capable of

---

65   Subsequent to this guidance the CA 1989 was amended to insert an additional right to direct payments – see para 12.8 below, and by omitting the words 'exceptional circumstances' – Children and Young Person's Act 2008 s24.
66   [2003] UKHL 57, [2003] 3 WLR 1194, (2003) 6 CCLR 500.
67   [2005] EWHC 2235 (Admin), (2006) 9 CCLR 58; and also applied in *Blackburn-Smith v Lambeth LBC* [2007] EWHC 767 (Admin).

being addressed by the specifically enforceable duty under the 1970 Act and those which cannot – and must therefore be addressed by the 17 target duty (or perhaps the CA 1989 s20 duty, see para 23.57 below). The second problem is ascertaining whether there is any practical difference between these two public law duties.

23.52   The first arises from an appreciation of the assessment process. As noted above (see chapter 4), the process is 'needs led'. If one takes, for example, the need of a family for respite (and the concomitant need of the disabled child for a family that did not break down under the pressure of not having respite), there are of course many ways of meeting that need. One way might be some arrangement in the home (for instance, a sitting service under the 1970 Act) and another would be for the child to spend a short period out of the home in residential respite: seldom will 'residential respite' care be the only way of addressing the need. If, however, a local authority refused to provide the latter service on the ground that it was merely in discharge of a target duty, it would not obviate the requirement to meet the assessed need where there was an alternative way of meeting it under an Act that gave rise to a specific duty – as, for instance, under the 1970 Act.

23.53   Not infrequently, however, the service difficulty encountered is that of a dearth of service providers available to meet an assessed need – for instance a need for respite or short break care. In such situations it may be that the parents of the disabled child could make the necessary arrangements themselves if they had direct payments – for instance, by arranging for one of their acquaintances or relations to provide the service (see para 12.35 or by paying for a short stay in residential respite care (see para 12.37 above). Section 17A of the 1989 Act (the duty to make direct payments) read in conjunction with the direct payment regulations (see para 12.37) strongly suggests that once an authority has decided that services need to be provided under section 17 for a disabled child then the authority is under a specifically enforceable duty to make direct payments in lieu of the services.

23.54   The second conceptual difficulty concerns the distinction in practice between the section 17 duty and the duty under section 2 of the 1970 Act: in practice this may be limited. Most obviously, the local authority must focus on the fact that section 17 imposes a duty – not a power: that target duties are not 'optional' or 'discretionary' obligations.[68] As the *Framework for assessing children in need* policy guidance states (at para 4.1) at the

---

68   In *LW: Re Judicial Review* [2010] NIQB 62, 19 May 2010 (considered at para 16.95 above) the need was for residential respite care pursuant to a similar target duty (article 15 of the Health and Social Services (NI) Order 1972). The court, however, concluded (para 38) that where a need for respite care has been identified adequate, effective and reasonable steps must be taken to ensure it is provided, including (if a particular respite care facility is unavailable) identifying alternative provision. If due to administrative inertia this does not happen and the authority advances 'no convincing evidence of reasonable efforts' to discharge its continuing statutory duty then, whether 'viewed through the prism of an absolute (i.e. unqualified) duty of provision or a duty to be measured by the criterion of reasonableness' it will be held to be in breach of its statutory duty (paras 48–49).

conclusion of an assessment the authority must identify 'whether and, if so, where intervention will be required to secure the well-being of the child' and that this must result in 'a realistic plan of action (including services to be provided), detailing who has responsibility for action, a timetable and a process for review'. Any decision not to provide a section 17 service to meet an assessed need, must be clearly reasoned; must not be based on a general exclusion or rigid limit; must be in accordance with the relevant guidance; and must have had due regard to the council's Equality Act 2010 duties (see para 2.32 above). The more severe the consequences of not meeting a need, the more 'anxiously' will the courts and the ombudsmen scrutinise the reasons given for the failure to meet that need,[69] and where a fundamental human right is engaged (eg the right to respect for personal dignity[70] or family life[71]) the more specific will the duty to meet that need become.

Respite care

23.55　As noted above, most respite care will be provided under section 2 of the 1970 Act (as a sitting service, an overnight 'in home' service or as a community-based day service, etc). Although this will trigger the specifically enforceable duties under the 1970 Act, technically this will be in discharge of a CA 1989 function (see para 9.152 above). In this context, the duty to provide respite care (when assessed as needed) set out in CA 1989 Sch 2, Part 1 para 6 (1)(c) is germane. This provision was inserted by the Children and Young Persons Act 2008 s25 – namely 'to assist individuals who provide care for such children to continue to do so, or to do so more effectively, by giving them breaks from caring'. Regulations[72] and guidance[73] accompany the new statutory duty. The regulations require local authorities:

- (reg 3) in determining whether support should be provided, to have regard to (apart from a risk of 'a caring breakdown') the other commitments of the carer and their wish to undertake education, training or any regular leisure activity (see para 16.72);
- (reg 4) to provide (so far as is reasonably practicable) 'a range of services which is sufficient to assist carers to continue to provide care or to do so more effectively' including day-time care and overnight care in their homes or elsewhere; educational or leisure activities for disabled children outside their homes; and services available to assist carers in the evenings, at weekends and during the school holidays.
- (reg 5) by 1 October 2011 to prepare and publish on their websites 'short breaks services statement' for carers in their area detailing the

---

69　See eg *R v Lambeth LBC ex p K* (2000) 3 CCLR 141.
70　*R (A and B, X and Y) v East Sussex CC* [2003] EWHC 167, (2003) 6 CCLR 194.
71　*R (Bernard) v Enfield LBC* [2002] EWHC 2282 (Admin), (2002) 5 CCLR 577.
72　Breaks for Carers of Disabled Children Regulations 2011 SI No 707.
73　Department for Children, Schools and Families (2010) *Short breaks: statutory guidance on how to safeguard and promote the welfare of disabled children using short breaks.*

range of services being provided; any criteria by which eligibility for those services will be assessed; and how the range of services is designed to meet the needs of carers in their area.

23.56   The provision of respite care by local authorities is also considered above at para 16.92 above – and see also para 4.43.

Residential respite care

23.57   Although respite/short break support for disabled children can generally be provided in home or community-based settings, not infrequently, what will be needed will be for the child to have a period away from the family home, and in such cases questions arise as to whether this service is provided under section 20 or section 17 of the 1989 Act. If provided under section 20 the child is a 'looked after' child and the accommodation provision is subject to significant regulatory obligations.[74] In general, however, a child provided with respite care accommodation is provided with the service under section 17. The 2010 guidance (chapter 2) explains how the distinction is to be drawn (and provides a helpful table – page 16). In summary, where the short break is provided in the child's own home (even if by an overnight carer) it will be provided under section 17. If, however, the care is provided for a continuous period of more than 24 hours away from the child's own home, it will be provided under section 20(4) and the child is looked after by the local authority for that period. In order to reduce the administrative burden on local authorities in relation to children attending successive and pre-planned respite care or this kind, a lighter regulatory obligation exists in England[75] where a child receives short breaks:[76]

- in the same setting; and
- no single placement lasts more than 17 days; and
- the total of short breaks in one year does not exceed 75 days.

Housing and residential care services

23.58   In *R v Tower Hamlets LBC ex p Bradford*[77] the court considered the housing and community care needs of a family which included a severely disabled mother and an 11-year-old son with special educational needs. Although the family members experienced particularly unpleasant harassment from their neighbours, their 'housing points' were insufficient to make them an 'overriding priority' for rehousing. A judicial review challenging

---

74 The Care Planning, Placement and Case Review (England) Regulations 2010 SI No 959 and the Placement of Children (Wales) Regulations 2007 SI No 310 (W27).

75 The Placement of Children (Wales) Regulations 2007 SI No 310 (W27) reg 14 provides for a similar exemption for a series of short-term placements at the same place where no single placement lasts for more than four weeks and the total duration of the placements does not to exceed 120 days in any period of 12 months.

76 The Care Planning, Placement and Case Review (England) Regulations 2010 SI No 959 reg 48.

77 (1997–98) 1 CCLR 294, QBD.

this decision was adjourned on grounds that the authority undertook various assessments, including under CA 1989 Part III. When considering its duty to provide accommodation under the Act, the authority effectively confined its attention to CA 1989 s20, the cross-heading to which section states 'provision of accommodation for children: general'. This section (which is in effect what, prior to 1989, used to be called 'voluntary care') only arises where there is no one with parental responsibility, or where the child is lost or abandoned or where the parents are prevented from providing suitable accommodation or care. Since these factors were not present, the authority declined to provide accommodation under Part III of the Act. Dyson J held that the authority had fundamentally misunderstood its accommodation powers under the Act; in that any housing would be provided under CA 1989 s17 (and not CA 1989 s20). Section 17 enables authorities to provide an almost unlimited range of services including, in appropriate cases, housing.

23.59   Subsequent to the *R v Tower Hamlets ex p Bradford* decision, considerable controversy arose concerning the extent of the housing obligation under CA 1989 s17, culminating in the House of Lords judgment in *R (G) v Barnet LBC*[78] where the majority concluded that there was only a target duty under CA 1989 s17 to provide this service. The position has now been put beyond doubt, by the amending of section 17(6)[79] expressly to include the provision of 'accommodation' as one of the general services that may be provided (and section 22 amended so as to exclude children provided with accommodation under section 17). Guidance on these amendments has been provided in England in LAC (2003)13.

23.60   As we have noted above (para 23.24) young people who have been accommodated under section 20 of the 1989 Act may, in certain situations, be entitled to the benefit of the 'children leaving care' provisions – whereas these rights do not accrue to children whose support derives from section 17. In *R (M) v Hammersmith and Fulham LBC*[80] the House of Lords held that a local authority could not avoid its obligations under the 'children leaving care' provisions simply by determining that the services it had provided were under section 17 (or some other statutory provision). Analysis of this complex issue (which has resulted in substantial litigation) is outside the scope of this text – and reference should be made to Wise et al, *Children in need: local support for children and families.*[81]

NHS services for disabled children

23.61   Disabled children are entitled to a variety of social care support services under the NHS Acts 2006. As noted above (para 9.178) these include home help and laundry services for which social services authorities

---

78 [2003] UKHL 57, [2003] 3 WLR 1194, (2003) 6 CCLR 500.
79 Effected by Adoption and Children Act 2002 s116.
80 [2008] UKHL 14, [2008] 1 WLR 535.
81 I Wise, S Broach, C Gallagher, A Pickup, B Silverstone and A Suterwalla, *Children in need: local authority support for children and families,* Legal Action Group, 2011, chapter 5.

are responsible under NHSA 2006 Sch 20. Since such services are 'community care services' (for the purposes of NHSCCA 1990 s46(3)) it follows that disabled children are entitled to have their needs assessed under the 1990 Act in addition to the CA 1989.

23.62   Disabled children are additionally entitled to NHS continuing health-care in certain situations and this issue is addressed further at para 14.196 above.

23.63   The NHS (like all local authority departments) is subject to the 2004 guidance *The national service framework for children, young people and maternity services* (NSF) (see para 1.61 above).[82] The *Standard for hospital services*[83] includes the following statement:

> 4.52 Disabled children have the same right to high quality services as any other child, though evidence suggests many are excluded from mainstream services . . . As more disabled children with complex needs survive for longer, they make up an increasing part of the work of children's hospital services. Hospitals need to recognise and meet the very particular needs of this group of patients and involve them and their parents in the planning of services.
>
> 4.55 There should be a multi-agency plan, developed and agreed with the disabled young person and their parents, and updated as needed . . . It should say who does what – GP, hospital, social services, therapy services, school, and respite setting.

and continues:[84]

> Children and young people should receive care that is integrated and co-ordinated around their particular needs, and the needs of their family. They, and their parents, should be treated with respect, and should be given support and information to enable them to understand and cope with the illness or injury, and the treatment needed. They should be encouraged to be active partners in decisions about their health and care, and, where possible, be able to exercise choice.
>
> Children, young people and their parents will participate in designing NHS and social care services that are readily accessible, respectful, empowering, follow best practice in obtaining consent and provide effective response to their needs.

23.64   The standard amplifies the above requirement (at para 3.16), stating:

> 3.16 Staff working with children and young people should have training in the necessary communication skills to enable them to work effectively with

---

82   Department for Education and Skills and Department of Health (2004) *National service framework for children, young people and maternity services*, TSO. The NSF aims to set standards for services for all children, including those who are disabled, across the next decade: it is probably best understood as setting benchmarks for what children and families ought to be able to expect in the way of best practice and service provision.

83   Department of Health (2004) *Getting the right start: national service framework for children standard for hospital services*, 'Hospital Standard Part One Child-Centred Services'.

84   Ibid, p13.

children, young people and parents, and to support them to be active partners in decision making. Ideally, this should include:

- How to listen to and communicate with children, young people, parents and carers, and the need to understand the extent and the limits of children's comprehension at various stages of development.
- Recognition of the role of parents in looking after their children in hospital
- Providing information that is factual, objective, and non-directive, about a child's condition, likely prognosis, treatment options, and likely outcomes.
- Giving bad news in a sensitive non-hurried fashion, with time offered for further consultation away from the ward environment.
- Enabling a child and family to exercise choice, taking account of age and competence to understand the implications.

Reviews and service reduction

23.65 The *Framework for assessing children in need* (para 4.36) stipulates that care plans that provide support for children and families in the community should be reviewed with family members 'at least every six months' and that a formal record of such reviews be retained. In the absence of good reasons, a failure to comply with this guidance will be maladministration.[85] Where an authority is considering reducing services (for instance, respite care) it will be maladministration to take such a step without first undertaking such an assessment.[86]

The transition into adulthood[87]

23.66 Negotiating transitions is a constant process for disabled children and their families. Dealing with a variety of different authorities and agencies, and frequently being caught up in funding and 'handover' disputes: disputes not only between public bodies, but not infrequently within them (for example, between children's services, adult services and the education section, or between secondary and primary health services and so on).

23.67 The CA 2004 requires English social services authorities to divide their functions into adult services and children's services departments and many Welsh authorities also have similar departmental divisions. While there may be good policy reasons for this division there is no significant justification for it in relation to the service provision entitlements of disabled children. Although in general services for disabled children under CA 1989 cease to be available when they reach the age of 18,[88] their

---

85 Complaint no 08 005 202 against Kent CC, 18 May 2009, para 41.
86 Complaint no 05/B/00611 against Northamptonshire CC, 30 November 2006 and see also para 4.40 above.
87 See generally, S Broach, L Clements and J Read, *Disabled children: a legal handbook*, Legal Action Group, 2010, chapter 10.
88 Subject to important exceptions, notably as a consequence of the Children (Leaving Care) Act 2000.

entitlement to services under CSDPA 1970 s2 and under NHSA 2006 Sch 20 para 3 remain. As we note at para 1.7 above policy guidance that accompanied the 2004 Act's reforms required that directors of adult social services and children's services in England,[89] have (amongst other things) 'adequate arrangements' in place 'to ensure that all young people with long-term social care needs have been assessed and, where eligible, receive a service which meets their needs throughout their transition to becoming adults'.

23.68   There are of course dangers in separating adult and child care services and these often surface when care responsibilities are being transferred from the disabled children's team to the adult social work team. All too often at this stage the quality of the service deteriorates significantly or the child is effectively lost to the system and ceases to receive any continuing care. Such a transfer of responsibility often occurs when the young person's special education provision is also coming to an end.

23.69   For the past 20 years there have been continuous expressions of grave concern[90] over the failure of social services authorities to manage the transition of disabled children into adulthood, which have been summarised in the following terms:

> Not untypically, councils simply fail to comply with their statutory responsibilities and even when the transition process is instigated, it is frequently characterised by delay, officer turnover, a lack of incisive action, broken undertakings, ignored complaints and a persistent failure to locate suitable placements (which may require a very specific and costly package of care) during which the authority loses the ability to look at the 'whole child' and his or her spectrum of needs – and becomes particularly insensitive to the impact these failures are having on the family carers.[91]

23.70 A 2007 CSCI report[92] for instance, called for 'urgent action' to tackle the 'considerable difficulties' faces by disabled young people and their families in the transition from children's to adult services and noted that for some the process was considered to be a 'nightmare'. The Department of Health has issued policy guidance[93] requiring social services authorities to have 'adequate arrangements' in place 'to ensure that all young people with long-term social care needs have been assessed and, where eligible,

---

89 Department of Health (2006) *Guidance on the statutory chief officer post of director of adult social services issued under s7(1) Local Authority Social Services Act 1970*; Department of Health (2006) *Best practice guidance on the role of the director of adult social services*.

90 A 2009 Public Services Ombudsman for Wales report illustrates another common problem – that of prolonged in action by the local authority followed by an ultimatum at the 11th hour that the family make a decision on a placement that they have not had time to investigate – see decision on complaints against Torfaen LHB, Gwent Healthcare NHS Trust and Torfaen CBC (report references 1712/200701931, 1712/200701932 and 1712/200702681) on 29 March 2009.

91 S Broach, L Clements and J Read, *Disabled children: a legal handbook*, Legal Action Group, 2010, para 10.7.

92 Commission for Social Care Inspection (2007) *Growing Up Matters: better transition planning for young people with complex needs*.

93 Department of Health (2006) *Guidance on the statutory chief officer post of director of adult social services issued under s7(1) Local Authority Social Services Act 1970*.

receive a service which meets their needs throughout their transition to becoming adults'.[94] In a follow up 2009 report[95] the Commission found that despite all their legal obligations and the extensive guidance, the majority of local authorities still were routinely failing disabled children and their families during the transition process and that only a third had developed any kind of joint protocol to ensure shared understanding of roles and responsibilities between the council and the other relevant agencies.

23.71   Statutory provisions exist which endeavour to ensure that there is a smooth handover of responsibility from the education section of an authority (responsible for special education provision) to the social services section. Disabled Persons (Services, Consultation and Representation) Act 1986 ss5 and 6 require education authorities to consult social services authorities to establish whether a child over the age of 14 who has been 'statemented' under Education Act 1996 Part IV, is likely to require support from the social services department when he or she leaves school. This duty has been reinforced by Education (Special Educational Needs) (England) (Consolidation) Regulations 2001 reg 21[96] which requires the contribution of social services departments and others to a transitional plan which the education department is required to prepare on the annual review of a statement made when the student attains the age of 14. The essential aim of such a plan is to ensure a smooth transition for the young person into adult life.

23.72   The CA 1989 guidance also stresses the social services' obligation to ensure such a smooth transition, stating:

> The SSD's provision of services to children with disabilities should involve an initial assessment of need, a continuing process of reassessment and review of the plan for the child. Continuity should not be broken for reasons which concern organisational or administrative convenience rather than the welfare of the child or young person. A smooth transition, when the young person reaches 18 . . . should be the objective.[97]

23.73   Paragraphs 135–140 of the Prioritising Needs Guidance[98] (see para 3.30 above) additionally states:

> Councils should have in place arrangements to ensure that young people

---

94   In similar vein the NSF Complex Disability Exemplar provides a detailed outline of what 'Standard 4 – Growing up into adulthood, smooth transition to adult services' demands in terms of good professional practice: Department of Health and Department for Education and Skills (2005) *The National Service Framework for Children, Young People and Maternity Services Complex Disability Exemplar*, pp50–55.

95   Commission for Social Care Inspection (2009) *Supporting disabled parents. A family or a fragmented approach?*

96   SI No No 3455; Education (Special Educational Needs) (Wales) Regulations 2002 SI No 152 (W20) reg 21.

97   Department of Health (1991) *The Children Act 1989 guidance and regulations Volume 6, 'Children with disabilities'*, para 5.4.

98   Department of Health (2010) *Prioritising need in the context of Putting People First: a whole system approach to eligibility for social care. Guidance on eligibility criteria for adult social care, England 2010* and see Welsh Assembly Government (2002) *Creating a unified and fair system for assessing and managing care* NAFWC 09/2002, p65–66.

with social care needs have every opportunity to lead as independent a life as possible and that they are not disadvantaged by the move from children's to adult services.

23.74   The *Special Educational Needs Code of Practice 2001* issued by the Department for Education and Skills in 2002[99] provides detailed guidance on the education and social services departments' responsibilities in developing and progressing the transitional plan of disabled pupils (paras 9.51–9.64).

23.75   Many children with learning disabilities experience particularly acute problems in negotiating the transfer from child care to adult care services. Accordingly the white paper *Valuing People* identifies young people moving from children's to adult services as a priority group who should have benefited from a person-centred approach by 2003.[100] The local government ombudsman has also expressed concern about acute shortfalls in service provision at the transition stage. She has reiterated that assessed needs must be met – regardless of the age of the service user – and that local authorities may not 'use available services as a starting point and just fit the people into them'.[101] In a complaint concerning this problem she illustrated her concerns by citing the following comments – made by professionals and parents – that 'once they become 18 it seems they have no interest in looking after them' and 'you hit adult services, it's like hitting a brick wall'.[102]

23.76   A 2003 complaint against East Sussex[103] concerned a young man with learning disabilities due to leave college. His parents wanted him to move to an independent residential provider for his post college needs (as many of his co-pupils were moving to this provider). The local authority assessed his needs and concluded (1) that this provider would meet his needs and (2) that there was no suitable alternative local provision available. The provider, however, indicated that the council should make a speedy decision as other students were also seeking the place identified. The council's internal policies required that the placement be approved by a series of funding panels which met throughout the year. The funding panel initially refused funding and placed the request on a 'service pending list'. As a consequence the placement ceased to be available and although the council made temporary arrangements, the young man's placement in the independent facility was delayed by two years. In finding

99   In Wales the equivalent (and very similar) code is Welsh Assembly, *Special Educational Needs Code of Practice for Wales* paras 9.51 et seq.
100   Circular HSC 2001/016: LAC(2001)23 para 33.
101   Complaint no 03/C/16371 against Stockton-on-Tees BC, 18 January 2005 citing *Valuing People*, para 4.17.
102   Complaint no 03/C/16371 against Stockton-on-Tees BC, 18 January 2005 paras 53 and 54.
103   Complaint no 00/B/18600 against East Sussex CC, 29 January 2003: and see also the not dissimilar report on Complaint no 02/C/17068 against Bolton MBC, 30 November 2004 where the ombudsman found that the service user was not in any way properly prepared for his return to the community on leaving school and that 'there is overwhelming evidence that' the council's reluctance to fund the parents' preferred option was because of the impact this would have 'on the Social Services agency budget'.

maladministration (and recommending over £30,000 compensation) the ombudsman held:

> . . . clearly the Council's Social Services budget is under heavy pressure . . . however, the Council knew of [the disabled person's] needs, has accepted its duty to fund the provision and was happy that the provision offered by [the independent provider] was suitable. Therefore it was unacceptable for it not to have made specific budgetary provision that would enable it to respond more quickly once a placement was offered.

23.77   For many disabled children and their families, there is also the transition to be negotiated between the different branches of the NHS – between children's healthcare and adult healthcare and their differing relationships with social services. In relation to this issue in England 2008 good practice guidance exists.[104]

Charging for children's services

Charging for domiciliary and community based services

23.78   As with most statutory adult care services, local authorities are empowered to charge for the services they provide under the CA 1989. The Act's charging provisions differ in a number of respects from those for adult service users (see chapter 10 above), most obviously in the fact that it is generally the carer's (ie, the parent's[105]) means which are assessed rather than the service user's.

23.79   CA 1989 s29(1) empowers the authority to recover 'such charge as they consider appropriate'. This is subject to the following restrictions:

- that no person can be charged while in receipt of income support, or of any element of child tax credit (other than the family element) or working tax credit or of an income-based jobseeker's allowance or of income-related employment and support allowance (section 29(3)); and
- that where the authority is satisfied that a person's means are insufficient for it to be reasonably practicable for them to pay the charge, the authority cannot require them to pay more than he or she can reasonably be expected to pay (section 29(2)). This provision follows closely the wording found in Health and Social Services and Social Security Adjudications Act 1983 s17, and reference should be made to para 10.10 where the issues of charge reduction or waiver are considered in detail.

23.80   The persons who can be charged are specified in CA 1989 s29(4), namely:

---

104   Department of Health and Department for Children, Schools and Families (2008) *Transition: moving on well – a good practice guide for health professionals and their partners on transition planning for young people with complex health needs or a disability.*

105   CA 1989 s17(8) states that for charging purposes the local authority can take into account the means of the parent and child.

a) where the service is provided for a child under sixteen, each of his parents;

b) where it is provided for a child who has reached the age of sixteen, the child himself; and

c) where it is provided for a member of the child's family, that member.

23.81 As with charges for adult non-accommodation services, authorities are empowered to recover outstanding charges 'summarily as a civil debt',[106] and where a service is assessed as being required, the authority must provide it even if the liable person refuses to pay the assessed charge. In practice few authorities do make charges for such services.

Charging for services under the Chronically Sick and Disabled Persons Act 1970

23.82 Local authorities are empowered to charge for services provided under CSDPA 1970 s2 on the same basis that they are empowered to charge for domiciliary services under CA 1989 s17. This question is considered further at para 10.77 above. In general few authorities do make charges for such services.

Charging for accommodation services under the Children Act 1989

23.83 CA 1989 Sch 2 Part III empowers (but does not oblige) local authorities to charge for the cost of accommodating children. The rules are the same as for non-accommodation services, save only that (in addition):

• the local authority cannot charge a sum greater than 'they would normally be prepared to pay if they had placed a similar child with local authority foster parents'; and

• provision is made for the local authority to serve what is known as a 'contribution notice' which it is able to enforce through the magistrates' court if necessary, which court can also arbitrate on any dispute as to the reasonableness of such a notice.

106   CA 1989 s29(5).

CHAPTER 24

Safeguarding adults from abuse

continued

Introduction

24.1 The law regulating the protection from abuse of vulnerable adults in England and Wales derives from a miscellany of legislation, guidance and ad hoc court interventions. Since 2000 the courts have developed a procedure of 'declaratory relief' in an effort to fill the statutory void – as Sedley J expressed it 'to speak where Parliament, although the more appropriate forum, was silent'.[1] In its recent review of the legal framework for adult social care, the Law Commission commented:

> The existing legal framework for adult protection is 'neither systematic nor coordinated, reflecting the sporadic development of safeguarding policy over the last 25 years'. Unlike in Scotland, there is no single or coherent statutory framework for adult protection in England and Wales. Instead, it must be discerned through reference to a wide range of law including general community care legislation and guidance, the Mental Health Act 1983, the Mental Capacity Act 2005, the Safeguarding Vulnerable Groups Act 2006, the inherent jurisdiction of the High Court, and the civil and criminal justice systems.[2]

Terminology

24.2 Concerns about the lack of clarity on the use of terms in this area are frequently raised. A discussion paper published by the Commission for Social Care Inspection in 2008 noted that there was 'no shared understanding of what "safeguarding adults" means' and the absence of generally accepted definitions for the terms 'safeguarding', 'abuse', 'harm' and 'vulnerable' contributed to 'the lack of clarity about roles and responsibilities in responding to situations where adults need assistance to stay safe'. This was considered to be 'unhelpful, confusing and inappropriate'.[3] The Law Commission also notes the distinction between safeguarding, which is generally considered to be a broad concept 'that extends to all aspects of a person's general welfare', and adult protection which concerns 'the investigation and intervention where it is suspected that abuse may have occurred'.[4]

24.3 There is widespread criticism of the term 'vulnerable adult'. This term is used in the statutory guidance issued in 2000 by the Department of Health (*No Secrets*)[5] and the Welsh Assembly (*In Safe Hands*),[6] which set out the procedures that local authorities should adopt to monitor and respond to concerns about adult abuse. The guidance defines a vulnerable adult as a person aged 18 years or over:

1 *Re F (Adult: Court's Jurisdiction)* [2000] 3 WLR 1740, (2000) 3 CCLR 210, CA.
2 Law Commission (2011) *Adult Social Care*, Law Com No 328 HC941, para 9.1.
3 Association of Directors of Adult Social Services (ADASS) (2011) *Raising voices, views on safeguarding adults* para 3.4 See also comments on the importance of terminology in *Safeguarding Adults 2011*.
4 Law Commission (2011) *Adult Social Care*, Law Com No 328 HC 941, paras 9.1–9.2.
5 Department of Health and Home Office (2000) *No Secrets: guidance on developing and implementing multi-agency policies and procedures to protect vulnerable adults from abuse.*
6 National Assembly for Wales (2000) *In Safe Hands*.

who is or may be in need of community care services by reason of mental or other disability, age or illness; and who is or may be unable to take care of him or herself, or unable to protect him or herself against significant harm or exploitation.

24.4   The term 'vulnerable adult' is considered unhelpful because it locates 'the cause of the abuse within the victim, rather than in placing the responsibility with the actions or omissions of others'.[7] It 'can also suggest that vulnerability is an inherent characteristic of a person and does not recognise that it might be the context, the setting or the place which makes a person vulnerable'. The Law Commission proposed that this term should be replaced by 'adults at risk'.[8] This would accord with the term used to describe those who come under the ambit of the Adult Support and Protection (Scotland) Act 2007.[9]

24.5   Definitions of abuse vary but one often quoted is that developed by Action on Elder Abuse, which has been adopted by the World Health Organization (it has also been suggested that this could be adapted to cover adults of all ages[10]):

> A single or repeated act or lack of appropriate action occurring within any relationship where there is an expectation of trust, which causes harm or distress to an older person.[11]

Safeguarding adults from abuse and community care law

24.6   The general legal framework for the protection of adults from abuse is wide ranging, extending to general criminal offences and areas such as consumer protection against rogue traders. This chapter therefore focuses on issues more closely associated with community care law. It first outlines the legal and policy context for safeguarding. It then considers the statutory measures that seek to protect adults from abuse within the field of health and social care, followed by a review of the legal and policy framework covering the action to be taken where suspected, or actual abuse, is identified. Proposals for reform in these areas are also high-

7   Association of Directors of Social Services (2005) *Safeguarding adults*: this point was also made by the Law Commission (footnote 2 above) para 9.21.
8   The Law Commission's proposed definition is given in Recommendation 40 at para. 9.51. See also the discussion on the definition of 'vulnerable adult' in Law Commission (2008) *Adult Social Care – Scoping Report*, paras 4.280–4.293. The Safeguarding Vulnerable Groups Act 2006 uses a different definition of 'vulnerable adult's: see para 24.23 below.
9   See section 3. The Act places a duty on councils to investigate in cases where an adult may be at risk, gives powers to enter premises where abuse of adults is thought to be taking place, creates banning orders to remove perpetrators from those settings, and establishes statutory adult protection committees.
10   Commission for Social Care Inspection (2008) *Raising voices, views on safeguarding adults*, para 3.8.
11   World Health Organization (2002) *Toronto declaration of global prevention of elder abuse*, 2002. See also *No Secrets* para 2.6.

lighted. Declaratory relief and the role of the High Court is also considered, followed by summaries of the key relevant criminal offences and provisions concerning vulnerable witnesses.

24.7   Other issues relevant to safeguarding are covered in separate chapters: information on the Mental Capacity Act (MCA) 2005 is provided in chapter 17 and for issues relating to access to information, data protection and confidentiality[12] see chapter 25. Specific safeguarding measures for children and young people are not covered.

Legal and policy context

The human rights and equality context

24.8   The Human Rights Act (HRA) 1998 is a 'key driver for safeguarding' as it requires respect for human rights and encourages high standards of practice by public bodies'.[13] It gives new impetus to the challenge posed by the widespread emotional, physical and sexual abuse of vulnerable adults,[14] not only by providing a cause of action in cases of abuse (see para 26.241 below) but also by providing a framework which can further the development of a culture where abuse is not tolerated.

24.9   Section 6 of HRA 1998 places a duty on public authorities to comply with the European Convention on Human Rights ('the Convention'). As highlighted in paras 26.252 and 26.260 below, Article 5 (right to liberty) and Article 8 (right to private and family life) of the ECHR are of direct relevance to the care and treatment of vulnerable adults.

24.10   Article 8 encompasses the individuals' right to autonomy. However, the requirement to respect the rights of individuals to make decisions for themselves is not excuse for inaction where an individual assessed as entitled to care and support, rejects such help. This point was highlighted in the joint report of the health service ombudsman and the local government ombudsman upholding a complaint concerning the care of a man with long-standing mental health problems who had become unwilling to receive the support offered to him. The ombudsmen noted that the man's care team wanted to respect his autonomy and independence but they had failed to address the clear risks of self-neglect. They concluded that it was not sufficient for the responsible local authority or NHS body to assert that person is 'a long standing, voluntary patient with capacity, entitled to reject assistance, which he did':

> We have not seen robust evidence that Mr B's capacity to make decisions was ever seriously considered or that there was discussion about the balance to be struck between an individual's autonomy and dignity. Mr B's

---

12   See also J Williams (2011) *Protection of older people in Wales: a guide to the law*, Older People's Commissioner for Wales, chapter 4: Confidentiality and data protection.

13   Commission for Social Care Inspection (2008) *Raising voices, views on safeguarding adults*, para 2.5.

14   Home Office (2000) *Setting the boundaries: reforming the law on sex offences*, para 0.17.

rights were clearly central in this matter but we have not seen evidence that the Trust or the Council had regard to or took specific account of human rights law or the provisions of the Mental Capacity Act 2005 in making their decisions.[15]

24.11   Article 3 (see para 26.247 below) is also relevant, in that it obliges states, not merely to refrain from subjecting anyone to degrading treatment, but also to take positive measures to ensure that no one is treated in this way. Accordingly in *Z and others v UK*[16] the European Court of Human Rights found that there had been a violation of Article 3 because a local authority 'had been aware of the serious ill-treatment . . . over a period of years . . . and failed to take any effective steps to bring it to an end'. In the court's opinion Article 3 (in conjunction with Article 1) required states:

> .#.#. to take measures designed to ensure that individuals . . . are not subjected to . . . degrading treatment . . . [which measures should] . . . provide effective protection, in particular, of children and other vulnerable persons and include reasonable steps to prevent ill-treatment of which the authorities had or ought to have had knowledge.

24.12   The case law on Article 3 has established that the courts and social services are obliged to use their powers to protect, not merely children, but also vulnerable adults[17] from abuse. Additionally, Article 3 requires states to take positive action to protect disabled people from harassment[18] and where credible evidence exists that an individual has suffered abuse while in the care of a public authority, to convene an independent and open investigation to be convened.[19]

24.13   The Equality Act 2010 public sector equality duty (see para 2.32 above) will also be of particular significance whenever a public body is developing or implementing safeguarding measures.

The need for reform

24.14   It could be argued that the current statutory and policy framework, if effectively administered, should be adequate to protect people who are in situations where they might be abused, since most forms of abuse contravene criminal law (eg amounting to theft or assault). Indeed it has been argued that having a different system for protection against abuse, creates its own problems by undermining the requirement that abusers should be punished under the criminal code, and accordingly that:

> Appropriate use of adult protection procedures should ensure that, just as any other citizen, a vulnerable adult has access to the criminal justice

---

15 Joint report by the Health Service Ombudsman and the Local Government Ombudsman (2011) concerning St Helens MBC and the five Boroughs Partnership NHS Trust, paras 114–115.
16 (2001) 34 EHRR 3.
17 *Re F (Adult: Court's jurisdiction)* [2000] 3 WLR 1740, (2000) 3 CCLR 210, CA.
18 See eg *Đorđević v Croatia* (pending) application no 41526/10 and *R (B) v DPP* [2009] EWHC 106 (Admin).
19 *Assenov v Bulgaria* (1998) 28 EHRR 652.

system. Otherwise, practice that results in only 'welfare' based responses to adult abuse decriminalises acts that in any other walk of life would be deemed a criminal offence and serves to justify oppressive and discriminatory responses on the part of organisations and practitioners.[20]

24.15   An alternative view is that because the framework for safeguarding adults is only set out in guidance, this has created a perception that compliance is optional.[21] Furthermore, whereas it 'has been known for many years that identifying and protecting children who need to be safeguarded from abusive situations is the responsibility of a wider constituency than the criminal justice' this is not the case for adults.[22] The majority of respondents (68 per cent) to the written consultation on *No Secrets* under-taken in 2008/9 to supported the need for safeguarding legislation.[23] The Law Commission recommendations for reform in relation to adult protection are discussed below (para 24.68 below).

24.16   While there may be differing opinions on how this is done, without doubt, there is an urgent need to address the serious failures within the health and social care sectors to provide adequate protection to adults who may be vulnerable to abuse. This has been made clear by series of reports, inquiries and media coverage. For example:

- A 2006 report into abuse of people with learning disabilities in the care of Cornwall Partnership NHS Trust highlighted the failure of senior management to address the abusive practices, such as physical, emotional and financial abuses, that had been taking place over many years.[24] Both the Cornwall report and the 2007 report concerning Sutton and Merton[25] suggested that although staff knew of the procedures for reporting abuse, they were largely unaware of what constituted abuse.
- A 2006 study of mistreatment of older people[26] found that about one in 40 people in the UK[27] aged 66 and over had been mistreated in their own homes (in the preceding year). When this prevalence of

---

20   D Galpin and J Parker 'Adult protection in mental health and inpatient settings' (2007) 9(2) *Journal of Adult Protection* 6.

21   M Flynn, 'How the NHS is Failing Vulnerable Adults' (2008) *Health Service Journal* 8 April.

22   Commission for Social Care Inspection (2008) *Raising voices, views on safeguarding adults.*

23   Department of Health (2009) *Safeguarding adults, report on the consultation on the review of 'No Secrets'*, para 11.

24   Commission for Social Care Inspection and Healthcare Commission (2006) *Joint investigation into the provision of services for people with learning disabilities at Cornwall Partnership NHS Trust.*

25   Healthcare Commission (2007) *Investigation into the provision of services for people with learning disabilities provided by Sutton and Merton Primary Care Trust*; and see also para 7.156 above.

26   M O'Keeffe et al (2007) *UK study of abuse and neglect of older people*, National Centre for Social Research and King's College London: this study used the definition of abuse developed by Action on Elder abuse, see para 24.5 above

27   Equating to about 227,000 people. For methodological reasons the study considers that it is likely to have underestimated the prevalence of abuse.

mistreatment (including both abuse and neglect) was broadened to include neighbours and acquaintances the prevalence increased to one in 25. The study estimated that only about 3 per cent of cases were picked up by adult protection services.[28]

- A 2011 BBC *Panorama* programme depicting a catalogue of serious and sustained abuse against people with learning disabilities in a locked ward of a private hospital.[29]

- A 2011 Equality and Human Rights Commission (EHRC) interim report of an inquiry into the home care of older people citing cases of 'people being left in bed for 17 hours or more between care visits; failure to wash people regularly and provide people with the support they need to eat and drink and people being left in soiled beds and clothes for long periods' while one in five of the older people who responded to the EHRC's call for evidence stated that they would not complain because they did not know how to, or for fear of repercussions.[30]

24.17   In May 2011, the Government set out its broad policy objectives in relation to safeguarding. It places safeguarding firmly within the personalisation agenda outlined in *A vision for adult social care: capable communities and active citizens* (see para 4.63 above).[31] Whilst the document is long on principles (empowerment, protection, prevention, proportionality, partnership and accountability) it is short on the detail of law reform. It confirms that *No Secrets* (see below) 'will remain as statutory guidance until at least 2013' and that (as recommended by the Law Commission) the government will to seek to provide a statutory basis for Safeguarding Adults Boards (see below).

24.18   While it is clear that the introduction of the legislation and guidance described in this chapter (and initiatives such as the Dignity in Care campaign[32]) are aimed at improving the protection of adults, it is legitimate to question the extent of the Westminster government's commitment to tackling adult abuse. As we note above, through its Prioritising Needs Guidance[33] (see para 3.206) it explicitly permits services to be limited to people whose needs are 'critical', but only describes 'serious' abuse and

---

28 At para 7.6.
29 See www.bbc.co.uk/news/uk-13548222 (accessed 18 July 2011). See also written statement of Paul Burstow MP, Minister of State (Care Services) outlining the steps to be taken in response to the abuse carried out at the Winterbourne View Hospital HC Deb, 7 June 2011, col 13WS.
30 www.equalityhumanrights.com/news/2011/june/inquiry-reveals-failure-to-protect-the-rights-of-older-people-receiving-care-at-home/ (accessed 20 June 2011).
31 Department of Health (2011) Gateway ref 14847.
32 Social Care Institute of Excellence: launched on 14 November 2006 with the aim to stimulate a national debate around dignity in care and create a care system where there is zero tolerance of abuse and disrespect of older people.
33 Department of Health (2010) *Prioritising need in the context of Putting People First: a whole system approach to eligibility for social care. Guidance on eligibility criteria for adult social care, England 2010.*

neglect as falling within that band (abuse and neglect only justifying a 'substantial' banding). The policy suggests therefore that the government only has zero tolerance of 'serious abuse'.[34]

Measures to protect adults from abuse

The vetting and barring scheme

24.19 The Safeguarding Vulnerable Groups Act (SVGA) 2006 was to have introduced an extensive 'vetting and barring' scheme for those wishing to work with children and/or vulnerable adults (whether paid or unpaid): protecting these vulnerable groups by stopping those who pose a known risk from working with them. This scheme was in response to the Bichard Inquiry report,[35] which found a range of flaws with the then existing arrangements for recruiting and vetting individuals wishing to work with these two groups.

24.20 The 2006 Act has (at September 2011) been partially implemented, with the bringing into force the provisions on barring individuals from working with children or vulnerable adults (see below). However, the provisions requiring those wanting to work with vulnerable groups to be registered and monitored to ensure their suitability to undertake such work (which had been subject to widespread criticism[36]) have not been brought into force, and indeed are to be abolished.[37]

24.21 At the time of writing (September 2011) proposals to 'scale back' the SVGA 2006 vetting and barring scheme are set out in the Protection of Freedoms Bill.[38] These include narrowing the scope of the barring provisions, abolishing the registration and monitoring system, the merging of the Criminal Records Bureau (CRB) and the Independent Safeguarding Authority (see below) into a body that will provide a 'barring and criminal records checking service' and enabling the 'portability of criminal records checks between jobs to cut down on bureaucracy'.

---

34 Welsh Assembly Government (2002) *Creating a unified and fair system for assessing and managing care,* 2002, in contrast treats all abuse as critical (para 5.16).

35 M Bichard (2004) *The Bichard Inquiry Report* HC653, established to enquire into child protection procedures following the conviction of Ian Huntley for the murders of Jessica Chapman and Holly Wells.

36 One of the concerns was that too many people would be required to register (for which there was a fee). Initially it was estimated that that around 11 million people would be required to register under the scheme – see HC Deb 27 October 2009 col 310W, although modifications reduced the estimated number to 9.3 million (see Home Office press release, 11 February 2011). See also Sir Roger Singleton, Chief Adviser on the Safety of Children, Chair of the Independent Safeguarding Authority, *Drawing the line, a report on the government's vetting and barring scheme,* December 2009.

37 For further information on the background to the proposed changes see House of Commons Library Research Paper 11/2, 23 February 2011.

38 Many of the provisions are based on the recommendations of the Home Office review (with the Departments of Health and Education), Vetting and Barring Scheme Remodelling Review – Report and Recommendations, February 2011.

Subject to parliamentary approval, these provisions are expected to become law by early 2012.[39]

24.22   The following paragraphs describe the current law.

Barring individuals from working with vulnerable groups

24.23   The Act establishes an Independent Safeguarding Authority (ISA) whose duty it is to oversee the vetting and barring scheme. The ISA decides on whether individuals should be prohibited from working with children and vulnerable adults and maintains two lists of those who have been barred, one in relation to children and one in relation to vulnerable adults (the 'ISA barring lists').[40] The SVGA 2006 includes a broad definition of 'vulnerable adult' which will include individuals aged 18 or over who are receiving health or social care.[41] The ISA barring lists replace the previous lists of individuals barred from working with vulnerable groups including the Protection of Vulnerable Adults (POVA) list established under the Care Standards Act 2000 Part 7.

24.24   Individuals placed on a barring list are prohibited from undertaking 'regulated activities' in relation to children and/or vulnerable adults – in essence this means they cannot work with children and/or vulnerable adults whether as an employee or a volunteer. The range of jobs and activities covered are wider than the previous lists, for example, the list for vulnerable adults applies to work undertaken in the NHS and prison sectors.[42] It is a criminal offence for individuals who have been barred from doing so, to seek to work with children and/or vulnerable adults.[43] Similarly it is a criminal offence to engage such a person to work with children and/or vulnerable adults.[44] The Protection of Freedoms Bill will introduce a duty on 'regulated activity providers' (which will include providers of health and social care) to check whether a person is barred before engaging them to work with children and/or vulnerable adults.

Duty to refer individuals to the Independent Safeguarding Authority (ISA)

24.25   The SVGA 2006 places a duty on employers, local authorities, professional regulators and inspection bodies to refer to the ISA any information on an individual working with children or vulnerable adults where they consider

39 See Home Office press release, 11 February 2011.
40 See SVGA 2006 s2 and Sch 3 Parts 1 and 2 for the criteria for determining whether a person should be barred from working with children (Part 1) or adults (part 2). See also ISA (2010) *Referral Guidance* p2.
41 SVGA 2006 s59. The new definition proposed in the Protection of Freedoms Bill (as amended in Public Bill Committee) covers those aged 18 or over who are receiving a range of support such as healthcare, personal care and assistance from a social worker (See clauses 64 and 65).
42 See SVGA Sch 4 Part 1 for 'regulated activities' in relation to children and Part 2 for 'regulated activities in relation to vulnerable adults. In essence the 'regulated activities' involve work that gives people the opportunity to have close contact with children and/ or vulnerable adults. It will therefore include those involved in regular contact with children and/or adults who use health or adult care services.
43 SVGA 2006 s7.
44 SVGA 2006 s9.

that person to have caused harm or pose a risk.[45] The ISA has provided guidance on the circumstances on when the duty to refer arises and the procedures for making the referral.[46] The ISA writes to those it is 'minded to bar', setting out the reasons for doing so and asking them to state why they should not be barred from working or volunteering with children and/ or vulnerable adults. Individuals have eight weeks to respond in writing to the ISA. If they are subsequently barred they will be notified in writing.

Challenging barring decisions

24.26   Save for those individuals who have committed certain serious criminal offences (who are automatically barred, without the right to make representations[47]) those whose names are included in either or both of the barred lists have the right of appeal to the Administrative Appeals Chamber of the Upper Tribunal against the ISA's decision to include them.

24.27   The procedures for referral and barring decisions under SGVA 2006 replace the procedure for placing workers on the POVA under the Care Standards Act 2000.[48] The Supreme Court found elements of this procedure to be incompatible with Articles 6 and 8 of the ECHR, namely the low threshold for inclusion on the provisional listing, alongside 'the draconian effect of provisional listing, coupled with the inevitable delay before a full merits hearing can be obtained'.[49]

24.28   Revised arrangements under SVGA 2006, which the Government had considered to be compatible with the Convention[50] have also been found wanting. In 2010 the High Court upheld a challenge by the Royal College of Nursing and others concerning the 'autobar with representations' element of the SVGA 2006 scheme. This requires the ISA to enter the names of those individuals convicted or cautioned for a wide range of offences on the barred lists automatically – ie before the individual has the opportunity to make representations on why their name should not be included. The court held that the absence of a right to make representations in advance was contrary to Articles 6 and 8 ECHR.[51] The Protection of Freedoms Bill seeks to address this breach by allowing for prior representations.[52]

---

45 See SVGA 2006 ss35–41.
46 See ISA (2010) *Referral guidance* V 2010–01, for an explanation of the referral requirements and procedures.
47 See SVGA 2006 Sch 3, Part 1 para 1 and Part 2 para 7 and Safeguarding Vulnerable Groups Act 2006 (Prescribed Criteria and Miscellaneous Provisions) Regulations 2009 SI No 37. Aspects of these provisions were the subject of legal challenge – see *R (Royal College of Nursing, OO, CW, AA and ER) v Secretary of State for the Home Department and Independent Safeguarding Authority* [2010] EWHC 2761 (Admin) and para 24.28 below.
48 CSA 2000 ss82 and 83.
49 *R (Wright and others) v Secretary of State for Health and another* [2009] UKHL 3.
50 See Ministry of Justice (2010) *Responding to human rights judgments. Government response to the Joint Committee on Human Rights* Fifteenth Report of Session 2009–10, July 2010 p27.
51 *R (Royal College of Nursing, OO, CW, AA and ER) v Secretary of State for the Home Department and Independent Safeguarding Authority* [2010] EWHC 2761 (Admin).
52 See clause 66 (4)–(8) of the Protection of Freedoms Bill (as amended in Public Bill Committee).

Criminal record checks

24.29 Providers of health and social care must ensure that they and their staff are suitable to undertake such work.[53] To do so they will need to initiate an enhanced CRB check.[54] This ascertains whether the person has any criminal convictions and if they have been barred from working with children[55] and/or vulnerable adults[56] (discussed above) and provides any other relevant police information.

24.30 Most such checks should be processed within four weeks. However, an expedited process, the 'Adult First Check', is available in relation to individuals wishing to work with vulnerable adults (replacing the 'POVA First'). This is only available where the provider would otherwise be unable to meet its statutory staffing levels. In essence, if the individual does not appear on the vulnerable adult barring list, he or she can be employed in advance of a full CRB disclosure.[57] In the meantime, that employee must be subject to stringent supervision.[58]

Disclosure and the Police Act 1997

24.31 The statutory provisions concerning the disclosure of information by the CRB are set out in Part 5 of the Police Act 1997.[59] The basis for determining what information to include in enhanced criminal record certificates was considered by the Supreme Court in *R (L) v Commissioner of Police of the Metropolis*.[60] In addition to records of convictions and cautions, the police are required to consider any other information which might be relevant and which ought to be included in the certificate. The Court held

53 See Health and Social Care Act 2008 (Regulated Activities) Regulations 2010 SI No 781 regs 4, 5, 6 and 21. See also Care Quality Commission (2010) *Guidance about Compliance: essential standards of quality and safety*. Outcome 12A. See also section 9 of SGVA 2006 (criminal offence to engage a person who is barred from doing so, to work with children and/or vulnerable adults).
54 For further information see: *CRB checks: Eligible positions guidance*, March 2011, NHS employment check standards published by NHS Employers, Jan 2011 and Care Quality Commission's guidance on CRB checks.
55 SVGA 2006 s113BA (suitability information relating to children).
56 SVGA 2006 s113BB (suitability information relating to vulnerable adults).
57 See *Request an ISA Adult First Check*: www.isaadultfirst.co.uk/guidance.aspx (accessed 8 June 2011).
58 See Care Quality Commission (2010) *Guidance about compliance: essential standards of quality and safety*, Outcome 12, Prompt 12A.
59 Previously Police Act 1997 s115 but this was replaced by sections 113A (in relation to standard CRB checks) and 113B (in relation to enhanced CRB checks), inserted by section 163(2) of the Serious Organised Crime and Police Act 2005. Section 113B (suitability information relating to vulnerable adults) was inserted by SVGA 2006 s63 and Sch 9 Part 2 para 14(1) and (4). See also Police Act 1997 (Enhanced Criminal Record Certificates) (Protection of Vulnerable Adults) Regulations 2002 SI No 446 as amended by SI 2009/1882.
60 [2009] UKSC 3. The court was concerned with the meaning and application of section 115(7) of the Police Act 1997. Although section 115 has been replaced, the Court noted that section 115(7) has been 're-enacted in virtually the same terms by sections 113B(3) and 113B(4) which were inserted into the 1997 Act by section 163(2) of the Serious Organised Crime and Police Act 2005' per Lord Hope at para 1 of the judgment.

that the approach to disclosure suggested by the Court of Appeal in 2004,[61] namely that non-criminal related information should be disclosed unless there is a good reason for not doing so, was misconceived since it 'encouraged the idea that priority must be given to the social need to protect the vulnerable as against the right to respect for private life of the applicant', whereas 'neither has precedence over the other'.[62] The court held that, in deciding whether to disclose the police must consider whether a) the information is relevant and reliable and b) in the light of the public interest and the likely impact on the person concerned, it is proportionate to provide the information. In some cases, such as where it is not certain whether the information is relevant, or the person might not have been given a fair opportunity to answer any allegation, police would be obliged to seek the views of the person concerned and take this into account.

24.32   The Protection of Freedoms Bill seeks to amend the Police Act 1997 to provide a more stringent test for determining whether additional information is to be included in the criminal record certificate. The chief officer must reasonably believe that the information is relevant and that it 'ought to be included in the certificate'.[63] The bill includes a range of further amendments to 1997 Act.[64]

Regulating the provision of health and social care

24.33   In England the Health and Social Care Act 2008 requires that all health and social care providers that carry out 'regulated activities'[65] are registered with the Care Quality Commission (CQC) (see paras 7.94 and 9.20 above). Such providers are monitored by the CQC to ensure that they are meeting their legal requirements, for which purpose the CQC has developed 'essential standards of quality and safety' (see paras 7.100 and 9.20 above)[66] which cover a range of themes such as 'personalised care, treatment and support' and 'safeguarding and safety' and will be used by the CQC to determine whether providers are complying with their legal obligations.

24.34   Outcome 7 of the CQC's essential standards focuses on 'Safeguarding people who use services from abuse' and is based on regulations which

61 *R (X) v Chief Constable of West Midlands Police* [2004] EWCA (Civ) 1068, [2005] 1 WLR 65.
62 Lord Hope, para 45 referring to *Campbell v MGN Ltd* [2004] UKHL 22, [2004] 2 AC 457 at para 12, per Lord Nicholls of Birkenhead.
63 Explanatory Notes para 298.
64 These derive in large measure from S Mason (2011) *A common sense approach: a review of the criminal records regime in England and Wales* (the Independent Advisor for Criminality Information Management).
65 Defined in the Health and Social Care Act 2008 (Regulated Activities) Regulations 2010 SI No 781, Schedule 1 including a range of health and social care such as personal care, nursing care and treatment of disease, disorder or injury.
66 Care Quality Commission (2010) *Guidance about compliance: essential standards of quality and safety. What providers should do to comply with the section 20 regulations under the Health and Social Care Act 2008* pursuant to Health and Social Care Act 2008 s23(1).

require providers to 'make suitable arrangements to ensure that service providers are safeguarded against abuse'.[67] However, the CQC notes that effective safeguarding requires compliance with a whole range of registration requirements, such as robust recruitment and vetting processes for staff.[68]

24.35   In Wales, the Assembly has issued similar guidelines (pursuant to the Care Standards Act 2000) to which the regulator, the Care and Social Services Inspectorate for Wales (CSSIW), works, namely – national minimum standards for care homes (see para 7.101 above) and for domiciliary care agencies (see para 9.14 above).

Additional measures to protect those perceived to be vulnerable

The Mental Capacity Act 2005

24.36   Although the MCA 2005 does not include the specific powers to protect vulnerable adults from abuse,[69] it has a significant role in relation to safeguarding. For example, the principles and the assessment of best interests detailed in sections 1 and 4 (see paras 17.5 and 17.31 above) are, as the CQC notes considerations that 'need to be embedded in everyday practice when safeguarding decisions are being considered'.[70]

24.37   Furthermore the following provisions will be of relevance: the powers of the Office of the Public Guardian to investigate cases of abuse; the power to appoint deputies (which could include local authorities) to take social welfare decisions in addition to financial decisions to ensure that the incapacitated person is adequately protected (see para 17.56 above); and the creation of a new criminal offence of ill-treating or wilfully neglecting people lacking capacity (see para 24.104 below).[71] The CQC also highlights the importance of the Deprivation of Liberty Safeguards under the MCA 2005 which apply to care homes and hospitals, noting that the CQC has a monitoring role in relation to the operation of these safeguards.[72]

---

67 Health and Social Care Act 2008 (Regulated Activities) Regulations 2009 SI No 781 reg 11. Abuse is defined as 'sexual abuse, physical or psychological ill-treatment; theft, misuse or misappropriation of money or property; or neglect and acts of omission which cause harm or place at risk of harm' (regulation 11(3)).
68 Care Quality Commission (2010) *Our Safeguarding Protocol*, para 4.3.
69 Despite the Law Commission's recommendations: see chapter 9: Public Protection for Vulnerable People at Risk, in The Law Commission (1995) *Mental Incapacity*, Law Com 231.
70 Care Quality Commission (2010) *Our Safeguarding Protocol* para 8.1.
71 See also the discussion of MCA 2005 – Department of Health (2009) *Safeguarding Adults, Report on the consultation on the review of 'No Secrets'* paras 2.24–2.27.
72 Care Quality Commission (2010) *Our Safeguarding Protocol* para 8.3 and see also para 17.49 above.

Guardianship

24.38 Mental Health Act (MHA) 1983 s7 provides for the circumstances in which a person can be made subject to guardianship.[73] The purpose of guardianship is 'to enable patients to receive care outside hospital when it cannot be provided without the use of compulsory powers'.[74] It can be applied where the guardian's powers 'and the structure imposed by guardianship, may assist relatives, friends and professionals to help a mentally disordered person manage in the community'.[75] The guardian has three specific powers:

1) to require the patient to reside at a place specified;
2) to require the patient to attend at specified places and times for medical treatment, occupation, education or training; and
3) to require access to the patient to be given.[76]

24.39 Individuals may only be received into guardianship if they are aged 16 or over, have a 'mental disorder', the mental disorder is 'of a nature or degree' which warrants their reception into guardianship and that this is necessary in the interests their welfare, or for the protection of other persons.[77] It follows that mental incapacity is not a necessary pre-requisite for the use of guardianship.

24.40 The term 'mental disorder' has a broad definition (MHA 1983 s1), namely: "mental disorder" means any disorder or disability of the mind'. However, in relation to persons with learning disabilities, guardianship can only be applied if their learning disability is 'associated with abnormally aggressive or seriously irresponsible conduct'.[78] Noting that this limitation on the application of guardianship 'removes a significant potential framework for the protection of adults with learning difficulties', the Law Commission in 2011 recommended that the government review the current application of guardianship to people with learning disabilities. Removing this qualification would:

> . . . enable professionals in an adult safeguarding situation to set conditions to protect the person – such as to allow professionals access to visit the person who is subject to guardianship and specifying where the person should live.[79]

24.41 In *Lewis v Gibson and MH*[80] it was held that there is no requirement that a local authority seek 'declaratory relief' (see para 24.76 below) in

---

73 For further information on guardianship see the Code of Practice to the Mental Health Act 1983, chapter 26 and the Reference Guide to the Mental Health Act 1983, chapter 19.
74 Code of Practice to the Mental Health Act 1983 (2008) para 26.2
75 Department of Health (2008) *Reference Guide to the Mental Health Act 1983* para 19.3.
76 MHA 1983 s8.
77 MHA 1983 s7(2).
78 See MHA 1983 s 1(2A) and (2B): see also *Re F (Mental Health Act: Guardianship)* [2000] 1 FLR 192, (1999) 2 CCLR 445, CA.
79 Law Commission (2011) *Adult Social Care*, Law Com No 328 HC 941, para 9.141; and see also Recommendation 46.
80 [2005] EWCA Civ 587, (2005) 8 CCLR 399.

preference to a guardianship order. However, when seeking to displace a nearest relative as a component of a guardianship application, it was essential (for the purposes of Articles 6 and 8 of the ECHR) that the patient be served and his or her capacity to act ascertained.

Adult protection

24.42   The governments in both England and Wales are proposing to legislate to provide new powers to protect adults at risk of abuse.[81] This section considers the legal and policy framework that exists currently, followed by a summary of the Law Commission's 2011 proposals for reform. To date, as the Law Commission notes:

> Unlike in Scotland, there is no statutory duty placed on local authorities in England and Wales to investigate cases of abuse or potential abuse, equivalent to the child protection measures contained in the Children Act 1989. Instead the legal framework for responding to cases of suspected adult abuse and identifying responsible agencies is provided for through a combination of the common law and local authority guidance.[82]

Local authority guidance

24.43   Although the 2000 adult protection guidance issued to local authorities, *No Secrets*[83] (in England) and *In Safe Hands*[84](in Wales) have been shown to be in need of reform,[85] they both continue to be the main statutory guidance for adult protection. *No Secrets* is to remain in place until, at least, 2013[86] and although the Welsh Government intends to 'revise and publish updated statutory guidance to replace *In Safe Hands*',[87] the timescale for this process (as at September 2011) is unclear.

24.44   *No Secrets* and *In Safe Hands* focus on processes such as:

- the clarification of the roles and responsibilities of the relevant agencies (eg social services, the police, NHS bodies);
- the development of multi disciplinary procedures for responding to

---

81   See Department of Health (2011) Statement 16 May 2011 pp4–5, and Welsh Assembly Government (2011) *Sustainable Social Services for Wales: a framework for action*, para 3.77.

82   Para 4.269.

83   Department of Health and Home Office (2000) *No Secrets: guidance on developing and implementing multi-agency policies and procedures to protect vulnerable adults from abuse.*

84   National Assembly for Wales (2000), *In Safe Hands.*

85   See (for England) Department of Health (2009) *Safeguarding Adults – report on the consultation on the review of 'No Secrets'* and (for Wales) J Magill, V Yeates and M Longley (2010) *Review of In Safe Hands: a review of the Welsh Assembly Government's guidance on the protection of vulnerable adults in Wales*, Welsh Institute for Health and Social Care, University of Glamorgan.

86   Department of Health statement, 16 May 2011.

87   Welsh Assembly Government (2011) *Sustainable Social Services for Wales: a framework for action*, para 3.76.

concerns and referrals, including joint protocols on such issues as information sharing;

- contract monitoring with independent providers;
- improvements to information for service users, carers and members of the public;
- the development of monitoring systems and training strategies.

24.45   While such processes are of value, *No Secrets* and *In Safe Hands* cover an area of law where there is currently no specific statute that confers powers and duties on local social services authorities.

24.46   A *national framework of standards for good practice and outcomes in adult protection work*, published by the Association of Directors of Social Services in 2005, has also had a significant positive influence.[88] These standards detail the responsibilities of safeguarding adult teams in relation to joint planning and capability, prevention of abuse and neglect, and responding to abuse and neglect – together with specific time frames. They were developed with the purpose of encouraging the 'development of consistent, high quality adult protection work across the country'. Although the standards are not mandatory, they reflect and promote good practice[89] and as such will be relevant considerations by courts, inquiries and ombudsmen if and when called upon to assess a local authority's performance in this field.

24.47   A 2010 review of *No Secrets* highlighted the 'absence of adult safeguarding systems within the NHS to ensure that healthcare incidents that raise safeguarding concerns are considered in the wider safeguarding arena'.[90] Accordingly the Department of Health has issued a range of guidance to encourage the development of robust safeguarding arrangements.[91]

24.48   That the lack of statutory framework for adult protection can lead to less significance being placed on adult protection, in comparison with child protection was one of the serious concerns raised by the Chair of the Serious Case Review into the murder of Steven Hoskin. She noted that in comparison to child protection measures 'safeguarding adults is a poor relation in terms of profile, funding and resources'. In addition, whereas the Children Act 2004 requires each local authority to establish local safeguarding boards, *No Secrets* only requires (at para 3.4) that 'agencies may consider there are merits in establishing a multi-agency management committee (adult protection) which is a standing committee of lead officers'.[92]

---

88 This document is described as being 'arguably the most important policy document since *No Secrets*' by the authors of the report into the prevalence of abuse (see note 26 above).

89 Association of Directors of Adult Social Services (ADASS) (2011) *Raising voices, views on safeguarding adults*.

90 Department of Health (2010) *Clinical governance and adult safeguarding processes*.

91 Listed at www.dh.gov.uk/en/Publicationsandstatistics/Publications/ PublicationsPolicyAndGuidance/DH_124882 (accessed 3 August 2011).

92 Cornwall Adult Protection Committee (2007) *The Murder of Steven Hoskin: a serious case review, executive summary* (December 2007) para 7.2.1.

24.49   The Law Commission seeks to address the lack of legislative backing to adult protection by including a range of adult protection provisions in its proposed single statutes for adult social care for each of England and Wales.[93] The non-mandatory status of local adult safeguarding boards is a particular concern. These boards are multi-agency partnerships, made up of statutory bodies and voluntary organisations, which aim to facilitate joint working in adult protection, through, for example, ensuring that multi-agency policies and procedures are in place, conducting serious case reviews and providing training and information. Despite their important role, they have no statutory basis. However, in the light of the Law Commission's recommendation the Department of Health has confirmed that local adult safeguarding boards will become mandatory in future legislation.[94]

Adult protection: the role of the regulators

24.50   The regulators of health and social care in England and Wales have a significant role in relation to safeguarding adults. However, the lack of a clear investigatory remit in cases where abuse against individuals is suspected may leave residents in care homes and other settings, such as private psychiatric hospitals, vulnerable to abuse.

24.51   Although the CQC regards safeguarding to be a 'priority area' and health and social care providers are required to inform it of any allegations of abuse,[95] the CQC's safeguarding protocol describes a supervisory, rather than a lead, role in the area of adult protection. It states that the CQC's function is 'primarily, as a regulator, to ensure that commissioners and providers of care have adequate systems in place' to ensure the safety of children and vulnerable adults.[96]

24.52   Where concerns about safeguarding suggest that there has been a breach of regulations or that the person registered to provide health or social care is not fit to do so, the CQC will consider what action it can take. The CQC powers are far reaching, ranging from the provision of advice and guidance to providers where there are minor concerns about compliance, to cancelling the registration and/or issuing criminal prosecutions against registered providers in cases where there are failures to comply with legal requirements or other serious concerns.[97] However, these powers focus on regulating the health and social care providers rather than responding to concerns about incidents of abuse against individual service users.

---

93 Law Commission (2011) *Adult Social Care*, Law Com No 326 HC941, Part 9.
94 Statement of Government Policy on Safeguarding, 16 May 2011: www.dh.gov.uk/ prod_consum_dh/groups/dh_digitalassets/documents/digitalasset/dh_126770.pdf
95 Outcome 20 Notification of other incidents, Prompt 20N, in CQC (2010) *Guidance on compliance: essential standards of quality and safety.*
96 CQC (2010) *Our safeguarding protocol.*
97 CQC (2010) *Our enforcement policy.*

24.53   The situation in Wales is similar. The CSSIW produces annual reports providing data on allegations of abuse against adults[98] and both regulators have highlighted the importance of adult protection and safeguarding and the need for much improvement in the health and social care sectors.[99] However, like the CQC, its comments focus on the adequacy of the response by other agencies to concerns about adult abuse. For example, CSSIW concluded that 'Most local authorities need to do more to provide a consistently effective service to protect vulnerable adults from abuse', while the Healthcare Inspectorate Wales's review of safeguarding arrangements in the NHS Wales found:

> Although NHS organisations have signed up to local safeguarding procedures, there is insufficient knowledge of the issues at an operational level and a lack of emphasis on the need to comply with the procedures.[100]

24.54   It may be that the regulatory bodies will take a more proactive role in the future. For example, the CQC has powers to carry out reviews and investigations into the provision of health or social care. It has 'a wide discretion about the circumstances which will lead to an investigation', which might be triggered by safeguarding issues such as serious injury or 'permanent unnecessary harm to people' and allegations of 'abuse, neglect or discrimination affecting people who use services, particularly those less able to speak for themselves or defend their rights'.[101]

24.55   The CQC announced that it was undertaking such a review following a 2011 BBC *Panorama* programme on the abuses that took place in a private hospital for people with learning disabilities.[102] The CQC acknowledged that it had failed to respond adequately to the concerns raised by former employee of the private hospital. However, it noted that as a safeguarding meeting had been set up, 'CQC took the view that the concerns were being examined.'[103] This raises a particular and serious concern with existing safeguarding procedures within health and care system, namely the need to ensure that prompt action is taken by a responsible authority. A similar failing was identified in a local government ombudsman's report upholding a complaint against Bristol City Council about the poor quality of care provided to an elderly woman with dementia. The council's delay in taking action to address the serious concerns with the care home identified by the CQC on two consecutive visits was considered to be maladministration.[104]

98   The report for 2009/10 is available at: http://wales.gov.uk/docs/cssiw/report/110701povaen.pdf

99   Joint statement of HIW and CSSIW, 30 March 2010 on the publication of National Inspection of Adult Protection All Wales Overview (CSSIW) and Safeguarding and Protecting Vulnerable Adults in Wales: a review of the arrangements in place across the Welsh National Health Service (HIW).

100 HIW (2010) *Safeguarding and protecting vulnerable adults in Wales: a review of the arrangements in place across the Welsh National Health Service* at para 3.1.

101 CQC (2010) *Our enforcement policy*, October 2010, p23.

102 Winterbourne View: see note 29 above.

103 CQC's statement on *Panorama*'s investigation 31 May 2011.

104 Report on an investigation into complaint no 09 005 944 against Bristol City Council 13 June 2011.

Whistleblowing

24.56   The Public Interest Disclosure Act 1998 should, in theory, give workers, who raise concerns about abuse and malpractice, protection from dismissal and victimisation. Covering all areas of employment, it can be of particular use where care workers are concerned about abusive practices experienced by service users within their organisation.

24.57   However, concerns about the lack of protection for whistleblowers, continue to be highlighted.[105] A report by Public Concern at Work, which analysed information received through its whistleblowing advice line, found that many workers in the care sector who had raised concerns reported that these were 'initially ignored, mishandled or denied by organisations' and the majority of whistleblowers are unaware of their organisation's whistleblowing policy.[106] Similarly, a survey of NHS hospital doctors in England and Wales by the British Medical Association (BMA) showed that while many doctors raised concerns about patient care, there was a low awareness of official whistleblowing policies in the workplace and of those that reported their concerns, nearly half were not told what had happened as a result of doing so. Reasons for not reporting concerns included fear for career prospects, and a lack of confidence in the outcomes of such processes.[107]

24.58   In its report on Patient Safety, the Health Committee of the House of Commons considered that '[a]n important measure of an organisation's safety culture is how it treats 'whistleblowing'. . . . Yet, in practice, it seems that many NHS staff fear the consequences of whistleblowing'. It quoted the results of the Royal College of Nursing's survey of its members, including that:

> 99% of registered nurses understood their professional responsibility to report worries about patient safety but fears about personal reprisals meant that only 43% would be confident to report concerns without thinking twice.[108]

24.59   The Committee noted that the information it had received indicated 'that the NHS remains largely unsupportive of whistleblowing'.[109] In June 2010, the Secretary of State for Health stated that the government intended to '. . . give teeth to the current safeguards for whistleblowers in

105 See eg Independent on Sunday, 'Whistle-blowers risk all while the chiefs do nothing', 5 June 2011. See also Complaint no 1999/200600720 against Carmarthenshire CC, 16 September 2009 para 357.
106 Speaking up for vulnerable adults: what the whistleblowers say, a report from Public Concern at Work, the whistleblowing advice line, April 2011.
107 BMA Survey: Speaking up for Patients Final Report Health Policy and Economic Research Unit, May 2009 See also the BMA's guide for medical students, February 2008.
108 House of Commons Health Committee (2009) Patient safety, Sixth Report of Session 2008–09 Vol 1, 18 June 2009, HC 151–11, paras 281–284: and see also The Shipman Inquiry, Fifth Report chapter 11, 2004 and Safeguarding patients. The Government's response to the recommendations of the Shipman Inquiry's Fifth Report, Cm 7015, February 2007, para 5.33.
109 Para 295.

the Public Interest Disclosure Act 1998' through various measures including 'reinforcing the NHS constitution to make clear the rights and responsibilities of NHS staff and their employers in respect of whistle-blowing' and 'issuing new guidance to the NHS about supporting and taking action on concerns raised by staff in the public interest'.[110] A consultation document on the *NHS Constitution and Whistleblowing* was issued by the Department of Health in October 2010.[111]

The role of the Office of the Public Guardian

24.60 The Public Guardian (supported by the Office of the Public Guardian (OPG)) is a creature of the MCA 2005[112] and is responsible for the administration of the registers of lasting powers of attorney, enduring powers of attorney and court appointed deputies (see para 17.56 above). The Public Guardian is, however, only responsible for supervising deputies and accordingly, will normally only investigate attorneys if representations have been made about the way they are carrying out their duties.[113]

24.61 The Public Guardian can send 'Court of Protection Visitors'[114] to visit people who may lack capacity and those who have formal powers to act on their behalf (ie attorneys and deputies). The code of practice comments that these Visitors 'have an important part to play in investigating possible abuse' but in addition they can 'check on the general well-being of the person who lacks capacity, and they can give support to attorneys and deputies who need help to carry out their duties'.[115] Furthermore attorneys and deputies must 'co-operate with the visitors and provide them with all relevant information'. If they fail to do so, 'the court can cancel their appointment, where it thinks that they have not acted in the person's best interests'.[116]

24.62 The Public Guardian has no direct powers of enforcement or sanction. Furthermore, the *Code of Practice to the Mental Capacity Act* states that the OPG will not always be the most appropriate organisation to investigate all complaints and that it would 'usually refer concerns about personal welfare LPAs or personal welfare deputies to the relevant agency', which in some cases might be the police.[117] However, the OPG has since issued its own safeguarding vulnerable adults policy which outlines a range of ways in which the OPG may be involved. This includes

110 House of Commons debates, 9 June 2010.
111 See www.dh.gov.uk/en/Consultations/Liveconsultations/DH_120349 (accessed 10 June 2010).
112 MCA 2005 s57. See also Lasting Powers of Attorney and Public Guardian Regulations 2007 SI No 1253.
113 MCA 2005 s58. See also the Code of Practice to the Mental Capacity Act, 2007, paras 14.12–14.14
114 There a two types of visitors: general and special – the Special Visitors are doctors with relevant expertise.
115 The Code of Practice, para. 14.11.
116 The MCA Code of Practice para 14.10.
117 See paras 14.19–14.21.

undertaking investigations into the actions of individuals acting on behalf of a person who lacks capacity, such as a deputy or registered attorney (lasting power of attorney (LPA) or enduring power of attorney (EPA)). It can also make applications to the Court of Protection for the suspension, discharge or replacement of a deputy or to cancel registration and revoke an EPA/LPA.[118]

24.63   A 2010 report from the OPG[119] shows that in the three years since the Act came into force, it received a total over 2,500 representations concerning the way in which deputies/attorneys were exercising their powers of which almost 1,200 were deemed to require a more formal in depth investigation. Most of these (1,080) were signposted to a third party such as the police or a social services department, but of those within the OPGs jurisdiction 194 court applications were made to discharge deputies/attorneys; 35 cases reported to the police; 31 formal censure letters from the PGO attorneys and 62 deputies were placed in a higher supervision level for ongoing monitoring.

The role of independent mental capacity advocates

24.64   The MCA 2005 established the Independent Mental Capacity Advocacy (IMCA) service. The role and scope of the IMCA service is detailed in regulations[120] and subject to guidance in the MCA Code of Practice. NHS bodies and local authorities are required to make arrangements for individuals to receive help from an IMCA if they lack capacity to make certain decisions (relating to serious medical treatment or changes of accommodation) and no relative or friend is able to assist them (considered further at para 17.67 above).[121]

24.65   Regulations also provide that, if such representation will be of benefit to the person, IMCAs may be appointed to represent individuals who lack capacity where an NHS body or local authority is contemplating taking adult protection measures.[122] Such appointments can be made, whether or not family, friends or others are involved.[123] Accompanying guidance to these regulations suggests that local authorities and NHS bodies should draw up a policy statement outlining who would most benefit from

---

118   OPG (2008) *Safeguarding vulnerable adults policy, November 2008.* See also OPG's 'Safeguarding Vulnerable Adults Procedures and Guidance' and the 'Office of the Public Guardian and Local Authorities: Working together to safeguard vulnerable adults'.

119   See www.justice.gov.uk/memorandum-mental-capacity-act.htm

120   Mental Capacity Act 2005 (Independent Mental Capacity Advocate) (General) Regulations 2006 No SI 1832; Mental Capacity Act 2005 (Independent Mental Capacity Advocate) (Expansion of Role) Regulations 2006 SI No 2883; Mental Capacity Act 2005 (Independent Mental Capacity Advocate) (Wales) Regulations 2007 SI No 852 (W77).

121   Sections 35–41. Note that the Health and Social Care Bill, published in January 2011, seeks to amend the MCA 2005 so that local authorities are directly responsible for arrangements for IMCAs.

122   Mental Capacity Act 2005 (Independent Mental Capacity Advocate) (Expansion of Role) Regulations 2006 SI No 2883 regs 3 and 4.

123   See Code of Practice para 10.66.

receiving support from an IMCA, and that this should be made widely available.[124] The guidance reminds councils and NHS bodies that if a person meets the qualifying criteria it would be unlawful for them not to consider exercising their power to instruct an IMCA.[125]

24.66   The Social Care Institute for Excellence has issued a practice guide for IMCAs involved in safeguarding adults proceedings. This points out that local authorities and NHS bodies that instruct an IMCA for adults at risk are legally required to have regard to any representations made by the IMCA when making decisions concerning protective measures and that IMCAs can make representations on any matter they feel is relevant to decisions concerning protective measures, including concerns about the investigation process or the involvement of the police.[126]

24.67   IMCAs must also be made available to individuals subject to the Deprivation of Liberty Safeguards (DOLS).[127] If they or their representative (not being a paid representative) request such assistance this must be provided. In addition, if the supervisory body considers that an IMCA is needed to enable the person subject to DOLS to exercise their rights, it must instruct an IMCA.[128] During its third year, 9,173 people received representation from the IMCA service, with 1,326 people being represented in adult protection proceedings and 1,214 IMCA instructions relating to the DOLS.[129]

The Law Commission's Review on Adult Protection

24.68   The legal framework for adult protection was considered by the Law Commission as part of its review of adult social care.[130] It recommended that legislation should provide that local social services authorities have the lead co-ordinating responsibility for safeguarding and:

> ... the statute will place a specific duty on social services authorities to investigate, or cause an investigation to take place, in individual cases. This should be worded to ensure that this duty can be discharged through a range of *pathways* or different routes through safeguarding. For example, the social services authority could undertake enquiries themselves, refer the matter to the appropriate agency or initiate a multi-agency investigation. The duty to investigate could also be delegated to the NHS,

---

124 Department of Health (2007) *Adult Protection Care Reviews and IMCAs.*
125 Department of Health (2007) *Adult Protection Care Reviews and IMCAs* para 10.
126 SCIE Guide 32: Practice guidance on the involvement of Independent Mental Capacity Advocates (IMCAs) in safeguarding adults: www.scie.org.uk/publications/guides/guide32/imcarole.asp (accessed 10 June 2011).
127 For further information about DOLS, see para 17.49 above.
128 See MCA 2005 s39D and the Code of Practice to DOLS para 7.37–7.41. See also *Hillingdon LBC v Steven Neary and others* [2011] EWHC 1377 (COP) in which the court highlighted the important role of the IMCA in such cases (para 194).
129 Department of Health (2010) *The Third Year of the Independent Mental Capacity Advocacy (IMCA) Service 2009 /10.*
130 Law Commission (2011) *Adult Social Care*, Law Com HC 941, Part 9.

as is currently the case, under the NHS Act 2006 and the NHS (Wales) Act 2006.[131]

24.69 To strengthen these provisions, the Law Commission recommended that the statute should include a general duty on agencies to co-operate, and an enhanced duty to co-operate in adult protection cases.[132] Furthermore, the Law Commission recommended that the statute should set out a range of functions for adult safeguarding boards, including to keep under review the procedures and practices of public bodies which relate to safeguarding adults and to give information or advice, or make proposals, to any public body on the exercise of functions which relate to safeguarding adults. It also proposed that the local social services authority should be given the lead role in establishing adult safeguarding boards and that the CQC, the Care and Social Services Inspectorate Wales and the Healthcare Inspectorate Wales should be given a power to nominate an appropriate representative to attend meetings.

24.70 Although the Law Commission had made a series of recommendations in relation to compulsory and emergency intervention in its 1995 report, *Mental Incapacity*,[133] it declined to include similar proposals in the report on adult social care on the basis such provisions had not been proposed by either the Westminster or the Welsh Governments.[134]

Misuse of adult protection procedures

24.71 While some consultees to the Law Commission's review on adult social care argued that the law was inadequate in this area and local authorities needed to have emergency powers to protect individuals from being abused or neglected,[135] others took a different view, reporting:

> . . . that local authorities are already heavy handed and too eager to intervene without proper legal authority to remove service users arbitrarily from domestic settings.[136]

24.72 A similar note of caution was made in *A Local Authority v A*. Munby LJ commented that while social workers needed to be alert to issues of concern and 'must act quickly and decisively' where these arise, they 'must guard against being seen as prying or snooping on the families who they are there to help and support':

> Nothing is more destructive of the 'working together' relationship which in this kind of context, as in others, is so vitally important than a perception by family carers that the local authority is being heavy-handed or worse.[137]

---

131 Para 9.16, referring to NHSA 2006 s75 and NHS(W)A 2006 s33.
132 Recommendation 45.
133 Law Commission (1995) *Mental Incapacity* Law Com No 231, February 1995.
134 See discussion at paras 9.52–9.59.
135 Some argued that such a review was necessary in the light of Article 16 CRPD (Freedom from exploitation, violence and abuse).
136 Paras 9.54–9.55.
137 [2010] EWHC 978 (Fam), (2010) 13 CCLR 404 at [98]: see also para 24.98 below.

24.73 Concerns about the misuse of adult protection measures have also been highlighted by the local government ombudsman. For example, the ombudsman found that the decision by Luton Borough Council to initiate adult protection procedures in relation to a disabled young man, during a time when there were on-going problems with various aspects of his care plan, amounted to maladministration. In addition to upholding the family's complaint that they had not received appropriate services from the council, the ombudsman stated:

> Quite apart from any procedural shortcomings, it beggars belief that the referral was made at all, and this was compounded by the fact that the family was informed far too late. I have no doubt that the family found the referral extremely hurtful, not least because it perceived itself as providing care for Shahid in the absence of any significant care provision by the Council. The adult protection referral and the delay in telling the family of it were maladministration by the Council, which caused the family distress and outrage when they found out.[138]

24.74 Similarly, the ombudsman admonished a social services panel for describing the action of a mother of two severely disabled, who due to the 'totally inappropriate accommodation where they could not be adequately bathed' had no option but to hose her sons down in the back garden, as being 'abusive'. Noting that the mother's parenting skills and her commitment to care for her sons had never been in question, the ombudsman considered that such comments were of 'breathtaking insensitivity' and it was maladministration for the panel to then fail to secure any immediate alternative.[139]

24.75 Another area of concern is the failure to respond adequately to allegations of abuse. The Public Services Ombudsman for Wales[140] detailed a catalogue of failures in the way that complaints about the abuse by staff of a day centre of a woman with learning disabilities was handled. The ombudsman concluded that this amounted to 'many instances of serious maladministration and service failure'. There was 'overwhelming evidence of pervasive management failure within the Learning Disabilities service at the time, characterised by a failure of leadership, a lack of accountability and, crucially, the failure to create and sustain a culture which valued the rights of service users and protect them against abuse.[141] This maladministration and service failure had caused considerable distress to the member of staff who had reported the abuse as well as other staff obliged to work in such an environment. It was particularly unjust for the users of the service who had been left at risk by the failure of the social services department.

---

138 Complaint no 07/B/07665 against Luton BC, 10 September 2008, para 37.
139 Complaint no 07C03887 against Bury MBC, 14 October 2009, para 43.
140 Complaint no. 1999/200600720 against Carmarthenshire CC, 16 September 2009.
141 Paras 356–358.

Declaratory relief and the role of the high court

24.76 Since the enactment of the HRA 1998, the higher courts have dynamically developed a number of latent common law doctrines and mechanisms in an effort to provide legal protection for vulnerable adults.

24.77   The MCA 2005 preserves the right of concerned parties to apply to the court for a declaration of 'best interests' (known as 'declaratory relief').[142] Such applications are made to the Court of Protection, which has the full powers of the High Court to make declarations on financial or welfare matters affecting people who lack capacity to make decisions. It also enables a concerned party to apply to be appointed an incapacitated person's 'deputy', and it can remove deputies and attorneys who are acting inappropriately.[143]

24.78   While the Court of Protection established under MCA 2005 has assumed the 'declaratory relief' jurisdiction developed by the High Court since 2000, its jurisdiction is limited to cases concerning people who lack mental capacity as defined under MCA 2005 (or cases in which the court is asked to determine whether the person lacks mental capacity). The Court of Appeal has also confirmed that, 'where it is necessary, lawful and proportionate', the High Court's 'inherent jurisdiction' has survived the introduction of MCA 2005. This means that the court can 'exercise its inherent jurisdiction in relation to mentally handicapped adults alongside, as appropriate, the Mental Capacity Act 2005', so long as this is not 'deployed so as to undermine the will of Parliament'.[144]

24.79   However, over the last decade the High Court (Family Division) had also developed its jurisdiction in relation to people who, although considered to have mental capacity, are otherwise vulnerable and in need of protection. With the introduction of MCA 2005 it was unclear as to whether the inherent jurisdiction could continue to be invoked in such cases. This question has now been resolved and is considered further at para 24.84 below.

Background – the development of declaratory relief

24.80 The High Court's declaratory relief procedure for vulnerable adults first found full expression in *Re F (Adult: court's jurisdiction)*.[145] The case concerned a young adult who lacked sufficient mental capacity to make informed decisions as to where she should live or who posed a risk to her safety. As a minor she had been neglected and exposed to abuse while in the care of her parents and had accordingly been made a ward of court and placed in specialist accommodation. The wardship came to an end on her 18th birthday and the local authority feared that without some form of

---

142 MCA 2005 s15.
143 See MCA 2005 ss16–20.
144 Lord Justice Wall endorsing the findings of Roderic Wood J, para 55 *City of Westminster v IC (By His Friend The Official Solicitor)* and *KC and NN* [2008] EWCA Civ 198, [2008] 2 FLR 267.
145 [2000] 3 WLR 1740, (2000) 3 CCLR 210, QBD.

fresh court order her mother would seek her return home where she would be at risk of further abuse. As Dame Butler-Sloss observed:

> There is an obvious gap in the framework of care for mentally incapacitated adults. If the court cannot act . . . this vulnerable young woman would be left at serious risk.[146]

24.81 To fill this gap, the court's solution was for it to 'grow' and 'shape'[147] the common law principle of 'necessity'. In the court's judgment, therefore, where a serious justiciable issue arose as to the best interests of an adult without the mental capacity to make the relevant decision, then the High Court was able to grant declarations (in the exercise of its inherent jurisdiction) as to what would be in that person's best interests.[148]

24.82 The courts have in subsequent judgments developed the principles established by *Re F* and, in so doing, have clarified the scope and availability of the declaratory jurisdiction.[149] This is an area in which the law continues to develop, particularly in the light of the HRA 1998.[150] The key issues are summarised below.

Requirement to seek the authority of the courts

24.83 The courts have emphasised that in some circumstances local authorities will be under a duty to take action to intervene in relation to the care of vulnerable adults, see, for example, *Re Z (Local Authority: duty)*[151] and *X and another v Hounslow LBC*.[152] However, save for cases where National Assistance Act s47 (see para 7.38 above) or the MHA 1983 applies, 'if a local authority seeks to control an incapacitated or vulnerable adult it must enlist the assistance of either the Court of Protection or the High Court.'[153]

The existence of mental incapacity or other barriers to decision making

24.84 Much of the early case law suggested that the court could only deploy its declaratory relief jurisdiction once it was established that the person in question was incapable (by reason of mental incapacity) of making the relevant decision – see, for instance, *Newham LBC v BS and S*.[154] However, in *A Local Authority v MA, NA and SA*,[155] Munby J held that incapacity was not essential. In his view the court could exercise its inherent jurisdiction:

---

146 [2000] 3 WLR 1740, (2000) 3 CCLR 210, QBD at 219.
147 [2000] 3 WLR 1740, (2000) 3 CCLR 210, QBD per Sedley LJ at 227B.
148 [2000] 3 WLR 1740, (2000) 3 CCLR 210, QBD at 218C–E.
149 Proceedings should be commenced in the High Court under CPR Part 8 – *M v B, A and S* [2005] EWHC 1681 (Fam), [2006] 1 FLR 117.
150 As predicted by Munby J, as he then was, in *In Re S (Adult Patient) (Inherent Jurisdiction: Family Life)* [2002] EWHC 2278 (Fam), [2003] 1 FLR 292 at [52].
151 [2004] EWHC 2817 (Fam), [2005] 1 FLR 740 at [19].
152 [2008] EWHC 1168 (QB)
153 *A v A Local Authority* [2010] EWHC 978 (COP) at [68].
154 [2003] EWHC 1909 (Fam), (2004) 7 CCLR 132.
155 [2005] EWHC 2942 (Fam), [2006] 1 FLR 867 at [55].

. . . in relation to a vulnerable adult who, even if not incapacitated by mental disorder or mental illness, is, or is reasonably believed to be, either (i) under constraint or (ii) subject to coercion or undue influence or (iii) for some other reason deprived of the capacity to make the relevant decision, or disabled from making a free choice, or incapacitated or disabled from giving or expressing a real and genuine consent.[156]

24.85   In coming to this conclusion Munby J cited an extensive case law,[157] including *Re G (an adult) (Mental capacity: court's jurisdiction)*[158] where the court held that G lacked capacity because of her 'father's ability to overbear [her] decision-making' ability. As a consequence G was placed by the court under a protective regime, which limited the father's access to her – and as a result she recovered her capacity to make decisions. The problem was, that if the court's power ceased when she recovered capacity, then she would fall under her father's power again – and so be caught in a rotating door. As Bennett J stated:

If the restrictions were lifted . . . it is probable that the situation would revert to what it was prior to March 2004. G's mental health would deteriorate to such an extent that she would again become incapacitated to take decisions about the matters referred to. Such a reversion would be disastrous for G.

24.86   In the circumstances the court held that incapacity was not an essential requirement for it to exercise its inherent jurisdiction.

24.87   These cases were decided prior to the introduction of MCA 2005. The question as to whether MCA 2005 and its accompanying code of practice had ousted the High Court's jurisdiction in relation to vulnerable adults was addressed in *A Local Authority v DL, ML and GRL*.[159] In this case the local authority wished to intervene to safeguard elderly parents from the threatening and abusive behaviour of their son, who lived with them. For the purposes of the proceedings it was accepted that the parents were mentally capable of making relevant decisions. Having given extensive consideration to relevant case law, in addition to reviewing the impact of the HRA 1998 and MCA 2005, Mrs Justice Theis DBE concluded that the High Court's inherent jurisdiction could still be invoked in relation to this group of people. However, the crucial factor is not whether the person is considered to be 'vulnerable':

Each case will, of course, have to be carefully considered on its own facts, but if there is evidence to suggest that an adult who does not suffer from any kind of mental incapacity that comes within the MCA but who is, or reasonably believed to be, incapacitated from making the relevant decision by reason of such things as constraint, coercion, undue influence or other vitiating factors they may be entitled to the protection of the inherent

156 In many respects this development follows the Law Commission's 1995 proposals in their original Mental Incapacity Bill which suggested (at clause 36) that the adult protection powers could be used where the person was (among other things) 'unable to protect himself against significant harm or serious exploitation'.
157 [2005] EWHC 2942 (Fam), [2006] 1 FLR 867 at [59]–[60].
158 [2004] EWHC 2222 (Fam).
159 [2011] EWHC 1022 (Fam).

jurisdiction (see: *SA (supra) para [79])*. This may, or may not, include a vulnerable adult.[160]

24.88   The court considered that the obligations on the state under the ECHR and the HRA 1998 required the retention of the inherent jurisdiction as by refusing to do so would, in effect, create 'a new "Bournewood gap". While the Court acknowledged that positive obligations to intervene in family life had, thus far, only arisen in relation to children and adults who lacked capacity, this did not preclude positive obligations arising in other circumstances. Whether such obligations arise will 'depend on the circumstances of each case and what the proportionate response is considered to be by the [local authority]'.[161] The court stressed that in cases where the inherent duty arises because the adult is deemed to have problems in making decisions for themselves, due to external forces, such as coercion:

> . . . the primary purpose is to create a situation where the person concerned can receive outside help free of coercion, to enable him or her to weigh things up and decide freely what he or she wishes to do.[162]

24.89   That the inherent jurisdiction could only be invoked for such purposes was emphasised in *LBL v RYJ and VJ*.[163] Macur J had 'no doubt' that the inherent jurisdiction could be used to 'supplement the protection afforded' by MCA 2005 but that this is only 'for those who, whilst "capacitous" for the purposes of the Act, are "incapacitated" by external forces – whatever they may be – outside their control from reaching a decision' in order to 'facilitate the process of unencumbered decision-making'. In so holding she specifically rejected the contention that 'the inherent jurisdiction of the court may be used in the case of a capacitous adult to impose a decision upon him/her whether as to welfare or finance'.[164]

A serious justiciable issue

24.90   A 'serious justiciable issue' which requires resolution must exist. The courts have not sought to define precisely what is meant by this phrase but have made clear that this will cover a broad range of issues – any genuine question as to what the best interests of a patient require or justify – extending 'to all that conduces to the incompetent adult's welfare and happiness, including companionship and his domestic and social environment'.[165] It will exist when the facts 'demonstrate a situation in which the doctrine of necessity might arise' (ie a matter that requires a resolution in the best interests of an adult who lacks mental capacity to

---

160   Para 53(4).
161   Para 53(6).
162   Para 53(7).
163   [2010] EWHC 2665 (CoP).
164   [2010] EWHC 2665 (CoP) at [62].
165   See *A v A Health Authority and another In re J (A Child) R (S) v Secretary of State for the Home Department* at [39]–[43].

decide for herself).[166] It is not the same as the threshold test for care proceedings under Children Act (CA) 1989 s31 so there is no requirement to establish risk of significant harm before intervening.[167]

What is the question that needs to be determined?

24.91   In *Newham LBC v BS and S*[168] a question arose as to whether the 'significant issue' that had to be determined was (a) if abuse had occurred; or (b) where the incapacitated person should live. The local authority applied for a declaration, basing its application on evidence that the disabled person's father drank excessively and had assaulted her. The court rejected this evidence, but nevertheless considered that an order should be made. In this respect Wall J considered that while there 'must be good reason for local authority intervention' and that there may be a need for the court to resolve disputed issues of fact: 'if their resolution is necessary to the decision as to what is in S's best interests. Findings of fact against [the father] . . . would plainly reflect upon his capacity properly to care for S.' He held:

> But it does not follow, in my judgment, that the proceedings must be dismissed simply because the factual basis upon which the local authority instituted them turns out to be mistaken, or because it cannot be established on the balance of probabilities. What matters (assuming always that mental incapacity is made out) is which outcome will be in S's best interests. There will plainly be cases which are very fact specific. There will be others in which the principal concern is the future, and the relative suitability of the plans which each party can put forward for both the short and the long term care of the mentally incapable adult. The instant case, in my judgment, is one of the cases in the latter category.

Best interests and the 'balance sheet' assessment

24.92   The meaning of best interests is considered at para 17.31 above. When exercising their declaratory powers, the courts have generally required a 'balance sheet' to be drawn up listing the potential benefits and 'disbenefits' that may flow from an intervention. This approach was identified by the Court of Appeal in *Re A (Medical treatment: male sterilisation)*,[169] in the following terms:

> The . . . judge . . . should draw up a balance sheet. The first entry should be of any factor or factors of actual benefit . . . Then on the other sheet the judge should write any counter-balancing disbenefits to the applicant . . . Then the judge should enter on each sheet the potential gains and losses in each instance making some estimate of the extent of the possibility that the gain or loss might accrue. At the end of that exercise the judge should be

---

166   *Re F (Adult: Court's jurisdiction)* [2000] 3 WLR 1740, (2000) 3 CCLR 210, QBD, per Butler Sloss LJ.
167   *Re S (Adult patient) (inherent jurisdiction: family life)* [2002] EWHC 2278 (Fam), [2003] 1 FLR 292, per Munby J at para 45.
168   [2003] EWHC 1909 (Fam), (2004) 7 CCLR 132.
169   [2000] 1 FLR 549 at 560F–H.

better placed to strike a balance between the sum of the certain and possible gains against the sum of the certain and possible losses. Obviously only if the account is in relatively significant credit will the judge conclude that the application is likely to advance the best interests of the claimant.

24.93 In the *Newham LBC* proceedings Wall J considered that the benefits of the daughter remaining with her father included his love for, and strong sense of duty towards, her and the fact that he had adequately provided for her in the recent past. The benefits of her moving to an independent residential care placement included the fact that her father (due to his age and poor health) would progressively find it difficult to care for her; that she could have contact with her siblings (who were not prepared to visit her at her father's house); and that the proposed care home would provide her with an opportunity for social contact with people of her own age group. In addition the court considered that the professional evidence was 'crucial': the social and health professionals were of the opinion that the care home placement was the better option. In the judge's opinion, therefore, the balance sheet came down firmly in favour of the care home placement.

24.94 The need for decision makers to 'balance the pros and cons of all relevant factors' is highlighted in the MCA Code of Practice (para 5.62) and is accordingly adopted by the Court of Protection.[170] The code also notes (para 5.64) that the decision maker will need to find a way of balancing the differing concerns and opinions of relatives and carers, adding that the decision-maker has the ultimate responsibility for working out the person's best interests. In *A local authority v C and others*,[171] the court stated:

> In practical terms best practice both in proceedings before the Court of Protection and generally is to apply a structured approach to the decision to be made. The decision maker draws up a notional balance sheet of welfare factors describing the benefits and detriments of the available courses of action having encouraged the person concerned to participate in the process and having ascertained wishes and feelings, beliefs and values and other considerations particular to the person including consulting with relevant third parties.

The proportionality of interventions

24.95 The 'benefits/disbenefits' assessment process will almost always relate to an issue of fundamental relevance to a disabled person's private and family life and their home – and thus require an examination of the proportionality of the proposed action from the perspective of Article 8 of the ECHR. In this context, it would appear that there are certain presumptions – for instance that the state interference will be the least restrictive and presumably that there should be no 'order' unless strictly necessary.[172]

170 See eg, *Re P (Adult patient: consent to medical treatment)* [2008] EWHC 1403 at [22].
171 [2011] EWHC 1539 (Admin) at para 59.
172 In this context, see the approach to a not dissimilar balancing exercise taken by Munby J in *R (A and B) v East Sussex CC (No 2)* [2003] EWHC 167 (Admin), (2003) 6 CCLR 194 at 226–232.

However, the courts have been reluctant to adopt such an approach in declaratory relief proceeding. For example, they have taken the view that there is no presumption that mentally incapacitated adults will be better off if they live with a family rather than in an institution. Nevertheless they have emphasised that the burden will be on the State (eg on a local authority) to establish, if it sought to do so, that it was the more appropriate person to look after the mentally incapacitated adult than his or her own family.[173]

24.96   The central importance of the Convention, and in particular Article 8, to decisions on where individuals who lack capacity should live, was emphasised in *Hillingdon LBC v Steven Neary and others,*[174] which concerned the local authority's decision to detain a young disabled man in a residential unit, despite the objections of his father (and main carer):

> Decisions about incapacitated people must always be determined by their best interests, but the starting point is their right to respect for their family life where it exists. The burden is always on the State to show that an incapacitated person's welfare cannot be sustained by living with and being looked after by his or her family, with or without outside support.

24.97   For a number of significant reasons, the court found that the local authority had breached the young man's rights under Article 8, the first being that the local authority had not considered the positive obligation to respect the right to family life and the requirement that in order to justify removing a children or vulnerable adults from their families 'can only be on the basis that the State is going to provide a better quality of care than that which they have hitherto been receiving'.[175] The court found:

> Nowhere in their very full records of Steven's year in care is there any mention of the supposition that he should be at home, other things being equal, or the disadvantages to him of living away from his family, still less an attempt to weigh those disadvantages against the supposed advantages of care elsewhere. No acknowledgement ever appears of the unique bond between Steven and his father, or of the priceless importance to a dependent person of the personal element in care by a parent rather than a stranger, however, committed. No attempt was made at the outset to carry out a genuinely balanced best interests assessment, nor was one attempted subsequently.[176]

Ex parte applications

24.98   Ex parte applications to the court may, in appropriate cases, be made without other parties being notified – for instance, in situations of urgency. In *B BC v S and S*[177] a nursing home was no longer willing or able to cope with an elderly resident, but his wife was known to be implacably

---

173   *Re S (Adult Patient) (Inherent Jurisdiction: Family Life)*, [2002] EWHC 2278 (Fam), [2003] 1 FLR 292. See also *A Local Authority v E* [2008] 1 FCR 389 at 412.
174   [2011] EWHC 1377 (COP).
175   Quoting from Munby LJ in *SA*.
176   [2011] EWHC 1377 (COP) at [154].
177   [2006] EWHC 2584 (Fam), (2006) 9 CCLR 596.

opposed to a temporary placement in hospital and the local authority had reached (in the court's opinion) the reasonable view that she would have tried to 'pre-empt a decision of the court by seeking to remove her husband from the nursing home'. However, the court expressed concern that practitioners were making without notice applications that were not necessary or appropriate, nor properly supported by appropriate evidence.[178] This concern was echoed by Munby LJ in *A Local Authority v A*:

> Too often, in my experience, local authorities seeking the assistance of the court in removing an incapacitated or vulnerable adult from their home against their wishes or against the wishes of the relatives or friends caring for them, apply ex parte (without notice) and, I have to say, too often such orders have been made by the court without any prior warning to those affected and in circumstances where such seeming heavy-handedness is not easy to justify and can too often turn out to be completely counter-productive . . .[179]

24.99 His Lordship went on to suggest that generally local authorities would 'only be justified in seeking a without notice order for the removal of an incapacitated or vulnerable adult in the kind of circumstances which in the case of a child would justify a without notice application for an emergency protection order'.[180]

The range of potential declarations

24.100 In the *Newham LBC* decision, Wall J made a declaration authorising the local authority to continue with the care home arrangement (with defined contact between the father and daughter). Additionally he declared that the authority was to consult her father about any future medical treatment/care arrangements she might require and that she be provided with an independent advocate.

24.101 Declarations can also be sought concerning future situations, provided they are rooted in a serious 'justiciable issue' and are not overly hypothetical.[181] In *Re S (Adult patient) (Inherent jurisdiction: family life)*[182] the local authority was concerned that it might have to return to the court – repeatedly – for additional declarations, given the difficult relationship that existed between it and the incapacitated person's father. The authority accordingly asked the court to declare that it had – in effect – proxy decision-making power on a range of social welfare questions. Munby J

---

178 [2006] EWHC 2584 (Fam), (2006) 9 CCLR 596 at [37].

179 [2010] EWHC 978 (Fam), (2010) 13 CCLR 404 at [99].

180 [2010] EWHC 978 (Fam), (2010) 13 CCLR 404, referring to *X Council v B (Emergency Protection Orders)* [2004] EWHC 2015 (Fam) and *Re X (Emergency Protection Orders)* [2006] EWHC 510 (Fam). These cases stressed that ex parte notices would only be appropriate if the case is genuinely one of emergency or other great urgency or if there are compelling reasons to believe that the child's welfare will be compromised if the parents are alerted in advance to what is going on.

181 See eg *R v Portsmouth Hospitals NHS Trust ex p Glass* (1999) 2 FLR 905, (1999) 50 BMLR 269 where the court held a future treatment decision to be too hypothetical.

182 [2002] EWHC 2278 (Fam), [2003] 1 FLR 292.

(as he then was) held that the court 'has jurisdiction to grant whatever relief in declaratory form is necessary to safeguard and promote the incapable adult's welfare and interests'.

Criminal offences

24.102 While it is debatable how far the possibility of being charged with a criminal offence deters people from abusing adults, over the last few years there has been an increase in the number of offences which are specific to adults who are in vulnerable situations or may be vulnerable to abuse.[183] These include provisions set out below.

Mental Health Act 1983 s127

24.103 Section 127 makes it an offence for managers of hospitals or care homes, or their staff, to ill-treat or wilfully neglect a patient (whether detained or not) who is receiving treatment for their mental disorder in that hospital or care home. This offence also applies to individuals receiving treatment for mental disorder when they are on the premises of the hospital or care home. In addition, it is an offence for any individual to ill-treat or wilfully neglect a mentally disordered person who is subject to their guardianship under MHA 1983, or otherwise in his or her custody or care. While this is potentially a wide-ranging provision, it is limited procedurally since proceedings can only be instigated by or with the permission of the Director of Public Prosecutions.

Mental Capacity Act 2005 s44

24.104 Section 44 makes it an offence for anyone caring for, or who is an attorney under a lasting power of attorney or enduring power of attorney, or is a deputy for a person who lacks capacity, to ill treat or wilfully neglect that person. The provision is limited to people who lack capacity (and accordingly narrower in scope than MHA 1983 s127 above) but is not restricted by a requirement to obtain leave before charges are laid. However, the Law Commission noted that at consultation events with police officers on its review of adult social care law, 'it was suggested that prosecutions were being dropped in practice because doctors cannot confirm or have not documented that the person lacks capacity'.[184]

24.105   In the case of *R v Dunn*[185] the Court of Appeal considered the relationship between section 44 and the test for capacity as set out in sections 2 and 3 of the Act. The appellant had been convicted for ill-treating three elderly residents of a care home, all of whom had dementia. She appealed on the basis that the recorder's direction to the jury had failed to focus

---

183 See also J Williams, *Protection of older people in Wales: a guide to the law*, chapter 5: The Criminal Justice System, Older People's Commissioner for Wales, 2011.
184 See para 9.144 and recommendation 46.
185 [2010] EWCA Crim 2935.

sufficiently on the capacity of each of the complainants to make decisions at the time at which the alleged ill-treatment took place. It was argued that the lack of reference to ' "the specific decision test of capacity" and "the specific time of decision requirement" resulted in a direction that was flawed because it was incomplete'.[186]

24.106   While acknowledging that the 'convoluted and complex' tests involved in sections 2 and 3 'do not appear to be entirely appropriate to defining the constituent elements of the criminal offence', the Court of Appeal considered that the purpose of section 44 was also significant: that everyone, who can no longer live an independent life and 'is a vulnerable individual living in a residential home, is entitled to be protected from ill-treatment if he or she lacks "capacity" as defined in the Act'. In rejecting the appellant's argument, the Court of Appeal held that:

> . . . it was open to the jury to conclude that the decisions about the care of each of these residents at the time when they were subjected to ill-treatment were being made for them by others, including the appellant, just because they lacked the capacity to make these decisions for themselves. For the purposes of section 2, this was 'the matter' envisaged in the legislation. On this basis the Recorder's direction properly expressed the issues which the jury was required to address and resolve by putting the direction clearly within the ambit of the language used in section 2.

> . . . In the context of long-term residential care, and on the facts of this particular case, it was unnecessary for the Recorder further to amplify his directions and complicate the position for the jury by referring in this part of his summing-up to any of the provisions of section 3, or for them to be incorporated into his directions. Therefore, the omission to incorporate them or to refer to the material contained in section 3 does not lead us to doubt the safety of the conviction of offences contrary to section 44 of the 2005 Act.

Fraud Act 2006 s4

24.107   Section 4 concerns 'fraud by abuse of position' and makes it an offence for a person who occupies a position where he or she is required to safeguard (or not act against) the financial interests of another person, to dishonestly abuse that position, with the intent of self-benefit or to benefit others.

Sexual Offences Act 2003 ss30–41

24.108   The Sexual Offences Act 2003 contains a range of provisions relating to people with mental disorder (bearing the same meaning as in the Mental Health Act (MHA) 1983). Sections 30–33 create offences that rely on the inability of the person to refuse the sexual activity on account of lack of capacity or where the person is unable to communicate refusal. Sections 34–37 relate to situations where the person suffering from a mental

---

186   The recorder had summarised the test for incapacity under section 2, but had not mentioned that this was to be assessed at the 'material time', nor had he included the test for determining whether a person is unable to make a decision as set out in section 3.

disorder is induced, threatened or deceived into sexual activity where the perpetrator knows or could reasonably be expected to know that the person suffered a mental disorder. Sections 38–41 relate to care workers where the assumption is that the worker must have known or reasonably expected to have known that the person had a mental disorder and do not rely on the inability of the victim to refuse.

Domestic Violence, Crime and Victims Act 2004 s5

24.109   Section 5 makes it an offence to cause or allow the death of a child or vulnerable adult and is designed to address the evidential problem of proving who in a household was actually responsible for causing or allowing the death to occur. In such circumstances a person is guilty of an offence if there was significant risk of serious physical harm, and the person either caused the victim's death, or was or ought to have been aware of the risk and failed to take steps to protect the victim, and the act occurred in circumstances that the person foresaw or ought to have foreseen. The definition of household includes people who do not live in the property but whose visits are sufficiently frequent for them to be counted as a member of such.[187]

Vulnerable witnesses

24.110   Many victims of crime, whose mental capacity is impaired, experience considerable difficulties in delivering their evidence. The report *Speaking Up For Justice*[188] made a number of recommendations aimed at encouraging and supporting vulnerable or intimidated witnesses to give their best evidence in criminal cases, many of which were enacted in Youth Justice and Criminal Evidence Act 1999 Part 2. This included the right of vulnerable witnesses to have the assistance of an intermediary when being interviewed or giving evidence (section 29).[189] The Ministry of Justice has issued guidance concerning the procedures.[190]

187   For further information see Home Office circular 9/2005.
188   Home Office, 1998.
189   The Crown Prosecution Service has a range of resources for victims and witnesses, including the special measures introduced under the 1999 Act. See www.cps.gov.uk/legal/s_to_u/special_measures/#Principle
190   Home Office (2011) *Achieving Best Evidence in Criminal Proceedings: Guidance for vulnerable or intimidated witnesses (including children)*: www.justice.gov.uk/guidance/docs/achieving-best-evidence-criminal-proceedings.pdf

CHAPTER 25

Access to personal information, data protection and confidentiality

Introduction

25.1   This chapter considers the right of access to personal information and the right to have one's personal information kept confidential. Clearly there is potential for these two rights to conflict and this chapter explores how the law regulates such situations. The right protected by the Freedom of Information Act 2000 (and other legislation) to obtain non-personal information from public bodies is considered in chapter 2 above (see for example, para 2.53).

25.2   Crucial to any analysis of the law of confidentiality is an appreciation that the right is not an 'absolute' one. It is qualified, and like all qualified rights requires a balance to be struck between competing interests and principles. In certain situations therefore the state is entitled to interfere with a person's 'privacy' provided the interference pursues a legitimate aim (for instance, the protection of the person or another) and the interference is not disproportionate. In terms, therefore, an understanding of the law requires an understanding of Article 8 of the European Convention on Human Rights ('the Convention') – the right (among other things) to respect for one's private life. At times, the right can only be 'respected' by a disclosure of confidential information – for instance, where a vulnerable person lacking capacity has been abused and the police need to be informed of this fact. In other situations the striking of a balance may require a limited disclosure. The local government ombudsman has held, for example, that while the confidential nature of risk assessments means that councils are not obliged to share them with service providers; this does not mean that they are under no duty to share information about (for instance) a service user's history of challenging behaviour.[1]

The legal framework

25.3   The striking of the balance has not been eased by the legal framework that has developed to regulate this important function. In essence there are three domains of the law that bear upon such decisions, namely:

- the Data Protection Act (DPA)1998;
- the Human Rights Act (HRA) 1998; and
- the common law.

25.4   The relevant provisions of DPA 1998, HRA 1998 and the common law are reviewed below. However, the interplay between them was considered in *R (S) v Plymouth City Council*.[2] The case concerned 'C', a 27-year-old man with learning and behavioural difficulties who had been assessed as lacking mental capacity to consent to the disclosure of information in his health and social services files to his mother (his nearest relative for the purposes of Mental Health Act 1983 s11). The local authority obtained a

---

1   Complaint no 04/C/16195 against Birmingham City Council, 23 March 2006.
2   [2002] EWCA Civ 388, [2002] 1 WLR 2583, (2002) 5 CCLR 251.

guardianship order in relation to C, since it believed that it was not in his best interests to live with his mother. The mother expressed concern about this action and in order to decide whether or not to object, she asked to see the relevant papers in his social services and healthcare files. The local authority refused, initially asserting that it could not disclose the information because it was confidential. Subsequently it shifted its position, accepting that it had power to disclose, but that this could not occur without very good reasons (and it considered that none existed). The Court of Appeal disagreed with this approach. Reviewing DPA 1998 it noted that although all the information that the mother was seeking was 'sensitive personal data' within the meaning of DPA 1998 s2(e), this did not mean that it could not be disclosed to third parties – since the Act permitted this in various situations, including:[3]

> . . . where it is necessary in order to protect the vital interests of the data subject or another person in a case where consent cannot be given by or on behalf of the data (Sched 3, para 3); or for the purpose of, or in connection with, any legal proceedings (including prospective legal proceedings) or for the purpose of obtaining legal advice, or where it is otherwise necessary for the purposes of establishing, exercising or defending legal rights (para 6); or where it is necessary for the administration of justice, or for the exercise of any functions conferred on any person by or under an enactment (at [7]).

25.5 In the circumstances therefore it considered that the Act provided little assistance and that the final decision on the disclosure of the confidential information[4] depended upon a careful analysis of the relevant common law and HRA 1998 principles – which required that 'a balance be struck between the public and private interests in maintaining the confidentiality of this information and the public and private interests in permitting, indeed requiring, its disclosure for certain purposes'.

25.6 Following a detailed analysis the court concluded as follows:

> 48. Hence both the common law and the Convention require that a balance be struck between the various interests involved. These are the confidentiality of the information sought; the proper administration of justice; the mother's right of access to legal advice to enable her to decide whether or not to exercise a right which is likely to lead to legal proceedings against her if she does so; the rights of both C and his mother to respect for their family life and adequate involvement in decision-making processes about it; C's right to respect for his private life; and the protection of C's health and welfare. In some cases there might also be an interest in the protection of other people, but that has not been seriously suggested here.

> 49. C's interest in protecting the confidentiality of personal information about himself must not be under-estimated. It is all too easy for professionals and parents to regard children and incapacitated adults as having no independent interests of their own: as objects rather than

---

3   [2002] EWCA Civ 388, [2002] 1 WLR 2583, (2002) 5 CCLR 251 at [27].
4   The court was of the view that it was overly simplistic to consider that all the information in the file was confidential, commenting at [33], 'some of it may not be confidential at all: straightforward descriptions of everyday life are not normally thought confidential'.

subjects. But we are not concerned here with the publication of information to the whole wide world. There is a clear distinction between disclosure to the media with a view to publication to all and sundry and disclosure in confidence to those with a proper interest in having the information in question. We are concerned here only with the latter. The issue is only whether the circle should be widened from those professionals with whom this information has already been shared (possibly without much conscious thought being given to the balance of interests involved) to include the person who is probably closest to him in fact as well as in law and who has a statutory role in his future and to those professionally advising her. C also has an interest in having his own wishes and feelings respected. It would be different in this case if he had the capacity to give or withhold consent to the disclosure: any objection from him would have to be weighed in the balance against the other interests, although as *W v Egdell*[5] shows, it would not be decisive. C also has an interest in being protected from a risk of harm to his health or welfare which would stem from disclosure; but it is important not to confuse a possible risk of harm to his health or welfare from being discharged from guardianship with a possible risk of harm from disclosing the information sought. As *Re D*[6] shows, he also has an interest in decisions about his future being properly informed.

50. That balance would not lead in every case to the disclosure of all the information a relative might possibly want, still less to a fishing exercise amongst the local authority's files. But in most cases it would lead to the disclosure of the basic statutory guardianship documentation. In this case it must also lead to the particular disclosure sought. There is no suggestion that C has any objection to his mother and her advisers being properly informed about his health and welfare. There is no suggestion of any risk to his health and welfare arising from this. The mother and her advisers have sought access to the information which her own psychiatric and social work experts need in order properly to advise her. That limits both the context and the content of disclosure in a way which strikes a proper balance between the competing interests.

25.7   In such cases, public bodies should analyse precisely why they are asserting 'confidentiality' and ask themselves whether this does indeed promote the best interests of the third party: is confidentiality being claimed to protect themselves rather than the disabled person? In its guidance on protecting vulnerable adults, *No Secrets*,[7] the Department of Health emphasised this point (at para 5.8), stating 'principles of confidentiality designed to safeguard and promote the interests of service users and patients should not be confused with those designed to protect the management interests of an organisation. These have a legitimate role but must never be allowed to conflict with the interests of service users and parents.'

5   [1990] 2 WLR 471, CA – see para 26.40 below.
6   *Re D (Minors) (Adoption reports: confidentiality)* [1995] 3 WLR 483, HL.
7   Department of Health and Home Office (2000) *No Secrets: guidance on developing and implementing multi-agency policies and procedures to protect vulnerable adults from abuse;* in National Assembly for Wales (2000) *In Safe Hands* (para 9.5) – see para 24.43 above.

Data Protection Act 1998

25.8   The DPA 1998 covers all social services and health records. It is not an easy Act and where possible courts tend to try to articulate the law using other reference points – principally the common law and Article 8 of the Convention (as did the Court of Appeal in the *Plymouth City Council* case). Indeed a former Lord Chancellor has observed that:

> The problem about the Data Protection Act is that it is almost incomprehensible. It is very difficult to understand. The precise limits of it are problematic. There are constant difficulties about what information you are allowed to share between departments for instance. I just think it needs to be looked at again at some stage to make it more simple.[8]

25.9   Legal guidance on the Act has been issued by the Information Commissioner,[9] in addition to which specific NHS[10] and social services guidance has been issued by the Department of Health. In the following section, paragraph references are to the social services guidance ('the guidance')[11] unless the context indicates otherwise.

25.10   The 1998 Act applies to all 'accessible public records', no matter when they were compiled, and includes electronic and manual data. An accessible public record is a record which contains any personal information held by the health body or social services department for the purposes of their health/social services functions, irrespective of when the information was recorded (DPA 1998 s68). The information held may include factual material as well as 'any expressions of opinion, and the intentions of the authority in relation to the individual' (guidance para 5.4).

25.11   The Act applies eight basic principles to the disclosure of information. These essentially require data to be processed fairly, legally, accurately and that the information be retained no longer than necessary; they restrict the transfer of data as well as unnecessary reprocessing of data; and require organisations holding such information to take appropriate measures to restrict unauthorised access to it.

25.12   Where joint records are held, for example, by social services and an NHS trust in a community mental health team, a request for access to that information can be made to either body (para 5.2) – the guidance stating that:

> Authorities and their partners in joint record holding will therefore need to have procedures in place to ensure that the data subject is aware that he/

---

8   Lord Falconer, as quoted in P Wintour, 'Fees pledge on information Act', *Guardian* 18 October 2004.

9   Information Commissioner (2009) *Guide to data protection*. The Commissioner's website (www.ico.gov.uk/) contains has extensive list of subject specific guidance on the DPA.

10   See eg Department of Health (2010) *Guidance for access to health records requests* and Department of Health (2003) *Confidentiality NHS Code of Practice*.

11   Department of Health (2000) *Data Protection Act 1998 – guidance to social services*. Virtually identical guidance was issued in Wales – Welsh Assembly Government (2000) *Data Protection Act 1998 – guidance to social services*.

she is not obliged to apply to all partners for access and to inform each other that access has been given.

25.13   The Act gives a right of access by individuals to any personal information held by the authority about them. Where the information concerns other individuals (for instance, a local authority file on an entire family) one member is not in general entitled to see information about another member without that person's consent (guidance paras 5.5–5.7). The Act permits the disclosure of information notwithstanding that it has been provided by a third party and that party has not consented to the disclosure. However, in deciding whether to agree to disclosure regard should be had to various factors, including the duty of confidence to the third party; the steps taken to obtain their consent (and whether they are capable of giving such consent); and the reasons for any refusal given by the third party (DPA 1998 s7(4); guidance para 5.7).

Access to information by or on behalf of children

25.14   The guidance (at paras 5.8 et seq) makes clear that where a person under 18 seeks access to their records the authority must decide whether or not they have 'sufficient understanding to do so', which means 'does he or she understand the nature of the request?'.[12] If the requisite capacity exists then the request for access should be complied with. If, however, insufficient understanding exists, the request may be made by a person with parental responsibility who can make the request on the child's behalf. Disclosure to parents in such cases should only occur after the authority has satisfied itself:

1)   that the child lacks capacity to make a valid application, or has capacity and has authorised the parent to make the application; and

2)   (where the child does not have capacity) that the request made by the parent on the child's behalf is in that child's interest (guidance para 5.9).

25.15   The advice accurately reflects the statutory and common law position. The Mental Capacity Act (MCA) 2005 s1 creates a presumption that all persons aged 16 or older have capacity to make decisions. The definition of parental responsibility in Children Act 1989 s3(1) includes the right of parents to consent on the child's behalf to a wide range of matters, including medical treatment.[13] In *Gillick v West Norfolk and Wisbech Area Health Authority*[14] the House of Lords had to consider when the parental right to make decisions on a child's behalf ended – for example, when the

---

12   For a review of the law concerning children's capacity to consent – see generally, S Broach, L Clements and J Read, *Disabled children: a legal handbook*, Legal Action Group, 2010, at paras 5.84–5.90.

13   See also Family Law Reform Act 1969 s8 and *Re W (A Minor) (Medical Treatment)* [1992] 3 WLR 758.

14   [1985] 3 WLR 830.

child achieved sufficient intelligence and understanding to make its own decision. The court held that it did, and cited with approval comments of Lord Denning,[15] namely:

> ... the legal right of a parent to the custody of a child ends at the 18th birthday: and even up till then, it is a dwindling right which the courts will hesitate to enforce against the wishes of the child, and the more so the older he is. It starts with a right of control and ends with little more than advice.

Requests made through another person (an agent)

25.16 Individuals with sufficient mental capacity are entitled to make their request for information via an agent. Paragraph 5.13 of the guidance states that agents should provide evidence (normally in writing) of their authority and confirm their identity and relationship to the individual; and that authorities (if satisfied that the agent is duly authorised) must treat the request as if it had been made by the individual concerned. Paragraph 5.14 accepts that some persons with profound physical impairments may not be able to give written consent to their agents and that in such cases the local authority should give the individual as much assistance as possible and ultimately need not always insist on permission in writing.

Access to information on behalf of an adult lacking mental capacity

25.17 A general outline of the law concerning adults who lack mental capacity is contained at chapter 18 above.

25.18 The DPA 1998 contains no special provisions concerning requests for access made on behalf of an adult who lacks sufficient understanding to make the request in his or her own name. The guidance, however, states (at para 5.11) that:

> ... if a person lacks capacity to manage their affairs, a person acting under an order of the Court of Protection or acting within the terms of a registered Enduring Power of Attorney can request access on her or his behalf.

25.19 Although the wording in this respect is an improvement on the draft guidance,[16] the failure of the Act to deal with this issue and the inadequacy of the guidance on this point has been the subject of criticism: as has the 'ambiguous, confused and scattered' nature of the guidance'.[17] However, these defects in the DPA 1998 are ameliorated to a degree by the approach the courts have taken in relation to the powers available under the

---

15 *Hewer v Bryant* [1970] 1 QB 357 at 369.
16 LASSL (99)16 para 2.12, which stated such requests could 'only' be made by such persons.
17 B Gray, C Robinson, D Seddon and A Roberts, 'Confidentiality smokescreens' and carers for people with mental health problems: the perspectives of professionals', (2008) *Health and Social Care in the Community* 16 (4), 378–387 at 386.

common law and consequent upon the implementation of HRA 1998 (as evidenced above in *R (S) v Plymouth City Council*[18] – see para 25.4 above).

25.20   The Code of Practice to the Mental Capacity Act (MCA) 2005 (see para 17.34 above) at chapter 16 contains useful information on the principles applicable to disclosure. It considers and gives examples of the situations where local authorities and health bodies are empowered to disclose information to third parties (even when these persons are not empowered by an enduring power of attorney, a lasting power of attorney or a deputy-ship) and includes:

> 16.19 Healthcare and social care staff may disclose information about somebody who lacks capacity only when it is in the best interests of the person concerned to do so, or when there is some other, lawful reason for them to do so.

> 16.20 The Act's requirement to consult relevant people when working out the best interests of a person who lacks capacity will encourage people to share the information that makes a consultation meaningful. But people who release information should be sure that they are acting lawfully and that they can justify releasing the information. They need to balance the person's right to privacy with what is in their best interests or the wider public interest . . .

> 16.21 Sometimes it will be fairly obvious that staff should disclose information. For example, a doctor would need to tell a new care worker about what drugs a person needs or what allergies the person has. This is clearly in the person's best interests.

> 16.22 Other information may need to be disclosed as part of the process of working out someone's best interests. A social worker might decide to reveal information about someone's past when discussing their best interests with a close family member. But staff should always bear in mind that the Act requires them to consider the wishes and feelings of the person who lacks capacity.

> 16.23 In both these cases, staff should only disclose as much information as is relevant to the decision to be made.

25.21   In 1991 practice guidance the Department of Health advised that advocates should in general be given access to relevant information concerning the person for whom they advocate and are enabled to consult with appropriate individuals in order to establish the best interests of that person.[19]

25.22   MCA 2005 s35(6) entitles independent mental capacity advocates (see para 17.67 above) to examine and take copies of (i) any health record, (ii) any record of, or held by, a local authority and compiled in connection with a social services function, and (iii) any record held by a person registered under the Care Standards Act 2000 Part 2 or the Health and Social Care Act 2008 Chapter 2 of Part 1 (see para 7.94 above) which the person

---

18 [2002] EWCA Civ 388, [2002] 1 WLR 2583, (2002) 5 CCLR 251.
19 *Care management and assessment practitioners guide*, HMSO, 1991, para 3.28.

holding the record considers may be relevant to the independent mental capacity advocate's investigation.

25.23   Research suggests that some professionals use 'confidentiality smoke-screens' as a way of withholding information from carers[20] where good practice requires that they anticipate such problems and (for instance) negotiate advance agreements when the disabled person has the capacity to consent and insight into their needs.[21] Guidance issued by the General Medical Council (GMC)[22] endorses this approach, advising (para 64):

> You should establish with the patient what information they want you to share, who with, and in what circumstances. This will be particularly important if the patient has fluctuating or diminished capacity or is likely to lose capacity, even temporarily. Early discussions of this nature can help to avoid disclosures that patients would object to. They can also help to avoid misunderstandings with, or causing offence to, anyone the patient would want information to be shared with.

25.24   The GMC guidance also advises (para 65) that where a patent lacks cap-acity that, unless they indicate otherwise, 'it is reasonable to assume that patients would want those closest to them to be kept informed of their general condition and prognosis'. The local government ombudsman has also suggested that this is a sound approach and that 'confidentiality' should not be used as a reason for not disclosing relevant information in such cases. In criticising a council for not sharing information with the parents of a 24-year-old man with serious learning difficulties, she commented:

> I accept that this would not be regular practice when the Council is looking after an adult: the privacy of the individual demands that the parents be kept at some distance. But [the user] had such a high level of dependency that the Council should have been willing to reconsider its approach to parental involvement in this case.[23]

Access procedures

25.25   DPA 1998 s7(2)(a) requires all requests for access to information to be in writing and section 7(8) requires the information to be disclosed 'promptly' and in any event within 40 days. All information must be disclosed, unless subject to any of the exceptions detailed below (most notably where the data includes information about another person).

20 B Gray, C Robinson, D Seddon and A Roberts, ' "Confidentiality smokescreens" and carers for people with mental health problems: the perspectives of professionals' (2008) *Health and Social Care in the Community* 16(4), 378–387.

21 See eg J Rapaport, S Bellringer, V Pinfold and P Huxley, 'Carers and confidentiality in mental healthcare' (2006) *Health and Social Care in the Community* 14, 357–365.

22 General Medical Council, 2009 *Confidentiality*, and see also *Carers and confidentiality in mental health. Issues involved in information-sharing*, Royal College of Psychiatrists, 2004.

23 Complaint no 97/C/4618 against Cheshire, 1999.

25.26   The information should not be altered in any way (guidance para 5.20) and should be the information which the authority held at the time of the request. Any amendment or deletion made between the time of request and supply should, however, be noted (if the changes would have occurred regardless of the request) (para 5.21). The Act contains procedures by which applicants can apply to have inaccurate information corrected.[24]

25.27   DPA 1998 s8(2) stipulates that the information should generally be provided in the form of a permanent copy although a copy need not be provided if is not possible, or would involve disproportionate effort or the applicant has agreed otherwise.

25.28   The 40-day period for disclosure is subject to certain restrictions, namely:

1)   Sufficient description of information sought. The applicant must provide the authority with sufficient information to enable it to identify the person about whom the information is sought and where that information is likely to be held. Authorities are permitted to provide a standard request form for this purpose but are not permitted to insist on its use (para 5.16).

2)   Payment of the appropriate fee. Authorities are permitted to charge a fee for the provision of information, which must not, however, exceed the statutory maximum of £10,[25] including the cost of supplying copies (special rules apply for access to manual health records for which the maximum fee is currently £50[26]). The guidance requires authorities to advise applicants promptly of the need to pay a fee (if one is charged) and advises that procedures should exist for waiving the fee where the applicant's means or any other circumstances dictate such a course (para 5.17). Since the 40-day period only commences when the fee has been paid it may be appropriate to include payment in the initial letter of request (see appendix C below for a precedent letter of request).

        The guidance advises (at para 2.18) that where authorities do not have the requested information, applicants should be informed as quickly as possible, and a decision then made as to whether the fee should be returned. In so deciding it should consider the applicant's circumstances, the effort involved in discovering that there was no data, and its own policy on charging.

3)   Repeated requests. Section 8(3) provides that access can be refused where the authority has previously complied with an identical or similar request from the applicant, unless a reasonable interval separates the requests.[27]

---

24 DPA 1998 s14 and see also paras 5.31 et seq of the guidance.
25 Data Protection (Subject Access) (Fees and Miscellaneous Provisions) Regulations 2000 SI No 191 reg 3.
26 Data Protection (Subject Access) (Fees and Miscellaneous Provisions) (Amendment) Regulations 2001 SI No 3223.
27 Para 5.19 of the guidance gives advice on what amounts to a 'reasonable interval'.

25.29 Not infrequently social services authorities suggest that the individual first view the data (eg files) in the presence of a social worker, before providing such copies as are required. It is very doubtful whether it is lawful for an authority to refuse to copy a file to an individual without their prior attendance to view it in the company of a social worker, since this imposes an extra non-statutory hurdle to access. Attendance at a social services office may be physically difficult for many service users and may be particularly daunting for the unassertive. If, however, the prior attendance requirement is put forward as good practice, to explain confusing or unclear aspects of the information and how it has been recorded, then, provided this does not significantly delay the provision of copies and provided proper consideration is given to difficulties service users may have in attending, such a requirement may be sustainable.

Third party information

25.30 DPA 1998 s7(4) states that where an authority is unable to comply with a request for information without disclosing information relating to another individual (who can be identified from that information), it is not obliged to comply with the request, unless, either:

a) the other individual has consented to the disclosure; or
b) it is reasonable in all the circumstances to comply with the request without the consent.

25.31 In deciding whether or not it is reasonable to make a disclosure without the third party's consent, section 7(6) requires the authority to have particular regard to the following factors:

a) any duty of confidentiality owed to that other individual;
b) any steps taken [by the authority] with a view to seeking the consent of the other individual;
c) whether the other individual is capable of giving consent;
d) any express refusal of consent by the other individual.

25.32 The guidance makes the following observations:

> 2.25 Section 7(6) is likely to be of particular relevance when a request is received for access to very old files and the possibility of tracing any third party is remote.
>
> 2.26 An authority should set itself a sensible timescale, within the 40 days allowed, in which to seek any third party consent. The 40 day period does not commence until the authority has received the written request, the appropriate fee, and if necessary, the further information required to satisfy itself as to the identity of the person making the request, and to locate the information sought.
>
> 2.27 If consent is not given by a third party within 40 days, an authority should give as much information as possible without identifying the third party (see DPA, section 7(5)). An authority should explain why some of the information requested has not been given. Where consent is or cannot be given and the authority considers it reasonable to comply with the

request without consent then the authority may be required to justify its actions . . .

2.28 Where the authority is satisfied that the data subject will not be able to identify the other individual (the third party source) from the information, taking into account any other information which the authority reasonably believes is likely to be in or to come into the possession of the [applicant] then the authority must provide the information.

26.32 In addition to the above factors, the statutory exemptions detailed below also apply to decisions about disclosure, most importantly where it is considered that disclosure could result in serious harm to the other individual. Indeed, if the third party is a social worker, access cannot be refused unless the 'serious harm test' applies (para 2.37).

Statutory exemptions from disclosure

25.33 DPA 1998 Part IV provides that authorities do not have to disclose information in certain situations. The principal grounds of relevance for the purposes of community care are (in summary):

1) The prevention or detection of crime (DPA 1998 s29). Where the authority considers that disclosure would be likely to prejudice criminal investigations, or crime prevention, it is exempt from the duty to disclose, although the guidance (para 3.37) advises that this only applies where there is a 'substantial chance' rather than a 'mere risk'.

2) Information about physical or mental health conditions (DPA 1998 s30(1)). Social services are prohibited from disclosing any information without first consulting an appropriate health professional[28] (normally this will be the person responsible for the person's current clinical care, eg a GP or psychiatrist) in connection with the matters to which the information relates. The relevant exemption order in relation to health information specifically permits the refusal of disclosure to the extent to which it would be likely to cause serious harm to the physical or mental health or condition of the data subject or any other person.[29]

3) Where disclosure is prevented by another enactment. This category includes such examples as adoption records and reports, parental order records and reports under Human Fertilisation and Embryology Act 1990 s30.[30]

4) Specific social services exemptions. Information held for the purposes of social work is exempt from disclosure if it would be likely to prejudice the carrying out of social work, by causing serious harm to

---

28 As defined in the relevant order, namely the Data Protection (Subject Access Modification) (Health) Order 2000 SI No 413 (as amended).

29 Data Protection (Subject Access Modification) (Health) Order 2000 SI No 413 (as amended) art 5.

30 These exemptions are listed in the Data Protection (Miscellaneous Subject Access Exemptions) Order 2000 SI No 419 (as amended).

the physical or mental health (or condition) of the applicant or another person.[31]

25.34 If any of these exemptions are to be relied upon, the applicant must be notified as soon as practicable and in writing, even where the decision has also been given in person; reasons should also be given (para 5.39).

Appeals procedure

25.35 If disclosure is refused the applicant may apply either to the Information Commissioner or to the courts; the choice of remedy is up to the applicant.

Caldicott Guardians – information management and sharing

25.36 Considerable concern has been expressed about the way the NHS and other statutory bodies respect the confidential information they store. As a result of this concern, in 1996 a review was commissioned by the Chief Medical Officer of England into the use of patient-identifiable information by the NHS in England and Wales with the aim of ensuring that confidentiality was not being compromised. The review was chaired by Dame Fiona Caldicott.

25.37 Her subsequent report[32] made a number of recommendations, including the need to raise awareness of confidentiality and information security requirements among all staff within the NHS; the need to track all data-flows within the NHS; the need for protocols to protect the exchange of patient-identifiable information between NHS and non-NHS bodies; and the appointment of a senior person, in every health organisation, to act as a guardian, responsible for safeguarding the confidentiality of patient information. This latter person has come to be known as a 'Caldicott Guardian' and the government has endeavoured to implement the recommendations of the report in a series of initiatives. Initially these were restricted to the NHS although recently the process has been extended to cover all English social services departments.[33] Updated guidance on the role of such guardians was issued by the Department of Health in 2010.[34]

The common law and the Human Rights Act 1998

25.38 As has been noted above, DPA 1998 is only one part of our domestic legal framework that seeks to both protect confidentiality and promote the right of access to personal information. The common law and HRA 1998

---

31 Data Protection (Subject Access Modification) (Social Work) Order 2000 SI No 415 (as amended).
32 The Caldicott Committee (1997) *Report on the review of patient-identifiable information.*
33 Department of Health (2002) *Implementing the Caldicott standard in social care* HSC 2002/003: LAC (2002)2.
34 Department of Health (2010) *The Caldicott Guardian Manual 2010.*

also play an important role in this respect, particularly in clarifying the principles that are relevant when the exercise of discretion to (or not to) disclose is being considered.

The common law

25.39   The common law has long recognised the concept of a person's right to confidentiality,[35] a right that arises 'when confidential information comes to the knowledge of the person (the confidant) in circumstances where he has notice or is held to have agreed that the information is confidential with the effect that it would be just in all the circumstances that he should be precluded from disclosing the information to others'.[36] The common law of confidentiality is based upon a presumption against disclosure to third parties.[37]

25.40   *W v Egdell*[38] concerned a doctor who disclosed a medical report commissioned from him by solicitors acting for a patient who was held in a secure hospital having killed a number of people. The patient applied to a tribunal with the eventual purpose of being discharged from detention. The doctor considered that the patient still posed a danger and although he stated this in his report, the solicitors decided not to disclose it. The doctor was so concerned about the potential risk that he gave a copy of the report to the hospital, which then copied it to the tribunal. The patient sued the doctor for breach of confidence.

25.41   In his judgment Bingham LJ accepted that the doctor owed a duty of confidence:

> He could not lawfully sell the contents of his report to a newspaper. Nor could he, without a breach of the law as well as professional etiquette, discuss the case in a learned article, or in his memoirs, or in gossiping with friends, unless he took the appropriate steps to conceal the identity of W.

25.42   However, the Court of Appeal concluded that the 'public interest' justified Dr Egdell's limited disclosure – his limited breach of the obligation of confidentiality.

25.43   In *Woolgar v Chief Constable of Sussex Police and the UKCC*[39] the Court of Appeal considered the extent of the 'public interest' defence and concluded that the disclosure of confidential information to a regulatory body (the UK Central Council for Nursing, Midwifery and Health Visiting) to assist it in its investigation of a matter which might affect the safety of patients, was sufficiently serious as to justify this action. The court came to a similar conclusion in *Brent LBC v SK and HK*[40] where it was held that an authority was entitled to disclose to another local authority confidential information about a care worker's assault on one of her children as there

---

35   *Prince Albert v Strange* (1849) 1 Mac and G 25.
36   *Attorney-General v Guardian Newspapers* [1988] 3 WLR 776, HL, per Lord Goff.
37   *R v Mid Glamorgan FHSA ex p Martin* [1995] 1 WLR 110.
38   [1990] 2 WLR 471, CA.
39   [2000] 1 WLR 25, CA and see also *R v Chief Constable of North Wales ex p AB* [1997] 3 WLR 724, (2000) 3 CCLR 25.
40   [2007] EWHC 1250 (Fam).

was a real risk of harm to vulnerable adults if this information was not disclosed. Likewise in *Maddock v Devon CC*[41] which concerned the disclosure of confidential information from the applicant's social services file to a university at which the applicant had obtained a place to study to become a social worker: the essence of the information being that she was potentially unsuited to that role.

The Human Rights Act 1998

25.44 In *A Health Authority v X*[42] the court had to determine whether it was permissible to order the disclosure of personal health records held by a GP practice to a health authority (investigating various alleged irregularities in the way the practice had been run). The court held that since the proposed disclosure of the records did amount to an interference with that patient's rights under Article 8 of the Convention, it could only be justified where:

1) the authority reasonably required them for its regulatory or administrative functions;
2) there was a compelling public interest in their disclosure; and
3) there was in place effective and adequate safeguards against abuse including safeguards of the particular patient's confidentiality and anonymity.

25.45 The demands of Article 8 were again considered in *H and L v A City Council and B City Council*[43] where a service user challenged a local authority decision to disclose information about him (including that he had been convicted of the indecent assault of a child) to a number of disabled people's organisations in which he had a role, and to his personal care assistants. The court undertook a proportionality review[44] and adopted the applicant's argument that there had to be a 'pressing need' for disclosure. In this case the local authority argued that this was a 'pressing need to protect children' – but the evidence was that the service user was not coming into contact with children and so this factor could not justify disclosure. The court also considered that in most cases, the local authority would only be acting proportionately if, before making its decision (as to disclosure), it had given the person an opportunity to comment on what it was proposing to do.

25.46   HRA 1998 s6 requires public authorities to act in conformity with Convention rights, including Article 8, which protects privacy. In a number of cases the European Court of Human Rights has confirmed that Article 8 is concerned both with the duty on the state to protect individuals from the unreasonable disclosure of publicly held confidential

41 [2004] EWHC 3494 (QB).
42 [2001] 2 FLR 673; upheld on appeal [2001] EWCA Civ 2014, [2002] 2 All ER 780, [2002] 1 FLR 1045.
43 [2011] EWCA Civ 403.
44 Relying heavily upon the approach adopted in *R (L) v Commissioner of Police of the Metropolis* [2009] UKSC 3, [2010] 1 AC 410, [2009] 3 WLR 1056.

information[45] as well as with the right of individuals to access such information.

25.47   In *Gaskin v UK*[46] the applicant sought access to his social services records. The request was refused in part on the ground that some of the information had originally been given in confidence and certain of the informants had not consented to their material being disclosed. The information was important to Mr Gaskin as he had spent almost all his life in care and he wanted it in order to understand his early childhood: essentially for his own sense of identity. His was a legitimate claim, as indeed was the refusal to divulge the information, which had been given to the local authority in confidence. The court concluded that Article 8 required a balancing of the conflicting interests in such a situation; and that this required an independent adjudication system to decide whether the papers should be disclosed. As no such system existed, it found a violation of Article 8.

25.48   It has been suggested that a useful checklist for determining whether a disclosure of confidential healthcare information is legally justified would include the following factors:[47]

1) Is the information in question of a confidential nature? For example, anonymised patient information is less likely to be given legal protection against disclosure.

2) Was the information imparted to the clinician on the understanding that it would not be disclosed, or only disclosed for limited reasons such as for diagnosis treatment and care? Most patients tell their doctors about themselves on the understanding that it will be communicated on a need-to-know basis to others involved in their care.

3) Has guidance issued by the relevant regulatory body (such as the GMC) been complied with?

4) Is there a legal requirement that information be disclosed? There are some legislative provisions requiring disclosure of medical records to health service, government or other bodies.

5) Is the legislation proportionate to any legitimate objective being sought?

6) Is access reasonably required to permit the body to carry out its legal functions? If there is another way to access the information that is needed, or if anonymised information would suffice, then the courts would be unlikely to sanction unconsented disclosure of patient records.

7) Are there adequate safeguards against abuse? The body seeking access to the records must be able to show that it would protect any information coming into its hands against further unauthorised disclosure.

---

45 See eg *Z v Finland* (1997) 25 EHRR 371 and *MS v Sweden* (1997) 3 BHRC 248.
46 (1989) 12 EHRR 36. See also *MG v UK* (2003) 36 EHRR 3, (2002) 5 CCLR 525.
47 Association of Community Health Councils for England and Wales Briefing Paper April 2002: arguably this checklist is of relevance – with the necessary modifications – for other professionally held information.

CHAPTER 26

Remedies

continued

continued

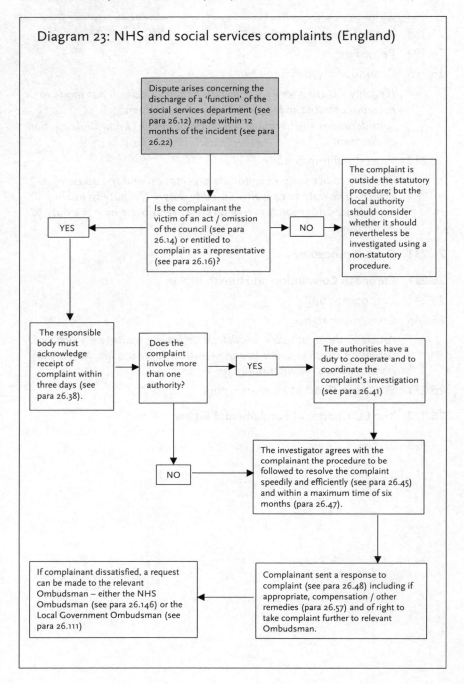

Diagram 23: NHS and social services complaints (England)

Introduction

26.1 Frequently the most effective way of resolving a community care dispute will be through informal contact with the local authority, NHS body, MP or a local councillor. Indeed, contact with the local media can also be a very effective way of remedying a problem. The law, however, provides six principal procedures by which a failure in the provision of community care services may be challenged. These are:

1) a complaint via the local authority complaints procedures;
2) a complaint via the NHS complaints procedures;
3) a complaint via the relevant ombudsman;
4) an application to the High Court for judicial review;
5) an application to the Secretary of State for Health or the Welsh Assembly to use their default powers;
6) an ordinary court application under Human Rights Act (HRA) 1998 s7.

26.2 A complainant will generally be expected to give the local authority or NHS body the opportunity to remedy the problem before the court, ombudsman or secretary of state concerned will be prepared to consider a complaint. In certain situations, the ombudsman or court will accept an application without the complaints process being utilised: these circumstances are discussed in the relevant sections below.

26.3 On a practical basis, the absence of a truly independent, cost-effective and timely remedy may be a significant difficulty for many users of NHS and/or social care services. Many users of such services find that, when facing a decision with which they disagree, the only remedy is the organisation's internal complaints process (and ultimately the relevant ombudsman) or judicial review proceedings in the High Court. The former is often perceived as an ineffective remedy, lacking independence and sometimes taking too long to resolve the disputed decision. The option of judicial review proceedings is often an inappropriate forum for resolving factual disputes and may also be inaccessible as a remedy on the grounds of cost (particularly where legal aid funding may not be available).

26.4 The community care review procedures contrast poorly with many other areas of decision making by the state, where a remedy is provided by means of a formalised appeal process, culminating in an appeal to a specialist tribunal.

26.5 Although the Law Commission, in its 2008 Scoping Report on Adult Social Care Law Reform[1] considered (amongst other things) the need for a tribunal to provide independent merits review of local authority community care decisions (analogous to that provided by the Special Education Needs and Disability Tribunal) in the event this aspect did not find its way into the Commission's subsequent consultation paper or final (2011) report.

---

1 Law Commission (2008) *Adult Social Care Scoping Paper* at para 4.348.

Local authority and NHS complaints in England

26.6   The Health and Social Care (Community Health and Standards) Act 2003 (HSC(CHS)A 2003) authorises the secretary of state in England and the Welsh Government to make regulations concerning the handling of NHS[2] and adult social services complaints.[3] The following information refers only to the position in England; the position in Wales is considered separately below (see para 26.86 below).

26.7   Until 2009, the NHS and the local authorities had separate complaints procedures, involving various stages with rigid time limits for those stages.[4] However, research commissioned by the Department of Health in 2005 found that the complaints processes for both health and social care were not easy to understand.[5] In brief, the complaints processes were seen as:

- too prescriptive and inflexible, not meeting the needs of the person making the complaint;
- fragmented, with different procedures to follow depending on what the problem is and with whom; and
- lacking the proper emphasis on resolving problems locally, quickly and effectively.[6]

The 2009 complaints process

26.8   As a consequence of these concerns, a new complaints process was introduced in England in 2009, by means of Regulations[7] (referred to in the following section as the '2009 Regulations') issued under HSC(CHS)A 2003 ss113 and 114. The Department of Health has issued best guidance on the new scheme (*Listening, Improving, Responding: a guide to better customer care*[8]) together with a series of 'Advice Sheets' aimed at complaints professionals.[9]

26.9   The new system lacks the various stages and specific timescales that characterised the previous arrangements. Instead, it requires the

2   HSC(CHS)A 2003 s114.
3   HSC(CHS)A 2003 s113.
4   The relevant regulations for local authority and NHS complaints were: Local Authority Social Services Complaints (England) Regulations 2006 SI No 1681 and National Health Service (Complaints) Regulations 2004 SI No 1768, as amended by the National Health Service (Complaints) Amendment Regulations 2006 SI No 2084.
5   Department of Health (2008) *Making Experiences Count: the proposed new arrangement for handling health and social care complaints, response to consultation*, p5.
6   Department of Health (2008) *Making Experiences Count: the proposed new arrangement for handling health and social care complaints, response to consultation*, p5.
7   The Local Authority Social Services and National Health Service Complaints (England) Regulations 2009 SI No 309, amended by the Local Authority Social Services and National Health Service Complaints (England) (Amendment) Regulations 2009 SI No 1768, cited as the '2009 Regulations'.
8   Department of Health (2009) *Listening, Responding, Improving – a guide to better customer care.*
9   Department of Health (2009) *Advice Sheet 1: Investigating Complaints; Advice Sheet 2: Joint working on complaints; and advice Sheet 3: Dealing with serious complaints.*

'responsible body'[10] to make arrangements for the handling and consideration of complaints[11]. These arrangements must be carried out in accordance with the 2009 Regulations, but these do not prescribe any particular process for doing so. The intention is that the new approach will enable organisations to develop more flexible and responsive complaints handling systems, focussing on the specific needs of the complainant with the aim of seeking a speedy local resolution. How complaints must handled and considered is further explored below.

26.10   The new complaints process is based on the six principles of good complaints handling, published by the parliamentary and health service ombudsman and endorsed by the local government ombudsman, namely:

- getting it right;
- being customer focused;
- being open and accountable;
- acting fairly and proportionately;
- putting things right;
- seeking continuous improvement.[12]

26.11   The Department of Health's view as to the new process is that it 'focuses on the complainant and enables organisations to tailor a flexible response that seeks to resolve the complainant's specific concerns'.[13] Whilst this is a laudable aim, it remains to be seen whether the 2009 complaints process will be successful in achieving it at a practical level.

What can be complained about?

26.12   In relation to local authorities, complaints may be made about the exercise of their social services functions[14] or where the authority has discharged any function under partnership arrangements made between the social services department and the NHS.[15] Complaints relate not only to the actions of the local authority – but also of their agents, for example, when the authority has made arrangements with another person or body (such as a care home or domiciliary care agency) to discharge its functions.[16]

26.13   In relation to the NHS, complaints may be made about the exercise of the functions of an NHS body[17] including functions under partnership

---

10 Reg 2(3) states that the 'responsible body' means a local authority, NHS body, primary care provider or independent provider.
11 See 2009 Regulations, reg 3(1).
12 Quoted in the Department of Health letter of 26 February 2009, introducing *'Listening, Improving, Responding: a guide to better customer care'.*
13 Department of Health (2008) *Making Experiences Count: the proposed new arrangement for handling health and social care complaints Response to consultation*, p5.
14 2009 Regulations reg 6(1)(a)(i) and see para 1.3 above.
15 See 2009 Regulations reg 6(1)(a)(ii).
16 2009 Regulations reg 6(1A), inserted by Local Authority Social Services and National Health Service Complaints (England) (Amendment) Regulations 2009 SI No 1768.
17 2009 Regulations reg 6(1)(b)(i).

arrangements made between the social services department and the NHS.[18] The 2009 Regulations also apply to complaints about the provision of services by primary care providers and independent providers, where those services have been commissioned by an NHS body.[19]

Who may complain?

26.14   There are two categories of persons who may make a complaint under the regulations. The first is a person who receives or who has received services from a responsible body (eg NHS patient or someone receiving social care services from the local authority).[20]

26.15   The second is described as someone 'who is affected, or likely to be affected, by the action, omission or decision of the responsible body which is the subject of the complaint'.[21] This latter category may therefore include, for example, carers or family of those receiving services from the NHS or the local authority, who would be able to make a complaint in their own right.

Representatives

26.16   Representatives may complain on behalf of a person in certain, specified circumstances. These include where the person:

- has died;
- is a child;
- is unable to make the complaint themselves because of a physical disability or a lack of capacity within the meaning of the Mental Capacity Act 2005 (MCA) 2005; or
- has appointed a representative to act on their behalf (this may or may not be a professional representative).

26.17   Where a representative makes a complaint on behalf of a child, the responsible body must not consider the complaint unless it is satisfied that there are reasonable grounds for the representative, rather than the child, making the complaint. If it is not satisfied, it must notify the representative in writing and state the reason(s) for its decision.[22] Such a situation might arise if, for example, the child is considered to have sufficient capacity to complain (see para 25.15 above) and is not in agreement with the complaint being made.

26.18   Where the responsible body is satisfied that the representative is not conducting the complaint in the best interests of the child or of a person lacking capacity under the MCA 2005, the complaint must cease to be considered under the 2009 Regulations. The representative must be notified

18   2009 Regulations reg 6(1)(b)(ii).
19   2009 Regulations reg 6(1)(c) and (d).
20   2009 Regulations reg 5(1)(a).
21   2009 Regulations reg 5(1)(b).
22   2009 Regulations reg 5(3).

by the responsible body of the decision in writing, with reason(s) for its decision.[23]

26.19   It appears almost inevitable that the complaints arrangements under the 2009 Regulations may still cause difficulties for representatives in some situations. For example, the NHS ombudsman upheld a complaint[24] (under the previous complaints system), which concerned a NHS trust's refusal to respond to a complaint made by a friend of a patient with dementia. The trust had cited 'patient confidentiality'; 'the Data Protection Act' and had agreed to 'take up the matters' with the patient's sister. The ombudsman held that:

> . . . while patient confidentiality is a legitimate consideration when deciding whether a representative is a suitable complainant, the Trust did not adequately explain to Mr P why it should not respond to his complaints. Nor did it demonstrate that it had adequately considered the NHS Complaints Regulations or the relevant legislation in reaching its decision. We found no evidence that the Trust had established whether Mr T was capable of providing consent for the release of confidential information to Mr P, or considered if Mr T had given implied consent to release. There was no evidence that the Trust had considered whether there was any overriding public interest reason for disclosing information to Mr P, or if any aspects of his complaint could be responded to without releasing confidential information.

26.20   Research highlights the importance of service users being supported in making complaints and that 'fear of the consequences' was by far the most commonly cited reason for service users not making formal complaints – fear of retaliatory action by the authority (for instance, the withdrawal of discretionary services).[25] Given these difficulties, authorities should be slow to question the good faith or 'standing' of a representative, particularly if the issue raised is one of importance.

26.21   These concerns have also been voiced by the Joint Committee on Human Rights in a 2007 report[26] which referred to the 'power imbalance' which exists between older people and those who care for them and the resultant reluctance to complain. It also noted that the Department of Health agreed that there was a fear of complaining in such situations.

Time limits for making a complaint

26.22   Complaints should usually be made within 12 months of the date of the incident which is the subject of a complaint or, alternatively, from the date upon which the complainant first became aware of the matter which is the subject of the complaint.[27]

---

23 2009 Regulations reg 5(4) and (5).
24 Parliamentary and Health Service Ombudsman (2008) *Annual Report 2007–08* Complaint against Bedfordshire and Luton Mental Health and Social Care Partnership NHS Trust Case Study 15 p37.
25 K Simons, *I'm not complaining, but . . .*, Joseph Rowntree Foundation, 1995.
26 Joint Committee on Human Rights (2007) *The human rights of older people in healthcare* HL Paper 156-I HC 378-I para 234 et seq.
27 2009 Regulations reg 12(1)(a) and (b).

26.23   The 12-month time limit may be extended where the responsible body is satisfied that the complainant had good reasons for not making the complaint within the time limit,[28] provided it is still possible to investigate the complaint effectively and fairly. Where a decision is made not to investigate, the complainant has the opportunity to approach the relevant ombudsman.[29]

26.24   Although the current guidance is silent as to the circumstances which might justify an extension, similar provisions existed in the previous complaints regulations and the earlier English guidance[30] addressed this question. It advised, for instance, that it might not be appropriate to apply the time limit where 'it would not be reasonable to expect the complainant to have made the complaint earlier and it would still be possible to consider the complaint in a way that would be effective and fair to those involved'. It gave as possible examples (among others) 'if a service user was particularly vulnerable and did not complain due to fear of reprisal' or 'where there is likely to be sufficient access to information or individuals involved at the time, to enable an effective and fair investigation to be carried out'.

Responsibility for the complaints arrangements

26.25 The local authority or NHS body must designate a 'responsible person', whose function is to ensure compliance with the 2009 Regulations and, in particular, that action is taken if necessary in the light of an outcome of a complaint.[31] This would involve, for example, ensuring that any training needs identified as being required during the investigation of the complaint would be provided, as well as ensuring that any undertakings given to the complainant are honoured.

26.26   The 2009 Regulations also specify who may be the 'responsible person', although their functions may be performed by any person authorised by the responsible body to act on their behalf.[32] In the case of a local authority or NHS body, the responsible person must be the chief executive officer. In other types of organisation, the responsible person must be, in broad terms, someone with decision-making powers within the organisation (eg chief executive, sole proprietor, partner, director).[33]

26.27   A 'complaints manager' must also be designated by the responsible body. Their role is to be responsible for managing the procedures for handling and considering complaints, in accordance with the procedures made under the 2009 Regulations.[34]

---

28 2009 Regulations reg 12(2)(a).
29 Department of Health (2008) *Making Experiences Count: the proposed new arrangement for handling health and social care complaints, response to consultation* at pp13 and 14.
30 Department of Health (2006) *learning from complaints: social services complaints procedure for adults* – see paras 3.3.2–3.3.3.
31 2009 Regulations reg 4(1)(b).
32 2009 Regulations reg 4(2).
33 2009 Regulations reg 4(4).
34 2009 Regulations reg 4(1)(b).

26.28   The functions of the complaints manager may be performed by any person authorised by the responsible person to act on behalf of the complaints manager.[35]

26.29   The complaints manager may be the same person as the responsible person, which is perhaps more likely to be the case in smaller organisations. Alternatively, they may be someone who is not an employee of the organisation, which would allow for the appointment of an external organisation to deal with complaints. A designated complaints manager from another responsible body may also act as the complaints manager for that organisation.[36] The local government ombudsman has expressed the view that a complaints system of this type can only function properly if the manager is of sufficient seniority to ensure that complaints are addressed with adequate commitment[37] and has commented as follows:

> In my view the Council's procedures for dealing with complaints are seriously flawed. There seems to be no officer of sufficient seniority to run the complaints system and to ensure that complaints are dealt with, not only within the statutory times, but also with sufficient commitment.[38]

Complaints excluded under the Regulations

26.30   There are a number of exclusions from the 2009 Regulations, some of which are 'technical' in nature,[39] whereas others are of more relevance to service users and their families. A complaint is excluded where it has been made orally and is resolved to the complainant's satisfaction no later than the next working day after it was made.[40] In addition, complaints which have previously been investigated are also excluded[41] (ie repeat complaints raising the same issues).

26.31   Where a responsible body makes a decision that a complaint is excluded, it must 'as soon as reasonably practicable notify the complainant in writing of its decision and the reasons for its decision'.[42] However, where the reason for the exclusion falls under regulation 8(c) (an oral complaint resolved by the next working day), there is no requirement to notify the complainant in writing of the decision to exclude.

26.32   The regulations also make it clear that, where a complainant makes a complaint which contains a part excluded for a reason listed in regulation 8, there is nothing to prevent the non-excluded part of the complaint being investigated in accordance with the 2009 Regulations.[43]

---

35 2009 Regulations reg 4(3).
36 2009 Regulations reg 4(5).
37 Complaint no 92/A/3725 against Haringey LBC.
38 Report no 94/C/2659 against Nottingham CC.
39 2009 Regulations reg 8(1) – eg a complaint made by a responsible body; a complaint by an NHS or local authority employee about any matter relating to their employment or where a responsible body has allegedly failed to disclose information under its Freedom of Information Act 2000 obligations.
40 2009 Regulations reg 8(1)(c).
41 2009 Regulations reg 8(1)(e).
42 2009 Regulations reg 8(2), inserted by Local Authority Social Services and National Health Service Complaints (England) Amendment Regulations 2009 SI No 1768.
43 2009 Regulations reg 8(3).

26.33   The 2009 Regulations do not, unlike their predecessors, specifically exclude complaints, where the complainant has stated in writing that they intend to take legal proceedings. The Department of Health has advised[44] that in such cases (or where there is a police investigation) good practice requires that discussions take place with the relevant legal advisers to establish whether the progression of the complaint may prejudice any subsequent legal action. If so, the complaint may be put on hold – with the complainant being advised of this and given reasons for the decision. The Department of Health's view, however, is that:

> . . . the default position in cases where the complainant has expressed an intention to take legal proceedings would be to seek to continue to resolve the complaint unless there are clear legal reasons not to do so.[45]

26.34   In similar vein there is no longer an exclusion relating to the investigation of complaints where disciplinary action is being considered or taken against a member of staff – provided the organisation has regard to good practice in respect of restrictions in supplying confidential/personal information to the complainant. However, although the complaints handling arrangements will operate alongside the disciplinary arrangements, the two arrangements will remain separate. Both of the above changes are justified on the basis that:

> In all cases, it will be important to ensure the potential implications for patient safety and/or organisational learning are investigated as quickly as possible, to allow urgent action to be taken to prevent similar incidents arising.[46]

26.35   Although direct payments and personal budgets do not form part of the new complaints procedure, both would be covered by the 2009 Regulations where the complaint is about the process of allocating a direct payment or a personal budget. The Department of Health's explanation for the exclusion is that 'the authority hands over money to the service user, and so decisions made by the service user are outside the [complaints] procedure'.[47]

Complaints handling and consideration

26.36   The process established by the responsible body must ensure that:

- complaints are dealt with efficiently;
- complaints are properly investigated;
- complainants are treated with respect and courtesy;
- complainants receive, so far as is reasonably practical, assistance to enable them to understand the complaints procedure or advice on where they may obtain such assistance;

44 See Department of Health (2010) *Clarification of the complaints regulations 2009.*
45 Department of Health (2010) *Clarification of the complaints regulations 2009.*
46 Department of Health (2010) *Clarification of the complaints regulations 2009.*
47 Department of Health (2009) *Reform of the complaints system:* Letter to NHS Chief Executives and Directors of Adult Social Care, with Key Messages. Gateway reference: 11380: 25 February 2009.

- complainants receive a timely and appropriate response;
- complainants are told the outcome of the investigation of their complaint; and
- action is taken if necessary in the light of the outcome of the complaint.[48]

Publicity

26.37 In addition, the responsible body must make information available to the public about its arrangements for dealing with complaints and also how further information about those arrangements may be obtained.[49]

The form of a complaint, and its acknowledgement

26.38 Although the 2009 Regulations do not prescribe how the complaints process itself must work, they set out in some detail the process to be followed by responsible bodies when in receipt of a complaint. A person may make a complaint orally, in writing or electronically.[50] Where the complaint is made orally, the responsible body to which the complaint is made must make a written record of the complaint and send a copy of that written record to the complainant.[51] The usual timescale for the responsible body to acknowledge the complaint is within three working days after the day it received the complaint.[52] The acknowledgement of the complaint may be made orally or in writing.[53]

Complaints made to another responsible body

26.39 The 2009 Regulations provide for detailed procedures to be followed where a person makes a complaint but inadvertently directs it to the wrong body, for example, the complaint is directed to a local authority but the subject of the complaint relates to an NHS body or an independent provider.

26.40 In this situation, where it appears to the responsible body (the first body) who receives the complaint that it would be a complaint to be handled in accordance with the 2009 Regulations by another responsible body (the second body), the first body sends it to the second. In these circumstances, the complainant is deemed to have made the complaint to the second body:[54] it is then the responsibility of the second body to acknowledge the complaint within three working days after the date on which it receives the complaint from the first body.[55] However, it is noted that the 2009 Regulations do not require the consent of the complainant when the first body decides to send the complaint to the second body.

48 2009 Regulations reg 3(2).
49 2009 Regulations reg 16(a) and (b).
50 2009 Regulations reg 13(1).
51 2009 Regulations reg 13(2).
52 2009 Regulations reg 13(3).
53 2009 Regulations reg 13(6).
54 2009 Regulations reg 6(5) and (6).
55 2009 Regulations reg 13(4).

Duty to co-operate

26.41   In 2007, the local government ombudsman published a special report[56] on the problems caused by the lack of a unified system to enable joint investigations into complaints that straddle (amongst other bodies) health and social services. The ombudsman also criticised authorities that insisted on complainants having to make separate NHS/social services complainants when they concerned the same facts.[57] In a number of earlier investigations the ombudsman had found maladministration where authorities had failed to have in place procedures to ensure that where a complaint raises matters that are outside the authority's remit, the complainant is directed to the appropriate body.[58]

26.42   This difficulty of complainants having to make multiple complaints was recognised during the consultation process[59] and is addressed in the 2009 Regulations, which create a formal 'duty to co-operate'.[60] The duty applies where a responsible body is considering a complaint, which contains material relating to a second responsible body. Where the complaint would fall to be handled by that second body, had the complaint be made directly to that second body, there is a duty to co-operate imposed upon both the first and second responsible bodies.

26.43   The bodies must co-operate for the purposes of co-ordinating the handling of the complaint and ensuring that the complainant receives a co-ordinated response to the complaint. In particular, each responsible body must agree which of the two bodies should take the lead in co-ordinating the handling of the complaint and communicating with the complainant. They must also provide each other with information relevant to the consideration of the complaint which is 'reasonably' requested by the other body and, further, attend or ensure it is reasonably represented at any meeting required in connection with the consideration of the complaint.[61]

Complaints involving other 'providers' or commissioners

26.44   The regulations deal with the procedures to be adopted where the responsible body considers that a complaint (or part of it) concerns another local authority or health body or relates to services provided by a 'provider' (ie a third party that was actually providing the services). In this respect the

56   Local Government Ombudsman (2007) *Special Report: Handling complaints about local partnerships.*
57   See Complaint no 97/A/4002 against Bexley LBC – where the ombudsman also stated (at para 134) that it was unreasonable to expect complainants to have to pursue separate complaints against each authority; and Complaint no 99/C/1276 against Northumberland CC where she approved a joint NHS/social services investigation (at para 61).
58   Complaint no 02/B/03622 against Harrow LBC, 22 June 2004.
59   Department of Health (2008) *Reform of health and social care complaints: Proposed changes to the legislative framework.*
60   2009 Regulations reg 9.
61   2009 Regulations reg 9.

Regulations are detailed, requiring the responsible body to keep the complainant fully informed as to what it is doing (and providing for time limits).[62]

Investigation of complaints

26.45 When the complaint is acknowledged by the responsible body, the complainant must be given the opportunity to discuss the manner in which the complaint is to be handled[63]. However, the 2009 Regulations are silent as to how complaints must be handled, other than to state that the responsible body 'must investigate the complaint in a manner appropriate to resolve it speedily and efficiently'.[64] It also provides that the complainant must be kept informed, 'as far as reasonably practicable, as to the progress of the investigation'.[65]

26.46 The 2009 Regulations, unlike the previous complaints system, do not provide for a rigid timetable to respond to the complaint. Instead, they allow for the complainant and the responsible body to discuss a 'response period' for the completion of the investigation and for the sending of a full response to the complaint. Where such a discussion does not take place, the responsible body is able to determine the response period itself and notify the complainant accordingly.[66]

26.47 The only time limit prescribed in the 2009 Regulations is for a maximum response period of six months from the date of the receipt of the complaint. This may be extended beyond six months, with the agreement of the complainant and the responsible body, where the agreement to extend the response period is made before the expiry of the six-month period[67]. However, where the response period is not met, the responsible body must notify the complainant in writing as to the reasons why, and it must send a full response 'as soon as is reasonably practicable' after the expiry of the response period.[68]

26.48 Once the investigation is concluded, the complainant must be sent a response 'as soon as is reasonably practicable', signed by the responsible person, which includes a report giving an explanation of how the complaint was investigated and its conclusions reached in relation to the complaint, including any matters where remedial action is needed. The response should also confirm whether such remedial action has been taken or is proposed to be taken and, further, advise the complainant of their right to take the matter to the relevant local government or health service ombudsman.[69]

62 See 2009 Regulations regs 7, 11 and 13.
63 2009 Regulations reg 13(7)).
64 2009 Regulations reg 14(1)(a).
65 2009 Regulations reg 14(1)(b).
66 2009 Regulations reg 13(7) and (8).
67 2009 Regulations reg 14(3).
68 2009 Regulations reg 14(4).
69 2009 Regulations reg 14(2).

26.49   The best practice guidance *Listening, Responding, Improving: a guide to better customer care* (referred to as the 'Guide' below)[70] states that 'the new approach ends the bureaucracy of the old system' and that 'organisations will be encouraged to ask people what they think of their care, to sort out problems more effectively and to use the opportunities to learn'.[71]

26.50   As part of the process of the investigation, the Guide makes it clear that the organisation should, when the complaint is first received, categorise the complaint, reviewing that category as the investigation proceeds. The seriousness of the complaint is to be assessed using a three-step process to gauge the impact of the complaints on those involved, the potential risks to the organisation (including the risk of litigation and adverse publicity) and the response required. The Guide cautions, 'It is also important to remember that a complaint can have a very different effect on an organisation compared with an individual', acknowledging that this is particularly important where the person is vulnerable for any reason.[72] In the context of about health and social care, it is perhaps difficult to envisage a situation where a person using such services is not vulnerable for one reason or another.

26.51   The Guide later provides examples of different types of incidents,[73] categorising as 'low' what it describes as 'simple, non-complex issues', for example, an event resulting in minor harm (eg cut or a strain) as well as things such as a lack of cleanliness, lost property, transport problems or missing medical records. Examples in the 'moderate' category are defined as an event resulting in moderate harm (eg fracture), as well as incorrect treatment, delayed discharge and medical errors.[74] Such incidents are often of enormous importance to the individuals concerned: it is difficult to envisage how the likely assessment of the incident by the organisation is not going to be at odds with the view of the complainant.

26.52   The Department of Health has also produced a series of Advice Sheets;[75] the first one is called 'Investigating Complaints'. It makes it clear that most complaints will be considered by someone from the organisation involved, who should be appropriately trained and independent of the service which is the subject of the complaint. It also notes that, for serious complaints, it may be necessary to involve an independent investigator.[76]

26.53   The Advice Sheet advises that complaints investigators must be clear about what they are investigating and also states, 'A key question to ask yourself before beginning any investigation is whether you will be able to

---

70   Department of Health (2009) *Listening, Responding, Improving – A guide to better customer care*.
71   Department of Health (2009) *Listening, Responding, Improving*, pp4–5.
72   Department of Health (2009) *Listening, Responding, Improving*, pp16–17.
73   Department of Health (2009) *Listening, Responding, Improving*, pp 18–19.
74   Department of Health (2009) *Listening, Responding, Improving*.
75   Department of Health (2009) *Advice Sheet 1: investigating complaints; Advice Sheet 2: joint working on complaints; and Advice Sheet 3: dealing with serious complaints*.
76   Department of Health (2009) *Advice Sheet 1: investigating complaints; Advice* at p1.

reach any robust conclusions', citing as an example a scenario where the complaint is solely about something said in conversation where there is no record of it nor any witnesses. In this situation, the Advice Sheet makes it clear that reaching a robust conclusion is unlikely and it suggests that mediation may be an appropriate, alternative route to resolving this complaint.[77] However, the Advice Sheet is silent about when and how to use mediation, but the Guide recommends its use where there is a risk of a relationship or communication breaking down.[78]

26.54   The Advice Sheet also recommends that 'the key to a good investigation is a good plan',[79] giving three key questions to define the investigation, as follows:

- What happened?
- What should have happened?
- What are the differences between those two things?[80]

26.55   The Advice Sheet also makes it clear that the investigator will need to understand the background information to the complaint, both from the complainant and also from the organisation (eg legal or policy requirements).[81] It also provides tips on obtaining evidence, including documentary evidence, interviews and, where appropriate, site inspections.[82]

The final response to the complaint

26.56   In terms of the final report itself, the Advice Sheet advises that both parties should have the chance to provide feedback, particularly to correct any factual inaccuracies before publication. It also notes that the 'purpose of the report is to record and explain the conclusions' reached by the complaint investigator and, further, that a good report is likely to be complete, relevant, logical, balanced and robust. It also makes it clear that a good report should not come as a surprise to anyone, recommending that it is a good idea to be open with both parties during the investigation.[83]

Remedies following a complaint

26.57   The Guide recognises that complainants will seek a range of remedies following a complaint and advises that 'complaints can be resolved more effectively if [it] is clear from the outset what the person complaining

---

77   Department of Health (2009) *Advice Sheet 1: investigating complaints; Advice* at p2.
78   See Department of Health (2009) *Listening, Responding, Improving – A guide to better customer care* at pp26–27.
79   Department of Health (2009) *Advice Sheet 1: investigating complaints* at p3.
80   Department of Health (2009) *Listening, Responding, Improving – A guide to better customer care.*
81   Department of Health (2009) *Listening, Responding, Improving – A guide to better customer care.*
82   Department of Health (2009) *Advice Sheet 1: investigating complaints* at p4.
83   Department of Health (2009) *Advice Sheet 1: investigating complaints* at p6.

expects as an outcome'.[84] Furthermore, the complainant has a right to a response which explains how their concerns have been resolved and what action has been taken.[85] A range of responses are of course possible and any remedy needs to be proportionate to the circumstances.

26.58   At pages 28–29 of the Guide, the advice of the local government ombudsman is quoted:

> There are some simple principles you can follow when you want to put things right. Whenever possible: put someone in the position they would have been if the fault had not occurred, make the remedy appropriate and proportionate to the harm suffered, take specific action if it's needed, offer compensation if appropriate and always apologise if you are at fault. Also consider whether any practices, procedures or policies should be reviewed.

Compensation

26.59   One of the defects of many early local authority complaints procedures was their disinclination to award compensation. Historically, this stemmed from a belief that this was not permitted by law. However, as a result of pressure from the ombudsman,[86] the government legislated to put this point beyond doubt: the Local Government Act (LGA) 2000 s92 provides that:

> (1) Where a relevant authority consider –
>   (a) that action taken by or on behalf of the authority in the exercise of their functions amounts to, or may amount to, maladministration, and
>   (b) that a person has been, or may have been, adversely affected by that action,
>   the authority may, if they think appropriate, make a payment to, or provide some other benefit for, that person.
>   . . .
> (3) In this section –
>   'action' includes failure to act,
>   'relevant authority' has the same meaning as in Part III of this Act.

26.60   Whilst the inclusion in the Guide of the comments of the local government ombudsman is appropriate and timely, the Guide is, on this question, significantly weaker than the now withdrawn 2006 guidance,[87] particularly in respect of the local authority's ability to grant financial redress. In the circumstances, it seems almost inevitable that local authorities will continue to be disinclined to award financial compensation as a resolution to a valid complaint.

26.61   However, the ombudsman is showing an increasing willingness to be robust on compensation claims and has expressed strong views about the

84 See Department of Health (2009) *Listening, Responding, Improving – a guide to better customer care* at pp28–29.
85 See Department of Health (2009) *Listening, Responding, Improving – a guide to better customer care* at pp28–29.
86 *Annual Report 1998/99* p7.
87 Department of Health (2006) *Learning from complaints: social services complaints procedure for adults,* para 6.3 et seq.

inadequacy of council proposals: for instance, a 2007 finding[88] that the authority should pay over £100,000 for a service failure and, in the same year, a finding that an offer of £4,000 to compensate a child for three years of council incompetence was 'derisory'.[89] The local government ombudsman has issued detailed and information practice guidance (in the following section referred to as the 'LGO guidance'), aimed at promoting greater consistency in the remedies recommended by local authorities.[90]

26.62   The LGO guidance notes that an appropriate remedy may require a number of separate elements, including recommendations as to specific action that should be taken and as to an apology. As a general principle, the remedy needs to be 'appropriate and proportionate to the injustice; it should, as far as possible, put the complainant in the position he or she would have been in but for the maladministration'. Where 'this cannot be achieved because of the passage of time or of events which have occurred ... financial compensation may be the only available approach'.[91]

26.63   On the question of compensation, the LGO guidance states that 'financial compensation may be appropriate, for example, if the council has taken the appropriate action but has delayed in doing so and the delay has caused injustice; or if there is no practical action which would provide a full and appropriate remedy; or if the complainant has sustained loss and suffering'. It suggests that the calculation of what is appropriate may include consideration of:

- The effect of the complainant's own action.
- Reimbursement to the complainant of any money which is owing but unpaid (ie unpaid housing benefit).
- Quantifiable loss: ie 'paying for the additional help the parents procured for a child with special educational needs because the council delayed in drawing up a statutory statement or providing the help'.
- Loss of a non-monetary benefit: ie 'a council tenant has been unable to use one of the rooms in his or her flat for a period because of lack of repair'.
- Loss of value: where something owned by the complainant has lost value.
- Lost opportunity: 'compensation for a lost opportunity may sometimes be a fairly small sum, because it is only the loss or opportunity which is certain and the actual outcome which would have obtained cannot be known'.
- Distress 'including stress, anxiety, frustration, uncertainty, worry, inconvenience or outrage'. 'This element may be a moderate sum of

---

88 Complaint no 05/C/11921 against Trafford MBC, 26 July 2007.
89 Complaint no 05/C/14043 against Birmingham CC, 13 March 2007, and see also Complaint no 05/C/11921 against Trafford MBC, 26 July 2007 which recommended that over £100,000 be paid for a service failure.
90 LGO (2005) *Guidance on good practice 6: remedies.*
91 LGO guidance p3.

no more than a few hundred pounds or less but in cases where the distress has been severe and/or prolonged, a more substantial sum may be justified.' The LGO guidance suggests that generally it 'could range from £50 (for example, for a period of uncertainty about the date or outcome of an assessment) to thousands of pounds in cases where, for example, allegations of abuse made against a complainant have not been investigated properly, or action requested by a complainant to prevent children from being abused has not happened'.[92]

- Professional fees in pursuing the dispute: while the LGO guidance advises that complainants usually do not need a solicitor or other professional to help them make a complaint, it may sometimes be appropriate. In such cases the recommendation may be for a contribution to costs rather than reimbursement of the whole of the expenditure.[93]

- Time and trouble in pursuing the complaint (but this should not be confused with the question of distress) (as above). The LGO guidance suggests that this element need not always be included (for instance, where minor failings in the complaints process have occurred) but in general complaints concerning social services complaints may be 'higher than the range of £50 to £250' to reflect the difficulty which a complainant with physical or mental health problems, or who is vulnerable for any other reason, may have in pursuing a complaint.[94]

- Offsetting compensation: in circumstances where the complainant owes money to the council (eg rent arrears) 'it would usually be appropriate for the compensation to be offset against the debt'.[95]

- Interest.[96]

- Formula: the LGO guidance advises that 'sometimes it may be appropriate to express a remedy, not as a sum of money, but as a formula which sets out how the council should itself calculate the requisite sum of money. Where relevant, this needs to include reference to any continuing problem so that the formula is designed to encompass the future as well as the past.[97]

Record keeping and reporting

26.64   The responsible body is required to maintain a record of each complaint received, including the subject matter and outcome of each complaint. In addition, where the responsible body agreed the response period (or any amended period) with the complainant, the monitored information will

---

92 LGO guidance p48.
93 However, where an accountant acting under an enduring power of attorney pursued a complaint, the ombudsman held that he was entitled to be paid at his professional rate, and recommended over £16,000 for this item alone: complaint no 00/C/03176 against Nottingham County and City Councils, 22 January 2002.
94 LGO guidance p49.
95 LGO guidance p50.
96 LGO guidance p50.
97 LGO guidance p50.

also included whether or not the report of the outcome of the investigation was sent within the required response time.[98]

26.65   In addition, the responsible body is required to produce an annual report, including the following information:

- the number of complaints received;
- the number of complaints which the responsible body decided were well founded;
- the number of complaints referred to the relevant ombudsman;
- a summary of the subject matter of complaints, including any matters of general importance arising out of those complaints, or the way in which the complaints were handled;
- a summary of any matters where action has been or is to be taken to improve services as a consequence of those complaints.[99]

Overlap with other local authority functions

26.66   In the context of local authorities, it is important to note that the 2009 Regulations relate to complaints about adult social care. They are therefore not applicable to complaints concerning education or housing (or indeed any other local authority function). Good administration requires, however, that any complaints process must incorporate the principles outlined in the LGO guidance on the operation of complaints procedures.[100]

26.67   A practical example of the consequences of these separate remedies can be seen in the 2009 complaint against the London Borough of Croydon, the local government ombudsman's expressed concern about the need for separate complaints in a social services and SEN matter, commenting that 'the legislation does not provide a single route of appeal where a child's inseparable social care and educational needs have not been adequately assessed or met'.[101]

26.68   Not infrequently, it may be unclear whether a complaint relates to a housing or social services function: for instance, a dispute concerning adaptations funded via a disabled facilities grant – or the provision of a house identified as needed in a care plan. The local government ombudsman has considered a number of such cases. In a complaint against Kirklees Metropolitan Council[102] she concluded:

---

98   2009 Regulations reg 17.
99   2009 Regulations reg 18(1).
100 Local Government Ombudsman (1992) *Good Practice 1: devising a complaints system*; see also Complaint no 94/C/2959 against Nottingham CC, 28 November 1994; Complaint no 97/C/1614 against Bury MBC, 1999, where the ombudsman accepted that part of the complaint lay outside the statutory complaints process but nevertheless warranted investigation, and commented, 'it is hard to identify any aspect of the Council's handling of Mr Redfern's complaints which was in the proper manner or in full accordance with the statutory complaints procedure and/or the Council's own written complaints procedure'.
101 Complaint nos 07B 04696 and 07B 10996 against Croydon LBC, 16 September 2009.
102 Complaint no 01/C/00627 against Kirklees MC, 28 January 2003, para 68.

There was confusion within the Council as to whether [the] complaint should be considered by the Housing or Social Services Department. From [the complainants'] point of view this was irrelevant, they simply wanted the complaint to be considered thoroughly and promptly. The Council should have been able to do that. Although officers say they made internal changes as a result of the complaint no remedy was offered to [the complainants] for the Council's acknowledged failings.

26.69   Likewise in a complaint against Sunderland City Council[103] she concluded:

I consider that [the complainant's] complaint about the failure to rehouse his family should also have been dealt with under the Social Services Statutory Complaints Procedure as the application arose out of a stated need in a Care Plan. The failure to consider the complaint under the statutory procedure was maladministration. This has caused injustice as it denied [the complainant] the opportunity of having his complaints properly addresses at an earlier date.

26.70   The previous (now superseded) English guidance[104] urged authorities to develop a 'seamless service' for complaints which straddle more than one departmental function within the local authority, that:

7.8.2 Building links with the local authority's other complaints procedures can be an essential way to develop the overall corporate obligation of the local authority to provide a high quality service. Local authorities are encouraged to offer a complete single response to complainants where possible, for example where a complainant has complaints relating to both a local authority's housing and social services functions.

7.8.3 The Complaints Manager responsible for social services should liaise with other staff as relevant. These members of staff should agree who will take the lead, to make sure that the complainant is kept informed and, wherever possible, gets a single reply that covers all aspects of his complaint.

Children procedures

26.71   In England, there is a separate complaints procedure for children and young people, as required by the Representations Procedure (England) Regulations 2006[105] and the accompanying statutory guidance.[106]

What can be complained about?

26.72   The 2006 Regulations provide for representations and/or complaints to be made 'about the actions, decisions or apparent failings of a local

---

103 Complaint nos 00/C/12118 and 00/C/12621 against Sunderland CC, 21 August 2002, para 252.
104 Department of Health (2006) *Learning from complaints: social services complaints procedure for adults.*
105 SI 2006 No 1738, cited as 'the 2006 Regulations'.
106 Department for Education and Skills (2006) *Getting the best from complaints: social care complaints and representations for children, young people and others,* cited as 'the 2006 guidance'.

authority's children's social services provision'.[107] This includes the discharge by an authority of any of its functions under Children Act (CA) 1989 Part III (services for children 'in need', including disabled children – see para 23.6). The 2006 guidance provides for a non-exhaustive list of matters which would fall within the 2006 Regulations including, for example, an unwelcome or disputed decision or the application of eligibility and assessment criteria.[108] The local government ombudsman has emphasised that the complaints procedure for children's services is a statutory duty such that it must be properly resourced by councils.[109]

Time limits for making a complaint

26.73 In general complaints need to be made within one year after the matters which are the subject of the complaint arose,[110] although provision exists to be extended at the local authority's discretion if it is still possible to consider the representations effectively and efficiently.[111]

Who may make a complaint?

26.74 A wide range of persons may make the complaint, including the child or young person themselves, anyone with parental responsibility and anyone the local authority considers has 'sufficient interest' in the child or young person's welfare to warrant his or her representations being considered by it. Complaints may also be made by a representative on the child or young person's behalf.[112] Where a child or young person wishes to make a complaint, local authorities are required to provide them with information about advocacy services and offer help to obtain an advocate.[113]

Outline of the complaints process

26.75 The handling and consideration of complaints consists of three stages:

- Stage 1 – Local resolution.
- Stage 2 – Investigation.
- Stage 3 – Review panel.

Stage 1: Local resolution

26.76 A complaint is made on the date on which it is first received by the local authority. The expectation is that the majority of complaints should be considered (and resolved) at Stage 1 although, where both parties agree,

---

107 2006 guidance para 2.1.2.
108 2006 guidance para 2.2.1.
109 See Complaint no 08 016 986 against Waltham Forest LBC, 21 October 2009, paras 70 and 82.
110 2006 guidance para 3.3.1.
111 2006 guidance paras 3.3.2 and 3.3.3.
112 2006 guidance paras 2.6–2.8.
113 2006 guidance paras 3.2.1 and 3.4.

the complaint can move directly to Stage 2. The timescale for this stage of the process is ten working days (with a further ten days for more complex complaints or additional time if an advocate is required).[114]

Stage 2: Investigation

26.77   Consideration of complaints at Stage 2 is normally achieved through an investigation conducted by an investigating officer (IO) and an independent person (IP). The 2006 guidance advises that 'consideration of the complaint at Stage 2 should be fair, thorough and transparent with clear and logical outcomes'.[115] An IO should be appointed by the authority to lead the investigation of the complaint and prepare a written report for adjudication by a senior manager. The IO may be employed by the authority (provided they are not part of the direct line management of the person or service complained of) or they may be brought in from outside the authority to deal with the complaint. An IP must be appointed to the investigation and part of their role is, amongst other things, to work alongside the IO to provide an independent and objective view to the investigation of complaints.[116]

26.78   Once the IO has completed his or her consideration of the complaint, he or she should write an investigation report, including:

- details of findings, conclusions and outcomes as against each point of complaint (ie 'upheld' or 'not upheld'); and
- recommendations on how to remedy any injustice to the complainant, as appropriate.[117]

26.79   Good practice recommends that the IP may also want to provide a report to the authority, after having read the final report prepared by the IO.[118] Once the IO has finished the report, a senior manager should act as 'adjudicating officer' and consider the complaints, the IO's findings, conclusions and recommendations, any report from the IP and the complainant's desired outcomes. The adjudicating officer should normally be a senior manager, reporting to the Director responsible for children's services. It is the role of the adjudicating officer to decide on the complaint and to prepare a response to the reports, specifying the action to be taken, with timescales for implementation: this is the 'adjudication'.[119]

26.80   The complainant must be notified of the decision and advised of the right to have the complaint considered by a review panel and of the time limit for so doing (20 working days).[120] The time limit for the completion of Stage 2 is 25 working days with a maximum extension to 65 days.

114   2006 guidance para 3.5.
115   2006 guidance para 3.6.3.
116   2006 guidance para 3.6.5 and annex 1.
117   2006 guidance para 3.7.1.
118   2006 guidance para 3.7.2.
119   2006 guidance paras 3.8.1–3.8.3.
120   2006 guidance para 3.8.6.

Stage 3 review panel

26.81 Where the complainant remains dissatisfied with the outcome of Stage 2 of the process, they have the right to proceed to a review panel hearing. The purpose of the panel is set out at para 3.10.1 of the 2006 Regulations and includes consideration of the adequacy of the Stage 2 investigation, amongst other things. However, it is noted that, as a general rule, the review panel should not reinvestigate the complaint.[121]

26.82 Complainants have the right to bring a representative to speak on their behalf but the 2006 guidance cautions against the need for having lawyers as representatives, stating 'the presence of lawyers can work against the spirit of openness and problem-solving'.[122]

26.83 The 2006 guidance makes it clear that the review panel must apply the civil standard proof, ie the 'balance of probabilities', and that it should be alert to the importance of providing a demonstrably fair and accessible process for all participants. Panels should be conducted in the presence of all the relevant parties with equity of access and representation for the complainant and local authority. It is also noted that it is important that the panel is customer focused in its approach to considering the complaint and child or young person-friendly.[123] Detailed information about the composition, attendance at and conduct of the review panels, as well as its deliberations and action after the review panel may be found at paragraphs 3.13–3.19 of the 2006 guidance.

26.84 The times limit for convening and holding the review panel is 30 working days, with a further five days allowed for the panel to issue its findings. The authority then has 15 days to respond to the findings.[124] The options for redress are those set out in LGA 2000 s92 (see para 26.59 above).

26.85 The 2006 guidance also provides guidance on matters similar to those considered above (para 26.37 above) under the 2009 Regulations. These include: publicity,[125] monitoring arrangements for local authorities[126] and relationships with other procedures,[127] including complaints involving both the NHS and social care as well as the relationship with other local authority complaints procedures (eg social care and housing).

Social care complaints: Wales

26.86 In Wales, the procedures for complaints involving adult social care and children's services are combined under the same policy guidance.[128] The

---

121 2006 guidance para 3.10.2.
122 2006 guidance para 3.10.3.
123 2006 guidance para 3.11.
124 2006 guidance para 3.19.
125 2006 guidance para 4.
126 2006 guidance para 5.
127 2006 guidance para 7.
128 Welsh Assembly Government (2006) *Listening and learning: a guide to handling complaints and representation in local authority social services in Wales.*

guidance, however, follows the procedures set out in two separate sets of Regulations.[129]

26.87   The procedures apply to any service provided (or commissioned) by the relevant social services authority The procedures are based on two key principles:

- Everyone who makes a complaint about social services in Wales has a right to be listened to properly. Their best interests must be safeguarded and promoted; their views, wishes and feelings must be heard; and their concerns should be resolved quickly and effectively.
- Complaints can highlight where services need changing. So good local authorities will want to learn from these concerns to improve services for everyone who uses them.

26.88   The Welsh complaints process follows a three-stage process, as summarised below.

Stage 1: Local resolution

26.89   The complainant raises their concerns with the social services department, which must try to resolve matters within ten working days although this timescale may be extended (by the complainant only) to 20 working days.

Stage 2: Formal consideration

26.90   At any time, the complainant has the right to ask the authority for a formal consideration of the complaint, usually involving an investigation by someone not involved with the service, and a report with findings, conclusions and recommendations must be produced. This stage should not usually take more than 25 working days, although it may be extended in certain circumstances.

Stage 3: Independent panel

26.91   Where the authority has failed to respond to the complainant's complaint, or where the complaint remains unresolved, the complainant has the right to have the complaint considered by a panel hearing. The panel membership and administrative arrangements will be completely independent of the authority and should meet within 20 working days of the request for a panel hearing.

26.92   The Welsh complaints process also provides for the complainant to take their complaint to the ombudsman after Stage 2, including any complaint about how the complaint has been handled. After Stage 3, the complainant may also take their complaint to the ombudsman, if dissatisfied with the outcome of Stage 2.

---

129   The Representation Procedure (Children) (Wales) Regulations 2005 SI No 3365 (W 262) and the Social Services Complaints Procedure (Wales) Regulations 2005 SI No 3366 (W 293).

NHS complaints: Wales

26.93 Complaints concerning the way in which NHS organisations in Wales deal with complaints, claims and incidents (known as 'concerns') are governed by National Health Service (Concerns, Complaints and Redress Arrangements) (Wales) Regulations 2011[130] (the '2011 Regulations' in the following section). These provide for a process of redress, using powers set out in the NHS Redress (Wales) Measure 2008 and for which there is also accompanying guidance (the 'PTR guidance' in the following section).[131]

26.94 General principles for the handling and investigations of 'concerns' (as they referred to in the 2011 Regulations) are set out in regulation 3(a)–(k).[132] The PTR guidance makes it clear (para 1.1) that the aim of the new NHS complaints process is to:

> ... provide a single, more integrated and supportive process for people to raise concerns which:
> • Is easier for people to access;
> • People can trust to deliver a fair outcome;
> • Recognises a person's individual needs (language, support, etc.);
> • Is fair in the way it treats people and staff;
> • Makes the best use of time and resources;
> • Pitches investigations at the right level of detail for the issue being looked at; and
> • Can show that lessons have been learnt.

What may be raised as a concern?

26.95 A concern may be raised provided it relates to the following:

• any matter connected with the exercise of the functions of a Welsh NHS body;
• a primary care provider, where its services are provided under a contract or arrangements with a Welsh NHS body;
• an independent provider where its services are provided under arrangements with a Welsh NHS body;
• any matter connected with the provision of services by a primary care provider under a contract or arrangements with the local health board.[133]

130 SI No 704.
131 Welsh Assembly Government (2011) *Putting things right: guidance on dealing with concerns about the NHS from 1April 2011* – the 'PTR Guidance'.
132 These include eg that concerns are properly investigated; that those who notify concerns are treated with respect and courtesy; that persons must be properly supported through the complaints process; and that redress is also considered in appropriate cases.
133 Further details as to what is included/excluded from the Regulations may be found in regs 13 and 14.

Who may raise a concern?

26.96   A range of people may raise a concern, including a person who has received services or 'any person who is affected, or likely to be affected by the action, omission or decision of a responsible body the exercise of whose functions is the subject of the concern'.[134] The 2011 Regulations also uses the concept of the responsible body and responsible officer in a very similar way to that used in the English 2009 Complaints Regulations.[135] Transitional arrangements are in place and are to be found at 2011 Regulations Part 10 regs 52–54.

Time limit for making a complaint

26.97   The time limit for the notifying of concerns is not later than 12 months after the date on which the subject matter of the complaint occurred or the date on which it came to the attention of the person raising the concern.[136] Again, similar provisions to those set out in the English 2009 Regulations apply to the question of whether a complaint may be considered outside of these time limits. Time may therefore be extended where 'good reasons for not notifying the concern within that time limit and, notwithstanding the delay, it is still possible to investigate the concern effectively and fairly'.[137]

How to make a complaint

26.98   Complaints may be made in a wide variety of ways, including by text[138] and paras 4.16–4.19 of the PTR guidance set out the steps which should be taken by the NHS, etc to provide information about the new procedures. This information must include details of the arrangements for advocacy to assist a person during the complaints process.[139] The 2011 Regulations have many similarities with their English counterparts, including provisions where a person's concerns involve other responsible bodies.[140]

The handling and investigation of complaints

26.99   The PTR guidance provides considerable detail on how the handling and investigation of the concern must be carried out, building on the requirements of Part 5 of the 2011 Regulations (see regs 22–24). Broadly,

---

134   2011 Regulations reg 12(a) and (b).
135   See paras 26.9 and 26,26 above.
136   2011 Regulations reg 15.
137   2011 Regulations reg 15.
138   Para 4.2 PTR guidance.
139   Para 4.29 PTR guidance, including assistance from the community health councils for anyone aged over 18 years and further provision for those with mental health problems, where mental capacity may be an issue, and for children and young persons.
140   2011 Regulations, Part 4 regs 17–21.

the notification of the concern must be acknowledged within two working days. The investigation should be completed within 30 working days, with a detailed written report being prepared, although this may be extended to six months or more in certain circumstances.

26.100 The outcome of the concern may be one or more of a range of options, for example, a written apology; the giving of an explanation; a report on the action which has or will be taken to prevent similar concerns arising and, where appropriate, financial redress.[141] Where the investigation reveals that there is a 'qualifying liability' under the Regulations and the value of that liability would not exceed £25,000, compensation may be paid to the individual without the need to go through court proceedings.

26.101 A 'qualifying liability', however, will apply only where the individual would have been able to sustain a claim following the usual tort principles: ie that the person's personal injury or loss arose because of a breach of the duty of care by the NHS body and, further, that the breach caused the harm suffered by the individual.[142] It is also noted that financial redress is not available under the qualifying liability rules where the treatment or service is provided by a 'primary care provider' (essentially GPs; dentists; persons providing ophthalmic services and pharmacists, who provide services under arrangements with local health boards).[143]

26.102 The provisions also address cases where a person has had treatment in England, Scotland or Northern Ireland on behalf of a Welsh NHS body including the arrangement for redress in such cases.[144]

26.103 Where a person is dissatisfied with the outcome of an investigation under the 2011 Regulations, they are entitled to pursue their concern with the public service ombudsman for Wales.

Independent and private sector providers

26.104 In England, although all health and adult social care providers must be registered with the Care Quality Commission (CQC) (see paras 7.94 above) to ensure that they meet the 'essential standards'.[145] The CQC as a regulatory body does not investigate complaints by individuals. Under the 2009 Regulations (see para 26.8 above) anyone whose health or social care is arranged or funded by a local authority or by the NHS is entitled to make complaint to the commissioning body, as well as utilising the provider's complaints procedures. Additionally, self-funders have the right to take their complaint to the local government ombudsman, if it has not been possible to resolve it directly with the provider (see para 26.16 below).

141 See 2011 Regulations Part 6 regs 27–29.
142 This point is emphasised clearly in the PTR guidance at paras 7.4 and 7.5.
143 Full details of the process to be followed is to be found in the PTR guidance at section 7 pp58–67.
144 See section 8 PTR guidance and 2011 Regulations Part 7 regs 34–48.
145 See paras 7.102 and 9.20.

26.105   In Wales the Care and Social Services Inspectorate for Wales (CSSIW) (see paras 7.101 and 9.14) exercises similar powers to the CQC and although it also deals with complaints about regulated providers[146] it too does not investigate complaints by individuals.

Patient advice and liaison service

26.106 *The NHS Plan,* 2000, announced the commitment to establish a patient advice and liaison service (PALS) in every English NHS trust by 2002.[147] PALS are a non-statutory advice service that: 'do not replace existing specialist advocacy services, such as mental health and learning disability advocacy. Rather, they are complementary to existing services. Providing information and on the spot help for patients, their families and carers, they are powerful lever for change and improvement.'[148] PALS are regulated by a Department of Health standards and evaluation framework[149] and their core functions include:

- being accessible to patients, their carers, friends and families;
- providing on-the-spot help in every trust with the power to negotiate immediate solutions or speedy resolutions of problems. PALS will listen and provide the relevant information and support to help resolve service users' concerns quickly and efficiently. It will liaise with staff and managers, and, where appropriate, with other PALS services, health and related organisations, to facilitate a resolution;
- acting as a gateway to appropriate independent advice and advocacy services, including the independent complaints advocacy services;
- providing accurate information to patients, carers and families.

Independent complaints advocacy service

26.107 National Health Service Act (NHSA) 2006 s248[150] obliges the secretary of state in England to 'arrange, to such extent as he considers necessary to meet all reasonable requirements' for the provision of independent complaints advocacy services (ICAS) to assist individuals making complaints against the NHS. ICAS replaced the service previously provided by community health councils (CHCs) in England. The service is provided on a regional basis by independent agencies that have been awarded contracts to deliver the service by the Department of Health. Patients who want to complain about NHS services can approach ICAS directly (or be directed

---

146   CSSIW (2008) *Complaint Procedure and Guidance for Handling Complaints in Regulated Services.*
147   Department of Health (2000) *The NHS Plan,* Cm 4818-I, para 10.17.
148   See www.dh.gov.uk 'Patient Advice and Liaison Services'.
149   Department of Health (2003) *PALS Core National Standards and Evaluation Framework.*
150   Previously Health and Social Care Act 2001 s12.

there by the PALS). Complaints managers at trust level are also expected to advise patients of the availability of this service and assist them in making contact.

26.108   In Wales CHCs continue to exist, and provide support and advocacy assistance to complainants: there is one CHC for every local health board.

Challenging discharge and continuing care decisions

26.109 The procedures for challenging hospital discharge and NHS continuing health care decisions are considered separately at paras 5.47 and 14.165 above.

The ombudsman process

26.110 There are a number of different ombudsmen in England and Wales whose task is to investigate complaints made against a range of government organisations. The role of each of the following ombudsmen is considered separately below:

- Local government ombudsman (LGO);
- Parliamentary and health services ombudsman (PHSO);
- Housing ombudsman service (HOS);
- Public services ombudsman for Wales (PSOW).

Local government ombudsman (LGO)

26.111 The Commissioners for Local Administration in England and Wales (generally known as the local government ombudsmen) were established and governed by LGA 1974 Part III.[151] As a result of the Public Services Ombudsman (Wales) Act 2005, Wales has a separate ombudsman system and this is considered at para 26.158 below.

26.112   By virtue of LGA 1974 s25 the LGOs in England are empowered to investigate (among other things) any local authority. LGA 1974 s26 provides that the LGO may investigate where members of the public claim or alleged that they have sustained injustice in consequence of maladministration and/or service failure[152] in connection with action taken by or on behalf of an authority. What is meant by the terms 'maladministration', 'service failure' and 'injustice' is considered further below.

26.113   There are three LGOs in England. Each of them deals with complaints from different parts of the country, but all new complaints (by telephone or in writing) go to the LGO Advice Team based in Coventry. The LGO website[153] contains copies of the complaint forms (which can also be

151   As amended by the Local Government and Public Involvement in Health Act 2007.
152   Introduced by Local Government and Public Involvement in Health Act 2007.
153   See www.lgo.org.uk.

obtained from Citizen's Advice Bureaux), previous relevant reports, publications and key addresses. Full copies of all the LGO investigation reports in England published since 2005 are available from the LGO website, arranged by subject headings under 'Complaint Outcomes'. In addition, the LGO publishes a very helpful Factsheets on a range of different types of social care complaints, available on its website.[154]

26.114   Only about 1 per cent of all complaints result in the LGO preparing a final report; the most significant reasons for a complaint not resulting in a report being: (1) it discloses no or insufficient evidence of maladministration (in about 46 per cent of cases); (2) a local settlement results (in about 27 per cent of cases); and (3) the complaint is outside the ombudsman's jurisdiction (in about 13–15 per cent of cases).[155]

26.115   In the 2008/09 Digest of Cases, the LGO identified common themes arising from its cases, across a range of different subject areas. These were:

- not taking into account the needs of service users;
- ignorance of, or failure to follow, policies and guidance;
- delays resulting in injustice;
- making assumptions; not checking information.[156]

26.116   Since October 2010, the role of the LGO has been extended, to provide an independent complaints review service for people who arrange and fund their own adult social care.[157] This includes those who are paying privately (ie self-funders) and also those whose care is funded by means of personal budgets. Usually, the LGO will only consider the complaint once the care provider's own complaints procedure has been concluded.

Definition of maladministration

26.117   As with judicial review (see para 26.160 below) the LGO's investigation is generally focused on how the decision was reached rather than the merits of the actual decision. In *R v Commissioner for Local Administration ex p Eastleigh BC*[158] Lord Donaldson MR commented:

> Maladministration is not defined in the 1974 Act, but its meaning was considered in *R v Local Comr for Administration for the North and East Area of England, ex p Bradford MCC* [1979] 2 All ER 881. All three judges (Lord Denning MR, Eveleigh LJ and Sir David Cairns) expressed themselves differently, but in substance each was saying the same thing, namely that administration and maladministration, in the context of a local authority, is

---

154   See www.lgo.org.uk/publications/fact-sheets/.
155   Percentages extracted from the *Annual Report 2009/10*.
156   See www.lgo.org.uk/publications/digest-of-cases/. These are no longer being published but the LGO's decisions are available under 'Complaint Outcomes' on the LGO website.
157   Health Act 2009 s35.
158   [1988] 3 WLR 113, CA.

concerned with the manner in which decisions by the authority are reached and the manner in which they are or are not implemented.

26.118 The Health Service Ombudsman in his annual report for 1993–94 (para 1.4) commented on the nature of maladministration in the following terms:

> The terms given by Mr Richard Crossman in 1966 were 'bias, neglect, inattention, delay, incompetence, ineptitude, perversity, turpitude, arbitrariness and so on'. I have added:
> - rudeness (though that is a matter of degree);
> - unwillingness to treat the complainant as a person with rights; refusal to answer reasonable questions;
> - neglecting to inform a complainant on request of his or her rights or entitlement;
> - knowingly giving advice which is misleading or inadequate;
> - ignoring valid advice or overruling considerations which would produce an uncomfortable result for the overruler;
> - offering no redress or manifestly disproportionate redress;
> - showing bias whether because of colour, sex or any other grounds;
> - omission to notify those who thereby lose a right of appeal;
> - refusal to inform adequately of the right of appeal;
> - faulty procedures; failure by management to monitor compliance with adequate procedures;
> - cavalier disregard of guidance which is intended to be followed in the interest of equitable treatment of those who use the service;
> - partiality; and
> - failure to mitigate the effects of rigid adherence to the letter of the law where that produces manifestly inequitable treatment'.

Definition of service failure

26.119 The Local Government and Public Involvement in Health Act 2007 (LGPIA 2007) amended the LGA 1974 to allow the LGO to investigate 'an alleged or apparent failure in a service which it was the authority's function to provide'[159] and also 'an alleged or apparent failure to provide such a service'.[160]

26.120 In most cases, the failure of a service provided by the authority or the failure to provide a service at all will also lead to a finding of maladministration against the authority. However, this is not always the case and, in some circumstances, maladministration will not be found or it is not necessary to invest resources in finding maladministration because the outcome of the investigation has provided an appropriate remedy to resolve the complaint.

26.121 An example of such a situation is provided on the LGO's website:[161] complaints made by 20 residents of recently constructed houses in a new road where the council made no refuse collections for a period of two

---

159 LGA 1974 s26(1)(a)
160 LGA 1974 s26(1)(b).
161 www.lgo.org.uk/guidance-on-jurisdiction/service-failure/.

months. Although the refuse service has now started, the complainants state that they had to make their own arrangements for some two months. The LGO notes that, although a finding of a service only failure would provide a quick remedy for the complainants, without investigating the question of maladministration, the disadvantage of such an approach is that there would not be any recommendations for change or improvements to prevent the same situation from happening in the future.

Injustice

26.122 In order for the LGO to investigate a complaint, there must be some injustice caused to the complainant. In other words, an authority may be responsible for potentially appalling maladministration or service failure but, in the absence of it causing injustice, the ombudsman is unable to investigate the issue.

26.123   There is no formal definition of 'injustice'. The LGO website[162] recommends that advisers consider the question: 'has the fault adversely affected your client in some way?' The adverse effect can include:

- hurt feelings, distress, worry or inconvenience;
- loss of right or amenity;
- not receiving a service;
- financial loss or unnecessary expense;
- time and trouble in pursuing a justified complaint.

LGO procedures

26.124 Complaints must in general be made in writing to the LGO within 12 months from the date on which the person aggrieved first had notice of the matters alleged in the complaint, although the LGO has an overall discretion to extend time if it is considered reasonable to do so (LGA 1974 s26B). This may be appropriate where, for example, 'someone may have been prevented from complaining due to a period of ill health, an inability to read or write English, or the mistaken belief that action would be taken to resolve their complaint'.[163]

26.125   The LGO cannot investigate a complaint unless it has first been drawn to the attention of the local authority in question, and that authority has been afforded an opportunity to investigate and reply to the complaint (LGA 1974 s26(5)(a)). In general, the ombudsman requires complainants to use the authority's complaints procedures before being prepared to investigate the matter.

26.126   By virtue of LGA 1974 s26(5)(b) where the LGO is satisfied that 'in the particular circumstances' it is not reasonable to expect the matter to be brought to the notice of the authority or, alternatively, for the authority to be allowed the opportunity to investigate the matter, the matter may be

162   See www.lgo.org.uk/guide-for-advisers/injustice.
163   See www.lgo.org.uk/guide-for-advisers/can-we-investigate/.

investigated by the LGO without the complaint having traversed the local authority's entire complaints process.

26.127   Helpful guidance[164] has been issued as to when the LGO may be prepared to consider a complaint without the completion of the authority's full complaints procedure – for example:

- where the matter is clearly urgent (eg complaints about education or homelessness);
- where the person's circumstances indicate a need for priority (eg complaints made by children or young people or an already disadvantaged complainant);
- where there has been unreasonable delay in investigating the complaint (generally if no progress has been made in 12 weeks); or
- where the LGO has good reason to believe that the council will not handle the complaint effectively.

26.128 The LGO has also stated in the past that that investigations will be undertaken before the statutory complaints process has been exhausted 'where there has been a breakdown of trust between the complainant and the authority, or where both sides agree that there is no point in completing a process which is unlikely to satisfy the complainant'.[165] Although not specifically referred to in the current guidance, this still appears to be a relevant ground for the exercise of the LGO's discretion in suitable cases.

The availability of an alternative remedy

26.129 Unless the LGO is satisfied that, in the particular circumstances, it is not reasonable to expect the aggrieved person to resort to such a remedy, complaints cannot be entertained where there exists an alternative remedy, for instance a right of appeal to a tribunal or to a minister of the Crown or a remedy by way of court proceedings.[166] Useful guidance about the ombudsman's jurisdiction, including the availability of alternative remedies, may be found on the LGO website.[167]

26.130   In respect of the alternative remedy of judicial review, the guidance available on the LGO website refers to judgment of Lord Justice Henry in the case of *R v Commission for Local Administration ex p Liverpool City Council*.[168] It provides the following in the exercise of discretion by the LGO as to whether judicial review may be available:[169]

- the allegation can best be investigated by the resources and powers of the ombudsman;
- the ombudsman is in a position to get to the bottom of the prima facie case of maladministration and the complainant would be unlikely

164 See www.lgo.org.uk/guide-for-advisers/council-response/
165 J White, 'Community care and the local government ombudsman for England' (2006) 9 CCLR 8.
166 LGA 1974 s26(6).
167 See www.lgo.org.uk/guidance-on-jurisdiction/
168 [2000] All ER (D) 235.
169 See www.lgo.org.uk/guidance-on-jurisdiction/alternative-right-remedy/

to reach that goal 'having regards to the weaknesses of the coercive fact
finding potential of judicial review . . . it would be very difficult, if not
impossible, for the complainants to obtain the necessary evidence in
judicial review proceedings';[170]

- the complainants are unlikely to have the means to pursue a remedy
through the courts;
- the ombudsman's investigation and report can provide a just remedy
when judicial review might fail to do so.

26.131   In addition, although not specifically referred to in the *Liverpool City
Council* case, the LGO has advised that other matters, such as whether it
would have been reasonable to expect the complainant to make an application for judicial review within the required time limit and, further, the
availability for legal aid funding for judicial review, are also to be considered by the LGO when exercising its discretion under LGA 1974
s26(6)(c).[171] It is also noted that the ombudsman has previously indicated
that 'in general' judicial review is not considered to provide a remedy 'that
is reasonable for most complainants to resort to'.[172]

Judicial review and the LGO procedures

26.132   As complaints to the LGO are only (in general) accepted if no effective
legal remedy is available, the judicial review and ombudsman procedures
are distinct and not 'alternative options'.[173] In *R v Commissioner for Local
Administration ex p PH*,[174] an applicant commenced judicial review proceedings against a local authority on the grounds that it had delayed
undertaking a special educational needs assessment. As a consequence
such an assessment took place. Subsequently she complained to the
ombudsman seeking compensation for the effect of the council's delay.
The ombudsman decided, under LGA 1974 s26(6), that the complaint
was outside his jurisdiction because the complainant had already sought a
judicial review of the council's actions. In upholding the ombudsman's
decision, Turner J held:

> It can hardly have been the intention of Parliament to have provided two
> remedies, one substantive by way of judicial review and one compensatory
> by was of the Local Commissioner . . . where a party has ventilated a
> grievance by way of judicial review it was not contemplated that they
> should enjoy and alternative, let alone an additional right by way of
> complaint to a local commissioner.

---

170   As per Lord Justice Henry, *R v Commission for Local Administration ex p Liverpool City
Council* [2000] All ER (D) 235 at [28].

171   See www.lgo.org.uk/guidance-on-jurisdiction/alternative-right-remedy/.

172   J White, 'Community care and the local government ombudsman for England' (2006)
9 CCLR 8 at 9.

173   Ombudsman decisions are, however, susceptible to judicial review; see eg *R v
Parliamentary Commissioner ex p Dyer* [1994] 1 WLR 621 and *R v Parliamentary
Commissioner ex p Bachin* (1999) EGCS 78.

174   [1999] COD 382, as cited in the *Annual Report 1998/99*, p7.

26.133 Prior judicial review proceedings will not, however, always be a bar to a subsequent ombudsman investigation. In *R (Goldsmith) v Wandsworth LBC*[175] the Court of Appeal quashed a local authority decision to require a resident to move to a nursing home (from her residential care home of many years). In order to avoid the contested move (pending the court decision) the resident's daughter had paid a private agency to provide her mother's nursing needs. On the Court of Appeal ruling that the local authority's decision making was irrational, the daughter complained to the ombudsman seeking to recover her expenditure on the nursing costs amounting to over £27,000 plus interest. The ombudsman upheld her complaint and recommended the compensation be paid in that sum.[176]

26.134   The fact that lawyers are involved and threatening legal action does not of itself make the Ombudsman process unavailable. A 2001 report concerned a council that delayed the provision of (assessed) services until threatened with a judicial review. A subsequent complaint concerning the delay was upheld and a compensation recommendation made by the ombudsman.[177]

The pros and cons of using the LGO

26.135 There are many advantages to a complainant in using the LGO procedures. They are free to the complainant; they can result in the award of significant sums in compensation and the authority is required to publicise the ombudsman's report (LGA 1974 s30). The ombudsman has access to all the relevant files and other records; can require the authority to furnish additional information; and has the same powers as the High Court in respect of the attendance and examination of witnesses and the production of documents (LGA 1974 s29). Complaints to the LGO are not subject to such short time limits as in judicial review.

26.136   The ombudsman is concerned with the factual basis of local authority decisions – whereas in judicial review the court is largely confined to a review of the decision's legality. The ombudsman is capable of undertaking a very detailed review of the relevant documentation, of interviewing all the participants to a decision (eg the director of social services, councillors as well as the staff in actual contact with service user/carers). This analysis frequently sees through protestations by an authority that its decision was not 'resource led'. Examples of this type of review can be found at paras 3.183, 4.50 and 23.76 above.

26.137   The disadvantages include the apparent reluctance of the LGO to accept many complaints;[178] the fact that less than 1 per cent of all complaints actually result in a final report; the length of time which it may take to complete the investigations (although this has shown considerable

---

175 [2004] EWCA Civ 1170, (2004) 7 CCLR 472 – see also para 3.229 above.
176 Complaint no 05/B/02414 against Wandsworth, 27 September 2006.
177 Complaint no 99/B/04621 against Cambridgeshire, 29 January 2001.
178 The LGO Annual Report for 2009/10 shows that, of 18,020 enquiries to the LGO Advice Team in Coventry, decisions were made on 10,309 cases forwarded to the LGO's offices during the last year (see pp12 and 15).

improvement, with more than half of all complaints being resolved within 13 weeks[179]) and the fact that, in general terms, ombudsman's recommendations are not binding on local authorities. However, whilst councils are not bound to comply with the recommendations, any failure that is based on irrational grounds will be vulnerable to be struck down in judicial review.[180] Furthermore, the ombudsman's recommendations are binding upon local authorities unless and until the authority applies for judicial review to quash the decision[181] (see *R (Bradley) v Secretary of State Work and Pensions*[182]).

26.138   Even so, each year, a very few such recommendations are not accepted by local authorities (or, even more occasionally, a council fails to implement and agreed settlement[183]). Trafford Metropolitan Borough Council is a example of such a recalcitrant authority. It refused to comply with recommendations made in a 2006 report[184] (concerning its decision to require the repayment of an improvement grant made to an elderly woman with significant mental health problems) and did so again in 2007 (concerning a serious failure in a disabled young persons transitional planning[185]). In the face of such a refusal, all that the ombudsman can do is issue a further critical report drawing attention to the failure. In the Trafford case this was done in 2007[186] in trenchant terms. Clearly when such a deadlock occurs (and it is not limited to English cases[187]) it is profoundly unsatisfactory for the complainant and evidence of the limitations of the process (compared to that of judicial review).

Compensation/other recommendations

26.139 The LGO will often recommend action in addition to an apology and compensation.[188] By way of example, a 2006 complaint against Blackpool Borough Council[189] included a recommendation that (among other things) the council should:

- offer Mrs Lloyd an appropriate form of tribute or memorial to her aunt (whose death had prompted the complaint) and bring that into effect within six months;
- formally adopt at member level a policy that ensures that risks to individual service users will be assessed as an integral part of the

179 *Annual Report 2009/10* p25.
180 See eg *R (Gallagher) v Basildon DC* [2010] EWHC 2824 (Admin).
181 *R (Bradley and others) v Secretary of State for Work and Pensions* [2008] EWCA Civ 36 [2009] QB 114, [2008] 3 WLR 1059 at [139] per Wall LJ.
182 [2007] EWHC 242 (Admin).
183 See eg Complaint no 08 004 517 against Corby BC, 17 September 2009.
184 Complaint no 04/C/17057 against Trafford MBC, 30 November 2006.
185 Further report concerning Complaint no 05/C/11921, 3 January 2008
186 Further report concerning complaint no 04/C/17057, 15 May 2007.
187 See eg the comments of the Public Service Ombudsman for Wales in his *Annual Report 2006/07* (p22) concerning the failure of Gwynedd Council.
188 Compensation may be significant: see Complaint no 09 014 026 against City of London, where a carer was awarded £50,880.00, representing the value of the respite care to which she had been entitled but which the council had failed to provide to her.
189 Complaint no 03/C/17141 against Blackpool BC, 23 February 2006.

response to both individual complaints and a known failure in home care services;

- ensure that there are adequate resources available to the contracts unit so that it can fulfil its role in monitoring contract performance;
- review complaint procedures and staff training to ensure the development of an appropriate customer care culture which recognises the difficulty and fears that vulnerable service users may have in making complaints.

26.140 Other examples include cases where the ombudsman has recommended that a council:

- commission and consider a report from its chief executive about the capacity of senior managers in the relevant services to provide leadership and a working environment that supports, values and responds effectively to 'front line' concerns about service failures and pressures;[190]
- create a fund of £5,000 to be spent on items or activities chosen by the other children in the family, in recognition of the effect on them of the strain caused to their mother, their restricted living space and witnessing their brothers' distress and indignity;[191]
- pay for a two-week UK summer holiday for the family.[192]

Overlap with the Health Service Ombudsman

26.141 A consultation document issued by the Cabinet Office in 2005[193] proposed reforms that would (among other things) address the problem of identifying whether a complaint should be investigated by the LGO or by the Health Service Ombudsman, in those situations where there were allegations of maladministration against both the local authority and the NHS.

26.142 In July 2007 the LGO published a special report[194] which addressed this issue in which it was noted that a regulatory reform order, due to come into force on 1 August 2007,[195] would remove the limitations on the Ombudsmen's ability to carry out joint investigations and issue joint reports.

26.143 The first investigation[196] under the Regulatory Reform Order concerned a failure in relation to the social care provision of a resident in a care home run by a local authority under functions devolved to it pursuant

190 Complaint no 07C03887 against Bury MBC, 14 October 2009, para 49.
191 Complaint no 07C03887 against Bury MBC, 14 October 2009, para 49.
192 Complaint no 04/C/16622 against Leeds CC, 4 May 2006, para 38.
193 Cabinet Office (2005) *Consultation paper: reform of public sector ombudsmen services in England.*
194 Local Government Ombudsman (2007) *Special report: handling complaints about local partnerships.*
195 Regulatory Reform (Collaboration etc between Ombudsman) Order 2007.
196 Complaint nos 03/A/04618 and HS-2608 against Buckinghamshire CC and Oxfordshire and Buckinghamshire Mental Health Partnership Trust (respectively), 17 March 2008.

to an agreement under Health and Social Care Act 2001 s31[197] agree-ment. The resident, who could not speak, was profoundly disabled requiring one-to-one attention for about 95 per cent of his waking time. His parents complained that (amongst other things) that they had to sub-sidise his care by paying for clothing, soft furnishings, day care activities, lunches, recreation and snacks. Furthermore, they also complained that staff did not have any commitment to their son's care (they alleged his dental health had been neglected; he was locked in his bedroom over-night; he had been found sitting in a chair cold, unwashed, unshaven and had clearly had an 'accident' as he and his clothes were covered in faeces and urine and that the staff had offered no explanation, apology or help).

26.144   In the opinion of both ombudsmen in their joint report, 'the greater a person's disability or communication difficulties, the greater the need for proper consideration to ensure the protection of basic rights such as human dignity' and that in the Articles 3, 8 and 14 of the European Convention on Human Rights were engaged. In consequence of the maladministration compensation totaling £32,000 was recommended to be paid, apportioned equally between the two bodies.

26.145   A subsequent (2009) report on a joint investigation by the LGO and the health service ombudsman concerned complaints brought by Mencap on behalf of the families of six people with learning disabilities who died whilst in NHS or local authority care.[198] The ombudsmen's overview summary was:

> The investigation reports illustrate some significant and distressing failures in service across both health and social care. They show the devastating impact of organisational behaviour which does not adapt to individual needs, or even consistently follow procedures designed to maintain a basic quality of service for everyone. They identify a lack of leadership and a failure to understand the law in relation to disability discrimination and human rights. This led to situations in which people with learning disabilities were treated less favourably than others, resulting in prolonged suffering and inappropriate care.

Parliamentary and Health Service Ombudsman

26.146 The Health Service Ombudsman (HSO) also fulfils the role of the Central Government (or Parliamentary) Ombudsman and is based in London. The HSO (sometimes also known as the NHS Ombudsman) has wide powers to investigate complaints concerning GPs, NHS trusts and health authorities, including clinical practice. These powers derive from the

---

197 Now NHSA 2006 s75/NHS(W)A 2006 s33.
198 *Six Lives: the provision of public services to people with learning difficulties* was laid before parliament on 23 March 2009. See www.ombudsman.org.uk/improving-public-service/reports-and-consultations/reports/health/six-lives-the-provision-of-public-services-to-people-with-learning-disabilities/11

Health Service Commissioners Act (HSCA) 1993 (as amended[199]) and provide (at section 3) for the Commissioner to investigate complaints made:

> ... by or on behalf of a person that he has sustained injustice or hardship in consequence of –
> (a) a failure in a service provided by a health service body,
> (b) a failure of such a body to provide a service which it was a function of the body to provide, or
> (c) maladministration connected with any other action taken by or on behalf of such a body.

26.147 HSCA 1993 s5 contained a general inhibition on the investigation of matters of clinical judgment. This was repealed by Health Service Commissioners (Amendment) Act 1996 s6. Accordingly the potential scope of the HSO's powers is wide. There are, however, limits, not least that she should restrict her investigations to the complaints that have been made and not (for instance) widen the scope of the investigation because she is concerned about separate or other issues.[200]

26.148   Complaints must concern issues of maladministration and/or service failure, leading to hardship or injustice. It must also be made in writing within one year of the date when the action complained about occurred. Details of the complaints procedures and past reports are accessible at the ombudsman's website.[201]

26.149   In general, the HSO cannot consider a complaint until the relevant NHS complaints procedures have been exhausted. Since 2009, a complainant who is remains dissatisfied at the outcome of the NHS investigation into their complaint is able to take the matter directly to the HSO. This has led to more than double the number of complaints being made (from 6,780 in 2008–09 to 14,429 in 2009–10).[202]

26.150   In October 2010, the HSO published the first in an annual series of reports[203] examining NHS complaints handling in England, covering the first full year of the new complaints system (see above). It shows that more complaints were received about hospital, specialist and teaching trusts than any other group,[204] followed by GPs.[205] The two most common reasons for complainants to be dissatisfied with the NHS were failings in clinical care and treatment and also the attitude of staff. The most common reasons for dissatisfaction with the NHS complaints handling procedures were a poor explanation or an incomplete response.

---

199 By the Health Service Commissioners (Amendment) Act 1996 and HSC(CHS)A 2003 Part 2 chapter 9.
200 *Cavanagh and others v Health Service Commissioner* [2005] EWCA Civ 1578, [2006] 1 WLR 1229.
201 www.ombudsman.org.uk.
202 *Annual Report 2009/2010*, published 15 July 2010 and available on the ombudsman's website: www.ombudsman.org.uk.
203 See *Listening and Learning: the ombudsman's review of complaint handling by the NHS in England 2009–10*. HC 482 18. October 2010 available on www.ombudsman.org.uk
204 6,304 complaints (44%), quoted in the Ombudsman Report.
205 2,419 complaints (17%), quoted in the Ombudsman Report.

26.151   In the foreword to the report, the HSO commented that the data published in the report pointed to a clear conclusion: 'The NHS needs to listen harder and learn more from complaints', before going on to observe that:

> When things do go wrong, an apology can be a powerful remedy; simple to deliver and costing nothing. If a mistake is not in dispute, the Ombudsman's input should not be necessary to ensure the NHS takes responsibility for the error. Too often it takes the involvement of my Office to secure an apology from the NHS, enabling those affected to move on with their lives.

26.152   The PHSO has published *The Ombudsman's Principles*,[206] which outline the approach the ombudsman believes public bodies should adopt when delivering good administration and customer service, including how to respond when things go wrong. The principles make clear that they are not a checklist and that the each complaint will be decided on its merits. Given the current time of financial austerity across all publicly funded services, the PHSO also provides some guidance on the question of limited resources:

> We also understand that the actions of public bodies are limited by their resources and all public bodies must spend money with care. There is often a balance between being sensitive to the needs of a customer and yet acting proportionately within available resources. Public bodies have to take decisions bearing in mind all the circumstances; delivering good service often means taking a broad and balanced view of all of the individuals or organisations that may be affected by decisions. However, finite resources should not be used as an excuse for poor service, poor administration, poor complaint handling or failing to provide a fair remedy.

26.153   The HSO has also issued a number of highly influential reports concerning the provision of NHS continuing care and these are considered separately at paras 14.16 and 14.26.

Housing Services Ombudsman (HOS)

26.154   The HOS was established under the Housing Act 1996 (amended by the Housing and Regeneration Act 2008), which requires all social housing providers to belong to the HOS.[207] Therefore, a tenant of a housing association has the right to complain to the HOS, rather than the LGO.

26.155   In common with the other ombudsman schemes, the HOS will consider complaints brought by a dissatisfied tenant after the final stage of the landlord's own complaint process has been completed. The HOS will investigate a complaint to establish what is 'fair in all the circumstances of the case'.

---

206   See www.ombudsman.org.uk/improving-public-service/ombudsmansprinciples.

207   Housing Ombudsman Service, 81 Aldwych, London, WC2B 4HN. Tel: 0300 111 300, www.housing-ombudsman.org.uk email: info@housing-ombudsman.org.uk.

26.156   Inevitably, there is overlap with the role of the LGO in respect of council housing, and in 2009 a protocol was agreed between the LGO and the HOS which allows for complaints made by social housing tenants to be directed to the appropriate ombudsman scheme, as well as providing for more collaborative working and sharing of information[208] for landlords.

26.157   Helpfully, all HOS decisions involving housing cases are collated in a single website.[209] There have been a number of decisions in respect of delays in the provision of disabled facilities grants (see, for example, para 15.107).

Public Services Ombudsman for Wales

26.158   The Office of Public Services Ombudsman for Wales came into being in April 2006, replacing the previous offices of the Local Government Ombudsman for Wales, Health Service Ombudsman for Wales, Welsh Administration Ombudsman and the Social Housing Ombudsman for Wales. These changes took effect as a consequence of the enactment of the Public Services Ombudsman (Wales) Act 2005. The ombudsman's office is on the outskirts of Bridgend in South Wales.[210]

26.159   The Public Services Ombudsman's most recent Annual Report confirms that, for the first time since its inception, the number of complaints about maladministration or service failure has fallen by 8 per cent from the previous year to 1,992. The vast majority of complaints relate to local councils, although the number is in fact falling, whilst the number of complaints against NHS bodies continues to increase.[211] The procedure for making complaints is similar to that for the separate ombudsman in England.

Judicial review

The nature of judicial review

26.160   'The basis of judicial review rests in the free-standing principle that every action of a public body must be justified by law.'[212] Judicial review is a procedure by which the High Court reviews the lawfulness of decisions made by public bodies, such as the departments of state, local authorities and NHS bodies. It is important to emphasise that the purpose of the court's scrutiny is not to consider the merits of the decision which is the

---

208   See LGO Annual Report 09/10 *Delivering Public Value* at p12.
209   www.housemark.co.uk/hmkb2.nsf/cdhp?openform.
210   Public Services Ombudsman for Wales, 1 Ffordd yr Hen Gae, Pencoed, CF35 5LJ, tel: 01656 641 150, website: www.ombudsman-wales.org.uk.
211   PSOW, Annual Report 2009/10 laid before the National Assembly for Wales on 25 June 2010; see www.ombudsman-wales.org.uk/en/publications/
212   Laws LJ in *R (Beeson) v Dorset County Council* [2003] UKHRR 353 at [17].

subject of the judicial review but to consider whether the public body made the decision in a lawful manner.

26.161   The High Court, through the use of judicial review, seeks to improve the way public bodies make decisions and thus contribute to a fairer and more open administrative system. It does not seek to usurp the powers of these bodies. It follows therefore that the court will only get involved if the aggrieved party acts swiftly and produces significant evidence, not only of a 'flawed' decision making process but also that as a consequence a real risk of injustice may result.

26.162   As judicial review is primarily concerned with process rather than merits, it follows that for many community care disputes of a factual nature, it has severe limitations as a remedy. As Collins J observed in *Gunter v South Western Staffordshire PCT*:

> Judicial review is an unsatisfactory means of dealing with cases . . . where there are judgments to be made and factual issues may be in dispute. At best, it can identify failures to have regard to material considerations and a need for a reconsideration. Very rarely if ever will it result in mandatory orders to the body which has the responsibility to reach the relevant decision.[213]

26.163   In general, the law allows private individuals or businesses to behave unreasonably or make capricious decisions: public bodies, however, have no such freedom. They must act reasonably in reaching decisions and, since October 2000, must not act in any way which is incompatible with the European Convention on Human Rights.[214] If the actions of the public body are found to be unreasonable or incompatible, and significant injustice results, the High Court may be prepared to quash the decision and require that it be considered again without the contaminant of unfairness.

26.164   What is 'reasonable' depends upon the nature of the decision and the context in which it is to be made. It will invariably require that, in reaching a decision, all relevant matters be considered; that all irrelevant matters are disregarded; that the body correctly applies the relevant law (including that it has the power to make the decision). In certain situations, reasonableness may require that prior to making a decision, consultation takes place with persons who are likely to be affected. Likewise, reasonableness may require that a particular decision-making procedure be followed, if affected parties have a 'legitimate expectation' that this will occur. Even if a public body adheres to all these principles, its ultimate decision will be capable of judicial challenge if it bears no sensible relationship to the material facts on which it was based (if it in essence 'defies logic') or if the decision amounts to an abuse of power. These matters are considered more detail below.

213   [2005] EWHC 1894 (Admin), (2006) 9 CCLR 121 at [19].
214   HRA 1998 s6.

Time limits

26.165 Since applications for a judicial review must generally be made promptly and in any event within three months of when the claim first arose,[215] it is vital that lawyers expert in this process be retained, if possible, and any action be commenced at the earliest opportunity. The time limits cannot be extended by the agreement of the parties[216] and the court will take a robust view when considering time limits.[217]

What is a public body?

26.166 In the context of community care, it is established law that decisions made by public bodies, such as a local authority or by the NHS, will be subject to judicial review. But what of decisions made by private or voluntary providers (such as independent nursing homes or voluntary sector day centres, etc)? In general terms, such decisions would not be susceptible to judicial review but the law is changing in this area.

26.167   In the case of *R (Weaver) v London and Quadrant Housing Trust*[218] the Court of Appeal decided that, although a registered social landlord, the trust had acted as a public authority for the purposes HRA 1998 s6(3)(b) in respect of the function of management and allocation of its housing stock. As such, its decision to terminate a tenancy was therefore amenable to judicial review. The extension of the meaning of 'public authority' (via Health and Social Care Act 2008 s145) for the purposes of the HRA 1998 is further considered at para 26.240 below.

26.168   As a general principle, a decision by a private or voluntary provider may therefore be subject to judicial review where the decision is authorised by an Act of Parliament; where the organisation is carrying out a 'public function' or where the decision is 'adopted' by the relevant public body. However, such decisions may, in any event, constitute a breach of private law rights (eg a breach of a contract with a nursing home) and be subject to the complaints or ombudsman processes described above.

The funding of judicial review proceedings

26.169 In general, this will require either legal aid funding[219] (and obtaining this can take not inconsiderable time) or access to significant resources –

---

215 CPR 54.5.
216 CPR 54.5(2).
217 See the decision in *R (Enfield LBC) v Secretary of State for Health, Barnet PCT, Enfield PCT and Haringey Teaching PCT* [2009] EWHC 743 (Admin) where, in an unusual case, the court refused the claimant's permission to bring judicial review proceedings where the authority had delayed making the judicial review application to allow the secretary of state's scrutiny procedure to be completed.
218 [2009] EWCA Civ 587.
219 Details of solicitors and advice agencies who undertake community care legal aid work in England and Wales may be found at: http://legaladviserfinder.justice.gov.uk/AdviserSearch.do.

although there is nothing to stop an individual seeking to take a judicial review without lawyers.[220]

26.170   Legal aid for judicial review claims in community care cases will be granted only where the Legal Services Commission (LSC) assesses the case as having sufficient merits and, further, where the individual has satisfied a means test and is found to be eligible on financial grounds. Legal aid for civil cases is currently subject to review by the Ministry of Justice (MoJ) and it is likely that the rules governing its availability will be subject to change.[221]

26.171   Judicial review proceedings follow the general costs principle that the 'losing' party pays the costs of the 'winning' party. Therefore, for those claimants who undertake judicial review proceedings (particularly those without the benefit of costs protection afforded by legal aid funding[222]), a significant consideration is the risk, if unsuccessful, of having to pay the costs of the other party.

26.172   Where judicial review proceedings have been issued and the parties wish to settle the case at an early stage, the general principle is that the defendant would only be expected to pay the claimant's costs if either (a) it should have been obvious from the issue of proceedings that the claim is likely to be successful at trial and/or (b) its conduct has been such that it would be appropriate to for it to pay all or a proportion of the applicant's costs.[223]

26.173   In certain situations, the court is prepared to consider limiting the sum an unsuccessful party may have to pay by making what is known as a 'protective costs order' (PCO). In *R (Corner House Research) v Secretary of State for Trade and Industry*,[224] the Court of Appeal set out the guidance to be considered by the courts when determining an application for a PCO. This includes matters such as: the issues are of general public importance; public interest requires that those issues should be resolved; the claimant has no private interest in the outcome of the case; having regard to the financial resources of the parties and the amount of costs likely to be involved, it is fair and just to make the order; if the order is not made, the claimant will probably discontinue the proceedings, and will be acting reasonably in so doing. A PCO may be granted at any stage during the proceedings. The court has very wide discretion as to the terms of the

---

220 The procedure is detailed in CPR Part 54, accessible at www.justice.gov.uk/guidance/courts-and-tribunals/courts/procedure-rules/civil/contents/parts/part54.htm#I-DA5ESIC. A useful guide to the process is J Manning (2004) *Judicial Review Proceedings: a practitioner's guide*, 2nd edn, Legal Action Group. Although High Court fees are substantial, procedures exist for these to be reduced or waived for applicants on low incomes.

221 For details of the proposed reforms, see *Proposals for the Reform of Legal Aid in England and Wales*, Consultation Paper CP12/10 November 2010 published by the Ministry of Justice.

222 See Access to Justice Act 1999 s11 and Community Legal Service (Costs) Regulations 2000 and Community Legal Services (Cost Protection) Regulations 2000 which broadly ensure that the losing legally aided party is not required to pay any more in costs than they are reasonably able to afford.

223 *R (Boxall) v Waltham Forest LBC* (2001) 4 CCLR 258 (Admin).

224 [2005] EWCA Civ 192.

PCO, being able to grant them where the court believes it is 'fair and just' to do so.[225]

Complaint to local authority monitoring officer

26.174 Where judicial review proceedings are contemplated, it is often advisable, as a preliminary step, to make a formal complaint to the local authority monitoring officer requesting that the impugned decision be reviewed. This may be in the form of (and constitute) the letter before action in appropriate cases. In general, the monitoring officer will be the senior legal officer of the authority.

26.175 The duties of the monitoring officer are set out in Local Government and Housing Act 1989 s5.[226] Section 5(2) provides that, if it at any time it appears to the monitoring officer that 'any proposal, decision or omission by the authority' (or any officer or committee of the authority) is likely to contravene 'any enactment or rule of law or of any code of practice made or approved by or under any enactment', then the monitoring officer must investigate this and prepare a report on the issue in question. Formerly, this obligation also applied to allegations that the authority's actions amounted to maladministration. The situation now, however, is that in such cases the monitoring officer has a power to investigate (which presumably it would be wise to do if the evidence provided were substantial) but not a duty – until such time as the LGO/PSO has 'conducted an investigation' in relation to the alleged maladministration.[227] Given that the duty to investigate and prepare a report is triggered by the monitoring officer receiving credible evidence that the law or a 'rule of law' has been (or will be) contravened, letters seeking the involvement of the monitoring officer should (if it be the case) be phrased in these terms.

Sufficient standing

26.176 In order to apply for judicial review, an applicant must have a 'sufficient interest' in the matter to which the application relates. The courts have recognised for some time that organisations, as well as individuals, may have a sufficient interest to bring judicial review proceedings.

26.177 In *R v Gloucestershire CC ex p RADAR*,[228] Carnwath J considered an application by the Royal Association for Disability and Rehabilitation (RADAR) for judicial review of a decision made by Gloucestershire County Council, relating to a general procedure which the council had adopted for the reassessment of the community care needs of disabled people, following on the earlier court decision in *R v Gloucestershire CC*

---

225 For recent PCO cases: see *R (Public Interest Lawyers) v Legal Services Commission* [2010] EWHC 3259 (Admin) (on the private interest point); *R (Garner) v Elmbridge BC* [2010] EWCA Civ 1006; *R (Badger Trust) v Welsh Ministers* [2010] EWCA Civ 1316.
226 As amended by LGA 2003 s113.
227 Local Government and Housing Act s2A.
228 (1997–98) 1 CCLR 476, QBD.

ex p Mahfood].[229] RADAR wished to challenge this general procedure and Carnwarth J found that this procedure was:

> . . . one which can, in my view, properly and conveniently be asserted by a body such as RADAR. It cannot be in anyone's interests that it should be left to each individual separately to assert that right. No doubt other individual test cases can be bought, but there is always a risk that if the particular individual loses his direct interest, either because his circumstances change or because the Authority carry out a reassessment, then the proceedings will prove abortive. In my view, RADAR has a sufficient interest to entitle it to a declaration as to the position as I have outlined it.

26.178 In *R (Evans) v The Lord Chancellor and Secretary of State for Justice*,[230] the claimant, a civil liberties campaigner, brought successful judicial review proceedings in respect of the government's decision to remove legal aid for cases brought 'in the public interest'. Although the question of whether or not the claimant had sufficient standing was not pursued by the defendants, it is a useful example of an interested third party being able to pursue an application for judicial review.[231]

An alternative remedy?

26.179 Judicial review is not available where the claimant has failed to pursue an equally convenient, expeditious and effective remedy. This will mean that, in the absence of cogent reasons, a claimant should first utilise the complaints procedures or seek to invoke an available 'default' remedy (see para 26.231 below). As a general rule, disputes which are primarily factual are best suited to the complaints process and disputes which concern the interpretation of directions or guidance may be suited to resolution via the default procedures.[232]

26.180   The court may be prepared to entertain a judicial review, notwithstanding that the applicant has not attempted to use the complaints or default procedures, if it can be shown that there are substantial reasons for believing that these remedies are not 'equally convenient, expeditious and effective'. Frequently this will be the case where:

- the matter in issue is a clear-cut dispute of a legal definition;
- what is in issue is a blanket practice or fixed policy;
- there is an urgent need for the service (ie a requirement for 'interim relief') or it can be otherwise shown that the complaints procedure would be incapable of adequately resolving the dispute.[233]

229 (1997–98) 1 CCLR 7, QBD.
230 [2011] EWHC 1146 (Admin).
231 As is the case of *R (Garner) v Elmbridge Borough Council and Ors* [2010] EWCA Civ 1006 (a planning issue). See also the decision of the Northern Ireland High Court in *JR1, Re Judicial Review* [2011] NIQB 5 where a narrower view of the definition of 'standing' was used where the claimant sought to bring a claim based solely on the HRA 1998, using the more restrictive 'victim' test.
232 *R v Westminster CC ex p P and others* (1997–98) 1 CCLR 486, CA and see also *R v Kirklees MBC ex p Good* (1997–98) 1 CCLR 506, QBD.
233 See R Gordon, *Community Care Assessments*, Longman, 1993, pp61 et seq.

26.181 In *R v Gloucestershire CC ex p RADAR*,[234] it was argued unsuccessfully that an application for judicial review could not be made until the alternative remedy of a local authority complaint under LASSA 1970 s7B had been pursued. Carnwath J held that in certain cases such a remedy might be appropriate, especially:

> ... where individual relief is being sought. However, in relation to a general issue of principle as to the authority's obligations in law ... I do not think that can be regarded as a suitable or alternative remedy to the procedure of judicial review.[235]

26.182 Likewise, in *R v Devon CC ex p Baker and others*,[236] such an argument (not only that an alternative remedy via the complaints procedure existed but also that, under LASSA 1970 s7D, the applicants should first have asked the secretary of state to use her default powers), was rejected on the grounds that:

> ... as the issue is entirely one in law in a developing field which is peculiarly appropriate for decisions by the Court rather than by the secretary of state, I would hold that the Applicants in the Durham case were not precluded from making their application for Judicial Review by the availability of another remedy; the case is one which it is proper for this Court to entertain.[237]

26.183 In *Cowl and others v Plymouth CC*,[238] the Court of Appeal spoke of the heavy obligation on lawyers in such disputes to resort to litigation only where it is unavoidable, stating '[i]f they cannot resolve the whole of the dispute by the use of the complaints procedure they should resolve the dispute so far as is practicable without involving litigation. At least in this way some of the expense and delay will be avoided'.[239]

26.184   In *R (Lloyd) v Barking and Dagenham LBC*,[240] the Court of Appeal held that it was not the appropriate forum to prescribe the degree of detail that should go into a care plan or the amount of consultation to be carried out with a patient's advisers. This judicial reluctance to use judicial review as a means of monitoring the performance of local authorities was noted by Munby J in *R (P, W, F and G) v Essex County Council*,[241] where he emphasised that: 'the Administrative Court exists to adjudicate upon specific challenges to discrete decisions. It does not exist to monitor and regulate the performance of public authorities.' This reluctance was

---

234 (1997–98) 1 CCLR 506, QBD.
235 See also *R v Hampshire CC ex p Ellerton* [1985] 1 WLR 749 and *R v Kent CC ex p Bruce* (1996) *Times* 8 February.
236 [1995] 1 All ER 73.
237 Per Dillon LJ at 87; and see also *R v Brent LBC ex p Sawyers* [1994] 1 FLR 203, CA.
238 [2001] EWCA Civ 1935, [2002] 1 WLR 803, (2002) 5 CCLR 42 at [27]. These views were reiterated by Maurice Kay J in *R (Dudley, Whitbread and others) v East Sussex CC* [2003] EWHC 1093 (Admin).
239 At [27].
240 [2001] EWCA Civ 533, (2001) 4 CCLR 196 at 205G; and also the comments of McCombe J in *R (F, J, S, R and others) v Wirral Borough Council* [2009] EWHC 1626 (Admin) at [75] et seq.
241 [2004] EWHC 2027 (Admin), see [30] at [33].

also expressed by Hallett LJ in *R (Ireneschild) v Lambeth LBC*,[242] when observing that 'Courts must be wary ... of expecting so much of hard pressed social workers that we risk taking them away, unnecessarily, from their front line duties' (at [57]).

26.185   Such disputes are often seen as best being resolved by the complaints process rather than by means of an application for judicial review. In *R (S) v Hampshire County Council*[243] (a case concerning the assessment under the CA 1989 where the claimant had previous experience of the relevant complaints process), for example, Walker J commented:

> For these reasons I conclude that the Council is right to say that L had an adequate alternative remedy which she should have followed. For that reason alone I would refuse permission to apply for judicial review in this case. I add that there was a complete failure to comply with the pre-action protocol in relation to the 2009 Assessment, and no attempt whatever to seek to avoid litigation. This, in my view, would also warrant peremptory refusal of permission. There was never any adequate opportunity for the Council to consider and respond to points of dispute before these proceedings were launched.

26.186   However, in *R (JL) v Islington LBC*[244] in response to the respondent's contention that the claimant should have exhausted the complaints process before pursuing a claim for judicial review, the judge observed:

> The claimants are indeed using the local authority complaints process to address the detailed issues that they wish to raise concerning the assessment and the care plan. Had they attempted to raise those matters in the judicial review proceedings, they would validly have met with the answer that they should first exhaust the complaints process as it constitutes a remedy which is not only available but also more appropriate to resolve such issues. However, if they are correct in arguing that the local authority has confined its consideration of how to meet JL's needs (or at least some aspects of them) to applying its eligibility criteria rather than identifying JL's actual needs and how they might be met for him, whatever progress may be made through the complaints process in relation to detail will not alter the fundamental parameters of the core assessment. Real change to the outcome in JL's case could only be achieved by a successful challenge to the eligibility criteria. As it is at least arguable that the assessment *was* confined by the eligibility criteria, the existence of the complaints procedure is not, in my view, a reason to refuse permission to bring the judicial review proceedings.

26.187   Furthermore, claimants should perhaps also be cautious of delaying an application for judicial review, particularly beyond the three-month time limit, in order to exercise alternative remedies where it is evident from the outset that the only appropriate remedy would be judicial review proceedings. In *R (Enfield LBC) v Secretary of State for Health*[245] the judge commented:

---

242 [2007] EWCA Civ 234.
243 [2009] EWHC 2537 (Admin) at [61].
244 [2009] EWHC 458 (Admin) at [31].
245 [2009] EWHC 743 (Admin) at [48].

In my judgment the question whether it is or is not reasonable to postpone making a claim for judicial review until after an alternative route of challenge has been exhausted, will depend on the facts and circumstances of the particular case. In many cases where a statutory regime for challenge to a decision of a public body exists, even if that challenge is an appeal on the merits, it will be appropriate to go down that route before applying for judicial review, which is traditionally viewed as a remedy of last resort. However there are some situations in which the only way, or the most appropriate way, for the complainant to achieve the desired result is to issue a claim for judicial review, and in such cases the obligation to act promptly cannot be ignored.

Judicial review procedure

26.188 The procedure for judicial review applications to the High Court are set out in the CPR Part 54 and the relevant practice direction.[246] The number of applications for permission for judicial review issued in the High Court (Administrative Division) in 2009 was 9,097, a 27 per cent increase on the corresponding figure of 7,200 for 2008.[247] Of the applications for permission for judicial review, 24 per cent were granted; of the 495 substantive applications for judicial review, 57 per cent were dismissed whilst 39 per cent were allowed.[248] It is fair to say that these statistics reveal that it is no easy task for a claimant to be successful in judicial review proceedings.

26.189 Most applications for judicial review start with the claimant sending a 'Judicial Review Pre-action Protocol' letter to the defendant, setting out the details of the decision being challenged, the factual background, the relevant law and the remedy sought. The defendant is allowed a period of 14 days to provide a 'Letter of Response', although this timescale may be shortened in very urgent cases. If this matter is extremely urgent, proceedings may be issued without the need to undertake the pre-action protocol procedure but, in community care matters, such circumstances are likely to be very rare.

26.190 If this process does not resolve the matter, it is only then that the claimant may proceed to the issue of an application for judicial review in the High Court. However, at this stage, the application is for permission to proceed to a full hearing for judicial review. This stage acts as a filter, where the court rejects unmeritorious or frivolous claims. Such decisions are usually made by consideration of the papers, although oral hearings may be held in certain circumstances.

26.191 If granted, a full hearing of the case will consist of oral arguments in respect of the substantive issues in the case after the submission of

---

246 The relevant rules and practice direction are available at www.justice.gov.uk/guidance/courts-and-tribunals/courts/procedure-rules/civil/index.htm

247 Judicial and Court Statistics 2009, available at www.justice.gov.uk/publications/docs/jcs-stats-2009–211010.pdf (see p150).

248 Judicial and Court Statistics 2009, available at www.justice.gov.uk/publications/docs/jcs-stats-2009–211010.pdf (see p158).

further written evidence, including the grounds of the judicial review. Witnesses are rarely called to give evidence and, as such cases do not involve the determination of factual matters, there is usually no order for disclosure of documents.

Remedies

26.192 It is emphasised that, in judicial review cases, remedies are discretionary: in other words, even where the court finds that the decision is unlawful, it is not obliged to grant any remedy to the successful claimant.

26.193   There are a range of orders which the court may make in judicial review proceedings and the court may make more than one order, depending on the case. These are as follows:

- Quashing order: this makes the decision being challenged completely invalid; the court will usually send the case back to the public body for the decision to be made again. This does not prevent the public body making the same decision (eg to close a day service centre) but it must do so in a lawful manner.
- Prohibiting order: such an order prevents a public body from doing something which is was intending to do which would be in breach of its powers (eg deport someone).
- Mandatory order: this order requires the public body to do something which it was obliged to do (eg carry out an assessment of a person's needs under NHS and Community Care Act 1990 s47).
- Declaration: this is not an order as such, as it does not tell the parties what they should do but it does advise the respective parties of their rights and obligations (eg that a proposed rule was unlawful). If either party then failure to comply with the declaration, it would be possible for the court to make other orders in any subsequent proceedings.
- Injunction: such an order may be made by the court to stop a public body from acting in an unlawful way or, alternatively, it may compel a public body to do something.
- Damages: the award of damages is unusual in judicial review proceedings.[249]

26.194 When contemplating judicial review proceedings, it is essential that prospective claimants are fully aware of the limitations of the judicial review, both in terms of its ability to consider the merits of a decision and also the limited nature of its remedies. It is perhaps not an option for the faint-hearted but, despite its shortcomings, judicial review is still a vital tool in ensuring that the decisions of public bodies are made in accordance with the law.[250]

---

249   Useful information and guides on various aspects of judicial review are available to the public at www.publiclawproject.org.uk.
250   For a practitioner's view of the practicalities of judicial review, see 'Beat the system' in the *Law Society Gazette* 14 April 2011 at pp14–16.

Grounds for judicial review

26.195 As noted above, judicial review generally concerns a challenge to the decision-making process (ie the procedure followed in coming to the decision) rather than to the decision itself. In such 'procedural' challenges, applicants are required to show some substantial flaw in the process by which the public body reached its decision. In certain cases, however, the court will entertain a 'substantive' challenge to the actual decision itself; for instance, on the basis that (given the process followed) the impugned decision is so absurd that in reaching it, the local authority must 'have taken leave of [its] senses'.[251]

26.196　　The principles underlying judicial review are sophisticated and multi-faceted; they are continually being refined and developed by the judiciary. Thus, when in *Kruse v Johnson*[252] the High Court indicated that it would be prepared to set aside local authority decisions which were 'manifestly unjust, partial, made in bad faith or so gratuitous and oppressive that no reasonable person could think them justified', it was merely outlining the type of situation which might provoke judicial intervention, not making any definitive statement of the potential grounds for review. Likewise, 50 years later, in *Associated Provincial Picture Houses v Wednesbury Corporation*[253] when Lord Greene described what are now the classic '*Wednesbury*' principles, he was again only sketching out examples of administrative behaviour which might attract judicial censure, not seeking to compile an exhaustive list. In his judgment, he instanced the following behaviour as being potentially justiciable:

- contravention of the law;
- a fettering of a discretion;
- unreasonableness in the sense of bad faith or dishonesty;
- failing to consider 'matters which he is bound to consider';
- failing to exclude matters which are irrelevant;
- reaching a decision that is 'so absurd that no sensible person could even dream that it lay within the powers of the authority'.

26.197 With the enactment of the HRA 1998, the courts have accepted that their traditional approach to administrative scrutiny may no longer be sufficient. In *R (Daly) v Secretary of State for the Home Department*,[254] Lord Steyn contrasted the traditional *Wednesbury* approach with the requirements of 'proportionality', in circumstances where a decision potentially engaged considerations of fundamental human rights. In his view although there was considerable overlap between the two approaches, they differed: not least that the doctrine of proportionality required courts to be more involved in assessing the evidence and determining the relative weight that should accorded to the competing interests and con-

---

251　*R v Secretary of State for the Environment ex p Nottinghamshire CC* [1986] AC 240 at 247, HL.
252　[1898] 2 QB 91.
253　[1948] 1 KB 223.
254　[2001] UKHL 26, [2001] 2 WLR 1622 at [27]–[28].

siderations – and that this had to be done in a broader range of cases, than merely ones involving extreme facts or situations.

26.198   The following subsections list some of the main principles which are used by the courts today, to test the validity of public law decisions. As indicated above, the labelling of these principles is not a taxonomic science, but merely an attempt to illustrate some of the more obvious characteristics of the jurisprudence in this field.

Illegality

26.199 A judicial review challenge on the grounds of illegality is based upon the notion that a 'decision-maker must understand correctly the law that regulates his decision-making power and give effect to it'.[255] Professor de Smith[256] separates administrative decisions which are flawed for illegality into those which are either beyond the power which authorises the making of the decision, or those which pursue an objective other than that for which the power to make the decision was conferred. Illegality may present itself in a number of guises, for instance, action by an authority which although within its power, has an ulterior and improper motive,[257] such as action designed to frustrate the purpose of a statute. Common examples are outlined below.

Ultra vires[258]

26.200 Social services and NHS bodies are statutory creatures and only able to act in accordance with the powers they have been given by statute. Accordingly, it is unlawful for a public body to act beyond its powers (ultra vires).

26.201   By way of example, certain actions are well established as being in general outside social services authority powers: for instance, the provision of nursing care by a registered nurse (see para 13.110 above) or the provision of residential accommodation to people entitled to NHS continuing care (see para 14.10 above).

26.202   In *R (Evans) v The Lord Chancellor and another*,[259] the claimant challenged new legal aid rules which prevented the granting of legal aid funding where the case was being brought 'in the public interest'. Evidence was adduced that part of the reason for the decision by the Lord Chancellor was founded in concerns expressed by the Ministry of Defence that adverse judgments in publicly funded cases concerning matters in Iraq or Afghanistan may damage the government's policy interests. The court held (at [25]–[29]):

> For the State to inhibit litigation by the denial of legal aid because the court's judgment might be unwelcome or apparently damaging would

255 *Council of Civil Service Unions v Minister for the Civil Service* [1985] AC 374 at 410, HL.
256 De Smith, Woolf and Jowell, *Judicial Review of Administrative Action*, 5th edn, Sweet and Maxwell, 1995.
257 De Smith, Woolf and Jowell, *Judicial Review of Administrative Action*, 5th edn, Sweet and Maxwell, 1995, p330 note 69.
258 Action which is outside the public body's legal powers.
259 [2011] EWHC 1146 (Admin).

constitute an attempt to influence the incidence of judicial decisions in the interests of government. It would therefore be frankly inimical to the rule of law . . . [and] . . . In those circumstances a legally inadmissible consideration was taken into account, and in my judgment the amendments must be quashed for that reason.

Misdirection of law

26.203 A decision may be challenged by way of judicial review if the authority can be shown to have misunderstood the relevant law in reaching its decision,[260] although the mere existence of a mistake of law does not vitiate the impugned decision unless it 'is a relevant error of law, ie, an error in the actual making of the decision which affected the decision itself'.

26.204   Given the confusing and complex nature of community care law, there is clearly wide scope for local authority decisions to be challenged on this ground. For instance, in *R v Tower Hamlets LBC ex p Bradford*[261] the court held that the authority had fundamentally misunderstood its powers under CA 1989 Part III and so quashed the decision it had reached.

26.205   An authority may make an error of law by misunderstanding the nature of its statutory obligation; it may, for instance, consider its obligation to be discretionary when it is in fact mandatory.

Decision not made in accordance with the facts

26.206 The decision made by the authority must be in accordance with (and supported by) the evidence. Authorities cannot simply 'go through the motions' by paying lip service to the evidence but in reality having no regard to the individual merits of the case.[262] Accordingly in *R v Avon CC ex p M*[263] Henry J overruled a decision by the social services authority which directly conflicted with a recommendation made by the panel. In so doing, he stated:

> The evidence before [the panel] had, as to the practicalities, been largely one way. The panel had directed themselves properly at law, and had arrived at a decision in line with the strength of the evidence before them . . . the strength, coherence and apparent persuasiveness of that decision had to be addressed head-on if it were to be set aside and not followed. These difficulties were not faced either by the Respondent's officers in their paper to the Social Services committee or by the Social Services committee themselves. Not to face them was either unintentional perversity on their part or showed a wrong appreciation of the legal standing of that decision. It seems to me that you do not properly reconsider a decision when, on the evidence, it is not seen that the decision was given the weight it deserved.

---

260 *R v Hull University Visitor ex p Page* [1993] AC 682 at 701–702, HL.
261 (1997–98) 1 CCLR 294, QBD; see para 24.53.
262 *Hemns v Wheller* [1948] 2 KB 61 and *Sagnata Investments v Norwich Corporation* [1971] 2 QB 614, CA.
263 (1999) 2 CCLR 185, QBD.

Relevant and irrelevant considerations

26.207 A basic tenet of the *Wednesbury* decision is that a decision maker must take into account all relevant considerations before making the decision and must ignore the irrelevant. Whether or not a consideration is 'relevant' is initially a question for the decision maker and as a general rule courts will only intervene if the failure to take it into account is either perverse or 'one which, on the true construction of the relevant statute, Parliament must have expressly or impliedly identified as being required to be considered'.[264]

26.208   In *R v Avon CC ex p M* (above), the court found that the authority, in deciding which residential placement to support, had ignored the applicant's psychological needs. In so doing it failed to take account of a relevant (and in the court's view a 'crucial') consideration. In addition, the authority had decided that the applicant's preferred home should not be funded because (among other reasons) such a funding decision would 'set a precedent'. In this context the judge held that this was a misleading consideration; essentially whether or not the decision set a precedent was irrelevant. The same principle applies to the LGO's decision[265] on a complaint against East Sussex County Council. The complaint concerned a panel's refusal to recommend the payment of compensation for benefits a service user lost as a result of wrong advice he received from the social services department. The LGO held that the refusal was based upon an irrelevant consideration (namely that it was the Benefits Agency, not the local authority, which was responsible for the payment of such benefits).

Fettering of discretion or duty

26.209 As noted above (para 26.196 above), public law duties cannot be frustrated by fixed or 'blanket' policies. The same holds true, even when the obligation is expressed as a 'power' rather than a 'duty'. Although an authority 'charged with exercising an administrative discretion is entitled to promulgate a policy or guidelines as an indication of a norm which is intended to be followed',[266] it is not entitled to fetter its discretion by approaching a decision with a predetermined policy as to how all cases falling within a particular class will be treated. Accordingly, in *R v Ealing LBC ex p Leaman*[267] Mann J held that where a disabled person had applied to a local authority under Chronically Sick and Disabled Persons Act (CSDPA) 1970 s2(1)(f) for financial assistance in taking a privately arranged holiday, it was an error of law for the authority to decline to consider the application on the ground that it would only grant such assistance for holidays which it itself had arranged or sponsored (as the

---

264 See *R (Ireneschild) v Lambeth LBC* [2007] EWCA Civ 234 at [41] where this quotation from *CREEDNZ v Governor-General* [1981] 1 NZLR 172 first adopted in *In re Findlay* [1985] AC 318 was cited with approval.
265 Complaint no 93/A/3738 against East Sussex CC.
266 See *R v Eastleigh BC ex p Betts* [1983] 2 AC 613, HL.
267 (1984) *Times* 10 February.

Act specifically allows for the support of holidays 'provided under arrangements made by the authority or otherwise'). On this principle, it would also be unlawful for an authority to have a fixed policy that it will not fund home help which consists solely of cleaning a house or ironing, etc (as no such limitation is imposed by CSDPA 1970 s2(1)(a)). Likewise, fixed policies by health or local authorities in relation to drug rehabilitation, which either confine such rehabilitation solely to funding detoxification (as opposed to harm minimisation or stabilisation) or where there is a fixed policy only to fund detoxification for a fixed and limited period, would again amount to a fettering of discretion (given, again, that no such limitations are imposed by the primary legislation).[268]

26.210   In *R v North West Lancashire Health Authority ex p A*,[269] the Court of Appeal held that the respondent's policy of not providing treatment for gender reassignment 'save in cases of overriding clinical need' was 'nonsense' since the authority considered that there was no effective treatment for the condition and, accordingly, an 'overriding clinical need' could not arise. Auld, LJ held:

> . . . the stance of the authority, coupled with the near uniformity of its reasons for rejecting each of the respondent's requests for funding was not a genuine application of a policy subject to individually determined exceptions of the sort considered acceptable by Lord Scarman in *Findlay*.[270] It is similar to the over-rigid application of the near 'blanket policy' questioned by Judge J in *R v Warwickshire County Council ex p Collymore* [1995] ELR 217, at 224 *et seq*:
>
> > 'which while in theory admitting exceptions, may not, in reality result in the proper consideration of each individual case on its merits'.

26.211   The court also made reference to *R v Bexley LBC ex p Jones*[271] where Leggatt LJ held:

> It is . . . legitimate for a statutory body . . . to adopt a policy designed to ensure a rational and consistent approach to the exercise of a statutory discretion in particular types of case. But it can only do so provided that the policy fairly admits of exceptions to it. In my judgment, the respondents effectively disabled themselves from considering individual cases and there has been no convincing evidence that at any material time they had an exceptions procedure worth the name. There is no indication that there was a genuine willingness to consider individual cases.

Unlawful delegation or dictation

26.212   Decision makers cannot avoid their duties by allowing themselves to be dictated to by, or simply accepting the decision of, another body.[272] Decision makers may not delegate their decisions to others unless they have

---

268   National Assistance Act 1948 s21, subject to the directions in LAC (93)10 appendix 1 para 2(6) and under NHSA 1977 Sch 8 para 2, subject to the secretary of state's directions in LAC (93)10 appendix 3 para 3(3)(g).
269   (1999) *Times*, 24 August.
270   *In re Findlay* [1985] 1 AC 316.
271   [1995] ELR 42, p55.
272   J Manning, *Judicial Review Proceedings*, 2nd edn, Legal Action Group, 2004, para 6.78.

specific power to do so and have done so properly. In the context of community care, for example, local authorities cannot ordinarily delegate their duty to undertake community care assessments (see para 3.49 above) or assessments of carers (see para 16.46).

Procedural impropriety

26.213 Procedural impropriety embraces a number of issues of natural justice.

The duty to act fairly

26.214 Decision makers must act fairly; must not be biased; must allow a party time to prepare his or her case; must ensure that a party has a proper opportunity to be heard; and, in appropriate situations, must give reasons for their decisions.

26.215   In *R (Montgomery) v Hertfordshire CC,*[273] for instance, the court held that the local authority had acted unlawfully because it had:

> . . . failed manifestly and flagrantly to comply with the fundamental principles of fairness. They had given no notice of their action, they did not explain the grounds of their action, they have not explained the basis of future fears based upon the past complaints and they have not given the claimant any opportunity before this decision was taken to respond to any such matters with effective representations.

Legitimate expectation and the abuse of power

26.216 The courts, initially, developed the notion of 'legitimate expectation' as a facet of 'procedural impropriety' or the requirement of administrative fairness. The courts are now extending the doctrine's reach to encompass substantive challenges. The basic principle, however, requires that if a public authority has committed itself to acting in a certain way it should meet that commitment in the absence of a good reason not to do so.[274] Put another way, it requires that no decision should be taken which will adversely affect an individual, without that person being given an opportunity to make representations as to why the particular benefit or advantage should not be withdrawn.[275]

26.217   In *R v North and East Devon Health Authority ex p Coughlan*[276] the Court of Appeal reviewed the development of the doctrine which it considered had 'emerged as a distinct application of the concept of abuse of power in relation to substantive as well as procedural benefits'. The court continued:

> Legitimate expectation may play different parts in different aspects of public law. The limits to its role have yet to be finally determined by the courts. Its application is still being developed on a case by case basis. Even where it reflects procedural expectations, for example concerning

273 [2005] EWHC 2026 (Admin) at [34].
274 *R (Goldsmith) v Wandsworth LBC* (2004) EWCA Civ 1170, (2004) 7 CCLR 472.
275 *Council of Civil Service Unions v Minister for the Civil Service* [1985] AC 374, HL.
276 [2000] 2 WLR 622, (1999) 2 CCLR 285, CA.

consultation, it may be affected by an overriding public interest. It may operate as an aspect of good administration, qualifying the intrinsic rationality of policy choices. And without injury to the *Wednesbury* doctrine it may furnish a proper basis for the application of the new established concept of abuse of power.[277]

and

... in relation to this category of legitimate expectation, we do not consider it necessary to explain the modern doctrine in *Wednesbury* terms, helpful though this is in terms of received jurisprudence ... We would prefer to regard the *Wednesbury* categories themselves as the major instances (not necessarily the sole ones ...) of how public power may be misused. Once it is recognised that conduct which is an abuse of power is contrary to law its existence must be for the court to determine.[278]

26.218 An example of legitimate expectation is found in *R (Theophilus) v Lewisham LBC*.[279] The claimant accepted a place to study law at a college in Dublin, after the authority informed her that she would receive student support if she studied anywhere in the European Union. The authority subsequently informed her that it had made an error and she was not entitled to support under the Education (Student Support) Regulations 2001.[280] This was correct, but the local authority continued to have power to fund the placement under LGA 2000 s2 (see para 1.68). On the basis of the legitimate expectation, created by the promise of grant support, the authority was held obliged to use its powers under the 2000 Act.

26.219 An authority may be released of its obligation to meet a person's legitimate expectation where the circumstances have changed after it gave its undertaking – *R (Lindley) v Tameside MBC*.[281]

The duty to consult

26.220 The principle of procedural propriety also appears, in certain situations, as a duty to consult. In *R v Devon CC and Durham CC ex p Baker*[282] it was stated that the duty:

... encompasses those cases in which it is held that a particular procedure, not otherwise required by law in the protection of an interest, must be followed consequent upon some specific promise or practice. Fairness requires that the public authority be held to it.

26.221 In this case, the court quashed a decision by Durham County Council to close various residential care homes because the authority had not properly consulted (see para 7.135). The court approved an earlier judgment[283] where the duty to consult was formulated as consisting of four parts, the requirements being:

277 [2000] 2 WLR 622, (1999) 2 CCLR 285 at 311, CA.
278 [2000] 2 WLR 622, (1999) 2 CCLR 285 at 315, CA.
279 [2002] EWHC 1371 (Admin), [2002] 3 All ER 851.
280 SI No 951.
281 [2006] EWHC 2296 (Admin).
282 [1995] 1 All ER 73, QBD.
283 *R v Brent LBC ex p Gunning* (1986) 84 LGR 168.

First that the consultation must be at a time when proposals are still at a formative stage. Second that the proposer must give sufficient reasons for any proposal to permit of intelligent consideration and response. Third . . . that adequate time must be given for consideration and response and, finally, . . . that the product of consultation must be conscientiously taken into account in finalising any statutory proposals.[284]

26.222 In England[285] public consultations should conform to the 'Code of Practice on Consultation'. The most recent edition of this document was published in 2008[286] which requires (amongst other things) that public bodies, when consulting must:[287]

- build a realistic timeframe for the consultation (12 weeks should be 'standard minimum period'), allowing plenty of time for each stage of the process;
- be clear as to who is being consulted, about what and for what specific purpose;
- ensure that the document is as simple and concise as possible (it should include a summary and clearly set out the questions it wishes to address);
- always distribute documents as widely as possible, using electronic means (but not at the exclusion of others);
- make sure all responses are carefully and open-mindedly analysed and the results made widely available, with an account of the views expressed and the reasons for decisions finally taken.

26.223 In *Eisai Ltd v NICE*,[288] the High Court held that NICE's engagement with the interested parties during the process of developing its guidance was, for legal purposes, a consultation exercise. A consultation exercise must be carried out fairly. How this is to be achieved was described in the *Eisai* case (at [44]) in its consideration of the Court of Appeal decision in *R v North and East Devon Health Authority ex p Coughlan*:[289] '[the consulting authority's] obligation is to let those who have a potential interest in the subject matter know in clear terms what the proposal is and exactly why it is under positive consideration, telling them enough (which may be a good deal) to enable them to make an intelligent response. The obligation, although it may be quite onerous, goes no further than this.' The court also applied the decision in *R v Secretary of State for Social Services ex p Association of Metropolitan Authorities*:[290]

284 [1995] 1 All ER 89 at 91.
285 The Welsh Assembly Government has similar approach to consultations – including the 12-week timeframe: http://wales.gov.uk/consultations/aboutconsultation;jsessionid=TKwkNTYbBJD5NspY5JdXGndTq0CgZyn1rKhs9SZhldvBH5SC1Lmp!1989468226?lang=en
286 Accessible at www.bis.gov.uk/files/file47158.pdf.
287 The following extract (which can be accessed at http://webarchive.nationalarchives.gov.uk/+/www.direct.gov.uk/en/Dl1/Directories/PublicConsultations/DG_10035668) is taken from the original Cabinet Office guidance (Cabinet Office, *Code of Practice on Written Consultation*, 2000).
288 [2007] EWHC 1941 (Admin).
289 [2001] QB 213.
290 [1986] 1 WLR 1.

> . . . the essence of consultation is the communication of a genuine invitation to give advice and a genuine receipt of that advice . . . it goes without saying that to achieve consultation sufficient information must be supplied by the consulting to the consulted party to enable it to tender helpful advice . . . By helpful advice, in this context, I mean sufficiently informed and considered information or advice about aspects of the form or substance of the proposals, or their implications for the consulted party, being aspects material to the implementation of the proposal as to which the [decision maker] might not be fully informed or advised as to which the party consulted might have relevant information or advice to offer.

26.224 The NHS has a duty (in both England and Wales) under NHSA 2006 s242[291] to consult and involve users and carers in the planning and provision of services, as well as in the development and consideration of proposals to reconfigure such services.

26.225   The courts have shown increasing impatience with cases alleging a lack of adequate consultation preceding decisions to close care homes (see para 7.144) and noted that this is always likely to be an imperfect art – particularly when service users have limited mental capacity. In *R (Grabham) v Northamptonshire CC*,[292] for example, Black J observed:

> It was inevitable, in my view, that consulting adults with learning disabilities would be a challenging process. Perfection will never be achieved in such an exercise. However the council give every appearance of having gone about it responsibly and they succeeded to a tolerable extent. I do not think that it can validly be argued that such flaws as there were invalidated the consultation.

26.226 Even if aspects of the consultation process are 'unfortunate', the court may exercise its discretion not to intervene where the overall process is fair and not fundamentally erroneous.[293]

Equality duty

26.227 The public sector equality duty under Equality Act 2010 s149 imposes (amongst other things) considerable consultation obligations on public bodies – and this is considered further at para 2.32.

The duty to act in accordance with mandatory or directory requirements

26.228 A further requirement of the duty to act fairly is that the decision maker must comply with procedures laid down by parliament. This is sometimes known as the duty to act in accordance with 'mandatory or directory requirements'. In *R v North Yorkshire CC ex p Hargreaves*,[294] it was accepted that the respondent authority, in assessing the applicant's sister's needs, failed to take into account the preferences of the sister, contrary to the mandatory (or directory) requirements set out in the 1990 policy

---

291 As amended by Local Government and Public Involvement in Health Act 2007 s233 (formerly Health and Social Care Act 2001 s11).
292 [2006] EWHC 3292 (Admin) at [64].
293 *Easyjet v Civil Aviation Authority* [2009] EWHC 1422 (Admin).
294 (1994) 30 September, QBD, CO/878/94.

guidance.[295] As the guidance was made under Local authority social Services Act (LASSA) 1970 s7(1), requiring authorities to act 'under' such guidance, a failure to do so rendered the decision unlawful. Dyson J held that the requirements of the 1990 policy guidance were mandatory and that the decision should, therefore, be quashed. See also *Secretary of State for Trade and Industry v Langridge*[296] where guidance was given on the principles to be applied in deciding whether a particular duty is mandatory or directory.

The duty to give reasons

26.229   Although there is no general duty on authorities to give reasons for their decisions, where the relevant statute, regulation or direction stipulates that reasons should be given, then the reasons must be 'proper, adequate and intelligible' and must deal with the substantial points raised by the complainant. An unparticularised assertion that 'on the evidence' the decision maker makes certain findings 'and recommends . . .' will be considered, in general, to be inadequate.[297] In the absence of an express provision requiring the giving of reasons, they may nevertheless be required, if, for instance, the decision would otherwise be unintelligible, or would contravene the minimum standards of fairness.[298]

26.230   In *R (Savva) v Royal Borough of Kensington and Chelsea*,[299] the Court of Appeal held that fairness required the respondent authority to explain how it had reached its final figure when calculating the amount of the appellant's personal budget. Although it was not a case where statute, the relevant regulations imposed a duty to provide reasons for the decision, the Court of Appeal held that it was one in which the common law required reasons to be given[300] and cited *Stefan v The General Medical Council (Medical Act 1983)*,[301] which sets out (at [21]–[24]) a helpful consideration of the developing law of the duty upon public bodies to give reasons for their decisions. In that case, the court held (at [32]): 'The extent and substance of the reasons must depend upon the circumstances. They need not be elaborate nor lengthy. But they should be such as to tell the parties in broad terms why the decision was reached.' However, the *Savva* case left open the question as to whether the duty to provide reasons could be satisfied by notice in a decision letter that reasons would be provided on request.[302]

---

295   Paras 3.16 and 3.25 of the guidance; and see also *R v Islington LBC ex p Rixon* (1997–98) 1 CCLR 119, QBD.
296   [1991] 2 WLR 1343.
297   *R v Secretary of State for Transport ex p Cumbria CC* [1983] RTR 129, QBD.
298   *R v Secretary of State for Home Department ex p Doody* [1993] 3 WLR 154, HL.
299   [2010] EWCA Civ 1209.
300   [2010] EWCA Civ 1209 at [19].
301   [1999] UKPC 10.
302   [1999] UKPC 10 at [23].

Default procedures

26.231 LASSA 1970 s7D[303] provides:

(1) If the secretary of state is satisfied that any local authority have failed without reasonable excuse, to comply with any of their duties which are social services functions[304] . . . he may make an order declaring that authority to be in default with respect to the duty in question.

(2) An order under subsection (1) may contain such directions for the purpose of ensuring that the duty is complied with within such period as may be specified in the order as appear to the secretary of state to be necessary.

(3) Any such direction shall, on the application of the secretary of state, be enforceable by mandamus.

26.232 On the face of it, a person aggrieved by a local authority decision may seek redress by making formal request to the secretary of state that he or she use this default power to remedy the particular injustice. In reality such executive powers are rarely if ever exercised. The power under LASSA 1970 s7D is no exception; it appears that it has never been used, and it is highly unlikely that, in anything but the most extreme of situations, it would be so exercised. The power can only be used where the authority has failed to exercise a 'duty' (rather than a 'power'); it only arises if the local authority has 'no reasonable excuse' for its failure; the secretary of state has to be 'satisfied' about the lack of any reasonable excuse; and even then he or she has wide discretion whether or not to take any such action.

26.233 In LASSL (96)12[305] the Department of Health set out its policy on responding to correspondence received from the public (as well as from MPs and corporate bodies). In general the department copies the correspondence to the relevant authority, but (at para 10):

... where the letter seems strongly to suggest that SSD policy or practice may be inconsistent in some significant respect with the law or Departmental guidance we will normally expect to reply substantively ourselves, but will refer the letter to the SSD for their observations before doing so.

26.234 In practice such an exchange, where the local authority is required to explain its position to the department, can prove to be an effective lever. There is some evidence that this action has, in the past at least, led to a resolution of various problems.[306]

26.235 In *R v Kent CC ex p Bruce*[307] it was held that the secretary of state was not a 'tribunal of fact' and in considering whether to exercise the default

---

303 Inserted by National Health Service and Community Care Act 1990 s50 and replacing an equivalent provision under National Assistance Act 1948 s36(1).

304 A function set out in LASSA 1970 Sch 1 other than a duty imposed by or under the CA 1989.

305 Department of Health (1997) *Correspondence on social services matters* LASSL 96(12).

306 See RADAR (2001) *Putting teeth into the Act* eg pp5 et seq, a report produced by RADAR on attempts made between 1970–81 to enforce CSDPA 1970 s2.

307 (1986) *Times* 8 February.

procedure 'must properly be concerned with whether the local authority had misdirected itself in law or formed an irrational view of the facts'. In *R v Devon CC ex p Baker and others*[308] an argument that the existence of the default procedure constituted an alternative remedy which thereby excluded the use of judicial review was, in this particular case, rejected (see para 7.159 above).[309]

26.236   In *R v Westminster CC ex p P and others*[310] four destitute asylum seekers challenged the policy of various London boroughs to accommodate them outside London. Simon Brown LJ, in rejecting the application (on grounds that there was an alternative remedy) held as follows:

> For my part I have reached the clear conclusion that the more 'convenient, expeditious and effective' course here is indeed that of applying to the secretary of state to exercise his default powers under s7D. This is par excellence an area of administration in which the Secretary of State rather than the courts should be closely involved. In the first place it is the secretary of state who funds the housing of asylum seekers under s21 of the 1948 Act. Secondly, it is the proper construction and application of his own directions and guidance which lie at the heart of the dispute. Thirdly, it was at the secretary of state's insistence that the appeal form the Court of Appeal's decision in *R v Westminster CC ex p M*,[311] which was to be heard by the House of Lords last month, was adjourned, specifically because the government are currently conducting a review of the treatment of asylum seekers and did not wish to risk a final judgment depriving asylum seekers of all protection until a decision had been made as to what (if any) alternative arrangements should be made.

European Convention on Human Rights

26.237 The following section makes reference to the case law of the European Court of Human Rights: all judgments of the court are accessible on the Council of Europe website.[312]

26.238   HRA 1998 s6, in general terms, makes it unlawful for a public body to act in such a way as to violate a person's 'convention rights'.[313] Section 6(3)(b) of the Act extends the definition of public authority to cover bodies that, although not public authorities, exercise functions of a 'public nature'. It was assumed at the time the Act came into force that this would mean that independent providers of community care services would be covered by the definition (for instance, care homes accommodating frail elderly residents at public expense or day centres run by charities under a contract with the local authority).

308 [1985] 1 All ER 73.
309 See also the case of *R (Enfield LBC) v Secretary of State for Health* [2009] EWHC 743 (Admin), where the claimant's decision to wait until the NHS default procedure was completed was criticised by the court (at [48]).
310 (1997–98) 1 CCLR 486, CA and see also *R v Kirklees MBC ex p Good* (1997–98) 1 CCLR 506, QBD.
311 *R v Westminster CC ex p M* (1997–98) 1 CCLR 85, CA
312 http://cmiskp.echr.coe.int/tkp197/search.asp?skin=hudoc-en
313 An 'act' for the purposes of s6 includes 'a failure to act' – HRA 1998 s6(6).

26.239   However, in *YL v Birmingham City Council and others*[314] (a case relating to a local authority funded resident of a private owned care home), the House of Lords applied a restrictive interpretation to the concept of 'public authority' such that independent providers of this kind were excluded from the reach of the Act. In the majority lords opinion (Lord Bingham and Baroness Hale dissenting), it considered that the arrangement of care and accommodation for those unable to arrange it themselves was an inherently public function – but not the actual provision of that care.[315]

26.240   As a result of the decision in *YL*, the government clarified the law by means of Health and Social Care Act 2008 s145, which provides that where a local authority arranges accommodation in a care home under National Assistance Act 1948 s21 or 26, it is to be taken for the purposes of HRA 1998 s3(b) to be exercising a function of a public nature in so doing. This enables those who are funded by the social services department under the 1948 Act (but not self-funders[316]) to be able to enforce their human rights under the Convention, even though they may be resident in a private care home.

Compensation

26.241   Where a violation of such a 'Convention right' by a public body is alleged to have occurred, an individual can institute court proceedings (HRA 1998 s7) for (among other things) compensation (HRA 1998 s8).

26.242   In *R (Bernard) v Enfield LBC*,[317] the court considered that the appropriate level of damages for violations of the 1998 Act was that which would have been awarded by the LGA. However, in *Anufrijeva and others v Southwark LBC*[318] the Court of Appeal cautioned against such an approach, without disagreeing with the damages awarded in the *Enfield* case (a total of £10,000 – see below). In *Anufrijeva*, the Court of Appeal suggested[319] that permission ought not to be given at the leave stage to proceed by way of judicial review unless the claimant satisfied the court that a complaint to the ombudsman was not more appropriate. Speaking in a personal capacity,[320] Collins J has expressed doubt as to whether this

---

314   [2007] UKHL 27, [2007] 3 WLR 112, (2007) 10 CCLR 505.
315   In a housing context, compare the judgment in *R (Weaver) v Quandrant Housing Trust* [2009] EWCA Civ 587 where the Court of Appeal reached the opposite conclusion: a registered social landlord, when serving a notice seeking possession upon a tenant, acted as a public authority for the purposes of the HRA 1998.
316   See comments of Baroness Thornton, House of Lords Hansard 22 May 2008: column GC636.
317   [2002] EWHC 2282 (Admin), (2002) 5 CCLR 577.
318   [2003] EWCA Civ 1406, [2004] 2 WLR 603, (2003) 6 CCLR 415 at [53]. See also *R (Greenfield) v Secretary of State for the Home Department* [2005] UKHL 14, [2005] 1 WLR 673 where the House of Lords endorsed the approach in *Anufrijeva* and *Andrews v Reading BC* [2004] EWHC 970 (Admin), [2004] 2 All ER(D) 319 where Collins J held that where a claim under the HRA 1998 does not depend upon proving maladministration, then *Anufrijeva* does not prevent the claim being issued in the county court or High Court.
319   *R (Anufrijeva) v Southwark LBC* [2003] EWCA Civ 1406, [2004] 2 WLR 603, (2003) 6 CCLR 415 at [81].
320   Collins J, 'Community care and the Administrative Court' (2006) 9 CCLR 5.

could in fact be correct since LGA 1974 s26(6)(c) states that the Local Government Ombudsman cannot act in respect of 'any action in respect of which the person aggrieved has or had a remedy by way of proceedings in any court of law'.

Convention rights

26.243 The Convention rights of most relevance in the context of community care law are Articles 2, 3 5, 8 and 14 of the European Convention on Human Rights. These Articles are considered elsewhere in this text[321] and what follows is merely a brief summary of the general scope of the rights.

26.244   Often a set of facts will suggest a violation of several Articles of the Convention. For instance, a 2008 Ombudsmen's complaint[322] concerned mistreatment of a profoundly disabled care home resident, who had been neglected such that he had been left locked in his bedroom overnight, had poor dental health and had been left in a chair for some time, cold, unwashed, unshaven and with his clothes covered in faeces and urine – with the staff offering no explanation, apology or help. These facts, in the opinion of the Ombudsmen engaged Articles 3, 8 and 14.

Article 2: the right to life

26.245 Article 2, although primarily negative in nature (ie requiring the state to refrain from arbitrarily killing people[323]), has been held to place a positive obligation on the state to protect life.[324] Cases are likely to occur concerning actions by health and social services authorities which might be harmful, such as the closure of dementia wards or residential care homes, as well as decisions not to provide treatment for people with serious illness, such as the decision in *R v Cambridge Health Authority ex p B*[325] considered at para 13.16 above).

26.246   Violations of the obligations under Article 2 have been found in cases such as the failure to protect a vulnerable prisoner from a dangerous cellmate.[326] The court has accepted that positive obligations require special measures to be taken to protect potentially suicidal patients[327] and may require individuals to be warned if exposed to any serious environmental or health risks.[328] The Commission has likewise considered the extent of

---

321   See for instance paras 7.170, 7.172, 4.71, 4.104, 17.47, 4.71, 21.17, 25.44, 18.39 and 24.9–24.12.

322   Complaint Nos 03/A/04618 and HS-2608 against Buckinghamshire County Council and Oxfordshire and Buckinghamshire Mental Health Partnership Trust (respectively) 17 March 2008.

323   *McCann v UK* (1995) 21 EHRR 97.

324   *Osman v UK* (1998) EHRR 245 at 305 – and see generally L Clements and J Read, *Disabled People and the Right to Life*, Routledge, 2007.

325   [1995] 1 WLR 898, CA.

326   *Edwards v UK* (2002) 35 EHRR 19.

327   *Keenan v UK* (2001) 33 EHRR 38 and also *Savage v South Essex Trust* [2009] 1 AC 681.

328   *LCB v UK* (1998) 27 EHRR 212.

the state's obligation to reduce the risks of a vaccination programme[329] or to fund a health service.[330] There are, however, limits to the obligation under Article 2; it cannot, for instance, be construed to provide a right for an incapacitated adult to have another assist her in dying (*Pretty v United Kingdom*[331]).

Article 3: degrading treatment

26.247 As with Article 2, Article 3 is also primarily negative in its scope – requiring states to refrain from subjecting anyone to torture, inhuman and degrading treatment. It too, however, has been held to place a positive obligation on the state to take reasonable measures to ensure no one is subjected to such treatment.

26.248 The court has emphasised that for treatment to be 'degrading' it must reach a minimum threshold of severity,[332] although it has indicated that this may be significantly lower for disabled[333] and elderly people.[334] Arbitrary and gross acts of discrimination may exceptionally be considered to violate Article 3, even in the absence of actual physical or mental harm.[335] The negative obligations under Article 3 are engaged by detention conditions,[336] corporal punishment[337] and poor prison conditions.[338] Extradition may violate Article 3 if the expelled person is thereby put at risk of degrading treatment: even (exceptionally) if solely a consequence of inadequate medical treatment in the receiving country.[339]

26.249 As noted above (para 24.12) Article 3 has been construed as creating a positive obligation on states to ensure that no one suffers from degrading treatment, and in this respect eligibility criteria cannot exclude services from persons at 'significant risk of harm' (see para 3.200). The case law on Article 3 has established that the courts and social services are obliged to use their powers to protect children[340] and vulnerable adults[341] from abuse. Where credible evidence exists that an individual has suffered abuse while in the care of a public authority, a positive obligation arises under Article 3 for an independent and

---

329 *Association X v UK* DR 14/31.
330 *Osman v UK* (1998) 29 EHRR 245.
331 (2002) 35 EHRR 1; and see also domestic proceedings at [2001] UKHL 61, [2001] 3 WLR 1598.
332 *Costello-Roberts v UK* (1993) 19 EHRR 112.
333 *Price v UK* (2001) 34 EHRR 1285, (2002) 5 CCLR 306.
334 See *Papon v France* [2001] Crim LR 917, an inadmissibility decision.
335 See *Cyprus v Turkey* (2002) 35 EHRR 30 and *Patel v UK (the East African Asians case)* (1981) 3 EHRR 76.
336 *McGlinchley v United Kingdom* (2003) 37 EHRR 41.
337 *Campbell and Cosans v UK* (1982) 2 EHRR 293.
338 *Napier v Scottish Ministers* (2001) *Times* 15 November and see also *Price v UK* (2001) 34 EHRR 1285, (2002) 5 CCLR 306.
339 *D v UK* (1997) 24 EHRR 423.
340 *Z and others v UK* (2002) 34 EHRR 97.
341 *In re F (Adult: Court's jurisdiction)* [2000] 3 WLR 1740, (2000) 3 CCLR 210, CA

open investigation to be convened[342] and for positive police/prosecution action to bring the perpetrators to justice.[343]

26.250   *Price v UK*[344] concerned a thalidomide-impaired applicant who in the course of debt recovery proceedings refused to answer questions put to her and was committed to prison for seven days for contempt of court. She alleged that she suffered degrading treatment as a result of the prison's inadequate facilities, but the UK government argued that any discomfort she experienced had not reached the minimum level of severity required by Article 3. The court, however, considered that the threshold depended 'on all the circumstances of the case, such as the duration of the treatment, its physical and mental effects and, in some cases, the sex, age and state of health of the victim', and after a thorough review it concluded:

> . . . that to detain a severely disabled person in conditions where she is dangerously cold, risks developing sores because her bed is too hard or unreachable, and is unable to go to the toilet or keep clean without the greatest of difficulty, constitutes degrading treatment contrary to Article 3.

26.251   Of particular interest was the concurring opinion of Judge Greve, in which she stated:

> It is obvious that restraining any non-disabled person to the applicant's level of ability to move and assist herself, for even a limited period of time, would amount to inhuman and degrading treatment – possibly torture. In a civilised country like the United Kingdom, society considers it not only appropriate but a basic humane concern to try to ameliorate and compensate for the disabilities faced by a person in the applicant's situation. In my opinion, these compensatory measures come to form part of the disabled person's bodily integrity.

Article 5: detention

26.252   Article 5(1) places a total prohibition upon a state's power to detain people except in six clearly defined instances, including under Article 5(1)(e) 'the lawful detention of persons for the prevention of the spreading of infectious diseases, of persons of unsound mind, alcoholics or drug addicts or vagrants'. A substantial body of case law exists concerning the Convention requirements that must be satisfied before a mental health service user can be legally detained, and the Mental Health Act 1983 was largely a response to a number of adverse Strasbourg judgements.[345] Increasingly, the court is requiring detention under this ground to be accompanied by a suitably therapeutic environment.[346]

---

342   *Assenov v Bulgaria* (1998) 28 EHRR 652.
343   See eg *R (B) v DPP* [2009] EWHC 106 (Admin) where a decision by the Crown Prosecution Service not to prosecute (because the victim had mental health problems) was held to violate Article 3 (and the court awarded the victim £8,000 compensation).
344   (2001) 34 EHRR 1285, (2002) 5 CCLR 306.
345   See eg *X v UK* (1981) 4 EHRR 188; *Ashingdane v UK* (1985) 7 EHRR 528; and *Winterwerp v Netherlands* (1979) 2 EHRR 387.
346   *Aerts v Belgium* (1998) 29 EHRR 50.

26.253   In *Winterwerp v Netherlands*[347] and a series of subsequent cases,[348] the court has laid down a number of factors which must be satisfied before the detention of a person of unsound mind is lawful within the meaning of the Convention, including:

1) The mental disorder must be reliably established by objective medical expertise.
2) The nature or degree of the disorder must be sufficiently extreme to justify the detention.
3) The detention should only last as long as the medical disorder (and its required severity) persists.
4) If the detention is potentially indefinite, then there must be a system of periodic reviews by a tribunal that has power to discharge.
5) The detention must be in a hospital, clinic or other appropriate institution authorised for the detention of such persons.[349]

26.254 Anyone detained for the purposes of Article 5 must be so detained 'in accordance with a procedure prescribed by law'. *HL v UK*[350] concerned a challenge in the European Court of Human Rights to a decision of the House of Lords, known as the *Bournewood* case.[351] The European Court held that the lack of any procedural protection for 'informally detained' patients violated Article 5(1) and it rejected the UK's argument that such people were not 'detained', stating:

> . . . the right to liberty is too important in a democratic society for a person to lose the benefit of Convention protection for the single reason that he may have given himself up to be taken into detention . . . especially when it is not disputed that that person is legally incapable of consenting to, or disagreeing with, the proposed action.

26.255 In the Strasbourg Court's opinion, he was detained because he was 'under continuous supervision and control and was not free to leave':[352] it was 'not determinative whether the ward was "locked" or "lockable" ': a person could be detained, 'even during a period when he was in an open ward with regular unescorted access to the unsecured hospital grounds and unescorted leave outside the hospital'.

26.256   The *Bournewood* decision led to the introduction of the Deprivation of Liberty Safeguards (DOLS) procedure as part of the Mental Capacity Act 2005 (see para 17.49). Since then, there have been a number of cases

---

347 (1979) 2 EHRR 387.
348 See eg *X v UK* (1981) 4 EHRR 188 and *Ashingdane v UK* (1985) 7 EHRR 528.
349 *Ashingdane v UK* (1985) 7 EHRR 528 at [44] and see *Aerts v Belgium* (1998) 29 EHRR 50 where the court found a violation of Article 5(1) in relation to the detention of the applicant in the psychiatric wing of a prison which was not an 'appropriate establishment' in view of the lack of qualified personnel.
350 (2005) 40 EHRR 32.
351 *R v Bournewood Community and Mental Health NHS Trust ex p L* [1998] 3 WLR 107, (1997–98) 1 CCLR 390, HL.
352 See also in this respect *JE v DE and Surrey CC* [2006] EWHC 3459 (Fam), (2007) 10 CCLR 149 where Munby J considered the crucial question to be whether or not the individual was objectively 'free to leave'.

where Article 5 has been alleged to have been breached as a result of an alleged failure of the DOLS process. In *A Local Authority v A (A Child)*,[353] in a case brought by a local authority where the court had to consider whether the circumstances of the defendants domestic care by their families in the family home involve a deprivation of liberty, engaging the protection of Article 5? At para 48, the court considered that, in determining whether there was a 'deprivation of liberty' within the meaning of and engaging the protection of Article 5(1) 'three conditions must be satisfied':

1) an objective element of 'a person's confinement to a certain limited place for a not negligible length of time';
2) a subjective element, namely that the person has not 'validly consented to the confinement in question'; and
3) the 'deprivation of liberty must be one for which the State is responsible'.

26.257 In this instance, the court held that there had not been a deprivation of the liberty and therefore no breach of Article 5 of the Convention. In the case of *G v E and others*,[354] the Court of Protection found that there had been a breach of DOLS, citing 'serious human rights breaches committed by the local authority' in respect of breaches of both Articles 5 and 8. In *Hillingdon LBC v Steven Neary*[355] (see para 24.96), a young man who lacked capacity to decide where to live, was placed in temporary respite care, following which the local authority refused to allow him to return home to his father, with whom he had lived all his life. The Court of Protection had no difficulty in finding that his rights under Article 5 had been breached.

Article 6: fair hearing

26.258 Article 6(1) entrenches the right of parties to a fair hearing when their civil rights are affected (or when charged with a criminal offence). It requires hearings to be before 'independent and impartial' tribunals and to be held within a 'reasonable time' which may require 'exceptional diligence' to ensure early listing.[356]

26.259   The right to a fair hearing may require the state to take positive action to ensure legal or advocacy assistance is available to a party under a disability. As the court observed in *Airey v Ireland*:[357]

> . . . the fulfilment of a duty under the Convention on occasion necessitates some positive action on the part of the State; in such circumstances, the State cannot simply remain passive . . . The obligation to secure an effective right of access to the courts falls into this category of duty.

---

353 [2010] EWHC 978 (Fam), (2010) 13 CCLR 404.
354 [2010] EWHC 621 (Fam).
355 [2011] EWHC 1377 (COP).
356 *H v UK* (1988) 10 EHRR 95; see also *P and D v UK* [1996] EHRLR 526.
357 (1979) 2 EHRR 305.

Article 8: private life, family and home

26.260 The court has consistently defined Article 8 as positive in nature.[358] This arises out of the presence of the word 'respect': rather than obliging states 'not to interfere' with private and family life, Article 8(1) provides that 'everyone has the right to respect for his private and family life, his home and his correspondence'. The demonstration of 'respect' is inherently positive in nature.

26.261   While family life, the home and correspondence have been given their everyday meanings, the concept of 'private life' has acquired an altogether more expansive interpretation, including a 'person's physical and psychological integrity' for which respect is due in order to 'ensure the development, without outside interference, of the personality of each individual in his relations with other human beings'.[359] Thus issues of sexual rights,[360] environmental pollution,[361] physical barriers to movement,[362] access to files[363] and information about one's illness[364] have been held to come within its reach.

26.262   Article 8 is a 'qualified right' in that state interference with the right is permitted, but only where the interference is 'lawful' and is done in a proportionate way in pursuance of a legitimate aim. Although Article 8(2) provides an exhaustive list of six legitimate aims, these are so widely drawn (including, for example, action which protects the rights and freedoms of others, action for economic reasons, or to protect morals or to prevent crime) that in general the court will have little difficulty in finding any 'interference' with Article 8(1) pursues a legitimate aim.

26.263   It is, however, in respect of the second limb of the test that public bodies have most difficulty. They must establish that what they did, not only had a legitimate aim, but also that it was 'proportionate'. Although there is substantial jurisprudence concerning the of concept of 'proportionality', the key principles of most relevance in a social welfare context concern the need for the action to be 'the least restrictive interference' commensurate with the legitimate aim pursued, and also that overall the action be 'balanced'.

26.264   In Gaskin v UK[365] the applicant sought access to his social services records. The request was refused in part on the ground that some of the information had originally been given in confidence and the law at that time did not permit disclosure of information where such third parties had not provided their consent to the disclosure. The information was important to Mr Gaskin as he had spent almost all his life in care and he wanted it for identity purposes. His was a legitimate claim, as indeed was

---

358 *Marckx v Belgium* (1979) 2 EHRR 330.
359 *Botta v Italy* (1998) 26 EHRR 241.
360 *Norris v Ireland* (1988) 13 EHRR 186.
361 *Hatton v UK* (2001) 34 EHRR 1.
362 *Botta v Italy* (1998) 26 EHRR 241.
363 *Gaskin v UK* (1989) 12 EHRR 36.
364 *McGinley and Egan v UK* (1998) 27 EHRR 1; and *LCB v UK* (1998) 27 EHRR 212.
365 (1989) 12 EHRR 36.

the refusal to divulge the information, which had been given to the local authority in confidence.

26.265   The court considered that the refusal to disclose pursued a legitimate aim (that of protecting the rights and freedoms of others) but was disproportionate. It was not the 'least restrictive interference'. The court considered that some of the 'third party' material could be disclosed without prejudicing the rights of others – for instance, if the person who had given the information had since died, or could not be traced, or if anyone reading the information would be unable to identity its author. It also considered that the blanket refusal was not 'balanced' since it meant that in such cases Mr Gaskin's claim always failed – and the concept of 'balance' requires that in certain situations the balance of interest might come down in favour of the person seeking disclosure. It was as a consequence of the *Gaskin* judgment that the changes in the Data Protection Act 1998 to accessing social services files were introduced (see para 25.47).

26.266   For many disabled people, their home is (in one form or another) in an institutional setting. Provided the stay has been for a reasonable length of time,[366] the care home or hospital ward, etc will be deemed the person's 'home' for the purposes of Article 8. Accordingly any attempt to move the resident will have to be justified as being proportionate. *R v North and East Devon Health Authority ex p Coughlan*[367] concerned an attempt by a health authority to move the applicant from her specialist NHS unit where she had lived for six years. Having regard to all the circumstances (which included the health authority's desire to close the facility for budgetary reasons) the court considered that the authority had failed to establish that such an interference with the applicant's Article 8 right was justified.

26.267   In a case against the NHS, *Gunter v South West Staffordshire PCT*[368] (see also para 14.150), the court held that the moving the claimant from her home would interfere with her right to respect for family life within Article 8. Collins J at [20] stated that:

> It is apparent that to remove Rachel from her home will interfere with her right to respect for her family life. Mr Wise has also relied on the positive need to give an enhanced degree of protection to the seriously disabled. This is in my view an unnecessary refinement. The interference with family life is obvious and so must be justified as proportionate. Cost is a factor which can properly be taken into account. But the evidence of the improvement in Rachel's condition, the obvious quality of life within her family environment and her expressed views that she does not want to move are all important factors which suggest that to remove her from her home will require clear justification'.

26.268   *R (Bernard) v Enfield LBC*[369] (see also para 15.29) concerned a disabled applicant and her family who through the local authority's failure to

---

366   In *O'Rourke v UK* (2001) 26 June, App no 39022/97, the court doubted that occupation of a hotel room for one month was sufficient and continuous enough to make it his 'home' for the purposes of Article 8.
367   [2000] 2 WLR 622, (1999) 2 CCLR 285.
368   [2005] EWHC 1894 (Admin).
369   [2002] EWHC 2282 (Admin), (2002) 5 CCLR 577.

assess her community care needs properly, and then provide the necessary services, had been forced to live in 'deplorable conditions' for over 20 months. Although the court held that this level of suffering had not attained the threshold required by Article 3, it considered that the council's failure to act on its assessments had the effect of condemning the applicant and her family to live in conditions which made it virtually impossible for them to have any meaningful private or family life – and on the facts found a violation of Article 8.

Article 14: discrimination

26.269 Article 14 can only be invoked in relation to one of the substantive rights set out in Articles 2–12 of the Convention and the protocols. Article 14 requires that in the delivery of the substantive rights, there be no discrimination. Discrimination is permissible under Article 14, if it is established that the measure has an objective and reasonable justification and is 'proportionate'.

26.270   Thus a violation of Article 14 can only occur in combination with another Article;[370] for instance, the inferior education rights of Roma children in the Czech Republic (compared with non-Roma children) were held to violate Article 14 in conjunction with Article 2 of the first protocol[371] (right to education). The court has further held that there is a positive obligation under Article 14 to combat invidious forms of discrimination such as racism,[372] and (probably) disability-related hate crime/harassment.[373]

European Court of Human Rights

26.271 A complaint can only be made to the European Court of Human Rights once all domestic remedies have been exhausted. The complainant must be an individual who claims to have suffered as a result of the measure in issue, and the complaint must be made within six months of the exhaustion of the last domestic remedy. The complaint must allege a violation of at least one of the principal Articles of the Convention (or the first protocol thereto).

The EU Charter of Fundamental Rights

26.272 The Charter of Fundamental Rights of the European Union[374] entered into force on 1 December 2009 (as a result of the Treaty of Lisbon). The UK

---

370 It may be that major improvement in this field will more likely flow from EU law, ie the Amsterdam Treaty amendments.
371 *DH v Czech Republic* Application no 57325/00 13 November 2007.
372 *Timishev v Russia* (2005) Application nos 55762/00 and 55974/00, 13 December 2005.
373 See *Đorđević v Croatia* (pending) Application no 41526/10.
374 The text of the Charter is accessible at www.europarl.europa.eu/charter/pdf/ text_en.pdf and for a discussion of its likely relevance, see the Select Committee on European Union (2008) *European Union: Tenth Report.* London: House of Lords at www.publications.parliament.uk/pa/ld200708/ldselect/ldeucom/62/6209.htm.

has negotiated an interpretative protocol to the Treaty – which has mistakenly been described by some as an 'opt out'. The UK intends the protocol to clarify that the Charter does not extend the ability of the European Court of Justice (or indeed any other court) to find that the UK law is 'inconsistent with the fundamental rights, freedoms and principles that it reaffirms'. In particular it states that Title IV of the Charter (which concerns amongst other things socio-economic rights) in itself does not create justiciable rights applicable in the UK.

26.273   The Charter (even prior to adoption) has been cited in a number of UK cases: in *R (A and B, X, Y) v East Sussex County Council* (2003),[375] for instance, Munby J referred to the Charter and observed:

> The Charter is not at present legally binding in our domestic law and is therefore not a source of law in the strict sense. But it can, in my judgment, properly be consulted insofar as it proclaims, reaffirms or elucidates the content of those human rights that are generally recognised throughout the European family of nations, in particular the nature and scope of those fundamental rights that are guaranteed by the Convention.

26.274   In many situations the rights protected by the Charter and the ECHR are very similar. This means that it will often be difficult to ascertain the provenance of a right – ie whether it derives from the Charter or the ECHR – and this will become more challenging as a result of the Lisbon Treaty's provision enabling the EU to accede to the European Convention on Human Rights. This intermixing of rights was evident in *R (S) v SS Home* (2010)[376] where the Charter's extensive citation was justified on the basis of its 'indirect influence as an aid to interpretation'.

375   [2003] EWHC 167 (Admin), (2003) 6 CCLR 194 at [73]–[74].
376   [2010] EWHC 705 (Admin) at [155].

APPENDICES

Legislation

NATIONAL ASSISTANCE ACT 1948 (EXTRACTS)

PART III: LOCAL AUTHORITY SERVICES

Provision of accommodation

Duty of local authorities to provide accommodation

21(1) Subject to and in accordance with the provisions of this Part of this Act, a local authority may with the approval of the Secretary of State, and to such extent as he may direct shall, make arrangements for providing–

(a) residential accommodation for persons aged eighteen or over who by reason of age, illness, disability or any other circumstances are in need of care and attention which is not otherwise available to them; and

(aa) residential accommodation for expectant and nursing mothers who are in need of care and attention which is not otherwise available to them.

(b) [*Repealed.*]

(1A) A person to whom section 115 of the Immigration and Asylum Act 1999 (exclusion from benefits) applies may not be provided with residential accommodation under subsection (1)(a) if his need for care and attention has arisen solely–

(a) because he is destitute; or

(b) because of the physical effects, or anticipated physical effects, of his being destitute.

(1B) Subsections (3) and (5) to (8) of section 95 of the Immigration and Asylum Act 1999, and paragraph 2 of Schedule 8 to that Act, apply for the purposes of subsection (1A) as they apply for the purposes of that section, but for the references in subsections (5) and (7) of that section and in that paragraph to the Secretary of State substitute references to a local authority.

(2) In making any such arrangements a local authority shall have regard to the welfare of all persons for whom accommodation is provided, and in particular to the need for providing accommodation of different descriptions suited to different descriptions of such persons as are mentioned in the last foregoing subsection.

(2A) In determining for the purposes of paragraph (a) or (aa) of subsection(1) of this section whether care and attention are otherwise available to a person, a local authority shall disregard so much of the person's resources as may be specified in, or determined in accordance with, regulations made by the Secretary of State for the purposes of this subsection.

(2B) In subsection (2A) of this section the reference to a person's resources is a reference to his resources within the meaning of regulations made for the purposes of that subsection.

(3) [*Repealed.*]

(4) Subject to the provisions of section 26 of this Act accommodation provided by

a local authority in the exercise of their functions under this section shall be provided in premises managed by the authority or, to such extent as may be determined in accordance with the arrangements under this section, in such premises managed by another local authority as may be agreed between the two authorities and on such terms, including terms as to the reimbursement of expenditure incurred by the said other authority, as may be so agreed.

(5) References in this Act to accommodation provided under this part thereof shall be construed as references to accommodation provided in accordance with this and the five next following sections, and as including references to board and other services, amenities and requisites provided in connection with the accommodation except where in the opinion of the authority managing the premises their provision is unnecessary.

(6) References in this Act to a local authority providing accommodation shall be construed, in any case where a local authority agree with another local authority for the provision of accommodation in premises managed by the said other authority, as references to the first-mentioned local authority.

(7) Without prejudice to the generality of the foregoing provisions of this section, a local authority may–
   (a) provide, in such cases as they may consider appropriate, for the conveyance of persons to and from premises in which accommodation is provided for them under this Part of the Act;
   (b) make arrangements for the provision on the premises in which the accommodation is being provided of such other services as appear to the authority to be required.

(8) Nothing in this section shall authorise or require a local authority to make any provision authorised or required to be made (whether by that or by any other authority) by or under any enactment not contained in this Part of this Act or authorised or required to be provided under the National Health Service Act 2006 or the National Health Service (Wales) Act 2006.

Charges to be made for accommodation (England and Wales)

22(1) Subject to section 26 of this Act, where a person is provided with accommodation under this Part of this Act the local authority providing the accommodation shall recover from him the amount of the payment which he is liable to make in accordance with the following provisions of this section.

(2) Subject to the following provisions of this section, the payment which a person is liable to make for any such accommodation shall be in accordance with a standard rate fixed for that accommodation by the authority managing the premises in which it is provided and that standard rate shall represent the full cost to the authority of providing that accommodation.

(3) Where a person for whom accommodation in premises managed by any local authority is provided, or proposed to be provided, under this Part of this Act satisfies the local authority that he is unable to pay therefore at the standard rate, the authority shall assess his ability to pay, and accordingly determine at what lower rate he shall be liable to pay for the accommodation: . . .

(4) In assessing for the purposes of the last foregoing subsection a person's ability to pay, a local authority shall assume that he will need for his personal requirements such sum per week as may be prescribed by the Minister, or such other sum as in special circumstances the authority may consider appropriate.

(4A) Regulations made for the purposes of subsection (4) of this section may prescribe different sums for different circumstances.

(5) In assessing as aforesaid a person's ability to pay, a local authority shall give effect to regulations made by the Secretary of State for the purposes of this subsection except that, until the first such regulations come into force, a local authority shall give effect to Part III of Schedule 1 to the Supplementary

Benefits Act 1976, as it had effect immediately before the amendments made by Schedule 2 to the Social Security Act 1980.

(5A) If they think fit, an authority managing premises in which accommodation is provided for a person shall have power on each occasion when they provide accommodation for him, irrespective of his means, to limit to such amount as appears to them reasonable for him to pay the payments required from him for his accommodation during a period commencing when they begin to provide the accommodation for him and ending not more than eight weeks after that.

(6) [*Repealed.*]
(7) [*Repealed.*]
(8) Where accommodation is provided by a local authority in premises managed by another local authority, the payment therefore under this section shall be made to the authority managing the premises and not to the authority providing accommodation, but the authority managing the premises shall account for the payment to the authority providing the accommodation.

(8A) This section shall have effect subject to any regulations under section 15 of the Community Care (Delayed Discharges etc) Act 2003 (power to require certain community care services and services for carers to be provided free of charge).

(9) [*Repealed.*]

Management of premises in which accommodation provided

23(1) Subject to the provisions of this Part of this Act, a local authority may make rules as to the conduct of premises under their management in which accommodation is provided under this Part of this Act and as to the preservation of order in the premises.

(2) Rules under this section may provide that where by reason of any change in a person's circumstances he is no longer qualified to receive accommodation under this Part of this Act or where a person has otherwise become unsuitable therefore he may be required by the local authority managing the premises to leave the premises in which the accommodation is provided.

(3) Rules under this section may provide for the waiving of part of the payments due under the last foregoing section where in compliance with the rules persons for whom accommodation is provided assist in the running of the premises.

Authority liable for provision of accommodation

24(1) The local authority empowered under this Part of this Act to provide residential accommodation for any person shall subject to the following provisions of this Part of this Act be the authority in whose area the person is ordinarily resident.

(2) [*Repealed.*]
(3) Where a person in the area of a local authority–
   (a) is a person with no settled residence, or
   (b) not being ordinarily resident in the area of the local authority, is in urgent need of residential accommodation under this Part of this Act,
   the authority shall have the like power to provide residential accommodation for him as if he were ordinarily resident in their area.

(4) Subject to and in accordance with the arrangements under section twenty-one of this Act, a local authority shall have power, as respects a person ordinarily resident in the area of another local authority, with the consent of that other authority to provide residential accommodation for him in any case where the authority would have a duty to provide such accommodation if he were ordinarily resident in their area.

(5) Where a person is provided with residential accommodation under this Part of this Act, he shall be deemed for the purposes of this Act to continue to

be ordinarily resident in the area in which he was ordinarily resident immediately before the residential accommodation was provided for him.

(6) For the purposes of the provision of residential accommodation under this Part, a patient ('P') for whom NHS accommodation is provided shall be deemed to be ordinarily resident in the area, if any, in which P was resident before the NHS accommodation was provided for P, whether or not P in fact continues to be ordinarily resident in that area.

(6A) In subsection (6) 'NHS accommodation' means–
   (a) accommodation (at a hospital or elsewhere) provided under the National Health Service Act 2006 or the National Health Service (Wales) Act 2006, or
   (b) accommodation provided under section 117 of the Mental Health Act 1983 by a Primary Care Trust or Local Health Board, other than accommodation so provided jointly with a local authority.

(6B) The reference in subsection (6A)(b) to accommodation provided by a Primary Care Trust includes a reference to accommodation–
   (a) in respect of which direct payments are made under regulations under section 12A(4) of the National Health Service Act 2006, and
   (b) which would be provided under section 117 of the Mental Health Act 1983 apart from the regulations.

25   [*Repealed.*]

Provision of accommodation in premises maintained by voluntary organisations (England and Wales)

26(1) Subject to subsections (1A) and (1C) below, arrangements under section 21 of this Act may include arrangements made with a voluntary organisation or with any other person who is not a local authority where–
   (a) that organisation or person manages premises which provide for reward accommodation falling within subsection (1)(a) or (aa) of that section, and
   (b) the arrangements are for the provision of such accommodation in those premises.

(1A) Arrangements must not be made by virtue of this section for the provision of accommodation together with nursing or personal care for persons such as are mentioned in section 3(2) of the Care Standards Act 2000 (care homes) unless–
   (a) the accommodation is to be provided, under the arrangements, in a care home (within the meaning of that Act) which is managed by the organisation or person in question; and
   (b) that organisation or person–
      (i) in the case of a home in England, is registered under Chapter 2 of Part 1 of the Health and Social Care Act 2008 in respect of a regulated activity (within the meaning of that Part) carried on in the home, or
      (ii) in the case of a home in Wales, is registered under Part 2 of the Care Standards Act 2000 in respect of the home.

(1C) Subject to subsection (1D) below, no arrangements may be made by virtue of this section for the provision of accommodation together with nursing without the consent of such Primary Care Trust or Local Health Board as may be determined in accordance with regulations.

(1D) Subsection (1C) above does not apply to the making by an authority of temporary arrangements for the accommodation of any person as a matter of urgency; but, as soon as practicable after any such temporary arrangements have been made, the authority shall seek the consent required by subsection (1C) above to the making of appropriate arrangements for the accommodation of the person concerned.

(1E) [*Repealed.*]

(2)   Any arrangements made by virtue of this section shall provide for the making by the local authority to the other party thereto of payments in respect of the accommodation provided at such rates as may be determined by or under the arrangements and subject to subsection (3A) below the local authority shall recover from each person for whom accommodation is provided under the arrangements the amount of the refund which he is liable to make in accordance with the following provisions of this section.

(3)   Subject to subsection (3A) below A person for whom accommodation is provided under any such arrangements shall, in lieu of being liable to make payment therefore in accordance with section twenty-two of this Act, refund to the local authority any payments made in respect of him under the last foregoing subsection:

Provided that where a person for whom accommodation is provided, or proposed to be provided, under any such arrangements satisfies the local authority that he is unable to make a refund at the full rate determined under that subsection, subsections (3) to (5) of section twenty-two of this Act shall, with the necessary modifications, apply as they apply where a person satisfies the local authority of his inability to pay at the standard rate as mentioned in the said subsection (3).

(3A) Where accommodation in any premises is provided for any person under arrangements made by virtue of this section and the local authority, the person concerned and the voluntary organisation or other person managing the premises (in this subsection referred to as 'the provider') agree that this subsection shall apply–

   (a)   so long as the person concerned makes the payments for which he is liable under paragraph (b) below, he shall not be liable to make any refund under subsection (3) above and the local authority shall not be liable to make any payment under subsection (2) above in respect of the accommodation provided for him;

   (b)   the person concerned shall be liable to pay to the provider such sums as he would otherwise (under subsection (3) above) be liable to pay by way of refund to the local authority; and

   (c)   the local authority shall be liable to pay to the provider the difference between the sums paid by virtue of paragraph (b) above and the payments which, but for paragraph (a) above, the authority would be liable to pay under subsection (2) above.

(4)   Subsection (5A) of the said section 22 shall, with the necessary modifications, apply for the purposes of the last foregoing subsection as it applies for the purposes of the said section 22.

(4AA) Subsections (2) to (4) shall have effect subject to any regulations under section 15 of the Community Care (Delayed Discharges etc) Act 2003 (power to require certain community care services and services for carers to be free of charge).

(4A) Section 21(5) of this Act shall have effect as respects accommodation provided under arrangements made by virtue of this section with the substitution for the reference to the authority managing the premises of a reference to the authority making the arrangements.

(5)   Where in any premises accommodation is being provided under this section in accordance with arrangements made by any local authority, any person authorised in that behalf by the authority may at all reasonable times enter and inspect the premises.

(6)   [*Repealed.*]

(7)   In this section the expression 'voluntary organisation' includes any association which is a housing association for the purposes of the Housing Act, 1936, or the Housing (Scotland) Acts, 1925 to 1946 and 'exempt body' means

an authority or body constituted by an Act of Parliament or incorporated by Royal Charter.

26A [*Repealed.*]
27 [*Repealed.*]
28 [*Repealed.*]

Welfare arrangements for blind, deaf, dumb and crippled persons, etc.

29 (1) A local authority may, with the approval of the Secretary of State, and to such extent as he may direct in relation to persons ordinarily resident in the area of the local authority shall make arrangements for promoting the welfare of persons to whom this section applies, that is to say persons aged eighteen or over who are blind, deaf or dumb, or who suffer from mental disorder of any description and other persons aged eighteen or over who are substantially and permanently handicapped by illness, injury, or congenital deformity or such other disabilities as may be prescribed by the Minister.

(2) [*Repealed.*]

(3) [*Repealed.*]

(4) Without prejudice to the generality of the provisions of subsection(1) of this section, arrangements may be made thereunder–

   (a) for informing persons to whom arrangements under that subsection relate of the services available for them thereunder;

   (b) for giving such persons instruction in their own homes or elsewhere in methods of overcoming the effects of their disabilities;

   (c) for providing workshops where such persons may be engaged (whether under a contract of service or otherwise) in suitable work, and hostels where persons engaged in the workshops, and other persons to whom arrangements under subsection(1) of this section relate and for whom work or training is being provided in pursuance of the Disabled Persons (Employment) Act, 1944, or the Employment and Training Act 1973 may live;

   (d) for providing persons to whom arrangements under subsection(1) of this section relate with suitable work (whether under a contract of service or otherwise) in their own homes or elsewhere;

   (e) for helping such persons in disposing of the produce of their work;

   (f) for providing such persons with recreational facilities in their own homes or elsewhere;

   (g) for compiling and maintaining classified registers of the persons to whom arrangements under subsection(1) of this section relate.

(4A) Where accommodation in a hostel is provided under paragraph (c) of subsection (4) of this section–

   (a) if the hostel is managed by a local authority, section 22 of this Act shall apply as it applies where accommodation is provided under section 21;

   (b) if the accommodation is provided in a hostel managed by a person other than a local authority under arrangements made with that person, subsections (2) to (4A) of section 26 of this Act shall apply as they apply where accommodation is provided under arrangements made by virtue of that section; and

   (c) section 32 of this Act shall apply as it applies where accommodation is provided under sections 21 to 26;

and in this subsection references to 'accommodation' include references to board and other services, amenities and requisites provided in connection with the accommodation, except where in the opinion of the authority managing the premises or, in the case mentioned in paragraph (b) above, the authority making the arrangements their provision is unnecessary.

(5) [*Repealed.*]

(6) Nothing in the foregoing provisions of this section shall authorise or require–

(a) the payment of money to persons to whom this section applies, other than persons for whom work is provided under arrangements made by virtue of paragraph (c) or paragraph (d) of subsection (4) of this section or who are engaged in work which they are enabled to perform in consequence of anything done in pursuance of arrangements made under this section; or

(b) the provision of any accommodation or services required to be provided under the National Health Service Act 2006 or the National Health Service (Wales) Act 2006. . .

(7) A person engaged in work in a workshop provided under paragraph (c) of subsection (4) of this section, or a person in receipt of a superannuation allowance granted on his retirement from engagement in any such workshop, shall be deemed for the purposes of this Act to continue to be ordinarily resident in the area in which he was ordinarily resident immediately before he was accepted for work in that workshop; and for the purposes of this subsection a course of training in such a workshop shall be deemed to be work in that workshop.

Voluntary organisations for disabled persons' welfare

30(1) A local authority may, in accordance with arrangements made under section 29 of this Act, employ as their agent for the purposes of that section any voluntary organisation or any person carrying on, professionally or by way of trade or business, activities which consist of or include the provision of services for any of the persons to whom section 29 above applies, being an organisation or person appearing to the authority to be capable of providing the service to which the arrangements apply.

(2) [*Repealed.*]

(3) [*Repealed.*]

Research

30A Without prejudice to any powers conferred on them by any other Act, –

(a) the Secretary of State may promote research into any matter relating to the functions of local authorities under this Part of this Act, and, in particular, may participate with or assist other persons in conducting such research; and

(b) a local authority may conduct or assist other persons in conducting research into any matter relating to the functions of local authorities under this Part of this Act.

31 [*Repealed.*]

FINANCIAL ADJUSTMENTS BETWEEN LOCAL AUTHORITIES

Adjustments between authority providing accommodation, etc and authority of area of residence

32(1) Any expenditure which apart from this section would fall to be borne by a local authority–

(a) in the provision under this Part of this Act of accommodation for a person ordinarily resident in the area of another local authority, or

(b) in the provision under section 29 of this Act of services for a person ordinarily so resident, or

(c) in providing under paragraph (*a*) of subsection (7) of section 22 of this Act for the conveyance of a person ordinarily resident as aforesaid,

shall be recoverable from the said other local authority and in this subsection any reference to another local authority includes a reference to a local authority in Scotland.

(2) For the purposes of paragraph (a) of the last foregoing subsection it shall be assumed that the expenditure incurred by a local authority in providing

accommodation for any person is, as respects accommodation provided in premises managed by a local authority, at the rate for the time being fixed for that accommodation under subsection (2) of section twenty-two of this Act, and, as respects accommodation provided pursuant to an arrangement made under section twenty-six of this Act, at the rate referred to in subsection (2) of that section.

(3) Any question arising under this Part as to a person's ordinary residence shall be determined by the Secretary of State or by the Welsh Ministers.

(4) The Secretary of State and the Welsh Ministers shall make and publish arrangements for determining which cases are to be dealt with by the Secretary of State and which are to be dealt with by the Welsh Ministers.

(5) Those arrangements may include provision for the Secretary of State and the Welsh Ministers to agree, in relation to any question that has arisen, which of them is to deal with the case.

LOCAL AND CENTRAL AUTHORITIES

Local Authorities for purposes of Part III

33(1) In this Part of this Act the expression 'local authority' means a council which is a local authority for the purposes of the Local Authority Social Services Act 1970 in England or Wales, and a council constituted under section 2 of the Local Government etc. (Scotland) Act 1994 in Scotland.

(2) [*Repealed.*]

HEALTH SERVICES AND PUBLIC HEALTH ACT 1968

Promotion by local authorities, of the welfare of old people

45(1) A local authority may with the approval of the Secretary of State, and to such extent as he may direct shall, make arrangements for promoting the welfare of old people.

(2) [*Repealed.*]

(3) A local authority may employ as their agent for the purposes of this section any voluntary organisation or any person carrying on, professionally or by way of trade or business, activities which consist of or include the provision of services for old people, being an organisation or person appearing to the authority to be capable of promoting the welfare of old people.

(4) No arrangements under this section shall provide–
   (a) for the payment of money to old people except in so far as the arrangements may provide for the remuneration of old people engaged in suitable work in accordance with the arrangements;
   (b) for making available any accommodation or services required to be provided under the National Health Service Act 2006 or the National Health Service (Wales) Act 2006.

(4A) No arrangements under this section may be given effect to in relation to a person to whom section 115 of the Immigration and Asylum Act 1999 (exclusion from benefits) applies solely–
   (a) because he is destitute; or
   (b) because of the physical effects, or anticipated physical effects, of his being destitute.

(4B) Subsections (3) and (5) to (8) of section 95 of the Immigration and Asylum Act 1999, and paragraph 2 of Schedule 8 to that Act, apply for the purposes of subsection (4A) as they apply for the purposes of that section, but for the references in subsections (5) and (7) of that section and in that paragraph to the Secretary of State substitute references to a local authority.

(5) The National Assistance Act 1948 shall have effect as if the following references included a reference to this section, that is to say,–
   (a) the reference, in section 32, to section 29 of that Act;
   (b) the references, in sections 35, 36,45, 52 to Part III of that Act;
   (c) the references, in sections 54, 56 and 59, to that Act.

(6) [*Repealed.*]

(7) [*Repealed.*]

(8) [*Repealed.*]

(9) The Health Visiting and Social Work (Training) Act 1962 shall have effect in relation to functions of local authorities under this section as it does in relation to functions of local authorities under Part III of the National Assistance Act 1948.

(10) [*Repealed.*]

(11) In this section 'local authority'(except where used in the expression 'public or local authority') means the council of a county, other than a metropolitan county or of a county borough, metropolitan district or London borough or the Common Council of the City of London, and 'voluntary organisation' means a body the activities of which are carried on otherwise than for profit but does not include any public or local authority.

(12) [*Repealed.*]

CHRONICALLY SICK AND DISABLED PERSONS ACT 1970 (EXTRACTS)

Information as to need for and existence of welfare services

1(1) It shall be the duty of every local authority having functions under section 29 of the National Assistance Act 1948 to inform themselves of the number of persons to whom that section applies within their area and of the need for the making by the authority of arrangements under that section for such persons.

(2) Every such local authority–

 (a) shall cause to be published from time to time at such times and in such manner as they consider appropriate general information as to the services provided under arrangements made by the authority under the said section 29 which are for the time being available in their area; and

 (b) shall ensure that any such person as aforesaid who uses any of those services is informed of any other service provided by the authority (whether under any such arrangements or not) which in the opinion of the authority is relevant to his needs and of any service provided by any other authority or organisation which in the opinion of the authority is so relevant and of which particulars are in the authority's possession.

(3) This section shall come into operation on such date as the Secretary of State may by order made by statutory instrument appoint.

Provision of welfare services

2(1) Where a local authority having functions under section 29 of the National Assistance Act 1948 are satisfied in the case of any person to whom that section applies who is ordinarily resident in their area that it is necessary in order to meet the needs of that person for that authority to make arrangements for all or any of the following matters, namely–

 (a) the provision of practical assistance for that person in his home;

 (b) the provision for that person of, or assistance to that person in obtaining, wireless, television, library or similar recreational facilities;

 (c) the provision for that person of lectures, games, outings or other recreational facilities outside his home or assistance to that person in taking advantage of educational facilities available to him;

 (d) the provision for that person of facilities for, or assistance in, travelling to and from his home for the purpose of participating in any services provided under arrangements made by the authority under the said section 29 or, with the approval of the authority, in any services provided otherwise than as aforesaid which are similar to services which could be provided under such arrangements;

 (e) the provision of assistance for that person in arranging for the carrying out of any works of adaptation in his home or the provision of any additional facilities designed to secure his greater safety, comfort or convenience;

 (f) facilitating the taking of holidays by that person, whether at holiday homes or otherwise and whether provided under arrangements made by the authority or otherwise;

 (g) the provision of meals for that person whether in his home or elsewhere;

 (h) the provision for that person of, or assistance to that person in obtaining, a telephone and any special equipment necessary to enable him to use a telephone,

 then, subject to the provisions of section 7(1) of the Local Authority Social Services Act 1970 (which requires local authorities in the exercise of certain functions, including functions under the said section 29, to act under the general guidance of the Secretary of State) and to the provisions of section 7A of that Act (which requires local authorities to exercise their social services functions in accordance with directions given by the Secretary of State) it shall be the duty of that authority to make those arrangements in exercise of their functions under the said section 29.

(2)   *Repealed.*

Application of Act to authorities having functions under the Children Act 1989

28A This Act applies with respect to disabled children in relation to whom a local authority have functions under Part III of the Children Act 1989 as it applies in relation to persons to whom section 29 of the National Assistance Act 1948 applies.

LOCAL AUTHORITY SOCIAL SERVICES ACT 1970 (EXTRACTS)

The director of social services

6(A1) A local authority in England shall appoint an officer, to be known as the director of adult social services, for the purposes of their social services functions, other than those for which the authority's director of children's services is responsible under section 18 of the Children Act 2004.

(1) A local authority in Wales shall appoint an officer, to be known as the director of social services, for the purposes of their social services functions.

(2) Two or more local authorities may, if they consider that the same person can efficiently discharge, for both or all of them, the functions of director of adult social services or (as the case may be) social services, concur in the appointment of a person as director of adult social services or (as the case may be) social services for both or all of those authorities.

(3) [*Repealed.*]
(4) [*Repealed.*]
(5) [*Repealed.*]
(6) A local authority which have appointed, or concurred in the appointment of, a director of social services, shall secure the provision of adequate staff for assisting him in the exercise of his functions.
(7) [*Repealed.*]
(8) [*Repealed.*]

Local authorities to exercise social services functions under guidance of Secretary of State[1]

7(1) Local authorities shall, in the exercise of their social services functions, including the exercise of any discretion conferred by any relevant enactment, act under the general guidance of the Secretary of State.

(2) [*Repealed.*]
(3) [*Repealed.*]

Directions by the Secretary of State as to exercise of social services functions[2]

7A(1) Without prejudice to section 7 of this Act, every local authority shall exercise their social services functions in accordance with such directions as may be given to them under this section by the Secretary of State.

(2) Directions under this section–
   (a) shall be given in writing; and
   (b) may be given to a particular authority, or to authorities of a particular class, or to authorities generally.

7B [*Repealed.*][3]

Inquiries

7C(1) The Secretary of State may cause an inquiry to be held in any case where, whether on representations made to him or otherwise, he considers it advisable to do so in connection with the exercise by any local authority of any of their social services functions (except in so far as those functions relate to persons under the age of eighteen).

---

1 See further, NHSA 2006 s77(11)(a), (12) and NHS(W)A 2006 s35(11)(a), (12) which provide, respectively, that in connection with the exercise by a body designated as Care Trust or an NHS Trust of any relevant social services functions under LA delegation arrangements this section shall apply to the body as if it were a local authority within the meaning of this Act.
2 See further, NHSA 2006 s77(11)(b), (12) and NHS(W)A 2006 s35(11)(b), (12) which provide, respectively, that in connection with the exercise by a body designated as Care Trust or an NHS Trust of any relevant social services functions under LA delegation arrangements this section shall apply to the body as if it were a local authority within the meaning of this Act.
3 Still in force in Wales.

(2)   Subsections (2) to (5) of section 250 of the Local Government Act 1972 (powers in relation to local inquiries) shall apply in relation to an inquiry under this section as they apply in relation to an inquiry under that section.

Default powers of Secretary of State as respects social services functions of local authorities

7D(1) If the Secretary of State is satisfied that any local authority have failed, without reasonable excuse to comply with any of their duties which are social services functions (other than a duty imposed by or under the Children Act 1989, section 1 or 2(4) of the Adoption (Intercountry Aspects) Act 1999 or the Adoption and Children Act 2002), he may make an order declaring that authority to be in default with respect to the duty in question.

(2)   An order under subsection(1) may contain such directions for the purpose of ensuring that the duty is complied with within such period as may be specified in the order as appear to the Secretary of State to be necessary.

(3)   Any such direction shall, on the application of the Secretary of State, be enforceable by mandamus.

Grants to local authorities in respect of social services for the mentally ill

7E   The Secretary of State may, with the approval of the Treasury, make grants out of money provided by Parliament towards any expenses of local authorities incurred in connection with the exercise of their social services functions in relation to persons suffering from mental illness.

MENTAL HEALTH ACT 1983

After-care

117(1) This section applies to persons who are detained under section 3 above, or admitted to a hospital in pursuance of a hospital order made under section 37 above, or transferred to a hospital in pursuance of a hospital direction made under section 45A above or a transfer direction made under section 47 or 48 above, and then cease to be detained and (whether or not immediately after so ceasing) leave hospital.

(2) It shall be the duty of the Primary Care Trust or Local Health Board and of the local social services authority to provide, in co-operation with relevant voluntary agencies, after-care services for any person to whom this section applies until such time as the Primary Care Trust or Local Health Board and the local social services authority are satisfied that the person concerned is no longer in need of such services; but they shall not be so satisfied in the case of a community patient while he remains such a patient.

(2A) [*Repealed.*]

(2B) Section 32 above shall apply for the purposes of this section as it applies for the purposes of Part II of this Act.

(2C) References in this Act to after-care services provided for a patient under this section include references to services provided for the patient–

(a) in respect of which direct payments are made under regulations under section 57 of the Health and Social Care Act 2001 or section 12A(4) of the National Health Service Act 2006, and

(b) which would be provided under this section apart from the regulations.

(3) In this section 'the Primary Care Trust or Local Health Board' means the Primary Care Trust or Local Health Board, and 'the local social services authority' means the local social services authority, for the area in which the person concerned is resident or to which he is sent on discharge by the hospital in which he was detained.

HEALTH AND SOCIAL SERVICES AND SOCIAL SECURITY ADJUDICATIONS ACT 1983 (EXTRACTS)

Part VII CHARGES FOR LOCAL AUTHORITY SERVICES

Charges for local authority services in England and Wales[4]

17(1) Subject to subsection (3) below, an authority in England providing a service to which this section applies may recover such charge (if any) for it as they consider reasonable.

(2) This section applies to services provided under the following enactments–

   (a) section 29 of the National Assistance Act 1948 (welfare arrangements for blind, deaf, dumb and crippled persons etc.);

   (b) section 45(1) of the Health Services and Public Health Act 1968 (welfare of old people);

   (c) Schedule 20 to the National Health Service Act 2006 (care of mothers and young children, prevention of illness and care and aftercare and home help and laundry facilities);

   (d) section 8 of the Residential Homes Act 1980 (meals and recreation for old people); and

   (e) paragraph 1 of Part II of Schedule 9 to this Act

   (f) section 2 of the Carers and Disabled Children Act 2000

   other than the provision of services for which payment may be required under section 22 or 26 of the National Assistance Act 1948.

(2A) Subject to subsection (3) below, an authority in Wales providing a service under section 2 of the Carers and Disabled Children Act 2000 in the form of residential care may recover such charge (if any) for it as they consider reasonable.

(3) If a person–

   (a) avails himself of a service to which this section applies, and

   (b) satisfies the authority providing the service that his means are insufficient for it to be reasonably practicable for him to pay for the service the amount which he would otherwise be obliged to pay for it,

   the authority shall not require him to pay more for it than it appears to them that it is reasonably practicable for him to pay.

(4) Any charge under this section may, without prejudice to any other method of recovery, be recovered summarily as a civil debt.

(5) This section has effect subject to any regulations under section 15 of the Community Care (Delayed Discharges etc) Act 2003 (power to require certain community care services and services for carers to be free of charge).

Recovery of sums due to local authority where persons in residential accommodation have disposed of assets

21(1) Subject to the following provisions of this section where–

   (a) a person avails himself of Part III accommodation; and

   (b) that person knowingly and with the intention of avoiding charges for the accommodation–

      (i) has transferred any asset to which this section applies to some other person or persons not more than six months before the date on which he begins to reside in such accommodation; or

      (ii) transfers any such asset to some other person or persons while residing in the accommodation; and

   (c) either–

      (i) the consideration for the transfer is less than the value of the asset; or

      (ii) there is no consideration for the transfer,

4 For Wales, see Welsh Charging Measure 2010.

the person or persons to whom the asset is transferred by the person availing himself of the accommodation shall be liable to pay to the local authority providing the accommodation or arranging for its provision the difference between the amount assessed as due to be paid for the accommodation by the person availing himself of it and the amount which the local authority receive from him for it.

(2) This section applies to cash and any other asset which falls to be taken into account for the purpose of assessing under section 22 of the National Assistance Act 1948 the ability to pay for the accommodation of the person availing himself of it.

(3) Subsection(1) above shall have effect in relation to a transfer by a person who leaves Part III accommodation and subsequently resumes residence in such accommodation as if the period of six months mentioned in paragraph (b)(i) were a period of six months before the date on which he resumed residence in such accommodation.

(3A) If the Secretary of State so directs, subsection(1) above shall not apply in such cases as may be specified in the direction.

(4) Where a person has transferred an asset to which this section applies to more than one person, the liability of each of the persons to whom it was transferred shall be in proportion to the benefit accruing to him from the transfer.

(5) A person's liability under this section shall not exceed the benefit accruing to him from the transfer.

(6) Subject to subsection (7) below, the value of any asset to which this section applies, other than cash, which has been transferred shall be taken to be the amount of the consideration which would have been realised for it if it had been sold on the open market by a willing seller at the time of the transfer.

(7) For the purpose of calculating the value of an asset under subsection (6) above there shall be deducted from the amount of the consideration–
   (a) the amount of any incumbrance on the asset; and
   (b) a reasonable amount in respect of the expenses of the sale.

(8) In this Part of this Act 'Part III accommodation' means accommodation provided under sections 21 to 26 of the National Assistance Act 1948, and, in the application of this Part of this Act to Scotland, means accommodation provided under the Social Work (Scotland) Act 1968 or section 25 (care and support services etc) of the Mental Health (Care and Treatment) (Scotland) Act 2003.

Arrears of contributions charged on interest in land in England and Wales

22(1) Subject to subsection (2) below, where a person who avails himself of Part III accommodation provided by a local authority in England, Wales or Scotland–
   (a) fails to pay any sum assessed as due to be paid by him for the accommodation; and
   (b) has a beneficial interest in land in England or Wales, the local authority may create a charge in their favour on his interest in the land.

(2) In the case of a person who has interests in more than one parcel of land the charge under this section shall be upon his interest in such one of the parcels as the local authority may determine.

(2A) In determining whether to exercise their power under subsection(1) above and in making any determination under subsection (2) above, the local authority shall comply with any directions given to them by the Secretary of State as to the exercise of those functions.

(3) [*Repealed.*]

(4) Subject to subsection (5) below, a charge under this section shall be in respect of any amount assessed as due to be paid which is outstanding from time to time.

(5)   The charge on the interest of an equitable joint tenant in land shall be in respect of an amount not exceeding the value of the interest that he would enjoy in the land if the joint tenancy were severed but the creation of such a charge shall not sever the joint tenancy.

(6)   On the death of an equitable joint tenant in land whose interest in the land is subject to a charge under this section–
   (a) if there are surviving joint tenants, their interests in the land; and
   (b) if the land vests in one person, or one person is entitled to have it vested in him, his interest in it,
   shall become subject to a charge for an amount not exceeding the amount of the charge to which the interest of the deceased joint tenant was subject by virtue of subsection (5) above.

(7)   A charge under this section shall be created by a declaration in writing made by the local authority.

(8)   Any such charge, other than a charge on the interest of an equitable joint tenant in land, shall in the case of unregistered land be a land charge of Class B within the meaning of section 2 of the Land Charges Act 1972 and in the case of registered land be a registrable charge taking effect as a charge by way of legal mortgage.

Interest on sums charged on or secured over interest in land

24(1) Any sum charged on or secured over an interest in land under this Part of this Act shall bear interest from the day after that on which the person for whom the local authority provided the accommodation dies.

(2)   The rate of interest shall be such reasonable rate as the Secretary of State may direct or, if no such direction is given, as the local authority may determine.

SCHEDULE 9

PART II: MEALS AND RECREATION FOR OLD PEOPLE

1 A district council or Welsh county council or county borough council shall have power to make such arrangements as they may from time to time determine for providing meals and recreation for old people in their homes or elsewhere and may employ as their agent for the purpose of this paragraph any voluntary organisation whose activities consist in or include the provision of meals or recreation for old people.

2 A district council or Welsh county council or county borough council may assist any such organisation as is referred to in paragraph 1 above to provide meals or recreation for old people–
   (a) by contributing to the funds of the organisation;
   (b) by permitting them to use premises belonging to the council on such terms as may be agreed; and
   (c) by making available furniture, vehicles or equipment (whether by way of gift or loan or otherwise) and the services of any staff who are employed by the council in connection with the premises or other things which they permit the organisation to use.

3(1) District councils or Welsh county councils or county borough councils shall exercise their functions under this Part of this Schedule (including any discretion conferred on them under it) in accordance with the provisions of any regulations of the Secretary of State made for the purposes of this paragraph; and without prejudice to the generality of this paragraph, regulations under this paragraph–
   (a) may provide for conferring on officers of the Secretary of State authorised under the regulations such powers of inspection as may be prescribed in relation to the exercise of functions under this Part of this Schedule by or by arrangement with or on behalf of district councils or Welsh county councils or county borough councils; and

(b) may make provision with respect to the qualifications of officers employed by district councils or Welsh county councils or county borough councils for the purposes of this Part of this Schedule or by voluntary organisations acting under arrangements with or on behalf of district councils or Welsh county councils or county borough councils for those purposes.

(2) The power to make regulations under this paragraph shall be exercisable by statutory instrument which shall be subject to annulment in pursuance of a resolution of either House of Parliament.

4 In this Part of this Schedule–

'functions' includes powers and duties; and

'voluntary organisation' means a body the activities of which are carried on otherwise than for profit, but does not include any public or local authority.

DISABLED PERSONS (SERVICES, CONSULTATION AND REPRESENTATION) ACT 1986 (EXTRACTS)

PART I: REPRESENTATION AND ASSESSMENT

Services under s2 of the 1970 Act: duty to consider needs of disabled persons

4 When requested to do so by–

    (a) a disabled person,

    (b) his authorised representative, or

    (c) any person who provides care for him in the circumstances mentioned in section 8,

a local authority shall decide whether the needs of the disabled person call for the provision by the authority of any services in accordance with section 2(1) of the 1970 Act (provision of welfare services).

Duty of local authority to take into account abilities of carer

8(1) Where–

    (a) a disabled person is living at home and receiving a substantial amount of care on a regular basis from another person (who is not a person employed to provide such care by any body in the exercise of its functions under any enactment), and

    (b) it falls to a local authority to decide whether the disabled person's needs call for the provision by them of any services for him under any of the welfare enactments,

the local authority shall, in deciding that question, have regard to the ability of that other person to continue to provide such care on a regular basis.

(2) Where that other person is unable to communicate, or (as the case may be) be communicated with, orally or in writing (or in each of those ways) by reason of any mental or physical incapacity, the local authority shall provide such services as, in their opinion, are necessary to ensure that any such incapacity does not prevent the authority from being properly informed as to the ability of that person to continue to provide care as mentioned in subsection (1).

(3) Section 3(7) shall apply for the purposes of subsection (2) above as it applies for the purposes of section 3(6), but as if any reference to the disabled person or his authorised representative were a reference to the person mentioned in subsection (2).

CHILDREN ACT 1989 (EXTRACTS)

PART III: LOCAL AUTHORITY SUPPORT FOR CHILDREN AND FAMILIES

Provision of services for children and their families

Provision of services for children in need, their families and others

17(1) It shall be the general duty of every local authority (in addition to the other duties imposed on them by this Part)–

    (a) to safeguard and promote the welfare of children within their area who are in need; and

    (b) so far as is consistent with that duty, to promote the upbringing of such children by their families,

by providing a range and level of services appropriate to those children's needs.

(2) For the purpose principally of facilitating the discharge of their general duty under this section, every local authority shall have the specific duties and powers set out in Part 1 of Schedule 2.

(3) Any service provided by an authority in the exercise of functions conferred on them by this section may be provided for the family of a particular child in need or for any member of his family, if it is provided with a view to safeguarding or promoting the child's welfare.

(4) The appropriate national authority may by order amend any provision of Part I of Schedule 2 or add any further duty or power to those for the time being mentioned there.

(4A) Before determining what (if any) services to provide for a particular child in need in the exercise of functions conferred on them by this section, a local authority shall, so far as is reasonably practicable and consistent with the child's welfare–

    (a) ascertain the child's wishes and feelings regarding the provision of those services; and

    (b) give due consideration (having regard to his age and understanding) to such wishes and feelings of the child as they have been able to ascertain.

(5) Every local authority–

    (a) shall facilitate the provision by others (including in particular voluntary organisations) of services which it is a function of the authority to provide by virtue of this section, or section 18, 20, 22A-22C, 23B to 23D, 24A or 24B; and

    (b) may make such arrangements as they see fit for any person to act on their behalf in the provision of any such service.

(6) The services provided by a local authority in the exercise of functions conferred on them by this section may include providing accommodation and giving assistance in kind or, in cash.

(7) Assistance may be unconditional or subject to conditions as to the repayment of the assistance or of its value (in whole or in part).

(8) Before giving any assistance or imposing any conditions, a local authority shall have regard to the means of the child concerned and of each of his parents.

(9) No person shall be liable to make any repayment of assistance or of its value at any time when he is in receipt of *income support under the Part VII of the Social Security Contributions and Benefits Act 1992,* of any element of child tax credit other than the family element, of working tax credit, of an income-based jobseeker's allowance or of an income-related employment and support allowance.

(10) For the purposes of this Part a child shall be taken to be in need if–

    (a) he is unlikely to achieve or maintain, or to have the opportunity of

achieving or maintaining, a reasonable standard of health or development without the provision for him of services by a local authority under
this Part;

(b) his health or development is likely to be significantly impaired, or further
impaired, without the provision for him of such services; or

(c) he is disabled,

and 'family', in relation to such a child, includes any person who has parental
responsibility for the child and any other person with whom he has been
living.

(11) For the purposes of this Part, a child is disabled if he is blind, deaf or dumb or
suffers from mental disorder of any kind or is substantially and permanently
handicapped by illness, injury or congenital deformity or such other disability
as may be prescribed; and in this Part–

'development' means physical, intellectual, emotional, social or behavioural
development; and

'health' means physical or mental health.

(12) The Treasury may by regulations prescribe circumstances in which a person
is to be treated for the purposes of this Part (or for such of those purposes as
are prescribed) as in receipt of any element of child tax credit other than the
family element or of working tax credit.

Direct payments

17A(1) The appropriate national authority may by regulations make provision for
and in connection with requiring or authorising the responsible authority in
the case of a person of a prescribed description who falls within subsection (2)
to make, with that person's consent, such payments to him as they may
determine in accordance with the regulations in respect of his securing the
provision of the service mentioned in that subsection.

(2) A person falls within this subsection if he is–

(a) a person with parental responsibility for a disabled child,

(b) a disabled person with parental responsibility for a child, or

(c) a disabled child aged 16 or 17,

and a local authority ('the responsible authority') have decided for the purposes of section 17 that the child's needs (or, if he is such a disabled child, his
needs) call for the provision by them of a service in exercise of functions
conferred on them under that section.

(3) Subsections (3) to (5) and (7) of section 57 of the 2001 Act shall apply, with any
necessary modifications, in relation to regulations under this section as they
apply in relation to regulations under that section.

(4) Regulations under this section shall provide that, where payments are made
under the regulations to a person falling within subsection (5)–

(a) the payments shall be made at the rate mentioned in subsection (4)(a) of
section 57 of the 2001 Act (as applied by subsection (3)); and

(b) subsection (4)(b) of that section shall not apply.

(5) A person falls within this subsection if he is–

(a) a person falling within subsection (2)(a) or (b) and the child in question is
aged 16 or 17, or

(b) a person who *is in receipt of income support under Part 7 of the Social
Security Contributions and Benefits Act 1992*, of any element of child tax
credit other than the family element, of working tax credit, of an income-
based jobseeker's allowance or of an income-related employment and
support allowance.

(6) In this section–

'the 2001 Act' means the Health and Social Care Act 2001;

'disabled' in relation to an adult has the same meaning as that given by
section 17(11) in relation to a child;

'prescribed' means specified in or determined in accordance with regulations under this section (and has the same meaning in the provisions of the 2001 Act mentioned in subsection (3) as they apply by virtue of that subsection).

Vouchers for persons with parental responsibility for disabled children

17B(1) The appropriate national authority may by regulations make provision for the issue by a local authority of vouchers to a person with parental responsibility for a disabled child.

(2) 'Voucher' means a document whereby, if the local authority agrees with the person with parental responsibility that it would help him care for the child if the person with parental responsibility had a break from caring, that person may secure the temporary provision of services for the child under section 17.

(3) The regulations may, in particular, provide–
   (a) for the value of a voucher to be expressed in terms of money, or of the delivery of a service for a period of time, or both;
   (b) for the person who supplies a service against a voucher, or for the arrangement under which it is supplied, to be approved by the local authority;
   (c) for a maximum period during which a service (or a service of a prescribed description) can be provided against a voucher.

Day care for pre-school and other children

18(1) Every local authority shall provide such day care for children in need within their area who are–
   (a) aged five or under; and
   (b) not yet attending schools,
as is appropriate.

(2) A local authority (in Wales) may provide day care for children within their area who satisfy the conditions mentioned in subsection (1)(a) and (b) even though they are not in need.

(3) A local authority may provide facilities (including training, advice, guidance and counselling) for those–
   (a) caring for children in day care; or
   (b) who at any time accompany such children while they are in day care.

(4) In this section 'day care' means any form of care or supervised activity provided for children during the day (whether or not it is provided on a regular basis).

(5) Every local authority shall provide for children in need within their area who are attending any school such care or supervised activities as is appropriate–
   (a) outside school hours; or
   (b) during school holidays.

(6) A local authority (in Wales) may provide such care or supervised activities for children within their area who are attending any school even though those children are not in need.

(7) In this section 'supervised activity' means an activity supervised by a responsible person.

PROVISION OF ACCOMMODATION FOR CHILDREN

Review of provision for day care, child minding, etc

19 [*Repealed.*]

Provision of accommodation for children: general

20(1) Every local authority shall provide accommodation for any child in need within their area who appears to them to require accommodation as a result of–

(a) there being no person who has parental responsibility for him;

(b) his being lost or having been abandoned; or

(c) the person who has been caring for him being prevented (whether or not permanently, and for whatever reason) from providing him with suitable accommodation or care.

(2) Where a local authority provide accommodation under subsection(1) for a child who is ordinarily resident in the area of another local authority, that other local authority may take over the provision of accommodation for the child within–

(a) three months of being notified in writing that the child is being provided with accommodation; or

(b) such other longer period as may be prescribed.

(3) Every local authority shall provide accommodation for any child in need within their area who has reached the age of sixteen and whose welfare the authority consider is likely to be seriously prejudiced if they do not provide him with accommodation.

(4) A local authority may provide accommodation for any child within their area (even though a person who has parental responsibility for him is able to provide him with accommodation) if they consider that to do so would safeguard or promote the child's welfare.

(5) A local authority may provide accommodation for any person who has reached the age of sixteen but is under twenty-one in any community home which takes children who have reached the age of sixteen if they consider that to do so would safeguard or promote his welfare.

(6) Before providing accommodation under this section, a local authority shall, so far as is reasonably practicable and consistent with the child's welfare–

(a) ascertain the child's wishes and feelings regarding the provision of accommodation; and

(b) give due consideration (having regard to his age and understanding) to such wishes and feelings of the child as they have been able to ascertain.

(7) A local authority may not provide accommodation under this section for any child if any person who–

(a) has parental responsibility for him; and

(b) is willing and able to–

(i) provide accommodation for him; or

(ii) arrange for accommodation to be provided for him,

objects.

(8) Any person who has parental responsibility for a child may at any time remove the child from accommodation provided by or on behalf of the local authority under this section.

(9) Subsections (7) and (8) do not apply while any person–

(a) in whose favour a residence order is in force with respect to the child;

(aa) who is a special guardian of the child; or

(b) who has care of the child by virtue of an order made in the exercise of the High Court's inherent jurisdiction with respect to children,

agrees to the child being looked after in accommodation provided by or on behalf of the local authority.

(10) Where there is more than one such person as is mentioned in subsection (9), all of them must agree.

(11) Subsections (7) and (8) do not apply where a child who has reached the age of sixteen agrees to being provided with accommodation under this section.

Provision of accommodation for children in police protection or detention or on remand, etc

21(1) Every local authority shall make provision for the reception and accommodation of children who are removed or kept away from home under Part V.

(2) Every local authority shall receive, and provide accommodation for, children–

(a) in police protection whom they are requested to receive under section 46(3)(f);

(b) whom they are requested to receive under section 38(6) of the Police and Criminal Evidence Act 1984;

(c) who are–

  (i) on remand under section 23(1) of the Children and Young Persons Act 1969;

  (ia) remanded to accommodation provided by or on behalf of a local authority by virtue of paragraph 4 of Schedule 1 or paragraph 6 of Schedule 8 to the Powers of Criminal Courts (Sentencing) Act 2000 (breach etc of referral orders and reparation orders);

  (ii) remanded to accommodation provided by or on behalf of a local authority by virtue of paragraph 21 of Schedule 2 to the Criminal Justice and Immigration Act 2008 (breach etc of youth rehabilitation orders);

  (iia) remanded to accommodation provided by or on behalf of a local authority by virtue of paragraph 10 of the Schedule to the Street Offences Act 1959 (breach of orders under section 1(2A) of that Act);

  (iii) the subject of a youth rehabilitation order imposing a local authority residence requirement or a youth rehabilitation order with fostering,

  and with respect to whom they are the designated authority.

(2A) In subsection (2)(c)(iii), the following terms have the same meanings as in Part 1 of the Criminal Justice and Immigration Act 2008 (see section 7 of that Act) –

'local authority residence requirement';

'youth rehabilitation order';

'youth rehabilitation order with fostering'.

(3) Where a child has been–

(a) removed under Part V; or

(b) detained under section 38 of the Police and Criminal Evidence Act 1984,

and he is not being provided with accommodation by a local authority or in a hospital vested in the Secretary of State, the Welsh Ministers or a Primary Care Trust, or otherwise made available pursuant to arrangements made by a Local Health Board or a Primary Care Trust, any reasonable expenses of accommodating him shall be recoverable from the local authority in whose area he is ordinarily resident.

Duties of local authorities in relation to children looked after by them

General duty of local authority in relation to children looked after by them

22(1) In this Act, any reference to a child who is looked after by a local authority is a reference to a child who is–

(a) in their care; or

(b) provided with accommodation by the authority in the exercise of any functions (in particular those under this Act) which are social services functions within the meaning of the Local Authority Social Services Act 1970 , apart from functions under sections 17, 23B and 24B.

(2) In subsection(1) 'accommodation' means accommodation which is provided for a continuous period of more than 24 hours.

(3) It shall be the duty of a local authority looking after any child–

(a) to safeguard and promote his welfare; and

(b) to make such use of services available for children cared for by their own parents as appears to the authority reasonable in his case.

(3A) The duty of a local authority under subsection (3)(a) to safeguard and promote the welfare of a child looked after by them includes in particular a duty to promote the child's educational achievement.

(4)   Before making any decision with respect to a child whom they are looking after, or proposing to look after, a local authority shall, so far as is reasonably practicable, ascertain the wishes and feelings of–
   (a) the child;
   (b) his parents;
   (c) any person who is not a parent of his but who has parental responsibility for him; and
   (d) any other person whose wishes and feelings the authority consider to be relevant,
   regarding the matter to be decided.

(5)   In making any such decision a local authority shall give due consideration–
   (a) having regard to his age and understanding, to such wishes and feelings of the child as they have been able to ascertain;
   (b) to such wishes and feelings of any person mentioned in subsection (4)(b) to (d) as they have been able to ascertain; and
   (c) to the child's religious persuasion, racial origin and cultural and lin-guistic background.

(6)   If it appears to a local authority that it is necessary, for the purpose of protect-ing members of the public from serious injury, to exercise their powers with respect to a child whom they are looking after in a manner which may not be consistent with their duties under this section, they may do so.

(7)   If the appropriate national authority considers it necessary, for the purpose of protecting members of the public from serious injury, to give directions to a local authority with respect to the exercise of their powers with respect to a child whom they are looking after, the appropriate national authority may give such directions to the local authority.

(8)   Where any such directions are given to an authority they shall comply with them even though doing so is inconsistent with their duties under this section.

Provision of accommodation for children in care
22A When a child is in the care of a local authority, it is their duty to provide the child with accommodation.

Maintenance of looked after children
22B It is the duty of a local authority to maintain a child they are looking after in other respects apart from the provision of accommodation.

Ways in which looked after children are to be accommodated and maintained
22C (1) This section applies where a local authority are looking after a child ('C').

(2)   The local authority must make arrangements for C to live with a person who falls within subsection (3) (but subject to subsection (4)).

(3)   A person ('P') falls within this subsection if–
   (a) P is a parent of C;
   (b) P is not a parent of C but has parental responsibility for C; or
   (c) in a case where C is in the care of the local authority and there was a residence order in force with respect to C immediately before the care order was made, P was a person in whose favour the residence order was made.

(4)   Subsection (2) does not require the local authority to make arrangements of the kind mentioned in that subsection if doing so–
   (a) would not be consistent with C's welfare; or
   (b) would not be reasonably practicable.

(5)   If the local authority are unable to make arrangements under subsection (2), they must place C in the placement which is, in their opinion, the most appropriate placement available.

(6) In subsection (5) 'placement' means–

    (a) placement with an individual who is a relative, friend or other person connected with C and who is also a local authority foster parent;

    (b) placement with a local authority foster parent who does not fall within paragraph (a);

    (c) placement in a children's home in respect of which a person is registered under Part 2 of the Care Standards Act 2000; or

    (d) subject to section 22D, placement in accordance with other arrangements which comply with any regulations made for the purposes of this section.

(7) In determining the most appropriate placement for C, the local authority must, subject to the other provisions of this Part (in particular, to their duties under section 22)–

    (a) give preference to a placement falling within paragraph (a) of subsection (6) over placements falling within the other paragraphs of that subsection;

    (b) comply, so far as is reasonably practicable in all the circumstances of C's case, with the requirements of subsection (8); and

    (c) comply with subsection (9) unless that is not reasonably practicable.

(8) The local authority must ensure that the placement is such that–

    (a) it allows C to live near C's home;

    (b) it does not disrupt C's education or training;

    (c) if C has a sibling for whom the local authority are also providing accommodation, it enables C and the sibling to live together;

    (d) if C is disabled, the accommodation provided is suitable to C's particular needs.

(9) The placement must be such that C is provided with accommodation within the local authority's area.

(10) The local authority may determine–

    (a) the terms of any arrangements they make under subsection (2) in relation to C (including terms as to payment); and

    (b) the terms on which they place C with a local authority foster parent (including terms as to payment but subject to any order made under section 49 of the Children Act 2004).

(11) The appropriate national authority may make regulations for, and in connection with, the purposes of this section.

(12) In this Act 'local authority foster parent' means a person who is approved as a local authority foster parent in accordance with regulations made by virtue of paragraph 12F of Schedule 2.

Review of child's case before making alternative arrangements for accommodation

22D (1)Where a local authority are providing accommodation for a child ('C') other than by arrangements under section 22C(6)(d), they must not make such arrangements for C unless they have decided to do so in consequence of a review of C's case carried out in accordance with regulations made under section 26.

(2) But subsection (1) does not prevent a local authority making arrangements for C under section 22C(6)(d) if they are satisfied that in order to safeguard C's welfare it is necessary–

    (a) to make such arrangements; and

    (b) to do so as a matter of urgency.

Children's homes provided by appropriate national authority

22E Where a local authority place a child they are looking after in a children's home provided, equipped and maintained by an appropriate national authority under section 82(5), they must do so on such terms as that national authority may from time to time determine.

Regulations as to children looked after by local authorities

22F Part 2 of Schedule 2 has effect for the purposes of making further provision as to children looked after by local authorities and in particular as to the regulations which may be made under section 22C(11).

General duty of local authority to secure sufficient accommodation for looked after children

22G (1)It is the general duty of a local authority to take steps that secure, so far as reasonably practicable, the outcome in subsection (2).

(2)   The outcome is that the local authority are able to provide the children mentioned in subsection (3) with accommodation that–
- (a) is within the authority's area; and
- (b) meets the needs of those children.

(3)   The children referred to in subsection (2) are those–
- (a) that the local authority are looking after,
- (b) in respect of whom the authority are unable to make arrangements under section 22C(2), and
- (c) whose circumstances are such that it would be consistent with their welfare for them to be provided with accommodation that is in the authority's area.

(4)   In taking steps to secure the outcome in subsection (2), the local authority must have regard to the benefit of having–
- (a) a number of accommodation providers in their area that is, in their opinion, sufficient to secure that outcome; and
- (b) a range of accommodation in their area capable of meeting different needs that is, in their opinion, sufficient to secure that outcome.

(5)   In this section 'accommodation providers' means–
local authority foster parents; and
children's homes in respect of which a person is registered under Part 2 of the Care Standards Act 2000.

23   [*Repealed.*]

Duty of local authority to ensure visits to, and contact with, looked after children and others

23ZA (1)This section applies to–
- (a) a child looked after by a local authority;
- (b) a child who was looked after by a local authority but who has ceased to be looked after by them as a result of prescribed circumstances.

(2)   It is the duty of the local authority–
- (a) to ensure that a person to whom this section applies is visited by a representative of the authority ('a representative');
- (b) to arrange for appropriate advice, support and assistance to be available to a person to whom this section applies who seeks it from them.

(3)   The duties imposed by subsection (2)–
- (a) are to be discharged in accordance with any regulations made for the purposes of this section by the appropriate national authority;
- (b) are subject to any requirement imposed by or under an enactment applicable to the place in which the person to whom this section applies is accommodated.

(4)   Regulations under this section for the purposes of subsection (3)(a) may make provision about–
- (a) the frequency of visits;
- (b) circumstances in which a person to whom this section applies must be visited by a representative; and
- (c) the functions of a representative.

(5) In choosing a representative a local authority must satisfy themselves that the person chosen has the necessary skills and experience to perform the functions of a representative.

23ZB Independent visitors for children looked after by a local authority

(1) A local authority looking after a child must appoint an independent person to be the child's visitor if–
   (a) the child falls within a description prescribed in regulations made by the appropriate national authority; or
   (b) in any other case, it appears to them that it would be in the child's interests to do so.

(2) A person appointed under this section must visit, befriend and advise the child.

(3) A person appointed under this section is entitled to recover from the appointing authority any reasonable expenses incurred by that person for the purposes of that person's functions under this section.

(4) A person's appointment as a visitor in pursuance of this section comes to an end if–
   (a) the child ceases to be looked after by the local authority;
   (b) the person resigns the appointment by giving notice in writing to the appointing authority; or
   (c) the authority give him notice in writing that they have terminated it.

(5) The ending of such an appointment does not affect any duty under this section to make a further appointment.

(6) Where a local authority propose to appoint a visitor for a child under this section, the appointment shall not be made if–
   (a) the child objects to it; and
   (b) the authority are satisfied that the child has sufficient understanding to make an informed decision.

(7) Where a visitor has been appointed for a child under this section, the local authority shall terminate the appointment if–
   (a) the child objects to its continuing; and
   (b) the authority are satisfied that the child has sufficient understanding to make an informed decision.

(8) If the local authority give effect to a child's objection under subsection (6) or (7) and the objection is to having anyone as the child's visitor, the authority does not have to propose to appoint another person under subsection (1) until the objection is withdrawn.

(9) The appropriate national authority may make regulations as to the circumstances in which a person is to be regarded for the purposes of this section as independent of the appointing authority.

Advice and assistance for certain children and young persons

The responsible authority and relevant children

23A(1) The responsible local authority shall have the functions set out in section 23B in respect of a relevant child.

(2) In subsection(1) 'relevant child' means (subject to subsection (3)) a child who–
   (a) is not being looked after by any local authority;
   (b) was, before last ceasing to be looked after, an eligible child for the purposes of paragraph 19B of Schedule 2; and
   (c) is aged sixteen or seventeen.

(3) The appropriate national authority may prescribe–
   (a) additional categories of relevant children; and
   (b) categories of children who are not to be relevant children despite falling within subsection (2).

(4)   In subsection(1) the 'responsible local authority' is the one which last looked after the child.

(5)   If under subsection (3)(a) the appropriate national authority prescribes a category of relevant children which includes children who do not fall within subsection (2)(b) (for example, because they were being looked after by a local authority in Scotland), the appropriate national authority may in the regulations also provide for which local authority is to be the responsible local authority for those children.

Additional functions of the responsible authority in respect of relevant children

23B(1) It is the duty of each local authority to take reasonable steps to keep in touch with a relevant child for whom they are the responsible authority, whether he is within their area or not.

(2)   It is the duty of each local authority to appoint a personal adviser for each relevant child (if they have not already done so under paragraph 19C of Schedule 2).

(3)   It is the duty of each local authority, in relation to any relevant child who does not already have a pathway plan prepared for the purposes of paragraph 19B of Schedule 2–
  (a)   to carry out an assessment of his needs with a view to determining what advice, assistance and support it would be appropriate for them to provide him under this Part; and
  (b)   to prepare a pathway plan for him.

(4)–(7)   [*Repealed.*]

(8)   The responsible local authority shall safeguard and promote the child's welfare and, unless they are satisfied that his welfare does not require it, support him by–
  (a)   maintaining him;
  (b)   providing him with or maintaining him in suitable accommodation; and
  (c)   providing support of such other descriptions as may be prescribed.

(9)   Support under subsection (8) may be in cash.

(10) The appropriate national authority may by regulations make provision about the meaning of 'suitable accommodation' and in particular about the suitability of landlords or other providers of accommodation.

(11) If the local authority have lost touch with a relevant child, despite taking reasonable steps to keep in touch, they must without delay–
  (a)   consider how to re-establish contact; and
  (b)   take reasonable steps to do so,
  and while the child is still a relevant child must continue to take such steps until they succeed.

(12) Subsections (7) to (9) of section 17 apply in relation to support given under this section as they apply in relation to assistance given under that section.

(13) Subsections (4) and (5) of section 22 apply in relation to any decision by a local authority for the purposes of this section as they apply in relation to the decisions referred to in that section.

Continuing functions in respect of former relevant children

23C(1) Each local authority shall have the duties provided for in this section towards–
  (a)   a person who has been a relevant child for the purposes of section 23A (and would be one if he were under eighteen), and in relation to whom they were the last responsible authority; and
  (b)   a person who was being looked after by them when he attained the age of eighteen, and immediately before ceasing to be looked after was an eligible child,
  and in this section such a person is referred to as a 'former relevant child'.

(2) It is the duty of the local authority to take reasonable steps–
    (a) to keep in touch with a former relevant child whether he is within their area or not; and
    (b) if they lose touch with him, to re-establish contact.

(3) It is the duty of the local authority–
    (a) to continue the appointment of a personal adviser for a former relevant child; and
    (b) to continue to keep his pathway plan under regular review.

(4) It is the duty of the local authority to give a former relevant child–
    (a) assistance of the kind referred to in section 24B(1), to the extent that his welfare requires it;
    (b) assistance of the kind referred to in section 24B(2), to the extent that his welfare and his educational or training needs require it;
    (c) other assistance, to the extent that his welfare requires it.

(5) The assistance given under subsection (4)(c) may be in kind or, in exceptional circumstances, in cash.

(5A) It is the duty of the local authority to pay the relevant amount to a former relevant child who pursues higher education in accordance with a pathway plan prepared for that person.

(5B) The appropriate national authority may by regulations–
    (a) prescribe the relevant amount for the purposes of subsection (5A);
    (b) prescribe the meaning of 'higher education' for those purposes;
    (c) make provision as to the payment of the relevant amount;
    (d) make provision as to the circumstances in which the relevant amount (or any part of it) may be recovered by the local authority from a former relevant child to whom a payment has been made.

(5C) The duty set out in subsection (5A) is without prejudice to that set out in subsection (4)(b).

(6) Subject to subsection (7), the duties set out in subsections (2), (3) and (4) subsist until the former relevant child reaches the age of twenty-one.

(7) If the former relevant child's pathway plan sets out a programme of education or training which extends beyond his twenty-first birthday–
    (a) the duty set out in subsection (4)(b) continues to subsist for so long as the former relevant child continues to pursue that programme; and
    (b) the duties set out in subsections (2) and (3) continue to subsist concurrently with that duty.

(8) For the purposes of subsection (7)(a) there shall be disregarded any interruption in a former relevant child's pursuance of a programme of education or training if the local authority are satisfied that he will resume it as soon as is reasonably practicable.

(9) Section 24B(5) applies in relation to a person being given assistance under subsection (4)(b), or who is in receipt of a payment under subsection 5A as it applies in relation to a person to whom section 24B(3) applies.

(10) Subsections (7) to (9) of section 17 apply in relation to assistance given under this section as they apply in relation to assistance given under that section.

Further assistance to pursue education or training

23CA (1)This section applies to a person if–
    (a) he is under the age of twenty-five or of such lesser age as may be prescribed by the appropriate national authority;
    (b) he is a former relevant child (within the meaning of section 23C) towards whom the duties imposed by subsections (2), (3) and (4) of that section no longer subsist; and
    (c) he has informed the responsible local authority that he is pursuing, or wishes to pursue, a programme of education or training.

(2) It is the duty of the responsible local authority to appoint a personal adviser for a person to whom this section applies.

(3) It is the duty of the responsible local authority–
   (a) to carry out an assessment of the needs of a person to whom this section applies with a view to determining what assistance (if any) it would be appropriate for them to provide to him under this section; and
   (b) to prepare a pathway plan for him.

(4) It is the duty of the responsible local authority to give assistance of a kind referred to subsection (5) to a person to whom this section applies to the extent that his educational or training needs require it.

(5) The kinds of assistance are–
   (a) contributing to expenses incurred by him in living near the place where he is, or will be, receiving education or training; or
   (b) making a grant to enable him to meet expenses connected with his education and training.

(6) If a person to whom this section applies pursues a programme of education or training in accordance with the pathway plan prepared for him, the duties of the local authority under this section (and under any provision applicable to the pathway plan prepared under this section for that person) subsist for as long as he continues to pursue that programme.

(7) For the purposes of subsection (6), the local authority may disregard any interruption in the person's pursuance of a programme of education or training if they are satisfied that he will resume it as soon as is reasonably practicable.

(8) Subsections (7) to (9) of section 17 apply to assistance given to a person under this section as they apply to assistance given to or in respect of a child under that section, but with the omission in subsection (8) of the words 'and of each of his parents'.

(9) Subsection (5) of section 24B applies to a person to whom this section applies as it applies to a person to whom subsection (3) of that section applies.

(10) Nothing in this section affects the duty imposed by subsection (5A) of section 23C to the extent that it subsists in relation to a person to whom this section applies; but the duty to make a payment under that subsection may be taken into account in the assessment of the person's needs under subsection (3)(a).

(11) In this section 'the responsible local authority' means, in relation to a person to whom this section applies, the local authority which had the duties provided for in section 23C towards him.

Personal advisers

23D(1) The appropriate national authority may by regulations require local authorities to appoint a personal adviser for children or young persons of a prescribed description who have reached the age of sixteen but not the age of twenty five who are not–
   (a) children who are relevant children for the purposes of section 23A;
   (b) the young persons referred to in section 23C;
   (c) the children referred to in paragraph 19C of Schedule 2; or
   (d) persons to whom section 23CA applies.

(2) Personal advisers appointed under or by virtue of this Part shall (in addition to any other functions) have such functions as the appropriate national authority prescribes.

Pathway plans

23E(1) In this Part, a reference to a 'pathway plan' is to a plan setting out–
   (a) in the case of a plan prepared under paragraph 19B of Schedule 2–

    (i) the advice, assistance and support which the local authority intend to provide a child under this Part, both while they are looking after him and later; and

    (ii) when they might cease to look after him; and

  (b) in the case of a plan prepared under section 23B or 23CA, the advice, assistance and support which the local authority intend to provide under this Part,

and dealing with such other matters (if any) as may be prescribed.

(1A) A local authority may carry out an assessment under section 23B(3) or 23CA(3) of a person's needs at the same time as any assessment of his needs is made under–

  (a) the Chronically Sick and Disabled Persons Act 1970;

  (b) Part 4 of the Education Act 1996 (in the case of an assessment under section 23B(3));

  (c) the Disabled Persons (Services, Consultation and Representation) Act 1986; or

  (d) any other enactment.

(1B) The appropriate national authority may by regulations make provision as to assessments for the purposes of section 23B(3) or 23CA.

(1C) Regulations under subsection (1B) may in particular make provision about–

  (a) who is to be consulted in relation to an assessment;

  (b) the way in which an assessment is to be carried out, by whom and when;

  (c) the recording of the results of an assessment;

  (d) the considerations to which a local authority are to have regard in carrying out an assessment.

(1D) A local authority shall keep each pathway plan prepared by them under section 23B or 23CA under review.

(2) The appropriate national authority may by regulations make provision about pathway plans and their review.

Persons qualifying for advice and assistance

24(1) In this Part 'a person qualifying for advice and assistance' means a person to whom subsection (1A) or (1B) applies–

(1A) This subsection applies to a person–

  (a) who has reached the age of sixteen but not the age of twenty-one;

  (b) with respect to whom a special guardianship order is in force (or, if he has reached the age of eighteen, was in force when he reached that age); and

  (c) who was, immediately before the making of that order, looked after by a local authority.

(1B) This subsection applies to a person to whom subsection (1A) does not apply, and who–

  (a) is under twenty-one; and

  (b) at any time after reaching the age of sixteen but while still a child was, but is no longer, looked after, accommodated or fostered.

(2) In subsection (1B)(1)(b), 'looked after, accommodated or fostered' means–

  (a) looked after by a local authority;

  (b) accommodated by or on behalf of a voluntary organisation;

  (c) accommodated in a private children's home;

  (d) accommodated for a consecutive period of at least three months–

    (i) by any Local Health Board, Special Health Authority, Primary Care Trust or local education authority, or

    (ii) in any care home or independent hospital or in any accommodation provided by a National Health Service trust or NHS Foundation Trust; or

  (e) privately fostered.

(3)   Subsection (2)(d) applies even if the period of three months mentioned there began before the child reached the age of sixteen.

(4)   In the case of a person qualifying for advice and assistance by virtue of sub-section (2)(a), it is the duty of the local authority which last looked after him to take such steps as they think appropriate to contact him at such times as they think appropriate with a view to discharging their functions under sections 24A and 24B.

(5)   In each of sections 24A and 24B, the local authority under the duty or having the power mentioned there ('the relevant authority') is–
(za) in the case of a person to whom subsection (1A) applies, a local authority determined in accordance with regulations made by the appropriate national authority;
(a)   in the case of a person qualifying for advice and assistance by virtue of subsection (2)(a), the local authority which last looked after him; or
(b)   in the case of any other person qualifying for advice and assistance, the local authority within whose area the person is (if he has asked for help of a kind which can be given under section 24A or 24B).

Advice and assistance

24A(1) The relevant authority shall consider whether the conditions in subsection (2) are satisfied in relation to a person qualifying for advice and assistance.

(2)   The conditions are that–
(a)   he needs help of a kind which they can give under this section or section 24B; and
(b)   in the case of a person to whom section 24(1A) applies, or to whom section 24(1B) applies and who was not being looked after by any local authority, they are satisfied that the person by whom he was being looked after does not have the necessary facilities for advising or befriending him.

(3)   If the conditions are satisfied–
(a)   they shall advise and befriend him if he is a person to whom section 24(1A) applies or he is a person to whom s24(1B) applies and was being looked after by a local authority or was accommodated by or on behalf of a voluntary organisation; and
(b)   in any other case they may do so.

(4)   Where as a result of this section a local authority are under a duty, or are em-powered, to advise and befriend a person, they may also give him assistance.

(5)   The assistance may be in kind and, in exceptional circumstances, assistance may be given–
(a)   by providing accommodation, if in the circumstances assistance may not be given in respect of the accommodation under section 24B, or
(b)   in cash.

(6)   Subsections (7) to (9) of section 17 apply in relation to assistance given under this section or section 24B as they apply in relation to assistance given under that section.

Employment, education and training

24B(1) The relevant local authority may give assistance to any person who quali-fies for advice and assistance by virtue of section 24(1A) or section 24(2)(a) by contributing to expenses incurred by him in living near the place where he is, or will be, employed or seeking employment.

(2)   The relevant local authority may give assistance to a person to whom sub-section (3) applies by–
(a)   contributing to expenses incurred by the person in question in living near the place where he is, or will be, receiving education or training; or
(b)   making a grant to enable him to meet expenses connected with his education or training.

(3) This subsection applies to any person who–
   (a) is under twenty-five; and
   (b) qualifies for advice and assistance by virtue of section 24(1A) or section 24(2)(a), or would have done so if he were under 21

(4) Where a local authority are assisting a person under subsection (2) they may disregard any interruption in his attendance on the course if he resumes it as soon as is reasonably practicable.

(5) Where the local authority are satisfied that a person to whom subsection (3) applies who is in full-time further or higher education needs accommodation during a vacation because his term-time accommodation is not available to him then, they shall give him assistance by–
   (a) providing him with suitable accommodation during the vacation; or
   (b) paying him enough to enable him to secure such accommodation himself.

(6) The Secretary of State may prescribe the meaning of 'full-time', 'further education', 'higher education' and 'vacation' for the purposes of subsection (5).

Information

24C(1) Where it appears to a local authority that a person–
   (a) with whom they are under a duty to keep in touch under section 23B, 23C or 24; or
   (b) whom they have been advising and befriending under section 24A; or
   (c) to whom they have been giving assistance under section 24B,
   proposes to live, or is living, in the area of another local authority, they must inform that other authority.

(2) Where a child who is accommodated–
   (a) by a voluntary organisation or in a private children's home;
   (b) by any Local Health Board, Special Health Authority, Primary Care Trust or local education authority in the exercise of education functions; or
   (c) in any care home or independent hospital or any accommodation provided by a National Health Service trust or NHS Foundation Trust,
   ceases to be so accommodated, after reaching the age of sixteen, the organisation, authority or (as the case may be) person carrying on the home shall inform the local authority within whose area the child proposes to live.

(3) Subsection (2) only applies, by virtue of paragraph (b) or (c), if the accommodation has been provided for a consecutive period of at least three months.

(4) In a case where a child was accommodated by a local authority in the exercise of education functions, subsection (2) applies only if the local authority who accommodated the child are different from the local authority within whose area the child proposes to live.

Representations: sections 23A to 24B

24D(1) Every local authority shall establish a procedure for considering representations (including complaints) made to them by–
   (a) a relevant child for the purposes of section 23A or a young person falling within section 23C;
   (b) a person qualifying for advice and assistance; or
   (c) a person falling within section 24B(2),
   about the discharge of their functions under this Part in relation to him.

(1A) Regulations may be made by the appropriate national authority imposing time limits on the making of representations under subsection (1).

(2) In considering representations under subsection (1), a local authority shall comply with regulations (if any) made by the appropriate national authority for the purposes of this subsection.

Secure accommodation

Use of accommodation for restricting liberty

25(1) Subject to the following provisions of this section, a child who is being looked after by a local authority may not be placed, and, if placed, may not be kept, in accommodation provided for the purpose of restricting liberty ('secure accommodation') unless it appears–

(a) that–

(i) he has a history of absconding and is likely to abscond from any other description of accommodation; and

(ii) if he absconds, he is likely to suffer significant harm; or

(b) that if he is kept in any other description of accommodation he is likely to injure himself or other persons.

(2) The appropriate national authority may by regulations–

(a) specify a maximum period–

(i) beyond which a child may not be kept in secure accommodation without the authority of the court; and

(ii) for which the court may authorise a child to be kept in secure accommodation;

(b) empower the court from time to time to authorise a child to be kept in secure accommodation for such further period as the regulations may specify; and

(c) provide that applications to the court under this section shall be ade only by local authorities.

(3) It shall be the duty of a court hearing an application under this section to determine whether any relevant criteria for keeping a child in secure accommodation are satisfied in his case.

(4) If a court determines that any such criteria are satisfied, it shall make an order authorising the child to be kept in secure accommodation and specifying the maximum period for which he may be so kept.

(5) On any adjournment of the hearing of an application under this section, a court may make an interim order permitting the child to be kept during the period of the adjournment in secure accommodation.

(6) No court shall exercise the powers conferred by this section in respect of a child who is not legally represented in that court unless, having been informed of his right to apply for representation funded by the Legal Services Commission as part of the Community Legal Service or Criminal Defence Service and having had the opportunity to do so, he refused or failed to apply.

(7) The appropriate national authority may by regulations provide that–

(a) this section shall or shall not apply to any description of children specified in the regulations;

(b) this section shall have effect in relation to children of a description specified in the regulations subject to such modifications as may be so specified;

(c) such other provisions as may be so specified shall have effect for the purpose of determining whether a child of a description specified in the regulations may be placed or kept in secure accommodation.

(8) The giving of an authorisation under this section shall not prejudice any power of any court in England and Wales or Scotland to give directions relating to the child to whom the authorisation relates.

(9) This section is subject to section 20(8).

Appointment of independent reviewing officer

25A (1)If a local authority are looking after a child, they must appoint an individual as the independent reviewing officer for that child's case.

(2) The initial appointment under subsection (1) must be made before the child's case is first reviewed in accordance with regulations made under section 26.

(3) If a vacancy arises in respect of a child's case, the local authority must make another appointment under subsection (1) as soon as is practicable.

(4) An appointee must be of a description prescribed in regulations made by the appropriate national authority.

Functions of the independent reviewing officer

25B (1)The independent reviewing officer must–

    (a) monitor the performance by the local authority of their functions in relation to the child's case;

    (b) participate, in accordance with regulations made by the appropriate national authority, in any review of the child's case;

    (c) ensure that any ascertained wishes and feelings of the child concerning the case are given due consideration by the local authority;

    (d) perform any other function which is prescribed in regulations made by the appropriate national authority.

(2) An independent reviewing officer's functions must be performed–

    (a) in such manner (if any) as may be prescribed in regulations made by the appropriate national authority; and

    (b) having regard to such guidance as that authority may issue in relation to the discharge of those functions.

(3) If the independent reviewing officer considers it appropriate to do so, the child's case may be referred by that officer to–

    (a) an officer of the Children and Family Court Advisory and Support Service; or

    (b) a Welsh family proceedings officer.

(4) If the independent reviewing officer is not an officer of the local authority, it is the duty of the authority–

    (a) to co-operate with that individual; and

    (b) to take all such reasonable steps as that individual may require of them to enable that individual's functions under this section to be performed satisfactorily.

Referred cases

25C (1)In relation to children whose cases are referred to officers under section 25B(3), the Lord Chancellor may by regulations–

    (a) extend any functions of the officers in respect of family proceedings (within the meaning of section 12 of the Criminal Justice and Court Services Act 2000) to other proceedings;

    (b) require any functions of the officers to be performed in the manner prescribed by the regulations.

(2) The power to make regulations in this section is exercisable in relation to functions of Welsh family proceedings officers only with the consent of the Welsh Ministers.

Supplemental
Review of cases and inquiries into representations

26(1) The appropriate national authority may make regulations requiring the case of each child who is being looked after by a local authority to be reviewed in accordance with the provisions of the regulations.

(2) The regulations may, in particular, make provision–

    (a) as to the manner in which each case is to be reviewed;

    (b) as to the considerations to which the local authority are to have regard in reviewing each case;

(c) as to the time when each case is first to be reviewed and the frequency of subsequent reviews;

(d) requiring the authority, before conducting any review, to seek the views of–

    (i)   the child;

    (ii) his parents;

    (iii) any person who is not a parent of his but who has parental responsibility for him; and

    (iv) any other person whose views the authority consider to be relevant,

including, in particular, the views of those persons in relation to any particular matter which is to be considered in the course of the review;

(e) requiring the authority, in the case of a child who is in their care–

    (i)   to keep the section 31A plan for the child under review and, if they are of the opinion that some change is required, to revise the plan, or make a new plan, accordingly,

(ii) to consider, whether an application should be made to discharge the care order;

(f) requiring the authority, in the case of a child in accommodation provided by the authority–

    (i)   if there is no plan for the future care of the child, to prepare one,

    (ii) if there is such a plan for the child, to keep it under review and, if they are of the opinion that some change is required, to revise the plan or make a new plan, accordingly,

    (iii) to consider, whether the accommodation accords with the requirements of this Part;

(g) requiring the authority to inform the child, so far as is reasonably practicable, of any steps he may take under this Act;

(h) requiring the authority to make arrangements, including arrangements with such other bodies providing services as it considers appropriate, to implement any decision which they propose to make in the course, or as a result, of the review;

(i) requiring the authority to notify details of the result of the review and of any decision taken by them in consequence of the review to–

    (i)   the child;

    (ii) his parents;

    (iii) any person who is not a parent of his but who has parental responsibility for him; and

    (iv) any other person whom they consider ought to be notified;

(j) requiring the authority to monitor the arrangements which they have made with a view to ensuring that they comply with the regulations.

(k) [*Repealed.*]

(2A)–(2D) [*Repealed.*]

(3)   Every local authority shall establish a procedure for considering any representations (including any complaint) made to them by–

(a) any child who is being looked after by them or who is not being looked after by them but is in need;

(b) a parent of his;

(c) any person who is not a parent of his but who has parental responsibility for him;

(d) any local authority foster parent;

(e) such other person as the authority consider has a sufficient interest in the child's welfare to warrant his representations being considered by them,

about the discharge by the authority of any of their qualifying functions in relation to the child.

(3A) The following are qualifying functions for the purposes of subsection (3)–

(a) functions under this Part,

    (b) such functions under Part 4 or 5 as are specified by the Secretary of State in regulations.

(3B) The duty under subsection (3) extends to representations (including complaints) made to the authority by–

    (a) any person mentioned in section 3(1) of the Adoption and Children Act 2002 (persons for whose needs provision is made by the Adoption Service) and any other person to whom arrangements for the provision of adoption support services (within the meaning of that Act) extend,

    (b) such other person as the authority consider has sufficient interest in a child who is or may be adopted to warrant his representations being considered by them,

about the discharge by the authority of such functions under the Adoption and Children Act 2002 as are specified by the appropriate national authority in regulations.

(3C) The duty under subsection (3) extends to any representations (including complaints) which are made to the authority by–

    (a) a child with respect to whom a special guardianship order is in force,

    (b) a special guardian or a parent of such a child,

    (c) any other person the authority consider has a sufficient interest in the welfare of such a child to warrant his representations being considered by them, or

    (d) any person who has applied for an assessment under section 14F(3) or (4),

about the discharge by the authority of such functions under section 14F as may be specified by the appropriate national authority in regulations.

(4) The procedure shall ensure that at least one person who is not a member or officer of the authority takes part in–

    (a) the consideration; and

    (b) any discussions which are held by the authority about the action (if any) to be taken in relation to the child in the light of the consideration,

But this subsection is subject to subsection (5A).

(4A) Regulations may be made by the Secretary of State imposing time limits on the making of representations under this section.

(5) In carrying out any consideration of representations under this section a local authority shall comply with any regulations made by the Secretary of State for the purpose of regulating the procedure to be followed.

(5A) Regulations under subsection (5) may provide that subsection (4) does not apply in relation to any consideration or discussion which takes place as part of a procedure for which provision is made by the regulations for the purpose of resolving informally the matters raised in the representations.

(6) The appropriate national authority may make regulations requiring local authorities to monitor the arrangements that they have made with a view to ensuring that they comply with any regulations made for the purposes of subsection (5).

(7) Where any representation has been considered under the procedure established by a local authority under this section, the authority shall–

    (a) have due regard to the findings of those considering the representation; and

    (b) take such steps as are reasonably practicable to notify (in writing)–

        (i) the person making the representation;

        (ii) the child (if the authority consider that he has sufficient understanding); and

        (iii) such other persons (if any) as appear to the authority to be likely to be affected,

of the authority's decision in the matter and their reasons for taking that decision and of any action which they have taken, or propose to take.

(8)   Every local authority shall give such publicity to their procedure for considering representations under this section as they consider appropriate.

26ZA [*Repealed.*]

Representations: further consideration (Wales)

26ZB(1) The Welsh Minister may by regulations make provision for the further
consideration of representations which have been considered by a local
authority in Wales under section 24D or section 26.

(2)   The regulations may in particular make provision–
   (a)   for the further consideration of a representation by an independent panel
         established under the regulations;
   (b)   about the procedure to be followed on the further consideration of a
         representation;
   (c)   for the making of recommendations about the action to be taken as the
         result of a representation;
   (d)   about the making of reports about a representation;
   (e)   about the action to be taken by the local authority concerned as a result of
         the further consideration of a representation;
   (f)   for a representation to be referred back to the local authority concerned
         for reconsideration by the authority.

(3)   The regulations may require–
   (a)   the making of a payment, in relation to the further consideration of a
         representation under this section, by any local authority in respect of
         whose functions the representation is made;
   (b)   any such payment to be–
         (i)   made to such person or body as may be specified in the regulations;
         (ii)   of such amount as may be specified in, or calculated or determined
                under, the regulations; and
   (c)   for an independent panel to review the amount chargeable under para-
         graph (a) in any particular case and, if the panel thinks fit, to substitute a
         lesser amount.

(4)   The regulations may also–
   (a)   provide for different parts or aspects of a representation to be treated
         differently;
   (b)   require the production of information or documents in order to enable a
         representation to be properly considered;
   (c)   authorise the disclosure of information or documents relevant to a repre-
         sentation to a person or body who is further considering a representation
         under the regulations;
   and any such disclosure may be authorised notwithstanding any rule of
   common law that would otherwise prohibit or restrict the disclosure.

Advocacy services

26A(1) Every local authority shall make arrangements for the provision of assistance to–
   (a)   persons who make or intend to make representations under section 24D;
         and
   (b)   children who make or intend to make representations under section 26.

(2)   The assistance provided under the arrangements shall include assistance by
way of representation.

(2A) he duty under subsection(1) includes a duty to make arrangements for the
provision of assistance where representations under section 24D or 26 are
further considered under section 26ZB.

(3)   The arrangements–
   (a)   shall secure that a person may not provide assistance if he is a person
         who is prevented from doing so by regulations made by the Secretary of
         State; and

(b) shall comply with any other provision made by the regulations in relation to the arrangements.

(4) The appropriate national authority may make regulations requiring local authorities to monitor the steps that they have taken with a view to ensuring that they comply with regulations made for the purposes of subsection (3).

(5) Every local authority shall give such publicity to their arrangements for the provision of assistance under this section as they consider appropriate.

Co-operation between authorities

27(1) Where it appears to a local authority that any authority mentioned in subsection (3) could, by taking any specified action, help in the exercise of any of their functions under this Part, they may request the help of that other authority specifying the action in question.

(2) An authority whose help is so requested shall comply with the request if it is compatible with their own statutory or other duties and obligations and does not unduly prejudice the discharge of any of their functions.

(3) The authorities are–
   (a) any local authority;
   (b) . . .;
   (c) any local housing authority;
   (d) any Local Health Board, Special Health Authority, Primary Care Trust, National Health Service trust or NHS Foundation Trust; and
   (e) any person authorised by the appropriate national authority for the purposes of this section.

(4) [*Repealed.*]

Consultation with local education authorities

28 [*Repealed.*]

Recoupment of cost of providing services, etc

29(1) Where a local authority provide any service under section 17 or 18, other than advice, guidance or counselling, they may recover from a person specified in subsection (4) such charge for the service as they consider reasonable.

(2) Where the authority are satisfied that that person's means are insufficient for it to be reasonably practicable for him to pay the charge, they shall not require him to pay more than he can reasonably be expected to pay.

(3) No person shall be liable to pay any charge under subsection(1) for a service provided under section 17 or section 18(1) or (5) at any time when he is in receipt *of income support under Part VII of the Social Security Contributions and Benefits Act 1992*, of an income-based jobseeker's allowance or of an income-related employment and support allowance.

(3A) No person shall be liable to pay any charge under subsection(1) for a service provided under section 18(2) or (6) at any time when he is in receipt *of income support under Part VII of the Social Security Contributions and Benefits Act 1992*, of an income-based jobseeker's allowance or of an income-related employment and support allowance.

(3B) No person shall be liable to pay any charge under subsection(1) for a service provided under section 18(2) or (6) at any time when–
   (a) he is in receipt of guarantee state pension credit under section 1(3)(a) of the State Pension Credit Act 2002, or
   (b) he is a member of a couple (within the meaning of that Act) the other member of which is in receipt of guarantee state pension credit.

(4) The persons are–
   (a) where the service is provided for a child under sixteen, each of his parents;
   (b) where it is provided for a child who has reached the age of sixteen, the child himself; and
   (c) where it is provided for a member of the child's family, that member.

(5)   Any charge under subsection(1) may, without prejudice to any other method of recovery, be recovered summarily as a civil debt.

(6)   Part III of Schedule 2 makes provision in connection with contributions towards the maintenance of children who are being looked after by local authorities and consists of the re-enactment with modifications of provisions in Part V of the Child Care Act 1980.

(7)   Where a local authority provide any accommodation under section 20(1) for a child who was (immediately before they began to look after him) ordinarily resident within the area of another local authority, they may recover from that other authority any reasonable expenses incurred by them in providing the accommodation and maintaining him.

(8)   Where a local authority provide accommodation under section 21(1) or (2)(a) or (b) for a child who is ordinarily resident within the area of another local authority and they are not maintaining him in–

(a)   a community home provided by them;

(b)   a controlled community home; or

(c)   a hospital vested in the Secretary of State or a Primary Care Trust or any other hospital made available pursuant to arrangements made by a Strategic Health Authority, a Local Health Board or a Primary Care Trust,

they may recover from that other authority any reasonable expenses incurred by them in providing the accommodation and maintaining him.

(9)   Except where subsection (10) applies, Where a local authority comply with any request under section 27(2) in relation to a child or other person who is not ordinarily resident within their area, they may recover from the local authority in whose area the child or person is ordinarily resident any reasonable expenses incurred by them in respect of that person.

(10) Where a local authority ('authority A') comply with any request under section 27(2) from another local authority ('authority B') in relation to a child or other person–

(a)   whose responsible authority is authority B for the purposes of section 23B or 23C; or

(b)   whom authority B are advising or befriending or to whom they are giving assistance by virtue of section 24(5)(a),

authority A may recover from authority B any reasonable expenses incurred by them in respect of that person.

NHS AND COMMUNITY CARE ACT 1990 (EXTRACTS)

PART III: COMMUNITY CARE: ENGLAND AND WALES

General provisions concerning community care services

Local authority plans for community care services

46(1) Each local authority–
- (a) shall, within such period after the day appointed for the coming into force of this section as the Secretary of State may direct, prepare and publish a plan for the provision of community care services in their area;
- (b) shall keep the plan prepared by them under paragraph (a) above and any further plans prepared by them under this section under review; and
- (c) shall, at such intervals as the Secretary of State may direct, prepare and publish modifications to the current plan, or if the case requires, a new plan.

(2) In carrying out any of their functions under paragraphs (a) to (c) of subsection(1) above, a local authority shall consult–
- (a) any Health Authority and Local Health Board the whole or any part of whose area lies within the area of the local authority;
- (b) [*Repealed.*]
- (c) in so far as any proposed plan, review or modifications of a plan may affect or be affected by the provision or availability of housing and the local authority is not itself a local housing authority, within the meaning of the Housing Act 1985, every such local housing authority whose area is within the area of the local authority;
- (d) such voluntary organisations as appear to the authority to represent the interests of persons who use or are likely to use any community care services within the area of the authority or the interests of private carers who, within that area, provide care to persons for whom, in the exercise of their social services functions, the local authority have a power or a duty to provide a service.
- (e) such voluntary housing agencies and other bodies as appear to the local authority to provide housing or community care services in their area; and
- (f) such other persons as the Secretary of State may direct.

(3) In this section–
'local authority' means the council of a county, a county borough, a metropolitan district or a London borough or the Common Council of the City of London; 'community care services' means services which a local authority may provide or arrange to be provided under any of the following provisions–
- (a) Part III of the National Assistance Act 1948;
- (b) section 45 of the Health Services and Public Health Act 1968;
- (c) section 254 of, and Schedule 20 to, the National Health Service Act 2006, and section 192 of, and Schedule 15 to, the National Health Service (Wales) Act 2006; and
- (d) section 117 of the Mental Health Act 1983; and
'private carer' means a person who is not employed to provide the care in question by any body in the exercise of its functions under any enactment.

Assessment of needs for community care services

47(1) Subject to subsections (5) and (6) below, where it appears to a local authority that any person for whom they may provide or arrange for the provision of community care services may be in need of any such services, the authority–

(a)   shall carry out an assessment of his needs for those services; and

(b)   having regard to the results of that assessment, shall then decide

whether his needs call for the provision by them of any such services.

(2)   If at any time during the assessment of the needs of any person under subsection (1)(a) above it appears to a local authority that he is a disabled person, the authority–

(a)   shall proceed to make such a decision as to the services he requires as is mentioned in section 4 of the Disabled Persons (Services, Consultation and Representation) Act 1986 without his requesting them to do so under that section; and

(b)   shall inform him that they will be doing so and of his rights under that Act.

(3)   If at any time during the assessment of the needs of any person under subsection (1)(a) above, it appears to a local authority–

(a)   that there may be a need for the provision to that person by such Primary Care Trust or Health Authority as may be determined in accordance with regulations of any services under the National Health Service Act 2006 or the National Health Service (Wales) Act 2006, or

(b)   that there may be a need for the provision to him of any services which fall within the functions of a local housing authority (within the meaning of the Housing Act 1985) which is not the local authority carrying out the assessment,

the local authority shall notify that Primary Care Trust, Health Authority or local housing authority and invite them to assist, to such extent as is reasonable in the circumstances, in the making of the assessment; and, in making their decision as to the provision of the services needed for the person in question, the local authority shall take into account any services which are likely to be made available for him by that Primary Care Trust, Health Authority or local housing authority.

(4)   The Secretary of State may give directions as to the manner in which an assessment under this section is to be carried out or the form it is to take but, subject to any such directions and to subsection (7) below, it shall be carried out in such manner and take such form as the local authority consider appropriate.

(5)   Nothing in this section shall prevent a local authority from temporarily providing or arranging for the provision of community care services for any person without carrying out a prior assessment of his needs in accordance with the preceding provisions of this section if, in the opinion of the authority, the condition of that person is such that he requires those services as a matter of urgency.

(6)   If, by virtue of subsection (5) above, community care services have been provided temporarily for any person as a matter of urgency, then, as soon as practicable thereafter, an assessment of his needs shall be made in accordance with the preceding provisions of this section.

(7)   This section is without prejudice to section 3 of the Disabled Persons (Services, Consultation and Representation) Act 1986.

(8)   In this section–

'disabled person' has the same meaning as in that Act; and

'local authority' and 'community care services' have the same meanings as in section 46 above.

CARERS (RECOGNITION AND SERVICES) ACT 1995

Assessment of ability of carers to provide care: England and Wales

1(1) Subject to subsection (3) below, in any case where–

    (a) a local authority carry out an assessment under section 47(1)(a) of the National Health Service and Community Care Act 1990 of the needs of a person ('the relevant person') for community care services, and

    (b) an individual ('the carer') provides or intends to provide a substantial amount of care on a regular basis for the relevant person,

the carer may request the local authority, before they make their decision as to whether the needs of the relevant person call for the provision of any services, to carry out an assessment of his ability to provide and to continue to provide care for the relevant person; and if he makes such a request, the local authority shall carry out such an assessment and shall take into account the results of that assessment in making that decision.

(2) Subject to subsection (3) below, in any case where–

    (a) a local authority assess the needs of a disabled child for the purposes of Part III of the Children Act 1989 or section 2 of the Chronically Sick and Disabled Persons Act 1970, and

    (b) an individual ('the carer') provides or intends to provide a substantial amount of care on a regular basis for the disabled child,

the carer may request the local authority, before they make their decision as to whether the needs of the disabled child call for the provision of any services, to carry out an assessment of his ability to provide and to continue to provide care for the disabled child; and if he makes such a request, the local authority shall carry out such an assessment and shall take into account the results of that assessment in making that decision.

(2A) For the purposes of an assessment under subsection(1) or (2), the local authority may take into account, so far as it considers it to be material, an assessment under section 1 or 6 of the Carers and Disabled Children Act 2000.

(2B) In any case where–

    (a) a local authority are carrying out an assessment mentioned in paragraph (a) of either subsection(1) or subsection (2) above in relation to the relevant person or (as the case may be) a disabled child, and

    (b) it appears to the local authority that an individual may be entitled to request (but has not requested) an assessment under the subsection in question of his ability to provide and to continue to provide care for the relevant person or the disabled child,

the local authority must inform the individual that he may be so entitled before they make their decision as to the needs of the relevant person or the disabled child.

(2C) An assessment under subsection(1) or (2) above must include consideration of whether the carer–

    (a) works or wishes to work,

    (b) is undertaking, or wishes to undertake, education, training or any leisure activity.

(3) No request may be made under subsection(1) or (2) above by an individual who provides or will provide the care in question–

    (a) by virtue of a contract of employment or other contract with any person; or

    (b) as a volunteer for a voluntary organisation.

(4) The Secretary of State may give directions as to the manner in which an assessment under subsection(1) or (2) above is to be carried out or the form it is to take but, subject to any such directions, it shall be carried out in such manner and take such form as the local authority consider appropriate.

(5)   Section 8 of the Disabled Persons (Services, Consultation and Representation) Act 1986 (duty of local authority to take into account ability of carers) shall not apply in any case where–

(a)   an assessment is made under subsection(1) above in respect of an individual who provides the care in question for a disabled person; or

(b)   an assessment is made under subsection (2) above.

(6)   In this section–

'community care services' has the meaning given by section 46(3) of the National Health Service and Community Care Act 1990;

'child' means a person under the age of eighteen;

'disabled child' means a child who is disabled within the meaning of Part III of the Children Act 1989;

'disabled person' means a person to whom section 29 of the National Assistance Act 1948 applies;

'local authority' has the meaning given by section 46(3) of the National Health Service and Community Care Act 1990; and

'voluntary organisation' has the same meaning as in the National Assistance Act 1948.

(7)   [*Repealed.*]

HOUSING GRANTS, CONSTRUCTION AND REGENERATION ACT 1996

Grants: purposes for which grant must or may be given

23(1) The purposes for which an application for a grant must be approved, subject to the provisions of this Chapter, are the following–

(a) facilitating access by the disabled occupant to and from–
   (i) the dwelling, qualifying houseboat or caravan, or
   (ii) the dwelling or the building in which the dwelling or, as the case may be, flat is situated;

(b) making–
   (i) the dwelling, qualifying houseboat or caravan, or
   (ii) the building,

safe for the disabled occupant and other persons residing with him;

(c) facilitating access by the disabled occupant to a room used or usable as the principal family room;

(d) facilitating access by the disabled occupant to, or providing for the disabled occupant, a room used or usable for sleeping;

(e) facilitating access by the disabled occupant to, or providing for the disabled occupant, a room in which there is a lavatory, or facilitating the use by the disabled occupant of such a facility;

(f) facilitating access by the disabled occupant to, or providing for the disabled occupant, a room in which there is a bath or shower (or both), or facilitating the use by the disabled occupant of such a facility;

(g) facilitating access by the disabled occupant to, or providing for the disabled occupant, a room in which there is a washhand basin, or facilitating the use by the disabled occupant of such a facility;

(h) facilitating the preparation and cooking of food by the disabled occupant;

(i) improving any heating system in the dwelling, qualifying houseboat or caravan to meet the needs of the disabled occupant or, if there is no existing heating system in the dwelling or any such system is unsuitable for use by the disabled occupant, providing a heating system there suitable to meet his needs;

(j) facilitating the use by the disabled occupant of a source of power, light or heat by altering the position of one or more means of access to or control of that source or by providing additional means of control;

(k) facilitating access and movement by the disabled occupant around the dwelling, qualifying houseboat or caravan in order to enable him to care for a person who is normally resident there and is in need of such care;

(l) such other purposes as may be specified by order of the Secretary of State.

(2) [*Repealed.*]

(3) If in the opinion of the local housing authority the relevant works are more or less extensive than is necessary to achieve any of the purposes set out in subsection (1), they may, with the consent of the applicant, treat the application as varied so that the relevant works are limited to or, as the case may be, include such works as seem to the authority to be necessary for that purpose.

Grants: approval of application

24(1) The local housing authority shall approve an application for a grant for purposes within section 23(1) subject to the following provisions.

(2) Where an authority entertain an owner's application for a grant made by a person who proposes to acquire a qualifying owner's interest, they shall not approve the application until they are satisfied that he has done so.

(3) A local housing authority shall not approve an application for a grant unless they are satisfied–

(a) that the relevant works are necessary and appropriate to meet the needs of the disabled occupant, and

(b) that it is reasonable and practicable to carry out the relevant works having regard to the age and condition of –

(i) the dwelling, qualifying houseboat or caravan, or

(ii) the building.

In considering the matters mentioned in paragraph (a) a local housing authority which is not itself a social services authority shall consult the social services authority.

(4) [*Repealed.*]

(5) A local housing authority shall not approve a common parts application for a grant unless they are satisfied that the applicant has a power or is under a duty to carry out the relevant works.

CARERS AND DISABLED CHILDREN ACT 2000 (EXTRACTS)

Right of carers to assessment

1(1) If an individual aged 16 or over ('the carer')–

(a) provides or intends to provide a substantial amount of care on a regular basis for another individual aged 18 or over ('the person cared for'); and

(b) asks a local authority to carry out an assessment of his ability to provide and to continue to provide care for the person cared for,

the local authority must carry out such an assessment if it is satisfied that the person cared for is someone for whom it may provide or arrange for the provision of community care services.

(2) For the purposes of such an assessment, the local authority may take into account, so far as it considers it to be material, an assessment under section 1(1) of the Carers (Recognition and Services) Act 1995.

(3) Subsection(1) does not apply if the individual provides or will provide the care in question–

(a) by virtue of a contract of employment or other contract with any person; or

(b) as a volunteer for a voluntary organisation.

(3A) An assessment under subsection(1) must include consideration of whether the carer–

(a) works or wishes to work,

(b) is undertaking, or wishes to undertake, education, training or any leisure activity.

(4) The Secretary of State (or, in relation to Wales, the National Assembly for Wales) may give directions as to the manner in which an assessment under subsection(1) is to be carried out or the form it is to take.

(5) Subject to any such directions, it is to be carried out in such manner, and is to take such form, as the local authority considers appropriate.

(6) In this section, 'voluntary organisation' has the same meaning as in the National Assistance Act 1948.

Services for carers

2(1) The local authority must consider the assessment and decide–

(a) whether the carer has needs in relation to the care which he provides or intends to provide;

(b) if so, whether they could be satisfied (wholly or partly) by services which the local authority may provide; and

(c) if they could be so satisfied, whether or not to provide services to the carer.

(2) The services referred to are any services which–

(a) the local authority sees fit to provide; and

(b) will in the local authority's view help the carer care for the person cared for, and may take the form of physical help or other forms of support.

(3) A service, although provided to the carer–

(a) may take the form of a service delivered to the person cared for if it is one which, if provided to him instead of to the carer, could fall within community care services and they both agree it is to be so delivered; but

(b) if a service is delivered to the person cared for it may not, except in prescribed circumstances, include anything of an intimate nature.

(4) Regulations may make provision about what is, or is not, of an intimate nature for the purposes of subsection (3).

Vouchers

3(1) Regulations may make provision for the issue of vouchers by local authorities.

(2) 'Voucher' means a document whereby, if the local authority agrees with the

carer that it would help him care for the person cared for if the carer had a break from caring, the person cared for may secure that services in lieu of the care which would otherwise have been provided to him by the carer are delivered temporarily to him by another person by way of community care services.

(3)   The regulations may, in particular, provide–

(a)   for the value of a voucher to be expressed in terms of money, or of the delivery of a service for a period of time, or both;

(b)   for the person who supplies a service against a voucher, or for the arrangement under which it is supplied, to be approved by the local authority;

(c)   for vouchers to be issued to the carer or to the person cared for;

(d)   for a maximum period during which a service (or a service of a prescribed description) can be provided against a voucher.

Assessments and services for both carer and person cared for

4(1)   In section 1 of the Carers (Recognition and Services) Act 1995 (which provides for carers to be assessed as to their ability to care in connection with an assessment of the needs of the individual cared for), after subsection (2) insert–

(2A)   For the purposes of an assessment under subsection(1) or (2), the local authority may take into account, so far as it considers it to be material, an assessment under section 1 or 6 of the Carers and Disabled Children Act 2000.'

(2)   Subsection (4) applies if the local authority–

(a)   is either providing services under this Act to the carer, or is providing community care services to or in respect of the person cared for (but not both); and

(b)   proposes to provide another service to (or in respect of) the one who is not receiving any such service,

and the new service, or any service already being provided, is one which could be provided either under this Act, or by way of community care services.

(3)   Subsection (4) also applies if–

(a)   the local authority is not providing services to the carer (under this Act) or to the person cared for (by way of community care services), but proposes to provide services to each of them following an assessment under section 1 and under section 47 of the National Health Service and Community Care Act 1990; or

(b)   the local authority is providing services both to the carer (under this Act) and to the person cared for (by way of community care services), and proposes to provide to either of them a new service,

and (in a paragraph (a) case) any of the services, or (in a paragraph (b) case) the new service, is one which could be provided either under this Act, or by way of community care services.

(4)   In the case of each such service, the local authority must decide whether the service is, or is in future, to be provided under this Act, or by way of community care services (and hence whether it is, or is in future, to be provided to the carer, or to the person cared for).

(5)   The local authority's decision under subsection (4) is to be made without regard to the means of the carer or of the person cared for.

5   [*Repealed.*]

Assessments: persons with parental responsibility for disabled children

6(1)   If a person with parental responsibility for a disabled child–

(a)   provides or intends to provide a substantial amount of care on a regular basis for the child; and

(b)   asks a local authority to carry out an assessment of his ability to provide and to continue to provide care for the child, the local authority must carry out such an assessment if it is satisfied that the child and his family are persons for whom it may provide or arrange for the provision of services under section 17 of the Children Act 1989 ('the 1989 Act').

(2) For the purposes of such an assessment, the local authority may take into account, so far as it considers it to be material, an assessment under section 1(2) of the Carers (Recognition and Services) Act 1995.

(2A) An assessment under subsection(1) must include consideration of whether the person with parental responsibility for the child–
   (a) works or wishes to work,
   (b) is undertaking, or wishes to undertake, education, training or any leisure activity.

(3) The Secretary of State (or, in relation to Wales, the National Assembly for Wales) may give directions as to the manner in which an assessment under subsection(1) is to be carried out or the form it is to take.

(4) Subject to any such directions, it is to be carried out in such manner, and is to take such form, as the local authority considers appropriate.

(5) The local authority must take the assessment into account when deciding what, if any, services to provide under section 17 of the 1989 Act.

(6) Terms used in this section have the same meaning as in Part III of the 1989 Act.

Duty to inform carers of right to assessment

6A(1) Subsection (2) applies if it appears to a local authority that it would be required to carry out a carer's assessment on being asked to do so by–
   (a) the carer, or
   (b) a person with parental responsibility for a disabled child ('the responsible person').

(2) The local authority must inform the carer or, as appropriate, the responsible person that he may be entitled to a carer's assessment (but this is subject to subsections (3) and (4)).

(3) Subsection (2) does not apply in relation to the carer if the local authority has previously–
   (a) carried out a carer's assessment for him in relation to the person cared for,
   (b) informed him that he may be entitled to a carer's assessment in relation to the person cared for, or
   (c) carried out an assessment of him under section 4(3) of the Community Care (Delayed Discharges, etc) Act 2003 in relation to the person cared for.

(4) Subsection (2) does not apply in relation to the responsible person if the local authority has previously carried out a carer's assessment for him in relation to the disabled child or informed him that he may be entitled to a carer's assessment in relation to the disabled child.

(5) In this section 'carer's assessment' means–
   (a) in the case of the carer, an assessment under section 1 of his ability to provide and to continue to provide care for the person cared for,
   (b) in the case of the responsible person, an assessment under section 6 of his ability to provide and to continue to provide care for the disabled child.

LOCAL GOVERNMENT ACT 2000 (EXTRACTS)

Promotion of well-being

2(1) Every local authority are to have power to do anything which they consider is likely to achieve any one or more of the following objects–

(a) the promotion or improvement of the economic well-being of their area,

(b) the promotion or improvement of the social well-being of their area, and

(c) the promotion or improvement of the environmental well-being of their area.

(2) The power under subsection(1) may be exercised in relation to or for the benefit of–

(a) the whole or any part of a local authority's area, or

(b) all or any persons resident or present in a local authority's area.

(3) In determining whether or how to exercise the power under subsection (1), a local authority must have regard to their strategy under section 4.

(3A) But, in the case of an eligible parish council, that is subject to section 4A.

(3B) In determining whether or how to exercise the power under subsection (1), a local authority in Wales must have regard to the community strategy for its area published under section 39(4) of the Local Government (Wales) Measure 2009 or, where the strategy has been amended following a review under section 41 of that Measure, the strategy most recently published under section 41(6).

(3C) The community strategy for the area of a community council is the strategy referred to in subsection (3B) that is published by the county council or county borough council in whose area lies the community or communities for which the community council is established.

(4) The power under subsection(1) includes power for a local authority to–

(a) incur expenditure,

(b) give financial assistance to any person,

(c) enter into arrangements or agreements with any person,

(d) co-operate with, or facilitate or co-ordinate the activities of, any person,

(e) exercise on behalf of any person any functions of that person, and

(f) provide staff, goods, services or accommodation to any person.

(5) The power under subsection(1) includes power for a local authority to do anything in relation to, or for the benefit of, any person or area situated outside their area if they consider that it is likely to achieve any one or more of the objects in that subsection.

(6) Nothing in subsection (4) or (5) affects the generality of the power under subsection (1).

Limits on power to promote well-being

3(1) The power under section 2(1) does not enable a local authority to do anything which they are unable to do by virtue of any prohibition, restriction or limitation on their powers which is contained in any enactment (whenever passed or made).

(2) The power under section 2(1) does not enable a local authority to raise money (whether by precepts, borrowing or otherwise).

(3) The Secretary of State may by order make provision preventing local authorities from doing, by virtue of section 2(1), anything which is specified, or is of a description specified, in the order.

(3A) The power under subsection (3) may be exercised in relation to–

(a) all local authorities,

(b) particular local authorities, or

(c) particular descriptions of local authority.

(4) Subject to subsection 4A, before making an order under subsection (3), the

Secretary of State must consult such representatives of local government and such other persons (if any) as he considers appropriate.

(4A) Subsection (4) does not apply to an order under this section which is made only for the purpose of amending an earlier order under this section–

(a) so as to extend the earlier order, or any provision of the earlier order, to a particular authority or to authorities of a particular description, or

(b) so that the earlier order, or any provision of the earlier order, ceases to apply to a particular authority or to authorities of a particular description.

(5) Before exercising the power under section 2(1), a local authority must have regard to any guidance for the time being issued by the Secretary of State about the exercise of that power.

(6) Before issuing any guidance under subsection (5), the Secretary of State must consult such representatives of local government and such other persons (if any) as he considers appropriate.

(7) In its application to Wales, this section has effect as if for any reference to the Secretary of State there were substituted a reference to the National Assembly for Wales.

(8) In this section 'enactment' includes an enactment comprised in subordinate legislation (within the meaning of the Interpretation Act 1978).

Payments in cases of maladministration, etc

92(1) Where a relevant authority consider–

(a) that action taken by or on behalf of the authority in the exercise of their functions amounts to, or may amount to, maladministration, and

(b) that a person has been, or may have been, adversely affected by that action,

the authority may, if they think appropriate, make a payment to, or provide some other benefit for, that person.

(2) Any function which is conferred on the Greater London Authority under this section is to be exercisable by the Mayor of London and the London Assembly acting jointly on behalf of the Authority.

(3) In this section–

'action' includes failure to act,

'relevant authority' has the same meaning as in Part III of this Act.

HEALTH AND SOCIAL CARE ACT 2001

Part IV SOCIAL CARE

Nursing care

Exclusion of nursing care from community care services

49(1) Nothing in the enactments relating to the provision of community care services shall authorise or require a local authority, in or in connection with the provision of any such services, to–

(a) provide for any person, or

(b) arrange for any person to be provided with,

nursing care by a registered nurse.

(2) In this section 'nursing care by a registered nurse' means any services provided by a registered nurse and involving–

(a) the provision of care, or

(b) the planning, supervision or delegation of the provision of care,

other than any services which, having regard to their nature and the circumstances in which they are provided, do not need to be provided by a registered nurse.

Direct payments

57(1) Regulations may make provision for and in connection with requiring or authorising the responsible authority in the case of a person of a prescribed description who falls within subsection (2) to make, with that person's consent, such payments to him as they may determine in accordance with the regulations in respect of his securing the provision of the service mentioned in paragraph (a) or (b) of that subsection.

(1A) Regulations may make provision for and in connection with requiring or authorising the responsible authority in the case of a person ('P') of a prescribed description–

(a) who falls within subsection (2)(a), and

(b) who falls within subsection (5A) or is reasonably believed by the authority to fall within that subsection,

to make, with the requisite consent, such payments as the authority may determine in accordance with the regulations to a suitable person other than P in respect of the other person's securing the provision for P of the service mentioned in subsection (2)(a).

(1B) In subsection (1A) 'the requisite consent' means–

(a) the consent of the other person; and

(b) where the other person is not a surrogate of P but there is at least one person who is a surrogate of P, the consent also of a surrogate of P.

(1C) For the purposes of subsection (1A), a person (whether or not an individual) is 'suitable' if–

(a) that person is a representative of P;

(b) that person is not a representative of P (or there is no-one who is a representative of P), but–

(i) a surrogate of P, and

(ii) the responsible authority,

consider that person to be a suitable person to receive the payments for the purpose of securing provision for P of the service concerned; or

(c) that person is not a representative of P (or there is no-one who is a representative of P), and there is no-one who is a surrogate of P, but the responsible authority considers that person to be a suitable person to receive the payments for that purpose.

(2) A person falls within this subsection if a local authority ('the responsible authority') have decided–

(a) under section 47 of the 1990 Act (assessment by local authorities of needs for community care services) that his needs call for the provision by them of a particular community care service (within the meaning of section 46 of that Act), or

(b) under section 2(1) of the Carers and Disabled Children Act 2000 (services for carers) to provide him with a particular service under that Act.

(3) Regulations under this section may, in particular, make provision–

(a) specifying circumstances in which the responsible authority are not required or authorised to make any payments under the regulations to a person or in respect of a person, whether those circumstances relate to the person in question or to the particular service mentioned in paragraph (a) or (b) of subsection (2);

(b) for any payments required or authorised by the regulations to be made to a person by the responsible authority ('direct payments') to be made to that person ('the payee') as gross payments or alternatively as net payments;

(c) for the responsible authority to make for the purposes of subsection (4) or (5) such determination as to–

(i) the payee's means in the case of direct payments under subsection (1) or, in the case of direct payments under subsection (1A), the means of the person ('the beneficiary') in respect of whom the payments are required or authorised to be made, and

(ii) the amount (if any) which it would be reasonably practicable for him to pay to the authority by way of reimbursement or contribution,

as may be prescribed;

(d) as to the conditions falling to be complied with by the payee in the case of direct payments under subsection (1), or by the payee or by the beneficiary in the case of direct payments under subsection (1A), which must or may be imposed by the responsible authority in relation to the direct payments (and any conditions which may not be so imposed);

(e) specifying circumstances in which the responsible authority–

(i) may or must terminate the making of direct payments,

(ii) may require repayment (whether by the payee in the case of direct payments under subsection (1), or by the payee or by the beneficiary in the case of direct payments under subsection (1A), or otherwise) of the whole or part of the direct payments;

(f) for any sum falling to be paid or repaid to the responsible authority by virtue of any condition or other requirement imposed in pursuance of the regulations to be recoverable as a debt due to the authority;

(g) displacing functions or obligations of the responsible authority with respect to the provision of the service mentioned in subsection (2)(a) or (b) only to such extent, and subject to such conditions, as may be prescribed;

(h) authorising direct payments to be made to any prescribed person on behalf of the payee;

(j) as to matters to which the responsible authority must, or may, have regard when making a decision for the purposes of a provision of the regulations;

(k) as to steps which the responsible authority must, or may, take before, or after, the authority makes a decision for the purposes of a provision of the regulations;

(l) specifying circumstances in which a person who has fallen within subsection (5A) but no longer does so (whether because of fluctuating capacity, or regaining or gaining of capacity) is to be treated, or may be treated, as falling within subsection (5A) for purposes of this section or for purposes of regulations under this section.

(4)   For the purposes of subsection (3)(b) 'gross payments' means payments–

(a)   which are made at such a rate as the authority estimate to be equivalent to the reasonable cost of securing the provision of the service concerned; but

(b)   which may be made subject to the condition that the payee in the case of direct payments under subsection (1), or the beneficiary in the case of direct payments under subsection (1A), pays to the responsible authority, by way of reimbursement, an amount or amounts determined under the regulations.

(5)   For the purposes of subsection (3)(b) 'net payments' means payments–

(a)   which are made on the basis that the payee will himself in the case of direct payments under subsection (1), or the beneficiary will in the case of direct payments under subsection (1A), pay an amount or amounts determined under the regulations by way of contribution towards the cost of securing the provision of the service concerned; and

(b)   which are accordingly made at such a rate below that mentioned in subsection (4)(a) as reflects any such contribution by the payee or (as the case may be) the beneficiary.

(5A)   A person falls within this subsection if the person lacks capacity, within the meaning of the Mental Capacity Act 2005, to consent to the making of direct payments.

(5B)   In this section 'representative', in relation to a person, means such other person (whether or not an individual) as may be prescribed.

(5C)   In this section 'surrogate', in relation to a person, means–

(a)   a deputy appointed for the person by the Court of Protection under section 16(2)(b) of the Mental Capacity Act 2005, or

(b)   a donee of a lasting power of attorney created by the person,

whose powers, as deputy or donee, consist of or include such powers as may be prescribed.

(6)   Regulations under this section shall provide that, where direct payments are made in respect of a service which, apart from the regulations, would be provided under section 117 of the Mental Health Act 1983 (after-care)–

(a)   the payments shall be made at the rate mentioned in subsection (4)(a); and

(b)   subsection (4)(b) shall not apply.

(7)   Regulations made for the purposes of subsection (3)(a) may provide that direct payments shall not be made in respect of the provision of residential accommodation for any person for a period in excess of a prescribed period.

(7A)   For the purposes of subsection (3)(d), the conditions that are to be taken to be conditions in relation to direct payments include, in particular, conditions in relation to–

(a)   the securing of the provision of the service concerned,

(b)   the provider of the service,

(c)   the person to whom payments are made in respect of the provision of the service, or

(d)   the provision of the service.

(7B)   Section 12 of the Social Care Charges (Wales) Measure 2010 makes further provision for and in connection with the determination of amounts by way of reimbursement as mentioned in subsection (4)(b) or contribution as mentioned in subsection (5)(a) in respect of chargeable services within the meaning of that Measure.

(8)   In this section 'prescribed' means specified in or determined in accordance with regulations under this section.

CARERS (EQUAL OPPORTUNITIES) ACT 2004

Co-operation between authorities

3(1) If a local authority requests an authority mentioned in subsection (5) to assist it in planning the provision of services to persons–

    (a) entitled to an assessment under any of the provisions mentioned in subsection (4), or

    (b) for whom those persons provide, or intend to provide, a substantial amount of care on a regular basis,

the authority mentioned in subsection (5) must give due consideration to the request.

(2) Subsection (3) applies if–

    (a) under a provision mentioned in subsection (4) a local authority is assessing, or has assessed, the ability of a person ('the carer') to provide and to continue to provide care for another person ('the person cared for'), and

    (b) the local authority forms the view that the carer's ability to provide and to continue to provide care for the person cared for might be enhanced by the provision of services (whether for the carer or the person cared for) by an authority mentioned in subsection (5).

(3) If the local authority requests such an authority to provide any such services the authority or person must give due consideration to the request.

(4) The provisions are–

    (a) section 1 of the Carers (Recognition and Services) Act 1995, and

    (b) sections 1 and 6 of the Carers and Disabled Children Act 2000.

(5) The authorities are–

    (a) any other local authority,

    (b) . . .

    (c) any local housing authority, and

    (d) any Special Health Authority, Local Health Board, Primary Care Trust, National Health Service Trust or NHS foundation trust.

(6) Subsections(1) and (3) do not apply in relation to any action which could be the subject of a request by the local authority to the authority mentioned in subsection (5) under section 27 of the Children Act 1989.

(7) In this section–

'local authority' has the same meaning as in section 46 of the National Health Service and Community Care Act 1990,

And, . . .

'local housing authority' has the same meaning as in the Housing Act 1985.

NHS ACT 2006 (EXTRACTS)

PART 1: PROMOTION AND PROVISION OF THE HEALTH SERVICE IN ENGLAND

The Secretary of State and the health service in England

Secretary of State's duty to promote health service

1(1) The Secretary of State must continue the promotion in England of a comprehensive health service designed to secure improvement–
  (a) in the physical and mental health of the people of England, and
  (b) in the prevention, diagnosis and treatment of illness.
(2) The Secretary of State must for that purpose provide or secure the provision of services in accordance with this Act.
(3) The services so provided must be free of charge except in so far as the making and recovery of charges is expressly provided for by or under any enactment, whenever passed.

General power to provide services

Secretary of State's general power

2(1) The Secretary of State may–
  (a) provide such services as he considers appropriate for the purpose of discharging any duty imposed on him by this Act, and
  (b) do anything else which is calculated to facilitate, or is conducive or incidental to, the discharge of such a duty.
(2) Subsection(1) does not affect–
  (a) the Secretary of State's powers apart from this section,
  (b) Chapter 1 of Part 7 (pharmaceutical services).

Secretary of State's duty as to provision of certain services

3(1) The Secretary of State must provide throughout England, to such extent as he considers necessary to meet all reasonable requirements–
  (a) hospital accommodation,
  (b) other accommodation for the purpose of any service provided under this Act,
  (c) medical, dental, ophthalmic, nursing and ambulance services,
  (d) such other services or facilities for the care of pregnant women, women who are breastfeeding and young children as he considers are appropriate as part of the health service,
  (e) such other services or facilities for the prevention of illness, the care of persons suffering from illness and the after-care of persons who have suffered from illness as he considers are appropriate as part of the health service,
  (f) such other services or facilities as are required for the diagnosis and treatment of illness.
(2) For the purposes of the duty in subsection (1), services provided under–
  (a) section 83(2)(primary medical services), section 99(2)(primary dental services) or section 115(4)(primary ophthalmic services),[3] or
  (b) a general medical services contract, a general dental services contract or a general ophthalmic services contract,
  must be regarded as provided by the Secretary of State.
(3) This section does not affect Chapter 1 of Part 7 (pharmaceutical services).

---

5 Not yet in force in relation to primary Ophthalmic Services.

Provision of services otherwise than by the Secretary of State

Secretary of State's arrangements with other bodies

12(1) The Secretary of State may arrange with any person or body to provide, or assist in providing, any service under this Act.

(2) Arrangements may be made under subsection(1) with voluntary organisations.

(3) The Secretary of State may make available any facilities provided by him for any service under this Act–

    (a) to any person or body carrying out any arrangements under subsection (1), or

    (b) to any voluntary organisation eligible for assistance under section 64 or section 65 of the Health Services and Public Health Act 1968 (c. 46).

(4) Where facilities are made available under subsection (3), the Secretary of State may make available the services of any person employed in connection with the facilities by–

    (a) the Secretary of State,

    (b) a Strategic Health Authority,

    (c) a Primary Care Trust,

    (d) a Special Health Authority, or

    (e) a Local Health Board.

(5) Powers under this section may be exercised on such terms as may be agreed, including terms as to the making of payments by or to the Secretary of State.

(6) Goods or materials may be made available either temporarily or permanently.

(7) Any power to supply goods or materials under this section includes–

    (a) a power to purchase and store them, and

    (b) a power to arrange with third parties for the supply of goods or materials by those third parties.

Direct payments for health care

12A (1)The Secretary of State may, for the purpose of securing the provision to a patient of anything to which this subsection applies, make payments, with the patient's consent, to the patient or to a person nominated by the patient.

(2) Subsection (1) applies to–

    (a) anything that the Secretary of State may or must provide under section 2(1) or 3(1);

    (b) anything for which the Secretary of State must arrange under paragraph 8 of Schedule 1;

    (c) vehicles that the Secretary of State may provide under paragraph 9 of that Schedule.

(3) Subsection (1) is subject to any provision made by regulations under section 12B.

(4) If regulations so provide, a Primary Care Trust may, for the purpose of securing the provision for a patient of services that the trust must provide under section 117 of the Mental Health Act 1983 (after-care), make payments, with the patient's consent, to the patient or to a person nominated by the patient.

(5) A payment under subsection (1) or under regulations under subsection (4) is referred to in this Part as a 'direct payment'.

(6) A direct payment may be made only in accordance with a pilot scheme under regulations made by virtue of section 12C.

Regulations about direct payments

12B (1)The Secretary of State may make regulations about direct payments.

(2) The regulations may in particular make provision–

    (a) as to circumstances in which, and descriptions of persons and services in respect of which, direct payments may or must be made;

(b) as to circumstances in which direct payments may or must be made to a person nominated by the patient;

(c) as to the making of direct payments (and, in particular, as to persons to whom payments may or must be made) where the patient lacks capacity to consent to the making of the payments;

(d) as to conditions that the Secretary of State or the Primary Care Trust must comply with before, after or at the time of making a direct payment;

(e) as to conditions that the patient or (if different) the payee may or must be required to comply with before, after, or at the time when a direct payment is made;

(f) as to the amount of any direct payment or how it is to be calculated;

(g) as to circumstances in which the Secretary of State or the Primary Care Trust may or must stop making direct payments;

(h) as to circumstances in which the Secretary of State or the Primary Care Trust may or must require all or part of a direct payment to be repaid, by the payee or otherwise;

(i) as to monitoring of the making of direct payments, of their use by the payee, or of services which they are used to secure;

(j) as to arrangements to be made by the Secretary of State or the Primary Care Trust for providing patients, payees or their representatives with information, advice or other support in connection with direct payments;

(k) for such support to be treated to any prescribed extent as a service in respect of which direct payments may be made.

(3) If the regulations make provision in the case of a person who lacks capacity to consent to direct payments being made, they may apply that provision, or make corresponding provision, with or without modifications, in the case of a person who has lacked that capacity but no longer does so (whether because of fluctuating capacity, or regaining or gaining capacity).

(4) The regulations may provide for a sum which must be repaid to the Secretary of State or the Primary Care Trust by virtue of a condition or other requirement imposed by or under the regulations to be recoverable as a debt due to the Secretary of State or the Primary Care Trust.

(5) The regulations may make provision–

(a) for a service in respect of which a direct payment has been made under section 12A(1) to be regarded, only to such extent and subject to such conditions as may be prescribed, as provided or arranged for by the Secretary of State under an enactment mentioned in section 12A(2);

(b) displacing functions or obligations of a Primary Care Trust with respect to the provision of after-care services under section 117 of the Mental Health Act 1983, only to such extent and subject to such conditions as may be prescribed.

(6) In this section–

(a) 'service' includes anything in respect of which direct payments may be made;

(b) references to a person lacking capacity are references to a person lacking capacity within the Service in England (ss 1–12D)/12C Direct payments pilot schemes

Direct payments pilot schemes

12C (1) Regulations under section 12B may provide for the Secretary of State to have power–

(a) to make pilot schemes in accordance with which direct payments may be made;

(b) to include in a pilot scheme, as respects payments to which the scheme applies, any provision within section 12B(2), subject to any provision made by the regulations.

(2) The regulations may in particular make provision, or provide for the pilot scheme to make provision, as to–
    (a) the geographical area in which a pilot scheme operates;
    (b) the revocation or amendment of a pilot scheme.

(3) A pilot scheme must, in accordance with the regulations, specify the period for which it has effect, subject to the extension of that period by the Secretary of State in accordance with the regulations.

(4) The regulations must make provision as to the review of a pilot scheme, or require the pilot scheme to include such provision.

(5) Provision as to the review of a pilot scheme may in particular include provision–
    (a) for a review to be carried out by an independent person;
    (b) for publication of the findings of a review;
    (c) as to matters to be considered on a review.

(6) Those matters may in particular include any of the following–
    (a) the administration of the scheme;
    (b) the effect of direct payments on the cost or quality of care received by patients;
    (c) the effect of direct payments on the behaviour of patients, carers or persons providing services in respect of which direct payments are made.

(7) After any review of one or more pilot schemes, the Secretary of State may make an order under subsection (8) or (10).

(8) An order under this subsection is an order making provision for either or both of the following–
    (a) repealing section 12A(6) and subsections (1) to (4) of this section;
    (b) amending, repealing, or otherwise modifying any other provision of this Act.

(9) An order may make provision within subsection (8)(b) only if it appears to the Secretary of State to be necessary or expedient for the purpose of facilitating the exercise of the powers conferred by section 12A(1) or by regulations under section 12A(4).

(10) An order under this subsection is an order repealing sections 12A, 12B, 12D and this section.

Arrangements with other bodies relating to direct payments

12D (1) The Secretary of State may arrange with any person or body to give assistance in connection with direct payments.

(2) Arrangements may be made under subsection (1) with voluntary organisations.

(3) Powers under this section may be exercised on such terms as may be agreed, including terms as to the making of payments by the Secretary of State

PART II: HEALTH SERVICE BODIES

Co-operation between NHS bodies

72 It is the duty of NHS bodies to co-operate with each other in exercising their functions.

Co-operation between NHS bodies and local authorities

82 In exercising their respective functions NHS bodies (on the one hand) and local authorities (on the other) must co-operate with one another in order to secure and advance the health and welfare of the people of England and Wales.

Local social service authorities

254(1) Subject to paragraphs (d) and (e) of section 3(1), the services described in Schedule 20 in relation to–

(a) care of mothers,
(b) prevention, care and after-care,
(c) home help and laundry facilities,
are functions exercisable by local social services authorities.

(2)   A local social services authority which provides premises, furniture or equipment for any of the purposes of this Act may permit the use of the premises, furniture or equipment by–
(a) any other local social services authority,
(b) any of the bodies established under this Act, or
(c) a local education authority.

(3)   The permission may be on such terms (including terms with respect to the services of any staff employed by the authority giving permission) as may be agreed.

(4)   A local social services authority may provide (or improve or furnish) residential accommodation for officers–
(a) employed by it for the purposes of any of its functions as a local social services authority, or
(b) employed by a voluntary organisation for the purposes of any services provided under this section and Schedule 20.

(5)   In this section and Schedule 20 'equipment' includes any machinery, apparatus or appliance, whether fixed or not, and any vehicle.

Power of Primary Care Trusts to make payments towards expenditure on community services

256(1) A Primary Care Trust may make payments to–
(a) a local social services authority towards expenditure incurred or to be incurred by it in connection with any social services functions (within the meaning of the Local Authority Social Services Act 1970), other than functions under section 3 of the Disabled Persons (Employment) Act 1958,
(b) a district council, or a Welsh county council or county borough council, towards expenditure incurred or to be incurred by it in connection with its functions under Part 2 of Schedule 9 to the Health and Social Services and Social Security Adjudications Act 1983 (c. 41)(meals and recreation for old people),
(c) a local authority (as defined in section 579(1) of the Education Act 1996), towards expenditure incurred or to be incurred by it in connection with its functions under the Education Acts (within the meaning of that Act), in so far as it performs those functions for the benefit of disabled persons,
(d) a local housing authority within the meaning of the Housing Act 1985, towards expenditure incurred or to be incurred by it in connection with its functions under Part 2 of that Act (provision of housing), or
(e) any of the bodies mentioned in subsection (2), in respect of expenditure incurred or to be incurred by it in connection with the provision of housing accommodation.

(2)   The bodies are–
(za) a private registered provider of social housing,
(a) a registered social landlord within the meaning of the Housing Act 1985 (see section 5(4) and (5) of that Act),
(b) the Homes and Communities Agency,
(ba) the Welsh new towns residuary body,
(c) a new town development corporation,
(d) an urban development corporation established under the Local Government, Planning and Land Act 1980,
(e) the Regulator of Social Housing.

(3) A Primary Care Trust may make payments to a local authority towards expenditure incurred or to be incurred by the authority in connection with the performance of any of the authority's functions which, in the opinion of the Primary Care Trust–
   (a) have an effect on the health of any individuals,
   (b) have an effect on, or are affected by, any NHS functions, or
   (c) are connected with any NHS functions.
(4) 'NHS functions' means functions exercised by an NHS body.
(5) A payment under this section may be made in respect of expenditure of a capital or of a revenue nature or in respect of both kinds of expenditure.
(6) The Secretary of State may by directions prescribe conditions relating to payments under this section or section 257.
(7) The conditions include, in particular, conditions requiring, in such circumstances as may be specified–
   (a) repayment of the whole or part of a payment under this section, or
   (b) in respect of property acquired with a payment under this section, payment of an amount representing the whole or part of an increase in the value of the property which has occurred since its acquisition.
(8) No payment may be made under this section in respect of any expenditure unless the conditions relating to it conform with the conditions prescribed under subsection (6) for payments of that description.
(9) 'A disabled person' is a person who has a physical or mental impairment which has a substantial and long-term adverse effect on his ability to carry out normal day-to-day activities or who has such other disability as may be prescribed.

Payments in respect of voluntary organisations under section 256

257(1) This section applies where the expenditure in respect of which a payment under section 256 is proposed to be made is expenditure in connection with services to be provided by a voluntary organisation.
(2) Where this section applies, the Primary Care Trust may make payments to the voluntary organisation towards the expenditure incurred or to be incurred by the organisation in connection with the provision of those services, instead of or in addition to making payments under section 256(1) or (3).
(3) Where this section applies–
   (a) a body falling within any of paragraphs (a) to (d) of section 256(1) which has received payments under the paragraph, and
   (b) a local authority which has received payments under section 256(3),
   may make out of the sums paid to it payments to the voluntary organisation towards expenditure incurred or to be incurred by the organisation in connection with the provision of those services.
(4) No payment may be made under subsection (2) or (3) except subject to conditions which conform with the conditions prescribed for payments of that description under section 256(6).

SCHEDULE 20: FURTHER PROVISION ABOUT LOCAL SOCIAL SERVICES AUTHORITIES

Care of mothers and young children

1 A local social services authority may, with the Secretary of State's approval, and to such extent as he may direct must, make arrangements for the care of pregnant women and women who are breast feeding (other than for the provision of residential accommodation for them).

Prevention, care and after-care

2(1) A local social services authority may, with the Secretary of State's approval, and to such extent as he may direct must, make the arrangements mentioned in sub-paragraph (2).

(2)   The arrangements are for the purpose of the prevention of illness, for the care of persons suffering from illness and for the after-care of persons who have been suffering from illness and in particular for–

    (a)   the provision, for persons whose care is undertaken with a view to preventing them from becoming ill, persons suffering from illness and persons who have been suffering from illness, of centres or other facilities for training them or keeping them suitably occupied and the equipment and maintenance of such centres,

    (b)   the provision, for the benefit of such persons as are mentioned in paragraph (a), of ancillary or supplemental services, and

    (c)   the exercise of the functions of the local social services authority in respect of persons suffering from mental disorder who are received into guardianship under Part 2 or 3 of the Mental Health Act 1983 (whether the guardianship of the authority or of other persons).

(3)   A local social services authority may not, and is not under a duty to, make under this paragraph arrangements to provide facilities for any of the purposes mentioned in section 15(1) of the Disabled Persons (Employment) Act 1944 .

(4)   No arrangements under this paragraph may provide for the payment of money to persons for whose benefit they are made, except in so far as they fall within sub-paragraph (5).

(5)   Arrangements fall within this sub-paragraph if–

    (a)   they provide for the remuneration of such persons engaged in suitable work in accordance with the arrangements of such amounts as the local social services authority considers appropriate in respect of their occasional personal expenses, and

    (b)   it appears to the authority that no such payment would otherwise be made.

(6)   No arrangements under this paragraph may be given effect to in relation to a person to whom section 115 of the Immigration and Asylum Act 1999 (exclusion from benefits) applies solely–

    (a)   because he is destitute, or

    (b)   because of the physical effects, or anticipated physical effects, of his being destitute.

(7)   Section 95(2) to (7) of that Act apply for the purposes of sub-paragraph (6); and for that purpose a reference to the Secretary of State in section 95(4) or (5) is a reference to a local social services authority.

(8)   The Secretary of State may make regulations as to the conduct of premises in which facilities are provided in pursuance of arrangements made under this paragraph for persons–

    (a)   who are or have been suffering from mental disorder within the meaning of the Mental Health Act 1983, or

    (b)   whose care is undertaken with a view to preventing them from becoming sufferers from mental disorder.

(9)   'Facilities' means facilities for training such persons or keeping them suitably occupied.

(10)   This paragraph does not apply in relation to persons under the age of 18.

(11)   No authority is authorised or may be required under this paragraph to provide residential accommodation for any person.

Home help and laundry facilities

3(1)   Each local social services authority–

    (a)   must provide or arrange for the provision of, on such a scale as is adequate for the needs of its area, of home help for households where such help is required owing to the presence of a person to whom sub-paragraph (2) applies, and

      (b) may provide or arrange for the provision of laundry facilities for house-holds for which home help is being, or can be, provided under paragraph (a).

(2) This sub-paragraph applies to any person who–
      (a) is suffering from illness,
      (b) is pregnant or has recently given birth,
      (c) is aged, or
      (d) handicapped as a result of having suffered from illness or by congenital deformity.

HEALTH AND SOCIAL CARE ACT 2008

Social care

Human Rights Act 1998: provision of certain social care to be public function

145 (1) A person ('P') who provides accommodation, together with nursing or personal care, in a care home for an individual under arrangements made with P under the relevant statutory provisions is to be taken for the purposes of subsection (3)(b) of section 6 of the Human Rights Act 1998 (acts of public authorities) to be exercising a function of a public nature in doing so.

(2) The 'relevant statutory provisions' are–
   (a) in relation to England and Wales, sections 21(1)(a) and 26 of the National Assistance Act 1948 ,
   (b) in relation to Scotland, section 12 or 13A of the Social Work (Scotland) Act 1968, and
   (c) in relation to Northern Ireland, Articles 15 and 36 of the Health and Personal Social Services (Northern Ireland) Order 1972.

(3) In subsection (1) 'care home'–
   (a) in relation to England and Wales, has the same meaning as in the Care Standards Act 2000, and
   (b) in relation to Northern Ireland, means a residential care home as defined by Article 10 of the Health and Personal Social Services (Quality, Improvement and Regulation) (Northern Ireland) Order 2003 or a nursing home as defined by Article 11 of that Order.

(4) In relation to Scotland, the reference in subsection (1) to the provision of accommodation, together with nursing or personal care, in a care home is to be read as a reference to the provision of accommodation, together with nursing, personal care or personal support, as a care home service as defined by section 2(3) of the Regulation of Care (Scotland) Act 2001.

(5) Subsection (1) does not apply to acts (within the meaning of section 6 of the Human Rights Act 1998) taking place before the coming into force of this section.

Regulations and directions

SECRETARY OF STATE'S APPROVALS AND DIRECTIONS UNDER SECTION 21(1) OF THE NATIONAL ASSISTANCE ACT 1948

(LAC(93)10 appendix 1)
The Secretary of State for Health, in exercise of the powers conferred on her by section 21(1) of the National Assistance Act 1948, hereby makes the following Approvals and Directions –

Commencement, interpretation and extent
1(1) These Approvals and Directions shall come into force on 1st April 1993.
(2) In these Approvals and Directions, unless the context otherwise requires, 'the Act' means the National Assistance Act 1948.
(3) The Interpretation Act 1978 applies to these Approvals and Direction as it applies to an Act of Parliament.
(4) These Approvals and Directions shall apply only to England and Wales.

Residential accommodation for persons in need of care and attention
2(1) The Secretary of State hereby –
    (a) approves the making by local authorities of arrangements under section 21(1)(a) of the Act in relation to persons with no settled residence and, to such extent as the authority may consider desirable, in relation to persons who are ordinarily resident in the area of another local authority, with the consent of that other authority; and
    (b) directs local authorities to make arrangements under section 21(1)(a) of the Act in relation to persons who are ordinarily resident in their area and other persons who are in urgent need thereof, to provide residential accommodation for persons aged 18 or over who by reason of age, illness, disability or any other circumstance are in need of care and attention not otherwise available to them.
(2) Without prejudice to the generality of sub-paragraph (1), the Secretary of State hereby directs local authorities to make arrangements under section 21(1)(a) of the Act to provide temporary accommodation for persons who are in urgent need thereof in circumstances where the need for that accommodation could not reasonably have been foreseen.
(3) Without prejudice to the generality of sub-paragraph (1), the Secretary of State hereby directs local authorities to make arrangements under section 21(1)(a) of the Act to provide accommodation –
    (a) in relation to persons who are or have been suffering from mental disorder, or
    (b) for the purposes of the prevention of mental disorder, for persons who are ordinarily resident in their area and for persons with no settled residence who are in the authority's area.

(4)   Without prejudice to the generality of sub-paragraph (1) and subject to section 24(4) of the Act, the Secretary of State hereby approves the making by local authorities of arrangements under section 21(1)(a) of the Act to provide residential accommodation –

    (a)   in relation to persons who are or have been suffering from mental disorder;

    or

    (b)   for the purposes of the prevention of mental disorder, for persons who are ordinarily resident in the area of another local authority but who following discharge from hospital have become resident in the authority's area.

(5)   Without prejudice to the generality of sub-paragraph (1), the Secretary of State hereby approves the making by local authorities of arrangements under section 21(1)(a) of the Act to provide accommodation to meet the needs of persons for –

    (a)   the prevention of illness;

    (b)   the care of those suffering from illness; and

    (c)   the aftercare of those so suffering.

(6)   Without prejudice to the generality of sub-paragraph (1), the Secretary of State hereby approves the making by local authorities of arrangements under section 21(1)(a) of the Act specifically for persons who are alcoholic or drug dependent.

Residential accommodation for expectant and nursing mothers

3 The Secretary of State hereby approves the making by local authorities of arrangements under section 21(1)(aa) of the Act to provide residential accommodation (in particular mother and baby homes) for expectant and nursing mothers (of any age) who are in need of care and attention which is not otherwise available to them.

Arrangements to provide services for residents

4 The Secretary of State hereby directs local authorities to make arrangements in relation to persons provided with accommodation under section 21(1) of the Act for all or any of the following purposes –

    (a)   for the welfare of all persons for whom accommodation is provided;

    (b)   for the supervision of the hygiene of the accommodation so provided;

    (c)   to enable persons for whom accommodation is provided to obtain –

        (i)   medical attention,

        (ii)   nursing attention during illnesses of a kind which are ordinarily nursed at home, and

        (iii)   the benefit of any services provided by the National Health Service of which they may from time to time be in need,

    but nothing in this paragraph shall require a local authority to make any provision authorised or required to be provided under the National Health Service Act 1977;

    (d)   for the provision of board and such other services, amenities and requisites provided in connection with the accommodation, except where in the opinion of the authority managing the premises their provision is unnecessary;

    (e)   to review regularly the provision made under the arrangements and to make such improvements as the authority considers necessary.

Arrangements for the conveyance of residents

5 The Secretary of State hereby approves the making by local authorities of arrangements under section 21(1) of the Act to provide, in such cases as the authority considers appropriate, for the conveyance of persons to and from premises in which accommodation is provided for them under Part III of the Act.

Duties in respect of residents in transferred accommodation

6(1) Where a person is provided with accommodation pursuant to section 21(1) of the Act, and –

    (a) the residential accommodation is local authority accommodation provided pursuant to section 21(4) of the 1948 Act; and

    (b) the local authority transfer the management of the residential accommodation to a voluntary organisation who –

        (i) manages it as a residential care home within the meaning of Part I of the Registered Homes Act 1984, and

        (ii) is registered under that Part or is not required to be so registered by virtue of being an exempt body; and

    (c) the person is accommodated in the residential accommodation immediately before and after the transfer, while that person remains accommodated in that residential accommodation, the local authority shall remain under a duty to make arrangements to provide accommodation for him after any transfer to which paragraph (b) of this subparagraph refers.

(2) For the purposes of paragraph (c) of sub-paragraph (1), a person shall be regarded as accommodated in residential accommodation if –

    (a) he is temporarily absent from such accommodation (including circumstances in which he is in hospital or on holiday);

    (b) before 1st April 1993, that accommodation was provided under paragraph 2(1) of Schedule 8 to the National Health Service Act 1977.

(3) Where immediately before these Approvals and Directions come into force a local authority was under a duty to provide a person with accommodation by virtue of –

    (a) the Secretary of State's former Directions under section 21(1) of the National Assistance Act 1948 contained in Annex 1 of Department of Health Circular LAC(91)12; or

    (b) the Secretary of State's former Directions under paragraph 2 of Schedule 8 to the National Health Service Act 1977 contained in Annex 2 of Department of Health Circular LAC(91)12,

while that person remains accommodated in that residential accommodation, the local authority shall remain under a duty to make arrangements to provide that person with accommodation from the date on which these Directions come into force.

Powers to make arrangements with other local authorities and voluntary organisations, etc

7 For the avoidance of doubt, these Approvals and Directions are without prejudice to any of the powers conferred on local authorities by section 21(4) and section 26(1) of the Act (arrangements with voluntary organisations, etc).

Dated 17/2/1993

SECRETARY OF STATE'S APPROVALS AND DIRECTIONS UNDER SECTION 29(1) OF THE NATIONAL ASSISTANCE ACT 1948

(LAC(93)10 Appendix 2)

The Secretary of State for Health, in exercise of the powers conferred on her by section 29(1) of the National Assistance Act 1948, hereby makes the following Approvals and Directions –

Commencement, interpretation and extent

1(1) These Approvals and Directions shall come into force on 1st April 1993.

(2) In these Approvals and Directions, unless the context otherwise requires, 'the Act' means the National Assistance Act 1948.

(3) The Interpretation Act 1978 applies to these Approvals and Directions as it applies to an Act of Parliament.

(4) These Approvals and Directions shall apply only to England and Wales.

Powers and duties to make welfare arrangements

2(1) The Secretary of State hereby approves the making by local authorities of arrangements under section 29(1) of the Act for all persons to whom that subsection applies and directs local authorities to make arrangements under section 29(1) of the Act in relation to persons who are ordinarily resident in their area for all or any of the following purposes –

   (a) to provide a social work service and such advice and support as may be needed for people in their own homes or elsewhere;

   (b) to provide, whether at centres or elsewhere, facilities for social rehabilitation and adjustment to disability including assistance in overcoming limitations of mobility or communication;

   (c) to provide, whether at centres or elsewhere, facilities for occupational, social, cultural and recreational activities and, where appropriate, the making of payments to persons for work undertaken by them.

(2) The Secretary of State hereby directs local authorities to make the arrangements referred to in section 29(4)(g) of the Act (compiling and maintaining registers) in relation to persons who are ordinarily resident in their area.

(3) The Secretary of State hereby approves the making by local authorities of arrangements under section 29(1) of the Act for all persons to whom that subsection applies for the following purposes –

   (a) to provide holiday homes;

   (b) to provide free or subsidised travel for all or any persons who do not otherwise qualify for travel concessions, but only in respect of travel arrangements for which concessions are available;

   (c) to assist a person in finding accommodation which will enable him to take advantage of any arrangements made under section 29(1) of the Act;

   (d) to contribute to the cost of employing a warden on welfare functions in warden assisted housing schemes;

   (e) to provide warden services for occupiers of private housing.

(4) Save as is otherwise provided for under this paragraph, the Secretary of State hereby approves the making by local authorities of all or any of the arrangements referred to in section 29(4) of the Act (welfare arrangements, etc.) for all persons to whom section 29(1) applies.

Welfare arrangements with another local authority

3 The Secretary of State hereby approves the making by local authorities of arrangements under section 29(1) of the Act, where appropriate, with another local authority for the provision of any of the services referred to in these Approvals and Directions.

Welfare arrangements with voluntary organisations and otherwise

4 For the avoidance of doubt, these Approvals and Directions are without prejudice to the powers conferred on local authorities by section 30(1) of the Act (voluntary organisations for disabled persons' welfare).

Dated 17/3/1993

SECRETARY OF STATE'S APPROVALS AND DIRECTIONS UNDER PARAGRAPHS 1 AND 2 OF SCHEDULE 8 TO THE NATIONAL HEALTH SERVICE ACT 1977

(LAC(93)10 Appendix 3)

The Secretary of State for Health, in exercise of the powers conferred on her by paragraphs 1(1) and 2(1) of Schedule 8 to the National Health Service Act 1977, hereby makes the following Approvals and Directions –

Commencement, interpretation and extent

1(1) These Approvals and Directions shall come into force on 1st April 1993.

(2) In these Approvals and Directions, unless the context otherwise requires, 'the Act' means the National Health Service Act 1977.

(3) The Interpretation Act 1978 applies to these Approvals and Directions as it applies to an Act of Parliament.

(4) For the avoidance of doubt, these Approvals and Directions apply only to England and Wales.

Services for expectant and nursing mothers

2 The Secretary of state hereby approves the making of arrangements under paragraph 1(1) of Schedule 8 to the Act for the care of expectant and nursing mothers (of any age) other than the provision of residential accommodation for them (services for the purpose of the prevention of illness etc.).

3(1) The Secretary of State hereby approves the making by local authorities of arrangements under paragraph 2(1) of Schedule 8 to the Act for the purpose of the prevention of illness, and the care of persons suffering from illness and for the aftercare of persons who have been so suffering and in particular for –

    (a) the provision, for persons whose care is undertaken with a view to preventing them becoming ill, persons suffering from illness and persons who have been so suffering, of centres or other facilities for training them or keeping them suitably occupied and the equipment and maintenance of such centres;

    (b) the provision, for the benefit of such persons as are mentioned in paragraph (a) above, of ancillary or supplemental services.

(2) The Secretary of State hereby directs local authorities to make arrangements under paragraph 2(1) of Schedule 8 to the Act for the purposes of the prevention of mental disorder, or in relation to persons who are or who have been suffering from mental disorder –

    (a) for the provision of centres (including training centres and day centres) or other facilities (including domiciliary facilities), whether in premises managed by the local authority or otherwise, for training or occupation of such persons;

    (b) for the appointment of sufficient social workers in their area to act as approved social workers for the purposes of the Mental Health Act 1983;

    (c) for the exercise of the functions of the authority in respect of persons suffering from mental disorder who are received into guardianship under Part II or III of the Mental Health Act 1983 (whether the guardianship of the local social services authority or of other persons);

    (d) for the provision of social work and related services to help in the identification, diagnosis, assessment and social treatment of mental disorder and to provide social work support and other domiciliary and care services to people living in their homes and elsewhere.

(3) Without prejudice to the generality of sub-paragraph (1), the Secretary of State hereby approves the making by local authorities of arrangements under paragraph 2(1) of Schedule 8 to the Act for the provision of –

(a) meals to be served at the centres or other facilities referred to in subparagraphs (1)(a) and (2)(a) above and meals-on-wheels for house-bound people not provided for –

    (i) under section 45(1) of the Health Services and Public Health Act 1968(a), or

    (ii) by a district council under paragraph 1 of Part II of Schedule 9 to the Health and Social Services and Social Security Adjudications Act 1983;

(b) remuneration for persons engaged in suitable work at the centres or other facilities referred to in sub-paragraphs (1)(a) and (2)(a) above, subject to paragraph 2(2)(a) of Schedule 8 to the Act;

(c) social services (including advice and support) for the purposes of preventing the impairment of physical or mental health of adults in families where such impairment is likely, and for the purposes of preventing the break-up of such families, or for assisting in their rehabilitation;

(d) night-sitter services;

(e) recuperative holidays;

(f) facilities for social and recreational activities;

(g) services specifically for persons who are alcoholic or drug-dependent.

Services made available by another local authority etc.

4 For the purposes of any arrangements made under these Approvals and Directions, the Secretary of State hereby approves the use by local authorities of services or facilities made available by another authority, voluntary body or person on such conditions as may be agreed, but in making such arrangements, a local authority shall have regard to the importance of services being provided as near to a person's home as is practicable.

Dated 17/3/1993

Signed on behalf of the Secretary of State for Health

NATIONAL ASSISTANCE ACT 1948 (CHOICE OF ACCOMMODATION) DIRECTIONS 1992

The Secretary of State in exercise of the powers conferred by section 7A of the Local Authority Social Services Act 1970 and of all other powers enabling her in that behalf hereby makes the following Directions –

Citation, commencement and extent

1(1) These Directions may be cited as the National Assistance Act 1948 (Choice of Accommodation) Directions 1992 and shall come into force on 1st April 1993.

(2) These Directions extend only to England.

Local authorities to provide preferred accommodation

2 Where a local authority have assessed a person under section 47 of the National Health Service and Community Care Act 1990 (assessment) and have decided that accommodation should be provided pursuant to section 21 of the National Assistance Act 1948 (provision of residential accommodation) the local authority shall, subject to paragraph 3 of these Directions, make arrangements for accommodation pursuant to section 21 for that person at the place of his choice within England and Wales (in these Directions called 'preferred accommodation') if he has indicated that he wishes to be accommodated in preferred accommodation.

3 Subject to paragraph 4 of these Directions the local authority shall only be required to make or continue to make arrangements for a person to be accommodated in his preferred accommodation if –

(a) the preferred accommodation appears to the authority to be suitable in relation to his needs as assessed by them;

(b) the cost of making arrangements for him at his preferred accommodation would not require the authority to pay more than they would usually expect to pay having regard to his assessed needs;

(c) the preferred accommodation is available;

(d) the persons in charge of the preferred accommodation provide it subject to the authority's usual terms and conditions, having regard to the nature of the accommodation, for providing accommodation for such a person under Part III of the National Assistance Act 1948.

GUIDANCE ON NATIONAL ASSISTANCE ACT 1948 (CHOICE OF ACCOMMODATION) DIRECTIONS 1992

NATIONAL ASSISTANCE (RESIDENTIAL ACCOMMODATION) (ADDITIONAL PAYMENTS AND ASSESSMENT OF RESOURCES) (AMENDMENT) (ENGLAND) REGULATIONS 2001

(LAC (2004) 20)

1 Summary

1.1 If, after an assessment of need, made in accordance with the General Principles of Assessment in LAC(2002)13 *Fair Access to Care Services*[1] and, where applicable, in accordance with a specific assessment framework[2] and discussion with the individual and their carers, a council decides to provide residential accommodation under section 21 of the National Assistance Act 1948 either permanently or temporarily (intermediate care or short term break or any interim care arrangement), it will make a placement on behalf of the individual in suitable accommodation. Nearly all placements under section 21 of the National Assistance Act 1948 are made in registered care homes. However, some adults are placed under section 21 of the National Assistance Act 1948 in unregistered settings where they need neither nursing care or personal care. While the detail of this guidance applies to registered care homes, the principles apply to adults placed in unregistered settings.

1. When the term 'residential care' is used in this guidance, it covers placements made on both a long-term and a temporary (which includes short-term care) basis to care homes, whether they provide nursing care or not.

1.3 If the individual concerned expresses a preference for particular accommodation ('preferred accommodation') within England and Wales, the council must arrange for care in that accommodation, provided:

- The accommodation is suitable in relation to the individual's assessed needs (see paragraphs 2.5.1 to 2.5.3)
- To do so would not cost the council more than what it would usually expect to pay for accommodation for someone with the individual's assessed needs see paragraphs 2.5.4 to 2.5.8). This is referred to throughout this guidance as the usual cost.

---

1 www.dh.gov.uk/en/Publicationsandstatistics/Publications/PublicationsPolicyAndGuidance/DH_4009653

2 Such as in HSC(2002)001 and LAC(2002)1 Single Assessment Process for Older People at www.dh.gov.uk/en/Publicationsandstatistics/Lettersandcirculars/LocalAuthorityCirculars/AllLocalAuthority/DH_4003997

- The accommodation is available (see paragraphs 2.5.9 and 2.5.15)
- The provider of the accommodation is willing to provide accommodation subject to the council's usual terms and conditions for such accommodation (see paragraphs 2.5.16 to 2.5.17)

1.4 If an individual requests it, the council must also arrange for care in accommodation more expensive than it would usually fund provided a third party or, in certain circumstances, the resident, is willing and able to pay the difference between the cost the council would usually expect to pay and the actual cost of the accommodation (to 'top up'). These are the only circumstances where either a third party or the resident may be asked to top up (see paragraph 3).

2   Preferred accommodation

2.1 As with all aspects of service provision, there should be a general presumption in favour of individuals being able to exercise reasonable choice over the service they receive. The limitations on councils' obligation to provide preferred accommodation set out in the Directions and the Regulations are not intended to deny individuals reasonable freedom of choice but to ensure that councils are able to fulfil their obligations for the quality of service provided and for value for money. The terms of the Directions and the Regulations are explained more fully below. Where, for any reason, a council decides not to arrange a place for someone in their preferred accommodation it must have a clear and reasonable justification for that decision which relates to the criteria of the Directions and is not in breach of the Regulations.

2.2 Arrangements under section 26(3A) of the National Assistance Act 1948 require the agreement of all parties. Individuals should not be refused their preferred accommodation without a full explanation from councils, in writing, of their reasons for doing so.

2.3 The location of the preferred accommodation need not be limited by the boundaries of the funding council. Councils are obliged to cater for placements falling within the Directions or the Regulations in any permitted care home within England or Wales. Any extension to this beyond England and Wales is subject to any future regulations governing cross-border placements (but see LAC(93)18 in respect of placements involving Scotland and the Department of Health/Welsh Assembly protocol on NHS funded nursing care for cross border placements).[3]

2.4 Funding councils may refer to their own usual costs when making placements in another council's area. However, because costs vary from area to area, if in order to meet a resident's assessed need it is necessary to place an individual in another area at a higher rate than the funding council's usual costs, the placing council should meet the additional cost itself.

2.5 The Directions state that a council must arrange for care in an individual's preferred accommodation subject to four considerations:

(a) Suitability of accommodation

2.5.1 Suitability will depend on the council's assessment of individual need. Each case must be considered on its merits.

2.5.2 Accommodation provided in a care home will not necessarily be suitable for the individual's needs simply because it satisfies registration standards. On the other hand, accommodation will not necessarily be unsuitable simply because it fails to conform to the council's preferred model of provision, or to meet to the letter a standard service specification laid down by the council.

2.5.3 The Directions and Regulations do not affect Section 26(1A) of the National Assistance Act 1948 as amended by the Care Standards Act

3 www.dh.gov.uk/en/Publicationsandstatistics/Lettersandcirculars/LocalAuthorityCirculars/AllLocalAuthority/DH_4004219

2000. Arrangements should not be made for the provision of accommodation together with nursing or personal care in a care home unless the accommodation to be provided is managed by an organisation or person who is registered under Part II of the Care Standards Act 2000. Similarly, the Directions and the Regulations do not require a council to contract with any accommodation where for any other reason it is prevented by law from doing so.

(b) Cost

2.5.4 One of the conditions associated with the provision of preferred accommodation is that such accommodation should not require the council to pay more than they would usually expect to pay, having regard to assessed needs (the 'usual cost'). This cost should be set by councils at the start of a financial or other planning period, or in response to significant changes in the cost of providing care, to be sufficient to meet the assessed care needs of supported residents in residential accommodation. A council should set more than one usual cost where the cost of providing residential accommodation to specific groups is different. In setting and reviewing their usual costs, councils should have due regard to the actual costs of providing care and other local factors. Councils should also have due regard to Best Value requirements under the Local Government Act 1999.

2.5.5 Individual residents should not be asked to pay more towards their accommodation because of market inadequacies or commissioning failures. Where an individual has not expressed a preference for more expensive accommodation, but there are not, for whatever reason, sufficient places available at a given time at the council's usual costs to meet the assessed care needs of supported residents, the council should make a placement in more expensive accommodation. In these circumstances, neither the resident nor a third party should be asked to contribute more than the resident would normally be expected to contribute and councils should make up the cost difference between the resident's assessed contribution and the accommodation's fees. Only when an individual has expressed a preference for more expensive accommodation than a council would usually expect to pay, can a third party or the resident be asked for a top up (see paragraph 3.1). Costs of accommodation should be compared on the basis of gross costs before income from charging. Given the different amounts that councils will recover from individuals by ways of charges, it would not be appropriate for a council to determine a usual net cost that it would expect to pay.

2.5.6 For the cost of placements in other councils' areas see paragraph 2.3.

2.5.7 Councils should not set arbitrary ceilings on the amount they expect to pay for an individual's residential care. Residents and third parties should not routinely be required to make up the difference between what the council will pay and the actual fees of a home. Councils have a statutory duty to provide residents with the level of service they could expect if the possibility of resident and third party contributions did not exist

2.5.8 Costs can vary according to the type of care provided. For example, the cost a council might usually expect to pay for short-term care might be different from its usual cost for long-term care. There are also a number of situations where there may be higher costs incurred in providing residential care, be it long or short-term. Examples include specialist care for specific user groups with high levels of need or where necessary to prepare special diets and provide additional facilities for medical or cultural reasons. Councils should be prepared to meet these higher costs in order to ensure an individual's needs are appropriately met.

(c) Availability

2.5.9   Generally, good commissioning[4] by councils should ensure there is sufficient capacity so individuals should not have to wait for their assessed (that is, eligible) needs to be met. However, waiting is occasionally inevitable, particularly when individuals have expressed a preference towards a particular care home where there are no current vacancies. Where individuals may need to wait at home or elsewhere, their access to the most appropriate (and possibly, preferred) service should be based solely on their assessed need, and councils should ensure that in the interim adequate alternative services are provided. Waiting for the preferred care home should not mean that the person's care needs are not met in the interim or that they wait in a setting unsuitable for their assessed needs, and this includes an acute hospital bed, until the most suitable or preferred accommodation becomes available. In view of the Community Care (Delayed Discharges etc.) Act 2003,[5] councils should have contingency arrangements in place, that address the likelihood that an individual's preferred accommodation will not always be readily available. These arrangements should meet the needs of the individual and sustain or improve their level of independence. For some, the appropriate interim arrangement could be an enhanced care package at home.

2.5.10   Councils should give individuals an indication of the likely duration of the interim arrangement. Councils should place the individual on the waiting list of the preferred accommodation and aim to move them into that accommodation as soon as possible. Information about how the waiting list is handled should be clear and the individual should be kept informed of progress. If the duration of the interim arrangement exceeds a reasonable time period, eg 12 weeks, the individual should be reassessed to ensure that the interim and preferred accommodation, are still able to meet the individual's assessed needs and to prevent any unnecessary moves between care homes that are unable to meet the individual's assessed needs. As part of this reassessment, individuals should also be asked if their preference is now to remain in the interim accommodation or whether they wish to continue waiting for their original preferred accommodation (see paragraph 2.5.14 for guidance on individuals who choose to remain in the interim accommodation).

2.5.11   Councils should ensure that while waiting in temporary residential accommodation, if an individual has to contribute towards their care costs it is in accordance with the National Assistance (Assessment of Resources) Regulations 1992. Individuals who are waiting in these circumstances should not be asked to pay more than their assessed financial contribution to meet the costs of these residential care services which have been arranged by the council to temporarily meet their assessed needs and councils should make up the cost difference between the resident's assessed contribution and the accommodation's fees. Only when an individual has expressed a preference for more expensive accommodation than a council would usually expect to pay, can a third party or the resident be asked for a top up (see paragraph 3.1).

4   In accordance with the principles set out in Building Capacity and Partnership in Care – An agreement between the statutory and independent social care, health care and housing sectors at www.dh.gov.uk/PublicationsAndStatistics/Publications/PublicationsPolicyAndGuidance/PublicationsPolicyAndGuidanceArticle/fs/en?CONTENT_ID=4006241&chk=BPcEi1
5   www.legislation.gov.uk/ukpga/2003/5/contents

2.5.12 Councils should take all reasonable steps to gain an individual's agreement to an interim care home or care package. Councils should make reasonable efforts to take account of the individual's desires and preferences. In doing this, councils should ascertain all relevant facts and take into account all the circumstances relevant to the person, and ensure that the individual (and their family or carers) understands the consequences of failing to come to an agreement. Where patients have been assessed as no longer requiring NHS continuing inpatient care, they do not have the right to occupy indefinitely an NHS bed. If an individual continues to unreasonably refuse the interim care home or care package, the council is entitled to consider that it has fulfilled its statutory duty to assess and offer services, and may then inform the individual, in writing, they will need to make their own arrangements. This position also applies to the unreasonable refusal of a permanent care home, not just the interim care home or care package. If at a later date further contact is made with social services regarding the individual, the council should re-open the care planning process, if it is satisfied that the individual's needs remain such to justify the provision of services and there is no longer reason to think that the individual will persist in refusing such services unreasonably. Councils should refer to Annex A of LAC(2003)21 – The Community Care (Delayed Discharges etc) Act 2003 Guidance for Implementation.[6] Councils may wish to take their own legal advice in such circumstances.

2.5.13 In all but a very small number of cases where an individual is being placed under Part II of the Mental Health Act 1983, individuals have the right to refuse to enter a care home. This includes patients who are awaiting discharge from hospital. In such cases the social services department should work with the person, his or her family and carers, and NHS partners, (and potentially housing partners), to explore alternative options, including a package of health and social care in the person's own home or suitable alternative accommodation.

2.5.14 In some cases, individuals who move into a care home for an interim period may choose to remain there, even if a place in their original preferred accommodation becomes available. If the care home is able to accept the individual on a long-term basis, they should be taken off the waiting list of their original preferred accommodation. If the cost of the interim care home is higher than the usual cost the council would expect to pay for their assessed need, upon making the choice to remain in that home, a third party or the resident could be approached for the total difference between the two rates. This should be clearly explained to individuals before they enter the home. See paragraph 3.2 for fuller details.

2.5.15 The Directions only apply to individuals whose care is being arranged by a council under Part 3 of the National Assistance Act 1948. For example, where hospital patients need to move to a different type of care, and social services are not involved, this is a matter for the NHS and the individual patient and the Directions do not apply. For good practice on handling these situations, see the Hospital Discharge Workbook.[7]

(d) Terms and conditions

2.5.16 In order to ensure that they are able to exercise proper control over the use of their funds, councils need to be able to impose certain con-

6 www.dh.gov.uk/en/Publicationsandstatistics/Lettersandcirculars/LocalAuthorityCirculars/AllLocalAuthority/DH_4065064

7 www.publications.doh.gov.uk/hospitaldischarge/index.htm

tractual conditions, for example, in relation to payment regimes, review, access, monitoring, audit, record keeping, information sharing, insurance, sub-contracting, etc.

2.5.17 The contractual conditions required of preferred accommodation should be broadly the same as those councils would impose on any other similar operation. Stricter conditions should never be used as a way of avoiding or deterring a placement. As with suitability, account should be taken of the nature and location of the accommodation. There may be occasions where it would be unreasonable for a council not to adapt its standard conditions and others where it would be unreasonable to expect it to do so. For example, councils should take into account the fact that care homes in other areas, or those that take residents from many areas, may have geared themselves to the normal requirements of other councils. Councils should be flexible in such circumstances and avoid adding to the administrative burden of care homes.

3   More expensive accommodation

3.1 The guidance set out in paragraphs 3.2 to 3.5.11, applies only where a resident explicitly chooses to enter accommodation other than that which the council offers them, and where that preferred accommodation is more expensive than the council would usually expect to pay.

3.2 In certain circumstances, councils can make placements in more expensive accommodation than they would usually expect to pay for, provided a resident or a third party is able and willing to make up the difference (to 'top up'). Residents that are subject to the 12 week property disregard or have agreed a deferred payments agreement with the council may make top-ups from specified resources on their own behalf. These are the only situations where the resident may top up. The most common arrangement is that a third party is providing the top-up. A third party in this case might be a relative, a friend, or any other source. For liable relatives see paragraph 3.5.10.

3.3 When setting its usual cost(s) a council should be able to demonstrate that this cost is sufficient to allow it to meet assessed care needs and to provide residents with the level of care services that they could reasonably expect to receive if the possibility of resident and third party contributions did not exist.

3.4 Councils should not seek resident or third party contributions in cases where the council itself decides to offer someone a place in more expensive accommodation in order to meet assessed needs, or for other reasons. Where there are no placements at the council's usual rate, councils should not leave individuals to make their own arrangements having determined that they need to enter residential accommodation and do not have care and attention otherwise available to them. In these instances, councils should make suitable alternative arrangements and seek no contribution from the individual other than their contribution as assessed under the National Assistance (Assessment of Resources) Regulations 1992. Councils must never encourage or otherwise imply that care home providers can or should seek further contributions from individuals in order to meet assessed needs.

3.5 This paragraph deals with considerations that apply where either residents or third parties are making further contributions to costs over and above the resident's assessed contribution under the National Assistance (Assessment of Resources) Regulations 1992.

(a) Responsibility for costs of accommodation

3.5.1 When making arrangements for residential care for an individual under the National Assistance Act 1948, a council is responsible for the full cost of that accommodation. Therefore, where a council places someone in more expensive accommodation, it must contract to pay the accommodation's fees in full. The resident's or the third party's contribution will be treated as part of the resident's income for charging purposes and the council will be able to recover it in that way. However, under a deferred payments agreement, where the resident is topping up against the value of their home, their top-up contribution is added to their deferred contribution.

3.5.2 Councils will be aware that under section 26(3A) of the National Assistance Act 1948 (as inserted by the NHS and Community Care Act 1990), it is open to them to agree with both the resident and the person in charge of their accommodation that, instead of paying a contribution to the council, the resident may pay the same amount direct to the accommodation, with the council paying the difference. In such a case, the third party would also pay the accommodation direct on behalf of the resident. However, it should be noted that even where there is such an agreement for the resident to make payments direct to the accommodation, the council continues to be liable to pay the full costs of the accommodation should either the resident or relative fail to pay the required amount.

3.5.3 Where top-ups are required from a resident or third party, the resident will therefore need to demonstrate that either they or the third party is able and willing to pay the difference between the council's usual rate and the accommodation's actual fees.

3.5.4 In order to safeguard both residents and councils from entering into top-up arrangements that are likely to fail, the resident or the third party must reasonably be expected to be able to continue to make top-up payments for the duration of the arrangements. Councils should, therefore, assure themselves that residents or third parties will have the resources to continue to make the required top-up payments. Councils should seek similar assurances when residents top-up against the value of their home when the home is subject to a deferred payments agreement. When the home is eventually sold, it should be possible for the resident or their estate to pay back the deferred contribution including the resident top-ups.

(b) The amount of the resident or third party top-up

3.5.5 The amount of resident or third party top-up payments should be the difference between the actual fee for the accommodation and the amount that otherwise the council would usually have expected to pay for someone with the individual's assessed needs. In determining the precise amounts in individual cases, the council will take account of the guidance give in paragraphs 2.5.4 to 2.5.8 above.

3.5.6 The amount of the resident or third party top-up should be calculated on gross costs; that is, the difference between the preferred accommodation's fees and the fees that a council would usually expect to pay. The fact that a resident might not have been able to meet the full cost of the accommodation that the council would otherwise have arranged does not affect their ability to benefit from the additional top-up payments.

(c) Price increases

3.5.7 Arrangements between the council, resident and third party will need to be reviewed from time to time to take account of changes to accommodation fees. There will also be changes to the council's usual cost, which should be reasonable and set in accordance with paragraphs 2.5.4 to 2.5.8. However, fees and usual costs may not change at the same rate, and residents and third parties should be told that there cannot be a guarantee that any increases in the accommodation's fees will automatically be shared evenly between the council and/or the resident or third party, should the particular accommodation's fees rise more quickly than the costs the council would usually expect to pay for similar individuals. A council may find it useful to agree with the resident (or third party) that the resident's (or third party's) contribution will be reviewed on a regular basis on the understanding that clear explanations for proposed increases are given. It is also important that individuals know when, and in what circumstances, the fees for their accommodation will be reviewed.

(d) Responsibilities of residents and third parties

3.5.8 Councils should make clear to residents and third parties, in writing, the basis on which arrangements are to be made when they seek to exercise their right to more expensive preferred accommodation. It should be clear from the outset to the resident, third party and person providing the accommodation that:

- failure to keep up top-up payments may result in the resident having to move to other accommodation unless, after an assessment of need, it is shown that assessed needs can only be met in the current accommodation. In these circumstances, councils should make up the cost difference between the resident's assessed contribution and the accommodation's fees. Where a resident's top-ups are being made against the value of property subject to a deferred payments agreement, a council will have assured itself from the outset that top-up payments are viable and recoverable when the home is sold;

- an increase in the resident's income will not necessarily lessen the need for a top-up contribution, since the resident's own income will be subject to means testing by the council in the normal way;

- a rise in the accommodation's fees will not automatically be shared equally between council, resident (if making a top-up), and third party.

(e) Suitability and Conditions

3.5.9 With reference to paragraphs 2.5.1 to 2.5.3 and 2.5.16 to 2.5.17 above, the criteria of suitability and willingness to provide on the basis of normal conditions should be applied in the same way as for other preferred accommodation. An exception to this is that it would be reasonable to expect providers entering this kind of arrangement to agree to do so on the basis that the council has the right, subject to notice, to terminate the contract should the resident's or third party's top-up payments cease to be adequate.

(f) Liable relatives

3.5.10 Liable relatives who are making maintenance contributions cannot act as third parties for the care of the relative to whose care they are already contributing under section 42 of the National Assistance Act 1948. This limitation does not apply to top-up arrangements agreed prior to 1 October 2001 with liable relatives. Neither does the limitation apply to liable relatives who are not making contributions under section 42 of the 1948 Act.

4   Individuals already resident in residential care

4.1 Individuals already placed by a council in residential accommodation, and those already in residential accommodation as self-funders but who, because of diminishing resources, are on the verge of needing council support, have the same rights under these Directions as those who have yet to be placed by the council. Any such individual who wishes to move to different or more expensive accommodation may seek to do so on the same basis as anyone about to enter residential care for the first time. Should a self-funder who is resident in a care home that is more expensive than a council would usually expect to pay later become the responsibility of the council due to diminishing funds, this may result in the resident having to move to other accommodation, unless, after an assessment of need, it is shown that assessed needs can only be met in the current accommodation. In these circumstances, neither the resident nor a third party should be asked for a top-up payment and councils should make up the cost difference between the resident's assessed contribution and the accommodation's fees.

5   Individuals who are unable to make their own choices

5.1   There will be cases in which prospective residents lack capacity to express a preference for themselves. It would be reasonable to expect councils to act on the preferences expressed by their advocate, carer or legal guardian in the same way that they would on the resident's own wishes, unless that would in the council's opinion be against the best interests of the resident.

6   Effect on contracting

6.1   Any block contract or other form of contract that a council may have with a provider should not serve to limit choice. An individual should not be limited to care homes that hold such contracts with the funding council, or cares homes that are run by councils. It would not be reasonable for a council to use as a test for the suitability of accommodation, its presence or absence from a previously compiled list of preferred suppliers. The Directions and Regulations do not, however, prevent an authority having a list of preferred providers with which it will contract where a potential resident expresses no preference for particular accommodation, nor from recommending such providers to prospective residents.

7   Information

7.1   Individuals, and/or those who represent them, need information on the options open to them if they are to be able to exercise genuine choice. They should be given fair and balanced information with which to make the best choice of accommodation for them. Councils should explain to individuals their rights under the Directions and the Regulations. Councils should also consider providing material in a range of forms including written leaflets in local community languages, Braille, on audio tape and in accessible language e.g. easy words, short sentences, large print and pictures (for those with learning disabilities). Councils should supply copies of the Directions and this guidance if requested in appropriate forms. They should work with local Primary Care Trusts (PCTs) and local hospitals to provide clear information to hospital patients as early as possible in their stay about what the council will be able to provide should they require short or long-term residential care at the end of their hospital stay. Individuals should be told explicitly that:

- they are free to choose any accommodation that is likely to meet their needs subject to the constraints set out in the Directions and the Regulations.
- they may allow the council to make a placement decision on their behalf; and
- they may choose from a preferred list (if the authority operates such a system).

7.2   Councils should ensure that individuals are informed that they have a choice of accommodation irrespective of whether they express a preference for particular accommodation. Individuals should also be told what will happen if the preferred accommodation is not available. Councils may also wish to cover the matters described in paragraph 2.5.12. Wherever possible, the individual should be encouraged to have a relative, carer or advocate present during the conversation. A written record of the conversation should be kept, in particular, recording any decisions taken or preferences expressed by the individual. This record should be shared with the individual.

8   Complaints

8.1   Complaints about the application of the Directions and the Regulations and decisions taken in individual cases will fall within the scope of councils' statutory complaints procedure. As in all aspects of their activity, councils should ensure that prospective residents are aware of and understand the existence of the complaints procedure and their rights under it.

Department of Health
14 October 2004

THE COMMUNITY CARE ASSESSMENT DIRECTIONS 2004

The Secretary of State for Health, in exercise of the powers conferred on him by section 47(4) of the National Health Service and Community Care Act 1990 hereby makes the following Directions:

Commencement, application and interpretation

1(1)   These Directions come into force on 1 September 2004 and apply to every local authority in England.

(2)   In these Directions—
'the Act' means the National Health Service and Community Care Act 1990;
'community care services' has the same meaning as in section 46(3) of the Act;
'local authority' has the same meaning as in section 46(3) of the Act.

Manner and form of assessment of needs for community care services

2(1)   In assessing the needs of a person under section 47(1) of the Act a local authority must comply with paragraphs (2) to (4).

(2)   The local authority must consult the person, consider whether the person has any carers and, where they think it appropriate, consult those carers.

(3)   The local authority must take all reasonable steps to reach agreement with the person and, where they think it appropriate, any carers of that person, on the community care services which they are considering providing to him to meet his needs.

(4)   The local authority must provide information to the person and, where they think it appropriate, any carers of that person, about the amount of the payment (if any) which the person will be liable to make in respect of the community care services which they are considering providing to him.

Signed by authority of the Secretary of State
26 August 2004
Craig Muir, Member of the Senior Civil Service
Department of Health

APPENDIX C

Precedents

PRECEDENT 1: COMMUNITY CARE ASSESSMENT REQUEST

To: Director of Social Services / Health Authority / NHS Trust etc
[*address*]

From: *Applicant's name*
[*address*]

Date:

Dear Director of Social Services

Community Care Assessment: Mr Albert Smith [*address*]

I am the [*solicitor/carer/agent/advocate*] for the above named who has asked that I assist him in obtaining an assessment of his needs for community care services under National Health Service and Community Care Act 1990 s47.

Mr Smith is [*insert*] years of age being born on [*insert if known*] and is a [*disabled/elderly/ill*] person, in that he

[*here detail as precisely as possible the impairments which have resulted in the applicant needing community care services*].
The help that Mr Smith currently envisages as being necessary, is

[*here detail if possible the services which are required*].

I understand that your care manager will wish to contact Mr Smith in order to investigate this complaint. He suggests that this be done by [*here give a telephone contact number and the time/days the client or carer etc are normally available or some other convenient way that contact can be made*]

Yours sincerely

PRECEDENT 2: ACCESS TO INFORMATION LETTER

To: Director of Social Services / PCT/ LHB/ NHS Trust etc
[*address*]

From: Applicant's name
[*address*]

Date:
Reference:

Access to personal information: Data Protection Act 1998 s7

I formally request that you give me access to the personal information held by your authority relating to my personal circumstances, by copying the relevant information to [*me*] [*my agent, namely . . .*] at [*insert address*].

The information I require to be disclosed is all personal information which your authority holds which relates to myself. [*If possible describe as precisely as possible the information that is sought, including for instance where the information is likely to be located, the nature of the information and the dates between which it was collected*].

I understand that I am entitled to receive this information within 40 days.

If you need further information from me, or a fee,[1] please let me know as soon as possible. If you do not normally handle these requests for your organisation, please pass this letter to your Data Protection Officer or another appropriate officer.

Please confirm receipt of this request.

Signed:

---

1 The 40-day period runs from the date of receipt of the request and any necessary fee. Accordingly, provision should be expedited if the fee is actually enclosed.

PRECEDENT 3: FORMAL COMPLAINT LETTER

To: Director of Social Services
[*address*]

From: Applicant's name
[*address*]

Date:

Dear Director of Adult Social Services

Formal complaint

I ask that you treat this letter as a formal complaint concerning the discharge by your authority of its functions in respect of [*myself*] [*the person for whom I care ~ Mr/Mrs/Ms etc. . .*]. I require the complaint to be investigated at the earliest opportunity

My complaint is:
[*here set out as precisely as possible*

(a) what it is that is being complained about
(b) the names of the key social workers who the complaints investigator will need to speak to;
(c) the dates of the relevant acts / omissions;
If possible also enclose copies of any relevant papers]
What I want to achieve by making this complaint is

[*here set out as precisely as possible what you want to be the result of your complaint: ie, an apology, a changed service provision, an alteration to practice, compensation, etc*]

I understand that your Complaints Manager will wish to contact me in order to investigate this complaint. I suggest that this be done by [*here give a telephone contact number and the time/days you are normally available or some other convenient way you can be contacted*]

I also understand that in investigating this complaint you may need to share information with other relevant parties /agencies and also to access my records. I confirm that I am in agreement to you taking this action – so far as it is strictly necessary, and accordingly give my consent to this, under the Data Protection Act 1998. [*if the complaint is in a representative capacity, then either attach a letter signed & dated by the person on whose behalf the complaint is made (agreeing for the information to be disclosed) or state that you believe the person lacks sufficient mental capacity to consent to this disclosure and you are of the opinion that such disclosure would be in his or her best interests, having regard to the advice in para 16.24–25 of the Mental Capacity Act 2005 Code of Practice at* www.justice.gov.uk/guidance/protecting-the-vulnerable/mental-capacity-act]

Signed:

Index